INDEX TO THE 1820 CENSUS OF KENTUCKY

INDEX TO THE 1820 CENSUS OF KENTUCKY

Compiled by

JEANNE ROBEY FELLDIN

& GLORIA KAY VANDIVER INMAN

CLEARFIELD

Reprinted for
Clearfield Company by
Genealogical Publishing Co.
Baltimore, Maryland
1996, 1999, 2002, 2007

ISBN-13: 978-0-8063-0937-8
ISBN-10: 0-8063-0937-7

Made in the United States of America

Library of Congress Catalogue Card Number 81-80889

HOW TO USE THIS BOOK

This index was transcribed from microfilm copies of the original handwritten census schedules Early census returns are especially difficult to read. Writing skills and styles differ from those in use today, and ink, the kind of paper used, even the microfilming technique affect legibility.

Although the 1820 Livingston County enumeration was among the worst we have ever seen, entries in several counties defied interpretation. Such entries will be found on the first page of the index, indicated by "——, ——", followed by the county and page number

Illiteracy was widespread in 1820. Frequently the census enumerator, himself poorly educated, was forced to guess at spellings. One page, written by one man, may have three or four different spellings of the same name. Therefore, the researcher must try all conceivable spellings when searching for an ancestor. In the case of two equally possible interpretations, names are either entered both ways or are cross-referenced. There are 300-400 of these double or cross-referenced entries.

The marshal, or census taker, was allowed only a few months in which to complete his enumeration. Can you imagine how many families must have been missed in early, migrant America? How many families were entered twice, or three times, as they travelled from county to county?

In addition to these common problems, we have the ever-present possibility of human error, both then and now. Although this index has been checked and re-checked, we are fully aware that errors have undoubtedly infiltrated the work. We hope the researcher will be understanding of the difficulties involved.

The 1820 Census reports the following data: Name of head of family; Place of residence; Number of free white males and females under 10 years of age, 10 and under 16, 16 and under 26, 26 and under 45, and 45 and upward; male and female slaves and free colored persons under 14 years, 14 and under 26, 26 and under 45, and 45 and upward; all other free persons, except Indians not taxed, persons (including slaves) engaged in agriculture, commerce, and manufacturing and trades.

"Although more than one set of numbers often appears on the schedules, the system of numbering, whether stamped or written . . . is generally that which (1) runs consecutively from the beginning to the end of the volume, and (2) appears to be consistent with the numbering for other volumes for the state. Where a schedule begins on a page not numbered, an 'A' number (36A, for example) has been used for identification . . . ."[1]

The above system has been used throughout this index. All unnumbered pages were given an 'A' number or, in one or two cases where two unnumbered pages occurred consecutively, a 'B' number. This means that a name may appear, for example, on page 36A while part of the information concerning this person appears on page 37.

Counties have been abbreviated as follows:

ADAIR	ADR
Columbia (city in Adair)	ADC
ALLEN	ALN
BARREN	BRN
BATH	BTH
BOONE	BNE
BOURBON	BBN
BRACKEN	BKN
BRECKINRIDGE	BRK
BULLITT	BLT
BUTLER	BTL
CALDWELL	CWL
CAMPBELL	CBL
CASEY	CSY
CHRISTIAN	CHN
CLARK	CLK
CLAY	CLY
CUMBERLAND	CLD
DAVIESS	DVS
ESTILL	ETL
FAYETTE	FTE
FLEMING	FLG
FLOYD	FLD
FRANKLIN	FKN
GALLATIN	GTN
GARRARD	GRD
GRANT	GRT
GRAYSON	GSN
GREEN	GRN
GREENUP	GNP
HARDIN	HRD
HARLAN	HRL
HARRISON	HAR
HART	HRT
HENDERSON	HND
HENRY	HRY
HOPKINS	HOP
JEFFERSON	JEF
JESSAMINE	JES
KNOX	KNX
LEWIS	LWS
LINCOLN	LNC
LIVINGSTON	LVG
LOGAN	LGN
MADISON	MAD
MASON	MAS
MERCER	MER

[1] National Archives Microcopy No. 33.

MONROE	MNR	SHELBY	SHE
MONTGOMERY	MTG	SIMPSON	SPN
MUHLENBURG	MBG	TODD	TOD
NELSON	NSN	TRIGG	TRG
NICHOLAS	NCH	UNION	UNN
OHIO	OHO	WARREN	WRN
OWEN	OWN	WASHINGTON	WAS
PENDLETON	PND	WAYNE	WYN
PULASKI	PUL	WHITLEY	WTY
ROCKCASTLE	RCK	WOODFORD	WDF
SCOTT	SCT		

Photocopies of specific pages of census records are provided for a fee by the *Correspondence Branch (NNCC), National Archives (GSA), Washington,* D.C. 20408. No form is now required. Use of GSA Request form 7029 has been discontinued.

As Val D. Greenwood points out in his *Researcher's Guide to American Genealogy,* there was a built-in "error factor" in the original census. We would like to add that there is a built-in *human* error factor in *any index.* Please be aware of both these deficiencies when shopping for your ancestor.

Your ancestor may have been in Kentucky in 1820, but, for one of many reasons, he may not be listed in this index. Over 70,000 heads of households are listed. We sincerely hope *your* ancestor is among them.

JEANNE ROBEY FELLDIN &
GLORIA KAY VANDIVER INMAN

Stagecoach, Texas, 10 February 1981

INDEX TO THE 1820 CENSUS OF KENTUCKY

Name	County	Page
(NO SURNAME), Aggy (Black)	FLG	34A
Amy	JEF	46
Andrew	LGN	38
Ben	MER	89
Ben (Free)	SHE	170
Benjamin	HAR	136
Betty	BRN	34
Black Bill (Free)	HRY	270
Bob (Free)	LGN	37
Clary (Blk)	MTG	299
Daniel	MAS	71
David	BRN	34
Dunmore (Free)	LGN	40
Easter (Slave)	FTE	62
Edward	MAS	74
Fanny (Free)	JES	81
Flanders (Blk Man)	MTG	226
Frank	MAS	53
Frank	HRT	158
Frank (A Free Negroe)	CLK	103
Frank (Free)	PUL	67A
Franklin	MAS	53
Frederick (White)	MBG	139A
Gedison?	HAR	170
George	LNC	59
George	FTE	60
George (A Free Negroe)	CLK	103
Gilbert (Owned By Jno. Bell	FTE	58
Hannah (Blk)	MTG	287
Harry (Free)	SHE	110A
Hunt (Slave)	FTE	62
Isaac	LNC	77
Isaac	GTN	120
Jacob	BBN	70
Jacob (A Man Of Color)	WAS	23A
Jacob (Free Blk)	LGN	28
Jacob (Freeman)	CHN	44A
Jean	LNC	47
Jemimy	WDF	96
Jenny	MER	99
Jinny (Black)	FLG	39A
John	MAS	75
John (Free)	LGN	40
Judiath	MAS	79
Kitty	FTE	60
Lydia (Free)	CLK	94
Mary	MAS	75
Matt	MAS	78
Milley	FTE	61
Milley	HRT	164
Milley (Slave)	FTE	62
Molborough	MER	103
Molly	WDF	97A
Nancy	MAS	72
Nancy (Oats Free Negroe)	CLK	107
Nancy (Black)	FLG	38A
Nancy (Free)	BBN	128
Ned (Free)	LGN	38
Ned (Free)	SHE	110A
Nelson	LNC	39
Nicholas (Free)	LGN	37
Parkey	MAD	154
Peggy	FTE	60
Priscilla	BRN	34
Rachel	HAR	160
Sally	FTE	61
Sally	MER	115
(NO SURNAME), Sam	FTE	60
Sarah (Blk Woman)	MTG	271
Sarah (Slave)	FTE	62
Suckey	FTE	61
Temay	FTE	60
Tom (Free)	SHE	110A
Tylor (A Woman Of Color)	WAS	86A
William	MAS	75
Zibe (Free)	PUL	60A
-------, Merick?	ALN	98
-------?, William	BLT	170
-----, -----	CWL	31
-----	FLD	43
-----	GRN	50
-----	GRN	69
-----	GRN	71
-----	GRN	73
-----	GRN	74
-----	GRN	76
-----	GRN	79
-----	BBN	96
-----	BBN	96
-----	CLD	158
-----	CLD	158
-----	WAS	38A
Christopher?	BKN	18
Ja---?	WAS	38A
James?	GRN	64
Mary?	WAS	38A
-----?, -----?	LVG	16
-----?	CHN	28
-----?	CHN	36
-----?	CHN	36
-----?	CHN	36
-----?	FLD	46
-----?	DVS	3A
-----?	DVS	4A
-----?	DVS	5A
-----?	DVS	6A
-----?	DVS	12A
-----?	CHN	35A
-----?	CHN	35A
Charles	GTN	117
H---?	CHN	33
Hezakiah	BKN	13
James	CHN	33A
James	CHN	34A
Jasper	JES	71
John I. / J.?	CHN	28A
John?	CHN	34
M.?	CHN	35A
Martin	CHN	36
Mary	MAD	174
Mite--?	CHN	32A
Noah	CBL	11A
Peggy	CHN	27A
Polley	CHN	35
Simeon	JES	71
Wm.	WAS	46A
-----BOTTOM, -----	CLD	159
-----DY?, Alexander	ALN	102
-----ES?, -----?	DVS	12A
-----MEN?, -----	CLD	160
-----RAN?, -----	CLD	160
-----RS?, ----- Sner.	CLD	160
-----TH?, John	CBL	10A
----?, Jacob	LVG	18
----ENSON?, -----?	DVS	13A
----LORD?, Ridley	BBN	96
----ON?, J---?	GRN	72
----R?, -----?	DVS	5A
----S?, -----?	DVS	3A
----SON?, John T.	FTE	64
---, Michael	ALN	104
---ADLING?, -----?, Jr.	DVS	4A
---AN?, -----?	DVS	3A
---ARD?, -----?	DVS	5A
---AS?, -----?	DVS	3A
---AY?, -----?	DVS	9A
---BANK?, Thomas	MNR	203
---DERS?, -----?	DVS	13A
---EN?, -----?	DVS	4A
---EY?, -----?	LGN	23
---IS?, -----?	DVS	3A
---LAND?, -----?	DVS	6A
---LER?, -----	CLD	157
---LETT?, -----?	LVG	18
---LEY?, -----?	DVS	3A
---LOR?, -----?	DVS	4A
---MAS?, -----?	DVS	4A
---NADA?, -----?	DVS	9A
---NETT?, -----?	DVS	4A
---NS?, -----?	DVS	4A
---NSTON, -----?, Senr.	DVS	5A
---OR?, -----	DVS	3A
---OSE?, -----	DVS	3A
---SON?, -----?	DVS	6A
Levi	GRN	79
---TE?, -----?	DVS	13A
---TH?, -----	DVS	7A
-----?	DVS	4A
-----?	DVS	4A
---TTS?, -----?	DVS	8A
---VIS?, -----?	DVS	9A
---W?, -----?	DVS	8A
---Y?, Thomas	FTE	57
--ANG?, John	BLT	158
--ARTER?, -----?	DVS	4A
--ARTON?, -----?	DVS	4A
--ATHERS?, James	WAS	49A
--BBLE?, -----?	DVS	3A
--BLE?, -----?, Jr.	DVS	3A
--CE?, -----?	DVS	6A
--CKSON?, -----?	DVS	3A
--ELD?, -----?	DVS	6A
--HNSTON?, -----?	DVS	5A
--IELD?, -----?	DVS	3A
--ITHY?, Lewis	CLK	86
--ITZ?, -----?	DVS	5A
--LENN?, -----?	DVS	9A
--LLEY?, -----?	DVS	6A
--LLOW?, Oliver	FTE	87
--MMINGS?, -----?	DVS	8A
--NNER?, -----?	DVS	7A
--OOM?, -----?	DVS	4A
--OW?, -----?	DVS	6A
--OWN?, -----?	DVS	3A
-----?	DVS	10A
--PLES?, -----?	DVS	4A
--RISTIAN?, -----?	DVS	5A
--RKER?, -----?	DVS	10A
--RTON?, -----?	DVS	6A
--SS?, -----?	DVS	4A
--THEWS?, -----?	DVS	4A
--TI--?, Frederick?	CBL	9A
--TTS?, -----?	DVS	8A
--URN?, John	OWN	99
--W?, -----?	DVS	5A
--WARD?, -----	DVS	5A
-----?	DVS	5A
-----?	DVS	5A
--WEL?, -----	CLD	159
--XON?, -----?	DVS	8A

Name	County	Page
--YLOR?, -----?	DVS	4A
-----?	DVS	6A
--YRES?, -----?	DVS	11A
-ACKSON?, -----?	DVS	3A
-ADDOCK?, -----?	DVS	3A
-ADY?, Benjamin	ALN	100
-ALL?, -----?	DVS	8A
-ALLACE?, -----?	DVS	6A
-ALLOWAY?, -----?	DVS	11A
-----?	DVS	11A
-ALUSHA?, -----?	CWL	42
-AMB?, -----?	DVS	8A
-AMBDIN?, John	BKN	16
-ANNER?, -----?	DVS	3A
-----?	DVS	7A
-ATES?, William	ETL	54
-AVIESS?, -----?	DVS	5A
-EARNS?, -----?	DVS	4A
-EARSON?, -----?	DVS	9A
-ELMS?, -----?, Jr.	DVS	4A
-ENTLEY?, -----?	DVS	3A
-EOMAN?, Richard	SHE	120A
-HAMBERLANE?, -----?	DVS	7A
-----?	DVS	7A
-ICHARD?, Whitley	BNE	48
-ICHARDSON, William	FTE	63
-IELD?, -----?	DVS	5A
-----?	DVS	5A
-ILEY?, -----?	DVS	4A
-----?	DVS	4A
-IMBLE?, Thomas	MTG	226
-IN-?, Hooper	BLT	172
-ITTLE?, -----?	DVS	8A
-LLEY-?, -----?	DVS	5A
-LOVER?, -----?	DVS	7A
-NYART?, Elizabeth	LWS	86A
-OBPRICE?, Christ	ALN	124
-OMES?, William	HRY	214
-OOLEY?, James	GRD	102A
-ORNEL?, -----?	DVS	11A
-OUITT?, Matthew	FTE	112
-OYCE?, Thomas	BLT	166
-PENCER, Thomas	FLD	46
-RADLING?, -----?	DVS	3A
-RIDDLE?, Jacob	BLT	164
-TETTON?, Benjamin	ALN	96
-THERTON?, -----?	DVS	6A
-----?	DVS	6A
-ULEY, John	BLT	170
-WAITS?, Elizabeth	FTE	73
A---N?, Micajah	HOP	230
A--, Jessee	ALN	110
AASBURY, Caleb	FLG	28A
ABBAY, Jonathan	MTG	259
ABBE, Benard	WAS	54A
ABBET, Jas.	HRY	250
ABBETT, Dennis	GTN	124
Jonathan	GTN	124
ABBIT, Geo.	HRY	240
ABBOT, Absalom	WYN	98A
James	BNE	50
Joseph	MBG	137
Joseph, Sr.	WYN	98A
William	BRN	1
William	MBG	137
William	BTH	162
Wm.	FKN	142
ABBOTT, Bevin	WDF	95
Elijah	BBN	134
Elleanor	SHE	162
Franky	SCT	125A
James	JEF	52
ABBOTT, James	HRY	196
Jno.	JEF	51
Jo./ Js.?	HRY	206
John	CBL	20A
John	CBL	23A
Jonathan	HRY	182
Joseph, Jr.	HRY	214
Joseph	SCT	124A
Js.	HRY	204
Susanna	HRY	180
Thomas	SHE	163
Will, Sr.	HRY	182
William	HRY	182
ABBRITTON, John	WRN	60A
ABDELL, George	HAR	186
ABEL, Jeremiah	ADR	4
Joseph	JEF	27
Robert	BRK	233
ABELL, Abner	WAS	29A
Elizebeth	WAS	29A
James	WAS	69A
Jesse	WAS	54A
Robert	NSN	176
Robt.	WAS	29A
Wm.	WAS	29A
ABERFIELD, Andrew	HRD	94
ABERNATHY, Blackstone	FTE	87
Rich. B.	BNE	2
ABLE, Benjamin	GSN	127A
Caleb	JEF	63
Edmund	NSN	194
Joseph	JEF	63
Saml.	HRD	28
Wm.	GRN	67
ABNER, Charles	MAD	122
Elisha	CLY	117
Enoch, Sr.	CLY	117
John	CLK	78
Menan	CLY	117
Wm.	RCK	75A
ABNEY, John K.	GRN	53
Joshua	BTL	317
Little Berry	ETL	37
Tucker	ETL	44
William	ETL	41
William	ETL	48
William	ETL	50
ABRAHAM, Gasper?	NSN	178
ABRAM, Henry	MAD	142
ABRAMS, Frances	LNC	71
Joseph	ETL	42
Joseph	ETL	44
ABRE-?, Cassandry	ADR	50
ABRELL, Jacob	ADR	4
James	ADR	4
John	ADR	4
ABSHEAR, John	ALN	104
ABSHER, Wm.	ADR	64
ABSHER?, Jacob	ALN	106
ABSHIER, John	FLD	19
ACERS, Henry	ETL	53
William	ETL	53
ACHISON, Jessee	BTH	180
ACKERMAN, Daniel	LGN	46
Daniel	BTH	154
Jacob	LGN	29
ACKLIN, Joseph	CBL	18A
ACKMAN, Henery	CBL	10A
William	CBL	10A
ACKMAN?, Jacob	HRD	54
ACKWORTH, Henry	BKN	11
ACLEY, Gibbins	WDF	104A
ACOCK, Allen	LGN	27
Henry	LGN	36
Robert	TOD	130A
ACOCK, William	LGN	36
ACRE, Abner	OWN	102
ACRES, -----?	DVS	7A
Adam	BBN	114
Henry	FTE	85
Jacob	BBN	106
John	HRD	42
John	ETL	54
John	BBN	122
Joseph	FTE	108
Josiah	HRD	44
Larkin N.	CHN	27A
ACRET?, Charles	HRY	180
ACRY, Candas, Mrs.	WYN	101A
John	WYN	101A
William	BNE	2
William	WYN	81A
ACTON, Aaron, Jr.	GRD	89A
Aaron	GRD	89A
Jams.	PUL	49A
Saml.	PUL	35A
Stephen	PUL	35A
William	GRD	89A
ACY, James	LVG	15
AD-INE?, Jacob	HRY	182
ADAIR, Benjamin T.	NCH	117A
Francis	NCH	112A
James	BBN	90
Jesse M.	BBN	98
John	TRG	7
John	TRG	7
John, Gen.	MER	85
Jos.	MAS	79
Joseph	BBN	108
Mansel	TRG	7
Richard	NCH	111A
Will	BBN	74
William	WRN	38A
William P.	NCH	126A
ADAM, Absalum	MAD	172
Thos.	PUL	37A
ADAMAS, Archibald	MER	85
ADAMS, -ym--?	WTY	119A
Aaron	GRT	139
Abraham	WAS	26A
Abram	GRD	104A
Abram	GRD	120A
Absalom	GTN	119
Absalom	HAR	178
Absolum	FTE	92
Alexander	LGN	37
Alexander	PUL	61A
Alexr.	NCH	115A
Andrew	BKN	16
Andw.	HRY	252
Ann	FTE	63
Anna	CBL	12A
Aron	HAR	154
Arthur	FLD	20
Banjamin	BLT	194
Benjamin	FLD	3
Benjamin	FLD	4
Benjamin	FTE	101
Benjamin	CLY	121
Benjamin	CSY	222
Berryman	MTG	291
Burwill	LGN	45
C., Mrs.?	MAS	59
Charles	FLD	8
Charles	LNC	63
Clement	LGN	46
Coonrod	WAS	26A
D.	HRY	261
Daniel	LNC	69
Daniel	HAR	178
Danl.	RCK	79A

Name	County	Page
ADAMS, Danl.	GRD	92A
Dav.	HRY	263
Dav., Capt.	HRY	249
David	MER	85
Dawsey	WDF	116A
Drury	TRG	12
Eleanor	HAR	176
Electius	NSN	208
Eli?	DVS	17A
Elijah	GRN	71
Elijah	RCK	79A
Elijah	GRD	84A
Elisha	MER	85
Elisha	DVS	19A
Elisha	WAS	33A
Elisha	RCK	83A
Eliza	LNC	73
Elizabeth	ALN	114
Elizabeth	NSN	208
Francis	JEF	40
Francis	MER	85
Francis	WRN	49A
Frederick	WRN	62A
Geo.	FKN	54
Geo.	FLG	72A
Geo.	GRD	118A
George	FLD	4
George	MER	85
George	FTE	99
George	UNN	146
George	HOP	228
George	CBL	14A
George	PUL	54A
George	GSN	127A
George	MBG	139A
Givin	HRY	206
Hannah	MTG	255
Harnes?	CLK	91
Henry	HAR	178
Henry	HRY	260
Henry	WAS	26A
Hugh	PUL	68A
Isaac	FLD	8
Isaac	CLD	148
Isaac	MTG	255
Isaac	SCT	98A
Isaac	SCT	120A
Isam	RCK	78A
Jac.	HRY	263
Jacob	WDF	92
James	HRD	8
James	LVG	15
James	LGN	39
James	GRN	56
James	GRN	67
James	CLK	71
James	HAR	164
James	HAR	176
James	HOP	228
James	BRK	233
James	CBL	9A
James	PUL	39A
James	PUL	40A
James	PUL	61A
James	SCT	98A
James	GRD	109A
James	NCH	114A
Jas.	CHN	41
Jas.	HRY	269
Jeremiah	SCT	134A
Jesse	FLD	4
Jesse	FLD	4
Jesse	BBN	136
Jesse	TRG	11A
Jesse	WRN	70A
Jesse	WTY	123A
ADAMS, Jessee	ETL	52
Jno.	CHN	38
Jno	HRY	26
Jno.	PUL	45A
Joel	MAD	90
Joel	HRY	192
Joel	PUL	46A
John	BRN	1
John	BNE	2
John	ADR	4
John	ADR	4
John	TRG	13
John	FLD	14
John	BKN	22
John	LGN	22
John	LGN	45
John	LNC	65
John	CLK	67
John	CLK	69
John	CLK	89
John	FTE	99
John	HRL	102
John	BBN	118
John	GTN	120
John	MAD	158
John	MAD	160
John	HAR	164
John	HAR	168
John	BRK	233
John	MTG	265
John	BTL	317
John, Sr.	LGN	44
John	FLG	43A
John	WAS	64A
John	WRN	65A
John	RCK	75A
John	RCK	82A
John	GRD	88A
John	SCT	93A
Joseph	MER	85
Joseph	MTG	245
Joseph	SPN	14A
Larcan	FTE	103
Larkin	BTH	216
Lettis	FLD	4
Leven	RCK	81A
Levin	BBN	118
Lewis	SCT	98A
Louisa	LNC	73
Luke	GRD	84A
Mabray	LGN	43
Mabray?	LGN	41
Margaret	FTE	100
Margaret	DVS	19A
Martha	MER	85
Martin	LGN	24
Martin	JEF	50
Mary	BBN	78
Mary	CLK	88
Mary	HOP	230
Massa	LNC	73
Mathew	BNE	2
Mathew	LVG	15
Mathew	GRD	84A
Matt., Jr.	MTG	243
Matt., Sr.	MTG	243
Matthew	FLD	8
Matthew	MTG	239
Matthias	BLT	188
Minter	CLK	75
Moses	FLD	4
Moses	SCT	100A
Nat	ADR	4
Nathan	CHN	41
Nathaniel	LVG	15
Nathaniel	CLK	90
ADAMS, Nathl.	BKN	18
Nimrod	PUL	47A
Otho	WAS	34A
Overton	GRD	98A
Patsy	LGN	43
Patsy	MER	85
Peter	MAD	162
Peter	WAS	63A
Polly	FTE	56
Randolph	WDF	95
Randolph	KNX	304
Reubin	GTN	120
Richard	NSN	208
Richd.	FLG	44A
Robert	BNE	2
Robert	CLK	73
Robert	WDF	93
Robert	MAD	118
Robert	HOP	228
Robt.	CWL	50
Robt.	FLG	38A
Sally	LNC	73
Saml.	FKN	106
Samuel	LGN	37
Sarah	LGN	43
Sarah	MAD	142
Silington?	RCK	83A
Silvester	FLD	7
Spencer	FLD	4
Spencer	MTG	287
Stephen	FLD	3
Stephen	FLD	4
Stephen	CLK	69
Thomas	BNE	2
Thomas	LGN	33
Thomas	HOP	228
Thomas	CBL	6A
Thomas	NCH	108A
Turril	SCT	99A
Ve-mus?	JES	79
Walter	GRD	91A
Walter	GRD	101A
William	BRN	1
William	BKN	4
William	FLD	7
William	TRG	13
William	JEF	50
William	CLK	68
William	FTE	70
William	GRN	73
William	MER	85
William	HAR	160
William	HAR	164
William	SHE	171
William	HAR	176
William	HAR	198
William	CHN	34A
William	GRD	85A
William	WYN	97A
William	WTY	123A
William B.	WRN	30A
Willis	GRD	114A
Wilson	MBG	143
Wilson	HOP	228
Wilson	GRD	98A
Wm.	TOD	132
Wm.	HRY	269
Wm.	PND	30A
Wm.	PUL	38A
Wm.	PUL	42A
Wm.	RCK	84A
Zadoc	CWL	50
ADAMSON, Danl.	BKN	22
Geo.	MAS	66
John	CWL	44
Jos.	MAS	54

INDEX TO THE 1820 CENSUS OF KENTUCKY

Name	County	Page
ADAMSON, Ruth	MAS	54
Simon	ADR	4
Wm.	MAS	66
ADAN, Simeon	SPN	20A
ADANY, James	JEF	53
ADCOCK, Edmund	SHE	171
George	SHE	171
George	SHE	173
Joel	GRD	96A
John C.	LVG	10
John M.	GRD	113A
ADDAMS, David	GNP	170A
John	GNP	170A
ADDINGTON, Henry	OHO	8A
ADDISON, Jonathan	LGN	40
Thos.	FKN	88
William	LGN	28
William	CLD	149
ADDLEMON, Aron	HAR	158
ADERNSON, Stephen	MAS	54
ADKERSON, Elisha	MBG	143A
John	WAS	48A
ADKIN-?, Thomas	WTY	120A
ADKIN, David	WTY	125A
Edmund B.	WDF	104
Jeramiah	WTY	121A
John	WDF	96
Talbot	WTY	126A
ADKIN?, Thomas	WTY	120A
ADKINS, -----?	WYN	99A
Able	MAD	178
Abner	DVS	17A
Amos	BTL	317
Bartlett	FLD	38
David	FLD	21
Edward	MER	85
Elias	BBN	122
Elijah	FLD	27
Elizabeth	BRK	233
Frederick	FLD	26
Gowin	HRY	260
Harrison	DVS	17A
Henery	GSN	127A
Howard	FLD	26
Isham	FLD	26
James	FLD	26
Jas.	PUL	40A
Jas.	PUL	50A
Jesse	FLD	25
Joel	FLD	26
John	ADR	4
John	FLD	45
John	GTN	120
John	GTN	129
Joseph	FLD	26
Lucas	FLD	26
Moses	FLD	26
Moses	HOP	228
Nathan	FLD	26
Nathaniel	FLD	25
Noton	FLD	38
Owen	PUL	46A
Roling	WYN	93A
Spencer	FLD	25
Thomas	FLD	40
William	FLD	25
Winright	FLD	25
Wm.	FLD	23
ADKINSON, James	LWS	93A
Richard	WYN	97A
Sally	MER	85
ADKISON, Jeremiah	BRK	233
John	BRK	231
Lewis	BRK	231
Pleasant	BRK	231
Samuel	BRK	231
ADLEY, Charles	CLD	156
Dority	ADR	26
Wm.	ADR	26
ADMAN, David	JEF	26
ADMIRE, Henry?	HRY	226
Jas.	HRY	244
Squire	HRY	226
AGEE, John	TOD	130
William	WYN	104A
AGIN, Thomas?	DVS	15A
William	WDF	117A
AGNEW, Robert	HND	9
Wyly	HND	11
AGNIEL, Camile?	GTN	127
AHULL?, Eliza	FTE	79
AIKEN, James	FTE	106
AIKIN, James	CLD	143
AIKINS, Garland	CLD	147
Joseph	CLD	144
Josiah	CLD	144
AILER, Abram	SCT	114A
AILESWORTH, Anney	HND	9
AILLES, Benjamin	GNP	170A
Benjamin	GNP	179A
AILLS, John	LWS	88A
William	LWS	87A
AINGEL, Jeremiah	LGN	29
AINGELL, William	LGN	29
AINS, Baley	WTY	127A
AINSWORTH, Charles	NCH	106A
AIRS?, Tho.	MAS	69
AITKEN, George	FTE	68
AKER, John	PUL	39A
AKERNAN?, John	KNX	312
AKERS, Abner	BRN	1
Bedd?	SHE	136A
Benjamin	SHE	136A
Drury	SHE	136A
Fenley	SHE	125A
George	MNR	209
John	CLD	156
Jonathan	FLD	32
Peter	FLG	78A
Solomon	FLD	32
Thomas	MNR	209
Valentine	FLD	32
William	FLD	32
AKERSON, Jno.	MAS	77
AKES, Peter	OWN	107
AKIN, George	HND	6
James	GRN	60
John, Senr.	WDF	125A
John	HND	7A
Joseph	GRN	51
Mary	SHE	153
Thomas	GRN	55
Thos.	HND	6
William, Esq.	MER	116
AKINS, Berryman	FTE	96
James	FLD	38
Susanna	SHE	153
William	WDF	94
AKIS, Mr.	RCK	82A
AKIS?, Frederick	RCK	76A
AKLE?, Susannah	BKN	24
AKLIN?, Joseph A.	PND	24A
ALAWAY?, Wm.	SHE	141A
ALBERSON, Benjamin	MAD	150
James	MAD	104
Reubin	MAD	130
Wm.	MAD	138
ALBERT, Philip	UNN	149
ALBIN, Absolom	OHO	5A
ALCORN, George	MAD	98
Jas.	MAS	77
Jessee	WYN	85A
ALCORN, Robert	GTN	120
William	ETL	50
ALDER, Geo.	HRY	267
ALDERSEN, Nancy	GRD	115A
ALDERSON, Aaron	HRT	152
Aaron, Sr.	HRT	152
Benjamin	WRN	33A
Henry	FTE	76
Will	ADR	4
ALDRIDGE, Annias	BRK	231
David	FLD	42
David	MTG	249
Elijah	MTG	249
Francis	WYN	90A
James	FLD	42
James	GRD	96A
John	CLK	95
John	GRD	83A
John P.	FTE	65
Malinda	LGN	34
Nathan	BRK	233
Nicholas	CLK	68
Peggy	FLD	42
Robert	FLD	42
Saml.	BRK	233
William	CLK	81
William	CLK	95
Wm.	BNE	2
Wm.	BRK	233
ALDRIDGE?, Mary	MAD	174
ALDRIGE, Francis	PUL	62A
Jno.	HRY	254
Milly	BTL	317
Nath.	RCK	80A
Thos.	HRY	262
ALE?, Thomas	NSN	211
ALEMBAUGH, Garrett	ETL	54
Peter	ETL	37
ALENUTS, Daniel	SPN	9A
ALEOM?, Henry	FKN	56
ALESBERRY, Chas. G.	CHN	33
ALESOM, John	TRG	8
ALEXANDER, -? Wm.	BBN	96
A.	MAS	53
Agness	HOP	230
Amze?	ALN	138
Andrew	ETL	50
Anis?	WYN	79A
Arch.	BKN	18
August	MAD	104
Baxter	TRG	3
Betsey	FTE	110
Charles	BRK	231
David	MTG	235
Ebenezer, Jr.	HOP	230
Ebenezer, Sr.	HOP	230
Edvin	SHE	162
Elenor	FLG	39A
Elizabeth	HRT	152
Gabriel	MER	115
Greenwood	CLD	137
Hugh	FKN	152
Hugh	SCT	121A
Hyram	ETL	39
Ingram	CLD	137
Isaac	MER	85
J. Martin, Junr.	CLD	167
Jacob	SCT	138A
James	ETL	39
James	BBN	62
James	MER	85
James	MER	85
James	BBN	108
James	ALN	138
James	MAD	144

Name	County	Page
ALEXANDER, James	SHE	149
James	BLT	174
James	NCH	122A
Jas.	FLG	54A
Jas.	FLG	75A
Jas.	FLG	79A
Jas.	GRD	93A
Jesse	BTH	174
Jesse T.	HRY	234
Jno. W.	CHN	43A
John	LVG	12
John	LGN	39
John	CLK	62
John	FTE	86
John	CLK	93
John	GTN	134
John	CLD	137
John	SHE	149
John	BTH	202
John	MTG	229
John	TRG	7A
John	FLG	30A
John	FLG	43A
John	NCH	116A
John D.	GTN	118
John R.	WDF	108A
Jonathan	SCT	97A
Jos.	FLG	28A
Joseph	HOP	230
Katherine	GNP	172A
M. Y.	BBN	112
Mahen?	ALN	138
Margaret	BKN	19
Martin	CLD	137
Mary	ALN	138
Mat	ALN	138
Mathew	LGN	44
Mathew	FLG	73A
Nancy	FTE	83
Peter	WDF	123A
Porter	GTN	134
Randolph	NCH	122A
Reuben	MER	85
Reuben	CLD	137
Richard	BRK	231
Robert	LGN	44
Robert	FTE	86
Robert	CLD	141
Robert	BTH	174
Robert	WDF	113A
Saml.	CHN	42A
Thomas	FTE	102
Thomas	CLD	137
Thomas	BTH	182
Thomas	NCH	116A
Thos.	CHN	31
Thos.	BRK	233
Travis	SCT	125A
Wesley	GTN	117
Will	GRD	96B
Will.	MTG	241
William	BNE	2
William	MER	85
William	MER	85
William	MER	85
William	GTN	117
William	BBN	126
Willis	ETL	53
Willis	CLD	137
Wilson	WDF	108A
Wm.	FLG	40A
Wm.	CHN	42A
Wm.	PUL	47A
Zacheus	NCH	124A
Zacius	FLG	75A
Zenas	TRG	3
ALEXR., Jonathan	SCT	97A
ALFORD, Charles	LNC	23
Jesse	GRD	104A
John	LNC	23
Morgan	GRD	100A
Payton	GRD	101A
ALFRED, Sarah	FTE	63
ALFREY, Isaac	MTG	239
James	NCH	116A
Samuel	BTH	214
ALFRY, Abram	BTH	214
ALGOOD, Joseph R.	HND	9A
Samuel	HND	9A
ALIFF, James	PUL	39A
ALISON, James	CLD	166
Joseph	SHE	172
ALL, Aquilla	BLT	178
James	NSN	175
ALL?, Thomas	NSN	211
ALLAN, Archd.	JEF	28
Archibald	JEF	21
Benjamin	CLK	92
Chilton	CLK	102
Duglass	CLK	97
Isaac	JEF	43
John	CLK	70
John G.	CLK	66
John S.	CLK	68
Joseph	CLK	97
Lewis	CLK	70
Thomas	CLK	70
Thomas	CLK	100
William	CLK	89
ALLAWAY, George	CSY	206
John, Sr.	BNE	50
ALLBAUGH, Amy	GRD	107A
ALLBORNE, Elizabeth	BBN	94
ALLBRIGHT, James	SCT	115A
John	HAR	132
ALLCOCK, Council	MBG	140A
Durin	MBG	142A
James	MBG	142A
Sarah	MBG	142A
ALLCORN, Geo.	CLY	130
George	PUL	65A
James	LVG	9
Nancy	LNC	63
Robert	CLK	88
ALLEE, Buford	MNR	205
John	MNR	217
Nicholas	MNR	205
William	MNR	203
William	MNR	205
ALLEGA, John	GRD	109A
ALLEGER, William	GRD	84A
ALLEN, ----t?	DVS	10A
Abel	WRN	50A
Abisha	HRD	56
Adamson	BBN	138
Ananias	ADR	4
Anderson	FKN	158
Andrew	SHE	118A
Andrew	SHE	123A
Ann	LGN	43
Ann	MTG	295
Ann	SHE	127A
Anne	BRN	1
Anne	CBL	12A
Asa	BBN	62
Asa	BBN	122
Bartlett F.	SHE	115A
Bayley	GSN	127A
Ben	HRD	14
Ben	TOD	134
Ben.	HRY	264
ALLEN, Benjamin	JEF	60
Benjamin	SHE	163
Benjamin	CSY	222
Benjamin	SHE	131A
Benjn.	MAS	57
Beverly	WDF	100
Charles	SHE	155
Charles	WRN	53A
Chas. H.	HRY	261
Chs.	FKN	158
Church	LNC	5
Daniel	WRN	49A
Davey	WAS	44A
David	BNE	2
David	BBN	122
David	CLD	142
David	HRT	152
David	BLT	164
David	NSN	213
David, Sr.	WYN	96A
David	PUL	61A
David	WYN	102A
Edmund	KNX	312
Elijah	LGN	30
Elijah	SHE	123A
Elisha	HRD	20
Elisha	FTE	68
Enas	WRN	71A
Enoch L.	LNC	79
Erasmus	GRD	113A
Francis	BNE	50
Gabriel	LNC	5
George	ALN	108
George	CLD	139
George	MTG	243
George	MTG	257
George?	FLD	41
Greenberry W.	FTE	82
Henry	FLG	37A
Hugh	BNE	50
Hugh	WDF	95
Isaac	BBN	122
Isam	FTE	74
Isham	FLD	7
James	ADR	4
James	LGN	33
James	BNE	50
James	GRN	52
James	FTE	112
James	SHE	155
James	SHE	160
James	NSN	181
James	HAR	204
James	CSY	208
James	MTG	226
James	MTG	259
James	MTG	273
James, Senr.	BNE	2
James (M. C.)	GRN	66
James	NCH	114A
James	SHE	115A
James D.	SHE	152
Jane	SHE	125A
Jas.	HRD	62
Jas.	MAS	71
Jas.	TOD	124A
Jeremiah	HRD	56
Jesse	OWN	105
Jesse	NCH	106A
Jno.	MAS	56
Jno.	MAS	59
Johathan	JEF	38
John	ADR	4
John	ADR	4
John	TRG	4
John	JEF	38

Name	County	Page
ALLEN, John	ADC	68
John, (River?)	CLD	159
John	FTE	104
John	BBN	136
John	CLD	142
John	BTH	160
John	BLT	174
John	NSN	199
John	MTG	226
John	HOP	230
John	KNX	298
John, Capt.	MER	85
John	WRN	53A
John	PUL	61A
John	WYN	89A
John	GRD	109A
John	WDF	114A
John	WDF	117A
John	NCH	119A
John	SHE	123A
John	SHE	123A
John	GSN	127A
John	SHE	137A
John L.	SHE	150
John M.	SHE	176
John R.	MTG	273
Jos.	FLG	39A
Joseph	GRN	63
Joseph	FTE	82
Joseph	MER	85
Joseph	BBN	112
Joseph	SHE	157
Joseph	BRK	227
Joseph	CBL	9A
Josias	SHE	148
Lee	ALN	108
Lee	SPN	23A
Malcomb	SCT	133A
Margret	GRN	71
Marshall	HRD	14
Mary	SHE	131A
Merriman?	FKN	158
Montgomery	SHE	139A
Moses	HAR	176
Nancy	MAS	58
Nat.	HRY	262
Nathan	CLD	137
Rebecah	LNC	7
Rennuls?	CHN	29
Richard	FLD	10
Richard	FTE	63
Richardson	FTE	78
Rob.	MAS	73
Robert	CLD	143
Robert	CSY	222
Robert H.	SHE	127A
Robert P.	SHE	110A
Royal	PUL	60A
Saml.	HRD	38
Saml.	BBN	116
Saml.	WAS	26A
Saml.	FLG	41A
Saml.	SCT	93A
Saml.	SHE	123A
Saml. S.	GRN	51
Sampson	CLD	142
Samuel	FLD	44
Samuel	BBN	126
Samuel	BRK	231
Samuel, Senr.	PUL	64A
Samuel	PUL	61A
Samuel	GRD	101A
Sarah	FLD	41
Solomon	MAS	85
Stephen	WRN	50A
Streahley?	BNE	2
ALLEN, Tabbitha	MER	85
Tandy	BBN	112
Theopilus	OHO	5A
Thomas	BNE	2
Thomas	FTE	78
Thomas	BLT	196
Thomas, Jr.	MER	85
Thomas, Maj.	MAS	85
Thomas	SPN	13A
Thomas	SHE	115A
Thos.	SHE	137A
Thos.	SHE	137A
Thos.	SHE	142A
Thos. O.?	BBN	96
Widow	BBN	96
Will	ADR	4
Will	MAS	77
Will	MAS	78
Will.	KNX	312
William	BRN	1
William	BNE	2
William	FLD	3
William	FLD	5
William	FTE	79
William	WDF	95
William	CLD	142
William	SHE	154
William	SHE	157
William	SHE	176
William	BRK	227
William	MTG	229
William	BRK	231
William, Sen.	BRN	1
William	OHO	5A
William	WRN	53A
William	WRN	71A
William C.	LGN	33
Wm.	HRD	34
Wm.	BBN	80
Wm.	BBN	82
Wm.	BRK	309
Wm., Jr.	HRD	18
Wm., Senr.	HRD	66
Wm.	WAS	59A
Wm.	GSN	127A
Wm.	SHE	144A
ALLEN?, John (Chas? Cr.)	WDF	95
ALLENDER, Edward T.	TOD	127A
ALLENSBERRY, Peter	MAD	132
ALLENSON?, John T.	FTE	64
ALLENSWORTH, Butler	CHN	41
Jas.	CHN	41
Jno.	CHN	38
Phillip	CHN	39
Wm.	CHN	38
ALLENTON, Isaac	BTH	216
Jacob	BTH	216
ALLENWORTH?, P.	TOD	131
ALLEXANDER, Jesse	GSN	127A
ALLEY / ATTEY?, John	BRN	1
ALLEY, David	BRN	1
David	FLD	32
John	WYN	99A
Jos.	TOD	131
William	BRN	1
William	FLD	32
Willis	TOD	131
ALLGOOD, Edmund	MAS	85
Edward	MER	85
ALLIGOODE, Geo.	HRY	240
ALLIGREE, Doctor	MAS	64
ALLIN, Charles W.	HND	9
ALLIN, David	WAS	18A
Henry	CHN	41A
John	CLY	111
John	WYN	85A
Joshua	CLY	130
Morris/ Mosus?	CLY	111
Patcy	CLY	111
Samuel	WYN	88A
Stephen	SHE	155
William	HND	9
Wm.	PND	31A
ALLINDER, Geo.	FLG	69A
ALLINGHAM, George	WRN	73A
ALLINGTON/ ALLINGTER?, Abraham	FLD	9
ALLINGTON, David	FLD	8
ALLION, William	BRK	233
ALLISBERRY, Thos.	CHN	44
ALLISON, Archabald	CLY	113
Asia	WTY	125A
David	BLT	192
Elijah	FLG	63A
Elizabeth	BBN	122
Henry	JEF	65
Henry	FKN	118
James	LGN	37
James	MTG	273
John	HRD	24
John	LGN	37
John	NCH	105
John	MTG	281
John	GNP	167A
Joseph	GNP	171A
Moses	SHE	177
Robert	LGN	44
Saml.	MAD	180
Samuel	MER	85
Samuel	MBG	140A
Stevenson	MTG	287
William	MTG	271
ALLMAN?, Robt.	LVG	5
ALLNUTT, Eleanor	LGN	43
ALLOCK, Joseph R.	WRN	69A
ALLONAY/ ALLONCEY?, John	HRY	178
ALLOWAY, Huldah	BNE	2
ALLSOBROOKS, James	LVG	14
ALLSPAUGH, Isaac	MER	85
ALMON, Samuel	HOP	228
ALMOND, Wyatt	WRN	46A
ALNETT?, Jesse	GTN	119
Ning	GTN	119
ALNETTE?, William	GTN	119
ALNURY?, Iasack	BTL	317
ALOER, Andrew	MAD	130
ALPHIN, Luke	CBL	10A
Ransom	CBL	10A
Zebulon	CBL	10A
ALPHRED?, William	FTE	101
ALPHREY, Absolam	FLG	46A
ALPREY, J---?	FLG	45A
John	FLG	45A
ALSBROOKS?, Robert?	TRG	8A
ALSBURY, Jonathan	SHE	153
Vincent	SHE	153
William	SHE	153
ALSMAN, Aaron	JES	78
Andrew	JES	69
Drury	JES	77
ALSOBROOK, Jno.	LVG	7
ALSOBROOKS, Huston	LVG	3
ALSOP, Allen	SHE	116A
B.	SHE	109A

Name	County	Page
ALSOP, Geo.	FKN	126
James	MER	85
James	SHE	116A
Spencer	FTE	63
Will	SCT	105A
ALSTAT?, Polley	CSY	214
ALSUP, James	KNX	306
ALTER?, Joseph	MTG	281
ALTICK, Henry	MAS	72
ALTICK?, Abraham	MBG	139
ALVERSON, Benj.	GRD	90A
John	LGN	45
John S.	GRD	88A
ALVES, Amelia	HND	9A
James	HND	11A
Jesse	SHE	128A
Thos.	SHE	123A
ALVEY, Charles	WAS	42A
Fanny?	UNN	150
George	BRK	231
John F.	UNN	154
Joseph	UNN	146
Robert	UNN	146
Thomas	BRK	231
ALVIS, John	FTE	84
ALVY, Benj.	WAS	62A
Henry	WAS	62A
James	WAS	62A
John	WAS	62A
Phill	WAS	62A
ALYPH?, David	WYN	79A
ALZER, John	CWL	43
ALZER?, Rob.	CWL	37
AMAS, John J.	DVS	19A
AMBER, Wm.	PND	15A
AMBERS, Nichilers	BNE	2
AMBERSON, William	HOP	228
AMBROSE, John	CLY	132
Matthias	NSN	186
Sandwich	OHO	5A
Thomas	PUL	58A
AMBROSS?, Joseph	CLY	116
AMENT, Gabriel	GRN	53
George	GRN	52
John	HRD	16
Philip	BBN	106
AMENT?, Henry	HRD	34
AMERS?, Frances	UNN	154
AMES, Caty	CLY	128
Saml.	HRT	152
AMICK, Nicholas	BRK	233
AMIN?, Frances	UNN	154
AMISS, Joseph	JEF	34
AMMERMAN, Albert	PND	16A
Daniel	BBN	60
David	BBN	84
John	BBN	84
John, Jr.	PND	16A
John	PND	16A
AMMERMON, Saml.	BBN	114
Wm.	BBN	84
AMMONS, Wm.	BRK	233
AMONS, John L.?	MAD	90
AMOS, Arasmus	HRT	152
Benjn.	HRT	152
Dito	BBN	92
Elijah	BBN	92
Francis	HRT	152
Gabl.	PND	31A
George	HRT	152
James	HRT	152
John	BTH	164
Mordica	HRT	152
Nicholas	BBN	130
Nicholas	BBN	130
Obediah	WRN	41A
AMOS, Polley	HRT	152
Ransom	HRT	152
Reuben, Senr.	WRN	41A
Reuben	WRN	39A
Robert	BLT	186
Thos.	BBN	130
Widow	BBN	88
William	HRT	152
AMOS?, C. W.	BKN	16
AMOSS, Asberry	JES	84
AMUS?, Frances	UNN	154
AMYA?, Peter	FLD	47
AMYX, Matthew	BRN	1
ANADALE, Wm.	SHE	118A
ANCELL, Maria	FKN	62
ANDERSEN, John	GRD	118A
ANDERSON, -----?	DVS	10A
----on?	DVS	10A
Abihu?	MTG	257
Abraham	WRN	31A
Abrm.	BNE	2
Absolom	HRD	36
Achely	RCK	78A
Alexander	TRG	8A
Alexr.	SCT	115A
Allen	UNN	150
Amos	GTN	125
Amos	OHO	9A
Andrew	WDF	93
Andrew	GRT	141
Archibald	NSN	213
Archillus	GRD	86A
Armistead	UNN	148
Asa	BBN	88
Austin	GRD	98A
Azer? R.	NSN	209
Baily	CWL	50
Barker T.	BRN	1
Benja.	ALN	112
Bob / Rob?	GRD	93A
C. C.?	MAS	63
Campbell	CLD	147
Charles	BKN	11
Charles	FLD	38
Charles	MAD	148
Charles P.	MTG	237
Chas.	MAS	67
Clabourn	MAS	69
Cornelius	CBL	7A
Cornelus	BTH	148
Cornelus	GRD	106A
Crofford	CWL	50
Danl.	CBL	8A
David	BRN	1
David	MTG	237
David	SPN	4A
David	SPN	12A
David	WRN	44A
Ed.	GRD	91A
Edward	BNE	2
Eli	MAS	64
Elias	MAS	64
Elijah	BNE	2
Elijah	FKN	90
Elizabeth	MAS	85
Elizabeth	MER	85
Elizabeth	BTH	204
Ezl.	GRD	116A
Frances	OHO	11A
Francis	HAR	204
Garland	RCK	78A
Geo.	MAS	60
Geo.	MAS	72
George	BNE	2
George	BNE	2
George	CLK	85
ANDERSON, George	BRK	233
George H.	HND	10
Hagerman?	NSN	218
Harrison	MER	85
Hedgeman	NSN	200
Henery	CBL	6A
Henry	BNE	2
Henry	BNE	2
Henry	BBN	104
Ince?	CWL	50
Isaac	MAD	98
Isaac	NSN	185
Isaac	WYN	97A
Isaac	SHE	131A
J. J.	MAS	70
James	BKN	2
James	FTE	56
James	FTE	69
James	CLK	87
James	MAD	114
James	GTN	132
James	UNN	154
James	HAR	158
James	HRY	208
James	NSN	210
James	BRK	231
James	MTG	237
James	MTG	265
James	GRD	84A
James	GRD	92A
James	GSN	127A
James	GNP	173A
James H.	GRD	90A
Jas.	HRY	270
Jas. W.	RCK	78A
Jeremiah	NSN	184
Jeremiah	HRY	210
Jessey	OHO	9A
Jno.	CWL	50
Jno. S.	TOD	131
Jno. W.	MAS	68
John	BRN	1
John	BNE	2
John	ADR	4
John	HRD	34
John	HRD	56
John	FTE	63
John	ADC	66
John	MER	85
John	JES	86
John, (B E)	MTG	289
John	CLK	102
John	ALN	126
John	CLD	153
John	CLD	161
John	BLT	166
John	BTH	198
John	HAR	202
John	NSN	210
John	NSN	212
John	CSY	214
John	HAR	214
John	HRY	232
John	MTG	237
John	KNX	296
John	MTG	297
John, Sr.	NSN	198
John	CBL	20A
John	WRN	32A
John	WRN	51A
John	WAS	79A
John	WYN	79A
John	NCH	103A
John D.	HND	10
John G.	HRY	202
John H.	BRN	1

Name	County	Page
ANDERSON, Jonithan	GSN	127A
Joseph	BRN	1
Joseph	BNE	2
Joseph	JEF	63
Joseph	MER	85
Joseph	FKN	90
Joseph	CBL	6A
Joseph	CBL	10A
Joseph	FLG	49A
Josiah	HRD	36
Josiah	CHN	36A
Jourdan	CWL	50
Js., Jr.	HRY	234
Judith	LGN	34
Larken	BKN	23
Leonard	LGN	37
Leonard	MAS	52
Margaret	NSN	209
Margaret, Mrs.	WYN	96A
Martha	BRN	1
Mason	BKN	13
Mathew	CLK	69
Mathias	GSN	127A
Meredith	BRN	1
Michael	HOP	272
Moses	WYN	99A
N. M.	TOD	130
Nancy	NSN	184
Nancy, Mrs.	WYN	103A
Nancy	SPN	17A
Nancy	SCT	119A
Nathan D.	BRK	227
Nicholas	MTG	265
Nimrod	FLD	6
Oliver	JES	86
P.	GRD	99A
P.	TOD	130A
Peter	ALN	120
Peter	ALN	134
Pinkney	WRN	67A
Polly	MTG	287
Presley	FKN	98
R. C., Jr.	JEF	26
Reason	NSN	193
Reuben	FKN	64
Reuben	BBN	120
Reubin	WDF	104A
Rheuben	HAR	158
Rhoda	FTE	59
Richard	JEF	45
Richd. C.	JEF	47
Robert	GRN	66
Robert	NSN	218
Robert	PUL	67A
Robt.	JEF	41
Robt.	ADC	68
Robt.	MAS	73
Rolen?	BKN	11
Rubin	GRN	62
Sally	LGN	31
Saml.	BRN	1
Saml.	SCT	116A
Samuel	BRN	1
Samuel	ALN	114
Samuel	CLD	138
Samuel	NSN	186
Sarah	MER	85
Sarah	HRY	208
Sarah	TRG	8A
Sarah	NCH	113A
Stokes	MAS	70
Susan	MTG	263
Theo.	GRD	92A
Tho.	HRY	232
Thomas	FTE	56
Thomas	MBG	141
ANDERSON, Thomas	HAR	204
Thomas	HOP	230
Thomas	MTG	237
Thomas	GRD	87A
Thomas D.	HND	3
Thos.	BNE	2
Ths.	MAS	66
Tolifarro	GRD	91A
Tranas?	MAS	73
Vincent	CWL	50
Walter	LNC	27
Western	HND	10A
Will	HRY	232
Will.	KNX	282
William	BRN	1
William	BRN	1
William	BNE	2
William	LVG	10
William	FTE	81
William	JES	86
William	MER	114
William	HAR	142
William	UNN	149
William	CLD	158
William	HAR	158
William	CLD	160
William	HAR	166
William	BTH	204
William	HAR	212
William	HAR	218
William	MTG	237
William	MTG	281
William, Jr.	LVG	11
William	CBL	5A
William	WRN	30A
William	GRD	84A
Wingate	MTG	251
Wm.	HRD	24
Wm.	LNC	33
Wm.	FKN	54
Wm.	MAS	73
Wm.	BBN	104
Wm.	ALN	134
Wm.	BBN	144
Wm.	MAD	178
Wm., Sen.	BRN	1
ANDERSON?, Jonathon	ALN	112
ANDESON, Andrew	ALN	112
Garland	GRN	66
ANDRE, Giles	LNC	37
ANDRES, Henry	MAD	106
ANDREW, Alexander	WYN	91A
Mark	WRN	36A
William	SPN	14A
ANDREWS, Abraham	FTE	78
Ann	WDF	107A
Christian	GRN	64
Jacob	FLG	32A
Jesse	LGN	34
John	FLG	67A
Jos.	TOD	129
Joseph	ALN	110
Martha	TOD	128A
Mary	JEF	42
Polly	BBN	132
Thomas	GRN	54
Thomas	FTE	93
Thos. D.	FLG	77A
William	MNR	213
ANDRSON, Catharine	JES	81
ANGEL, John	FTE	110
John	GRD	96B
Willis	CLK	66
ANGELL, George, Jr.	PND	24A
ANGELL, George, Sr.	PND	24A
Milly	PND	24A
William	PND	16A
ANGLEGON?, William	BNE	2
ANGLETON, John	SCT	111A
ANGLIN, James	CLY	132
John	GNP	175A
ANKARD?, William	CBL	17A
ANKERMON, Andrew	BRK	231
ANKLIN, David	MAS	78
ANNESS, John	GRT	146
John B.	SCT	112A
William	GRT	146
ANNO, Will	MAS	69
ANSEL, Nancy	CHN	33A
ANSLEY?, Wm.	FLG	76A
ANSMINGAR, Philip	SHE	152
ANSON, Henry	LGN	34
ANSTON, Francis	SPN	15A
ANTHER?, David	LWS	86A
ANTHONY, Adam	NSN	178
Daniel	JES	77
Jacob	MBG	141A
Joseph	ALN	106
Joseph	CLK	107
Mehitabel	HAR	218
William	HND	3
ANTLE, Henry	HRY	268
Jacob	CLD	156
John	CLD	156
ANTLES, Benj.	SCT	117A
Henrey	SCT	117A
Jas.	SCT	117A
Jerry	SCT	117A
Peter	SCT	117A
ANTMELL?, James	MAS	52
Tho.	MAS	52
ANTONY, Joseph	FLG	30A
ANTROBUS?, Benjamin	NCH	127A
John	NCH	109A
ANTWILL?, James	MAS	52
Tho.	MAS	52
APLEGATE, Abra.	MAS	70
Ben	MAS	68
Richd.	MAS	70
APLIN?, Henry	MGB	137A
APPERSON, Richd.	FKN	104
APPLE, John	CSY	208
APPLEBY, John	CLD	153
Philip	LNC	53
Temperence	CLD	152
APPLEGATE, Benj.	FLG	25A
Benjamin	SHE	152
Daniel	HRY	253
Elisha	JEF	22
Isaac	MAS	62
James	GNP	172A
Jno.	MAS	62
John	SCT	93A
John	GNP	172A
Joseph	JEF	23
Lena	BLT	184
Milton	HRY	253
P. W.	MAS	64
Saml.	JEF	26
Saml.	JEF	33
Tho.	MAS	65
Tunis	JEF	33
William	BLT	170
APPLETON, William	FTE	76
APPLING, Joel	SPN	13A
Thomas	SPN	15A
ARAMS, John	HRY	208
ARBERRY, Robert	ETL	49

Name	County	Page
ARBUCKLE, James	BKN	15
James	CWL	33
Saml.	BKN	8
Saml.	FKN	160
Saml.	CHN	42A
Saml.	GRD	93A
Thos.	CHN	41
ARCHABLE, Adam	GSN	127A
ARCHER, Benjamin	GTN	124
Edmd.	JEF	50
Elizabeth	NCH	119A
John	JEF	68
John	WTY	110A
Jos.	SHE	126A
Meredith	UNN	153
Moses	CWL	34
Sampson	NCH	112A
ARD, Jacob	WYN	83A
John	WYN	88A
Reubin	WYN	88A
ARDEREY, James	NCH	109A
James	NCH	123A
Robert	NCH	123A
ARDERY, John	BBN	110
John	BBN	118
William	HAR	182
ARDRY, Alexr.	BBN	132
John	BBN	130
ARGO, Alexr.	FLG	67A
Purnell	FLG	67A
ARIGHT?, John	MAD	158
ARINGTON, Jourdan	SHE	111A
Wootson	SHE	130A
ARKMAN?, Jacob	HRD	54
ARLIDGE, Jonathan	HOP	228
ARMES, Abigal	FLD	4
ARMITAGE, William	CLK	62
ARMON, Tho.	PUL	49A
ARMS, Daniel	BRK	231
Micajah	CH	231
ARMSTEAD, John	FTE	86
John	GTN	131
Peter F.	FKN	80
ARMSTRONG, -----	CWL	32
-----?	CWL	41
----.	CWL	32
--at.?	CWL	32
--mes?	CWL	43
Abel	MER	85
Alex.	LVG	8
Alexander	MER	85
Alexr.	FLG	64A
Alexr.	FLG	64A
Ambrose	FTE	106
Andrew	FTE	97
Andrew	MTG	299
Benjamin	SHE	152
Benjn.	ADR	4
C.	JEF	26
Daniel	SHE	138A
David	GTN	122
David	SPN	3A
George	SHE	140A
Henry	FLG	48A
Irvin	HAR	184
Isaac	FKN	72
James	BKN	23
James	WDF	101
James	MER	116
James	FKN	132
James	UNN	154
James	HAR	200
James	BTH	212
James	HOP	230
James	CBL	13A
James	WRN	35A

Name	County	Page
ARMSTRONG, James B./ R.?	MER	116
Jno.	MAS	76
John	LGN	28
John	CHN	36
John	WDF	93
John	FTE	106
John	TOD	133
John	CLD	164
John	SHE	164
John, Jr./ Sr.?	WDF	100
John	CBL	13A
John	FLG	61A
John	WDF	99A
John	SCT	107A
Johnston	MAS	76
Lanty, Maj.	MER	85
Levi	SHE	175
Logan	CWL	38
M.	CHN	29
Mary	MER	85
Mason	MAD	96
Plimkart?	BBN	110
Rebecca	BRK	231
Robert	HOP	228
Robert	MTG	273
Robt.	SCT	101A
Rowley	BRN	1
Saml.	SCT	92A
Samuel	LGN	37
Samuel	CLK	67
Samuel	SHE	138A
Thomas	JEF	34
Will.	FLG	61A
William	TRG	10
William	LGN	23
William	FTE	68
William	MER	85
William	FTE	106
William	GTN	119
William	HAR	164
William	HAR	166
William	NCH	129A
Wm.	BKN	18
Wm.	CWL	38
Wm.	CWL	50
Wm. E.	MAS	65
Wm.?	CWL	41
ARMSTRONG?, Wm.	FKN	118
ARNALD, Elizebeth	WDF	96
Wiott	WDF	96
Younger	WDF	96
ARNEL?, Rebecky	MAD	122
ARNET, Joseph	HND	10A
Margret	WDF	98A
Saml.	NCH	117A
William	HND	11A
ARNET?, Rebecky	MAD	122
ARNETT, Andrew	JES	85
Burns	JES	83
David	LNC	53
Elias	HRL	102
Henry	GRN	56
James	MBG	139A
John	JES	72
Joseph	GRN	55
Leven	JES	78
Reuben	FLD	5
Stephen	FLD	5
Thomas	BTH	182
ARNETZ, Rebecca	BTH	170
ARNOLD, Aaron	CHN	38
Abs.	GRD	118A
Adam	JEF	39
Adam, Jnr.	JEF	32
Ann	FKN	152

Name	County	Page
ARNOLD, Barnet	FKN	118
Benj.	FKN	102
Bennet	BTL	317
Charles	HRD	60
Chas.	FLG	31A
David	JES	87
David	LWS	91A
Elijah	BBN	62
Elijah	BBN	114
Erbin?	BTL	317
George	HRD	74
Hannah	MBG	138
Henry	CLK	91
Humphry	GRD	92A
Isaac	BNE	2
Isaac	GRD	103A
Jacob	HRD	34
James	WDF	98
James	CLD	139
James	CBL	4A
Jane	HAR	216
Jas.	BBN	78
Jas.	PUL	40A
Jeremiah	MBG	138
Jno.	MAS	77
Jno.	FKN	130
John	LGN	40
John	HRD	56
John	BBN	114
John	GTN	126
John	SHE	163
John	BTL	317
John	CBL	7A
John	FLG	31A
John	GRD	93A
John E.	LGN	41
Joseph	MBG	138
Josiah	MBG	138
Lewis	FKN	98
Lewis	WDF	102A
Lewis H.	NCH	123A
Lewis M.	CLD	143
Lot	BTL	317
N. H.	GRN	52
Nancy	WDF	97
Patsey	FKN	152
Peter	LWS	91A
Presley	FKN	98
Reuben	MTG	277
Reubin	BTL	317
Saml.	MAS	74
Saml.	FKN	134
Samuel	BNE	2
Samuel	LGN	42
Samuel	GTN	118
Samuel	HAR	180
Sarah	BBN	94
Susannah	JEF	49
Thomas	GTN	118
Thomas	BBN	146
Thompson	FLG	32A
Thos.	BBN	62
Thos.	FKN	98
Thos.	FKN	102
Thos.	BBN	122
Weedon	LGN	41
Westley	MTG	251
Will	BBN	68
William	BNE	50
William	MBG	138
William	GRT	145
Willis	WRN	46A
Wm.	BBN	118
Wm.	GRT	149
Ziba?	SHE	114A
ARNOLDS, Samuel	BTL	317

Name	County	Page
ARNSPIGER, Christian	JES	90
Henry	JES	76
John	JES	76
Michael	JES	93
Samuel	JES	90
ARNSPIGER?, Christopher	JES	76
ARON, Joseph	LVG	11
AROWSMITH, John	GTN	135
Thomas	GTN	135
ARRASMITH, Abner	BTH	196
William	BTH	170
ARRENDEL, James	HOP	228
ARROWSMITH, Jas.	SCT	105A
John	BBN	62
Widow	BBN	64
ART, Robt.	SCT	109A
Thos.	FLG	38A
Wm.	FLG	37A
ARTEBERRY?, Sally	DVS	18A
ARTEBURN, Harrison	JEF	45
Saml.	JEF	44
Wm.	JEF	40
ARTENBURY, Richard	OHO	6A
ARTERBERRY, ---an?	DVS	12A
---el?	DVS	12A
Edward?	DVS	12A
Elisha	HRT	152
Isaiah	HRT	152
Jessee	HRT	152
Michael	HRT	152
Thomas	HRT	152
Thomas	HRT	152
ARTERBURN, Elijah	JEF	60
Jno.	JEF	60
Vincent	JEF	60
Wm.	JEF	60
ARTHER, Barnabass	WAS	27A
Wm.	WAS	25A
Wm.	WAS	26A
Wm.	WAS	26A
ARTHERTON, Jabez	NSN	204
ARTHUR, Aaron	WTY	111A
Ambrose	KNX	286
James	GNP	177A
John	KNX	306
Nicholas	GTN	121
Stephen	MTG	257
Thos., Jr.	KNX	284
Thos., Sr.	KNX	284
Zephanius	GNP	176A
ARTINBURY, David	OHO	6A
ARTMAN, Adam	GSN	127A
ARTUS, Jas.	MAS	79
Jno.	MAS	70
Mathew	MAS	73
ARUNDALE, Cader	MBG	136
ARVEN, John	MAD	146
ARVIN, Jemison	ETL	52
AS-ENE?, William	MER	114
ASBELL, John	ETL	44
John	MAD	128
Joseph	MAD	134
Ross	MAD	134
Thomas	ETL	44
William	ETL	44
Wm.	MAD	128
ASBERRY, Elijah	HAR	180
Hannah	HAR	210
Henry	HAR	180
John	CLD	154
John N./h.?	HAR	180
Thomas	HAR	204
William	CLD	161
William	HAR	182
ASBERRY, William	HAR	188
ASBRIDGE, Martin	LGN	47
ASBURRY, Thos.	SCT	93A
ASBURY, Ammey	PND	25A
Henry	FLG	36A
Joseph	GRN	58
Landman	FLG	24A
Roly	MAS	56
Roly	MAS	60
ASBY, James?/ Jane?	HAR	138
Thomas	GTN	135
ASCUA?, Isaac	OHO	5A
ASCUE, John	CLD	142
Jonathan	GRD	94A
ASCUE?, Christopher	BRN	1
ASH, Buckner	UNN	151
Chas.	HRD	76
Edwd.	HRD	76
George	GSN	127A
Henry	HRD	48
Henry	NSN	218
John	BLT	190
John	MGB	137A
Littleton	BTH	204
Mary	BLT	190
Nancy	BLT	190
Saml.	HRD	66
Sarah	MGB	137A
Wm.	HRD	18
ASHBAUGH, David	GSN	127A
Frederick	NSN	176
John	GSN	127A
ASHBEY, M. G.	MAD	178
ASHBROOK, Aaron	HAR	206
Andrew	HAR	202
Felix	HAR	206
Frederick	WRN	74A
John	BRK	231
Levi	CLK	97
Levi	BRK	231
Thomas	NCH	116A
ASHBROOKS, James	PUL	63A
ASHBURNE, Henry	LGN	44
James	LGN	46
John	CLK	72
ASHBURNS, James	BNE	2
ASHBY, -----?	DVS	6A
Abraham, Jr.?	HOP	228
Abram	SHE	171
Absalom, Sr.	HOP	228
Alexander	HOP	230
Argile	HOP	230
Beda	SHE	118A
Benjamin	SHE	176
Bounds	HOP	228
C.	JEF	27
Charlotte	SHE	156
Daniel	HOP	230
David	OHO	6A
David	SHE	114A
Enoch R.	HOP	228
Fielding	SHE	156
Hankison	SHE	173
Henry	HOP	228
Jeremiah	HOP	230
Jessee	HOP	230
John	HOP	230
John L.	HOP	228
John M.	HOP	272
Jonathan	HND	6A
Lettice	SHE	171
Nathaniel	HOP	230
Peter	HOP	230
Peter	OHO	7A
ASHBY, Robert	HOP	228
Robert	SHE	118A
Silas	SHE	171
Stephen	HOP	228
Thomas	OHO	7A
Thomas	SHE	118A
Tinson	SHE	130A
William	HOP	228
William	OHO	8A
Willis	JEF	27
Willoughby	HOP	228
ASHCRAFT, Abishar	HRD	38
Absolom	BRK	231
Amos	GRT	141
Daniel	GSN	127A
Elijah	BRK	231
Elisha	HRD	12
Ichabod	GRT	141
Jacob	HRD	48
Jacob	GRT	141
Jacob	HAR	180
James	ETL	53
James	GRT	141
Jediah	GRT	141
Jediah	GSN	127A
John	HRD	16
Nimrod	NCH	105
Uriah	HAR	190
ASHENHURST, Ralph	CLD	142
ASHER, Bartlett	JEF	45
Benjamin C.	HOP	228
Charles	MER	85
Danl.	JEF	43
Dillian, Sr.	CLY	116
Dillion, Jr.	CLY	116
James	JEF	53
James	JEF	61
John	MER	85
John, Jr.	JEF	53
John, Sr.	JEF	53
Robert	FTE	89
Robert	CLY	125
Silas/ Lilas?	HOP	230
Wm.	JEF	41
Wm.	JEF	57
Wm.	MAD	160
ASHERST?, -m.?	CWL	39
Danl.?	CWL	39
Wm. A.	CWL	39
ASHFORD, Jno. E.	FKN	72
John	WDF	102
John	ALN	130
Tho.	ALN	136
Thomas	WDF	102
Thomas M.?	WDF	101A
Westley	WDF	102
William	WDF	102
ASHIN?, William	GRT	142
ASHLEY, Dad.?	CWL	35
Hannah	LGN	35
James P.	NCH	129A
Joel	WDF	120A
John	ADR	4
John	CWL	35
John?	CWL	36
Josiah	CLK	71
Stephen	CWL	36
Tho.	ALN	128
William	LGN	4/
ASHLEY?, (See Ashby)	SHE	171
ASHLOCK, John	WRN	31A
William	HOP	228
ASHLY, Benjamain J.	MAD	124
James	BTL	317

Name	County	Page
ASHLY, Silus	BTH	212
Thomas	BTH	158
ASHMORE, Walter	HOP	230
Walter E.	BBN	122
William	BTL	317
ASHPAW?, Jacob	HAR	188
Joseph	HAR	180
ASHTON, Richard	FTE	70
ASHURST, Henry	PUL	46A
Josiah	BBN	108
Robert	HAR	170
ASHWORTH, John	HRT	152
ASKER, Dillion	CLY	111
ASKEW, George	FTE	88
ASKIN, Richd.	JEF	30
ASKIN?, William	GRT	142
ASKING, Edward	GSN	127A
ASKINS, Courtney	BRK	231
John	BRK	233
John	WAS	46A
John	GRD	121A
Josiah	WAS	45A
Peggy	GRD	121A
Thos.	BKN	18
William	BRK	233
ASKUE, William	LGN	32
ASNABACK, Jacob?	CWL	42
ASTEN, James	BRN	1
ASTON, Jink	GRN	53
ATCHER, Christopher	HRD	32
ATCHERSEN, Hamilton	FTE	100
ATCHERSON, John	FTE	99
John	FTE	99
William	FTE	101
ATCHESON, Elisabeth	HAR	160
Jno.	MAS	58
ATCHISON, George	SHE	158
Henry	FLG	58A
James	SHE	154
Jere.	FLG	43A
Kisiah	BTH	170
Polly	BTH	178
Siles	BTH	194
William	BTH	194
ATHERSON?, Absolem	ADR	4
Joshua	ADR	4
ATHERSTON, Caleb	MAS	59
ATHERTON, Henry	SHE	143A
Wm.	HRD	76
Wm.	SHE	143A
ATHEY, Robt.	BBN	106
William	CBL	8A
ATHRINGTON, Peter	HRD	16
ATHY, Elisha	JEF	34
ATKENSON?, Absolem	ADR	4
Joshua	ADR	4
ATKINS, Absolum	SCT	101A
Alexr.	SCT	124A
James	CLK	80
Jas., Senr.	SCT	102A
Jas.	SCT	115A
Jas.	SCT	131A
Joseph	ADR	4
Joseph	MER	85
Nathanl.	BBN	114
Robt.	SCT	127A
Rolin	ADR	4
Thomas B.	NCH	116A
Will	ADR	4
Will.	SCT	131A
Will.	SCT	138A
ATKINSON, Alexander	JEF	66
ATKINSON, Amos	CHN	30A
Edward	BNE	2
Ellis	MAD	140
Frederick	BRN	1
George	HND	3
John	CWL	43
John	BTH	148
John E.	GRN	56
Johnson	BRN	1
Josiah	WAS	80A
Jubel	MAD	154
Maryann	BTH	156
Mathew	HND	12
Pleasant	MAD	144
Sherwood W.	LGN	25
Spencer	GRN	56
Wm.	MAD	136
ATLEE?, Joseph	MTG	281
ATRMAN, Jacob	GSN	127A
ATTA?, Joseph	MTG	281
ATTAWAY, J.	TOD	132A
ATTERBERRY, Charles	GSN	127A
Elijah	BRN	1
Happy	GSN	127A
Melchesideck	GSN	127A
Michael	GSN	127A
Thomas	BRN	1
ATTERBURY, Solomon	GSN	127A
ATTICK?, Abraham	MBG	139
ATTISON, Andrew	JES	72
ATTWOOD, Jesse	HRD	26
John	HRD	46
ATWELL, Hugh	BKN	9
John	GRN	61
Joseph	NSN	176
Richd.	HRT	152
ATWOOD, George	HRD	36
James	ALN	134
James	ALN	134
James	WDF	121A
Jno.	ALN	134
R. B.	GRN	51
Wm.	ADR	4
AUBERRY, Craven	HRD	58
P. C.	HRY	220
AUBRY, John	HRD	56
AUD, Ambrose	NSN	213
Anna	BLT	194
James	BRK	233
Philip	NSN	224
Robt. C.	ALN	110
Thomas	NSN	179
AUD?, Jessee	ALN	110
AUGUSTUS, David	JEF	39
Jas.	JEF	36
John	JEF	40
Springer	JEF	42
AULGER, Jeremiah	PUL	63A
AULICH, Charles	PND	21A
AULLE?, Henery	ADR	4
AULT, Federick	BNE	2
AUSBERN, Edwd.	WAS	71A
Nicolass	WAS	56A
Walter	WAS	71A
Wm.	WAS	64A
AUSBURN, Hiram	FLD	40
Salley	FLD	17
AUSTIN-?, B.	GRD	83A
AUSTIN, Alexander	OHO	11A
Brooks	OHO	3A
Charles	MNR	199
David	JEF	32
Elizath.	SCT	104A
Frances	OHO	11A
George	CHN	33
AUSTIN, James	WAS	64A
Jas.	MAS	71
Jeremiah	HRD	56
Jno. B.	HAR	136
John	JEF	57
John	MNR	209
John, Jr.	JEF	57
John	OHO	4A
John	GRD	117A
Molly	UNN	153
Nat	GRD	99A
Obadiah	BBN	136
Pleasant	CLD	156
Thomas	GRD	110A
Warrack	OHO	4A
Will	MAS	79
Wm.	JEF	34
Wm.	JEF	57
Zachariah	OHO	3A
AUSTIND, Jonas	GRD	102B
AUSTINS, Benjamin	MER	85
AUTERY, John	OHO	8A
AUTHER?, David	LWS	86A
AUTIBEN?, Amos	CLK	90
AUTROB--?, John	NCH	109A
AUTTE?, Jno.	HRY	253
AUXER, Daniel	FLD	29
John	FLD	36
Nathaniel	FLD	23
Samuel	FLD	29
AUXTAN, Robert	OHO	10A
AVAIRS, Asa	CWL	50
AVERA, Jacob	SPN	14A
AVERALL, Jacob	FLD	47
AVERALL?, John	HRD	26
AVERY, John	WAS	25A
John	WAS	85A
William	GRN	63
Zacheriah	BRK	231
AVET, Richard	BRK	231
AVEY, John	CWL	46
AVIT, Andrew	BRK	231
AVUS?, Mary	NSN	191
AWBERRY, Henry	FTE	84
AWE?, Michl.	CWL	50
AWKARD?, William	CBL	17A
AXTON, Balis	OHO	7A
Henry C.	OHO	7A
Isom	OHO	7A
Philip	OHO	7A
William	BRK	231
AYDLETT, John	PND	16A
AYERS, John	SHE	160
Leander	HAR	186
Rilike?	HAR	136
Samuel	BBN	62
Thos.	BBN	78
Wm.	BBN	78
AYLER, Banjamin	BNE	2
Henry	BNE	2
Michael	BNE	2
William	BNE	2
AYRE, George	FTE	79
AYRES, Agga	HRY	254
Benjamin	FTE	66
Daniel C.	GTN	131
Edmund	LGN	38
James	WDF	117A
Lewis	GTN	131
Peter	CBL	21A
Samuel	FTE	57
Walter	WDF	110A
AYREZ, Elias	JEF	19
AYTON, Henery	ADR	4
B----?, Charles	GTN	119

B----?, William CHN 27A
B---ELL?, David HRY 204
B---N?, Robert NSN 204
B---ON?, Henry ALN 96
B--ILER?, Jacob ALN 140
B--SSEY?, Will. SCT 117A
BABB, Arthur HOP 234
  Wiley LVG 12
BABBS, Wm. FLG 57A
BABCOCK, Benjamin CBL 9A
  William HAR 154
BABER, George MER 87
  Isaac JEF 45
  John CLK 87
  Jonathan CLK 91
  Joseph WAS 31A
  Obediah CLK 87
  Robert PUL 67A
  Stanley CLK 91
BACCHUS, Ezra BLT 184
BACH, Henry JES 86
BACK, Charles WYN 96A
  Charles WYN 102A
  Elizabeth HRL 104
  Enoch GRD 107A
  Henry HRL 104
  Jacob WYN 81A
  James GRD 107A
  Jo. GRD 107A
  John HRL 104
  John, Sr. WYN 94A
  John WYN 84A
BACKER?, Jerotice? MTG 247
BACON, Burwell FTE 108
  Edmond WRN 48A
  Jno. G. MAS 57
  John CBL 7A
  John C. OWN 107
  Lankston FKN 64
  Lyddall FKN 104
  Mary FKN 114
BACUM, James GNP 178A
  James GNP 179A
BACY, Elijah SHE 133A
  Richard SHE 132A
BADDEN, Stephen -.? WAS 55A
BADDERS/ BADDEN?, Moses CBL 10A
BADDERS, Moses BBN 122
BADDUS, Finnes MTG 279
BADGER-?, David CBL 7A
BADGER, David MTG 283
  John H. MER 86
  Joshua MER 86
BADLY, Amy MER 116
BADMAN, William CLY 116
BADY?, Benjamin ALN 100
  Thomas GNP 171A
BAGBY, Daniel BRN 4
  Frederick LGN 29
  Jas. MAS 71
  John BRN 2
  John SCT 123A
  Landon BRN 2
  Nathaniel MTG 269
  Price LGN 29
  Robert LWS 89A
  Sylvanus M. BRN 2
  William LWS 89A
BAGGESS?, Robt. BNE 8
BAGLE, Wm. MAS 70
BAGLEY?, Carr B. FLG 35A
BAGS?, Jno. JEF 66
BAGSBEY, Bennet ALN 140
  Charles CBL 15A
BAGSBEY, Jessee CBL 10A
  Robert CBL 10A
  William CBL 10A
BAGWELL, Archabald LGN 39
  Jany? JES 78
  John SCT 108A
  John SHE 136A
BAIL, Andrew BNE 46
BAILEIE, Samuel BKN 26
BAILER, Jno. FKN 58
BAILEY, Abner FKN 82
  Abram, Jr. FKN 120
  Abram, Sr. FKN 120
  Andrew HRL 102
  Ann LNC 5
  Augustine HAR 160
  Benj. FKN 104
  Benjamin FLD 7
  Benjamin HAR 188
  Callum BRN 5
  Carlton SCT 98A
  Carob LNC 2
  Charles C. HRD 32
  Daniel LGN 39
  David SHE 176
  Delila LNC 31
  Dennett D. MBG 135
  Doct.? MAS 74
  Edward LNC 5
  Elexious SHE 158
  Elijah LNC 53
  Elisha ADR 6
  Elizabeth SHE 167
  Gabriel LGN 29
  Geo. W. SCT 117A
  George LGN 35
  Harmon LGN 38
  James LNC 33
  James HOP 232
  Jane LGN 31
  Jas. MAS 66
  Jesse FKN 76
  Jno. MAS 73
  John FLD 7
  John HRD 14
  John FTE 87
  John HRL 102
  John HRL 102
  John HRL 102
  John MNR 191
  John SCT 98A
  John R. FTE 104
  Joseph FLD 7
  Joseph HRD 56
  Joshua LWS 89A
  Julius BRN 3
  Lemuel FLD 5
  Margar. LNC 33
  Margaret LGN 31
  Martin, Sr. MNR 193
  Nimrod HRL 102
  Prior FLD 7
  Richard BRN 2
  Richard R. HOP 236
  Robert SHE 114A
  Samuel BRN 3
  Shelar FKN 80
  Simon SHE 174
  Stephen GTN 132
  Tho. MAS 74
  Thomas LNC 31
  Thomas CLD 137
  Thos. SHE 123A
  Thos. SCT 136A
  Thos. T. ADR 8
  Thos.? BRK 241
BAILEY, W. W. ADR 8
  Wiley WRN 33A
  Will LNC 31
  William HRL 102
  William SHE 174
  Wm. FKN 160
  Wm. H. BRN 4
  Wm. L. ADR 6
  Wm. Wm.? ADR 8
BAILIS?, William UNN 153
BAILISS, Jno. LVG 2
BAILY, Bowden MAS 72
  David JES 87
  Geo. MAS 62
  Henry MAS 62
  Isaac HRY 178
  Jessee BTH 182
  John BBN 120
  John BTH 184
  John, Jr. BTH 180
  Nancy BTH 212
  Thos. MAD 164
  Warran BTH 198
  William BBN 108
  William NSN 219
  Wm. ADR 8
  Wm. S. CWL 46
BAILYE, King MAD 138
BAIN, Britton SPN 18A
  George WDF 121A
  Johnson HRY 204
  Lewis HRY 204
  Lindsey HRY 204
  Peter MNR 195
BAINBRIDGE, Darius LGN 40
  Edwd. T. JEF 23
  John W. WAS 78A
  Peter BRN 33
BAINE, George SHE 141A
  James SHE 141A
  Wm. SHE 141A
BAINN?, Sarah JEF 22
BAINSTER?, John NCH 113A
BAINURN?, James PND 22A
BAIRD, -----? DVS 8A
  Andrew BRN 2
  Andrew HAR 146
  Bazillia LGN 33
  David LGN 35
  David MAS 61
  David ALN 92
  James HRD 74
  James HAR 146
  James LWS 96A
  James SHE 135A
  John HRD 80
  John ALN 92
  John SHE 126A
  John GSN 129A
  John MBG 136A
  John SHE 136A
  Robt. BRK 243
  Saml. LNC 11
  Taylor HRD 72
  Thos. SHE 137A
  William BRN 2
  William LNC 11
  Wm. GSN 129A
BAITMAN, Eliza. KNX 314
  Malinda KNX 304
BAITY, Mary BBN 82
BAKER, -----? DVS 11A
  Abner CLY 111
  Abraham BKN 6
  Abraham WDF 117A
  Abram GRD 94A

Name	County	Page
BAKER, Alex?	BBN	96
Andrew	OWN	101
Andrew	MAD	128
Andw.	PUL	49A
Aron, Jun.	BKN	9
Aron, Sr.	BKN	22
Baily	CWL	37
Bazel	MAD	142
Bazel, Sr.	MAD	142
Bazle	MAD	134
Beckworth	FKN	120
Beckworth	FKN	160
Benjamin	BBN	126
Benjamin	UNN	153
Blake	CWL	33
Bowling	CLY	124
Bowling, Sr.	CLY	130
Bradock	MAD	132
Brice	KNX	294
Charles	JEF	46
Charles	MAD	92
Charles	CLY	117
Claibourne	MAD	170
Cricy	MAD	170
Cuthbert	CLK	71
Daniel	CWL	58
David	MAD	98
David	FTE	101
David	CBL	18A
David	FLG	36A
Dudly	JES	80
Edward	WYN	80A
Edward	WYN	99A
Elias	MAD	124
Elias	HAR	184
Elizabeth	CBL	16A
Elizabeth	FLG	78A
Esquier	WAS	47A
Francis	FLG	33A
Fransis B.	TRG	8
Freeman	CWL	33
Geo.	JEF	46
George	CLY	116
George W.	ETL	54
Green	GRD	111A
Hennery	CSY	222
Henry	HRY	182
Henry	WAS	21A
Humphrey	GNP	172A
Indi---?	GSN	131
Isaac	NSN	189
Isaac	HRY	267
Isaac	NCH	125A
Jacob	NCH	125A
Jacob S.	MBG	139A
Jahu	PUL	54A
James	FLD	14
James	CWL	50
James	CWL	50
James	CWL	58
James	GTN	118
James	CLY	130
James	MAD	140
James	CLD	145
James	HOP	232
James, Jr.	HOP	234
James	CBL	17A
James	WYN	85A
James	GRD	105A
James	NCH	124A
Jehue	FTE	65
Jesse	GTN	120
Jessee	BKN	9
Jno.	MAS	57
Jno.	MAS	67
Jno.	FKN	96
BAKER, Jno.	HRY	263
Job.	CHN	42A
Joel	MAD	134
John	CWL	36
John	FTE	67
John	WDF	97
John	CLY	111
John	GTN	117
John	CLY	128
John	CLY	130
John	CLD	143
John	CLD	145
John	HAR	194
John	CSY	212
John	KNX	292
John, Jr.	CBL	19A
John	CBL	17A
John	WAS	25A
John	WRN	39A
John	RCK	80A
John	RCK	80A
John	WYN	94A
John	GRD	111A
John	NCH	112A
John	NCH	126A
John	SHE	142A
John C.	CLY	112
John D.	CLY	125
John H.	BRN	2
Jonathan	GTN	117
Jonathan	WRN	43A
Joseph	JEF	21
Joseph	GTN	117
Joseph	MTG	285
Joseph	KNX	294
Joseph	WRN	53A
Joseph	WYN	88A
Joseph	GRD	101A
Joseph	NCH	125A
Josias	BRN	2
Julyather	GRD	111A
Larkin	PUL	38A
Laurence	CHN	34
Margret	FLG	36A
Martin	MER	88
Martin	BBN	126
Martin	GRD	108A
Mary	GTN	120
Mary	MAD	164
Mary	HOP	230
Mary	WDF	98A
Mary	NCH	126A
Matthew	CBL	16A
Michael	MAD	150
Miles	HOP	232
Moses	BNE	8
Moses	MTG	259
Moses, Jr.	GTN	117
Moses, Jr.	GTN	131
Moses, Sr.	GTN	126
Nancy	JES	80
Nicholas	WDF	97
Nicholas	CBL	18A
Obed	CLD	143
Peter	JES	92
Peter	HAR	194
Polly	PUL	50A
Reason	MAD	132
Reason	MAD	142
Reuben	FKN	146
Richard	HOP	234
Robert	TRG	10
Robert	LGN	39
Robert	CLY	111
Robt.	HRY	250
Salley	MAD	106
BAKER, Sally L. B.	LGN	24
Saml.	CBL	17A
Samuel	LGN	39
Samuel	CLD	147
Sarah	CLD	145
Seth	CWL	33
Thomas	LVG	15
Thomas	LNC	33
Thomas	BBN	130
Thomas	CLD	147
Thomas	HND	8A
Thomas	NCH	125A
Thos.	JEF	65
Urich	CWL	35
Vach?	MAD	168
Wamsly	MAD	142
Wamsly	MAD	174
Will.	KNX	294
William	LGN	39
William	FTE	79
William	CLY	116
William	CLD	145
William	LWS	98A
William	WYN	98A
William	WTY	122A
William	NCH	126A
Wm.	HRD	52
Wm.	BBN	90
Wm.	BBN	132
Wm.	BBN	138
Wm.	WAS	20A
Wm.	PND	22A
Wm.	PUL	50A
Wm.	FLG	56A
Zebedee	MAD	106
BAKER?, Abraham	NCH	119A
Jos.	TOD	125
BAKETT?, ---se?	NCH	126A
BAKEWELL, Thos.	JEF	27
BAKEY, Rodolphus	BLT	192
BAKLEY, William	FTE	65
BAL-?, Samuel	HOP	232
BALAIN, James	NSN	217
BALANCE, Henry R.	LGN	47
Polly, Mrs.	CLK	95
Willis	MER	117
BALCHER, Elizabeth	CLD	146
John	CLD	141
Peter	CLD	149
BALDEN, Jabez	HND	3
BALDIN, Amos	MER	89
BALDING, Sary	FKN	92
BALDOCK, Jas.	SCT	97A
Leucy	CSY	222
Levy	LNC	77
Richard	CSY	228
BALDOCK?, William	CSY	208
BALDWIN, Caleb	GTN	130
Daniel	BNE	6
Edward	HOP	232
Garrison	MAS	68
Hiram	HOP	232
Ira	SCT	94A
Ishman/ Isham?	HOP	234
James	MER	89
Jeremiah	FTE	89
Jerry	SCT	125A
Jno.	MAS	72
John	SCT	102A
Kinsey	NSN	205
Leonard	CHN	46
Luke	HND	10A
Moses	FTE	89
Polly	PUL	43A
Saml.	MAS	56
Samuel	NSN	216

BALDWIN, Thomas NSN 207
Thomas NSN 219
William MTG 259
BALEE, Joel SHE 137A
Peter SHE 136A
BALEE?, A? SHE 136A
BALES, Eden CLY 130
Hocking CLY 132
James S. TRG 3A
John GRN 72
John CLY 116
Lila? ADR 8
Lilie? ADR 8
Russel GTN 133
BALES?, Debora FTE 63
Jacob, Jr. GRN 78
BALEY, Benjn. GRN 80
Benjn. ALN 136
Callvin H. MER 88
Carr HRL 102
David GRN 79
David WRN 34A
Ezekial WTY 124A
Golven? HRL 102
Hezekiah WAS 27A
John CLY 118
Lewes GRD 111A
Robert GRN 79
Ruben GRN 62
Stephin WAS 24A
Vinsent ADR 8
BALEY?, John B. LGN 43
BALIE, John R. TRG 5
BALINGER, Frances FTE 58
Henry GRD 108A
BALINTINE, Willis B. CWL 36
BALIS, Charles HAR 186
Richard HAR 204
BALIS?, Jacob, Jr. GRN 78
BALL, --? MAS 58
Aaron MAS 65
Allin ADR 10
Benjamin BNE 4
Bennet MER 87
Bennett HRL 102
Catharine LWS 92A
Daniel LNC 45
Danl. O. LNC 37
Edmund WDF 95A
Edward P. CBL 21A
Humphrey UNN 148
James HRL 102
James GTN 118
James NSN 189
James GRD 87A
Jane GTN 129
Jas. GRD 95A
Jessy HRL 102
John FTE 92
John MAD 102
John BRK 239
John H. CWL 46
Lettecy? MNR 213
Lewis LNC 41
Mary LNC 35
Moses FLD 34
Moses HRL 102
Munford LNC 35
Polly GRD 112A
Richard GRD 101A
Robert GRN 70
Rubin GRN 64
Saml. FLG 23A
Samuel PUL 60A
Secretary FTE 109
BALL, Vallentine CBL 10A
William FTE 104
William GTN 131
William CBL 10A
William P. LWS 90A
Willm. LNC 29
BALL?, Jno. ADR 8
BALLA, Mary BTH 190
BALLAD, Margaret, Mrs. WYN 102A
BALLANCE, Ahaz LGN 44
BALLANGER, John SCT 100A
BALLARD, A. E. FLG 79A
Benjamin LGN 35
Benjn. SCT 119A
Bentley HRD 26
Beverley OWN 100
Blann SHE 142A
Charles CLD 141
Curtis HAR 150
David MAD 104
Edward MAD 114
Elza? CLK 65
Evan CBL 11A
Geo. SCT 125A
George MAD 172
Henry MAD 102
Hiram FTE 107
James SHE 159
James NSN 187
James MTG 251
James SHE 126A
James B. MAD 134
Jesse SHE 158
John JEF 26
John CLK 90
John NSN 188
John WYN 104A
John P. MAD 134
Johnson WDF 107A
Joseph WYN 102A
Larken MAD 100
Lewis LGN 32
Mary NSN 188
Nicholas MAD 104
Percevell? WRN 51A
Philip CLK 80
Tho. M. HRY 222
William CLK 90
William WYN 102A
BALLENGER, Edward BRN 2
Jane LNC 81
John MAD 132
Wm. MAS 77
BALLEW, Absalom CLD 154
Alfred CLD 154
Cleveland CLD 154
William CLD 154
BALLINGALL, David NCH 107A
BALLINGER, Achl. GRD 104A
Danl. ADR 8
Edward NCH 119A
Elizabeth ADR 8
James F. KNX 304
Jeremiah BKN 13
Jessee CBL 13A
John ADR 6
John, Sr. CBL 13A
John CBL 14A
Richd. KNX 278
Thos. HRD 64
William WTY 115A
William NCH 126A
Willis MAS 79
BALOR?, John NSN 195
BALSICK?, John E. GRD 109A
BALSLEY, George B. BNE 4
BALT?, Jno. ADR 8
BALWIN, Jas. MAS 80
BAMARD, Pleasant SPN 6A
Zadoc SPN 6A
BAMSTER?, John NCH 113A
BANAMOND?, John BNE 2
BANDLE, William WYN 99A
BANDURANT, Joseph BTH 202
BANDY, (See Bundy) BRK
George BRK 239
Thos. C. BRK 235
Wm. BRK 239
BANE, George LWS 92A
John CWL 55
Richard LWS 92A
BANER, Moses MAS 72
BANES, John MAD 108
Samuel MAD 162
BANETT, Joseph, Sr. MAD 128
BANFIELD?, Thomas GNP 169A
BANISTER, --gh? CWL 43
E. CWL 34
Elizebeth WAS 50A
John, Sr. NCH 109A
William FLD 21
BANK, Vandiver ADR 3
BANK?, Ephraim M. HOP 236
John MER 116
BANKS, Cuth. MTG 295
D. C. JEF 27
Harper GRD 95A
Jarrod FKN 130
John JEF 39
John GRD 101A
Lynn GRD 90A
Rivers LGN 30
Sally FKN 132
Samuel SHE 161
William FLD 3
Williams GRD 112A
BANMAN, ---.? CWL 42
BANMORE?, John CBL 7A
BANNEL, Jonathan MER 88
BANNESTER, Enoch CBL 9A
BANNING, Benoni CLD 155
Clark CLD 152
Jeremiah CLD 155
Thomas W. CLD 155
BANNION?, James O.? CLD 138
William O.? CLD 140
BANNISTER, Augustus CBL 8A
Daniel CBL 9A
BANNON, Daniel MAD 110
BANS, William, Esq. WYN 88A
Yancy LVG 3
BANTA, Albert HRY 257
Andrew BBN 70
Dan. HRY 261
Henry BBN 70
Henry, Senr. BBN 72
Henry P. HRY 257
Jno. HRY 262
Pet. HRY 262
Pet., Jr. HRY 257
Pet. A. HRY 261
Pet. W. HRY 262
Peter, Sr. HRY 255
BANTHUM, Sam. MAS 55
BANTON, George GRD 88A
Henry GRD 92A
John LNC 67

Name	County	Page
BANTON, John	FLG	29A
Squire	MER	115
William	FTE	58
BANTON?, James	NCH	112A
William	NCH	112A
BANTY, Henry	MAD	114
BAR, William	OWN	99
BARBEE/ BARBER?, Elias	GRN	60
BARBEE, Daniel	MER	116
Dr.	BBN	146
Elijah	BBN	68
Ire?	UNN	152
Jesse	BBN	70
Jessee	FTE	86
Joseph	FTE	66
Nathl.	SCT	122A
Sameth	BLT	186
BARBER, Edward	BRN	5
Edward	BTH	194
Edwd.	MAS	66
Ezekiel	MER	87
John	KNX	304
Joshua, Col.	MER	87
Lander	BBN	124
Moses	MAD	94
Thomas	MTG	279
BARBIE, James	JEF	44
BARBOUR, Ambrose	HND	3
Ambrous	WAS	21A
Chas. V.	JEF	28
Elizbeth	HND	9A
James	MER	116
John	PUL	61A
Phill	WAS	78A
Phillip C. S.	JEF	64
Richd.	JEF	52
Robert	PUL	67A
Samuel	PUL	61A
Tho. T.	JEF	57
Thos.	JEF	50
William T.	SHE	154
Wm.	WAS	21A
BARBY, John	SHE	169
Robert	BTH	154
BARBY?, Francis	SHE	151
BARCLAY, Eli	WRN	35A
Geo.	PUL	48A
Geo. W	JEF	19
Joshua G.	JEF	37
Samuel	WRN	46A
BARD, Ebinezer	NSN	179
James	NSN	193
Stephen	NSN	185
Stephen	NSN	217
BARD?, William	NSN	178
BARDAY, James	BBN	122
William	BLT	190
BARDEN, Levi	HND	3
Richd.	JEF	24
BAREFIELD, Thomas	MBG	139
BAREMORE?, John	BNE	2
BARES, Balaam	TRG	11
BARET?, Samuel	GRN	79
BARETT?, Fisher	GRN	73
BARFIELD, Reding	HOP	234
BARGER, Abraham	CLY	126
Geo.	BRK	241
George	ADR	8
Jno.	ADR	8
John	ADR	14
John	CLY	119
John	BRK	239
John, Sr.	BRK	241
Josiah	ADR	6
BARGO, Andrew	GTN	132
BARGO, John	GTN	129
BARHAM, Daniel	LGN	34
James	LGN	43
James F.	LGN	47
William	LGN	42
BARICKMAN, Jonathan	JEF	64
BARINSCRAFT, Thos.	BBN	140
BARKER, Aaron	NSN	200
Ann	FTE	81
Annanias	LGN	42
Brooky	BLT	176
Chas.	TOD	127
Cornelius	LGN	27
Danl.	FTE	70
Elias	ETL	47
George	SCT	114A
Henry	MER	86
Henry	LWS	99A
James	ETL	53
James R.	WRN	73A
Jane	FTE	109
Jesse	OWN	105
Jno.	JEF	44
John	LGN	32
John	WAS	65A
John	PUL	66A
John H.	PND	21A
John N.	TOD	126A
Joseph	BKN	13
Joseph	FTE	63
Joseph	FTE	81
Leonard	FTE	68
Letty	FTE	112
Perry	LGN	42
Samuel	DVS	16A
Silas	BTH	186
Stephen	ETL	53
Stephen A.	FLG	56A
Thomas	BBN	104
Thomas	UNN	147
Thos.	JEF	55
Thos.	BBN	132
Thos.	SHE	132A
William	LGN	30
William	LGN	43
William	ETL	53
William	NSN	200
Wm.	JEF	31
Wm.	ALN	108
Wm.	BBN	136
Wm.	HRY	243
Wm. C.	JEF	20
BARKER?, Jerotice?	MTG	247
BARKLEY, James	BRK	237
James	LWS	96A
Mathew	SCT	132A
Robt.	SCT	132A
Thomas	MNR	201
Thos. S.	SCT	137A
William	CLK	69
William	LWS	96A
BARKLOW, Benjamin	GNP	175A
Ruth	GNP	170A
BARKLY, Lazerus	BTH	168
Robert	BTH	168
BARKS, Charles	WAS	43A
Floyd	MER	88
BARKSDALE, D.	TOD	131
BARKSHIAR, Jeremiah	GTN	127
BARKSHIRE, Dickey	GRT	139
Joel	BNE	6
Johnse?	HAR	132
Mary	HAR	186
Wm.	BNE	6
BARKSHORE, John	BNE	4
BARKWELL, Joseph	BNE	4
BARLEE, John	GRN	74
BARLET, Henry	SCT	119A
BARLEY?, Francis	SHE	151
BARLIS?, William	UNN	153
BARLOW, Aaron	BNE	6
Ambrose	MNR	199
Christopher	HRD	50
Daniel	BNE	6
Eliphalet	HAR	184
Enoch	SCT	139A
Jacob	WAS	49A
Jacob M.	WAS	76A
James	MNR	215
James (Free Man)	BBN	128
Jas.	LVG	4
Jesse	HAR	216
Jno.	PUL	49A
John, Jr.	NCH	110A
John, Sr.	NCH	111A
John	WAS	76A
Joseph	BNE	6
Joshua	BRN	3
Joshua	HAR	182
Julius	NSN	199
Lewis	LVG	6
Rebecca	BNE	6
Robert T.	BRN	2
Thom.	CWL	50
Thomas	HAR	154
Thomas	NCH	108A
Thos.	BBN	92
Thos.	SCT	101A
Wilbert	BRK	235
William	NCH	123A
BARNABY, Geo.	FLG	59A
BARNARD, -----?	CWL	44
Charles	ADR	14
George	HND	3
Ignatious	OHO	9A
John	MTG	269
John, Jr.	MTG	277
John	SPN	25A
Jonathan	MTG	269
Peter	ADR	14
Silas	OHO	9A
William	MTG	281
Wm.	OHO	9A
BARNATT, John H.	CSY	220
BARNER, Francis	LGN	35
John	LGN	24
Joshua	SPN	18A
William	LGN	24
Willie I./ J.?	LGN	23
BARNES, Aaron	FTE	87
Ann	FLG	35A
Beal	CLK	67
Brinsley	FTE	104
Daniel	BBN	120
Davd.	PUL	47A
David?	CWL	32
Edward	ETL	52
Elias	MAD	182
Elijah	FTE	88
Elijah	NSN	181
Elijah, Sr?	PUL	43A
Elisha	LVG	8
Enoch	PUL	40A
Ephraim	FLG	68A
George	BLT	172
George	NSN	175
James	ETL	52
James	HAR	146
James	TRG	6A
Jane	HAR	156

BARNES, Jas. LVG 9
Jas./ Jos.? C. GRD 116A
Jno. HAR 146
Jno. PUL 43A
Jno. W. HAR 146
John MAD 114
John HAR 182
John OHO 4A
John TRG 6A
John H. ETL 37
Jos. FLG 37A
Joseph OHO 3A
Joshua FLG 41A
Matthew WTY 117A
Moses FTE 102
Nancy ETL 39
Nathan MAD 156
Newcomb LVG 5
Nimrod ADR 8
Noble BTH 178
Numan FKN 144
Oliver HAR 152
Patsy? GSN 131
Philip BTH 204
Richard WDF 124A
Richd. JEF 21
Richd.? CWL 46
Robert CLK 68
Robert (Overseer) CLK 101
Robt. PUL 49A
Robt. FLG 57A
Roston WDF 115A
Rueben TRG 6
Samuel NSN 182
Sherwood LVG 6
Soloman TRG 6A
Soloman TRG 6A
Stephen? CWL 32
Thomas LVG 15
Thomas FTE 104
Thomas BTL 317
Thos. GSN 129A
William TRG 4
William CHN 30
William LGN 43
William CLK 78
William CBL 3A
Wm. ADR 8
Wm. FKN 142
Wm. PUL 36A
Wm. TOD 131A
BARNES?, Alfr--? CLK 106
Neriah, Jr. FLG 33A
BARNET, Abner TOD 128A
Elijah CLY 132
James ADR 14
Jno. G. HRY 249
Robert CHN 36
Thos. CHN 33
Wm. CHN 33
BARNET?, Wm. CHN 45
BARNETT, -----? CWL 42
---man? DVS 13A
Abner MTG 275
Absalom MNR 215
Alex BBN 60
Alexander MAD 136
Alexander, Jr. MAD 164
Alexander OHO 3A
Alexander M. MAD 130
Ambrose NCH 111A
Andrew GRN 67
Ann LNC 5
Benjamin BBN 120
Cathrine HND 7
BARNETT, Daniel JES 93
David NSN 200
Edward LNC 19
Elizabeth LGN 33
Enoch D. SPN 16A
Geoe. BBN 82
George MTG 235
George NCH 112A
Gilbert FLD 20
Henry ETL 42
Jacob OHO 11A
James LGN 33
James LGN 35
James CWL 50
James GRN 68
James JES 72
James MAD 96
James HRL 102
James BBN 128
James HAR 166
James SHE 168
James HAR 192
James WRN 69A
James NCH 120A
Jane MAD 126
Jane OHO 5A
Jason MTG 273
Jeremiah ETL 51
Jesse LGN 32
Jno. CWL 50
John CWL 33
John LGN 44
John MNR 215
John, Jr. NCH 116A
John HND 10A
John NCH 110A
John NCH 111A
John NCH 116A
Joseph HND 10
Joseph FTE 69
Joseph, Junr. OHO 5A
Joseph OHO 3A
Lewis ETL 49
Mary P. MTG 275
Moses HAR 188
Nancy WRN 60A
Nathan ADR 14
Nathaniel FLD 31
Newel? WYN 82A
Nimrod SCT 114A
Pall? PND 26A
Paul PND 29A
Peter HAR 166
Phelix OHO 11A
Richard HAR 164
Robert LNC 17
Robert OHO 4A
Ruth CWL 50
Salley FLD 36
Scuyler LNC 27
Scuyler LNC 65
Spencer NCH 128A
Tho. BBN 92
Thomas WRN 65A
Thomas WRN 73A
W. C. LNC 61
Will MAS 72
William BRN 5
William LGN 37
William GRN 68
William HRT 153
William WRN 65A
William NCH 107A
William NCH 116A
Willm. LNC 31
Wm. JEF 53
BARNETT, Wm. MAD 124
Wm. B. CWL 50
BARNETT?, Henry WRN 49A
James MTG 299
BARNETTE, Susanna MNR 215
BARNEY, Harriott HRD 82
James MER 87
John GNP 175A
Thomas GNP 170A
BARNHAM, John WRN 68A
BARNHART, John ALN 96
BARNHILL, Cleamency SCT 98A
James HRY 192
Jas. SCT 98A
Joseph HRY 192
Robert SHE 156
Robt. SCT 98A
Saml. SCT 98A
Saml. SCT 123A
William HRY 192
BARNHOUSE, William WRN 40A
BARNIT, William GRD 120A
BARNS, Adam PUL 45A
Amos PUL 56A
Archibald HRD 74
Bengamon GTN 129
Charles WYN 91A
Charles L. WDF 98
Daniel BRK 241
Elijah PUL 44A
Elijah PUL 46A
Frances, Jr. GTN 128
Francis, Sr. GTN 128
Henrietta BTH 210
Henry OHO 5A
James MAD 108
James WYN 100A
James L. MER 89
Jno. HRY 266
John MER 87
John WDF 103
John BTH 212
Joseph MER 89
Joshuay WAS 61A
Josiah WYN 88A
Nichodemus WYN 82A
Phillemon BTH 208
Reuben FKN 158
Richd. RCK 77A
Sam. HRY 264
Samuel SPN 11A
Shadrach GTN 129
Shadrach GTN 129
Thos. HRY 262
Weaver OHO 4A
William BTH 212
Zachariah MER 89
BARNS?, Stephen ALN 96
BARNSIDES, Robert MAD 130
BARNY, Jas. CHN 42
BARON?, Elisabeth FKN 104
BARR, George JES 84
Henry FLD 19
James B. CLK 106
John JES 82
John SHE 155
John HRY 222
Mary JEF 63
Richard WRN 60A
Robert FTE 89
Robert NCH 124A
Robt. BKN 23
Silas SPN 7A
Thomas FTE 85
Thomas FTE 86

Name	County	Page
BARR, Thomas T.	FTE	62
William	MNR	197
BARR?, Thos. C.	CLK	104
BARRATT, Richd.	OHO	11A
BARRELL, Christopher	JEF	24
BARREN, Josiah	GSN	129A
Wm.	ADR	60
BARRET, Isom	CLY	121
Jesse	CLY	112
John	GRN	52
Murrel	CLY	117
Peggy	BRK	227
Robt.	GRN	54
William	CLD	138
William	CLD	166
BARRET?, Wm.	CHN	45
BARRETE, Will	HRY	232
BARRETT, Daniel	GTN	128
Elijah	LWS	87A
Elizabeth	OHO	4A
Francis	CLD	148
James	WYN	82A
James W.	GRN	79
Joseph	HAR	168
Joshua	OHO	11A
Peter	HAR	200
Squire M.	WRN	51A
Thomas	CLD	167
William	OHO	8A
BARRICK, Russall	WRN	56A
BARRIGER, William	SHE	167
BARRIS, Pleasant	SHE	139A
BARRMORE?, John	CBL	7A
BARRON, Aaron	PUL	65A
Augustine	UNN	147
Green	CHN	43
Jno.	PUL	48A
Jno.	PUL	48A
John	HRD	16
William, Senr.	PUL	65A
BARROW, Augustin	MTG	285
Daniel, Sen.	WYN	87A
Daniel	WYN	87A
David	WYN	87A
Hinchen G.	CLK	82
James	LGN	29
James	PUL	59A
Jesse	PUL	59A
Judith	MTG	285
Sarah	MTG	253
William	UNN	154
William	MTG	231
William	PUL	58A
BARRUTT, Saml.	CWL	50
BARRY, James T.	BTH	174
Richd.	RCK	75A
Rosey	CHN	40
William	GTN	122
William T.	FTE	62
BARRY?, William T.	FTE	95
BARSSOE?, James	ADC	68
BART?, John	GRD	94A
BARTAN, Dabbey	CSY	208
John	CSY	208
BARTEE, Payton	GRD	102B
BARTELOW, Abm.	JEF	46
BARTEN, Clark	GSN	128A
BARTHE, Andrew	MAD	178
BARTIN, John	CLY	124
Valentine	BNE	6
BARTLET, David	FTE	96
Ebenezer	FLG	38A
Edmund	CLD	155
Elijah	HRT	153
Elijah	HRT	155
BARTLET, Elizabeth	DVS	16A
John	JES	81
John, Jr.	MAD	126
John, Sr.	MAD	126
Nancy	HRY	262
Peter	MAD	126
Spencer	BBN	132
William	HOP	234
BARTLETT, ----ge?	DVS	12A
----se?	DVS	12A
Burgess	FTE	83
Edmund, Jr.	HRY	194
Edmund, Sr.	HRY	194
Haines	NCH	118A
Hary?	HRY	218
Hiram	CLK	96
James	JEF	46
James	BBN	92
James	HRY	220
Jeffrey	NCH	118A
Jno.	FKN	100
John	MTG	285
John, Jr.	JEF	37
John, Sr.	JEF	37
John	SCT	119A
Joshua	CLK	68
Martha	JES	82
Mary	JES	81
Reuben	BKN	6
Saml.	HRY	255
Samuel	JES	84
Samuel	NCH	118A
Solomon	MNR	195
Thos.	FKN	82
Will.	SCT	110A
William, Sr.	NCH	118A
Willis	FKN	98
Willis	FKN	100
Wm.	HRY	264
BARTLEY, Edmond	MAS	77
James	GNP	166A
Jos./ Jas.?	HRY	269
Matilda	MAS	77
Will	MAS	53
William, Jr.	CLK	100
William, Senr.	CLK	100
BARTLOW, Isaac	CBL	22A
Margaret	WDF	121A
BARTON, Abm. S.	FTE	66
Abner	BRN	2
Ann	GRD	114A
Berry	WRN	69A
David	BBN	120
Elijah	BBN	60
Elizabeth	WRN	69A
George	WRN	66A
Henry	KNX	302
Jacob	BRN	5
James	BRN	2
James	GRN	79
James	HAR	186
James	KNX	300
James, Jr.	BRN	4
Jno.	MAS	56
Joel	WDF	102
John	FTE	90
John	WDF	99
John	HOP	232
John	PND	31A
John	GRD	110A
Joseph	TRG	13
Joshua	BBN	130
Manoah	BRN	3
Nicholas	BBN	92
Richd.	MAS	67
Robert, Capt.	MER	86
BARTON, Samuel	BRN	4
Sarah	BNE	8
Stephen	HAR	188
Taylor	CBL	14A
Will., Jr.	KNX	302
Will., Sr.	KNX	302
William	TRG	13
William	CBL	17A
Wm.	BBN	118
BARTON?, John	WAS	83A
BARTTELL, David	CLK	79
David, Senr.	CLK	79
BASCO, Rachel	CHN	43
BASEY, Elias	NSN	219
William	MER	88
BASH, Thomas	GTN	124
BASHAM, Angles	BRK	243
Bartlet, Sr.	BRK	237
Bartlett, Jr.	BRK	237
Bartlett, Jr.	BRK	237
James	BRK	239
Littlebery	BRK	243
Micajah	BRK	233
Obediah	BRK	235
Wm.	BRK	235
BASHAN, Peter, Snr.	BTH	218
BASHAW, Eppa	HRY	266
Peter, Jr.	BTH	218
Sarah T.	SHE	120A
BASHEARS, Isaac	HOP	234
Jeremiah	HOP	234
Si-tha?	HOP	234
BASHER, Edwd.	MAS	59
BASIL, John	NCH	127A
BASKETT, Henry M.	SHE	161
James	NCH	111A
Job	SHE	133A
John	NCH	103A
John	SHE	116A
Martin	SHE	168
Martin	NCH	103A
Thomas	SHE	175
Thomas	SHE	112A
William	SHE	116A
Wm.	SHE	114A
BASNETT, Wm.	JEF	39
BASS, Absalom	BLT	192
Ailsey	MBG	139A
Eliza	GRN	79
Elizabeth	BRN	4
Isaac	BRN	4
Jordan	CHN	30A
Josiah	GRN	79
Matthew	BLT	180
Mosley	GRN	58
Nathan	BRN	2
Nedham	MBG	140A
Nilson	ALN	144
Patcy	BRN	4
Peter	GRN	55
Robertson	FKN	68
Thomas	GRN	79
Tyre	GRN	55
BASS?, Jno.	JEF	66
BASSET, Abner	DVS	17A
BASSETT, Amos	HAR	180
Amoss	LWS	86A
David	MAS	64
David	CBL	15A
Elijah	MAS	56
James	OWN	99
James	HAR	182
Jedediah	BNE	8
John	GRD	96B
John	LWS	88A

BASSFORD, John BTH 220
BASSICK?, John BKN 14
BASSNETT, Isaac CLK 86
BAST, George MER 116
BAST?, John GRD 94A
BASY, Lisbon HRY 268
BASYE, Elezemon BBN 120
  Thos. BBN 120
BATCHELLOR, Jessee BNE 6
BATCHELOR,
    Littleberry FKN 66
BATCHER, Wm. GSN 129A
BATE, James L.? JEF 46
BATE?, Jno. JEF 51
BATEMAN, Sally FLG 77A
  Thos. FLG 25A
  Thos. SHE 142A
  Wm. FLG 24A
BATEMAN?, John FLG 25A
BATES, Anne MER 87
  Charles MBG 136
  Ephraim FTE 108
  Esquire? WAS 26A
  George MBG 136
  Humphrey GRD 115A
  Isaac GRD 109A
  James BKN 9
  James FTE 98
  James HRT 155
  James DVS 16A
  James WAS 25A
  Jarrel H. BRK 237
  John BNE 8
  John JEF 33
  John CLY 126
  Matthew WAS 26A
  Polley MAD 124
  Robert CLD 137
  Royal WYN 94A
  Sarah BNE 8
  Sarah MAD 124
  Simean MBG 136
  Thomas WYN 96A
  Thos. MAD 124
  Warren BBN 118
  Wiley BNE 8
  William BNE 4
  Willis BNE 4
  Willis BKN 9
  Wm. BRK 235
BATES?, Danl. CLY 111
  Debora FTE 63
BATEY, Arther SPN 8A
BATH?, Thompson ADR 6
BATHE, John BBN 64
BATHURIM?, Benj. RCK 76A
BATISTE, John LNC 57
BATLELL?, Thos. WAS 27A
BATMAN, Isaac JEF 66
BATS, William MER 87
BATSEL, John NSN 195
  Nathaniel NSN 180
  Smith NSN 196
BATT?, Jno. ADR 8
BATTERSHELL, Nancy CLK 87
BATTERTON, Henry BBN 126
  Moses BBN 126
  Saml. BBN 128
BATTICE?, John JEF 30
BATTLES, Lucy FTE 61
  Reubin CBL 20A
BATTLETON, Abram MAD 116
BATTO, James TRG 7
BATTS, Richd. HRY 252
  William TRG 6A
BATTS?, Nancy HRY 252
BATTSON, Joseph BBN 126
  Robt. BBN 90
BATTZELL, Geo. FKN 60
BATY, Joseph GSN 129A
  Wm. GSN 128A
BAUFIELD?, Thomas GNP 169A
BAUGH, Abram GRD 96B
  Adam PUL 60A
  Henry PUL 68A
  Jacob, Jr. PUL 60A
  Jacob, Senr. PUL 68A
  John LGN 38
  Philemon BRN 2
  Rosanna BRN 2
  Samuel LGN 31
  Thomas SHE 177
  William BRN 2
  William MAD 116
  Wm. A. MAD 124
BAUGHCUM?, Icom? BTL 317
BAUGHMAN, Eliz. HRL 104
BAUGHMON, John HRL 104
BAUGHUS?, Martin FKN 156
BAUHAM?, Nathaniel LWS 95A
BAULDING, William LVG 12
BAULDING?, James LVG 12
BAUM, Sarah JEF 22
BAUTH?, James MAD 100
BAW, Geo. FKN 128
BAWELS?, Isaac WDF 94
BAWL, John GNP 176A
BAWLAND, William WDF 94A
BAXDAL, John MER 87
BAXTER, Benjamin MAD 94
  Bethel ETL 50
  Edmund NCH 125A
  Edward MAD 156
  Ephraim ETL 42
  Fran. HRY 240
  George CLK 93
  George MAD 156
  Jacob SCT 139A
  James ADR 10
  James JEF 41
  James JES 78
  James JES 87
  James JES 88
  Jas. HRY 240
  Jesse HRY 240
  Jessee CLK 94
  Jno. HRY 240
  John CLK 78
  John CLK 93
  John MAD 148
  John WDF 95A
  John SCT 128A
  John G. MAD 176
  John M. CLK 79
  Jonathan HRD 54
  Joshua MAD 162
  Kenaday JES 87
  Levi MNR 207
  Reubin FTE 86
  Saml. JEF 43
  Samuel FTE 102
  Samuel FTE 102
  Samuel MTG 237
  Thomas FTE 88
  William LVG 15
  William CLK 71
  William HAR 158
  William CBL 3A
  Wm. HRY 240
BAXTLY, Levi JEF 57
BAXTON?, Samuel JES 72
BAXTOR?, Samuel JES 72
BAY, Joseph MTG 265
BAYER, Jacob HRY 210
BAYLEE, Jacob SHE 148
BAYLES, Benjn. MAS 79
  Catharine MAS 71
  Isra MAS 71
  Mary MAS 71
  Nathan BBN 74
  Saml. MAS 71
BAYLESS, E. JEF 20
BAYLEY, Jessey MAD 90
  Martin, Jr. MNR 211
  Noah ALN 96
  Robert CSY 224
  Thos. HRD 46
  William MNR 193
BAYLEY?, Carr B. FLG 35A
BAYLOR, Dorsey HRD 74
  Geo W. BBN 144
  Isaac CBL 11A
  John G. W. LGN 31
  John W. BBN 146
  R. T. TOD 131A
  Robert LGN 43
  Walker BBN 136
  Wm. HRD 72
BAYNE, Henry H. WAS 52A
  John HRD 88
  Robt. KNX 288
  Thos HRD 86
  Wm. HRD 72
BAYNES, Jno. LVG 4
BAYS, Edward SHE 156
  John OHO 7A
BAYSINGER, Gasf-- BRK 235
  Michel BRK 235
  Val / Vol? BRK 243
  Valentine HND 10A
BAYSMAN, John HAR 198
BAZAN?, John BLT 184
BAZIL, Samuel FLD 30
BCRAFT?, Benjamin BTH 218
BE---?, Daniel CHN 32
BE-K, Mary FTE 57
BEABOUT?, Ben HRY 204
BEACH, Asa BNE 4
  Baley FTE 101
  Jabez FTE 69
  James FTE 59
  William FTE 101
BEACHAM, -----? SHE 131A
  Betsey FTE 107
  Isaac SHE 131A
  Joshua SPN 20A
  Stephen SPN 17A
BEACHAMP, Joseph GRN 67
  Thomas SPN 23A
BEACHUM, Sarah WDF 92
BEADDLES, John LNC 57
  Rice LNC 57
BEADES, William H. CLK 80
BEADLE, Betsey SCT 137A
  Daniel BRK 239
  Elizath. SCT 104A
  Nathan BRK 235
  Samuel BTH 194
  William BTH 216
BEADLES, John MER 86
  Joseph WRN 30A
  Leaton? MER 87
BEAGH?, John HAR 152
  Joseph HAR 152
  Solomon HAR 152
BEAGLE, Elijah JES 82
  James HAR 148
  Solomon HAR 152

BEAGLE?, John HAR 152
Joseph HAR 152
BEAIRD, Wm. MAS 78
BEAKEN, John HAR 202
BEAL, Frederick BKN 15
John BTH 186
Jourden BNE 46
Pennal MAS 76
Samuel CLK 71
Thomas BNE 4
William G. CLK 107
BEALE, Pricilla FLG 30A
BEALER, Cordelia FTE 76
BEALL, Daniel BNE 4
Jesse WAS 58A
John CBL 20A
Middleton LGN 35
Norborne B. JEF 42
Richard WAS 18A
Samuel T. NSN 179
Walter LGN 30
William M. WAS 17A
Zadock LGN 45
BEALMARE, Samuel NSN 182
BEALS, Caleb HRD 46
BEAM, Coonrad? WAS 44A
George SHE 119A
Jacob NSN 187
Jacob WAS 44A
Saml. W. SCT 116A
BEAMAN, Daniel, Jr. BNE 6
Daniel, Sr. BNE 6
BEAMAN?, Filo JEF 27
BEAMES, Fielden GRN 55
BEAMON, John BNE 6
Joshua BNE 6
BEAMS, James WTY 110A
Jesse WTY 122A
Jessee GRN 63
BEAN, Bend. WAS 75A
Charles CLK 98
Clotilda NSN 193
Dory JEF 62
Elizabeth NSN 178
Francis BLT 192
Isaac TOD 129A
Jacob BRN 4
Jno.? R. LVG 6
John CLK 93
Leonard OHO 3A
Mary JEF 63
Mary HRY 250
Patterson FTE 61
Ransome MNR 197
Widw. A. CWL 43
William CLK 67
William FTE 67
BEANE, Abner FTE 63
James HAR 200
Joshua HAR 200
William HAR 212
BEAR, Adam BRK 241
Adam, Sr. BRK 235
George BRK 239
BEARD, Alexr., Jr. BRN 3
Alexr., Sen. BRN 3
Archibald BTH 174
Charles SHE 169
David SPN 9A
George BTH 170
George W. GTN 131
Henry FTE 101
Henry BTH 174
Hugh S. ADR 8
James ADR 4
BEARD, James, Junr. OHO 8A
James OHO 8A
James R. SPN 21A
Jno. ADR 3
John BRN 3
John ADR 6
John LVG 10
John CLD 147
John CHN 31A
John WAS 62A
Joseph FTE 102
Joseph BLT 188
Joseph WAS 42A
Josiah GRN 66
Lewis WTY 113A
Marth BTH 170
Peggy BLT 194
Phebe, Mrs. WYN 85A
Samuel D. BTH 174
Sarah, Mrs. GRT 140
Simon LVG 5
Thomas GRT 144
Thomas OHO 8A
Thomas OHO 11A
William HRL 104
BEARD?, Lewis (Crossed Out) WTY 117A
BEARDEN, Philip LVG 4
BEARDIN, John TRG 11
BEARDING, --.? CWL 42
John CWL 44
BEASLEY, Catharine WDF 116A
Charles WDF 115A
Cornelius BRN 5
Edmund FTE 97
Eli/ Elj.? GRD 108A
Thomas GRD 120A
William WDF 114A
Willis LNC 19
BEASLY, James GRD 85A
John BTL 317
William BTL 317
BEASLY?, Ezekiel MAS 71
BEATEY?, Milard? BKN 20
BEATTIE, Edwd. TOD 128
BEATTY, Adam MAS 69
Danl. LVG 7
David MTG 261
Elizabeth FTE 105
Henry ETL 51
James PUL 55A
John BBN 110
John MTG 245
John PUL 55A
John PUL 63A
Polly MTG 245
Samuel ETL 51
Samuel LWS 89A
Thomas MTG 229
Thomas MTG 233
Will. LVG 7
William MTG 245
BEATY, Alexander CLD 148
David FLD 23
Geo. SCT 127A
James LNC 57
James GTN 120
James CLD 148
James SHE 157
John SCT 91A
Joseph SCT 138A
Martin WYN 79A
Robert FTE 68
Will SCT 103A
William GTN 120
BEATY, William CLD 148
BEAUCAMP, Peter R. WRN 74A
BEAUCHAM, Isaac WDF 122A
BEAUCHAMP, Jereboham WAS 87A
Jno. FKN 124
John BRK 241
Newel NSN 185
R. P. BRN 2
William DVS 15A
BEAVEN?, Rabecca NSN 184
BEAVER, Abraham HAR 158
Isham CLK 72
Michael HAR 166
Peter FTE 73
The Ironworks BTH 220
BEAVERS, Abraham FLD 28
John BRN 4
Wm. HRD 10
BEAVIN?, Benjamin NSN 209
BEAZLEY, Aquis WDF 99
Lewis WDF 99A
BEBOW?, Thos. MAD 114
BECHAM, Coleman C. SHE 120A
BECK, ----? LVG 17
Aaron WYN 89A
Ariah? -? FLG 72A
Elihu CLD 138
James WRN 42A
Jeremiah MAS 62
John BBN 70
Joseph WYN 89A
Joseph WYN 101A
Moses CLD 145
Quiller BBN 70
Silas CLD 145
Siles MAD 102
Thos. CWL 44
Winston MAD 102
BECK?, Asa MAD 128
Saml. FLG 59A
BECKAM, James SHE 134A
John HND 11A
BECKE, James LVG 17
BECKELHIMER, Saml. MAD 124
BECKER, Joseph LVG 15
BECKERS, William HAR 148
BECKET, Elizabeth BBN 122
John BBN 68
Josiah CLD 145
Umphrey FLG 29A
Wm. WAS 60A
BECKETT, Antony WAS 60A
Henry WAS 60A
John HAR 178
Joseph HAR 178
Saml. WAS 55A
Saml. R. PND 26A
Thos. WAS 60A
BECKHAM, Alexander SHE 139A
Hugh BBN 92
John CLK 71
John WRN 56A
John WRN 68A
Simon FKN 56
William WRN 56A
BECKINGHAM, Wm. CWL 50
BECKITT, Nelson PND 19A
BECKLEY, Henry SHE 161
Jno. HRY 261
John W. SHE 152
Levi SHE 152
BECKMAN, David WYN 90A
Michael WYN 90A
BECKNALE, Thos. MAD 134
BECKNALL, Samuel MAD 106

Name	County	Page
BECKNELL, Linsfield	ETL	50
BECKNER, Fredrick	FLG	68A
Henry	FLG	76A
Jacob	FLG	59A
Jacob	FLG	76A
John	FLG	71A
BECKSTON, Samuel	OHO	4A
BECKWELL, Martin	MAD	96
BECKWISTH?, John	BLT	164
BECKWITH, Bennedict	HRD	26
John W.	BLT	174
W.	JEF	23
BECRAFT, Jonathan	BBN	80
William	MTG	237
BECRAFT?, Benjamin	BTH	202
Benjamin, Sr.	BTH	208
BECTELL, Henry	BLT	168
John	BLT	168
BEDDOW, Henry	LNC	3
Thomas	LNC	73
Thos.	FKN	142
BEDFORD, Archibald	BBN	108
Benjamin	BBN	108
Benjamin	BBN	124
Benjamin	LWS	88A
Henry	BBN	108
John	HAR	184
John	NSN	206
John C.	MNR	195
Lilliby?	NSN	218
Little B.	BBN	84
Little Berry	BBN	108
Rebeka	MNR	213
Shed.	JEF	27
Stephen	MNR	213
Thomas	LWS	86A
Zachh.	BNE	4
BEDING/ BEDINGER?, Henry	LWS	97A
BEDINGER, Danile P.	NCH	117A
BEDWELL, Daniel	LGN	45
BEEBOUT / BECBOUT?, Peter	FLG	36A
BEEBOUT, Benj.	FLG	56A
Danl.	FLG	65A
BEECH, James	GRD	102A
John	MAD	124
Rufus	CWL	36
BEECHLER, John	GRD	116A
Saml.	GRD	116A
BEEDEN, J. W.	JEF	25
BEEDING?, Milley	NCH	112A
BEEGLE, Thomas	CBL	23A
BEEK?, Asa	MAD	128
BEEKERS?, William	HAR	148
BEEL, Andrew	BTL	319
BEEL?, John	ADR	18
BEELER, Geo.	JEF	32
Geo.	JEF	37
John C.	JEF	32
BEELER?, Christopher	NSN	191
John	NSN	195
BEEMISH, George	CBL	7A
BEEMS, Richd.	FLG	69A
BEEN, Ben	MAS	72
Fantly	MAS	61
Jno.	MAS	67
Leonard	MAS	72
Richd.	HRY	259
Will	MAS	72
BEESLEY, Hiram	HRY	268
BEESLY, Sarah	FTE	98
BEESON, Jessee	CBL	9A
John W.	WYN	81A
Lurana, Mrs.	WYN	80A
BEET, Elenor	FLG	35A
BEETEM, Adam	HRY	268
BEGAN?, Jesse	HAR	140
BEGLEY, Henry, Jr.	CLY	128
John	CLY	127
Thomas	CLY	128
William	CLY	131
BEIRD, James	SPN	13A
Willis	SPN	13A
BEITOL?, Peter	BRK	235
BEL--E?, James	FLD	23
BELART, David	FTE	70
BELCHER, George	FLD	38
George	MER	88
Robert	CLK	83
BELCHY, James	MAD	126
Thos.	MAD	126
BELEN?, Elisha	WRN	54A
BELER, G. W.	GRD	98A
BELEW, Elizabeth	SHE	149
George	WYN	92A
James	PND	28A
John	GNP	178A
Linney	PND	28A
Samuel	PND	27A
Shelton	WYN	92A
BELFORD, Nathan	CHN	42
BELIN?, Elisha	WRN	54A
BELK, John	ADR	8
BELL, -----?	DVS	10A
----in?	DVS	10A
--.?	HRY	230
-i-inson	BBN	110
And-.?	CWL	50
Archibald, Senr.	BBN	124
Asa	FTE	95
Asa	BBN	118
Asa	BLT	184
Baily	CLK	82
Benj.	FLG	31A
Burwill	HND	5
Carter	FLG	34A
Celah	HND	10A
Chas.	MAS	74
Chs., Jr.	MAS	64
Clement	FKN	82
Daniel	FKN	110
Daniel	WDF	119A
David	FTE	90
David	MER	116
David	HRY	230
Disey	CSY	220
Edward	NCH	105
Elijah	RCK	77A
Eliz.	HRY	253
Elizabeth	TRG	7
Fr.	MAS	72
Frances	CSY	212
Francis	SPN	22A
Francis	WYN	100A
George	CWL	33
George	GRN	63
George	GRN	80
Hannah	HRY	178
Henry	JEF	58
Henry	MER	89
Henry	HRT	155
Henry D.	BBN	126
Henry S.	NSN	217
Isaac	SHE	165
Isabella	SHE	153
Jabes	OHO	8A
BELL, Jacob	HRT	153
James	JEF	31
James	CWL	42
James	LGN	43
James	CLK	66
James	FTE	97
James	SHE	154
James	SPN	5A
James	SPN	5A
James	HND	10A
James	WYN	95A
James	WYN	100A
James	NCH	110A
James	NCH	121A
Jane	NSN	206
Jane	NCH	117A
Jas.	RCK	82A
Jas.	SCT	136A
Jeffersen	GNP	167A
Jno.	FTE	58
Jno.	JEF	62
John	ADR	6
John	JEF	26
John	LGN	39
John	LGN	45
John	FTE	65
John	HRD	86
John	FTE	90
John	CLY	132
John	HAR	196
John	NSN	206
John	WAS	39A
John	WRN	45A
John	PUL	68A
John	LWS	91A
John	LWS	93A
John	WYN	95A
John	WYN	100A
John	SHE	127A
John A.	HRY	204
John T.	LNC	2
Jonathan	NSN	207
Joseph	HRY	208
Joseph	HRY	230
Joseph	WYN	95A
Joseph	SCT	97A
Josiah	MBG	141
Josiah	HAR	196
Kinchen	HND	5
Leonard	CLK	76
Lucy	JEF	62
Mary	BBN	80
Mary	FKN	108
Nancy	DVS	17A
Nancy?	DVS	14A
Patrick	JEF	65
Patterson	JEF	22
Patterson B.	HRY	228
Peter	NSN	191
Pulaski B.	HRY	178
R.?	SHE	143A
Richd.	MAS	67
Robert	JEF	42
Robert	FTE	99
Robert	MBG	135A
Robert T.	WDF	108A
Robt.	HRD	30
Saml.	SHE	137A
Samuel	BRN	3
Samuel	SPN	19A
Samuel	GNP	165A
Sarah	BRN	3
Silas	WYN	83A
Stephen	NSN	206
Thomas	HRT	155
Thomas	SHE	170

BELL, Thomas SHE 170
Thomas MBG 141A
Thomas GNP 165A
Thomas A. NSN 201
Thos. BBN 64
Thos., Senr. BBN 78
Thos. C. FLG 24A
W. W. ADR 8
Washington MAS 72
Will MAS 67
William BRN 2
William ETL 47
William FTE 66
William MER 89
William CSY 214
William MTG 259
William, Sr. WYN 104A
William WRN 47A
William WYN 95A
William WDF 112A
William MBG 139A
William C. FTE 67
William? DVS 14A
Williams WYN 102A
Wm. BRN 3
Wm. CWL 50
Wm. BBN 70
Wm. FLG 62A
Wm. SHE 143A
Wm. Wm.? ADR 8
BELL?, Archd. BBN 114
John ADR 18
Rachel FTE 66
BELLAMY, John LGN 31
BELLAR, Eli WRN 31A
BELLENSWORTH, Charles ADR 10
BELLENSWORTH?, Jno ADR 10
BELLERSWORTH?, Charles ADR 10
Jno. ADR 10
BELLEW, Edward SHE 166
Thos. PND 28A
BELLIS, Jacob NCH 119A
Peter, Jr. MER 87
Peter, Sr. MER 87
BELLIS?, Philip NCH 125A
BELLOMY, Reuben R. ETL 50
BELLOWS, Henry SCT 108A
Mary SCT 108A
Wm. BBN 120
BELLS, Bennajah A. BRK 301
Lovel BLT 172
BELLUE, Charles BRK 233
John BRK 235
John BRK 239
BELLVILLE, Samuel CBL 22A
BELMEAR, Daniel V. UNN 151
William UNN 150
BELNAP, Elijah HRT 153
Jas. HRD 64
Jesse HRD 92
Jonas HRT 153
Jonas, Sr. HRT 155
BELOW, Massa UNN 154
BELOW?, Sary HRL 104
BELSHE, Robert, Esq. WYN 103A
BELT, Dennes FLG 76A
Fielding FLG 71A
John SCT 116A
Jos. FLG 32A
Jos. C. FLG 41A
Joseph FKN 88
Josiah JEF 59
R. W. GRD 110A
BELT, Thos. FLG 32A
Wigginson OHO 10A
BELTCHER, Berry GRN 77
BEMER, Jno. MAS 61
BENBOUT?, Ben HRY 204
BENBROOK, Jas. CWL 50
John SPN 13A
Nathan SPN 21A
Zecal? SPN 18A
BENDER, Jno. MAS 80
BENEAR, Wm. BBN 120
BENEDICK, Jenjn. ALN 136
BENEDICT, Jacob LNC 61
BENETT, Elijah CWL 39
BENETT?, Fisher GRN 73
BENFORD, Daniel MER 88
John MER 88
BENGE, Anne WTY 111A
David CLY 130
Joel MAD 172
John CLY 124
William CLY 113
BENHAM, Danl. CHN 44A
Nathaniel LWS 95A
BENIFEE, Robert MTG 257
Strode MTG 291
BENING, Anthony CLK 84
BENINGFIELD, John GRN 70
Rubin GRN 70
BENINGTON, David NCH 123A
Nehimiah NCH 123A
BENIT, Stephen CWL 38
Stephen CWL 39
BENITT, James GRD 112A
BENJAMIN, Black BNE 8
BENK?, John MER 116
BENLEY?, Nathaniel GRN 77
BENNEL?, Bond ADR 6
BENNET, Aaron BNE 2
Anna BTH 176
Bartlet SCT 96A
Catharine FKN 128
Elisha MAD 160
Elisha BTL 317
George WDF 97
James FKN 112
Jno. ADR 3
Jno. FKN 132
Jno. CHN 41A
John WTY 110A
John GRD 118A
Johnson HRD 14
Joseph MAD 92
Levi BNE 4
Moses MAD 150
Nelly HRD 14
Richard OWN 100
Richd. FKN 132
Samuel NSN 219
William BRN 2
BENNETT, Abrah SHE 153
Asa SHE 170
Asa OHO 8A
Bazil SHE 134A
Benj. BRK 243
Catharine GTN 127
Daniel SHE 134A
David OHO 6A
Edmond ETL 44
Edward HND 10
Elizabeth ETL 54
Enoch MAS 72
Enoch SHE 134A
Gabriel MNR 191
Hiram C. JEF 35
James BRN 2
BENNETT, James HAR 140
James BRK 243
James OHO 9A
Jeffreys OHO 8A
Jesse CHN 28A
Jno. BKN 26
Jno., Junr. OHO 6A
Jno., Snr. OHO 7A
John ETL 49
John ALN 100
John MAD 116
John MNR 191
John PND 15A
John SHE 135A
Joseph GTN 117
Joseph OHO 10A
Joshua ETL 54
Levi KNX 300
Lidia MBG 139A
Marques NSN 176
Moses GTN 127
Moses CSY 212
Nathan LVG 15
Phill WAS 46A
Phillip MBG 139A
Reuben HRY 224
Reuben OHO 3A
Reuben C. GRT 142
Richard MNR 191
Richd. BBN 76
Robert FTE 82
Sam OHO 11A
Samuel WRN 37A
Samuel MBG 140A
Silus C. LWS 92A
Thomas LGN 46
Thomas, Junr. OHO 9A
Thomas OHO 9A
Thos. LVG 6
Timothy, Jr. GTN 135
Timothy, Sr. GTN 135
Titus OHO 10A
Tunis MAS 61
Walter TRG 14A
Will MAS 70
William LGN 46
William HAR 140
Wm. MAD 92
Wm. HRT 155
Zenes? HAR 132
BENNETT?, James MTG 299
Wm. BBN 76
BENNEY, John CBL 2A
BENNING, Isaic WRN 75A
James FTE 88
Perkins FTE 87
BENNINGTON, John MER 87
Thomas CSY 220
Thos. FLG 73A
BENNIT, ----n? W. CWL 37
Danl. JEF 59
Isaac CHN 42A
Jas. JEF 65
BENNITT, Anna HRY 226
Evans HND 11
William HAR 140
BENOHAM, Joseph MER 88
BENSENHOFER, John BNE 6
BENSON, Mrs. JEF 28
Amos MAD 118
Chichester SHE 141A
Daniel JEF 64
Enoch B. UNN 147
James BTH 216
James BTH 218
Martin BTL 319

Name	County	Page
BENSON,		
Martin	CBL	16A
Reubin	CBL	12A
BENTHAL, Seth	WDF	105
BENTHALL, Thomas	UNN	149
BENTLEY, Daniel	MAD	152
Ephraim	LNC	45
Frances	FTE	85
James	WAS	53A
John	FLD	15
John, Jr.	MAD	148
John	HND	9A
Lenard	MAD	94
Levy	LNC	45
Lewis	FLD	15
Mary	MAD	152
Mikael	FLG	39A
Reubin	FTE	85
Samuel	FLD	15
Samuel	WDF	96
Solomon	FLD	15
Thomas	FLD	15
Thomas	CLD	140
Thomas	CBL	16A
William	HND	9A
Wm.	MAD	94
Wm.	MAD	178
Wm. N.	JEF	20
BENTLY, Benjamin	FLD	15
John, Sr.	MAD	148
John	WAS	46A
Saml.	MAD	116
William	MAD	116
BENTON, Benjn.	OHO	8A
David	CWL	34
Elijah	HRY	220
Erasmus	SCT	108A
George	OHO	4A
Hezekiah	MTG	279
Hiram	MAD	120
Isaiah	CWL	33
James	MAD	120
James	HRY	216
James	HRY	220
Jeremh.	CWL	34
Jessee	ETL	51
John	MER	88
John	MER	88
Richard	ETL	50
Richard	MTG	237
Robert	ETL	44
Samuel	HAR	142
W., Sr.	HRY	234
William	MBG	135
BENTON?, Allen	OHO	6A
BENTZ, Andrew	OHO	6A
BER-OT, Ann	GTN	134
BERCKENRIDGE, Francis P.	BTH	204
BERDIT, Wm.	WAS	75A
BERDY, Wm.	WAS	49A
BERGEN, George	SHE	158
John	SHE	171
Thomas	LNC	5
BERGENSTEEN, Hugh M.	BRN	3
Ro. P.	BRN	3
BERGER, Peter	CLD	146
BERGOIN, Evan	FLG	59A
BERING, Cornelius	BBN	106
BERING?, Chas.	BBN	130
BERK, John, Jr.	FLG	71A
John, Sr.	FLG	71A
John	FLG	71A
Moses	FLG	71A
Saml.	FLG	71A
BERK, Stephen	FLG	71A
BERKELY, Spencer	BBN	118
BERKHART, A. B.	NSN	219
BERKHEAD, Abraham	NSN	196
Eleaser	NSN	196
Philip	NSN	196
BERKLEY, ----?	HND	10A
Benjamin	LGN	34
Hugh	BLT	154
Jonathan	NSN	207
Micaijah	BNE	8
BERMON?, Charles	HRY	186
BERNAN, Toliver	CHN	43A
BERNARD, Absolem	ADR	8
Jesse B.	LGN	36
John B.	GTN	124
Jos.	HRY	252
Philadelphia	GTN	124
BERNEL?, Bond	ADR	6
BERNS, William	WRN	69A
Wm.	FLG	72A
BERNUM, John	LNC	51
BERREY, James	MAD	120
BERRIMAN, Thomas	MER	89
BERRY, Achilus	MAD	156
Alcy/ Aley?	CBL	15A
Allen	WDF	118A
Anna	BTH	150
Bazzel	BBN	138
Ben	HRD	18
Benjamin	FTE	109
Benjamin	BBN	120
Benjamin	HOP	236
Benjamin, Jr.	WDF	119A
Benjamin, Sen.	WDF	118A
Burnberry	MAS	60
Daniel	LGN	24
David	CHN	29A
Edward	CLK	70
Elijah	MAS	67
Eliz.	MAS	67
Elizabeth	HOP	232
Ephraim	LNC	75
Ephraim	WRN	56A
Francis	BTL	317
Francis	WAS	85A
Francis	NCH	125A
Franklin	ADR	8
Garrard	MAD	120
Geo.	FKN	116
Geo.	SCT	134A
Geo. C.	SCT	137A
George	BRN	3
George	ADR	60
George	BBN	66
George	FTE	100
George	UNN	149
George	WYN	79A
George H.	BNE	6
Harry	MAS	66
Henry	FKN	118
Henry D.	ALN	104
Holdsworth	MAS	55
Hubbard	CBL	2A
Isaac	FLD	45
Isaac	FLD	45
Isaac	BBN	120
James	MAD	112
James	HOP	230
James	WRN	68A
Jane	MAS	66
Jesse	LNC	23
Jesse	BBN	112
Jno.	LVG	2
Jno.	HAR	140
Jno. J.	HRY	265
BERRY, Jno. M.	TOD	129A
Joel	MAS	63
John	FLD	45
John	GTN	124
John	TOD	134
John	MBG	142
John	UNN	150
John	HRY	216
John	MTG	257
John	WTY	122A
Jos.	MAS	64
Joseph	BRN	5
Joseph	GRN	69
Joseph, Dr.	BBN	112
Joseph, Sen.	BRN	5
Joseph	NCH	120A
Jubal	FLD	45
L. S.	LNC	13
Lewis	CLK	69
Lewis A.	WDF	105
Mary	BRN	4
Mary	WDF	118A
Naomi	WAS	18A
Peter	BRK	235
Reuben	MAS	69
Reuben	UNN	150
Reuben	HAR	202
Reuben	HOP	230
Reuben	MTG	249
Reuben, Sr.	HOP	236
Reubin	FTE	109
Richard	BRN	2
Richard	FTE	112
Richard	WAS	75A
Richd.	WAS	54A
Robert	NCH	112A
Rubin	FLG	27A
Saml.	HRD	60
Samuel	WDF	118A
Samuel	NCH	123A
Silas	SCT	118A
Thomas	GRN	64
Thomas	CLK	86
Thomas	CLK	89
Thomas	BBN	128
Thomas	HOP	232
Thomas (S. Creek)	CLK	92
Thomas T.	CLK	71
Thompson.	BRN	2
Widw. J.	CWL	43
Will	ADR	6
Will	MAS	68
Will	MAS	72
Will, Jr.	MAS	67
William	LNC	23
William	GRN	65
William	CLK	70
William	UNN	150
William	MNR	213
Wm.	PND	28A
Wm. F.	MAS	59
BERRY?, -----?	GRN	80
James S.	NSN	193
Jno.	HAR	140
BERRYMAN, Ann	ETL	52
Gilson	FTE	91
James	SCT	98A
James S.	WDF	104
Jared B.	OHO	3A
John	ETL	52
John H.	FTE	108
John N.	SHE	152
Josiah	BBN	114
Josiah	OHO	3A
Margaret	FTE	108

Name	County	Page
BERRYMAN, Samuel	FTE	86
William	NSN	219
William	WRN	64A
Wm.	HRD	70
BERT?, Henry	JEF	46
BERTHOND, Nicholas	JEF	30
BERTON, Charles	SPN	20A
Elijah	KNX	280
John	WAS	81A
Julus	WAS	82A
Thomas	CLD	139
BERY, William	HOP	230
BESHANG, John	HRD	14
BESHEARS, Jesse	FLD	7
BESS, Adam	BLT	178
Cornelius	BLT	190
BESSETT, Mary	NSN	190
Rachel	NSN	191
BEST, Banks	GRD	103A
David	CLK	62
Ebnzr.	GRD	123A
Elijah	HRD	38
Henry	JEF	46
James	CLK	62
Jas.	MAS	72
Joseph	PND	21A
Josiah E.	HRD	28
Samuel	LNC	45
Thos.	PND	16A
BEST?, John	BKN	19
BETHEL, Joshua	MAD	146
Samuel	MAD	124
William	NSN	183
BETHELL, James	HND	6
BETHERDS, Henry S.	BBN	94
BETISWORTH, James K.	WRN	43A
BETTENSWORTH?, Charles	ADR	10
Jno.	ADR	10
BETTERES?, John	SCT	96A
BETTERSWORTH, John	MAD	152
Marey?	MAD	152
William	BRN	33
BETTERSWORTH?, Charles	ADR	10
Jno.	ADR	10
BETTES, Marshall	MAS	63
Wm. E.	MAS	63
BETTESS, Harris	FTE	103
BETTIS, Hyatt	LVG	15
Roger	FLG	27A
BETTISWORTH, Jesse	WRN	74A
BETTS, James (Crossed Out)	SCT	101A
James	SCT	94A
John	OWN	105
Jos.	SCT	123A
Joseph, Sr.	SCT	123A
Marmaduke	OWN	100
Thos.	SCT	137A
BETTS?, Thompson	ADR	6
BETTYSWORTH, Fielding	WRN	73A
BETYSWORTH, Richard	WRN	44A
BEUFORD, John	BBN	104
BEUFORD?, Ambrose	BBN	102
BEVEAN?, Charles	CLK	93
BEVEN?, Bend.	WAS	58A
BEVENS, James	LWS	94A
Noah	NCH	110A
BEVERLY, Anna	JEF	32
Stephen	GRT	144
BEVIN, Benj. F.	WAS	54A
Edward	WAS	40A
BEVIN, James H.	LWS	88A
Simeon	LNC	2
BEVINS, John	SHE	116A
BEVY, Benjn.	CWL	50
BEYAR?, Jesse	HAR	140
BEYL, William	NSN	219
BIANSTETTER, Frederick	BRN	2
BIAS, John S.	TOD	131A
BIBB, ----?	GRN	65
Benjamin	TRG	5
David	OWN	105
Elijah	JES	87
Geo. M.	FKN	56
George D.	LNC	59
Henry G.	LGN	22
James	BBN	62
James	BBN	122
James	MNR	205
John	OWN	105
John B.	LGN	24
Martin	LNC	57
R--?, Sr. (At Farm)	LGN	28
Richard, Jr.	LGN	24
Richd., Sr.	LGN	23
Robert	MNR	205
Thomas	HRD	12
Thomas	LNC	15
Wright E.	LGN	22
BIBBINS, Elijah	KNX	312
BIBBS, Thomas	OWN	101
BIBEE / BIBER?, John	CLK	90
BIBEE, Ann	CLK	91
James	CLK	91
Neily	CLK	91
William	CLK	65
William	CLK	69
BIBEY, Benj.	RCK	77A
BICE, Cornelius	SHE	166
Everet	MER	88
Jacob	MER	87
Nicholas	MER	88
BICHENSTAFF, Molley	MAD	116
BICKERS, Joel	MER	89
Uriel	SCT	119A
BICKLEY, John	MTG	257
Will	MAS	73
BICKSLER, Jacob	SHE	138A
John	SHE	138A
BICKUM?, John	WDF	100
BIDDLE, Caleb	BBN	62
Richard	BBN	110
BIDDLECOM, Richd., Jr.	HRD	44
BIDDLECOME, Asher	HRD	44
Richd., Senr.	HRD	56
BIDWELL, Daniel	LGN	33
Levi	MBG	135
BIERLY, Harman	KNX	280
BIERS, A.	JEF	28
BIGELO, Joseph	HRT	153
BIGELOW, Hiram	BNE	8
BIGERS, Gorden	MAS	66
James	MNR	191
M. Mrs.?	MAS	66
Wm.? M.	MAS	66
BIGGER, Joseph	SPN	9A
Landis	CLK	68
BIGGERS, Richard	WAS	35A
William	MTG	239
BIGGERSTAFF, Aaron	CLD	140
John	CLD	140
Samuel, Junr.	CLD	140
BIGGERSTAFF, Samuel, Senr.	CLD	140
Thomas	MBG	135A
William	CLD	140
BIGGINS, David	JES	84
BIGGIRS, Wm.	WAS	23A
BIGGS, Andrew	HAR	140
Andrew	SHE	135A
Andrew	GNP	178A
Andrew	GNP	179A
Benjamin	BLT	176
Benjn.	GRN	70
Burrel W.	WDF	117A
Duglass	GNP	166A
Elijah	SPN	7A
John	ADR	14
John	GRN	58
John	MTG	267
Joseph B.	LGN	23
Peter	HND	13
Robt. P.	GNP	167A
Sally	BLT	192
Stephen	HRT	155
Will	ADR	6
BIGHAM, David	CWL	38
John?	CWL	42
Mathews	CWL	42
Mathews	CWL	43
Sally?	CWL	42
Wm.	FLG	38A
BIGS, Thomas	BNE	2
BIKINS, John	ALN	106
BILBO, Archibald, Maj.	MER	87
John	MER	87
William	MER	87
BILBREW, Thomas	MBG	138A
BILDERBACK, Ephraim	LWS	89A
Jacob	SHE	131A
William	LWS	89A
BILES, Ann	FKN	144
Joseph	FKN	142
William	LVG	15
BILESTON, John	BRN	3
BILL, Daniel S.	BRK	227
BILL?, Archd.	BBN	114
BILLETTER, Ann, Mrs.	GRT	144
Daniel	GRT	145
Joel	GRT	144
John	GRT	143
Mark	GRT	145
BILLEW, Andrew	HRT	155
BILLINGS, Abraham, Junr.	MBG	141A
Abraham	MGB	137A
Arden	MBG	137
BILLINGSLEY, John	WRN	70A
BINCH, Walter	NSN	219
BINCH?, Henry	NSN	189
BINGAMON, Henery	ADR	6
Polly	LNC	47
BINGHAM, Elijah	HRL	102
George	CLD	159
Henry	GRN	50
John	HRL	102
John	HRL	102
Jos.	GRD	84A
Reuben	GRT	147
Thomas	MER	88
Thomas	DVS	18A
William	HRL	102
BINGMAN, Jacob	FTE	83
BINNS, Daniel	CLD	149
Towns	CLD	149

Name	County	Page
BIRAM, Feilding	BTH	198
Henry	MAD	96
William	LGN	44
BIRCH---, Joshua	ALN	102
BIRCH, George	CLK	70
James	FTE	110
John	ETL	42
John	BTH	204
John S.	JEF	36
Moza	LNC	77
Nichodemus	SPN	5A
Thomas E.	HAR	214
BIRCHET, Bartlet	PUL	50A
BIRCHFIELD, Aby?	BTL	317
Larkin	BTL	317
Thomas	BTL	317
BIRCKET?, Bartlet	PUL	50A
BIRD, Abraham S.	ALN	140
Abram	FTE	96
Abram	SHE	173
Austin	UNN	151
Frances	CBL	7A
George	NSN	216
Hugh	SCT	115A
Isaiah	WTY	120A
Jacob	CWL	44
Jacob, Junr.	HRD	72
Jacob, Senr.	HRD	72
James	BLT	174
James	HOP	232
Jenny?	HRD	40
Jermy?	HRD	40
John	BRN	5
John	HRD	72
John	BBN	134
John	MAD	148
John	CBL	18A
John M.	TOD	129A
Lee	SCT	128A
Pruscilla	WDF	102
Robert	BRN	3
Robert (Crossed Out)	WTY	117A
Robert	WTY	112A
Robt.	HRT	155
Saml.	GRD	96B
Sarah	HRT	155
Thomas	BRN	4
Thomas	WTY	110A
William	BRN	4
William	HRT	155
BIRDSALE, Warren	LVG	13
William	LVG	13
BIRDSONG, Henry	SPN	4A
James	MNR	205
William	MNR	205
BIRDSONS?, -m.?	CWL	42
BIRDWELL, Alexander	MNR	193
James	MNR	197
William	MNR	215
BIRDWHISTLE, William	MER	89
BIRK, Robert	FKN	114
BIRKHART, George	NSN	208
William	NSN	208
BIRKHEAD, Abraham	NSN	216
William H.	BLT	178
BIRRES, Jacob	MAD	100
BIRT, Joseph	FKN	82
BISH, George	MBG	138A
BISHAN?, Wm.	BBN	82
BISHAW?, Wm.	BBN	82
BISHONG, George	MNR	211
John	MNR	205
BISHOP, Benjamin	CLK	66
BISHOP, Charles	HOP	234
Charles H.	NCH	122A
Daniel	NSN	210
Daniel	NCH	107A
Eli	HOP	234
Elisha	HRY	258
Enos	PUL	38A
Erasmos	OHO	8A
Geo.	FLG	40A
George	ETL	41
Greenberry	MER	89
Henry	HOP	232
Henry	NCH	118A
Isaac	BBN	86
Jacob	MER	88
Jacob	NSN	198
Jacob	FLG	41A
James, Jr.	HOP	232
James Sr.	HOP	230
John	JES	77
John	CLK	78
John	HAR	192
Jonathan	PUL	68A
Jos.	PUL	49A
Joshua	HRY	257
Joshua	OHO	10A
Joshua	WRN	45A
Joshua M.	HRY	257
Josiah	HAR	208
Laurence	BLT	182
Laven	BBN	80
Lemuel	NCH	122A
Lonry	BRN	2
Malon	WTY	127A
Miller	ETL	41
Purnell	FTE	61
Rachel?	MER	88
Rebecca	TRG	8
Richd.	HRD	28
Richd.	BBN	82
Robert H.	FTE	99
Sally	UNN	149
Saml.	CLY	117
Solomon, --?	NSN	222
Solomon	NSN	197
Solomon	NSN	199
Stephen	ETL	42
Susanna	NSN	197
Terril	HAR	194
Thomas	SHE	177
Thomas	MNR	195
Thomas	NSN	199
Thos.	HRY	267
Thos.	PUL	40A
Valentine	MER	88
William	CLY	117
William	HOP	234
William	PUL	66A
William	WTY	110A
BISSETT, Thomas	UNN	150
BISWICK, George	MER	87
BITER, James	CLD	149
BITNER, Nicholas	SCT	121A
BITTLE, John	CWL	50
BIVAN, John	TOD	129A
BIVEN, Alexander	BRK	241
Benjamin	BRK	235
Charles	BRK	239
Henry	BRK	237
Leonard	NSN	219
Leonard	BRK	239
Richard	NSN	219
Richard	WDF	93A
Saml.	BRK	243
Sophia	BRK	239
Thos.	BRK	243
BIVEN, Walter	BRK	239
BIVENS, --h-?	CWL	40
Benjamin	WDF	112A
John	FLD	34
John	GRD	121A
Thomas	FLD	39
Truman	MAD	130
BIVI--?, Julian	WDF	108A
BIVIN, Henry	NSN	222
BIXLER, David	LNC	39
BLACBURN, James	MAD	140
BLACK, Alexander	FTE	110
Alexander?	DVS	14A
Alexr.	KNX	2/8
Andrew	MAD	92
Andrew	WRN	37A
Ann	BBN	62
Ann	BBN	114
Archibald	KNX	296
Daniel	LVG	11
Daniel	PUL	66A
David	JEF	25
David	KNX	292
Drosula	BKN	14
Elizabeth	BKN	13
Elizabeth	PUL	68A
Frances	CBL	8A
George	BNE	6
George	MTG	231
Henry W.	MBG	141A
Hezakiah	FKN	64
Hugh	MER	87
James	BRN	1
James	BNE	6
James	WDF	101
Jane	CWL	38
Jas. D.	SCT	103A
Jeremiah	MNR	213
Jno.	JEF	31
Jno.	FKN	118
Jno.	HRY	251
John	MER	89
John	MAD	90
John	BBN	114
John	BBN	120
John	MNR	213
John	KNX	302
John	HND	9A
John	PUL	68A
John	SCT	118A
John	SHE	137A
Joseph	CBL	18A
Josiah	SPN	20A
Judy	CHN	44A
Marium	GNP	172A
Moses	HRT	153
Moses	PUL	61A
Nathaniel	PUL	64A
Peter	GRN	74
Robert	WDF	101
Robert	OHO	6A
Rudolph	BKN	13
Saml.	KNX	312
Saml.?	CWL	39
Samuel	BBN	94
Samuel	HAR	156
Samuel	SHE	140A
Sarah	PUL	68A
Stephen	JEF	34
Thos., Jr.	BRK	237
Thos., Sr.	BRK	241
Will	BBN	96
William	LVG	15
William	LGN	32
Wm.	BKN	14
Wm.	MAD	158

BLACK?, Benjamin? BNE 8
Mary BKN 8
BLACKABY?, Wm. O. BKN 26
BLACKALEY?, Wm. O. BKN 26
BLACKBURN, Alexander GTN 135
Benj. BKN 26
Benjamin NCH 118A
Churchil J./ I.? WDF 104A
David HAR 136
Edward M. WDF 111A
George WDF 108A
Hudson FLD 25
James MAD 138
James HAR 198
John HAR 208
John HRY 228
Jonathan WDF 110A
Julius SCT 116A
Julius NCH 117A
Nancey NCH 118A
Prudence WDF 110A
Rankin HAR 198
Robert HAR 178
Saml. BKN 16
Saml. MAS 63
Tho. MAS 67
Thomas FLD 23
Thomas D. GTN 131
Thos. SCT 134A
William B. WDF 104A
William N. SHE 176
Wm. BKN 16
Zebulon? CWL 32
BLACKBURN?, James ALN 108
Robt. ALN 96
BLACKEBY, Thadeus LNC 37
Thomas LNC 45
BLACKELY, Jeduthan BKN 4
BLACKETER, Alexr. MER 87
David MER 87
Henry MER 87
John, Jr. MER 87
John, Sr. MER 87
William MER 87
BLACKFORD, Benjamin JES 95
Ephraim WRN 38A
BLACKLEDGE, Ichabod PUL 55A
John PUL 56A
BLACKLOCK, Edward OHO 4A
Thomas NSN 179
Thos. NSN 219
Thos. GSN 129A
BLACKMAN, Frank GTN 122
BLACKMORE, Js. HRY 234
Owen SHE 125A
BLACKSTONE, Letty LNC 59
BLACKWELL, Armstead CLK 96
Benjamin MAD 130
Betey HRY 254
Catharine SHE 167
Edmond BRK 233
Geo. LVG 4
James ETL 47
James BRK 233
Jarret BRK 233
John LVG 15
John ETL 52
John UNN 151
Levy ETL 52
Mary GRD 111A
Patsy MBG 136
BLACKWELL, Richard FTE 73
Robert FKN 160
Robt. HRT 152
Robt. GRD 84A
Tho. ALN 112
Thomas UNN 153
Thornton HAR 156
William ETL 52
William ALN 92
William CLK 96
William UNN 151
Zach. GRD 88A
BLACKWOMAN, Rose FKN 58
BLACKWOOD, Joseph, Maj. MER 89
BLACWELL, Randolph MAD 172
BLADES, Eli SHE 156
BLADES?, Saml. BKN 19
Selby BKN 20
BLAGG, Calep SPN 7A
BLAGRAVES, Banister MER 86
BLAIN, Allexdr. LNC 15
Ann LNC 33
George BRN 2
James FKN 80
Jno. LNC 27
Martin CSY 204
Michael GSN 128A
Thomas CSY 204
Thomas CSY 210
William PUL 56A
Wm. BRK 237
BLAIR, (See Blain) LNC 63
Alexander NCH 109A
Andrew HRT 155
Charles HRL 102
Elizabeth JEF 66
Elizabeth HRT 153
Francis P. FKN 56
George FLD 35
Hannah HAR 134
James ADR 64
James GTN 123
James NSN 177
James NSN 201
James G. HAR 176
Jas. C. JEF 19
Jesse FLD 8
John FLD 21
John LNC 77
John CLD 144
John HOP 234
John WRN 49A
John FLG 70A
John R. HAR 198
Joseph LGN 23
Joseph HRL 104
Mancy WDF 103
Nancy HRL 104
Saml HAR 146
Samuel FTE 101
Sarah HRT 155
Sarah FLG 40A
Thomas NSN 180
Thos. FLG 36A
William HAR 134
William W. FTE 57
Wm. FLG 40A
Wm. FLG 70A
Wm. D. SHE 109A
BLAKE, Archibald WTY 122A
Bartholomew BRK 237
Benj. WTY 122A
George MTG 237
James JEF 44
BLAKE, James MER 88
James WYN 90A
John SCT 105A
Martin JEF 20
Martin JEF 24
Peter SHE 150
Polly MTG 261
Robt. BBN 78
Sarah MER 86
Sarah SHE 166
William SHE 156
William WTY 122A
BLAKELEY, Charles TRG 13A
James TRG 14
Jno. MAS 73
John UNN 154
Tho. MAS 63
William UNN 154
BLAKELY, Benj. KNX 278
Charles KNX 288
Charles WTY 112A
Jesse (Crossed Out) WTY 118A
Jesse WTY 113A
Saml. CHN 41A
BLAKELY?, Charles (Crossed Out) WTY 117A
BLAKEMAN, Aaron JES 86
Daniel GRN 68
George JES 86
James GRN 53
Jane JES 71
John JES 71
BLAKEMON, Aaron GRN 61
BLAKEMORE, John WRN 74A
BLAKENY, Wm. BBN 94
BLAKEY, Beverley K. WRN 75A
Fields CHN 29A
George LGN 36
James M. WRN 35A
William WRN 75A
BLAKINBAKER, Jeremh. JEF 48
BLAKLY, Thos. KNX 288
BLAKY, Thomas MNR 213
William GRN 60
BLALOCK, William WRN 69A
BLAN--T?, Jacob TRG 13
BLAN?, Reuben PUL 65A
BLANCHAD, Thomas LGN 42
BLANCHARD, Asa FTE 57
Greenberry LGN 43
William LGN 32
Willis LGN 44
BLAND, Ann WAS 36A
Ben MAS 76
Calvin MAS 56
Chas. GRD 104A
Eli MNR 193
J. B. JEF 26
James NSN 200
Jas. HRD 64
John CLD 141
John CLD 153
John NSN 185
John WAS 32A
Nancy WAS 30A
Osborn, Jr. MNR 193
Osburnd, Sr. MNR 193
Saml. ADR 10
Samuel NSN 199
Thomas GRD 83A
Thos. WAS 35A
Warren MNR 195
William NSN 198

BLANDFORD, Benedict BLT 194
Benjamin BLT 154
Edward BLT 192
Edwd. HRD 68
Francis D. BLT 194
George BLT 192
Henry L. WAS 87A
Nat WAS 56A
Richard BLT 192
Thos. WAS 38A
Walter BLT 154
BLANE, Jacob HRD 86
Silvain GTN 123
Tho. GRD 111A
BLANFORD, Aquiler WAS 50A
Catharine UNN 154
Francis NSN 184
John B. BRK 237
BLANKENBAKER, Lewis SHE 140A
Nicholas SHE 140A
Solomon SHE 140A
BLANKENSHIP, Barnet / Barret? ALN 142
Danl. GNP 172A
Elijah MAD 98
Fanny CLD 157
Hudson CLD 155
Jane CLD 145
Jesse CLD 157
John GRT 143
John CLD 157
Levi LGN 34
Lewis GNP 174A
Noel CLD 157
William CLD 161
BLANKINBAKER, David JEF 63
Hannah JEF 48
Jacob JEF 63
Saml. JEF 49
Thos. JEF 63
BLANKINSHIP, James GRN 52
Joel ALN 116
Obediah FLD 39
William FLD 37
Wm. GNP 169A
BLANTON, Abraham GSN 128A
Ann WDF 109A
Burdit A. TRG 4A
Carter FKN 74
Elijah GRD 108A
Harison FKN 108
Henry GTN 120
James F. MER 116
Jane GTN 123
Jessee JEF 66
John HRL 102
Joshua GRD 104A
Nancy WDF 99A
Sally FTE 91
Thos. CHN 42
Vincent HRL 102
William MER 88
William HRL 104
William GTN 120
Willis FKN 160
BLARE, Joseph WAS 56A
Mary WAS 56A
Richard WAS 56A
BLARE?, Rueben PUL 65A
Wm. B. FLG 71A
BLASINGEM, Thos. C. BKN 11
BLASINGIM, Buckley BKN 9
BLAYDES, Francis SHE 167
Francis, Sr. SHE 168
Francis R. SHE 158
George SHE 175
John SHE 160
William SHE 160
BLAYDS, Walker J./I.? GRN 55
BLAYLOCK, Jer. RCK 81A
BLEAK, James MAD 128
BLEAKLEY, Robert HRD 96
BLEDSO, Volentine BKN 22
BLEDSOE, Abra. MAS 53
Abram GTN 123
Benjamin CLD 158
Benjn. MAS 52
Edwd. SCT 109A
Elijah WYN 87A
H. BBN 146
Isaac GTN 133
Jesse BBN 142
John CHN 28
John FTE 82
John S. GTN 123
Joseph CLY 124
Joseph CLD 158
M. O. GRD 115A
Moses GTN 133
Richard FTE 86
Will SCT 121A
Will. KNX 304
Willis CLY 127
Winefried GTN 117
BLESS, Will MAS 57
BLETCHOR?, Thomas CLK 74
BLEVIN, James OHO 8A
John OHO 8A
William OHO 7A
BLEVINS, Abraham WYN 95A
Benj. RCK 82A
Charles GRN 78
Daniel GRN 77
Elisha WTY 122A
James JEF 60
James WYN 101A
James WYN 102A
John JEF 44
John WTY 122A
Johnathan WYN 95A
Lemuel JEF 55
Saml. JEF 35
Stephan WTY 122A
William WYN 104A
BLEW, John HOP 232
BLEWET, Edward WRN 62A
Eli WRN 62A
BLEWETT?, Thomas WRN 62A
BLIMOE?, Bery BRK 241
Thos., Jr. BRK 241
BLINCOE, James NSN 185
Jas. HRD 94
BLINCOE?, Bery BRK 241
Thos., Jr. BRK 241
BLINOE?, Thos., Sr. BRK 241
BLISIT, George HRT 153
BLISS, Pliny CBL 4A
Stephen LWS 98A
William LWS 98A
BLISSARD, Josh LGN 28
BLIWETT?, Thomas WRN 62A
BLOCKER, David GTN 123
Sely CHN 43
BLOODSWORTH, William LWS 97A
BLOOM, Isaac CBL 12A
BLOOMER, Daniel GNP 165A
Henry H. GNP 171A
BLOUNT, Andrew NCH 121A
Beverly JEF 34
Eatha NCH 119A
Hezekiah NCH 121A
Miles LNC 59
BLOYD, Bivy GRN 55
Purnell PUL 67A
BLUE, David UNN 154
David FLG 28A
Hary FTE 58
Jacob BBN 62
James UNN 154
John UNN 147
John UNN 149
Margaret TOD 125A
Richard UNN 146
Rolley FTE 60
Solomon UNN 151
Wm. FLG 54A
BLUERN?, Jesse OWN 100
BLUFORD?, Ambrose BBN 102
BLUM?, Jesse OWN 100
Joab OWN 100
BLUMER, Abraham CBL 15A
Peter PUL 62A
BLUNFORD, Lewis BRK 243
BLUNT, Bartho. FTE 57
Henry GTN 117
John GRN 58
Joseph JEF 44
Levy GRN 59
Sally WDF 103
Thomas HRT 153
BLYTHE, Charles ETL 39
James FTE 62
Jno. ETL 39
John RCK 79A
Martha CHN 36
Robert ETL 41
Samuel CHN 36
Samuel FTE 85
Stephen TRG 13A
William FTE 82
BO-LS?, Mary MAD 136
BOADS, Wm. MAD 130
BOARD, Elijah BRK 235
Ezekel BRK 237
Henderson BRK 235
James BRK 235
James, Jr. BRK 237
Joel BRK 237
Jubal BRK 237
Micajah BRK 235
Nehemiah BRK 235
Philip BLT 192
Reuben BRK 239
Richard BRK 235
Stephen BRK 235
Wm. BRK 237
BOARDMAN, Benjamin NCH 125A
Elizabeth BBN 72
James WDF 103
William NCH 125A
BOAS, John SCT 120A
BOATMAN, Elijah WRN 58A
Francis WRN 58A
Henry LNC 79
Henry NCH 114A
Jessee JES 69
John LNC 79
John LWS 94A
Richard CLD 156
Robert JES 69

Name	County	Page
BOATMAN, Robert	JES	86
William	JES	86
William	NCH	107A
BOATS, Wm.	BKN	13
BOAZ, James	BBN	72
BOBB, Dorothy	FTE	65
BOBBETT, John	CHN	36
Mary	CBL	11A
Stephen	CHN	33A
BOBBIT, Wm.	PUL	43A
BOBBS, Danil	FTE	79
BOBIT, James	PUL	39A
BOCOCK, Wm. W.	GNP	167A
BODELL, James	PUL	42A
BODIN, John	BRK	237
BODINE, C-----ame?	NSN	224
Catharine	NSN	224
Cornelius	NSN	181
Elizabeth	NSN	206
Jacob	WDF	105A
John	LGN	41
BODINE?, Elizabeth	NSN	200
Isaac	NSN	200
BODINGER, George M.	NCH	117A
BODKIN, John	BTH	216
John	KNX	278
BODKINS, William	HAR	158
BODLEY, Thomas	FTE	63
BOGAN, James	SPN	12A
Levi	SPN	12A
Samuel	SPN	11A
William	SPN	12A
BOGARD, Cornelius	BLT	162
George	BLT	178
John	BLT	178
BOGART, Isaac	MER	89
BOGEE?, Andrew	MAD	96
BOGER, John	GRN	71
BOGGESS, Jno.	FKN	156
John	BNE	6
Joseph	FKN	158
Josiah	CLK	87
Lemuel	MGB	137A
Margaret	BNE	8
Peter	MBG	141A
Richard	MBG	141
Robert	MBG	141
Robert	NCH	106A
Thomas	LWS	97A
Vincent	FKN	158
Warren	MBG	141
BOGGESS?, Robt.	BNE	8
BOGGS, Alexander	FKN	60
Brazillea	SHE	139A
John, Jr.	MAD	164
John, Sr.	MAD	128
Joseph	MAD	128
Robert	FTE	84
William	BNE	6
William	CLK	107
BOGGUS?, William	BBN	108
BOGLE, Robert H.	WYN	90A
BOGS, Charles	CLK	96
Delilah	HRL	104
William	CLK	95
BOHALL, Jos.	HRD	40
BOHANNAN, Judy	FKN	62
Ostin	FKN	114
BOHANNON, Abram	SHE	151
Betssey	LNC	63
David	MNR	199
Deborah	JEF	44
Elijah	JEF	52
Elliott	WDF	94A
Francis	JEF	52

Name	County	Page
BOHANNON, Geo.	JEF	55
Jermon	WDF	94A
Julious	JEF	58
Larkin	JEF	52
Patty	BRN	3
Richd. B.	WDF	126A
Simian	WDF	94A
BOHON, Benjamin	MER	86
Elijah	MER	86
George	MER	86
John, Jr.	MER	86
John, Sr.	MER	86
Thomas	SHE	166
Walter	MER	86
William, Esq.	MER	86
William R.	MER	86
BOID, Abner	TRG	7A
Abraham	TRG	7
Archer	TRG	6A
Ebenezar	TRG	7A
John	TRG	7
Josiah	TRG	7A
Robert	TRG	7A
BOIDN?, Zeruiah	MNR	207
BOIL, Hugh	SPN	8A
BOILS, James	GSN	129A
BOISSEAU, Patrick	BRN	33
BOISSEAW, Daniel	SPN	6A
John	SPN	6A
BOLAND, Widow	LVG	15
John	CWL	43
Moses	BNE	2
BOLD, James	NSN	213
John	NSN	213
BOLDOCK, Anney	CSY	228
Reuben	CSY	228
BOLDOCK?, William	CSY	208
BOLEN, Jordon	HAR	148
William	HAR	152
Wm.	JEF	55
BOLENGER, Henry	MAS	78
BOLER, Archer	JEF	55
Fountain	JEF	48
John	JEF	52
Mordica	FKN	86
Theodric	FKN	88
Thos.	JEF	27
BOLERIGHT, James	JES	94
BOLES, Fulton	CBL	20A
Henery	CBL	20A
John	MER	86
John	UNN	149
John	CBL	18A
Robert	HAR	154
Samuel	NCH	128A
Sary	HRL	102
Thomas	CLD	151
William	CLY	117
BOLEY, Henry	NSN	219
James	BRK	241
John	HRT	153
BOLIN, Archibald	CHN	29A
Isam	KNX	312
James	CHN	29A
Jimms?	GTN	125
John	FLD	28
John O.	GTN	125
John S.	GTN	119
Jos.	KNX	312
Sish/ Lish?	WTY	111A
Stephen	WTY	127A
William	GTN	127
BOLING, James	CWL	36
BOLINGER, Jos.	CHN	39
BOLLETT?, Nicy	FLG	27A
BOLLIN, George	LVG	15

Name	County	Page
BOLLINGER, Masseys?	LVG	15
BOLLON?, John	WAS	40A
BOLLONG, Joel, Sr?	SCT	107A
BOLLS, Austin	CHN	44
BOLSON, John	SCT	95A
BOLT, Isaac	GNP	167A
James	GNP	176A
BOLT?, Jno.	ADR	8
BOLTIN?, Peyton	LNC	13
BOLTON, Amos	LVG	2
Aqu.	JEF	21
John	CWL	39
John	GTN	119
John	MAD	162
BOLY, George	NSN	222
BOLZ?, Peter	HRY	192
BOMAN, Geo.	GRD	108A
John	WAS	49A
John	WYN	97A
L-----?	RCK	82A
Roswell,	WAS	70A
Sarah A.	WAS	60A
BOMANS, Isaac	GRN	77
BOMBO, Thomas	HRT	153
BOMGARDNER, Geo.	JEF	39
BOMGARNER, Aaron	LGN	40
BOMON, Henry	WAS	35A
BOMONT, William	GRD	102B
BONAM?, Ameriah	FLG	54A
Saml.	MAS	71
BOND, ---.? B.	CWL	43
Anthony	FKN	144
Charles	FLD	34
Danl.	CWL	34
Ealenor	NCH	121A
Elizabeth	CLD	152
Isaac	WYN	88A
James S.	FKN	142
Jno.	HAR	144
Jno.	FKN	156
Joel	WYN	85A
John	HRY	234
Joseph	WYN	85A
Lenard	WAS	20A
Robert	BRN	3
Solomon	HRY	234
Thom.	CWL	50
Thomas	CWL	58
William	HAR	144
William	WYN	87A
William	WYN	88A
Winfry	CWL	37
Wm.	CWL	50
Wm.	FKN	142
Wm., Sr.	FKN	144
Wm.	SHE	130A
Zach.	CWL	34
BOND?, Bazil	GNP	176A
BONDS, John	GTN	132
John	SPN	22A
Robert	GTN	131
Thos.	CHN	29A
Thos.	SCT	116A
Walker	SCT	116A
Will	SCT	112A
William	GTN	132
BONDURANT, Benjamin	SHE	173
Benjm.	SHE	161
Geo. D.	SHE	161
James	MAD	174
Jos	SHE	161
Joseph	MTG	225
Robt. M.	SHE	161
Thomas	SHE	167

Name	County	Page
BONE, Asana?	TOD	130A
Hugh	HOP	232
James	HOP	232
John	MBG	142A
Mark	HOP	232
Trifonia	MBG	135
BONEL?, Bazil	GNP	176A
BONER, Barnibus	PND	27A
Charles	PND	17A
John	LNC	79
BONER?, Edward	NSN	204
BONIFIELD, John	CLK	69
Marine?	CLK	72
BONN, Thos.	BBN	110
BONNEL?, Joseph	JES	82
BONNER, J. I.?	TOD	132
John	PND	26A
Mary	PND	26A
Moses Q.?	ALN	92
BONODURANT, Joseph W.	SHE	160
BONTA, Henry	MER	87
Henry	MER	88
Jacob	MER	88
Lambert	MER	88
Peter	MER	87
Polly	MER	87
BONTZ, James	NSN	219
BONWELL?, Thomas	BKN	2
BOOCHER, James	LNC	33
BOOGS, James	MAD	158
BOOHER, John	MER	89
Nicholas	MER	89
BOOIE, Archibald	TRG	14
BOOK, Henry	HND	10A
Mary	HND	11A
BOOK?, Saml.	FLG	59A
BOOKE, Samuel	BTH	202
BOOKER, Daniel	GRN	58
Edward	SHE	162
Elizabeth	SHE	165
Isaac	JEF	61
Jacob	HRD	62
Jno.	ADR	6
Jno.	JEF	46
John P.	SHE	165
Parom	SHE	165
Paul J.	WAS	75A
Richard	SHE	166
Saml.	WAS	75A
Simon	GRT	144
William	SPN	12A
Wm. B.	WAS	79A
BOOKOUT, John	WYN	88A
John	WYN	98A
Joseph	WYN	98A
BOOKS, Jonathan	MAD	120
BOOLES, Jas.	CHN	44A
BOON, Abner	HAR	168
Ann	TOD	126A
Bend.	WAS	44A
Charles	HRD	94
Charles	WAS	44A
Cornelious	WAS	44A
Enoch	HRD	60
George G.	FTE	81
Isaiah	WDF	105A
Israel	WYN	85A
Jacob	MAS	78
James	BBN	108
James	WAS	44A
Jessee	WYN	94A
Joab	HAR	152
John	HRD	94
John	WRN	66A
John L.	SHE	154
BOON, Joseph, Snr.	BTH	192
Joseph	BTH	192
Josiah	SHE	155
Mary H.	WAS	75A
Mosses	WDF	101
Samuel	FTE	81
Thomas	LGN	30
Thomas	WRN	66A
Walter	NSN	189
William	FTE	79
BOONE, Edward	SHE	157
George	SHE	164
George, Senr.	CLK	79
Joseph	WAS	41A
BOONE?, Solomon	BLT	152
BOOTEN?, Walker	WRN	47A
BOOTH, Anderson	CLK	86
Federick	WDF	100
Isaac	BTH	196
James	HRD	22
James	WDF	102
Jno.	BRN	3
John	BNE	8
Thos.	HND	9
Wm.	JEF	43
BOOTH?, Franklin?	BKN	15
BOOTHE, Benjamimn	SHE	161
David	BBN	78
David, Senr.	BBN	78
Elijah	FLG	36A
John	SPN	14A
Joseph	BKN	26
Peter	SHE	161
Rodolphey	BLT	192
Saml.	BBN	68
Stephen	SHE	160
Thos.	JEF	27
William, Jr.	MER	86
William, Sr.	MER	86
Wm.	BBN	136
BOOTS, Bartus, Jr.	FKN	96
Bartus, Sn.	FKN	96
Isaac	BLT	158
John	BLT	158
Joseph	FKN	92
Sally	FKN	92
BOOWN?, Scott	BBN	64
BOOYER, Joseph	ADR	8
BOOYIER, Jno.	ADR	8
BOOZ, John	WDF	116A
William	WDF	115A
BORAH, George	BTL	317
Jacob	BTL	317
Michael	BTL	317
BORALLY, P. D.	GRD	108A
BORAM, Isaac	GTN	123
Jos.	TOD	130
BORD, James	MER	86
Philip	MER	86
BORDERS, Archibald	FLD	24
Catharine	FLD	24
David	BRN	4
Henry	BRN	4
Henry	WAS	75A
Hezekiah	FLD	24
John	FLD	22
Mat	WAS	74A
Michael	FLD	22
Peter	BRN	4
Thomas	LGN	36
BORDERS?, George	NSN	197
BORGAS, John	FTE	93
BORIN, Hozeah	TRG	5A
BORIN?, Stephen	TRG	5A
BORNER, Robt.	BRK	235
BOROUGH, Thomas	GNP	171A
BORTON?, George	SCT	105A
BOSCLEY?, Joseph	WRN	66A
BOSE?, Saml.	MAD	132
BOSELEY?, Joseph	WRN	66A
BOSEY, William	HAR	138
BOSHART, Jacob	FTE	66
BOSIER, Wm.	OHO	5A
BOSLEY, Benedict	NCH	108A
Berry	LNC	43
Charles	MER	87
Elisha	WAS	35A
Gidian	WAS	65A
Isaac	SHE	152
James	SHE	133A
John, Dr.	MER	88
Sarah	LNC	43
Walter	BBN	88
BOSLY, Elija	WAS	30A
BOSOWELL, Hartwell	HAR	220
BOSSEL?, Elijah	SCT	96A
BOSSILER?, Jacob	ALN	140
BOSSWELL?, John	BNE	4
BOST, Catharine	LNC	45
David	LNC	45
Valentine	LNC	45
BOST?, Peter	GRD	90A
BOSTHLEWAIT, Richard	LVG	12
BOSTICK, Elizabeth	BBN	130
Ezra?	HND	10A
Hezakiah	BKN	5
John	HND	10A
Margaret	BRN	3
BOSTIE, Catherine	BLT	168
BOSTON, James	JEF	60
James	GRN	71
Jonas	WYN	84A
Lydia	BBN	60
Reuben	MER	89
BOSWELL, Bushrod	FTE	67
Craven	HND	11A
Eleanor	OHO	3A
George	FTE	56
George	SHE	123A
George	SHE	128A
Harrison	KNX	296
Henry	OHO	3A
John	LNC	11
John	SHE	131A
Joseph	FTE	58
Thomas	LNC	11
Thomas E. & Co.	FTE	56
Will	HRY	186
Will	SCT	111A
William	HAR	154
William	HAR	166
BOSWORTH, B.	FTE	108
B.	FTE	108
BOTEN / BOTER?, Frederick	UNN	151
BOTH--?, Dave	RCK	78A
BOTH?, Thompson	ADR	6
BOTHEL, Samuel	SPN	9A
BOTHERN?, Dave	RCK	78A
BOTHUM?, Dave W.	RCK	78A
BOTHURN?, Dave	RCK	78A
BOTKINS, Richard	WTY	121A
BOTTOM, Anderson	HND	10A
Jacob	MER	86
John	MER	86
Martin	MER	86
Micajah	MER	86
Thomas	MER	86
Turner, Jr.	MER	86
Turner, Sr.	MER	86

Name	County	Page
BOTTOM, William, Jr.	MER	86
William, Sr.	MER	86
William S.	MER	86
Wilson	HND	11
BOTTOMS, Abner	GRN	75
Edmund	MER	86
Eliza	GRN	73
William	BLT	154
BOTTONS, Martin	WAS	81A
BOTTS, Archabalde	BTH	202
Catharine	MTG	265
Charles	NSN	186
Charles	MTG	239
Geo. W.	FLG	78A
Jno.	MAS	57
Jno.	MAS	62
Jno.	HRY	250
John	SHE	168
John	BTH	202
John	FLG	56A
Joseph	BNE	4
Joshua	BNE	4
Joshua	MTG	267
Lawrence	MTG	265
Moses	BTH	202
Robert	MTG	265
Roland	BNE	4
Seth	FLG	73A
Thomas	BTH	206
Thomas	MTG	297
William	BNE	4
BOUCHER, Gabriel	ALN	100
James	WDF	121A
Peter	ALN	122
Richard	BKN	28
BOUGE, Elihu	HRD	94
John	HRD	92
BOUGH, Fredrick	BTH	208
BOUGHMAN, Asahel	BKN	23
Henry	LNC	49
BOUGHNER, Peter	BKN	8
BOULDEN, Jesse	NCH	105
BOULDIN, Mary Anne	MER	86
BOULTON, James	BLT	192
Joel	OWN	99
Maryann	LGN	24
BOUNEY, Joseph	FLD	25
BOURLAND, Benjamin	HOP	234
John	HOP	234
William	HOP	234
BOURN, David	CLD	151
Jessee	FKN	132
John	OWN	103
Richd.	FKN	126
William	OWN	104
BOURN?, William	MER	88
BOURNE, Abner	JES	79
Ambrose	TOD	126A
Andrew	JES	69
Daniel	JES	96
Elijah	JES	79
George	JES	72
Hannah	JES	77
James	MTG	239
John	JES	79
Morton	JES	73
Moses	JES	77
Susanna	FKN	126
Walker	MTG	235
William	JES	79
Wm.	SHE	119A
BOURNE?, Moses	JES	77
BOUSLEY?, James	CSY	218
BOUSS?, Michael C.	CLD	144
BOUTA, Peter	MER	88
BOUY?, John	HAR	180
BOW, Henry	CLD	164
Jesse	CLD	162
John	CLD	162
Nathaniel	CLD	162
BOWAN, Adam	FLD	24
David	GRN	71
Robt.	GRN	69
BOWDEN, John	UNN	146
BOWDRY, Lettice	WDF	116A
Lewis	WDF	115A
Saml. P.	BRN	2
BOWEN, A.	CHN	27A
Andrew	FLG	52A
Benjamin	WRN	40A
Elenor	BBN	132
Franc-s	GRD	88A
Francis	HAR	192
Frederick	MTG	259
Isaac	BKN	24
Jacob	BLT	176
John	LVG	15
Laben	HRD	36
Micajh.	CWL	32
Milby	BBN	92
Morgan	LVG	15
Parker	FTE	66
Samuel A.	HND	3
Thomas	SHE	157
Thomas	BLT	182
William	NCH	118A
Wm.	FLG	51A
BOWENS, Nancey	SCT	110A
BOWER, G. M.	SCT	91A
Jacob	LGN	37
John	BBN	132
Michael	SCT	122A
Nicholas	BBN	132
Robt.	BBN	132
Solomon	BBN	132
BOWERS, Chs.	JEF	61
James	CBL	3A
Saml.	PND	27A
William	WRN	34A
BOWES?, Daniel	FTE	105
BOWHALL, George	HND	9
BOWING, William R.	HND	11
BOWLAND, James	CWL	50
R---?	CWL	50
Wm.	SHE	142A
BOWLEN, Elizaber	MAD	174
John	OHO	10A
Wm.	SHE	126A
Wm.	SHE	129A
BOWLER, Benjamin	MAD	152
Daniel	MAD	166
John	FTE	92
John	MAD	166
Larker	MAD	120
Richd.	FKN	80
William	CLK	75
William	FTE	75
BOWLES, Ally	WAS	29A
David	BBN	114
Hannah	BBN	86
Hugh	BBN	86
J. B.	JEF	19
John	BRN	5
John	LGN	47
Joseph	WAS	73A
Mary	MNR	201
Nathl. N.	BRN	4
Nelson	BBN	86
Polly	WAS	81A
Robt.	BBN	86
Robt.	BBN	114
BOWLES, Stephen	BBN	68
Thos.	BBN	92
Thos.	SHE	128A
Walter	SCT	105A
William	BRN	2
William	BBN	126
William	MNR	201
BOWLESS, Thomas	WRN	33A
BOWLIN, Elizabeth	WTY	121A
James	CSY	220
Jarred	HRD	28
Jemima	MER	86
John	HRD	72
John	CSY	220
Thomas	CLK	92
Wm.	HRD	18
BOWLING, Benjn.	ADR	6
Christo.	CLY	127
Dread	MER	87
Elijah	CLY	126
Henry	FTE	76
James	CLY	116
James	WAS	81A
James	WAS	82A
Jas	MAS	63
Jesse, Jr.	CLY	126
Jesse, Sr.	CLY	126
John	CLY	126
John	CLY	126
John	HRT	152
John	NSN	178
John, Sr.	CLY	120
Joseph	HRD	92
Justus	CLY	126
Mary	MAS	72
Richard &?	MER	87
Robert	BBN	140
Susan	HRT	155
Thomas	BBN	108
William B.	CLY	126
Wm.	WAS	81A
BOWLS, Jessee	BBN	86
Thos. R.	BBN	80
William	ETL	54
William	WAS	45A
BOWLWARE, Ramsey	WDF	114A
BOWMAN, Abraham	JEF	51
Abraham	FTE	104
Abraham	FTE	112
Canelius	CLY	111
Casper	BKN	9
Chas.	SHE	136A
Cornelus	CLY	113
Daniel	CLD	151
David	JES	96
E. W.	CLY	124
Edwd.	CLY	112
Edwd.	CLY	122
Elijah	FLD	3
Elijah	CLY	111
Elijah	CLY	113
Elisha	CLY	112
Elisha	BLT	172
Granville	CLD	167
Jacob	BLT	158
Jacob	PUL	39A
Jacob	SCT	111A
John	BKN	14
John	MER	88
John	CLY	112
John	TOD	131
John	UNN	150
John	OHO	10A
Joseph	JES	93
Joseph	FTE	104
Joseph	BLT	174

Name	County	Page
BOWMAN, Judah	WAS	23A
Margaret	CHN	44A
Milly M.	MBG	135
Nicholas	ETL	53
Peter	JES	76
Pleasant	CLD	163
Robt.	HRD	26
Schadrach	NCH	114A
Thomas	CLY	122
Thos.	HRD	70
William	FTE	64
William	MER	88
William	CSY	210
Wm.	OHO	10A
BOWMAN?, Jacob	CLY	122
John, Esqr.	MER	88
Joseph	JES	93
Robert	WDF	119A
BOWMAR, Herman	WDF	122A
John	HRT	153
Talbot	LNC	11
BOWMER, John	PUL	65A
BOWMER?, Joseph	JES	93
BOWMON?, Charles	HRY	186
BOWNAN, William	HRT	153
BOWNAR, John	HRT	153
BOWNER, William	FTE	101
BOWOR?, Alex.	BKN	14
BOWREN, Alfr--?	CLK	107
BOWREN?, Cornelius	CLK	101
BOWRNE, Benjamin	SHE	119A
Charles	SHE	119A
George	SHE	119A
BOWROUGH, John	MAD	102
BOWS, John	FTE	107
BOWSMAN?, John	FLG	79A
BOWYER, --lentine?	CWL	43
Henry	FKN	136
John	FTE	111
Nat.? P.	CWL	43
BOX, Betsy	KNX	312
Saml.	KNX	312
BOY---?, Saml.	JEF	54
BOYAKIN?, Solomon	MBG	136
BOYARS, Phillip	JEF	60
BOYCE, Allen	FLG	57A
Jesse	WRN	35A
John	FTE	90
Nicholas	HOP	230
Richard	LGN	33
Robert	MER	86
Thos.	SCT	110A
Will	SCT	110A
William	JES	84
BOYD, -----?	CWL	40
Aaron	CHN	33
Abner	CHN	41A
Andrew	BTH	184
Andrew	HAR	214
Ann	SHE	132A
Archibald	LWS	91A
Charles	BTH	188
Darcus	BTH	192
David	CHN	33
Drury B.	BTH	188
Edward	LWS	94A
Elijah	MBG	136
Elisha	MER	116
Elizabeth	HND	10A
Francis	CHN	32A
Geo.	CWL	44
George	SHE	167
George	LWS	88A
Hardy	CHN	32A
Henry	LGN	46
Henry	HND	6A
BOYD, Heron	BRN	3
Hiram	BRN	2
Hugh	HRL	102
Hugh	SCT	104A
James	LVG	8
James	FTE	88
James	CLD	157
James	HRY	178
James	LWS	94A
James	LWS	96A
James	SHE	133A
Jeremiah	PND	27A
Jessee	FLG	65A
Jno.	BKN	28
Jno.	MAS	72
Jno.	MAS	74
Jno.	HRY	240
John	CHN	29
John	LGN	30
John	LGN	37
John	FTE	95
John	CLD	149
John	HAR	200
John	MNR	215
John	HRY	216
John, Jr.	NCH	116A
John, Sr.	NCH	116A
John	CBL	15A
John	PND	27A
John	FLG	65A
John	LWS	98A
John	SHE	134A
John C.	BNE	6
John G.	ETL	51
John M.	TOD	132
John S.	HAR	216
Joshua	SHE	168
Lemuel	BRN	4
Martha	FTE	112
Matthew	LWS	94A
Moses	BTH	184
Nancy	PUL	50A
Philip	GNP	171A
Polly	HAR	214
R.	BBN	144
Rankin	HAR	154
Richard	BTH	166
Robert	HAR	196
Robert	WTY	127A
Robert	GNP	171A
Robt.	LVG	2
Robt.	PUL	44A
Sally	BRN	5
Saml.	PUL	44A
Saml.	PUL	50A
Saml.	NCH	115A
Saml.	SHE	122A
Samuel	LWS	96A
Samuel	WTY	115A
Spence	BTH	178
Spencer?, Sr.	BTH	202
Thomas	FTE	106
Thomas	BTH	156
Thomas	MTG	261
Thomas	CBL	20A
Thomas D.	MNR	215
Thos.	BKN	23
Will.	SCT	117A
William	CLD	157
William	BTH	162
William	SHE	168
William	LWS	95A
William	LWS	96A
William	NCH	116A
Wm.	BRN	4
Wm.	CHN	33
BOYD, Wm.	FKN	124
Wm.	SHE	132A
Wm. G.	SHE	127A
BOYD?, John	FLG	73A
BOYED, Andrew	GRD	106A
BOYER, Adam	PUL	62A
Jacob	LNC	3
Jacob	HRY	255
John G.	FTE	56
Martin	CHN	42A
Michael	BBN	114
BOYERS, Frederick	JEF	56
Michael	BNE	8
Phillip	JEF	64
Samuel	WTY	124A
BOYL, Margart?	NSN	208
BOYLE, Alexr.	GRD	92A
David	TOD	128
Edward	WDF	112A
Henry	BLT	188
James	MNR	211
James	MTG	291
John	LGN	43
John	UNN	146
John	HAR	152
John, Judge	MER	88
John, Sr.	GRD	116A
John	FLG	25A
BOYLS?, Mary	MAD	136
BOYLSTON, Bartlett	WRN	56A
Benjamin	WRN	55A
BOYTTEN?, Saml.	JEF	54
BOZARTH, Jonithan	GSN	128A
Terry/ Jerry?	GSN	128A
BOZARTH?, Joseph	TRG	14A
BOZE?, James	MAD	108
BOZIER, Fanny	CHN	43A
BR---N?, Wm.	ALN	140
BR--TS?, Durham	WAS	18A
BRAATELY, Layton	BBN	120
BRACH / BRACK?, James	CSY	208
BRACHER, Allen	BRN	4
John	WTY	124A
Nannah	SPN	22A
Seth	BRN	4
BRACKEN, Charles	HAR	216
Charles	WAS	22A
James	BTH	204
Nancy	BTH	184
Walter	BTH	204
BRACKET, John	KNX	314
John, Sr.	KNX	286
BRACKETT, Elizath	HRY	200
Polly	SHE	169
Thomas	MBG	136
BRACKETTE, Burwell	HND	6
BRACKIN, Theophilis	BTH	202
BRACKIN?, John	BRK	241
BRADA, John	HOP	232
BRADBERRY, James	HAR	140
BRADBURN, Mary	MER	116
Richard D.	WAS	82A
Widw.	CWL	33
Wm. C.	ALN	106
BRADDOCK, General	HRD	94
BRADEN, Aron	WAS	33A
Bartleson	HRD	36
Elijah	JEF	48
Will	SCT	110A
BRADEY, Philip	FTE	61
BRADFORD, Adam	WAS	29A
Alexr.	SCT	132A
Austin	SCT	138A
Benjn.	SCT	111A

Name	County	Page
BRADFORD, Charles	FTE	69
Daniel	FTE	70
Daniel	SCT	93A
Elizth.	SCT	111A
Enoch	SCT	129A
Fielding	SCT	128A
Garland	FLG	68A
James	BKN	19
James	WAS	29A
John	FTE	68
John	PND	16A
John	PND	27A
Nancy	SPN	14A
Thos. H.	SCT	128A
Wm.	BKN	8
Wm.	PND	16A
BRADFORD?, John B.	BBN	136
BRADHAM, Edward	FLD	30
BRADIN, Joseph	ETL	53
BRADLEY, Andrew	CLY	129
Ben.	CHN	45
Beverley	BRN	3
Charles	HOP	232
Charles	WDF	122A
Daniel	BBN	66
Dennis	FTE	84
Elijah	HRD	84
Elish	BTH	194
George	BRN	3
George	FLD	31
George	NCH	106A
Henry	CLK	90
Hiram	MTG	279
Hiram	WRN	76A
James	BRN	4
Jesse	FLD	5
Jno.	CHN	44
Joel	BRN	3
John	LVG	15
John	BBN	66
John	GTN	128
John	MTG	279
John	GRD	95A
John	SCT	120A
John W.	SCT	128A
Johnson	BNE	46
Leonard K.	FTE	81
Mildred	FTE	62
Milly	TOD	131A
Reubin	PUL	38A
Richard	CLD	154
Richd.	BRN	3
Richd.	PUL	49A
Robert	NCH	106A
Samuel	BTH	206
Stephen	BNE	46
Terry	FTE	81
Thomas	GTN	128
Thos.	FKN	86
Thos.	SCT	127A
William	FTE	83
William	HOP	232
William	WRN	39A
Willis	SCT	107A
Wm.	ADR	8
Wm.	BBN	70
Wm.	HRD	84
Wm.	PUL	49A
Wm.	SHE	139A
BRADLY, Edward R.	CHN	28A
Elisha	BBN	66
Isaah	BTH	212
James	CHN	32
Jas./ Jos.?	HRY	255
Oney / Oncy?	CHN	32
Samuel	CHN	32
BRADLY, William	CHN	33A
BRADSBARY, John	NSN	208
BRADSBERRY, Joel	NSN	218
BRADSBERT, E--za?	JEF	26
BRADSHAW, -----?	LVG	15
-am-.	CWL	44
Anderson	MTG	261
Benjamin	MER	88
Benjamine	JES	89
Catharine	JES	89
Charles	LGN	31
Clabourn	MER	88
Clemons	BKN	19
David	BTH	192
David	NCH	126A
Elijah	ADR	18
Elizabeth	BTH	174
Felden	ADR	8
Gideon	ADR	18
Isaac	ADR	56
Isaak	ADR	54
James	MER	88
James	SHE	110A
Jas.	BTH	150
John	CWL	50
John	BBN	102
John	SHE	168
John	MTG	241
Larnner?	MER	88
Obediah	ADR	18
Robt.	GNP	170A
Seth	BRN	3
Shadrach	MER	88
Steth	ADR	18
Thomas	HRT	152
Thomas	BTH	174
Thomas	SHE	126A
William	LGN	23
William	HOP	234
William	MTG	247
William	NCH	118A
Wm.	ADR	3
BRADSWAW, Edward	CHN	39
BRADY, Charles	CBL	9A
Henry	WAS	69A
James	SCT	120A
Jamima	SHE	125A
John	BNE	4
John, Jr.	GRD	88A
John, Sr.	GRD	88A
John A.	MER	87
Michael	CBL	9A
Patrick	NCH	117A
BRAFFORD, Samuel	FLD	36
BRAGG, Elizabeth	MTG	243
Ezechial	ADR	8
Gabriel	BRN	4
Joel	MAS	54
Thomas	LWS	95A
BRAIDY, Tho. A.	LNC	9
BRAINBRIDGE, A.	TOD	128
BRAKE, Bennet	CLD	155
Jacob	CLD	156
Joshua	CLD	157
William	CLD	157
William	CLD	162
BRAMBELL, Alexdr.	MAS	60
Saml.	MAS	60
BRAMBLE, Abra.	MAS	65
David	FLG	27A
Johnathan	FLG	48A
BRAMBLET, Henry	BBN	66
Will	SCT	109A
Wm.	BBN	78
Wm.	BBN	80
BRAMBLETT, John	OWN	100
BRAMBLETT, Martin	OWN	99
BRAMELL, Hanson	MAS	66
Jno	MAS	66
BRAMER, Jeremiah	BTH	210
Robt.	FLG	43A
BRAMER?, Saml.	FLG	42A
BRAMLET, Ambrose	CLD	148
James	CLD	150
Lewis	BBN	64
BRAMMEL, Nathan	BLT	152
BRAMWELL, Elisha	MAS	66
Will	MAS	66
BRAN/ BRAW?, Wm.	CWL	58
BRANAM, Will	MAS	58
BRANCH, Nelson	CWL	43
Pleasant	NCH	124A
BRANCHCOMB, David	WYN	98A
John, Sr.	WYN	98A
Thomas	WYN	98A
BRAND, John	FTE	63
Reason W.	BBN	84
Richard	BBN	112
Richd.	BBN	84
Thos.	FLG	73A
William	HND	5
BRAND?, ---	BBN	96
BRANDENBERRY/ BRANDENBURG?, David	CLK	82
BRANDENBURG, Absolem	ETL	50
Absolom	HRD	12
Henry	HRD	10
Jonathan	HRD	10
Joseph	ETL	53
Samuel	ETL	53
Solomn.	HRD	12
Solomn.	HRD	22
BRANDIMAN?, Abraham	MNR	199
BRANDON, Benjamin	HAR	144
George	CWL	50
James	MNR	209
John	MNR	191
Peter	BLT	166
BRANENBURG, John	FLG	24A
BRANER?, Jacob	BNE	4
BRANHAM, Ambrose	JEF	34
Benj.	HRY	241
Beverley	SCT	120A
David	FLD	32
Geo.	SCT	116A
Harben? M.	BBN	114
Henry	SCT	125A
Jas.	SCT	124A
Jas.	SCT	130A
Jas. S.	SCT	93A
John	SCT	93A
John	SCT	122A
Joseph	NCH	116A
Mrs.	BBN	138
Ricd., Jr.	JEF	58
Richard	CLD	145
Richd.	JEF	55
Sanford	SCT	132A
Simeon	SCT	131A
Tairney/ Turner?	SCT	93A
Tavener	WDF	103A
Tavner	OWN	99
Wm.	WAS	72A
Wm.	WAS	72A
BRANHAM?, Ben.	FLD	27
David	FLD	40
Isham	FLD	28
John	FLD	28
Turner	FLD	32

Name	County	Page
BRANHAM?, William	FLD	32
BRANIGAN, Tho.	MAS	59
BRANK, Ephraim M.	HOP	236
Robt.	GRD	111A
BRANN, Joseph	PND	17A
BRANNAN, John	WRN	76A
BRANNER?, Elizabeth	HAR	166
BRANNIN, Daniel	HRY	176
Richd.	SCT	92A
BRANNOM, Thos.	ADR	10
BRANNON, (No Given Name)	HRL	102
David	BKN	13
John	BTL	317
BRANNUM, Martin (Crossed Out)	WTY	118A
Martin	WTY	113A
BRANOCK, Robert	HAR	184
BRANOM, John	GNP	168A
BRANOUR?, Peter	NSN	195
BRANSAM?, Archibald	FKN	118
BRANSCOMB, Robert	LGN	41
BRANSFORD, Thomas	BRN	2
BRANSOM?, John	CSY	212
BRANSON, Armintiad	HOP	236
Hannah	HOP	236
Henry	HRL	102
Liner	HOP	236
Thomas	LGN	41
BRANSON?, Elizabeth	HAR	166
Jacob	FTE	70
BRANSTETTER, John	BRN	5
Mary	BRN	5
Michael	BRN	3
*BRANT, Christopher	SHE	133A
Henry	SHE	159
John	SHE	133A
Mathias	SHE	129A
BRANTLEY, Josiah	LGN	43
BRANTLY, Will.	LVG	7
BRASFIELD, James E.	MAD	90
James L.	MAD	156
William	CLK	101
BRASHAW, Benj.	CHN	41
BRASHEAN?, James	NSN	219
BRASHEAR, Benjamin	BLT	162
Ignatius	BLT	162
Isaah	WYN	93A
James	NSN	223
Levi	NSN	223
Lilbourne	LGN	36
Marsham	BLT	174
Richard	BLT	162
Robert	JEF	32
William	BLT	164
BRASHEARE, Edward	GSN	128A
BRASHEARS, Absalom	WYN	93A
Bett	GTN	122
John	SCT	139A
Joseph	GTN	122
Levey	SCT	123A
Rezin	GTN	122
Robert	BTH	152
Robert	WYN	93A
Saml.	SCT	97A
Saml.	SCT	117A
Thos.	BKN	16
BRASHEIR, Walter	FTE	66
BRASHER, Aquilla	HOP	234
Elijah	HOP	234
BRASHERARS, Thomas	HRD	16
BRASIER, Thomas	CHN	29
BRASLEY, John	WDF	100
BRASS, Peter	FKN	152
BRASSFIELD, James	CLK	68
Lewis	WDF	95
Thomas W.	WTY	118A
Wiley R.	CLK	101
BRASSTELOW?, John	MER	87
BRASURE, Thomas	CWL	37
BRATCHER, Amas	BTL	317
David	GSN	129A
David	GSN	129A
John, Snr.	GSN	129A
John	GSN	129A
Thos.	GSN	129A
Wm.	GSN	129A
Wm.	GSN	129A
BRATHWAITE, Elizh.	OHO	7A
BRATIKER, Saml.	GSN	128A
BRATON, James	MAD	162
BRATTEN, Jas.	MAS	56
Jerem.?	CWL	39
Jno.	MAS	56
Robt. G.	FKN	88
Wm.	FKN	74
BRATTIN, Peter	BNE	4
BRATTON, Adam	WRN	43A
Archibald	WRN	43A
David	WRN	71A
George	WRN	42A
Hugh	LGN	45
Hugh	CWL	50
James	TRG	3A
John	LGN	46
John	MAD	158
John	TRG	8A
Nancy	GRN	71
Robert	CLK	66
Silvester	MAD	90
William	GRN	71
William	WRN	42A
BRAUDY, Thos.	WAS	32A
BRAUGHTON, John	CLK	102
BRAUHAM?, Ben.	FLD	27
Mrs.	BBN	138
BRAUN, Rebecca	BNE	6
BRAUNS?, Jas.	MAS	81
BRAVEBOY, Sarah	TRG	12A
BRAWDIS?, Beverley	CHN	46
BRAWHILL, John N.	KNX	290
BRAWN?, Joshua	ALN	96
BRAWNER, Amila	GRD	117A
Edward	FKN	110
Henry	MAS	62
Isaac	WRN	62A
Jno.	HRY	261
Jno., Jr.	ADR	8
John, Ser.	ADR	6
Noah	GRD	117A
Thomas	JES	80
BRAY, Abraham	GSN	128A
Benj.	PUL	39A
Benj.	PUL	49A
Edward	MNR	201
Henry	JES	71
John	NSN	216
Littlebury	KNX	314
Nathan	PUL	35A
Richard	MNR	191
Saml.	JEF	36
Thomas	LVG	15
BRAYFIELD, Jno.	MAS	55
BRAYNT, Thomas	GRD	113A
BRAZIER, Aquilla	LVG	11
Joseph	LVG	4
BREADING, David	CHN	45
Jno.	CHN	43A
BREAST, John	BBN	84
BREATHILL, Elizabeth	LGN	28
Wm., (Exors Of)	LGN	28
BREATHILL?, Cardwell	LGN	25
BREATHITT, John	LGN	22
BREATHITT?, Cardwell	LGN	25
Elizabeth	LGN	28
Wm, (Exors. Of)	LGN	28
BRECKEN?, Wm.	WAS	38A
BRECKENRAGS?, Margarett	BBN	74
BRECKENRIDGE, Alxr.	BBN	106
Elizabeth	FTE	76
Geoe.	BBN	80
Henry	JEF	26
James	BBN	78
James	MER	89
James	BBN	106
Jas. D.	JEF	26
John	FTE	75
John	BBN	80
John	BBN	106
Jos. C.	FTE	66
Linn	BBN	112
Mary	FTE	73
Polly	NCH	120A
BRECKINRIDGE, Mary	BTH	148
Robt.	JEF	21
William	FTE	93
BREDEN, Jacob	BRN	5
Jo.	GRD	97A
BREDING?, Milley	NCH	112A
BREDWELL, David	NSN	223
George	BLT	182
Lewis	NSN	183
Noah	NSN	219
Presley	NSN	219
BREED, Nathan	MNR	217
BREEDING, Alxr.	ADR	6
Alxr.	ADR	20
B. B.?	SHE	139A
David	ADR	6
Eligah	CBL	10A
Elijah	SHE	139A
George	ADR	6
Henry	SHE	139A
J./ I.?	SHE	139A
James	ADR	6
Jno.	ADR	6
John	GTN	135
Jos.	ADR	6
Preston	SCT	112A
William	GTN	134
BREEDLOVE, David	SPN	14A
John	MAD	146
John	WTY	115A
Martin	WRN	64A
Thos.	SPN	14A
William	WRN	63A
BREEDON, Abraham	CSY	224
BREEDWELL, Fielding -.?	FTE	60
Mary	FKN	90
Saml.	MAD	150
BREEZE, Jno.	MAS	59
Jno., Jr.	MAS	59
Reason	HAR	182
BREMER, John	NSN	209
BREMLET, Nathaniel	CLD	148
BRENHAM, Daniel	FKN	62
Robert	FKN	60
BRENNBLET?, Jubal	BRK	241

* [Also see Brent/Brant?]

BRENNER, Jacob,
  Sr. BRK 239
BRENNER?, Saml. FLG 42A
BRENT/ BRANT?,
  John HRY 184
BRENT, George HND 3
  Hugh BBN 146
  Richd. BBN 144
  Thos. SCT 102A
  Will. SCT 108A
  William HRY 196
BRENT?, James HRY 194
BRENTON, Briant WAS 24A
  James WRN 70A
BRENTS, Peter CLD 164
  Saml. GRN 51
BRESHERS, Joseph BRK 237
  Polly BRK 239
BRETTENHAM, Jerman WDF 96A
BREVARD, Benj. FLG 74A
  Josa. FLG 36A
BREW, Peter BRK 235
BREWBAKER, Abram GNP 177A
BREWER, -----a? NSN 186
  Abraham MER 87
  Abraham MER 89
  Asael LWS 91A
  Ben HRD 78
  Catharine NSN 213
  Daniel MER 89
  Edward LWS 96A
  Garrot MER 86
  Geo. TOD 128
  Henry CHN 32
  Henry CHN 31A
  Jesse CHN 31A
  John HRD 44
  John MER 87
  John MBG 139
  John SHE 157
  John SHE 132A
  John A. MER 89
  Jonathan HAR 160
  Mark HRD 52
  Merridith CHN 42
  Peter HRD 80
  Pious NSN 177
  Samuel MER 87
  Thos. HRY 266
  William GRN 70
  Wm. HRD 44
  Wm. HRY 261
BREWER?, William JES 80
BREWIN, Daniel FKN 146
  Danl. CHN 42A
BRIAN, Barton NSN 219
  Ignatus NSN 191
  Lewis NSN 216
  William NSN 218
BRIANT, -----? DVS 11A
  --hariah? DVS 13A
  Aaron NSN 214
  Allen WAS 52A
  Alvus? MER 86
  Alxr. ADR 8
  Bailey LWS 97A
  Daniel LWS 97A
  Elhanen? NSN 201
  Frances SHE 130A
  George ADR 6
  Jams? CWL 50
  Jesse CLD 137
  John MER 88
  John SHE 136A
  Joseph UNN 150
  Josiah FLD 12
BRIANT, Mary WAS 83A
  Nancy JEF 20
  Peter SHE 140A
  Rhody WAS 25A
  Saml. PUL 42A
  Solomon HOP 232
  Thos. SHE 130A
  Thos. SHE 140A
  Will ADR 6
  William MER 87
  William CSY 224
  Wm. WAS 63A
BRIANT?, Abner PUL 38A
BRICE, Benona BBN 112
  James LVG 7
  Saml. BBN 112
  Thomas BRK 233
BRICE?, Eliza GRN 75
BRICKERS?, Wm. WAS 38A
BRICKEY,
  Christopher BRK 241
BRICKHAM?, Dudley CHN 36A
BRICKHOUSE,
  William FTE 84
BRICKIN, W. ADR 10
BRIDGEFAMER?,
  George WYN 82A
BRIDGEFARNER?,
  George WYN 82A
BRIDGEFORD, James FKN 82
  Richard WDF 112A
BRIDGES, Absolem LNC 47
  Ben CWL 50
  Benj. JEF 20
  Benj., Jr. JEF 23
  Cathne. FLG 79A
  David BNE 4
  Drewry TRG 7
  Drury WRN 49A
  Elizabeth MTG 247
  Geo. JEF 54
  George BTH 154
  Hyram BTH 156
  Isam JEF 25
  James MER 86
  James ALN 102
  James MTG 247
  Jeremiah BRN 4
  Jessee GRN 70
  Jno. LVG 8
  John BNE 6
  John CWL 50
  John FTE 69
  John MER 86
  John BBN 102
  John L., Esqr. MER 88
  Jonothan ALN 136
  Joseph BNE 6
  Joseph BTH 164
  Lewis MAS 77
  Martha BRN 4
  Mastin MER 115
  Nancy BBN 102
  P. CWL 33
  Stephen LGN 34
  Stephen LGN 46
  Tabitha NSN 216
  Thomas BRN 4
  Thomas, Sen. BRN 4
  William MER 86
  William TRG 3A
  William WRN 54A
  Willis BTH 158
  Wm. BRN 4
  Wm. BBN 102
  Wm. FLG 57A
BRIDGES, Zecheriah ALN 130
BRIDGEWATERS,
  Elias NSN 219
  Isaac SHE 134A
BRIDGFARMER,
  Martin CLD 155
BRIDGWATER,
  Jonathan ADR 8
  Nat ADR 8
  Will ADR 6
BRIDGWATERS, Wm. JEF 59
BRIDLINGER?, John JEF 33
BRIDWELL, Stephen MTG 229
BRIGES, John CWL 50
BRIGGS, Andrew NSN 181
  Benj. LNC 17
  Benjamin NSN 176
  Daniel WYN 101A
  David WRN 29A
  Ebenezer UNN 147
  Elizabeth WRN 31A
  Jacob FLD 31
  James WRN 31A
  John FLD 44
  John WRN 75A
  Lucinda LWS 90A
  Margret FTE 64
  Mariah? WRN 62A
  Menah? WRN 62A
  Moses CLD 137
  Robert WRN 30A
  Thomas, Sr. WYN 101A
BRIGHT----?, Thos. BKN 20
BRIGHT, Albert FTE 78
  Daniel CHN 35
  Davey WAS 27A
  Dennis GTN 126
  George GRN 74
  George ALN 126
  Henry LNC 65
  Jacob RCK 84A
  James CLK 68
  James ALN 120
  James GRD 117A
  Jno. JEF 51
  Jno. ALN 128
  John LNC 13
  John MER 88
  John FLG 23A
  John A. JEF 22
  John H. UNN 147
  Lydia MER 89
  Milly HAR 156
  Solomon FKN 116
  Thomas FTE 78
  Thomas GRD 117A
  Tobias ALN 126
  William BTL 317
BRILES, Daniel MER 86
  Fountain MER 86
  Julius MER 87
  Machael MER 87
  Thomas MER 86
  William MER 87
BRILEY, John MNR 197
  William CLD 142
BRIM, Churchill MER 88
  David CHN 40
  Richard SHE 154
  Susannah MER 89
BRIMM, John GRD 101A
BRINDLY, John JEF 34
BRINEGAR, Jacob ETL 54
  John CLK 69
  John CLK 82
  Linville FTE 91

Name	County	Page
BRINEGAR,		
Margarett	CLK	101
Morgan	CLK	101
Samuel	CLK	101
Thomas	ETL	45
BRINEGEN?, Jacob	CLK	100
BRINER, John	NSN	219
BRINEY, Henry	NSN	197
BRINGLE, John	WAS	85A
BRINGMAN, John	JEF	34
Margaret	JEF	34
BRINGMAN?, Mary	JEF	47
BRINK, Hibert	FTE	104
Phillip	FTE	87
Robert	UNN	149
BRINKER, Jacob	BBN	110
Jos.	HRY	234
BRINKLY, Hudson	CHN	32
BRINLEY, J----, ?		
-.?	CWL	44
BRINN?, Phillip	FTE	106
BRINNER, Frederick	JEF	49
Jno.	JEF	49
BRINSON, Jno.	PUL	36A
John	HAR	188
Jonathan	ALN	128
Moses?	ALN	128
Stout	ALN	128
Thomas	HAR	188
William	HAR	188
BRINTLINGER,		
Andrew	JEF	47
BRINTON, Elizabeth	NCH	115A
Henry	GTN	126
James	CSY	218
Robert	GTN	127
Robert	NCH	115A
BRISBAN, Wm.	CHN	41A
BRISBANE, Jno.	CHN	39
BRISBY, James	JES	75
James	JES	75
Leonard	WDF	95A
BRISCO-?, James	FTE	106
BRISCO, James	FKN	90
BRISCOE, Geo. H.,		
Col.	MER	86
Gerard W.	BLT	192
Harrison	BLT	176
Henry	JEF	39
Hezekiah	JEF	37
James	JEF	37
James	SHE	113A
Jas. M.	SCT	134A
Jer.	SHE	116A
Jeremiah, Maj.	MER	87
John, Esq.	MER	87
John	SHE	109A
John	SCT	125A
Katharine	SHE	116A
Margaret	SHE	112A
Robert	JEF	43
Robert, Jr.	NSN	217
Robert P.	NSN	183
Samuel	BLT	182
Walter	HRD	8
Warner	SHE	112A
Williamson	SHE	113A
BRISCOW, Edward	WAS	22A
Ira	WAS	22A
BRISENDINE, Lewis	FKN	126
BRISON, Joseph	WDF	105
BRISSY, John	BBN	136
BRISTE?, Levan	ADR	18
BRISTO, John	BTH	158
BRISTOE, Elijah	CLD	152
Gasper	SHE	134A
BRISTOE, Gideon	SHE	117A
Isaac	BTL	317
James	SHE	143A
Nathaniel	SHE	117A
William	CLD	142
William	CLD	154
BRISTOL, Sarah	SHE	175
BRISTOW, A.	TOD	128
James	BBN	110
John	CLK	87
BRITAIN, Parks	RCK	77A
Wm.	CHN	32
BRITE, Albert	SHE	110A
Albertus	SHE	150
Hopkins	SHE	150
Jepthah	SHE	150
Jessee	GTN	125
Jno., Dr.	HRY	241
BRITE?, Henson	NSN	222
BRITLEY?, Thomas	NSN	201
BRITON, Samuel	MER	86
BRITON?, William	NSN	212
BRITT, Benjamin	BRN	4
Henry	GTN	130
Obidiah	BRN	2
Thos.	SHE	127A
William	BRN	4
Wm.	HRY	266
BRITTAIN, George	HRL	102
Hesekiah	KNX	280
Jonathan	HOP	232
Levi	KNX	300
William	KNX	300
BRITTON, Cinthia		
Anna	WRN	70A
John	GRN	66
John	SHE	132A
Joseph	WRN	61A
Saml.	SHE	143A
William	SHE	149
BRO---?, Joseph	ALN	98
BROAD, William	GTN	131
BROADDUS, Wm.	TOD	130A
BROADDY, Thomas	BRN	2
BROADUS, Edward	MAD	122
Hudson	MAD	124
James	MAD	126
John	MAD	100
John	MAD	112
John	MAD	132
Omitia	MAD	164
Paschal	JES	78
Richard	MAD	122
Thos.	MAD	144
Thos.	KNX	314
BROADWELL, Asberry	HAR	220
Samuel	HAR	210
William	HAR	210
BROCK, Aaron	HRL	104
Amon	HRL	102
Betsy	LNC	25
Daniel	MAD	180
George	LNC	25
Henry	BKN	28
Henry	JEF	64
Henry	FKN	74
Henry, Snr.	JEF	35
Henry B.	GTN	131
James	HRL	102
James	PUL	53A
Jesse	HRL	104
Jessey	HRL	102
John	BRN	4
John	CLK	73
John	GTN	131
John	CSY	210
BROCK, John, Sr.	GTN	131
Joseph	FTE	109
Joshua	RCK	80A
Mashac	PUL	63A
Peggy	LGN	2/
Phebe	PUL	66A
Richd.	LNC	27
Shelton	MAD	142
Thos.	ADR	20
BROCKMAN, Ambres	ADR	8
Ambrose	BRN	4
Andrew	BNE	4
Durrett	GRN	58
Elijah	LVG	2
Elijah	SCT	99A
Elizabeth	BNE	4
Jas.	MAS	56
John	ADR	54
John	GRN	75
John	SCT	99A
Jos.	TOD	132A
Lydia	FTE	77
Moses	BNE	4
Samuel	GRN	75
Stephen	CLK	69
Tandy	MAS	56
William	BNE	4
Wm. Mason	BRN	4
BRODERICK, Jas.	MAS	70
BRODNAL?, Henry B.	LGN	22
BRODNER, David	JES	85
BRODUS, Robt. L.	SHE	129A
BROGAN, John	CBL	13A
BROKAW, Abraham	MER	86
Peter	MER	86
BROKE, Geo.	RCK	82A
BROMLEY, Moses	GTN	120
Thomas	GTN	120
BROMSER?,		
Bennadicton	MAD	148
BRONAUGH, George	JES	80
Mary	MAS	70
BRONER, Nathen	MAS	67
BRONNER, John	MAD	102
BRONOUGH, Tho.	LNC	55
Wm.	LNC	55
BRONSON?, Jacob	FTE	70
BRONSTON, Thos. S.	MAD	132
BROOK, Magret	LGN	31
Thomas	SHE	110A
Zachariah	NCH	127A
BROOK?, Hiram	HRL	104
BROOKBANK, John	SCT	124A
Mary	SHE	139A
BROOKE, Benjamin	MAD	142
BROOKES, George	CSY	212
BROOKHART, David	JEF	35
Hannah	JEF	36
Hannah	GTN	128
BROOKIN, Alvin	SCT	119A
Levina	SCT	120A
BROOKING, Jno.	HRY	255
Mary Ann	WDF	114A
Robert	CLK	98
Robert E.	CLK	102
Samuel S.	WRN	74A
Thomas A.	LGN	46
Vivion	NCH	105
BROOKINS, Charles	MAD	90
John M.	CHN	35
BROOKS, Mrs.	MAS	71
Alexander	WDF	109A
Ann	LNC	47
Archer	MTG	271
Boaz	MAS	59
Cary	TOD	129

BROOKS, David BKN 18
David BLT 180
Eli-.? T. CWL 44
Elisha SHE 132A
George HRT 153
Henry OWN 105
Henry MAD 154
Henry MAD 154
James HRT 152
James NSN 191
James BTL 317
James A. BTH 186
James R. GTN 130
Jesse CWL 46
Jessee HOP 234
Jessee WYN 103A
Jno. S. OHO 9A
Joel BNE 8
John HRT 153
John MAD 154
John BTL 317
John, Jr. MAD 156
John GRD 92A
John LWS 98A
Joseph JEF 32
Joseph A. BLT 180
Joshua CLD 145
Joshua SHE 131A
Larkin CHN 44A
Larry MTG 261
Lynch MAD 118
Miles HRT 155
Nancy CHN 44A
Paul SHE 124A
Samuel GRN 72
Squire JEF 37
Tho. HRY 188
Thomas CLD 147
Thomas BTL 317
Thomas, Jr. CWL 43
Thomas WRN 39A
Thomas WYN 85A
Thos. MAD 120
Thos.? CWL 35
Will SCT 92A
William CLD 137
William HAR 148
William HRT 155
William HOP 232
William BTL 317
William BTL 317
William CBL 13A
William WAS 33A
William WYN 88A
BROOKSHIRE, Benjamin CLK 75
Charles CLK 75
Henry CLD 156
Hugh CLK 75
Jessee CLK 65
Manering? CLK 73
BROOKY, Robert SHE 176
BROOMFIELD, Henry GNP 171A
James JES 94
Joel JES 86
Moses JES 71
Obed JES 77
BROON?, John BTL 319
BROONER, Henry JES 93
BROSIER, Laurence CHN 29
BROSLIN?, Joab ALN 138
BROSMAN, Man JEF 21
BROTHER, Henry BTH 186
BROTHERS, Abraham MTG 277
James WAS 53A
John NSN 219
BROTHERS, John MTG 275
John MTG 279
John WAS 55A
Polly MTG 277
Samuel SHE 119A
Thomas CLD 142
BROUGH, Hopple SHE 137A
Peter MAS 54
BROUGHTON, Jesse KNX 292
Job SHE 164
Jobe KNX 292
Will. KNX 294
Woodred KNX 292
BROUGTON, William B. JES 96
BROWDER, Ishum HOP 232
John HOP 236
BROWEN, Greenlee LGN 33
BROWIN?, James BKN 16
BROWN, -----? DVS 4A
-----? DVS 6A
-----? J. CWL 41
----am? DVS 13A
----et? DVS 13A
---es? DVS 12A
---l.? CWL 41
--thur? CWL 41
A. I./ J.? GRD 113A
Abr., Sr. GRD 114A
Abr. GRD 100A
Abraham CLD 154
Abs. GRD 92A
Adam OHO 4A
Alexander BTH 162
Alexander OHO 7A
Alexd. WAS 65A
Allen ALN 138
Alsey ALN 138
Andrew BRK 237
Andrew CHN 35A
Andrew WRN 47A
Ann NCH 113A
Araba GRD 113A
Archd. BBN 74
Archubul WAS 24A
Armstead MER 89
Armstead NSN 193
Armstead OHO 7A
Armsted GRD 96B
Austin BTL 317
Baily LNC 81
Barg.? HRY 269
Barney HRY 270
Barton SHE 128A
Basil NSN 219
Bazl. GRD 114A
Ben HRD 46
Ben. FKN 154
Benj. WAS 50A
Benj. WAS 63A
Benj. WAS 65A
Benjamin HOP 234
Benjamin GNP 178A
Bently LGN 31
Berry FLD 41
Berry FKN 154
Betssy LNC 75
Beverley NCH 117A
Beverly GRD 114A
Caleb HRD 24
Caleb HRD 24
Caleb LNC 59
Caleb MBG 142A
Catharine CHN 41A
Catharine WAS 74A
Caty FKN 112
BROWN, Chafen WAS 31A
Charles HND 9
Charles MER 88
Charles HOP 230
Charles GRD 119A
Christopher ADR 8
Coleman CWL 31
Coleman CWL 33
Coleman HAR 132
Constant WDF 105
Dabney CLD 138
Daniel FLD 14
Daniel GRN 50
Daniel FKN 154
Daniel BTH 174
Daniel BTH 178
Daniel HOP 236
Daniel BRK 239
Daniel NCH 119A
Daniel SHE 125A
Daniel SHE 128A
Daniel E. FKN 78
Danl. FLG 39A
Danl. FLG 56A
Danl. SCT 112A
David LVG 7
David LVG 15
David CWL 40
David SHE 162
Dawson WDF 116A
Demarcus HRY 261
Dixon HRD 28
Drury ALN 138
Edward MAD 108
Edward MBG 142
Edwin MER 87
Eleazer LWS 95A
Eli GSN 129A
Elias, Junr. WRN 50A
Elias WRN 50A
Elijah GRN 69
Elijah CLK 81
Elijah MER 86
Elisabeth FKN 80
Elisabeth FKN 162
Elisha LNC 77
Elisha BTH 202
Elisher ADR 54
Eliza MAS 53
Elizabeth ADR 8
Elizabeth ETL 42
Elizabeth MER 87
Elizabeth WRN 56A
Elliott WDF 107A
Ervin HAR 164
Evan NSN 184
Evans MER 89
Evinton JEF 34
Ezakel CSY 208
Ezekiah WYN 104A
Ezekiel LNC 43
Ezekiel SCT 136A
Ezekl. SCT 128A
Francis HAR 144
Francis A. FLD 23
Frank FTE 58
Franky HRY 270
Fred K. GRD 90A
Frederick HRD 48
Fredrick WAS 85A
G. R. A. BRK 239
Geo. JEF 61
Geo. FKN 124
Geo. SCT 91A
George LGN 27
George FTE 77

Name	County	Page
BROWN, George	MER	87
George	FTE	106
George	MAD	170
George	NSN	181
George	BTH	214
George	WYN	104A
George H.	LGN	23
George J.	JES	96
George P.	LVG	15
George R.	FLD	31
George S.	JEF	27
Gideon	BRK	229
Green	HOP	234
H. E.	SCT	136A
Hannah	GSN	129A
Harmon	WYN	104A
Harry	FKN	122
Harvy	GRD	100A
Henderson	MER	88
Henry	ALN	142
Henry	SHE	168
Henry	KNX	298
Henry	WAS	68A
Henry	GRD	87A
Henry	SCT	105A
Henry O.	HAR	216
Hezekiah	LGN	40
Hobson	HOP	234
Howard	NSN	218
Hugh	MAD	116
Hugh	TOD	133
Hugh	ALN	144
Hugh	BLT	166
Ignatius	SHE	128A
Isaac	HRD	56
Isaac	HRT	152
Isaac	WAS	26A
J. S.	MAS	61
Jacob	CLD	150
James	FLD	10
James	FLD	29
James	JEF	40
James	CWL	50
James	CWL	58
James	BBN	60
James	GRN	62
James	JEF	62
James	MER	89
James	FTE	110
James	FKN	136
James	BBN	138
James	CLD	138
James	BTH	152
James	UNN	152
James	HAR	160
James	CLD	165
James	HAR	202
James	MNR	207
James, Jr.	MER	87
James, Sr.	MER	87
James, Sr.	WYN	85A
James	OHO	9A
James	OHO	9A
James	OHO	10A
James	WRN	50A
James	WYN	84A
James	WYN	95A
James	GRD	107A
James	SHE	118A
James D.	WDF	96A
James H.	GRN	62
James H.	NSN	212
James L.	BBN	112
James M.	NSN	176
James W.	FLD	47
Jane	BTH	214
BROWN, Jas.	HRD	26
Jas.	MAS	67
Jas.	HRD	80
Jas.	ALN	130
Jasiah	HAR	170
Jehu	CLD	138
Jeremiah	HRD	28
Jeremiah	OHO	9A
Jeremiah	WAS	26A
Jeremian	MER	88
Jesse	HRD	12
Jesse	CLD	164
Jessee	FKN	154
Jessee	HOP	232
Jno.	CWL	50
Jno.	FKN	54
Jno.	MAS	76
Jno.	FKN	126
Jno.	HRY	270
Jno. P.	JEF	57
Jo.	GRD	113A
Joel	ADR	28
Joel	GTN	131
John	FLD	3
John	BNE	4
John	BNE	8
John	HND	10
John	FLD	13
John	FLD	14
John	FLD	22
John	CHN	34
John	FLD	35
John	CWL	42
John	HRD	42
John	CWL	43
John	JEF	48
John	GRN	57
John	GRN	68
John	MER	87
John	MER	88
John	MER	88
John	MER	89
John, (Free)	LGN	24
John	CLK	100
John	MAD	112
John	GTN	120
John	GTN	125
John	TOD	129
John	MAD	130
John	CLD	139
John	GRT	142
John	NSN	184
John	NSN	211
John	BTH	214
John	HRY	216
John	MTG	233
John	HOP	234
John, Jr.	SPN	11A
John, Jr.	WDF	123A
John, Jr.?	GRD	117A
John, Sr.	SPN	11A
John	OHO	4A
John	CBL	13A
John	WAS	22A
John	PND	23A
John	WAS	23A
John	WAS	24A
John	WAS	31A
John	WRN	50A
John	FLG	74A
John	RCK	76A
John	WYN	82A
John	WYN	84A
John	GRD	86A
John	WYN	100A
John	SCT	101A
BROWN, John	GRD	104A
John	NCH	106A
John	SCT	122A
John	NCH	123A
John	WDF	123A
John	GSN	128A
John L.	NSN	218
John N.	FTE	111
John N.	WTY	126A
John S./ T.?	BBN	124
John T.	NSN	212
John T. S.	HRD	96
Jonathan W.	GTN	131
Jones	ALN	130
Jos.	CWL	46
Jos.	FLG	30A
Joseph	BNE	4
Joseph	LVG	13
Joseph	LVG	15
Joseph	CWL	50
Joseph	HAR	150
Joseph	BLT	156
Joseph	CLD	161
Joseph	NSN	176
Joseph	NSN	207
Joseph	BTH	208
Joseph	GRD	100A
Joseph S.	WAS	19A
Joshua	CWL	50
Joshua	FTE	100
Joshua	MAD	170
Joshua	MNR	191
Joshua	NSN	194
Josiah	WYN	87A
Judy	GRD	90A
Keah	FKN	122
L., Mrs.	FLG	23A
Larkin	MTG	251
Lazarus	HOP	234
Leonard	HOP	234
Leroy	GRD	102B
Letty / Lilly?	NSN	178
Levanson	CLK	95
Leven	FKN	124
Lewis	HRT	153
Lewis	BLT	154
Lewis	CLD	155
Lewis	WTY	120A
Lowdon	PUL	44A
Lyda	SCT	112A
M.	RCK	83A
Major	CBL	5A
Margaret	GNP	170A
Martha	TOD	130A
Mary	JES	73
Mary	WDF	103
Mary	WRN	32A
Mary	FLG	64A
Mathew	BTH	152
Maurice	LNC	17
Milly/ Molly?	WAS	29A
Mordica	NSN	218
Moses	SPN	12A
Nancy	WAS	26A
Nat	HRD	32
Nathan	CHN	34
Nathan	BBN	64
Nathaniel	JEF	44
Nathaniel	HRT	155
Nathaniel	NSN	205
Neri	BRN	2
Nicholas	WRN	47A
Nichs.	JEF	33
Oliver	WDF	96A
Patrick	GSN	129A
Peter	NSN	184

Name	County	Page
BROWN, Peter	NSN	198
Pettis?	HOP	232
Peyton	ADR	3
Peyton	BTL	319
Peyton, Sr.	BTL	319
Polly	SPN	14A
Polly	NCH	118A
Preston? W.	FKN	60
R. M.	GRD	105A
Ralph	SHE	118A
Raphial	WAS	34A
Richard	ADR	62
Richard	GTN	133
Richard	BTH	198
Richardson	MER	87
Richd.	BTL	317
Robert	FLD	27
Robert	JEF	36
Robert	FKN	62
Robert	GRT	142
Robert	OHO	8A
Robert	OHO	11A
Robert S.	HOP	232
Robt.	FKN	68
Robt.	FKN	88
Robt.	HRT	155
Robt.	BRK	239
Robt.	GNP	169A
Roland	KNX	286
S. M.	JEF	24
Sally, Mrs.	WYN	104A
Sally	GRD	119A
Saml.	LVG	7
Saml.	HRD	70
Saml.	GRD	108A
Saml.	SCT	111A
Saml.	SCT	126A
Samuel	GRN	65
Samuel	HRD	68
Samuel	HAR	144
Samuel	BLT	152
Samuel	CLD	154
Samuel	BLT	156
Samuel	NSN	184
Samuel	NSN	204
Samuel, Sr.	LVG	11
Samuel	OHO	4A
Samuel	SPN	11A
Samuel D.	NCH	125A
Samuel, Doc.	MNR	215
Sanders	CLD	148
Sarah	SPN	9A
Scott	FKN	150
Shadrick	HRD	60
Solomon	MAS	61
Solomon	GNP	165A
Spill? C., Jr.	HOP	234
Spill? C., Sr.	HOP	234
Stephen	LNC	79
Stephen	FKN	124
Stephen	MNR	199
Stephen	OHO	6A
Susan	NSN	219
Susana	BRK	239
Swelston?	BLT	180
Tho.	ALN	110
Thomas	LVG	13
Thomas	BKN	23
Thomas	GRN	59
Thomas	GRN	65
Thomas	LNC	75
Thomas	MER	89
Thomas	GTN	120
Thomas	CSY	208
Thomas, Jr.	MNR	207
Thomas, Sr.	MNR	207
BROWN, Thomas	WYN	81A
Thomas	GRD	89A
Thomas	SHE	123A
Thomas C.	FLD	36
Thomas?	HND	10A
Thornton	BKN	16
Thos.	BNE	4
Thos.	HRD	22
Thos.	JEF	33
Thos.	CHN	44
Thos.	MAD	172
Thos.	HRY	241
Thos.	SCT	108A
Thos.	GSN	128A
Timothy	CHN	34
Travers	FKN	136
Tut	HOP	234
Upssen?	MAD	152
Vincent	UNN	152
W. Jr.?	GRD	112A
Wiley	ALN	140
Will	JEF	28
Will	BBN	62
Will	SCT	93A
Will.	LVG	5
Will.	SCT	114A
Will.	SCT	139A
William	BNE	6
William	LVG	11
William	LVG	15
William	CHN	32
William	LGN	36
William	LGN	46
William	CLK	88
William	MER	88
William	GTN	120
William	HAR	134
William	BTH	152
William	CLD	153
William	SHE	153
William	BLT	158
William	SHE	166
William	BTH	214
William	HAR	214
William	HOP	234
William	HOP	236
William, Jr.	LVG	13
William	WAS	19A
William	WRN	47A
William	WYN	84A
William	GRD	100A
William	GRD	108A
William	GRD	108A
William	NCH	113A
William	GRD	115A
William	WTY	119A
Willis	ALN	140
Windle	JEF	36
Wm.	JEF	30
Wm.	JEF	40
Wm.	JEF	42
Wm.	CWL	50
Wm.	JEF	61
Wm.	HRD	72
Wm.	FKN	126
Wm.	HRT	153
Wm.	OHO	6A
Wm.	OHO	9A
Wm.	WAS	31A
Wm.	WAS	38A
Wm.	FLG	55A
Wm.	SHE	114A
Wm.	GSN	128A
Wm.	SHE	128A
Wm.	SHE	141A
Zachariah	CLD	138
BROWN?, Jas	MAS	81
Joshua	ALN	96
Joshua	ALN	98
Scott	BBN	64
William	BKN	16
BROWNERY?, Margret	WAS	70A
BROWNFIELD, George	HRD	22
James	TRG	10
James	HAR	186
John	HRD	86
John	HAR	202
John	CBL	19A
William	CBL	14A
Wm.	HRD	20
BROWNIN?, Elias	GTN	127
BROWNING, Basil	FLG	23A
Benj.	FLG	33A
Calob	PND	29A
Charles	MNR	195
Daniel	MNR	197
David	LGN	45
Edwd.	MAS	53
Elias	CLK	81
Elijah G.	CLK	105
F. L.	ADR	8
Francis	WAS	85A
George	LGN	43
Henry	CLK	95
J.	MAS	53
Jacob	BBN	90
James	CLK	87
James	BBN	116
James	BBN	132
James	HAR	166
James	PND	22A
James	WAS	85A
Jeremiah	FLG	36A
Jesse	SCT	121A
John	CLY	117
Joseph	BRN	5
Joshua	HOP	232
L. W.	MAS	70
Levi D.	FLG	30A
Lucy	BBN	120
Meshac	FLG	25A
Micajah	HAR	178
Reuben	LGN	44
Saml.	WAS	85A
Tho.	MAS	63
Toliver	PND	21A
William	BRN	33
William	MNR	195
William F.	LGN	44
Wm.	FLG	23A
Wm.	FLG	67A
BROWNLE, Jane C.	GRN	52
BROWNLEE, Andrew C.	GRN	60
Charles	GRN	53
John	GRN	60
BROY, Elijah	GTN	121
BRUCE, -----?	CLK	66
Abner	HOP	234
Alexander	WRN	32A
Alexander	LWS	87A
Ambrose	CLK	62
Benjamin	FTE	70
Cader	HOP	234
Duning	HOP	232
Eli	CLK	81
Ezekial	WTY	115A
George W.	LWS	88A
Hanry	FLG	36A
Horatio	LWS	87A
James	CLK	62
James	BRK	243

Name	County	Page
BRUCE, John	BNE	4
John	FTE	65
John	HAR	218
John	HOP	236
John	LWS	87A
John	GRD	94A
Major	WTY	115A
Mathew	UNN	154
Milly	HOP	234
Peter	MBG	138
Polly	BBN	114
Richard W.	HND	9
Richd. P.	GRD	101A
Waddle, G.	JES	96
William	LNC	37
Wm.	HRY	263
BRUEHER?, John	BRK	241
BRUEN, Joseph	FTE	70
Richd.	MAS	55
BRUER?, Abriham	WAS	83A
BRUFF, James	LVG	6
Mary	LVG	2
Rody	TOD	127A
BRUFFS, Tho. H.	ALN	110
BRUIER?, Jacob	GTN	133
BRUINGTON?, Geo.	BRK	237
BRUM?, Phillip	FTE	106
BRUMBACK, John	FTE	85
John	GRT	139
John	MAD	174
Martin	SHE	133A
Paul	GRT	139
Peter	SHE	133A
BRUMBARGER, John	FTE	101
BRUMBLE, Leven	WAS	44A
BRUMER, Benjamin	CLD	163
Robert	CLD	145
BRUMFIELD, -----?	DVS	8A
Chas.	HRD	80
Elizabeth	MER	87
James	WAS	28A
James	GNP	176A
Joel H.	HRT	155
John	MNR	197
John	BRK	235
John	LWS	95A
Richard	HRD	50
Sarah	MER	87
William	MER	87
William	MER	87
Wm.	HRD	32
BRUMIGIN, Jarvis	BTH	178
Jeremiah	BTH	162
Thomas	BTH	160
BRUMK, John, Junr.	HRD	82
BRUMLEY, Daniel	SHE	111A
Samuel	SHE	111A
Wm.	JEF	62
BRUMLY, Benj.	BKN	18
BRUMMET, Riece	KNX	298
BRUMMET?, Owin	WYN	88A
BRUMNER?, William	JES	80
William	JES	80
BRUNBACK, Charles	MAD	162
BRUNDRIDGE, Solomon	GTN	134
BRUNDRIGE, Marget	GTN	134
BRUNER, Adam	BRK	237
Charles	BRK	235
Christan	JES	86
Geo.	BRK	241
Geo.	BRK	241
Geo.	BRK	243
George	JES	85
Henry	BRK	239
Jacob	BRK	243
BRUNER, Jacob, Jr.	BRK	239
Jacob, Sen.	BNE	4
James	SHE	125A
John	CLK	105
John	BRK	241
John, Sr.	BRK	241
John T.	BRK	241
Leonard	BRK	241
Mary	BRK	243
Michel	BRK	233
Michel	BRK	241
Moses	BNE	4
Peter	BRK	239
Peter	BRK	241
Peter	BRK	241
Peter	BRK	243
BRUNK, Christopher	GSN	129A
David	GRN	53
Jacob	HRT	153
Noah	CHN	43A
Wm.	GSN	128A
BRUNNER?, William	JES	80
BRUNT, Alexander	ALN	138
Henry	SHE	128A
BRUNTA, Sally	CLD	151
BRUNTS?, Jno.	LVG	5
BRUNTY, Robert	GSN	129A
BRURY, Zack	WAS	44A
BRUSAN?, Charles	BBN	106
BRUSH, Caty	UNN	153
Chs.	RCK	84A
James	FLD	42
James	SHE	160
John	SHE	160
Thomas	UNN	153
William	WYN	100A
Wm.	PUL	48A
Wm.	PUL	48A
Wm.	PUL	49A
BRUSH?, Richard	PUL	39A
BRUSK?, Richard	PUL	39A
BRUSON, Wm.	GNP	176A
BRUSTER, Alexander	LVG	8
Benjn.	GSN	128A
Comfort	GSN	129A
Davis	GSN	128A
Mary	FLD	39
BRUTON, David	MAD	96
David	WYN	98A
Enoch	MAD	112
George	WYN	97A
Phillip	WYN	97A
William	WYN	97A
BRYAN, Alexander	BBN	68
Banack?	HRY	196
Daniel	FTE	100
Dav.	HRY	266
David	CHN	34A
Ed'd	HRY	269
Elijah	SCT	93A
Ezekiel	CHN	34A
Jas.	HRY	243
Joel	SHE	155
John	CHN	27A
John	CHN	28A
John P.	MBG	143
Joseph	SHE	148
Lewis H.	CLK	66
Luke	PND	30A
Milly	HRY	263
Morgan	HRY	256
Sanl.	CHN	43A
Thomas L.	OWN	99
Thos.	HRY	269
Thos.	PND	19A
William	HAR	200
BRYAN, Wm.	JEF	36
Wm.	PND	17A
BRYAN?, Stephen	MAD	182
BRYANS, Wm.	MAS	58
BRYANT, Abijah	LGN	35
Absalom	WTY	125A
Andrew	BBN	68
Ann	LGN	30
Archibald	LGN	38
Benjamin	JES	92
Burrel	BRN	5
Chas.	HRD	52
Clifton	FTE	66
Daniel	LGN	38
David	GRN	75
David	JES	81
David	FTE	89
Ed	GRD	95A
Edward	LGN	35
Eli	LGN	42
Eliza.	JEF	53
Elizabeth	LGN	35
Enoch	FTE	86
Gabriel	FLD	11
Geo.	BBN	106
Geo.	GRD	96A
George	FTE	87
Hampdon	CBL	17A
Harrison	LGN	25
Henry A.	SPN	15A
Hiram	SPN	15A
James	FTE	87
James	JES	92
James	CLD	154
Jas.	BBN	70
Jas.	GRD	95A
Jas. A.	BBN	70
Jeremiah	ETL	45
Jesse	BRN	5
Jesse	FTE	89
Jessee	JEF	57
Jno.	FKN	146
Jno.	GRD	100A
John	FTE	60
John	ADR	64
John	GRD	86A
John	GRD	99A
Joseph	JEF	52
Joseph	FTE	87
Josiah	GRN	65
Laurence	CHN	36A
Lewis	JES	93
Lewis	FLG	35A
Luke	GRD	84A
Michael	ETL	39
Morgan	JEF	57
Nicholas	BBN	104
Peter	MAS	77
Peter	WTY	122A
Price	GRN	75
Ricd.	JEF	54
Richard	FTE	85
Richd.	GRN	70
Robert	LNC	45
Robert	LNC	75
Robt.	WRN	75A
Sally	GRD	90A
Sally?	WTY	126A
Saml.	JEF	52
Saml.	RCK	84A
Samuel	SHE	162
Samuel	CBL	17A
Sarah	LNC	43
Stephen	FKN	100
Thomas	ETL	54
Thomas	OHO	8A

BRYANT, Thomas SPN 15A
Thos. FKN 76
Thos. PUL 36A
Will GRD 91A
William JES 88
William FTE 95
Wm., Jr. BBN 146
Wm. S. BBN 146
BRYARLY, Geo. MAS 58
Saml. MAS 71
BRYDON, Robert. FKN 90
BRYE, George CSY 214
BRYERS, Catharine JES 84
Ricd. JEF 57
Wm. JEF 56
BRYINING, Jacob JES 90
BRYNE, Andrew JEF 43
BRYON, John GNP 166A
Rachael GNP 168A
BRYSON, Abnerr CLD 157
David LWS 86A
Edmond CBL 4A
Robert CLD 157
Thos. SCT 132A
BUCEY, Benjamin LVG 13
Jacob SHE 170
Mathew SHE 170
BUCHANAN, Andrew BBN 60
David LVG 8
Edwd. J. PUL 37A
James NCH 106A
Jane LGN 32
Nancy HRY 262
Robt. PUL 35A
BUCHANNAN, James PUL 61A
Wilshire BRK 233
BUCHANNON, George LGN 38
James SPN 13A
John SHE 151
BUCHANNON?, Robert FTE 110
BUCHANON, Henry GNP 178A
Henry GNP 179A
Wm. GNP 165A
BUCHARNON?, Robert FTE 110
BUCHART, Joseph HRT 152
BUCHEEN?, Jno. ADR 8
BUCHUM?, James JEF 53
BUCK--ER?, Cornelius LVG 4
BUCK, Charles UNN 153
Charles WDF 115A
James RCK 75A
Jas. HRY 267
Jno. PUL 40A
Peter C. WDF 104A
William C. UNN 153
BUCKALOW, Isaac N./ V.? LGN 34
BUCKAM?, Coleman CSY 210
BUCKANNON, Nathiel? BRK 243
BUCKEEN?, Jno. ADR 8
BUCKER, Lewis D. SCT 96A
BUCKHALTER, John LGN 41
BUCKHAM, Andrew HOP 232
BUCKHANAN, Alexr. GRN 62
Catey GRN 62
David GRN 62
John GRN 56
John GRN 62
William GRN 64
William GTN 129
BUCKHANNON, James MER 89
Jas. FLG 69A
John MER 86
John ALN 126
BUCKHANNON, John WDF 107A
Levy WDF 101
Robt. HRY 222
Semian? WDF 99A
Smith HRY 222
Spencer BBN 106
William SHE 152
Wm. BBN 104
BUCKHANNON?, Mary HRY 210
BUCKHART, Jacob ETL 46
BUCKINGHAM, Peter ADR 16
Rebecca FKN 146
BUCKLE, Harden FLG 23A
BUCKLER, Henry WAS 57A
Rachel WAS 60A
Ricd. WAS 62A
Robert NCH 107A
Stephen NCH 106A
BUCKLES, John HRD 8
Robert MBG 136A
William MBG 136A
BUCKLEW, J. C. JEF 28
BUCKLEY, Asel GTN 125
Jerry? FKN 148
John SHE 138A
Saml. MAD 152
Samuel WDF 120A
William LVG 10
William MER 87
Wm. FLG 68A
BUCKLY, Abraham BKN 16
Thomas M. HRY 176
BUCKMAN, Clement UNN 150
Ebenezer SHE 117A
John UNN 153
Joseph WAS 19A
William NSN 222
BUCKMOND, Charles WAS 61A
John WAS 34A
Joseph WAS 61A
BUCKNER, Archibald CHN 44A
Avery JEF 66
Aylett H. HRT 155
Ballard JEF 68
Benjamine H. CLK 101
Elizabeth BBN 124
Gabriel GRN 52
Geo. CHN 45A
Geo. M. CLK 66
Henry BNE 46
Henry FTE 91
Henry NCH 107A
Henry W. HRT 153
Horace HRD 44
James GRN 65
James GRN 76
James CHN 44A
John GRN 76
John CHN 44A
John C. SCT 93A
Liley A. JEF 66
Martha CHN 45
Moses SHE 135A
Peter B. CLK 93
Polly FKN 56
Richd. A. GRN 52
Robt. JEF 52
Saml. NCH 120A
Saml. P. JEF 48
Thomas CBL 3A
Thornton GRN 73
Thos. BKN 8
Thos. JEF 54
Thos. SHE 135A
Walker BBN 84
William GRN 67
BUCKNER, William GRN 73
Wm. JEF 25
Wm. BKN 28
BUCKNER?, Phillip BKN 20
BUCKSTANE, Wm. MAS 56
BUCY, Isaac SHE 170
Jacob SHE 135A
BUDD, John BLT 186
Joseph BLT 186
BUDWHISTLE, William CBL 5A
BUEL, A. D. JEF 21
BUFORD, Abraham HAR 158
Abram SCT 108A
Betsy MNR 197
Elijah BRN 2
Hillery GRD 104A
James GRD 82A
Jas./ Jos.? SCT 137A
John GRD 86A
John WDF 125A
Mathew SHE 168
Simeon BRN 3
Simeon SHE 152
Simeon WDF 111A
Thomas GRD 83A
W. RCK 83A
William WDF 111A
BUGG, -----? CWL 40
Elizabeth HND 9
James HND 9
Mary T. HND 10A
BUHANNAN, Jno. MAS 78
BUKHART?, (See Birkhart) NSN 208
BUKHEAD?, Abraham NSN 216
BULCY?, William GRN 78
BULER?, Armsted MAD 94
BULEY, Christopher HRD 68
Jesse BRN 4
John HRD 68
Jos. HRD 68
BULEY?, William GRN 78
BULL, Edward SHE 141A
Isiah LVG 6
John P. HAR 220
Richd. KNX 284
Robert SHE 176
BULL?, Isaiah PUL 49A
Rachel FTE 66
BULLARD, Joseph TRG 14
Katharine SHE 110A
Leah CLD 149
Reuben SHE 110A
BULLER, Wm. BBN 122
BULLETT, Cuthbert SHE 168
BULLIER, Jas. JEF 30
BULLIGHER, H. TOD 132A
BULLIN, Jacob LVG 15
BULLINGTON, Josiah ADR 6
BULLINGTON?, John MER 88
BULLITT, Cuthbert JEF 19
Thos. JEF 19
William, Sr. JEF 36
William C. JEF 37
BULLOCK, Boldin PUL 38A
David SHE 176
David SHE 176
David KNX 310
David W. ETL 46
Edmund FTE 84
Edward, Maj. MER 117
Elizabeth WRN 44A
Garland GTN 122
J. B. CHN 42
James PUL 68A

Name	County	Page
BULLOCK, James P.	CLK	102
Jesse	PUL	49A
Jno.	MAS	57
John	BNE	4
John	NSN	201
John	KNX	310
John	WRN	48A
John H.	SHE	110A
John P.	BBN	122
Lewis	MAS	58
Nathaniel	FTE	82
Rebecca	WAS	57A
Richd.	JEF	46
Robt.	MAS	61
Sally	PUL	46A
Stephen	BNE	4
Thomas	WDF	103
Waller	FTE	86
Will	MAS	61
Wingfield	SHE	176
Wm.	PUL	38A
BULLOK, Nathan	BNE	4
BUMBARGER, Frederick	UNN	153
BUMBARGER?, Michael	HAR	166
BUMGARDNER, Chs.	HRT	155
Jacob	HRT	152
Wm.	HRT	152
BUMINGTON, Wm.	BNE	6
BUMP, Nathan	PND	31A
BUMPUS, Augustus	LVG	6
BUMSEY, Edward	CHN	40
BUNCH, Archibald	CLD	137
Charles	WRN	36A
Davis	CLK	89
George	CLY	125
George	WRN	64A
Henry	CLK	86
Hyram	HND	3
Israel	CLD	153
James	MER	114
James	CLD	153
James	WRN	36A
Lydda	CLD	151
Nancy	MTG	289
Nancy	WRN	64A
Rawdon	CLD	161
Sally, Mrs.	WYN	88A
Samuel	CLY	125
Simeon	WRN	64A
Simion	WRN	66A
Solomon	WTY	123A
Wm. C.	OHO	7A
Zacariah	HRD	70
BUNDIN, Jams	BTL	319
BUNDREN, Edward	MAD	146
BUNDRUM, Thos.	BNE	6
BUNDY, (See Bandy)	BRK	
Ambrose	BRK	239
George	CLD	150
Reubin	MAD	124
BUNDY?, Reuben	BRK	237
Richard	BRK	237
BUNDZ?, Rachel	FTE	67
BUNGER, (See Burger)	HRD	66
Jacob	HRD	8
BUNK, Marah	WTY	122A
BUNKER?, Geo.	JEF	45
BUNNEL, Jeremiah	HRT	152
BUNNELL, Peter	GRN	59
Samuel	MER	89
BUNS, Samuel	MAD	102
BUNSELL?, David	HRY	204
BUNTIN, Andrew	FKN	138
BUNTIN, James	FKN	138
Jno.	FKN	140
BUNTON, Andrew	MER	88
Andrew	NCH	119A
Elijah	FLD	15
George	MER	88
Isaac	FLD	12
James	CLY	129
Robert	WDF	101A
Samuel	MER	89
William	MER	89
BUNTON?, William	NCH	112A
BUNYARD, Ephraim	WYN	98A
Saml.	ADR	6
BUNYARD?, Samul	ADR	62
BUOY, John	PND	30A
Robt.	PND	29A
BURAM?, Thompson	MAD	178
BURBAGE, Geo.	SCT	125A
Robt.	SCT	124A
Thos. H.	SCT	124A
BURBANK, Stephen	HND	3
BURBRAGE, Linchfield	CLK	94
BURBRIDGE, Elijah	WDF	109A
Jeremiah	ADR	6
Robert	BTH	166
Rolen	BTH	166
Wm.	ADR	8
BURBRIGE, William	BTH	180
BURCH, Alexr.	HRD	76
Ben	HRD	36
Benjn.	OHO	4A
Francis	HRD	76
Francis Anne	WRN	31A
George	GRD	119A
Henry	JES	97
John	GTN	133
John	BTH	202
John	GRD	86A
John H.	HRD	76
Joseph	SCT	126A
Leonard	HRD	68
Likia A.	BLT	188
Oliver	HRD	76
Robert	ETL	50
Samuel	JES	81
Samuel	BLT	194
Samuel	GSN	129A
Stapleton C.	BRN	1
BURCH?, Melton	SCT	134A
BURCHAM, David	HRD	56
Henry	HRD	32
BURCHELL, Isaac	JES	71
BURCHET, Isel	WYN	103A
John	CLD	152
BURCHETT, Armstead	FLD	30
Benjamin	FLD	33
Benjamin	FLD	45
Drury	FLD	30
John	FLD	42
Thomas	FLD	33
BURCHFIED, Adam	FLD	3
BURCHFIELD, Elias	NCH	112A
Jno.	FKN	102
John L.	OWN	100
Meshac	WRN	35A
BURCHUM, Isaac	CBL	22A
BURD, John	BRK	239
John, Sr.	BRK	241
Joshua	CLY	117
Richd.	CLY	131
BURDELL?, John	BLT	188
BURDEN, Benjamin	BTL	317
James	NCH	105
Saml.	NCH	105
BURDEN, Theophilus	GTN	135
William	BTL	317
BURDET, Enoch	GRD	112A
John	WAS	69A
BURDETT, Gracy	GRD	116A
John	BLT	188
Nelson	GRD	82A
BURDETT?, John	BLT	188
BURDICK, David	CBL	23A
BURDICT, Spencer	LNC	67
BURDID, Lewis	BRK	239
BURDIN, Charles	NCH	105
Chs.	PUL	46A
Elijah	PUL	46A
BURDINE, L.	GRD	102B
BURDIT, Mary	BRK	237
Richard	BRK	239
Stephen	BRK	237
BURDIT?, Joshua	MER	88
BURDITT, Jos.	GRD	86A
William	LNC	19
William	BLT	184
BURFORD, Wm.	FKN	142
BURGAN, Charles	MAD	112
David C.	MER	87
Garret	HRY	257
Isaac	MAD	162
James	MAD	116
Peter	HRY	257
Thos.	MAD	162
BURGE, Beverly B.	WRN	36A
James	WRN	35A
Robertson	PUL	62A
Woody	SHE	109A
BURGE?, Daniel	GRN	68
BURGEN, Dines	MAD	162
Wm.	WAS	48A
BURGER, Henry	HRD	58
Philip	HRD	66
Philip, Junr	HRD	58
(Also see Bunger)	HRD	
BURGERS, Heny/Herry?	BBN	146
BURGES, Henry	TOD	126A
Jessee	GTN	125
Thos.	MAD	120
BURGESS, Dempsa?	LVG	2
Edward	FLD	21
Edwd.	SCT	115A
Garland	FLD	24
Henry	FLD	21
Jno.	HAR	138
John	FLD	21
John	CHN	44A
Joshua	MAS	58
Osgood	MAS	53
Phill	MAS	74
Timothy	LNC	13
William	FLD	46
BURGHER, Charles	BTL	317
Joseph	WRN	31A
Manson/mauson	ETL	42
Nicholas	ETL	41
BURGIN, George J./I.?	WDF	93
John	ETL	52
BURGINEY?, Jacob	JEF	36
BURHAM, John	CSY	212
BURHAM?, Coleman	CSY	210
BURK-?, Thompson	GRD	120A
BURK, Abram	FLG	35A
Alex.	FKN	114
Benjamin, Sen.	WYN	99A
Geo.	JEF	59
Henry, Jr.	PUL	38A
Jacob	ADR	6
Jno.	PUL	39A

Name	County	Page
BURK, John	SCT	138A
Joshua	BBN	112
Joshua	PUL	35A
Martin	SCT	136A
Mc Kinney	PUL	47A
Mitchel	MAD	122
Richard	SHE	166
Robert	GTN	117
Robt.	BBN	138
Robt.	SCT	138A
Thomas	WYN	80A
Thos.	PUL	49A
William	CBL	6A
BURK?, Jas.	HRY	267
Mathias	FKN	150
Samuel	JES	80
BURKAM?, Milton?	CSY	204
BURKE, Edmund	CHN	33A
George	NCH	108A
James	MTG	265
James	NCH	119A
John M.	NSN	184
Peter	MTG	233
Samuel	SHE	116A
William	NSN	178
BURKELOW, John	UNN	152
William	UNN	152
BURKES, Roland	CSY	206
BURKETT, Bazel	BLT	154
Ely	BLT	188
Mildred	JES	97
BURKHART, Geo.	HRL	102
George, Senr.	HRD	86
Henry	HRD	18
Solomon	HRL	102
BURKHEAD, Thos.	GSN	128A
BURKHEART, George	HRD	82
BURKHILL, Jesse	WAS	86A
BURKITT, John	BKN	13
BURKS, Allen	MER	88
Berry	MER	88
Charles	WAS	17A
Christopher	BLT	184
David	FLD	43
David J.?/ I.?	LGN	42
Edmund	MER	88
Floyed	GRD	107A
George	MER	89
Henry	PUL	35A
Jas.	JEF	37
Jno.	JEF	32
Jno., Sen.	BRN	3
John	JEF	37
John	CLK	82
John	MER	88
John	MER	89
John, Jr.	BRN	2
Levy	MER	89
Matthew	SHE	124A
Nathaniel	LGN	42
Saml.	HND	10
Silas	GRN	58
Sussanna, Mrs.	WYN	99A
Thomas	BRN	3
BURLEY, Ralph	HRD	82
Wm.	HRD	86
BURNAM, John	ETL	44
BURNAW?, George	NCH	114A
BURNE, Patrick	JEF	30
BURNER?, Abraham	HRT	153
BURNES, Andrew	ETL	47
Dennis	BTH	184
Garret	HAR	210
Jacob	WAS	51A
Saml.	FKN	130
BURNET, Absolom	GSN	128A
BURNET, Godfrey	HRD	28
Isaac	WYN	99A
Isaac	GSN	129A
John	GSN	128A
Mathew	GSN	128A
Mikajah	MAD	142
Robert	CLD	139
Roling	WYN	94A
Saml.	GNP	169A
Thos.	GSN	128A
BURNETT, Benjamin	MER	117
Corneilus	TRG	4A
Corneilus	TRG	4A
Henry	SHE	176
James C.	SHE	124A
John	NSN	180
John	SHE	122A
Joseph	ALN	100
Nicholas	WTY	124A
Robert	WRN	51A
Robt.	WAS	28A
Thomas	HRY	208
William	FLD	17
William	ETL	50
William, Jr.	ETL	48
William, Sr.	ETL	48
Wm.	SHE	118A
BURNETT?, Henry	WRN	49A
BURNHAM, Bennett	WRN	73A
George G.	WYN	91A
BURNITT, John	WAS	32A
BURNLEY, Wm.	PND	24A
BURNS, Andrew	CLY	115
Arther	BRK	239
Brice	CLY	115
Daniel	LVG	15
Danl.	HRD	40
David	FTE	97
Dennis	CLY	130
Edward	WRN	67A
Elizabeth	FTE	77
Gabriel	LWS	86A
Horatio	PUL	61A
Isaac	MER	86
Jacob	WAS	83A
James	GRN	61
James	HRL	104
James	GRT	140
James	GRT	144
James	NCH	125A
James A.	BNE	8
Jeremiah	GNP	176A
Jno.	HAR	164
John	JEF	30
John	CLY	115
John, Jr.	NCH	126A
John, Sr.	NCH	126A
John	WAS	75A
Joseph	WAS	75A
Lawrance	WAS	45A
Mary	GTN	133
Mary	LWS	98A
Mathew	NCH	114A
Matthew	BRK	237
Philip	MER	86
Phill	WAS	69A
Robert	NCH	118A
Rolin	GNP	176A
Samuel	GRT	140
Samuel	LWS	86A
Tarrance	HAR	180
Tho.	ALN	96
Thomas	GRN	61
Thomas	FTE	70
Thomas	GRT	144
Thomas	WDF	112A
BURNS, Thos. T.	SCT	92A
William	FTE	108
William	CLY	115
William	GTN	133
William	HAR	188
William	LWS	86A
William	NCH	127A
Wm.	WAS	34A
BURNS?, Charles	GTN	119
Saml.	NCH	118A
BURNSIDES, Nany	GRD	112A
Robt.	GRD	122A
BURNSIDS, James	GRD	100A
BURNT, Henry	SHE	176
BUROWS, Thomas	ETL	47
BURR, William	LGN	39
BURRAS, Thos.	CHN	45
BURRES, Charles	MAD	110
Ridgley	FLG	27A
BURRESS, Andrew	WRN	38A
Basil	FLG	27A
Benj.	FLG	30A
Elizabeth	FLG	63A
Henry	FLG	69A
Isaac	FLG	27A
John	JEF	58
John	FLG	47A
Mathew	FLG	28A
Nancy	GTN	134
Seth	FLG	41A
Wm., Sr.	FLG	23A
Wm.	FLG	23A
Wm.	FLG	30A
Zadock	FLG	28A
BURRIMOND, Will	WAS	21A
BURRIS, Benja.	GRT	147
Boaz?	BTL	319
Charles	BTL	317
Charles	LWS	97A
Edmund, Jr.	MER	89
Edmund, Sr.	MER	89
Jacob	ALN	112
James R.	WAS	48A
Job	HRD	22
John	GRT	146
John	BTL	317
Nathaniel	MER	89
Nathl.	TOD	126
Roger	TOD	126
Saml.	NCH	118A
Sarah	HRD	58
Tho.	ALN	114
Wm.	HRD	52
BURRIS?, Jeremiah	GNP	176A
Rolin	GNP	176A
BURRISS, Henry	LWS	89A
Jacob	NCH	117A
John	GRD	100A
Joseph	LWS	93A
Nathaniel	LWS	93A
Ruth	LWS	97A
BURRNS?, (See Burrus)	CLK	99
BURROS, Jas. G.	BBN	70
Mary	BBN	70
BURROSS?, Geo.	MAS	59
BURROWES, Absolum	FTE	90
Clement	FTE	91
BURROWS, --ry?	CWL	36
Betsey	SCT	116A
Betsy	SCT	124A
Geo.	MAS	55
Geo.	MAS	63
George	UNN	149
Jonathan	MTG	279
Nathan	FTE	58

BURROWS, Saml. MAS 72
Will SCT 120A
Will. SCT 110A
Wm. HRY 241
BURRUS, Robt. HRT 155
Thomas, Jr. CLK 85
Thomas, Senr. CLK 85
Thomas SHE 138A
William CLK 68
BURRUS?, Lancaster WRN 76A
Michael CLK 99
Thomas CLK 98
BURRUSS, Peter WRN 42A
BURRY, Edward WAS 76A
Phill WAS 70A
BURT, Andw. HRY 249
Benjn. SCT 138A
Elizabeth BNE 6
John SCT 120A
Will. SCT 124A
BURTCH, Darius/ Davius? CBL 16A
BURTLE, Susannah GSN 129A
BURTLES, Benjin. GSN 128A
James GSN 128A
Wm. GSN 129A
BURTON, Abraham JES 92
Abraham MAD 168
Abram SHE 148
Allen MAD 170
Allen GRD 109A
Amabrose MER 88
Archibd. LNC 29
Arthur PUL 54A
Benjamin PUL 53A
Bob GRD 102B
Charles ALN 120
Cuthbert ALN 120
Drury ALN 120
Elizabeth, Mrs. WYN 89A
Elizabeth PUL 64A
George PUL 62A
James K. PUL 54A
Jane SHE 167
Jarrett MAS 55
Jeremiah JEF 52
Jesse PUL 53A
Jesse GRD 85A
Jessee MAD 168
Jno. MAS 55
John JEF 42
John ALN 94
John SHE 167
John, Senr. PUL 53A
John PUL 54A
John D. GRD 85A
John M. HRY 234
Joseph GRN 54
Joseph MER 88
Josiah NCH 126A
Laban GRD 94A
Lewis SCT 127A
Margaret GNP 170A
Martha SHE 163
Moses MAS 57
Presley WDF 103
Prettyman SHE 163
R. H. ADC 68
Richard MAD 114
Robert PUL 53A
Robert WYN 89A
Robt. GRD 91A
Saml. PUL 40A
Samuel PUL 54A
Walthel NSN 192
Will. SCT 104A

BURTON, William FLD 7
William FLD 24
William JES 92
William SHE 157
William D. PUL 54A
William L. PUL 66A
Wm. MAD 158
BURTON?, Alan OHO 6A
BURTTES?, (See Burtles) GSN 129A
BURWELL, John JES 89
BURWELL?, Wm. HRD 34
BURYON, John FLD 13
BUSAND, Jesse HRD 66
Wm. HRD 86
BUSBEE, Lewis FTE 66
BUSBY, Charles NCH 103A
Isaac BTH 166
Jacob NCH 103A
James FTE 74
James BTH 184
John MTG 269
Martin ADR 6
Mathew, Jr. NCH 103A
Mathew, Sr. NCH 103A
Rawly BTH 182
Robt. ADR 6
Schamel HRD 22
Wm. FLG 65A
BUSCH, Clifton R. SCT 106A
BUSCH?, Melton SCT 134A
BUSEY, James FTE 64
Jno. FKN 140
BUSH/ BUSK?, John CWL 33
Wm. CWL 33
BUSH, Aaron GNP 174A
Armbrose CLK 79
Charles HRY 212
Christopher HRD 66
Drury CLY 114
Elkana MAD 134
George BRN 3
George GNP 172A
Henry HRT 155
Isaac BRN 3
James BRN 4
James CLK 69
James PND 21A
Jeremiah CLK 80
Jeremiah GNP 174A
John BNE 2
John ETL 39
John HRD 66
John HRT 152
John, Jr. GNP 174A
John GNP 174A
John H. CWL 37
John V. CLK 65
Jonathan CLK 84
Joseph CLK 92
Joseph GNP 172A
Joshua MAD 172
Joshua PUL 51A
Matthew ETL 39
Moses CLK 91
Nancy LGN 35
Nelson CLK 90
Patterson HND 12
Phil. BNE 52
Philip SPN 17A
Philip S. BNE 46
Pleasant CLK 90
Rachel CLK 77
Robert ETL 39
Robert V. CLK 85
Rowland FTE 91

BUSH, Samuel CLD 157
Thacker CLK 102
Thomas HRT 152
Thomas T. CLK 72
Tilman MAD 162
Walton BRN 3
William MNR 209
William W. CLK 64
Wm. HRD 74
Wm. T. BRN 2
Zackariah CLK 78
BUSH?, Ann PND 30A
Ann PND 30A
Jeremiah CLD 161
John CLD 161
Mathias FKN 150
BUSHONG, Andrew MNR 205
Henry MNR 193
BUSHREE, Anthomy FTE 58
BUSICK, Leven GRT 145
BUSKIL, John HOP 272
BUSKIRK, Ann MAS 52
John SHE 110A
Lawrence GRT 139
Lewis GRT 139
Thomas GRT 139
BUSLEY, Elijah GRD 104A
BUSON, Isaac HOP 234
BUSSEY, John SCT 112A
BUSSING, John GRD 82A
BUSSLE, William BNE 4
BUSTARD?, John JEF 21
BUSTER, Benjamin WRN 51A
Clandins PUL 56A
David KNX 314
Francis PUL 54A
Jno. PUL 41A
John PUL 37A
Joshua WYN 79A
Michael PUL 56A
William, Junr. PUL 56A
William, Senr. PUL 56A
Wm. PUL 44A
BUSTLE, John BBN 76
BUTCHER, George BKN 13
George BTH 182
Henry WRN 37A
Isaac GTN 124
Isaac BTH 192
James BTH 184
Jno. MAS 54
John CSY 220
Polly FKN 64
Samuel BTH 184
William C. BTH 184
William? DVS 16A
Wm. RCK 75A
BUTCHER?, Thomas CLK 74
BUTE?, Thomas BNE 6
Thomas, Senr. BNE 6
BUTER?, Armsted MAD 94
BUTLER, (See Butter) MTG 271
Anthony LGN 27
Bazel GNP 166A
Caleb WDF 97A
Charles WRN 58A
Chas. FLG 35A
Clifford GNP 174A
Colier TOD 128A
Cornelius SCT 114A
Delilee BTH 192
Douglas BTL 317
Edward BRK 241
Edward SPN 3A
Edward A. HAR 220

Name	County	Page
BUTLER, Eleaner	ADR	6
Enoch	HRT	153
Frances	BBN	112
Geo.	FKN	120
Geo. S?.	JEF	19
George	SPN	17A
Ichabud	BBN	112
Izrael	GNP	174A
Jacob	MTG	271
James	ADR	8
James	FLD	30
James	GRN	78
James	HRT	153
James	HAR	188
James	BRK	237
James	SPN	18A
James C.	WDF	97A
James?	BRK	243
Jas.	SCT	125A
Jesse	BTH	192
Joel	HRT	153
Joel	GSN	128A
John	BRN	2
John	ADR	10
John	BTH	200
John	WRN	53A
John	GNP	174A
John D.	LGN	23
Joseph	BNE	6
Joseph	MTG	235
Joseph	HND	7A
Joseph	SPN	17A
Joseph D.	NCH	129A
Joshua	ADR	71
Julian	FTE	61
Letty	FLG	79A
Lucy	FKN	120
Man?	FKN	68
Margret	FLG	62A
Mary	MER	86
Micheal	JEF	30
Nathan	ADR	6
Nathan	HRT	153
Nathan	BTH	192
Owen	TRG	3A
Pearcival	GTN	123
Peter	WRN	53A
Richard	GTN	122
Richd.	JEF	21
Saml.	HND	7
Samuel	MER	86
Samuel	WDF	97A
Samule	MBG	138
Seamon	HRT	153
Shubel	HRT	155
Sidner / Sidney?	ADR	6
Tabitha	BBN	102
Thomas	JES	86
Thomas L.	GTN	123
Tobias	JEF	66
Will	ADR	6
Will	BBN	62
Will	SCT	122A
William	MER	86
William	CLD	147
William	HRT	153
William	HRT	153
William	MNR	215
William O.	GTN	123
Wm.	BRN	4
Wm.	BBN	112
Wm.	HRY	265
Wm.	PND	23A
BUTLER?, Edward	MTG	275
W--.?	CWL	41
Wm.	BRK	235
BUTNER, Edward	JES	78
John	MAD	148
Wm.	MAD	132
BUTOL?, Peter	BRK	235
BUTRAM, Andrew	WYN	100A
Betsey, Mrs.	WYN	90A
Hiel	WYN	83A
Jacob	WYN	90A
James	WYN	100A
John	WYN	99A
Larkin	WYN	100A
Nealy	WYN	94A
William	WYN	97A
William	WYN	97A
BUTRUM, John	MNR	209
William	MNR	209
BUTRY, William	CLY	121
BUTS, Saml.	FKN	136
BUTT, Addison	PUL	61A
Ambrose	PUL	49A
Betteshazer	PUL	54A
Edmund	MTG	255
Jacob	MTG	251
Jeremiah	MTG	263
Richard	LNC	23
Samuel	MTG	263
Vance	UNN	153
William	BNE	6
BUTTER, (See Butler)	MTG	271
Thomas	JES	94
Thos.	MAD	94
BUTTER?, (See Butler)	NCH	129A
Edward	MTG	275
BUTTERFIELD, Wm. S.	HRD	90
BUTTON, Elias	BRN	3
Jacob	MNR	195
John	HRY	226
Will	HRY	228
Wm.	JEF	59
Zacheus	MNR	205
BUTTON?, John (Near Huffmans)	BRN	5
BUTTRAM, Jeremiah	MAD	118
BUTTS, Jacob	LGN	44
John	WRN	63A
William	GTN	129
BUTTS?, Thompson	ADR	6
William, Senr.	GTN	128
BUWNER?, William	JES	80
BUZAN, William	BLT	178
BUZZARD, Anna	HAR	202
Daniel	HAR	192
John	HAR	200
Solomon	FTE	68
BYARS, Edmund	GRD	102B
John	MER	88
John	GRD	102B
BYAS, Elizabeth	GRN	53
BYBEE, Betsey	BRN	5
Buford	BRN	2
Byram	BRN	5
Byrum (Near Thomas Shirley's)	BRN	5
Jno. Jno's Son	BRN	5
Jno. Sherods Son	BRN	3
Joseph	BRN	5
Lee	BRN	2
Neal Mc Can / Mc Carr?	BRN	5
Pleasant	BRN	5
Sherad	MNR	205
BYBEE, Sherod	BRN	2
Thomas	ETL	45
William	MNR	205
BYE, Jonas	BRK	243
BYERS, Aaron	WYN	95A
Elizabeth	NCH	129A
Henry	HRY	262
Jacob	HAR	146
James	GSN	128A
Jas.	FLG	43A
John	HAR	170
John	NCH	112A
John	GSN	128A
Nathan	JEF	38
Richard	WYN	80A
Will	MAS	59
Wm.	ALN	140
BYLUE, Abraham	LWS	98A
John	LWS	94A
Paul	LWS	93A
BYRAM/ BYRANE?, Lucy	MAS	60
BYRAM, Augustin	NCH	115A
James	MAD	174
Salley	MAD	168
Valentine	BTH	172
BYRD, Agnes	SPN	5A
Mitchell	CLK	90
BYRES, Jacob	BKN	20
John	BKN	15
Masie	FTE	64
BYRN, Ignatus	NSN	181
BYRNE, Augustine	LGN	23
Henry	FKN	64
BYRNES, Enoch	BTH	158
BYRNS, Denis	OWN	104
Ignatious	OWN	104
Nicholas	BTH	168
BYRUM, John, Jr.	BRN	5
John, Senr.	BRN	5
BYTHE, David	LNC	79
William	MAD	150
Wm.	LNC	79
C----GI-?, James	LVG	15
C----LAND?, Ralph	CHN	41
C----TON?, Archibald	ETL	45
C---?, Tonn.?	OHO	6A
C---FORD?, Henry	SHE	148
C-A-BY?, Jno.?	ADR	60
C-RODE?, William	FTE	66
CAAR, Peter	FKN	150
CAAR?, Reuben	FKN	114
CABANISS, Charles	GRN	52
George L.	GRN	58
John M.	GRN	52
CABBELL, John	CSY	224
Samuel	CSY	224
Samuel J.	CSY	216
William	CSY	224
CABEL, Isaac	HRY	178
Will	ADR	14
CABELL, Joseph	HND	9
CABLE, Federick	WDF	92
CACKE?, Stephen	WAS	19A
CADWELL, John	CHN	44
Wm.	CHN	44
CADY, Jonathan	CBL	6A
CAFFEY, James	WAS	33A
CAFTON?, Nehemiah	CSY	206
CAGGE?, Harry T.?	RCK	82A
CAGGESHALL, John P.	MER	117
CAGILL, Elijah	MAS	67
CAGLE, Sampson	ALN	120

CAHILL, Jas. MAS 71
  Laurance MAS 67
  Oliver MAS 72
  William FTE 66
CAHOE, Eliza WAS 73A
CAIL, David MAD 116
CAIN, Asail CBL 8A
  Catherine KNX 300
  Daniel KNX 296
  Daniel KNX 312
  Henry NSN 207
  Henry HOP 238
  Howel BRK 245
  Isaac CBL 15A
  Jacob GNP 178A
  James NSN 212
  John CWL 34
  John ETL 43
  John KNX 278
  John GSN 133A
  John MBG 140A
  John GNP 178A
  Nathan NSN 207
  Patrick GSN 132A
  Peter KNX 280
  Rhoda CLD 165
  Sally CHN 30
  Thomas CLD 165
  Washington WAS 82A
  William CLD 165
  William PUL 66A
CAINE?, James NCH 121A
CAINES?, Margaret FTE 105
CAINS, Job FLD 20
  Richard FLD 20
CAIR?, James WAS 66A
CAIRY, John FTE 79
  Lewis FTE 96
  Robert FTE 88
  William WYN 96A
CAISEY, Wm. BKN 16
CAKE?, Richard WDF 96A
CALAHAN, Charles GNP 178A
CALANCEE?, John NSN 178
CALAWAY, Chesley OHO 10A
CALBERT, Francis SPN 15A
  Mansall? MAS 60
  Shelton? SPN 15A
CALBRAITH, Eleanor MTG 241
CALDEHOON, James ADR 10
CALDER, Abram BTL 319
CALDHOON, James GRN 67
CALDHOUN, William WYN 96A
CALDWELL, Widow LVG 15
  A. LGN 23
  Alexander CBL 19A
  Alexander NCH 114A
  Allen WDF 118A
  Andrew FTE 69
  Andrew FTE 77
  Beverly GRN 54
  Chas. CHN 40A
  D. LGN 23
  David CWL 38
  David GRN 70
  David MER 91
  David HAR 132
  David NCH 112A
  David NCH 113A
  David NCH 114A
  Davis MER 91
  Eliza GRN 52
  Eliza GRN 72
  Ephraim BTH 148
  Francis CWL 39
  George MER 91

CALDWELL, George BTL 319
  Henry SPN 5A
  Henry SPN 20A
  James NSN 175
  James BLT 194
  James, Esqr. MER 90
  James WAS 19A
  James NCH 114A
  James WDF 118A
  James NCH 121A
  James C. WDF 113A
  Jno., Sen. ADR 10
  John HRD 8
  John TRG 14
  John FTE 69
  John BTH 150
  John BLT 170
  John NSN 223
  John, Jr. CBL 18A
  John PND 16A
  John CBL 18A
  John SPN 21A
  John NCH 115A
  Jos. MAS 60
  Jos. P. CHN 46
  Joseph TRG 14
  Joseph BTH 148
  Joseph NCH 113A
  Joseph SCT 119A
  Josiah LNC 33
  Martha WDF 118A
  Mary HAR 176
  Oliver MTG 231
  Phebe LGN 35
  Polly LNC 19
  Rob. CWL 44
  Robbert CBL 18A
  Robert MAD 180
  Robert MTG 226
  Robert, Sr. NCH 113A
  Robert NCH 114A
  Robert GNP 165A
  Robt. ADR 50
  Saml. HND 10A
  Samuel LGN 23
  Samuel GRN 64
  Samuel FTE 93
  Samuel W. MER 91
  Susan FTE 105
  Thomas GRN 72
  Thomas HAR 138
  Thomas BLT 160
  Thomas NCH 113A
  Thomas NCH 114A
  Thomas NCH 121A
  Thos. JEF 62
  Walter BTH 174
  William JES 69
  William HRL 104
  William BTH 152
  William NSN 192
  William, Jr. NCH 114A
  William CBL 19A
  William NCH 114A
  Willis ADR 10
  Wm. ADR 10
  Wm. ADR 12
  Wm. BBN 122
  Wm., Jr. ADR 12
  Wm. PND 22A
  Wm. T. WAS 87A
CALEB, Lewis FKN 64
CALEMES, Spencer
    N. CHN 34A
CALHOON, -----? DVS 10A
  -----? DVS 11A

CALHOON, -----? DVS 11A
  David CLY 119
  Elizabeth WAS 54A
  Henry P. WAS 54A
  John CSY 212
  John OHO 3A
  John WAS 77A
  Mary LWS 98A
  Robert FLD 13
  Thomas CLY 119
CALHOUN, -----? LVG 3
  John MER 116
  John WYN 96A
  Pharibee, Mrs. WYN 96A
CALICUTT, Willim. LNC 63
CALISON, Robt. CHN 43
CALK, Francis SCT 91A
  Thomas MTG 251
CALL, Daniel BBN 64
  Daniel BBN 112
  George W. LGN 23
  Hannah BBN 70
  John BBN 112
  Samuel BBN 64
  Widow BBN 62
  Wm. BBN 70
  Wm. BBN 122
CALLAHAM, Edwd. CLY 114
CALLAHAN, Anderson FLG 70A
  David MAD 104
  Edward SPN 24A
  Edwd. FLG 71A
  Elizabeth MAD 106
  John FLG 75A
  Saml. W. FLG 70A
CALLANDER, Jas. HRY 254
CALLANT, Thomas HAR 202
CALLAWAY, Abraham HAR 142
  James SHE 150
CALLAY, A. CHN 44
CALLCEY, Polley MAD 156
CALLDRON?, Baldwin CBL 2A
CALLEN, Lucy MAS 54
CALLENDER, Philip GTN 119
CALLENS?, Zach ADR 10
CALLERMAN, John FLG 70A
CALLES, Horatio BBN 102
CALLESMAN, Susan FLG 67A
CALLICUT, Harrison ADR 28
CALLIHAN, Daniel MNR 191
CALLIN, John CBL 14A
CALLIS, William HAR 170
CALLIWAY, Edmund CHN 41
CALLOE, Elizabeth MAD 146
CALLOWAY, John HRY 216
  John NCH 110A
  John T. WRN 29A
  Stephen WRN 44A
  Thos. JEF 65
CALLY, Allen GNP 167A
CALMES, George CLK 89
  Spencer CLK 89
  William CLK 89
CALMIS, Marquis WDF 94
CALOWAY, Stephen WRN 44A
CALRISE, Peleg FTE 93
CALTERSON?, See
    Catterson? GTN 120
CALTON?, James GTN 131
CALUM?, Thomas O. ETL 40
CALVER, Daniel NSN 189
CALVERT, --encer? CWL 40
  Allen MAS 60
  Ann W. LWS 87A
  Basil LWS 95A
  Bennett G. MBG 135

CALVERT, Cecelius BBN 102
Celas B. OWN 100
Elias CWL 39
Elizabeth BNE 8
Ezekiel MAS 66
Geo. BBN 102
Isaac SCT 126A
Jarrett MAS 57
Jas. MAS 63
Jean MAS 60
Jeremiah SCT 104A
Jno. MAS 75
John BRN 7
John BBN 102
John WAS 23A
John SCT 125A
John T. CWL 39
Joseph SHE 160
Mansel CWL 33
Page FLG 56A
Presley SCT 108A
Richard NSN 212
Rubin MBG 138
Thomas R. NSN 212
Thos. GSN 131
Will MAS 60
William H. LWS 86A
Willis BNE 46
Wm. MAS 52
Wm. FLG 55A
CALVERTS, Richard NSN 204
CALVIN, Jas. MAS 71
John FLD 35
Luther MAS 70
Robt. BNE 8
CALWELL, Johno., Jun. WYN 87A
CAM---N, Benidict WAS 19A
CAMAGA?, James CLY 128
CAMBDEN, Betssey LNC 41
Richard LNC 41
Sarah LNC 2
William LNC 41
CAMBELL, Bell/ Bill? MAS 58
Geo. MAS 79
Jesse GNP 168A
Jno. MAS 54
Jno. MAS 69
Johnson GNP 168A
Nancy CLY 130
Saml. MAS 70
Saml. MAS 71
Will MAS 68
Will. SCT 129A
William JES 92
CAMBLE, Jas. MAS 74
CAMBRIDGE, George BKN 16
Wm. BKN 13
Wm., Jun. BKN 13
CAMBRON, Charles WAS 66A
John WAS 57A
Lenard WAS 56A
Lucy WAS 70A
Melbrun NSN 186
Thos. WAS 71A
Wm. WAS 64A
Zephanah WAS 41A
CAMBRON?, Benidict WAS 19A
CAMBSON?, Benidict WAS 19A
CAMDEN, George JEF 24
CAMEL, Daniel K. FKN 94
James CLY 127
John, Jr. CLY 127
John, Sr. CLY 127
Mathew HAR 152
CAMEL, William CLY 126
William HAR 156
CAMEL?, Jno. A. FKN 54
Peggy FKN 130
CAMELL, Mich. CWL 52
Phebe GRD 115A
CAMERON, Archibald SHE 152
Daniel JES 85
James JEF 37
John BLT 184
Labern JES 79
Samuel HAR 188
CAMIAL?, Thomas D. CBL 23A
CAMICK, Hannah FTE 67
Lewis MER 92
CAMINGORE, John MER 91
CAMMACK, Beverley GTN 131
Christopher FKN 54
Hannah SCT 125A
James MER 91
Lomax FLG 42A
CAMMEL, Moses GRD 111A
William GRD 105A
CAMMICK, John MER 91
CAMP., Ambrose JEF 43
CAMP, Harden WRN 51A
Joseph WRN 51A
Thos. CWL 31
CAMPBEL, Ezechial ADR 12
Jacob GTN 124
CAMPBELL, ----- GRN 74
----- CLD 157
----- CLD 157
----- CLD 157
----- CLD 158
-----? CWL 40
-ecky? DVS 12A
Aaron LGN 37
Abraham MNR 199
Adam GRN 60
Alexander FTE 105
Alexander MBG 141
Alexander WTY 123A
Alexr. FLG 26A
Alexr. SCT 128A
Allen FLD 6
Allen LGN 25
Ambrose ETL 39
Andrew OHO 5A
Andw. FLG 27A
Ann LGN 39
Archd. FTE 62
Archd. FLG 26A
Archibald M. LGN 44
Arthur WRN 61A
Arthur L. JEF 42
Ben. P. CHN 44
Benjamin CLD 147
Charles BNE 10
Charles BBN 114
Charles WRN 46A
Clark JEF 68
Collin CHN 30A
Daniel CHN 29
Daniel HOP 238
David MER 90
David KNX 286
David FLG 25A
David WRN 73A
David MBG 142A
David S. TRG 11A
Duncan GTN 121
Edley MAD 172
Elener ETL 43
Elizabeth FTE 110
Ewd. BKN 23
CAMPBELL, Francis NCH 106A
George CHN 27A
George SHE 126A
Gilbert BNE 8
H. HRY 232
Hiram OWN 103
Hiram KNX 302
Hugh BBN 80
Hugh BBN 114
Hugh SHE 149
Hugh W. NCH 108A
James LVG 12
James LGN 27
James GRN 60
James MER 91
James MER 92
James JES 93
James CLK 99
James FTE 112
James BBN 120
James MBG 141
James SHE 149
James CLD 152
James CLD 154
James HRY 180
James HRY 196
James HAR 198
James MTG 297
James KNX 302
James, Jr. MNR 199
James, Sr. MNR 199
James PUL 56A
James WTY 114A
James WTY 124A
James NCH 125A
James MGB 137A
Jas. FLG 26A
Jas. TOD 131A
Jas. W. FLG 36A
Jeramiah WTY 121A
Jeses? MAD 114
Jno. CHN 44
Jno. CWL 52
Jno. FKN 68
John ADR 12
John LGN 36
John LGN 40
John BBN 66
John JES 76
John BBN 78
John JES 94
John CLK 99
John MAD 154
John HRY 196
John CSY 210
John KNX 302
John TRG 6A
John TRG 11A
John CBL 21A
John WRN 28A
John LWS 88A
John NCH 119A
John SCT 120A
John NCH 127A
John NCH 129A
John G. BBN 124
John H. CLK 82
John R. MTG 295
Joseph CLK 71
Joseph TRG 14A
Joseph LWS 93A
Joseph NCH 108A
Joshua BTH 172
Josiah ADR 12
Josias NCH 115A
Levi KNX 302

Name	County	Page
CAMPBELL, Lewis	BBN	86
Linsy	CWL	31
Mary	LGN	39
Mathew	JES	89
Mathew	HRY	178
Mathew	GSN	132A
Michel	GRN	67
Moses	MNR	199
Moses	HOP	238
Nancy	TOD	132A
Nat	WAS	35A
Nathan	JES	93
Nathaniel	HAR	218
Patrick	CWL	36
Peter	JES	93
Polly	LGN	36
Polly L.	CHN	41A
Rebecca	GRN	60
Reubin	CWL	31
Rice	MBG	142
Richard	HAR	216
Richd.	WAS	22A
Richd.	WAS	31A
Robert	FTE	86
Robert	FTE	86
Robert	LWS	90A
Robert	NCH	108A
Robert	NCH	116A
Robt. M.	ADC	66
Rodgers	CLD	152
Saml.	LNC	15
Saml.	MAD	140
Samuel	TRG	10
Samuel	OWN	105
Samuel	CLD	147
Samuel	WDF	118A
Sancsey	BNE	10
Tandy	WRN	66A
Thomas	LGN	36
Thomas	ETL	37
Thomas	LGN	46
Thomas	PUL	63A
Thos. P.	SCT	132A
Victoria	FTE	64
Will	SCT	107A
Will	SCT	120A
Will., Sr.	KNX	302
Will. Jr.	KNX	302
William	LVG	5
William	FLD	22
William	LGN	36
William	LGN	46
William	JES	94
William	JES	96
William	SHE	152
William	MTG	297
William	CBL	6A
William	LWS	88A
William	NCH	108A
William	NCH	119A
William	WTY	124A
William	MBG	142A
William C.	MBG	140A
Williamson	BTH	176
Willie	CHN	42
Wm.	ADR	10
Wm.	MAD	140
Wm.	MAD	160
Wm.	OHO	5A
Wm.	SHE	126A
Wm. H.	FLG	77A
Wm.?	CWL	39
CAMPBELL?, Charles	LVG	15
David	JES	83
David M.?	MBG	140A
James M.	JES	87
CAMPBLE, David	WDF	104A
Joannah	WDF	94
John	WDF	101A
CAMPDEN, George	JEF	43
CAMPER, Charles W.	OWN	103
Elisha	LNC	39
Henry	FTE	90
William	FTE	91
CAMPFIELD, Thomas	FTE	109
CAMPION, Kerion	JEF	24
CAMPLAIN, Edward	MAD	164
CAMPLE, William	CLY	125
CAMPLIN, James	CLK	107
Will.	KNX	282
CAMPTON, Joseph	SHE	135A
Tho.	MAS	74
CAMRON, George	CHN	29
James	FLD	44
Peter	FLG	33A
Will.	SCT	101A
CANADA, -----?	DVS	12A
Isaac	DVS	19A
Jessee	WYN	87A
John	BTH	192
Joshua	WYN	93A
Moses	WYN	97A
Robert	WYN	85A
CANADAY, Elijah	GRN	78
Ezekiel	OHO	10A
CANADY, George?	CWL	36
James?	CWL	36
Peter	CWL	35
Rob.	CWL	35
Thos.	CWL	35
Z--hh.?	CWL	41
CANAFAX, Wm.	RCK	75A
CANAGA?, William	GRT	145
CANARD, David	ADR	6
George	ADR	18
CANARD?, James, Jr.	BBN	142
CANARY, Abraham	WAS	35A
Michael	MER	91
CANATSEY?, Barbary	ADR	14
CANBRELL?, Joseph	BNE	8
CANBY, Benj. H.	BNE	10
CANDELL?, Thomas	SPN	17A
CANDLE?, Moses	CWL	52
CANE, (See Cave)	CHN	40
Cely?	CHN	42
Jno.	CHN	40
CANE?, Benjamin	BNE	8
Casper	MAS	54
Edwd.	MAS	54
CANELL?, Dorathy	CHN	32
Joseph	FLG	43A
William	CHN	28A
CANES?, James	MAD	174
CANHAM, Levi	WAS	69A
CANIDAY, Joseph	BNE	8
CANIFAX, Radford	PUL	43A
CANINE?, Andw.	HRY	261
CANLOCK?, George	ALN	120
CANN, Jean	BTH	168
CANNADAY, James	CSY	212
Jerm.?	BRK	245
John	CSY	212
John	CSY	226
Robert	CSY	212
Ruth	FLD	39
William	CSY	212
CANNADY, Archibald	HND	13
CANNAN, Elijah	CSY	204
John	CSY	204
Josiah	CSY	204
CANNBRON?, Stephen	NSN	176
CANNEFAX, Jos.	PUL	43A
CANNELL, James	BLT	156
CANNON, Abbey	TOD	128
Bird	GRN	61
Edward	BRK	247
Furna	HND	10A
Izeral	WAS	35A
James	HRT	154
Jesse?	SCT	94A
John	GRN	54
John	GRT	142
John	WRN	42A
John	SCT	92A
John	SCT	95A
John H.	BRK	247
Laws W.	SHE	142A
Neibable?	BTH	158
Newton	SCT	139A
Rebeckah	HND	11
Saml.	BRK	245
Silas (Crossed Out)	SCT	101A
Silas	SCT	94A
Thomas	LNC	5/
Thos.	JEF	40
Will.	SCT	94A
William	TRG	10
William	HND	11
William	WRN	56A
Zadock	JES	78
CANNON?, Elijah	BRK	247
James	CSY	222
CANON, Alexander	GRN	54
Constance, Mrs.	CLK	107
George	BTH	176
John	CWL	33
John	CWL	35
Nathn.?	CWL	43
Tarlton	CWL	33
CANOTE, Jacob	MAD	104
CANOVER, Daminicus	WDF	93
CANPBELL, Duncan	CWL	52
CANSY?, Rebecca	FTE	78
CANTER, Truman	MTG	265
William	MTG	265
CANTERBEREY?, Nimord	GNP	166A
CANTERBERRY, Benjamin	GNP	165A
John	GNP	168A
Reuben	GNP	168A
CANTERBURY, Asa	FLG	43A
CANTON, Nancy	MER	90
CANTRAL, Caleb	HRT	156
CANTRELL, Abraham	FLD	38
James	GRN	76
John	FLD	35
Joseph, Colo.	BBN	114
Polley	GRN	77
Thomas	GRN	76
CANTRILL, Polling?	GRN	76
Zebulon	BTH	196
CANYERS, William	GRT	140
CAPE, John	CLD	153
CAPE?, Thos.	KNX	282
CAPERTON, Wm. H.	MAD	178
CAPEWELL, Charles	SPN	20A
CAPIHEIFER, Samuel	WYN	86A
CAPLE, Andrew	JEF	38
CAPLINER, Daniel	SHE	156
CAPLINGER, George	FTE	106
Henry	SHE	149
Henry	SHE	156
Henry	SHE	160
Jacob	SCT	93A
John	WRN	68A

Name	County	Page
CAPPS, Henry	MNR	215
CAPS, Lancaster	WRN	47A
CAPS?, Caleb	CLK	80
John	FTE	91
CAR, William	WYN	87A
CARAGAN, Arthur	CLD	141
Joseph	CLD	137
CARAWAY, James	CWL	43
CARBY, John	FTE	66
CARDEL, H. M.	MAS	79
CARDEN, Archabald	LGN	41
Reubin	BRN	6
CARDER, Burket	JEF	61
Jno.	JEF	56
Peter	HAR	132
CARDEWELL, Jno. R.	FKN	146
CARDIN, Archibald	HRT	154
Nancy	GRN	55
CARDWELL, George	MER	92
George	BLT	166
George	SHE	176
Jack, Capt.	MER	92
James	MER	92
Jesse	SHE	125A
John	MER	92
John, Capt.	MER	92
Perin	HOP	236
Sally	MER	92
Sarah	SHE	169
Wilcher	MER	92
William	BLT	162
Wm.	SHE	143A
CARDWILL, Jacob	SHE	159
CARE, Jno.	MAS	68
Will	MAS	73
CARE?, Edwd.	MAS	54
James	MAS	56
CARELL, Bartlet	BTH	192
CARER, John	CSY	206
CARERY?, John	WRN	30A
CAREW, Jno.	MAS	57
CAREY, Elizabeth	CLK	87
Hugh	JEF	22
John	CLK	72
John	MER	89
Joseph	JEF	35
Joseph	JEF	58
Ludwell	FTE	94
Moses	MER	90
Thomas	GTN	131
CAREY?, Charles M.	UNN	154
James	GRN	54
Levi	GRD	119A
CARGIL, Daniel C.	HOP	236
CARGILL, Thom.	CWL	52
CARGLE, John	HOP	238
CARGMILES, James	HAR	132
CARIER, Isaac	GRD	112A
Sol	GRD	112A
CARIG, Elijah	BNE	10
Thomas	CLD	140
CARINDER, David	WYN	89A
CARINGER, Andrew	BTL	319
CARINGTON, John P.	NSN	178
CARITHERS, Adam	SHE	134A
Nancy	SHE	134A
Stephen	SHE	134A
William	NSN	223
CARK?, James	CSY	218
CARLAN, Hugh	FTE	65
CARLE, George	KNX	294
CARLEN, John	SHE	130A
Matthias	SHE	132A
CARLILE, George	WDF	103A
James	GRN	56
James	GRN	61
CARLILE, James	GRN	75
John	GRN	61
John	GRN	75
John	HRT	154
John H.	WAS	77A
Sarah	GRN	75
CARLIN, Joseph	NCH	119A
Thos.	SHE	139A
Will	MAS	56
CARLISLE, Alexander	CBL	11A
Bazil	FKN	150
Daniel	FTE	78
James	CWL	33
James	CBL	11A
Jas., Junr.	HRD	54
Jas., Senr.	HRD	54
John	CBL	11A
Mathew	LGN	29
Robert	FTE	98
Samuel	CBL	3A
Thomas	HOP	236
William	CBL	11A
CARLOCK?, George	ALN	120
CARLTON, Edmond	GRT	142
James	BNE	46
James?	BRK	243
Kimbol	HRD	66
Thomas	GRT	142
CARMACK, Geo.	CHN	39
Jonathan	CBL	22A
CARMAN, Caleb	HRD	86
Isaac	SHE	164
Nancy, Mrs.	WYN	102A
William	HAR	218
CARMAN?, See Cannan	CSY	204
CARMICKLE, Andrew	HRD	70
John	HRD	44
Peter	HRD	48
Wm.	HRD	48
CARMINE, Cornelius	SHE	163
CARMON, Joshua	SHE	164
CARNAGA, Francis	BTH	212
Rebekah	HAR	212
Stephen	HAR	212
CARNAGA?, James	CLY	128
CARNAGEY, John	SCT	112A
Will	SCT	101A
CARNAGY, Will	SCT	99A
CARNAHAM, James	HRY	176
CARNAHAN, James	HOP	238
John	HOP	236
William	HOP	240
CARNAHAN?, Jas.	HAR	150
CARNAS, Peter	SHE	164
CARNE, Asa	SHE	114A
CARNE?, James	NCH	121A
CARNEHAN, Thos.	SHE	137A
CARNES, Henry	BRK	247
Josiah	LNC	2
Robert	HAR	144
CARNEY, -----?	CWL	36
Danl.	CWL	32
David	CBL	2A
John	CWL	32
CARNEYHAM, Robbert	CBL	22A
CARNINE, Peter	SHE	154
Ralph	SHE	157
Richard	SHE	154
CARNS, Zachariah	GSN	131
CARNY, Martha	MAD	122
Thos.	PND	30A
CAROTHERS, Gabriel	HAR	208
John	FTE	111
Thomas	HAR	208
CARPENDER, C.	TOD	129A
J.	TOD	129
J./ I.?	TOD	129A
CARPENTER, Absalem	BTH	176
Andrew	BRN	6
Catharine	CSY	212
Catherine	ALN	142
Conrod	LNC	33
Daniel	BTH	190
Fielding	MAD	92
Fielding	CLY	119
George	LNC	27
George	SHE	113A
H.	TOD	131
Henry	LNC	27
Jacob	CSY	212
James	MBG	138
James	CLD	155
Jas. P.	RCK	77A
Jeny	GRD	119A
Jeremiah	BNE	8
Jerry	GRD	110A
Jesse	CLD	152
Jesse	SHE	140A
Job	GRD	91A
Joel	JEF	61
Joel	BLT	178
John	GRN	65
John	ALN	94
John	CLK	96
John	BTH	200
John, Jr.	GRN	72
John, Sr.	GRN	72
John	WDF	99A
Jonathan	BNE	8
Jonathan	WDF	99A
Michael	BLT	158
Michael	BTH	190
Moses	MAD	116
N.	TOD	130A
Nathan	GRN	72
Nathan	CBL	20A
Richd.	FLG	34A
Robt.	GRD	111A
Rufus	GRD	111A
Samuel	NSN	175
Sarah	GRD	91A
Steph	ALN	142
Thos.	MAD	108
William	BNE	8
Wm.	FLG	23A
Z.	GRD	119A
Zacheus	SHE	140A
CARPINTER, Danl.	FLG	29A
Henry	FLG	49A
John	FLG	48A
Simon	FLG	33A
CARR, Abraham	LWS	92A
Andrew	GRN	71
Andrew	WYN	87A
Aron	SPN	11A
Benj.	SCT	114A
Burton W.	GRN	57
Canaday	GNP	176A
Charles	FTE	70
Charles	FTE	85
Charles	FTE	99
Daniel	LWS	91A
David	HRD	16
Edwd.	HRD	70
Elijah	JEF	60
Elizabeth, Mrs.	WYN	87A
Geo.	BBN	132
George	CLK	62
Hanah	LNC	63
Harvey	BBN	124

Name	County	Page
CARR, Henry	HAR	132
Hiram	BRK	245
Isaac	FLG	69A
James	BKN	18
James	JEF	60
James	BBN	66
James	FTE	69
James, Senr.	BBN	124
James	LWS	86A
James H.	BBN	106
Jas.	HRY	259
Jas.	HRY	264
John	JEF	64
John	JES	80
John	CLK	99
John	SHE	136A
John H.	MTG	295
Jonathan	SPN	11A
Joseph	TRG	5
Joseph	BBN	130
Joseph	HAR	160
Larkin	WDF	120A
Lucas	WDF	93
Margaret	CHN	40A
Mary	GTN	132
Moses	SPN	11A
Nancy	BRN	7
Nathan	HAR	150
Nathaniel G.	WDF	104A
Richard	MER	92
Ruthy	GSN	132A
Samuel	BTH	216
Samuel -.?	UNN	147
Tho.	MAS	71
Thomas	JES	87
Thomas	FTE	89
Thomas, Sr.	WDF	118A
Thomas	TRG	4A
Walter	FTE	103
Will.	LVG	5
Wm	HRD	22
CARR?, Abraham	BRK	247
Ezekiel	HAR	148
Robert	HAR	150
CARRACO, Thomas	GTN	129
CARRANT?, John	BBN	130
CARRAWAY, Jas.	JEF	26
CARREL, Saml.	FKN	152
Samul	SHE	176
CARREL?, Perry	WDF	99
CARRELL?, Dorathy	CHN	32
Joseph	FLG	43A
William	CHN	28A
CARRENS?, Wm.	BKN	13
CARRICK, ---w.?	CWL	41
Elizabeth	FTE	77
John	CWL	38
Robert	FTE	77
CARRICO, Alex	WAS	71A
Amelia	SHE	120A
Bazel	SHE	123A
Bend.	WAS	71A
Cornelious	WAS	63A
Francis	WAS	71A
Joan	WAS	73A
Joseph	WAS	71A
Katharine	SHE	123A
Levi	WAS	71A
Levi	SHE	119A
Mathew	WAS	42A
Stanley	WAS	72A
Susan	WAS	71A
Thomas	SHE	123A
Vincent	SHE	120A
Wm.	WAS	41A
CARRICO?, Joseph	WAS	70A
CARRICOE, James	BLT	180
James	BLT	190
CARRIER, Henry	GRD	84A
Jno.	ALN	136
CARRINE?, Andw.	HRY	261
CARRINGTON,		
Archibald	HND	9
Asa	MTG	285
Jessee	LWS	86A
Milly	MTG	283
Randall	MTG	235
Thomas	MTG	235
Timothy	BTH	218
William, Senr.	LWS	90A
William	LWS	89A
William	LWS	97A
CARRINGTON?, Joel	BBN	74
CARRIS, Henry	SHE	109A
CARROL, Demsey	SCT	139A
Jacob	SCT	96A
James	JES	85
John	JES	76
John, Jr.	JES	86
Thomas	JES	95
Thomas	WDF	112A
CARROLL, Andrew	MAS	59
Catharine	WRN	37A
Daniel	MER	91
Elizabeth	MAS	76
James	JEF	22
Jane	MAS	77
Jas.	HRD	94
John	CHN	44
John	WRN	41A
John B.	CHN	44
Joseph	CLK	80
Loudon	CBL	18A
Nancy	HRD	54
Thomas	CBL	18A
Wm.	BBN	138
CARRUTH, Thomas	MNR	199
Walter	MNR	199
CARRY, Danl.	JEF	61
Marry	SCT	94A
CARRY?, Thomas	NSN	207
Thomas	NSN	207
CARSNER, John	FTE	99
CARSON, --dw.	CWL	40
Agnes	CBL	15A
Alex	TOD	130A
Chs. C.	RCK	76A
David	RCK	78A
Elizabeth	CSY	226
George R.	SHE	154
Isaac	HRY	264
Isabella	FTE	100
James	JES	81
Jas.	HRD	26
John	BNE	50
John	HRD	92
John	CBL	15A
John	WYN	96A
John	LWS	98A
John P.	BTL	319
Polly	RCK	83A
Robert	GRN	55
Roger	WYN	86A
Saml.	RCK	77A
Samuel	SHE	143A
Thomas, Jr.	BTL	319
Thomas, Sr.	BTL	319
William	HAR	204
William	BTL	334
William, Sr.	BTL	319
William	CBL	15A
William	WRN	67A
CARSON, Willian	BTL	319
Wm.	RCK	77A
CARSON?, James	CSY	222
CARSWELL,		
Catherine	FTE	65
John	BLT	158
Peter	BLT	164
CART--?, William	BLT	162
CART, Leonard	BRK	243
CARTENHOUR, John	SCT	139A
CARTER, Alexander	LWS	95A
Allen	MAD	166
Alsy	WDF	98
Ann	FKN	84
Ann	OHO	4A
Arthur	BBN	96
Barbary	TRG	3A
Ben	WAS	30A
Benjamin	SHE	113A
Betsy	ADR	12
Braxton, Capt.	WYN	92A
Charles	LNC	59
Charles	CLD	138
Charles	PUL	66A
Charles L. A.	JES	86
Danl.	JEF	32
Danl.	HRT	155
Danl.	FLG	38A
David	FLD	20
E. Charles	GSN	131
Elisha	LNC	61
Elisha	WRN	43A
Elizabeth	MER	92
Elizabeth	SHE	156
Elizabeth	MAD	172
Ezekiel	HOP	238
Garland	SPN	12A
Geo.	GRD	106A
George	BRN	7
George	LNC	33
George	PUL	55A
Goodlow	WDF	104A
Henry	BRN	5
Henry	OWN	101
Henry	HOP	236
Henry, Esqr.	OWN	105
Henry	FLG	32A
Hugh	OHO	8A
Isaac	KNX	290
Jack	WDF	105
Jacob	HRD	18
James	BRN	6
James	BRN	7
James	MER	117
James	CLD	142
James	MAD	166
James	HRY	194
James	NCH	122A
James T.	GRN	52
Jas.	FLG	38A
Jas.	FLG	66A
Jas. B.	FLG	78A
Jesse	LNC	31
Jesse	LNC	79
Jesse	MER	92
Jessee	JEF	45
Jno.	MAS	73
Jno.	FKN	146
Job	CLD	154
Joel	BRK	245
Joel	BRK	247
John	ADR	12
John	BBN	94
John	FTE	94
John	CLD	151
John	NSN	185

Name	County	Page
CARTER, John	MNR	201
John	NSN	205
John	HOP	238
John	MTG	245
John, Esq.	WYN	83A
John, Jr.	BNE	8
John, Jr.?	NCH	121A
John, Sen.	BNE	10
John	FLG	29A
John	WAS	36A
John	WYN	92A
John B.	WDF	99A
John M.	WDF	99A
John R.	JEF	34
Jos.	GRD	83A
Joseph	BKN	2
Joseph	BNE	8
Joseph	GRN	61
Joseph	CLD	154
Joseph	SHE	156
Joseph	BTH	180
Joseph	MNR	201
Joseph	BRK	245
Joseph, Jr.	BTH	190
Joseph	WAS	58A
Joseph	GNP	174A
Joshua	JES	69
Joshua D.	FKN	156
Joshua D.	FKN	158
Josiah	CLD	137
Landon	BRN	7
Levi	BKN	14
Margaret	NSN	205
Martin	MER	92
Mashae?	BLT	168
Mathias	FKN	146
Moses	HOP	238
Nancy	MBG	139
Nancy	CLD	154
Nicholas	NSN	186
Peter	LNC	9
Peter E.	LNC	61
Philip	BRN	7
Richard	SHE	127A
Richard F.	BRK	245
Richd.	GRD	96B
Ritche	HAR	166
Robert	CLK	83
Robert	FTE	94
Robt, Jr.	HRT	156
Robt.	BNE	10
Robt.	GRN	66
Robt., Sr.	HRT	156
Saml.	HRD	78
Samuel	HRD	92
Samuel	CLD	138
Samuel	HAR	176
Sarah, Mrs.	CLK	106
Sol.	KNX	288
Sol.	GRD	112A
Solomon	BKN	14
Solomon	LNC	33
Solomon	MTG	225
Thomas	GRN	60
Thomas	FTE	94
Thomas	OWN	101
Thomas	CLD	138
Thos.	MAS	58
Thos.	BBN	78
Thos.	FKN	92
Thos?	CWL	32
Tilman	MER	91
Trend	CLD	150
Walker	JEF	20
Walker	JEF	28
Washington	BLT	168
CARTER, Will	GRD	85A
William	BRN	5
William	CLD	139
William	CLD	148
William	MNR	201
William	MTG	243
William	OHO	4A
William	WYN	91A
William A.	MTG	279
William C.	PUL	55A
Wm.	BKN	22
Wm.	MAD	118
Zach	JEF	51
CARTER?, Henry	MAD	142
CARTMEL, John.	HAR	206
CARTMELL, Elijah	FTE	103
CARTMILL, Andrew	BTH	220
David	BTH	160
Jacob	NSN	210
John	BTH	174
Nicholas	NSN	209
Thomas	BTH	166
Thos.	JEF	44
CARTO?, Abijah	MAS	78
CARTRIGHT, Christianna	CHN	45
Eljah	GNP	172A
Joseph	ADR	10
Levi	GNP	170A
Peter	CHN	44A
Thomas	GNP	172A
CARTTER?, John	CSY	206
CARTWELL, George	BKN	19
CARTWRIGHT, Benneh? E.	CWL	50
Jas. A.	CWL	44
Justn.?	CWL	52
CARTY, James	CLD	148
William	CLD	148
William	CBL	18A
CARUTHERS, Hugh	LVG	10
CARVER, Archilus	MAD	104
Bartholomew	BRN	7
Cornelius	BRN	7
James	FTE	91
James	MAD	104
James	MNR	209
John	BRN	7
John	GRD	110A
Johnson	GNP	173A
Moman?	MAD	104
Thos.	FKN	128
Thos.	FKN	160
William	BRN	7
William	MER	90
William	CLD	162
CARVEY, Peter	WRN	29A
CARWFORD, John	FLG	62A
CARY, Daniel	MER	89
Ebenezer	MER	89
Ebenezer P.	MER	89
Edward	CLD	151
Henry	CLD	151
James	CHN	41A
James H.	BBN	116
Miles	MBG	143A
Nathaneel	CLD	150
Wilson	CLD	143
CAS---?, Henry	GRN	56
CASADY, Jerimie?	ALN	122
Jesse	FLD	8
CASAL?, David	MER	90
CASAT?, David	MER	90
CASE, Benj.	WAS	49A
Beverley	CSY	214
Delila	BBN	106
CASE, Deward	BKN	9
George	MTG	257
Horatio	BKN	23
James	BKN	20
James	HRD	90
John	BNE	8
John	CSY	214
Joseph	BKN	9
Joseph	BBN	106
Joseph	OHO	10A
Shadrack	BKN	4
Theophilus	MTG	231
William, Sr.	MTG	257
CASE?, Green	CLK	77
Thomas	BKN	8
CASEBIER, Jacob	MBG	141A
William	MBG	141A
CASEE?, Benjamin	GNP	177A
CASEMAN, William	JES	86
CASETY, Jacob	BTH	180
CASEY, Archibald	HAR	218
Burbridge	JEF	54
Clapham?	CLK	98
David	GSN	131
David, Sn.?	GSN	131
Green	ADR	14
Henery	GSN	131
James	HAR	200
Jno.	FKN	120
John	HND	12
John	BRK	247
John	WRN	71A
John	GSN	132A
John D.	GRN	58
Joseph	CBL	12A
Josiah	FKN	82
Moses P.	FTE	61
Peter	UNN	146
Randolph	LVG	13
Riley	JEF	62
Samuel	WRN	71A
Stephen	GRD	99A
Thomas	HAR	190
William B.	MTG	253
CASEY?, James	GRN	54
John	BBN	138
Levi	GRD	119A
CASH, --ward?	CWL	42
Archibald	CLK	105
Isaiah	MBG	142A
James	NSN	197
James	PUL	44A
Jno.	MAS	53
Jno.	PUL	47A
John	NSN	197
John	MBG	142A
Larkin	PUL	44A
Lawson	CWL	38
Nelson	SHE	162
Samuel	LGN	34
Thomas	CLD	164
Walter?	RCK	83A
Warren	HRD	64
Willis	CWL	44
Wm.	GSN	131
Wm.	PUL	47A
CASH?, Elizebeth	WAS	72A
CASHBROOKE, Jno.	MAS	58
CASHMAN, Peter	BRK	247
CASHMAN?, Martin	BRK	247
CASHON?, Thomas	BTH	182
CASHOT?, Felix F.	NSN	176
CASHWALLER, Christeener	MER	91
CASHWELL, John	LNC	9
CASITY, David	BTH	190

CASITY, Elizabeth BTH 190
Isaac BTH 200
Isaac BTH 214
John BTH 200
John BTH 214
John BTH 214
Jonathan BTH 200
Peter BTH 214
Reuben BTH 214
Stephen BTH 198
Stephen BTH 214
CASKEY, Allen WAS 33A
John FLD 8
John WAS 33A
Thomas FLD 8
CASKY, Robert ADR 50
Robt. ADR 12
CASLERIGIM?, James LVG 15
CASLEY?, Nicholas GRT 142
CASLIN, Andrew JEF 55
CASODY, Wm. ALN 124
CASON, Granvill HAR 132
John HAR 142
Nelson HAR 160
Will. SCT 132A
CASPER?, John CLK 98
Peter CLK 98
CASS, Samuel WRN 61A
CASS?, James FLD 6
CASSADAY, Martin PUL 45A
CASSADY, Daniel MER 92
Joel ADR 18
Mc Man? FLG 70A
CASSAT, Jacob MER 90
CASSELL, Abrm. FTE 66
Benjamin FTE 68
Henry FTE 68
Jacob FTE 70
CASSELL?, Abraham JES 83
CASSEY, Henry CBL 7A
CASSIDAY, Ths. JEF 47
CASSIDY, James NCH 108A
Jeremiah NCH 113A
Peter FLG 44A
Thos. FLG 45A
CASSILL, Robert SHE 119A
CASSITY, William BTH 200
William NCH 116A
CASSWELL, John HRT 156
CAST, Amon CLK 70
James CLK 96
Robert CLK 80
CASTEAL?, Zacariah HRD 20
CASTEEL, John CLY 114
John MNR 193
Joseph MNR 195
CASTELL, John, Jr. MNR 195
CASTELLO, Margaret, Mrs. WYN 84A
CASTELO, Thomas WYN 86A
CASTER, Conrad HRD 20
CASTINE, Henry WDF 118A
Paul HRD 72
CASTLE, Abraham JES 83
Bazil FLD 36
David FTE 105
John FLD 24
John WDF 99
Nathan FLD 36
Robert HND 12
Zedekiah FLD 24
CASTLEBERRY, ----.? CWL 32
CASTLEBERY, Flemin? CWL 34
CASTLEBURY, James HOP 238
CASTLEBURY, Nathan HOP 238
William M. HOP 238
CASTLEDINE, John MTG 241
CASTLEMAN, Aug. HRY 264
Gen. FKN 66
Jas. HRD 28
Jno. FKN 84
Lewis FKN 54
Lewis WDF 96
CASTO?, Abijah MAS 78
CASWELL, John, Sr. HRT 155
Samuel HAR 192
Thomas HRT 154
Wm. GSN 132A
CATALET, Nathanel HRD 64
CATCHING, Benj. KNX 288
Saymore KNX 288
CATES, Abner HOP 236
Alexander HOP 238
Benjamin HOP 238
John GRN 69
John HOP 236
John Sr. HOP 238
Richard ETL 42
CATHALL, Joshua JEF 34
CATHEY, Andrew UNN 149
William LGN 39
CATHON?, Laforce SHE 133A
CATLEN, Dory WAS 32A
Nancy WAS 32A
CATLET, Francis FKN 136
James JES 86
John JES 69
Peter BNE 10
CATLETT, Calones? UNN 146
Elijah SHE 148
George UNN 146
George F. UNN 149
Horatio GNP 168A
John FLG 34A
Peter UNN 146
Thos. B. SCT 124A
CATLETT?, Fanny FTE 70
CATLIN, Dory WAS 65A
John WAS 31A
John T. WAS 30A
Wm. WAS 65A
CATMAN, Benjamin CLK 89
Tubman CLK 89
CATO, Henry TRG 14
Nathan CHN 44
CATON, George D. MER 90
Jemima MER 90
CATRON?, Peter WYN 80A
CATSON?, Peter WYN 80A
CATTERSON, Polley GTN 119
CATTERSON?, James GTN 120
William GTN 120
CATTLETT, Elisha BTH 186
CATTON, Bur-l.? KNX 306
CAUDELL?, Thomas SPN 17A
CAUDILL, Abner FLD 14
Henry FLD 3
Matthew FLD 4
Sampson FLD 4
Stephen FLD 3
Stephen FLD 15
Thomas FLD 4
William FLD 35
CAUDLE, William HRL 104
CAUDLE?, Moses CWL 52
CAUDRY, Mary FTE 76
CAUGHEY, David BTL 319
James NCH 105
John NCH 105
CAUGHMAN, David FTE 98
CAUGHRAN, John MAD 174
Saml. MAD 132
CAUGREN, James MAD 138
CAULESS?, Lewis WRN 64A
CAULEY, James GRD 122A
CAULTER, Mark WAS 18A
CAURY?, Jno. FKN 60
CAUSBY, John WAS 85A
CAUSY?, Rebecca FTE 78
CAVANAH, Chas. CHN 35
David HOP 238
Wm. CHN 35
CAVANAUGH, Phillip S. FTE 111
CAVE, (See Cane) CHN 40
(See Case) MTG 257
Abner GRN 53
Jeremiah BNE 10
John WDF 95A
Polly BNE 10
Thomas GRN 59
Thomas GRN 74
Uriel BNE 10
William MTG 241
William, Jr. BNE 46
Wm. JEF 57
Wm., Senr. BNE 10
CAVE?, Benjamin BNE 8
Wm.? BKN 22
CAVEN?, Thomas GRN 59
CAVENAUGH, Fielding FTE 111
Leroy CLK 77
CAVENDER, Jas. SCT 112A
Jas. SCT 117A
Joseph CHN 33
Nancy FTE 75
CAVENS, Absolum SCT 103A
J. T. FTE 61
CAVERS?, Thomas GRN 59
CAVERY?, John WRN 30A
CAVETT, Thomas GTN 131
CAVIN, William GTN 125
CAVINS, John FTE 100
Will SCT 101A
CAWKINS, Isaac HRD 42
CAWLEY, Sallathiel GRN 68
CAWOOD, Berry HRL 106
John HRL 104
Joseph HRL 104
CAWSEY, Joseph CSY 204
CAWTHORN, Asa CLK 91
CAWTHRON, Benja. JEF 39
Tarlton JEF 24
CAY?, (See Coy) HRD 76
CAYCE, Chas. SHE 139A
Chas. SHE 140A
Riley SHE 140A
CAYTON, Abel WRN 48A
Philip GTN 121
William WRN 48A
Wm. ALN 132
CAYWOOD, Acquilla BTH 184
Isaac BBN 66
Thomas O. BTH 184
CEALY, Anna MAS 63
CEARBY?, Jon ADR 60
CEARLOCK, John D. SPN 8A
CEARSEY, Jery WAS 49A
CECIL?, Kinsey B. FLD 31
CECKE?, Stephen WAS 19A
CEDARS, Bennett FTE 81
CEEKE?, Stephen WAS 19A
CEESEE?, Benjamin GNP 177A
CELEY, Courtley JEF 27
CELIA, (Free) BRK 229

CELLISON, Willm. LNC 69
CEMONS?, Charles WAS 33A
CENTER, Willis ALN 138
CENTNER?, Jacob MER 116
CEPEL?, James S. NSN 189
John NSN 189
CERBIN?, Zacheriah BTH 198
CERK, Elenor WAS 40A
CESOSS?, Will MAS 59
CESSEL?, James S. NSN 189
John NSN 189
Joseph NSN 187
CESSELL, Thos. WAS 61A
CESSELL?, Ben WAS 40A
Matthew WAS 42A
Silvester WAS 39A
Wm. WAS 42A
Zack WAS 40A
CESSILL, Elizebeth WAS 45A
CESSILL?, Elias UNN 147
Je--idnah? WAS 75A
CH-LEY?, John NCH 112A
CHADDIC, John BLT 174
CHADDICK, John BLT 160
CHADOWEN, John W. WAS 43A
CHADWELL, Geo. HRY 253
George JES 92
Jas. HRY 255
CHADWICK, Israel NCH 111A
John GNP 168A
CHADWIK, John GTN 129
CHAFFAN, Aaron HRD 20
CHAFFIN, Elias CWL 52
CHAFIN,
Christopher FLD 42
David FLD 46
James FLD 45
John FLD 46
Jourdan FLD 45
Milley FLD 46
Simon FLD 45
CHAFIN?, John FLD 20
CHAINEY, Benony BBN 88
John BBN 86
CHALAS, Ezekiah MAD 160
Hugh MAD 160
Wiley MAD 160
CHALEN?, William FTE 66
CHALFAN, Judith HRD 62
CHALFANT, Amos BKN 26
Francis HAR 186
Thos. BKN 24
CHALFIN, John HRD 28
CHALKLEY, Benjamin CLD 145
CHALPANT?, Wm. BKN 8
CHAMBERLAIN,
Benjn. BNE 8
Charles CLD 138
George CLD 138
Griffin CLD 147
John FTE 68
Prudence CLD 138
Thomas ETL 51
William ETL 54
William MNR 203
Zeb MER 91
CHAMBERLAND,
Daviss ADR 14
Young HRT 156
CHAMBERLIN,
Feald--y? WAS 68A
Jno. MAS 63
Jno. MAS 71
Joseph WAS 68A
Silas WAS 68A
Thos. WAS 68A
CHAMBERS, ---on? DVS 10A
Ahemaz? NSN 195
Andrew ETL 44
Arthur FTE 76
Asa HRD 10
Benj. S. SCT 127A
D. S. JEF 19
David MER 90
Edmund FKN 122
Edward BRN 7
G. W. JEF 28
Geo. FKN 160
George ADR 4
Hugh ADR 12
James HAR 134
James HAR 170
James HAR 206
Jas. SCT 125A
Jiles BRK 247
Jno. MAS 77
Jno. MAS 80
Jno. FKN 122
Jos. MAS 76
Lemuel W. SHE 170
Martha HAR 158
Mary MTG 245
Maxwell FTE 107
May HRY 228
Richard FLD 42
Robert FTE 76
Robt. S. BNE 46
Rowland WDF 92
Saml. HAR 158
Tho. ALN 94
Thomas FTE 107
Uriel SCT 92A
Walker MTG 249
William FTE 107
William H. MER 92
Wm. JEF 40
Wm. RCK 81A
CHAMBLIN, Geo. BBN 102
Wm. BBN 142
CHAMP, Moley BBN 94
Robert NCH 125A
Robt. BBN 94
Thomas NCH 125A
Thos. BBN 134
Wm. MAD 172
CHAMPER, Christian JEF 64
CHAMPION, Drury LVG 7
Edward WDF 102
James LVG 2
Mary LVG 8
Nancy WAS 45A
Tho. CWL 44
William LVG 3
Willis LVG 3
CHANCE, Benjamin, Sr. WYN 97A
Ezekiel WYN 97A
Thomas WYN 96A
William LGN 45
William WYN 97A
CHANCELOR, Jno. MAS 73
William BTL 319
CHANCELOR?, Levi GSN 132A
CHANCY, John CLK 80
CHANDLER, Mrs.? --ch.? MAS 66
CWL 41
Ase CHN 34
Benjamin CLD 139
Britten MAS 66
Charity CLD 139
Chs. CWL 44
Claburn HAR 140
CHANDLER, Edmond GRT 147
Edwd. WAS 67A
George R HAR 170
Henry JES 82
Horathio GRN 75
Isaac MAS 56
Israel HAR 184
J--.? CWL 41
James FTE 87
James HRT 156
James WAS 67A
John CHN 34
John GRN 74
John CLY 130
John CLD 139
John HAR 184
John HOP 238
Levi BTH 212
Manson LNC 29
Martin HRT 156
Mary CWL 44
Richard WAS 32A
Robert MAD 138
Samuel CHN 34
Sarah WAS 67A
Susan WAS 67A
Thomas HRY 200
Walter GNP 174A
William HAR 162
William BLT 194
Wm. CWL 44
Wm. MAD 138
Wm. WAS 39A
Wm.? MAS 66
Zach CWL 44
CHANDOIN?, (See Chaudoin) GRN
CHANEY, Elijah SPN 13A
Greenberry FLD 40
James SPN 12A
James LWS 92A
Jno. PUL 50A
John CLK 78
Moses SPN 6A
Nathan CLK 78
Obediah GRN 69
Sarah GNP 177A
William SPN 24A
CHANLER, Wm. HRY 266
CHANY, Phillip HND 13
CHAPEEZ, Benjamin HRD 96
CHAPEL, Harrison FKN 98
CHAPELL, George CLY 120
CHAPIN, Amariah BNE 50
L.? R. MAS 67
Lucius FLG 35A
CHAPLINE, Abraham, Capt. MER 92
Isaac MER 92
James BLT 156
CHAPMAN, A. BTL 319
Aaron GRN 70
Antony CHN 28
Archible HAR 162
Benjamin LGN 42
Benjn. BNE 10
David MNR 205
David WRN 68A
Edmund WDF 121A
Geo. MAS 60
Hanah WDF 100A
Henry FLG 57A
Isaac FLD 21
James LNC 69
James HRL 106
James MNR 201

Name	County	Page
CHAPMAN, James	OHO	7A
Jesse	WRN	67A
John	FLD	41
John	MNR	217
John, Jr.	MNR	211
John	WRN	66A
John A.	BNE	8
John S.	UNN	149
Joseph	LWS	93A
Joshua	OHO	8A
Josiah	GNP	169A
Mary	FLG	27A
Moses	OHO	10A
Nancy	SPN	21A
Neal	BRN	6
Oralanda	CBL	16A
Patience	FLD	21
Peyton	ADR	10
Purrir	BTH	174
Reuben	GNP	169A
Richard	LNC	69
Robert	HAR	178
Robert	MNR	205
Thomas	BNE	8
William	BRN	6
William	GTN	121
William	UNN	154
William	LWS	93A
William C.	UNN	153
Willice H.	HRT	156
Willis	OHO	9A
Wm.	OHO	9A
Wm.	FLG	23A
Wm.?	CWL	38
Zacariah	LWS	93A
CHAPPEL, John	SCT	117A
Stephen	HOP	238
Thos. L.	SCT	126A
CHAPPELL, James	BLT	170
Jesse	HRD	54
Jesse	LNC	71
Richd.	CHN	42A
William	BLT	154
CHAPPLE, Jas.	FLG	71A
CHARD?, John	RCK	79A
CHARLES, James	MTG	283
Philip	ETL	44
Rachael	BLT	196
William	BLT	158
William B.	NSN	184
CHARLTIN, Lucy	RCK	83A
CHARTER, Elizabeth	PUL	64A
Jonathan	BRN	7
CHARVET, Lucian	GTN	123
CHASE, Josiah	BNE	10
CHASON, John	SPN	8A
CHASTAIN, Jesse	WRN	55A
John	WRN	52A
CHASTEAN, Geo.	HRY	216
CHASTEEN, Elija	BTH	204
Elizabeth	BTH	204
Jacob	LGN	43
John	MAD	132
John L.	HRD	28
William	LGN	38
Wm.	ADR	10
Wm.	MAD	110
CHASTEN, Thomas	SPN	5A
CHASTINE, Peter	HRT	154
CHATHAM, Benjamin	MER	89
James	MER	91
Josiah	MAD	148
Thomas	HRY	194
CHATMAN, Jeremiah	SPN	24A
CHATTEEN?, Jessee, Jr.	WYN	97A

Name	County	Page
CHATTEN, Thomas	WRN	74A
CHATTOM?, David	ALN	114
CHAUDOIN, Andrew	GRN	55
David	GRN	55
Francis	GRN	55
John J.	GRN	58
Thomas?	GRN	52
CHAUDOWEN, Andrew	HRT	155
John M.	HRT	154
CHAUNCY, Wiley	CLD	161
CHAYNE, Jackson	PUL	47A
CHEAK, Nancy	CHN	43A
Silas	CHN	34A
Wm.	CHN	43
CHEANEY, Ambrose	BBN	88
Heritage	BBN	88
John	NCH	116A
Leonard	FTE	107
Rachael	BBN	88
William	NCH	103A
CHEARLOCK, John	SPN	22A
CHEATHAM, David	MTG	287
Edward	HND	10
James	MTG	249
John	MTG	287
Lenard	WAS	78A
Leonard	MTG	261
Maj.	TOD	126A
William	BRN	33
CHECK?, Willis	BKN	20
Wm.	BKN	10
CHEEK, Alexander	BKN	14
Henery	ADR	50
John	CWL	44
John?	CWL	42
N.	SHE	123A
CHEEKS, ---iah?	CWL	36
Benjamin	WYN	100A
David, Sr.	WYN	101A
CHEER, John	CHN	40
CHEESMAN, Wm.	MAS	70
CHEETHAM, Christopher	CLD	144
Christopher	CLD	144
Edward	CLD	151
Hezekiah	CLD	144
Josiah	CLD	167
Owen	CLD	147
Richardson	CLD	144
Samuel	CLD	167
William	CLD	151
CHENAULT, Anderson	MAD	100
CHENCELOR?, John	BTL	319
CHENOWITH, Arthur	JEF	41
Arthur	HRD	58
Isaac	HRD	14
John T.	GTN	123
Margaret	SHE	152
Miles	HRD	28
Nicholas R.	GTN	124
William	NSN	194
CHENUTE, Abe	RCK	79A
CHEPIN?, Jonathan	BLT	194
CHERRY, Alexander	SPN	12A
James	GRN	63
John	CBL	7A
Nicholas	CBL	18A
Polley	GTN	133
Rob.?	CWL	37
Saml.	WRN	35A
William	WRN	28A
CHERSENT?, James	MAD	132
CHESER, Robert	MAD	92
CHESHER, William	WTY	115A
CHESHIRE, John B.	HRD	52
CHESNEY, John	CSY	226

Name	County	Page
CHESNUT, Benj.	CLY	124
Edmund	KNX	310
John	HRD	68
Saml.	CWL	46
Samuel	CLK	84
Samuel	CLY	116
CHESNUTT, Jas.	TOD	129A
S.	TOD	129A
CHESSIN?, Jonathan	BLT	194
CHESTNUT, Abrah.	KNX	314
CHESTNY, John	PUL	66A
CHETUM, Archbd.	LNC	5
Leonard	LNC	5
CHEW, Richard	JEF	48
Samuel	FTE	107
Samuel	BTH	220
Thos.	SCT	120A
CHEWNING, Jesse	BRN	6
CHEYNE, Archibald R.	PUL	57A
Hiram	PUL	53A
CHICK, James, Jr.	KNX	286
James, Sr.	KNX	290
Reubin	LGN	43
Silas	KNX	286
Susannah	MER	92
CHILDERS, Abraham	FLD	13
Abraham	FLD	38
Elisha	CLY	131
Francis D.	SPN	13A
Goolsbery	GRD	91A
Jno. -?	HAR	138
Lindsey	FTE	94
Samuel	WRN	39A
Soloman	PND	25A
Wm. G.	PND	20A
CHILDRES(STRAY), Henry	GRT	140
CHILDRES, Harman	GRT	141
Harry	GRT	141
Henry	GRT	143
Henry (Stray)	GRT	140
John	CWL	46
Joseph	GRT	141
Joshua	GRT	143
Major	GRT	143
Reuben	GRT	143
Robert, Jr.	GRT	143
Robert, Senr.	GRT	143
Susanna	GRT	141
Thomas	GRT	140
William	CLD	138
William	GRT	141
CHILDRESS, Aarchabald	ADR	50
Jacob	BTL	319
James	BTL	319
Joshua	MER	117
Royal	ADR	12
William	MER	91
William	BTL	319
CHILDS, Richd.	CWL	35
Richd.?	CWL	36
CHILES, David	MAS	58
Elizabeth	MER	91
Garland	MAS	58
Jno.	FKN	72
John	FTE	93
Joseph	FKN	162
Lewis C.	BKN	28
Phebe	SHE	167
Richard	FTE	89
Sally	FKN	56
T. C.	SHE	143A
Tarlton W.	CLK	79
Thomas	MER	91

Name	County	Page
CHILES, Uriah	HAR	142
William	NSN	214
William	MTG	295
CHILES?, Henry	CLK	97
CHILTON, Geo.	HRY	250
Jno.	HRY	250
CHILTS, John	GRN	59
CHINA, Jacob	GTN	122
CHINAULT, Christopher	NSN	186
David	MAD	120
Stephen	BRK	227
Wm.	MAD	90
CHINAULT?, Thos.	BRK	245
CHININTS?, George	NSN	222
CHINN, A.	BBN	136
Benjamin	GNP	166A
Christopher	MER	115
Dudley	FLG	34A
Eli	HAR	158
Elijah	MAS	66
Geo.	MAS	56
George	HAR	158
James	MER	92
Jno.	HAR	158
Joseph	BBN	118
R. S.	BBN	112
Rawleigh	MAS	66
Richard H.	FTE	62
Sarah	FTE	79
Thomas	HAR	166
William B.	BBN	112
CHINOWETH, Samuel	LGN	27
CHINOWITH, ----m?	DVS	9A
Abram.	JEF	45
Jacob	BTL	319
James	GNP	171A
Jonathan	BTL	319
Saml.	SCT	91A
CHINWITT?, Thos.	BRK	245
CHIPLEY, Jane	HAR	150
Stephen	FTE	70
CHIPMAN, Alice, Mrs.	GRT	144
Draper	BTH	172
James	SCT	96A
Perry	GRT	142
CHISHAM, Benjn.	GRN	74
Gabriel	GRN	74
John S.	GRN	60
CHISM, Benjamin	JES	92
Benjn.	SCT	101A
Elij.	HRY	255
Gabriel	GSN	132A
Geo.	SCT	116A
George	MNR	193
I./ J.? Thos.	GSN	131
James	JEF	36
James	CLK	78
Jas.	SCT	115A
John	HRD	38
John	CLK	88
John	SPN	17A
John	SCT	116A
Michael	MNR	195
Phebe	MNR	201
Richd.	HRD	38
Samuel	MTG	255
Thomas	CLK	91
Thomas	CLK	98
Urial	JES	92
William	MNR	217
Wm.	GSN	132A
CHISMAN, Jacob	CHN	36
CHISTY, Elijah	SPN	20A
CHISUM, William	JEF	30
CHITTY, Joseph	MAD	138
CHITWOOD, Danl.	PUL	41A
Jas., Sr.	PUL	41A
Jas.	PUL	41A
John R.	GNP	170A
John R.	GNP	179A
Lazarus	PUL	41A
Pleasant	PUL	41A
Shadk., Sr.	PUL	41A
Shadk.	PUL	41A
CHNOWEATH, Will	MAS	64
CHOAT, Edwd.	FLG	53A
Richd.	FLG	53A
CHOATE, Herod	SPN	16A
Samuel	BTH	208
CHOOLEY, Ruben	WAS	23A
Wm.	WAS	28A
CHOPPELL?, Abraham	BLT	152
CHOWNING, John	BBN	116
Laramore?	MAS	62
Patsy	BBN	116
Robt.	SCT	126A
Walker	SCT	103A
CHR-T--?, Elizabeth, Mrs.	WYN	89A
CHRISLER, Ambrose	BNE	10
David, Jr.	BNE	10
David, Sr.	BNE	10
John	BNE	10
Leonard	BNE	10
Lewis	BNE	10
CHRISMAN, Abraham	FTE	88
Barbary	WDF	113A
George, Junr.	CHN	33A
George	CHN	33A
Henry	CHN	41
Isaac, Col.	WYN	83A
James	GTN	119
John	CHN	33A
John	WYN	106A
Joseph	CLD	142
Michael	CHN	36
CHRISP, William	LNC	71
William	WYN	92A
CHRISTAIN, Gilbert	HOP	238
CHRISTENBERRY, Wm.	BNE	10
CHRISTENSON, Robt.	ADR	12
CHRISTIAN, Andrew	FTE	82
Benjamin	WYN	86A
Durry	WRN	33A
Elizabeth	BRN	7
J./ I.?	TOD	130A
James	OHO	11A
James	OHO	11A
John	HND	10
John	GRN	65
John	FTE	68
John	FTE	81
Judith	FTE	109
Martin S.	SHE	164
Mathew	UNN	148
Paul	SCT	134A
Thomas	FTE	83
Thos.	WAS	31A
Titus?	WRN	75A
William	FTE	81
William	WRN	33A
CHRISTLEER, John	CBL	7A
CHRISTMAN, Elijah	LGN	37
George	JES	81
George T.	JES	85
Hugh	JES	78
Joseph	JES	73
Joseph	JES	87
Nathaniel	CLD	142
CHRISTMAS, Richd.	BTL	319
Richd.	BTL	319
CHRISTOPHER, Ambrose	MAD	114
Ebanezer	JEF	32
James	LNC	75
James	MAD	148
Jas.	CWL	52
Lewis	LNC	55
Sarah	MAD	100
William	WDF	99
William	WDF	114A
CHRISTOSAN, Isaac	CSY	220
CHRISTOSON, Thomas	CSY	222
CHRISTOSTON, John	CSY	220
CHRISTUSON, Christopher	MER	90
James	MER	90
Samuel	MER	90
CHRISTY, Ambrose	CLK	77
Andrew	WRN	56A
David	BNE	8
Israel	SHE	174
John	CLK	91
Peter	JEF	46
William	SHE	174
CHRISWELL, John Y.	KNX	282
William	WYN	94A
CHRONICK, Christopher	LNC	81
CHRYSTAL, John	FTE	95
CHUDWELL?, George	JES	92
CHUNING, Charles	JES	76
CHUONING?, Thomas S.	TRG	5A
CHURCH, Eleanor	BRN	6
James	FKN	94
Jesse?	RCK	84A
Joel	CLY	119
John	FTE	84
Joral?	FLD	13
Joshua G.?	CWL	44
Robert	HND	10
Robt.	FKN	94
Thomas	BRN	6
Thomas	LNC	39
Thomas	FTE	103
Thomas	FKN	104
Thomas	CBL	10A
Wm.	FKN	94
Wm.	FKN	106
CHURCHILL, Alvah	GTN	121
Armstead	HRD	86
Armstead H.	HRD	96
George	SHE	169
Henry	JEF	39
John	HRD	66
John	DVS	19A
Mary	SHE	118A
Saml.	JEF	31
CHURCHWELL?, Molley	MAD	126
CINCH, Saml.	WAS	67A
CINNAMOND, John	SHE	148
CIPEL?, Joseph	NSN	187
CISHINER, Henry	LNC	73
Sarah	LNC	79
CISNA, Elizabeth	MBG	135A
Wm.	HRD	18
CISSEL, Elias	UNN	149
Wilford	SCT	133A
CISSON, John	JES	88
CISTER?, James	MAD	120
CITY, John	GTN	122
CIUTSENGER, Salley	WAS	86A
CIVENS?, John	CSY	220

CIVERS, Same.? WAS 40A
CLABOURN, White GSN 131
CLACK, John BRN 6
John SPN 17A
Moses FLG 45A
Sterling SPN 7A
CLAGET, Allen GSN 131
Charles GSN 131
Henery GSN 131
CLAGGETT, James H. WDF 123A
Mary WDF 109A
CLAGHORN, M. HRL 104
Robert HRL 104
CLAGITT, J. W. TOD 124A
CLAIBOURN, Milo BRN 34
CLAK, Chas. B. CHN 46
CLAMER, James CSY 222
CLAMORE, Thomas CSY 222
CLAMPET, Henry CLK 106
CLAMPETT, Moses SHE 167
CLANCEY, Mathew M. FLG 25A
CLANCY, James HRL 104
Wm. FLG 28A
CLANTON, Henry LGN 39
Samuel LGN 39
Sterling LGN 41
CLAPOLE,
Corneliums HAR 160
CLAPTON, David HRT 156
John HRT 154
John, Sr. HRT 154
CLAR-?, Samuel CHN 33A
CLARE, Daniel PUL 52A
Thos. PUL 48A
CLAREY, Joshua LWS 91A
CLARK, -----? DVS 9A
Abner JES 92
Abner GRD 100A
Abram GRN 74
Alexander FLD 29
Alexander MER 117
Alexander MGB 137A
Allouesce? NSN 191
Amos OWN 104
Ann RCK 84A
Asa SHE 150
Ben. HRY 251
Benedict NSN 179
Benj. WAS 50A
Benjamin BRN 6
Benjamin FTE 105
Benjamin CLD 158
Benjamin MAD 174
Benjamin NSN 186
Benjamin BLT 188
Benjamin MBG 142A
Benjamin W. BRN 6
Betsey SCT 114A
Bowling CLK 98
Carter FLD 42
Cary GNP 175A
Catharine FTE 104
Catherine FTE 62
Charles CLK 86
Charles BRK 243
Chas. HRY 256
Chas., Sr. HRY 251
Christopher MAD 172
Christopher BRK 247
Christopher WRN 63A
Chs. HRY 253
Clement NSN 199
Daniel FLD 29
Daniel BLT 188
Danl. FLG 38A
Davey WAS 38A
CLARK, David ADR 12
David MAD 108
David CLY 116
David UNN 150
David HOP 238
David, Dr. MER 90
David OHO 5A
David GRD 103A
Davis NSN 186
Dison NSN 213
Drury ADR 18
E., Mrs.? MAS 55
Edward MAD 180
Edward BTL 319
Elias LVG 15
Elijah GTN 125
Eliza SCT 91A
Elizabeth FTE 87
Elizabeth SHE 171
Elizabeth GSN 132A
Ellis HOP 236
Enoch FTE 64
Everard BRN 6
F. D. MAS 75
Fiddy GRN 75
Frances BTH 184
Francis MER 90
Francis SHE 167
Geo. HRY 253
George HND 3
George LNC 25
George FTE 101
George HRT 156
George SPN 3A
George LWS 95A
Georoge HOP 238
Hannah FTE 110
Henry CWL 34
Henry CWL 37
Henry LNC 47
Henry OWN 104
Henry CLD 150
Henry, Jr. CHN 40
Henry A. BRK 247
Henry W. UNN 146
Heny, Sr.? CHN 40
Icabod SCT 133A
Ignatus MAD 130
Isaac JEF 31
Isaac GRN 57
Jacob BRN 7
Jacob GRN 58
James BRN 7
James CLK 72
James MER 90
James MER 91
James JES 96
James CLK 103
James GTN 131
James GRT 141
James BLT 182
James NSN 189
James BLT 190
James BTH 218
James (Stoner) CLK 83
James SPN 14A
James PND 26A
James H. GRN 72
Jams. PUL 36A
Jane FTE 64
Jane CLK 88
Jas. CHN 42A
Jas. W. MAS 53
Jehu GRD 82A
Jessee ADR 12
Jessee JEF 43
CLARK, Jno. CHN 40
Jno. CHN 42
Jno. ALN 134
Jno. HRY 265
Jno. PUL 45A
John BRN 7
John FLD 28
John JEF 40
John GRN 68
John FTE 74
John GRN 75
John MER 90
John MER 92
John BBN 136
John UNN 151
John BLT 184
John BTH 218
John BRK 243
John BRK 245
John HOP 270
John BTL 319
John, Jr. SHE 166
John, Junr.? ALN 106
John, Sr. SHE 166
John GRD 96B
John SPN 6A
John WAS 84A
John LWS 89A
John GRD 122A
John GNP 172A
John B. FLG 39A
John H. & Co. JEF 23
John S. GRN 50
Jonathan BRN 6
Jos. MAS 54
Jos. CHN 44A
Joseph BRN 7
Joseph FKN 152
Joseph CLD 167
Joseph CBL 20A
Joseph WAS 53A
Joseph WAS 65A
Joseph SHE 111A
Joseph GSN 132A
Joshua CBL 12A
Josiah GTN 124
Kitty GRT 146
Lamma? WTY 127A
Lanslott SCT 112A
Lewis PND 28A
Lewis PUL 56A
Mary HRD 56
Matthew FKN 122
Merriat? HRT 156
Micajah CHN 40
Micajah SPN 4A
Micajah SPN 5A
Michael FKN 90
Michl. FTE 58
Mildred BRK 245
Moses HRT 154
Nancy MAS 71
Nathaniel BLT 164
Nathaniel BLT 188
Peter WTY 126A
Peter W. PUL 52A
Phillip D. BTH 186
Phineas SCT 117A
Polly CLD 154
Rachel NSN 223
Reuben LNC 5
Reuben BRN 7
Reuben CLD 154
Richard NSN 199
Richard BRK 245
Richard LWS 90A

CLARK, Robert MAD 132
Robert WYN 85A
Robert GRD 107A
Robert WDF 121A
Robert MBG 133A
Rubin GRD 103A
Sally ETL 45
Saml. TOD 133
Samuel FLD 29
Samuel CLD 141
Samuel HOP 238
Samuel WYN 102A
Samuel MBG 133A
Sarah GRN 62
Schuyler PUL 52A
Shederick WAS 64A
Solimon ADR 10
Susan LVG 8
Susanna FTE 90
Tho. MAS 74
Thomas FTE 86
Thomas MER 91
Thomas NSN 196
Thomas HOP 238
Thomas GRD 103A
Thomas A. JES 69
Thomas D. NSN 200
Thos. PUL 37A
Thos. WAS 49A
Thos. TOD 125A
Will ADR 10
Will GRD 96B
William LVG 13
William CLK 83
William MER 90
William WDF 93
William CLY 116
William SHE 161
William NSN 199
William, Sen. UNN 151
William, Sr. OWN 105
William, Sr. UNN 151
William SPN 3A
William PND 29A
William PUL 57A
William GRD 85A
William D. OWN 104
William S. HAR 210
Wm. GRN 57
Wm. ALN 134
Wm. MAD 150
Wm., Jr. BBN 102
Wm., Senr. BBN 124
Wm. For Jno. Lowrey & Co. FTE 61
Wm.? E. MAS 55
Woodson? MAD 104
Zac SHE 119A
CLARK?, Patious? HAR 164
Wm. WAS 29A
CLARKE, Abner BKN 9
Abner LGN 47
Adin? HRD 78
Benjamin CBL 17A
Benjamin SHE 138A
Bowlin CHN 28A
Bowling WRN 37A
Charles LGN 28
Daniel CBL 23A
David HAR 190
David, Junr. CHN 33A
David, Senr. CHN 33A
David SHE 115A
Edmd. HRY 216
Elisha SHE 125A
Elizabeth OWN 100
CLARKE, Fielding BTH 208
Frances NSN 208
Hannah CBL 20A
Hector LGN 23
Ichabod CBL 23A
Isaac HAR 198
Jacob HRY 228
James LGN 39
James BBN 108
James CSY 222
James MTG 273
Jeremiah NCH 127A
John LGN 32
John LGN 37
John NCH 120A
John SHE 131A
John D. SHE 115A
John H. JEF 23
John H. WRN 75A
John M. LGN 43
Johnathan CHN 35
Joseph MTG 231
Joseph WRN 63A
Josiah SHE 138A
Ludlow JEF 46
Milly HRD 78
N. JEF 22
Nancy NCH 117A
Obadiah SHE 138A
Phillip BKN 10
Richard SHE 128A
Robert BBN 122
Samuel CLK 62
Samuel MTG 239
Samuel CBL 23A
Samuel NCH 122A
Singleton NCH 120A
Thomas HRD 12
Thomas LGN 39
Thomas HAR 216
Thomas MTG 277
Thomas NCH 120A
Wacker BKN 18
William LGN 39
William MAD 116
William MTG 233
William CBL 17A
William CHN 33A
William WRN 44A
William NCH 117A
Willis MTG 229
Wm. SHE 138A
Wm. A. HRD 70
Wm. M. SHE 125A
Wm. S. SHE 138A
CLARKSON, Anselm BBN 104
Charles L. BBN 100
Charles L. BBN 142
David, Jr. BBN 144
David PND 16A
Drury MER 90
James M. BBN 136
Jas. F. HRD 64
John SHE 152
Joshua WDF 97
Julius BBN 106
Julius W. BBN 108
L. H. B. BBN 142
N. J. BBN 148
N. L. BBN 98
Peter BBN 142
R. L. BBN 106
Thomas CSY 220
William SHE 152
CLARKSTON, Absalem MAD 144
Edward WAS 20A
CLARKSTON, William? DVS 12A
CLARRY, Wm. GSN 133A
CLARY, Garrett FLG 31A
Joseph FLG 31A
Richd. FLG 31A
Robt. ALN 118
CLASPELL, John WRN 46A
CLASPILL, Sarah WRN 46A
CLASSER, Lenard BTH 200
Michael BTH 200
CLASSNER, Nicholas NSN 208
CLATON, John ALN 116
CLATTER, Henry MAS 62
CLATTERBUCK, Reuben SHE 168
CLAUNCH, Barnard OHO 8A
David LGN 28
Jacob MER 117
Matthew MER 90
William MER 90
CLAVELL, Elizabeth BTH 172
William BTH 172
CLAVENGER, Asa LGN 44
Reuben CLD 152
CLAW, Nathaniel WDF 118A
CLAWS, Henry CLK 64
CLAWSON, Richard CLK 71
William WDF 103A
CLAXTON, Achilles OWN 100
CLAXTON?, John FTE 112
CLAY, Abraham FTE 83
Barnet HND 3
Caleb FLD 8
Charles V. HND 10
George TOD 128A
Green MAD 176
Henry FTE 86
Henry BBN 106
Henry BBN 108
James HND 9A
John BBN 126
Jourdan FLD 25
L. B. BBN 124
Nester? DVS 14A
Porter FKN 62
Thomas DVS 14A
Thos. HND 9A
William NCH 116A
Zekiel LVG 10
CLAY?, Edward ALN 104
CLAYBROOK, Edwd. MAS 52
Thos. WAS 41A
CLAYCOMB, Conrad BRK 245
Frederic BRK 247
John BRK 245
Peter BRK 245
CLAYPOLE, Jeremiah WRN 60A
Jesse BBN 132
Jesse BBN 132
John WRN 60A
John WRN 71A
Stephen WRN 60A
CLAYPOTE, George WRN 71A
CLAYTON, -uel? CWL 34
Ambrose SCT 129A
Augustine WRN 54A
Austin WRN 47A
Charles BTH 212
Coleman NCH 109A
Daniel LGN 36
David SHE 118A
Deby BTH 166
Edwin BRN 5
Foster WRN 54A
Francis CWL 34

CLAYTON, Francis, Jr. CWL 34
Franky BRN 5
George BTH 198
Henry CLD 158
James ALN 132
James? CWL 40
Jasper BTH 188
Jesse CWL 43
Jno. MAS 55
John MAD 106
John NSN 189
John BRK 247
John SHE 117A
John? G. CWL 32
Moses CWL 43
Pettus? O. LGN 28
Rachel HAR 220
Richard CLD 158
Robert WRN 54A
Saml. PND 26A
Tho. MAS 54
Thomas LGN 36
Thomas WRN 57A
Thomas P. GRN 66
Thornton LGN 47
Thos. LVG 4
Thos. L. HRY 190
Will HRY 176
William NSN 189
William WRN 54A
William NCH 129A
Wm. CWL 41
CLAYTON?, Jno.? CWL 58
CLAYWELL, Shadrack CLD 155
Shadrack CLD 165
CLEAR, Allen LNC 3
CLEAREY?, Joseph BKN 23
CLEAVELAND, Henry W. CLK 79
Jesse BRK 243
Jesse H. BRK 227
William CLK 79
CLEAVES, Wm.? CWL 32
CLEAVLAND, George JES 75
CLEEKE?, John MTG 273
CLEFFORD, John V. LGN 44
CLEFT?, William HOP 240
CLELAND, Thomas, Revd. MER 92
CLELLAND, Horatio BRN 33
CLEM, Adam GTN 126
Isaac GTN 126
Jacob GTN 126
John CLK 89
John GTN 126
Joseph CLK 89
CLEM?, Jno. PUL 38A
Mabel, Mrs. WYN 90A
CLEMANS, William CSY 220
CLEMANT, Benjn. PND 27A
Webster G. ETL 51
CLEMENS, Gust. HRY 251
Jos. PUL 40A
Stephen FTE 112
CLEMENT, John SCT 126A
Nachel BRN 6
CLEMENT?, Thos. BBN 96
CLEMENTS, Benedict NSN 210
David LNC 61
David MTG 273
Edward H. UNN 154
Elizabeth LNC 75
Francis HRD 72
Jas. HRD 72
John MTG 269
CLEMENTS, John R. UNN 149
Leonard UNN 147
Oswell NSN 210
Philip MTG 273
Roger MTG 229
Samual NSN 210
Wm. R. LNC 37
Zachariah MTG 247
CLEMINGS, Benjamin FLD 9
CLEMINS, Emely MAD 122
Nancy GRD 120A
Thomas WYN 106A
William GRD 106A
CLEMMENS, -----? LVG 12
CLEMMENT, Isaac HAR 182
CLEMMINS, C. A. GRD 87A
H. GRD 84A
CLEMMONS, Christena WRN 42A
Elenor WRN 56A
Feberick MAD 134
Francis CLY 118
Henery ADR 12
Henry HAR 152
Isham SHE 131A
James ADR 12
James CHN 44
James MNR 205
Joseph ADR 12
Samuel NSN 209
Thomas HAR 152
Willson BLT 152
CLEMONDS, (See Clmonds) WAS 85A
John WAS 66A
CLEMONS, Allen FKN 98
Barnet FKN 98
Basil GRN 70
Charles WAS 33A
Gesham LVG 5
Jacob BRK 245
Jeremiah, Esq. MER 92
Jeremiah, Esq. MER 116
John ADR 12
William CLY 130
Wm. HRT 154
CLENDENIN, Thos. BBN 116
CLENDENING, Geo. BBN 118
CLENDENNON, George BBN 74
CLENEAY, Vincent MAS 75
CLENGMAN?, Jno.? CWL 58
CLENINDEN, Thos. BBN 122
CLERDEN?, Arthur MAS 53
CLERK, Albin OHO 10A
John HAR 148
Joseph OHO 10A
CLERN?, Jno. PUL 38A
CLEVELAND, Adam JEF 54
Eli FTE 85
Eli HAR 166
Geo. BBN 136
James CBL 7A
John BBN 136
John WDF 96A
John SHE 135A
Micajah HAR 140
Rachel CBL 7A
Robert MAD 126
William HAR 168
Zatted? JES 86
CLEVENGER, Alexander FLD 38
Nathan FLG 69A
CLEVER, Benjamin GSN 131
John GSN 131
Wm. GSN 131
CLEVER, Wm. GSN 132A
CLEVINGER, Uriah MGB 137A
CLEYWELL, Tyse? LVG 15
CLIA-?, George ADR 14
CLIAN?, George ADR 12
CLICE?, William MTG 243
CLICK, John BNE 8
John FLD 17
Mary Anne BTL 319
CLICKER?, Thos. WAS 29A
CLICKETT, Euphen FTE 102
Thomas FTE 102
CLICKINBEARD, Nancy BTH 152
CLIFF, Horatio CBL 21A
CLIFFORD, -----? DVS 7A
Edward HAR 138
James HAR 146
Patric FTE 57
Robert HAR 138
Sarah FTE 63
William CBL 15A
CLIFT, Abner MAS 60
Ben MAS 66
George MAD 132
Henson MAS 72
Newton MAS 68
William HOP 240
CLIFTON, Charles SHE 162
Edmond GRT 144
George SHE 166
Harden MAD 96
Henry GTN 125
Isaiah CSY 228
Job CSY 228
Josiah CSY 212
Juhugh FLG 36A
Nathaniel HAR 206
Noah OWN 100
Sarah HAR 200
Wm. WAS 59A
CLIMEN?, Thomas FTE 108
CLIMENS, George GRD 102B
CLIMINTS?, George NSN 222
CLIMMINS, Geo. GRD 106A
CLINE, Daniel BBN 118
David HRY 226
James HRY 206
Jno. HAR 152
Jno. HRY 265
Mary FLG 43A
Mathias BKN 8
Michael PUL 60A
N. SHE 112A
Wm. FLG 43A
CLINES, Aaron SHE 171
Hiram FTE 83
Jacob SHE 171
Jesse SHE 171
John SHE 171
Peter SHE 168
CLINGMAN, George SPN 19A
Henry WRN 65A
CLINKENBEARD, John CLK 99
William CLK 99
CLINKINGBEAN, John BBN 86
CLINKINGBEARD, Isaac BBN 114
John CBL 21A
CLINTON, -----? CWL 40
Archd. GRD 86A
George GRD 86A
James GRD 86A
John WDF 98
Jos. HRY 243
Moses FKN 80

Name	County	Page
CLINTON, Saml.	SCT	124A
CLINTON?, John	FTE	112
CLMONDS, Wm.	WAS	85A
CLOAK, Benjamin	WDF	117A
CLOID, James	LNC	65
James	CLD	143
Saml.	WAS	60A
Samuel	CLD	140
Thomas	CLD	139
CLONCH, Jno.	PUL	48A
CLONCH?, Christo.	PUL	47A
CLONDUS, Pitman	MER	91
CLOPTON, Wm.	MAD	154
CLORE, Israel	BNE	10
Levi	BNE	10
Michael	BNE	10
CLOSE, Charles	WRN	32A
John	GRN	72
John W.	HRT	154
CLOUCH?, (See Clonch)	PUL	48A
Wm.	PUL	40A
CLOUD, Caleb W.	FTE	67
Daniel	BNE	10
Jane	BNE	10
Jason	CWL	58
Robert	FTE	73
William	BNE	10
CLOUGH, Elizabeth	BTH	152
Price	HAR	182
Thomas	HAR	182
William	HAR	182
CLOUSE, George	GRD	89A
CLOW, Elizabeth	BBN	134
John	BBN	134
CLOWD, Anne	WRN	61A
CLOWDY, Norman	WRN	68A
CLOYD, Elinor	GRN	75
Jesse	PUL	61A
John	LNC	61
John	MAD	130
John	MNR	213
CLUB, Lucy	MAD	110
Mc Kinsey	MAD	126
William	BTH	198
CLUBB, Eliz.	HRY	240
CLUBBS, Susana	BRK	247
CLUER, Davey	WAS	41A
CLUKE?, John	MTG	273
CLUNEN?, Thomas	FTE	108
CLUSTER, Michael	CBL	13A
CLUTTER, John	PND	26A
CLYCK?, James	CSY	218
CLYMER, James	HRT	156
CLYNE, Isacc	PUL	61A
Jacob	WTY	124A
John	WYN	82A
Peter	PUL	57A
CLYTON?, Beverly?	LVG	15
CN--O-AY, David	ALN	106
CO---?, Elijah	LVG	15
CO--E?, William	BKN	11
COAL, John	NSN	223
Joshua	JEF	59
Samuel	MER	91
William	GTN	131
COALERY?, Barba?	HAR	140
COALMAN, Thos.	CHN	39
COALNEY, (See Coatney)	HAR	162
COALNEY?, Charles	HAR	146
COALTEN, Morriss	CSY	212
COALTER, Wm.	FLG	24A
COALTER?, Matthias	CSY	218
Morriss	CSY	212
COAP, David	FLG	30A
COAP, Joseph	FLG	30A
COAT, William	BLT	192
COATES, Richd.	SCT	130A
COATNEY, Agnes	HAR	168
Elijah	FLG	39A
Henderson	HAR	146
James	HAR	162
James	HAR	162
Jno.	HAR	162
Jno.	HAR	168
John	NSN	198
John	GRD	96A
Robert	HAR	162
Saml.	HAR	146
Wallace	HAR	162
COATNY, Danl.	HAR	168
COATS, Celia	GRD	89A
Charles	ADR	10
Dav. G.	HRY	241
George	HRT	155
Henry	MAD	110
Kinsey	ADR	10
Peter	MAD	152
Tho. P.	HRY	212
Thomas	CLD	153
Thomas	HRT	156
COATTER, Matthias	CSY	218
COBB, -----?	CWL	42
---w.?	CWL	42
A----?	RCK	83A
Ambros, Jr.	KNX	292
Ambrose	CLY	114
Ambrose, Sr.	KNX	292
Asa	OWN	99
David	FTE	64
Elisha	OWN	99
Gideon P./ D.?	CWL	46
Howel	HOP	240
Jesse	ETL	39
John	CWL	46
John	JES	78
John B.	GRN	52
Martin	KNX	292
Mary	MBG	142
Phillip	FLG	45A
Saml.	MAD	150
Saml.	KNX	296
Saml., Jr.	FLG	45A
Saml., Snr.	FLG	45A
Thomas	OWN	102
Thos.	KNX	290
Warner	OHO	6A
William, Esqr.	OWN	101
William W.	GRN	54
COBBS, John M.	HAR	216
Livingston	FKN	142
Robert Z?.	HND	3
COBLE, Michael	HRT	154
COBLIN, Wm.	HRY	269
COBOURN, Jacob	FLD	41
COBUL, Liddy	GSN	133A
COBUN, James	GNP	168A
COBURN, James	MER	91
Jas. W.	MAS	75
Jno.	MAS	60
Saml. W.	SCT	131A
Samuel	FLD	44
Wilson	MAS	78
COCANOUGHER, Jacob	WAS	80A
COCHRAL, Peter	BBN	140
COCHRAN, Andrew	BRN	6
Andrew	LGN	38
Dennis	BRN	6
George	MER	92
James	MER	91
Jas.	JEF	58
COCHRAN, Jas.	FLG	41A
John, Capt.	MER	116
John	FLG	24A
John	WRN	32A
John	FLG	34A
John	FLG	79A
Peter	HAR	212
Robert	SHE	131A
Thomas	FTE	74
William	FTE	78
COCHRANS, Thos.	LVG	3
COCHRARN, Preston	CSY	214
COCHRELL, Benjamin	FTE	81
John	BTH	200
COCK, Charles	WYN	79A
Henry D.	MAD	180
James	SHE	121A
Jessee	WYN	79A
Mordica	CHN	44A
COCK?, James	BTH	210
COCKE, Jno. W.	CHN	43A
Thos.	FKN	142
Thos.	CHN	43A
Thos. J.	WAS	41A
COCKEL?, Anderson	ALN	94
COCKERAL, Simon	ETL	46
William	ETL	46
COCKERALL, Prestley	WRN	40A
William	UNN	153
COCKIRELL, John	NCH	109A
COCKRAIN, John	OHO	9A
COCKRALL, John J.	LGN	42
COCKRAM, Jesse	LVG	15
Jno. Y.	LVG	9
COCKRAN, Eli, Jr.	CWL	52
Jas.	FLG	69A
John	JEF	33
Thom.	CWL	52
COCKREHAM, Daniel	SPN	20A
COCKRELL, Elizabeth	FTE	84
Jeremiah	FLD	6
John	FTE	88
John	CLY	114
Joseph	CLY	112
Shelton	FTE	104
COCKRIL, J. J.	ALN	126
Josph	ALN	136
Lewis	SPN	7A
Wm.	ALN	124
Wm.	ALN	136
COCKRILL, John	TOD	127
Thos.	TOD	127
COCKRUM, Bryan	MBG	136A
COCKS, Henry	CHN	40A
James	LNC	37
James	WYN	97A
Maberry	WYN	97A
CODINGTON, John	BRN	6
CODY, John	FLD	3
COE, Jane	NSN	222
John	CLD	160
Rebecca	BRN	7
COE?, Pearson	CLD	157
COEWELL, Benjamin	LVG	10
COFER, George	BBN	108
Joel	GTN	133
COFFEE, Ambrose	MTG	243
Ananias	ADR	12
Cleveland	WRN	55A
Eligah	CBL	12A
Elijah	FLD	1A
Ely	ADR	12
Felden	ADR	12
Hayse	ADR	12

Name	County	Page
COFFEE, James	SPN	14A
Joel	ADR	12
Joel	CLD	150
Joel, Jr.	ADR	12
John	CLD	150
Nat	ADR	12
Nathan	SPN	14A
Nebuzaraden	SPN	14A
Polly	PUL	63A
Salathial	ADR	64
Saul/ Sail?	PUL	57A
William	FLD	1A
COFFEE?, -----?	DVS	6A
COFFER, Elijah	FTE	97
Joseph	CLD	160
COFFETT, Jacob	KNX	286
James	KNX	286
John Sr.	KNX	294
COFFEY, Benjamin	WYN	90A
Eli	WYN	79A
Jesse	CSY	204
Joel	WYN	84A
Lewis	WYN	84A
Martin	WYN	88A
Marvel	WYN	83A
Molley	CSY	204
Rutherford	WYN	91A
COFFIELD, Isaac	LVG	3
COFFIN, Christopher	BNE	8
COFFMAN, Absolem	HOP	238
Adam	LGN	27
Christian	JES	76
Daniel	KNX	288
Henry	HOP	240
Isaac, Jr.	HOP	240
Issac, Sr.	HOP	240
Jacob	LGN	36
Jacob	MAD	138
Jacob	NSN	197
John	JEF	49
Leonard	LGN	32
Mary	MER	91
COFFON, Isaac N.	SHE	114A
COFIELD, Polly	TRG	8A
COFMAN, Benjamin	MBG	138A
Jacob	CSY	216
Jno.	FKN	140
Nelly	FKN	162
COFMON, Polly	WAS	23A
COFRIN?, William	LWS	87A
COFTON?, Samuel	ALN	94
COGDAL, John	HRT	154
Joseph	HRT	156
Wm.	HRT	154
COGER, Elizabeth	JES	74
James	WYN	94A
John	WYN	99A
Nicholas, Sen.	WYN	91A
Thos.	WYN	94A
COGHIL, Frederick	GTN	125
Zachariah	GTN	125
COGHILL, Catharine	MER	92
Coleman T.	MER	92
James	GTN	125
John	SHE	113A
Littleton	MER	92
Reuben	MER	92
COGIL, John	LNC	71
Stephen	LNC	71
COGIN, William	WYN	98A
COGSDELL, John	GNP	176A
COGSWELL, James	BBN	74
Jetediah	FLG	46A
Joel	FLG	46A
John	FLG	46A
COGSWELL, William	HAR	166
COGWELL, Nemrod	WDF	97
COHEN, Samuel	BBN	112
COHEN?, Elijah	LVG	15
COHENN?, Samul	ADR	64
COHERN, James, Sr.	WYN	92A
Thomas	WYN	92A
William	WYN	92A
COHERN?, Samul	ADR	64
COHN, Stephen	CLK	92
COHO, John	HRD	14
COHOON, Daniel	TRG	6
David	TRG	3A
Joel	TRG	6
John	TRG	6
Joseah	TRG	6
COHORN, Elijah	JEF	38
Wm.	BBN	124
COHORN?, James	BLT	194
COHRON, Molly	BTL	319
COIK?, James	BTH	210
COIL, George	BTH	202
Jacob	BBN	118
James, Sr.	WYN	98A
James	WAS	34A
Patrick	WYN	98A
Peter	BTH	186
William	WYN	98A
COIN?, Brice	LVG	10
COINER?, John	JES	72
COKE, Wm.	BRK	249
COKELY, William	GRN	56
COKER, Jacob	LVG	3
Martin	LWS	86A
Thomas	HRL	104
COKINDOFFER, David	NSN	219
COKRON, Eli	CWL	52
COLBERT, Alex	ALN	112
Alexander	UNN	147
Catharine	FTE	106
George A.	ALN	92
Israel	MER	117
James	CBL	21A
Jesse	NCH	119A
Jessee	FTE	94
Levi	FTE	108
Margaret	HRY	198
Richard	MER	90
Samuel	LGN	45
COLBERT?, William	ALN	116
COLBURN, Jerathaniel	MAS	60
Oliver	MAS	74
COLCLAISURE, John	FLG	67A
COLCLAZIER, David	BTH	192
Polly	BTH	192
COLCORD, Jonathan	BBN	60
COLDIRON, Coonrod	HRL	106
Geo.	HRL	104
John	HRL	106
COLDWELL, Andrew	FLG	33A
Isaac	SPN	23A
COLE, ---rd?	DVS	6A
Amos	WRN	59A
Barnett	LNC	63
Benj. J.	BNE	8
Benjn.	MAS	62
Benjn., Jr.	MAS	62
David	CLD	144
Dianna	SHE	176
Ebenezer	WRN	32A
Elijah	FKN	146
Elizabeth	HRD	74
Frances	TRG	12
Francis	HRD	58
Geo.	HRY	263
COLE, Harbin	HRD	36
Isaac	UNN	149
Isabella	FLD	1A
Jacob	CBL	7A
Jacob	SHE	134A
James	ALN	114
James	CLD	144
James H.	WRN	49A
Jehu	NCH	122A
Jessee	CLK	106
Jno.	PUL	42A
John	ALN	140
John	WAS	36A
John	WRN	58A
Jos.	FLG	61A
Leroy	HAR	214
Margaret	LVG	10
Mary	ALN	114
Richard	WDF	112A
Robert	MTG	265
Sampson	ALN	114
Samuel	CLD	152
Tobias	GNP	178A
Tobias	GNP	179A
Will	MAS	64
William	LGN	37
William	LGN	40
William	ETL	49
William	SHE	166
William	CLD	167
William S.	BTL	319
Wm.	JEF	42
Wm.	FKN	146
Wm. H.	BRN	6
COLEGROVE, Francis	GNP	166A
Jeremiah	GNP	166A
COLEMAN, Alexander	FLD	40
Benjamin	HRD	86
Betty	JEF	46
Charity	FLD	31
Charlott	FLD	31
Covington	HAR	176
Curtis	TRG	14A
Daniel	GTN	127
Daniel	GSN	131
Danl.	HRY	184
Drury	WRN	36A
Edward	HAR	132
Edward S.	FKN	68
Elizabeth	HAR	176
Farish	BKN	16
Francis	PND	29A
George	BTH	208
George	OHO	8A
Henry	JEF	65
Henry	OHO	6A
James	TRG	11
James	FTE	74
James	HAR	214
James	WDF	94A
James	WDF	126A
Jas.	TOD	128
Jeremiah	JES	86
Jno. E.	LVG	6
John	FTE	88
John	TOD	128
John	BLT	178
John H.	HAR	214
Jos.?	CHN	46
Joseph	BRN	7
Joshua	KNX	282
Josiah	HRD	32
Lindsey	FTE	88
Mary	TRG	8
Mary	HAR	132
Nancy, Mrs.	GRT	145

COLEMAN, Nathan NSN 187
Philip BRN 7
Richard FLD 26
Robert GTN 129
Robert TOD 132A
Robert E. MER 92
Saml. TOD 128
Sarah BKN 16
Thomas BRN 6
Thomas WRN 68A
Thomas WDF 115A
Will. KNX 280
William LGN 39
William LGN 40
William ETL 41
William HAR 142
Wyatt GTN 128
Wyatt HAR 210
COLES, Josh CHN 46
COLGAN?, James M.? CLD 141
COLGIN, Susanna SHE 166
COLHOUN, John, Jr. WRN 73A
COLIER, Isaac SHE 167
John JEF 44
William JES 96
COLINS, Aaron HRL 106
COLKINGS, Daniel G. BNE 10
COLLADISON, Reuben LGN 34
COLLARD, Elijah GSN 131
Joseph GSN 132A
COLLCLZIER, Philip BTH 192
COLLENS, D. W. CHN 44A
Lucy SHE 115A
COLLENS?, Zach ADR 10
COLLES, Geo. MAS 61
COLLET, Samuel WYN 87A
Wm. MAD 98
COLLET?, William CLY 116
COLLETT, Isaac HRY 244
John SHE 109A
Joseph JEF 33
COLLETT?, James WRN 42A
COLLEY, Andrew CHN 34A
John CWL 52
Jonathan BRK 247
Larkin CWL 52
Wm. BRK 245
COLLIER, Claborne HND 9
Coleman A. NCH 109A
Daniel NSN 211
George JEF 46
Hamlett? NCH 126A
Isaiah PND 22A
Isham, Mas. GRT 146
James LNC 73
James GTN 127
Jeremiah FLD 43
John JEF 55
John FLD 7
John MAD 128
Lewis SHE 132A
Micajah FLD 37
Michael SHE 176
Nathaniel SHE 134A
Perry GRT 139
Stephen FLD 37
Thomas NSN 211
Thos. SHE 129A
William MER 90
William HAR 138
William NCH 103A
Wm. PND 24A
Zephry? MER 90
COLLIN, Franklin BBN 116
COLLINGIM, Will. KNX 310
COLLINGS, Paul NSN 188
COLLINGS?, John NSN 181
COLLINS, ----ah? NCH 126A
Aaron HRL 106
Abraham SHE 117A
Adam BLT 168
Alexander MTG 261
Anos FLG 75A
Aquilla MAS 55
Bartlett GRT 140
Benjamin BLT 186
Bradley FLD 40
David CWL 58
David BLT 166
David KNX 290
Dillard? CLK 84
Edmd. MAS 54
Edmund FKN 72
Edmund NCH 105
Edward FLD 23
Edwd. MAS 55
Elijah MAS 52
Elisha LGN 42
Elisha BLT 176
Elisha SCT 125A
Eliz. FLG 76A
Eliza JEF 21
Fillith CLY 111
Foster BBN 94
Francis MAS 55
George FLD 42
George FLD 42
George BLT 176
Hannah? NCH 126A
Henry HRL 106
Henry ALN 138
Henry MBG 141
Isaac BKN 26
Isaac MAS 67
Isaac BLT 160
Isaiah KNX 286
Jacob SHE 153
James ADR 14
James FLD 14
James OWN 105
James FTE 108
James SHE 148
James MTG 275
James MTG 293
James PND 21A
Jas. JEF 19
Jas. FLG 76A
Jas. FLG 76A
Jas. B. BNE 10
Jasper WDF 93A
Jeremiah UNN 152
Jeremiah WDF 117A
Jeremiah WDF 119A
Jno. MAS 52
John HND 8
John JEF 61
John MAD 104
John CLD 138
John BLT 168
John CHN 29A
John FLG 49A
John FLG 73A
John WYN 102A
John SHE 117A
John WDF 118A
Jos., Sr. SHE 149
Joseph SHE 148
Joseph MAD 150
Joseph WDF 96A
Joseph M. BLT 186
Joshua FKN 92
COLLINS, Josiah BBN 86
Josiah MAD 162
Josiah BTH 188
Levi SHE 150
Levi KNX 284
Lewis JES 74
Marthy CHN 40
Meridith FLD 40
Michael ETL 54
Milly FKN 128
Nancy HND 8
Ralph GRT 147
Reuben FLD 33
Rezen B. WRN 30A
Richard BNE 46
Richard WRN 65A
Richd. FKN 128
Richd. SCT 138A
Richd. A. PND 18A
Robert FTE 91
Robert FKN 124
Sally CHN 29
Sally PND 24A
Sol. KNX 284
Sol. RCK 80A
Spencer SHE 136A
Stephen ETL 40
Stephen CBL 8A
Stephen FLG 38A
Thomas JES 73
Thomas WDF 93A
Thomas WYN 96A
Thomas NCH 106A
Thos. BKN 24
Thos. MAS 70
Thos. FKN 126
Thos. P. SCT 125A
Uriah JES 73
Valentine FLD 3
Whitfield WDF 118A
Will MAS 73
William FLD 17
William FTE 92
William FTE 92
William BLT 158
William BLT 186
William MTG 231
William WRN 65A
William WRN 69A
William SHE 117A
Willis CLK 106
Willis BTH 180
Wm. MAD 104
Wm. ALN 132
Wm. PUL 40A
Wm. FLG 73A
Wm. SHE 120A
COLLINSWORTH, Thomas FLD 8
COLLISON, Bennett HAR 134
COLLIVER, Polly MTG 279
Richard MTG 279
Thomas MTG 277
COLLOMS, Jno. MAS 63
COLLS?, Daniel OWN 100
COLLUNS?, Danl., Jr. CLY 116
COLLY, Charles MAD 158
Deberah JES 91
Jacob CHN 44
Seth BTL 319
Wm. CHN 44
COLMAN, Archabald HOP 238
Steph. HRY 270
Stephen FLD 31
Thomas UNN 153

COLMAN, Thos. ADR 18
William ALN 102
Wm. H. CHN 42
COLMES---L?, T. D. JEF 22
COLMIN, Saml. BBN 132
COLQUETT?, Ransom E. OWN 101
COLQUITT?, Ransom E. OWN 101
COLREDGE, Samuel FTE 63
COLSON, Ann SCT 109A
James HRL 106
Joel TRG 6
John HRL 106
Sander TRG 6
COLSTAN, Susan JEF 26
COLSTON, Jno. HRY 265
COLTER, Arch. TOD 129
James MAD 180
John TOD 124A
Robt. JEF 26
COLTON?, Benjamin BRN 7
Francis FKN 148
COLTORS?, James LVG 15
COLUMBRA?, Henry MAD 172
COLVERT, George LGN 33
Margrit WAS 22A
COLVIN, Aaron CHN 31
Aaron TOD 133
Bennet BKN 19
Charles LNC 67
Charles CBL 18A
Elijah LNC 37
Elizabeth CBL 18A
George PND 28A
Henry, Jr. PND 26A
Henry PND 26A
James BBN 132
John BBN 132
John GNP 166A
Joseph LNC 37
Luke HRD 50
Raleigh HAR 182
Samuel BRN 7
William HAR 182
Wm. HRD 56
COLVIN?, John HRD 56
COLYAR, Aaron GRD 102A
Alexr., Jr. GRD 89A
Alexr. GRD 101A
John GRD 104A
Moses GRD 95A
Robt. GRD 104A
Sol. GRD 104A
COLYER, Chs., Jr. PUL 37A
Chs. PUL 46A
Chs. RCK 76A
Jno. PUL 37A
John, Sr. RCK 75A
John RCK 75A
Richd. PUL 35A
Richd. PUL 46A
Richd. RCK 76A
Stephen RCK 80A
Stephen RCK 81A
Wm. RCK 82A
COLYR, John RCK 84A
COMAC?, Andrew NSN 221
COMB?, Andrew WDF 99A
COMBER, Mastin? MNR 209
COMBEST, Samuel PUL 57A
Ute FLG 40A
COMBS, Adair HRT 155
Anderson MBG 138A
Benjamin CLK 94
Cuthbert CLK 65
COMBS, Cuthbert, Jr. CLK 81
Edward FTE 74
Elijah CLY 124
Ennis MTG 295
George MER 91
George CLY 125
Hardin CLY 125
Henry, Sr. CLY 124
Henry, Sr. CLY 125
Huston WRN 74A
Jacob MER 92
James FKN 84
Jeremiah FLD 13
Jeremiah CLY 124
Jeremiah CLY 125
Jesse CLY 120
Jesse CLY 125
Jessee MBG 138A
John BRN 6
John FLD 13
John CLK 102
John CLY 132
John NSN 183
John MNR 217
John HOP 236
John MTG 239
John SPN 11A
John A.?, Jr. CLK 79
John H. CLK 80
Joseph CLK 82
Mason CLY 125
Mathew CLY 130
Nelson NSN 204
Nicholas, Jr. CLY 124
Nicholson CLY 124
Richard TRG 13A
Sally FLD 13
Saml. CLY 124
Samuel A. CLK 103
Shadrick CLY 121
Stephen MNR 205
Thomas BRN 7
Thos. FLG 75A
William FLD 13
William GRN 78
William CLY 111
William CLY 121
William CLY 125
William CLY 131
William BTH 156
William PUL 59A
William R. CLK 98
Jonah HRY 190
COMELY, James GRD 97A
Jas., Sr.? GRD 90A
COMER, Mildred WAS 22A
Robert WYN 101A
COMES, Dolly BTL 319
Ignatious HND 3
Ignatious BRK 245
Jacob HND 3
Joseph BTL 319
COMFERT, Daniel LGN 24
COMFORT, John SPN 12A
William LGN 44
COMINGON, John, Sr. MER 90
COMINGORE, Abraham MER 91
David B. MER 92
Samuel MER 91
COMINGOW, Henry MER 90
COMINS, Asa SPN 6A
James SPN 23A
Jesse SPN 7A
Richard SPN 7A
COMLEY, Sabert GRD 90A
COMMAN, Abraham JES 84
COMMIC?, James ETL 40
COMMONDUAN?, Nicholas JEF 30
COMMONDUM?, Nicholas JEF 30
COMPTON, Elias H. JEF 25
John GRN 77
John WRN 54A
Thomas HOP 236
William GRN 79
COMSEY?, Robert LGN 28
CON, James, Sen. WYN 83A
CONAHAN?, Jas. HAR 150
CONALLY, Widow LVG 15
CONATHY, James GTN 131
CONATZEN, Nicholas, Sr. WYN 99A
CONATZER, Leanner, Mrs. WYN 100A
CONAWAY, Acquller BBN 88
Amos BBN 92
Michael LWS 91A
Miles LWS 91A
Richard LWS 91A
Richard LWS 92A
Samuel LWS 92A
Wm. BBN 92
CONCKLIN, David GSN 132A
CONDER, David MER 91
John WAS 24A
Peter MER 91
CONDER?, John WAS 82A
Martain CSY 218
CONDERN, Jesse CWL 52
CONDITT, Mary OHO 9A
Timothy OHO 6A
Usual OHO 9A
CONDRA, William MNR 209
CONDRAN, Stewart CHN 43
Wm. CHN 43
CONDRE, Elifus LNC 59
CONDUFF, Christopher HRD 46
Jas. HRD 46
CONDY, Adam CBL 9A
CONE, Nancey, Mrs. CLK 95
CONELLEY, Thompson CBL 11A
CONES?, Flurnoy/Flinnoy? CBL 17A
Jacob CBL 19A
James CBL 19A
John CBL 19A
Robbert CBL 19A
CONEY, John WRN 57A
CONGLETON, William FLD 12
Wm. BBN 68
CONHERMIGHT, Isaac CSY 214
CONHERWRIGHT, William CSY 214
CONHILL, Siles E. JEF 41
CONIWAY, Thos. GSN 133A
CONKLIN, Eliza JEF 24
CONKWRIGHT?, Abraham ETL 52
CONLAN, Patk. JEF 27
CONLEE, Mary BRN 7
Wm. HRT 156
CONLEY, Adams & MTG 295
Alexander FTE 109
Alexander MTG 259
Bartlett NSN 210
Daniel SHE 171
Daniel NSN 208
David FLD 22

CONLEY, David FLD 35
Edmond FLD 35
Henry FLD 35
Henry FLD 35
James MTG 291
James SHE 122A
Jane MTG 247
John FLD 31
John FLD 35
John NSN 191
John NSN 208
John MTG 273
Joseph FLD 31
Joseph MNR 193
Martha? NSN 210
Michael NSN 198
Sampson FLD 32
Sanford, Sr. SHE 171
Thomas FLD 38
Thomas MTG 259
William SHE 171
CONLEY?, Michael NSN 210
CONLY, Charles WYN 89A
CONN, Benjamin CLD 142
Fancis? SHE 136A
Hezekiah UNN 154
Jas. HRY 270
John BBN 136
Joseph OWN 103
Richard HRY 214
Thomas BLT 186
William HRY 214
Wm. BBN 136
CONN?, Hugh JEF 62
Saml. JEF 55
CONNAL, Hiram BRK 247
CONNALLY, Reuben WRN 50A
CONNAWAY, Peter FTE 73
Peter FTE 74
CONNEL, James GSN 132A
Jesse, Sr. GTN 128
William GTN 127
CONNELL, Edward FTE 61
George HRY 186
James FTE 103
James HRY 212
Jessee, Jr. GTN 128
Walter FTE 69
CONNELLEY, Jas. SCT 133A
CONNELLY, Alexander CBL 3A
Jesse SHE 115A
Rice SHE 129A
Robt. BNE 8
Sanford SHE 168
Thomas BNE 8
Wm. JEF 34
Wm. SHE 114A
CONNELY, Francis MAD 132
James SHE 119A
CONNER, Abner HAR 188
Benj. CHN 34
Caleb GRD 84A
Daniel BTH 186
Dillard CSY 222
Elizabeth GRN 62
Francis LGN 27
Francis FTE 74
Harrison FTE 90
Irum HOP 236
Isaac HOP 236
Isaac PND 29A
Jacob HOP 236
James BNE 8
John MAD 98
Laurence CLD 155

CONNER, Lewis BNE 8
Philamin HAR 170
Philemon BNE 10
Phillimon SHE 109A
Reuben BNE 8
Samuel MER 92
Samuel GTN 121
Tarence SHE 150
Thomas CSY 212
William BTH 186
William MTG 267
Wm. BNE 8
Wm. ALN 124
CONNER?, James JES 97
James R. JES 97
CONNERLY, Levi LWS 89A
CONNETT, William C. FTE 78
CONNIERS?, Jno. HAR 154
CONNOLLY, Robt., Sen. BNE 8
Sarah SHE 123A
CONNOR, Clement MTG 261
John HRD 12
CONNOT, Elijah JEF 25
CONNOVER, Wm. ADR 10
CONOR, Livingston GRN 73
CONOVER, James FTE 70
John V. GTN 124
Joseph GRT 142
Robert GRN 52
William GTN 121
CONOVER?, Peter WDF 98A
CONOWAY, Hugh GTN 120
Robt. ALN 144
Tho. ALN 138
CONOWAY?, Jemy / James? ALN 138
CONQUEST, Betwey FTE 111
CONRAD?, Andrew NSN 221
CONROD, Joseph GNP 177A
CONSTABLE, Robert WAS 27A
CONSTANT, Edward HRD 88
Isaac CLK 66
John FLG 68A
Wm. HRT 154
CONSTANTINE, Thomas SHE 177
Wm. FKN 118
CONVICTS, (71, No Names Given) FKN 66
CONWAY, Jno. MAS 58
John GTN 131
John, Sr. NCH 103A
John HND 9A
M. W. MAS 58
Miles MAS 60
William GTN 131
William NCH 110A
CONWAY?, Martin JES 76
CONWELL, Jos. MAS 76
William WYN 81A
CONYER, Mordicai WRN 55A
CONYERS, Azariah NCH 129A
Dennis PND 25A
James CHN 45
James PND 25A
Wm. HRT 156
CONYERS?, Isaac BTH 158
CONYIER, John BTH 194
COO-HINFRAM?, Vinson ALN 100
COOCH?, Deadrick CSY 218
COODER?, Wm. ALN 104
COOFMAN, Henry HRD 44
COOGLE?, John HRD 42

COOK, --dry? CWL 40
-llen? CWL 37
Abel WDF 107A
Abraham BTH 162
Abram SHE 174
Alexander MAD 90
Alexander MAD 152
Amos MAD 108
Anthony LNC 63
Aron BLT 196
Benjamin HAR 164
Benjamin NSN 177
C. H. JEF 23
Catharine GRN 51
Catharine SHE 151
Clayton FLD 8
David, Jr. LNC 49
Edward N. WRN 31A
Elizabeth JES 75
Frances ALN 134
George BRN 6
George LNC 77
George BTL 313
George BTL 319
Gibbs WYN 92A
Grove GRD 122A
Henry BRN 6
Henry FLD 23
Henry LNC 63
Henry BTH 166
Henry HOP 236
Hosea FKN 68
Isaac SCT 99A
Isham SHE 110A
Jacob MNR 199
James CWL 35
James CWL 39
James BTH 188
James BTL 319
James SPN 5A
James WAS 19A
James WAS 42A
James WAS 87A
James WYN 93A
James SHE 113A
James? CWL 40
Jane PUL 64A
Jas. HRD 62
Jas. HRD 84
Jerem. CWL 52
Jesse LVG 12
Jesse SHE 151
Jno. LVG 4
Joel BTH 218
John JES 84
John BTH 160
John HAR 164
John WYN 102A
John NCH 119A
John SCT 120A
John GSN 132A
John B. GRN 52
Johnston HOP 236
Joseph HAR 152
Joseph TRG 3A
Joseph SPN 6A
Joshua PUL 65A
Joshua WYN 92A
Jussey? MAD 104
Laucinda FKN 58
Lavinia LVG 4
Lewis WAS 19A
Lewis WAS 87A
Loftis RCK 78A
Martin B. NCH 107A

Name	County	Page
COOK,		
Mathew	SCT	110A
Meredith	GRD	107A
Moses	BRN	6
Nancy	HAR	164
Nicholas	GSN	131
Payton?	GRD	89A
Peter	NCH	116A
Philip	JES	87
Reubin	CWL	35
Richard	PUL	58A
Richard	WYN	100A
Richd.	FKN	110
Robert	LVG	12
Robert	UNN	151
Robt.	SCT	121A
Ruth	TRG	8A
Seth	SHE	151
Stephen	HOP	238
Thomas	CWL	34
Thomas	FTE	111
Thomas	CLD	153
Thomas	SHE	135A
Thos.	WAS	86A
William	LVG	15
William	JES	81
William	FTE	98
William	GRT	143
William	CLD	147
William	SPN	11A
William	GRD	82A
William	GRD	89A
William	NCH	110A
Windell	HRD	94
Wm.	HRT	156
Wm.	RCK	80A
Wm.	SHE	114A
Wm. B.	BRN	7
COOK?, John	FTE	78
COOKE, Alexander	HRY	202
Aron	LNC	75
Augustin	TRG	11A
Catherine B.	FTE	64
David	LNC	49
Elizebeth	HAR	162
George W.	MTG	249
Isaac	BBN	132
Jno.	MAS	65
John	LNC	49
John	WRN	76A
John W.	WRN	73A
Joseph	MTG	233
Littleton	MAS	69
Norb. B.	WDF	126A
Valentine	LGN	43
Wilds	MTG	235
COOKENDORFER, John	PND	31A
COOKEY, Jonathan	GNP	165A
COOKS, Peyton	WRN	52A
COOKSEY, Fanney?	ADR	30
Harrison	WRN	61A
Isaac D.	FLD	45
Ledston S.	LGN	42
Lucy	WRN	62A
Somersett	LGN	32
Warren	WRN	69A
William	CLD	137
William	CLD	140
COOKSY, John	CLD	161
COOL, Jacob	CLK	88
COOLEDGE, Nathaniel	MAD	180
COOLEY, James	MAD	98
John	ADR	12
John	HRD	44
John	MER	91
COOLEY, John	CSY	216
John, Jr.	CSY	216
John	SHE	135A
Matthew	MER	91
COOLLY, William	HRY	202
COOLY, Da--?	ADR	14
Ham?	RCK	84A
James	ADR	14
James	LVG	15
Mathew	LVG	15
COOMBS, Tassy?	HRD	28
Thos.	HRD	26
COOMES, Charles	NSN	193
Enoch	NSN	198
Francis	NSN	205
Ignatus	NSN	198
Richard	NSN	205
Walter	NSN	181
William	NSN	198
William?	DVS	12A
COON, Christopher	BTH	216
Jacob	HAR	166
James	BBN	118
Jno.	HAR	158
John	TOD	125A
Micheal	JEF	32
Solomon	HAR	166
COON?, Brice	LVG	10
COONE/COONS?, Nancy	BTH	200
COONEY, Ann	JEF	23
James	BRN	7
James	MER	89
John	BRN	6
COONFIELD, Isaac	HRY	206
COONRAD, Henry	FLG	51A
Henry	FLG	52A
COONROD, Benjamin	HAR	160
Catharine	HAR	160
George	GSN	132A
Isaac	HAR	150
Jacob	HAR	144
Joseph	CBL	15A
Samuel	HAR	160
Valentine	JEF	42
William	GRT	141
Wm.	JEF	36
COONS, Adam	BLT	180
Ben	HRY	224
George	FTE	74
Henry	FTE	90
Henry	FTE	95
Henry	MTG	239
James	BBN	130
Jno.	CHN	44A
John	FTE	91
John	MTG	233
Joseph	HRY	224
Martin	FTE	90
Martin	BBN	102
Samuel	FTE	68
Thomas	FTE	90
William	WDF	98
William	HRY	224
Wm.	JEF	50
COOPEER, Robert	ETL	48
COOPEN, Caty	MAD	104
John	MAD	104
COOPER, -----?	WYN	91A
Adam	BTH	178
Adam, Jr.	BTH	184
Archibald	CLK	87
Asa	PUL	36A
Austin	WAS	35A
Benjamin	SHE	122A
Bennett	MNR	197
COOPER, C. C.	MAS	76
Caleb	PUL	68A
Charles	BTH	186
Charles	FLG	51A
Chas.	SHE	130A
Conner	SHE	131A
Cornelieus	GSN	131
Cornelius	OHO	3A
Daniel	WYN	90A
Danl.	SCT	105A
David	MAS	79
David	GRT	139
David	SHE	153
David	TRG	6A
Edward	PUL	55A
Elza	BNE	10
Ennis?	CWL	38
Fielding	HAR	196
Frederic	WYN	90A
Frederic	WYN	101A
George	MTG	226
George	MTG	243
George	CBL	13A
George B.	PUL	56A
Henry	MTG	243
Henry, Capt.	WYN	90A
Henry	OHO	9A
Hugh	MAS	71
Isaac	MAS	69
Isaac	WYN	96A
J. L.	SHE	132A
Jacob	KNX	296
Jacob	FLG	31A
James	BNE	10
James	LGN	41
James	JEF	42
James	CHN	44
James	ALN	128
James	SHE	153
James	SHE	160
James	PUL	58A
James H.	LWS	87A
Jamima	SHE	135A
Jas.	MAS	74
Jesse	MAS	74
Jessee	JEF	45
Jessey	SPN	5A
Jno.	CHN	43
Job.	OHO	11A
John	LVG	15
John	ETL	53
John	NSN	201
John	BTL	319
John	SPN	5A
John	OHO	6A
John	FLG	44A
John	WRN	58A
John	WYN	90A
John	SHE	124A
Jonathan	ETL	48
Jonathan	CLY	120
Jonathn.	HRY	243
Joseph	LNC	25
Joseph	CLK	71
Joseph	SCT	138A
Joshua	DVS	18A
Laydon?	SPN	15A
Levi	PUL	64A
Levin	JEF	42
Levin, Jr.	JEF	42
Lewis	BNE	8
Malichi	PUL	62A
Mark	SPN	6A
Martha, Mrs.	GRT	147
Mary	CWL	34
Mary, Mrs.	CLK	64

COOPER, Micagah BKN 13
Milton PUL 57A
Murdoch LWS 86A
Nancy HND 9
Nathaniel NSN 187
Nathaniel WYN 86A
Nicholas MAS 62
Phill. WAS 36A
Priscilla CHN 35A
Rebeca? BRK 247
Robert MER 91
Robert BTL 319
Roberth CLK 72
Rubin BTH 214
Saml. MAS 62
Saml. SCT 121A
Saml. SCT 138A
Samuel BNE 8
Samuel GTN 130
Sherod CLY 116
Spencer FTE 113
Spencer LWS 96A
Tacy CWL 38
Thomas SHE 153
Thos. FLG 78A
William LVG 15
William LGN 32
William SHE 154
William CLD 160
William MTG 251
William, Capt. WYN 90A
William FLD 1A
William SPN 14A
William CBL 20A
William PUL 59A
William GRD 103A
Wm. JEF 30
Wm. JEF 31
Wm. OHO 10A
COOPER?, Martin CHN 36
COOPERIDER, Henry HRY 243
Jacob HRY 243
COOPPER, Elizabeth FTE 76
COOTS, Shepherd SHE 127A
Wilson SHE 127A
COOXEY?, Tho. ALN 106
COPAGE, Rhodin FTE 86
COPART?, Henry JEF 26
COPE, Andrew CLY 114
David MBG 140A
Jesse HRL 104
John MBG 140
Martin MBG 141
William MBG 142
Wily CLY 118
Wm. D. SHE 128A
COPELAND, Ab-.? CWL 50
Elizabeth, Mrs. WYN 97A
John LGN 40
John JEF 64
Thomas HND 6A
Thos. JEF 25
William LGN 45
COPELEN, John HRT 154
COPELIN, John SPN 14A
COPER, Peter WAS 40A
COPES, Southy LWS 89A
COPHER, Abram FKN 148
COPHER?, Laurence HRD 28
COPLAND, Abel HND 6A
Lot CLD 148
COPLEN, Moses BLT 170
COPLEY, James FLD 41
Joseph FLD 25
Nancy FLD 42
Thomas FLD 42

COPLINGER, Adam SHE 154
COPPAGE, Alex. WAS 26A
Alexander HAR 184
Fielding PND 30A
John SCT 120A
Mary HAR 184
Rodern? HAR 164
Travis WAS 25A
Wm. WAS 24A
COPPAGE?, Alexander WAS 27A
James WAS 26A
COPPER, Richard ETL 54
William FTE 78
CORAM, Armstrong GRN 64
Rada, Mrs. BKN 26
CORBAN, Sam. HRY 268
CORBEN, Igs.? WAS 74A
Stephen BBN 138
CORBET, Catharine UNN 146
Elisha NSN 192
James WYN 87A
John WAS 72A
Saml. HND 6A
CORBETT, Saul? WAS 40A
CORBIN, (See Cerbin?) BTH 198
Benjn. BBN 136
Ellin NCH 117A
Henry SCT 114A
James CLK 70
James MTG 289
James PND 24A
John JES 80
John CBL 21A
John SCT 125A
John C. LVG 15
Lewis BBN 142
Martin BTH 198
Nancy MER 91
Nathan BBN 62
Nathan BBN 136
Philip HAR 152
Susanna BBN 138
William WDF 103A
CORBIT, William HOP 238
CORBY, Dabny C. WAS 77A
CORCKET, Robert BTH 166
CORD, (See Curd) LVG 22
Cavil FLG 38A
Geo. FLG 40A
Jacob FLG 39A
James FTE 77
Milkey FLG 39A
Night? WRN 72A
Phillip MAS 56
Zacius FLG 39A
CORDEN, Edward, Sr. WYN 95A
CORDER, Benj. WAS 69A
John HAR 210
Stephen WYN 95A
William ALN 110
Wm. S. HRD 32
CORDER?, Wm. ALN 104
CORDIAL, Isham MTG 291
CORDINGLY, Jno. MAS 78
William LWS 97A
CORDOO, George LWS 98A
CORDREY, C. TOD 133
Chas. TOD 133
Jas. TOD 133
John TOD 133
CORE?, Casper MAS 54
Edwd. MAS 54
COREM, Champ WRN 57A

CORENOR?, John GRN 63
CORETHERS, James JES 74
COREWINE, Geo. MAS 78
COREY, Edward SHE 157
CORILL?, Levi HAR 202
CORKLE?, Jos. M. FLG 26A
CORLILE, William GRN 73
CORLS?, Richd. HRY 230
CORMAN, Daniel ALN 92
CORMANY, Jacob PUL 48A
CORMINY?, John ADR 12
CORMWELL, Peter JEF 65
Wm. JEF 65
CORN, -----? DVS 15A
Aaron? LVG 6
Basil MER 92
Hannah GSN 132A
Hazel LVG 3
Joseph GTN 135
Solomon MER 92
Timothy MER 89
Wm. GSN 132A
CORNAC?, Andrew NSN 221
CORNATSY, Sampson ADR 14
CORNEL?, Jno. A. FKN 54
CORNELIOUS, Abner JES 77
CORNELISON, Andrew MAD 116
Coonrod MAD 158
Elcey MAD 166
John ETL 49
John ETL 49
John MAD 130
Richard MAD 128
Wm. MAD 138
CORNELIUS, Absalom BNE 10
B. John GSN 132A
George BNE 50
John BNE 10
John LGN 42
John CLY 117
John CBL 11A
John CHN 33A
Livi CHN 45
Robert BNE 10
CORNELL, Martin NSN 222
CORNELUS, John GRD 96A
CORNER, Geo. JEF 37
Jno. HAR 162
CORNES?, James JES 97
James R. JES 97
CORNET, Archabald CLY 125
Nathl. CLY 113
Robt. CLY 125
Roger CLY 125
Saml. CLY 122
William CLY 121
William, Jr. CLY 122
CORNETT, Literal LNC 57
Parks LNC 57
CORNETT?, John FLD 13
CORNHESS?, Lesse? MAS 54
CORNIC?, Richard BBN 66
CORNING?, John ADR 12
CORNISH, Jame? WDF 96A
CORNMAN, George JES 90
CORNMAN?, George JES 93
CORNN?, Cay RCK 83A
CORNOG, David FLG 40A
CORNSTALK, Eph--- BRK 247
CORNSTUBBLE, Samuel SHE 150
CORNSTUBLE, Stephen HRD 38
CORNWALL, Edward WRN 69A
James JEF 46
Jarvis ALN 110

Name	County	Page
CORNWELL, D.	TOD	134
D.	TOD	130A
Elisha	ALN	110
Jacob	BLT	178
Nancy	BLT	182
Nimrod	MER	90
Solomon	BLT	182
Thomas	FLG	61A
W.	TOD	130
CORODER, Lewis	HRD	46
CORONE, Augustine	LWS	95A
CORRES?, Flurnoy/ Flinnoy?	CBL	17A
CORRIGAN?, Jno.	MAS	52
CORRINGTON?, Joel	BBN	74
CORRY, Moses	CBL	2A
CORSBY, Jno.	MAS	70
CORSIGAN?, Jno.	MAS	52
CORSON, Julia	BNE	10
CORT, Daniel	CBL	15A
CORTIZ, John	BBN	142
CORTTOWN?, John	ALN	104
CORUM, Jesse	GNP	178A
Jesse	GNP	179A
CORUTHERS, Joseph	LVG	3
CORVAN?, Hugh	NCH	120A
CORVEY?, John	HAR	194
Joseph	HAR	192
CORVINE?, Geo., Jr.	MAS	70
CORWAY, Jacob	JES	93
CORWAY?, Martin	JES	76
CORWIN, David	BRK	229
CORWINE, Amos	MAS	77
Amos, Jr?	MAS	77
Joab	MAS	77
CORYELL, C.	MAS	68
COSBY/ COSLY?, Anne	NSN	191
COSBY, Archd.	HRY	178
Archelaus	WRN	58A
Austin	MAD	110
Duglass	GRD	115A
Forts?	JEF	27
Francis	HND	10A
John	MER	92
John	WRN	58A
Meredith	BLT	184
Stith	CWL	43
Stith	CWL	52
William H.	WDF	126A
Winfield	MAD	110
Wm.	SHE	127A
COSBY?, Charles	MAD	110
COSENOR?, John	GRN	63
COSLEY?, Nicholas	GRT	142
COSLY, (See Cosby)	MAD	110
COSSART?, Henry	JEF	26
COSTIGIN, William	BTH	168
COTERAL, Henry	HRT	156
John	HRT	156
Joshua	HRT	154
COTES, Allen	MAD	106
John	WRN	50A
COTHE?, Wm.	BKN	11
COTHON?, Laforce	SHE	133A
COTHRAN, Robert	MAD	124
COTHREN, Charles	MAD	148
COTINGHAM, Polly	LWS	97A
COTNEY, Elias	PND	25A
COTRELL, Abel	SHE	130A
Henry	KNX	298
John	KNX	298
Jos.	SHE	130A
Reuben	SHE	133A
Richard	SHE	128A
COTRILL, Thomas, Jr.	NCH	103A
COTT, Henry	JEF	31
COTTEL?, William	CLY	116
COTTEN, Jacob Matson	JEF	38
COTTENGIM, July N.	KNX	312
COTTER, Edmund	NSN	217
COTTINGHAM, Isaac	NCH	116A
Thomas	NCH	114A
Thomas	NCH	116A
Wm.	NCH	128A
COTTINGIM, Charles	HND	10
COTTLE, Joseph	FLD	9
Uriah	FLD	9
COTTON, Charles	WDF	105
Daniel	NSN	192
Dinah	FTE	85
George	FTE	87
George T.	WDF	125A
Henry	FTE	87
Henry	NSN	179
Jane	FTE	85
Jesse	HAR	182
John	FTE	105
John J.	CLK	73
Jonathan	NSN	205
Littleberry	CWL	43
Lucy	FTE	58
Nathaniel	NSN	192
Polly	GRD	118A
Ralph	NSN	194
Temple	NSN	206
Thomas	HAR	182
William	CLK	75
William	PUL	61A
Wm.	CHN	35
Wm.?	CWL	41
COTTON?, Benjamin	BRN	7
James	LVG	15
COTTRILL, Thomas, Sr.	NCH	105
COTTY, Edward	LWS	92A
COUCH, Jacob	PUL	60A
Jas.	CLY	127
Lindley	PUL	35A
Martin	CLY	127
COUCHMAN, Ann	BBN	80
Benjamin	BBN	80
Frederic	CLK	95
John	CLK	83
Margaret	BBN	116
Peter	BBN	80
COULSEN, Jesse	HAR	154
COULSON, John	HAR	154
Thomas	TRG	3A
COULTER, A.	TOD	129
Joseph	CLK	103
Starling	MER	90
Thomas	MER	90
COUN, John	JEF	58
Levi	FLD	27
Martin	WYN	83A
Saml.	JEF	55
COUN?, Hugh	JEF	62
Joseph M.?	MBG	140A
Stephen T.	WYN	88A
COUNCE?, Lewis	HAR	162
COUNER?, Lewis	HAR	160
COUNING, Jas.	MAS	58
COUNTS, William	MNR	205
COUR, George	BNE	8
James	BTL	319
COURNIERS?, Jno.	HAR	154
COURR?, John	MAD	122
COURSE, Charly	JEF	31
COURTLAND?, Ralph	CHN	41
COURTNEY, Henry	CLK	78
Jno.	MAS	52
Jonas	CHN	35
Lewis	CLK	92
Robt.	MAS	68
Tho.	MAS	52
Tho.	MAS	58
Thomas	CLK	77
COURTNY, Mathew	MAS	57
COURTS, Frances	BRN	33
Walter H.	BRN	7
Wm.	BRN	6
COUSINS, Daniel	HAR	188
COUTLER?, John	CSY	206
COUTS, Aaron	WRN	65A
Christley	WRN	69A
COVART, Cornelius	MER	90
Daniel	MER	90
David	MER	91
Isaac	MER	90
Isaac	MER	92
John	MER	92
Simon	MER	92
COVENS?, William	SCT	105A
COVENTON, Famgtn.?	CWL	52
COVERDALE, Eli	NCH	112A
COVES?, (See Cones?)	CBL	19A
COVILL?, Levi	HAR	200
COVINGTON, Abel	JEF	35
Benjamine	SPN	21A
Charles	ETL	39
Elijah M.	WRN	68A
Francis	WRN	63A
James	WRN	36A
Joseph	WRN	36A
Luke	SCT	115A
Luke	SCT	120A
M.	CHN	38
Nathaniel	WRN	64A
Peter B.	WRN	36A
Philip	HOP	236
Robert	MAD	158
Stephen	HAR	206
Thomas	FTE	104
Wm.	MAD	122
COVINTON, Francis	BTH	156
COWAN, Andrew	CLD	147
David	CLD	146
David G.	MER	116
Isaac	PUL	62A
Isaac	NCH	109A
James	PUL	55A
James	WYN	86A
Jeremiah	UNN	153
John	MER	91
John	CLD	147
John	PUL	54A
Margaret	MER	91
Mary	TRG	6
Robert	PUL	62A
Samuel	CLD	147
Samuel	PUL	56A
Thomas	MER	116
William	MER	92
William G.	PUL	57A
COWAN?, Hugh	NCH	120A
John	HRY	176
COWARDIN, Peter G.	WRN	74A
COWDEN, James	SCT	100A
COWDER, Saml.	JEF	36
COWDIN, James	ALN	120
COWEN, Hugh	BBN	66
Hugh	BBN	114
Joseph	HND	3

COWEN, Levicia WRN 69A
William WRN 70A
COWER-?, John TRG 13
COWER?, John MAD 122
COWERY?, Joseph HAR 192
COWGILL, Geo. MAS 56
Henry MBG 143
Joseph CBL 9A
Ralph FKN 150
COWHERD, James GRN 53
John SHE 152
Reuben SHE 152
William SHE 162
Yelverton GRN 55
COWIN, Samuel WYN 86A
William WYN 89A
COWIN?, William LVG 15
COWING, Peter SPN 22A
COWLES, Henry WRN 41A
Vincent WRN 41A
COWLEY, Abraham TRG 14A
Richard SHE 158
COWN?, Hugh JEF 62
COWNON?, Deminicus? ADR 64
COWNOVER, J. C. ADR 10
Levi ADR 12
Peter T. ADR 10
COWNOVR, Garret ADR 14
COWSER, John LVG 10
COX, ----t? DVS 3A
Alexander OHO 5A
Allen WYN 87A
Ambros FKN 138
Amos HRY 251
Amos KNX 290
Andrew GTN 129
Antony WAS 50A
Asher UNN 154
Benj. FKN 92
Benj. WAS 21A
Benjamin MER 92
Benjamin SHE 159
Benjamin S. BTH 206
Berry BRK 245
Beverley HRT 154
Burwell WRN 34A
Camuel LWS 88A
Charles ETL 50
Charles LWS 94A
Charles L. ADR 10
Chasteen BRN 5
Daniel FTE 76
Danl. MAS 61
David SHE 158
David NSN 209
David BRK 229
David WAS 26A
David WYN 86A
Edward SHE 130A
Edwd. MAS 78
Elias PUL 58A
Eligah CSY 214
Elisha BNE 50
Elisha CLD 151
Elizebeth WDF 94A
Enoch MAS 61
Enoch WTY 123A
Enos TRG 5A
Ezekial PUL 62A
Ezekiel LWS 95A
Federick KNX 290
Flory FLD 41
Frederick WRN 30A
Gabriel SHE 159
Gabriel NSN 209
COX, Gabriel E. NSN 176
Gale? KNX 282
Garland HRY 258
Geo. MAS 78
George WYN 87A
Gersham TRG 11
Hannah SCT 113A
Henry OHO 5A
Horatio LNC 43
Isaac NSN 210
Isaac R. BRK 245
Jacob PUL 52A
Jacob M. FKN 92
James ADR 10
James ETL 51
James HRT 154
James, Jr. GTN 122
James, Sr. GTN 122
James OHO 8A
James PUL 36A
James WRN 49A
James WDF 94A
James R. MNR 209
James? BRK 243
Jane WTY 116A
Jarvan SPN 9A
Jas. FLG 73A
Jas. SCT 113A
Jeremiah OHO 8A
Jeremiah GSN 132A
Jesse TRG 5
Jesse BRN 6
Jessey MAD 98
Jno. FKN 96
Jno. HAR 166
John FLD 12
John CWL 34
John ETL 37
John FLD 41
John HRD 42
John GRN 68
John FTE 70
John JES 76
John GRT 144
John BRK 245
John OHO 4A
John CBL 12A
John WRN 34A
John FLG 70A
John LWS 88A
John GRD 95A
John H. JEF 43
John P. GRN 53
Joiles? HRL 104
Jonathan LGN 32
Jonathan WRN 32A
Jonathan SHE 119A
Jos. SHE 142A
Joseph MAD 150
Joseph, Junr. SCT 100A
Joseph, Junr. SCT 129A
Joseph, Senr. SCT 100A
Joseph OHO 9A
Joseph MGB 137A
Lazarus GTN 129
Lemuel SPN 3A
Littleberry GRN 70
Margarett LNC 45
Mary TRG 5A
Matt HRY 251
Matthew LNC 43
Michajah CSY 214
Moses (Hatter) BRN 6
Moses (Little) BRN 6
Nathan WTY 123A
Noah KNX 290
COX, Pheneas (Son Of Jno.) WRN 34A
Pheneas WRN 33A
Philip BBN 66
Phillip WRN 34A
Richard JEF 43
Richard LNC 43
Robert GRN 59
Robert PUL 66A
Rose HRT 156
Russel, Jr. MER 92
Russel, Sr. MER 92
Samuel MER 90
Samuel, Jr. WTY 119A
Samuel, Sr. WTY 124A
Samuel WRN 30A
Samuel LWS 94A
Samuel LWS 98A
Samul GRT 142
Sarah JEF 23
Solomon BTH 206
Solomon SPN 11A
Sowgel? FKN 82
Stephen (Crossed Out) WTY 117A
Stephen WTY 112A
Susannah MER 90
Temperence HOP 236
Thomas LNC 25
Thomas GTN 122
Thomas WTY 123A
Thos. FKN 88
Thos. MAD 160
Uelsill FLD 15
Will MAS 59
William FTE 66
William FTE 77
William MER 90
William JES 96
William CLD 153
William CSY 216
William OHO 8A
William WRN 33A
William LWS 88A
Wm. BRK 245
Wm. W. FKN 90
Wyatt HOP 236
Zackariah WTY 121A
COX?, (See Case) CSY 214
Green CLK 77
Henry HRY 240
James S. BLT 172
COXE, Peter MTG 297
Richard MTG 277
COY, ----? CWL 36
Amos HRD 76
Christopher MAD 162
Daniel MAD 124
Danl. HRD 76
John NSN 191
Moses HRD 76
Phebe HRD 76
Saml. MAD 108
Saml. GRD 110A
Stephen MAD 158
Thos. MAD 144
Wm. HRD 76
Wm. MAD 136
COY?, Henry HRY 240
Samuel GRD 116A
William GRD 116A
COYL, Alfred ETL 44
James NSN 189
Jessee ETL 44
Nancy ETL 44
COYLE, Cornelius FTE 58

Name	County	Page
COYLE, Delila	BLT	182
John	BLT	182
William	WYN	81A
COZINE, Cornelius, Jr.	MER	90
Cornelius, Sr.	MER	90
Garret	MER	91
John	MER	91
John J.	MER	91
Peter C.	MER	90
Peter V., Lt.	MER	89
Polly	MER	92
CRAAN?, James	BLT	162
CRAB, Richd. M.	HRT	156
CRABB-, John	GRD	117A
CRABB, Jeremiah	SHE	150
CRABSTER, Peter	JEF	35
CRABTREE, -----?	DVS	9A
----h?	DVS	9A
Abraham	CLD	161
Ben.	CHN	32A
Hiram	MNR	201
Iraah/ Isaah?	HOP	238
James	CHN	35
James	GRN	70
James	HOP	238
James, Junr.	CHN	35
James, Senr.	CHN	35
John	LVG	11
John	MBG	143A
Joseph	HOP	238
Mark	WYN	82A
Mary	LVG	10
Mary	OHO	5A
Reece	FLD	23
Richd.	GRN	70
William	CLD	165
CRABTREE?, -----?	DVS	9A
-----?	DVS	10A
CRACE, George	FLD	7
CRACE?, Peter	FLD	4
CRACRAFT, John	GNP	173A
Jos.	CAR	56
Mary	FLG	58A
Reuben	MAS	56
Saml.	MAS	56
Tho.	MAS	67
William	BTH	150
Zadoch	FLG	65A
CRACROFT, Charles	GNP	173A
CRADDOCK, Archer	BRN	6
James	HRT	154
Jessee	HRT	154
John	HRT	154
Nathl.	BRN	7
Richard C.	BRN	6
Robert	GRN	61
Robert	WRN	30A
Wm.	HRT	154
CRADICK, John	BBN	114
CRADIE, William	HOP	236
CRADLEBOW, Wm.	MAD	122
CRAE?, Elsay?	ADC	68
CRAFFORD, James	JES	83
Josep	BTH	196
CRAFT, David	CHN	36
Michal	CLD	157
CRAFT?, (See Croft?)	FLD	4
CRAFTON, Anthony	SHE	114A
Anthony	SHE	138A
James	WRN	64A
Polly	SHE	115A
CRAGEN, Alfred	PND	27A
CRAGG, John	GSN	132A
Saml.	HRD	34
CRAGMILES, Matthew	GTN	119
CRAIG, Andrew	JEF	49
Andrew	HRL	106
Andrew	WRN	51A
Benjamin	GTN	123
Benjn.	BNE	10
Betsey	LNC	9
Charles	MER	92
Cyrus	GTN	123
David	LNC	11
David	KNX	292
David	PND	22A
Donaldson	MTG	267
Elijah	MAS	52
Elijah	SCT	94A
Fed	GRD	95A
Francis	BNE	8
Garland D.	MBG	141
George	HRL	106
Hawkins	JES	73
James	FLD	12
James	GRN	75
James	WDF	96
James	TOD	132
James	HAR	144
James	BTH	148
James	CLD	149
James	SHE	125A
Jerimaah	GTN	123
Jno.	MAS	52
Jno.	HAR	160
Joel	JEF	57
John	TRG	6
John	LNC	11
John	CWL	39
John	MER	92
John	FTE	94
John	GTN	123
John	GSN	131
John	CLD	141
John	HAR	204
John	MTG	255
John	TRG	5A
John	WYN	103A
John	SCT	132A
John D.	SCT	135A
John H.	BNE	10
John W.	JEF	31
Joseph	FTE	109
Larkin	SCT	124A
Levi	GTN	123
Lewis	MAS	68
Lewis	GTN	122
Lewis	WDF	120A
Lewis H.	GTN	123
Margaret	FTE	102
Nathl.	SCT	124A
Philip	BNE	10
Reuben	SCT	137A
Richard	TOD	128A
Robbert	CBL	20A
Robert	FLD	9
Robert	GRN	67
Robert	GRN	75
Robert	GRN	77
Robert	FTE	95
Robert	HAR	156
Robt.	ADR	12
Robt.	BTH	180
Saml.	LNC	9
Saml.	FLG	44A
Samuel	MER	92
Samuel	HOP	240
Samuel H.	JES	82
Sarah	MBG	141
Sluman	GTN	121
CRAIG, Thomas	ADR	64
Thomas	GTN	123
Toliver	SCT	130A
Twyman	GTN	122
Whitfield	BKN	26
William	LNC	2
William	HRL	106
William	CLD	139
William	BTH	148
William	HAR	160
William	HAR	168
William	MTG	267
William, Jun.	LNC	2
William M.	WDF	104
CRAIG?, Wm.?	CWL	40
CRAIGE, Elijah W.	FTE	60
CRAIGMILES, Agness	LGN	42
CRAIL, Wilson	PND	22A
CRAIN, Jno.	PUL	42A
Samuel	TRG	5
Wm.	PND	31A
CRAIN?, Saml., Jr.?	FLG	58A
Saml., Snr.	FLG	58A
CRAINSHAW, John	SHE	150
Lewis	SHE	142A
CRAISE?, Wm.	BRK	247
CRALE, James	GRN	53
CRALL, Christian	JES	88
CRALLY, Renner	BKN	8
CRAME?, Jessee	NSN	196
John	NSN	196
CRAMMER, Geo.	SCT	111A
CRANDALL, Benj.	JEF	27
CRANDELL, Lemuel	BLT	178
Thomas	BLT	178
CRANDLE, Azariah	MTG	247
Samuel R.	GRD	87A
CRANE, Aaron	FTE	98
Abraham	JES	80
Anderson	HRT	156
Armistead	LGN	45
Cary	MER	90
David	MER	90
Francis	MER	90
Geo.	FKN	120
George	HRT	154
Jas.	FLG	52A
John	MER	90
Joseph	HRY	220
Lewis	FLG	74A
Nathaniel	MER	90
Nelson	MER	90
Saml., Jr.	FLG	70A
Simeon	MTG	247
Tarlton	MER	90
Thomas	MER	90
Thomas G.	MER	90
William	LGN	44
Wm.	FLG	74A
CRANE?, Jesse	NSN	219
John	NSN	219
CRANK, James	KNX	286
Nathaniel	FLD	29
Wm.	GNP	178A
CRAPPER, Bela, Jr.	HRY	252
Bela, Sr.	HRY	252
Jas.	HRY	252
Laban	NCH	112A
Leven	SCT	127A
Noble	HRY	208
Provy?	HRY	242
CRASK, James	SHE	149
CRAULEY, Wm.	SHE	112A
CRAVANS, Jesse L.	WTY	119A
CRAVEN, Hiram	ADR	10

Name	County	Page
CRAVENS, Abrahan	CHN	42
Benjamin	BNE	10
Elijah	CHN	42A
Iry	WYN	104A
Jeremiah	BNE	10
Jno.	ADR	10
Jno.	CWL	52
Joseph	CWL	52
Robert	CHN	28A
Robt.	ADC	66
Widw.?	CWL	44
William	TRG	11
William	MTG	273
CRAVENS?, Nancy	ADR	64
CRAVER, Geo.	BBN	116
CRAVINS, Aaron	JES	87
Archabald	JES	87
Armon	FTE	109
Cornelius	FLG	67A
David	JES	87
Elijah	CWL	52
Elisha	JES	82
James	JES	87
Jeremiah	JES	80
Jerrimiah	CHN	44A
John	JES	87
John	FTE	109
Thomas	JES	82
CRAVSON, Saml.	SHE	132A
CRAWFORD, Adams	PUL	42A
Alexander	FTE	83
Alexander B.	NCH	127A
Alexr.	JEF	38
Alexr.	PUL	42A
Betsey	SCT	103A
Catherine	FTE	66
Charles	SHE	163
Elenor	MER	92
Ephraim	NSN	182
Frances	LVG	7
Gideon	ETL	45
Hezekiah	FTE	78
Jacob	FLG	74A
James	LVG	7
James	MER	91
James	GTN	124
James	HRY	186
James	MNR	193
James	WRN	60A
Jane	HRY	257
Jas.	FLG	58A
Jas. B.	SCT	93A
John	HRD	36
John	SHE	151
John	SHE	152
John	MTG	273
John	KNX	296
John	CBL	16A
John	WAS	30A
John	LWS	98A
John	NCH	125A
John H.	WRN	54A
Jonathan	LWS	92A
Joseph	ETL	51
Josiah	NSN	182
Martha	CLD	160
Mary	BLT	188
Mary	NCH	112A
Nathan	SHE	137A
Orson	ETL	41
Phebe	MER	92
Rachael	WRN	60A
Richard	LWS	98A
Robt.	HRY	256
Saml.	CWL	33
Samuel	MER	90
CRAWFORD, Samuel	OHO	4A
Susan	ETL	44
Thomas	MER	90
Thomas, Sr.?	MER	90
Thomas I./ J.?	MER	117
Valentine	ETL	49
William	NSN	196
William	LWS	97A
William	NCH	112A
Wm.	HRD	90
Wm.	BRK	245
Wm.	SHE	137A
CRAWFORD?, Henry	SHE	148
Saml.	BRK	245
CRAWL, Jacob	JES	83
CRAWLEY, Asa	ADR	50
Peggy	MNR	203
Saml.	ADR	12
Samuel	FTE	97
Washington	ADR	50
CRAWLY, Anderson	SPN	5A
Aqulla	HRY	269
CRAWLY?, Abner	ADR	10
CRAWTY?, Abner	ADR	10
CRAY, Edward	NCH	128A
Martin	NCH	128A
CRAYBLE, Jonathan	HRD	84
CRAYCRAFT, Thos.	WAS	17A
CRAYTON, Henry	SCT	96A
CREADY, David	HRD	16
Thos.	HRD	76
CREAGER, Daniel	HRD	8
CREAL, Phillip	HRD	86
CREASON, John	MTG	225
CREASY, Pleasant	CLD	138
CREED, Elijah	WDF	116A
John	ETL	41
CREEK, Abraham	BRN	6
David	BRN	6
John	MNR	209
CREEKBAUGHM, Jacob	JES	81
CREEKBAUM, Jno.	MAS	68
CREEKMON, Thomas	SPN	23A
CREEKMORE, Bachalor R.	WTY	119A
Balentine	WTY	119A
Charles G.	WTY	124A
Richard	SPN	12A
Robert	WTY	127A
Thomas	LGN	46
William B.	WTY	114A
CREEKMURE, William	SPN	12A
CREEKPAUN?, Michael	GNP	171A
CREEL, Durhan	ADR	10
Elijah	HRT	154
John	ADR	10
Simeon	ADR	10
CREEL?, Charles	GRN	52
Elijah	GRN	52
CREESON, William	CLD	161
CREESY, John	CLD	141
Joseph	CLD	141
Thomas	CLD	141
CREMAR, Moses	JEF	57
CRENDEN?, William	MNR	215
CRENNE?, Jesse	NSN	196
John	NSN	196
CRENSHAW, Abner	HND	13
Benjamin	BRN	6
Bluford	BLT	160
Corneilus	TRG	4A
Cosby	BLT	178
Dabney	BRN	7
J. T.	HRY	234
Joel	SCT	102A
CRENSHAW, John	CWL	52
Joseph	HND	12
Milly	BRN	6
Nelson	BLT	176
Nicholas	MTG	229
Overton	BLT	156
Thomas	BRN	6
Thomas	BBN	134
Thompson	BRN	6
Thos.	HND	13
CRESS, Valintine	NCH	128A
CRESSWELL, Dav.	HRY	249
Edward D.	NCH	114A
Robt.	HRY	263
CREST, Nicholas	BLT	190
Nicholas	NSN	210
CREST?, Henry	BLT	192
CREWDSON, George	LGN	38
James	LGN	38
Thomas	LGN	38
CREWS, ---riah?	DVS	14A
Andrew	MNR	205
David	MNR	205
David, Jr.	MAD	92
David, Jr.	MAD	92
David D.	MAD	92
Edward	MAD	128
Elijah	HRD	28
James	MER	92
Matthew	BRN	5
Nancy	BRN	6
Redman	MNR	201
Richard	MAD	154
Sarah	WRN	39A
Stanley	MAD	150
Thos.	MAD	148
William	HND	12
Wm.	MAD	164
CRICHFIELD, M.	GRD	103A
Nick	GRD	103A
CRICHFILD, John	GRD	103A
CRIDER, Daniel	LVG	13
Jacob	LVG	13
Jacob, Jr.	LVG	13
Samuel	LVG	13
CRIFFEY?, James	FKN	156
CRIGLAR, Lewis	BNE	10
Richd.	BNE	10
CRIGLER, Abraham	BLT	164
John	MAD	124
Lewis	BNE	8
CRIM, Enoc	CLK	92
James	FTE	82
Jason	MTG	269
Joseph	FTE	96
Martin	SHE	170
Moses	SHE	170
Stephen	WAS	82A
William	MTG	269
CRIM?, Ambrose	CLK	66
Elias	CLK	94
CRIMM, Fielding	FTE	87
CRIMM?, John	HRY	224
CRING, John	BTH	216
CRINNE?, Jessee	NSN	196
John	NSN	196
CRISLER, John	BNE	8
Michael	BNE	8
Wm. M.	BNE	10
CRISMAN, Jacob	FLG	68A
Jacob	FLG	68A
Mathias	FLG	69A
Mathias	FLG	69A
CRISP, Ancil	FLD	27
Jefferson	WAS	32A
John	WAS	32A

CRISP, Susanna FLD 27
William MNR 211
CRISS, Humfrey WAS 76A
CRISSMAN, Mary SHE 117A
CRIST, George SHE 132A
Henry SHE 135A
Wm. SHE 132A
CRIST?, Henry BLT 192
CRISTELL, Wm. FLG 49A
CRISTENSON, Elisha ADR 12
Thos. ADR 14
CRISTLER, Elias JEF 53
Fielden JEF 53
Joshua JEF 53
CRISTOPHER, Crowell BNE 10
CRISTY, Simeon BNE 10
CRISWELL, Anna BLT 196
Elijah ALN 96
Robt. BRK 247
Samuel LWS 87A
CRITCH, John HRL 104
John HRL 104
Jonathan HRL 104
Thomas HRL 104
CRITCHER, James FKN 122
Jno. FKN 122
CRITCHET, Caleb CBL 3A
CRITCHLAW?, Jno. MAS 52
CRITCHLOW, John GTN 126
CRITH, Jacob FKN 104
CRITINGTON, John JEF 22
CRITMAN, Malaihi TRG 12A
CRITMES?, John? CWL 32
CRITTENDEN, Chas. W. SCT 108A
Jno. FKN 56
CRITTENDER, Henry WDF 125A
CRITTENDON, Richd. H. HRY 232
CRO-?, John OHO 3A
CROAKE, Richard HAR 218
CROASTHWAITE, Thos. BBN 114
CROCKET, David CLD 149
James CLK 100
John CLK 100
John BTH 166
John GRD 112A
Newbowl FTE 74
Robert CLD 149
Saml. B. FKN 54
Samuel CLK 100
CROCKETT, Anthony FKN 152
Hamilton FKN 152
John W. SPN 3A
Joseph JES 72
Joseph JES 82
Robert JES 72
William WYN 79A
Wm. R. FKN 120
CROCKSELL, William BRN 6
CROFFORD, Joshua MAS 81
William SHE 155
William SHE 177
CROFMAN?, Henry HRD 44
CROFT, John HOP 238
CROFT?, Archilaus FLD 4
James FLD 4
John FLD 4
CROGHAN, Wm. JEF 22
Wm. JEF 46
CROKE, Robert W. SHE 119A
CROLEY, Polly WTY 112A
Prior HOP 240
William WTY 127A
CROMELL, Rachel FTE 77
CROMER, George KNX 314
John KNX 314
CROMER?, D. RCK 79A
CROMWELL, Benjamin FTE 111
Garrard LGN 34
Jereh. JEF 65
Joseph HAR 216
Joshua HRD 24
Joshua FTE 75
Levi HRD 56
Nicholas G. SHE 118A
Ruthy JES 97
CRONICK, Philip LNC 49
CRONLEY, E. & Co. GRD 82A
CRONWELL, Chs. JEF 51
Danl. JEF 65
CROOK, Hezakiah FKN 128
Jabez GRD 90A
John MAD 112
John SHE 161
M.? W. CLY 116
Olly ETL 49
Phebe SHE 151
Robert GRT 143
William GRT 143
CROOKS, Abraham GNP 167A
James BTH 154
Jas. SCT 106A
John JEF 42
John BTH 178
John WYN 88A
Robert B. ETL 39
Uzal BTH 154
CROOKSHANKS, A. MAS 77
CROSBY, Alexr. MAS 71
Chas. MAS 64
John SCT 115A
Jos. MAS 57
Robt. MAS 53
Simion GTN 124
CROSBY?, George SHE 160
CROSCALL?, Jas. JEF 21
CROSE, Adam NCH 121A
Andrew NCH 121A
CROSE?, Solomon BTH 152
CROSLEY?, George SHE 160
CROSLIN, Benjamin BKN 5
CROSORT, Isaiah CLD 137
CROSS, Abm. BBN 104
Alexander MBG 133A
Geo. TOD 125
Gibbons CLD 147
Hezekiah BLT 190
James BRN 7
John JEF 51
John FTE 75
John, Sr. TOD 126A
John FLG 31A
Jonathan BBN 68
Joseph WDF 126A
Joshua BRN 7
Joshua MAD 118
Levi BBN 102
Mary BBN 68
Robert CLD 144
Solomon PUL 59A
Squire MAD 122
William BRN 7
William ADR 10
William CLD 144
William MBG 140A
Wm. HRY 244
Zachariah LGN 30
CROSS?, Joseph JES 75
CROSSFIELD, Jno. FKN 136
CROSSMAN?, Henry HRD 44
CROSSTHWAIT, Abm. MTG 279
CROSTHWAIT, Perry HAR 220
Samuel WRN 73A
CROUCH, Charles MGB 137A
Chas. TOD 129A
David BBN 68
David SPN 19A
David NCH 125A
Elias NCH 124A
Elijah CLD 148
Francis ETL 51
James CLD 150
John GRN 76
John CLD 148
John NCH 124A
John TOD 129A
Jonathan NCH 124A
Jonithan BTH 218
Jonothan, Jr. BTH 218
Joseph NCH 122A
Nancy HAR 154
Richard LGN 31
Richard W. HND 3
Robert WAS 79A
Thos. CWL 37
Will BBN 68
William CLD 151
William BTH 206
CROUCHER, Wm. MAD 142
CROUDERS?, George WAS 34A
CROUSE, George FTE 101
John BBN 126
Peter FTE 96
CROW, Andrew JEF 55
Bazil BLT 158
Benj. LNC 53
Benjamin LNC 77
Benjamin BBN 102
Charles SHE 115A
Daniel ETL 41
Daniel CLK 78
David JES 76
David CLK 78
Edward BLT 174
Eli BBN 102
Elijah OHO 4A
Ely CHN 31A
Fanny JES 76
Geo. FLG 65A
Henry (Free) CLK 95
Henry OHO 10A
Jacob LGN 39
Jacob MER 90
James LNC 55
James OHO 7A
Joab ETL 41
John CLK 62
John NSN 219
John HOP 236
John HOP 236
John, Jr. CLK 78
John, Senr. CLK 78
John DVS 14A
John F. SHE 143A
Joseph SHE 164
Joseph OHO 10A
Joshua CHN 44
Leonard BBN 102
Levi LVG 9
Moses? CWL 41
Philip NSN 223
Robt. CHN 39
Saml. PUL 39A
Samuel BLT 174
Susan, Miss JEF 24

CROW, Thos. JEF 54
Thos. PUL 48A
Walker MER 91
Walter LNC 75
William OHO 7A
Willm. LNC 53
Wm. ALN 110
Wm.? CWL 32
CROWAN?, Will NSN 223
CROWCHER, Robert JES 94
CROWCHER?, Huston JES 76
CROWDER, Anthony FTE 97
Bennit? ALN 122
James GTN 120
James HND 9A
John GTN 120
Matthew WAS 59A
Phillip GRN 75
Ruben WAS 59A
Saml. CWL 31
Sterling JES 71
William GTN 120
CROWDUS, George WAS 22A
CROWELL, Ada BNE 10
Calvin MAS 78
CROWHITE, Elijah CLK 102
CROWLEY, Alfred MAS 55
CROWNOVER, Gilbert FLG 25A
CROWSON, Elijah SCT 103A
CROZIER, John NSN 178
CRUCHELOE?, William BLT 152
CRUCHER, Thos. MAD 172
CRUCHERVILLE, James CBL 23A
CRUD, Elijah, Sr. WDF 96
CRUISE, Clara HRD 88
George MNR 193
CRUISE?, John FLD 17
Wm. BRK 247
CRUM, Adam FLD 27
Frederick FLD 27
Henry FLD 30
Jacob FLD 30
John, Sr. CLY 132
Michael FLD 30
Ralph, Sr. BRK 247
Thomas LNC 49
CRUM?, Charles BRK 245
Elias CLK 94
John FLD 17
Ralph, Jr. BRK 243
CRUMB, John CLY 112
CRUMBAUGH, Conrod LGN 24
Danl. SCT 113A
Henry SCT 113A
Jacob FKN 64
John LGN 25
John FTE 110
Solomon SCT 127A
William W. LGN 25
CRUME, John BRK 247
CRUME?, Jesse NSN 196
Jesse NSN 219
John NSN 196
John NSN 219
CRUMEL?, Jessee NSN 196
John NSN 196
CRUMLEY, Saml. HRT 154
CRUMMEY, George CBL 2A
CRUMP, Archer HRT 156
Daniel MER 92
David HRT 156
Elisha NCH 127A
Holly GNP 175A
Joel GRN 63
CRUMP, Joseph BBN 92
Joshua HRT 155
Patrick BBN 92
Romeo HRT 154
Thos. WAS 22A
Turner TOD 131
Widow BBN 82
Wm. T. BBN 66
CRUMPTON, --ury? CWL 42
CRUMS?, Danl. RCK 83A
CRUMWELL, Richard JES 95
CRUN?, Ambrose CLK 66
CRUPPER, John FLG 36A
CRUS, Amey MAD 124
CRUSE, Anderson MAD 162
Isaac LVG 9
James LVG 5
James MAD 94
Ledy MAD 124
Littlebury WAS 24A
Richd. LVG 9
CRUSENBERRY, M. CWL 37
CRUSH, William WYN 106A
CRUTCHELOE, John BLT 154
CRUTCHER, Charles LNC 25
Henry BRN 33
Henry FKN 78
Isaac WDF 107A
Jas. HRD 96
Martha FKN 78
Matthew LWS 96A
Norvel HRD 64
Reuben FKN 76
Saml. LNC 29
Seiburt SHE 131A
CRUTCHFIELD, Benjamin F. MER 116
Coburn? WYN 89A
Geo. SCT 105A
Martin CLK 75
Nancey FKN 108
Nicholas CLK 95
Richard CLK 75
Richard D. MER 91
Wm. TOD 127A
CRUTCHLOW, Moses HAR 186
CRUTHERS, Geo. FLG 48A
CRUZ, Peter UNN 150
CRYDER?, -----? CWL 40
John?, Jr. CWL 40
CUDD, Martha TRG 7A
CUFFEY, Samuel GSN 133A
CULBERSON, -----? MAS 76
B. Robert GSN 132A
David LNC 39
Jas. MAS 53
Jas. FLG 78A
John MBG 135A
M. John GSN 131
CULBERTH, (See Cutberth) WTY 110A
CULBERTON, Lee TOD 129A
CULBERTSON, Alexander FTE 105
Alexander BBN 130
Allen CBL 13A
David CLK 87
James CBL 13A
Joseph BBN 128
Robbert CBL 13A
William CBL 13A
CULL, Ann FLG 54A
James SHE 125A
John HRY 190
John WAS 81A
Samuel GTN 119
CULL, Thos. WAS 17A
CULLAMS, Jas. MAS 63
CULLENS, Charles FTE 107
CULLEY, James HRT 154
Matthew M. HRT 154
CULLIN, Charles SCT 92A
CULLINS, Charles WRN 29A
James FTE 99
Sarah WRN 29A
William BRN 5
CULLOM, Alvan WYN 106A
Edward N. WYN 106A
Francis WYN 102A
Richard WYN 84A
William WYN 84A
CULLOP?, John PUL 60A
CULLUM, Francis BNE 10
Susanna MAD 128
CULLY, John HRD 66
Mathew HRD 46
Thos. HRD 30
Thos. HRD 64
William FTE 106
CULP, Daniel BRN 33
David BRN 7
John BRN 7
Mary BKN 22
Mary NCH 127A
Tilman GNP 173A
CULPEPPER, William HND 12
CULTON, Elizabeth MER 91
CULUM?, Thomas O.? ETL 40
CULVER, John ETL 43
John NSN 222
John GNP 170A
Ranson RCK 80A
Sarah BLT 190
CULVER?, Robert UNN 147
CUMBERS, Jas. MAS 55
CUMINGON, John M. MER 90
CUMINGORE, Henry, Jr. MER 91
Henry, Sr. MER 91
CUMINGS, Matthew, Jr. FKN 130
Matthew, Sr. FKN 130
Wm. FKN 130
CUMINS, Danl. RCK 78A
John RCK 79A
Moses BRK 249
Nelson BRK 247
Prestley BRK 249
CUMINS?, Moses RCK 79A
William ALN 94
CUMMENS, Charles FTE 67
CUMMIKLE, Jas. JEF 66
CUMMING, Daniel MTG 247
Uriah CLY 118
CUMMINGHAM, R. TOD 124A
William MER 92
CUMMINGS, Andrew BBN 140
Christopher BKN 6
James BBN 140
Jno. FKN 146
Joseph HAR 136
Thomas CLK 64
Washington CLK 64
William CLK 65
CUMMINS, Alexander MER 92
Andrew CLD 137
Benjamin CLK 83
Casey CBL 2A
Cornelius JEF 37
Daniel BBN 60
David JEF 33
Jacob BBN 132

Name	County	Page
CUMMINS, James	JEF	34
James	MER	92
James	CLY	116
James	MAD	142
John	JEF	33
John	JEF	37
John	BBN	146
John	SPN	24A
John B.	BBN	120
Joshua	MER	92
Michael	NSN	198
Rebeca	LWS	88A
Robt. B.	BBN	116
Saml.	BRN	5
Samuel	BLT	166
Samuel	LWS	88A
Silas	CLD	139
Simon	BBN	74
Stephen	RCK	78A
Thomas	LNC	77
Thomas	HAR	170
Thos.	BBN	120
William	HAR	138
William	HAR	142
William	WTY	115A
Wm.	JEF	23
Wm.	JEF	33
Wm.	BBN	116
Wm.	BBN	132
CUMMONS, Robt.	MAS	65
CUMPTON, Burris	GRD	108A
Caty	ADR	14
Ebenezer	ADR	14
Edw.?	WAS	61A
Joel	HRT	154
Joel	BRK	245
John	MBG	136
John	BRK	249
Micajah	ADR	14
Robert	MER	90
Samuel	HOP	238
Will	ADR	14
Wm.	BRK	243
Wm. S?.	WAS	61A
CUMSTOCK, Isaac	KNX	278
Joseph	WTY	119A
CUNDEFF, Bryan	MBG	136A
CUNDIF, Greenbury	WAS	59A
Meshack	WAS	22A
CUNDIFF, Benjamin	PUL	58A
Frail	WYN	92A
George, Senr.	PUL	55A
Isaac	MBG	138
Jno.	PUL	37A
John	CLY	112
John	MBG	141
John G.	PUL	55A
Rebecca	PUL	66A
Richard	PUL	57A
William	CSY	204
CUNDITH, John	BLT	190
CUNDUFF, John	HRD	8
John	CSY	206
Richard	ADR	3
Shad	ADR	12
CUNE, Michael D.	BKN	6
Robert	MAD	154
CUNICES?, Jacob	MAD	108
CUNINGHAM, Isaac	CLK	87
John	CWL	52
John	BTH	148
John	WDF	99A
Thomas	FLD	7
Thomas	CSY	214
Thomas	WDF	99A
William	HND	7A
CUNNIGHAM, Robert	CLK	100
CUNNING, J./ I.?		
L.	GRD	94A
Uriah	FLD	6
CUNNINGHAM, Andrew	WAS	31A
Braken	BRK	247
C. W.	PUL	69
David	CBL	4A
Edward	BLT	186
Elizabeth	NCH	127A
Ephraim	CSY	220
Francis	MER	92
Hugh	ETL	52
Hugh	WDF	100
J.	JEF	23
J.	TOD	130
Jacob	MER	92
James	CWL	52
James	WDF	100
James	HAR	134
James	BLT	176
James	BTH	182
James	BRK	249
Jas.	TOD	125
Jas.	FLG	33A
Jas.	SCT	109A
Jno.	ADR	14
Jno.	JES	95
John	LGN	37
John	BBN	104
John	GRT	139
John	GSN	132A
John N.	HOP	238
Jonathan	FLD	12
Jones	BRK	247
Joseph	MER	89
Joseph	CSY	216
M.	TOD	130
Margaret	FTE	105
Mariah	MER	92
Mathew	GSN	131
Nancy (Crossed Out)	WTY	117A
Nancy	WTY	112A
Robert	BBN	124
Robert	WAS	18A
Robt. M.	FTE	63
Sarah	GSN	132A
Sarry	FKN	54
Thos.	FLG	33A
Vancy/ Vaney?	GSN	132A
Walter	MER	92
William	TRG	13
William	MER	89
William	HAR	198
William	CBL	9A
William	WDF	97A
Wm.	GSN	131
Wm.	SHE	141A
CUPP, Peter	MAS	77
Phillip	MAS	62
CUPP?, Mrs?/ Wm.?	MAS	62
CUPPY, Aaron	NSN	186
Aaron	NSN	219
John	NSN	223
CURBY, John	SCT	124A
Zachariah	SCT	115A
CURD, Aaron	MER	91
Benjamin	MER	91
Daniel	BRN	6
Daniel	JES	89
Edmund	LGN	30
Edward	LGN	28
Fanny	TRG	4
Fanny	FTE	104
James	JES	94
CURD, James	TRG	7A
Jesse	BRN	6
John	LGN	43
John	CHN	46
Jonathan	TRG	5A
Joseph	LGN	30
Joseph	MER	92
Mary	MER	91
Merriman B.	JES	89
Newton	MER	91
Samuel H.	LGN	23
Stephen	CHN	40
William	LGN	29
Woodford	JEF	59
CURD?, Richard	LGN	22
Spencer	LGN	22
Willis	MER	116
CURDMAN, John	SPN	6A
CURENS, James	MER	92
CURETON, Nat.	HRY	260
CURL, Anne	BRN	6
Jno.	JEF	58
John	BBN	102
Morogan	MAD	154
CURLE, Clayton	MAD	178
CURLE?, Archibald	MAD	126
CURLEW, James	CWL	43
CURLIN, James	TRG	12
John	TRG	12A
CURMETT, John	FLD	46
Reuben	FLD	46
CURNEAL, Fleming	HOP	236
CURRAN, Thomas	NSN	183
CURRENCE?, Mathew	LGN	27
CURRENS, Jos.	FLG	67A
CURRENT, Elijah	BBN	132
Thomas	BBN	132
Thos.	BBN	132
CURRENT?, John	BBN	130
CURRIN, Thomas	NSN	209
CURRY, Alexr.	SCT	121A
Bath	GRN	61
Benjn.?	CWL	50
Charles	GRN	58
Charles	GRN	58
Danl.	JEF	62
David	FTE	86
Edward	JEF	62
Edward	UNN	152
George	GRN	61
James	CWL	50
James	HAR	132
James	HAR	166
James, Jr.	MER	89
James, Sr.	MER	90
Jas.	MAS	66
Jno.	HAR	164
John	GRN	53
John	JEF	62
John	MER	90
John, Sr.	MER	92
John	SCT	136A
Nicholas	GRT	143
Robert	MER	89
Robert, Jr.	UNN	148
Robert, Sen.	UNN	148
Robt.	ADR	10
Saml.	LNC	31
Samuel	MER	89
Thos.	CWL	46
Thos.	JEF	62
Will	SCT	102A
William	FTE	85
William	MER	89
William	OWN	100
William	GTN	122

Name	County	Page
CURRY, William, Sr.	MER	89
William	WDF	95A
Wm.	GRN	58
CURRY?, Henry S.	GNP	175A
CURTES, Elijah	LNC	37
CURTIS, Ann	MAS	55
Benjamin	CLK	74
Danl.	FTE	67
David	BRK	245
Filden	MNR	197
Geo.	MAS	56
Jacob	FTE	78
James	HOP	238
Joel	HRY	206
John	CLK	65
John	CLK	74
John	MNR	197
Moses	MNR	197
Peter	GRD	102A
Russell	TRG	13
Saml.	CLY	114
Seth	NCH	107A
Theodocia	CLK	74
Thomas	CLK	74
Thos.	SCT	101A
William	CLK	74
William J.	MNR	197
Wm.	MAS	52
CURTLEY, Jas.	JEF	57
CURTNER, Peter	MBG	135
CURTRIGHT, Cornelius	BBN	104
Danl.	BBN	106
John	BBN	104
Saml.	BBN	104
CURTUS, George B.	WDF	100
Will	MAS	68
CURTZ, George	NSN	201
CURTZ?, Elizabeth	NSN	201
CURZAD, John	FLD	46
CUSCADEN/ CUSCADER?, James	NCH	103A
CUSEE?, Benjamin	GNP	177A
CUSHENBERRY, Cosly	MAD	112
CUSHING--NY, David	ALN	124
CUSHINGS, Elijah	ALN	126
CUSHMAN, David	MAS	52
Morris	MAS	58
Thomas	BNE	8
CUSICK, Ignatius	UNN	154
Robert	HAR	138
CUSICK?, Francis	WAS	43A
James	WAS	43A
CUSMAN, John	FLG	71A
CUSS?, David	BTH	208
CUSSINS, Jesse	WAS	85A
CUSTARD, Amelia	HAR	208
Benjamin	CBL	16A
Conrad	HAR	212
Coonrod	CBL	17A
CUSTER, Elisha	BNE	8
CUSTER?, Elizabeth	BBN	140
CUTBERTH, David	WTY	110A
CUTBERTH?, James	WTY	110A
CUTLER, Martin	GTN	135
CUTLISS, David	WRN	47A
CUTRIGHT, John	HRD	82
Saml.	HRD	72
CUTSENGER, Jacob	WAS	86A
John	WAS	51A
Mical	WAS	80A
CUTTON, John	KNX	294
CYPHERS, Aaron	FLD	15
D-----?, Joseph	LVG	16
D-----A?, James	WDF	99A
William	WDF	99A
D----?, William	LVG	16
D-ARINGTON?, Miles	ALN	94
DA--LL?, George	NCH	125A
DABNEY, John	WYN	81A
John	SHE	131A
John Q.?	MAD	120
Jubal?	WYN	102A
Nathan	WYN	102A
Wm.	SHE	120A
DACON, John	NSN	217
DACREY?, John	ADR	16
DACSEY?, John	ADR	16
DADD?, Milly	HRY	266
DADE, John	NSN	201
DADESMAN, Jacob	NSN	204
John	NSN	204
Matthias	NSN	204
DADISMAN, ----ge?	DVS	10A
DAFRON?, Rody	WYN	102A
DAGG-?, ---g--ah?	FLD	42
DAGLEY, Benjamin	PUL	58A
DAGNER, Pet.	HRY	249
DAILEY, Chas.	FLG	67A
Danl.	FLG	67A
Elijah	HRD	94
Elizabeth	HRD	14
John	HAR	180
John	FLG	67A
Laurence	FTE	102
Mary	HAR	188
Ru--?	GTN	132
Sarah	GTN	132
Wm.	FKN	92
DAILY, Jno.	MAS	55
John	MER	93
John	HRY	222
John	BRK	249
Ralph	BKN	5
DAISY, Ishmael	BBN	88
DALE, Abraham	GSN	133A
Abram	WDF	98
David	JES	95
Elijah	WDF	115A
G.	JEF	27
George	WDF	102A
George W.	HRD	36
Isaac	BRN	8
James	MTG	273
John	JEF	25
John	SHE	148
John	FLG	35A
John P.	BNE	12
Leroy	WDF	115A
Margaret	BRN	8
Philip	GSN	133A
Polly	WDF	98
Rawleigh	WDF	116A
Reuben	BRN	8
Reuben	SHE	134A
Robert	MTG	275
Susan	BTH	164
Thos.	SHE	137A
Uriah	FLG	50A
William	BRN	8
William, Sr.	WDF	98
William	WDF	116A
DALES?, Thomas	GRD	114A
DALEY, Benj.	WAS	57A
Chas.	FLG	64A
John	WAS	57A
DALK?, Oliver	CHN	35A
DALLAM, Richd. B.	BTL	321
Saml.	JEF	24
DALLAM?, Richd. B.	BTL	334
DALLAN, John	JEF	26
DALLANE?, Jane	LGN	24
DALLARN?, ---k?	CHN	46
A. T.?	CHN	46
DALLASS?, Jos.	CHN	46
DALLUM, William S.	FTE	62
DALLY?, Richard	JES	73
DALNEY, Isaac W.	JEF	35
DALTON, Beryman	LGN	36
Jesse	WRN	58A
Joseph	LNC	13
Lewis	LGN	25
Terisa	JEF	42
William	WRN	56A
DALY, Elizabeth	GNP	172A
DALY?, Thomas	GRD	114A
DAMAL, Christopher	GNP	169A
DAME, Jacob	MBG	138
DAMON, Solomon	CBL	9A
DAMOND, (Free)	ADR	70
DAMPEER?, Henry	NCH	122A
DAMRALL, Thomas	CBL	21A
DAMRALL?, David	CBL	19A
DAMRON, Jessey	MAD	154
Moses	FLD	28
Richard	FLD	28
Samuel	FLD	28
DAMSTER?, Plesent	WAS	65A
DAMTIC?, Paul	CLK	107
DANCE, John	PND	24A
Peter	SPN	6A
Wm.	PND	24A
DANCE?, Thos	PND	19A
DANFFORD?, James	LVG	16
DANFORTH, Asa	FKN	114
Joseph	JEF	20
DANIEL, Abner G.	MAD	178
Beverly	MTG	291
Burrell	JEF	58
Carter	CLK	88
Charles	LVG	2
Charles	GRT	139
Charles	CBL	2A
Coleman	JEF	24
Edmond	MAD	138
Elijah	TRG	13A
Estrige	MTG	253
Gambol	LVG	2
Garret	CBL	17A
Garrett	LGN	33
Garrett	CBL	17A
George	TRG	13
George	FLD	36
Henry	MTG	299
Isham	FLD	24
J./ I.?	SHE	109A
James	CLK	107
James	TRG	4A
James M.	MTG	291
Jeremiah	CLD	151
Jesse	MTG	235
Jno.	LVG	4
Joel	HND	6A
John	TRG	14
John	LGN	30
John	JEF	60
John	JES	88
John	CLK	92
John	HRL	106
John	HAR	196
John	MNR	201
John	SHE	109A
John N.	MTG	285
Leonard	SHE	137A
Nathaniel	FTE	102

Name	County	Page
DANIEL, Peter	BRK	251
Peter	CBL	17A
Philip	HRL	106
Reubin	HRD	20
Robert	MTG	287
Robinson	HAR	214
Spencer	KNX	300
Spillsberry	WYN	100A
Thomas	FLD	36
Thos.	JEF	60
Traverse	CBL	17A
Vivion	MTG	295
Walker	SHE	177
Will.	LVG	8
William	GRN	79
William	TRG	4A
William	CBL	17A
William	WYN	100A
Wm.	BNE	12
Wm.	BNE	12
Wm.	TOD	132
Wm.	WAS	49A
Wm.	SHE	113A
DANIELS, Henery	CBL	5A
Rutha	CBL	20A
DANIPEER?, Henry	NCH	122A
DANKS, John	LGN	43
Wm.	CWL	46
DANLEY, David	CBL	23A
John	CLK	89
DANNALDSON, Wm.	MAS	70
DANNEL, Ann	OHO	3A
William B.	OHO	11A
DANNER, Samuel	MBG	139
DANNERILY, Stephen	ADR	12
DANNICK?, Samuel	WRN	61A
DANT, J. F.	JEF	27
James	NSN	182
John	WAS	57A
Joseph	WAS	54A
Joseph	WAS	57A
DANT?, Thomas	NSN	181
DANTON, Kily	BKN	9
DARBY, Danl.?	CWL	41
Denton	SPN	14A
Joseph W.	LNC	19
DARCLIS?, Saml.	JEF	24
DARCUS, Saml.	JEF	43
DARDEN, John	CLD	164
DARE, Goodall	SCT	129A
Isaac	SCT	102A
Mrs.	JEF	23
DARIG?, Snead?	LVG	15
DARK, Job	JEF	45
DARLES, Tho.	MAS	54
DARN-I--?, J./ I.?	CWL	46
DARNABY, Edward	FTE	95
George	FTE	91
James	FTE	91
John	FTE	91
William	FTE	91
DARNABY?, Edward	FTE	89
DARNAL, George	GRD	87A
Henzey/ Henry?	BBN	74
Johnathan	PUL	47A
Levi	LWS	95A
Thomas	BBN	120
Thos., Jr.	BBN	74
DARNALD, Adam	MER	93
Joseph	LNC	75
Mary Ann	LNC	71
Nelson	LNC	73
Zenis	JES	78
DARNALL, Amos	MTG	233
Daniel	MTG	239
Hannah	BBN	66
DARNALL, Henry	MTG	269
Isaac	MTG	281
John	MTG	269
Levi	BBN	116
Marian	MTG	279
Samuel	MTG	295
Thos.	CWL	34
William	MNR	205
William	SPN	18A
DARNALL?, David	CBL	19A
DARNE, Thomas P.	SHE	118A
DARNEL, Lewis	SHE	126A
DARNELL, Abijah	BBN	68
Heny	CWL	52
Isaac, Senr.	BBN	70
James	LGN	28
Jane	WDF	124A
Mary	BBN	82
Thos.	BBN	68
Uriah	BBN	74
Wm.	HRY	252
DARNIAL, Edward	WDF	94A
Jacob	WDF	94A
Joseph	WDF	94A
DARNOLD, Chas.	FLG	74A
Ezekael	FLG	75A
Isaac	FLG	74A
Martin	BNE	12
Nicholas	LGN	42
DARR, John	WDF	120A
William	WDF	121A
DARRENT?, Preston	SHE	123A
DARRINGER, Docia	HRY	251
Martin	HRY	261
DARSE, Parmelei?	HRD	80
DARSEY, L. P.	MAS	79
DARST, Daniel	GSN	133A
John	GSN	133A
DATE, Jane	MTG	245
DATRAM?, William	GRN	63
DAUBENSPECK, Hannah	HAR	210
DAUGERTY, John	SHE	122A
DAUGHERLY, Edward	BLT	182
DAUGHERTY, Arthur	FKN	122
Daniel	WDF	103A
David	HRD	52
Elizabeth	JEF	32
George	PUL	56A
Henry	PND	17A
Hugh	BBN	72
James	FKN	86
James	PND	28A
Jas.	HRD	48
Jas.	RCK	75A
Jas.	SCT	107A
Jas.	SCT	133A
Jas.	SCT	138A
John	LNC	15
John, Sr.	PND	27A
John	RCK	77A
Joseph	SHE	163
Joseph	PND	27A
Peter	WRN	31A
Redman	MER	114
Samuel	HRD	34
Samuel	MER	93
Susan	LNC	15
Tom	MER	93
William	MER	93
Wm.	LNC	15
Wm.	ADR	16
Wm.	HRD	44
Wm., Jr.	HRD	28
Wm.	PND	21A
DAUGHHETEE?, Isaac	ETL	49
DAUGHHETEE?, Moses	ETL	50
Thomas	ETL	50
DAUGHHETTE?, Nancy	ETL	43
DAUGHRITY, Noble	WAS	34A
Wm.	WAS	34A
DAUGHTER, Presley	TRG	10
DAUGRITY, Matthew	WAS	32A
DAUHERTY, Sarah	MAD	174
DAUKINS?, Martha	FLG	33A
DAULEY?, William	NCH	113A
DAULTON, Geo.	MAS	78
Jane	MAS	75
Mary	MAS	78
DAUSON, George	NSN	185
DAV--?, Michael	NSN	183
DAVAGE, Reason	CHN	28
DAVASS, David	CBL	23A
DAVEISS, Robert	MER	93
DAVENPORT, Adrian	UNN	148
Alexander	UNN	148
B.	TOD	127A
Elizabeth	MER	116
Fortunatus	JES	94
John	CLK	76
John	MER	93
John	UNN	152
Marmaduke	FTE	85
Robert	OHO	8A
Samuel	MER	93
William	FTE	83
William	MER	95
DAVES, Asher C.	TRG	4A
DAVES?, William	MBG	138
DAVICE, Jno.	HRY	257
John	CLD	156
Peter	CLD	155
Robert	CLD	155
William	CLD	139
Williamson	CLD	139
DAVID, Abraham	HRD	88
Beverly	CLK	71
Edward	HRD	88
Henry	BBN	116
Henry, Senr.	BBN	130
Henry	WRN	63A
Jacob	HRD	90
Jacob	BBN	140
Jean	MAS	62
Joab	HAR	158
John	HRD	88
Michael	MAS	79
Richard	HRD	88
Sally	HRD	88
DAVIDGE, Henry	GTN	121
DAVIDSON, Abner	GRD	102B
Abr'am	BRN	8
Alex B.	CWL	39
Alexander	BRN	9
Benjamin	BRN	8
C. B.	TOD	131
Caleb	BRN	8
David	OWN	105
Elijah	BRN	8
Ellis	WRN	52A
George	JES	69
George	LNC	81
George	WRN	29A
George	GNP	166A
Henry	PUL	59A
Hezekiah	HRT	157
Isaac	BRN	8
James	LNC	2
James	GRN	51
James	CLY	112
James	MAD	114
James	SCT	102A

DAVIDSON, James NCH 126A
James H. LGN 23
Jas. B. HRD 40
John LNC 49
John CLY 115
John MAD 126
John, Sen. BRN 8
John WRN 71A
John NCH 109A
John NCH 129A
Joseph WDF 95A
Mary BRN 9
Michael LNC 2
Moses MAD 114
Polly LNC 81
Reuben SCT 101A
Richard JES 80
Robert LWS 95A
Robt. GNP 167A
Saml. LNC 5
Samuel GTN 117
Samuel CLY 131
Sarah WRN 66A
Silas CLY 127
Thomas BRN 8
Thomas BTH 208
Thomas NCH 112A
White CLY 127
William BRN 8
Wm. BRK 227
Wm. GNP 171A
DAVIE, Ambrose CHN 41
Thomas FLD 39
DAVIES, Giddeon OHO 9A
James OWN 100
Jonathan OWN 102
Sandwich OHO 7A
Solomon OHO 11A
Thomas OHO 7A
William OWN 102
DAVIES?, Ingham? CWL 46
DAVIESS, John CBL 13A
John DVS 17A
Joseph CBL 13A
Matthew LNC 41
Saml. LNC 73
Samuel LNC 47
William CBL 9A
DAVINNE, Saml. CHN 30
DAVINPORT, Charles JES 97
John SPN 20A
Mary SPN 24A
DAVIS, -----? DVS 7A
-----? DVS 7A
-----? DVS 7A
-----? DVS 11A
-----? DVS 13A
A. B. TOD 131
Abijah WDF 123A
Abner UNN 149
Abner BTL 321
Abraham SPN 16A
Abram GSN 134A
Agnes UNN 154
Alexander NCH 105
Alexander LWS 93A
Ann SHE 168
Aquilla UNN 146
Archibald GTN 130
Arthur BRN 9
Arthur H. CWL 52
Asa FLG 60A
Asel, Sr.? GRD 116A
Asel WRN 48A
Ashley GTN 121
Azeriah GSN 134A
DAVIS, Barney BBN 80
Basil FLG 33A
Baylor FTE 104
Benedict UNN 150
Benj. CLY 114
Benjamin FTE 92
Benjamin HAR 180
Benjamin MTG 235
Benjamin HOP 240
Benjamin MTG 249
Benjamin BTL 319
Benjn. MAS 62
Benjn. SCT 98A
Benjn. SCT 122A
Brinkley FLG 31A
Caroline JEF 62
Catharine LWS 92A
Catherine, Mrs. WYN 92A
Chares MNR 193
Charity JEF 54
Charles HND 7
Charles HAR 192
Charles NSN 207
Charles HOP 240
Charles SHE 129A
Clement CHN 29A
Danl. MAS 70
Danl.? CWL 41
David LVG 8
David BKN 16
David BTH 188
David LWS 87A
David GNP 176A
Dennis FTE 111
Edward UNN 148
Edward MAD 150
Edward GRD 102B
Edward GSN 134A
Eli BBN 90
Eli SHE 159
Eli BTH 190
Eli FLG 30A
Elias FLG 55A
Elihue HRT 157
Elijah CLK 88
Elijah NSN 180
Elijah SCT 129A
Elizabeth HRL 106
Elizabeth MBG 138
Elizabith GNP 178A
Elnathan MNR 197
Enoch MTG 229
Ephraim SHE 137A
Ester GNP 168A
Evan FLD 13
Evan JEF 52
Fielding PND 30A
Fielding WDF 99A
Forrest OHO 5A
Francis SHE 133A
Fry JEF 30
G. W. JEF 25
Gabriel SPN 16A
Geo. BBN 144
Geo. BBN 146
Geo. SCT 123A
George BRN 9
George ETL 46
George HAR 146
George HRT 157
George WAS 40A
George GSN 134A
George G. HRY 182
George M.? GNP 166A
George W. LGN 40
Gerrard FTE 80
DAVIS, Golsly GRN 53
Hardin BRN 9
Harrison LGN 46
Harrison HOP 240
Henry FLD 6
Henry LGN 40
Henry MAD 102
Henry MAD 120
Henry WDF 103A
Hezekiah OHO 4A
Hitchebud JEF 62
Ignatious BTH 192
Ingram SCT 121A
Isaac MAD 126
Isaac NSN 204
Isaac NSN 205
Isaac MGB 137A
Isham WRN 31A
Israel GTN 130
Israel WRN 70A
Israel GSN 134A
Jacob CLK 99
Jacob WAS 46A
James LVG 3
James FLD 10
James BNE 12
James FLD 13
James FLD 38
James JES 77
James FKN 80
James BBN 120
James SHE 153
James MAD 168
James HAR 192
James MNR 213
James MTG 237
James HOP 240
James MTG 281
James KNX 308
James WRN 42A
James WRN 57A
James NCH 110A
James WTY 111A
James SHE 129A
James SHE 133A
James GNP 170A
James D. SHE 137A
James E. FTE 67
James L. HOP 240
James M. SHE 129A
James? CWL 32
Jas. CHN 39
Jas. SCT 131A
Jemima FLG 26A
Jeremiah WYN 85A
Jesse WRN 64A
Jessee MBG 137
Jessee FLG 62A
Jno. MAS 74
Job GNP 166A
John BRN 7
John FLD 14
John FLD 32
John JEF 37
John FLD 38
John JEF 38
John HRD 54
John MER 93
John HRL 106
John BBN 128
John MAD 136
John UNN 150
John UNN 154
John HRT 157
John NSN 191
John BTH 192

Name	County	Page
DAVIS, John	NSN	212
John	NSN	217
John	MTG	226
John	BRK	249
John	KNX	290
John, Jr.	MER	93
John, Sr.	MER	93
John, Sr.	TRG	4A
John, Sr.	WYN	102A
John	TRG	4A
John	HND	9A
John	SPN	12A
John	FLG	32A
John	FLG	32A
John	WRN	42A
John	PUL	63A
John	WRN	70A
John	WYN	82A
John	LWS	91A
John	SCT	94A
John	WYN	98A
John	SCT	108A
John	SCT	110A
John	WTY	111A
John	SCT	119A
John	SHE	122A
John	SHE	125A
John	SHE	126A
John	GSN	133A
John B.	WDF	122A
John W.	SHE	176
Jonathan	NSN	207
Jonathan W.	LGN	35
Jos.	CHN	39
Jos.	FLG	52A
Jos.	FLG	62A
Jos.	FLG	79A
Joseph	FLD	21
Joseph	MAD	96
Joseph	GTN	122
Joseph	GTN	122
Joseph	MAD	130
Joseph	BTH	192
Joseph	NSN	217
Joseph, Jr.	HOP	240
Joseph, Sr.	HOP	240
Joseph	SHE	120A
Joseph	WDF	122A
Joseph H.	SCT	103A
Joshua	MAD	96
Joshua	MAD	152
Joshua	MNR	193
Joshua	NCH	116A
Joshua H.	UNN	146
Josiah	SHE	127A
Josua	GSN	135A
Jupson?	BRK	251
Lamach	MTG	259
Laurence	MAD	96
Lemuel	FKN	140
Levi	HAR	152
Livi	CWL	52
Lodawick	SCT	108A
Lot	SHE	120A
Lucy	SCT	109A
Luke	BTH	184
Luke	BTH	192
Martin	MAD	102
Mary	GRD	111A
Mary	SHE	114A
Mary	MBG	140A
Mathew	MAS	65
Mathias?	FLD	10
Mathus	CLK	90
Matthias	LWS	92A
Maxfield	MTG	243

Name	County	Page
DAVIS, Milly	MER	95
Morgan	MNR	211
Morton	BTH	220
Moses	LVG	10
Moses	JEF	25
Moses	MNR	213
Moses L.	HRD	26
Nancy	HOP	240
Nathan	JEF	51
Nathan	MTG	235
Ned	GRD	112A
Noah / Nash?	CWL	46
Noah	WDF	113A
Norton	GRN	57
Peter	GRN	67
Peter	FTE	103
Peter	FKN	138
Peter	BTH	186
Philemon B.	WDF	110A
Philip	TRG	12A
Phill	WAS	40A
Phillimon	BRK	249
Phillip	SCT	100A
Polly	MER	93
Presley	SHE	127A
Pressley	ETL	46
R. Wm.	GSN	134A
Randall	MBG	135
Reese	SHE	153
Rezin, Jr.	GRN	71
Rezin, Sr.	GRN	71
Rezin	LWS	91A
Richard	CLK	91
Richard F.	CLK	90
Richd.	CWL	31
Robert	FLD	13
Robert	NSN	210
Robert	HND	8A
Robert	GSN	134A
Robt.	BRK	249
Robt.	BTL	319
Ruben	SCT	109A
Salley	FLD	13
Salley	GTN	127
Saml.	MAS	74
Saml.	BRK	249
Samuel	FLD	21
Samuel	MER	93
Samuel	MER	93
Samuel	GRD	101A
Samuel D.	GTN	122
Scintha	FLG	33A
Shadrach	LGN	41
Simon	NSN	182
Simon	NSN	206
Simon	MTG	226
Solomon	SCT	115A
Squire	JEF	39
Susannah	MER	93
Susannah	MTG	299
Theodorus	GSN	134A
Thomas	LGN	38
Thomas	HRD	56
Thomas	MER	93
Thomas	SHE	153
Thomas	SHE	171
Thomas	HAR	212
Thomas	HOP	240
Thomas	LWS	92A
Thomas	WDF	98A
Thomas	WDF	103A
Thomas	WDF	109A
Thomas	NCH	124A
Thomas	MBG	143A
Thomas G.	HOP	272
Thos.	JEF	54

Name	County	Page
DAVIS, Thos.	BRK	249
Thos.	KNX	280
Thos.	CHN	40A
Thos.	FLG	45A
Travis	NSN	183
Travis	NSN	205
Vincent	NSN	207
Wade	BRK	251
Walter	MAS	64
Warren	SHE	155
Will.	SCT	113A
William	BRN	8
William	HND	11
William	FLD	39
William	FTE	92
William	MER	93
William	HRL	106
William	SHE	152
William	UNN	154
William	NSN	205
William	NSN	207
William	HOP	240
William	BTL	319
William	WRN	43A
William	PUL	58A
William	LWS	90A
William	LWS	91A
William	WYN	102A
William	WYN	103A
William	WTY	110A
William	WDF	112A
William	GRD	116A
William	MBG	135A
William J./ I.?	NSN	205
William P.	HOP	240
Willin	LWS	87A
Winniford	NSN	201
Wm.	CWL	52
Wm.	HRD	88
Wm.	MAD	108
Wm.	BBN	124
Wm.	BRK	253
Wm.	FLG	46A
Wm.	WAS	47A
Wm.	FLG	54A
Wm.	SHE	126A
Wm.	GSN	134A
Wm. C.	TOD	130A
Wm. R.	SHE	142A
Zachariah	FLD	22
DAVIS?, -----?	DVS	5A
Asahel	GRD	102B
Edward	GSN	134A
Humphrey	BBN	86
William	MBG	138
William	HOP	240
DAVISE, Charlotte	HRY	268
DAVISON, Daniel	CLY	126
Elias	WAS	78A
George	ADR	16
John	ADR	16
Joseph	ADR	16
Mary	NSN	189
Robt.	ADR	16
DAVISON?, Wm.	BKN	22
DAVISS, Absolem	ADR	16
Anthony	ADR	3
Berry	ADR	14
George	CSY	218
Hannah	JES	87
Henry	JES	76
J. P.	ADR	16
James	JES	75
John	LNC	3
Landan	CSY	228
Larkin	JES	91

DAVISS, Mary MER 93
Robert CSY 206
Samuel JES 75
Samuel, Capt. MER 115
Suson? ADR 16
William JES 79
DAVISSON, Josiah GNP 166A
Reuben GNP 166A
DAVITT?, Frederic CLK 86
DAVY, Gabriel TRG 12A
DAWHERITY?, Stephen ADR 14
DAWHONEY, Rodes ADR 16
DAWKINS, Polly HRY 220
DAWNER, Benj. TOD 132
DAWNS?, Israel GSN 133A
DAWON, Joseph, Jr. HOP 240
DAWS, Edward OHO 10A
Henry OHO 10A
Isaac GRD 84A
DAWS?, Edward GSN 134A
Ingham? CWL 46
DAWSEY, Wm. BBN 106
DAWSON, Aaron GRN 76
Abraham MAS 56
Armstrong BBN 104
Bailey SHE 172
Christopher CLK 67
Chs. FKN 148
Elijah LNC 63
Elijah SHE 166
Gabrl. BBN 104
George SHE 136A
H. MAS 76
Jacob CLK 98
James LVG 8
James JEF 37
James MER 117
Jno. FKN 158
John TRG 8
John HRD 10
John BBN 104
John HRT 156
John SHE 166
John NCH 103A
John WDF 114A
Joseph, Sr. HOP 240
Moses FLD 40
Nathl. GNP 166A
Peter HAR 218
Richard TRG 4A
Richard WDF 102A
Richd. FKN 142
Robt. MAS 79
S., Mrs.? MAS 56
Stephen GNP 172A
Stephen N. LGN 29
Thomas TRG 8
Thomas NSN 200
Vincent FLD 30
William LGN 42
William LGN 47
William CLD 160
William, Jr. WDF 102A
William, Sr. WDF 99A
Wm.? S. MAS 56
DAWSON?, Benjamin CSY 224
William FTE 91
DAY, Ackley FLG 55A
Allen FLD 12
Arch JEF 51
Archibald FLD 8
Asa BKN 10
Caty BTH 184
Daniel BTH 216
David WTY 116A
DAY, Henry LGN 44
Horatio WRN 35A
Isaac CLK 79
Isaac, Jun. BKN 14
Isaac (--?) BKN 10
Jacob FLD 9
Jacob ALN 126
James FLD 12
James, Jr. GTN 122
James, Sr. GTN 122
Jane FLG 64A
Jno. J. MAS 79
John FLD 10
John FLD 12
John FLD 12
John GRN 74
John HRL 106
John HAR 164
John WRN 59A
John WTY 116A
John GSN 134A
John GNP 169A
Joseph BKN 15
Joseph GRN 63
Joseph GRN 66
Joseph FTE 70
Joseph GTN 122
Joseph GSN 133A
Joshua FLD 8
Lewis HAR 142
Lewis HAR 160
Lewis FLG 77A
Madison HAR 160
Peggy WTY 121A
Peter FLD 10
Polly FLG 37A
Reuben FLD 12
Travis FLD 9
Truman FLG 61A
Valentine GRD 97A
William GTN 122
William WTY 116A
Wm. MAD 166
Wm. FLG 59A
DAYHOFF, Fredric SHE 134A
DAYLEY, Wm. MAD 168
DAYLOR, Dibby JES 77
DAYTON, Garrett BBN 144
John CLY 114
Lewis CLY 114
DAZEY, Elijah NCH 109A
Jasper NCH 128A
Jonathan NCH 128A
Lemuel NCH 128A
DE CLARY, Peter JEF 27
DE GALLON, Henry JEF 25
DE GATTON?, Henry JEF 25
DE HART, Acklin GRT 141
Robinson JEF 24
DE MARSLEY, Andw. Lecog? JEF 25
DE PAW, Peter LNC 57
DE ZAY, G. JEF 30
DEABORN, Jonathan HAR 218
DEACON, James A. BLT 190
DEADMAN, James FTE 104
Lewis FTE 101
Richmond FTE 111
Thomas FTE 67
DEAKINS, James SHE 174
John SHE 174
DEAL, Catharine NCH 119A
David FLD 26
Isaac NCH 109A
John NSN 193
Nancy FTE 107
DEAL, William FLD 26
DEALE, James MAD 144
DEALS, John BLT 160
DEALY, Tho. MAS 65
DEAN, Abraham KNX 292
Amos FLD 20
Daniel GTN 130
Ebenezer WRN 30A
Edward CLK 101
Ellis CLK 96
George CLK 68
James CLK 97
James WYN 91A
Jeremiah CLK 97
Job FLD 33
John BRN 9
John FLD 33
John WDF 100
John GTN 123
John WRN 75A
Joseph NCH 116A
Nancy BTH 170
Robt. HRY 212
Saml. LNC 69
Thomas WDF 100A
Thos. WAS 34A
William GTN 129
Zacheus GTN 121
DEANE, James JES 91
Peter F. JES 74
Philip JES 96
DEARBON, Stephen WAS 20A
DEARE, Ruben WAS 25A
DEARENGER, John WDF 98A
DEARIN, Richd. GRN 59
DEARIN?, Daniel GRN 62
DEARING, Anne, Mrs. WYN 98A
Danl. FLG 58A
Elisha ALN 134
Francis FLG 56A
George ALN 94
George T. BRN 33
Simeon B. SCT 91A
Walker WDF 107A
Wm. ALN 120
Wm. FLG 55A
DEARINGER, Jacob WDF 101
John WDF 101
Joseph WDF 98A
Martin WDF 98A
Micheal WDF 101
Polly WDF 101
DEARMAN, Wm. FLG 59A
DEARMET, James GTN 125
DEARNIN?, Flenin? RCK 77A
Jno. RCK 82A
John RCK 82A
DEAS, Mark CLY 113
DEASE, Luke CWL 52
DEASON, Benj. TOD 134
DEATHERIDGE, Holeman LGN 35
Milly LGN 35
DEATHERIDGE?, Wm. MAD 160
DEATLEY, Jemima NCH 113A
DEATLY, Wm. FLG 24A
DEATON, Sylas OHO 7A
DEATS, Michael BLT 194
DEAVENPORT, William CSY 224
DEAVENPORTE, Hennery CSY 226
John CSY 226
Thomas CSY 228
William CSY 226

DEAVER, Richd. FKN 68
  Thos. HRD 48
DEAVERS, Clem GRN 63
  John SCT 112A
DEAVOURS, James FTE 78
  John FTE 78
DEBARA, Jessee CLK 64
DEBARD, Ephriam CLK 81
DEBAUN, Joseph MER 93
  Samuel MER 93
DEBELL, Elizabeth LWS 92A
  Joel FLG 29A
  John FLG 28A
  John WRN 63A
  Mary FLG 29A
DEBENPORT, Clem GRN 66
  John GRN 66
  Presly GRN 66
DEBILL, Wm. FLG 31A
DEBORD, James PUL 42A
  Jonathan PUL 39A
  Reuben RCK 79A
  Wm. PUL 40A
DEBRELL, Charles WYN 87A
  John L. WYN 89A
DEBRULER, John BBN 106
DEBRULER?, James
    C. HAR 220
DEBURLER?, Jacob HAR 186
DECK, John, Esq. WYN 88A
DECK?, Wm. GSN 133A
DECKER, Abner WYN 81A
  Barnet GSN 133A
  Caliss GSN 134A
  Ezekiael GSN 133A
  George WYN 81A
  Henery GSN 135A
  Jacob V. NSN 187
  John, Snr. GSN 134A
  John GSN 133A
  John GSN 134A
  M. Lodick GSN 134A
  Michael HRD 24
  Thomas WYN 91A
  Wm. PUL 47A
DECKIN?, Joseph HOP 240
DECOARSEY, Leonard CBL 12A
  William CBL 18A
DECRUT, Joseph CLK 106
DEDHAM, John HRT 157
DEDMAN, Bartlett MTG 297
  Elijah SHE 153
  John JES 74
  Peter WDF 94
DEEBO, Henry BLT 188
DEEDS, Charles TOD 131
DEEING?, Jane JEF 27
DEEK?, Wm. GSN 133A
DEEM, William HAR 168
DEEMS, Rosina HAR 166
DEEN, Ambrose GRD 107A
  Obediah CBL 15A
  Robbert CBL 13A
  Thomas CBL 15A
  Wm. MAD 180
DEEN?, (See Dun?) WAS 76A
  Jonathan HND 9
  Joshua MAD 158
DEENE, Henry, Jr. BRK 249
  Henry, Jr. BRK 251
DEER, Andrew BNE 12
  Bernard LWS 91A
  Joel BNE 12
  John BNE 12
  K--? JEF 48
  Lewis LNC 65
DEER, Richd. MAS 53
  Simeon BNE 12
DEER?, Andrew BKN 19
DEERING, Bayless MBG 140
DEESE, Denson TRG 6
DEESON, William TRG 7
DEFEVERS, John HRT 157
DEFOROE, Stephen LNC 41
DEGARNET, James MAD 110
DEGARNETT, Abijah HAR 138
DEGERNET?, John BRK 249
DEGRAFFENREID,
    Tabitha CLD 139
  William CLD 141
DEGREFFENREID,
    John CLD 139
DEHART, Elijah JEF 53
  John WYN 79A
  Nathan WYN 96A
  Wm. JEF 53
  Wm. PND 23A
DEHAVEN, Isaac BRK 249
  Isaac SCT 101A
  Jacob SCT 123A
DEHAVIN, Chris. JEF 65
DEHONEY, Rhodes OWN 100
  Thomas SCT 106A
DEHONY?, Chapman ADR 14
DEHOUSE, Geo. GRD 98A
  James GRD 99A
DEITTY, John TOD 127A
DEJUNETT, Elias HRY 222
  J--.? HRY 224
DELANA, John LNC 39
  Matthias LNC 39
DELANEY, John NCH 111A
  Joseph WRN 35A
DELANY, Abner BBN 120
  Abraham LNC 39
  Danl. BBN 112
  Edward JES 82
  Elijah MAS 62
  George W. UNN 154
  Harris SCT 128A
  Henry F. UNN 147
  James LNC 39
  Joseph LNC 39
  Joseph R. UNN 150
  Nancy UNN 150
  Will. SCT 118A
  Willis F. UNN 154
DELAY, Edward NCH 122A
  Henry BBN 68
  Jas. BBN 80
  John BTH 152
  John NCH 121A
  Saul BTH 152
DELIHA, Saml. HAR 132
DELIHAL?, Thos. L. WAS 65A
DELINAN?, Andrew BKN 8
DELINDER, Jesse GTN 132
DELONG, George FLD 23
DELP, Elijah GRD 106A
DELPH, Aaron BNE 12
  Adam BNE 12
  Joel BNE 12
  Merrymond WRN 50A
  Samuel BNE 12
DELPLH, John BNE 12
DELWIT?, Mary CLD 161
DELZELL, Abram NCH 124A
  Thomas NCH 122A
DEMAIR?, Winny FKN 92
DEMAR, Francis G. JEF 51
  Joshua JEF 51
DEMARE, Edward NSN 195
DEMAREE, Cornelius MER 93
  Cornelius MER 93
  Jacob SHE 173
  John SHE 173
  John A. SHE 173
  Peter MER 95
  Peter SHE 174
  Rachel SHE 174
  Samuel SHE 174
DEMARU?, David GTN 124
DEMAWAY, Dollson BBN 134
DEMENT, Jarrett GTN 125
  Richd. MAS 77
  Saml. FLG 26A
DEMING?, A./ H.? JEF 21
DEMINT, Elias GTN 132
  Henry GTN 132
  William GTN 125
DEMIT, Joshua BBN 130
  Wm. S. JEF 62
DEMMITT, Jas. MAS 69
  Moses MAS 69
DEMOSS, Ase JES 76
  Charles CBL 21A
  Jas. FLG 68A
  Job CBL 16A
  Lewis FLG 60A
  Peter PND 21A
  Polly FLG 68A
DEMOSS?, John BKN 11
DEMOT, Peter MER 93
DEMOTT, Daniel MER 93
  Laurance HRY 257
  Lawrence MER 93
DEMPSEE, Patrick CBL 5A
DEMPSEY, Coleman FKN 100
DENESON, John B. GRN 61
DENHAM, Alexander PUL 55A
  Elizabeth PUL 64A
  Harden WRN 42A
  Isaac N. BRN 8
  John MNR 197
  Margaret BRN 8
  Obediah PUL 55A
  Peter BRN 8
  Thomas PUL 57A
  Wm. MAD 134
DENHEART,
    Christian JEF 59
DENING, Micajah SPN 18A
DENIS, Josiah GSN 134A
DENISON, Benjn. HRT 157
  Danl. FLG 37A
  George CBL 15A
  Isaac HRT 157
  John CLD 154
  Lawton BNE 12
  Wm. GSN 133A
  Zacheriah HRT 157
  Zadock HRT 157
DENITT?, Elizabeth CBL 5A
DENKIN, John WAS 59A
DENMAN?, Peter MTG 226
DENNEL, John OHO 5A
DENNEY, Artimesia WAS 87A
  Saml. MAD 154
DENNEY?, James HRL 106
DENNING, A./ H.? JEF 21
  David SPN 8A
  Ezekiel CWL 37
  John SPN 10A
DENNING?, Robert MAD 160
DENNINGTON, Wm. CWL 52
DENNIS, Eli P. BBN 146
  Elisha GRD 102B
  Jesse FKN 74

Name	County	Page
DENNIS, John	HND	7
John	WDF	109A
Jonathan	WAS	51A
Mathew	FTE	65
Richd.	WAS	48A
Samuel	BTH	216
Samuel Y.	BTH	218
DENNISON, Adam	JEF	46
David	FTE	97
Samuel	BRN	9
DENNISS, Abraham	MBG	141A
DENNISSON, Danl.	BBN	104
James	BBN	104
John	BBN	104
DENNY, Benjamin	WYN	90A
Benjamin	WYN	98A
Charles, Jr.	WYN	93A
Charles, Sr.	WYN	83A
George	GRD	97A
Henry	WYN	95A
J. W.	JEF	24
Jerh.	PUL	41A
John	WYN	95A
John	WYN	101A
Lewis	SCT	116A
Mathew	WYN	93A
Samuel	BRN	33
William	WYN	101A
Wm.	GSN	134A
DENNY?, Levy	RCK	79A
DENSFORD, James	JEF	44
John	JEF	43
DENSON, Ophal	JEF	62
DENT, William	BLT	190
William	WRN	68A
Wm.	BRK	251
DENTON, David	WRN	55A
Dorcas	CLD	155
Geo.	GRD	113A
Henry	GRD	116A
Isaac	CLD	151
Isaac	WYN	84A
James	GTN	129
John	LNC	47
John	WAS	41A
John	GRD	108A
John	GRD	115A
John Sr.	GRD	96A
Joseph	LGN	28
Joseph	LNC	41
Joseph	BTH	196
Mary	LGN	38
Reubin	HND	11A
Saml.	HND	11A
Samuel	HOP	240
Sarah	BTH	196
Sarah	HND	10A
West	BTH	196
William	LNC	47
William	BTH	196
DEPENPORT?, Samuel	ETL	40
DEPEW, A. R.	MAS	79
Abram	BNE	12
DEPOYSTER, John	BTL	319
DEPP, Joel	BRN	33
Peter	BRN	8
Peter	BRN	33
William	BRN	9
DEPREAST?, Robert	HRL	106
DEPRIEST, John	UNN	154
DEPUYSTER, Thomas	WRN	34A
DERBY, James	BTH	216
DERHA, (See Desha)	MAS	73
DERHAM, Elijah	WTY	112A
James	LNC	57
John	HRT	157
DERHAM, John	WDF	112A
DERINGTON, Wilkins	SPN	10A
DERIXSON, Ephraim	BBN	114
DERNAL, Anderson	SPN	21A
DERNIT?, Richd.	BBN	132
DEROSETT, James	FLD	47
DERRYFIELD, Enos	FLD	20
DERSE?, Zacariah	HRD	58
DERYBERRY, John	SPN	10A
DESARN?, Frank	CLY	124
DESFORGES, Stephen H.	FTE	60
DESHA, John	BBN	72
DESHA?, Benjm.	MAS	73
Jos.	MAS	73
DESHAY, John	GSN	134A
DESHAZER, Henry	LNC	61
DESKINS, Daniel	BTH	174
John	FLD	42
DESMUKS, Will	GRD	94A
DESPER, Overton	TOD	134
DESRANGES, Jerome	FTE	61
DESSENPORT?, Samuel	ETL	40
DETHARADGE, Philamon	MAD	122
DETHERAGE, Isaac	FKN	134
James	SPN	13A
Lewis	SPN	13A
Mary	SHE	113A
P.	TOD	131A
DETHERDGE, Byrd	MAD	154
DETHERIDGE, John	SPN	16A
DEULANEY, Elijah	BNE	12
DEULANY, Susan	BNE	12
DEVANPORT, Abram	CLK	88
Patsey	TRG	4
DEVENPORT, Alice	WDF	115A
Elias	MAD	148
Fortunatus	WRN	28A
James	WDF	119A
Jas.	SCT	118A
John	WDF	119A
Osburn	WYN	95A
Richard	TRG	11A
Richard	WRN	36A
Thos.	FLG	27A
Wm.	CHN	39
Wm.	MAD	118
Zechariah	WTY	110A
DEVER, Henry E.	CHN	33
John, Jr.	MAD	164
John, Sr.	MAD	164
John	WAS	27A
Will	MAS	68
William	CHN	29A
DEVERN, John	FTE	58
DEVERS, John	NCH	105
Jos.	TOD	130A
Michael	NCH	105
DEVIN, James	LNC	7
DEVINS, Sally	WDF	100A
DEVIRE?, Stephen	LWS	98A
DEVITT?, Elizabeth	CBL	5A
DEVORE, David	FTE	85
Henry	BKN	16
Jeremiah	BKN	16
John	FTE	93
John	GNP	176A
Joseph	NSN	213
Moses	FTE	95
Samuel	FTE	93
Wm.	BKN	16
DEVORS, Michl.	BBN	78
DEVOUIN?, Jno.	ALN	136
DEVOUR, Harrison	BRK	251
DEVOUR, John	HRT	157
DEW, William F.	TRG	7
DEWBERRY, John	CLD	138
DEWEES, Farmer	FTE	58
Jesse	CLD	152
Mildred, Mrs.	GRT	144
William, Mas.	GRT	146
DEWEESE, Cornelius	BRN	8
David	BRN	8
Elisha	BRN	8
Henry	BTL	321
John	BTL	321
Samuel	BRN	8
DEWESE, Benjin.	GSN	133A
Daniel	GSN	133A
Edward	GSN	133A
Jane	KNX	314
Lewis	CLY	119
W. John	GSN	134A
Will.	KNX	306
DEWETT, Abraham	NSN	195
DEWHITT, William	MBG	143
DEWIT, Bennet	HRD	58
DEWITT, Aaron	GRN	69
Ann	HRD	76
Benjamin	BTH	214
Danl.	MAS	69
Henry	FLG	47A
Isaac	HRD	76
Jacob	HRD	76
Jacob	NCH	111A
James	NSN	195
Jno.	FKN	144
John	NSN	194
Nancy	NSN	194
Tarlton	HRY	212
DEWS, John	SCT	127A
Samuel	WRN	63A
DEZERN?, Nathaniel	HND	9A
DIAL, Alex.	LVG	6
Benjamin	BRK	251
James	WRN	67A
Thomas	WRN	32A
Wm. F.	WRN	51A
DIAL?, Isaac	WRN	50A
Samuel	WRN	50A
DIARMET, John	GTN	130
Thomas	GTN	130
DIBBY, Ignatious	GSN	134A
DICAS, Andrew	TOD	127
Hugh	TOD	132
John	TOD	132
DICE, Benjn.	ADR	16
DICK, Alexander	PUL	60A
Archibald	BRN	9
Archibald	PUL	61A
Coonrod	SPN	12A
Jacob	JEF	64
John, Senr.	PUL	67A
John	SPN	12A
John	PUL	61A
Peter	SPN	12A
Philip	JEF	57
Samuel	PUL	60A
DICKEN, ----t?	DVS	7A
Christopher	DVS	18A
Ephraim	MNR	193
Henry	SCT	113A
DICKENS, James	BNE	12
Richard	BNE	12
Stephen	BTH	172
DICKENSON, Saml.	JEF	23
Thomas	BRN	7
Thomas	BRN	8
William	BRN	8
DICKERSON, Archiba	CBL	14A

DICKERSON, Ben WAS 20A
Cephias? MNR 217
David JES 78
David KNX 282
Elisha CLK 105
Ezekiel ETL 40
Fanny MER 93
Fountain JES 69
Francis GRN 52
Griffith CLY 118
Henry MNR 215
Jacob FTE 74
James MNR 201
Jeremiah JES 79
John BBN 102
John R. MNR 217
Lewis JES 69
Mary CBL 10A
Samuel CBL 10A
Solomon MNR 217
William JES 69
William NSN 196
William CBL 10A
William WYN 84A
DICKESON, Catherine BLT 168
Thomas FTE 70
DICKEY, Adam MTG 271
Alexander BBN 116
David LVG 5
Ebenezer SPN 12A
Elisha BRN 8
Jamison D. WRN 46A
Jas. HRD 64
Jas. FLG 23A
John CHN 41A
John S. GRN 73
Robert MTG 231
Robert MTG 281
Thomas MTG 239
Will. LVG 5
William WRN 45A
DICKIN, Joseph HOP 240
Joseph CBL 20A
Simeon MER 93
Thos. WAS 68A
DICKINSON, Joel WRN 57A
John WRN 57A
Mary WRN 56A
Mary WRN 64A
Teague JEF 43
Valentine WRN 57A
Wm. CHN 45
DICKISON, Elizabeth NCH 123A
Noah BKN 8
DICKS, Joseph CBL 22A
William CBL 22A
DICKSON, David HAR 144
Greenberry WYN 80A
Henry FLD 36
Hiram TRG 6
Jno. HAR 138
John WYN 80A
Rutha UNN 154
Sally BTH 170
Thos. MAD 102
Tilman LVG 10
William FTE 77
William ALN 100
DICKY, Ann WDF 113A
Hays MER 95
James LVG 12
Michael WDF 113A
Robert WAS 83A
Saml. KNX 296
DICKY, William MER 93
DICTUM, Richard CBL 14A
DIDDLE, Wm. ADR 14
DIDLAKE, George B. CLK 102
Robert CLK 96
DIE, Fentelroy WAS 86A
Isaac CBL 16A
DIER, John WAS 34A
John WAS 34A
DIGBEY, William CBL 16A
DIGGINS, Betsey FTE 60
DIGGS, Barby MAD 162
Colo? MAD 128
DIGLAW?, Jas. MAS 58
DIGMAN, Peter MAS 73
DIKE, William PUL 62A
DIKE?, Nelson JES 96
DIKES, John, Snr. GSN 133A
John GSN 133A
DILBACK, Abram BTL 319
Jacob UNN 151
Polly BTL 319
DILCE, Nelson JES 96
DILINESS?, Michael BKN 11
DILINGHAM, Henry MAD 118
DILLAN, Mary MAS 63
DILLARD, Jas. HRD 30
Lewis CHN 28
Ryland T. CLK 105
Wm. CHN 35A
DILLEN, Mary SHE 115A
DILLER, Jere. JEF 24
DILLERFORD, John BKN 13
DILLINER?, John GTN 120
DILLINGER, Jacob MAD 142
DILLINGHAM, Drison CSY 224
James CWL 34
Jos. CWL 34
Lott CSY 224
Michael WRN 56A
Vachael L. MBG 143A
Vachel WRN 56A
William HOP 240
DILLINNER, Wm. MAD 130
DILLION, Henry HRL 106
DILLMAN, Andrew JES 93
DILLOE, Rachel SHE 173
DILLON, --ward? JES 86
Abner FLG 63A
Abrah FLG 67A
Amos FLG 63A
David UNN 154
Eli FLG 69A
Henry LGN 41
Isaiah FLG 63A
James FKN 152
James SHE 175
John FLG 63A
John D. FTE 55
Thomas B. GTN 119
DILLS, Abraham HAR 206
Casniah? HRT 157
Charles HAR 206
David HAR 202
Harman HAR 206
John UNN 151
John HAR 212
Thomas GRN 56
William FLD 39
DILLY, Elizabeth BRN 9
DILMAN, Andrew BKN 15
Ann? GTN 129
Frederick BKN 11
DILS, Elijah HAR 138
Saml. HAR 138
DILTS?, John CBL 20A
DILWORTH, Thomas WRN 76A
DIN---DY?, Wm. ALN 130
DINGEMAN, Jacob CHN 29
DINGLE, Edwd. SCT 139A
Richd. SCT 111A
William NCH 108A
DINKIN?, Marvel ALN 98
DINNINGHAM, Champness CSY 224
DINSMORE, Henry, Jr. NCH 123A
Henry NCH 123A
John FLG 59A
John WYN 96A
John NCH 127A
Robt. FLG 60A
Thomas ETL 42
DINWIDDEE, Wm. BBN 110
DINWIDDI, James MAD 170
Thos. MAD 174
Wm. MAD 166
DINWIDDIE, David LNC 25
Eliz. HRY 266
Hanah LNC 33
John LNC 7
Robert FKN 138
Thos., Jr. SCT 126A
Thos. SCT 126A
Wm. LNC 25
DINWIDDY, Wm. HRD 20
DINWIDE, James MAD 136
DINWIDI, Robert MAD 124
DINWIDY, Tho. ALN 144
Wm. ALN 144
DIRHAM, James KNX 310
Jesse KNX 284
Will. KNX 310
DISHER, Christopher BKN 19
Peter MAS 54
DISHMAN, J---? SPN 15A
James WRN 63A
Jeffery WYN 99A
Jeremiah SPN 15A
John FTE 56
William BRN 8
William FTE 108
Wm. CHN 43
DISMORE, Henry, Jr. NSN 218
John NSN 217
DISMUKES, Joseph MER 93
Willis (Free) LGN 37
DISON, (See Dixon) HAR 136
John MNR 199
DITT, Sarah ALN 144
DITTERLINE, Will. LVG 5
DITTO, Henry, Junr. HRD 56
Henry, Senr. HRD 74
William HRD 12
DITTOE, (See Dilloe) SHE 173
Abram SHE 162
William SHE 172
DITWORTH, John CWL 43
DIVINE, Andrew MER 93
David MER 93
George MER 93
James MER 93
John MER 93
Joseph MER 93
Nathan MTG 299
Roger FKN 58
Samuel MER 93
DIVINS, Esther BKN 23

Name	County	Page
DIX, Jno.	MAS	71
Severn	MAS	77
Thos.	BKN	11
DIXON, Alexander	HRL	106
Aron	FLG	63A
Bur.? Om?	BNE	12
Ebenezer	MTG	287
Geo.	FLG	28A
George	HAR	136
Henry	BNE	12
Henry	HND	11A
James	CLY	119
James	HAR	184
Jas.	FLG	28A
Jessee	MBG	139
Jno.	FKN	86
John	FLD	3
John	BNE	12
John	HRL	106
John	FLG	28A
Joseph	NSN	191
Richard R.	HAR	176
Robert	LWS	98A
Roswell	HAR	134
Thomas	MNR	197
Thos.	FLG	28A
William	FLD	24
William E.	BTL	321
Wynn	HND	10A
DIXSON, Mrs.	MAS	78
Benjn.	MAS	75
David	MAS	75
George	CLK	86
Henry	WRN	47A
Hollensby	WRN	47A
James	LWS	93A
John	WRN	46A
Will	MAS	70
DO--NG?, Abednigo	WYN	91A
DO--THAN?, Hawkins	BTH	218
Thomas	BTH	218
DOAK, David	ADR	14
DOAKES, David	BKN	5
DOANE, Benjamin	HAR	176
William	HAR	176
DOATY, Elijah	BRK	251
DOBBINS, -----?	CWL	41
-----?	DVS	12A
James	CWL	43
John	LVG	14
DOBBINS?, -----?	DVS	12A
DOBBS, David	ALN	138
Henry	ALN	104
James	WAS	27A
John	ALN	114
John, Sr.	WYN	95A
William, Jr.	WYN	98A
William	WYN	95A
DOBSON, George L./ S.?	CLK	94
James	GRN	62
Joseph	GRN	61
Tho.	ALN	122
DOBYNS, Apollis C.	FLG	24A
Berry	MAS	64
Chas.	MAS	66
Danl.	MAS	57
Edwd.	MAS	64
Enoch	MAS	69
Jas.	FLG	24A
Lanson?	MAS	52
Leroy	MAS	55
Lew	MBG	143A
Sally	HOP	240
Tho.	MAS	58
DOCKERY, Richard P	HOP	240

Name	County	Page
DOCKINS, Wm.	JEF	59
DOCREY?, John	ADR	16
Robert	MAD	168
DOCSEY?, John	ADR	16
DODD, Daniel	SHE	124A
David	BTH	162
Edward	JEF	37
Geo.	JEF	68
Henry	GRD	92A
James	BRN	9
James, Jr.	BRN	8
James	GRD	102B
Jno.	LNC	57
Jno.	FKN	94
John	BRN	8
John	FTE	86
John	MAD	136
John, Jas. Son	BRN	7
John, Jr.	JEF	39
Lewis	SPN	6A
Margaret	BRN	9
Margaret	WRN	59A
Mary	NSN	219
Pablo?	BBN	90
Richard	NSN	219
Thomas	FTE	99
Thos.	JEF	50
Wm.	FKN	90
DODD?, Milly	HRY	266
DODDS, Albert?	CWL	40
Francis?	CWL	40
Henry	CWL	39
James	LVG	5
Jane	LVG	6
John	CWL	39
John	LNC	55
William	WRN	71A
DODDY, James	HRT	157
John	BRN	8
DODGE, Dorcas, Mrs.	CLK	104
Jno.	CWL	52
Malicke?	HAR	180
Richard	UNN	152
DODSON, Dilingham	ALN	98
Dorcas	HAR	190
Elias	JEF	50
Elijah	CLY	114
Isaac	MTG	281
DOEG?, John	LGN	33
DOERCY?, Robert	MAD	168
DOFFICE?, Harald	SPN	10A
DOGAN, Jerrett	HRY	268
Lovell H.	PUL	45A
Samuel	PUL	63A
DOGE, Richd.	CWL	52
DOGGET, George	BBN	124
Richd.	FLG	38A
DOGGETT, Benjamin	BBN	66
DOGHEAD, Henry	BTH	196
Prestley	SHE	112A
Thomas	BTH	196
Wm.	SHE	112A
DOHARTY, Robert	WRN	32A
DOHERDY, Johnest?	BTH	192
DOHERTY, Andrew	WYN	86A
Daniel	BTL	321
John	BTL	321
Owen	MAS	54
Thomas	BTL	321
DOHONEY, Jas., Senr.	SCT	122A
Jas.	SCT	130A
Jas.	SCT	133A
Thos.	ADR	16
Willis	SCT	122A

Name	County	Page
DOIL, Mathew	WAS	20A
Richd. G.	HRT	157
Saml.	HRT	157
DOKE, Alexander	WRN	69A
James	JES	73
John H.	WRN	69A
Robert	JES	73
Thomas	MER	93
William	MER	93
DOLALSON, Joseph	JEF	64
DOLAN, William	FTE	70
DOLANSON, Robert	JEF	43
DOLES, Thomas	TRG	12
DOLIN, Edward	WYN	95A
DOLLARHIDE, Thomas	PUL	56A
DOLLAS?, William	NCH	113A
DOLLENS, Mathew	BNE	12
DOLLERHIDE, John	CBL	6A
DOLLINS, James	LNC	79
Reuben	LNC	35
William	LNC	3
Wm.	BNE	12
DOLLIS, Henry	FLG	36A
Susan	FLG	36A
DOLLITSON, Andrew	LVG	8
DOLLY, Owen	MAS	52
DOLLY?, Richard	JES	73
DOLLYHITE, Francy	BLT	180
DOLSON, Stephen	CBL	22A
DOLTON, Elijah	PUL	58A
George	ALN	116
George	PUL	54A
James	ALN	116
John	CBL	20A
Tho.	ALN	116
Wm.	JEF	32
DOLTON?, Isham	MAD	126
DOME, Daniel	GRN	63
DONAHOO, James	WRN	36A
DONALDSON, Alex.	BTH	168
Cary	WRN	75A
James	GTN	125
John	CLK	100
John	BTH	168
Prestley	WRN	75A
William	CLK	71
DONALSON, Robert	MAD	128
William	BLT	178
DONALSON?, John	JEF	43
DONAM, John M.	BRN	8
DONAN, David C.	HRT	156
DONATHAN, Nelson	BTH	202
DONAVAN, James	PND	15A
DONAVON, Joseph	LWS	92A
Thomas	LWS	92A
DONAWAY, Amy	ETL	52
Chas.	PND	30A
Isaac	ETL	51
John	ETL	52
William	ETL	54
DONDUETT?, Nathaniel	TRG	6A
DONE?, Abner	HAR	158
DONEGHY, Hugh, Sr.	MER	93
James	MER	93
DONEGHY?, Hugh, Jr.	MER	117
Paul	MER	116
DONELL, John	RCK	82A
DONELSON, Barbary	BTH	162
Jas.	BTH	150
DONEVAN, Gilbert	BKN	4
DONIPHAN, Anderson	MAS	54
George	BKN	24
DONITHAN, John	BTH	214
DONLEY, Cornelius	SCT	106A

Name	County	Page
DONLEY, Hugh	ETL	40
T.	TOD	125
Thomas	CLK	74
William C.	LGN	24
DONNALDSON, James W.	WRN	39A
DONNALLY, Patk.	JEF	47
DONNELL, Robert	NCH	124A
Thomas	NCH	124A
DONNELLY, James	SHE	160
DONNOHUE, Hugh	LGN	37
DONOHO, Jessey	MAD	92
Major	FTE	107
Rice	MAD	106
Robert	MAD	108
DONOHOO, Patrick	NSN	209
DONOHOO?, Daniel	NSN	188
DONOHOOE?, Mathew	BTH	202
DONOLDSON, Wm.	MAS	55
DONOLSON, Henly	BNE	12
DONOVAN, Alexr.	MAS	69
Chasn?	WRN	75A
Cornelius	BBN	72
Jacob	BKN	14
Jacob F.	BKN	14
James	BKN	16
James	BBN	74
Jeremiah	MER	93
Tho. M.	MAS	60
Will	MAS	53
DONOVON, Leonard	NCH	124A
DONOWAY, Jno.	MAS	72
DOOD / DORD?, Ferdinand	BKN	9
DOOD?, Dorothy	FTE	90
DOOLEN, Permelia	BLT	194
DOOLEY, Elizabeth	CLK	97
Enoch	LVG	8
George	LNC	35
Henry	CLK	82
Jacob	GRD	111A
John	CLK	97
Obadiah	CLK	97
Obid	CLK	97
Stephen	CLK	97
DOOLIN, Alex?	WRN	31A
Elizabeth	FTE	82
John	BTL	321
Lodd / Loda?	CHN	32A
Mary	PUL	48A
Thos.	PUL	36A
DOOLING?, Daniel	LVG	15
Jesse	LVG	15
William	LVG	15
DOOLY, Catharine	FKN	122
Gideon	MAD	154
Jacob	MAD	158
Jobe	MAD	158
Nancy	FKN	128
Sedy	ADR	16
DOOM, Benjamin	NSN	177
Edmond	NSN	180
Jacob	CWL	52
Sarah	CWL	38
DOOMS, David	CWL	38
Henry	CWL	43
DOORN?, Jesse C.	TOD	132A
DORAN, Richard	NSN	191
DORCH, Isaac	HND	12
DORDOUGH, James	HAR	150
DOREGHTY, Robert	WAS	20A
DOREN, John	GSN	133A
DORIN, Patrick	WAS	63A
Phillip	MAS	61
DORIS?, William	HOP	240
DORITHY?, Lewis	CLK	86
DORITY, William	CLK	73
DORLAND?, Abraham	NCH	125A
DORMAN, Matthew	GTN	120
Thos.	FLG	24A
DORNIGIN, Patrick	FTE	92
DORR?, Daniel	FTE	110
DORREL?, James	BTH	182
DORRELL?, Will	GRD	84A
DORRIS, John	HND	9
Samuel	SPN	23A
DORROW, John	NCH	118A
William, Sr.	NCH	119A
William	NCH	119A
DORROW?, James	NCH	115A
DORSAN, Benjamin	FTE	94
John	FTE	96
Thomas	FTE	96
DORSE, Aaron	SHE	167
DORSE?, Abner	HAR	158
DORSEL?, James	BTH	182
DORSEN, Jeremiah	HRT	157
Thomas	HRT	156
DORSEY, Beal	HRD	42
Caleb	JEF	44
Charles	BRK	251
Chs. G.	JEF	54
Corborn N.	JEF	63
Edward	WAS	18A
Edwd.	FLG	79A
Elias	SHE	162
Henry C.	JEF	44
Jeremiah	BRN	9
John	FLG	73A
Johnsy	WAS	45A
Jos. J. / I.?	FLG	73A
Levin	JEF	60
Nimrod	JEF	58
Reason	FTE	77
Richd.	HRD	20
Richd.	WAS	45A
Robt.	HRT	156
Sarah	HRD	54
Thos.	HRD	18
Westley	JEF	62
DORSON, James	FTE	92
Jonathan	ALN	142
Samuel	SHE	163
DORSON?, Ana-?	ALN	132
Nimrod	HRL	106
DORTO-?, Edward	FLD	36
DORTON, George	SHE	168
Lewis	SHE	168
Moses	KNX	284
DORY, James	BKN	9
John	BKN	9
DOSIER, Lenard	MAD	160
Richard	MAD	164
DOSIER?, Lucy	FKN	108
DOSS, Ambrose	CLD	142
Ambrose	WRN	52A
Azariah	MBG	133A
Jane	SPN	12A
Joel	PUL	68A
Moses	PUL	55A
Nancy, Mrs.	WYN	104A
Rhoda	CLD	162
William	WYN	99A
DOSSET, John	HOP	240
Thomas	HOP	242
DOSSEY, Noah	HND	10
DOSSON, Joseph	BTH	180
DOSWELL, Peyton	HND	8A
DOTSAN, Jos. N.	BRK	251
DOTSON, Chs.	PUL	40A
Daniel	NCH	110A
Eli	SHE	139A
DOTSON, Elijah	NCH	106A
George, Sen.	WYN	85A
George	WYN	79A
Isaac	NSN	197
James	WYN	84A
James	NCH	120A
Jer.	SHE	130A
Jonathan	NSN	197
Leonard	WYN	93A
Martha	NCH	120A
Martin	CHN	40A
Mary	KNX	284
Robert	WYN	93A
Westly	NSN	197
William	NSN	197
DOTTON?, Isham	MAD	126
DOTTSON, Jeremiah	LNC	81
Lambert	LNC	7
Thomas	LNC	65
DOTTY, Elijah	HRD	40
DOTY, Azriah	GRD	116A
Jesse	GRD	85A
John	GRD	85A
DOUBLE, Joseph	BNE	12
DOUCH, Wm.	GNP	173A
DOUCKY, Celia	LVG	6
DOUD?, Hezekiah	HAR	156
James	HAR	156
DOUGAN, Mary	HRD	52
DOUGE?, James	GRN	71
DOUGHERTY, Alexr.	MAS	60
Andrew	FLG	64A
Charles	CLD	153
Chas.	HRD	52
Chas.	MAS	69
Daniel	WRN	57A
Elizabeth	CLD	137
James	BKN	20
James	GTN	119
James H.	MNR	213
Jas.	HRD	54
Jas., Junr.	HRD	54
Jesse	NCH	117A
John	HRD	50
John	HRD	72
John	JES	88
John	NCH	117A
John	NCH	129A
Michael	BRN	8
Michael	MAS	68
Michl.	HRY	198
Philip	WDF	112A
Robert	BRN	9
Robt. S.	HRY	180
Saml.	BBN	76
Thomas	WDF	103
Thos.	FLG	63A
DOUGHLAS, Reton	BTH	180
DOUGHTY, James	WRN	56A
John	NCH	127A
Preston	WRN	53A
Skellman	NCH	114A
Stephen	WRN	56A
Thomas	NCH	118A
Widow	BBN	74
William	NCH	111A
Wm.	BBN	96
DOUGLAS, Alexander	HAR	216
Andrew	SHE	135A
Jas.	HRY	268
John	HAR	218
Jonathan	HAR	220
Wm.	GNP	177A
DOUGLASS, Charles	GRN	60
Charles, Jr.	GRN	60
David	MTG	245

Name	County	Page
DOUGLASS, Geo.	MAS	63
Hezekiah	WDF	113A
Jeremiah	SCT	106A
Jno.	PUL	37A
Jonathan	BTL	321
Joseph	SCT	91A
Richard	HAR	182
Robert	GRN	74
Samuel	BRN	9
Tho.	PUL	47A
William	BRN	8
William	MER	93
William	FTE	107
William	BTH	202
William	MTG	267
DOUITT, Peter	CLK	86
DOUITT?, Frederic	CLK	86
DOULEY?, George	HAR	166
DOUNING, Caty	SHE	130A
DOUP, Danl.	JEF	40
George	JEF	40
DOUTHARD, Benjamin K.?	SHE	115A
DOUTHART, Thomas	CSY	212
DOUTHET, Silas	FKN	84
DOUTHETT, Lewis	CLK	90
DOUWNARD?, Thos.	BKN	19
DOVE, Henry	PUL	64A
DOVER, Abraham	JEF	51
Absolem	HND	7
Jacob	GRN	64
John	JEF	43
DOVIN?, Benjamin	NSN	177
DOWAN, Mrs.	MAS	71
Susan	MAS	70
DOWDALL, Barnett W.	HRY	196
Timothey	HRY	188
Wm.	HRD	56
DOWDEL, John	WAS	76A
DOWDELL, Thomas	HRD	54
DOWDEN, James, Jr.	MAD	144
Jno.	MAS	61
William	FTE	67
DOWDON, Nathaniel	SHE	172
DOWEL, Ambrose	PUL	49A
David	ALN	106
Elijah	BRK	249
George	BRK	249
John	BRK	251
Littlebury	BRK	251
Micajah	BRK	249
Nemiah, Jr.	BRK	251
Nemiah, Sr.	BRK	251
Nimrod	BRK	249
Richd.	PUL	43A
Thos.	BRK	251
DOWELL, Fielding	WYN	91A
Harrison	GRN	66
James	HRD	24
Reubin	WYN	101A
DOWELL?, Will	GRD	84A
DOWENS, Jos.	MAS	70
DOWIN, Hannah, Mrs.	WYN	89A
DOWIS, Isaac	KNX	304
Jesse	KNX	300
Rebecca	KNX	300
DOWIS?, Mary	KNX	290
DOWKINGS, Jno.	HRY	244
DOWLING, William	FTE	79
DOWLS, Thomas	FTE	107
Wm.	FKN	96
DOWNARD, David	CBL	15A
Samuel	HAR	212
DOWNARD?, Adam	BKN	19
DOWNES, Wm.	HRD	24
DOWNEY, Abraham, Senr.	WRN	62A
Alex	CWL	35
Alexr.	LGN	39
Jaley/ Joley?	CLK	103
James	LNC	23
James	MER	93
James	MTG	263
Jesse	SPN	15A
Job	TOD	128A
Martin	WRN	62A
Polly	MNR	199
Samuel	HOP	242
Sarah	NCH	119A
William	CSY	208
DOWNEY?, Abraham, Jr.	WRN	62A
DOWNING, Alexander	HAR	220
Benjamin	MNR	199
Clary	FTE	60
Elisha	MBG	142A
Francis	FTE	60
Francis	FTE	83
Francis	SCT	107A
Geo.	FKN	58
Jane	MAS	71
Jno.	MAS	64
Jno.	MAS	71
Jno.	HRY	251
John	JEF	35
John	FTE	63
John	JES	96
John	GRD	100A
John	SCT	138A
John	MBG	140A
Jos.	MAS	70
Joseph	FTE	66
Joseph	FTE	75
Joseph	MBG	139A
Nancy	MAS	71
Reason	MAS	70
Richard	FTE	67
Sarah	MNR	199
Stephen	MBG	143
Will	GRD	105A
William	FTE	85
DOWNINGS, Tho.	MAS	64
DOWNS, -----?	DVS	9A
Abraham	MTG	251
Andrew	BRN	9
Benjamin	FTE	105
Benoni P.	JES	72
Burrell	BRN	9
Francis E./ C.?	NSN	187
Henry	WDF	103
Jacob	MTG	283
John	SHE	170
John	NSN	182
John, Jr.	NSN	222
John	FLG	29A
John	GNP	175A
Jonathan	NSN	193
Peter	GSN	134A
Richard	GSN	133A
Robert, Jr.	MTG	257
Robert, Sr.	MTG	255
Susan	CHN	34
Susannah	JES	90
Thomas	BTH	192
Thomas	DVS	15A
William	GTN	121
Zacheriah	BRN	9
Zacheriah	HRT	157
DOWNS?, (See Dawns?)	GSN	133A
DOWNTON, Richd.	FTE	95
Thomas	FTE	86
DOWNY, Abraham, Junr.	WRN	62A
Alexander	CHN	34A
George	ADR	16
DOWTAIN, Wm.	MAS	61
DOWTHART, Jno.	HRY	251
Mary	HRY	251
DOYAL, Allen	ALN	98
Gregory	WRN	50A
DOYEL, Farmer	SHE	165
DOYEL?, Isaac	WRN	50A
Samuel	WRN	50A
DOYL, Alexander	LVG	10
DOYLE, Chas.	MAS	77
James	SCT	130A
John	LGN	40
John	WRN	44A
John	FLG	50A
John	WRN	50A
Theo-.?	FLG	76A
William	CBL	8A
DOZER, James	LWS	98A
John	WDF	99
DOZIER, Evans	CBL	2A
James J.	BLT	174
John	CLK	64
John	MBG	135
William	CLK	102
Zackariah, Senr.	CLK	64
DRACE, Daniel	KNX	290
DRAFFIN, R.	TOD	134
R., Jr.	TOD	132A
Wm.	TOD	134
DRAGOO, Jane	BLT	194
John	NSN	194
DRAIN, Robert	BTH	196
Stephen	SHE	150
DRAK, John G.	BTL	321
DRAKE, Abrm. S.	FTE	59
Allbritain	MBG	142
Allen	HRD	62
Ann	JES	93
Asa	MAS	66
Benj.	SHE	139A
Berry	BRN	9
Brexton	HRD	54
Carter	CSY	210
Charles	FLD	26
Charles	BLT	184
Chas.	HRD	54
Cornelious	MAS	66
Edward	ADR	16
Edward	FTE	109
Jacob	MAS	66
Jessee	CBL	23A
Jno.	MAS	53
Jno.	MAS	71
John	JEF	25
John	JEF	63
Juliana	JES	82
Michael	FLD	26
Mosley C.	MBG	142
Nancy	BLT	170
Peggy	JES	93
Peter	FLD	20
Rachell	SCT	100A
Sally	HRD	10
Samuel	MBG	138
Silas	MBG	142
Tarlton	WRN	30A
Taylor	LGN	47
Thos.	ADR	16
Thos.	HRY	250
Will Henry	FTE	80

DRAKE, William HRD 10
William WRN 51A
Wm. ADR 16
DRANE, Anthony BRN 9
Ed.,, Dr. HRY 241
George WAS 31A
Joel WAS 32A
Joseph WAS 67A
Stephen WAS 32A
Thomas O. LGN 29
Thos. WAS 32A
Walter WAS 32A
Wm. WAS 67A
DRANE?, Theodore L. HRY 210
DRAPER, Jno. HAR 166
John CLD 164
Martin HAR 162
Thos. CWL 37
Wm. BNE 12
DREDEN, Jno. MAS 62
DRENEN, John SCT 97A
DRENNON, Hugh FLG 65A
Saml. CWL 52
Thos. FLG 62A
DRENNONS, John CWL 31
DREON, George LGN 45
Henry LGN 45
DREON?, William LGN 35
DRESDEN, Stephen MAS 65
DREURY?, Levy RCK 78A
DREVN?, William LGN 35
DREW, Clementine LGN 25
Francis W. LGN 41
John MER 93
DREWIN?, William GRN 60
DRIESDALE, John CBL 18A
DRIMENSEL?, Anthoney FTE 59
DRINNARD?, Joshua BBN 132
DRINNING, William SPN 10A
DRISDALE, James MTG 283
DRISKEL, David GTN 124
David GTN 129
Davis GTN 124
Timothy GTN 124
DRISKELL, Dennis FKN 142
Joseph LVG 15
Nancy BRK 251
Peter MAS 57
Wm. BRK 251
DRISKILL, David FKN 158
James LVG 15
John TOD 130A
DRIVER, Francis SCT 101A
Polly MNR 209
DROWDUS, Judith WAS 22A
William WAS 22A
DRUING, Richard GNP 175A
DRUMMON?, William CSY 222
DRUMMOND, David HAR 208
Parker NCH 111A
DRUMMONDS, Amos NCH 128A
DRURY, Charles NSN 209
Daniel LVG 15
Elias HRD 30
Ignatus NSN 209
Jas. HRD 92
John UNN 149
Mary NSN 211
Michal MNR 193
Samuel HRD 92
Thos. WAS 73A
Wm. LNC 27
DRURY?, -----? LVG 16
DRY, George ALN 122
DRYDEN, Jane HAR 168
Martha NCH 128A
William WTY 120A
DRYSDAL, Reubin JES 94
DRYSDALE, James CBL 18A
DU--?, Mary ADR 16
DUANE, Patrick NSN 210
DUAY, Thomas BTL 321
DUBERLY, William JEF 31
DUBONG, Wm JEF 30
DUBREE, Benjamin BLT 158
Giles BLT 158
DUCAN, Hewitt SCT 94A
DUCHER?, William WDF 107A
DUCK, Dd. BBN 138
James PUL 57A
Josiah, Senr. PUL 64A
Josiah PUL 58A
DUCKER, Abraham SHE 109A
Benjamin LGN 23
Enoch WDF 104
James SHE 124A
John, Jr. CBL 14A
John, Sr. CBL 14A
Nathnl. PND 27A
DUCKERMAN, William WDF 104
DUCKET, John WRN 59A
DUCKETT, Caleb HRY 206
Isaac BBN 88
William NCH 124A
DUCKHAM, Prior CWL 35
Thos. FKN 70
DUCKWORTH, Absolem CWL 33
Elijah HRD 18
George GRN 76
George BTH 154
George W. BTH 154
Isaac GRN 77
John GRN 76
John BTH 148
Simon BTH 154
William MTG 275
DUCT?, William HAR 148
DUCTT?, John BBN 110
DUDERY, Conrod LNC 67
Saml. LNC 81
DUDGEON, James BNE 12
Wm. M. BNE 12
DUDGEONS, William LNC 71
DUDLESON, Nelson GRD 110A
DUDLEY, A. TOD 131A
Ambrose FTE 89
Ambrose FTE 90
Benjamin W. FTE 62
Dotson NCH 105
Elijah FLG 23A
Elisabeth FKN 62
Gardner CWL 52
James FTE 89
Jephthat FKN 60
John GRN 80
John CLK 105
John NCH 129A
Lucy FTE 91
Peter FKN 66
Robert LGN 33
Robert MGB 137A
Robt. BBN 120
Robt., Capt. CHN 44A
William GRN 80
William E. FTE 89
Wm. ADR 50
Wm. FLG 23A
Wm. TOD 131A
Wm.? CWL 37
DUELT?, John BBN 110
DUERSON, Lucy MAD 98
Thos. JEF 50
Wm. JEF 50
DUERSON?, William FTE 91
DUESE, Peter CLY 132
DUET?, William HAR 148
DUETT?, John BBN 110
DUFF, Daniel FLD 8
Daniel MTG 297
Danl. CLY 114
Fieling ALN 132
Hubbard ALN 132
John BRN 8
John KNX 294
John GRD 119A
M. B. JEF 25
Nathaniel WRN 58A
Patrick JEF 35
Patrick, Sr. JEF 36
Robert SPN 22A
Ths. JEF 47
Will MAS 53
William MNR 201
DUFFEE, Moses MAS 65
DUFFER, Chas. HRY 252
DUFFY, Allen FLG 72A
Lewis HRD 66
DUFNER, Jacob HRD 16
DUFRIEND, Paul SCT 132A
DUGAN, David BRK 251
George NSN 199
George NSN 213
Henson NSN 206
Hilery/Hiling? BRK 251
Hugh CBL 7A
James BNE 12
John NSN 201
Owen NSN 197
Richard BNE 12
Sarah SHE 117A
Thomas NSN 180
Thomas NSN 197
DUGANS, Revd. Bishop NSN 223
DUGEON, William GRN 62
DUGGER, Daniel KNX 308
William WTY 111A
William WTY 120A
DUGGINS, Alexr. GRD 106A
Vincent WAS 51A
DUGGLASS, Ann HAR 160
DUGINS, Elizabeth GRD 89A
DUGLAS, Nathan GRD 95A
Saml. MAD 164
Thos. H. MAD 176
DUGLASS, Elizabeth GNP 177A
George CSY 208
Gilson B. BRK 251
Joseph WAS 29A
Milly ADR 16
Peyton BTH 168
William HAR 164
DUHAMEL, Jacob JEF 21
DUHY, John R. WRN 30A
DUING?, Jane JEF 27
DUKE, Alexr. MAS 57
Basil MAS 80
Ben JEF 26
Charles GRN 64
Christian HAR 152
George BRN 8
Greenberry LGN 34
Henry MAD 162
James WAS 68A
John OHO 11A
John CHN 30A

Name	County	Page
DUKE, John B.	MTG	297
Mary	FLG	67A
Mathew	CLK	69
Michael	CLK	100
Phillip	CHN	40
Thomas	BRN	8
Wm.	OHO	5A
DUKEMONIER, John	FTE	70
DUKES, Benjamin	MBG	142
Jacob	MBG	142
Sampson	MBG	143A
Samuel	MBG	142
Young	MBG	142
DULAND, John	HOP	240
DULANEY, John	WRN	33A
Thomson	WRN	33A
DULANY, Will.	SCT	115A
William	LVG	13
DULAPP, Joneth	TOD	131A
DULEN, Edward	SHE	122A
Wm.	SHE	118A
DULEY, Jas.	SCT	128A
John	SHE	120A
Robert	SHE	117A
Saml.	SHE	121A
Saml.	SHE	121A
Thos.	SCT	127A
DULICK, Daniel	BNE	12
Joseph	BNE	12
DULIN, Edwd.	FLG	23A
Wm.	FLG	26A
DULY, Philip	HRD	56
Saml	HRD	62
Thos.	HRD	20
Wm.	HRD	94
Zedock	FLG	62A
DUM?, Mary	ADR	16
Wm.	JEF	26
DUMARSLEY, -.? Lecog?	JEF	31
DUMASS, Armildah	FTE	98
DUMFORD?, Soloman	CLK	74
DUMIT, George	GNP	171A
George	GNP	171A
Robert	GNP	174A
DUN, Alsey	ALN	114
DUN?, James	WAS	76A
John H.	WAS	76A
Jonathan	HND	9
Joshua	MAD	158
Thos.	BBN	134
DUNAGAN, Hiram	SHE	177
Isaac	WYN	87A
James	WYN	88A
DUNAGIN, Solomon	JEF	64
DUNAHAN?, Daniel	CLK	88
DUNAIR?, Winny	FKN	92
DUNAPHAN, Epram	FLG	75A
DUNAVAN, Jacob	CHN	28A
DUNAVEN, Daniel	CHN	35
Thomas	CHN	35
DUNAVN?, Cornelus	ADR	62
DUNAWAY, Benjamin	CLK	64
Benjamin	CLK	78
Isaac	FLG	49A
James	BBN	136
Jno.	HRY	253
Sam.	HRY	260
William	LNC	39
DUNBAR, Alexander	FLD	47
Elizabeth	BLT	168
Ephraim	CLK	103
John	ADR	16
John	ADR	16
John	SHE	135A
Nath.?	CWL	34
DUNBAR, Rubin	ADR	16
Thos.	MAD	112
William	HAR	166
DUNBAR?, Ashley	ALN	114
DUNBO-?, Thomas	JES	97
DUNCAN, ---les? Y.	DVS	18A
Agness	LNC	55
Alamander	GNP	166A
Alexr.	PUL	40A
Alexr.	PUL	47A
Allen	SHE	161
Alsaborn?	JES	92
Anderson	MAD	160
Andrew	MTG	269
Archibald	HAR	190
Asahel	CWL	52
Benj.	LNC	65
Benjamin	HOP	240
Benjamin	DVS	17A
Benjamin	NCH	106A
Charles	JEF	45
Charles	GNP	171A
Coleman	JEF	45
Coleman	NSN	206
Colon?	SCT	108A
Daniel	PUL	53A
Danl.	BBN	144
David	FTE	82
David	GRD	85A
David	WYN	88A
Edward	MER	93
Edward	MAD	100
Elias	PND	20A
Elisha	HRD	50
Elisha	HRD	88
Eliza	TRG	5
Elizabeth	CLK	91
Elizabeth	BBN	108
Elizabeth	HRY	230
Elizabeth	FLG	36A
Elizabith	LGN	43
Ennis	MAS	67
Ennis	MAS	79
Enoch	PND	30A
Gabriel	MAD	148
George	LGN	44
George	NSN	206
George, Senr.	WYN	79A
George S.	WYN	84A
Harvey B.	WTY	111A
Heathy	BRK	251
Henry	BTH	156
Howsan	LNC	55
Isaac	MAD	122
Isaac	NSN	222
James	ADR	16
James	JEF	43
James	CLK	92
James	BBN	108
James	GTN	132
James	BRK	249
James B.	CLK	105
James M.	LGN	44
James W.	BRK	249
Jesse	SHE	161
John	ADR	14
John	BNE	14
John	HRD	24
John	LGN	30
John	BBN	90
John	MER	93
John	CLK	100
John	MAD	102
John	BBN	108
John	CLD	156
John	MAD	172
DUNCAN, John	MAD	172
John	NSN	200
John	HOP	240
John	DVS	15A
John	DVS	16A
John	PUL	53A
John	WYN	80A
John	WTY	111A
John W.	CLK	80
Johnston	LNC	37
Jos.	LNC	57
Jos.	MAS	78
Jos. C.	CHN	43A
Joseph	BRN	8
Joseph	CLK	97
Joseph	BBN	136
Joseph	SHE	170
Joseph	HAR	190
Joseph	SPN	23A
Joseph	GNP	166A
Joseph	GNP	171A
Leroy	GNP	171A
Mandford	SPN	6A
Martin	FLG	36A
Martin	SHE	125A
Mary	DVS	15A
Mathew	BBN	106
Matthew J.	NSN	195
Moses	LNC	75
Nancy	BTH	156
Nimrod	LGN	43
Nimrod	SHE	170
Peter	SCT	104A
Purcen	KNX	304
Reuben	HRY	200
Richd.	WRN	62A
Robert	BRN	33
Robert	JES	84
Robert?	DVS	18A
Rogers	BBN	134
Sally	RCK	80A
Saml.	LNC	15
Saml.	CWL	53
Samuel	FTE	82
Samuel	DVS	17A
Sarah	MAD	122
Sarah	HAR	144
Seth	CLK	103
Seth	NSN	195
Shadrick	HRD	28
Squire	LGN	45
Squire	HAR	168
Ste. C.	GRD	113A
Tho.	MAS	78
Tho.	GRD	112A
Thomas	BRN	8
Thomas	NSN	181
Thomas	NSN	217
Thos.	BBN	118
Traverse	MTG	257
Walter	MAS	60
Washington	BBN	134
Will	GRD	102A
William	LGN	37
William	JES	86
William	GTN	132
William	HAR	190
William	HRY	198
William	NSN	205
William	DVS	15A
William	WYN	93A
Willis	HRY	202
Willis	DVS	16A
Willis	PND	18A
Wm.	CWL	52
Wm.	BBN	124

DUNCAN, Wm. BRK 249
Wm. BRK 251
Wm. BRK 251
Wm. D. JEF 19
Wm.? CWL 36
Zachariah LGN 40
DUNCAN?, Wm. BRK 249
DUNCASTER, Charles NSN 187
DUNCECOMB, Samuel SPN 9A
DUNCELER, Charles LGN 44
DUNCUN, Edmund WRN 35A
Ruth BRK 249
DUND?, Mary ADR 16
DUNE, Albert MTG 261
DUNEGAN, Acre HRT 156
DUNELL/ DUNETT?, William HRY 194
DUNELL?, Paul MTG 297
DUNETT?, Francis HRY 218
Josiah HRY 178
DUNEVAN, Peter HRT 157
DUNGAM, Geo. PUL 40A
DUNGAN, Thomas HAR 160
DUNGANS, Jeremiah PUL 67A
DUNGAR, (No Other Name Given) BNE 12
DUNGARTIN, Allen SHE 132A
DUNHAM, Amos MTG 281
John MAD 90
John WRN 66A
Parker MAD 110
Philip R. MAD 148
Saml. MAD 110
Timothy WRN 64A
DUNHAMER?, Joseph JEF 66
DUNIGAN, Thos. CWL 38
DUNING, Hardiman CWL 35
Jeremiah HOP 240
Jonath CWL 35
Shadh. CWL 35
DUNING?, -aham? CWL 44
DUNIT?, Richd. BBN 132
DUNIVAN, David CWL 46
DUNKEN, Tol.? / Job? HRY 243
DUNKEN?, Ashley ALN 114
DUNKESON, Josiah CHN 32A
Thomas, Sr. CHN 36
DUNKIN, Benj. WAS 86A
Benjamin FKN 142
John CWL 36
DUNKLIN, Jos.? CWL 41
DUNLAP, Alexander WDF 99
Andrew JEF 24
Ben TOD 134
Elizabeth FTE 63
Elizabeth MER 93
George FTE 83
Henry P. FLG 75A
James HAR 186
John MER 93
John CLD 139
Nancy FKN 66
Rebecca FTE 83
William FTE 83
William FTE 112
William MTG 259
William CBL 21A
DUNLAVA, Anthony MER 117
DUNLAVY, Martha MTG 263
DUNN, --e. Mary CWL 42
Alex CWL 40
Alexander JES 76
Alexander GTN 125
Anderson CLK 89
Andrew CWL 52
DUNN, Angl.? GRD 116A
Ann GSN 134A
Archibald HAR 196
Ben GRD 113A
Benajah, Jnr. HAR 184
Benajah, Snr. HAR 186
Benjamin HAR 148
Edward HAR 150
Edwin LGN 32
Elijah HAR 150
Elizabeth HRD 74
Elizabeth FTE 103
Elizabeth, Senr. HRD 74
Erasmus GRD 88A
Furrow CWL 52
George HRY 192
Henry FLG 62A
Hosea SHE 174
Isham CLK 89
James FTE 108
James MAD 154
James SHE 173
James HAR 184
Jane MER 93
Jas HRD 14
Jas. L.? HRY 240
Jeremiah CLK 89
Jesse HRY 243
Jesse WRN 38A
Jessee HOP 240
Jno. CWL 52
Jno. CWL 52
Jno. MAS 57
Jno. HAR 138
John JEF 27
John LGN 45
John CLK 90
John JES 92
John SHE 152
John BLT 162
John HRY 186
John MTG 291
John GRD 88A
John GRD 113A
John A. GRD 102A
Johnson CWL 42
Joseph HOP 240
Josephus FTE 103
Julius WRN 41A
Justice HAR 184
Levi HAR 162
Lewis LGN 32
Lewis WRN 53A
Mary GSN 134A
Matth. CWL 52
Moses GSN 133A
Nathan MAD 116
Nathaniel JES 82
Phillip FTE 85
Robt. HRD 74
S. BBN 136
Saml. JEF 58
Sarah HAR 148
Sarah WRN 53A
Thos. JEF 49
Walter GRD 87A
William BKN 4
William MTG 287
William WRN 53A
William GRD 87A
William C. FTE 103
Willy GRD 117A
Winney FTE 108
Wm. BKN 11
Wm. MAD 154
DUNN?, Alexander HRY 192
DUNN?, George HRY 194
Jno. HRY 243
Robert HRY 192
Wm. JEF 26
Wm. GNP 168A
DUNNAGAN, Thomas, Jr. BRN 33
Thomas, Sr. BRN 8
William WDF 117A
DUNNAVANT, Dan'l BRN 8
DUNNETT, Captain FTE 58
DUNNING, ----is? CWL 37
--ad-.? CWL 36
--ahum? CWL 35
--therington? CWL 34
Effy HRY 267
Ezekiel? CWL 35
George UNN 151
James CWL 35
Jesse CWL 35
John CWL 35
John R. UNN 151
Wm. CWL 34
DUNNINGTON, Bird CWL 52
Francis WDF 101
DUNSITH?, David FLG 57A
DUNVILLE, Richard HOP 242
DUNWIDDE, John BBN 132
Wm. BBN 114
DUNWIDDEE?, Jos. B. CHN 46
DUNWOODIE, James JES 80
DUNWOODY, John JEF 20
DUNYARD?, Soloman CLK 74
DUPEA, Moses GNP 177A
DUPED/ DUPEEL?, Wm. GNP 173A
DUPEY, Benjamin SHE 176
James BRK 251
Salley CSY 208
DUPEY?, Wm. HRD 12
DUPIE, Wm, Senr. CHN 32
DUPIECE?, Asher ADR 14
DUPREE, Tho. HRY 204
DUPREY, James SHE 111A
Nancy HRY 263
Starke? SHE 111A
DUPREY?, John HRY 226
DUPRY, Minter HRY 208
DUPUEE?, Asher ADR 12
DUPUY, James WDF 119A
Joel M. WDF 117A
Mary WDF 119A
Samuel SHE 176
DURALL, David MGB 137A
Martha MBG 135A
DURAY, John NCH 105
DURBAN, Christopher N. HRD 56
Daniel HAR 182
John HRD 64
Jos. HRD 24
Samuel HRD 62
DURBEN, John GSN 134A
Thos. GSN 134A
DURBICK?, Michael BKN 20
DURBIN, Christopher K. MAD 158
Philip MAD 92
DURCE?, Jacob NCH 122A
DURHAM, Benjamin MER 93
Danl. CHN 41
George BRN 8
Henry ALN 138
Isaac CHN 30
James GRN 76

Name	County	Page
DURHAM, James, Jr.	MER	93
James, Sr.	MER	93
John	MER	93
John	ALN	120
John	WYN	94A
Martha	MER	93
Mastin/ Martin?	WYN	84A
Saml.	GRN	67
Saml.	GRN	76
Thomas	MER	93
Washington	ALN	138
William	GRN	76
DURIAM?, Wm.	BRK	249
DURIE, Peter	HRD	46
Saml	HRD	66
DURING, Robt.	FKN	132
DURINGTON, Walter	SPN	10A
DURNAL, John	WAS	83A
DURPIN, George	WDF	126A
DURRETT, A.	GRN	67
Aqulla	GRN	64
Henry	MAS	70
John	GRN	53
Larkin	GRN	54
Richd.	MAS	64
Sarah	GRN	53
Woodson	MAS	64
DURRETT?, R.	TOD	126
DUSHINS, John	LWS	89A
DUSKEY, James	MAD	102
DUTTON, David	PUL	57A
William	SHE	176
DUTY, Daniel	BTH	158
Jas.	HRD	52
John	BTH	166
William	SCT	91A
DUVAL, Dicy	LVG	6
Gabrel	NSN	219
Jacob	NSN	219
James	LVG	6
John	WDF	99A
Lewis	CLD	146
Robert K.	BRN	9
William P.	NSN	223
DUVALL, Alexander	OHO	5A
Archibald B.	LGN	41
Benjamin	MBG	143A
Benjn.	OHO	5A
Claburn	UNN	154
Claibourne	LGN	30
Claudius	LGN	42
Cornelius, Jr.	SCT	120A
Cornelius	SCT	103A
Cornls.	LGN	41
Danl.	PND	29A
Dennis	BLT	160
George	WDF	93
Henry	FLG	40A
Howard	MBG	143A
James	BTH	166
John	SCT	129A
John L.	BLT	156
John R.	CLK	70
Lewis	BLT	160
Lewis	MBG	143A
Lucius C.	UNN	154
Lucy	CLK	100
Marune?	SCT	103A
Nicholas	OHO	5A
Notley	HND	11
Shepherd	LGN	41
Silas	MAS	59
Thomas	HRD	72
Thomas	FTE	104
Thompson	CLK	79
William	WDF	98A
DUVOIS, Stephen	OHO	9A
DUZAN-?, Jacob	FLG	40A
DUZAN, Abra.	MAS	58
Ben	MAS	72
E.	MAS	69
Elenor	LWS	93A
Peter	MAS	62
Wm.	MAS	62
Wm.	FLG	40A
DUZAN?, Alexander	BKN	15
DWIER, Jeremiah	JEF	21
DYAL, Alexander	LWS	98A
John	LWS	88A
Jos.	FLG	46A
DYAS, Thomas	BNE	50
DYE, Allen	MER	93
Beathatanner?	CSY	228
Benjamin	UNN	152
David	MAS	74
Fantleroy	GRN	73
Isaac	PUL	67A
Jacob	PUL	67A
James	GRN	73
Jno.	MAS	56
Jno.	MAS	61
Job	HRD	30
John	JEF	27
John	SHE	176
Joseph	NCH	115A
Martin	GRN	73
Mount	MAS	63
Peter	FLG	34A
Robt.	MAS	61
Shadrach	PUL	61A
Will	MAS	56
William	PUL	67A
DYER, ----?	CWL	40
Francis	FLD	19
Francis	FLD	22
James	LNC	13
John	LVG	2
John	TRG	13
Manoah	WRN	66A
Sarah	TOD	126
Wiley	GNP	165A
William	FLD	8
William	NCH	128A
Wm.	GNP	167A
DYER?, William	UNN	147
DYKES, Isham	FLD	5
James	FLD	5
John	BBN	106
Robert	NCH	129A
Stephen	CLK	79
Wm.	BBN	106
DYSANT, John B.	RCK	76A
DYSART, Johnston	RCK	76A
Saml.	RCK	76A
DYSON, Bennet	UNN	151
Francis	UNN	151
Hezekiah	SCT	119A
Thomas	UNN	152
EADANS, Annuy	CSY	216
John	BLT	160
EADE, James	PUL	66A
EADER, Henry	FTE	99
EADES, Charles	WYN	81A
Drury	MTG	225
Gabriel	WYN	79A
Jacob	WYN	80A
John	FTE	60
John	HAR	212
John	LWS	95A
Joseph	OWN	104
Thomas	BBN	108
EADLEN, Bend.?	WAS	38A
John	WAS	72A
Saml.	WAS	80A
Zack	WAS	73A
EADLIN, Charles F.	WAS	41A
Lewis	NSN	189
EADONS, Elias	CSY	226
Salley	CSY	228
William	CSY	226
EADS, George	GRN	66
John	GRN	66
Jonathan	GTN	117
Rebeca	GRN	66
Robert	GRN	66
Thomas	GRN	66
William	HAR	162
EADSON, George	LGN	43
EAGLIN, John	OWN	102
Peggy	GTN	121
EAKEN, Alexander	SHE	111A
EAKIN, Alexander	SHE	111A
EALES, Daniel	BBN	124
James	BBN	118
James	BBN	124
EALEY, Edwd.	SCT	104A
Geo.	SCT	124A
Henry	SCT	116A
EALLY, Beverly	SHE	142A
EANIS?, Thomas	BBN	104
EAPS, Parky?	CWL	37
EARBY, William	SPN	24A
EARICKSON, James	JEF	31
Saml.	JEF	38
EARINGTON?, John	OWN	103
EARL, Ann	HOP	242
Edward H?	HOP	242
James	PUL	62A
Jonathan	BNE	14
Samuel B.	HOP	242
Samuel H.	HOP	242
EARLES, Abraham	CBL	3A
Jesse	CLD	155
John	CSY	216
John	PND	21A
John	PND	31A
Joshua	CSY	216
Rodam	CBL	17A
Wm.	PND	31A
Wyat	GRN	65
EARLES?, James	CSY	214
Samuel	CSY	214
EARLEY, Daniel	FKN	134
John	FLG	36A
Joseph	CWL	32
Joseph	WTY	121A
Mathias	CWL	35
Robert	WTY	110A
Whitfield	BNE	14
EARLEY?, Leonard	JES	71
EARLS, Saml.	FLG	69A
EARLY, David	FLG	33A
James	CWL	37
James	CWL	43
James	MAD	110
Jas.	MAS	74
Thomas	CLY	119
Willy	MAS	58
EARLY?, James	CSY	214
EARLYWINE, Daniel	NCH	110A
George	NCH	111A
Jacob	NCH	110A
Mary	NCH	110A
William	NCH	111A
EARNES, William	LNC	61
EARNEST, Aron	SPN	11A
Henry	SPN	11A

EARNEST, Jane SPN 12A
Joseph WRN 65A
Pheby SPN 12A
Thomas WRN 41A
William SPN 11A
EARP, Joel BBN 90
Joshua SCT 97A
Josiah PUL 39A
Simon NCH 112A
Walter BTL 321
EARRL, Susanna BBN 112
EARTHENHOUSE,
Coonrod JES 90
John JES 90
EASLEY, --rham CWL 32
-anl.? CWL 32
Jesse CLD 154
Joseph SHE 109A
Wm. ALN 106
Wootson SHE 110A
EASLEY?, Leonard JES 71
EASLIN, John HRY 196
EASLIN?, Tho. HRY 196
EASLY, Pleasant JES 91
EASOM, James PUL 36A
EASONS, Charles JEF 49
EAST, ---.? B. CWL 41
David LNC 23
James GRD 116A
John CWL 42
Joseph LNC 2
Joseph LNC 23
Neel LNC 23
Nimrod LNC 23
Robert JES 97
Sigh GRD 85A
EASTACE?, Geo. MAS 60
EASTAN, Edwd. MAS 78
EASTAN?, Geo. MAS 60
EASTBURN?, John NSN 216
EASTEN, Austin,
Rev. BBN 132
Zachariah BBN 132
EASTEP/ EASTESS?,
Joel FLD 32
EASTEP, Cornelius FLD 28
Elisabeth FLD 30
Shadrack FLD 29
EASTEP?, Samuel FLD 19
EASTER, Byrd? MAD 130
David PUL 38A
Samuel BBN 66
EASTER?, Jane MAD 140
EASTERDAY, Lewis GTN 128
Thomas GTN 128
EASTERLING,
William FLD 10
EASTERS, Biddy GRN 68
EASTES, Abraham CLK 66
Joel SHE 152
John D. GRN 70
Royal GRN 56
Thomas A. GRN 67
EASTES?, Eliza GRN 74
EASTHAM, Ann FTE 76
Edward LNC 61
James FTE 78
William SCT 93A
EASTIN, Augustine FTE 91
Elizabeth BBN 70
Henry CLK 75
Robert MAD 128
EASTIN?, (See
Easlin?) HRY 196
Tho. HRY 196
EASTIS, Elisha CLK 79
EASTIS, Robert CLK 79
Will SCT 116A
EASTLEY, C. -.? GRD 112A
EASTON, Hannah MER 116
James W. JES 96
Wm. MAD 146
EASTONE, Frances MAD 146
EASTWOOD, Abram HND 6A
James HND 6A
EATHER?, Permelia SCT 123A
EATHERINGTON, Mary FLG 29A
EATON, Anne GTN 120
Benjamin MTG 277
Benjamin WTY 111A
Chas. FLG 68A
David BRN 10
Franky ETL 40
George SHE 111A
Henry WRN 49A
Jacob NCH 106A
James BRN 10
John BRN 10
John CWL 53
John GTN 117
John BTH 162
John, Jr. BRN 10
John WDF 115A
John WTY 120A
Jonathan CLK 91
Joseph WDF 99
Leonard BRN 10
Will FLG 52A
William WRN 50A
Wm. G. JEF 61
Zackariah CLK 91
EAVES, John S. MBG 143
William GTN 124
William MBG 135A
EAVINGER, John JEF 45
EAZTEN, Nathan JEF 34
EBERLEY, Jacob FTE 69
EBY, Abm. MBG 137
ECCLES, Henry MER 115
Jane MER 95
John, Esqr. MER 95
Samuel MER 95
ECHERT, Jacob JEF 36
ECKELS, Jas. FLG 78A
ECKERT, Mary CBL 22A
ECKLAR, John HAR 176
Samuel HAR 218
Ulery HAR 184
ECKLES, Charles SCT 93A
ECKOLS, Isaac SHE 128A
ECTON, Betsy GRD 89A
Horratio CLK 69
ECTON?, Smallwood CLK 65
Thomas CLK 72
ED---TON?, Thomas MNR 195
EDDEN, Robert WAS 19A
EDDEN?, Henry WAS 63A
EDDINGS, Benjamin WDF 109A
EDDINS, John UNN 151
EDDLEMAN, Leonard HAR 158
Peter FTE 82
Robert FTE 81
EDDLEN?, Salley WAS 69A
EDDS, Barnett MBG 142A
Carrel MBG 141A
John RCK 77A
Lewis MBG 140A
Samuel MBG 139A
William HAR 162
EDDY, Saml. HRY 218
William HRY 218
EDELIN, John WRN 67A
EDELIN, Joseph NSN 189
Leonard NSN 181
Lewis NSN 184
EDEN, Jeremiah BTH 184
Phillip CLD 158
EDENS, Eliah CWL 53
Ezekiel CWL 53
Pheriby MBG 135A
EDER, Thos. GSN 135A
EDERINGTON, Thos. ADR 18
EDES, John LNC 73
Joseph HND 9A
Robert HND 10
EDES?, Walter MAD 158
EDGAR, Alexander FTE 84
Geo. MAS 59
James HRT 157
Jno. T. MAS 77
John, Jr. HRT 157
John, Sr. HRT 157
Johston HRT 157
Josiah HRT 157
Saml. HRT 157
Saml. S. CHN 40
EDGE, Benjamin FTE 110
Jacob WYN 103A
Jonathan ETL 43
Saml. MAD 120
Thomas ETL 54
EDGEMOND, Kimble WYN 89A
EDGER, Archibald HAR 166
Edmond HAR 164
Henry HAR 144
Jno. HAR 168
EDGES, Caleb OHO 9A
Eliza. OHO 9A
Ezekiel OHO 9A
Josiah OHO 9A
Peggy SCT 98A
EDINGS, Joseph WDF 103
EDLIN, Jas. HRD 48
Jno. JEF 50
John HRD 48
Wm. HRD 94
EDMENSON, Tho. GRD 95A
EDMINS, John CBL 15A
Lewis CBL 14A
William CBL 14A
EDMINSON, Clary GRD 118A
Margaret FTE 91
Robt. GRD 106A
EDMISTON, James HOP 242
John HOP 242
William HAR 178
EDMON, Gamon WAS 51A
EDMONDS, Eli CBL 11A
Thomas GNP 168A
EDMONDSON, Jno.,
Jr. JEF 55
Thos. CHN 39
EDMONSON, James CLK 76
James WAS 66A
John JEF 59
Thomas MER 115
Will. SCT 114A
Wilson WAS 41A
Wm. WAS 37A
EDMUNDS, Benj. WAS 38A
James BRN 10
James WRN 71A
James GRD 97A
John BRN 10
William BRN 9
EDMUNDSON, James MER 95
Thos. BNE 14
EDMUNSON, Wm. MTG 299

EDMUSON, William WYN 83A
EDMUSSON, Robert WYN 79A
EDMUSTON, J. TOD 127A
EDRINGTON, Benj. FKN 76
George GRN 54
John GRN 62
Mary GRN 58
Price WDF 107A
William GRN 61
EDRINGTON?, John OWN 103
EDS?, George HRL 106
EDSEL, Benjn. HRT 157
EDSON, Jno. HRY 260
EDSTER?, Jane MAD 140
EDTCALF, Ignatus NSN 184
EDWARD, Aaron ADR 18
Edwd. B. WAS 66A
Elisha BRK 253
Isaac NSN 207
John F. WAS 68A
Samuel M. MBG 133A
EDWARDS, Adam BBN 62
Ambrose GRD 103A
Amos LGN 22
Amos (On His Farm) LGN 27
Andrew WRN 41A
Arthur KNX 292
Asa LVG 3
Benjamin FKN 130
Benjamin TOD 131
Benjn. NCH 114A
Bennet HRY 241
Bernard TOD 128A
Briton M. MBG 133A
Brown KNX 306
Cader BRN 9
Cader K. BRN 9
Chas. JEF 26
Cornilius WDF 96A
David LGN 29
E. B. TOD 127A
Edmond SHE 140A
Edward CHN 32
Elijah BRN 10
Elijah SHE 150
Elizabeth SHE 160
Emmanual CSY 210
Francis HAR 146
Geo. BBN 116
George LNC 23
Gustavus G. LGN 22
Henry CHN 39
Henry SPN 8A
Hezekiah L.? UNN 146
Hugh SPN 7A
Hugh H. SPN 8A
Isaac BRN 10
Isaac CHN 32
Isaac SHE 121A
Isham CSY 210
J. ADR 18
James BRN 10
James CWL 34
James LNC 35
James JEF 46
James JES 71
James BBN 142
James WDF 121A
James GSN 135A
Jesse GRT 144
Jesse PUL 38A
Jessee RCK 77A
Jno. ADR 18
Jno. CWL 53
Jno. HRY 268
EDWARDS, Jno. M. LNC 7
John BRN 9
John BRN 10
John JEF 37
John BNE 46
John GRN 58
John JES 69
John LNC 69
John JES 71
John GRN 79
John BBN 136
John BBN 142
John UNN 149
John MAD 154
John KNX 292
John, Jr. GRN 79
John SPN 8A
John CBL 21A
John PUL 65A
John WYN 89A
John WYN 97A
John WYN 102A
John WDF 122A
Jonah WAS 30A
Jonathan HAR 148
Joseph FLD 46
Joseph BTH 150
Langham CSY 210
Leroy SHE 168
Lewis MER 95
Lewis GSN 135A
Lucy GRD 97A
Margaret CLD 160
Mathew GRD 105A
Merdeith HND 5
Meridith FLD 20
Moses FKN 120
Moses GSN 135A
Nancy NSN 212
Patsey WDF 93
Peter LNC 7
Peter WYN 97A
Presley LGN 24
Robert HND 8
Robert BRN 9
Robert LWS 96A
Robert NCH 107A
Simian WDF 96
Stouten DVS 15A
Thomas BRN 9
Thomas GRN 64
Thomas SHE 121A
Thomas TOD 129A
Thos. JEF 32
Turner DVS 18A
Uria HRY 241
Uriah CBL 19A
Wiley WDF 124A
Will. KNX 292
William LGN 42
William FTE 65
William FTE 94
William HAR 146
William CSY 212
William, Sen. BRN 10
William GRD 105A
William WTY 123A
Wm. JEF 35
Wm. JEF 50
Wm., (Near Lyons) BRN 10
Wm. TOD 131
Wm. HRY 268
Wm. H., Alexr's Son BRN 9
Wm. Jr. M. BRN 9
EDWARDS?, Oliver ALN 94
EDWRDS, Hickman CSY 214
EDY, (Blank) JEF 19
EEARLS, Mathew ADR 18
Thos. ADR 18
EGBERT, David FKN 140
John WDF 116A
EGERTON, Ben GRD 121A
Benj., Jr.? GRD 108A
Polly GRD 122A
Will GRD 108A
EGGLESTON, Amos CBL 12A
EGLER, Henry HAR 140
Jacob HAR 140
EGLESTON, Ebenezer BKN 16
EGNAR, Benjamin FTE 103
EGNEW, Isaac HAR 182
James HAR 178
EIDSON, James BRK 253
Pleasant BRK 253
William OHO 4A
ELAM, Benjamin FKN 150
Lewellen BTL 321
Samuel BTL 321
ELAN, Thomas G. NSN 191
Thomas R. NSN 212
ELBERT, Henry D. SCT 108A
Saml. C. JEF 35
ELDER, -m-. CWL 32
Andrew MAD 140
Ann FTE 70
Ann WAS 56A
Ann C. JEF 30
Arnold BRK 253
David MAD 132
Geo. LVG 7
Guy WAS 55A
James LVG 5
James WAS 39A
James WAS 84A
Jesse PUL 59A
John BRK 253
Mathew LNC 63
Mathew FTE 68
Peter MNR 195
Phebe JEF 34
Robert LNC 63
Robert WAS 46A
Robot. LVG 7
Saml. LVG 5
Saml. BRK 253
Saml., Sr. LVG 5
Sarah LNC 63
Sarah LNC 63
Silvester WAS 87A
Thomas LVG 5
Will. LVG 5
William CSY 208
Wm., Sr. BRK 253
Wm. W. BRK 253
ELDER?, Alexander MAD 152
ELDRIDGE, (John-crossed Out) S. HRL 106
Jas. HRL 106
Jenney FLD 3
John HRL 106
Peyton BBN 78
ELDRIGE, Thos. BBN 86
ELEDGE, Edward CLK 88
Louvicy CLK 88
ELERSON?, Amus GRN 66
ELEXANDER, Benjamin SHE 111A
ELEY, Edward GTN 122
ELGAN, Gustavus CLK 81

ELGIN, Agness BBN 136
Federick WDF 101A
George LNC 47
Hezekiah S.? FTE 94
Joseph SCT 100A
William A. WDF 102
ELIE?, Michal CHN 43
ELIM, Godfrey CLD 142
ELINGTON, David GNP 168A
Plesant GNP 167A
ELINORE?, Matthew LNC 73
ELIOT, Asael? KNX 304
Francis KNX 300
John MAD 158
Sarah KNX 308
William BTL 321
Zacheriah BTL 321
ELIOTT, Rebecca FKN 130
Wm. GSN 135A
ELISON, William WTY 123A
ELKIN, Benjamin MER 95
Ezekiel CLK 103
Isaiah WDF 101A
James CLK 62
Robert CLK 103
Sary FKN 140
Zackarieh CLK 70
ELKINS, Alete? MAD 126
Drewry PUL 35A
Jas. CLY 127
Jesse? RCK 83A
Joshua MBG 142
Reuben H. RCK 84A
William GRN 52
ELLEN, John WYN 92A
ELLER, George WYN 88A
ELLERTON, Thos. WAS 64A
ELLES, Linsey ADR 18
ELLESS, Elizabeth CSY 216
Isaac CSY 214
John CSY 212
ELLET, Danl. CLY 118
Jesse CLY 118
Thomas CLY 118
ELLETT, Edwd. FLG 61A
Jas. FLG 48A
John FLG 47A
John FLG 49A
Thos., Jr. FLG 52A
Thos., Snr. FLG 53A
William GTN 126
ELLEXANDER, James SHE 142A
John SHE 142A
ELLIDGE, Elijah FLD 11
France BTH 172
James FLD 12
ELLIN, Solomon JEF 31
ELLINGTON, Hezekiah CLD 163
Jesse CLD 151
ELLINGWOOD, Harry SHE 139A
ELLINSWORTH, Bartholomew JEF 49
Thos. JEF 49
ELLIOT, Bruk./Burk.? PUL 59A
David MAD 130
Dorson? MAD 94
Elizabeth BKN 15
Heydon PUL 59A
James FTE 55
John HAR 216
John PUL 66A
John SHE 142A
Reubin BKN 15
Saml. BKN 5
ELLIOT, William BRN 10
ELLIOTT, ----- NCH 124A
Alxr. ADR 16
Andrew WDF 94
Andrew BRK 253
Archibald FKN 130
Babary CSY 208
Barner? BRK 253
Benjamin OWN 99
Chas. SHE 132A
Danl. LNC 17
Edward GTN 135
Elijah ETL 41
Elijah BBN 144
Ephraim FLD 22
Ezekiel H. MBG 140
Francis SHE 132A
Galen R. PUL 52A
George ADR 16
George HRD 38
George CLD 146
George WAS 68A
George GRD 122A
George W. HAR 182
Hamilton FLG 44A
Jacob BRK 253
James FLD 8
James WDF 94
James WDF 113A
James NCH 124A
Jas. SCT 132A
Jno. FKN 130
Jno. FKN 138
John JEF 24
John HRD 58
John HRD 78
John WDF 95
John SHE 163
John WAS 23A
John SCT 109A
John MBG 133A
Johnston CSY 208
Joseph HRD 40
Mary CLK 98
Nancy SHE 136A
Richard FTE 99
Richd. WAS 23A
Robert WDF 94
Robert NCH 128A
Robert M. NCH 128A
Robt. SHE 132A
Samuel FTE 73
Samuel WDF 95
Samuel CLD 146
Stephen WAS 55A
Thomas CLD 148
Thos. JEF 58
Thos. SCT 95A
Thos. C. WAS 42A
Ths. MAS 74
Uriah WDF 103A
William JEF 34
William NSN 192
William NSN 212
William HAR 216
William WDF 116A
Wm. BKN 11
Wm. JEF 58
Wm. HRD 82
Wm. BBN 110
Wm., Jr. BKN 22
Wm. WAS 31A
ELLIS, --ram CWL 32
Asa BRN 10
Augustin MER 95
Barthalomew WRN 67A
ELLIS, Benjamin HAR 190
Benjamin WRN 31A
Charles CLY 114
Charles MBG 138
Charles SHE 154
Charles MTG 261
Christopher CLD 156
Daniel MER 95
David BBN 102
David SHE 111A
Dudley CBL 21A
Dunrus? OWN 99
Eleazer BRN 10
Eleazer OWN 99
Elijah MAS 68
Elisabeth FKN 106
Elizabeth SHE 157
Elizabeth PND 30A
Geo. WYN 96A
George BNE 14
George CBL 10A
George PUL 59A
Grrot MER 95
Harrison MAS 64
Henry BBN 86
Henry GTN 122
Henry PND 31A
Hezekiah FTE 88
Hezekiah FTE 96
Isaacs SHE 130A
Israel OWN 104
J. P. BBN 54
Jacob FKN 118
James BKN 10
James BBN 92
James BBN 94
James MER 95
James WRN 29A
James NCH 117A
James A. GTN 122
James P. BBN 98
James P. BBN 100
Jas. MAS 80
Jesse OWN 99
Jesse CLD 155
Jesse WDF 123A
Jno. B. HRY 258
Joel CLD 142
John BKN 4
John BRN 10
John BNE 46
John BBN 116
John ALN 138
John CBL 9A
John CBL 17A
John PND 20A
John SCT 109A
John WDF 124A
Jonath. HRY 258
Joseph MAD 122
Joseph SHE 173
Lander? RCK 83A
Leonard HRY 258
Lewis FTE 96
Mary SHE 155
Milly SHE 174
Nelson R. BNE 14
Obadiah SCT 110A
Owen BTH 196
Owin WDF 108A
Peter, Sr. WYN 96A
Richard SHE 174
Robert BBN 102
Robert TOD 129
Saml. BBN 120
Saml. SHE 155

ELLIS, Samuel LVG 13
Stephen ALN 140
Steven PND 30A
Tho. MAS 79
Tho. ALN 114
Tho. RCK 83A
Thomas LNC 49
Thomas FTE 95
Thomas FTE 96
Thomas SHE 153
Thomas SHE 161
Thomas FLD 1A
Thornton MAS 68
Thos. BBN 88
Thos. SHE 130A
William FTE 88
William WDF 94
William SHE 155
William SHE 159
William, Jr. MER 95
William, Sr. MER 95
William, Sr. SHE 174
William CBL 7A
William PND 21A
William WDF 108A
Wm. JEF 21
Wm. BBN 142
Wm. MAD 166
Wm. BRK 253
Wm. HRY 258
Wm. PND 30A
Wm. SHE 129A
ELLIS?, Joel GTN 133
ELLISON, Akis MBG 140
Bayler MAD 106
Benja. GRT 142
Daniel T. WDF 105
Hugh SHE 152
Hugh SCT 130A
Jacob FKN 132
James GRT 142
James MAD 158
Jessee MBG 135
John MAD 108
John GTN 133
John WRN 35A
Jos. TOD 129
Lewis CLD 145
M. TOD 132
Reuben TOD 127
Robert FKN 132
Robert GRT 142
Robert SPN 14A
Sam TOD 128A
Thomas BNE 14
Thos. JEF 23
William FTE 75
ELLISTON, Amos LNC 5
ELLMORE, James JES 73
John JES 83
ELLSBERRY, Wm. BBN 114
ELLUNBAUGH?, John JES 78
ELLY?, Thomas HRY 178
ELMORE, Athanasius BRN 10
Edward BRN 10
Edward MAD 126
Elizabeth, Mrs. WYN 101A
James BRN 10
Jesse BRN 10
John BRN 10
John LNC 79
John GSN 135A
Martin/ Mastin? GSN 135A
Nelley HRT 157
Patsey FTE 109
Peter GRN 79
ELMORE, Shapley LNC 79
Thos. GRN 79
Travis GRN 60
Travis GRN 62
ELMORE?, Matthew LNC 73
ELMS, William BTL 321
ELROD, Jas. MAS 58
Jeremiah WRN 65A
Jeremiah WYN 80A
Michael PUL 58A
ELROY?, Abraham M. WAS 35A
James M. WAS 33A
Samuel M. WAS 33A
ELSBURY, Ben. HRY 267
Benjamin CLK 68
ELSER?, Alexander MAD 152
ELSEY, John GTN 117
ELSON, Cornelius LWS 99A
Nicholas LWS 89A
Nicholas LWS 99A
Richard LWS 90A
Richard T. LWS 95A
ELSTON, Alexander MAD 156
Ben. HRY 256
Dav. HRY 255
Jno. HRY 256
Jos. HRY 255
Wm. HRY 255
Wm. T. MAD 158
ELSTON?, David GTN 126
Jonathan JEF 63
ELSUM, Richard CLY 113
William CLY 117
ELSWICK, Bradley FLD 25
John FLD 38
Joseph FLD 38
William FLD 38
ELSWORTH, Phebe WRN 68A
ELUM, Edmund WYN 104A
ELUM?, Wallis / Waltis? FLD 10
ELUSON?, Amus GRN 66
ELY, Anthony HRL 106
Edward LGN 29
James LNC 35
James MER 116
Lawrence LGN 29
Roody CLK 98
ELZY, Elzy JEF 32
EMBERTON, John MNR 191
Richard MNR 197
Walter W. B. MNR 197
EMBOY?, Jane ADR 18
EMBREE, Caleb CLK 87
Colby MNR 211
Elisha CLD 151
Joel CLK 65
John LNC 39
John CLK 64
Polly LNC 49
EMBRY, Heny GRN 67
Joel MAD 166
Joseph MAD 100
Samuel GRN 72
Talton MAD 164
Wm. GRN 59
EMBRY?, Jane ADR 18
EMERSON, Ash SCT 138A
Benjn. SCT 129A
Hugh SCT 122A
James CLK 68
Jas. SCT 116A
John GRN 53
John SCT 120A
John M. CLD 166
Manuel ADR 64
EMERSON, Polley SCT 116A
Simpson CLK 92
Thomas PUL 58A
Thomas M. CLD 166
Will. SCT 124A
EMERY, Adam HRD 62
Cader MAD 144
Isaac HRD 58
John KNX 284
Joseph HRD 26
EMMERSON, Henry FTE 86
James LNC 53
John LNC 53
John WRN 56A
John WYN 92A
Judith BRN 10
Pleasant BRN 9
Reubin FTE 86
Walter, Col. WYN 86A
Zachariah BRN 10
EMMERT?, Phillip MNR 211
EMMERY, William BRN 10
William LGN 36
EMMES?, Luther BNE 14
EMMET, Wm. ADR 62
EMMETT, Richard S. LGN 24
Silas CBL 18A
EMMIT, Zach ADR 16
EMMIT?, Alexander BTH 218
EMMITT, Josiah LGN 24
William BNE 14
EMMMONS, Uriah MAS 65
EMMONS, Elijah FLG 50A
Jos. FLG 55A
Nancy LGN 32
Richard NSN 199
Richard G. LGN 32
Sinclear FLG 55A
William FTE 100
Wm. FLG 55A
EMREY, Burel GRD 94A
EMRY, Will GRD 94A
ENDICOTT, James HAR 208
James HAR 208
John HAR 212
John HAR 218
Joseph NCH 103A
Lewis HRY 259
Mary HAR 210
Moses HAR 208
Moses, Jr. HAR 208
Thomas HAR 210
Wm. HRY 260
ENDICUT, Joseph WDF 120A
Samuel WDF 120A
ENERINE, Jonathan MAD 122
ENGLAND, Augt. GRD 121A
Daid BTH 198
Elisha MNR 207
James GRD 107A
Jesse BTH 198
Jessee ADR 18
John KNX 280
Jonat ADR 18
Jos. JEF 50
Joseph FLD 37
Josiah ADR 18
Mary KNX 280
Nat. ADR 18
William MNR 205
ENGLANT, John GSN 135A
ENGLE, George, Jr. KNX 300
George, Snr KNX 300
Jacob KNX 302
John KNX 300
Peter KNX 278

Name	County	Page
ENGLE, Philip	KNX	302
ENGLEMON, Saml.	LNC	45
Simon	LNC	39
ENGLES, John	FTE	65
ENGLETON, -enry?	CWL	40
ENGLISH, Asa	FLG	76A
Betsey	FTE	111
Frances	FLG	72A
George	CLD	148
James	GTN	126
James	CLD	147
Jas.	FLG	40A
John	BTH	188
John	GSN	135A
Leven	HRY	250
Mahala	FKN	56
Noah	HRD	22
Robert	HAR	164
Robt.	HRD	62
Sary?	MAD	174
Silas	HRD	46
Thomas	HRY	200
William	HAR	164
William	BTL	321
Wm., Jr.	FLG	71A
Wm., Sen.	FLG	72A
Wm.	GSN	135A
ENIS, James	GRD	102B
ENLOE, Benjamin	MNR	199
Enoch	MNR	199
James	MNR	199
Thos.	HRD	30
ENLOW, Abraham	HRD	86
Abrm.	HRD	40
Jesse	NCH	107A
ENNEY, James	SPN	5A
ENNIS, George	WRN	63A
Henry	FTE	78
James	FTE	78
James	GTN	121
James	WDF	95A
Jno.	JEF	21
John	BRN	9
John, Senr.	WRN	65A
John	WRN	65A
Widw.	CWL	46
Will.	SCT	112A
William	BRN	10
ENNIS?, Thomas	BBN	104
ENOCH, David	JEF	52
Isaac	JEF	65
Thos.	JEF	52
ENOCHS, Garrett	SHE	153
Jones	SHE	153
ENOS, Abner	CLK	84
ENOX, Abraham	FLD	22
ENSIGN, Justice	BBN	128
ENSOR, James	GSN	135A
ENSOR?, George	WAS	64A
ENTRITKEN?, John	CWL	53
ENYAND?, Abraham?	MNR	213
ENYARD?, Wright	MNR	213
ENYART?, Elizabeth	LWS	86A
ENZOR, Tho.	MAS	59
EOFF, Jno.	PUL	39A
EPELAND?, Daniel	BRN	10
EPERSON, Barnett	CLK	87
John	CLK	85
EPISON, Cornelious	JES	88
EPISON?, Cornelious	JES	88
EPLER?, George	WDF	119A
EPLIN, Lewis	MBG	135A
EPPERLEY, George	WYN	81A
EPPERSON, Arthur	BBN	130
Charles	MAD	126
EPPERSON, Charles	WRN	65A
Chesley	FTE	87
David	LNC	59
David	MER	95
Eliza	LNC	63
Francis	FTE	87
Francis	SHE	151
George L.	WRN	69A
James	SHE	171
James	MTG	235
Jesse	LNC	9
John	SHE	158
John	SHE	173
Nancy	FTE	102
Peter	BRN	10
Peter	BTH	206
Richd.	HRT	157
Robert	MTG	265
Robert	DVS	15A
Thomas	FTE	84
Thos.	MAD	144
Wm.	ADR	18
EPPESON, James	BTH	178
EPPISON, Richard	JES	78
EPPLEY, Jacob	LGN	45
ERBA, William	MER	95
ERNEST, Jacob	SPN	25A
ERSKINE, Jere	HRD	32
ERTON?, Nathan	JEF	35
ERVAN, Richard	SHE	115A
Samuel	SHE	115A
ERVIN, Elizabeth	BRK	253
Francis	CLY	131
James	BKN	10
Jared	BTH	154
Joseph	WRN	52A
Mathew	GRD	110A
Sterlin?	GRD	92A
Thomas	GRD	110A
Thos.	CHN	35
Williamson	GRD	105A
ERVIN?, Robert	BTH	204
ERVINE, Benjamin	PUL	61A
ERWIN, Elias	BTH	162
Jane	MTG	285
John	MER	116
John	BTH	186
Jos.	PUL	48A
Robt.	GRN	66
Wm.	BKN	6
Wm., Sr.	GRN	59
ERWINE, Jos.	HRY	270
Robt.	HRY	261
Squire	HRY	270
Wm.	HRY	255
Wm.	HRY	263
ESAM, James	FTE	82
Richard	FTE	99
ESHAM, Thomas	BNE	14
William	LWS	89A
ESKERIDGE, George	GSN	135A
Joseph	GSN	135A
Robt.	GSN	135A
ESKIN, John	HRY	224
ESKRIDGE, William H.	HAR	148
ESLICK, Francis	BTL	321
ESMAN, John	MNR	193
ESMAN?, Thomas	MNR	193
ESOM, Edward	GNP	176A
Gideon	MBG	142A
John	PUL	65A
ESON?, John H.	GRD	100A
ESSEM?, Mabel, Mrs.	WYN	90A
ESSEX, Joseph	NSN	195
ESSEX, Thomas	HAR	192
Thomas	NSN	195
ESTEL, Stephen	SCT	102A
ESTELL, Will, Jr.	FLG	42A
Wm., Snr.	FLG	42A
Wm.	FLG	51A
ESTEP, James	FLD	39
Shad	HRL	106
ESTER, Ephraim	CLD	151
ESTER?, James	MAD	120
ESTES, Abraham	LNC	23
Brasel	ETL	41
Clement	BBN	110
Elisha	MAD	120
George	BRN	10
James	FTE	111
Jno. C.	ADR	18
Jno. Y.	ADR	18
John	TRG	4
John	LNC	23
John	MAD	124
John H.	MAD	122
Marshall	BRN	10
Martha	BRN	10
Peter	ADR	18
Peter	FTE	81
Robt.	BBN	76
Thomas	LNC	59
Thomas	WRN	35A
Thos.	SCT	104A
William	DVS	15A
Willis	LNC	21
Wm.	ADR	18
ESTIL, Daneil?	MAD	124
ESTILL, James	MAD	162
John	SCT	113A
Samuel, Jr.	MAD	96
Samuel, Sr.	MAD	162
Thos.	SCT	99A
Wallace	MAD	172
ESTIN, Reuben	MTG	275
Reubin J./ I.?	MAD	138
ESTIS, Fielding	HRY	186
Geo. W.	HRY	186
John	HAR	202
Lettn.?	HRY	186
Middleton	FTE	93
Will M.	HRY	186
ESTON, James	JEF	35
Nathan	JEF	35
ETHEREGE, Neley	TRG	12A
ETHERIDGE, Samuel	LGN	35
ETHERINGTON, Ben	GSN	135A
Reuben	FKN	98
ETHERRIDGE, George	SPN	9A
ETHERTON, Benjamin	NSN	195
Henry	SHE	111A
Joshua	CLY	130
ETHERTON?, James	JES	79
ETHINGTON, Field.	HRY	265
Jno.	HRY	244
Loveday	HRY	244
Wm.	HRY	265
ETHRINGTON, Cajor	FTE	75
ETON, James	BTH	170
EUBANK, Ambrose	CLK	67
Edward W.	BRN	33
Elizabeth	SPN	22A
Harrison	CLK	93
John	MNR	201
Joseph	BRN	9
Robert	SHE	154
Stephen	CLK	81
Susanna	BRN	9
William	NCH	105
EUBANK?, Thomas	MNR	205

EUBANKS, Henry BRN 10
James WAS 57A
James WAS 57A
James PUL 62A
John LNC 29
John SPN 22A
Joseph NCH 105
Thomas MTG 289
EUDAILEY, Elisha GTN 117
EULAP, (See Eulass) SCT 108A
EULASS, Jacob SCT 108A
EUSALEY, James CSY 214
EUSOR?, Stephen WAS 72A
EVANS, ---ams? DVS 10A
Abraham BKN 24
Adam FTE 81
Alexander BRN 9
Alexr. MAS 70
Ambros GRD 120A
Belain C.? FTE 84
Ben. CWL 38
Bennett H. NCH 106A
Christopher BTL 321
Davd. PUL 36A
David FLD 19
David BLT 160
David HAR 194
David, Jun. MBG 136A
David, Senr. MBG 141A
David CBL 10A
David NCH 114A
Edward NSN 183
Edwd. CLY 113
Elijah KNX 312
Elizth. SCT 106A
Enoch PUL 42A
Evan FLD 36
Evan FKN 68
Evan FLG 50A
Evan LWS 90A
Ferrell FLD 39
Francis JEF 60
Francis SHE 166
Francis BTH 182
Gabriel FLG 48A
George BTL 321
Gilead NCH 111A
Harris BTL 321
Henry MAD 112
Henry OHO 11A
Henry WDF 125A
Hugh MER 95
Isaac MTG 265
Isaac SCT 117A
Isabella FLD 29
Jacob BLT 160
James CLK 87
James PUL 42A
James LWS 90A
James NCH 126A
James MGB 137A
James MBG 141A
Jane MTG 241
Jesse MTG 257
Jno. PUL 42A
Jno. PUL 48A
John JEF 25
John ETL 41
John JES 95
John CLK 97
John MAD 104
John CLY 122
John BTH 182
John MTG 253
John MTG 263
EVANS, John KNX 286
John, Sr. RCK 75A
John FLD 1A
John PUL 36A
John FLG 53A
John WRN 59A
John RCK 75A
John RCK 79A
John GRD 94A
John SCT 108A
John NCH 114A
John GRD 115A
John SCT 131A
John MBG 135A
John J. ETL 44
John? ETL 40
Joseph NSN 183
Joseph FLG 31A
Joseph GRD 88A
Joshua FTE 90
Josiah PUL 51B
Josiah PUL 35A
Josiah PUL 51A
Lititia, Mrs. GRT 144
Love MAD 90
Mabray CLK 82
Mabray, Jr. CLK 87
Margaret DVS 16A
Mary MER 95
Mary BRK 253
Michael NCH 124A
Nancy BRN 10
Nancy BLT 196
Nathaniel JES 75
Nathaniel MER 95
Nicholas CLK 97
Paul CLK 62
Peter CLK 62
Rachael WRN 68A
Rachel PUL 42A
Rebecca GRD 101A
Rice JEF 59
Richard FTE 87
Richard MAD 90
Richard FLD 1A
Richard LWS 90A
Robert WDF 94A
Robt. SCT 130A
Rody FLG 32A
Saml. PUL 42A
Samuel BLT 162
Samuel PUL 51A
Samuel WDF 103A
Samuel D. WDF 96
Samule BKN 26
Scioto FLG 29A
Silas CLK 71
Susan LVG 12
Susanna HRY 249
Taylor FKN 114
Thomas BRN 9
Thomas BTH 182
Thos. JEF 46
Thos. HRD 74
Walter HAR 194
Will MAS 73
Will. KNX 288
Will., Jr. KNX 286
William BRN 9
William BRN 10
William CLK 69
William JES 75
William MBG 140
William SHE 156
William, Mas.? GRT 144
Wm. BRK 253
EVANS, Wm. FLG 31A
Wm. PUL 39A
Zachariah PUL 42A
Zech. HRY 247
EVATT, John ETL 41
EVE, Abraham FTE 98
Elizabeth SCT 96A
John BNE 14
Joseph KNX 278
EVENS, Alxr. ADR 16
Benjn. ADR 18
Eleanor JEF 24
Redmon NSN 199
Stephen MAD 120
Thos. ADR 18
Will., Sr. KNX 286
EVERAGE, Joel CLY 124
EVERBY?, John MNR 199
EVEREL, M. D. SCT 138A
EVERET, Aaron HOP 242
Craven SCT 126A
Sydner HOP 242
EVERETS, Augustin A. LNC 2
EVERETT, Jesse BRN 9
Joseph MER 95
Samuel BRN 9
William BRN 9
Wm. JEF 20
EVERHEART, Marten WAS 39A
EVERITT, Isaac CBL 10A
John D. LWS 93A
Saml. D. MTG 295
EVERLY, Henry MER 95
Jacob MER 95
Jessee MBG 136
EVERMAN, Andrew MTG 277
Arthur BBN 66
Jacob GNP 174A
John BBN 114
John GNP 172A
Michael MTG 277
Michael, Sr. MTG 277
Moses GNP 174A
Samuel MTG 277
Wm. GNP 172A
EVERMONTE, Jacob CLK 78
EVERN?, James WAS 48A
Wm. WAS 43A
EVERSALL, Wm. JEF 31
EVERSOLE, Abraham CLY 127
John CLY 128
Peter CLY 114
Woolery CLY 126
EVERT, Thomas WRN 37A
EVES, Soloman CHN 40A
EVINGER, David JEF 42
Geo. JEF 36
Geo., Sr. JEF 42
EVINS, Andrew PUL 59A
Frankey GNP 172A
James BTH 216
John GNP 165A
Thomas BTH 200
EWALT, Samuel BBN 112
EWARD, John NCH 127A
EWART, Henry BBN 138
EWATT?, John BBN 140
EWELL, Jessee CLK 62
Leighton KNX 282
Leroy MAS 60
William CLK 62
EWENS, Wm. ADR 18
EWERS?, Wm. ADR 18
EWIN / EWING?, Robt. FLG 40A

EWIN?, Robert BTH 204
EWING, Adla? CHN 43
Andrew ADR 16
Anne CLD 147
Chatham LGN 36
Diana FTE 84
F. M. TOD 125
Ford LGN 31
George, Col. WYN 92A
Henry WRN 43A
J./ I.? B. S. TOD 131
James HRY 212
James BTL 321
Jno. MAS 65
John, Junr. LGN 35
John PND 17A
John WRN 30A
John SCT 122A
John L. MER 95
Joseph SCT 127A
Matthew CLD 147
Phillemon SCT 91A
Putmun BTH 180
Reuben LGN 28
Robartus LGN 30
Robert LGN 39
Robert CLD 147
Robt. M. SCT 93A
Rosey DVS 17A
Saml. SCT 139A
Samuel LGN 35
Samuel BTL 321
Samuel, Esqr. MER 95
Thos. WAS 81A
Timothy MTG 257
Urbin LGN 28
Will. SCT 107A
William LGN 42
William GRN 50
William BTL 321
Wm. GSN 135A
Wm. M. BNE 14
Young CHN 45
EYLER, Daniel OHO 8A
EYLOR, Jacob H./ W.? OHO 8A
EYLOUR?, John OHO 5A
EYSON, Tho. MAS 62
EZEL, Balam HND 9A
Berryman HND 9A
EZELL, -----? TRG 8
Balaam TRG 13
Gilliam TRG 8
Lewis TRG 7A
William TRG 7A

F----?, John? CWL 39
F---ISH?, William HAR 142
F--GHER, Christopher GNP 175A
F--LAS?, James WAS 72A
James WAS 72A
John WAS 72A
Phill WAS 72A
F-NNIN?, David FLD 10
FABERR, Robt. GNP 169A
FADIS, James KNX 280
FAG, James CSY 212
FAGAN, John BKN 14
John LWS 91A
FAGANS, Zacheriah BBN 106
FAHARTY, Bartholomew NSN 208
FAHERTY, Mary NSN 208
Owen NSN 208
Patrick NSN 208
FAHNESTOCK, Benjn. BBN 146
FAIN, John JES 77
Joseph JES 86
Martin JES 77
Sally JES 78
William JES 77
FAIRCHILD, Abiud? FLD 35
Michael ETL 40
FAIRMAN, Richard MER 115
FAIRVILLE, Joseph MBG 138A
FAIT?, Saml. MAS 60
FAITH, ----am? DVS 9A
FALCONER, J. N. TOD 126A
FALKNER, Jamaes JES 93
Samuel ADR 20
Samuel GRN 53
Thomas FTE 81
FALL, William LGN 32
FALLEN, William WRN 68A
FALLENASH?, James, Mas. GRT 147
Thomas, Mas. GRT 147
FALLENASK?, James GRT 147
FALLING, David BKN 5
FALLS, Tarns SCT 123A
FAMILY, Nancy MER 95
FANCHER, John BRN 11
FANING, Akillus BTH 208
John BTH 214
Josiah BTH 218
FANNEN, Michael MAS 55
FANNING, Joseph MTG 259
FANNY, Catherine CLK 78
FANON, John GNP 176A
FANT, Will. P. SCT 124A
FANT?, Armsted MAS 80
FANTRESS, Pleasant OHO 6A
William OHO 6A
FAR, James JEF 53
FARCHILDS, Ebenezer WYN 94A
FARDING?, Dudley ETL 43
FARE, James M. LNC 31
FAREWELL, Nathan JEF 31
FARGASON, Abraham FTE 74
FARGUSON, James SHE 121A
Jas. SCT 116A
FARIES, M. A. SCT 92A
FARIS,
Eli-h? WTY 119A
Elijah FLG 66A
Ephraim C. PUL 52A
Ephram FLG 74A
Hiram L. WTY 119A
Isaac BRN 11
Jas., Snr. FLG 50A
Jas. FLG 51A
Jas. FLG 74A
Jessee HRT 158
Job FLG 50A
John FLG 32A
John FLG 49A
John FLG 78A
John T. BRN 11
Levi FLG 56A
Major WAS 84A
Michael MAD 156
Moses RCK 81A
Robert D. HND 3
Thos. FLG 32A
FARISH, John BRN 11
Joshua GRN 65
Reuben LVG 2
FARLAND, -----? DVS 5A
FARLEIGH, Andrew HRD 66
Wm. HRD 66
FARLEY, Clay BRN 11
Daniel GTN 127
Danl. HRY 214
Farris HRL 108
Jeremiah LVG 10
Jno. HRY 244
William OHO 7A
Wm. HRY 267
FARLIE, Peter GRD 102A
FARLY, John HRY 204
Jos. F. HRY 214
William HRY 214
FARMER, Widow H. LVG 16
---id? DVS 11A
Abraham HOP 244
Absolum UNN 154
Benj. FKN 162
Benjamin MNR 213
Charles BKN 4
Conrod SPN 7A
Eli P. SHE 122A
Eliz. HRY 244
Hen. HRY 260
Henry LNC 5
Henry PUL 37A
James GRN 75
James UNN 151
James HND 6A
Jas. HRD 66
Jeremiah BNE 14
Jeremiah GNP 177A
Jesse TOD 129
John LVG 16
John LGN 34
John HRD 76
John CLK 90
John NSN 195
John SHE 123A
John H. LVG 16
Joshua GNP 176A
Leonard CWL 58
Lewis HRL 108
Mary GRN 75
Otho BLT 168
Saml. BKN 8
Sarah SHE 123A
Stephen HRL 108
Thos. BBN 62
Wm. HRY 244
FARNEY, Hudson ETL 43
FARNSLEY, David JEF 38
James JEF 38
James JEF 43
FAROW, George JES 83
FARQUAR, Wm. JEF 27
FARR, John MAD 102
FARRA, John WDF 97A
FARRANTS, David SCT 96A
FARRAR, Edward SPN 9A
FARREL, Thomas CSY 210
FARREN?, Catharine M.? MAS 57
FARRIER, Joseph SCT 118A
FARRIS, Elija WAS 87A
George LNC 25
George KNX 314
Gilbert KNX 308
Isaac KNX 282
Isham KNX 308
Isham, Snr KNX 310
James LNC 69
James J. KNX 310
James M. KNX 310
John CLK 68
John KNX 304
John, Snr KNX 308

FARRIS, Lally KNX 310
Mariah KNX 308
Moses RCK 79A
Nathan LNC 69
Stephen LNC 19
William LNC 49
FARRISS, Isaac MAD 162
FARROW, Aaron FTE 97
Alexander MTG 231
Amos JES 79
Assa FTE 64
Henretta FLG 27A
Isaac MTG 289
Jno. MAS 61
Jno. MAS 72
John JES 96
John JES 97
Jos. M. MAS 59
Joseph T. CLK 91
Kenaz MTG 295
Peregrine MTG 231
Thos. FLG 27A
Wm. FLG 27A
FARTHING, Abner LGN 44
Abner HAR 152
John MAD 108
Mary LNC 71
Richard WRN 28A
William MTG 285
FARZIER, William FLD 17
FASE?, Prudence WTY 113A
FAST?, Elizabeth BBN 106
Nathan TRG 4
FAU?, W. H. S. MAS 80
FAUGHT, Gasper FKN 110
Powell OWN 100
FAUKNER, James, Sr. WTY 120A
FAULCONER, John MER 95
Martin SPN 10A
Sarah SPN 10A
FAULKNER, Achillas HRY 202
Alexander BRN 11
Benjamin TRG 13
Daniel WTY 120A
David BRN 11
Francis WTY 115A
George WTY 116A
James HRY 202
James WTY 116A
James D. HRY 204
John BRN 11
John GRD 115A
Jonas MTG 257
Joseph FTE 104
Lewis FTE 101
Mary LGN 29
Mary HND 9A
Nelson FTE 104
Nicholas SCT 125A
Peter GRD 85A
Pleasant LGN 29
Robert GRT 144
Thomas GRD 123A
William MTG 255
FAUNTLEROY, William M. LGN 39
FAUQUIER, George UNN 152
FAUT, Nelson FLG 58A
FAVIS, (See Faris) MAD 156
FAVORINS?, Silas JES 87
FAVOUR, John FTE 98
FAVOURS?, Silas JES 87
FAWN, James CWL 53
Jno. CWL 53
John CWL 37
FAWN, Lewis CWL 53
Wm. CWL 43
FAWT, William OHO 11A
FAY, James BNE 50
FEAGAN, George LGN 40
FEAGLEY, Peter BTL 321
FEAIR, Absalom / Abraham? CSY 210
Aron CSY 220
Edmund CSY 220
Edmund, Jun. CSY 222
FEALMAN?, Thos. BKN 20
FEAR, John HAR 152
John MTG 283
William FTE 99
William HAR 152
FEARES, James FTE 65
FEARIS, George LWS 95A
FEARMAN, Jane NCH 123A
FEARS, Archbald BTL 321
John PUL 35A
Thos. HRD 70
FEATHER, Jacob GRN 77
William BNE 14
FEATHERHITE, Andrew CSY 206
FEATHERKILL, George NSN 217
FEATHERSTON, Burwell FTE 98
Carolus FTE 99
James FTE 99
Jeremiah FTE 98
FEDERICK, Augustus JEF 49
Geo. A. JEF 48
Saml. JEF 40
FEE?, Geo. BKN 8
John BKN 18
John, Sr. BKN 18
FEEBACK, David NCH 110A
Gilbert NCH 110A
Jacob NCH 111A
John NCH 110A
Mary NCH 110A
FEEMSTER, Samuel MTG 297
FEES, Jacob ADR 20
FEGAN, Henry MAS 59
FEGETT, Caty ADR 20
FEIGLEY, Saml. MAD 130
FEILOR?, Telly HRL 108
FELAND, John LNC 33
Thomas LNC 49
Wm. LNC 11
FELCHER, Peter JEF 42
FELIX, Mary WDF 104
FELKINS, John ADR 20
John CLD 155
Martin CLD 155
FELL, Edward CHN 32
John CHN 32
FELLOWS, Henry UNN 146
Jonathan HND 11
FELMANT?, Jacob WRN 75A
FELPS, Cary ADR 62
Elizabeth BTH 214
FELTS, Archibald LGN 42
John LGN 44
FELTS?, Tilman WRN 62A
FELTY, Polly BTL 321
FEMESTER, John ADR 54
FENIX, Federick SPN 3A
John SPN 3A
Robert SPN 3A
FENIX?, David LWS 96A
FENLEY, Isaac JEF 46
FENLY, J.?/ G. SHE 141A
FENLY?, Tho. HRY 210
FENNEL, Geo. FKN 112
Jas. SCT 124A
FENTON, Caleb FLG 32A
Enoch MAS 64
John BKN 10
John ADR 20
Josa.? FLG 23A
Polly GRD 118A
Thomas GRD 102B
Zacariah LNC 27
FENTON?, (See Tenton) FLG 35A
FENTRESS, John MBG 135
Volentine BRK 253
FENWICK, Benj. WAS 60A
Ignat. M. SCT 105A
Susan WAS 71A
Wm. FKN 64
FENWINK, Enoch GSN 136A
Henery GSN 136A
FERCE?, Jessee HRY 216
FERELL, Wm. HRD 80
FERGERSON, Henry WAS 22A
John WAS 35A
Wm. B. WAS 47A
FERGUS, James, Junr. CLD 161
James, Senr. CLD 161
John CLD 161
FERGUSON, Abner KNX 306
Andrew BLT 172
Benjamin CLD 148
Catharine HRD 96
Champion CLD 148
Charles? LVG 16
David HRT 158
David PUL 58A
H----? LVG 16
Hugh JEF 25
Hugh HRT 158
J. HRY 228
James HRT 158
James PND 23A
Jesse PND 16A
John FLD 7
John BRN 11
John JEF 24
John JEF 26
John JEF 51
John FTE 90
John MBG 135
John CLD 145
John UNN 153
John HRT 158
John BLT 176
John TRG 8A
John MBG 135A
Joseph NSN 196
Josiah MTG 273
Lewis BRN 11
Martin LVG 9
Mary MBG 135A
Richard FLD 9
Richard BLT 176
Richd. JEF 21
Robert MNR 211
Robt. HRT 158
Saml. JEF 51
Thomas FTE 87
Thomas LWS 97A
Widow -.? LVG 16
William FLD 28
William CLK 105
William GTN 121
William CLD 145

Name	County	Page
FERGUSON, William	MTG	297
William, Junr.	CLD	145
William	FLD	1A
William	MBG	139A
Wilson	NSN	201
Wm.	JEF	26
FERIS, Absalom	CLD	165
Samuel	CLD	165
FERREL, ----a?	DVS	11A
Archibald	MAD	96
Cristina	MAD	146
Thos.	MAD	152
William	CSY	212
FERRELL, Edmund	BRN	12
Isaac	FTE	109
Jas.	FLG	59A
London	FTE	60
Michael	GRT	140
FERRIL, Ann	ALN	134
Charles	ALN	134
Enoch	PUL	46A
George	CLK	69
John	CLD	151
Thomas	CLK	77
William	CLD	148
FERRILL, John	LVG	10
William	LVG	10
FERRIS, Micajah	MAD	172
Pheby	MAD	140
Thos.	MAD	124
FERRISS, Dudley	MAD	176
FERRY, James	GSN	136A
John H.	JEF	25
FESLER, John	CLK	97
FESTER, John	GTN	123
FETHERINGILL, Elias	JEF	48
Jos.	JEF	52
Wm.	JEF	53
FETHERNGILL, Jno.	JEF	55
Mary	JEF	55
Reubin	JEF	54
FETTERS, Daniel	LWS	95A
Michael	LWS	94A
FEWEL, Henry	CHN	40A
James	SHE	157
John	SHE	157
Nancy	HRD	10
Polley	CSY	220
FEWELL, Abner	HAR	178
Elijah	HRD	54
John	FLG	26A
R------	ETL	43
Wm.	JEF	68
FI-?, David	HRL	108
FIAGLEY?, John	BTL	323
FIBEL, Frederic	SHE	156
FICKLAND, Charles	BTH	208
John	BTH	206
Thomas	BTH	202
FICKLIN, Asa	SCT	131A
Danl.	FLG	56A
Esther	ALN	132
Jarrett	MER	95
John H.	SCT	129A
Jos. K.	MAS	78
William	MTG	297
FIDLER, Jno.	FKN	136
Martin	BLT	184
Nancy	FKN	136
William	CHN	44
William	FTE	103
William	BLT	184
FIEDS, Ezekiel H.	MAD	178
FIELD, -----?	DVS	5A
-----?	DVS	6A
FIELD, -----?	DVS	6A
----ah?	DVS	6A
Abraham	JEF	41
Abraham	BLT	174
Abraham	NCH	124A
Aquilla	OHO	3A
Ezekiel	SHE	115A
Henry	BLT	162
James	MNR	207
John	JEF	41
John	ADC	68
John	BBN	120
Larkin	BBN	140
Reubin	JEF	39
Robert	BRN	10
Tarlton	ETL	40
William	JEF	36
William	ETL	40
William	NSN	206
William	OHO	5A
Zackariah	CLK	92
FIELD?, John	BKN	6
FIELDEN, John M.	SHE	137A
FIELDER, George	NCH	106A
John	NCH	106A
FIELDERS, William	CLK	96
FIELDING, James	LNC	45
James	WRN	61A
Joseph	WRN	61A
Nancy	LNC	77
William	WRN	55A
FIELDING?, John M.	LVG	16
FIELDS, ---kston	FLD	42
Abner	JEF	42
Abram	SCT	117A
Ambrose	MAS	57
Anderson	HRL	108
Arel?	HRL	108
Charles	BKN	19
Curtis	MAD	166
Daniel	MER	95
Davis	HRL	108
E., Mrs.?	MAS	53
Ezekiel	HRD	54
G.	MAS	54
Henry	MER	95
James	MER	95
Jas.	SCT	118A
Jesse	CLD	142
John	CLY	125
John	PND	22A
Joseph	BNE	14
Joseph	SCT	118A
Levin	BKN	13
Lewis	JEF	33
Lewis	HRY	206
Mathaw	HRL	108
Mathew	PND	21A
Mehaley?	SHE	140A
Obediah	WYN	96A
Obediah	WYN	102A
Richard	HAR	168
Rosanna	MNR	207
Sabery?	HRL	108
Sally	MER	116
Samuel	MER	95
Stephen	CLY	114
Steven	PUL	41A
Will	MAS	57
William	GRN	61
William	MER	95
William	PUL	64A
Willis	WDF	117A
Wm.	FLG	39A
Wm.? E.	MAS	53
FIERS?, Drury	GRN	65
FIFE, Ben	MAS	72
David	JEF	36
Jas.	FLG	71A
John	HRD	44
Johnathan	FLG	36A
Jonathan	MAS	58
Patk	JEF	23
Perry	MAS	53
Perry	MAS	70
FIFER, Betsy	JES	71
Jacob	NCH	103A
John	HOP	242
FIG, Willm.	LNC	57
FIGG, Benjamin	SHE	121A
Eli	SHE	122A
James	SHE	118A
John	FTE	99
John	NSN	195
Robert	BTL	321
Robt	BTL	313
Wm.	SHE	120A
Wm.	SHE	120A
FIGG?, Benj.	SHE	121A
FIGGINS, Aaron	MTG	275
Danl.	BKN	20
Garrod	CLK	97
James	BKN	4
Mr.?	BKN	18
FIGHT, Catharine	FKN	94
Jacob	NCH	128A
FIGHT?, Jacob	NCH	105
John	NCH	105
FIGHTMASTER, Frederick	BTH	190
George	HAR	160
John	HAR	146
Philip	HAR	162
FIGLEY, Abraham	SHE	119A
David	SHE	132A
John	OHO	10A
FIKE, Elijah	LGN	36
Lucy	SPN	9A
FILES, Absalum	MAD	142
Thomas H.	MBG	138A
FILSON, Ebenezer	HAR	132
Jas.	FLG	42A
Saml.	FLG	61A
Wm.	FKN	144
Wm.	FLG	73A
FIN, Evin	GNP	176A
FIN?, John, Sr.	BKN	18
FINCH, Mrs.	MAS	74
Abram	BRK	255
Absolom	MNR	199
Danil	CWL	53
Isaac	HRD	10
James	NSN	184
James	HOP	242
James	BRK	253
Jeremiah C.	WDF	120A
John	HRD	40
John	NSN	184
Walter	BRK	255
William	WDF	121A
William P.	LGN	37
Wm.	BBN	60
FINCHER?, Elias	CLY	117
William	CLK	77
William H.	CLY	117
FINCK, John	NSN	186
FINDLAY, Jno.	CHN	32
FINDLEY, Geo.	JEF	41
Howard	HOP	242
James	HAR	220
James	WTY	115A
John	MER	116

FINDLEY, Jonothan ALN 106
Mary HAR 156
Samuel LNC 11
Sarah MAS 63
Thos. ALN 106
FINDULL, Benjamin WRN 72A
FINE, Jacob JEF 60
FINELL, Nimrod L. CLK 67
FINESON?, James TRG 8A
FINEY, Jno. P. CHN 41
FINK, Daniel LWS 97A
John SHE 113A
FINLAY, Andrew CHN 31
FINLEY, Alex? CWL 40
Dabney CHN 45
David FLG 71A
Geo. JEF 36
George TOD 130A
Isaac HRT 158
James SHE 163
James C. LGN 23
John JEF 55
John FLG 71A
John SCT 111A
John B. SCT 114A
John G. JEF 32
John H.? JEF 46
Richd. JEF 55
Saml. HRT 158
Saml. SCT 123A
Susan SCT 139A
William LGN 38
William F. SHE 172
Wm. CHN 42A
FINLY, John JES 95
Thomas HRY 194
FINN, James ADR 64
Mashack SPN 20A
Peter ADR 62
Scarlet MTG 285
Thos. JEF 36
Wm. ADR 64
FINN?, Richard ADR 64
FINNED?, Joshua MAD 120
FINNELL, Benjamin BNE 14
Benjamin MER 95
James BNE 14
Johnson GRD 85A
Robert BNE 14
FINNEY, Alexr. TOD 125
James GRD 92A
Jno. ALN 126
Morgan ALN 128
Wm. ALN 128
FINNIE, Elijah UNN 154
Mary UNN 154
FINNY, Elizabeth JES 79
FINSLEY?, James ADR 54
FIPP, John BBN 104
FIPPS, Daniel HOP 244
George HOP 242
John HOP 244
Thomas GTN 117
William HOP 244
FIRBUE?, Jane HAR 132
FIREE?, Jessee HRY 216
FIRMAN, Aaron BBN 112
James BBN 120
Mary BBN 114
FIRMAN?, John MTG 291
FIRST, William LGN 23
FISEL?, Benjamin HAR 162
FISH, David GTN 132
James RCK 76A
John RCK 76A
Robt. H. SCT 121A
FISH, Tho. RCK 78A
Will RCK 77A
William CBL 14A
FISHBACK, Charles HRD 60
Charlotte SHE 165
Frederick BKN 8
George HAR 158
Jacob CLK 94
James FTE 62
Jessee CLK 87
John JES 85
John ALN 126
Martin BKN 14
Wm. JEF 65
FISHBEIN, Peter ALN 142
FISHEL, Michl. FTE 61
FISHER, Adam MAS 61
Adam MER 95
Alexander CLK 87
Barnard MER 95
Benjamin, Esqr. MER 95
Caleb MER 95
Daniel CBL 21A
David BRN 12
David FTE 69
David CBL 21A
Elias MER 95
Elijah MER 95
Ezekiel MER 95
Henry ETL 52
Henry CLY 122
James BRN 11
James JEF 43
James CBL 11A
Jeremiah MER 116
John BRN 11
John ETL 49
John FTE 63
John FTE 69
John GRN 72
John BTH 206
John BRK 253
John WRN 53A
John B. MTG 289
Joseph MER 95
Lewis HND 10A
Margaret BBN 134
Matthias PUL 60A
Meredith W. UNN 152
Nathan BBN 134
Peter BBN 146
Rebeca JES 84
Saml. MAS 55
Samuel FTE 95
Stephen LNC 75
Thomas MER 95
Thomas B. GRN 74
Thos. TOD 127
Thos. A. JEF 22
William BRN 12
William FTE 95
William L. HAR 210
Wm. BBN 82
Wm., Jr. BRK 253
Wm., Sr. BRK 253
Wm. H. GRN 69
Zachariah SHE 169
Zerobable NCH 126A
Readding HRY 192
FISHER?, Joseph, Jr. MTG 226
FISHLI?, John JEF 20
FISK, Henry MTG 233
FISKE, David CBL 14A
John CBL 14A
FITCH, Benjamin LWS 97A
FITCH, Collins FTE 80
F. B. JEF 23
Henry FLG 25A
James LWS 96A
Joseph LWS 97A
Salathael FLG 25A
Thos. FLG 25A
FITCHPATRICK, Wm. MAD 138
FITGERRALD, Francis JES 72
FITSGERROLD, Thos. WAS 58A
FITSJARELL, Isham MNR 191
William MNR 191
FITSJARRELL (See Fizjerral & Fitzjerral) MNR 191
FITZ-GERRALD, Jos. HRY 241
FITZCHEW, Lucy SHE 110A
FITZCHPATRICHES, John CSY 210
FITZCHPATRICK, James CSY 210
Thomas CSY 210
FITZGARRALD, George MBG 142A
Wilson MBG 135A
FITZGEARL, Davis HOP 242
FITZGERALD, -aml.? CWL 53
Ben. MAS 69
Benjn. MAS 63
D. MAS 74
Danl. FLG 25A
Moses MAS 74
S.? MAS 74
Silas SHE 158
Venable ETL 47
Wm. SHE 125A
FITZGERALDS, James SHE 174
FITZGERRALD, Jas. FLG 33A
FITZHUGH, Ann LGN 36
Coal JEF 64
George LGN 40
Henry LGN 36
Henry LGN 42
John LGN 36
Peter LGN 40
Robert LGN 40
Thomas LGN 36
FITZIMMINS, Jno. HRY 265
FITZJARREL, Jessee FTE 111
FITZJERALD, James PUL 63A
John PUL 57A
Tho. MAS 66
FITZJERRAL, John MNR 193
FITZJERRALD, Daniel FKN 116
Susanna BRN 17
FITZPATRICK, Chas. MAS 52
Dennis SHE 158
George PUL 55A
James NCH 122A
John FLD 32
John FLD 35
John FLD 38
John, Senr. PUL 55A
Jonathan FLD 32
Richd. HAR 166
Samuel PUL 58A
Thomas FLD 38
William FLD 21
William FTE 107
FITZSIMMONS, Patrick SHE 174
Richd. SHE 162
Thos. SHE 161
FITZWATER, John HAR 186

FITZWATER, Stephen HAR 198
FIZER?, David PUL 61A
FIZJERALL?, Jesse MNR 191
FLACK / FLASK?,
  John GTN 122
FLACK, James TOD 131
  James MAD 140
  John A. LNC 2
  William LNC 73
FLAGET?, B. J.,
  Rt. Revd.
  (Crossed Out) NSN 186
FLANAGAN, Charles BRK 253
FLANDERS, Ezekiel GNP 173A
  George HRD 18
  Jacob HRD 24
FLANERY, Danl. B. LVG 5
  Isaac LVG 7
FLANIGAN, John CBL 10A
  Margaret NSN 177
  Peter CLK 105
  S----? LVG 16
  Saml./ Jame? MAD 160
FLANIGIN, Austin WAS 70A
  Briant ADR 20
  John ADR 20
  Patsey ADR 20
  Torrance WAS 61A
FLANNAGAN, C. B. FTE 68
FLANNERY, Patsy LVG 12
FLARAH, William BTH 172
FLARETY, Roger NSN 210
FLAT, John HRT 158
FLAT?, Wm. GSN 136A
FLATHER, Benjamin MAD 144
FLATHERS, Edward MAD 144
  John MAD 142
FLECHER?, James GRD 94A
FLECKER?, James GRD 94A
FLEECE, Charles LNC 43
  John LNC 43
  John, Dr. MER 116
  Nicholas LNC 2
FLEENER, Samuel WYN 83A
FLEET?, William NCH 118A
FLEETWOOD, Adam FLD 13
  Isaac FLD 38
  Isaac CLY 132
  John FLD 14
  Thomas CLY 132
FLEMING/
  FLENNING?,
  Elizabeth CLK 89
FLEMING, Andw. PND 28A
  Francis MAS 76
  George BTH 152
  James MAD 92
  James FTE 108
  Jas. FLG 42A
  Jno. MAS 62
  John HAR 190
  John D. FLG 74A
  Leonard J./ I.? WDF 92
  Margaret CBL 10A
  Robert FLD 43
  Sarah SCT 100A
  Stephen MAS 66
  Stephen, Jr. MAS 66
  Susan FTE 95
  Thos. W. FLG 78A
  William BTH 150
FLEMMING, James BBN 64
  Patrick BBN 88
FLEMON, David BTL 323
FLENAGAN, John
  (Crossed Out) WTY 117A

FLENAGAN, John WTY 113A
FLENER, Moses BTL 321
FLENOR/FLENON?,
  Adam BTL 321
FLERNOY, James ADR 20
FLEST?, William NCH 118A
FLETCHALL, J. TOD 127A
FLETCHER, Abraham MAD 106
  Barton HRT 158
  Betsy ADR 20
  Elias CLD 146
  Elijah FLG 43A
  Elizabeth BTH 162
  Fanny CLD 146
  George FLD 5
  Green ADR 20
  Horatio HRD 58
  Jacob BTH 210
  James JES 79
  James MAD 92
  James CLD 146
  James HRT 158
  James MTG 233
  James SPN 9A
  Jas. CHN 43A
  Jilson MTG 273
  John LGN 40
  John CLK 82
  John TOD 127
  John CLD 149
  John KNX 284
  John MTG 287
  Joseph LNC 29
  Lewis LGN 35
  Mary FLD 5
  Matthew CLD 146
  Mercy MAD 116
  Nancy BTH 188
  Richard TRG 7A
  Robt. ADR 18
  Robt. HRD 60
  Thomas UNN 149
  Thomas BTH 176
  Thomas BTH 223
  Thos. HRD 60
  Washington BRN 12
  Washington CSY 220
  William LGN 34
  William HRL 108
  William CLD 149
  William MTG 271
  Wm. HRD 20
FLETCHUR, Polly CWL 53
FLETT, John CLK 101
FLICK, Chrstopher SHE 138A
FLICK?, Elizabeth BLT 192
  John BLT 152
FLID, Martha MAD 172
FLIN, John JEF 24
  Lofkin MNR 213
  Michael CLK 71
  William MNR 211
FLINN, -----? LVG 11
  Andrew ETL 39
  Arthur FLG 63A
  Benjn. MAS 53
  Catherine KNX 296
  Jno. MAS 53
  Jno. MAS 71
  John CLK 71
  John CLK 76
  Laughlin CLD 160
  Levy ETL 50
  M. JEF 25
  Nancy ETL 39
FLINN?, Ezekiel CLK 72

FLINN?, John PND 21A
FLINT, ---.? W. CWL 41
  E. CWL 38
  John CSY 204
  Martin JEF 56
  Simeon BNE 14
  Stephen CSY 206
  Thomas LGN 44
  Wm. JEF 56
FLIPPEN, Isaac MNR 209
  James MNR 207
  Jesse MNR 209
  Thomas MNR 207
FLOCKER, C. JEF 23
  John, Jnr. JEF 30
FLOID, Elizabeth TRG 4
  Elizabeth TRG 4
  Lawrance WAS 65A
FLOOD, Benjamin SHE 152
  Joseph SHE 162
  Joshua SHE 161
  Martha MTG 237
  Washington BRK 227
  William SHE 158
FLORA, Adam WRN 40A
  George WRN 40A
  James CBL 22A
FLORAH, John WDF 94
FLORAR?, Matthew CSY 218
FLOREM?, William WDF 99
FLORENCE, Moses HAR 202
  Nicholas HAR 202
  William HAR 202
  Willis B. NSN 177
FLORO, John LWS 93A
FLORRENCE, James BNE 14
  John BNE 14
FLORY, Godwin LNC 13
  Jacob FTE 84
FLOURNOY, David SCT 137A
  Francis FTE 109
  Hoy ETL 45
  James WAS 54A
  Lawrence ETL 45
  Mathew FTE 75
  Mathew W. JES 96
  Mathis WAS 50A
  Nancy MER 95
  Theodocia FTE 102
FLOVIN?, William JEF 37
FLOWERS, Austin GSN 136A
  Macajah WRN 55A
  Rebekah CLD 159
  Rolland LNC 67
  Thomas CLD 159
  Thos. ADR 20
  William CLD 159
FLOWIN?, William JEF 37
FLOYD, Abram, Jr.? PUL 44A
  Abrham. PUL 44A
  Ambrose HRY 260
  Aron MAD 148
  Benj. LNC 21
  Chs. JEF 32
  David GTN 130
  Elij. HRY 260
  Enoch WRN 37A
  G. R. C. JEF 45
  Henry LGN 28
  Henry C. UNN 150
  Henry H. UNN 150
  Jno. PUL 44A
  John LNC 21
  John UNN 150
  John C. UNN 150
  Jonathan MAD 148

Name	County	Page
FLOYD, Levi	SHE	116A
Matthew	BNE	14
Nathaniel I./ J.?	UNN	150
Nathl.	JEF	47
Robt.	ALN	106
Saml.	HRY	240
Samuel	BNE	14
Singleton	LNC	21
Thomas	LGN	28
Thos.	PUL	48A
Washington	GTN	130
William	BLT	156
FLOYD?, George	GRD	100A
FLOYED, Jesse	GSN	136A
John	GRD	102B
John	GRD	89A
Thomas	GRD	122A
FLOYET, Rt. Revd. Bishop	NSN	223
FLUALLEN, Henry	BTL	321
FLUM?, Ezekiel	CLK	72
FLURNOY, John	BNE	50
FLUTY, Ezekiel	MTG	293
Francis	CLK	91
John	CLK	73
John	CLK	74
FO-WOOD, Saml.	JEF	58
FOANS, John	BTH	170
FOARD, Jacob	FTE	70
FOBBLE?, Geo.	MAS	77
FODD, Abel	HAR	150
FODERY, Joseph	CLK	86
FODGE, Frederic	CLD	137
John	CLD	137
John	CLD	142
FOGARSON, Elizabeth	SHE	110A
FOGG, J.	JEF	23
FOGISH?, Peter	LVG	16
FOGLE, Charles	OHO	6A
John A.	WAS	37A
Joseph	WAS	37A
Robert H.	WAS	37A
FOLDEN, Mary	ADR	64
Wm.	ADR	64
FOLEY, Elijah	LNC	77
Elijah	FTE	101
James	HOP	242
James	WRN	64A
Jane	FTE	101
John	CWL	53
John	LNC	79
John	FLG	50A
Mary	FTE	97
Mason	CWL	53
Moses	LNC	79
Moses, Sr.	KNX	304
Spencer	LNC	79
Thomas	HOP	242
William	FTE	101
FOLIER, Isaac	MER	95
FOLKS, John	CWL	53
John	MBG	142A
Stephen	NCH	112A
FOLLER, Thos., Jr.	KNX	306
FOLLIER, James C.	MER	95
FOLLIS, Geo.	HRY	257
Mary	ALN	112
Richard	HRY	198
FOLLOWELL, Abriham	WAS	24A
Markas	WAS	24A
FOLLY, Danl.	MAS	65
FOLSTON, (See Tolston)	MAD	100
Elisha	MAD	102
FOLY, Elijah	MER	95
FONTAIN, Edmd? H.	JEF	59
FONTAINE, Aaron	JEF	45
FONTLEROY, John, Maj.	MER	95
FOOKS, Benjamin	HAR	184
Garrard	BBN	70
FOOKS?, William	HAR	136
FOOT, Jane	MAD	126
FOP?, John	CHN	32
FORB?, John	HRD	90
FORBES, Ely	CHN	31A
James	BRN	11
James	GRN	71
James	HRT	158
Jane	HRT	158
Jesse	CHN	31A
Jonathan	LNC	69
Mongomery	WYN	89A
Reuben	LNC	69
FORBIS, Isaac	RCK	81A
FORBISH, Mary	CHN	36A
FORBUS, Anne	CLD	140
May	HRY	216
FORBUSH, John	CLY	124
John T.	MAD	160
Thomas B.	CLK	71
Wm.	CLY	124
FORCE, (See Foree)		
Jno.	HRY	270
Nancy	SHE	172
Peter, Sr.	HRY	234
FORCE?, (See Foree?)		
Jesse	HRY	247
Silas	HRY	247
Thos.	HRY	247
FORD, --hn?	CWL	42
--sse?	LVG	4
Abner	HRY	254
Absalem	WRN	28A
Absolom	WDF	95
Ann	OHO	10A
Bailey	CWL	53
Baily	SCT	127A
Ben.	CHN	32A
Benj.	WAS	33A
Benj.	SCT	138A
Benjamin	WRN	38A
Benjn. B.	SCT	137A
Charity	JEF	33
Chas.	BBN	136
Danl.	CWL	53
Dilling	CWL	53
Elijah	CWL	53
Elisha	SHE	160
Elizabeth	GRN	56
Elizabeth	BBN	124
Elizebeth	WAS	33A
Frederick	LNC	45
George	HRT	158
H. -.?	HRY	230
Isaac	CLD	149
Isaac	TRG	8A
Jacob	MAD	136
James	LVG	9
James	BBN	124
James	SHE	151
James	OHO	11A
James	WRN	28A
James	WDF	114A
Jared	HAR	216
Jerret	HRY	254
Jesse	CWL	53
Jno.	FKN	94
Jno.	HRY	253
FORD, Jno.	HRY	254
John	BRN	11
John	CWL	38
John	HRD	88
John	BBN	124
John	GRT	141
John	SHE	150
John	SHE	158
John	HAR	176
John	TRG	3A
John	OHO	7A
John	PND	20A
John	PUL	53A
John	WDF	103A
John	GRD	104A
John G.	NSN	189
Joseph	HRD	46
Joseph	GRT	142
Joseph	OHO	8A
Joseph	WAS	33A
Lewis	MTG	225
Lewis	WAS	36A
Lewis	SCT	133A
Lydia	FTE	79
Margaret	MER	116
Martin	SCT	124A
Mary	FLD	46
Moses	HRD	26
Nancey	FKN	136
Nancy	GRD	90A
Nathaniel	FTE	77
Patrick H.	WRN	76A
Peter	BRN	11
Phillip	CHN	42A
Reub.	HRY	262
Reuben	FKN	78
Reuben	PUL	60A
Robert	NCH	108A
Robert	SHE	131A
Saml.	HRY	212
Spencer	SHE	150
Stephen	MAD	162
Thom.	CWL	53
Thomas	WDF	114A
Warner	HRY	254
Will.	SCT	133A
William	FTE	108
William	BBN	112
William	CLD	150
William	SHE	151
William	SHE	160
William	HRY	210
William, Jr.	HRY	230
William D.	LGN	31
Wm.	CWL	38
Wm.	CWL	53
Wm.	HRT	158
Wm., Jr.	CWL	38
Zachariah	PUL	63A
FORD?, Armsted	MAS	80
FORDE, Daniel	GRD	101A
Rubin	GRD	120A
Timothy	GRD	120A
William	GRD	120A
FORDEN, John	BBN	62
FORE, Joseph	LVG	16
Joseph	SHE	172
Peter	KNX	296
Peter G.	CHN	43
FOREE, Elizth.	HRY	184
Hezekiah	SHE	158
John	SHE	162
Jos. L.	SHE	126A
Peter	SHE	173
William P.	SHE	159
FOREE?, (See Force &Force?)		

FOREE?, Jno. L. HRY 256
Peter, Junr.? HRY 184
FOREMAN, Joseph NSN 216
Joseph, Sr. NSN 216
Thomas NSN 220
FOREST, Dennis HAR 208
Gresham HAR 210
FORESTER, John BRN 11
FORESYTHE, James BTH 208
FOREWORTHY?, Thomas CLK 62
FORGA, James MTG 277
FORGASON, Hugh ALN 102
John BTL 321
Vivian? BTH 206
FORGESON, James BTL 321
John BTL 321
Jonathan BTL 321
Paul BTL 321
William BTL 321
FORGEY, Hugh BBN 78
James LGN 32
FORGUSON, Hossy/ Hopy? FLG 53A
John FLG 40A
FORGY, James BTL 321
Samuel C. BTL 321
FORHAN, Nehemiah MBG 139A
FORISTER?, David GTN 125
FORKER, Thomas BLT 174
FORKNER, B. CHN 45
Henry ETL 43
James ETL 41
Richd. HAR 150
William HAR 164
Wm. ETL 43
FORKNER?, Rheuben HAR 150
FORMAN, E. MAS 80
Elizabeth BBN 62
Elizabeth BBN 74
Hamilton MTG 253
John LWS 88A
Jos. MAS 67
Joseph BBN 74
Saml. MAS 55
Thos. MAS 80
FORQUER, Jas. HRY 252
FORREST, Johiel? GRN 68
Richard WAS 18A
Thos. WAS 37A
FORRISTER, Hezekiah HRL 108
John HRL 108
FORROWMAN?, Tho. MAS 57
FORSETER, Edmund MBG 139
FORSITHE, Sol. GRD 119A
Thomas GRD 122A
FORSSEE, Geo. FKN 82
Wm. FKN 88
FORSTON, Frederick WDF 114A
FORSYTH, Augustus FTE 95
David JEF 52
Elisabeht BTL 323
Jas. JEF 58
Robt. JEF 52
Thos. JEF 19
FORSYTHE, Isaac BBN 124
Jacob HAR 178
James LNC 81
John MAD 140
John PND 26A
John NCH 126A
Joseph BTL 321
Matthew MER 95
Oliver BBN 132
Robert PND 19A
FORSYTHE, William LVG 16
FORT, Christopher LWS 90A
David LVG 4
Frederick WRN 48A
French WRN 52A
Garey? CHN 43
Jessee CHN 43
Joseph LGN 33
Micajah CHN 43
William WRN 42A
FORT?, John HRD 90
FORTENBURY, Jacob LNC 19
Wm. LNC 19
FORTER, Jno. ALN 112
John WRN 28A
FORTER?,
(See Foster?)
Danl. GRD 109A
James, Jr. NCH 127A
John CBL 21A
FORTNER, A--/ Ann? KNX 292
Jesse CLY 127
John KNX 294
John KNX 314
Jonas BTH 218
Jonas KNX 284
Porter WRN 32A
FORTUNE, Benjamin GTN 130
Michael MTG 267
Thomas BTH 204
Vincent MTG 247
William SPN 3A
FORWOOD, Hannah JEF 66
FOSHER, John WRN 31A
FOSS?, John CHN 32
FOSSEE?, Stephen JES 74
FOSSETT, Conelias LWS 96A
Robt. GRN 64
FOSTEN?, Jeremiah BBN 102
FOSTER/ FORTER?, John HRY 198
FOSTER, Abner WAS 49A
Alex. HRY 267
Archd. JEF 50
Archd. G. JEF 50
Arthur FLG 59A
Asa BBN 106
Bartlett BRN 11
Carter WRN 58A
Chares WYN 99A
Cornelius SPN 12A
David NCH 123A
David T. BTH 176
Drusilla MTG 247
Edmund LGN 31
Edmund WRN 70A
Elizabth CLD 160
Elzabeth NSN 206
Frederic WYN 93A
Gabl. TOD 124A
George G. LGN 43
Henry NCH 117A
Hezekiah WDF 107A
Hugh FTE 58
Isaac MAS 57
Isaac SCT 130A
Ivans HAR 186
James LVG 4
James BRN 11
James LGN 35
James LGN 43
James, Jr. BRN 11
James C. LGN 47
Jeremiah BTH 212
Jesse BBN 102
FOSTER, Jno. FKN 54
Job GNP 175A
John BRN 11
John CLK 66
John BBN 102
John MAD 110
John GRT 139
John HAR 186
John NSN 198
John, Jr. WYN 95A
John WRN 28A
John WRN 44A
John WRN 65A
John WDF 108A
John GNP 173A
Johnan. FLG 59A
Joshua CLY 114
Josiah GRN 61
Nancy LGN 29
Nancy SCT 109A
Nathan CHN 30
Nathaniel FKN 120
Nathaniel MTG 289
Paten? CLK 86
Patsey MAD 106
Peter OHO 3A
Phebe, Mrs. WYN 93A
Pleasant JES 86
Presly MAS 71
Rebecca FLG 62A
Richard BNE 14
Richard MAD 102
Robert BRN 10
Robert GTN 121
Robert MTG 273
Saml. BRK 255
Samuel LVG 13
Samuel BNE 14
Samuel BBN 74
Samuel HAR 184
Samuel GNP 173A
Susanna MAD 160
Tandy MAD 100
Thoma BBN 112
Thomas LGN 28
Thomas JES 76
Thomas FTE 91
Thomas WDF 93
Thomas GTN 117
Thomas HAR 186
Thomas WDF 108A
Thos. JEF 50
Weeden MAS 57
William FTE 83
William CLK 86
William GTN 132
William HRY 204
William SPN 12A
Wingfield BRN 11
Wm. HRD 92
Wm. MAD 100
Wm. WAS 86A
Zenus? FLG 62A
FOSTER?, Abner ALN 116
Dabney ALN 132
Danl. GRD 109A
James, Jr. NCH 127A
James NCH 126A
James J. ALN 130
Jeremiah BBN 102
Joel ALN 116
John CBL 21A
Jon ALN 130
Jud ALN 114
Nathl. FLG 79A
Peter B. ALN 130

FOSTER?, William ALN 116
FOSWOOD, Saml. JEF 58
FOTHERGALE, David BBN 102
FOTHERGILL, Jane FTE 93
FOUCH, Isaac JEF 36
James BTH 172
Wm., Snr. FLG 56A
Wm. FLG 52A
FOUCHEE, Wm. HRD 72
FOUCHEIR, John B. FTE 63
FOUDRAY, Wm. FLG 55A
FOUE?, (See Force & Foree?) HRY 247
FOUGHT, Leonard FKN 108
FOUGLE?, Christian HRD 94
FOULAND, Mary SPN 20A
FOULEY, William OHO 9A
FOULKS, John LGN 30
Joseph LGN 42
FOUNTAIN, James SHE 153
FOURMAN, Benjamin SHE 135A
Jos. SHE 135A
Joseph SHE 119A
Thos. SHE 135A
FOURTH, Josiah ALN 104
Larking ALN 98
FOUSHEE, Daniel NSN 181
John GSN 136A
FOUST, Lewis ADR 20
FOWEL, Bury MAD 92
FOWKE, William WRN 35A
FOWLER, --os.? CWL 39
Alexander BTH 198
Benjamin BNE 14
Bernard NSN 185
Bernard NSN 224
Bernard? TRG 8A
Charles BBN 142
Elictious? WAS 21A
Eligah CBL 2A
Elijah JES 96
Elizebeth WAS 71A
Ewd. HRT 158
Isaac KNX 306
Jacob CBL 5A
James HAR 188
James WAS 35A
Jas. HRD 76
Jeremiah MAD 148
Jeremiah CLD 157
Jesse KNX 308
John FTE 62
John CLK 88
John SHE 174
John WAS 29A
Jonas CBL 15A
Jos. CWL 37
Joseph BNE 14
Joseph ETL 42
Lewis LGN 34
Mary TRG 3A
Matthew HRT 158
Mordica CWL 43
Moses MAS 79
Nelly LVG 12
Robbert CBL 6A
Robbert CBL 23A
Robt. GRD 89A
Saml. SCT 95A
Samue BRN 0
Samuel TRG 3A
Thomas CLK 76
Thomas WAS 28A
Thos., Sr. KNX 306
Widw. CWL 38
William TRG 6A
FOWLER, Wm. WAS 51A
Zachariah MAD 148
Zachariah NSN 193
Zefeniah MAD 148
FOWLGER, John FLG 56A
Robt. FLG 61A
FOX, Abram ADR 20
Abram ADR 20
Allen HOP 242
Arthur MAS 52
Arthur WRN 37A
Benj. KNX 278
Benjamin CLK 87
Catharine MAD 152
Charles MAD 122
Daniel, Jr. HOP 242
Daniel, Sr. HOP 242
Gates CSY 224
Geo. S. FLG 31A
Isham R. MAD 150
Jacob BLT 178
James LVG 16
James CLK 90
James HAR 146
James HOP 242
James KNX 278
Jeremiah HOP 244
Jesse MTG 229
John BRN 11
John MAD 124
John NSN 217
John MTG 226
John WYN 93A
Jonathan CLY 116
Michael HRD 38
Morris SHE 109A
Nathan HOP 242
Newton TOD 133
Nichol. KNX 278
Noah HOP 242
Philip BLT 184
Prudence (Crossed Out) WTY 118A
Richard WDF 126A
Saml. MAD 100
Saml. MAD 116
Sarah JEF 24
Sarah WRN 37A
Thos. MAD 162
Titus HOP 242
William CLK 90
William PUL 52A
Wm. FLG 79A
FOX?, Prudence WTY 113A
FOXWORTHEY, Jno. MAS 66
Saml. FLG 29A
Thos. FLG 29A
Wm., Jr. FLG 30A
Wm. FLG 29A
FOXWORTHY, George NSN 186
James NSN 220
Vincent MTG 289
FOXWORTHY?, Enock CLK 70
Thomas CLK 62
FOY, David JEF 25
Frederick PND 31A
FOY?, (See Coy?) GRD 116A
FR--ER, Robert FTE 57
FRA--EN?, James ADC 66
FRADENBURGH, Isaac, Jr. CBL 9A
Isaac CBL 5A
Isaac CBL 7A
Jacob CBL 6A
FRAGIER?, Alex JEF 46
FRAIKES, Conrod HRD 12
FRAIL?, John CBL 10A
FRAILEY, Daniel HOP 242
FRAIM, William BLT 166
FRAIM?, George BLT 168
FRAIN, Esther FTE 110
FRAINKLIN, Conrad CSY 220
FRAISE, Frederick BRK 255
Michel BRK 255
FRAISER, Henry MNR 197
FRAISER?, James CBL 3A
FRAISERE? (See Frazies?) MNR 207
FRAKER, Michael, Jr. WRN 34A
Michael, Senr. WRN 61A
FRAKES, Barnabas MTG 273
Daniel BRK 255
Danil, Sr. BRK 255
John BBN 112
John BRK 255
Joseph, Sr. MTG 231
Nathan MTG 257
Polly BRK 255
Wm. BKN 8
FRALEY, Mary ALN 114
FRALEY?, Reuben FLD 5
FRAME, A.? B.
James GSN 136A
Samuel MTG 253
Sarrah GSN 136A
William BTH 188
FRAMEL?, William CLY 112
FRANCE--?, Alexander CLK 76
FRANCE, Danl. TOD 133
John HRD 40
Micajah BRN 11
Michael MBG 138A
Wm. BBN 114
FRANCE?, John MTG 267
FRANCES, Elisabeth FLD 45
Henry LNC 69
James CLY 131
Robt. GRD 107A
William BTH 150
FRANCIS, Bartlett BRN 11
Daniel FTE 84
David JES 77
Frederick BRN 11
Jessee CLK 88
John NSN 197
John WYN 89A
John?, Jr. CWL 36
John?, Sr. CWL 36
Joseph FKN 78
Lewis MAD 148
Malachi BRN 11
Morgan BBN 72
Osbern JES 85
Perril? MAD 132
Stephen TOD 127
Thomas JES 76
Thos. MAD 134
Vincent JES 85
William WYN 90A
Wm. BBN 76
James BBN 104
FRANCIS?, Patterson NCH 108A
FRANCISCO, John WDF 92
FRANE?, John MTG 267
FRANK, Elizabeth BRK 255
Fre. MAS 78
Geo. BRK 255
George -? BRK 253
Henry BKN 13

FRANK, Peter BRN 33
FRANKIN, Jasper LVG 3
FRANKLIN, Absalum CHN 40A
Barnard MAD 140
Bennet HRD 8
Claiborn, Jr. MER 95
Claibourn, Sr. MER 95
Edmond HOP 242
Edward GTN 121
Elisha WYN 91A
Frederick NCH 115A
Henry FTE 92
James MER 95
James NSN 207
James WRN 51A
James WYN 90A
James W. CLK 64
John BRN 11
John BRN 11
John FLD 30
John CLD 140
John NCH 115A
John A. MTG 289
Josep BKN 0
Lewis BRN 11
Martin WRN 51A
Nathan MAS 79
Reuben BRN 11
Reubin CLK 78
Rosanna MER 95
Stephen BRN 11
Stephen FTE 92
Thomas HRY 186
William DVS 19A
FRANKLING, Absalom TRG 3A
FRANKS, Elizabeth, Mrs. GRT 140
Jacob GRT 140
John GRT 140
Joshua CLD 148
Thos. HRY 268
William BNE 14
William GRT 140
FRANKUM, Joseph ADR 18
FRANKUM?, Wm. ADR 30
FRANS, Henry BRK 255
John BRK 255
Madison BRK 255
FRANSIS, Henry TRG 8
FRARY, Mary MER 95
FRASER, John HND 5
William, Jr. HND 10
William, Sr. HND 10
FRASEUR, John R. GNP 167A
FRASHEUR, James R. FKN 158
Jeremiah FKN 144
Robt. FKN 158
FRASIER, John MER 95
FRASURE, Katharine SHE 110A
FRATER, John BBN 64
FRAWELL, John CLK 105
FRAWER, John CBL 7A
FRAWNER, Mary WDF 111A
FRAY, Moses BNE 14
FRAZEE, Aaron MAS 62
Ephraim MAS 64
Jas. MAS 79
Moses MAS 64
Saml. MAS 54
Saml. MAS 68
FRAZEE?, Joseph BKN 13
FRAZER, Alexander FTE 64
Alexander MTG 281
FRAZER, Alexander SPN 6A
Charles C. FTE 110
Geo. MAS 69
George LVG 3
George HAR 136
Haston FLD 45
James LVG 2
James BRN 11
James MTG 273
James DVS 16A
Joel HAR 142
John LGN 23
John CWL 35
John FLG 53A
John FLG 73A
Sela HRY 259
William, Junr. CLD 166
Wm. S. CHN 44A
FRAZER?, Will MAS 65
FRAZIER, Alfred NSN 223
George WRN 34A
James OWN 105
James HAR 214
James C. LGN 36
Jas. SCT 124A
Jeremiah JES 76
Joel C. HAR 220
John HAR 214
Jonathan FLD 3
Jos. C. TOD 126
Josiah SCT 105A
Martin JES 76
Mary FTE 112
Micajah FLD 41
Robert PUL 63A
Stanwix? FLD 17
Thos. SCT 97A
William CLK 77
Wilson HAR 176
FRAZIER?, Alex JEF 39
Thos. CWL 46
FRAZIES?, Benjamin MNR 207
James, Sr. MNR 207
FRAZOR, John CBL 6A
Joseph CBL 13A
William CBL 6A
FRAZUER, James, Jr. MNR 201
FRAZURE, John WDF 119A
FREDERICK, Geo. JEF 40
Jno. JEF 49
John JEF 62
John KNX 294
Stephen KNX 286
FREDERIM?, F. GRD 82A
FREE, Nicholas ADR 20
FREEDLY, Jacob JEF 63
FREELAND, Joseph FTE 78
Robert BTH 182
FREEMAN, -ich.? CWL 42
Aron KNX 308
Barnet GNP 176A
Charles Y. FKN 160
Eli GTN 123
Fleming BRN 11
Geo. FKN 160
George BRN 10
George CLY 118
George CLY 122
Jaley MAD 154
John BRN 11
John JEF 37
John KNX 282
John WRN 45A
John P. LGN 40
Jonathan MAD 130
FREEMAN, Moab MAD 164
Moses MER 95
Nancy HRD 38
Nathaniel MAD 154
Robert, Jr. BRN 11
Robert, Sr. BRN 10
Thomas HRT 158
William BTH 156
William CSY 210
William MTG 247
William HND 8A
William J. MAD 154
Wm. HRD 38
Wm. MAD 116
FREER, Solmn. CWL 41
Wm. CWL 39
FREIGLEY?, John BTL 323
FREILEY, Adam MNR 217
Elizabeth MNR 215
Nicholas MNR 215
FREILEY?, Edward MNR 191
FRELAND, John FLG 56A
Robt. L. FLG 26A
FRENCH, Curtiss BNE 14
Edmund OHO 9A
Elisha HRD 24
Ephrain MER 95
Hannah MAD 144
Henry, Jr. MER 95
Henry, Sr. MER 95
Hugh ADR 18
Hugh ADR 20
Ignatius HRD 52
James MTG 257
Jas. MAS 67
Jno. MAS 58
John TRG 4
John ADR 20
John JEF 32
John LGN 34
John MER 95
John WRN 42A
John WYN 91A
Joseph WRN 66A
L. B. ADR 20
Margaret OHO 4A
Marshal JEF 20
Marshall JEF 28
Martin HRD 52
Mary JEF 36
Noah BNE 14
Ralph HRD 52
Roahton MAD 100
Robt. CWL 39
Simon CHN 38
Stephen HRD 52
Susanah HRD 52
Thos. HRD 52
William MER 95
William GTN 130
William NSN 189
Wm. CWL 34
Wm. RCK 84A
Wm. SHE 140A
FREND, Joel CLD 164
FRESH, Benjamin LNC 75
FRESH?, Francis GTN 130
FRETWELL, Richd. CHN 44
FRIDDLE?, Jacob BLT 164
FRIED, Jacob GTN 123
FRIEL?, Benjamin HAR 162
FRIELDS, --omas DVS 14A
FRIELDS?, ---derson? DVS 14A
--erly? DVS 11A
FRIEND, Andrew GSN 136A

FRIEND, Chas. HRD 82
George ETL 50
Isaac HRD 82
Jacob GNP 166A
Jesse GSN 136A
Jonathan GNP 166A
Nancy ETL 44
Nelly? GTN 122
FRIER, Cristener MAD 172
John PND 18A
FRIGATE, Reuben BTH 166
FRILEY, Daniel GNP 165A
Federick GNP 167A
FRILIY?, Isaac GNP 169A
FRILLY?, Isaac FLD 22
FRILY, Martin HND 8A
FRISBEE, Johnathan S. WYN 106A
FRISBEY, Isaac FTE 65
FRISBEY?, John FLD 12
FRISEUS?, George ETL 39
FRISH, Nicholas LGN 35
FRISLER, Henry JES 90
Peter JES 90
Peter, Dr. JES 90
FRISTOD, Jesse MAS 63
FRISTOE, Danl. TOD 132
Richd. MAS 65
Rob.? L. CWL 36
Thos. MAS 59
FRITH, Thomas GRD 97A
FRITS?, William CHN 35A
FRITTS, Michael CLK 72
FRITZLIN, George WDF 126A
FRIVET?, Fredrick CHN 41
FRIZELL, Henry LGN 22
Robert LGN 30
FRIZLE, Widw. CWL 37
FRIZZLE, Archibald LWS 86A
Dawson LWS 87A
Jacob LWS 87A
William LWS 86A
FROGG, Lucrecia CLD 158
William, Junr. CLD 158
FROGG?, William Senr. CLD 150
FROGGET, William BRN 12
FROMAN, Abrm. HRD 32
Absalom BLT 164
Arthur JES 85
Isaac BLT 168
FROST, Elizabeth FTE 65
Ichabold FTE 60
James WYN 81A
James WDF 97A
Jedediah ALN 92
John JES 92
Joseph ALN 92
Joseph CBL 2A
Simeon JES 74
Stephen JES 92
FROWMAN, Jacob WAS 47A
FROWMAN?, Elijah WDF 101A
FRUIT, James CHN 35
Thomas CHN 35
FRUNNELS?, Daniel BBN 130
FRWET?, Fredrick CHN 41
FRY-EAN?, John NSN 192
FRY, Aaron FTE 95
Abraham JEF 55
Abraham HAR 164
Barbary JES 95
Benjamin HAR 158
Daniel NSN 201
Danl. CLY 127
Edward WDF 101
FRY, Eli ALN 118
Elijah SHE 117A
Ferdinan LWS 95A
George BNE 14
George FTE 97
George, Jr. CLK 105
George, Senr. CLK 76
George LWS 95A
Henry FTE 95
Henry, Sr. WYN 101A
Henry SHE 110A
Isaac, Sr. SHE 117A
Isaac SHE 114A
Jacob SHE 111A
Jacob SHE 120A
John FTE 61
John JES 87
John FTE 107
John LWS 87A
John WYN 93A
John NCH 110A
John E. NSN 201
Joshua GRD 116A
Martin SHE 120A
Mary? HAR 164
Michael ETL 48
Michael HAR 168
Michael WYN 93A
Mima MER 114
Peter WYN 92A
Solomon SHE 112A
Susan FTE 95
Thomas W. MER 95
Thos. W. TOD 125A
Voluntine PUL 62A
William HAR 164
William HAR 170
William A. JES 89
FRY?, Andrew BKN 4
Noah GTN 119
FRYAT, Edwd. WAS 38A
FRYE, Abm. BBN 142
John CSY 206
FRYER, David MTG 291
Jane GTN 118
Robt. M. BTH 180
Tapley GRN 54
Walter, Sr. PND 31A
Walter PND 31A
FRYER?, Resin CWL 31
FRYLEY, Benjamin ETL 45
FRYMAN, George NCH 103A
Henry HAR 194
Jacob NCH 103A
Philip HAR 194
Philip NCH 103A
FRYMER, John BRK 255
FRYMIER, Polly BRK 255
FRYREAR, Francis HRD 44
Jere HRD 14
FUBACK?, (See Feeback) NCH 110A
FUEL, Benjamin MER 95
FUEL?, Ephraim HAR 162
FUGATE, Benj. CLY 132
Charles CLY 130
Eli CLY 119
George HOP 244
Henry CLY 131
James Senr. NCH 124A
John H. PND 17A
Jonathan CLY 118
Lewis HOP 242
Martin CLY 132
Martin HOP 242
Martin PND 18A
FUGATE, Randolph BTH 220
William NSN 193
Wm. PND 23A
Zachariah CLY 132
Zachariah HOP 242
FUGATT, Andrew S. GNP 169A
FUGET, Mary BBN 138
FUGIT, Benjamin FLD 45
James FLD 10
James FLD 10
FUHER?, Henery CBL 21A
FULCHER, A. TOD 134
John BRN 11
Richard BRN 11
Tho. MAS 56
FULDS, Joseph WAS 19A
FULFORD, A. H. CLY 117
FULKENSON, Abigal NSN 211
Philip NSN 211
FULKERSON, Abraham MER 95
Ful? GSN 136A
John GSN 136A
Peter GSN 136A
Philip GSN 136A
William MER 115
FULKESON, Federick LVG 7
FULKINSON, Adam OHO 8A
Fuleard OHO 8A
Jacob OHO 8A
John OHO 8A
FULKS, Arthur GNP 169A
Gabriel HRL 108
John FLD 26
Joseph GNP 169A
Obadiah GNP 169A
Ralph BTH 210
FULLALOVE, Anthony MAD 102
James S. MAD 182
Larkin MAD 102
Salley MAD 152
Wm. MAD 112
FULLENTON, Thomas TRG 7A
FULLER, Allsee TRG 7
Daniel CHN 33A
Darius SHE 156
Gilbert HRY 264
Green BTL 323
Jacob E. CWL 38
John BKN 6
Jones BTL 321
Joseph BKN 9
Joseph CBL 5A
Joseph NCH 111A
Nathaniel BKN 19
Stephen MAS 65
Will MAS 62
Wm. S. HRY 264
FULLERTON, David CLY 113
FULLILOVE, John BNE 14
FULLINWIDER, Abram SHE 165
Henry SHE 154
Jacob SHE 154
FULTNER?, Henry CLY 128
FULTON, Ben HRD 70
Daniel HRD 44
David SHE 124A
Elizabeth FLG 42A
Hugh MAS 72
Jacob SHE 151
Jane FLG 34A
Jos. MAS 68
Nathaniel SPN 10A
Samuel NCH 108A
Samuel MBG 136A
FULTON?, James GNP 165A
FUNDLEY, William LNC 71

FUNK, Abn. HRY 222
Adam WRN 58A
Alexr. HRD 16
Jacob JEF 46
Jacob WAS 69A
Joseph WAS 65A
Peter JEF 45
Peter JES 89
FUNKHOUSER, L. Wm. GSN 136A
FUNLANON?, Michl. CWL 38
FUNRTR--?, Humphrey MAD 134
FUQUA, David BNE 14
Elizabeth HND 7
John HND 7
John M. GNP 172A
Joseph HRT 157
Moses GNP 167A
Stephen LGN 35
Thomas MTG 281
William BNE 14
William MTG 281
Wm. GNP 172A
FUQUAY, Henry BLT 164
John HRY 212
Joseph HOP 242
Obeh. W. FLG 67A
Saml. HRY 212
Washington BNE 14
FURBUSH, Mary LGN 47
William LGN 45
FURGARSON, Joshua C. SHE 117A
Wm. SHE 117A
FURGASON, Alexander HOP 242
Henry HAR 196
Samuel FTE 75
Thomas HAR 216
FURGERSON, Hugh FKN 150
James WRN 31A
John CHN 40A
Thomas WRN 53A
William CLY 127
FURGERSON?, Nancy ADR 20
FURGUSON, ---lvester? HRY 214
Bryant FTE 98
Henry FLG 71A
John FTE 89
John FLG 43A
Martha MER 95
R. HRY 214
FURLEY, John ADR 20
FURLY?, Francis HRY 182
FURMAN?, James CHN 29
FURNACE, William WRN 29A
FURNER?, Cornelius WRN 31A
FURNES, Benjamin GTN 135
FURNES?, Cornelius WRN 31A
FURNEY, Betsey GRD 107A
John GRD 107A
FURNICE, Wm. JEF 55
FURNIS?, James, Sr. GTN 134
FURNISH, James GTN 134
Joel GTN 135
William HAR 142
FURNISH?, John GTN 134
FURNSTER?, Samuel MTG 297
FURQUERN?, James CLD 144
FURR, Arlinncy? WDF 97
Edwd. FLG 32A
French GRD 89A
Jacob FLG 26A
Joseph JES 91
FURR, Will/ Wile? FLG 29A
FURS?, Drury GRN 65
FURSLEY?, James ADR 54
FURY?, Obadiah HAR 140
FUSTON?, Betsey, Mrs. WYN 103A
FUTCHER?, Wm. FKN 108
FUTERALL, John TRG 6A
Nathan TRG 8A
Thomas TRG 6A
Winburn TRG 5A
FUTHY, Benjamin FTE 69
FUTRELL, Daniel TRG 12A
FUTTNER?, Henry CLY 128
FYFFE, James LWS 97A

G-----?, Jane CBL 17A
G----?, Lander JEF 58
Thos. J./ I.? SHE 127A
G----ER?, David WTY 113A
G---?, Alex BBN 96
G---N?, David LVG 16
G---NER?, David WTY 113A
G---ON?, William LVG 16
G--AN?, James CWL 46
G--N?, Richard A. LVG 16
G--PY?, William LVG 16
GAAR, Adam HRT 159
GABARY, Rhoda LNC 17
GABBARD, Edwd. CLY 115
Edwd. CLY 122
George MER 96
Henry MER 96
Henry CLD 147
Jacob CLY 130
Jacob, Jr. CLY 115
James DVS 15A
John MER 96
John DVS 14A
John DVS 17A
Matthias MER 96
Michael MER 96
Michael CLY 113
Michael CLD 151
Peter MER 96
William DVS 17A
GABBART, George CSY 222
John CLD 148
Thomas CSY 226
GABBERT, George WAS 28A
John WAS 61A
GABBOARD, James LNC 59
GABBORD, George LNC 57
GABLE, John HRD 16
GABLE?, Ben HRD 76
GABRALL, Elizabeth JES 79
GABREATH?, Hervey CLD 153
Larken W. CLD 153
GAD---?, Reese CBL 19A
GADARD, Francis OWN 104
GADBERRY, Thomas BRN 12
Wm. ADR 24
GADBURY, Christeney CSY 226
Samuel CSY 228
GADD, Thos. RCK 75A
GADDIE, Eliza GRN 73
GADDIS, Gege GRN 70
GADDISS, John CSY 206
GADDY, Barnet CLK 74
Francis GRN 59
George GRN 69
George, Jr. GRN 53
Silus HRT 158
Thomas ETL 51
Wm. HRT 159
GADLER, George FLD 30
GADLEY?, John ALN 126
GADSBURY, John LGN 34
GAFFIN, Otho NCH 126A
GAFNEY, John GRD 119A
GAGAR?, Elijah JEF 52
GAGER, Wm. JEF 68
GAGER?, Joel, Sr. JEF 35
GAGGARD, Dabney CHN 42
GAILBREATH, Robert JEF 40
GAILEY, Benjamin SHE 165
Elizabeth SHE 164
Hugh SHE 165
James SHE 164
Samuel SHE 165
GAINES, Abner BNE 16
Bernard FTE 62
Churchill BNE 46
Daniel FTE 111
Francis FTE 77
Francis H. GNP 171A
Gabriel FTE 110
Gabriel P. FTE 89
George BNE 14
Harvey J. SCT 137A
James BNE 16
James WDF 123A
James M. BNE 16
Jas. SCT 134A
John P. BNE 16
John W. WRN 58A
Oliver SCT 92A
Richard BNE 14
Richard CHN 28A
Richd. LNC 5
Robert WDF 123A
Samuel FTE 105
Thomas MTG 267
William BNE 14
William F. LGN 30
Wm. M. BNE 14
GAINESS, James CHN 29
GAINEY, Matthew MBG 135
Matthew MBG 133A
GAINS, Barnard HRY 254
Caty OWN 102
Edward ALN 104
Gabriel MER 96
Geo. HRY 254
Jno. R. HAR 164
John CLK 85
John CLK 91
Richard HAR 168
Werly? JES 75
William MER 96
William GRD 96B
Wm. HRY 249
Wm.? ALN 96
GAINS?, Thomas L. LGN 37
GAITHER, Abner ADC 68
Greenberry NSN 198
Greenberry A. HRD 96
Harriet? NSN 178
John R. BLT 166
Nat ADC 66
GALAGER, Miles BBN 144
GALAGHER, Charles MER 96
GALAPSIE?, William LWS 96A
GALASPE, Gerge MAD 164
Joshua MAD 124
GALASPI?, Margaret, Mrs. WYN 96A
GALASPY, John OHO 5A
GALAWAY, Elijah BKN 9
GALBREATH, Dav. HRY 268
Robert CLD 166

GALBREATH, Wm. HRY 268
Wm., Jr. HRY 253
GALBRETH, Danl. CHN 39
Danl. CHN 40
Jas. CHN 38
Jas./ Jos.? HRY 259
Jno. CHN 38
Macam? CHN 39
GALE, Henry UNN 146
John GTN 120
John BBN 124
John E. WDF 122A
Josiah GTN 133
Judith WDF 122A
Robert F. WDF 122A
GALEPSIE?, William LWS 96A
GALION, Thomas WTY 110A
GALISPI, Wilson MAD 136
GALL?, Jonathan WRN 36A
GALLAGER, Chas. MAS 76
GALLAGHER, Jno. MAS 54
John FLG 37A
GALLAHER,
Jas./Jos.? HRD 18
Patrick LGN 30
Thos. HRD 18
GALLASPE,
Elizabeth MAD 124
GALLASPIE, Isaiah FLG 55A
GALLAWAY, ----.? CWL 34
Daniel GRN 59
Isam GRN 65
John WAS 31A
Joseph BBN 146
Robt. BRK 257
GALLEGER, Caleb BKN 2
GALLHAM, Amos CHN 41
GALLIARD?, Jno. M. MAS 81
GALLIGHER, Elen FLG 65A
Isaac FLG 33A
GALLIHACKER,
Patrick CBL 19A
GALLION, Elijah FLD 12
GALLIWAY, John MAD 170
GALLOP, Enoch MTG 233
GALLOWAY, -----? DVS 9A
-ariah? DVS 10A
Archibald HND 8
Daniel MER 97
Edmund HND 7
Elizabeth BRN 12
Frankey HND 8
James MER 97
Jas. SCT 103A
John HND 12
John BRN 13
John SCT 134A
John G. FLD 27
Obadiah HND 7
Robert BTH 156
Saml. SCT 103A
Thos. PUL 40A
William WDF 98A
GALLOWAY?, -----? DVS 9A
GALOWAY, Uriah HND 8
GALSPSIE?, William LWS 96A
GALT, David FLG 51A
Matthew FKN 148
Wm. C. JEF 19
GAMBLE, Bradley LGN 36
Henry LGN 35
Jesse LGN 36
Josiah BBN 86
Martha CHN 31
Mary CBL 5A
Saml. LVG 16
GAMBLE, Saml. CLK 71
William LGN 36
William LGN 36
Wm. JEF 27
GAMBLIN, James HOP 244
John HOP 246
Joshua HOP 246
William HOP 246
GAMBOL, Wm. CHN 31A
GAMBREL?, Anne GTN 132
GAMBRELL, John CLY 128
William CLY 116
GAMES, Margrett PND 26A
Wm. H. BNE 50
GAMES?, Absolum SCT 123A
GAMMON, Jessee MBG 136A
GAMON, Richard D. GNP 172A
Saml. W. GNP 176A
GAMS, Thomas, Jr. GRN 59
GAN---ETY?, Martin BRK 257
GANARD?, James,
Jr. BBN 142
Thomas BBN 134
GANAWAY, Isaac BRK 255
GANAWAY?, Wm. BRK 255
GANDY?, David GNP 176A
GANER?, John RCK 81A
GANES, Joseph MAD 104
Richd. FKN 132
Thomas GRN 79
Thos. FKN 96
Thos. FKN 132
Will. KNX 308
GANES?, Francis GRN 69
GANET?, Lemuel CHN 28A
Thos. WAS 39A
GANETT, Loving HRY 212
GANETT?, Reason NSN 213
Saml. BBN 136
Waller L. NSN 186
William MTG 229
GANIWAY, John GSN 137A
Sarah GSN 137A
GANN, Thomas WYN 92A
GANNEL?, Richd. SCT 126A
GANNETT?, (See
Garrett?) WDF 95
GANNON, Danby M. GTN 129
Daniel FLD 34
James FLD 28
James WAS 39A
William FLD 28
GANNY, Uriah ALN 104
GANNY?, Burket G. FKN 106
GANO, Aaron CBL 5A
John S. CBL 4A
GANOE, Danl. SCT 110A
Will SCT 110A
GANOLE?, David BLT 166
GANT, John BNE 16
John HOP 244
Robert BNE 16
Thomas HOP 246
GANT?, Archibald CHN 46
GANY?, Cheek TRG 3A
GARD, Jesse TRG 4
GARDEN, Silas JEF 37
GARDENER, John MNR 209
John A. BTL 323
GARDENNER, Mary MAD 180
GARDENR, James MAD 140
GARDINER,
Churchwell MTG 287
James MTG 263
John CLK 92
Joseph MTG 287
GARDNEER, James NSN 216
GARDNER, Alexander HRT 158
Aron FLG 50A
Arthur SCT 97A
Asa B. WRN 49A
Auth. FLG 54A
Ben HRD 62
Bennet SCT 97A
Chas. FLG 50A
Clemont WAS 42A
Daniel WRN 49A
David TRG 4A
Edmond HRT 159
Elias CLK 98
Elias H. CLK 98
Elisha HRT 158
Elizabeth FTE 79
George MAD 174
Henrietta NSN 217
Isidore NSN 217
James NSN 220
James PND 26A
James WAS 44A
James WDF 104A
James P. HOP 244
John HRD 26
John HRT 158
John MAD 168
Joseph SCT 107A
Mason WDF 93A
Nancy GTN 127
Nelson MAD 130
Nicholas FLG 50A
Nugent FTE 64
Rhal.? WAS 54A
Richard BRN 13
Robt. FLG 55A
Saml. P. HRD 32
Silas NSN 220
Thomas CLK 66
Thompson BRN 13
Thos. WAS 55A
William BRN 13
William WRN 49A
William WDF 104A
William WDF 126A
Wm. MAD 96
Wm. HRT 159
Wm. HRT 159
Zachariah MAD 94
GARDNER?,
Catharine NSN 214
GARE, Joseph WAS 25A
Lewis WAS 25A
Solomon WAS 25A
GAREHART, Adam FLD 17
John FLD 41
Joseph FLD 41
William FLD 44
GARH?, B. R.? MAS 69
Michael MAS 65
GARITY, John ETL 39
GARLAND, Ambrose WTY 115A
Jas. RCK 79A
Jesse LNC 77
John BNE 16
John KNX 292
Lewis KNX 292
Robert WRN 62A
Sol. KNX 292
Thomas WRN 62A
GARLINGHOUSE,
Gamerel? HRT 158
James HRT 158
James HRT 158
GARMAN, Adam CLD 143

GARMAN, Anne CLD 143
George CLD 143
John CLD 143
GARNER, Abigal B. BTH 202
Andrew B. BTH 202
David, Jr. WYN 90A
David, Sr. WYN 101A
David, Sr.? WYN 90A
Henry, Sen. WYN 80A
Henry WYN 81A
Jacob BTH 202
Jacob B. BTH 202
James CLK 84
Jeremiah LGN 23
John CWL 53
John BBN 64
John BBN 76
John WRN 65A
John WRN 73A
John WYN 81A
Jonathan CLK 90
Parish ADR 22
Parish ADR 22
Thomas WTY 112A
Thomas SHE 113A
Thos. MAD 154
Vincent PUL 62A
William BBN 112
GARNES?, Absolum SCT 123A
GARNET, Anthony CHN 45A
Oliver CLD 146
Reubin HRD 12
Reubin WDF 94
GARNET?, Leonard FTE 87
GARNETT, Anderson WDF 114A
Andrew HAR 196
Benj. SHE 123A
Edmund BNE 16
Elijah BNE 46
Geo. MAS 56
James WDF 109A
Jeremiah BNE 16
John BRN 12
John GTN 119
Larkin HAR 196
Lewis FTE 82
Richard BRN 12
Robert BRN 13
Robert BNE 16
Sarah JES 82
Silas MTG 269
Thomas BBN 124
Walter? GTN 131
Wesley M. KNX 278
William BNE 16
William MTG 297
William WDF 124A
Willis W. SHE 137A
GARNETT?, (See Garrett?) WDF 95
GARNITT, Zachariah JES 91
GARR, Benjamin MER 96
Benjamin BLT 160
John MER 96
Lawrence MER 96
Nicholas JEF 48
GARR?, Michael MAS 65
GARRARD, Danl. CLY 119
Edward JES 81
Elijah JES 87
James BBN 134
John PND 30A
Larkin JES 92
Stephen BBN 94
Thomas CBL 21A
Wm., Jr. BBN 144
GARRARD?, James, Jr. BBN 142
Thomas BBN 134
GARRARDS, Eenry (Estate) HND 9
GARRET, Danl. CWL 38
Ignatius GNP 171A
Isaac CHN 38
John CLD 165
Mansel? WYN 101A
Robert ADR 22
Sina CLD 156
Thomas CLD 164
William CLD 142
GARRET?, Lemuel CHN 28A
Thos. WAS 39A
GARRETT, -anl.? CWL 36
Antony? CBL 8A
Ashton MTG 297
Benjamin PUL 63A
Danl. HRY 190
Elizabeth SHE 130A
Finley MTG 289
Fleming J./ I.? FTE 81
Francis GTN 124
Henry FTE 81
J. TOD 132
James MTG 287
Jas. T. TOD 124A
John CWL 42
John HRY 186
John MTG 285
John WAS 28A
Morice SHE 116A
Murdock T. MTG 257
Nimrod MTG 271
Robert MTG 289
Silas JEF 41
Thomas J. FTE 67
William FTE 59
William HAR 142
Wm. JEF 39
GARRETT?, Hugh WDF 100
John WDF 95
Reason NSN 213
Saml. BBN 136
Waller L. NSN 186
William WDF 95
William MTG 229
GARRIS, Benjamin HOP 246
Sikes MBG 140
GARRISON, Benjamin BRN 12
Elwell FTE 84
Geo. MAS 68
George HRT 159
H. A. ALN 110
Jacob CBL 8A
James HRT 159
John BRN 12
John JES 81
John M. ALN 112
Levi SPN 17A
Mark ALN 102
Mary MAD 122
Mathew WRN 50A
Robt. SHE 136A
Salsberry GSN 137A
Samuel ALN 102
Shadrack BRN 13
GARRISSON, James BKN 4
GARRITT, Thomas J./ I.? MTG 299
GARROT, Edmond ALN 138
Henry SPN 18A
Peter MER 97
GARROTE, Coonrod JEF 33
GARROTT, Elimelech FLD 27
John HND 9
Midleton FLD 30
GART?, Michael MAS 65
GARTH, Ben HRY 216
Catharin TOD 133
Daniel LWS 87A
David HRY 216
John SCT 139A
Rodes WYN 106A
Thomas BBN 140
William HRY 216
William HRY 216
GARTHRIGHT, John SHE 156
GARTON, Ann HAR 160
Anthony HAR 162
Wm. TOD 131A
GARTRELL, Richard JES 79
GARVEY, Jno. FKN 158
Job GTN 117
Samuel GTN 117
GARVIN, David MER 96
David HRT 159
Isaac LNC 17
John MBG 135
John NSN 212
Saml. FLG 53A
Samuel MER 96
GARVIN?, Johnson FLG 53A
GARY, Frederick HOP 272
Wm. MAD 162
GARYER?, Benjn. OHO 8A
GASESINGER, Jacob OHO 5A
GASEWAY, James SHE 121A
John SHE 121A
Nicholas SHE 121A
Samuel SHE 120A
GASH, Thomas MER 96
GASH?, B. R.? MAS 69
Michael MAS 65
GASKENS, Frances LVG 2
GASS, David MAD 104
James CLK 80
James MAD 94
James MER 117
John BBN 142
Wm. MAD 112
GASSAGE, Charles GRT 140
GASSAWAY, Benjamin BRN 33
Mary BRN 13
Nicholas BRN 13
Samuel BRN 13
Uriah HRD 82
GASTINEAU, Geo. PUL 47A
Job PUL 37A
GASTON, Hugh KNX 308
James PUL 39A
Robt. KNX 308
William CHN 29A
GASWAY, Samuel BLT 166
GATELY, Thomas SPN 21A
Widw. CWL 44
GATER, Beil SPN 23A
Johnny SPN 23A
GATES, David MAD 96
Elijah SHE 173
Elijah GRD 113A
George MBG 141
Isaac JEF 44
James BRK 257
John MBG 142
John BRK 257
Joseph CLD 164
Levi HRD 78
Michael TOD 129A
Nathan CWL 39

GATES, Patience MAD 144
Philip SPN 12A
Robert CLD 165
Salley MAD 142
Sally MER 96
Squir JEF 53
Will. MAS 52
William MER 96
William MNR 195
GATESKILL, Ann, Mrs. CLK 97
John S. CLK 66
William CLK 97
GATEWOOD, Claburn FTE 104
Elizabeth FTE 104
Fielding LGN 36
Fullington WRN 74A
Henry GRN 50
Hugh S. GTN 124
James MTG 283
James WRN 74A
Jas. JEF 25
John CWL 32
John ALN 102
John SCT 101A
Joseph CLK 85
Larkin FKN 106
Leonard JEF 38
Peter FTE 89
Peter FTE 104
Reuben HRY 202
Richard JES 82
Robert JES 75
Robt. A. FTE 61
Tho. R. HRY 188
Thomas FTE 111
Thomas R. FTE 112
GATHER, Edwd. B. WAS 78A
GATHRITE, Saml. SHE 129A
GATLIFF, Aron KNX 304
Charles WTY 120A
Cornelius WTY 114A
James WTY 116A
Moses WTY 119A
Reese WTY 118A
GATLIN, Alexd. CWL 58
Jessee HOP 246
GATRELL, Dennis WYN 101A
GATSON, James CLK 93
William CLK 97
GATTEN, Charles GSN 137A
James GSN 137A
Thos. GSN 137A
GATTIN?, Jessee HOP 246
GATTNEY?, Wm. ALN 98
GATTON, Samuel NSN 220
Sylvester SHE 132A
Tho. ALN 132
Thomas BNE 16
GATY, Harriett JEF 27
GAUCEY?, James GNP 168A
James GNP 168A
GAUFFORD?, Benjm. BBN 112
GAUGE, James GRT 146
GAUGH, Ignatius SCT 105A
James SCT 98A
Jeremiah WAS 18A
John B. SCT 104A
GAUGH?, Saml.? CWL 36
Wm. WAS 20A
GAUGHF, Charles WAS 44A
Igs. WAS 43A
GAULT, David LWS 92A
William LWS 93A
GAUNT, Anthony FTE 64
James GTN 129
GAUNT, John GTN 123
John W. WRN 74A
Marshal GTN 124
Reuben GTN 132
Will. SCT 94A
GAUPH, Phillip GRT 145
GAUTIER, Nicholas LGN 29
GAWTH, Thos. JEF 23
GAY, Allen LVG 10
Allexdr. LNC 25
Benjamin CLK 98
James WDF 93
James, Jr. CLK 70
James, Senr. CLK 99
John CHN 31
John, Jr. WDF 99
John TOD 124A
Rebickah MAD 176
Thos. WAS 25A
GAYE?, Alexandra CSY 212
GAYER?, Adam GSN 137A
GAYLE, Geo. FKN 60
James FKN 74
Jas., Jr. ADR 66
Margaret SCT 108A
Nancy SCT 108A
GAYLE?, Geo. FKN 54
GEA, Anthony GTN 127
GEAR, Samuel S. GTN 129
GEARHART, Peter CLD 140
GEARS, Jas. BBN 76
GEARVES?, Henry FTE 59
GEBERT, Jacob BRK 257
GEBRON, Turner GRN 74
GEE, James SHE 112A
John MAD 116
John CSY 218
John B. MNR 213
John S. BRN 12
Lucy MNR 213
Mary FTE 79
Mary SHE 112A
Parker MAD 166
Robert JES 85
Wm. SHE 125A
GEEHAN, Jane TRG 3A
GEERS, Jesse NCH 120A
William FTE 59
GEETER, Elbert FTE 101
Fielding FTE 88
John FTE 87
Little FTE 102
GEGRAM?, Abraham MTG 267
GEHIN?, Jno. LVG 3
GEHON?, George CWL 35
GEIGER, Frederick, Jr. JEF 33
GEIGR?, Thos. J. SHE 127A
GEISER, Daniel MER 117
GELKY, Allen NSN 188
David NSN 188
John NSN 188
John, Jr./ Sr.? NSN 188
GELLEPEN?, Jno. MAS 77
GELPIN, George HRY 230
GELVEN, Hugh ADR 20
GENER, John CBL 17A
GENNER, Saml. HRD 34
GENNINGS, Hanly B. WRN 43A
Stubin PND 27A
GENOWINE, Jacob JEF 40
John JEF 42
Peter JEF 49
GENT, David MNR 199
Jesse, Jr. MNR 199
Jesse, Sr.? MNR 199
GENT, John MNR 199
Thomas MNR 199
GENTLE, John CLD 156
William CLD 162
GENTLE?, Stephen LVG 16
GENTRY, Alhtha? MNR 217
Benage MAD 130
Blaxton BLT 184
Davd. RCK 84A
David ETL 44
George MNR 207
Henry BLT 172
Isham LNC 77
James FTE 96
James BLT 162
James MNR 191
James, Jr. CLK 66
John CWL 53
John BLT 184
Joseph BLT 166
Joseph OHO 4A
Joseph O. GRN 57
Martin HRD 56
Martin BLT 164
Martin BLT 184
Moses GRN 56
Nicholas BLT 164
Rich ADR 22
Richd. RCK 83A
Robt ADR 22
Samuel BLT 182
Sarah MNR 217
Shelton OHO 6A
Wm. PUL 43A
Wyatt BLT 166
Zach ADR 22
GENTRY?, Martin, Jr.? MAD 90
GEOGHAGEN, John H. HRD 50
GEOGHEGAN, Denton HRD 66
GEORGE, Aaron CWL 41
Alexander FLD 33
Alfred WRN 65A
Baily BTH 174
Daniel GRN 52
Edward, Esqr. OWN 105
Ellis SCT 123A
Euticia LVG 13
Fielding SHE 168
Gabriel HAR 166
Isaac HRY 240
James GRD 85A
James GRD 102A
James? CWL 41
Jane FLD 29
John LNC 71
John CLK 86
John MER 96
John? CWL 41
Leonard JEF 25
Leroy? WDF 107A
Moses SHE 162
Parnach? HAR 166
Presley SHE 166
Robert HRL 108
Robert KNX 284
Sarah FKN 130
Thos. FKN 76
Whitson CLK 77
Widw. CWL 46
Widw.? CWL 41
William BNE 16
William LNC 73
William JES 74
William HAR 166
Wm. HRD 70

Name	County	Page
GEORGE?, William	BTH	212
GEOSS?, Joseph	JES	75
GERALD, Elisha	CBL	12A
GERANER?, David	WTY	113A
GERDEN, Elisha	WAS	65A
Hugh	WAS	64A
Joel	WAS	64A
Wm.	WAS	64A
GERDON, Wm.	WAS	64A
GERHAM, Lanaford/ Landford?	BBN	142
GERHART, Thos.	ADR	22
GERRALD, Ancil	FLD	27
Carrell	FLD	27
Dempsa?	LVG	9
William	FLD	30
GERRARD, Wm.	FKN	76
GERT?, Wm.	WAS	20A
GERTON, George	WAS	28A
Sally	WAS	26A
GESFORD?, Joel	CSY	222
GESS, James	OWN	103
William	ETL	52
GEST, John	FTE	84
Nathaneil	WYN	80A
Sarah	FTE	82
William	FTE	82
GEST?, Wm.	WAS	20A
GETERS, Burwel	WRN	75A
Henry	WRN	75A
GETSTRAP?, Nancy	RCK	81A
GETTNER, Abm.	BBN	110
Catherine	BBN	110
GETTON, Charles	PND	31A
James, Sr.	PND	31A
James	PND	31A
John	PND	31A
Robt.	PND	31A
Wm.	PND	30A
Wm.	PND	30A
Wm.	PND	31A
, John	PND	19A
GETZ, Elizabeth	JEF	31
GEURAND, Burtrand	HOP	246
GEVATKINS?, Horace D.	HND	10A
GEVDEON, John	MTG	253
GEVEDON, Joseph, Jr.	SHE	151
Joseph B.	SHE	151
GEWELL, Jeremiah	JEF	64
John	JEF	30
Simeon	JEF	64
GEYER, Frederick	JEF	45
Jacob	JEF	40
GEYS?, Ben	ADR	22
GHANT, Robt.	SHE	140A
Wm.	SHE	140A
GHINN?, Jno.	HAR	150
GHOLSON, Benjamin	WYN	79A
James	CLD	139
Jas.	SCT	110A
John	WYN	84A
Nancy	CLD	142
Samuel, Jr.	LVG	16
Samuel, Sr.	LVG	16
Wm. S.	GNP	175A
GHORT?, John	FLD	7
GHOST?, John	FLD	7
GIBB, John H.	JEF	45
GIBBENS, Wm.	SHE	125A
GIBBINS, Arthur E., Esqr.	WAS	19A
David	JEF	59
Francis	BRN	12
Thos.	JEF	61
GIBBONS, Cloe	MAS	52
Elizabeth	CLD	146
Isaac	GRN	64
John R.	UNN	146
Jonathan	CBL	10A
Thomas	FTE	62
GIBBS, Alexander	JEF	58
Anne, Mrs.	WYN	102A
Benj.	WAS	76A
George F.	WAS	80A
James	FKN	74
James	GNP	175A
James L.?	SHE	141A
Jerry	GRD	84A
John	LGN	37
John	CLK	85
John	ALN	98
John	WRN	35A
John	WYN	81A
John	GRD	85A
John	GRD	92A
John	GNP	175A
Julius	SCT	132A
Nathan H.	FLD	6
Sampson T.	SHE	124A
Smith	LGN	31
Thomas	BRN	13
William	NSN	199
Wm. P.	WAS	17A
GIBNEY, Alexander	FTE	65
GIBSON, -----?	HND	13
-----?	DVS	8A
Andrew	BKN	11
Archerbald	WTY	110A
Archibald	FLD	14
Baley	HND	10
Campbell	MTG	239
Catha	LNC	19
Danl.	HRT	159
David	GTN	121
Elisha	SHE	121A
Ezekiel	FLD	14
Ezekiel	FLD	43
Geo.	MAS	76
George S.	ALN	136
Henry	BLT	184
Isaac	KNX	286
Isaiah	MER	96
Jacob, Jr.	BRN	13
Jacob, Sen.	BRN	13
Jacob	SPN	8A
Jacob	SPN	24A
James	FLD	14
James	BKN	15
James	GRN	63
James	GRN	75
James	FTE	103
James	GRT	139
James	HRY	188
James	MTG	233
James, Snr	KNX	298
James	SPN	20A
James	SPN	20A
James	GRD	121A
Jesse	LVG	7
Jesse	KNX	284
Jesse	WTY	116A
Jno.	ALN	112
Jno. L.	ALN	130
Jno. S.	ALN	136
John	FLD	14
John	ADR	24
John	CHN	36
John	JES	89
John	MER	96
John	WDF	101
GIBSON, John	FTE	102
John	GTN	120
John	GTN	121
John, Junr.	PUL	56A
John, Senr.	PUL	56A
John	SPN	18A
John	SCT	98A
John	SCT	103A
John	SCT	110A
John	WTY	116A
Johnson	HRD	50
Joshua	BNE	16
Lewis	KNX	298
M.	CHN	36
Major	KNX	284
Martin	FLD	3
Martin	PUL	55A
Pitman	CHN	36
Polly, Mrs.	CLK	94
Randolph	ALN	104
Robert	GRT	140
Robt.	MAS	67
Samuel	MTG	251
Sarah	PUL	48A
Silas	SPN	20A
Thomas	HRT	159
Thomas	HOP	244
Thomas	PUL	55A
Thomas	GRD	120A
Usial?	CLY	114
Valentine	KNX	296
William	HND	8
William	FLD	14
William	FLD	40
William	FTE	103
William	FTE	103
William	GRT	139
William	NSN	176
William	MTG	261
William	WDF	108A
William	GRD	121A
William B.	NSN	196
Willima	CLY	121
Wm.	ALN	104
Zachariah	FLD	3
GIDCOMB, Anne	BTL	323
John	BTL	323
GIDDENS, James	BRN	33
Reuben	FLD	34
Richard	FLD	34
GIDDING, Peter	LWS	96A
GIDDINGS, Kinsey	WAS	63A
GIDDINS, Albin	UNN	149
James	HRY	204
GIDENS, George	HRT	159
GIER, John	MAD	160
Williamson	MAD	164
GIFFINS, James	MAD	114
GIFFORD, Elijah	CSY	206
Joshua	MAS	66
GIGER, Henry	GNP	166A
GILASPIE, Gabl.	BBN	68
GILBERT, (See Gillbert)	MAD	112
Anthony H.	LGN	40
Benja.	LVG	5
Benjamin	LGN	41
Benjamin	LGN	47
Benjamin	MAD	112
Byrd	LGN	42
Charles	LGN	41
Elias	LWS	95A
Elijah	WYN	92A
Enoch	WYN	92A
Felix	CLY	132
George	GRD	120A

Name	County	Page
GILBERT, Henery	CBL	17A
Henry	FTE	78
Isaac	MAD	112
Isham	LNC	35
James	LVG	4
James	HRD	22
James	WYN	81A
Joel	CWL	53
John	CLY	132
Larkin?	TRG	6
Martin	LGN	42
Mary	LNC	35
Mordica	BRK	255
Morton	LVG	5
Nicholas	BTH	180
Robt.	LVG	5
Saml.	MAD	118
Saml., Sr.	MAD	122
Silas	LGN	41
Stephen	MAD	132
Thos.	WAS	61A
Wm.	TOD	130
GILBREATH, Geo.	MAS	72
Joseph	JEF	37
GILBRETH, Andrew	ADR	22
GILCHRIST, Robert	UNN	154
GILCRESS, Sylvanes	ADC	68
GILE, James	JES	72
GILERT, Silas	LGN	37
GILES, Daniel	FTE	62
Elijah	MAD	142
John	BKN	6
John	BRN	12
John	BLT	168
Richard	MNR	213
William	HAR	134
GILESPY, Lewis	MAD	92
GILHAM, John	LGN	41
Marcus	LGN	28
Robt.	BKN	6
GILILAND, Wm.	CWL	38
GILKERSON, Geo.	MAS	60
James	WAS	63A
Matthew	MER	97
Thomas	MER	97
William	MER	97
Wm.	FLG	54A
GILKEY, Edward	GNP	166A
Polly	MTG	253
Thomas S.	MTG	226
William	MTG	267
GILKINSEN, John	GNP	168A
GILKINSON, James	GNP	177A
GILKISON, John	BTH	170
GILKY, James	CHN	36
Jon	ADR	22
GILL, Aaron	PUL	44A
Alxr.	ADR	22
Benjamin	FTE	88
Cornelius	NSN	192
Edward	BRN	12
Edwd.	MAS	70
Erasmus	BBN	134
George	WDF	99
George	SHE	111A
Helen	HRD	62
Isaac	HOP	272
James	LGN	29
James, Jr.	SHE	117A
James	SHE	117A
Jas.	MAS	70
Jemimah	WDF	102A
Jno.	PUL	44A
John	MER	97
John	WDF	99
John	FLG	30A
GILL, John	GRD	97A
Joshua	LNC	55
Peter R.	BTH	180
Phillip	MER	96
Rachel	MER	97
Richd.	GRD	118A
Saml.	GRD	85A
Samuel C.	BTH	214
Susan	GRN	79
Tho.	JEF	65
Will	GRD	94A
William	UNN	148
Wm.	HRT	159
Wm.	PUL	44A
GILL?, Catsby	FKN	108
GILLAM, Jas.	MAS	59
John	SCT	126A
Mary	FTE	106
Thomas	FTE	108
GILLAM?, William	FTE	65
GILLANY, James	WDF	109A
GILLASPIE, James	GRD	82A
Martin	CLK	96
Mathew	SPN	9A
William	SHE	157
GILLASPY, Geo.	HRY	186
James	HRY	186
John	BRN	13
John	SHE	155
William	HRY	186
GILLBERT, Aquila?	MAD	112
GILLCEES?, Geo.	MAS	58
GILLEHAM, Clement	WAS	18A
GILLEHAN?, Mark	WAS	80A
GILLELAND, James	BRN	13
John	BRN	13
Mary	BRN	13
GILLEN, Daniel	MTG	247
Thomas	MTG	277
GILLERLAND, William	DVS	19A
GILLESPIE, James	LGN	34
James	FTE	79
John	MTG	275
Simon	MTG	275
Simon, Jr.	MTG	273
William	FTE	81
GILLESS?, Joseph	WTY	125A
GILLIAM, Cornelius	BRN	12
William	TRG	3
GILLIAN, John	CBL	23A
Robbert	CBL	20A
GILLIAND, John S.	BRK	257
GILLIARD, James	CHN	30A
GILLICK, Thomas	CBL	21A
GILLILAN, John	SPN	25A
GILLILAND, Harvy	PUL	35A
James	HRD	8
Tho.	JEF	62
Thomas	HOP	246
Thos.	HRD	66
GILLILIN, Samuel	SPN	13A
GILLIS, John	BNE	16
Sarah	WAS	48A
GILLISON, Jane?	HAR	136
GILLISPIE, Geo. E.	SCT	134A
J.	TOD	126
John R.	FTE	96
Mary	MER	96
Mary	MER	116
William	FTE	81
Wm.	CWL	34
GILLISPY?, Philip	MAD	90
GILLMAN, Ben	HRD	32
Sarah	JES	93
GILLMAWR?, David	HRD	30
GILLMORE, George	FTE	82
Mathew	BTH	204
Robt.	MAS	63
Will.	MAS	63
William	WDF	116A
GILLOCK, James	BRN	12
John	BBN	118
Laurence	BRN	12
Robert	BRN	13
Samuel	BRN	13
William	BRN	12
GILLS, And.	ALN	136
GILLUM, A. B.	TOD	125A
Amos	TRG	4A
Chs.	HRY	214
Danl.	HRY	214
James	GTN	125
Jas.	SCT	115A
Jesse	HRL	108
John	TRG	8
John	MAD	176
John	SCT	115A
John D.	MAD	164
Martin	HRL	108
Thos.	SCT	115A
William	HRL	108
Wm.	MAD	140
GILMAN, George	MER	117
Samuel	JEF	37
Timothy	JEF	45
GILMAN?, D.	TOD	127
GILMER, David	FTE	69
James	MER	96
Jane	ADR	22
Janes	ADR	22
Jno.	CHN	40
Nicholas	CHN	40
W.	ADR	22
GILMON, James	MER	96
Martha	PUL	35A
GILMOORE, James	BNE	16
Joseph	BNE	46
GILMORE, A.	TOD	133
Alexander	ADR	22
Andrew	WRN	60A
Betsy	MER	116
Enoch	FLD	12
George	HOP	244
James	FLD	12
Jas.	CHN	45
John	GRN	64
Joseph	LGN	46
Martha	MTG	281
Patrick	WRN	60A
Richard	WRN	60A
Robert	PUL	53A
Thomas	LVG	16
Thomas	ADR	22
William	FLD	8
GILNEATH?, Benj.	WTY	126A
Gideon	WTY	114A
GILPIN, James	ADR	22
W.	ADR	22
William	WDF	120A
GILPIN?, Joseph	CLK	67
GILSON, Alexander	BKN	10
GILSSIN?, Joseph	CLK	67
GILSTRAP, Bright	WYN	96A
Elisabeth	BTL	323
Lewis	WYN	96A
GILTINER?, Francis	GTN	131
GILVEN, James	MTG	275
GIMBLEN, David	LGN	32
Samuel	MNR	213
GINEY, Alex. D.	JEF	44
GINN, Aaron	MAS	77

Name	County	Page
GINN, James	BKN	10
James	GTN	129
Jas.	MAS	69
John	CBL	4A
Thomas	BKN	18
William	LWS	97A
Wm.	BKN	14
GINNESS?, Thos. M.	MAS	60
GINNIS?, Elias	JEF	31
GINTEN?, James	UNN	148
GIPSON, Archibald	WYN	99A
David	TOD	132A
Fle---an?	CSY	220
Geo.	TOD	134
George	SPN	19A
George	WYN	99A
Henry	HRL	108
Henry	TOD	132A
Hugh	TOD	126A
J.	TOD	132A
Jacob	CSY	220
John	SPN	23A
John	TOD	126A
Martin	BLT	174
Milly	TOD	128
N.	TOD	132
Nancy	FTE	76
Nathan	MER	96
Robert	WYN	79A
Ruben	HRL	108
Stephen	CLY	116
Thomas	FTE	104
Thomas	WYN	89A
Wm.	CWL	53
GIRD, William	SCT	96A
GIRDLER, James	PUL	56A
Joseph	PUL	58A
GIRDNER, Joseph	KNX	288
GIRGGSBY?, Smith	NSN	217
GIRON, Mathuun	FTE	61
GIRTEN, John	UNN	153
GIRTEN?, James	UNN	148
GISH, Barberry	MBG	138A
George	MBG	139
John	MBG	138A
Joseph	MBG	140
Lydia	HOP	246
Samuel	HOP	244
Thomas	CLK	99
GIST, Billy	FTE	58
John	MNR	207
Joseph	BRN	13
Joseph	MNR	195
Nathaniel	UNN	152
Rezin H.	MTG	259
William	FTE	103
Willliam	MNR	207
GITKEY?, -m.?	CWL	43
GITTHENS?, John	GNP	167A
GITTINER?, Francis	GTN	131
GITTINGS, Jas.	HRD	20
GITTINS, William	UNN	154
GIVAN?, James	CWL	46
GIVANS, Will.	FLG	69A
GIVATKINS?, Horace D.	HND	10A
GIVE, Reuben	BKN	6
GIVEN, James	LVG	16
James	LWS	92A
Jos. R.	CWL	44
William	FTE	98
GIVENS, Alexander	GTN	128
Alexdr.	LNC	15
Allen	BTL	323
Dickson	LVG	2
Eleazer	HOP	242
GIVENS, George	LNC	35
George	NSN	216
George, Sr.	LNC	59
Hannah	LNC	61
Hiram	UNN	146
James	LNC	17
James	LNC	61
James	HOP	244
John	LNC	11
John	HAR	158
John	HOP	244
John, Co.	LVG	13
Martha	LNC	15
Mathew	HAR	156
Richard	CLK	91
Robert	LNC	15
Robert, Sr.	LNC	15
Ruth	HAR	158
Samuel	UNN	147
Thomas	HOP	244
William	HOP	244
GIVIN, William	HRY	188
GIVINS, Alexr.	BBN	140
George	FTE	90
Margarett	BBN	94
Matthew	SHE	137A
Wm. D.	HRD	58
GIVONS, James R.	BBN	120
GLACKEN, Andrew	BNE	16
William	BNE	16
GLACKIN, Will.	LVG	8
GLADALL, Ben	JEF	26
GLADDISH, Richard	WRN	33A
Wright	WRN	33A
GLANTON, Burwill	WDF	93
John	WDF	99A
GLASBROOK, James	WAS	29A
GLASCOCK, Ann	BKN	15
Maddin	WRN	70A
GLASCOCKE, Whorton	WAS	30A
Wm.	WAS	77A
GLASGOW, Frances	NSN	209
George	NSN	209
John	MAD	140
Samuel	HOP	246
Thomas	NSN	209
GLASPEY, W. James	GSN	137A
GLASPIE, Alexr.	HRY	268
GLASS, Alex.	LVG	8
Belfield	OWN	104
Benjamin	BRN	13
Benjamin	OWN	101
David	FTE	108
David	NSN	207
Davis	NSN	198
Flem.	SCT	103A
Geo.	FLG	26A
George	CWL	35
James	CWL	35
James	CWL	35
James	NSN	206
James	NSN	212
James	WRN	40A
Jas.	LVG	8
Jehu	OWN	104
John	GTN	128
John	SHE	157
John, Esqr.	OWN	102
Joseph	JEF	34
Robert	SHE	172
Royal	BLT	156
Saml.	SCT	129A
Sarah	LVG	4
Thomas J./ I.?	NCH	109A
Thos.	JEF	27
Will.	SCT	127A
GLASS, Will.	SCT	132A
Zachariah	CHN	27A
GLASSBROOK, Mary	SPN	17A
GLASSCOCK, Abraham	NCH	117A
Cena	HRD	60
Danl.	MAS	79
Enoch	HRD	50
Geo.	BRK	257
Geo.	FLG	29A
Grigory	BRK	257
John	BRK	229
John	FLG	27A
Micajah	NSN	213
Newman	FLG	27A
Peter	MAS	79
Thomas	LGN	37
Will.	MAS	58
Wm.	BRK	255
GLASSCOK, Asa	FLG	34A
GLASSGOW, Allen	NSN	175
GLASSON?, Jesse	HRL	108
GLAUGHLIN?, M. D.	MAS	73
GLAVES, Thos.	PND	16A
GLAVES?, Michael	PND	17A
GLAZEBROOK, James	MER	96
Jerdin?	SPN	17A
John	BRN	13
William	BRN	12
GLEAN, Adam	BRK	257
GLEEN, Nehemiah	LNC	43
GLEN, James	SHE	126A
GLEN?, Jesse	HRL	108
GLENN, -----? M.	DVS	5A
---ey?	DVS	10A
---liam?	DVS	10A
Andrew	MBG	138
Archd., Jr.	FLG	72A
Archd., Sen.	FLG	72A
Fleming	SCT	112A
Henry	MBG	143
Henry	FLG	72A
Hugh	MAD	140
James	SCT	112A
James	TOD	131A
Jerry	SCT	127A
John	GTN	130
John	BLT	154
Martin	MAD	114
Mary	JEF	31
Minor	SCT	112A
Moses	MBG	136A
Robert	MGB	137A
Robt.	MAS	72
Saml.	CWL	36
Simeon	NCH	127A
Thomas F.	MBG	140
Whitehead	PUL	62A
William	SHE	160
William	MNR	193
William	MTG	289
GLENN?, Danl.	ADR	22
GLIDEWELL, Nash	CLD	165
GLIN?, Jesse	HRL	108
GLINN, Anna	PND	30A
Jo. K.	PND	15A
Joseph K.	PND	31A
Nancy	PND	30A
GLOOYER?, Richard	ALN	142
GLORE, Abraham	JEF	56
Adam	CBL	9A
Alex	JEF	58
Benjamin	JEF	68
Elijah	JEF	54
Francis	JEF	58
Gideon	BNE	16
Jeremiah	BNE	16

Name	County	Page
GLORE, Lawrence	JEF	64
Nathaniel	CBL	9A
Oliver	BNE	16
Rosanna	JEF	60
Simeon	CBL	6A
Susan	FTE	73
GLORE?, Larcan	FTE	73
GLOVER, -----?	DVS	8A
Charles	HRD	58
Charles	MTG	226
Chesley, Sr.	MTG	251
E.	JEF	26
Isabella	BRN	12
Jesse	MTG	249
John	JEF	51
John	MAS	66
John	FTE	88
John, Esqr.	MER	97
Peter G.	MTG	251
Richard	BRN	13
Robert	MTG	225
Samuel	MTG	237
William	BRN	12
William	MER	97
Zachariah	MTG	249
GLOVER?, Michael	PND	17A
GLOVIER, Betssey	LNC	71
GLOVYRS?, Richera	ALN	142
GOAD, John	HOP	244
Peter	HOP	246
GOAN, Isaac	SHE	138A
GOATTY, John	BRK	257
GOBEN, Elizabeth	SHE	171
John	SHE	141A
GOBIN, James	HND	3
Wm.	JEF	39
GOBLE, Aram A.	GNP	175A
Ephraim	GNP	166A
Wm.	GNP	175A
GOBLE?, Ben	HRD	76
GODARD, John	SCT	110A
Michail	SCT	135A
Thos.	SCT	135A
GODBY, --hn?	DVS	14A
Wm.	PUL	35A
GODDARD, Benj.	FLG	49A
John	FLG	27A
John	FLG	49A
Jos.	FLG	49A
Porter	FLG	49A
GODDARG?, Wm.	FLG	79A
GODDEN, Hugh	MAD	182
James	MAD	180
GODDIN, Jarred	HRD	32
GODFREY, Edward	MER	96
John	MER	97
Robert	MER	97
GODLEY?, John	ALN	126
GODLSMITH, Owen	BLT	154
GODMAN, Allen	HAR	138
John	SCT	112A
Samuel	HAR	156
William	NCH	124A
Zachariah	PND	18A
GODSEY, Daniel	PUL	63A
Samul	ADR	22
GOE, John	SHE	151
William	SHE	151
GOEN, Amanuel, (Free Man Of Collr.)	BBN	84
GOFF, Abram	PUL	36A
Aron	MAD	144
Caleb	MER	96
Dory	BLT	176
Edward	BLT	178
GOFF, Elijah	GRN	55
George	SHE	118A
James	MAD	164
James	SHE	122A
Jno.	PUL	43A
John B.	SHE	118A
Moses	MAD	170
Thomas	CLK	86
Wm.	HRT	159
Zachariah	MAD	144
GOFF?, Elisha	CLK	64
GOFORTH, Thomas	JES	85
GOFT?, Mary	MAS	73
GOGGEN?, Jubilee	LVG	16
GOGGIN, Bourne	PUL	69
Bourne, Esq.	PUL	51B
William	CLD	148
GOGGIN?, Richard	PUL	54A
GOGGINS, Robert	MAD	164
Stephen	MAD	94
GOHEIN, James	SPN	5A
GOIN, Anstar	MAD	176
Francis	MAD	168
Jeremiah	MAD	98
Wm.	MAD	164
GOING, Gilbert	HAR	144
Jack	LVG	2
Jno.	LVG	2
Mercer	LVG	2
GOINS, Berry	KNX	304
Charles	GTN	133
Galloway	GTN	133
Isaiah	KNX	306
GOLDEN, Jarret	MAS	67
John	PND	28A
Stephen	KNX	298
GOLDIN, William, Jr.	BNE	16
William, Sr.	BNE	16
GOLDON, A.	MAS	68
GOLDSBERRY, Jonithan	GSN	137A
GOLDSBURG, Martin	PUL	52A
GOLDSBY?, Jas.?	CWL	41
GOLDSMITH, James	SHE	114A
John	BLT	166
Reubin	HRD	64
Saml.	HRD	64
GOLDSMITH?, John?	BLT	170
GOLEMAN, Thos.	FKN	100
GOLIER, Susan/ Guson?	GNP	173A
GOLLAHER, F.	TOD	129A
GOLLIHUE, Peter	FLD	23
GOLLISPY?, Philip	MAD	90
GOLLOHOR, Randolph	BLT	176
GOLSBURY, Jno.	GRD	96A
John	GRD	86A
Mack	GRD	96B
GOLSBY?, Edward	GRN	56
GOLSLEY, Stephen	GRN	53
GOLSLY, Edward	GRN	56
James	GRN	78
GOLSON?, ----y? C.	CWL	44
GONCE, George	NCH	110A
John	NCH	110A
Phillip	JEF	58
GONCE?, Samuel	NCH	110A
Samuel	NCH	110A
GONTERMAN?, George	BLT	158
GONTS?, Rhodolph	BBN	124
GOOCH, Chas.	MAS	53
Claibourn	LNC	15
Gideon	MBG	143
Gidion	MAD	108
James	LNC	19
GOOCH, James	JES	69
John	LNC	41
Judith	LNC	13
Linah	LNC	41
Rolland	LNC	15
Thomas	LNC	41
Thomas	LNC	65
William	LNC	9
GOOD, Jacob	SHE	153
Nathan	MER	96
GOODACRE, Thos.?	CWL	32
GOODALL, Clarisa	MNR	207
John	MNR	215
Lodowichk	MNR	207
Thomas	MNR	207
Turner	BRN	12
GOODBAR, John	MTG	247
GOODBREAD, Nancy	SPN	18A
GOODDING, David	FLG	49A
Saml.	FLG	48A
GOODE, Alfred	ADR	22
Benj.	LNC	61
Benjamin	LGN	39
Benjamin	TRG	13A
Danl.	LNC	61
Flemin	ADR	22
John	ADR	24
John	CSY	220
John	TRG	13A
John C.	WRN	42A
Joseph	LNC	61
Mickajeh	CSY	220
Nathan	CSY	218
Richard	HRY	220
Robert	WRN	42A
Robt	ADR	24
Tymothey	CSY	216
William	CSY	210
Willm.	LNC	61
Wm.	LNC	15
GOODEN, Alexd.	KNX	290
Hesekiah	KNX	286
James	BRN	12
John	KNX	290
Joseph	KNX	290
Thomas	SHE	119A
Thos.	KNX	290
GOODIN, Isaac	HRD	18
James	HRD	36
Thomas	HRD	18
GOODING, Abram	FLG	28A
Daniel	BTH	206
John	TRG	14
John	CWL	35
Julius	CBL	2A
Richard	WYN	91A
Samuel	TRG	14
Samuel	TRG	13A
GOODLAW, Dorothy	WDF	93
GOODLET, Ebenezer E.	BTL	313
James	MER	97
GOODLIT, Ebanezar E.	BTL	323
GOODLOE?, Wm.	MAD	166
GOODLOW, Henry	HOP	244
John	HOP	244
Nancy	FTE	103
GOODMAN, Amos	HRT	159
Anderson	MNR	199
Ansel	ADR	20
Ansel	ADR	24
Arthur	HRT	158
Charles	BRN	13
Charles, Jr.	BRN	13
Elijah	BTL	323

GOODMAN, George MNR 205
J. TOD 125
Jacob, Jr. MNR 199
Jacob, Sr. MNR 215
Jessee MAD 168
Joel JEF 56
John BRN 13
John ADR 20
John MER 96
John CLD 164
John MNR 215
John WTY 112A
Johnson BRN 13
Marcus ADR 22
Mildred BRN 12
Nathan BBN 112
Richard BRN 12
Richard BRN 13
Robert LGN 47
Solomon MNR 199
Stephen HRT 159
Wm. PUL 40A
GOODMARY, Elijah CWL 53
GOODNIGHT, Abram SHE 149
Abram, Jr. SHE 149
Edward MER 96
Elizabeth GTN 134
George HAR 160
Isaac WRN 59A
Jacob LNC 63
James SHE 175
John CSY 214
John, Jr. MER 96
John, Sr. MER 96
Michael MER 96
Michael MBG 133A
Micheal JEF 54
Thomas FTE 96
GOODPASTER,
Bufford BTH 160
John BTH 190
Joseph BTH 190
Michael BTH 160
GOODPASTURE,
Abraham BTH 210
Polly BTH 210
GOODRAM, James WRN 70A
GOODRICH, George HRY 214
James FKN 152
John WYN 88A
GOODRICK, Benjamin NCH 112A
GOODRIDGE,
Fountain BNE 16
Jane WDF 123A
Walter BNE 16
Wm. BNE 16
GOODRIGE, Moses GNP 170A
GOODRITCH,
Elizabeth CLK 77
GOODRUM, James WAS 57A
Wilford WAS 57A
GOODSLOE?, Wm. MAD 166
GOODSON, Josiah CLD 152
Samuel CLD 152
William LGN 42
William, Junr. CLD 142
William, Senr. CLD 142
GOODSPEED, Gideon GTN 123
GOODWIN, Amos JEF 39
Andrew ADR 20
Benjamin GTN 121
Benjamin GTN 133
Daniel GTN 130
Daniel M? LGN 43
Enoch BTH 184
John BRN 12
GOODWIN, John WRN 38A
John SHE 119A
Jos. MAS 76
Josep G. FTE 85
Lewis / Louis? BRN 13
Loyd K. FTE 87
Morgan SPN 5A
Nancy FTE 96
Patrick MTG 279
Robert HRY 200
S. S. JEF 20
Simeon S. JEF 41
Thomas BRN 12
Thomas JES 80
Will MAS 59
GOODWIN?, James ALN 110
John PND 26A
GOODWINE, James MAD 132
GOOLMAN, Abraham CLK 83
Charles CLK 73
Frederick JEF 63
Isaac CLK 66
GOOMAN, Ejah CWL 53
GOOR, Joseph FKN 104
GOOSE, Catherine JEF 49
Jacob JEF 36
GOOSEBY, Tarleton JEF 62
GOOSEE, Susanna HRY 270
GOPT?, Mary MAS 73
GORAN?, James CHN 29A
GORCHAM, John C. OWN 104
GORDAN, Benjamin CLK 67
Caty GRD 112A
David GRD 85A
Geo. MAS 65
James WRN 44A
Saml. CHN 41
GORDEN, Benja. ALN 122
Christopher NSN 212
David CLK 74
Jas. FLG 75A
John CLK 74
John HOP 244
John FLG 75A
Jos. FLG 76A
Rob ADR 24
Uriah TRG 4
William CLK 66
William HOP 244
Wm. ADR 24
Wm. FLG 72A
GORDEN?, Silas JEF 37
GORDLY, John FTE 100
GORDON, Archibald MER 97
Charles H. MER 96
Christopher LGN 40
Daniel LGN 31
David MAD 94
David SHE 170
David HRY 230
Elisha FTE 69
Elizabeth MAS 53
Geo. HRY 266
George H. TRG 7
Jessee WYN 87A
Jno. MAS 53
Jno. D. FKN 134
John LGN 33
John LGN 37
John CWL 44
John FTE 65
Joseph LGN 37
Laurance HRY 266
Lewis MAS 71
Randall MTG 255
Samuel LGN 40
GORDON, Thos. CWL 46
William CHN 35
William MER 97
William HAR 168
William MTG 243
Wm. SHE 130A
GORE, ---aning? CWL 32
Ashford D. TRG 10
Benjamin MTG 257
Benjamin F. SHE 176
Christian LNC 75
Eleazar TRG 3
Isaac HRD 50
James BRN 13
James CWL 46
James HOP 244
John TRG 4
John CLK 92
John FLG 44A
Jonathan BLT 174
Jonathan NSN 185
Joshua CWL 46
Mat. CWL 37
Michael TRG 3
Notly CWL 37
Thomas NSN 205
Thos. SHE 123A
Wm. GSN 137A
GORE?, Andrew MER 114
GOREN, John, Jr. MNR 215
John WRN 72A
GORHAM, George FTE 77
Harry T. BBN 146
John FTE 111
John A. SCT 92A
Joshua LGN 28
Mary ALN 102
William LGN 38
GORIN, Henry TOD 124A
GORIN?, Franklin BRN 33
John, Senr. BRN 12
GORINE, J./ I.? D. TOD 131
GORLEE, Saml. HRY 228
GORLEY, Jemima KNX 290
Robert WRN 39A
GORMAN, Danl. FLG 59A
Isaac MNR 199
Jane GNP 166A
John FLG 57A
GORNEY?, Armstead CBL 18A
Benjamin CBL 18A
Frederick CBL 18A
Henery CBL 18A
James CBL 18A
John CBL 17A
William CBL 20A
GORR?, Henry NSN 179
GORREL, Thomas BTH 192
GORREL?, James BTH 182
John BTH 180
GORRELL, Benjamin LGN 27
James LGN 27
GORSEL?, James BTH 182
GORSHUGE, Chas. MAS 63
GOSER, Peter GRD 88A
GOSHAN?, William LVG 16
GOSLIN, Jos. FLG 72A
Nathl. FLG 26A
GOSNELL, Benjamin HAR 204
John HAR 204
William HAR 204
GOSNEY, Alfred JEF 54
Jas. JEF 54
Jno. JEF 54
Nimrod CBL 17A
Wm. JEF 54

GOSNEY?, (See Gorney) CBL 18A
John CBL 17A
GOSS, Henry FTE 111
Kincheon MBG 141A
Sally SPN 12A
GOSSAM, William WRN 44A
GOSSEL, Elijah SCT 96A
GOSSET, Mary CLY 126
GOSSETT, Abraham HAR 146
Ann PUL 63A
Jacob CLK 84
John MBG 139
Mathias CLK 84
Reuben PUL 58A
Samuel CLK 84
Stanley PUL 63A
Wm. CWL 41
GOSSOM, John HRY 220
GOTHARD, John GTN 129
GOTLY, George WAS 65A
GOTT, Cornelius WRN 61A
Cornelius WRN 64A
John WRN 45A
John D. WRN 68A
Jonathan WRN 45A
Peter WRN 61A
Richard SHE 163
Richard WRN 45A
Robert SHE 166
Robert SHE 167
Sutton WRN 45A
Thomas SHE 165
William SHE 167
GOUCE?, Phillip JEF 58
GOUDA--?, Wm. FLG 79A
GOUDY, Samuel WAS 37A
GOUGE, William ADR 22
GOUGH, Cornelius WDF 126A
Isaac BTL 323
James WDF 111A
Jesse BTL 323
John SHE 156
Mason HRY 258
Michl. FTE 60
William BTL 323
William, Jr. SHE 156
William, Sr. SHE 156
GOULD, Jacob JEF 23
GOULDER, Christopher GRN 59
GOULDINS, George CBL 7A
GOUN?, Franklin BRN 33
GOUNG?, Walter JEF 35
GOUTERMAN?, George BLT 158
GOUTS?, Rhodolph BBN 124
GOUTTY, Thos. BRK 257
Wm. BRK 255
GOVEL?, Samuel NCH 110A
GOVER, Jno. PUL 42A
Jno. PUL 44A
GOW?, Andrew MER 114
Fanny MAS 73
GOWDY, James BKN 24
GOWEL, Merry WDF 100A
GOWEN, James WRN 47A
Lu---ca? BTH 170
GOWER, Stanly P. FKN 58
GOWERLY, Hugh TRG 8
GOWERS, Jacob FKN 54
GOWIN, Macage WDF 122A
GOYER?, Adam GSN 137A
GRA-ING?, Reubin BKN 20
GRABLE, David OWN 101
Philip BLT 158
Samuel A. MBG 140
GRACE, Allin TRG 8A
Clemant CHN 31A
Elkanah HOP 244
George TRG 3A
Greenbury CHN 30
Ilijah HOP 246
Joseph CHN 30A
Nancy CHN 30A
Thomas CWL 58
Thomas FTE 93
William CHN 30A
GRACE?, Nath. CHN 46
GRACY, George CWL 46
GRADDY, Louis HOP 244
GRADEN, George CBL 18A
GRADY, Benjamin FTE 100
Jesse WDF 120A
Leonard HND 7A
Reuben TOD 124A
Samuel FTE 73
Tamson SHE 148
Thomas H. LGN 40
William FTE 106
William WDF 120A
GRAFFORD, Thos. BBN 82
GRAFFORT, John NCH 124A
GRAFFORT?, Thomas BBN 122
GRAFT, David NSN 184
GRAFTON, James SHE 131A
Philip SHE 119A
GRAGG, Jessey MAD 118
Jno. PUL 44A
Robert WYN 94A
Samuel NCH 122A
GRAHAM, Adam H. BTH 206
Alexander WRN 73A
Andrew BLT 152
Christopher, Dr. MER 114
Clement UNN 148
Elijah ETL 44
Elizabeth LWS 96A
Enoch GRD 115A
George SHE 109A
H. R. MAS 54
Henry MAS 77
I. F.? SHE 143A
Isaac HRD 92
James ETL 44
James LWS 95A
James C. BLT 174
James M. BTH 147
James M. BTH 220
James M. BTH 223
Jane UNN 148
Jas. TOD 128A
Jno. MAS 74
Jno. TOD 128A
John FLD 30
John ETL 44
John BLT 174
Jonathan HRD 92
Jos. SHE 139A
Joseph W. BBN 66
Larkin WRN 69A
Levi LGN 43
Levi, Jr. LGN 28
M. TOD 130
Merrick HRD 88
Moses GRD 107A
Moses SHE 135A
Nathl. FLG 63A
R. JEF 26
R. C. TOD 129A
Richard LGN 45
Robert BBN 102
Robert WRN 42A
GRAHAM, Robert WRN 61A
Saml. BTH 182
Samuel BLT 162
Samuel C. UNN 154
Sarah WRN 41A
Sarah GRD 120A
Susana HRD 58
Thomas LGN 42
William CLY 128
William E. WRN 73A
Wm. HRD 88
GRAHAM?, William BLT 172
GRANGER, John HAR 160
GRANT, Daniel BBN 118
Daniel OHO 4A
Danl. FLG 68A
Eligah CBL 17A
Geo. MAS 69
George WAS 45A
Jacob SHE 169
James FTE 90
Jas. MAS 73
Jas. W. SCT 91A
Jesse M. GNP 168A
John BKN 8
John BNE 16
John MER 96
John BBN 118
John, Jr. BBN 140
John CBL 3A
John SCT 96A
John SCT 117A
John V. FLD 39
Joshua CHN 33A
Joshua D. SHE 143A
M. V. GRD 91A
Micheal ADR 22
Milton SHE 177
Peter MAS 78
Robert LWS 86A
Robt. M. PND 15A
Samuel M. FTE 78
Squire CBL 13A
Thomas FTE 60
Thos. JEF 51
William FLD 39
William MER 96
William BLT 182
William OHO 4A
William CBL 14A
Wm. BRK 257
GRANTHAM, Isaac HND 10
James HND 10A
John HND 13
GRAREY, William CBL 23A
GRASHAM, John BRN 13
GRASHAN, Isaac GRD 88A
GRASHEAR, Robert CLY 121
GRASS?, Danl. HRD 44
GRASTZ?, Sarshal? CWL 33
GRATZ, Benjamin FTE 66
GRAUL, Danl. MAS 76
GRAVAT, George CLK 75
GRAVE, Jacob SPN 19A
GRAVE?, Preston CWL 42
GRAVEL, John WAS 20A
GRAVEN, Anderson CHN 32A
GRAVES, A-? FTE 77
Absalom BNE 16
Absalom, Jr. BNE 16
Bartlett, Junr. CBL 3A
Bartlett CBL 6A
Bartlett L. BRN 12
Benjamin CBL 23A
David BBN 72
David SHE 121A

Name	County	Page
GRAVES, Edmond	SHE	121A
Edmund	BNE	16
Elijah	FTE	77
Fanny	FTE	88
Francis	GRN	53
George	FTE	88
George N.	WAS	42A
Harrison	CLK	92
Hawes	FTE	88
Henry B.	LVG	16
James	BNE	16
James	JES	79
James	FTE	92
James	BBN	128
Jesse A.	WAS	40A
Jno.	ADR	4
Jno.	FKN	86
John	BNE	14
John	BBN	64
John	HRD	74
John	FTE	76
John	FTE	76
John	CLD	143
John	GRT	146
John	WAS	73A
John	WDF	95A
John	WYN	100A
John	SHE	126A
John C.	FTE	96
John S.	MBG	135A
Jos.	MAS	63
Jos. P.	TOD	134
Joseph	FTE	96
Joseph, Jun.	BNE	16
Joseph, Sen.	BNE	16
Joseph	WAS	73A
Lance	WRN	36A
Mical	SPN	19A
Nathan	MER	96
Nelson	WDF	92
Polly	FTE	92
Polly	FKN	152
Reson?	WAS	55A
Reuben	BNE	16
Richard	LVG	16
Richard	WDF	112A
Richard	SHE	116A
Richard	SHE	121A
Robt.	PUL	47A
Sally	MER	97
Saml.	SHE	121A
Samuel	FTE	76
Sarah	GRT	146
Thomas	HAR	214
Thomas C.	CLD	159
Thomas N.	BBN	124
Thos.	WAS	82A
Thos. H.	SCT	92A
Uriah	WAS	82A
W. O.	TOD	134
William	FLD	24
William	MER	115
William	GRD	122A
William B.	NCH	126A
William W.	FTE	79
Williamson	CLY	129
Willis	BNE	46
Wm.	ALN	104
Wm., Jr.	WAS	81A
Wm.	WAS	55A
Wm.	RCK	79A
Wm.	WAS	81A
Zacariah	FTE	77
GRAVES?, James	FTE	56
GRAVETT, Thomas	WDF	109A
GRAVIL, David	WRN	39A
GRAVIT, Geo. S.	FKN	88
GRAVOT, Ellis	CLK	95
GRAW?, Nath.	CHN	46
GRAY, ---.?	CWL	42
-arret, Senr.	CWL	43
Abigal	JES	72
Andrew	MTG	275
Archibald	LGN	32
Caty	FLG	59A
Charles	FTE	69
Charles	BTL	323
Charles, Sr.	WYN	101A
Charles	WYN	103A
Daniel	LVG	16
Daniel	SPN	7A
Daniel	CHN	32A
David	JES	79
David	GRT	144
David	FLG	47A
David	NCH	115A
Edward	BRN	13
Elias	GNP	170A
Elijah	MAS	74
Elish	FLG	64A
Elizabeth	MTG	283
Francis	HAR	154
French S.	UNN	146
Gadi	CLY	118
Geo.	JEF	43
George	FTE	88
Gipson	CWL	53
Gipson, Sr.	CWL	53
Hardin	JES	69
Henry	MER	97
Isaac	CWL	53
Isaac	WDF	102
Isaac	TRG	12A
Isaac	NCH	108A
James	BNE	14
James	CWL	36
James	FKN	54
James	BBN	90
James	MER	96
James	HAR	214
James, Senr.	CLK	93
James	NCH	108A
James	SHE	114A
James	GNP	170A
Jas.	HRD	84
Jas. R.	TOD	124A
Jessee	WYN	101A
Jno	HRY	268
John	CWL	53
John	FTE	75
John	MER	96
John	ALN	108
John	TOD	126
John	BBN	128
John, Jr.	MER	96
John, Sr.	MER	96
John	CBL	3A
John	CHN	35A
John	CHN	44A
John	FLG	47A
John	WRN	70A
John	SCT	94A
John	SCT	106A
John	GNP	170A
John B.	BBN	144
John D.	GTN	130
John P.	CWL	43
John T.	JEF	19
Jonathan	HRD	68
Jonathan	WDF	102A
Jos.	CHN	43A
Joseph	LGN	23
GRAY, Joseph	FKN	104
Joseph	HAR	196
Joseph	WRN	46A
Joseph	SHE	128A
Kitty	NCH	108A
Lee	HRY	240
Loyed	GSN	137A
Mark	ETL	45
Mary	GNP	170A
Mathew	MAS	58
Miles	CHN	27A
Milton	WDF	102A
Nathaniel	LVG	2
Nathl.	SCT	104A
Peter	ALN	96
Presley	LVG	2
Presley	GTN	128
Rawdon	CWL	53
Reuben	HRT	158
Richard	FTE	106
Rob.	CWL	43
Robert	FTE	57
Robert	MER	96
Robert	NSN	209
Robert	SHE	121A
Robert	SHE	121A
Russell	HOP	244
Samuel	LGN	36
Samuel	MER	97
Samuel	HAR	196
Samuel	HOP	244
Sarah	BBN	94
Sary	HRL	108
Stanford	NSN	191
Stephen	NSN	180
Stephen	HOP	246
Stout	HRT	158
Thomas	HRD	12
Thomas	FTE	61
Thomas	MER	116
Thos.	HRD	30
Thos., Sr.	HRD	20
Will	ADR	22
Will	MAS	76
Will.	LVG	7
William	LGN	22
William	GRN	52
William	FTE	75
William	HAR	154
William	GRD	83A
William	NCH	114A
William	NCH	115A
William F.	CHN	46
William S.	GTN	127
Wm.	BBN	128
Wm.	BBN	132
Wm.	CHN	29A
Wm.	WAS	41A
Wm.	WAS	80A
Wm.	SHE	121A
Wm.	GSN	137A
GRAY?, Lititia, Mrs.	WYN	79A
GRAYDON, Richd.	BKN	18
GRAYER, George	OHO	9A
GRAYHAM, Arthus	NSN	209
Berry	GRN	59
Charles	SPN	9A
George	WAS	54A
George	WAS	68A
Green	ALN	98
Hampton	GRN	73
James	CSY	212
James	NCH	109A
James	GSN	137A
Jane	HOP	244

Name	County	Page
GRAYHAM, Jane	FLG	57A
Jane	WAS	68A
Jas.	FLG	64A
Jerry	GRN	78
Jno.	CHN	38
John	GRN	68
John	WAS	52A
John	FLG	57A
John	WAS	68A
John	WYN	90A
Johnson	GRN	56
Lawren	GSN	137A
Margaret	BRN	12
Nancy	GSN	137A
Peyton R.	MER	97
Richard	HOP	244
Robert	SPN	20A
Samuel	SHE	175
Sarah	NSN	198
Will.	SCT	138A
William	SHE	162
William	NSN	198
Wm.	FKN	76
Wm.	HRT	159
Wm.	FLG	64A
GRAYHAN, Amus	WAS	83A
John	WAS	83A
GRAYMON, Frederick	BKN	11
GRAYSON, Alfred W.	NSN	178
Benjamin	NSN	175
Elizabeth	JEF	30
John	BRN	13
John	FLG	44A
Peter W.	NSN	177
Robt. H.	JEF	45
GREANSLATE?, John	GNP	173A
GREAR, Aqulla	GRN	79
GREATHOUSE, Harmon	HND	12
Harmon	NSN	194
Isaac	SHE	152
Isaac	WRN	57A
Levi	WRN	46A
Michael	BLT	168
Samuel	WRN	53A
Will	MAS	72
William	BLT	184
William	WRN	58A
GREATSENGER, Geo.	JEF	24
GREEG, Aron	BKN	14
GREEK, Peter	BRK	257
GREELKEY?, Elizabeth	UNN	147
GREEN, -----	GRN	72
--pps?	FKN	94
Absolem	GNP	168A
Amelia	MER	96
Andrew	BNE	16
Austin	HND	9
B. George	GSN	137A
Beale	MTG	279
Ben	GRD	113A
Ben.	HRY	243
Benj.	FKN	92
Charles	MER	96
Daniel O.	MAD	124
Danl.	JEF	48
David	BNE	16
Davis	WRN	49A
Delpha	LVG	6
Duff, Dr.	MER	116
Edmond	PND	29A
Edmund	CHN	29
Edw.	JEF	27
Edward	ADR	22
Edward	BTL	323
Elihu	MAD	118
GREEN, Elijah	HRL	108
Elijah	FKN	126
Elisha	HRL	108
Elizabeth	HRD	76
Elizabeth	CLD	138
Elizabeth	CBL	20A
Elizabeth	FLG	34A
Equilla	WRN	52A
Fielding	FLG	44A
Frances	WAS	64A
Francis W.	JEF	36
Gardener	CLD	138
Garrett	ETL	52
Garrett	HAR	156
George	LVG	13
George	OWN	104
George	NSN	217
George	KNX	282
George, Junr.	CLD	150
George, Senr.	CLD	150
George	WRN	50A
George B.	BTL	323
Golesbury	FLG	62A
Hannah	HRD	60
Harison	GRD	121A
Henery	ADR	20
Henry	ETL	52
Henry	OWN	101
Henry	CHN	36A
Henry	WAS	55A
Henry	SCT	119A
Henry E.	GNP	178A
Henry E.	GNP	179A
Isaac	BRK	255
Isaac, Sr.	HRY	243
Isaac F.	HRY	243
James	BRN	12
James, (Near James Foster's)	BRN	13
James	MAD	104
James	HRL	108
James	NSN	178
James	WAS	74A
James	GRD	94A
James B.	MER	96
Jas.	HRY	240
Jeremiah	FKN	98
Jessee	PND	29A
Jno.	MAS	63
Jno.	FKN	74
Jno.	HRY	240
Jno.	HRY	257
Joel	MER	96
John	BNE	16
John	HRD	18
John	LNC	55
John	BBN	80
John	KNX	280
John, Sr.	HND	10
John	FLG	34A
John	WRN	50A
John	WRN	51A
John	WRN	51A
John	GSN	137A
Jonah	JEF	48
Jos.	HRY	244
Joseph	JEF	40
Joseph	FTE	62
Joshua	BLT	192
Josiah	FKN	98
Leven	NSN	200
Lewis	HRL	108
Luther	GNP	169A
Martin	MAD	156
Martin	FLG	41A
GREEN, Martin	WDF	100A
Mathew	HRD	8
Nathaniel	MBG	142A
Oliver	CBL	2A
Patrick	NSN	208
Paul	HRY	253
Peter	HND	4A
Polly	MER	96
Rabecca	NSN	201
Rebecca	FTE	61
Richard	HOP	244
Richd.	HRY	243
Robert	BNE	16
Robert	MNR	213
Robert	WAS	74A
Robert	WYN	81A
Robt.	BBN	86
Robt.?	MAS	59
Saml.	JEF	48
Saml.	KNX	314
Saml. R.	MAD	96
Sarah	HND	11A
Sarah	WDF	119A
Susanna	NSN	217
Thadeus	MTG	269
Thomas	BRN	12
Thomas	BNE	46
Thomas	SHE	148
Thompson	HND	5A
Thos.	CHN	42
Thos.	KNX	314
Thos.	WAS	74A
Thos.	GSN	137A
Thos.	GSN	137A
Wilford	WAS	39A
William	BNE	16
William	LGN	29
William	BNE	50
William	MER	96
William	HRL	108
William	HAR	160
William	WYN	82A
William	WYN	92A
William	WDF	121A
Willis	MER	96
Wm.	JEF	48
Wm.	MAD	124
Wm.	HRY	263
Wm.	FLG	29A
Wm.	FLG	44A
Wm. P.	BBN	88
Wm. P.	PND	20A
Zacariah	BTH	170
Zachariah	NSN	204
Zachr.	GRD	100A
GREEN?, Charlotte	LVG	3
Edward	CLK	67
Equilla	WRN	52A
Joseph	JEF	39
Levi	WRN	52A
Nathaniel	BNE	14
Robert	JES	80
William	WYN	101A
GREENALCH, John	MAD	94
GREENE, Anne	GTN	128
Chas. R.?	SHE	143A
Elizabeth	SHE	115A
H.	JES	95
John	GTN	131
Thos.	SHE	137A
GREENE?, Lander	JEF	58
GREENELL, Stephen	HRD	24
GREENEWALT, Anthony	HRD	68
Danl.	HRD	28
David	HRD	74

Name	County	Page
GREENEWALT, Eve	HRD	92
Jacob	HRD	92
John	HRD	92
Joseph	HRD	92
Luke	HRD	24
GREENEWOOD, Francis	GTN	131
GREENFIELD, Burges	CHN	28
Sam	TOD	124A
T. G.	TOD	133
Tho.	JEF	39
Wm.	TOD	125
GREENHA-GH?, Roger	MAD	178
GREENING, John	FTE	107
Robert	FTE	80
Robert	FTE	111
GREENLEA, David	KNX	304
GREENLEY, Francis	MER	96
GREENSTREET, John	GRN	60
Peter	HRT	159
GREENUP, John	MNR	191
John	WYN	85A
John	WYN	86A
John	SCT	125A
Sally	FKN	58
Saml.	SCT	124A
Thomas	MNR	191
GREENWAD?, John	TRG	4A
GREENWALL, Robt.	HRY	262
GREENWELL, Benedic	BRK	257
Elizabeth	NSN	191
Ellin	NSN	191
Henry	SCT	97A
Ignatus	NSN	179
John	GRN	67
John	NSN	194
John	NSN	216
Joseph	BLT	176
Joshua	NSN	179
Phillip	SCT	102A
Robt.	HRD	74
Robt.	WAS	56A
Robt.	SCT	97A
Samuel	UNN	150
GREENWOOD, Bartl.	LNC	13
Henry F.	BRN	33
John	LNC	51
John T.	JES	88
Nimrod, Capt.	MER	96
Philip	HRD	60
Samuel	MTG	267
Walcut	OHO	10A
William	SHE	167
GREER, Elisha	OWN	103
Hannah	LGN	35
Henry	BRK	257
Isaac	LGN	37
James	CWL	53
Jas.	SCT	103A
John	BRN	12
John	SCT	100A
Joseph	NSN	205
Lawrence	HRD	38
Lawrence, Jr.	BRK	257
Lawrence, Sr.	BRK	257
Luke	HRD	54
Moses	HOP	244
Robt.	SCT	131A
Sally	LGN	35
Smith	WRN	51A
William	BRN	12
GREER?, Charlotte	LVG	3
GREERS?, Liberty	GRN	52
GREEWELL?, Wilfred	BRK	257
GREEWOOD, Thos.	BRK	257
GREGERY, Ja--?	ADR	22
GREGG, Abner	FLG	75A
Cl---?	CLK	98
David	SHE	148
David	HAR	154
David L.	HRY	176
Harvy	HRY	241
James	FTE	105
John	BKN	13
John	SHE	148
Joseph	FLG	40A
Patsey	MTG	263
Saml.	SCT	106A
Sarah	FTE	105
Soloman, Sr.	FLG	68A
Soloman	FLG	68A
GREGG?, John	BBN	134
GREGGORY, Uriah	WAS	87A
GREGGSBY, John	NSN	183
GREGORY, Asa	SHE	163
David	BNE	18
Flemming	WYN	79A
Godfrey	WAS	47A
Hiram	WYN	95A
James	BNE	18
James	WAS	25A
James	WAS	47A
Jessee	BNE	16
John	CLY	113
John	BBN	128
John	KNX	284
John	WAS	46A
John	WDF	111A
Joseph	FKN	102
Joseph	UNN	149
Joseph	WRN	45A
Leroy	WAS	50A
Lewis	GRT	143
M. L./ S.?	WAS	19A
May	HRY	216
Mesheck	WYN	106A
Mordecai	WYN	95A
Peter	BNE	16
Richard	WAS	86A
Robert	KNX	306
Saml.	CWL	53
Smith	WAS	46A
Thos.	CWL	44
Thos.	KNX	294
William	BNE	18
William	BTH	194
GRENARD, Wm.	FLG	38A
GRENING?, Thomas	CLK	98
GRENNWELL, Jas.	HRD	48
GRENWELL, Ralph	NSN	184
GREOGERY, John	OHO	6A
GRESHAM, Eli	LGN	29
Jno.	JEF	41
Job	LNC	51
John	LNC	49
John	SCT	106A
Thos.	JEF	41
Willm.	LNC	65
Wm.	RCK	86A
GRESTY, James	NSN	191
GREWELL, Asa	HAR	184
Isaac	HAR	178
John	HAR	186
GREY, Andrew	BTH	196
Ebenezer	BTH	174
Isaac	BTH	150
James	KNX	306
Jane	JEF	30
Joshua	KNX	306
Mary	KNX	308
William	CLD	138
GREYHAH, Geo. W.	FKN	68
GREYHAM, David	FKN	68
Francis	FKN	108
James	CSY	226
Robert	CSY	226
Sely A.	FKN	64
GRIBBIN, James	WAS	33A
John	WAS	32A
GRIBBINS, John	WAS	30A
GRICE, Thomas	FTE	60
GRIDER, Elizabeth	ADR	22
Frederick	ADR	64
Henry	WRN	43A
Jacob	MNR	191
Jacob H.	MNR	207
James	ADR	22
Jesse	WRN	43A
John	ADR	64
John	GTN	131
John	WRN	43A
Martin	ADR	22
Martin	MNR	195
Martin	WRN	35A
Moses	ADR	62
Silas	ADR	22
Tobias	MNR	201
Wm.	ADR	64
GRIDLEY, Enock	CBL	3A
GRIEN?, William	WYN	101A
GRIER, Joseph	NSN	180
GRIEVS, John, Jnr.	GSN	137A
John	GSN	137A
Nathaniel	GSN	137A
GRIFFE?, John	HRD	72
GRIFFEN, Burgess	GRN	69
Sherwood	GRN	69
GRIFFETH, Bird	CWL	53
George	CWL	53
Jno.	MAS	77
Masrhall	BRK	257
Willaby	FLG	61A
GRIFFEY, Burrus/ Burrns?	FKN	140
Joseph	FKN	140
GRIFFEY?, James	FKN	156
GRIFFIN, Anthoney	ALN	128
Anthony	HND	9A
Aron	BBN	144
Aron	SPN	18A
Bazil	PUL	35A
Berry	MAS	59
Betsey	LWS	87A
Clabourn	WTY	122A
Clim.	SCT	110A
Coleman	TOD	128A
Comn?	CHN	30A
Eddy	HND	9A
Elias	JES	72
Elijah	HRD	66
Elizabeth	BLT	190
Fountain	HND	8
Gabriel	HAR	200
Hannah	SPN	18A
Henry	TOD	128A
James	FKN	138
Jas.	PUL	43A
Jas.	SCT	111A
Jesse	CLD	158
Jno.	FKN	138
Jno.	PUL	49A
John	LVG	16
John	MBG	136
Joseph	CLD	152
Joseph	GNP	178A
Joseph	GNP	179A
Leroy	MAS	67
Levi	FTE	95

GRIFFIN, Mathias BNE 16
Rachal SPN 20A
Reason BLT 192
Richard, Sr. MTG 289
Robert FKN 138
Robert HAR 192
Robt. BBN 138
Saml. HRD 72
Saml. S. KNX 280
Sollomon RCK 78A
Solomon PUL 45A
Squire PUL 43A
Terry MTG 233
W. A. LNC 35
Washington SHE 168
Will SCT 110A
William LVG 16
William CLD 152
William SHE 166
Wm. JEF 52
Wm. PUL 44A
Wm. S. FKN 54
Zachariah CLY 129
GRIFFING, Anthony CLK 88
Benjamin CBL 5A
Jeramiah CBL 7A
William BTH 204
GRIFFING?, Benjamin CBL 14A
Robert CLK 106
GRIFFINS?, Benjamin CBL 14A
GRIFFIS, Hezekiah K. LWS 88A
GRIFFIT, Aron KNX 310
James KNX 310
GRIFFITH, Abel FLD 30
Benjamin SHE 174
Caleb SHE 172
David FLD 30
Eli CWL 35
Horatio CHN 45
Isaac SCT 113A
James MBG 133A
Jesse FLD 42
Jesse BBN 122
Jessey MAD 148
Jno. MAS 74
John BBN 78
John HRL 108
John BBN 130
John HOP 244
Joshua DVS 18A
Mary BBN 78
Mary BBN 120
Mary HAR 182
Mary CBL 11A
Mordica I./ J?. SHE 159
Patterson? CLK 62
Robert FLD 30
Robert SHE 173
Salley SCT 119A
Saml. BBN 72
Samuel HAR 192
Thos. MAD 114
Thos. HRY 263
Uriah BBN 110
Wells? CWL 37
William HAR 144
William CBL 10A
William? R.? DVS 19A
Wm. E. MAS 63
Zaphaniah NCH 105
GRIFFITH?, ----- DVS 7A
James? NCH 126A
John CBL 10A
GRIFFITH?, Thomas? NCH 126A
GRIFFRY, Wm. MAD 142
GRIFFY, Goe.? CHN 40A
Joseph SCT 98A
Patrick PND 29A
GRIFITH, ---ney? WTY 126A
GRIGERY, Jesse CSY 208
GRIGG, Fielden? ETL 52
James HAR 136
John CLK 65
John CBL 16A
Minor ETL 42
Minus? CLK 65
Rachel, Mrs. CLK 65
Wm. PND 19A
GRIGGS, Daniel BRN 13
John FTE 75
Joseph NSN 192
Joseph SCT 113A
Wm. ALN 132
Wm. TOD 133
GRIGGSBY, John FTE 103
GRIGGSLY, Elijah NSN 220
John NSN 216
Nathanel NSN 200
Redmon NSN 206
GRIGGSLY?, Smith NSN 217
GRIGORA?, James BTH 198
GRIGORY, Absolem ALN 100
Thos. BRK 257
Wm. BRK 255
GRIGSBY, ----h? DVS 14A
----nah? DVS 14A
Benjamin CLK 66
David FLG 50A
Jesse LGN 28
Jesse LGN 29
John BRN 12
John HND 12
John HRD 40
John CLY 124
Lewis CLK 70
Nimrod HND 11
Redmond HRD 32
Saml. GRD 102B
Thos. CLY 125
Tolliver HND 12
Wilkinson SHE 136A
GRIGSLY, James CLK 76
GRIGSLY?, Elijah NSN 216
James WAS 66A
GRIM, Frederick LWS 96A
GRIM?, Charles GRN 65
Edward CLK 67
John GRN 58
GRIMES, Amanuel GSN 137A
Barnabas MAS 65
Benjamin LVG 12
Betsey MAD 140
Charles FTE 85
Christian NCH 122A
David MAS 73
Edward BTH 176
Edward NSN 217
Edwd. H. BBN 106
Elias JEF 47
Elizabeth BBN 110
Ephraim WYN 104A
George CLK 100
Hiram LWS 96A
James JEF 47
James GTN 119
James UNN 153
James BTL 323
James LWS 96A
Jno. MAS 73
GRIMES, Jno. FKN 162
John JEF 39
John FTE 84
John FTE 88
John BBN 106
John SHE 176
John, Jr. UNN 153
John, Sen. UNN 153
John A. MAD 180
Jonathan CLD 142
Leonard HRY 210
Margarett LNC 71
Mary FTE 75
Mary BTH 196
Mathew GSN 137A
Nancy GRD 112A
Nicholas BBN 106
Phillip BBN 104
Sylvester BBN 106
Thomas MER 114
Ths. JEF 47
Verlindy MAD 170
William FTE 82
William UNN 153
William BTH 158
Wm. MAD 158
GRIMMAL?, Solomon WRN 55A
GRIMSLEY, David WRN 57A
Mariah BNE 16
Nelson CBL 7A
Payton R. FLG 42A
Wm. R. WAS 78A
GRINDLE, James WYN 81A
GRINDSTAFF, Drewry KNX 296
George JES 85
Michael KNX 296
Micheal JES 85
Susan GRD 89A
GRINDSTEAD, Wm. MAS 76
GRINES, Easlen BTL 323
GRINING, James CLK 80
GRINNEL, John GRN 74
Richd. GRN 74
GRINSLEY, Silas BNE 16
GRINSTAFF, Henry GRD 89A
Isaac GRD 106A
Jacob GRD 112A
GRINSTEAD, Bartholomew WRN 57A
David WRN 56A
Henry BRN 33
James BRN 13
John BBN 64
Philip BRN 12
Richard WRN 46A
Richard WRN 56A
Robert FTE 64
GRINSTED, Jessee HRT 159
GRINTER?, Francis LGN 32
GRINTOR, James LGN 38
John LGN 38
John H. LGN 38
Robert LGN 38
Samuel LGN 38
GRISAM, Ben GRD 83A
GRISHAM, David FTE 64
George CHN 41A
John SCT 110A
Wm. MAD 132
GRISHAM?, Uriah RCK 81A
GRISON, Robert GRD 86A
GRISSOM, John ADR 20
Tho. ALN 116
GRISTY?, Ben HRD 78
GRISUM, John ETL 48
GRITTEN, Aaron MER 97

Name	County	Page
GRITTEN, Amos	MER	96
William	MER	97
GRITTON, Jesse	MER	96
John	MER	96
John	MER	97
Levy	MER	96
GRIVES, James	FTE	84
GRIZZLE, Elim	CBL	12A
GROAF?, John	JEF	52
GROAT, Matty	LWS	95A
GROCE, Edmund?	HRL	108
GROCE?, Jacob	FLG	71A
GROGHIGAN, John	NCH	127A
Michael	NCH	123A
GROIN?, Andrew	BNE	50
GROMER, Alexr.	GRD	90A
David	GRD	90A
Fredk., Sr.?	GRD	118A
Garret	MAD	168
Isaac	GRD	110A
Samuel	GRD	113A
Wm.	MAD	144
GROOM, -----?	TOD	134
Benjamine	CLK	95
Bright	TOD	134
Enoch M.	MNR	207
George	SHE	171
Isaac	BBN	122
James	TRG	8
James	CLK	96
Richard	CLK	86
Robert	CLK	95
Sarah	CLK	86
William	CLK	86
GROOM?, ----.?	CWL	37
GROOMER, Fredk., Jr.	GRD	113A
John	GRD	102B
GROOMES, Moses	MTG	299
GROOMS, Horatio	OWN	103
Jesse	MER	115
Nancy	FTE	68
William	SHE	176
GROOVER, William	BTH	166
GROSE, Jacob	BLT	158
GROSS, Abram	BRK	257
Duval	CLD	151
Henry	CLD	155
Jacob	CLD	151
Jacob	BTL	323
James	BTL	323
John	WYN	82A
Peter	CLD	145
Simon	CLD	151
GROSS?, Danl.	HRD	44
GROSSENOR, Elizabeth	NCH	103A
Richard	NCH	103A
GROSSHEART, Adam	JEF	32
GROUNDS, Robert	WRN	57A
GROVE, Abram	BNE	16
George	CLD	137
John	MTG	247
Joseph	JEF	31
Martin	JEF	52
GROVEOR, Jonathan	LWS	97A
Thomas	LWS	97A
GROVER, Jas.	MAS	62
Joel	JES	85
Jos.	MAS	70
GROVER?, Benj.	BKN	8
GROVES, --ed-.?	CWL	40
Asa	CHN	44
Daniel	CLK	73
Daniel	MGB	137A
Donavan	PND	21A
GROVES, Elizabeth	MGB	137A
Francy	CLK	87
Fred	FLG	77A
Henry	GRN	54
Joseph	MBG	141
Josiah	FTE	67
Richard	CLK	89
Robt.	PND	21A
Sarah	CLK	89
Sarah	FLG	28A
Sarah	FLG	62A
GRUB, William	NSN	220
GRUBB, George	FLD	46
James	BNE	16
John	WRN	34A
Philip	BTL	323
Wm.	HRD	16
GRUBBS, (No Given Name)	JEF	26
Chrisley	WTY	111A
Huston	CWL	53
Isaac	CWL	35
Jacob	WYN	80A
John	LGN	36
John	CWL	53
John	MER	97
Moody	WRN	74A
Sarah	BRN	12
Thom.	CWL	53
Thomas	LGN	24
Thomas	ETL	37
William	HAR	218
Wm.	CWL	53
GRUBEL?, John	BRK	257
GRUBLE, James	WDF	104
GRUBS, Hickerson	MAD	166
James	BTH	208
Jessey	MAD	166
GRUFFORD?, Benjm.	BBN	112
GRUGAN, Paul	HRY	266
GRULKEY?, Elizabeth	UNN	147
GRUM, Johnathn.	CWL	38
GRUMBLY, John	TOD	126A
GRUMER / GRUMES?, John	CBL	4A
GRUNDY, ----am?	BLT	156
Felix B.	WAS	39A
George	WAS	20A
Robert	WAS	28A
Saml.	WAS	85A
Wm.	OHO	9A
Wm.	WAS	79A
GRUNHILL, Wm.	WAS	74A
GRUNINGS?, Polly	FLD	13
GRUNWELL, Bennet	SCT	106A
GRYDER, John	CLD	154
Joseph	CLD	156
Joshua	CLD	155
Martin	CLD	158
Valentine	CLD	158
GRYMAN?, John	MNR	195
GUARANT, Charles	MTG	247
GUARDENER, Saml.	HND	7
GUAYTAR?, John	MAD	180
GUD-ELL?, Andrew	BTH	148
GUDGEL, Allen	BTH	178
GUDGELL, Andrew	FKN	132
Jacob, Jr.?	FKN	156
Jacob, Sr.	FKN	154
Jno.	FKN	124
GUELES?, Harvah?/ Haneah?	GSN	137A
GUESENDARY?, James	CHN	38
GUESS, Elzabeth	NSN	204
James?	CWL	40
GUESS, Jonas	NSN	205
Pinkill H.	MER	96
Wm.?	CWL	40
GUESS?, Jesse	WAS	54A
GUFFEE?, Alexander	LGN	42
GUFFEY, Ephraim	WYN	103A
Henry, Sr.	WYN	102A
Henry	WYN	101A
Henry	WYN	104A
John, Jr.	WYN	81A
John, Jr.	WYN	102A
John, Sr.	WYN	102A
Thomas	CBL	22A
Willaby	WTY	110A
William	WYN	83A
William	WYN	103A
GUFFIN, Andrew	BKN	14
GUFFY, James	BTL	323
GUIBERT, H.	JEF	19
GUILER?, Saml.	HND	13
GUILKEY?, Elizabeth	UNN	147
GUILL, Nathaniel	BRN	12
GUILLILAND, Elizabeth	SHE	141A
Robert	SHE	139A
Sarah	SHE	141A
Wm.	SHE	139A
GUIM?, Ishmael	BLT	188
GUIN, Andrew	WAS	31A
Joseph	WYN	102A
Randolph	TRG	11A
Thos.	BRK	257
GUIN?, William	GRD	111A
GUINN, James	FKN	90
Jno.	FKN	90
John	CLK	72
Margaret	NSN	201
GUINN?, Hiram	MAD	142
GUINNESS, Danl.	BBN	132
GUIREY?, Wm.	ADC	68
GUIRY, Wm.	GRN	68
GUJS?, Ben	ADR	22
GULASPI, James, Capt.	WYN	86A
GULLET, Wm.	PUL	35A
GULLETT?, James	FLD	7
Jesse	FLD	7
John	FLD	4
William	FLD	4
William	FLD	4
GULLEY, Enoch	MAD	168
John	MAD	168
John	LWS	99A
Thos.	MAD	168
Willis	MAD	168
GULLION, Benjamin	GTN	125
Elizabel	GTN	125
George	GTN	125
James	GTN	130
Jeremiah	GTN	125
Joseph	GTN	130
GULLY, Drury	GRD	102A
James	GRD	113A
Johnston	HOP	246
William	GRD	113A
GUM, Abraham	CLY	117
Elias	CLY	129
Jacob	HRT	159
Jehu	MNR	209
Jesse	MNR	195
Jessee	HRT	159
John	MNR	209
Shepherd	HRD	16
William	CLY	117
William, Jr.	CLY	117

Name	County	Page
GUM?, Charles	GRN	65
John	GRN	58
GUN---ETY?, Martin	BRK	257
GUN?, -----?	CWL	40
Charles	GRN	65
GUNBRAMAN, Henery	GSN	137A
GUNI--?, Robert	GTN	122
GUNN, James	SHE	136A
John	SHE	136A
Wm. Q?.	SHE	136A
GUNNEL, Allen	CHN	43A
GUNNEL?, Richd.	SCT	126A
GUNNELL, Anderson	PUL	63A
GUNROD?, John	BNE	16
GUNSAUL, James	HAR	188
GUNSAUL?, Thomas	HAR	188
GUNTER, Davidson	JES	69
James	WAS	24A
John	LNC	51
GUNTER?, Francis	LGN	32
Thomas	WRN	49A
GUNTREMAN, John	SHE	134A
GUNTRYMAN, Wm.	HRD	54
GUPTON, Garland	CLD	166
Pheby	GRN	55
Temperance	LGN	30
Turner	LGN	44
GURLEY, Daniel	GRT	142
GURN?, Charles	GRN	65
Jessee	HRT	159
GURSENDARY?, James	CHN	38
GUTCHERSON?, Enoch	JEF	52
GUTHERY, Nathaniel	MAD	142
Stephen	ADR	22
GUTHREY, Benjamin	WDF	121A
Benjamin	WDF	122A
Caleb	WDF	110A
James	WDF	111A
Robert	WDF	111A
Thomas, Jr.	WDF	111A
Thomas	WDF	111A
GUTHRIE, Adam	CLD	157
Alexander	OWN	99
Benjamin	HRY	216
Edmund	NSN	204
Edmund	NSN	212
George	CLD	157
James	JEF	43
James	MER	96
James	CLD	157
Jesse	HAR	200
John	MER	97
Thomas	CLD	157
William, Esqr.	MER	96
GUTRIDGE, John	MAD	150
GUTTON, Joseph R.	BLT	194
GUY, Henry	CLY	126
Jno.	FKN	158
Mathew	CLK	75
Reuben	CLK	65
Richard	ALN	92
William	ALN	92
GUYMAN?, John	MNR	195
GUYN, Robert	WDF	101A
GUYNN, Peter	MER	96
GUYTON, Saml.	HRY	224
GUZZLE, Solomon	CBL	8A
GWALTNEY, Benj.	LNC	47
GWATHENY, John	JEF	36
Joseph	JEF	63
Robert	JEF	63
GWATHMEY, Temple	JEF	26
GWATHMEY?, Geo.	JEF	26
GWATHMY?, Owen	JEF	56
GWIN, Henry	JEF	25
Joseph	WDF	111A
GWIN?, Henry	LGN	23
GWINN, Abra.	JEF	51
James	CLD	146
GWINN?, Elias	JEF	33
Lander	JEF	58
GYER, Frederick	TRG	7
Henry	TRG	7
GYNAND, Julius	GTN	134
Samuel	GTN	134
H---------?, Nathaniel	ALN	104
H---?, John F.	CWL	39
H---Y?, Simon	FTE	56
H--LAWEY?, Joseph	FTE	55
H-HER?, John	BRN	16
H-R---?, Andrew	ALN	94
H-STUTER?, Joseph	FTE	70
HA---?, Danl.	FLG	47A
HABEL, Saml.	FLG	71A
HACER, Saml.	BBN	146
HACHET, Thomas	GRD	87A
HACHNA / HACKNA?, Enoch	FTE	111
HACKE, Philip	WRN	39A
HACKEDY, James	MAD	126
HACKER, Drury	BRK	261
John	CLY	116
Vallentine	CLY	129
HACKET, Jacob	MAD	160
Peter	MAD	90
Wm.	MAD	156
HACKETT, Bazel	MAD	90
James	SHE	175
James	WDF	109A
HACKLER, Rasannah	WTY	112A
Rosannah (Crossed Out)	WTY	117A
HACKLEY, Frances	FKN	136
James S.	FKN	136
John	NSN	181
Joseph	LNC	43
Lot	MER	99
Ricd.	RCK	78A
Richard	LNC	43
Samuel	NSN	193
William	BTH	164
HACKLEY?, James	GSN	138A
HACKLY, Elizabeth	BTH	168
George	NSN	216
HACKMAN, Clara, Mrs.	BBN	138
HACKNEY, John	WDF	97
Saml.	GRD	106A
Thomas	LGN	46
HACKWITH, Jeremiah	FLD	31
John	FLD	28
Thomas	FLD	28
HACKWORTH, Joseph	SHE	116A
HADDEN, Elisabeth	BTL	323
Elisha	LGN	40
Margaret	LGN	29
Robert E.	OWN	103
Samuel	MTG	257
Thomas	BTL	323
Thos.	TOD	130
Wm. W.	TOD	124A
HADDIX, Coleby	CLY	132
Henley	CLY	131
John	CLY	131
Nancy	CLY	119
William	CLY	119
HADDOX, Mary	LGN	45
Zackeriah	KNX	294
HADDY?, Saml.	LVG	16
HADEN, Barnabey	FLG	43A
HADEN, Ben.	HRY	252
E., Mrs.?	MAS	53
Elisha	MAS	55
Elisha	TOD	130A
Henley	TRG	14
James	LGN	30
James C.	MTG	267
John	MTG	283
Jos.	TOD	124A
Rebecca	SCT	102A
Sally	LGN	47
Will	SCT	102A
William	LGN	47
William D.	MTG	245
Wm.? E.	MAS	53
HADERSTEER, David	CSY	218
HADIN, Joel	CHN	42A
Nancy	TOD	131A
Samuel	LGN	47
HADLEY, Josiah	MTG	277
Sam, Jr.	TOD	124A
Sam, Sr.	TOD	124A
HADON, Bartholomew	WYN	80A
Elisa	FKN	74
John	MAD	110
John	WYN	85A
HAFF?, Abraham	SHE	128A
Luke	SHE	127A
Luke	SHE	129A
HAFFIELD, Benjamin	BKN	2
HAFFORD, Charles	HOP	250
HAFLEY, Jacob	CSY	216
HAFNETTOM, Andrew	MAD	118
HAGAN, (See Hydon?)	NSN	210
Alexander	MTG	235
Arthur	MNR	217
Arthur, Sr?	MNR	217
Basil	NSN	210
Catharine	NSN	222
Charles	JEF	19
Clement	NSN	188
David	CLK	91
Edward	NSN	209
Electius?	NSN	182
Elizabeth	NSN	209
Enoch	NSN	189
Henry	BLT	190
Ignatus	NSN	189
John	NSN	188
John	MNR	217
Jonas	MNR	217
Joseph	NSN	179
Nicholas	HRD	34
Ralph	NSN	211
Randolph	NSN	183
Richard	NSN	205
Robert	NSN	182
Robert	NSN	201
Thomas	NSN	184
Thomas C.	NSN	193
Walter	NSN	201
Wm.	ALN	98
HAGAN?, William	JES	71
William	GRT	145
HAGANS, Leonard	NSN	181
Samuel	MAD	96
Sarah	BRN	16
HAGAR, James	FLD	29
Mary	FLD	29
HAGARMAN, Betsy	MNR	211
Tunes	SHE	135A
HAGEN, Christopher	WAS	74A
Henry	WAS	33A
Henry	WAS	54A
Wm.	WAS	36A

HAGEN, Wm. WAS 44A
Wm. WAS 85A
HAGENS, Campbell ALN 100
HAGER, Christian WDF 99
David WDF 99
HAGER?, James BRK 261
John C. BRK 261
HAGERMON?, Joseph WRN 63A
HAGERTY, Samuel CLK 95
HAGGAN, Nathan CHN 41A
HAGGARD, Bartell CLK 90
Benj. RCK 77A
Benjamin CLD 143
David CLK 73
David CLK 86
David CLK 93
David MAD 164
Dorsan CHN 41A
Ezekiel E. WRN 75A
James HRL 110
Jas. CHN 41A
John CLK 72
John JES 86
John, Jr. CLK 81
John RCK 77A
Levi CLD 143
Martin CLK 75
Martin, Senr. CLK 80
Nancy CLD 160
Pleasant CLK 74
Rice GRD 107A
Richm? HRL 110
Wm., Jr. MAD 134
Wm., Sr. MAD 134
HAGGARDY, Robt. KNX 314
HAGGARTY, John FTE 93
John HAR 204
HAGGE?, Harry RCK 82A
HAGGERTEY, William MER 98
HAGGIN, James FTE 60
John, Jr. MER 98
John, Sr. MER 98
Samuel FTE 105
Sarah? T. MER 115
HAGGINS, Isaac GRN 54
Solomon BBN 140
HAGIN, John ETL 39
John WAS 62A
HAGINS, John FLD 4
Thomas FLD 6
William FLD 4
HAGLAND, Johnson FTE 73
HAGOOD, Buckner R. TOD 125
R. TOD 127
HAGUE, Thomas FTE 111
HAGUE?, Samuel MER 115
HAHN, Josep NSN 0
Margaret NSN 177
Samuel NSN 177
William NSN 176
HAIBACK, Volantine HRD 78
HAIL, -----? DVS 10A
Ben. PUL 45A
Deram? SPN 9A
Edward HND 6A
Gatewood SPN 3A
John SPN 7A
John PUL 53A
Joseph MER 97
Laboun PUL 63A
Mary MER 97
Nancy MER 97
Pleasant BRK 259
Thomas MER 97
Thomas SPN 3A
William MER 97
HAIL, Wm. BRK 263
HAILE, Nancy MNR 203
HAILER?, George RCK 75A
HAILEY, Abner BKN 4
Bar. RCK 80A
HAIN?, William GRN 79
HAINEN?, William NSN 194
HAINES?, David MAS 67
David RCK 78A
Richd. RCK 79A
HAINLINE, John MTG 229
HAINLINE?, Jesse MTG 269
HAINS, Abam GTN 128
Davd. RCK 82A
Joseph LWS 95A
Josiah OHO 4A
Robert TOD 131
HAINS?, Lis. RCK 80A
HAIR, Jonas LWS 89A
N----n? GTN 119
HAIRES?, John HRD 34
HAIS, Solomon SPN 12A
HAISLIP, Henry (Crossed Out) WTY 117A
Henry WTY 113A
Joel (Crossed Out) WTY 117A
Joel WTY 113A
Robert (Crossed Out) WTY 118A
Robert WTY 113A
HAITSTOCK, Cha. MAS 62
HAIZLE, Caleb HRT 160
HAKE, Jonathan WRN 39A
HALBERT, Henry LWS 86A
James BLT 174
John JEF 43
John LWS 86A
Ralph NSN 186
William NSN 186
HALBROOKS, William BRN 16
HALCOMB, Charlotte MER 115
Eliz. GRD 96B
HALCUP, Henry WAS 46A
HALDERMAN, Davis BLT 184
HALE/ HALL?, Amos CLK 96
Edward CLK 74
Peter A. GRN 68
William CLK 96
HALE, --chariah FLD 41
Abram FLG 68A
Benjamin FLD 5
George SCT 119A
Gideon SHE 174
James WYN 88A
Jesse CWL 34
Jesse CWL 35
John FLD 30
John CWL 31
John WYN 88A
Joseph FLD 44
Nancy WDF 109A
Nathan JEF 51
Nathan CWL 54
Nathn.? CWL 35
Peter FLD 44
Randolph GRD 104A
Stephen PUL 45A
Tho. PUL 42A
HALE?, Caleb BBN 82
David E. OHO 7A
John LGN 28
John BBN 106
Lucy WRN 55A
Thomas BLT 194
William LVG 11
HALEKER?, Barnett BRN 16
HALES, Hugh KNX 278
James KNX 278
James, Jr. KNX 312
HALETT, Richard CLK 100
Robertson CLK 101
William CLK 91
HALEY, Ambrose FTE 93
Bartlett LNC 13
Benj. LNC 9
Benjamin FTE 81
Benjamin FTE 94
Carter GNP 179A
Carter/ Cather? GNP 178A
Danl. HAR 156
Edmund, Capt. MER 98
George RCK 76A
Henry B. BRN 14
James FTE 73
James FTE 82
John FTE 81
John TRG 14A
John RCK 77A
Johnson FTE 76
Lucy TOD 125
Maximilian BRN 14
Nancy WRN 47A
Robt. CLY 130
Silias LNC 13
Spencer SHE 125A
William MER 98
HALFAKER, Isaac WYN 81A
John WYN 81A
HALFPENNY, John CLK 102
HALL, ----. CWL 32
Aaron MTG 295
Adam ADR 28
Adam OHO 7A
Adam WYN 93A
Aeley ETL 42
Andrew LNC 53
Andrew W. FTE 101
Ann LGN 25
Anson OHO 6A
Anthony FLD 14
Arta ETL 50
Asa BLT 182
Austin BLT 156
Bainbridge SHE 166
Bannister HRY 241
Barnett OHO 6A
Basil MTG 269
Benjamin UNN 152
Benjamin SHE 167
Benjamin WRN 72A
Benjamin NCH 113A
Bennet GSN 138A
Beverly JEF 33
Beverly JEF 41
Braxton SCT 104A
Caleb JEF 41
Caleb NSN 194
Caleb HOP 248
Charles BLT 176
Chesley LGN 34
Christopher BRK 261
Clifton BLT 156
Cornelius TOD 125
D., Sr. GRD 88A
Danl. HAR 144
David BLT 182
David OHO 4A
David WYN 92A
David WYN 93A
David GRD 113A
Derias BBN 82

HALL, Drury BRK 263
Drury WTY 111A
Eddy BRN 15
Edmund BRN 33
Edward HRY 180
Edward MTG 243
Edwd. JEF 50
Edwd. S. TOD 132A
Elihu NCH 107A
Elijah JEF 52
Elijah MTG 265
Elijah NCH 113A
Eliz. HRY 252
Elizabeth LGN 32
Elizabeth MER 99
Elizabeth BBN 146
Equillar MNR 213
Frances HND 10
Francis SHE 167
Frans. HRY 204
Garsham BKN 13
George MER 99
George WYN 91A
George WDF 113A
Green MTG 291
Henry LGN 41
Henry MER 97
Henry BBN 126
Henry HAR 144
Henry NCH 112A
Hitty? RCK 80A
Hugh WDF 102
Isabella SCT 106A
Isham FLD 40
J., Mrs.? MAS 57
Jacob BBN 86
Jacob MER 97
James BRN 15
James JEF 33
James CLK 70
James CLK 83
James HRL 110
James GTN 124
James BBN 136
James HAR 180
James BLT 188
James MNR 213
James, Jr. NCH 123A
James, Senr. NCH 107A
James OHO 7A
James WYN 93A
James WYN 93A
James WYN 104A
James? CWL 41
Jane FTE 98
Jane SCT 102A
Jas. JEF 64
Jas. CHN 44A
Jas. RCK 80A
Jas. W. HRD 60
Jeremiah FKN 106
Jesse FLD 30
Jesse CLY 132
Jessee WYN 103A
Jno. HAR 170
Jno. HRY 252
Jno. HRY 262
Joel WAS 19A
John BRN 17
John ADR 26
John LGN 28
John LGN 36
John FLD 40
John JEF 40
John CWL 43
John LNC 65
HALL, John HRD 80
John FTE 98
John MER 98
John FTE 102
John MAD 120
John CLY 130
John HRT 160
John BLT 166
John SHE 176
John BLT 186
John NSN 210
John MTG 237
John MTG 243
John BRK 263
John, Jr. WYN 104A
John, Junr. OHO 6A
John, Sr. WYN 104A
John OHO 6A
John TOD 130A
John MBG 138A
John SCT 138A
John GNP 176A
John B. LNC 51
John C. JEF 33
John C. LGN 39
John S. GTN 124
John W. SHE 113A
Jos. JEF 50
Joseph LNC 5
Joseph JEF 59
Joseph BBN 106
Joseph MNR 213
Joshua BBN 102
Joshua HAR 162
L. F. BBN 98
Labsley WRN 35A
Lawrence NCH 120A
Leonard BRN 17
Levi HRD 16
Levi F. BBN 72
Lewis WRN 33A
Londy/ Loudy? LVG 7
Mahlon BBN 86
Malon? BTH 180
Martha MTG 289
Martin? CWL 41
Matthew PUL 59A
Maze MAD 118
Mchial?, WDF 97
Micajah ETL 42
Micajah TOD 130
Michael HRT 160
Michael W. BRN 14
Mingo OHO 3A
Moses SHE 169
Moses, Jr. NCH 108A
Moses, Sen. NCH 109A
Moses WYN 93A
Moses SHE 127A
N. P. FLG 79A
Nathan GTN 128
Neale? WRN 47A
Palmer BRN 14
Patsey? BRK 263
Peter TOD 134
Phillip HRD 86
Phillip WYN 81A
Polly NCH 120A
Ransom CBL 20A
Reuben CLK 82
Richd. JEF 26
Richd. HAR 144
Robert LGN 38
Robert CHN 32A
Robert NCH 107A
Robt BBN 62
HALL, Robt. BRK 261
Robt. SHE 142A
Sam. HRY 250
Saml. NCH 113A
Samuel FLD 29
Samuel CLK 78
Samuel FTE 86
Samuel BBN 112
Samuel HAR 144
Samuel HAR 214
Sarah HAR 162
Shadrack BLT 154
Sigh GRD 98A
Silvester BRK 263
Simeon BLT 182
Squire HRY 249
Stephen BBN 146
Stephen H. GTN 134
Tharp LNC 9
Theophilas BBN 104
Thomas GRN 57
Thomas CLK 90
Thomas FTE 91
Thomas MER 98
Thomas HAR 220
Thomas MTG 243
Thomas MTG 293
Thomas CBL 7A
Thos. FKN 106
Thos. G. PND 15A
Urila MTG 289
W. Philip GSN 138A
Will SCT 106A
Will. KNX 308
William LVG 11
William FLD 14
William BRN 15
William ETL 44
William FTE 73
William MER 98
William BBN 102
William UNN 148
William MNR 213
William MNR 213
William, Sr.? GRD 110A
William SPN 22A
William CHN 28A
William PUL 68A
William WYN 82A
William GRD 98A
William GRD 110A
William NCH 112A
William Sr. WYN 97A
Williams MER 98
Willis WDF 114A
Winny BRN 17
Wm. FKN 124
Wm. HRY 252
Wm. PUL 36A
Wm. S. CHN 41A
Wm.? J. MAS 57
Zach JEF 52
HALL?, Caleb BBN 82
David E. OHO 7A
Elisha MAD 116
John BBN 106
Thomas BLT 194
William HAR 180
William, Jr. ETL 44
HALLACK, Benjn. BBN 106
HALLARD, John MAD 118
HALLAWAY, Jno. HRY 241
HALLER, Isaac JEF 22
Lewis WDF 104
HALLER?, Benjamin FTE 56
HALLES, Susanna MAD 124

HALLET, Solomon NSN 177
HALLEY, Benjamin MTG 291
James CLK 98
John MTG 259
Nancy MAD 172
Samuel MTG 293
HALLOWAY, John? CWL 36
HALLOWELL, -----? CWL 41
HALLS, Nathon H. WAS 77A
HALLSA, Jos. PUL 40A
Jos. PUL 49A
HALLY?, John MAD 152
HALO, Chas. W. SCT 136A
HALOWDAY, Charles ALN 120
HALSELL, Benjamin MNR 211
HALSELL?, Turner MNR 195
HALSEY, Elizabth CLY 115
HALSTEAD, Daniel FTE 68
John D. FTE 68
HALSTED, A. B. JEF 19
HALSY, Elizabeth GRN 70
HALT, Ben ADR 42
Thos. ADR 42
Wm. B. BRK 259
HALVY?, Peter LWS 94A
HALY, Coleman GRD 96B
HALYARD, John CLK 92
HALZ, Nancy BBN 142
HAM, Drury LNC 41
Elijah JES 75
George GRD 102A
John PUL 52A
Josiah RCK 79A
Matthew MBG 135A
Samuel BNE 20
HAM?, Catherine NCH 126A
Elizabeth NCH 126A
Ezekel RCK 77A
Jacob NCH 127A
James BKN 11
Johah RCK 83A
John LGN 47
John, Jr. NCH 127A
John, Senr. NCH 126A
Michael, Jr. NCH 127A
Michael NCH 109A
Saml. NCH 127A
Thomas BTH 186
William GRN 79
Wm. JEF 59
HAMAH?, John GNP 174A
HAMAMONS, Mary WDF 92
HAMAN, John GRN 59
HAMB---?, James CHN 35
HAMBLETON, ---ken? WAS 69A
Alexander WAS 53A
Allen WAS 28A
Archibald BTH 160
Clemont WAS 70A
Daniel BTH 166
Edward WAS 70A
Hance HRD 20
Isam WAS 28A
James WAS 27A
John A. FLG 58A
Patrick WAS 70A
Robertson BTH 220
Thos. MAD 164
Walter WAS 78A
William BTH 148
William BTH 150
William OHO 5A
HAMBLIN, Benjamin WTY 118A
Dant KNX 298
George SHE 154
George KNX 298
HAMBLIN, John WTY 125A
Peter KNX 298
Vincent KNX 298
HAMBORG?, George BKN 22
HAMBRAKE, Jesse SCT 103A
HAMBRICK, Adam MBG 137
Elender HRY 253
Gilson MAS 55
Jessee LWS 91A
Lewis FLG 31A
Thomas ETL 44
William OWN 99
HAMBRIGHT, Daniel LGN 31
James SPN 10A
HAMBY, Isaac CHN 29
Jerry, Junr. CHN 29
Jėsse CHN 29
Susan HOP 250
HAMBY?, James CHN 29
HAMEL, John BRN 14
HAMELTAN, E. Mrs.? MAS 65
Wm.? E. MAS 65
HAMELTON, James MAD 178
James NSN 181
James M. HND 4A
Jno. MAS 53
Robert MNR 195
Samuel NCH 122A
HAMEN?, (See Hansen?) FLG 47A
William NSN 194
HAMER, James CBL 11A
HAMES, Robt. TOD 129
HAMES?, David MAS 67
HAMET?, James BRN 16
HAMETT?, Benjn. CHN 28A
HAMILLOW?, Charles LVG 16
HAMILTAN, Geo. MAS 65
HAMILTON, -----? CWL 44
----el? DVS 10A
Abner BRN 14
Alexander BNE 20
Andrew FKN 116
Andrew MTG 245
Anthony L. LVG 13
Asa BNE 18
Baxter MER 98
Ben ADR 26
Benjamin FLD 19
Benjamin BTL 323
Charity NCH 122A
Charles BRK 259
Charlote FTE 58
Chas. SCT 113A
Danl. FLG 65A
David FLD 32
David WDF 121A
E. L. GRN 60
Edw. BRK 261
Edward H. BLT 154
Elizabeth BRN 15
Ellis HRY 249
George CLK 69
George FTE 74
George BLT 196
George HAR 214
George T HAR 214
Guy WDF 103A
Hannah, Mrs. WYN 90A
Henry ETL 37
Isabella WDF 103A
Isham G. BNE 20
James BNE 18
James ADR 26
James FTE 58
James CLK 83
HAMILTON, James JES 84
James FKN 94
James HRY 222
James NCH 109A
James NCH 115A
James NCH 123A
Jas. PUL 42A
Jas. FLG 68A
Jas. S. FLG 59A
Jason NCH 109A
Jesse WRN 38A
Jno. LVG 8
Jno. ADR 26
Jno. MAS 62
Jno. HAR 158
John BKN 14
John BKN 15
John BNE 18
John FLD 19
John BNE 20
John CWL 36
John GRN 65
John FTE 68
John LNC 79
John BBN 122
John MNR 205
John HAR 206
John HRY 222
John PND 20A
John FLG 33A
John WYN 90A
John NCH 107A
John WDF 113A
John NCH 128A
John C. HAR 218
John H. BBN 120
John O. GTN 119
Joseph MER 98
Joseph HAR 196
Joseph WYN 90A
Joseph D. LGN 23
Justin HRT 160
Margaret FTE 111
Margarett HAR 148
Mary CBL 7A
Maurice CBL 7A
Micajah MER 99
Nancy HAR 220
Nathen CWL 36
Patrick MAD 120
Polly NCH 120A
Reuben FKN 122
Reuben BLT 168
Robert JES 71
Robert NCH 122A
Saml. BKN 2
Saml., Jr. BKN 14
Saml. SCT 114A
Samuel FLD 37
Samul BNE 18
Sarah WDF 126A
Thomas FLD 32
Thomas LNC 53
Thomas FTE 75
Thomas HAR 144
Thomas CLD 156
Thomas MNR 205
Thomas CBL 14A
Thos. ADR 26
Will. LVG 8
William BNE 18
William BNE 18
William LNC 49
William GRN 59
William JES 73
William CLK 86

HAMILTON, William HAR 158
William CBL 14A
William WDF 108A
William NCH 109A
Willim. LNC 65
Willm. LNC 79
Wm. ADR 26
Wm. HRY 240
Wm. PUL 36A
HAMILTON?, Polly NCH 126A
HAMLIN, Charles LWS 90A
Rodger LWS 93A
William LWS 89A
HAMLINE?, Jacob MTG 226
Jesse MTG 269
HAMM, Jos. FLG 47A
HAMMACK, Ephraim MAD 136
Jane MAD 168
HAMMAND?, Richard M. LGN 23
HAMMER, Frederick MNR 215
Henry HRD 50
John MNR 197
John F. MNR 191
Peter MNR 195
Richard MNR 191
Wm. HRD 58
HAMMERLY, James PND 25A
HAMMET, William WRN 30A
HAMMETT, Danl. S. JEF 22
Isaac CBL 2A
Saml. MAS 54
HAMMILTON, James HAR 164
Mary HAR 164
HAMMITT, R. MAS 54
HAMMOCK, Agnes KNX 278
Benjamin UNN 149
Jno. PUL 38A
William UNN 149
HAMMON, Conelius MAD 180
James GTN 129
William GRN 76
HAMMON?, Jno. ADR 28
Jno. ADR 28
Nancy ADR 28
HAMMOND, Eli E. LGN 46
Eli, (Exor. Of S. Hannah LGN 33
Elizah WRN 38A
Fielden JEF 54
Geo. JEF 54
George CLD 156
Hutchen JEF 54
James NSN 181
James NSN 199
James MTG 291
Jervas S. SPN 3A
Job. LGN 46
Lewis FKN 94
Margaret HRY 251
Phil. MTG 253
Richd. BKN 28
Rose MAS 52
Silas GRD 82A
Tho. MAS 52
Thomas LNC 51
Thomas SPN 6A
Thos. S. NSN 210
William SPN 6A
Wm. CWL 54
Wm. MTG 247
HAMMONDS, James OWN 99
James A. WRN 46A
John LNC 49
John WRN 61A
John PUL 64A
HAMMONDS, Thomas OWN 99
William WRN 37A
Wm. CHN 34
HAMMONS, Bery WTY 125A
Caleb FLG 77A
Charles WDF 102
Edwin KNX 292
Ezra WDF 97A
James KNX 292
Jane NSN 199
John KNX 278
John FLG 75A
John LWS 93A
John WDF 99A
Obd?, Jr. KNX 280
Obd?, Sr. KNX 280
Peter, Jr. KNX 278
Peter, Sr. KNX 278
Polly WDF 99A
Thomas W. LGN 46
HAMNER, Henry MER 98
Jesse MER 98
John MER 97
HAMON, Joseph FLD 4
Martin CWL 44
William FLD 4
HAMON?, John FLD 1A
HAMOND, Christ-.? CWL 36
John G. CWL 43
Joshua CWL 38
HAMONS, Edward FLD 6
HAMPER, Joel BBN 102
HAMPTON, Abijah MNR 201
Amos WRN 55A
Andrew JES 74
Benjamin WRN 29A
Charles HOP 248
Charles BTL 323
David JEF 53
David CLK 91
David NSN 192
Elizabeth GNP 175A
Ephram JEF 48
Geo. GRD 113A
George CLK 92
George FTE 99
Green WYN 92A
Henry MAS 63
James GTN 121
James, Jr. GTN 122
James, Sr. GTN 122
James WRN 61A
Jas. FLG 61A
Jesse FTE 70
Jesse WRN 52A
Jessee CLK 91
Joel CBL 21A
Joel WRN 51A
John CLK 102
John MTG 263
John BTL 323
John OHO 5A
John FLG 33A
John WRN 52A
Jonathan WRN 28A
Joseph LWS 94A
Joshua WRN 52A
Lybern ADR 4
Martha JES 92
Moses CLK 91
Obadiah CLK 95
Oliver JEF 53
Polly LGN 42
Preston FKN 106
Preston GRT 142
Rowland JEF 48
HAMPTON, Samuel GTN 122
Samuel LWS 95A
Sarah GRT 146
Susy BTL 325
Thomas HAR 148
Thomas BTL 325
Turner FLD 13
William CLK 92
William WRN 55A
Wilson CLK 74
Wm. FKN 98
HAMSLEY, Henry WRN 40A
HAMTELL?, Thos. FLG 53A
HAMTON, Lewis HAR 150
HAN-ERRY?, Thomas TRG 12
HANABY?, Jerry, Senr. CHN 29
HANAH, Hugh CHN 45
HANALEY, James WAS 41A
HANALY?, Alexander WAS 17A
HANBACK, William FTE 95
HANBERRY, John TRG 12
HANBERRY?, Thomas TRG 12
HANCE, John BBN 68
Richd. BBN 68
HANCEFORD, Thomas LNC 73
William LNC 3
Wm. T. BBN 86
HANCOCK, Anderson MER 97
Benjamin WYN 103A
Elizabeth GRD 121A
Geo. MAS 77
Henry JEF 58
Isaac P. HOP 250
James FKN 102
James NSN 180
Jessee WYN 103A
Jo. GRD 107A
John HND 11A
John CHN 36A
Joshua HND 9
Major WYN 79A
Major WYN 97A
Micajah HND 11A
Obed. WDF 121A
Robt. HRY 266
Scarett G. HND 12
Sillanus HND 9A
Simon HRY 220
Thos. CWL 33
William HND 11
William HND 12
William JES 89
William WDF 94
William WYN 97A
Williamson MER 98
Wm. JEF 64
HANCOCKE, Sally WAS 29A
HAND, Jacob CHN 29A
Monarck? WAS 53A
Robt. BBN 138
Thomas SHE 115A
Uriah SHE 119A
HAND?, Elias MAS 59
John?, Jr. PND 23A
Lanan? RCK 84A
HANDCOCK, Charles SPN 20A
Hiram ADR 26
Simon ADR 26
Wm., Sr. ADR 26
Wm. Jr. ADR 26
HANDLEY, ---el? DVS 8A
David WRN 67A
George DVS 19A
James WAS 41A
Sally LNC 29

Name	County	Page
HANDLEY, Samuel	MBG	135A
Wilo.?	LVG	7
Wm.	WAS	65A
HANDLEY?,		
Alexander	WAS	17A
HANDLY, -andy?	JES	80
John	WAS	36A
John H.	JES	69
Phebe	WAS	39A
Wm.	WAS	39A
HANDSFORD, John W.	HRD	62
Wm.	HRD	52
HANDY, Betsey	FTE	61
James	GRN	57
Jesse	BRN	15
John	CHN	29
Will.	SCT	121A
HANDY?, Peter	HRY	194
HANE?, Joseph	GNP	171A
HANEBY, Jane	JES	71
HANELY, Elijah	BTL	325
George, Jr.	MAD	146
George, Sr.	MAD	146
Jacob	BTL	325
Wm.	MAD	146
HANER?, John	MAD	90
HANES, Amelia	SCT	106A
Christopher	ALN	136
Evan	MAD	150
Henry	BRK	261
John	RCK	80A
Joseph	KNX	284
Lewis	WRN	46A
Robert	MAD	94
Temple	PUL	45A
Thos.	PUL	45A
William	WYN	79A
HANESWORTH, Henry	HRY	222
HANEY, Christopher	ALN	116
Geo.	JEF	65
Henry	GNP	168A
James	BBN	64
James	FTE	92
James, Senr.	PUL	58A
James	PUL	58A
John	FLD	24
John	BBN	116
Lucy	FTE	109
Polly	MTG	273
William	FLD	21
HANEY?, Jesse	ADR	24
Richd.	RCK	79A
HANGE?, John	JEF	62
HANIKIN, Jacob	FLG	38A
HANIKIN?,		
Christian	FLG	38A
HANISH, Wm.	ALN	136
HANISH?, Dianah	ALN	136
HANKEN, George	SHE	112A
Gilbert	SHE	109A
Wm.	SHE	112A
HANKIN, Henry	SHE	138A
HANKINS/ HARKINS?,		
Moses	HRY	198
HANKINS, Barnaba	HOP	248
John	HOP	250
Richard	WYN	87A
Timothy	HOP	248
HANKINS?, Daniel	CHN	29
Wm.	CHN	30
HANKLE, James	MER	97
HANKLEY, Royal	MER	98
HANKS, Abner	HRY	258
Elijah	WDF	105A
Fielding	FLD	11
Geo.	FKN	144
HANKS, James	HRD	74
Jno.	HRY	254
John	MTG	231
John	HOP	248
John W.	MAD	100
Joshua	HOP	248
Pitman	FKN	146
Polly	MTG	245
Samuel	ETL	39
Sedner?	WDF	98
Thomas	GTN	127
Thomas	HOP	248
Turner	FKN	156
Wm.	BRK	259
Wm.	OHO	9A
Wm.	GSN	138A
HANKS?, Absalam	CLK	68
HANLEY, Redmon	BKN	8
Thos.	HND	9
HANLY, John	BTH	214
HANN, Anthony, Dr.	MER	98
John	RCK	77A
John	GRD	86A
Thos.	BBN	122
William	MTG	237
HANN?, John	RCK	84A
HANNA, Adam	SHE	162
Ebenezer	FLD	33
Edwd.	MAS	58
James	FLD	23
Joseph	FLD	19
Martha	SHE	154
Robert	CHN	45
Samuel	FLD	23
Samuel	FLD	31
Thomas	SHE	173
Wm.	SHE	143A
HANNAH, (Free)	BBN	90
Abraham	WDF	103A
Andrew	SCT	101A
Caleb	HAR	166
Elizabeth	MER	99
Gabriel	GNP	175A
Hugh	LWS	91A
Jno.	FKN	68
John	MER	99
John	LWS	92A
John	NCH	127A
John	GNP	169A
Joseph	BBN	116
Robt.	GNP	175A
Roland	SCT	92A
S. (Eli		
Hammon-exor.)	LGN	33
Saml	HAR	166
Townley	GNP	175A
Wallis	UNN	150
William	LWS	91A
William	LWS	92A
Wm.	GNP	175A
HANNAH?, Samuel	WYN	96A
HANNAN, John	LGN	34
Margarett	HAR	142
HANNAN?, David	HAR	162
HANNER, James	WAS	45A
John	WAS	45A
Sollomon	WAS	45A
HANNON, Ama?	GSN	139A
John	HRY	212
HANNON?, Zebulon	BKN	23
HANNS?, Simeon	CBL	15A
HANNUM, John	HRD	90
HANON?, Solomon	GNP	168A
HANOR, Harman	WRN	66A
HANS, Geo.	JEF	41
HANSAN, Andrew	CHN	42A
HANSAN, Dicy	CHN	42A
John	CHN	42A
HANSBOROUGH, Ann	JEF	62
HANSBROUGH, Enoch	SHE	166
Joel	SHE	166
John	SHE	124A
Joseph	MTG	229
Morias?	SHE	124A
Peter	LGN	27
Wm.	SHE	119A
HANSEN, William	LVG	13
HANSEN?, Danl.	FLG	47A
Perry	FLG	47A
Saml.	FLG	47A
HANSFORD, Ben.	PUL	50A
Jno.	PUL	46A
Thos.	PUL	41A
HANSHAW, Joseph	SPN	3A
HANSHEW, Andrew	FLD	31
HANSLETT?, Thos.	FLG	53A
HANSLEY?, Tho.	HRY	204
HANSON, Anthony	MER	115
Jno.	MAS	66
John	BKN	5
Paul, Sr.	LVG	9
Sarah	NCH	105
William	FTE	67
Willis	WRN	34A
HANSON?, Paul, Jr.	LVG	9
Samuel	CLK	103
HANSTELL?, Thos.	FLG	53A
HANTHOM, Charles	MAD	144
HANY, Robt	ADR	28
HANY?, Grove	NSN	198
William T.	FTE	95
HANZ?, Hooper	BLT	172
HAPHERD, Wm.	FKN	74
HAPPIALE?, Peter	BKN	8
HAPPY, Elijah	FTE	98
Rebecca	FTE	65
HARBARGER, Joseph	BTH	156
HARBAUGH, Jacob	MBG	137
HARBER, Elisha	TRG	14
Thos.	MAD	162
HARBERSON, James	MER	98
Nancy	MER	98
HARBERT, Henry	NCH	108A
John	NCH	108A
John	NCH	108A
Paul	JEF	58
Wm.	FLG	46A
HARBETT, Thomas	HAR	150
HARBIN, Henry	WAS	72A
HARBIN?, John B.	FTE	68
HARBISON, Anne	BRN	14
John	BRN	14
John	SHE	172
Martha D.	SHE	163
Matthew	BRN	15
Samuel	SHE	143A
William	SHE	162
HARBOLD, Jno., Jr.	JEF	65
Leonard	JEF	35
HARBOUGH, Henry	JES	83
HARBOUR, Jeremiah	MER	98
Thomas	NCH	106A
HARCOAT, Richard	HAR	200
HARCOURT, Alexr.	BBN	144
John	BBN	118
HARD--?, Henry	FLG	72A
HARD, William,		
Maj.	MER	115
HARDAWAY, Richard	BRK	259
HARDCASTLE, James	WRN	59A
Jno.	ALN	132
Riley	WRN	59A

HARDCASTLE, Shadrack WRN 59A
William WRN 59A
HARDECK, Michel MAD 116
HARDEMAN, Wm. OHO 10A
HARDEN, Charles CLK 84
Daniel S. BBN 118
Elihu HAR 190
Geo. W. SCT 91A
George GRD 88A
Hannah MAD 142
James MAD 132
James CLD 153
Jemima MAD 142
John LVG 16
Joseph G. MNR 215
Marke SHE 127A
Nathan SHE 141A
Presly BTH 188
Thomas HAR 190
Thos. BBN 128
Vachel JEF 38
Wm. MAD 144
HARDENBROOK, John MER 98
HARDESTEY, Charles WAS 73A
HARDESTY, Benjn. BBN 102
Caleb NSN 207
Charles WAS 86A
Elezibeth WAS 40A
Francis BBN 104
Henry FTE 91
Henry NSN 220
Jacob BNE 18
Kenyez BBN 118
Saml. BBN 106
Thomas CLK 71
Uriah BNE 50
Wm. BBN 110
HARDGROVE, Jno. PUL 45A
Polly MTG 245
HARDI?, Lucius WDF 95
HARDICK, Cary? ADR 28
George ADR 28
Henry BBN 124
HARDIN, Absolum LVG 3
Alexander SHE 157
Alf. G. JEF 27
Alxr. ADR 3
Ann JEF 57
Asa ADR 26
Ben NSN 223
Benjamin OWN 104
Benoni WAS 46A
Bob GRD 109A
Charles GTN 133
Cuthbert BRN 14
Daniel HRY 251
Daniel BRK 259
David MNR 205
Davis SPN 14A
Elias LGN 42
Elizebeth WAS 46A
George OWN 106
George HOP 248
Hardy HRD 88
Henry LVG 8
Henry LNC 75
Henry BRK 259
Henry WAS 53A
Henry C. SHE 148
Isaac HAR 176
Isaac BRK 227
James LNC 9
James OWN 105
James PUL 40A
James G. FTE 65
HARDIN, Joel BRK 261
John ADR 28
John FLD 41
John GRD 102B
John WAS 20A
John C. WAS 61A
John E. BRK 227
Joseph ADR 26
Joseph HRD 88
Lewis OWN 100
Lewis BTH 182
Marcus BRN 14
Mark HRD 88
Mark WAS 17A
Mark WAS 56A
Mark WAS 87A
Martin HRD 8
Martin BRN 14
Martin WAS 20A
Martin WAS 47A
Martin D. FKN 76
Mason SHE 150
Mordica WAS 53A
Moses WAS 41A
Nathaniel HOP 250
Nicholas ADR 24
Nicholas HOP 250
Peter WAS 47A
Richd FKN 142
Robt. BRK 263
Saul HRT 160
Thomas GTN 129
Thompson CLK 65
Wesley FKN 126
William SHE 176
William HAR 180
William WYN 83A
Wm. JEF 35
Wm. JEF 65
Wm. HRD 88
Wm., Sen. BRK 229
Wm. (Exors Of) LGN 42
Worren? WAS 63A
HARDING, Aaron GRN 67
Able GRN 75
Jacob CBL 4A
Jno. MAS 67
John JEF 56
John JEF 68
John GRN 71
John BBN 146
John, Jr. BBN 72
John, Senr. BBN 72
Jonathan HAR 220
Lida GRN 74
Rebecca JEF 68
Saml. GRN 71
Sarah GRN 64
Stephen GRN 66
Thomas GRN 75
HARDISTER, Christopher HND 12
Henry HND 12
James BRK 261
Jeptha PUL 38A
Jessee HND 12
Richard BRK 261
Salley MAD 104
Thos. PUL 38A
HARDISTON, Benijah LGN 30
Gabirel LGN 28
John LGN 45
HARDISTY, Charles WAS 67A
Jerimiah WAS 60A
John WAS 62A
Thomas MER 116
HARDMAN, Edward FKN 106
Jonathan BLT 190
HARDMON?, Robt. ADR 24
HARDON, John MNR 191
HARDWAY, Jos. E. HRD 14
HARDWIC, Willis TOD 126A
HARDWICH, Christopher FKN 110
HARDWICK, Charles SHE 151
Jno. PUL 41A
Joanah BBN 62
John ADR 26
John MER 98
John MAD 142
John MAD 154
Lucy MTG 289
Robert HRY 220
Wm. TOD 126A
HARDY, Andrew LGN 37
Andrew SPN 15A
Armistead NCH 107A
Arnold SCT 107A
Benjamin BRN 17
Casper SCT 132A
George HRT 160
Henry UNN 153
Henry SCT 122A
Isham HRT 160
James G. BRN 15
Joseph GTN 124
Pliny BBN 144
Richd. S. JEF 52
Saml. BKN 16
Samuel ALN 116
Thomas WRN 29A
Will SCT 97A
HARE, Daniel WRN 74A
James LNC 13
Jno. LNC 7
Willis HOP 248
HAREGROVES, George TRG 7A
John TRG 7
William TRG 7A
Willis TRG 5
HARENS?, Simeon CBL 15A
HAREWOOD, James SCT 122A
John SCT 118A
HARFORD, Thomas SHE 173
HARGAN, Jas. HRD 54
Michael HRD 50
HARGATE, Peter MAS 52
HARGET, Danl. FLG 54A
Israel FLG 54A
HARGIN, George HRY 232
HARGIN?, George HRY 206
HARGIS, Abraham CHN 42
Abram PUL 48A
Isaac CHN 42
Jno. PUL 47A
John TRG 4A
John GNP 168A
Tho. PUL 50A
Thomas CLD 140
Wm. PUL 38A
HARGRAVE, Zachariah MER 98
HARGRAVES, Leml. TOD 124A
HARGROVE, Robert LGN 34
Wm. CHN 34A
HARIESON?, William CHN 28
HARING, Elizabeth CHN 43
HARIS, Richmund GRD 94A
HARK, Andrew GSN 138A
Thomas GRN 78
HARKINGS, Daniel NSN 210
HARKINS, James CHN 30A

Name	County	Page
HARKLEY?, James	GSN	138A
HARL, Baldwin	MAS	52
Hypocratus	HRD	74
John	HRD	72
Leander	MAS	53
HARLAN, Elijah	MER	98
Elijah	TOD	132A
George	TRG	10
George	CHN	44A
George C.	MER	98
James	TRG	10
Jehu	MER	98
Matthew	CHN	39
Sarah	MER	98
Silas	MER	98
Wm.	TOD	130
HARLAND, Aaron	MNR	205
Elijah	MNR	191
Ennis	MNR	205
Jacob	BRN	14
Joel	MNR	215
John	MNR	191
Levi	TRG	3
Samuel	MNR	217
Thomas	MNR	215
HARLESS, Daniel	HND	13
Joseph	FLD	38
HARLEWOOD, Daniel	MER	98
HARLEY, Daniel	MER	98
Gatesfield	LVG	13
John	MER	98
John	MER	98
Joshua	SCT	131A
Leonard	SHE	167
HARLIN, Al-gis?	WAS	54A
David	BTL	323
Elijah G.	JEF	30
George	LNC	45
Henry	LNC	45
John	BTL	323
Nathl.	MAS	80
HARLON, Michael	BRN	15
HARLOW, Anderson	BRN	14
Archd.	HRY	243
Bartholomew	MER	97
Claibourn	BRN	14
E.	HRY	261
George	FTE	84
George Barton	MNR	195
Hezekiah	MER	97
Jesse	BRN	14
Lewis	HRT	159
Nathaniel	MAD	156
Nelson	MAD	118
Randol	HRT	161
Sirwood?	HRY	267
Thomas	BRN	14
Thomas	MER	97
Tyler	HRY	261
Wm. D.	BRN	14
HARM?, John	RCK	84A
HARMAN, Jackson	FLG	69A
Jesse	BBN	132
John	LVG	13
John	ALN	108
John	BTH	214
Lewis	SHE	114A
Nancy	HRY	198
Peter	HAR	202
Rosanna	FLD	30
HARMAN?, David	HAR	162
Micajah	WRN	70A
Nancy	ADR	28
HARMASON, John	JEF	44
HARMER?, Nical	WAS	22A
HARMERSON, Henry	JEF	45
HARMES?, Alex.	HRY	244
HARMIN, Michael	HOP	248
HARMON, -an-.?	CWL	36
Anderson	WYN	97A
Benjamin S.	WRN	67A
Charles	GRD	98A
George	SPN	25A
Henry	GTN	126
Henry	HOP	250
Isaac	ADR	24
Isaac	HND	6A
Jacob	BTH	216
Jacob	WTY	124A
Jacob	MBG	133A
John	ADR	24
John	JEF	31
Lettuce	PUL	50A
Nicholas	HOP	248
Peter	MER	98
Philip	MTG	257
Robt.	FLG	70A
Saml.	BKN	18
Thos.	FLG	69A
Valentine	BKN	9
Valentine	WTY	114A
Wm.	FLG	60A
Wm.	GNP	173A
HARMON?, John	HRY	212
HARMOND, Jacob	GRD	99A
Lewis	WYN	92A
Rece	GRD	99A
HARMOND?, John	BKN	26
HARMS?, Hezekiah	HRT	160
HARN, Wm.	GNP	172A
HARN?, (See Ham?)	NCH	126A
Ezekel	RCK	77A
Johah	RCK	38A
Michael	NCH	109A
William	GRN	79
Wm.	JEF	59
HARNAH?, John	GNP	174A
HARNBY?, James	CHN	29
HARNDEN, John	WRN	35A
HARNED, Wm.	HRD	56
HARNELL, Ben	CWL	52
HARNESS, Jacob	BBN	76
Richard	BRN	16
HARNET, Enos	HRD	18
HARNETT?, Benjn.	CHN	28A
Nathal	BRK	263
HARNEY, Hiram	NCH	105
James	BBN	66
James F.	WRN	68A
Rowland	NCH	105
Samuel A.	NCH	125A
Thomas	NCH	107A
William	FTE	75
HARNID, Jonathan	NSN	192
HARNID?, Benjamin	NSN	192
John	NSN	192
Joseph	NSN	192
HARNIS?, David H.	WDF	95
Hezekiah	HRT	160
Thomas	HRT	160
HARNON?, John	FLD	1A
HARP, Abram	FTE	95
Alin	PUL	45A
Bayer	NSN	216
Benajer	KNX	300
Conrod	FTE	92
David	FTE	92
George	FTE	95
Henry	FKN	110
James	FKN	110
Joel	GRN	76
John	FTE	95
HARP, Ritchard	BBN	74
Susanna	LGN	33
Tobias	KNX	300
Will.	KNX	298
Zachariah	NSN	216
HARPENDING, Joshua?	CWL	42
HARPER, -----?	CWL	36
-----?	CWL	39
Absalom	BRN	15
Adam	WDF	111A
Asa	CLD	152
Billips	BKN	6
Bryant	LVG	16
Charles	MTG	287
Daniel	LGN	34
David	BTL	325
Ebenezer	SCT	113A
Everitt	MBG	140A
Francis	GRN	54
Hance	HRT	160
Hennery	CSY	220
Henry	WAS	31A
Henry	WDF	111A
Hezekiah	SHE	173
Isaac	CWL	33
Isaac	HRT	159
James	CLD	150
James	MTG	249
Jesse	SPN	6A
Joel B.	SHE	120A
John	BRN	15
John	BBN	106
John	MBG	137
John	MTG	287
John	WDF	111A
John D.	MBG	137
Johnathan	HRT	161
Lewis	CWL	36
Margerit	WDF	113A
Martin	FLD	10
Mary	HRT	161
Mary	FLG	75A
Matthew	HRT	160
Micheal	WDF	108A
Nathan	MBG	140
Nicholas	MTG	249
Pleasant	MER	98
Robert	TOD	129A
Robt.	FLG	73A
Saml.	HRT	160
Saml.	HRT	161
Silus	HRT	161
Stephen	FLD	17
Stephen	HRT	159
Thomas	LGN	27
Thomas	MTG	249
Turner	MAD	164
Vicy	CHN	43
Widw.	CWL	33
William	CBL	16A
William	WDF	111A
William	WDF	113A
William S.	WDF	93A
Wm.	HRT	161
HARPER?, Daniel	WDF	92
HARPOLE, Henry	WRN	64A
Jacob	WRN	64A
John	WRN	64A
HARPUTH?, John	CWL	37
HARR, Mathew M.	WRN	73A
HARRAH, James	MTG	237
HARRALD, John	WRN	39A
Lewis	WRN	75A
HARRDIN, Henry	JEF	60
HARREL, Absalom	SHE	158

HARREL, Isaac NSN 186
James NSN 199
John SHE 158
John BTL 323
Mildred SHE 158
Moses NSN 199
HARRELL, Bendict SHE 118A
Thos. SHE 118A
HARRELSON, William BTL 323
HARRIES, Jestenian OHO 3A
HARRIFORD, William WRN 54A
HARRILSON, Anderson HOP 246
HARRINGTON, Joseph SHE 167
Thos. HND 12
HARRIOTT, Ephraim BBN 116
John BBN 64
HARRIS, -----? DVS 13A
----n? DVS 7A
Abraham MAD 106
Alan HRY 254
Alexander SPN 11A
Alexis MTG 279
Alford MAD 124
Ann FKN 58
Ann MAS 62
Aron UNN 149
Arthur SHE 125A
Baley SHE 112A
Barton MER 98
Ben HRD 44
Ben. CHN 44
Benjamin CLK 99
Benjamin HRL 110
Benjamin PUL 65A
Bowls ETL 43
Caleb GTN 134
Carington ETL 41
Charles HRD 68
Charles MTG 293
Charles CBL 17A
Charles WYN 90A
Christopher MAD 164
Christopher SPN 15A
Christopher PUL 67A
Chs. JEF 49
Clabourn BBN 122
Dabney PUL 58A
Dan. HRY 269
Daniel ETL 51
Danl. PND 24A
Dav. HRY 216
Dav. HRY 264
David LVG 9
David ALN 100
David ALN 112
David MAD 118
David WDF 98A
David K. FLD 47
Di-gui--? MER 98
Edward FKN 140
Edward WYN 87A
Edwd. MAS 81
Edwd., Jr. MAS 81
Elijah CLK 105
Elijah KNX 306
Elizabeth MER 114
Elizabeth MAD 120
Elizabeth SPN 12A
Enoch WRN 32A
Foster FTE 104
Frances BRN 33
Francis BBN 62
Francis MNR 217
George FTE 69
George, Junr. WRN 64A
HARRIS, George SPN 11A
George CBL 14A
George WRN 64A
George GSN 138A
George F. LNC 79
Gillum TRG 3A
Graves WRN 67A
Henry BRN 16
Henry MAD 92
Henry MER 99
Henry MAD 106
Henry MAD 152
Hosea HAR 162
James JES 71
James FTE 107
James MNR 195
James WRN 58A
James GRD 86A
James SHE 124A
James P. FLD 47
Jas. HRY 264
Jessey MAD 90
Jno. PUL 45A
John BRN 14
John FLD 30
John LGN 36
John HRD 58
John JES 90
John MAD 94
John MAD 108
John HRL 110
John CLY 122
John MBG 137
John UNN 150
John HRY 216
John MNR 217
John, Jr. MNR 217
John SPN 11A
John CBL 17A
John WDF 125A
John NCH 129A
John H. SCT 111A
John J. LGN 41
John M. WRN 65A
Jonath. HRY 262
Jonathan SHE 157
Jonithan GSN 138A
Jordan CWL 37
Joseph MER 99
Joshua SHE 159
Josiah MAD 160
Mahu HRD 58
Margret MAD 122
Mary LGN 37
Mary WDF 103
Mary DVS 17A
Mary MBG 139A
Milly FTE 79
Moses ADR 24
Nancy HRD 72
Nancy MAD 170
Nathan HRL 110
Nathan BLT 194
Nathan GRD 86A
Nathan GSN 138A
Nathan M. UNN 152
Nathaniel JES 83
Nathaniel UNN 149
Nicholas WYN 90A
Orange MER 99
Overton FKN 120
Overton MAD 166
Overton BLT 184
Overton TOD 131A
Polly HRD 78
Rachel HRD 90
HARRIS, Randolph FTE 105
Reubin? CWL 37
Rice JES 90
Richard CLD 138
Richard WRN 36A
Richd. BBN 72
Robert BRN 14
Robert ALN 108
Robert MAD 118
Robert WRN 62A
Roland MBG 133A
Ruth MER 98
Sam M. TOD 133
Sam. HRY 262
Saml. CLY 116
Saml. NCH 113A
Saml. P. MAD 148
Samuel FLD 43
Samuel FTE 74
Samuel MAD 158
Samuel GSN 139A
Shederick WAS 53A
Simeon BLT 184
Sophia BBN 88
Susanna GRT 147
Taylor LGN 41
Tho. JEF 59
Thomas ETL 49
Thomas FTE 84
Thomas JES 90
Thomas CBL 2A
Thomas WRN 32A
Thomas GSN 139A
Thos. FKN 140
Thos. CHN 42A
Thos. D. CHN 35
Thos. G. S. HRD 30
Tyne MAD 114
Tyre GRD 119A
Walter MER 98
Webb FKN 140
Weber? MAD 160
Will. SCT 104A
William BRN 16
William FLD 35
William LGN 39
William ETL 43
William JES 87
William JES 90
William SHE 173
William MNR 217
William HOP 248
William MTG 261
William SPN 11A
William WRN 64A
William WDF 104A
Wm. BRN 16
Wm. BRN 17
Wm. HRD 78
Wm. FKN 114
Wm. MAD 132
Wm. SHE 136A
Wm. H. CHN 44
Zecheriah BLT 156
Zedekiah BLT 182
HARRIS?, David RCK 78A
David H. WDF 95
John (Miller) WDF 103
John RCK 80A
Lis. RCK 80A
Moses ALN 98
HARRISMAN, Peter FTE 102
HARRISN?, William NSN 194
HARRISON, Adison CHN 42
Alexander BBN 124
Anthony A. PUL 54A

HARRISON, B. I./
  J.? JEF 23
  Balus HRT 160
  Ben. CHN 35A
  Benj. O.? CWL 38
  Benjamin CLK 85
  Burr HRD 36
  Cabell FTE 93
  Carter H. FTE 113
  Charles WYN 85A
  Charles L. JEF 38
  Cuthbert HRD 40
  Cuthbert NSN 193
  Cuthbert LWS 97A
  Damoni? MAS 59
  Daniel CLK 83
  Danl. CHN 40
  Davis CHN 35A
  Edwd. P. FTE 62
  Elisha CLY 129
  Elisha MAD 142
  Elizabeth NSN 193
  Ezekiel CHN 39
  Ezekiel, Snr. CHN 40
  Federick T. MAD 178
  Fielding TRG 4
  Garret GNP 172A
  Garret G. GNP 172A
  George GTN 132
  Grove NSN 210
  Henery CBL 4A
  Henry WDF 95A
  Isaac MBG 139A
  J. P. JEF 25
  J. W. TOD 128
  Jack LVG 8
  James JES 83
  James BTH 184
  James MNR 205
  James SCT 127A
  Jeremiah OWN 103
  John HND 7
  John JEF 22
  John ADR 62
  John FTE 64
  John HRL 110
  John BBN 120
  John NSN 199
  John KNX 280
  John HND 9A
  John CHN 29A
  John LWS 97A
  John SHE 113A
  Joshua CLD 150
  Joshua SHE 152
  Josiah CHN 44
  Luke MER 99
  Major CBL 13A
  Micajah MTG 295
  Milly LNC 17
  Nancy CWL 38
  Penelope FTE 62
  Peyton LGN 36
  R. TOD 133
  Reuben SHE 162
  Reuben, Jr. BRN 15
  Reuben, Senr. BRN 15
  Reuben CHN 28A
  Rich. ALN 106
  Richard CBL 19A
  Robert BRN 16
  Robert CHN 31
  Robert HAR 200
  Robert WRN 44A
  Robert C. FTE 112
  Robert C. CHN 29A
HARRISON, Robin CHN 42A
  Robt. CHN 39
  Saml. MAS 65
  Saml. FLG 25A
  Samuel MER 99
  Samuel MER 99
  Sarah MAS 60
  Tho. ALN 104
  Thomas MER 116
  Thomas CBL 14A
  Thomas LWS 97A
  Thos. WAS 66A
  Thos. G. WAS 35A
  Tunis CHN 42A
  William LVG 11
  William OWN 103
  William GRT 146
  William NSN 200
  William, Jr. LGN 24
  William, Jr. LGN 25
  William (At Do.) LGN 28
  William CBL 8A
  William SPN 24A
  Wm. ADR 24
  Wm. GSN 138A
  Zachariah CBL 19A
HARRISON?, Andrew ALN 106
  William CHN 28
HARRISS, Alexr. GRN 54
  Benjamin NSN 181
  Charles GRN 61
  James? GRN 63
  John GRN 63
  Thomas GRN 59
  Thomas GRN 75
HARRISSON, Geo. BBN 104
  Robert BBN 140
HARROD, Anne MER 98
  Barnett HRY 266
  Ben. HRY 266
  James BRN 15
  Jno. HRY 266
  Jno. HRY 266
  Richd. FKN 112
HARROLD, Parker CWL 54
HARROW, Daniel MTG 271
  Danl. FLG 64A
  James, Sr. MTG 245
  John MTG 245
  Joseph MTG 285
  Margret FLG 65A
  Robt. FLG 65A
  William MTG 245
HARROW?, Zebulon BKN 23
HARROWBOUGH, Henry JES 79
HARRY, Charles BKN 5
  Danl. BKN 5
  Evan LWS 96A
  Jessee BKN 15
  John NCH 113A
  Saml. CHN 42A
HARRYMAN, Job JEF 41
HARSELL, Anthony FTE 86
HARSHA, William OHO 7A
HARSHAR, James OHO 11A
HARSHFIELD, John BLT 152
  Martin BLT 152
  Martin BLT 170
HARSHY?, Hugh BRN 16
HARSKILL, David A. BRK 261
HARSON?, Mary FTE 106
HART, Aaron HRD 8
  Aaron MNR 209
  Aaron GSN 139A
  Alfred CWL 35
  Amos HRD 90
HART, Amy JEF 34
  Ann HND 13
  Beazley PUL 66A
  Benjamin MTG 271
  Charles, Jr. MER 97
  Charles, Sr. MER 97
  Charles WYN 92A
  Childers WYN 92A
  Danl. T. JEF 34
  David MER 97
  David BTH 208
  David FLG 26A
  Ed GRD 96A
  Elijah FLG 57A
  Ezekiel BLT 154
  Gabriel SPN 11A
  Geo. BRK 261
  Henry BLT 154
  Henry BTH 210
  Henry SPN 11A
  Hezekiah HRD 92
  Hezekiah WYN 93A
  Israel, Senr. PUL 66A
  Jack LNC 33
  James MTG 231
  John BRN 16
  John CWL 31
  John CLK 77
  John HRD 86
  John MER 114
  John MAD 146
  John BTH 172
  John, Sen. ALN 128
  John HND 11A
  John FLG 26A
  John GRD 123A
  Josiah HRD 68
  Josiah CLK 72
  Mary BLT 196
  Miles GSN 139A
  Minor FTE 86
  Molly FTE 110
  Moses GRN 80
  Nancy PND 22A
  Nathaniel WDF 125A
  Nathl. MAS 67
  Nicholas PND 22A
  Olive GNP 172A
  Oliver FTE 65
  Pleasant MER 98
  Reubin MAD 140
  Ricard MAD 140
  Richard G. HND 7
  Robert WYN 92A
  Robt. CWL 31
  Ruchd. FLG 57A
  Samuel MER 114
  Samuel BTH 210
  Silas HRD 92
  Solomon UNN 151
  Susanna FTE 62
  Thomas P. FTE 110
  Thos. HND 13
  William HND 11
  William BNE 20
  Wm. JEF 32
HART?, Jonathan ADR 24
  William BTH 174
HARTER, Caty BBN 134
  John BBN 130
HARTGROVE, James PUL 62A
  Thomas MER 117
  Wm. WAS 31A
HARTGROVE?, Joseph BTL 323
  Samuel, Sen.? BTL 323
HARTIN, Henry C. LWS 93A

Name	County	Page
HARTLEY, Benj.	FLG	49A
David	HRD	14
Jacob	HRD	16
John, Junr.	HRD	74
John	GNP	172A
Jos.	HRD	42
William	NCH	114A
HARTLY, Daniel	SHE	162
HARTMAN, Abraham	SHE	117A
HARTNESS, Sally	SCT	96A
HARTSOCK, Isaac	HAR	180
Peter	BKN	18
HARTT, Geo.	BRK	263
HARTZ?, William	BTH	174
HARVELL?, B. Henery	GSN	138A
HARVEY, Betsy	ADR	26
Calvin	GNP	174A
Danl.	ADR	24
James	ADR	26
James	CLD	137
Jno.	FKN	66
Joel	CHN	41
John	BNE	20
John	ADR	26
John	HRD	58
John	CLD	138
John, Jr.	HOP	246
John, Sr.	HOP	248
John	HND	10A
John	CBL	20A
John S.	HOP	246
Robt.	ADR	24
Wilson	CLD	138
Winston	HOP	246
HARVIE, Austin	BRN	15
Charles	BRN	33
Joseph	BRN	15
Thomas	BRN	15
HARVY, Andrew	CLY	130
Danl.	ADR	26
John	BKN	8
John	ADR	26
Naurace?	MAD	108
HARVY?, Mills	NCH	105
HARWICK, George	GNP	165A
Wm. A.	CHN	43
HARWOOD, Leven	LGN	41
Nathan	CBL	13A
Samuel H.	SHE	127A
Sarah	CBL	21A
Wm. W.?	BRK	259
HAS, Wm.	WAS	64A
HASARD, Martin	GRN	62
William	GRN	67
HASELL, Ignatious	GRN	57
HASELLWOOD, Cliff	GRN	69
HASH?, James	GRN	80
Thomas	GRN	78
HASHALL?, David	BNE	50
HASHFIELD, Henry	BRK	263
HASKELL, Isaack	GTN	135
HASKIN, Joseph	MER	115
HASKINS, Creed	GRN	54
William	LGN	39
HASKINS?, James C.	HRT	159
John	WDF	101A
HASLERIG, Hanah	SHE	133A
Wm.	SHE	137A
HASLIP, Robert	GSN	138A
HASSLER, Daniel	SPN	14A
HASTA?, Leven	PUL	43A
HASTAND, Daniel	MNR	217
Henry	MNR	197
John	MNR	217
HASTINGS, John	LWS	92A
HASTINGS, Joseph	JEF	20
Wm.	FKN	82
HASTY, Clemant	GNP	171A
Elisa	BTH	200
John	BTH	216
Levi	PUL	47A
Robt.	PUL	47A
HASTY?, William	BTH	188
HATCH, Saml.	WAS	55A
HATCHER, Agness	CHN	38
Archibald	OHO	9A
Hellary	WRN	63A
Henry	GRN	64
Hopkins	ADR	26
Jer	ADR	26
John	FLD	27
Richard	HRD	48
Robert	LGN	32
Samuel	MTG	291
HATCHER?, Barnett	BRN	16
HATCHET, Benjamin	NSN	198
HATCHWORTH, William	CSY	218
HATER, Corneliaus	MAS	75
HATFIELD, Ale?	WYN	100A
Charles	GSN	138A
David	GSN	139A
Edward	GSN	138A
Jeremiah	FLD	29
John	CLD	146
John	HAR	178
John	GSN	139A
Joseph	FLD	39
Nathaniel	NSN	213
Reuben	KNX	302
Samuel	FLD	29
Stanley	WTY	126A
Valentine	FLD	39
W.	ADR	26
HATHAWAY, James	CBL	7A
Jno.	MAS	61
John	CBL	7A
Jonathan	MTG	247
Philip	MTG	247
HATHMAN, Benjn.	MAD	110
Jonathan	MAD	108
HATLER, Michael	ALN	100
Philip, Jr.	BRN	16
Wm.	ALN	100
HATTEN, Adam	CLK	86
Henry	WAS	80A
James	BRN	33
John	WAS	80A
Samuel	MAD	164
Thomas	CLK	79
Wiley	WAS	80A
HATTENHOW, John	CBL	16A
HATTER, James	FTE	82
HATTER?, James	ALN	142
Philip	ALN	142
HATTIN, Benjamin	CLK	62
John	CLK	88
Thomas	CLK	94
William	CLK	62
William	CLK	94
HATTON, David	GNP	168A
Ephraim	MTG	291
John	GNP	167A
Nancy	FLD	11
William	MTG	287
HATTON?, James	ALN	142
HATZEL, George	JEF	26
HAUCER?, Danl.	FLG	47A
HAUCHIN, John	MER	99
HAUGE?, John	JEF	62
HAUGHEY, Tho.	MAS	67
HAUKS?, Absalam	CLK	68
HAUL?, Joseph	GNP	171A
HAUN, Adam	SCT	104A
Henry	SCT	104A
John	SCT	104A
HAUN?, John	RCK	84A
HAUSKINS?, William	GRD	117A
HAUSNEY?, Richard	CLK	68
HAUSON, Samuel	CLK	103
HAUSON?, Paul, Jr.	LVG	9
HAVANS, George	BBN	76
HAVE, John	JEF	37
HAVE?, Joseph	GNP	171A
HAVENDER, Joseph	MTG	249
HAVENS, Joel	FLG	42A
John	WYN	106A
John	GNP	173A
William, Jr.	CBL	16A
William, Sr.	CBL	16A
HAVER, David O.	FTE	67
HAVER?, Jacob	BBN	96
HAVINS, Joseph	WYN	106A
HAVINS?, Thos.	FLG	24A
HAW, Edward	WDF	94
HAWES, Isaac	JEF	54
John	JEF	34
Peter	JEF	41
Richard	JEF	42
HAWES?, Jacob	BBN	96
HAWKENS, John	MAD	156
HAWKENSMITH?, John H.	SCT	124A
HAWKER, Nicholas	MAD	114
Nicholas	OHO	4A
Philip	OHO	4A
Samuel	MER	98
Weaver	OHO	4A
HAWKERSMITH, Henry	SCT	120A
Jacob	SCT	130A
Will.	SCT	130A
HAWKERSMITH?, John H.	SCT	124A
HAWKIN?, John	GSN	139A
HAWKINGS, Jas.	HRY	269
Jno.	HRY	269
Richd.	HRY	269
Silas	HRY	269
HAWKINS, ---den?	MAD	144
Abner	SHE	134A
Abraham	MER	99
Andrew	MER	99
Ann	MAD	146
Ann	FKN	154
Ann	HAR	160
Areulus	FKN	124
Augustus F.	WDF	125A
Benjamin	CHN	34
Benjamin	MER	99
Benjamin	OWN	100
Bery	BRK	259
David	HRD	56
Elijah	FKN	132
Elijah	SCT	109A
Elisha	FKN	152
Elisha	FKN	154
Eliz.	ALN	136
Fielden	BRK	261
Francis	MER	99
Francis G.	WDF	110A
Gabriel	BNE	20
Gregery	FLG	68A
Gregory F.	BTH	172
Harden	WDF	99
Harman	OWN	106
Henry	JEF	43
Henry	HRD	56

HAWKINS, Henry	BBN 138	HAWKINS, Wm.	FKN 66	HAYDON, Bland	GTN 123
Isaac	BTH 172	Wm.	WAS 30A	Edward	NSN 176
Isham	BRN 16	Wm. B.	FKN 128	Elijah	BRN 14
James	MAD 114	Wm. R.	FKN 152	Elijah	BBN 80
James	BTH 148	Wood	FKN 62	Enoch	BBN 72
James	HRT 160	HAWKINS?, Daniel	CHN 29	Garnett	HAR 156
James	BTH 170	William	GRD 117A	George	NSN 187
James	WDF 94A	Wm.	CHN 30	Jacob	BBN 80
James	WDF 101A	HAWKS, Fredrick?	GRN 75	James	FKN 100
Jamison	BNE 18	George	GRN 56	James	FKN 100
Jarvis H.	MER 99	George	WDF 102A	James	BRK 261
Jehu	BRN 14	Joseph	GRN 78	James	BRK 263
Jiley	JES 94	HAWLEY, David	HRT 159	James, Jr.	BNE 20
Jno.?	CHN 46	Hezekiah	JEF 64	James, Sen.	BNE 20
John	LNC 23	HAWLIT?, William	BNE 20	Jarvis	BNE 20
John	JEF 50	HAWS, Alexr.	FLG 50A	Jeremiah	BNE 20
John	HRD 56	Azreal	FLD 33	Jessee	JES 73
John	MAD 90	Caty	SHE 116A	Jno.	HAR 160
John	JES 94	Grizzle	FKN 58	John	BRN 33
John	GTN 121	John	FLD 21	John	JES 90
John	GTN 126	John	MBG 136	John	WDF 104
John	HRT 159	John	BTL 323	Jonathan	LWS 95A
John	BTH 170	John	SHE 116A	Lewis	NSN 197
John, Jr.	BNE 18	Richard	FTE 62	Mary	JES 82
John, Sen.	BNE 18	Samuel	BTL 325	Stanislaus	NSN 186
John, Snr.	BTH 172	Stephen	MAD 164	Thomas	JES 89
John	CBL 5A	Thomas	GTN 122	Thos.	FKN 100
John	WDF 101A	HAWTHORN, Dav.	HRY 264	Thos.	WAS 46A
John	WDF 124A	Jas./ Jos.?	HRY 259	William	BNE 20
Joseph	BNE 18	Joseph	HND 10A	William	JES 73
Joseph	FTE 96	Robert	MNR 199	William	NSN 182
Joseph	WDF 98	Robt.	JEF 34	Wm.	FKN 100
Joseph	WDF 105A	HAY, Ad?	RCK 77A	Wm. B.	BNE 20
Joshua	WRN 50A	Alexr.	MAS 72	HAYER?, James	BRK 261
L. J.	CHN 46	George	FTE 61	John C.	BRK 261
Lucy	LGN 37	James	JEF 43	HAYERMON?, Joseph	WRN 63A
Margaret	FTE 97	James S.	LGN 23	HAYES, Aaron	MNR 191
Martin	SCT 128A	John	ETL 47	Allen	MNR 195
Mary	BTH 196	John	CLY 132	Jane	SHE 164
Moses	JES 97	Kenyard	MBG 141A	John B.	CLK 76
Moses	FKN 124	Michal	HND 9A	Robert	GRN 75
Moses	FKN 154	Peter	CHN 43A	Thomas	BBN 142
Moses	BTH 212	Sally	BTL 323	Thomas	NSN 182
Nathan	MER 99	Walter	NSN 187	Thos.	CHN 44
Nathaniel	WDF 100A	William	BTL 325	William	FTE 88
Nicholas	MAD 96	HAY?, Joseph	UNN 148	HAYGAN, Hugh	ALN 98
Perry	GTN 121	HAYCRAFT, James	GSN 138A	HAYGOOD, Hetty	LGN 36
Peterson	BRK 259	Jas.	HRD 30	HAYMAKER, Betsey	JEF 58
Phileman	BNE 20	John	OHO 8A	HAYMAN, Hezekiah	CBL 2A
Rebecca	FKN 128	Saml., Senr.	HRD 66	HAYNE, Simeon	FTE 77
Reuben	MER 99	HAYDEN, ---.? C.	CWL 43	HAYNES, ----iam?	DVS 13A
Robert	TRG 10	Bazzel	WAS 33A	Adam	CWL 54
Roddy?	FKN 128	Benjn.	BBN 144	Charles	OHO 6A
Sally	WDF 96	Elenor	WAS 53A	Charles G.	OHO 10A
Saml.	HRT 160	Elizabeth	MER 97	Christo.	LVG 5
Saml.	NCH 118A	Elizebeth	WAS 71A	Christopher	WRN 53A
Samuel	TRG 13	Jacob	HRD 44	Dudley	BRK 261
Smith	FKN 154	James	WAS 62A	Ephraim	HND 11A
Tho.	ALN 134	Jas.	HRD 72	Frederick	MBG 138A
Tho.	ALN 134	Jas.	HRY 254	Henry	HAR 214
Thomas	BNE 18	Jeremiah	CLK 93	Isaac	MAD 164
Thomas	JES 94	Joseph	WAS 20A	Isaiah	CSY 224
Thomas	JES 94	Joseph	WAS 87A	James	MAD 106
Thomas	GRT 143	Mary	NCH 121A	James, Jr.	ADR 26
Thomas W.	FTE 69	Nathaniel	BBN 134	James, Sen	ADR 26
Thos.	MAD 138	Nathin O.	CHN 42A	John	ADR 26
Walker	FTE 97	Noah	WDF 104A	John	OHO 10A
Walter	BTH 218	Richard	CLK 82	John	WRN 58A
Warner	FTE 65	Samuel, Jr.	CLK 79	John	WYN 82A
William	ETL 41	Samuel, Sr.	CLK 79	John B.	OHO 6A
William	CLD 141	Samuel	OHO 7A	Michael	SCT 98A
William	BTH 170	Wilford	WAS 51A	Peter	OHO 11A
William	WDF 123A	Wm.	HRD 22	Reuben	CSY 228
William W.	WDF 109A	Wm.	WAS 54A	Thos.	JEF 21
Willis	WDF 122A	HAYDON, Abner	HAR 142	William	GRD 96B
Wm.	HRD 56	Benjamin	FKN 100	Wm.	BRK 259

HAYNS, Bethlehem FKN 100
Richd. FKN 72
HAYS, -----? CWL 42
-----? CWL 42
Alexander OWN 103
Alexander CLD 151
Archibald FKN 108
Arthur MAD 152
Betsey FTE 112
Charles ADC 66
Charles, Sr. GRD 105A
Charles PUL 62A
Charles GRD 105A
Claybourn MNR 201
Do---ck WAS 59A
Elias MAD 152
Elizabeth JEF 33
Gabriel WYN 104A
Henry BRN 16
Hercules HRD 54
Hugh, Jr. LNC 81
Hugh, Sr. LNC 81
Isaac WAS 31A
Isaac PUL 60A
Isack WAS 83A
James ADR 24
James MTG 297
James, Junr. WRN 68A
James, Senr. WRN 69A
James WRN 46A
Jas. JEF 51
Jas. FLG 64A
Jemima MNR 205
Jeremiah WRN 67A
John JEF 41
John FLD 43
John FTE 97
John MER 98
John CBL 9A
John WRN 45A
John WRN 45A
John WAS 76A
John NCH 119A
John NCH 119A
John GNP 176A
Joseph UNN 152
Joseph CHN 35A
Joseph CHN 35A
Joshia? WAS 66A
Justice? WAS 66A
Lernon? PUL 37A
Nancy MAD 174
P. MAS 76
Patrick MAS 78
Richd. SCT 117A
Robert MAD 164
Saml. CWL 54
Saml. MAD 166
Samuel LGN 29
Samuel LGN 30
Samuel WRN 45A
Samuel PUL 57A
Samuel WRN 68A
Shadrach WRN 68A
Stark, Sr. WAS 29A
Susan FLG 66A
Tavenor CLY 118
Thomas GRD 84A
Thos., Jr. BRK 263
Thos., Sr. BRK 263
Walter BBN 134
Wiley MAD 152
William LNC 47
William MER 99
William CLY 115
William, Junr. WRN 45A
HAYS, William, Senr. WRN 45A
Wm. HRD 30
Wm. PUL 48A
Wm. WAS 50A
Wm. WAS 65A
Wm. H. WAS 47A
Wm. R. WAS 51A
HAYS?, William MNR 201
HAYSE, Allexander GSN 139A
James JES 83
James HRY 220
James GSN 139A
John GSN 139A
John GSN 139A
Nat ADR 26
Wm. GSN 139A
Wm. GSN 139A
HAYSELWOOD, Joseph CSY 220
HAYSLICK, Elijah MER 115
HAYWOOD, George DVS 15A
James DVS 15A
John HRD 96
Lewis FLD 32
HAYWORTH, John CWL 44
HAYZEN?, Daniel LVG 13
HAZE, Alexander KNX 282
David B. CLK 79
HAZELE/ HAZELL?, John N. GRN 56
Richd. GRN 56
HAZELL, Alfred GRN 72
Caleb HRD 64
Richard GRN 55
Richd., Sr. GRN 65
William GRN 55
HAZELRIGG, John BBN 108
HAZERD, Henry H. WDF 98
HAZLE, Abraham FLD 22
Jesse SCT 111A
John D. BBN 106
HAZLERIG, Eli BTH 150
HAZLERIGG, Alexander FTE 84
Charles CLK 89
Elijah CLK 90
Joshua BTH 174
William CLK 66
HAZLEWOOD, Clifton GRT 144
Jerry SCT 126A
John GRT 145
Luke LNC 5
Randolph LNC 69
Wyatt CLY 124
HAZLIP, Robt. HRT 160
HAZZARD, Elisha JEF 52
Jas. JEF 51
Michael JEF 51
HAZZLEWOOD, Richard WAS 21A
HE--?, Joseph TRG 8A
HE-D?, -----? DVS 10A
HEAD, ----n? DVS 13A
Benj. FKN 82
Benj. FKN 86
Benj. FKN 98
Benja. JEF 35
Benjm. SCT 117A
Bigger BLT 164
Bigger J./ I.? WAS 19A
Chs. B. JEF 58
Edward L. LVG 6
Edward L. WAS 40A
Francis NSN 220
Greenberry BLT 176
Hadley HRY 192
HEAD, Henry R. BLT 176
James WAS 66A
Jesse MER 115
John WAS 18A
John E. BLT 176
John L. MTG 297
Milly FKN 108
Nancy CLD 155
Reith? NSN 177
Thompson MER 99
Thos. WAS 17A
Wm. FKN 86
Wm. E. WAS 77A
Zachr. JEF 59
James HRY 192
HEADDLESON, John FLG 24A
HEADEN, Abraham SHE 112A
Abraham SHE 115A
Elisha SHE 114A
Isaac SHE 116A
Jacob SHE 114A
Jacob SHE 138A
James SHE 113A
Joseph SHE 112A
Oliver SHE 116A
Samuel SHE 109A
Simon SHE 116A
HEADGES, Wm. WAS 47A
HEADINGBERG, James V. FTE 64
Peter FTE 59
HEADINGTON, Abel FTE 70
Nicholas BLT 190
Wm. JEF 20
HEADLEY, James FTE 100
HEADRICK, Geo. FLG 67A
Jacob FLG 66A
Jacob FLG 69A
Jno., Jr. FLG 59A
John FLG 59A
Jos. FLG 56A
Mikael? FLG 67A
Walter HRD 88
HEADS, H. James OHO 7A
HEADSPETH, James GRN 77
Joel SPN 25A
HEADSPITH, Hollan? GRN 73
Lemuel? GRN 73
HEADY, Stilwell SHE 139A
Thomas NSN 206
HEAFNER, Geo. JEF 36
HEANE?, John HRD 34
HEARD, Daniel M. LGN 23
George WRN 30A
William GRD 100A
HEARINGTON, James SPN 6A
Stephen SPN 21A
HEARN, Andrew FKN 74
Athelbert UNN 154
Edward OWN 101
Jacob OWN 103
Samuel GTN 132
Thomas H. OWN 101
HEARNDON, Wm. CHN 45
HEARNDON?, Ned. FKN 546
HEART, John WTY 110A
HEART?, John ALN 128
HEARTHWAY, John DVS 19A
HEARTZ, Richard BTH 172
HEASE?, Charles BBN 104
HEATEN, Jas. FLG 51A
HEATER, George WRN 73A
HEATH, Ephraim SPN 23A
Hartwell JES 69
James LWS 87A
Philip PUL 41A

HEATH, Richard WRN 48A
Wiland LVG 11
William JES 80
Wm. PUL 36A
HEATH?, Jesse HAR 166
Richd., Jnr. HAR 166
Richd., Snr. HAR 166
HEATHERINGTON, Jacob CHN 32A
HEATHERLY, John HRT 159
Nathan HRT 160
HEATHHORNE, Francis SHE 125A
HEATHMAN, Geo., Senr. BBN 112
Joseph MAD 108
HEATON, William WTY 111A
Windford LNC 57
Wm. HRY 240
HEAVENHILL, George GSN 138A
William NSN 182
HEAVEREN, Bery BRK 259
Robt. BRK 259
HEAVINGTON, James SPN 25A
Thomas SPN 17A
HEAVNER, Christopher WRN 39A
John WRN 41A
HECK, George BKN 16
Henry MBG 143
John, Sen. BKN 28
Joseph MBG 135A
HECKLIN, Thomas UNN 146
HEDDEN, Elezar BLT 168
John HRD 30
HEDDINGTON, Zebulon HAR 202
HEDDLESTON, James BBN 126
Wm. HRD 22
HEDDY?, Elizabeth NSN 220
HEDELSON, Will MAS 80
HEDGE, Thos. LVG 2
HEDGEMAN, Fanny FKN 60
HEDGER, Elisabeth HAR 148
Jacob HAR 150
Jonathan HAR 220
Joseph MER 99
Reuben HAR 148
Samuel MER 99
Stephen MTG 267
Thomas MER 99
William WDF 97
Zecheriah HAR 148
HEDGER?, Joseph HAR 156
Rheuben HAR 162
HEDGERS, Lemuel M. FKN 110
HEDGES, Caleb WAS 18A
Jackson HRD 10
James BBN 122
James W. UNN 154
John BBN 124
Joseph BBN 66
Joseph BBN 120
Joseph BLT 166
Joseph WRN 59A
Levi FLG 46A
Peter BBN 124
Robt. FKN 104
Samuel BBN 112
Samuel P. BNE 20
HEDGMAN, Levi MAS 57
HEDINGTON, Layburn FTE 103
HEDRICK, Jacob BBN 74
Jacob BBN 74
Jacob GRD 107A
John CLY 126
HEDRICK, Jos. GRD 117A
Jos.? GRD 109A
Michl. LNC 3
Nicholas FLG 60A
HEEDSPITH, David MNR 211
Giles MNR 211
HEERINGTON, William CSY 218
HEETER?, George ALN 110
HEETH, Elizabeth HND 9A
HEFLER, Elizabeth NSN 193
Jacob NSN 193
HEFLIN, Birdie? HAR 148
Elijah FLG 42A
Gustavus MTG 273
Lewis MTG 277
Reubin MTG 279
Rubin FLG 24A
William MTG 277
Wm. WAS 52A
HEFTON, ----.? CWL 41
HEGDON, Erasmus NSN 177
HEGGEN?, Johnathan HAR 150
HEGWOOD, William HRY 216
HEIATT, Saml. MAS 66
HEIFNER, Coonrod JES 76
David JEF 36
Peter JES 76
HEIFUE?, George ALN 104
HEINDON?, Henery CBL 14A
HEIPUE?, George ALN 104
HEISS, Bledsoes MTG 259
HEISSUE?, George ALN 104
HEITH, Nathan MAS 76
HEITHMAN?, Geo. BBN 106
HEITS, Nathan JEF 57
HELDSON?, Phillip FTE 105
HELER?, Cornelius GTN 121
HELIN, Thomas LNC 2
HELLER?, Robert LVG 12
HELLOMS, Charles CBL 7A
Lewis CBL 20A
HELLOSS?, Joseph BLT 174
HELM, Allexander LNC 61
Benjamin HRD 94
Charles WAS 18A
Chas. HRD 96
Francis CBL 3A
George LNC 9
George HRD 74
George, Sr. LNC 9
Henry P. HRD 60
Jane HRD 94
John BNE 20
John JEF 54
John BRK 261
John, Jr. JEF 54
Joseph LNC 13
Joseph LNC 39
Lydia SHE 127A
Marqius LNC 61
Meridith JEF 54
Moses BTL 323
William HRY 186
HELM?, Henery ADR 26
HELMES, Peter MTG 233
HELMS, Charles WAS 24A
George CLD 157
Henry CLD 156
James CLD 156
Leonard GRN 65
Maberry GRN 65
Rubin GRN 65
Saml. FLG 30A
Wm. GRN 65
HELMS?, -----?, Se DVS 4A
HELMSTUTLER, Peter KNX 296
HELPHINSTINE, J. P. J. (I. P. I.?) FLG 53A
John FLG 52A
P. H. FLG 53A
Peter FLG 53A
HELSTAD, Asahel GNP 169A
HELTERBRANDT?, Joseph LGN 41
HELTON, Arthur KNX 300
Henry KNX 302
James, Sr. KNX 292
James WTY 121A
John HRL 110
Nathaniel BRN 14
Peter, Jr. KNX 300
Peter, Sr. KNX 300
Shadruck HRL 110
Susan, Mrs. WYN 84A
Thomas GRN 80
Will. KNX 292
William NSN 213
HELTSLEY, John MBG 140A
HELUM?, Thomas WDF 98A
HELVE?, Cornelius GTN 121
HELVY, Chas. MAS 65
HEMAN?, Wm.? CWL 36
HEMBERLIN?, John WAS 35A
HEMBREE?, John HOP 250
HEMBRY?, Mashack ALN 112
HEMBY, Thos. HND 11
William HND 11
HEMCOCK, Charles HRY 188
HEMINGWAY, Samuel DVS 17A
HEMPHILL, Robert LVG 10
Robt. CHN 32
HEMTREE, John HOP 250
HENAGE, George FTE 96
HENAGEN, Henery WYN 85A
HENAR?, Robert NCH 115A
HENAS, James WAS 49A
HENCELY, James JEF 61
HENCOCK, ----1? DVS 8A
Bartlet FKN 92
Benj. FKN 98
Benjamin MBG 143A
Jno. FKN 148
John SHE 148
Lewis FKN 148
Thos. FKN 96
Will. SCT 102A
William W. MBG 143A
HENDERLIDER, Michael, Jr. JEF 56
Michael, Sr. JEF 56
HENDERSHOTT, J. SCT 91A
HENDERSON, Abraham MAD 120
Alexr. HRY 253
Alexr. FLG 28A
Alexr. FLG 34A
Andrew LGN 41
Andrew LGN 46
Andrew LWS 98A
Archid. SCT 94A
Archid. SCT 129A
Barnabas GTN 127
Benj. BKN 13
Bennett SPN 4A
Charles MER 117
Charles OHO 3A
Daniel MAD 166
David FTE 63
David FLG 31A
David WAS 51A
Dinah (Free) BBN 84

HENDERSON, Duncan HRY 178
Edward JES 77
Eleven BTH 206
Francis LWS 98A
Geo. FLG 32A
Geo. GNP 171A
Geo. W. GNP 171A
Isaac MAD 132
Isaac CHN 31A
Isaiah LGN 35
J. S. RCK 89
James LGN 46
James CLK 78
James FTE 79
James GTN 121
James SHE 151
James, Jr. BRK 263
James, Sr. BRK 263
James WAS 49A
James GRD 110A
James GRD 115A
James GNP 171A
James W. FTE 105
Jas. MAS 63
Jas. HRY 270
Joel CHN 32
John BNE 18
John CHN 32
John FTE 96
John MER 98
John MER 116
John ALN 118
John MAD 120
John MTG 259
John BRK 263
John GRD 102B
John TRG 8A
John FLG 29A
John NCH 128A
Jones MTG 241
Jones SCT 98A
Jos. FLG 28A
Joseph BRN 16
Joseph GTN 121
Joseph MAD 128
Joseph WRN 64A
Josiah LGN 47
Js.?/ Is.? HRY 176
Kerns G. LGN 37
Mariam ADR 28
Mary CHN 32
Michael LGN 46
Nathl. GRT 143
Nelly RCK 83A
Patty LGN 35
Peter WYN 91A
Polly L. KNX 314
Rachael LGN 35
Richard HAR 132
Robert NCH 121A
Robt. GNP 171A
Rolen WAS 25A
Sally RCK 83A
Saml. BBN 82
Samuel FTE 96
Samuel WRN 71A
Thomas MER 98
Thomas BBN 110
Thomas, Senr. LWS 99A
Thomas LWS 99A
Thos. CWL 38
Thos. HRD 86
Thos. SCT 129A
W. GRD 112A
Widw. CWL 38
Widw. A. CWL 44
HENDERSON, William GRN 68
William SPN 9A
William LWS 93A
Wm. MAD 166
Wm. BRK 263
Wm. CHN 31A
Wm. GRD 84A
Wm. T. HRY 270
HENDERSON?, Alex. RCK 81A
Robt. ADR 24
HENDIX, Coonrod ETL 43
HENDORSON?, Alexander MAD 178
HENDREN, David MAD 164
Elijah WDF 92
Elisha MAD 164
James GTN 121
James MAD 168
John MAD 138
Russel MAD 168
Taylor WDF 92
HENDRICK, Byrd D. WRN 53A
Edwd. SCT 114A
James SPN 6A
James WRN 41A
James WRN 46A
John, Jr. SPN 18A
John, Sr. SPN 18A
John WRN 44A
John WRN 52A
John WRN 71A
Obediah WRN 41A
Robt. WRN 74A
Squire WRN 60A
Thomas WRN 44A
Thomas WRN 60A
William BTL 313
William SPN 18A
William B. BTL 323
HENDRICKS, Abraham, Jr. SPN 24A
Abraham, Sr. SPN 24A
Anthony CLK 93
Benjamin LGN 41
Daniel SPN 22A
Danl. HRD 28
Danl. JEF 53
Frederick JEF 47
Henry SPN 3A
Henry SPN 24A
Jacob SPN 19A
Jacob WRN 34A
James SPN 19A
James SPN 22A
James SPN 25A
James WAS 83A
John SPN 21A
John SPN 24A
John C. SPN 18A
Joseph HAR 202
Joseph SPN 21A
Joseph WDF 100A
Kitty WDF 98A
Mary SPN 19A
Moses LGN 25
Peter SPN 22A
Peter SPN 25A
Robt. CBL 10A
Samuel SPN 24A
Starvis LGN 38
Tobias HRD 14
William R. SPN 21A
Wm. BRN 16
HENDRICKSON, Aaron MER 97
Daniel LWS 99A
John LWS 94A
HENDRICKSON, Leprate (Big) MER 97
Leprate (Little) MER 97
O---? LWS 93A
William LWS 93A
HENDRIX, Abraham BTH 188
Abraham BTH 192
Allen ETL 51
Andrew ETL 37
Calven BRK 261
Enoch FLG 65A
Frederick NCH 127A
George HAR 152
Henry FKN 88
Jacob FKN 106
John ETL 50
John HAR 200
John HAR 218
John SPN 6A
John NCH 120A
Joseph JES 97
Lucey BRK 263
Nancy ETL 43
Peggy RCK 84A
Peter BTH 158
Phillip FLG 55A
Reuben HAR 148
Rhudy? HRY 228
Thomas BTH 188
Wm. FLG 76A
HENDRIXON, Ez. HRL 110
Isaac ADR 3
Isaac ADR 26
Jno. FKN 72
John ADR 24
John ADR 28
Joshua HRL 110
Josiah ADR 24
Micheal ADR 24
Rubin HRL 110
Thos. HRL 110
Wm. HRL 110
HENDRIXSON, James PUL 61A
John CLY 120
Samuel PUL 56A
Thomas PUL 61A
HENDRON, David MAD 158
Eanon MAD 110
John MAD 96
Nimrod MAD 108
Phantley MBG 136A
Wm. MAD 110
HENDS, Benjamin WYN 87A
Levi, Sen. WYN 86A
HENERSON, Henry BKN 22
HENERY, Jack GSN 138A
Sarah MAD 172
HENING, Anna HAR 146
Daniel HAR 206
HENKLEY, Otis JEF 22
HENLEY, John FTE 82
Ozborne FTE 70
HENLY, Henry BNE 20
John BNE 18
Joshua SPN 7A
Peter PUL 57A
HENNING, Saml. JEF 60
HENNING?, William HAR 164
HENNIS?, Benj. FLG 26A
HENNON, Abel WRN 44A
John WRN 44A
HENRICKS, Michl. PND 20A
Philip PND 18A
HENRIX, Abraham SPN 4A
HENRY, Alexander M. HOP 248

HENRY, Belfield GRN 55
Benjamin HAR 142
Benjamin SHE 135A
Chopta-? NSN 214
Danl. CHN 42
Danl., Jr. CHN 45A
David BBN 82
David MER 117
Elizabeth LGN 45
George HAR 196
George NCH 125A
Hugh BBN 70
Isaac ETL 51
Jacob BBN 70
Jacob FTE 75
Jacob WRN 39A
James BBN 78
James HAR 148
James PND 18A
James NCH 124A
James P. FTE 68
Jas. MAS 62
Jas. RCK 77A
Jesse BRN 14
Jno. MAS 59
Jno. MAS 62
Jno. HAR 150
Joel WDF 120A
John FLD 12
John BBN 62
John FTE 64
John BBN 70
John FTE 86
John GTN 130
John HAR 186
John HAR 204
John HOP 248
John SCT 112A
John SHE 137A
Joseph BBN 136
Joseph HRY 212
Joseph HOP 248
Kitty ETL 51
Lewis FLD 15
M. W. CHN 42A
Noah MTG 285
Richard FTE 64
Richard GTN 130
Robert LGN 44
Robt. GRN 72
Robt. GRD 96B
Robt. GRD 103A
Robt. P. CHN 41A
Saml. FLG 23A
Saml. SHE 131A
Samuel MER 117
Samuel D. NCH 112A
Steward SHE 143A
Thomas HAR 150
Thos. CHN 42
Will GRD 96A
William FTE 73
William GTN 123
William HAR 150
William HAR 152
William HOP 248
William WYN 100A
William WYN 103A
William? GRN 78
Wm. CHN 41
Wm. BBN 82
Zachariah WDF 125A
HENSEY, John BBN 122
HENSHAW, Adam S. UNN 153
HENSLEY, Ann FTE 65
Benj. FKN 56
HENSLEY, Clifton BNE 20
Elijah FLD 33
Elijah MTG 243
Fielding MTG 293
George FLD 3
George GNP 167A
James FLD 34
John FLD 39
Joseph, Esqr. MTG 229
Joseph GNP 176A
Lewis WDF 93
Lewis HAR 168
Nicholas WDF 93
Saml. HRT 160
Samuel GTN 131
Samuel GNP 167A
Westley MTG 295
William MTG 249
William HND 9A
Wm. FKN 120
HENSLY, Ben. HRY 256
Wm. FKN 134
HENSLY?, Garnett M. ETL 54
HENSON, Abner HOP 250
Bartlet HOP 250
Bath CWL 54
Benjamin BLT 176
Elisha CSY 228
Francis MAD 176
Geo. MAS 57
George HAR 152
Isaac CLY 129
Isaac KNX 314
Jacob MAS 71
James CWL 38
James CWL 54
James CLY 131
Jesse MAS 53
Jesse CWL 54
Jesse, Jr. CWL 54
Jessee WYN 100A
John CWL 54
John CLY 132
John SPN 19A
John PND 23A
Joseph PUL 67A
Mary SPN 18A
Paul CLY 121
Phil. CWL 54
Robert FTE 91
Saml. PND 23A
Susannah HAR 146
Will. KNX 296
Wm. CWL 54
HENTON, Casper WDF 109A
Thomas WDF 109A
Thos. CSY 208
HENTON?, Jane BBN 134
HENTS?, Martin UNN 148
HENY, Elisha BBN 80
HERALD, Kader? LVG 6
Robert WRN 33A
Turney CLD 159
Widw. CWL 33
HERBERD, Jeremiah WAS 80A
HERBERT, Geo. MAS 76
Jonah CBL 2A
Jonah CBL 4A
Thomas CBL 20A
HERD, Ra---? WAS 44A
Thomas HAR 144
HERDMAN, George LGN 31
HERENDON, Hanton MAD 160
Nathaniel MAD 96
Wm. CHN 40A
HERIFORD, George WYN 92A
HERIN, Alexander HOP 248
Heli HOP 250
James HOP 248
John HOP 250
Matthew HOP 246
Reubin HOP 246
Thomas HOP 248
William, Sr. HOP 246
William Jr. HOP 246
HERINGTON, John SPN 18A
HERL?, Geo. BRK 263
HERMAN, F. TOD 126
HERN, Aron MAD 156
Clement BBN 136
Jarred LWS 91A
Larkin MAD 154
Lucy MAD 172
Mary LWS 93A
Thompson MAD 156
HERNDEN, James SPN 7A
HERNDON, Alva FKN 130
Boswell SCT 118A
Caddis GRN 73
David SCT 124A
Edwd. SCT 134A
Elisha LGN 29
Elisha FKN 116
George LGN 33
George R. LGN 45
James OWN 100
James W. SHE 140A
Jas. CHN 39
Joel SCT 135A
John BRN 15
John TOD 127
John SCT 138A
John SHE 140A
John T. GRT 145
Joseph LGN 47
Joseph SCT 121A
Mason & MTG 295
Polly CBL 8A
Richd. KNX 304
Richd. W. SCT 137A
Robert LGN 33
Thomas NCH 118A
Thos. HRY 267
Thos. SCT 124A
Thos. SCT 125A
Thos. H. HND 4A
William GRN 50
Zachah. SCT 137A
Zachariah FTE 86
HERNENDON, George MAD 138
HEROD, William BKN 14
HERRAL?, Nancy BRK 263
HERRALD, Decon HRY 262
James SHE 161
Jas. HRY 262
Jas., Jr. HRY 262
Wm. HRY 262
HERRALDSON, Ezakiel WRN 29A
HERRAN, Rewben CSY 206
HERREL, Noah GSN 138A
HERRELD, Levi SHE 114A
HERRELL, Enoch FLD 29
Mary SHE 122A
Nathan FLD 30
Robert FLD 46
William FLD 38
HERREN, James SHE 133A
Nelly GRN 70
Susen FTE 89
HERRENDEN, David HRD 68

HERRENDON, Eligah CBL 22A
John CBL 22A
John CBL 22A
HERRIER?, Samuel NSN 205
HERRIK, Thos. BBN 108
HERRIN, Augustin GRD 86A
George GRD 105A
Isaac PUL 39A
Isaac PUL 40A
Jane PUL 48A
Jesse PUL 40A
John BBN 122
John FLG 30A
Thos. BBN 62
William -.? MBG 136
Wm. PUL 48A
HERRIN?, James HRY 188
Joseph LVG 16
Samuel NSN 205
HERRING, Daniel SHE 150
Edmond SCT 136A
Geo. HRY 260
George HAR 168
James SHE 150
John TOD 129
Terrel GRD 87A
William BRN 17
William GRT 147
HERRINGTON, Jno. HAR 152
John NCH 103A
Jonathan SHE 167
Nathaniel WRN 48A
William LVG 11
HERRIS, West LVG 14
HERROD, Bailey BNE 20
E. HRY 266
James BNE 18
James HRD 46
Thomas BNE 18
William BNE 20
HERROLD, Jeremiah LGN 36
HERRONIMUS, Benjamin CLK 83
HERSPERGER, Adam MER 115
HERTTER, Geo. MAS 65
HERVY, James LNC 47
James MNR 203
William LNC 47
HERVY?, Nancy MNR 197
HERZAL, Nancy BRK 263
HESLER, Jacob OWN 103
John H. FLG 78A
L., Miss. MAS 66
Wm. FLG 32A
HESS, Henry FTE 70
Henry SCT 103A
John SCT 120A
HESSE, Jacob WRN 67A
John WRN 67A
HESSEE?, Edward BLT 182
HESSIN, John CBL 14A
HESSONG, Jacob GTN 122
HESTER, Francis BRN 15
John BNE 18
John FLG 77A
Nathin CHN 41
Polly SPN 10A
William SPN 10A
HETER, Frederick ALN 124
John G. WDF 105
HETHEBY?, Leonard MAD 128
HETHELY?, Leonard MAD 128
HETHERLY, James B. MAD 130
HETHERTON, Jeremiah JES 83
HETHLIN, Prudenc MAD 140
HETHRINGTON, James LVG 7
HETTSLEY, Michael MBG 138
HETZLEY?, Elizabeth MBG 140A
HEVER?, James ALN 122
HEWES, John JEF 27
HEWETT, John M. JES 96
Thomas WDF 104A
HEWIT, John BRK 259
HEWIT?, Russell UNN 150
HEWITT, John M. SCT 91A
Josephus SCT 94A
HEWLAND?, John MAD 100
HEWLETT, Alfred HOP 246
Ambrose JES 88
Fanny JES 84
Jane HOP 250
Jno. JEF 54
John JES 88
Lemuel HOP 250
Marvel HOP 250
William SHE 164
HEWLING, Jas. CHN 41A
HEWS, Hugh R. BNE 48
Richard LVG 11
Richard LVG 12
William LVG 11
HEYDON, Elisha SPN 16A
Samuel SPN 15A
William SPN 16A
HIAT, Joseph MAD 170
HIATT, Allen WDF 98
Allen FLG 42A
Ben. RCK 77A
John UNN 154
Thatcher? FLG 42A
Wm. FLG 42A
Wm. P. RCK 75A
HIATT?, Aron UNN 153
HIBBARD, Jed KNX 312
John KNX 280
HIBBITS, William CLD 149
HIBBS, Isaac HRD 26
Isaac HOP 250
John PUL 64A
Jona LVG 4
Jonathan NSN 220
Joseph NSN 220
Nathan HOP 248
William NSN 220
William HOP 246
HIBBS?, Js. HRY 232
HIBES?, Js. HRY 232
HIBLER, Daniel BBN 112
Joseph BBN 84
Joseph BBN 112
Wm. BBN 84
HIBS, Cristiana HRD 62
John HRD 62
HICK'S, Mary WRN 49A
HICK, Wm. BKN 10
HICK?, Jacob BKN 2
HICKASON, Able FLG 51A
Chas. FLG 56A
HICKEN, Wm. HRY 260
HICKENBOTTOM, Andrew WYN 101A
Kenady FLG 36A
HICKERSON, John WAS 86A
Joseph WAS 52A
Wm. WAS 72A
HICKEY, Thomas FTE 66
William FTE 84
William WTY 126A
HICKINBOTTOM, Larkin WRN 51A
HICKLAND, Charles BTH 198
HICKLIN, James HOP 250
James WDF 102A
Mary BBN 60
HICKMAN, Adam MAS 55
Benj. FKN 62
Benjamin HAR 190
D. B. MAS 81
Dd. BBN 146
Elisa FKN 60
Elliott WRN 60A
Esom WRN 71A
George LGN 41
Grills? WRN 71A
Hugh S. HAR 190
James BRN 15
James LNC 43
James SHE 169
James L. CLK 83
Jesse MAS 73
Jessee ALN 126
Jno. MAS 73
Joel CLK 95
John LGN 43
John WRN 66A
John B. CLY 130
John L. BBN 112
John W. FTE 85
Joseph ALN 110
Joseph SHE 172
Lewis FTE 82
Ralph SHE 169
Reuben CSY 208
Richard CLK 93
Richard, Jr. CLK 82
Sarah MAS 55
William LNC 43
William LGN 45
William CLK 101
William SHE 169
William WRN 35A
William WRN 66A
Wm. FKN 80
Wm. BBN 84
Wm. FKN 124
Wm. BBN 146
HICKS, ---om-.? CWL 36
Abraham FTE 78
Allen CLD 156
Allen GRD 109A
Anthony LNC 67
Bailey RCK 79A
Beverly SCT 120A
Beverly A. SCT 123A
George MAD 98
Greenberry MNR 211
Hanah TRG 8A
Hannah, Mrs. WYN 84A
Henry M. TRG 8A
Isaac CWL 38
Jacob WYN 82A
James ADR 38
James CWL 43
James SHE 159
James, Jr. HND 13
James, Sr. HND 8
James WRN 37A
James G. BRN 14
Jesse SHE 159
Jesse BRK 227
John LNC 67
John JES 71
John FTE 105
John CLD 156
John SHE 164
John HND 10A

HICKS, John SCT 107A
John C. HRD 22
John G. FLG 72A
Jos. GRD 107A
Joseph ADR 26
Joseph JES 71
Joshua CLK 106
Moses CBL 9A
Nat GRD 98A
Nathaniel LWS 98A
Rebecca HRD 90
Robert CLY 125
Robert WDF 103A
Samuel FTE 76
Sarah MER 98
Tabitha, Mrs. WYN 90A
Thomas SHE 159
Thos. HRD 64
Thos. MAD 112
Thos. S. SCT 123A
Walker HRD 30
Walter L. MER 98
William HND 6
William JES 71
William FTE 76
William FTE 76
William SHE 164
William WYN 81A
Wm. MAD 118
Wm. FLG 43A
HICKS?, Moses FTE 105
HICKSON, Peyton LVG 4
HICKSON?, James HRD 14
HIDD?, Henry NSN 214
HIDE, Benjamin BRN 16
James L. GNP 173A
Jesse KNX 310
HIEATT, Mrs. MAS 78
Benjn. MAS 52
Benjn., Sr.? MAS 53
Elisha MAS 60
Jno. MAS 53
Stephen MAS 52
HIETT, Shadrach MTG 255
HIFTON?, Saml.? CWL 41
HIGBEE, Elisha JES 82
Jeremiah BBN 116
John FTE 101
Joseph JES 81
Joseph JES 93
Obediah JES 93
Peter JES 82
HIGBY, Vincent LGN 33
HIGDEN, B. Eliazor GSN 139A
Frances GSN 139A
Ignatious GSN 139A
James GSN 138A
Lucy WAS 55A
Peter WAS 78A
HIGDON, Gabriel BRN 13
James NSN 213
James NSN 214
John BRN 13
Joseph BRN 13
Leonard NSN 216
Peter NSN 214
Thomas NSN 216
HIGGASON, Supre? GRN 58
Thomas GRN 56
HIGGERSON, Ezecal SPN 16A
HIGGINBOTHAM,
Jaly? JES 72
HIGGINBOTHEM,
Ralph FTE 63
HIGGINBOTTOM,
Charles CLD 156
HIGGINBOTTOM,
Elizabeth CLD 156
John CLD 154
Robert CLD 154
HIGGINS, A. S. FTE 110
Abraham MER 98
Daniel GRN 69
David GRN 75
Durret CLD 158
George BTH 180
Gideon W. MER 99
J. TOD 132
James UNN 146
James MTG 225
James DVS 19A
James PUL 61A
Jno. MAS 80
Joel CLY 112
John MER 115
John TOD 132
John BTH 180
John KNX 278
John, Jr. MTG 229
John CBL 15A
John PUL 61A
John GNP 176A
John M. GNP 170A
John S. LNC 81
Moses MTG 235
Polly UNN 154
Richard FTE 65
Richd. FLG 25A
Robert MTG 275
Robt. CHN 41
Saml. MAS 71
Thomas FTE 55
Thomas MTG 275
William FTE 90
William FTE 98
William MER 99
William MTG 231
Wm. BBN 138
HIGGINS?, Aaron MTG 275
HIGGINSON, George HND 11
George, Jr. HND 11A
HIGGS, Isaac GSN 138A
Rodham HRY 250
HIGH, Levina MNR 201
Mark MNR 201
Mikael FLG 75A
HIGHBARGER, Joseph MER 99
HIGHBAUGH, George HRT 160
Henry HRT 159
HIGHBORGS, Adam LVG 16
HIGHDIVER, Wm. BBN 114
HIGHFILL, Benjamin MER 99
Jeremiah PND 20A
HIGHLANDER, George NCH 107A
HIGHLEY, Thomas MBG 135A
HIGHSMITH, Jas. HRY 244
HIGHT, Thomas MER 98
HIGHTON, James LNC 79
HIGHTOWER, George CBL 11A
H. TOD 127
Jane WRN 28A
John WRN 28A
John WRN 70A
John B. BRK 263
Joshua JES 93
Rawleigh CBL 11A
HIGINBOTH, Emanuel GRD 90A
HIGINBOTTOM, Peter BTL 323
HIGINBOTTON,
Curtis L. BTL 323
HIGNIGHT, Moses KNX 292
HIGS, Isaac GSN 139A
HIKES, Geo. JEF 40
Geo., Jr. JEF 40
Jacob JEF 40
John JEF 40
HILAND, Dewman? BBN 70
HILBERT, Henry H. MBG 133A
HILBURN, John BRN 17
William BRN 16
HILDRETH, Aquilla BBN 142
James BBN 106
John BBN 106
John NCH 118A
Sarah NCH 118A
HILDRIDGE, Peter CWL 38
HILDRITH, Jessee BBN 86
John BBN 86
Mary BBN 94
Rachael BBN 94
Reese BBN 86
HILE, Andrew SCT 123A
HILER, David GRT 142
HILES, Christian MAS 57
Christian SCT 121A
Jno. MAS 57
John SCT 122A
John S. SCT 115A
Paulser SCT 114A
HILES?, Adam HAR 168
HILIARD, Alex. CWL 39
HILL/HILE?,
Burrill CWL 58
HILL, -----? MNR 205
Abm. BBN 138
Andrew LVG 8
Archibald MAD 100
Atkenson NSN 186
Barber CLD 163
Benjamin CLD 145
Benjamin SHE 120A
Benjn. MAS 55
Brook JEF 19
Charles NSN 220
Clary FTE 82
Clemont BRN 16
Clemont WAS 70A
Daniel BBN 118
Daniel LWS 94A
David LVG 11
Demcy MBG 143A
Edward FLD 19
Edward CLD 166
Edward, Junr. CLD 144
Elijah ALN 120
Eliz. CWL 44
Elzy NCH 124A
Ephraim HRT 160
Ezekial? CBL 10A
Francis MNR 213
Fredrick WAS 85A
Gabriel WYN 83A
Garland CHN 41A
Gebriel ADR 20
George HOP 248
George MBG 139A
George W. MER 99
Green JES 85
Green TOD 124A
Halcut ALN 96
Holley MAD 168
Humphrey, Jr. ETL 51
Humphrey, Sr. ETL 51
Humphry MAS 62
Ira BBN 126
Isaac BRN 14
James BRN 15
James ADR 24

HILL, James CWL 44
James ETL 49
James GRN 65
James GRN 67
James FTE 82
James BTH 148
James HRT 161
James SHE 166
James HRY 194
James HOP 246
James WRN 28A
James WRN 31A
James NCH 113A
James D. BTL 323
Jane SHE 169
Jarret MAD 134
Jesse GRD 102A
Jesse H. MNR 195
Jno. MAS 61
Jno. CHN 41A
Joel, Jr. MAD 100
Joel, Sr. MAD 100
Joel CBL 2A
John HRD 44
John ADR 64
John JES 79
John RCK 89
John ALN 96
John WDF 96
John FTE 108
John MAD 112
John MAD 146
John MAD 164
John HAR 198
John HOP 248
John BTL 325
John GRD 102B
John PND 23A
John PUL 58A
John WAS 72A
John GRD 113A
John NCH 115A
John MBG 133A
John SHE 135A
John B. MER 117
John N. WAS 66A
John P. TOD 126A
Jonathan HRD 96
Jonathan HRY 184
Joseph LVG 16
Joseph NSN 185
Julius MBG 143A
Leonard CLK 67
Madison FLD 37
Margaret GRD 90A
Matthew HAR 186
Morgan H. SCT 93A
Nancy MER 99
Nathan MAS 55
Nathan JES 88
Nelson HRT 160
Otho NCH 106A
Parmela FTE 65
Polly MBG 139A
Rebekah HAR 186
Richard NCH 103A
Richard MBG 143A
Robert GTN 126
Robert HRY 198
Robt. MAS 68
Robt. BBN 118
Robt., Jr. BBN 140
Rubin GRN 65
Sally FTE 87
Sally CLD 145
Samuel LGN 30
HILL, Samuel GRD 100A
Sarah LVG 11
Simon NSN 220
Spencer? FLD 22
Sterling MBG 143A
Sullet GSN 138A
Thomas MBG 139
Thomas BTH 148
Thomas CLD 155
Thomas WRN 60A
Thos. CWL 54
Thos. MAS 77
Thos. WAS 44A
Thos. H. CWL 54
Travers N?. HOP 272
W. Allen GSN 138A
Walter WYN 96A
West WRN 60A
William LNC 39
William LNC 59
William CLK 84
William BLT 160
William BTL 323
William CBL 2A
William DVS 17A
Wm. HRD 52
Wm. MAD 100
Wm. ALN 108
Wm. BBN 128
Wm. HRY 270
Wm., Jr. MAD 102
Wm., Sr. MAD 102
Wm. WAS 48A
Wm. RCK 75A
Zadoch ADR 24
Zekiel PND 23A
HILL?, Adam ETL 40
HILLACOST, Conrad FLG 69A
Isaac FLG 70A
Jacob FLG 70A
Soloman FLG 76A
HILLAGOSS?, John FLG 70A
HILLARD, Henry MTG 239
HILLER, Simon HRD 86
HILLES, Samuel LWS 95A
HILLHOUSE, Jas. LVG 7
HILLHOUSE?, Fanny? LVG 16
Will LVG 16
HILLIAR, Jessee CBL 13A
HILLIARD, Bartlet GRN 52
Saml. HRD 42
HILLICOST, William LWS 90A
HILLIS, Abram FLG 62A
Jas. FLG 24A
John CLD 137
Wm. FLG 24A
HILLIS?, Robert LVG 12
HILLIWAY, Gregory ETL 40
HILLIX?, James FTE 84
HILLMAN, Henry MAS 55
Henry MAS 71
Jas. MAS 55
John ALN 134
HILLOCK, James NCH 111A
HILLORY, Francis HAR 180
HILLY, Geo. HRY 247
HILLYER, James HND 4A
HILTON, Alexr. HRD 60
Benjamin FLD 20
Daniel WAS 85A
Jesse FLD 20
Jesse SPN 24A
John SPN 24A
Joseph SPN 24A
Level? FTE 63
Margrit WDF 101
HILTON, Moore SPN 13A
Rhodrick FLD 20
Thomas GRN 66
William F. BLT 176
HILTON?, Thomas NSN 220
HILY?, William BTH 194
HIMER, Sol B. GRD 122A
HINAR?, Robert NCH 115A
HINCHEE, William SPN 16A
HINCKSTON, Samuel HAR 142
HINCLE, Randle CLY 132
HIND, John R. HAR 200
Ladack?, Junr HRD 12
Saml. HRT 160
William BNE 20
Zadack, Sr. HRD 12
HINDE, John W. CLK 87
HINDMAN, Matthew HRT 161
Nancy BRN 14
William HRY 230
William NCH 120A
Wm. CWL 43
Wm., Sen BRN 16
HINDRICKS, James NSN 192
HINDS, George WYN 85A
James BTH 188
John BTH 188
Joseph, Mrs. WYN 86A
Saml., Jun. WYN 87A
Samuel, Sen. WYN 87A
Stephen MAD 106
HINDSMAN, Robt. FLG 62A
HINES, Hardy MBG 140
Henry WRN 37A
James WRN 30A
John WRN 35A
John LWS 96A
Jonathan JES 88
Joseph MAD 136
Pleasant WRN 32A
Rebecca GRD 85A
Spencer MBG 140A
Tho. GRD 116A
Thomas WRN 30A
William WRN 31A
HINKLE, Abner JEF 31
Charles SHE 153
Charles SHE 154
Enoch NCH 121A
Gasper SHE 154
Jacob JEF 43
Jane NCH 125A
Jno. PUL 43A
John JEF 27
Saml. JEF 53
William CLD 148
Windle JEF 52
HINKLEY, --th? CBL 23A
HINKSTON, John HAR 142
HINSON, James TOD 132A
HINTON, Asher SCT 117A
Benj. FLG 23A
Dempsa LVG 9
Elijah ALN 102
Ezekiel NCH 114A
George ALN 122
George SHE 110A
Hardy WRN 59A
Hezekiah FLG 25A
James HAR 168
Jas. FLG 48A
Jerimiah ALN 108
Jesse LGN 38
Jethro LVG 13
John HRD 16
John FLG 30A

Name	County	Page
HINTON, John B.	SHE	115A
Margret	LGN	40
Margret	LGN	45
Mary	SHE	166
Meshack	WAS	57A
Moore	ALN	100
Nachel	BRK	261
Rachel	GSN	139A
Ruey	FLG	48A
Shederick	WAS	62A
Solomon	SCT	114A
Thos.	BKN	4
Veachel	FLG	25A
Will.	SCT	117A
HINTON?, Jane	BBN	134
HIOR, Robert	GTN	126
HIOTT, M.	SHE	109A
HIRD, Raphial	WAS	53A
HIRL?, Geo.	BRK	263
HISE, George	MER	98
Nancy	LGN	23
HISER, Benjamin	BRN	15
John	BRN	15
Nathaniel	GRN	56
HISLE, William, Jr.?	CLK	62
HISSEL, Thos.	MAD	128
HISSEN?, Elisabeth	HAR	144
HISTEL, Benjamin	MAD	130
HITCH, Clement	BRN	14
John	MER	98
Wiseman	HAR	180
HITCH?, Joseph	PND	19A
HITCHCOCK, Abel	BBN	134
Asel	BBN	134
John	FLD	36
HITCHMAN, Samuel	ETL	40
HITE, Abraham	JEF	36
Henry	CLK	68
Henry	MER	99
Jacob	JEF	21
James	JEF	35
James	JEF	36
Joel	JEF	64
John	LGN	40
John	SHE	154
John	SHE	117A
Joseph	LGN	41
Joseph	JEF	42
Joseph	SHE	116A
Lewis	JEF	42
Peter	UNN	150
Samuel	LGN	40
Thomas	NSN	178
Wm.	JEF	44
Wm.	SHE	132A
HITE?, Samuel	FTE	107
HITEN, Richd.	PUL	41A
HITEN?, Stephen H.	FLG	54A
HITER, Adam	FKN	86
Benjamin	WDF	100
Charles	WDF	100
HITER?, James	JES	82
HITON, James	HAR	162
HITT, Aaron	MAS	56
Chas.	FLG	77A
J. S.	BBN	126
Nathan	WDF	95
Thompson	MAS	56
Will	MAS	56
Wm.	FLG	77A
HITTELL?, Sampson	MAD	132
HITTERS?, Thomas	NSN	220
HIX, Eleanor	CHN	34A
James	HAR	184
Nat	ALN	116
HIX, Samuel	JES	89
Thomas	BTH	218
HIXSLEY?, Amos	OHO	10A
HIXSON, Nathl.	MAS	56
Thos.	MAS	68
HIZER, Jacob	HRT	159
Polly	BBN	146
HIZZEN?, Elizabeth	HAR	144
HO--NG---?, Merrick	ALN	98
HOAGLAND, Mary	GTN	131
Moses T.	GTN	131
Solomon S.	FTE	70
HOAK, Jacob	CBL	3A
HOARD, John	GTN	117
Richd.	GRN	74
Thos.	CHN	41A
HOARED, John	BNE	20
HOASKINS, Aquiler	WAS	37A
James	WAS	68A
Joseph	WAS	52A
Josiah	WAS	80A
Randolph	WAS	70A
Thos.	WAS	80A
Vincent	WAS	38A
HOASTEN?, Anthony	SCT	123A
HOBART, Joseph	CWL	54
HOBBS, ---ah?	DVS	9A
B. H.	FLG	70A
Bazil N.	JEF	35
Eli	NSN	200
Ezekiel	BLT	176
Hinson	SHE	141A
Horatio	SHE	166
Jacob	FTE	89
James	JEF	62
Jared	HRD	26
Jeremiah	MAS	55
Jesse	WAS	86A
John	NSN	216
John	WYN	99A
Joseph	FKN	100
Joshua	NSN	200
Joshua	NSN	208
Joshua	NSN	216
Mary	JEF	35
Nathan	NSN	201
Nicholas	OHO	5A
Samuel	NSN	200
Solomon	OHO	11A
Thomas	HRL	110
Thomas	NSN	201
Thomas, Jnr.	HRL	110
Vachel	NSN	185
Will	MAS	66
Zack	WAS	52A
HOBBY, Wm.	CWL	32
HOBDAY, John	PND	20A
HOBDY?, Thomas	OHO	4A
HOBKINS?, Wm.	JEF	20
HOBNER, F.	JEF	27
HOBS, Joseph	MER	98
Nicholas	HRD	62
HOBSON, Geo. B.	CHN	40
Harry	CHN	44
Henry	CHN	45
John	CHN	41A
Jonathan	WRN	73A
Jos.	CHN	40
Morgan	CHN	40
Saml.	CHN	43
Will	GRN	51
HOCKADAY, Amelia, Mrs.	CLK	102
John	GNP	170A
William	CLK	106
HOCKER, Alfred	LNC	5
George	LNC	9
John	LNC	15
Joseph	LNC	15
Philip L.	LNC	17
Philip S.	LNC	19
R. W.	LNC	13
Saml.	LNC	17
Will	LNC	31
HOCKERSMITH, Conrod	LGN	22
David	JES	79
Isaac	JES	88
Isac	JES	79
Jacob	ETL	50
John	LGN	24
John	MAD	134
Squire	LNC	3
HOCKINGS, -----?	DVS	4A
--thew?	DVS	14A
Nicholas	CLK	90
HOCKINS, ---on?	DVS	14A
HODBERRY?, Wm.	GSN	139A
HODGE, Alexander	FTE	87
Allen	LVG	9
Amos	OHO	6A
Benjamin	HAR	132
Charety	SPN	14A
David	LGN	33
Dosiah?	LVG	16
Drury	CWL	54
Drury	CLY	118
Elizabeth	MTG	289
Federick	HRT	160
George	SPN	13A
Henry, Jr.	LVG	9
Henry, Sr.	LVG	5
James	CLY	115
James	KNX	292
James	WRN	71A
John C. M.	BTL	323
Mashack	CLY	115
Portlock?	CWL	43
Robt.	LVG	3
Samuel	TRG	12A
Shadrick	CLY	115
Soloman	MAS	55
William	LVG	2
William	MTG	289
William	SPN	3A
William	OHO	6A
Wm.	FLG	78A
HODGE?, James	WRN	60A
HODGEN, Payten	HRT	161
HODGERS, Amos	SHE	157
Jesse	SHE	177
HODGES, Aby	TRG	12
Andrew	WRN	66A
Daniel	FTE	92
David	LGN	37
Emarey	CSY	208
Gavin	BBN	102
Jesse	LGN	42
Jesse	MTG	226
Jessey	MAD	146
Jno.	CWL	54
John	BNE	20
John	LGN	34
John	NSN	205
John	NSN	220
Mosses	LNC	21
Robert	TOD	125
Samuel	NSN	212
Welcom	CSY	228
Will	MAS	59
William	LVG	4

HODGES, William BNE 20
William ALN 106
William CSY 212
William SHE 113A
HODGINS, Jacob HRD 82
John HRD 86
HODGS, James LVG 2
HODSON, John B. WDF 110A
HOE, Thomas B. MER 114
HOE?, Moses BRK 263
HOEBACK, Isaac HRD 88
John HRD 28
John HRD 80
Michael HRD 32
HOFF, John FLD 41
HOFF?, Abraham SHE 128A
Luke SHE 127A
Luke SHE 129A
HOFFMAN, Abrm. HRD 32
Barnet CLD 151
George GRT 144
Isaac HRD 70
John HRD 12
John, Jr. BBN 102
John, Senr. BBN 102
Michael BBN 110
William FLD 26
HOGAN, David HRL 110
David GNP 168A
Elendor SHE 127A
Elijah BNE 18
Isaac SHE 128A
James GRN 72
James SPN 4A
James GRD 99A
John LGN 33
John GRD 120A
Lewis/ Luces? GRD 114A
Martin LGN 33
Nancy SCT 97A
Nathan GRN 72
Prosser GRN 71
Samuel GRD 101A
William BNE 18
William LGN 33
William ALN 104
William SPN 4A
Wm. MAD 92
Young CWL 58
Zachariah GRT 143
HOGAN?, William GRT 145
HOGE, Anderson LNC 61
Milburn WAS 20A
HOGEN, Thomas CHN 30
HOGG, Andrew CSY 204
Drewry CSY 204
Elijah OHO 4A
Elisabeth HAR 142
James FLD 3
James OHO 3A
John CSY 204
Reuben BRN 16
Robert HAR 142
Stephen FLD 4
William BRN 16
William MNR 207
HOGGARD, Biass LVG 9
Jno. LVG 9
HOGGINS, Wm. BBN 120
HOGIN, Wm. WAS 85A
HOGLAN, Abraham NSN 208
HOGLAND, Aron HRY 202
Elias HRY 206
Jas. HRY 243
Moses HRY 228
HOGLIN, William WDF 93
HOGLY, Isaac GRN 75
HOGMIRE, Benjn. SCT 119A
Thos. SCT 118A
HOGSHEAD, James JES 87
Jas. FLG 37A
Wm. FKN 154
HOGUE, Aaron MER 99
Burrel SCT 91A
Sampson MER 98
William MER 99
William NCH 124A
HOGUE?, Samuel MER 115
HOHAINER?, George GRD 102B
HOHAMER?, George GRD 102B
HOIBECK?, Volantine HRD 78
HOKE, Adam JEF 40
Geo. JEF 48
Geo. JEF 49
Jacob JEF 47
Jas. JEF 53
Leonard JEF 41
Peter JEF 40
Peter, Jr. JEF 63
Saml. JEF 48
Solomon JEF 41
HOLADAY, Elliot CLK 79
Joseph CLK 79
Stephen CLK 94
HOLAM, Edward M. NSN 176
HOLAND, John GRD 90A
HOLAWAY, John (H. C.) CLK 68
John (H. Crick) CLK 89
Thomas CLK 94
HOLBERT, James WDF 95A
John NSN 197
Noah GTN 135
Stephen LWS 89A
Thomas HRD 54
Thomas NSN 196
HOLBROOKS, John FLD 19
Randal FLD 19
William FLD 19
HOLCOM, Mark WYN 85A
Mary SPN 15A
Nathaniel SPN 5A
HOLCOMB, Charles SPN 22A
Hiram SPN 9A
Preston SPN 22A
HOLCRAFT, Geo. HRY 261
Seley SCT 115A
HOLDEN, Benj. SCT 114A
Calib SCT 138A
James SCT 121A
Jas. SCT 114A
John WRN 50A
John SCT 138A
Richard S. WDF 105
Thomas HRD 8
Will., Jr. SCT 114A
Will., Senr. SCT 137A
HOLDER, Beadley WRN 39A
Benjamin FTE 85
Davis BRN 16
Elijah FTE 83
Fancis MAD 154
Fielding BRN 16
Gary MTG 289
James WYN 79A
John GSN 139A
Ricard C. MAD 178
Shederick HOP 246
Wm. ALN 142
HOLDERBY, James HOP 250
HOLDERMAN, Jacob HRT 160
HOLDERMAN, Jacob CSY 216
HOLDRETH, Joseph BBN 108
Ratchet? BBN 116
HOLDSEN, Jacob HRD 68
HOLE?, John WYN 90A
HOLEBROOK, John FLD 3
Ranal FLD 3
William ETL 40
William OWN 99
HOLEBROOKS, Colby OWN 99
James OWN 100
HOLEMAN, Absalom CWL 33
Andrew SCT 94A
Cornelius WDF 118A
Daniel MAD 148
Henry GTN 121
Jacob CHN 29A
John ETL 42
John GTN 120
John KNX 310
Reuben FKN 144
Reubin FTE 97
Richard MER 99
Thomas MER 99
William ETL 52
William GTN 121
William BTL 325
Wm. FKN 58
HOLESCLAW, James NSN 220
HOLESHOUSER, John NSN 184
HOLESTON, Jas., Jnr. JEF 54
HOLFEETE?, Thos. CHN 46
HOLFUTE?, Thos. CHN 46
HOLIDAY, Benjamin GTN 119
George GNP 168A
Moses GTN 121
Salley GTN 121
Wm. GNP 168A
HOLIMAN, Mary FTE 106
HOLINGSWORTH, James SHE 142A
HOLIWAY, Robt. FKN 114
HOLLADAY, Thomas NCH 116A
William NCH 117A
HOLLAGAN, John MER 99
HOLLAND, -----? CWL 41
Aaron SCT 122A
Abisha CBL 4A
Abraham TRG 8A
Anthony HAR 206
Augustin W. TRG 10
Bazel TRG 6
Benj., Jr. FLG 63A
Benj., Snr. FLG 63A
Charles MNR 209
Drewry C. TRG 6
Edward WDF 94A
Ezekiel WRN 65A
George BRN 33
George ETL 46
Gracey TRG 14A
Henry WAS 58A
James TRG 8
Jno. CWL 54
Jno. CWL 54
John TRG 8
John, Jr. MER 98
John, Sr. MER 98
Jonas M. SHE 121A
Mary FLG 39A
Michael TOD 131
Nancey SCT 133A
Thos. TOD 130A
Whitmel TRG 12

Name	County	Page
HOLLAND, Will.	SCT	108A
William	BTH	158
William	WTY	110A
Zadock	FLG	57A
HOLLAND?, John	ETL	46
HOLLARWAY?, Spencer	JES	95
HOLLAWAY, Jacob	WRN	35A
James	JES	92
James	HRT	160
HOLLENWORTH, Jonathan	CLY	112
William	CLY	112
HOLLER, John F.	NCH	110A
HOLLERDAY, Zach.	ADR	3
HOLLET?, Solomon	CLD	144
HOLLEY, Absalom	SHE	149
Joel	WAS	22A
John	CBL	2A
HOLLIDAY, John	MAD	110
John	BBN	126
HOLLIDY, William	FLD	44
HOLLIN, Major	SPN	19A
HOLLINGBECK, Henry	FTE	89
HOLLINGSHEAD, James	DVS	19A
HOLLINGSWORTH, J.	TOD	130
Joseph	SHE	148
HOLLINGWORTH, Robert	SHE	160
HOLLINSWORTH, Beasley	PUL	49A
J. G.	TOD	130
HOLLIS, Benj. O.	BKN	20
Fielden	JEF	38
James W.	SHE	112A
John	SHE	175
John P.	GTN	131
John W.	JEF	38
Lewis	JEF	55
Ruth	JEF	32
Ruth	JEF	38
Thos.	JEF	32
Vencen &?	JEF	47
Vincent	JEF	46
Wm.	BKN	10
Wm.	JEF	32
Wm.	JEF	32
HOLLIWAY, John, Sr.	ETL	40
HOLLMAN, Danl.	HRD	30
HOLLOCK, Benjamin	BBN	148
HOLLOMAN, John	UNN	149
HOLLON, John B.	GRN	73
HOLLONWORTH, Isaac	CLY	130
John	CLY	111
HOLLOWAY, Charles	JEF	34
Dave?	ALN	108
David	HND	13
Geo.	BBN	116
George	WDF	110A
James	UNN	146
Joel	LGN	45
John	HND	10
Judith	SHE	126A
Laban	ALN	108
Robert	MNR	193
S. W.	MAS	69
Sally	ADR	66
Saml. W.?	MAS	58
Samuel	BRN	15
Thomas	MNR	207
William	HND	12
William	LGN	45
Wm. B.	SHE	137A
HOLLOWELL, Whitby	TRG	12
HOLLOWMAN, James	ALN	106
William	HOP	248
HOLLSCLAW?, James	BLT	152
HOLLY, Henry	BTH	212
Horace	FTE	65
Samuel	SHE	171
Thompson	BBN	128
HOLMAN, Daniel	MTG	253
Henry	BRN	15
Jacob	HOP	246
James	HOP	246
James C.	LVG	8
John	BRN	15
John	CWL	33
John	CWL	33
Philip	HOP	246
Sally	WRN	55A
Thos.	CWL	37
Wm.	HRY	259
HOLMARK, -----? Castleman	DVS	4A
Castleman	HND	8A
HOLMES, Alexander	PUL	65A
Ann	HRD	12
Charles	LVG	16
Daniel	NCH	127A
Elias	WRN	31A
Elizabeth	NSN	195
Isaac	GRD	99A
Jacob	MNR	207
James	BLT	174
James, Sr.	SHE	173
James L.	SHE	173
Jane	JEF	26
Jesse	SHE	173
John	LVG	16
John	MER	98
John	HAR	204
John	MTG	291
Robt.	SCT	133A
Thomas	HAR	178
W. H.	GRD	83A
William	ETL	46
HOLMES?, Moses	JEF	43
HOLMS, Andrew	SHE	110A
Bryan	MBG	139
David	FLG	73A
Gabriel	HND	4A
Jacob	GRD	96A
John	MAD	96
John	MAD	96
John	MAD	110
John	SHE	142A
John C.	MAD	96
Joseph	MAD	108
Nicholas	BRK	259
Samuel	LNC	3
Sarah	BBN	84
Thos.	MAD	168
Wm.	SHE	139A
HOLSAPPLE, Caty	CLD	150
HOLSCLAW, Abner	GRD	95A
Elijah	GRD	112A
Elizabeth	PUL	62A
Jacob	BNE	18
Jacob	GRD	117A
Jesse	GRD	117A
HOLSEY, Edward	NSN	188
Thomas	ETL	40
William	CLK	94
HOLSTEIN, John	HRD	20
Thos.	HRD	22
HOLSTON, Robert	WAS	47A
HOLT, -----	CLD	159
Benja.	JEF	49
Berryman	ADR	62
Dauswell	CLD	163
HOLT, David	HAR	158
Francis	WYN	95A
Henery	GSN	139A
Henry	FLD	42
Henry	SHE	122A
Isaac	JEF	49
Isaac E.	JEF	43
Jas. T.	HRD	62
Jno.	PUL	41A
John	FLD	42
Joseph	HAR	158
Kannon	SHE	122A
Lucy	GRD	88A
Nathan	FLD	41
Patsy C.	LVG	16
Polly	MER	99
Rachul	JEF	49
Richard	LNC	61
Samuel	LGN	32
Thomas	HAR	156
Thomas	HRT	160
Thomas	WYN	95A
Wm.	ADR	64
HOLT?, Elisha	MAD	116
John W.	BRK	261
Ziba?	GTN	130
HOLTER, Alexr.	JEF	32
HOLTON, Abner	BKN	5
Elijah	HAR	190
Jno.	FKN	82
S., Mrs.	MAS	70
HOLTON?, Jesse	MAS	53
Will, Sr.	MAS	53
HOLTSCLAW, Benjamin	NSN	207
HOLTZCLAW, Benj.	LNC	67
Henry	BRN	15
Henry, Jr.	BRN	15
James	BRN	15
HOLVY?, Peter	LWS	94A
HOLWORTH, John	HRY	204
HOLYFIELD, William	HND	6A
HOLZCLAW, Jesse	BBN	104
HOMAN, Mark	BLT	188
Matthew	BLT	188
HOMBS, Nathon	WAS	60A
HOMER, Will.	SCT	127A
HOMES, Edmund	GRD	87A
Hugh	ADR	24
William	WYN	94A
HOMESLEY, Benjamin	CLD	166
HON?, Daniel	NCH	125A
Jonas	NCH	121A
Peter	NCH	120A
HONAKER, Isaac	BTL	325
James	FLD	28
John	WRN	39A
HONCH, William	CLY	122
HONIKER, John	FTE	98
HONNIKER, John	FTE	98
HONOR, Francis	JEF	28
HONORE?, John A.	JEF	22
HONSLEY?, Tho.	HRY	204
HOOBERRY?, Wm.	GSN	139A
HOOD, Andrew	ETL	37
Andrew	GNP	177A
Edward	BTL	323
George	GRN	58
Heath Horn?	WTY	112A
Jas.	FLG	26A
Jesse	ADR	24
John	BTL	323
John	FLG	37A
John	RCK	78A
Luke	CLK	82
Saml.	FLG	33A

HOOD, Sarah GNP 177A
Thomas BRN 16
Wm. FLG 26A
HOODROOK?, Robert PUL 55A
HOOF, Jacob CSY 218
Jonathan CSY 222
HOOGE?, James WRN 60A
HOOK, Belitha NCH 125A
Geo. FLG 36A
John BKN 16
Mc Kinney NCH 112A
Thomas NCH 122A
HOOKER, George R. KNX 284
Jno. FKN 102
Robert HOP 250
HOON?, Robt. BBN 146
HOOPER, Joseph CLD 159
Samuel UNN 150
Samuel CBL 21A
Samuel H. SHE 165
Terry BTL 325
William FTE 88
William GTN 128
HOOPWOOD, Moses SHE 165
HOORE?, Robt. BBN 146
HOOSER, David TOD 128A
Wm. TOD 128A
HOOTEN, Frederick CLY 124
James ETL 39
Manuel ALN 118
Nicholas CLK 77
Sarah CLY 127
William CLK 84
HOOTON, James ALN 118
John MAD 142
Joseph ALN 118
Thomas MTG 235
Thos. MAD 92
HOOTS, Henry CLD 159
HOOVER, Andrew JES 94
David JES 76
George OHO 5A
Henry WDF 124A
Jacob GRN 61
Jacob FTE 76
Jacob JES 76
Jacob CLY 119
Jacob OHO 5A
Joseph BNE 18
Lawrence OWN 99
Leonard OHO 5A
Marion? JES 93
Mason? JES 93
Math--? FTE 105
Paulter HRD 58
Peter JES 85
Peter LWS 95A
HOOY, Lewis HRY 264
Wm. HRY 244
HOPE, Ezra SHE 169
George CLK 89
James MBG 137
Michael MER 98
Richard MER 98
William SHE 172
William BTH 186
William WDF 104A
HOPE?, James HRL 110
James HRL 110
HOPEWELL, (No Other Given) BLT 166
John NSN 185
Samauel LGN 25
Samuel BLT 166
William BLT 176
Wilmoth BLT 168
HOPGOOD, Daniel UNN 146
John UNN 146
HOPKINS, Benjamin FTE 77
Cynthia NSN 209
David FLG 44A
David FLG 63A
Dennis CLD 145
Dennis, Jr.? WYN 103A
Dennis, Sr. WYN 103A
Dennis WYN 87A
Edmund HND 11
Elijah CLD 145
Elizabeth HND 8
Elizah. FLG 75A
Ephraim LGN 37
Ezekiel BBN 86
Frances, Jr. BTH 192
Francis BTH 160
Garner FLD 8
George W. NCH 123A
Henry BTH 188
Isaac FLG 63A
Jacob B. HND 4A
James W. BNE 20
Jenithan? CBL 18A
John SCT 107A
John NCH 124A
Jos. FLG 63A
Joseph A. NCH 112A
Joshua WYN 103A
Josiah NCH 108A
Joslin NCH 115A
Luther CBL 5A
Peter BTH 192
Richd. SCT 111A
Robert NCH 113A
Saml. HND 7
Saml. G. HND 12
Samuel CLD 149
Samuel CLD 149
Samuel CBL 17A
Selby BBN 90
Tho. MAS 77
Thos. CHN 40
Thos. SCT 111A
W. ADR 26
William NSN 209
William MTG 297
William CBL 2A
William NCH 108A
William NCH 115A
HOPPEER, Thomas ETL 49
HOPPEN, Jas. FLG 46A
HOPPER, Achillis SPN 23A
Anderson CHN 43A
Blackgrove KNX 296
Darby MNR 197
Darby SPN 6A
David MAD 162
David WRN 66A
Elijah BBN 124
Elijah FLG 35A
Harris KNX 290
Jacob KNX 292
Jane MAS 66
John LNC 21
John CWL 37
John MAD 128
John MAD 158
John CBL 11A
John CHN 40A
Jos., Jr. GRD 82A
Joseph ADR 60
Joseph BTH 152
Joshua ADR 28
Levi FLG 46A
HOPPER, Lucy FKN 94
Mc Micken FLG 34A
Nancy MER 98
Nancy SPN 19A
Raleigh KNX 280
Robt. HRT 159
Samuel ETL 41
Will. KNX 304
Wm. ADR 28
Wm. TOD 128
Wm. FLG 46A
HOPSON, Henry, Senr. CHN 29A
Henry CHN 36A
Nevil CHN 35
Tho. ALN 124
William TRG 13A
William TRG 13A
Wm. CHN 33
Zecheriah ALN 126
HOPTON, Stephan BTL 323
HOPWOOD, C. A. GRD 98A
James MTG 255
HOR?, Moses BRK 263
HORD, Aaron HRL 110
Andrew HRL 110
Benjamin CHN 35
Edwd. MAS 74
Edwin MAS 74
Francis P. JES 96
John HRL 110
Rhoden MAS 74
Samuel HRL 110
Tho. MAS 69
Willis JEF 62
Willis GNP 172A
HORD?, Elias MAS 59
HORDE, Ezekiel CHN 33
HORIN?, William MTG 267
HORINE, George BLT 152
Henry JES 85
Jacob JES 84
Jacob BLT 164
Nancy MER 99
Saml. NSN 175
HORN, Aaaron ETL 41
Aaron ETL 53
Chapman KNX 296
Chirs., Jnr KNX 284
Christopher, Sr. KNX 282
David GSN 138A
Elijah ETL 44
Jacob MER 97
John MER 97
Joseph MTG 269
Joseph, Sr. MTG 291
Mathew ETL 42
Michael MER 97
Nathan SPN 13A
Patrick MER 98
Phillip MER 97
Pricilla HRD 68
Reddick LGN 46
Thomas HRL 110
William, Jr. ETL 54
William, Sr. ETL 53
HORN?, Thomas BTH 186
HORNADA, Major BRN 34
HORNBACK, Abraham BTH 210
Adam FLG 47A
Adam NCH 116A
Buckner GSN 139A
Daniel HRD 84
Daniel GSN 138A
Isaac HRD 18
Jacob HRD 48

Name	County	Page
HORNBACK, Jacob	HRD	48
Jacob	BTH	158
James	CLK	101
John	BTH	194
Levi	CLK	101
Mary	BBN	124
Michael	BBN	88
Nancy	BBN	126
Soloman	CLK	88
HORNBECK, Abraham	BLT	166
John	BLT	154
Samuel	BLT	162
Solomon	BLT	176
Solomon	BLT	176
William	BLT	160
HORNBOY?, Mashack	ALN	112
HORNBRUCKE?, Washington	GRN	72
HORNBUCKLE, -.?	MAS	75
Alfred	FLG	34A
Geo.	MAS	60
Wm.	FLG	41A
HORNE, J. Elias?	BBN	106
HORNELL?, John	HRD	84
HORNER, Saml.	JEF	59
Samuel	BLT	172
Samuel	NSN	220
HORNIN-TON?, Nathaniel	ALN	104
HORNSBARGER, Ephraim	TRG	13
HORNSBY, Jos.	SHE	139A
Thos.	CLY	127
Thos.	SHE	139A
HORR?, (See Hon?)	NCH	125A
HORREL?, James	PUL	67A
Mary	NSN	183
HORRIL, Clever C.	ADR	3
HORRILL, Cornelius	SHE	123A
HORSELY, Burrel	BRK	259
Christopher	BRK	261
Henderson	BRK	261
James	JEF	65
Levi	BRK	259
Mary	BRK	261
HORSEMAN, Isaiah	SCT	96A
Joseph	BTH	176
Zecheriah	OHO	6A
HORSLEY, Andrew	BNE	18
Elijah	BNE	20
James	GNP	170A
Nicholas C.	HND	4A
Taylor	GNP	174A
Wm., Jr.	GNP	172A
Wm.	GNP	172A
HORTEN, Samuel	GSN	138A
HORTON, Anthony	WRN	70A
Augustus	GRN	69
Betsey	GRD	118A
Betsy	LNC	19
Daniel	WRN	70A
Edward W.	BBN	78
Hugh	MAD	136
Isaiah	MBG	140
James	WRN	70A
Joseph	BNE	18
Justice	CBL	5A
Leonard	GRD	110A
Reubin	WRN	70A
Will	BBN	64
HOSE?, Bryan	ALN	98
HOSEA, Thomas	CLD	144
HOSECK?, Alex.	LVG	10
HOSEE, Jas.	LVG	7
HOSHALL?, David	BNE	50
HOSKINS/ HORKINS?,	HRY	188
HOSKINS, Aquilla	BLT	158
Daniel	MAD	132
George	HRL	110
Harrison	MAD	132
Hugh	BLT	194
Hugh	BRK	259
Isaac	LVG	16
John	HRL	110
John	CLY	119
John	MAD	144
Jos.	SHE	141A
Josias	BLT	152
Levy	HRL	110
Robt.	BRK	263
Rubin	HRL	110
Saml.	LVG	16
Samuel	LGN	27
Thomas	HRL	110
Thomas	HRL	110
William	JES	79
Woodrough	HND	4A
HOSKINS?, James C.	HRT	159
HOSKINSON, David	HRD	34
HOSLEY, Mathew	FLG	46A
HOSMAN, William	UNN	154
HOSTETLER, Adam	SHE	116A
HOSTETTER, Abraham	SHE	138A
Tomas	SHE	115A
HOTTET?, Solomon	CLD	144
HOTTON, Catharine	FKN	90
Enoch	MAS	53
James	FKN	90
Jno.	MAS	64
Will	MAS	52
HOTTON?, Jessee	MAS	53
Will, Senr.	MAS	53
HOTZCLAW, Archibald	FTE	90
HOU?, Jonas	NCH	121A
Peter	NCH	120A
HOUCHEN?, John	GSN	139A
HOUCHENS, Robt.	ALN	128
HOUCHER?, Charles, Junr.	WRN	48A
HOUCHIER, John	WRN	49A
HOUCHIN, -----?	DVS	12A
Francis	WRN	48A
John, Junr.	WRN	49A
HOUCK, Aquilla	BKN	23
HOUGH, Charles	OHO	4A
Goldsbury	OHO	6A
John	MER	97
John	OHO	6A
Jos.	HRD	44
Moses	BLT	188
Moses C.?	BLT	172
Peter	MER	98
Richard, Esqr.	MER	97
Richard	OHO	6A
Samuel	MER	97
Thomas	MER	97
William	MER	97
William, Capt.	MER	97
Wm	HRD	44
Wm.	OHO	9A
Wm.	OHO	10A
HOUGH?, Thomas	PND	28A
HOUGHLAND, James	MBG	135
HOUGHMAN, John	JEF	46
HOUGHTON, Aaron	MAS	61
Charles	LWS	96A
John	FTE	77
Livingston	FLD	3
Reuben	FTE	77
HOUGLAND, Abraham	MBG	135
William	UNN	154
HOUK, Felix	WYN	86A
Fred	RCK	84A
John	BRN	13
Michael	BRN	14
Michael	BRN	17
N.	RCK	78A
HOULMAN, James	CBL	5A
Squire	CBL	5A
William	CBL	16A
HOUNSHELL, A.	PND	18A
HOUSE, Andrew	BBN	64
Charles	CLY	115
George	BBN	70
James	PUL	66A
John	BNE	20
John	ETL	41
John	BBN	64
John	CLY	126
John	GRD	88A
Joseph	BTH	204
Margaret	CBL	5A
Mathias	GRD	88A
Robt.	BTL	323
Simeon	JEF	34
Thomas	CLK	75
William	CLY	115
William	BTH	182
William	BTL	323
Willie	LGN	40
HOUSELY, Leathy?	NSN	175
Robert	NSN	178
HOUSELY?, Sarah	NSN	191
HOUSEMAN, Stephen	MBG	142A
HOUSEN?, Wm.	ALN	102
HOUSEWORTH, Abram	SHE	148
HOUSLEY, Albern? S.	WAS	38A
Thom.	CWL	54
Wm.	WAS	37A
HOUSLEY?, Isaac	FLD	13
HOUSTEN, Stephen	SCT	113A
HOUSTIN, George J./ I.?	BKN	6
HOUSTON, A. G.	FLG	78A
Bob, (Free Man)	BBN	80
Chas. C.	SCT	123A
George	PND	19A
James	BBN	114
James	HAR	162
Joseph	BKN	11
Joseph	JEF	20
Levi	BKN	10
Levi	BBN	116
Peter	BBN	64
Saml.	BBN	78
Wm. J.	JEF	34
HOUSTON?, Anthony	SCT	123A
HOUTEN, Joab	FLG	37A
HOUTS, Jacob	LVG	2
Thos.	WAS	77A
HOUVERIN?, Thos.	BKN	22
HOVEL?, James	PUL	67A
HOVERMILL, Fredrick	BTH	200
HOVIS, John	GRN	75
HOW, Abra	MAS	67
Christopher	BBN	102
David	BNE	20
Edward	FTE	65
Edward	FKN	100
James	BNE	18
James	FKN	94
James	BRK	263
Jno.	FKN	92
John N.	GNP	170A
John W.	GNP	169A

HOW, Samuel BTH 176
William F. HND 9
HOWARD, -----?, Sr. DVS 5A
-----? DVS 5A
Abraham TRG 8
Allen WRN 69A
Andrew NSN 208
Arcd. JEF 62
Bazzel SCT 97A
Benjamin HRL 110
Benjamin MAD 164
Benjamin WRN 49A
Broody CWL 33
Charles WDF 105
Charles WAS 57A
Chitester? JES 95
Christopher BRN 15
Christophere BRK 259
Cornelias HND 12
David LGN 42
David G. LVG 4
Eli FLG 45A
Elisha BBN 126
Elizabeth ALN 106
Elizabeth NSN 197
Fleet JES 95
Frederick BTH 160
Geo. JEF 63
George FLD 22
George BLT 158
George MTG 297
George GSN 138A
Gideon FLG 59A
Gideon NCH 106A
Greenberry BBN 76
Grover CWL 33
Harman? MNR 195
Henry MAS 56
Henry WRN 46A
Henry FLG 58A
Henry WAS 61A
Henry H. MAD 92
Ignatious MAD 110
Isaac WDF 99
Isham GRD 84A
James FLD 5
James FLD 5
James MAD 104
James CLD 148
James MTG 261
James BTL 313
James BTL 323
James WAS 44A
James M. GRN 73
James S. BBN 60
Jas. HRD 48
Jesse MNR 195
Jno. B. CWL 54
John FLD 5
John BRN 15
John JEF 40
John BBN 68
John ALN 94
John HRD 94
John WDF 100
John ALN 104
John HRL 110
John MNR 195
John MTG 287
John BTL 323
John WRN 60A
John B. MTG 231
John J. BTH 176
Joseph BKN 9
Joseph JEF 44
HOWARD, Joseph MTG 231
Joshua NCH 108A
Leroy WDF 96A
Mary BTH 188
Mathew NCH 113A
Mordica JES 81
Moses FLD 1A
Nancy NSN 199
Nathan BBN 128
Nathan MNR 197
Obediah MNR 207
Owen CWL 33
Perris BBN 128
Philip CLK 75
Portman? WYN 100A
Richard HRD 34
Richd. WAS 55A
Robert S. MNR 215
Robt. MAS 60
Ruth FLG 58A
Saml. NCH 117A
Samuel LWS 89A
Sarah JES 95
Sarah FTE 96
Steven CWL 54
Thomas TRG 4
Thomas LNC 39
Thomas NSN 208
Thomas MTG 265
Thomas FLD 1A
Thomas NCH 103A
Thompson JES 96
Thos. C. MAD 180
Unis FLG 43A
Vincent WDF 100
William FLD 5
William BNE 18
William CLK 62
William SHE 166
William MNR 217
William SPN 4A
William WAS 17A
Wm. CWL 35
Wm. BRK 261
Wm. SHE 133A
HOWARD?, -----? DVS 5A
HOWCHEN, Benjn. HRT 160
Charles HRT 160
John D. HRT 160
HOWCHIN, Jessee JES 71
HOWDESHELL, Nancy SPN 24A
HOWDESHELT, Elizabeth BRN 14
HOWE, Abraham HRD 44
Ann NCH 113A
David, Senr. FLG 51A
David FLG 74A
David D. FLG 74A
Electius FLD 36
Isaac P. MTG 245
Jacob CLK 102
James GRN 71
James GRT 146
James GNP 175A
John HRD 28
Jos. FLG 51A
Joseph CBL 16A
Joseph GNP 170A
Joseph P. MTG 259
Robt. FLG 51A
Rudolph LGN 42
Saml. FLG 51A
Saml. FLG 74A
Saml. NCH 123A
Thos. FLG 52A
Washington FLG 74A
HOWE, William FTE 78
HOWEL, David SHE 126A
Henry HOP 250
James BRN 15
James HOP 246
James PUL 42A
John BRN 14
John SHE 133A
Leonard BBN 114
Raleigh ALN 140
Stephen SHE 149
Vincent HOP 248
HOWELL, Absher? HRD 14
Amas? HRD 14
Berry ETL 49
Butler BBN 102
C. D. FTE 63
Charles GRN 66
Charles NSN 182
Chas. HRD 78
Clayborn HRD 38
Daniel S. NSN 176
Danl. BKN 14
David MTG 279
Easter SPN 10A
Fanny GRN 71
Hardy TRG 7A
Isaac MTG 279
Jacob HRD 78
James WRN 71A
Jas. H. HRD 80
John LGN 43
John JES 72
John HRD 78
John OHO 10A
John DVS 16A
John CHN 29A
Laban HRD 38
Nancy ETL 44
Nat HRD 78
Phillison ETL 53
Richd. JEF 64
Samuel NSN 200
Samuel NSN 213
Stephen FLD 32
Thomas FLD 32
Thomas WRN 60A
William JES 77
William HAR 218
William WRN 33A
HOWER?, Jonathan NCH 120A
HOWERAN, Jno. MAS 62
HOWERTON, Anderson SHE 127A
James FLD 12
James SHE 127A
John FLD 12
Nathan FLD 9
William FLD 12
Wm. SHE 127A
HOWES, Richard NCH 123A
HOWES?, Jonathan NCH 120A
HOWESTON, Francis SPN 10A
HOWETH?, Elizabeth WRN 75A
HOWEY, Jas. HRD 46
HOWINGTON, John GSN 139A
Joseph GSN 139A
HOWITZ?, John M. BKN 6
HOWK, John, Jr. ETL 52
John, Sr. ETL 52
HOWKINS, Thomas HAR 132
HOWLAND, Isaac W. MER 117
HOWLE, James WRN 28A
HOWLET, George BNE 18
John BNE 18
HOWLETT, John BLT 156
HOWLEY, Dennis FKN 102

HOWLIT?, William BNE 20
HOWS, Reuben BBN 72
HOWSER, Abraham JES 90
Henry JES 89
John JES 75
Nicholas MNR 199
Nicholas MNR 215
Thomas MNR 209
Warner MNR 199
HOWSLEY, Marmaduke OHO 9A
HOWSON, Ann MAS 73
HOWTON, Abraham HOP 248
David HOP 248
Jonathan HOP 248
Louis HOP 248
HOWTTOWER, Merrimon BNE 20
HOY, John SPN 4A
Jones ETL 49
Thomas SPN 4A
HOY?, Joseph UNN 148
HOYT, Jonathan LWS 89A
Marget GTN 132
Samuel LGN 22
HU-ILL, David FTE 82
HUBANKS, John FLG 39A
Larrance? FLG 27A
Wm., Jr. FLG 24A
Wm., Sr. FLG 24A
HUBARD, Carter GRN 67
HUBART, John GRD 109A
Jos. GRD 109A
William GRD 109A
HUBBAND?, Nathaniel MAD 102
HUBBARD, Albert E. BLT 188
Austin S. NSN 177
B. JEF 22
Behcfeler? NSN 188
Benj. CLY 129
Diner GRN 52
Eli WYN 95A
J. H. JEF 20
James MAS 56
James CLY 128
James CBL 21A
Joel BRK 263
John BRN 14
John BRN 16
John LWS 90A
John GRD 93A
Matthew CLY 128
Moses CLY 117
Moses GRD 93A
Theadric NSN 216
Thomas ETL 41
Thomas NSN 188
Thos. CLY 128
William CLY 132
HUBBART, Daniel MAD 148
HUBBELL, Wm. PUL 43A
HUBBERT, ---nah? MAD 124
Elinor FKN 54
George MAD 124
HUBBLE, Erastus BNE 20
Levi PUL 38A
Levi PUL 40A
Will SCT 121A
HUBBOARD, Catharine HOP 248
Liner HOP 248
Nathaniel HOP 248
HUBBS, Jacob BLT 180
Jonathan HRD 90
Stephen KNX 302
Will. KNX 302
HUBERRT, Duret? MAD 128
HUBERT, John MAD 128
HUCBEY, John BRK 259
HUCHESON, Philip GRD 108A
Randolph GRD 95A
HUCHISON, Chas. GRD 92A
John GRD 106A
HUCKABY, Joseph BRN 16
Nathan BRN 16
Thomas BRN 16
Wm. BRN 16
HUCKEBY, Joshua LNC 49
HUCKINGS, Tho. RCK 80A
HUDDLESTON, John FTE 94
John M. HAR 206
William HAR 216
HUDELDON, Hance NCH 120A
HUDELSON, David NCH 123A
James NCH 128A
William NCH 125A
HUDERSON?, (See Henderson) RCK 83A
HUDESON?, (See Henderson) RCK 38A
HUDGEN, John HRT 161
HUDGEONS, Allexander LNC 69
Ambrose LNC 7
Danl. LNC 7
John LNC 67
Medley ADR 24
Moses ADR 28
Patsey LNC 7
Wm. ADR 28
HUDGINS, John WYN 89A
Wm. FKN 72
HUDNELL?, James WRN 37A
HUDNUT?, Elias P. FLG 78A
HUDNUTT, J. H. MAS 79
HUDS?, James ALN 138
HUDSON, -----? DVS 5A
Arasha GRD 89A
Arnold BRK 261
Bayle MAS 78
Benj. GRD 85A
Daniel PUL 62A
David JES 79
David OHO 10A
Drury GRN 55
Elijah BNE 20
Evans NCH 128A
Henry PUL 53A
Jacob CLK 91
James HRD 12
James ADR 24
James FTE 83
James BBN 118
James PUL 53A
Jane BRN 16
Jesse SPN 20A
Jessee FTE 85
John BRN 16
John JEF 53
John JEF 61
John FTE 81
John CLD 152
John CBL 3A
John PUL 54A
John P. GRN 72
Joseph OHO 10A
Joshua JES 72
Levi PUL 44A
Littleton SPN 15A
Martin OHO 5A
Mary CLK 101
Michael NCH 112A
HUDSON, Moses SHE 175
Noah PUL 59A
Obediah SCT 109A
Patsy PUL 53A
Pleasant GRN 71
Rawleigh WDF 115A
Reubin FTE 83
Robert MAD 166
Robert PUL 54A
Robert PUL 64A
Robert WDF 102A
Saml. MAS 69
Saml. SCT 105A
Simon MAD 150
Thomas OHO 4A
Thomas WDF 102A
Will HRY 190
Will GRD 112A
Will. KNX 278
William, Jr. OWN 102
William, Sr. OWN 102
William PUL 53A
William P. DVS 18A
Wm. E. OHO 11A
HUDSON?, Caty SHE 121A
HUDSPETH, Thomas WRN 66A
William SPN 4A
HUDSPITH, John MNR 195
William MNR 207
HUDUSON?, Alex. RCK 81A
HUEL, William F. SPN 8A
HUES?, John GNP 176A
HUETS?, Martin UNN 148
HUEY, Saml. PND 15A
HUFF, Abner CLD 150
Benjamin BRK 259
Daniel CLD 146
George RCK 75A
Isaac WYN 92A
Jemima CLD 149
Jno. FKN 88
John GRN 71
John BTH 172
Leonard CLY 126
Phillip WYN 84A
Saml. FLG 37A
Samuel CLD 146
William CLY 124
William, Junr. CLD 146
William, Senr. CLD 146
HUFF?, Richard SHE 111A
HUFFAKER, Christopher WYN 80A
Jacob WYN 94A
HUFFMAN, Aaron PUL 54A
Aaron GNP 175A
Ambrose BRN 14
Ambrose, Jr. BRN 15
Barnett BRN 14
Ben HRD 50
Cornelius BRN 15
David NSN 204
Edward BRN 14
Elam BRN 14
Elias CBL 9A
Ephraim PUL 63A
Fountain BNE 18
George HRD 20
George NSN 204
Godfrey WRN 45A
Henry BRN 15
Henry FTE 94
Henry GRD 100A
Jacob HAR 146
Jacob HAR 152
Jacob GNP 172A

Name	County	Page
HUFFMAN, James	BTH	162
James	GRD	97A
James A.	MTG	271
Jesse	BRN	15
John	BKN	11
John	HRD	38
John	NSN	204
John	GRD	104A
John	GRD	107A
John R.	BTH	150
Julius	BRN	17
Peter	NSN	204
Peter, Jr.	BRN	15
Peter, Sr.	BRN	17
Peter	NCH	116A
Sampson	CBL	9A
Soliman	BNE	18
Thomas	MTG	297
William	GRD	83A
William	GRD	96A
Wm.	PND	25A
Zachariah	CBL	9A
HUFFORD, Barbary	SCT	111A
David	SCT	111A
Elizebeth	WDF	96A
Jacob	SCT	112A
John	WDF	100A
Solomon	WDF	100
HUFFORD?, Jno.	HAR	164
HUFFSTETLER, Barny	NCH	129A
HUFFSTUTLER, John	LGN	39
Solomon	LGN	36
HUFFSTUTTER, John	NCH	107A
HUFFT?, Joseph	KNX	288
HUFINE?, George	ALN	104
HUFMAN, Christopher	NSN	204
Ed	GRD	95A
Elijah	PUL	66A
Henry	GRD	112A
Huston	GRD	114A
John	LWS	94A
John	GRD	95A
Nimrod	MNR	205
Philip	FKN	112
Will	GRD	111A
HUGALEY, John	MAD	152
HUGGEND?, John	RCK	79A
HUGGINS, Caty	FTE	65
Edwd.	SCT	103A
James	LVG	4
Jeremiah	LVG	4
Jno.	LVG	4
John?	CWL	41
Reuben	BRN	14
Will.	LVG	4
William	LVG	11
HUGGS, Elizabeth	LVG	4
HUGHARD, Edward	BTH	162
Thomas	BTH	154
HUGHART, John	MTG	237
HUGHES, Abijah	FKN	74
Abner	HRD	58
Absalom	BRN	16
Andrew	LVG	5
Andrew	WAS	42A
Andrew S.	NCH	129A
Bell	NSN	199
Benjamin	BLT	174
Charles	TRG	12
Cornelius	BNE	18
David	TRG	12
Edward	WAS	64A
Eli	BBN	146
Elizabeth	CLD	139
Fielding	OWN	102
HUGHES, Francis	WAS	42A
Hezekiah	NSN	185
Hiram	PUL	59A
Isaac	NCH	118A
James	NSN	207
James	MTG	247
James, Jr.	NCH	112A
James	SPN	3A
James	WAS	31A
James	PUL	42A
James	WAS	61A
James	WAS	78A
James R.	WAS	79A
James T.	UNN	148
Jas.	JEF	19
Jas.	FLG	65A
Jas.	SCT	117A
Jesse	BBN	116
Jno.	HAR	158
Jno.	PUL	47A
John	BNE	18
John	JEF	43
John, (F. R.)	BBN	128
John	BBN	112
John	GRT	142
John	NSN	206
John	MTG	237
John, Jr.	JEF	38
John, Jr.	OWN	102
John, Sr.	OWN	102
John, Sr.	WAS	17A
John	WAS	78A
John	SCT	118A
John	NCH	129A
Joseph	LVG	9
Laban	HAR	204
Letty	HRY	196
Mary	FKN	64
Mary J.	BNE	18
Mason	BBN	128
Michael	BNE	18
Nathan	OWN	102
Otho	BBN	146
Peter	FTE	87
Pratt	BBN	114
Richard	FTE	83
Ruben	WAS	67A
T.	JEF	22
Thomas	BBN	112
Thomas	CHN	27A
Thomas	LWS	95A
Thomas W.	BNE	46
Toliver	NCH	118A
Will	NSN	204
William	OWN	102
William	BBN	112
William	NSN	183
William	NCH	109A
William	NCH	109A
Willis	HRY	188
Wm.	BBN	146
Wm.	WAS	61A
Wm.	FLG	69A
HUGHEY, -----?	DVS	13A
Jno.	MAS	52
Ro.,, Judge	LVG	5
Samuel	BNE	20
Spencer R.	BNE	18
HUGHINE?, Christian	SPN	17A
HUGHS, Absalom	BTH	218
Ann	BTH	148
Anne, Mrs.	WYN	84A
Barnabas	MER	116
Barnabas	OHO	10A
Blacky	ADR	24
HUGHS, Bowling	MER	98
Caroline	BBN	62
Cynthia	LGN	43
Edward	LGN	38
Elender	ETL	44
Elizabeth	BBN	76
Frances	LNC	11
Gabriel	LNC	59
Gabriel	SHE	158
George	ADR	26
George	MER	99
Hardin	PUL	40A
Hugh	GTN	131
Isaac	GRD	116A
Ishmael	MBG	141
Jacob	FTE	92
James	BBN	84
James	JES	92
James	SHE	163
James	GRD	102A
James	GRD	116A
Jessee	BBN	86
Jessee	MBG	133A
John	LNC	33
John	CWL	38
John	LGN	42
John	JES	82
John	MBG	140A
Joseph	JES	75
Joseph	JES	92
Lucy	BTH	154
Matthew	LGN	41
Meriett?	JES	74
Ralph	OHO	10A
Reubin	BTH	154
Richardson P.	MNR	199
Robt.	BBN	66
Robt.	FLG	25A
Rowland	LGN	42
Sally	GRN	61
Stephen	MER	99
Thomas	JES	91
Thomas	MER	98
Thomas	SHE	167
Thomas	MNR	213
Thomas	WRN	28A
Thos.	ADR	28
Thos.	FLG	62A
Wiley	ALN	132
William	LNC	11
William	JES	92
William	BTH	156
Wm., Jr.	LNC	11
Wm.	GRD	117A
HUGHS?, John	BBN	134
HUGHSTON, Mathew	BTH	174
HUGHY, John	CWL	34
John?	CWL	41
Lazarus	CHN	34A
HUGLEY, Alexr.	HRY	265
Chas.	HRY	259
HUGONSON?, Alex.	JEF	42
HUITS?, Martin	UNN	148
HUKER, Geo.	MAS	74
HUKEY, Daniel	FTE	94
HUKILL, David	FTE	90
Nathen	MAS	77
HUKILL?, John	FTE	79
HUKINS, Abra.	MAS	58
HULAND, Ambrose	ETL	51
Wm.	ETL	52
HULAND?, Taylor	ETL	50
HULCE, Richd., Jr.	FLG	33A
Richd., Sr.	FLG	33A
HULET, Moses	CLD	145
HULETT, Adison	GRD	88A

HULETT, Benjamin FTE 92
Benjamin FTE 92
Jessee CLK 81
Jno. MAS 68
Joseph FTE 93
Richard FTE 92
Ruben GRD 88A
Wiatt FTE 92
HULEY, Joel SHE 122A
Randol FTE 76
HULING, Jonathan CBL 2A
Marcus ADR 28
HULL, Carter WAS 46A
Catherine FTE 68
Daniel CLD 151
Henry CLD 151
Jacob FTE 100
Jesse CLD 151
John BNE 20
John FTE 68
Margaret HAR 140
Moses CLD 151
Randel ADR 44
Saml. MAS 75
William CLD 151
HULL?, John WAS 46A
William, Jr. ETL 44
Willis WAS 46A
HULON, Margaret MAD 110
HULS?, John GNP 176A
HULSE, John CLK 88
Josiah BRK 263
Robt. BRK 263
Wm. BBN 92
HUMBERT, Henry FTE 59
HUMBLE, Esquire HAR 212
Nancy MER 98
Noah HAR 144
Paul JEF 40
Robert WDF 98A
Uriah JEF 40
HUMBRIGHT, John LGN 31
HUME, Benjamin MAD 180
Chas. GRD 90A
Dudley FKN 58
Elza BNE 18
Enoch WRN 49A
Henry F. LGN 46
John CLK 99
John CBL 15A
John P. BNE 18
Larken MAD 122
Lewis BNE 20
Prue B. GRT 145
Rewbin MAD 114
Richard CBL 11A
Sarah PND 22A
Susanna MAD 122
Thomas CBL 15A
William CBL 11A
Wm. MAD 172
HUME?, S. B. PND 16A
HUMES, Frederick LNC 27
G. BBN 112
Geo. SCT 113A
James FTE 76
John GRD 91A
Thomas LNC 53
HUMFLEET?, Christian HAR 164
HUMFRIES, Eliza WAS 73A
HUMFRIS, Rolley WAS 86A
HUMLONG?, George BKN 22
HUMMAN, John MAD 122
HUMMER, Ann LGN 43
HUMPH--S?, Elizabe BBN 138
HUMPHARY, Samuel NSN 196
HUMPHRES, Davd. PUL 47A
John LVG 16
HUMPHREY, ----l? DVS 8A
----m? DVS 8A
Anderson SHE 155
Benjn. OHO 9A
David CSY 204
Gilford BBN 140
Hartt? BRK 261
Holeman HRY 214
Hugh GNP 177A
James GTN 126
John NSN 200
John CSY 206
Simon NSN 197
Thos. NSN 187
HUMPHREYES, Charles FTE 55
HUMPHREYS, Benja. JEF 54
Benjamin WRN 54A
Catharine FTE 87
Charles MER 115
David HAR 214
Eli SHE 119A
George WRN 54A
Harrison FLG 54A
Jas. HRD 24
Jas. FLG 52A
John BBN 60
John HAR 156
John HRT 161
John FLG 53A
John WRN 73A
Joseph NCH 107A
Reuben HRY 176
Saml. HRD 34
Saml., Jr. FLG 53A
Saml. FLG 53A
Thos. BBN 94
Wm. FLG 53A
HUMPHRIES, Absalom TRG 11
George HRD 42
John TRG 10
Mary FKN 70
Thomas TRG 4
HUMPHRIS, Davd. PUL 39A
Elijah JEF 41
HUMPHRY, Richard HRY 226
Thos. HRD 62
Wm. HRD 62
HUMRICK, Nimrod FTE 91
HUNBY, Wm. BKN 6
HUNDLEY, Jesse WAS 22A
John B. BRN 17
HUNDLY, Elisha WAS 65A
Sherwood W. BLT 196
HUNDON?, Henery CBL 14A
HUNGATE, Akillas WAS 29A
Charles MER 97
Elizabeth MER 97
Wm. WAS 51A
HUNGERFORD, Wm. FLG 61A
HUNLEY, John FTE 103
John W. JEF 40
Ransom FTE 87
Wm. SHE 109A
HUNLY, Abner SPN 20A
Dav. HRY 256
HUNNICUTT, John FTE 111
HUNPHILL, James JES 78
HUNPHRY, Geo. PUL 49A
HUNSAKER, Andrew MBG 136
Christina MBG 136A
John MBG 136A
HUNSFORD, Henry WRN 28A
HUNT, -----? DVS 8A
Aaron HRD 90
Abel BRN 14
Abraham WYN 90A
Absalom BTH 182
Absulam FLG 57A
Albin ADR 24
Ambros GRN 76
Andrew HRD 18
Archabald SPN 19A
Basel FLG 42A
Benjn. MAS 62
Celia LGN 31
Charles ADR 24
Daniel MBG 137
Elijah MBG 137
Enoch FTE 82
Ezekael FLG 42A
Gasham MBG 137
George FTE 83
George GTN 128
George WDF 115A
Henry BRN 16
Henry SHE 149
Hiram FLG 46A
Israel NCH 124A
James LNC 47
James FTE 77
James MER 97
James MER 98
James ALN 138
James MTG 283
Jas. FLG 46A
Jeremiah BTH 184
Jesse SPN 23A
Jno. FKN 142
Jno. PUL 47A
John BRN 16
John FLD 26
John FTE 92
John ALN 106
John SHE 159
John, Senr. MBG 136
John SPN 19A
John FLG 36A
John FLG 57A
John MBG 141A
John W. FTE 68
Jonathan HRD 12
Jonathan BRN 16
Jonathan FKN 56
Jonathan CLK 81
Jonathan CLY 128
Jonathan, Jr. BRN 16
Jonathan MBG 141A
Labern GRN 76
Lewis BTH 182
Moses SPN 18A
Nathan MTG 285
Nehemiah CBL 19A
Owen MBG 136
Reubin FLG 46A
Reubin FLG 58A
Richard LNC 47
Robert LNC 73
Robert PUL 59A
Robinson MTG 285
Rubin BTH 216
Sally LNC 71
Samuel GTN 118
Simeon GRN 76
Thomas SPN 18A
Uel FLG 46A
Will, Jr. ADR 24
William MBG 142
William SHE 154

HUNT, William SPN 19A
William PUL 58A
William G. FTE 57
Willson JES 93
Wilson FTE 100
Wilson BBN 110
Wm., Sr. ADR 24
HUNT?, -----? DVS 8A
Bartho. FTE 57
John MER 98
Jonathan ADR 24
HUNTER, Abigail LGN 45
Abigal OHO 7A
Absalom WDF 117A
Alexander NSN 187
Andrew LGN 45
Ann GRN 74
Barbary FLG 69A
Carter SHE 116A
Charles JES 80
Charles SHE 116A
Chs. FKN 150
Daniel MAD 106
Daniel SHE 153
David HOP 250
Elinder ALN 128
Eliphalel NSN 216
Elizabeth LGN 25
Francis KNX 294
George FTE 86
George CSY 210
Henry SHE 112A
Hiram LGN 40
Jacob GTN 119
James HND 10
James CLK 87
James FTE 110
James FKN 118
James WYN 84A
James SHE 125A
Jas. MAS 70
Jno. MAS 70
John CWL 34
John FTE 75
John JES 84
John JES 87
John MAD 134
John MAD 134
John SHE 153
John CLD 160
John FLG 39A
John S. SCT 135A
Jos. B. TOD 130A
Joseph JES 80
Joseph SHE 152
Joseph MNR 213
Josiah FTE 73
Judith, Mrs. WYN 84A
Levi KNX 294
Lydia CHN 35A
Michael HND 5
Rachel FTE 83
Reuben OHO 9A
Richard FTE 83
Robt. HRY 241
Sally JES 78
Sally CLD 140
Sally CLD 142
Saml. HND 5
Saml. BRK 263
Saml. GRD 117A
Samuel JES 80
Samuel SHE 120A
Solomon LGN 40
Susan LNC 79
Thomas SHE 153
HUNTER, Thomas NSN 224
Thomas PUL 59A
Thos. SHE 124A
Titus MBG 136A
William LGN 45
William CLK 68
William JES 78
William SHE 156
William SHE 167
William LWS 86A
William WYN 101A
William WYN 103A
William L. WDF 125A
Willis SHE 125A
Wm. FKN 60
Zachariah MER 98
HUNTER?, Saml. C. BKN 11
Wm. FLG 38A
HUNTING, George SHE 119A
HUNTON, Ludwell WRN 33A
Thomas LNC 2
HUNTSAKER, George MBG 136A
HUNTSINGER, Jacob OHO 8A
HUNTSMAN, Benj. LNC 9
Henry ALN 118
Lemuel SPN 11A
Peter ALN 118
Robt. FLG 47A
William LNC 19
HUNZMAN, John FTE 77
HUP?, John WAS 57A
HUPPT?, Joseph KNX 288
HURBY, John JEF 23
HURBY?, Jesse, Senr. WRN 67A
Leonard WRN 67A
HURD, Frances MBG 139A
James, Junr. CLD 143
James, Senr. CLD 143
William CLY 114
HURDIN, John WAS 20A
HURDMON?, Robt. ADR 24
HURENDON, Haywood JEF 54
HURLEY, Isaiah HAR 214
James NCH 103A
Moses LVG 3
Samuel FLD 14
HURLY?, Jesse, Senr. WRN 67A
HURRAGIN?, Winney WAS 22A
HURRY?, Jenry GNP 175A
HURSHMAN, Geo. BBN 104
HURST, Absalum DVS 15A
Elisha FLD 6
George WDF 95
Harmon LWS 91A
Henry FLD 6
Henry FLG 52A
Henry FLG 55A
Henry SCT 102A
Jams. FLG 50A
John MAS 61
John FTE 77
John FLG 50A
John WAS 78A
Michl. HRY 210
Nancy FLG 54A
Peter WDF 93A
Sandy FLG 48A
Valentine DVS 16A
William TRG 11
William DVS 16A
Wm. FLG 57A
HURT, Abram TOD 130
Henry GRD 103A
James WYN 80A
HURT, Jane GRD 110A
John FTE 90
John CLD 143
John WRN 61A
John WYN 80A
Joseph, Senr. WYN 80A
Joseph, Sr. WYN 100A
Lewis WRN 35A
Mourning FKN 88
Thomas TOD 129
William, Sr. WYN 96A
HURTS?, Martin UNN 148
HUSBAND, Jas. RCK 79A
HUSBANDS, George BTL 325
Harmon CHN 29
John WAS 68A
Very MER 98
HUSE, Armistead CLK 73
Dudley ADR 24
HUSH?, James GRN 80
HUSHMAN, Henry HAR 164
HUSKETH, Nathaniel LGN 46
HUSS, George LGN 47
Jacob LGN 47
John HRD 86
Michael LGN 35
HUSS?, Richard SHE 111A
HUSSEY, John LVG 12
HUST/ HURT?, Field. HRY 268
HUST, Harmon CLY 131
HUSTEN, Isaac HRT 159
Jessee HRT 161
Wm. HRT 160
HUSTON, -----m? DVS 10A
---nin? DVS 10A
Archib. LNC 25
Archibald BNE 50
Benjamin NSN 199
David NSN 201
James OHO 7A
Jno. JEF 31
John FTE 88
John GTN 133
John NSN 199
John NSN 207
Jonathan NSN 199
Joseph BLT 158
Joseph NSN 212
Joseph NSN 213
Margaret BRK 227
Mary BTH 158
Maxwell BLT 174
Robert TRG 13
Robert FTE 109
Robert OHO 8A
Robt. BRK 227
Starling JEF 33
Stephen LNC 25
Thales LNC 3
Thomas NSN 199
William FTE 112
William CLY 116
William NSN 207
HUSTON?, William FTE 57
HUTCH, James GNP 173A
HUTCHASON, H. B. GRN 56
Mary GRN 70
Mathew GRN 64
Saml. GRN 55
Thomas GRN 55
William GRN 59
HUTCHCRAFT, Thomas BBN 112
HUTCHENS, Thos. SCT 109A
Thos. SCT 115A
HUTCHENSON, Archib SCT 139A

HUTCHENSON, Hiram SCT 96A
Jas. SCT 134A
HUTCHERSON, Clem JES 69
Elijah WYN 80A
Elizabeth BLT 168
John JEF 65
Joseph WYN 80A
Samuel WYN 86A
Thomas WYN 80A
Vincent HND 11
HUTCHERSON?, Enoch JEF 52
HUTCHESON, Amy HOP 246
Benjamin HAR 132
James HRD 92
John CSY 210
John HOP 250
Luke CLD 154
Thomas CSY 218
HUTCHINES, Samuel SPN 4A
HUTCHINGS, James SPN 7A
Richard LGN 38
HUTCHINGSON,
Robert LGN 41
Samuel LGN 41
William LGN 41
HUTCHINS, Cader CLK 106
James T. CLD 141
Jessee CLK 106
John CLD 141
John CLD 143
John CLD 145
Richard CLK 98
Thom. CWL 54
Will SCT 109A
HUTCHINSON, Alex. BNE 18
Hannah BBN 142
Hiram JEF 37
James BBN 118
Jas. HRD 64
Joseph LNC 57
Lewis LNC 79
Peter BBN 140
Saml. JEF 37
Samuel BBN 126
Thom? LNC 59
William FTE 112
William, Capt. BBN 112
Wm. LNC 79
Wm. BBN 142
HUTCHISON, ---ob? CWL 36
Andrew WDF 98A
Carter CBL 10A
Danl. BKN 15
David BKN 19
Jas. FLG 27A
Jno. HAR 142
Jos. BRK 261
William GRT 140
William HAR 142
William HAR 146
HUTER?, George ALN 110
HUTSELL, Geo. BBN 104
Isaac BBN 102
Jacob NCH 120A
John FTE 91
Mathias C. NCH 127A
HUTSON, Abram FLG 75A
Alexander MTG 249
Andrew MTG 253
Benjamin MTG 267
Jno. LVG 6
John MBG 140
John BTL 325
Thomas MTG 267
HUTT, Corbin BBN 94
Francis ADR 64
HUTTON, Benj. FLG 26A
Cornelius WDF 112A
James FKN 148
John JES 81
Joseph HAR 132
Saml. FLG 26A
Thomas HAR 140
HUTTS, James MTG 285
HUXSTUDLER/
HUXSTUDLET?,
Phoebe HAR 180
HYATT, Benj. LNC 69
Elijah GRD 86A
Frederick LNC 69
Gilbert? LVG 16
John LNC 7
John GRD 94A
Lewis FKN 146
Reubin GRD 100A
Shadrack HAR 190
Thomas D. NCH 107A
William GRD 98A
Wilson GRD 99A
Wm. LNC 5
HYDE, John CHN 30A
HYDON?, (See
Higdon) NSN 216
William NSN 210
HYER, Alexander C. BNE 18
HYETT, Tho. MAS 57
HYGHT, Partrick CSY 204
HYMAN, Jno. MAS 65
HYNDMAN?, James FTE 55
HYNES, -----? DVS 9A
-----? DVS 9A
Isaac HRD 64
James LGN 28
James BLT 160
Kotley SPN 16A
Samuel FTE 97
Toney? NSN 178
HYNES?, William PUL 61A
HYRES?, William PUL 61A
HYRONEMOUS, John SPN 11A
HYSONG, Jacob FLG 72A
Peter FLG 72A
HYTON, William MTG 239
I--EN?, Oliver FTE 60
ICE, Elizabeth NSN 194
James NSN 194
Robert NSN 194
IGLEHEART, Dennis OHO 10A
Jacob OHO 4A
James OHO 9A
John OHO 9A
Levi OHO 6A
IGO, Jacob LGN 34
John MAD 116
IGOE?, Wm. MAD 90
IGOR?, Wm. MAD 90
ILES, Samuel PND 21A
Thomas CBL 21A
ILIFF, John FLD 36
Samuel BNE 22
Stephen BNE 22
IMCO, Mordicai LGN 30
IMLER, William MBG 135A
IMMEL, Thos. HRY 268
INABNET?, Jos. PUL 35A
INDICUT, Joseph FLD 41
INDMAN, Archabald DVS 19A
INDOW?, Abraham CHN 41A
INDRY?, Harvy CLK 98
Martin CLK 98
INGHUFF, Frederick CBL 8A
INGLE, Henry FLD 14
William HRY 210
Wm. JEF 60
INGLER, David,
Jun. MBG 137
David, Sen. MBG 137
INGLES, Abraham HAR 182
Andrew FTE 103
Boon BBN 144
James BBN 102
Peter HAR 182
Thos. SCT 126A
INGLES?, Joseph HAR 138
INGLETON, Sally MER 100
INGRAHAM, Griffin LGN 43
INGRAM, Abraham BTH 214
Ben ADR 28
Charlton CWL 34
Garret ADR 28
George GRN 64
Hannah KNX 290
Henry NSN 207
Hiram FLD 12
James BNE 20
James HRD 58
James WYN 84A
Jer, Jr. ADR 30
Jer, Sen. ADR 28
John ADR 28
John MNR 195
John NSN 220
Johnson KNX 304
Jonathan SPN 13A
Milton CWL 34
N. CWL 33
Nimrod WYN 84A
Patsy PUL 65A
Saml. BKN 13
Saml. MAS 72
Samuel FTE 65
Samuel GRT 145
Samuel WYN 84A
Samul DVS 18A
Shadrack CWL 54
Thomas WRN 53A
Thos. JEF 56
Thos. CLY 122
Winefred LGN 40
Wm. CWL 54
Wm. CWL 54
Wm. WAS 53A
Wyatte H. HND 4A
INGRAM?, Abraham MTG 267
INGRHAM, Barton HAR 218
Jeremiah HAR 220
INGRUM, Isaac FLD 12
Isaac MBG 140A
William ETL 53
Wm. SHE 114A
INLON?, Henry BBN 122
INLOW, A. B. S. FLG 74A
Jas. FLG 74A
INLOW?, Henry BBN 122
INMAN, Elisha WTY 120A
Henry D. LGN 34
Susanna LGN 30
INMOND, Jesse WAS 41A
INNES, Henry BBN 106
Hugh FKN 104
INNIS, Chas. MAS 55
Will. SCT 123A
INNMAN, James MBG 135
INPIN?, Barbary NSN 193
INSKEEP, Joseph FTE 93
INSKO?, Saml. BKN 14
INSSIN?, Barbary NSN 193

Name	County	Page
INTORD?, Benjn.	ALN	142
INYARD, John	LNC	25
Silas	HRD	94
IRELAND, Alexr.	JEF	33
Andrew	OWN	102
Jas.	MAS	73
Jno.	FKN	72
John	SCT	118A
John R.	SCT	113A
Partrick	HRT	161
Saml.	HRY	255
Thomas	NCH	118A
Wm.	HRD	86
IRON, Archibald	GNP	169A
IRONS, Hanes	BLT	164
IRVIN, Alexr.	GRN	69
Andrew	BBN	62
David	KNX	286
David	NCH	121A
Elisha	PND	26A
George	NCH	118A
James	JES	86
James	JES	94
James	MBG	139A
Jas.	CHN	42
John	ADR	28
John	JES	69
John	FTE	83
John	WDF	104
John	SHE	174
John	NCH	108A
John	WTY	121A
John M.	BBN	130
Joshua	BBN	134
Lawrence	FTE	79
Loyd	BBN	68
Robert	FTE	87
Robert	KNX	284
Samuel L.	MER	99
Thomas	BBN	64
Thomas, Senr.	MBG	139A
Thos.	BBN	68
William	BRN	17
William	FTE	85
IRVINE, Benjamin	MAD	140
Benjamin F.	MAD	114
Bryson	MAD	138
David	MAD	180
Edmond	MAD	178
Elizabeth	CLD	148
Jesse	LGN	37
John	CLD	148
Nancy	MAD	164
Samuel	MAD	124
William	LGN	35
William	CLD	148
Wm.	TOD	127A
IRWIN, Abraham	MER	99
Alexander	LWS	98A
Ben	HRD	44
Benjamin	BLT	190
Francis	OHO	5A
Jno.	CWL	54
John, Jr.	NSN	218
John	OHO	6A
John	LWS	97A
John M. C.	WDF	108A
Joseph	NSN	183
Joseph	BLT	194
Moses	LWS	97A
Prudence	MER	99
Samuel	CLK	83
Thompson	JEF	24
William	FTE	105
William	BLT	194
IRWINE, Abner	FTE	58
IRWINE, George	HRD	36
Isaac	HRD	28
ISAAC, Wm. Y.	PUL	48A
ISAACH, Sutten	MAS	77
ISAACKS, Elisha	WAS	24A
Jesse	SHE	114A
John, Jr.	WAS	21A
John, Sr.	WAS	24A
Saml.	ADR	28
ISAACS, Arn / Ann?	ADR	30
Gabrial	WTY	117A
Godfrey	ETL	53
Godfrey, Sr.	CLY	129
Godfrey, Sr.	CLY	130
Jacob	ADR	62
Jessee	HRT	161
Saml.	CLY	132
Saml.	HRT	161
William	FLD	43
ISABELL, Henry	WRN	42A
Livingstone	WRN	40A
ISAM, George	CLY	122
Henry	WAS	81A
Wm.	WAS	81A
ISBEL, Jno	ADR	28
ISBEL?, Thomas	JES	77
ISBELL, Geo.	TOD	132
James	BBN	64
James	WRN	42A
Jason	WRN	71A
John	WRN	43A
Temple	WRN	60A
William	JES	80
William	WRN	33A
ISBELL?, Joseph	MAD	134
ISENOGLE, Christian	BNE	20
ISGRIGG, Daniel	HAR	208
Michael	HAR	208
William	HAR	208
ISGRIGG?, Henry	HAR	182
Matson	HAR	198
ISHAM, Russell	DVS	17A
ISHMAEL, Benjamin	NCH	119A
John	NCH	119A
ISHMAEL?, James	NCH	108A
ISHMELL, Thos.	FLG	54A
ISHUM, Joseph	BBN	126
Unied?	BBN	94
ISOM, Edmon	TRG	14
ISON, Archibald	FLD	22
Chas., Sr.	GRD	121A
Jacob	LVG	4
James	GRD	114A
James	GRD	121A
John	GRD	101A
John, B,	GRD	121A
Michael	GRD	109A
Michael	GRD	121A
Nelson	GRD	121A
William	GRD	121A
Chas.	GRD	121A
ISRAEL, Wm.	BBN	110
ISUM, Gabl.	CHN	44
IVANS, Moses	MAD	108
IVENS, Charles	BBN	140
IVERS, Margaret	SHE	140A
IVEY, James	LGN	36
IVEY?, John	FTE	57
IVINS, Majr.	BBN	92
Thomas	BTH	174
IVY, Absalom	OWN	101
Jarrard	TOD	128A
IZZELL, Gilum	CHN	40A
J---TMAN, George	CSY	204
J--EN?, Oliver	FTE	60
JA--?, Charles	HRY	204
JABIM?, Chas.	JEF	20
JAC--ON?, Lucy	FTE	60
JACK, John	GTN	121
Joseph	NSN	220
Rachel	LWS	93A
Robert	GSN	140A
William	NSN	220
JACKLEY, Bruen	MAS	52
JACKMAN, Elijah	MER	99
James	CLD	157
John	JES	96
John	CLD	154
Jos.	GRD	111A
Mary	CLD	160
Reuben	LGN	24
Saml.	GRD	86A
Thomas	MER	99
William, Junr.	CLD	155
William, Senr.	CLD	157
JACKMOND, Joseph	WAS	24A
JACKS, Thomas	BTH	154
William	MTG	275
William M.	BTH	154
JACKSON, Alexander	GTN	132
Alexr.	SCT	117A
Amos	HRY	266
Amy	HOP	252
Ann	HAR	180
Ann	WDF	96A
Archabald	JES	84
Archibald	WRN	72A
Beckley	HOP	252
Benjamin	LGN	40
Benoni	LGN	35
Burrel	CWL	34
Charles	HRY	204
Charles	SPN	15A
Charles	GNP	173A
Chesterfield	WRN	33A
Christopher	HOP	252
Christopher	OHO	3A
D.	BBN	116
Daniel	HAR	180
Daniel L.	OHO	4A
David	JES	69
David	WDF	104
Dempsey	FLG	37A
Edwd.	MAS	55
Elias	OHO	3A
Elijah	HRD	44
Elijah	JES	85
Elijah	CLD	161
Elizabeth	SPN	15A
Elsey	MAD	132
Ephraim	LNC	81
Ezekiel	CLD	160
Frances	LNC	5
Francis	WAS	23A
Francis	WDF	107A
Francis	SHE	131A
Francis	SHE	143A
Francis F.	CLK	71
G. W. George	GSN	140A
Gabriel	HRL	112
Gabriel	OHO	3A
Geo.	GRD	91A
George	GTN	132
George	BTH	204
George	NSN	210
Gibson	KNX	294
Henry	HAR	180
Henry	FLG	76A
Hugh	GTN	133
Iaiah?	JES	83

JACKSON, Isaac HRD 54
Isaac MNR 191
Isaac MNR 199
Isaah HOP 252
Isaiah HRD 54
Isaiah FLG 76A
Isham JES 83
Jacob GTN 133
Jacob FLG 76A
James BRN 17
James HRL 112
James WAS 34A
James WYN 95A
Jared CLD 142
Jas. HRY 240
Jas. FLG 66A
Jas. SCT 126A
Jeremiah BTH 184
Jesse BBN 108
Jessee ETL 52
Jessee MBG 140A
Jno CHN 45
Jno. PUL 35A
Jno. C. FKN 100
Joel HRY 270
John LVG 13
John HRD 52
John GRN 59
John JES 84
John JES 86
John MER 99
John BBN 108
John CLD 140
John BLT 158
John BLT 192
John BTH 202
John MTG 239
John KNX 282
John, Dr. BBN 108
John, Sr. BTH 202
John WRN 33A
John WRN 66A
John FLG 73A
John FLG 76A
John RCK 79A
John SHE 129A
John SHE 130A
John SHE 130A
John B. WYN 79A
Jonathan HAR 186
Jos. PUL 35A
Joseph BBN 60
Joseph BBN 60
Joseph HAR 180
Joshua HAR 156
Josiah CLK 74
Josiah UNN 151
Jourd-? ALN 98
Julius C. OHO 4A
Lemuel SPN 15A
Leroy WRN 33A
Lewis LNC 43
Lewis FLG 60A
M.?, Mrs.? MAS 56
Madred? SHE 130A
Martin MNR 199
Martin GRD 121A
Mary HRL 112
Mary WRN 63A
Micajer KNX 294
Michl. LNC 9
Mordicai GTN 134
Moses GTN 132
Nathan HOP 252
Nathl. SHE 148
Needum MNR 199
JACKSON, Polly BLT 192
Ray CBL 20A
Reuben FKN 100
Richard B. NSN 180
Robt. SCT 107A
Robt. SCT 122A
Roda SCT 99A
Rubin GRN 57
Saml. FLG 45A
Sammuel BBN 144
Samuel LVG 11
Samuel HAR 182
Simon OWN 100
Thomas BBN 94
Thomas BTH 204
Thomas NSN 220
Thomas WYN 95A
Thos. CWL 37
Thos., Sr. FLG 66A
Thos. FLG 66A
Vachel GTN 125
Wiley LVG 3
William JES 97
William HAR 186
William MNR 201
William BTH 208
William HRY 220
William SPN 23A
William WAS 23A
William WRN 66A
William WDF 107A
Wm HRD 14
Wm. BBN 92
Wm. MAD 132
Wm., Jr. ADR 30
Wm., Sen. ADR 30
Wm. R? ALN 94
Wm.? M. MAS 56
JACKSTON, John WAS 35A
JACO, Nancy CBL 13A
JACO?, Theodore SCT 123A
JACOB, Arnold CWL 37
Isaac CLK 71
Samuel CLK 98
JACOBS, Mrs. JEF 28
Baylor MAD 98
Carter FLD 44
Claudius FLD 44
Daniel CLK 99
George CLK 103
George CLY 119
Greenbury FTE 93
Harrison BRK 267
Hukerson? C. GTN 120
James SHE 112A
Jeremiah NSN 207
Joel MAD 98
John BNE 22
John FLD 44
John MAD 98
John MAD 120
John, Junr. SCT 109A
John, Senr. SCT 109A
John FLG 33A
John SHE 111A
John J. JEF 24
Martin GTN 120
Martin SHE 112A
Mathew JES 77
Maurice MAD 96
Moses GRT 139
Robt. SCT 100A
Rowley FLD 41
William FLD 44
William HAR 164
Wm. BKN 23
JACOBS, Wm. JEF 62
JACOBSON, Maltz/ Waltz &? JEF 27
JACOBY, Ralph BBN 112
JACOCOBS, Zachariah BBN 134
JACOP, Ben. CHN 46
JACOWAY, Archibald WTY 114A
JAFERS?, Jeremiah GSN 140A
JAGER, Samuel FTE 68
JAGERS, Levi HRT 161
Nathan HRT 161
William HRT 161
JAINES?, George MBG 142
JAMERSON, Saml. D. HRT 161
JAMES, Aaron MER 100
Baley JEF 63
Bej? SCT 96A
Berryman? MAS 69
Beverly MAS 55
Charles SHE 151
Charles B. LGN 43
Criswell HAR 136
Daniel FKN 106
Danl. F. PUL 48A
David MBG 139
David MTG 253
Edward GNP 174A
Elijah WRN 47A
Elisha BLT 156
Fanney PUL 35A
Foster? BTL 325
George MAD 150
George GNP 171A
Gidean HOP 250
Henry TRG 10
Henry PUL 45A
Hezekiah BTL 313
Hezekiah BTL 325
Isaac L. LGN 46
James MNR 201
James WRN 55A
James SCT 99A
Jno. HRY 256
Joel BLT 164
John FLD 41
John LGN 42
John BBN 126
John BBN 126
John MAD 144
John MAD 150
John SHE 155
John MAD 160
John BLT 176
John MNR 207
John MTG 267
John OHO 7A
John PUL 35A
John GNP 174A
Jonathan MAD 138
Joseph WDF 100
Joseph CLY 118
Joseph OHO 4A
Joseph M., Sr? PUL 35A
Kelley GTN 127
Levi BBN 90
Martha BRN 17
Michal. R. SCT 105A
Motley? OHO 6A
Nathan HAR 196
Rachael LNC 71
Richard BLT 180
Richard BLT 182
Robert MER 100
Ruth NCH 122A
Saml. JEF 38

JAMES, Samuel FLD 33
Samuel, Jr. MER 100
Samuel, Sr. MER 100
Samuel CBL 2A
Tho. MAS 53
Tho., Sr. MAS 55
Thomas BRN 17
Thomas LNC 43
Thomas ADR 64
Thomas BBN 136
Thomas UNN 147
Thomas NSN 197
Thos. MAS 58
Thos. HRY 251
Thos., Sr. HRY 256
Thos. M. BBN 138
Tobias MTG 257
Wiley SCT 99A
Will SCT 122A
Will. SCT 99A
Will. SCT 128A
William LVG 13
William MER 100
William, Jr. CBL 8A
William OHO 6A
Wm. ADR 62
Wm. BBN 90
Wm. MAD 102
JAMES?, Berry ADR 32
George MBG 142
Ishmael NCH 108A
JAMESON, Benj. C. KNX 278
George BRN 17
George BTH 166
George (Near Prewets Knob) BRN 17
James BRN 17
James MTG 237
Jno. LVG 2
Jno., (Blue Spi-?) BRN 17
John MTG 259
John, Senr. BRN 17
Margaret MTG 289
Robert BRN 17
Sarah MTG 271
Thomas MTG 245
Thomas MTG 245
Thos. LVG 2
Will. LVG 3
William BRN 17
William BTH 204
William MTG 289
JAMESON?, James HAR 142
James HAR 142
Townsend HAR 136
JAMISON, Abram SHE 169
Abram, Jr. SHE 169
Aggy FTE 58
Andrew LGN 30
Benoni HAR 188
Bird LVG 8
David CLD 149
David MTG 233
Edward CBL 3A
Elisabeth FLD 23
George JES 75
Henry LGN 30
James NCH 125A
John BBN 88
John NCH 125A
Martin JES 71
Nathan PUL 56A
T. TOD 124A
William WRN 57A
JAMISON?, Samuel J. NCH 112A
JANE, Ebenezar PND 28A
Wm. T.? HRY 240
JANE?, Joseph JEF 44
JANES, Jos. MAS 57
Wm. GNP 169A
JANES?, Joathan FLD 12
Thomas FLD 12
JANMAN?, Thos. MAD 112
JANUARY, A. M. MAS 76
Ephraigm JES 92
Ephraigm JES 92
James B. FTE 74
John MBG 143
Peter WDF 101A
Robert A. LGN 22
Saml. MAS 59
T. H. MAS 76
Thomas FTE 63
JAPAR?, Lewis NSN 185
JAQUIT, Isaac CBL 18A
JARBER, James GSN 140A
William NSN 189
JARBER?, Charles NSN 185
JARBO, Jeremiah NSN 220
John NSN 220
Joseph NSN 220
Joseph? DVS 13A
JARBO?, John NSN 216
JARBOE, Benedict BRK 265
James BRK 265
Janet BRK 265
John WAS 69A
Robert GRN 74
Walter WAS 70A
JARBOE?, John A. WAS 63A
Mark WAS 42A
Saml. BRK 265
JARETT, Thomas LVG 16
JARMAN, Henry BRK 265
John MAD 170
Wm. MAD 150
JARRALL, Anne MER 100
JARRARD, Jacob MAD 144
John TOD 126A
JARRELL, Ellis OWN 99
James HRY 214
JARRET, Joel BRK 265
Thos. BRK 265
JARROTT, Nicholas LGN 33
JARVES, Robert SHE 142A
JARVIS, Danl. FLG 29A
Edward, Junr. MBG 139A
Edward, Senr. MBG 139A
Jabis GRN 58
John GRN 55
John LWS 87A
John MBG 136A
Joloman FLG 52A
Joshua FLG 31A
Josiah MBG 142A
Peter CLY 118
Reason FLG 34A
Soloman FLG 68A
Thomas PUL 68A
Wm. BRK 265
Wm. PND 25A
JASPER, Abraham PUL 59A
Achillis PUL 59A
Andrew PUL 64A
Charles PUL 52A
John PUL 53A
Nicholas PUL 58A
Thomas PUL 55A
JASS?, Wm. JEF 56
JAWMAN?, Thos. MAD 112
JAY, John LVG 16
JEAGUE, John JEF 33
JEAN, Gilly CLD 152
JEANES, Alexr. D. MTG 283
John MTG 283
William MTG 269
JECOBY, Nancy FLG 65A
JEDD?, Sally FTE 99
JEFERS, William GRD 117A
JEFFER, Wm. MAD 142
JEFFERIES, Isham HRD 50
Thos. TOD 125A
JEFFERRESS, Anderson WAS 46A
JEFFERRISS, John WAS 77A
JEFFERRISS?, Elisha WAS 66A
William WAS 65A
JEFFERS, David GSN 140A
James GSN 140A
Robert JES 93
Thomas JES 76
Thos. GSN 140A
Tolifar GRD 109A
Wm. CWL 58
Wm. GSN 140A
JEFFERSON, Harry GRD 91A
Isaac BBN 132
Jesse MAS 56
Perry MAS 56
William GRD 86A
JEFFORD, John DVS 17A
JEFFORDS, John GNP 177A
Rufus GNP 177A
JEFFRES, Ambrose SHE 137A
David SHE 130A
Goan? SHE 112A
JEFFREYS, John FTE 73
JEFFRIES, Enoch MTG 281
Frederick MAS 61
James MER 117
James SHE 173
John SHE 162
Nancy MTG 281
Thomas SHE 151
Will HRY 218
JEFFRYS, Jeffry GRN 57
John GRN 58
JEFFS, Joseph FKN 150
JELF?, James WDF 101
Thomas WDF 100
JEMERSON, David, Jr. BBN 84
David, Senr. BBN 84
JEMESON, Alexander SHE 169
Ellender HAR 156
Joseph HAR 156
JEMISON, David, Jr. BBN 62
Henry FKN 112
John BBN 62
Will MAS 57
JEMMERSON?, John MAD 118
JEMSON, Rufus CBL 3A
Sylvanus CBL 6A
JENINGS, Charles HND 11A
James BRK 265
Wm. BRK 265
JENINGS?, James NSN 220
JENIS?, Isack WAS 85A
JENKENS, John SHE 115A
JENKINGS, Edward NSN 214
Margaret NSN 194
Richard NSN 196
JENKINS, Abel MER 99
Alfred FTE 83
Allison HRD 90

JENKINS, Amos MBG 141
Bartlett SHE 115A
Bath CWL 54
Bath 2nd CWL 54
Charles MAD 102
Danl. MAS 57
Danl. MAS 67
David FTE 100
David GRD 121A
Ditto &? HRD 82
Elijah MTG 257
Eliza CWL 54
Ezekiel HRD 54
Fanny CLD 139
Hamilton FTE 84
Henry GRD 96A
Ignatius HRD 28
James FTE 81
James WAS 63A
Jehue HRD 48
Joel LGN 28
John HRD 36
John HRD 70
John HAR 196
John G. GTN 120
Joseph LGN 38
Lewis JEF 23
Lewis HRD 36
Mary HRD 54
Merwood FKN 94
Nathan HOP 250
Philip HRD 48
Philip HRD 70
Richard FTE 82
Robert FLD 38
Sally BRN 17
Sarah CWL 54
Thomas MER 100
Thomas GRD 96B
Thomas SHE 117A
Thos. FKN 94
Whitnal? CWL 34
Wiley HOP 250
William FTE 82
William HRL 112
William HOP 250
William WRN 40A
Wm. MAS 65
Wm. MAD 170
JENNET, James MAD 134
JENNING, Berreman SHE 141A
David SHE 121A
John MAD 90
Thos. SHE 126A
JENNINGS, Alexr. GRD 84A
And. BKN 26
Anne GTN 132
Augt. GRD 96A
Baylor GRD 100A
Daniel WAS 38A
Elisha CWL 54
Elizabeth GRD 86A
Elkahah HAR 160
Ezekiel MTG 229
Isaah MAD 96
J./ I.? B. GRD 97A
Jacob CWL 37
James CWL 35
James LWS 99A
Jane GRD 99A
John TRG 13A
Joshua HRY 226
Louis HOP 250
Payton GTN 132
Peter JEF 30
Robert MAD 108
JENNINGS, Saml. GRD 86A
Thomas C. MER 100
William MER 99
William BLT 186
William GRD 86A
Wm. CWL 54
Wm. MAD 108
Wm. TOD 131
Wm. SHE 130A
JENTERY, William HND 11
JENTRY, Benagah MAD 164
Benjamin CSY 224
Christopher MAD 138
David MAD 124
Elizabeth MAD 172
James MAD 138
Jane MAD 134
John MAD 122
John MAD 164
Joseph MAD 138
Josiah MAD 166
Martin, Jr. MAD 154
Pleasant GTN 120
Pleasant MAD 158
Richard MAD 134
Richard MAD 172
Wesley ADR 32
Wm. MAD 156
JEPSON, Samuel C. SPN 8A
Willis SPN 8A
JEREMIAH, Dugan HAR 138
JERRALD FITZ, Susanna BRN 17
JERRALD, Jane FLD 27
Polley FLD 27
JERREL, Zachary BNE 20
JESFURD?, Joshua ADR 30
JESPERD?, Joshua ADR 30
JESS?, Isaac WDF 97A
JESSE, John B. WDF 118A
Richard WDF 99
Richard C. WDF 94
Samuel WDF 118A
Tho. H. LNC 57
Thomas WDF 93A
Thomas WDF 121A
Thomas M. WDF 124A
JESSEE, James JES 92
Thos. ADR 20
JESSUP, Samuel FTE 93
JESTER, John WDF 120A
JET, Isaac MAD 154
Neomi HRT 161
JETER, Anderson GRN 56
Barnet TOD 125
Elijah JEF 60
Elizabeth JES 83
Thos. JEF 60
Wm. JEF 35
Wm. TOD 125
JETS, Saml. BKN 4
Thomas BKN 4
JETT, Elijah WAS 19A
James BRN 17
James JES 71
Lucy GTN 122
Porter BKN 8
Preston JEF 61
Richard WDF 112A
Stephen LNC 31
Stephen CLY 121
Washington GTN 124
William GTN 122
William B. HND 4A
JETTON, Zebulon CWL 34
JEWEL, Allen BBN 70
JEWEL, Barrel FKN 136
Elihue FKN 136
Enos NSN 220
George GTN 128
Isaac SHE 134A
Jacob SHE 132A
Jonathan BRN 17
Joseph CLD 151
Nancy CLD 149
Peter BBN 66
Robert BRN 17
Saml. SHE 136A
Thomas CLD 153
Wm. FKN 140
Wm. SHE 132A
JEWELL, David JEF 32
Elisha JES 94
John JES 94
Sandford NSN 220
Smallwood JEF 41
William BLT 164
JIMESON, John GSN 140A
JIMMERSON, David FLG 58A
David FLG 58A
John FLG 58A
Nancy MAD 172
JIMMERSON?, David M.? FLG 59A
JIMMESON, John FLG 58A
JININGS, Joseph ALN 120
Laban ALN 124
Solomon OWN 106
JINISON?, Berley BRK 265
JINKENS, Amos MNR 207
Henry MNR 207
Jeremiah MNR 207
Samuel MNR 207
Uriah MNR 207
JINKINS, -----? CWL 42
Abraham MNR 197
Amos HAR 200
Arthur? CWL 35
Edward WYN 101A
Hedgman WDF 96A
Henry SCT 116A
Henry H. SCT 106A
Isaac GSN 140A
Jesse BTL 325
John SHE 167
John BTL 325
John WDF 96A
Jonathan GRD 106A
Matthew CBL 11A
Sam. HRY 268
Simon WRN 43A
Thomas BTL 325
Thos. C. SCT 97A
Will. GRD 106A
William HAR 168
William BTL 325
William CBL 3A
Wm. CWL 44
Wm. MAS 71
Zackariah WDF 96A
JINNET, Hezekiah SPN 4A
JINNINGS, Alexr. GRN 72
Isreal MAS 61
JINNINGS?, Hatsel NSN 182
JOB, Andrew JEF 28
Danl. JEF 44
John JEF 28
Wm. JEF 55
JOBE, Thomas BRN 17
JOBSON, William S. HRY 224
JOHES, Haydon? HRY 182
JOHISON?, John LVG 16

Name	County	Page
JOHN, Able	MAS	61
James W.	BLT	180
Johnson	SCT	116A
JOHNES, John	WRN	34A
JOHNS, Abraham	CBL	18A
Anderson	CLK	66
Archible	MAD	146
Benjamin	WRN	30A
Daniel	MAD	166
David	CBL	18A
Elisha	HRT	161
Jacob	ETL	47
Jacob	CBL	18A
Robert	BRN	17
Thomas	FLD	27
Thomas	HAR	150
Thomas	GRD	93A
Wm.	ADR	30
Wm.	CHN	43A
JOHNSON, -----?	CWL	41
-olo.?	CWL	34
Ab.	BBN	114
Able	FKN	116
Abs.	CWL	54
Absalom	NSN	180
Abslom.	CWL	54
Absolum	CLY	117
Adam	BTL	325
Adam	GRD	103A
Alexander	CLD	165
Andrew	BNE	22
Andrew	FLD	24
Andrew	FLD	46
Andrew	WYN	92A
Andrew	SCT	121A
Andrew	GSN	140A
Andrew	GNP	167A
Anthony	MER	99
Archibald	MAS	62
Aron	KNX	312
Arter/ Artes?	GSN	140A
Arthur	FLG	43A
Asa	GRN	56
Asa	GTN	131
Barnabas	FLD	34
Barnabis A.	BTH	194
Barton	ALN	140
Basil	FLG	47A
Ben	HRY	206
Ben.	CHN	28A
Benj.	FLG	47A
Benjamin	BNE	46
Benjamin	BBN	70
Benjamin	BTH	206
Benjamin C.	WRN	72A
Benjamin D.	FTE	88
Benjn.	ALN	118
Benjn.	SCT	137A
Bob	FTE	61
Cave	BNE	20
Charles	OWN	101
Charles	CHN	34A
Charles	SCT	111A
Chas.?	CWL	36
Clemen	OHO	6A
Clemons	NSN	189
Daniel	FKN	150
Daniel	KNX	304
Daniel	BTL	325
Daniel	GSN	140A
Daniel	GSN	140A
Danl.	SCT	120A
David	FLD	46
David	MER	99
David	SHE	152
David	FKN	156
JOHNSON, David	HAR	184
David	WDF	97A
Delilah	KNX	280
Dilmus	CHN	30
Dorcas	FTE	95
Earles	SCT	124A
Ebenezer	FLG	43A
Edward	HAR	184
Edward	BRK	267
Edwd. P.	SCT	120A
Eli	FLD	43
Elias	FLD	22
Elias	NSN	191
Elias	NSN	220
Elijah	BRK	265
Elijah	FLG	35A
Elijah	FLG	79A
Elijah	MBG	138A
Elinor	FKN	116
Eliphalet	GSN	140A
Elisabeth	FKN	66
Elisha	HRD	36
Elisha	FKN	58
Elizabeth	FTE	88
Elizabeth	MER	100
Elizabeth	UNN	154
Elizabeth	CLD	165
Elizabeth	PND	24A
Elizabeth	SCT	102A
Elizabeth	MBG	136A
Enoch	SCT	127A
Ephraim	BLT	196
Ez.	HRL	112
Fauntley	WDF	115A
Flemming	GTN	129
Garrot	MER	99
Geo.	SCT	91A
Geo. T.	FKN	132
George	LVG	16
George	BNE	22
George	GRN	70
George	WDF	103
George	CLD	152
George	NSN	214
George	KNX	286
Henry	MAS	74
Henry	FTE	75
Henry	WDF	105
Henry	ALN	140
Henry	WDF	122A
Henry	GNP	175A
Hezekiah	BNE	22
Holeman	JES	94
Howell	TRG	12A
Hy?	SCT	101A
Isaac	CWL	54
Isaac	FTE	97
Isaac	SHE	157
Isaac	CLD	161
Isaac	BLT	162
Isaac	MNR	205
Isaac	BTH	218
Isaac	KNX	304
Isaac	SCT	98A
Isaac	SCT	100A
Isaac	WYN	102A
Isaac	WYN	104A
Isaac	WDF	122A
Isaac	GSN	140A
Isabela	MNR	201
Isham	NCH	123A
J./ I.? W.	GRD	95A
Jack	HRY	253
Jacob	FLD	7
Jacob	GRT	145
James	LGN	30
JOHNSON, James	HRD	36
James	GRN	56
James	FTE	76
James	FTE	95
James	FTE	100
James	MER	100
James	CLY	132
James	FKN	142
James	BBN	144
James	UNN	151
James	SHE	162
James	NSN	178
James	MNR	195
James	HAR	202
James	BTH	204
James	HAR	204
James	KNX	286
James	BTL	325
James, Sen.	WYN	86A
James	OHO	11A
James	TRG	13A
James	PND	21A
James	WYN	89A
James	WYN	93A
James	NCH	122A
James	NCH	123A
James I./ J.?	WYN	86A
Jane	HAR	206
Jas.	JEF	55
Jas.	HRY	249
Jas.	FLG	39A
Jas.	FLG	69A
Jas.	SCT	116A
Jas.	SCT	130A
Jas. M.	SCT	97A
Jeptha	CWL	39
Jesse	HRL	112
Jno.	MAS	55
Jno.	HRY	257
Jno.	HRY	261
Jno.	HRY	263
Joel	KNX	278
Joel	SCT	134A
John	HRD	14
John	ETL	46
John	FTE	59
John	FTE	90
John	MAD	90
John	MER	100
John	FTE	107
John	FTE	111
John	CLY	122
John	SHE	164
John	BLT	170
John	HAR	198
John	HAR	200
John	MNR	201
John	BTH	206
John	BRK	265
John, Jr.	BRK	265
John (Near Hugh Mc Comb's's)	BRN	17
John	FLG	47A
John	WRN	74A
John	WTY	110A
John	SCT	111A
John	GRD	122A
John	SCT	125A
John	SCT	126A
John	TOD	128A
John	MGB	137A
John	GSN	140A
John	GSN	140A
John	GNP	173A
John C.?	GRD	90A
John D.	WDF	109A

Name	County	Page
JOHNSON, John G.	JEF	59
John J.	SCT	127A
John M.	GTN	128
John P.	HAR	200
John S.	SCT	116A
John T.	SCT	91A
Jonathan	NCH	116A
Jos.	HRD	26
Jose	MNR	193
Joseph	BLT	160
Joseph	KNX	282
Joseph	KNX	312
Joseph	BTL	325
Joseph	WDF	111A
Joseph	SCT	120A
Joseph G.	GNP	166A
Joseph R.	MNR	203
Joshua	SHE	166
Josua	GSN	140A
L. W.	CHN	28A
Laban	NCH	128A
Lard.	CWL	54
Laurance	HRY	258
Le Roy	FTE	66
Leonard B.	MNR	215
Levey	SCT	119A
Levi	CWL	54
Levi	GNP	175A
Lewis	FLG	43A
Luke	LNC	35
Luther	SPN	14A
Margaret	ALN	122
Marquis	OHO	7A
Martha	FTE	90
Mary	FTE	88
Mary	FKN	108
Mary	FKN	122
Mary	GTN	127
Mary	GSN	140A
Mathew	ALN	140
Mathew	HRY	234
Mathew	SCT	132A
Moses	BLT	156
Moses	NSN	218
Moses	OHO	8A
Nat	ALN	124
Nathaniel	GTN	132
Nelson	PND	24A
Nicholas	FTE	70
Os.	FLG	60A
Patrick	FLD	14
Patrick	FLD	43
Peter	FLG	75A
Philip	BLT	156
Philip	SHE	157
Philip	OHO	5A
Pleasant S.	WYN	86A
Polly	BTH	194
Presley	OWN	104
Rebecca, Mrs.	WYN	86A
Rebecka	GTN	117
Richard	NSN	197
Richard	WDF	123A
Richd.	CWL	37
Richd. M.	SCT	130A
Robert	BNE	20
Robert	MER	100
Robert	WDF	105
Robert	CLY	113
Robert	NSN	187
Robert	MNR	195
Robert	NCH	110A
S. M.	MAS	64
Saml.	CWL	34
Saml.	LNC	35
Saml.	BBN	110
JOHNSON, Saml.	CHN	30A
Saml.	FLG	68A
Sampson	GTN	124
Samuel	BNE	22
Samuel	CLY	113
Samuel	BLT	162
Samuel	WDF	95A
Sandford	HRY	256
Sarah	CHN	33A
Silas	WDF	97A
Solomon	FTE	75
Srah	BBN	114
Susanna	MNR	201
Tho.	ALN	118
Tho.	ALN	122
Tho. W.	ALN	118
Thomas	FLD	14
Thomas	FLD	14
Thomas	HRD	16
Thomas	BNE	22
Thomas	FLD	37
Thomas	FLD	37
Thomas	FTE	101
Thomas	CLY	119
Thomas	CLD	143
Thomas	MNR	201
Thomas	NSN	220
Thomas	NCH	111A
Thomas	WDF	125A
Thompson	UNN	154
Thos.	HRY	249
Thos.	HRY	250
Thos.	SCT	127A
Thos.	SCT	132A
Thos.	SCT	138A
Thos. M.	GRN	70
Uriah	MNR	191
Will	MAS	55
Will	MAS	64
Will	SCT	101A
Will H.	HRY	232
Will.	KNX	312
Will.	SCT	98A
Will.	SCT	130A
Will.	SCT	135A
William	TRG	14
William	BNE	22
William	FLD	37
William	FLD	43
William	MER	100
William	WDF	104
William	BLT	158
William	NSN	179
William	NSN	191
William	MNR	201
William	HRY	204
William	HAR	212
William	HAR	214
William	BTL	325
William	WYN	93A
William	WDF	96A
William	NCH	109A
William	WTY	112A
William	NCH	116A
William C.	GTN	119
William S.	SHE	169
William S.	SHE	177
Williamson	WRN	34A
Willis	HRY	249
Wm.	CHN	36
Wm.	CHN	44
Wm.	FKN	62
Wm.	FKN	134
Wm.	BBN	138
Wm.	ALN	140
Wm.	MAD	174
JOHNSON, Wm.	BRK	265
Wm., Jr.	BRK	265
Wm.	PND	25A
Wm. T.?	FKN	116
Zacariah	FTE	75
Zachariah	CLY	129
Zachariah	GTN	132
JOHNSON?, John	LVG	16
JOHNSTON, -----?	DVS	5A
-----?	DVS	5A
-----? W.?	DVS	19A
Allin	WRN	66A
Anthy.	MAS	75
Archibald	SHE	172
Armura	BTH	212
Arthur	JEF	43
Ben W.	JEF	38
Benja.	JEF	45
Benja.	SHE	140A
Benja. L.	SHE	141A
Benjamin	MAD	146
Benjamin	MTG	265
Benjamin	WRN	49A
Bryan	JEF	39
Calvan	SPN	4A
Cornelius	CBL	7A
Daniel	MTG	277
David	BTH	212
David	MTG	277
David	SHE	118A
Delicia	WRN	71A
Dixon	SHE	118A
Edward	MAD	156
Elisha	HRD	88
Elizabeth	WRN	67A
Enos	HRD	42
Frances	JEF	35
Francis	WRN	36A
Francis W.	GRN	67
Ga. J.	JEF	26
Geo.	JEF	38
Geo.	JEF	43
George	BKN	16
Henry	HRD	76
Henry	MAD	98
Hugh	MTG	291
Hugh	WRN	61A
Igs.?	WAS	41A
Isaac	ADR	58
Isaac	HRT	162
Jacob	MTG	271
James	BKN	22
James	LGN	31
James	LGN	32
James	MAD	118
James	MAD	162
James	SHE	175
James	BTH	216
James	WRN	49A
James	SHE	118A
James	SHE	125A
James J./ I.?	LGN	29
Jas.	ADR	50
Jas.	MAS	53
Jas.	MAS	77
Jessee	LGN	33
Jessee	HRT	161
Jessey	MAD	100
Jno.	MAS	79
John	HRD	8
John	HRD	12
John	LGN	32
John	HRD	52
John	GRN	59
John	LNC	61
John	GRN	63

Name	County	Page
JOHNSTON, John	MAD	140
John	MBG	142
John	MAD	170
John	BTH	216
John	HOP	250
John	MTG	293
John	WAS	54A
John	WAS	76A
John	LWS	86A
John	LWS	90A
Jones	SHE	173
Joseph	LGN	33
Joseph	LGN	45
Joseph	SHE	118A
Lampson	CSY	216
Lanta	SHE	118A
Lanta	SHE	118A
Levi	MTG	275
Lewis	ADR	4
Liddia	SHE	175
Maj. M.	LNC	25
Matthew	HRD	52
Matthew	MAD	114
Matthew	WAS	54A
Matthew	WAS	72A
Mjor?	MAD	128
Nancy	LGN	34
Pearson	JEF	44
Peteway	WRN	28A
Philip	MAD	158
Philip	SHE	163
Polly	LNC	69
Reubin	WRN	55A
Richard	MAD	156
Robert	ADR	30
Robert	MAD	130
Robert	HOP	250
Robt	ADR	30
Robt.	HRD	74
Robt.	RCK	81A
Samuel	LGN	31
Samuel	MTG	235
Samuel	HOP	250
Sarah	SHE	163
Silvanas	WRN	46A
Starling	MAD	100
Stephen	MAD	108
Tandy, Jr.	WRN	66A
Tandy	WRN	65A
Thomas	SHE	175
Thomas	WRN	45A
Thos.	ADR	16
Thos.	CWL	36
Thos.	JEF	62
Thos. B.	ADR	28
W. B.	MAS	58
William	LGN	33
William	LGN	36
William	GRN	67
William	CLK	82
William	HAR	158
William	SHE	163
William	CBL	3A
William	WRN	49A
William	WRN	62A
Willm.	LNC	67
Wm.	MAD	114
Wm.	MAD	146
Wm.	WAS	43A
Wm.	SHE	111A
Wm.	SHE	120A
Zack	WAS	78A
JOHNSTON?, -----?, Jr.	DVS	5A
-----?	DVS	7A
JOHNSTONE, Jane	FTE	63
JOHSTON?, James?	CLK	85
JOINDER?, Thomas	LVG	12
JOINER, Amos	MNR	199
Israel	TRG	7A
Johnathan	LVG	3
Jonas	CWL	37
Thomas	TRG	8
William	TRG	7A
Wm.	CWL	37
JOLLEY, Nelson	BRK	265
Petter	PND	26A
JOLLIFF, James, Jr.	BRN	17
James, Senr.	BRN	17
JOLLY, James	NCH	115A
John	BBN	90
John	LWS	92A
John	NCH	115A
Saml.	BRK	265
Solomon	HAR	180
Susannah	GSN	140A
JOLLY?, David	LWS	92A
JONAS, Thomas	SPN	16A
JONAS?, Robert, Jr.	GTN	132
JONATHAN, Peter	LNC	2
JONES, ---.?	CWL	42
---.?	CWL	42
---.?	CWL	42
Aaron	NSN	197
Abm.	BBN	110
Abner	GRN	63
Abner	WYN	90A
Abraham	BRN	17
Abraham	FTE	90
Abraham	MAD	166
Abraham	WRN	70A
Abram	GRD	115A
Adam	HND	8A
Adis	FLD	17
Affia	BBN	146
Alexander	HRT	161
Alexander, Sr.	NSN	176
Allen	MAS	54
Allen	CSY	218
Allen	SPN	8A
Allin	SPN	4A
Alvan	WYN	81A
Ambrose	FLD	9
Andrew	BTH	210
Ann	FLG	32A
Anthony D.	CHN	40
Aquilla	HRD	88
Armstead	SCT	131A
Arthur	CSY	220
Asa	FTE	80
Asa	FKN	110
Asa	SHE	151
Bartholomew	LGN	29
Ben.	HRY	265
Benj.	FKN	106
Benj. M.	CWL	40
Benja.	JEF	49
Benja.	SHE	125A
Benja. W.	JEF	65
Benjamin	BNE	22
Benjamin	BBN	62
Benjamin	BTH	156
Benjamin	SHE	169
Benjamin	WYN	99A
Benjamine	WRN	40A
Benjn.	BBN	142
Bethia	WRN	40A
Betsey	MER	99
Betsey	MAD	140
Burril	TOD	127
JONES, Cadwaler	BTH	190
Cadwallader	BRN	17
Caleb	PUL	59A
Charles	TRG	13
Charles	ADC	68
Charles	OWN	101
Charles	BLT	174
Charles	BTH	190
Charles, Sen.	ADR	30
Charls	ADR	30
Chas.?	CWL	42
Christopher	MER	114
Christopher	DVS	19A
Chrles L.	CHN	40
Claybourn	MNR	213
Cyrus	GNP	173A
Daniel	BBN	126
Daniel	CLY	131
Daniel	HRY	243
Daniel	WRN	74A
Daniel	SHE	141A
Daniel M.	SPN	17A
Danl.	JEF	63
Darlin?	KNX	312
David	ADR	30
David	ADR	30
David	CWL	54
David	FTE	82
David	MER	117
David	CLD	149
David	CSY	206
David, Esq.	MER	100
David	GNP	173A
David T.	HOP	252
Drury	NCH	123A
Dudley	CWL	54
Dudley	MTG	269
Dumas	HAR	210
Dynold	FLG	33A
E. Moses	GSN	140A
Edmond	SHE	120A
Edmund	HRL	112
Edward	CLK	85
Edward	SHE	141A
Edwd.	HRD	34
Edwd.	BBN	104
Eleazer	BRN	17
Elija	BTH	220
Elijah	GRN	73
Elijah	HRL	112
Elijah	WRN	49A
Elizabeth	HRL	112
Elizabeth	BRK	265
Elizbeth	CWL	54
Elliot	WYN	80A
Elz?	RCK	81A
Evan	LNC	29
Evin, Junr.	HAR	134
Evin, Senr.	HAR	134
F. Phillip	HRT	161
Fanny / Tanny?	GRN	72
Fielding	FKN	86
Fielding	UNN	148
Fleming	MNR	213
Fleming	FLG	32A
Fountain	WRN	76A
Frances	BBN	104
Francis	BTH	154
Francis	GRD	106A
Frederick	TRG	8A
Gabriel	HRL	112
Gabriel	CLY	120
Gabril	MAD	126
Garden	BBN	116
Garrard	BBN	108
Geo.	HRY	228

Name	County	Page
JONES, George	GTN	125
George	TOD	127
George	HAR	134
George	CLD	146
George	HRT	161
George	BLT	170
George	MAD	174
George	BLT	186
George	KNX	294
George	WYN	103A
George W.	HRT	162
Giles	CLK	86
H-----?	ALN	112
Hampton	HND	11A
Henry	HND	11
Henry	GRN	56
Henry	BLT	166
Henry	CHN	41A
Henry	SCT	119A
Henry H.	SHE	143A
Hezekiah	JEF	19
Igana?	NCH	124A
Irvine	MAD	152
Isaac	BBN	104
Isaac	CLY	118
Isaac	CLY	129
Isaac	HAR	196
Isham	WTY	119A
Isreal	HRY	263
Jacob	BRN	17
Jacob	BBN	134
Jacob	BBN	142
Jacob	SHE	169
Jacob	HAR	188
Jacob?	NCH	103A
James	HND	9
James	LNC	29
James	MER	99
James, --?	WYN	83A
James	BBN	104
James	GTN	125
James	BTH	154
James	CLD	159
James	BTH	174
James	BLT	178
James	MTG	247
James	BRK	265
James	MTG	275
James, Jr.	WYN	91A
James, Sr.	WYN	96A
James	OHO	10A
James	TRG	11A
James	DVS	14A
James	WRN	33A
James	WYN	79A
James	SCT	104A
James	SHE	121A
James	WTY	127A
James	GSN	141A
James	GSN	141A
James M.	UNN	153
Jane	CLD	149
Jas.	MAS	53
Jas.	HRY	240
Jas., Jr.	FLG	26A
Jas., Snr.	FLG	28A
Jas.	FLG	44A
Jas.	FLG	50A
Jas.	RCK	76A
Jason D.	LVG	9
Jesse	MAS	65
Jesse	MAS	65
Jesse	MER	99
Jesse	MER	100
Jesse	BLT	166
Jesse	MTG	229
JONES, Jesse, Jr.	BLT	186
Jesse	SPN	16A
Jesse	SPN	17A
Jesse	WRN	48A
Jessee	MBG	135A
Jessey	MAD	126
Jessey	MAD	150
Jno.	CWL	54
Jno.	MAS	61
Jno.	FKN	76
Jno.	FKN	146
Jno. W.	JEF	49
John	FLD	10
John	BNE	22
John	LNC	29
John	CWL	32
John	JEF	32
John	JEF	38
John	CWL	39
John	ETL	51
John	CWL	54
John	GRN	59
John	HRD	60
John	FTE	69
John	CLK	75
John	BBN	76
John	FTE	94
John	MER	99
John	MER	100
John	MER	100
John	FTE	112
John	HRL	112
John	CLY	119
John	CLY	121
John	CLY	121
John	GTN	123
John	CLY	126
John	HAR	134
John	CLD	140
John	MAD	144
John	CLD	152
John	BTH	156
John	BLT	190
John	BTH	192
John	NSN	194
John	BTH	196
John	MNR	197
John	HAR	204
John	HAR	210
John	HRY	230
John, Jr.	CSY	210
John, Jr.	CSY	210
John, Sr.	MER	100
John	TRG	13A
John	FLG	32A
John	FLG	73A
John	WYN	80A
John	GRD	103A
John	GRD	114A
John	NCH	117A
John	SCT	119A
John	GSN	141A
John	SHE	141A
John	GNP	173A
John A.	HND	10A
John H.	SCT	133A
John L.	JEF	63
John L.	SHE	159
John L.	SHE	174
John R.	WAS	52A
John R.	WAS	76A
John S.	SHE	126A
John W.	BBN	120
Johnathan	WYN	103A
Johnathan	WYN	104A
Jonath.	HRY	256
JONES, Jonathan	CLD	149
Jonathan	SPN	10A
Jonathan	PUL	39A
Jos.	CWL	33
Joseph	TRG	3
Joseph	MAS	76
Joseph	JES	97
Joseph	MAD	100
Joseph	BBN	110
Joseph	FTE	112
Joseph	CLY	118
Joseph	GTN	120
Joseph	GTN	121
Joseph	NSN	206
Joseph	MTG	225
Joseph	MTG	237
Joseph, Sr.	GTN	120
Joseph	FLG	51A
Joseph	SCT	119A
Joseph	SCT	127A
Joshua	FLD	41
Joshua	BBN	92
Joshua	MER	99
Joshua	MAD	114
Joshua	SHE	166
Joshua	HAR	216
Joshua	PND	16A
Joshua	PND	18A
Joshua	PUL	68A
Josiah	SHE	152
Labon	CLK	80
Landy	CLD	164
Lemuel	MNR	193
Lemuel?	TRG	7A
Lenard	WAS	70A
Leonard	DVS	18A
Leroy	BNE	22
Levi	HND	9A
Levi	PUL	43A
Levi	FLG	44A
Levin	ADR	30
Levy	ETL	40
Lewis	TRG	3
Lewis	BRN	17
Lewis	JES	94
Lewis	CLY	121
Lewis	HAR	134
Lewis	MAD	152
Lewis	HRT	161
Lewis	CHN	41A
Littleberry	MNR	201
Lowry	SHE	169
Lunsford	GRD	89A
Margaret	MAD	122
Marshal	HAR	158
Martha	FLG	63A
Martin	GSN	141A
Mary	HAR	136
Mary	FLG	32A
Mathew	BTH	202
Matthew	MTG	243
Matthew	MTG	253
Merrit S.	MAD	180
Michael	BRN	33
Michael	CSY	204
Michael	WRN	57A
Milly	CLD	149
Morgan	GRN	79
Moses	CLY	121
Moses	HRY	232
Moses	NCH	103A
Moses	GNP	173A
Moss	MER	100
Nancy	FLD	32
Nathan	SCT	99A
Nathaniel	GSN	140A

JONES, Nelson R. FTE 58
Newman SPN 6A
Newman SPN 25A
Newton C. CSY 210
Nicholas CLK 80
P. P. ADC 68
Peter CWL 54
Peter GRN 63
Peter MBG 135
Peter MAD 148
Peter WRN 39A
Peter LWS 89A
Peter SCT 119A
Phebe JEF 32
Philip LGN 33
Philip, Sn. GSN 141A
Philip GSN 141A
Phoebe GTN 119
Rachel SHE 164
Rebecca CLK 93
Redmond HRD 62
Reuben MER 99
Rial HRL 112
Richard FLD 7
Richard HND 13
Richard LGN 30
Richard CLK 90
Richard ALN 112
Richard HAR 186
Richard TRG 12A
Richard WAS 85A
Richard L. SHE 132A
Richardson SHE 130A
Richd. BBN 104
Robert TRG 13
Robert GRN 58
Robert FTE 82
Robert OWN 104
Robert CSY 224
Robert KNX 312
Robert W. MER 100
Robt. ADR 28
Robt. ADR 28
Robt. (A Negro) JEF 65
Robt.? CWL 42
Rodham SHE 121A
Roger FTE 81
Rosanna UNN 147
Rubin FLG 44A
Saml. CWL 33
Saml. CHN 40
Saml. HRY 252
Saml. BRK 265
Saml. CHN 41A
Saml. FLG 48A
Saml. FLG 77A
Saml. A. MAD 90
Sampson BRN 17
Samuel FTE 95
Samuel MER 99
Samuel MER 100
Samuel GTN 125
Samuel BTH 156
Samuel BTH 158
Samuel BTH 168
Samuel WRN 55A
Samuel D. MAD 146
Sarah GRN 73
Silas SHE 164
Simon WTY 116A
Simon WTY 127A
Sol. HRY 252
Souarin? CSY 210
Stafford SCT 119A
Steph. HRY 247
Stephen JEF 38
JONES, Stephen HRL 112
Stephen FLG 41A
Stephen FLG 77A
Stephne FLG 65A
Strother MBG 143A
Sturdy? HRD 62
Susanna MNR 207
Susannah NCH 123A
Tarlton WRN 47A
Thala.? HRY 252
Tho. RCK 81A
Thomas BNE 22
Thomas ETL 47
Thomas CWL 54
Thomas CLK 70
Thomas OWN 101
Thomas BBN 102
Thomas GTN 119
Thomas HAR 140
Thomas SHE 150
Thomas BTH 154
Thomas HRT 161
Thomas HRY 200
Thomas HOP 250
Thomas MTG 271
Thomas SPN 17A
Thomas WRN 61A
Thomas WYN 82A
Thomas SHE 121A
Thomas GSN 140A
Thomas E. CSY 206
Thomas G. CLK 101
Thornton OWN 101
Thos. BKN 9
Thos. HND 10
Thos. JEF 20
Thos. CWL 33
Thos. GRN 69
Thos. BBN 114
Thos. HRY 260
Thos. FLG 32A
Thos. FLG 34A
Thos. CHN 41A
Thos. WAS 52A
Thos. FLG 61A
Thos. FLG 77A
Thos. A.? CLK 103
Thos? D. HND 11A
Timothy TRG 7A
Umphrey MAD 156
Walter LGN 23
Walter ADR 28
Washington BLT 172
Watkins HRT 161
Wayman HND 12
Wharton BBN 108
Wiley CLY 120
Wiley B. TOD 125
Will SCT 99A
Will SCT 102A
Will. TOD 127
William TRG 3
William FLD 10
William HND 10
William HND 13
William TRG 14
William FLD 22
William GRN 65
William GRN 68
William GRN 77
William JES 88
William FTE 94
William MER 99
William OWN 105
William CLY 129
William HAR 132
JONES, William UNN 153
William HRT 161
William SHE 169
William BLT 174
William MNR 195
William MNR 205
William MNR 213
William HOP 252
William, Sr. CBL 8A
William CHN 31A
William WRN 41A
William WRN 44A
William WRN 52A
William WYN 80A
William WYN 82A
William WTY 113A
William NCH 122A
William WTY 123A
William NCH 124A
William WTY 124A
William S. BLT 178
William S. NSN 194
Willis MBG 142
Wm. ADR 28
Wm. ADR 28
Wm. JEF 32
Wm. CWL 33
Wm. CWL 34
Wm. CWL 54
Wm. CWL 58
Wm. FKN 96
Wm. BBN 104
Wm. BBN 116
Wm. MAD 178
Wm. HRY 256
Wm. HRY 259
Wm. BRK 265
Wm. OHO 9A
Wm. PND 24A
Wm. WAS 36A
Wm. FLG 38A
Wm. FLG 52A
Wm. RCK 81A
Wm. SHE 120A
Wm. B. FLG 65A
Wm. R. HRD 46
Woodford HOP 250
Wyatt HRY 190
Younger BLT 186
Zacariah HRD 36
Zaccariah HRL 112
Zachariah WDF 124A
Zadock CSY 208
Wm. GSN 140A
JONES?, Allen ADR 32
Joathan FLD 12
Thomas FLD 12
JONIER, Rebecca CLK 106
JONS?, Aurlen / Amben? ADR 30
JONSON, Washington GRD 98A
JONSTON, Alexander M. CLK 65
Michael LNC 47
JOPLING?, Edwana W. MAD 136
JORDAN, -----? DVS 9A
-----? DVS 9A
-----? DVS 10A
Efferilla CLK 92
Garrot MER 100
Geo. FKN 138
John BRN 17
John MER 100
John MAD 144
John BLT 188

JORDAN, Jos., Jr. BKN 10
Patrick MER 100
Peter MER 100
Peter, Col. MER 100
Saml. BRN 17
Samuel CLD 160
Thos., Sr. BKN 10
JORDEN, Arther HND 9A
Henry GNP 166A
Jas. FLG 49A
Polly FLG 49A
Thos. FLG 49A
Wm., Jr. GNP 171A
JORDON, Charles BRK 265
Edward BRK 267
Saml. BRK 265
Wm., Ser. GNP 172A
Woodsen BRK 265
JOREY?, Allen ADR 32
JORIGG?, James CSY 206
JOSEPH, (Free) ADR 70
Sarah HRD 94
William FLD 13
JOSEY, John C. MBG 143A
JOSLIN, Benjamin CSY 222
John J. CSY 210
Rebecca GRD 119A
JOST?, Christian FLD 24
JOUETT, Charles TRG 11
John BTH 202
JOUITT?, Matthew FTE 112
JOURDAN, Hiram FLD 45
Jesse FLD 45
Jonas FLD 45
Samuel CLD 159
Samuel HAR 218
William CLD 159
JOYCE, George BLT 154
Richard BLT 152
JOYES, Thos. JEF 30
JUD, Harvey JEF 35
John ADR 28
Joseph ADR 28
Nat ADR 28
Squre ADR 28
JUDAH, Amos MTG 235
Samuel MTG 226
JUDD, Boswell C. HND 4A
Danl. MAS 62
Jno. MAS 62
Nathan GRN 61
Robert GRN 57
Timothy HRY 178
JUDKINS, Jas. TOD 133
Samuel LGN 33
JUDRY?, Harvy CLK 98
Martin CLK 98
JUDY, David CLK 83
Winepark CLK 84
JUETT, John SCT 112A
Joseph GRT 146
JUITT, Jack WAS 77A
JULIAN, Chs. FKN 120
Saml. HND 11A
JUMP, John BBN 130
John GRT 144
John, Jr. GRT 144
John, Senr. GRT 144
Joseph GRT 144
Robert F. GRT 142
Valentine GRT 144
William GRT 142
William GRT 144
JUMUYS?, Hatsel? NSN 182
JUNE?, Henry OWN 105
JUNEL, Andrew HND 13
JUNIPER, Ned FTE 61
JUNKENS, Jacob MNR 207
JUNKINS, Noble BNE 22
JUPIN?, Barbary NSN 193
Freeborn NSN 183
Lewis NSN 185
JUSKS?, Danl. BKN 4
Joseph BKN 4
JUSSIN?, Barbary NSN 193
Freeborn NSN 183
JUSTI--?, Hugh -. ALN 94
JUSTICE, Archebald FLD 43
Edmond FLD 17
Ezra FLD 26
George FLD 26
Israel FLD 17
Jarral / Isrral? ALN 108
John FLD 17
John FLD 20
John FLD 25
Peyton FLD 25
Simeon FLD 26
Simeon FLD 43
Simson FLD 17
Thomas FLD 25
Tubal/ Jubal? FLD 23
Wm.? FLD 23
JUSTON, Buchner WRN 70A
JUSTONE, Jno. FKN 116
JUVINALL?, David FLG 38A

K--HTER?, Danl. BKN 20
K--N?, Oliver FTE 60
KAGUN, Arthur MNR 191
KAIN, Jas. JEF 58
KALFUS, Henry F. JEF 63
KALOGG, Isaac BBN 86
KAMINSKY, J. C. JEF 19
KAMPLIN, Zeph. BBN 132
KANAN, William BNE 22
KANARD, David ADR 30
KANE, Michael HRD 70
Patrick LVG 5
Thomas FTE 59
Will. LVG 5
KANE?, Richd. BKN 9
KANOTE, John MAD 128
John MAD 128
KARAC, Walter CLK 105
KARIAC?, Jno. LVG 7
KARNES, Elizabeth ADR 14
John ADR 56
Ralph ADR 30
KARNS, John BNE 22
John ADR 32
KARR, James GTN 124
Jno. HRY 249
John MAD 124
KAS, James CLK 64
KASH, Caleb FLD 11
James FLD 11
KAUKWELL, John SCT 131A
KAVANAUGH, Charles MAD 132
Elizabeth MAD 136
Philamon MAD 132
Thomas CBL 15A
Wm. MAD 124
KAVENAUGH, Wm. FKN 160
KAY, James CHN 45
James FTE 106
John FTE 100
Mary FTE 111
Robert FTE 90
KAYE, Reed &? JEF 26
KAYLE, Wm. JEF 45
KAYS, Francis HRT 162
KAYS, George MNR 205
John HRT 162
John WRN 48A
William WRN 48A
KAYS?, William MNR 201
KAYSTON, Thos. MAD 94
KAYWOOD, Asa FLG 76A
Erasmus FLG 39A
Stephen FLG 75A
Thos. FLG 39A
KEAGAN, Patrick FTE 98
KEAL, Thos. WAS 84A
KEAN, Benjamin SHE 110A
Fleming SHE 140A
Francis GRN 79
Francis CLD 156
John CLD 156
Nicholas CLD 156
Patrick NSN 206
Polly CLD 165
Sarah WDF 97A
KEARNEY, Wm. JEF 65
Wm., Jr. JEF 50
KEARSEY, William SHE 176
KEAS, Isaac CLK 70
KEASTON?, William FTE 57
KEATH, Garnett HAR 154
John DVS 18A
KEATH?, Jesse HAR 166
Richd., Jnr. HAR 166
Richd., Snr. HAR 166
KEATON, John HRY 180
William HRY 208
Wm. JEF 51
KEAWN, Andrew BTL 325
John BTL 325
William BTL 325
KEE, Henry MAD 140
Martin GSN 141A
KEECH, Chas. FLG 39A
KEEL, Abraham WRN 63A
Geo. FLG 69A
Jacob FLG 69A
Jas. WRN 73A
Jesse WRN 68A
John WRN 73A
KEELER, Thadius CBL 2A
KEELER?, George MTG 283
KEELIN?, Wm.? CWL 36
KEELING, Edmund TOD 127
James HRT 162
John UNN 153
Leonard MTG 295
Wm HRD 28
KEEN, Greenup? SCT 102A
John LNC 11
John FTE 108
Jonathan CBL 16A
Oliver FTE 112
Rachel LNC 11
Sanford FTE 65
Sanford FTE 112
Thos. JEF 30
KEENAN, Patrick OHO 6A
KEENE, Aaron CBL 16A
Edward SPN 8A
John CBL 10A
Joseph CBL 10A
Ricd. T. SCT 106A
Vachel SCT 126A
Will B. SCT 103A
KEENE?, (See Kune?) GTN 134
KEENNELL, George MAD 102
KEENY, Henry PUL 60A
Jas. PUL 46A

KEENY, Moses PUL 57A
KEEREE?, Benjamin B. HOP 252
KEES, William HAR 178
KEESER?, Adam FTE 79
KEETEN, John CLD 146
Jospeh FLD 22
William FLD 21
William CLD 146
KEETER?, George MTG 283
KEETH, George SCT 120A
Walter BBN 86
KEETING, --ch-.? CWL 41
--s.? CWL 41
KEETING?, Wm. HRD 28
KEETON, Abraham FLD 10
Allin WYN 94A
Hezekh. SCT 130A
Hezekiah SCT 124A
Isaac FLD 10
James WYN 91A
Joel WYN 99A
John FLD 19
Julius WYN 99A
Miles WYN 99A
Nelson FLD 19
Peter, Sr. WYN 91A
William WYN 91A
Wm. HRT 162
KEETON?, Barney FLD 10
KEETS, Obadiah HND 8
KEEZEE, Avara FLD 36
Elias FLD 20
Richard FLD 36
KEIGER, John FTE 63
KEIGHTOR, John BBN 126
KEIRNES?, William BTH 160
KEISER?, Benjamin FTE 59
KEITH, A. D. BKN 24
Adam HAR 182
Edwd. BBN 138
Enos HRD 72
Gabriel MTG 257
Henry HAR 180
Henry MBG 136A
Isaac FLG 66A
James MBG 138
John MBG 138
John WRN 50A
John FLG 66A
John WYN 93A
John NCH 114A
Jonathan HRD 60
Joseph MBG 138
Peyton R. MAS 75
Tho. MAS 67
Uriah MTG 263
William HRD 10
William MBG 138
William HAR 188
Wm. HRD 82
KEITH?, George BKN 13
James W. CLK 105
KEITHLY, John BTH 194
Joseph BBN 130
KEIZOR?, John CBL 10A
KELLAR, Abraham H. JEF 64
Abram JEF 42
Isaac JEF 44
Moses JEF 42
Rebecca JEF 64
KELLEN?, Joseph JEF 32
KELLER, Abm. BBN 142
Duvalt PUL 53A
Elizabeth JES 82
Frederick GSN 141A
KELLER, George GSN 141A
Isaac FKN 100
Jacob JES 82
Jacob GSN 141A
John FTE 100
John MER 100
Leonard HRD 70
Michael LGN 39
Saml. GSN 141A
Valentine MER 100
KELLERSON, Jos. ADR 30
Robt. ADR 30
KELLEY, -----? DVS 8A
Abraham CBL 7A
Benjn. OHO 4A
Cornilious WAS 76A
Dan. HRY 251
Daniel WAS 76A
Edwd. SCT 128A
Elizabeth BRN 18
George P. SCT 121A
Giles BRN 18
Isaac HRL 112
James ALN 124
James HAR 218
Jane MAD 120
Jesse MTG 249
John FLD 13
John FLD 13
John BRN 18
John OWN 101
John MTG 265
John WAS 63A
John MBG 139A
Johnathan HRL 112
Joseph MER 100
Joseph? MAD 118
Marton GRN 57
Mathew GRN 73
Matthias HRL 112
Moses CBL 10A
Reuben BRN 18
Robt. HRT 162
Thomas FLD 45
Thomas GTN 125
Thomas GNP 167A
Walter BRN 18
Will. SCT 127A
Will. SCT 128A
William MER 100
William H. FLD 27
Wm. SHE 129A
Wm. L. WAS 41A
Zachiriah BRK 267
KELLIN, Theophis.? CWL 38
Wills CWL 44
KELLIS, Clem M. HRY 222
Frances BBN 142
Sarah BBN 140
KELLISON, Absalom GRD 87A
KELLTY, William NSN 182
KELLUM, John LWS 88A
Richard LWS 98A
KELLY, (Blank) JEF 27
-irey? CWL 43
Alexander MTG 233
Alexander MTG 269
Amos HRY 251
Andrew ETL 53
Andrew WDF 101A
Basel NSN 187
Beckham LNC 9
Benj. CHN 41
Benjn. H. OHO 7A
Betsy MNR 205
Caleb MNR 201
KELLY, Chas. CWL 33
Chas.? CWL 36
Daniel FKN 114
Dennis WRN 50A
Elias WYN 93A
Elijah GSN 141A
Elzabeth NSN 176
Frederick GSN 141A
George, Sr. WYN 101A
George WAS 57A
Gideon HRD 60
Griffing CLK 80
Henry FTE 66
Henry LWS 97A
Isaac LNC 33
Jacob HRY 251
Jacob HRY 256
James FTE 65
James CLK 69
James HRY 232
James MTG 245
James OHO 8A
Jane FTE 108
Jas. FLG 35A
Jessee BNE 22
Jno. HRY 244
Jno. PUL 36A
John FLD 14
John CWL 37
John JEF 41
John ETL 49
John, Jr. SPN 19A
John, Sr. SPN 18A
John WRN 35A
John PUL 65A
John FLG 74A
John WYN 81A
John LWS 92A
John GRD 122A
John GSN 141A
John R. NSN 187
Jonathan HRL 112
Jos. CHN 41
Jos. PUL 36A
Jos./ Jas.? HRY 250
Joseph CLK 80
Joseph KNX 298
Joseph SPN 22A
Marshall WRN 68A
Martin L. SPN 9A
Nancy WRN 50A
Peggy LNC 79
Philip JES 72
Richard MTG 233
Robert WAS 38A
Saml. JEF 53
Saml. BBN 122
Saml. HRY 251
Saml. HRY 251
Samuel ETL 44
Samuel PUL 61A
Susanna NSN 187
Thomas BNE 22
Thomas NSN 197
Thomas WRN 49A
Thomas NCH 103A
Thos. JEF 25
Valand? MAS 58
Will. MAS 64
William NSN 177
William MTG 265
William LWS 92A
William LWS 93A
William R. OHO 7A
Wm. BBN 114
Wm. HRY 251

Name	County	Page
KELLY, Francis	FLG	39A
KELMS, Hirum	BRK	267
Jinsey	BRK	267
Wm.	BRK	267
KELSAW, John	ETL	40
KELSEY, Alexander	WYN	93A
Hugh B.	BRN	18
John	BRN	18
William	HRT	162
KELSO, Isaac	CBL	14A
Jane	CLD	138
Wm.	BKN	18
KELSOE, Andrew	ADR	30
Charles	HAR	214
James	MNR	199
John	ADR	30
John, Jr.	BTH	200
John, Jr.	MTG	255
John, Sr.	BTH	200
John, Sr.	MTG	255
Robert	GTN	127
Robert	BTH	166
Robt.	ADR	30
Thos.	ADR	30
Walker	BTH	178
KELTINER?, John	ADR	30
KELTNER, Micheal	ADR	30
Micheal	ADR	54
KEMBROUGH, Robert H.	NCH	128A
KEMP, Charles	PND	20A
Edw., Jr.	PND	26A
Edward	LVG	12
Edward, Jr.	PND	19A
Edward	PND	29A
James	BKN	5
John	WRN	48A
Marshal	ADR	3
William	WDF	95A
Willis	MAD	158
Wm.	HRD	44
KEMPE/ KEMPER?, William	GRD	108A
KEMPER, A. S.	GRD	113A
Benjamin	GTN	119
Burditt	GRD	87A
Henry	FLG	29A
Joel	HRY	224
John	GRD	102B
Jonathan	GTN	119
Nancy	GRD	117A
Nimrod	GTN	120
Nimrod	GTN	126
Reuben	MTG	226
Thomas	MBG	136
Thornton	GRD	116A
Westley	BLT	172
William	MTG	281
KEMPLE, Adam K.	FTE	77
KEN--Y?, William	FTE	98
KENADAY, Andrew	PND	20A
Robert	CLK	106
KENADY, James	PUL	43A
KENDAL, Aaron	MAS	53
Jeremiah, Sr.	BRK	267
KENDALL, (See Kindall)	NSN	
Amos	FKN	66
Baily A.	NSN	180
Elijah	FKN	84
Enoch	HRD	22
Enoch	DVS	16A
Jacob	NSN	183
Jeremiah	FKN	84
John V.	JEF	27
Joseph	BBN	118
KENDALL, Joseph	BBN	134
Peter	HRD	90
Rolla	JEF	39
Stephen	NSN	183
Sterne	GRT	139
William	NSN	180
KENDELL, Jas.	TOD	131A
KENDLE, Peter	FLG	61A
Rolly	FLG	56A
KENDOLL, John	GTN	119
John	GTN	129
KENDRICK, Abraham	MAS	67
Benjn.	BBN	136
Danl. B.	SCT	112A
Jacob	SCT	121A
John	BBN	118
John	LWS	86A
Joseph	BBN	136
Mitchel	SCT	102A
Turner	CSY	226
Walter	JEF	21
Will.	SCT	112A
Winifred	SCT	112A
Wm.	WAS	52A
Wm.	WAS	87A
Wm.	SHE	138A
KENEDAY, Elliott	MAS	59
KENEDY, Chas.	CWL	55
David, Sr.	GRD	119A
James	BNE	22
Jno.	CWL	55
Joseph	BNE	22
Moses	UNN	148
KENER, Abraham	CHN	44A
KENERDY, James	BBN	64
Nathan	BBN	96
Wm.	BBN	80
KENEY, John	JES	88
KENEY?, Miridith	GRD	122A
KENHAM?, William	WRN	65A
KENINGHAM, Milly	GRD	116A
KENISTER, Henry	JEF	58
KENLER?, Lewis	LVG	16
KENLY, John	MAD	144
KENNADY, Daniel	BLT	160
Jesse	GRT	140
John	GRT	140
Js.	HRY	198
Mathew	WDF	101A
KENNARD, James	FLD	7
James	LWS	98A
Joseph	MAD	94
William	LWS	98A
Wm.	MAS	73
KENNEDAY, George	BLT	162
James	ETL	54
Jno.	JEF	42
John	ETL	54
Priscilla	NSN	205
Richard L.	ETL	54
KENNEDY, Abasalom	WRN	50A
Andrew	MAD	98
Andrew	GRD	96A
Arthur	MAD	94
Benjamin	FTE	94
Blatt	CBL	5A
Charles	WDF	100
D.	MIT	101A
David	LVG	11
David	HOP	252
David, Sen.	NCH	111A
Eli	BBN	116
Esther	BBN	108
Henry	HRD	22
James	MER	100
James	CBL	21A
KENNEDY, Jas.	GRD	96A
Jesse	BBN	108
Jo., Sr.?	GRD	96A
John	HRD	26
John	LGN	29
John	HRD	38
John	MER	100
John	FTE	111
John	BBN	134
John, Jr.	LGN	29
Joseph	BBN	116
Joseph	MAD	176
Joseph	CBL	5A
Mathew	FTE	65
Philip	MER	100
Saml.	HRD	22
Samuel	HRD	12
Thomas, Jr.	CBL	10A
Thomas	CBL	3A
Thomas	GRD	120A
Thos.	HRD	20
Wahington	BBN	108
Will.	LVG	8
William	WRN	50A
KENNER, David	GNP	166A
Radhum?	LGN	28
Rodham	LGN	29
Sarah	FLG	29A
KENNERBY, John	LGN	45
KENNERDAY, William	JES	93
KENNERLEY?, Philip	LGN	45
KENNETT, Ann	WAS	28A
Joseph	BLT	186
Joshua D.	BLT	184
Press G.	PND	15A
Wm. C.	PND	15A
KENNETZER, Christopher	MAD	104
Wm.	MAD	106
KENNEY, A., Dr.	BBN	128
David	GNP	168A
Eli	BBN	60
John	GSN	141A
Margaretta	BBN	60
Thos.	SCT	135A
Wm.	GRN	53
KENNIDY, John	WDF	97A
KENNING?, Jno.	HAR	164
KENNINGHAM, John	MAD	150
Lyne S.	KNX	284
KENNISON, John R.	BLT	162
KENNON, Robert	CLK	97
Wm.	FLG	62A
KENNY, Fras.	HAR	150
John	BBN	116
Matthew	FTE	88
Moses	FTE	83
Moses	FTE	102
Moses	HAR	142
Patsey	MTG	257
Robert P.	CLK	66
KENON, John G.	HAR	220
KENRICK, Bennedict	FTE	60
KENSER?, Frederic	PUL	66A
KENT, David	FTE	86
David	FTE	86
Henry	FTE	86
Isaac	WYN	79A
Samuel T.	GTN	131
KENTON, Jno.	MAS	58
William	NCH	105
KENYON, Will.	SCT	120A
Wm.	MAS	76
KEOWN, Elizabeth	WRN	39A
Nathan	WRN	37A
KEPHART, Henry	BTH	216

KEPLINGER, John BBN 134
Philip BBN 120
KERBY, David WRN 67A
David WRN 69A
Elisha MAD 136
Elisha MAD 164
Francis JES 91
Henry JES 94
Isaiah WRN 69A
James HND 12
James PND 20A
Jesse WRN 67A
John NCH 128A
Leonard WRN 69A
Leonard GRD 109A
Nancy MAS 71
Nancy BBN 136
Richard M. JES 91
Richd. BBN 136
Samuel, (Son Of Sa--?) WRN 69A
Samuel WRN 67A
Samuel WRN 69A
Susanna UNN 152
William WRN 67A
Wm. MAD 150
Wm. PND 18A
KERCHERVILL, James CBL 14A
KERCHEVAL, Jno. MAS 63
John NSN 177
Tho. MAS 69
KERCHWALL, William, Jr. LGN 28
William, Sr. LGN 28
KERFOOT?, Saml. HRD 66
KERK, Nathl. FLG 73A
Nelson FLG 71A
Wm. FLG 30A
Wm. FLG 49A
KERL?, Adam HAR 176
KERLE, Richard BBN 120
KERLIN, Geo. HRY 257
Jos. HRY 260
Peter HRY 244
Peter HRY 269
KERNES, Alxr. ADR 30
Margaret HAR 196
KERNS, Adam, Jr. NCH 113A
John CLD 144
Polly CLD 157
Thos. ADR 30
KERNS?, Simeon NCH 120A
KERR, Armstrong GRN 62
David LGN 29
David SCT 136A
Gilbert MAD 150
Henry MAD 156
James BKN 26
James LGN 44
James MAD 118
John LGN 32
John MNR 195
John R. BRN 18
Nathaniel GSN 141A
Robert LGN 45
Saml. MAD 122
Saml. MAD 156
Will SCT 106A
William GRN 62
Wm. MAD 164
Wm. MAD 170
KERREY?, Miridith GRD 122A
KERRICK, Benjamin H. SHE 120A
Edward BNE 46
James SHE 118A
KERRICK, Jos. SHE 124A
KERRY, David WDF 109A
KERRY?, Martin MNR 207
William MNR 201
KERSEY, Claborn JES 86
James, Senr. NCH 115A
James NCH 18A
John GRN 68
John NCH 18A
KERSHAW, John BTH 176
KERTLY, Willis MBG 137
KES?, Thomas BTH 212
KESINGER, Isaac HRT 162
Joseph HRT 162
Peter HRT 162
Solloman HRT 162
Sollomon HRT 162
William HRT 162
KESLER, Abram FKN 110
Lewis SHE 151
KESSICK, Henry FLG 43A
KESSLER, Daniel GRN 66
KESTER, John SHE 134A
John SHE 134A
John SHE 134A
KESTERSON, George CWL 35
John CWL 35
KETCHAM, Joseph SHE 151
KETHERS, Betsy KNX 312
KETHERWOOD, Charles HAR 188
KETHLY, Jacob SPN 5A
KETLETT, Dickson BBN 126
KETRICH, Roswell PND 27A
KETTINGER, William MBG 135
KEUSLER?, Thomas HAR 140
KEVIL?, Thos.? CWL 42
KEY, Chesley D. HND 7
James CLD 138
Jas. MAS 53
Jesse MER 100
Marshall MAS 81
Marshall CLK 87
Price CLK 87
Theophilus CLD 137
Thos. MAS 53
William BRN 18
Zaccheus HAR 194
KEY?, Thomas BLT 170
KEYHOE, Thomas FKN 68
KEYKENDOLL, Simon UNN 152
KEYS, Adam R. FTE 94
Charles GRD 102B
John LGN 34
John CHN 33A
John GRD 100A
John GRD 102A
Wesley W. LGN 32
William CHN 33A
KEYSER, John HOP 252
KEYSUCKER, Geo. JEF 32
KEYWOOD, Jeremiah BRK 267
KIBBY, Joseph UNN 152
Moses GNP 171A
Wm. H. BBN 136
KIBLER, Michael FTE 86
KICKSON?, James HRD 14
KID, Harman CSY 214
Moses LNC 27
Zacariah LNC 43
KIDD, Allen H. MAD 136
Edmund FTE 85
Elias, Capt. WYN 91A
Elliot MAD 114
Larkin WYN 91A
Phillip FTE 87
KIDD, Ramon HND 13
Richard WYN 84A
Sarah CLK 88
Shered? WYN 91A
Walker FTE 82
William, Sr.? WYN 91A
William N. JES 75
Winny? WDF 96
KIDDER, John HRD 12
KIDNEY, Wm. BBN 144
KIDRELL, Susan WAS 53A
KIDWEL, Truman GTN 133
KIDWELL, Darky KNX 306
Drury MAD 108
James MAD 110
James MNR 207
Jas. FLG 23A
John MAD 162
John MNR 193
Jonathan MAD 110
Jonith MAD 110
Leonard MAD 100
Levi MAD 166
Matthew MNR 191
Ruty JES 78
Stephen MAD 110
Thos. MAD 106
Vinsen MAD 106
William MNR 193
William BTH 208
Wm. BBN 134
KIETH, Bennitt HND 7A
Jacob HAR 188
Philip HAR 204
KIETLEY, Ibby MTG 267
KIETLEY?, Simion? HAR 156
KIGEE?, John PUL 54A
KIGER, Jacob FKN 94
KIGGINS, Thomas BTH 188
KIGHTLY, Abraham JEF 59
KIKEN, Abra. JEF 65
KILANDER?, Phillip BKN 19
KILBURN, W. RCK 78A
KILBY, John SCT 135A
Saml. FKN 142
KILD, Wm. JEF 41
KILD?, John JEF 33
KILDEY, James HRT 162
KILGORE, --dw.? J. CWL 37
Benjamin CBL 11A
David CWL 42
David CWL 43
Hung CWL 36
Jemison CBL 15A
John CBL 11A
Jonthn. CWL 58
Wm. CWL 31
KILGOUR, Anthy. MAS 68
Jos. MAS 65
Robt. MAS 69
KILGOUX?, Chas. MAS 58
KILLAM, Asa HRD 86
Peter NCH 128A
KILLEN, John SHE 132A
Sally HRD 78
KILLEN?, Joseph JEF 32
KILLENBARGER?, Jos. BRK 267
KILLEY, Charity MAD 108
Jas. SCT 123A
Robert E. MAD 178
KILLGORE, John HND 10A
Thos. HND 8
KILLON?, James MTG 226
KILLOUGH, David HOP 252
KILLPATRICK, Josep LVG 10

KILPATRICK, James WRN 38A
John FTE 56
KILWELL, Wm. JEF 64
KILY?, William BTH 194
KILYON, John BTH 180
Mikael FLG 44A
KIMBALL, Auk? MAD 94
KIMBELL, James MAD 112
KIMBERLAIN, George BLT 152
Sarah HRD 84
KIMBERLAND, Abraham HRY 210
Danl. HRY 210
Jno. HRY 261
KIMBLE, Abraham WRN 53A
David MTG 225
Willis JEF 53
KIMBLE?, Thomas MTG 226
KIMBLER, Moses BBN 114
KIMBOL, Charles WRN 54A
KIMBOLE, Hezekiah WRN 53A
Thomas WRN 54A
KIMBREL, George SPN 24A
Samuel SPN 24A
KIMBRO, John WRN 62A
KIMBROUGH, A. TOD 126
Aaron TOD 130
N. TOD 130A
T. TOD 128
Thomas G HAR 220
Thos. TOD 126A
William HAR 210
KIMBROW, Richard HRD 14
KIMEL, Benjaman BTL 325
Philip BTL 325
KIMER, Henry BBN 114
KIMES, Jaco? BBN 112
Jacob BBN 62
Will BBN 62
KIMES?, Stephen BBN 112
KIMINGS?, Samuel ALN 98
KIMLEY, Andrew MBG 136A
Francis MGB 137A
KIMMEL, David MBG 137
KIMMION, Nicholas BKN 16
KIMS?, George NCH 120A
KINBLE, Harnon/Hamon? GSN 141A
KINCADE, Sarah HAR 166
Wm. SHE 144A
KINCAID, Edward ETL 37
Hugh BBN 136
James LGN 28
James ETL 54
Jas. HRD 78
Jas., Jr. RCK 79A
Jas. RCK 77A
John LNC 2
John MAD 116
John LWS 96A
Joseph MAD 126
Mathew SHE 155
Polly SHE 155
Robt. HRD 48
Robt., Junr. HRD 90
Thos. MAD 134
William T. LGN 47
Wm. M. LNC 11
KINCHELOE, Elias NSN 179
Lewis B. MBG 139
Peter MBG 133A
Thos. BRK 227
William MBG 140
KINCHER, Peter GSN 141A
KINCHLOE, Jesse SHE 123A
KINDAL, Jeremiah, BRK 267
KINDALL, (See Kendall) NSN
Hele? NSN 179
John SHE 175
William SHE 175
William NSN 179
William NSN 217
Wm. JEF 42
KINDEL, Sanford WYN 88A
KINDER, Barnabis BTH 212
Jacob SHE 154
John SHE 154
Nathaniel MAD 130
Peter SHE 154
Peter WYN 88A
Samuel WYN 87A
Sanl. MAD 168
William WYN 87A
KINDEY?, Polly HRY 230
KINDLE, John HAR 148
Lewis HAR 148
Romley JEF 38
Saml. HAR 148
William HAR 148
KINDLEY, David MER 100
James MER 100
KINDOLL, George GTN 127
Noah GTN 130
Reason FKN 110
Yelley GTN 130
KINDRED, Edward CLK 84
Edward WRN 54A
James FTE 101
KINDREW, Martin MAD 134
Wm. MAD 134
KINDRICK, James HAR 168
KINEART?, John NCH 126A
KINER, David CHN 38
KINER?, George NCH 120A
KINERY, Joseph MNR 205
KING, Abner NSN 216
Abraham HRY 180
Abram LVG 6
Abram GTN 130
Aguta ALN 142
Alexander BLT 182
Amstred PND 26A
Ann BRK 267
Ann SHE 125A
Arthur HRT 162
Asa GSN 141A
Benjamin LGN 36
Benjn. CWL 46
Beryman HRY 196
Charles MAD 164
Chs. B. JEF 20
Daniel LGN 40
Daniel BLT 170
Daniel HAR 198
Daniel DVS 15A
Ebsand, Sr.? GRD 101A
Edd. HRY 266
Edmund WRN 35A
Edward JES 85
Edwards CLD 167
Eli FTE 78
Elijah ADR 50
Elijah HND 7A
Elisha WRN 74A
English CSY 204
Francis MNR 201
Geo. HRY 255
George LGN 41
George CLD 139
George HND 7A
George B. HAR 180
KING, Henry MAD 148
Henry BLT 170
Henry, Jr. BLT 168
Herbert LNC 2
Hiby/Hiley? BRK 267
Higason CLD 154
Isaac WTY 120A
Jacob LVG 16
Jacob NSN 189
James ADR 30
James CLD 147
James BRK 267
James PND 15A
James D. WRN 62A
Jeremiah JES 76
Jeremiah CLK 78
Jesse BTH 162
Jesse HAR 192
John LNC 5
John LNC 7
John BRN 18
John BKN 19
John BKN 22
John BKN 26
John FLD 26
John LGN 27
John ETL 42
John JEF 45
John ETL 52
John CLK 71
John HRD 74
John MAD 102
John BBN 106
John GTN 127
John CLD 156
John SHE 162
John SHE 162
John CBL 13A
John PUL 53A
John WDF 93A
John E. CLD 150
Johnson MNR 209
Joseph BKN 16
Joseph CLY 115
Joseph HAR 198
Joshua LGN 37
Joshua HAR 198
Levin? LGN 28
Major ETL 39
Malinda? BKN 13
Martin JEF 42
Martin NSN 201
Milton, Clk. C. C. CLD 166
Montjoy NSN 197
Nancy ETL 48
Nath. RCK 79A
Nathan ETL 44
Nathaniel LGN 47
Ned GRD 96B
Nelson BLT 182
Osburn GTN 127
Peter HRD 24
Pricilla LGN 33
Richard HAR 140
Richard CLD 158
Richard HAR 198
Richd. BKN 11
Robert LNC 19
Robert GTN 127
Robert HAR 192
Robt. BKN 5
Robt. ALN 98
Rodham LGN 36
Russel GRD 101A
Samuel FLD 26

Name	County	Page
KING, Silais M.	HAR	198
Smith	GTN	127
Smith	SHE	128A
Smith	GNP	175A
Stephen	JES	84
Thomas	LVG	11
Thomas	LNC	19
Thomas	SHE	162
Thomas	HRY	210
Thomas	SHE	127A
Thomas B.	GNP	166A
Thos.	JEF	38
Thos.	JEF	46
Thos.	SHE	139A
Trueman	CBL	13A
Valentine	BLT	186
Will	MAS	64
William	FLD	26
William	GTN	126
William	CLD	156
William	BLT	182
William	NSN	198
William	PUL	66A
William	GRD	101A
William F.	GTN	117
Wm	BRK	267
Wm.	CWL	46
Wm., Jun.	BKN	22
Wm., Sr.	BKN	16
Wm.	PND	16A
Wm.	PUL	50A
Zach	ADR	30
KING?, Hooper	BLT	172
KINGERY, Andrew	MNR	205
Jacob	MNR	201
KINGSTON, Ephraim	LGN	34
Nicholas	MNR	193
KINISON?, Saml.	BRK	267
KINKADE, George	BTH	184
KINKAID, Abigal	BTH	202
Andrew	BTH	152
Archabalde	BTH	200
Archibald	BTH	152
David	BTH	148
John	BTH	152
John	BTH	188
Margaret	BTH	152
Thomas	BTH	202
William	BTH	174
KINKEAD, Charles	CLK	76
Love	CHN	42
Robert	CLK	82
KINKIAD, Archabald	WDF	104
James	WDF	103A
John	WDF	104
John, Sr.	WDF	103A
John	WDF	113A
Joseph	WDF	104
Robert	WDF	93A
Robert	WDF	126A
William	WDF	103A
KINMAN, David	GRT	145
David	HAR	150
Jeremiah	HAR	150
John	GRT	145
Samuel	GRT	145
William	HAR	150
KINNEDY, Robert	NCH	119A
KINNERSON, John	JEF	38
KINNEY, David	GRN	55
Edwd. D.	SCT	126A
George	SHE	143A
Isaac	BKN	15
John	GRN	66
Joseph	FKN	112
Thomas	GRN	58
KINNEY, Wenden?	BKN	5
KINNY?, Richard	WDF	100
KINSEY, David	LVG	7
James	LVG	7
Jesse	WAS	20A
KINSLER, James	HAR	134
KINSLER?, Thomas	HAR	140
KINSLEY, James	GTN	132
KINSLOW, Aaron	BRN	18
Adam	BRN	18
Ambrose	BRN	18
Joshua	BRN	18
Mrs.	BRN	18
KIPART, Abm.	HRY	269
Dan.	HRY	269
Geo.	HRY	259
Geo.	HRY	269
Jacob	HRY	256
Mary	HRY	269
KIPER, Frederick	GSN	141A
Jacob	GSN	141A
KIPHART, Abm.	HRY	262
Betey	HRY	254
Jno.	HRY	254
Jno.	HRY	262
Wm.	HRY	262
KIRBY, Charles	PND	16A
Francis	RCK	79A
Jesse	HRD	8
Jesse	RCK	84A
Jessee	MBG	143A
John	WDF	102
John	SCT	120A
Ricd.	RCK	80A
Zachariah	SCT	103A
KIRCHEVAL, George	SHE	124A
KIRCHEVALL, John	SCT	107A
KIRK, -----?	DVS	3A
Alexander	FLD	11
Anthony	SHE	148
Benjm.	MAS	70
Daniel	WAS	68A
Daniel?	DVS	13A
Danl.	CWL	55
Elijah	FKN	118
Elizabeth	BLT	180
Geo.	MAS	69
Geo., Jr.	MAS	71
James	MTG	243
James	WAS	17A
Jerard	LVG	6
Jeremiah	BLT	180
Jesse	WAS	17A
John	FTE	91
John	TOD	131A
Matthew	MTG	233
Nicholas	MNR	197
Richd.	MAS	61
Robt.	LVG	6
Tho.	MAS	52
Tho., Jr.	MAS	52
Thornsburry	GNP	166A
Thos.	KNX	312
Vincent	HRY	180
Will	MAS	69
William	BLT	180
William B.	BTH	148
William B.	MTG	269
KIRKENDOLL, Richd.	GRD	91A
KIRKHAM, --lly?	DVS	12A
--muel?	DVS	12A
James?	DVS	12A
KIRKLAND, Abraham	MER	117
Isaac	MER	100
John, Jr.	MER	100
John, Sr.	MER	100
KIRKLAND, Joseph	MER	100
William	LGN	39
William	MER	100
KIRKLIN, David	CHN	40A
KIRKMAN, Geo.	TOD	127A
Thomas	CHN	35
Thos.	KNX	292
KIRKPATRIACK, Moses	MNR	193
KIRKPATRICK, Anna	MER	100
C.	BBN	110
David	LNC	35
Elihu	MNR	193
Gabriel	HRD	50
George	HAR	200
Hannah	BBN	120
Hannah	GSN	141A
Hugh	MNR	193
James	MTG	241
James	MTG	291
Jas.	HRD	86
Mathew	WRN	74A
William	CLD	163
William	LWS	95A
KIRKPRTAICK?, Sarah	MNR	213
KIRKWOOD, David	PND	17A
Hugh	HOP	252
John	LVG	13
John	HOP	252
Will	JEF	22
KIRLEY, John	MAD	178
KIRLIN, Jos.	HRY	267
KIRLING, Thomas	CSY	218
KIRLRING, Charles	CSY	218
KIRPMAN?, John	HAR	192
KIRTLEY, E. L.	GRN	60
Elijah	BNE	46
Elijah, Jr.	BNE	22
James	BRN	18
Jeremiah	BNE	46
John	BRN	18
John	BNE	22
Pleasant	GRN	60
Robert	BNE	22
Thodosha	WDF	125A
William	BNE	22
William	GRN	72
KIRTLEY?, Simion?	HAR	156
Sophiah	HAR	156
KIRTLY, Benjamin	JES	91
Mary	BNE	22
KISE, Elias	FTE	109
William	FTE	110
KISE?, John	FTE	76
KISER, John	FTE	74
KISLER, Joseph	JEF	25
KISNER, Jacob	FLD	27
KITCHEM, Joseph	GRN	72
KITCHEN, Andrew	GNP	168A
Antony	WAS	37A
James	MTG	271
James	GNP	169A
John	BLT	160
John	SCT	109A
John	GNP	168A
KITCHENS, Thomas	BTL	325
KITCHLINE, Peter	HRD	12
KITCHUM, Joseph	ETL	53
KITE, George	BNE	22
George	BNE	22
George, Jr.	BNE	22
John	BNE	22
William	BNE	22
KITE?, John	JEF	31
KITES, James	BNE	22

KITETY, Abraham MAD 110
KITHERWOOD, Saml. HAR 132
KITS, Nancy SPN 21A
KITSON, Jas. HRY 251
Jas. HRY 262
William SHE 151
KITTINGER, Jacob MBG 138A
Martin MBG 138A
KITTS, Jacob CBL 7A
KIZEE, Benjamin PUL 65A
George PUL 65A
Robert PUL 65A
KIZEE?, John PUL 54A
KIZER, Henry GNP 175A
Jacob FTE 110
Jacob BBN 134
James GNP 165A
Jocob GNP 176A
John BBN 118
John HRY 232
John, Senr. BBN 142
Joseph BBN 134
KLEET, Lewis CBL 12A
KLEETE, Frederick CBL 15A
KLEINDSMITH, Edwd. JEF 21
KLINE, John WRN 39A
KLINESMITH, Malach BNE 22
KLIZER, Geo., Jr. BBN 110
Henry BBN 110
Joseph BBN 110
KNAVE, Francis WDF 95A
John WDF 93
KNEELING?, Lowery BBN 134
KNETZER, Chas. MAS 71
Mary A. MAS 65
KNIFLY, Philip ADR 30
KNIGHT, Andr. MAS 73
Charles SHE 151
David CHN 36A
Elijah FLG 24A
George SHE 143A
George H. LGN 41
Isaac ADR 64
James JES 73
James GTN 117
James CHN 36A
Jas. FLG 79A
John LVG 10
John SHE 151
John, Junr. CHN 30A
John, Senr. CHN 30A
John FLG 41A
John SHE 132A
Jos. SHE 143A
Knight CHN 36
Mary SHE 171
Radden LGN 47
Robert B. LGN 41
Shadrach HAR 208
Simons CHN 36A
Thos. FLG 25A
William GTN 117
William HOP 252
Wm. FLG 23A
Woodson FKN 98
Zacheriah CLD 158
KNIGHTEN, Jessee MBG 141A
KNOK, Sarah WAS 66A
KNOTT, Clem WAS 73A
Francis WAS 62A
James NSN 213
James WAS 62A
James WAS 62A
James P. WAS 77A
Joseph WAS 64A
Ralph NSN 182
KNOTT, Thos. WAS 60A
KNOTTS, James NSN 222
Jonathan NSN 198
KNOW, James GTN 132
KNOWLES, Joshua WRN 71A
Mathew WRN 71A
Will MAS 62
KNOX, Abner MER 100
Alexander GTN 133
Benjamin JES 83
David, Esq. MER 100
David NCH 124A
Elizabeth PUL 65A
George C. NSN 177
Hugh HND 8A
Jacob PUL 39A
James, Jr. GTN 132
James SHE 129A
John HAR 176
John BTL 325
Nehimiah HOP 252
Robert FKN 116
Salley SCT 126A
Samuel JES 72
Samuel NCH 124A
Stokeley LGN 46
Thomas MTG 291
KNUCKOLS, George W. SHE 176
KOHENHASS?, Henry CLK 101
KOKERSON, John JEF 32
KOMERS?, Benja. JEF 54
KONNER, Nancy KNX 284
KOOGH, John GTN 118
KOONROD, Thomas HRT 162
KORNERS, Benja. JEF 54
KOTT?, Henry WAS 59A
KOUNS, John GNP 176A
John C. GNP 178A
John C. GNP 179A
KOUNS?, Letitia MTG 241
KOUNZ, Jacob GNP 165A
KRECKLE, Frances FTE 69
KREPS, Jacob HRT 162
KRILEIGH, Frances CBL 5A
Jacob CBL 5A
KROUTT, Henery CBL 6A
Jacob CBL 11A
John CBL 12A
Michael CBL 12A
KUN, John BNE 22
KUNE?, Charles GTN 134
William GTN 134
KURBY?, (See Hurby) WRN 67A
KURKE?, Alexander MAD 94
KURRAGIN?, Winney WAS 22A
KURRY, Thomas BNE 22
KUTLEY?, Elijah RCK 77A
KUYKENDALL, Abram BTL 325
Josiah BTL 325
Mark BTL 325
Matthew, Jr. BTL 325
Matthew, Sr. BTL 325
Moses BTL 325
KUZOR?, John CBL 10A
KWAITS?, Elizabeth FTE 73
KYLE, Alexr. SCT 139A
John MER 100
Rachel SCT 97A
Robbert CBL 5A
Samuel FTE 73
Thomas MER 100
KYLER, Joseph, Sr.? GRD 97A
Will GRD 100A
L----, Elijah HRT 163
Robt. BKN 19
L--?, Francis BKN 2
L--K?, Jacob WRN 59A
L--NALL?, Tho. MAS 66
L-E?, Dolly FTE 61
L-WRY?, George FTE 85
LA COMPT?, Isaac HRY 262
LA MASTER, Jas. HRY 267
Jas., Sr. HRY 260
Jas., Sr. HRY 267
Wm. HRY 260
LA--?, Luke CHN 33
LA--ENS?, Peter ALN 96
LABB, William CSY 220
LABERTREE, Asher MER 117
LABORD, Rhoda MTG 265
LACCY, John SCT 114A
LACEFIELD, Andrew GRN 67
Ezekiel NSN 206
Gillum GRN 58
Jacob SHE 165
John MNR 203
LACEWELL, Daniel HND 10
William HND 10
LACEY, Elijah FKN 148
James FLD 23
Jane LVG 13
Jessee JEF 58
John B. FLD 1A
Levi MTG 249
Mark FLD 11
Philemon H. MTG 225
William FLD 11
LACHER, Lewis BNE 24
LACKER?, G. L. CHN 46
LACKEY, Alexander FLD 17
Alexander MAD 138
Andrew MAD 112
Gabriel LNC 31
James MAD 112
Saml., Jr. MAD 140
Saml., Sr. MAD 140
LACKLAND, Alfred JEF 36
Aron CLK 90
Fielding CLK 101
John SCT 128A
LACKY, Andrew, Jr. ETL 47
Andrew, Sr. ETL 39
Elias ETL 39
Hugh CLD 150
James ETL 47
James CLD 154
Thomas ETL 47
Thos. NSN 177
Will GRD 114A
William ETL 47
LACY, Alexander FLD 11
Bartholomew CHN 32A
Batt C. NSN 199
Ben. CHN 32
Ben., Junr. CHN 31A
Benjamin LGN 47
Burley? WRN 35A
Burwell LGN 47
David CHN 32
Edward WDF 104A
Elizabeth CHN 31A
Elkanah LGN 47
George CHN 29A
Henry CLD 143
Jephtha HOP 254
Jessee JEF 57
Jessee CHN 44A
John ETL 46
John GNP 177A

LACY, Joseph BBN 90
Kenner LGN 47
Moses CHN 30
Philup CHN 32A
Walter MAS 56
William NSN 200
LACY?, Ami BBN 130
Arubah FKN 102
LAD, Thomas HND 5
LADD, Benjamin, Jr. TRG 13A
Benjamin TRG 13A
Davis CHN 44
Elijah TRG 14
Francis TRG 14
Jacob CLK 71
James BBN 122
John TRG 13A
Robert G. MNR 215
William TRG 13A
William GRD 92A
LADISAN, Lewis BLT 180
LADY?, Philip ETL 53
LAFAN?, James CWL 43
LAFERTY, Thomas CLK 67
LAFFERTY, Alexander CLD 138
James HAR 156
John MER 101
Samuel CLD 141
Zepheriah HAR 162
LAFFETTE, Alexandria WRN 46A
LAFFOON, John B. HOP 252
Reatherford HOP 254
William HOP 252
LAFFOON?, James FTE 97
LAFOLLET, Isaac HRD 22
John HRD 26
Usual HRD 16
LAFTLEY, Benjn. OHO 10A
LAFTLY?, John OHO 9A
LAGE?, Hennery CSY 210
LAGRANGE, Peter MER 100
LAHUGH, John GSN 142A
LAID, James PND 31A
LAIL, Jno. HAR 156
LAILL, Peter GRT 140
LAIN, Dutton ADR 32
John ADR 32
Moses BRN 18
Robert BRN 18
Thomas BRN 18
William GRD 101A
Wm. ADR 32
Wm. BRK 269
LAIN?, Samuel FLD 43
LAINE, Daniel CSY 216
Edmund CSY 216
LAIR, Charles HAR 212
David GRD 85A
Geo. GRD 97A
James GRD 105A
Jesse GRD 85A
John HAR 212
John, Jr. HAR 212
Mathias HAR 142
Matthias BRN 19
Matthias HAR 212
William HAR 212
William GRD 114A
LAIRD, James LWS 89A
John S. LWS 90A
Samuel FTE 78
LAIRY, Wm. CHN 40A
LAITON, Thomas TRG 5A
LAKANAL, Joseph GTN 123
LAKE, Aron BRK 269
Joseph HAR 160
LAKE?, Danl. HAR 152
LAKEN / LAHEN?, Meridith GTN 123
LAKIN, Benj. FLG 24A
Benjamin WDF 125A
LAKINSTER, James BNE 24
Lockey BNE 24
Robert BNE 24
William BNE 24
LAKINSTER?, Jacob BNE 24
LALE?, Lewis JEF 37
LALES, George BNE 24
LALLAY?, John HRY 226
LAM, Benjamin CLK 73
James CLK 74
LAMAR, Marian? T. BRK 269
Polly CWL 55
LAMASTER, Benjamin BTH 156
Elijah BTH 188
Hugh SHE 140A
Richard BTH 192
LAMASTERS, Isaac BTH 156
Richard WRN 38A
Thomas LGN 47
LAMB, -----? DVS 12A
---.? CWL 32
---n? DVS 8A
--ingstan? CWL 32
-artin? CWL 32
Basil MAS 58
Basil MAS 67
Benjamin CSY 208
Charlotte OHO 5A
Edward HAR 218
Elijah JEF 45
Jacob HRY 255
Jacob PUL 63A
James LVG 11
James MER 101
James TOD 131
James TRG 5A
John CWL 32
John CWL 41
John CWL 44
John MAD 92
Jonathan CWL 55
Jonathan SPN 13A
Josiah JEF 24
Lemuel CBL 7A
Levi CWL 55
M.?, Mr.? MAS 56
Manson FTE 87
Manuel CWL 55
Matthew MAD 142
Milly GRD 117A
Moses BBN 112
Moses HOP 254
Pendleton MAD 160
Pennal CWL 55
Saml. HAR 132
Susan MER 101
Thomas CSY 214
Travis TOD 132A
Will MAS 67
Wm.? M.? MAS 56
LAMB?, Richard MAD 128
LAMBDIN?, John BKN 16
LAMBERT, -uba? HND 4A
Andrew MTG 293
Anthony HND 7A
Benjamin OWN 102
Davey WAS 50A
David WRN 69A
LAMBERT, Evans HND 9A
Garrett HRD 86
George MAD 140
Hiram NSN 208
Hugh KNX 290
Janet NSN 214
Jeremiah HRD 86
Joel HND 4A
John WAS 50A
Jorden HND 7
Mary PUL 66A
Mathias MAD 140
Moses SHE 175
Polly GRD 119A
Rivers WRN 70A
Ruben HRL 112
Shadrach WRN 61A
Starling MER 101
William MER 100
William HND 7A
LAMBERTSON, T. BKN 26
LAMBETH, David SPN 18A
LAMDEN, William T. DVS 19A
LAMKIN, David HRT 162
Presley T. WDF 97
LAMKINS, Charles H. HAR 144
Jere HRT 162
Nancy HRT 162
LAMME, James BBN 114
Jessee FTE 104
Mary FTE 104
Nancy NCH 120A
LAMMONS, James ETL 53
John BBN 116
LAMPKIN, George WAS 75A
John B. JES 91
Wm. WAS 75A
LAMPTON, Edmond BRK 267
Henry BRK 269
John, Jr. CLK 70
John, Senr. CLK 70
Joshua BRK 269
Lewis ADC 68
Mark JEF 28
Saml. JEF 30
Thos. C. BRK 269
Wharton S. BRN 33
William DVS 19A
Wm. JEF 26
LANAM?, John/ Jehu? BBN 114
LANAN?, Henry BBN 114
LANBUT?, John RCK 80A
LANCASTER, Ben. PND 29A
Delany MAD 118
Eligah CBL 2A
Henry TRG 14
Jeremiah WAS 52A
John WAS 54A
Joseph WAS 79A
Levi TRG 6
Littleton MAD 150
Moses HRY 184
Rachel BTH 188
Ralph NSN 194
Rapheal WAS 78A
Reuben SCT 119A
Reubin CBL 13A
Robert FTE 85
Robert SHE 154
Thos. PND 17A
Will. BKN 26
Wm. HRT 162
Wm. PND 23A
LANCE, George MTG 253

LANCE?, William N. CLK 102
LANCEFORD?, Nelly LNC 55
LANCHART?, James MAD 126
LANCHARTE, Christopher CSY 222
LANCHEART, Henry FTE 69
LAND, Henry CWL 31
Henry JES 78
James JES 78
James MAD 128
Jessee MAD 168
John MAD 110
John MAD 138
John MAD 170
John J./ I.? MAD 170
Polley MAD 168
Richard MAD 170
Thomas SPN 24A
Thos. MAD 168
Thos., Sr. MAD 114
Ursly MAD 146
William JES 78
LAND?, Moses MAD 140
LANDCASTER, John JES 74
LANDEMAN, Jacob FTE 77
LANDER, Henry CHN 42
Henry CLK 69
Henry BRK 227
Henry TRG 14A
Jacob BRK 269
Jno. CHN 41A
Jno. S., Jr. CHN 41A
Nathal. BRK 271
Richard BRK 269
Thos. L. BRK 269
Wm. CHN 41A
LANDERS, Abraham CSY 214
Abram GRN 64
Charles BBN 122
Clark GRN 67
Clark C. MAS 57
Daniel MBG 140A
Francis WYN 89A
Hanah WDF 96A
Jacob MBG 137
Jeremiah TRG 12A
Jno. HRY 244
John ALN 122
John WAS 59A
John MBG 140A
Kimbro HRY 244
Louis FTE 74
Peter GRN 64
Robert GTN 131
Thos. L. BRK 309
Wm. BBN 114
Zachariah WYN 83A
LANDERS?, Joel FTE 102
LANDIS, John MBG 140A
LANDMAN, Ep? JEF 25
Griffin JEF 40
LANDON, George BKN 15
LANDRAM, James OHO 4A
James WRN 58A
LANDRIGE, John GRN 66
LANDRITH, David LGN 36
LANDRUM, Hawkins WAS 44A
James WAS 50A
John BRN 18
John GRT 141
Nancy SCT 104A
Nelson BRN 18
Reubin CLK 67
William BRN 19
William WRN 69A
LANDRURCY?, Francis BKN 18
LANDSAN, William FLD 6
LANDSBERRY, Mary WAS 87A
LANDSBY, James WDF 100A
LANDSDEN, Eli M. HOP 252
LANDSDOWN, Nancy HRL 112
LANE, Aaron MNR 201
Benjamin S. BRN 18
Betsey HRD 90
Bird MNR 209
Daniel SHE 110A
David LWS 94A
Edward FKN 150
Elisha SHE 151
Felix FKN 150
Garland FKN 150
Garret BTL 325
Greenwood ALN 144
Hastin FKN 150
Isham MAD 126
Jacob HRD 90
James GRN 59
James MAD 90
James LWS 95A
James H. MTG 231
Jesse SPN 21A
Joel CLK 64
John MNR 193
John MTG 247
Joseph LWS 95A
Letitia MTG 247
Martin MAD 128
Mirna?, Mrs. WYN 97A
Moses MNR 209
Robert G. BTH 148
Samuel HRL 112
Samuel SPN 21A
Samuel LWS 95A
Sarah SHE 143A
Sary HRL 112
Tabitha SHE 133A
Thomas MNR 209
Thomas WYN 97A
Thomas NCH 125A
Thomas G. JES 96
Thos. MAS 72
Tilman MNR 217
William GRN 55
LANE?, Hilley MNR 201
LANEGOW?, Elizabeth MTG 273
LANEHART, Isaac MAD 156
LANEHART?, James MAD 126
LANEN?, Meridith GTN 123
LANER, Fred G. JEF 31
LANERE, Collins SPN 4A
LANEY, Culbert M. SPN 22A
Isaac SPN 22A
Thomas SPN 22A
William HAR 220
LANFIELD, Wm. GRD 119A
LANFIELD?, Wm. BRK 269
LANG, -oses? DVS 13A
James PUL 40A
Smith GRN 76
LANG?, Joseph GRN 68
Sarah CLK 91
Wm. CHN 42
LANGATE?, Dixon GRT 145
LANGDON, Edmond SHE 131A
James PUL 49A
John PUL 56A
John PUL 62A
Rosswell HRD 14
Samuel WYN 83A
LANGE?, Anthony JEF 22
LANGFORD, Ivy PUL 62A
LANGFORD, James WAS 25A
Lois? RCK 84A
Nancy RCK 80A
R. V.? RCK 78A
LANGHORNE, Jno. T. MAS 78
Morris MAS 78
LANGLEY, Abraham HAR 182
Charles GSN 142A
David GTN 128
David MBG 141
George W. MBG 141
Isaac MBG 136
James GSN 142A
Jeremiah MBG 143A
John TRG 11A
John WAS 72A
John GSN 142A
Rob. CWL 44
Walter C. HND 11A
LANGLY, James KNX 314
Jesse TRG 11A
Johnathn. CWL 44
Miles KNX 308
LANGSDALE, Robert GTN 121
LANGSDON, Charles BLT 154
John BLT 180
Royal BLT 168
LANGSFORD, Nicholas NSN 213
LANGSTON, Ahab LGN 34
Dicy LGN 34
Hiram LGN 34
James WYN 106A
John LGN 34
William LGN 34
LANGWELL, Peter GRN 71
Thomas PUL 68A
Timothy GRN 70
LANHAM, Catharine CSY 206
Clement WAS 18A
Green MAD 146
John MAD 146
John CSY 220
John WAS 69A
Nathon WAS 67A
Notley WAS 69A
Stephen MAD 156
Stephen WAS 67A
Thos. MAD 146
Thos. MAD 148
William CSY 222
Wm. MAD 156
Zacariah MAD 94
Zack WAS 69A
LANHAM?, James MAD 118
LANIM?, Elias OHO 6A
LANKAM?, James MAD 118
LANKFORD, Larkin FKN 140
Thos. BBN 86
Walker PUL 45A
LANKSTONE, Abm. BBN 122
LANKTON, Lewis BRK 269
LANNDER, Isaac WRN 59A
LANNFORD?, Benjamin D. WRN 62A
LANSBERRY, Elisha WAS 87A
LANSDAL, Waters T. G. WAS 34A
LANSDALE, David NSN 178
Hester BTH 190
W. M. GRN 51
LANSDELL, Jesse OWN 103
LANSDONE, Zachariah LGN 46
LANSDOWN, George BTH 186
LANSON?, Jearmiah BKN 22

LANTAM, Alexander MAD 118
LANTER, Jessee HND 9A
LANTERN?, Jacob HAR 152
Larkin HAR 152
LANTES?, James MTG 283
LANTHREM?, Burch? JES 96
LANTHRUM?, Burch? JES 96
LANTRISS, Sharach CHN 29
LANTZ, Martin BNE 22
LANY, Samuel CHN 28A
LAPIN, Hamilton FTE 110
LAPPINGTON, Abrah. JEF 51
LAPRADE, William LGN 46
LAPSLEY, John -? GRD 114A
Joseph B. WRN 68A
LAPSLEY?, Charlotte MER 101
LAPSLY, James ADR 32
Joseph ADR 32
LARABE, Solomon CBL 23A
LARAWAY, John JEF 46
LARCE?, Jas. FLG 43A
LARCH, Abraham WRN 72A
LARCHER, Joseph WYN 84A
LARD, Hezekiah HRT 163
James HOP 254
Jessee HRT 163
Joseph HRT 163
LARD?, Jas. FLG 43A
LARE, Andrew LNC 37
Hubbard LNC 37
Thomas LNC 63
LARE?, Moses MAD 140
LAREMORE, James GRN 56
Phillip GRN 56
Robert GRN 71
LAREW, Peter LVG 8
LARGE, Joseph GNP 167A
Nancy GNP 167A
Robert FLD 15
Thomas FLD 15
LARIMORE, Abraham MAD 112
Hugh HAR 210
LARK, Robert CLD 139
LARKER, John MBG 141
LARKIN, Elizabeth HRD 28
George LGN 45
Jos. MAS 79
LARLEY?, Manoah? ADR 38
LARMON, Edward LGN 37
LARNE?, Saml HRD 16
LAROIN?, Sam ALN 132
LARR, Danl. HRY 202
John HRY 202
LARR?, Jesse HRY 200
LARRANCE?, George CSY 220
LARRENCE, Archibald WRN 57A
Richard WRN 58A
Rodham WRN 59A
Wallis WRN 57A
LARRINCE, Willis WRN 57A
LARRY?, Samuel CHN 28A
LARSH, Jonathan LWS 95A
LARUE, Jacob, Jr. HRD 30
Jacob, Senr. HRD 86
Jacob W. HRD 96
Jas. HRD 74
Squire HRD 18
Wm. HRD 72
LARVIN?, Sam ALN 132
LARY, Dennis BBN 104
Joseph BBN 104
LARY?, Ami BBN 130
LASBROOKE, Wm. MAS 79
LASBY, Saml. SCT 116A
LASELY, Peter BRK 269
Wm. BRK 271
LASETOR, Enus TRG 6A
Joab TRG 6
LASH, Adam HRD 16
David UNN 153
Jonathan MAS 73
LASHBROOKS, George BLT 178
James BLT 186
John BLT 164
Samuel BLT 166
Thomas BLT 186
LASHLEY, Frances GSN 142A
Jemmima GSN 142A
John GSN 142A
Robert GSN 142A
LASHURE, John GRD 118A
LASLETT, William F. WDF 112A
LASLEY, Amos WTY 121A
James GRN 55
Manoah, Sr.? GRN 58
Thomas GRN 67
LASLEY?, Manoah? ADR 38
LASSEN, Thomas FTE 56
LASSON, Barnell SHE 126A
Wm. SHE 126A
LASSWELL, Ben HRD 62
Jesse HRD 54
LAST?, Nathan TRG 4
LASTLY, James WYN 91A
LASURE, Jo.?, Sr. GRD 92A
Joseph GRD 85A
LASWON, Daniel JES 72
LATCHELL/ LATCHETT?, Eves FTE 76
LATHAM, Bazle TOD 130
Elijah TOD 130
Jer. TOD 130
John BKN 6
John LGN 32
Richd. MAS 66
Richd. MAS 70
William CLK 85
LATHERM, Geo. FLG 54A
LATHOM, George GTN 117
LATHRUM, Jas. BBN 84
John BBN 84
John, Senr. BBN 84
LATIMER, Baker HAR 154
Wm. PND 25A
LATIMORE, Samuel MER 100
LATON, David FKN 150
LATON?, Wm. H. FLG 47A
LATRELL, James SHE 166
LATTA?, Jno. FKN 150
LATTY, Alexander GTN 126
Mary WDF 126A
LAU--ENS?, Peter ALN 96
LAUBENS?, Peter ALN 96
LAUDELL, Zachariah LGN 33
LAUFIELD?, Wm. BRK 269
LAUGHERTY, James HAR 212
LAUGHEY?, James NSN 183
Thomas NSN 183
LAUGHLANE, Benjamn. CLK 74
Nancy CLK 65
LAUGHLEN, --m-s? WTY 127A
James GTN 122
James? WTY 127A
LAUGHLIN, -----? CWL 40
-----? CWL 40
----d? CWL 40
Benj. BKN 19
LAUGHLIN, Hiram CWL 37
John BBN 64
John HAR 168
Johnson CWL 33
Joseph D. WTY 114A
Thomas WTY 125A
Wm. CWL 39
LAUGLEY?, James NSN 183
Thomas NSN 183
LAUGLIN, John CLK 93
LAUR, Masez NSN 210
LAURANCE, David HND 7
Isaac FLG 47A
Jno. MAS 57
Nancy MNR 205
LAURANS?, Nathaniel NSN 185
LAURENCE, Charles KNX 306
Henderson LNC 75
Henry JEF 57
Hugh LNC 53
James GRN 55
James JES 85
John CLD 138
Martha PUL 66A
Richd. KNX 306
Samuel GTN 127
Samuel S./ L.? FTE 92
William T. MBG 139
LAURENCE?, Elizabeth S?. JEF 55
LAUSON, Allen WTY 127A
Isham WTY 127A
James GRD 98A
John WAS 81A
Nathan WTY 112A
LAUTER?, James MTG 283
LAUWELL?, Chandler WAS 83A
Jacob BRK 271
LAVELY, William BLT 156
LAVENDER, George CWL 55
John LNC 49
LAVICY?, James GTN 135
LAVILLE, Joseph -? JEF 44
LAW--F-R-?, Dicea FLD 29
LAW, Absolam CLK 64
Daniel CLK 64
Jno. MAS 61
LAW?, Jesse HRY 200
LAWDON, Berry MER 100
LAWELL, Peter FTE 91
LAWES, Thos. JEF 35
Wm. JEF 24
LAWHAM, Ausbern WAS 41A
LAWHON, Benj. FKN 152
LAWLER, Bennett SHE 125A
David BBN 138
Nicholas SHE 170
LAWLES, James SPN 16A
Samuel SPN 16A
LAWLESS, August ADR 32
Benjamin WRN 44A
Bird WAS 24A
Edward ADR 32
Henry GRT 143
James ADR 32
Jessee ADR 32
John ADR 32
John, Jr. GRT 145
John, Senr. GRT 145
Peter GRD 109A
Reuben ADR 32
Saml. JEF 46
William GRD 100A
LAWNY, (Free) ADR 70
LAWRANCE, Isaac, J FLG 49A

Name	County	Page
LAWRANCE, John	WAS	21A
William	BTL	325
LAWRANCE?, David	WAS	21A
LAWRENCE, Anthony	JES	87
Benja.	JEF	34
Byram	WRN	30A
Geo.	FKN	78
George	MER	101
Henry	CLK	64
Henry	SPN	8A
Humphrey	TRG	7
Isaac	FKN	146
James	TRG	7
James	SHE	173
James	NSN	214
John	JEF	31
John	MAD	178
John	CBL	6A
John B.	CLK	87
Levin	JEF	60
Meredith	CLK	87
Robert	JEF	58
Saml.	JEF	35
Thomas	CLK	87
Thomas	SHE	173
Thomas	BTL	325
William	NCH	124A
Wm.	FKN	72
LAWS, Cassaander	GTN	126
Edmund	KNX	306
Geo.	FKN	86
Hill. & Co.	JEF	24
Jeremiah	MER	101
John	SHE	170
Thomas	MER	101
Thos.	JEF	24
Thos.	KNX	290
William	FTE	103
Wm.	PUL	37A
Wm. C.	JEF	34
LAWSON, Aaron	GRD	98A
Adam	WRN	70A
Catlett	MER	101
Chesley	WAS	81A
David	CWL	55
Edwd.	SCT	107A
George	HRD	42
Henry	HRD	82
Isaac	HRD	38
Jacob	FLG	63A
Jacob	WAS	82A
James	FLD	10
Jas.	HRD	60
John	FLD	7
John	MER	101
John	KNX	292
John	FLG	66A
Joseph	FLD	10
Joshua-?	WAS	80A
Nathon	WAS	81A
Peter	LGN	25
Phillip	CLD	161
Richd.	SCT	104A
Robt.	SHE	136A
Thos.	HRY	267
Travis	FLD	12
Walter	MBG	143
William	LWS	98A
Wm.	HRD	64
Wm.	HRY	267
Wm.	FLG	66A
Zack	WAS	81A
LAWTON, Thomas	WRN	31A
LAX, Carter	ETL	50
Timothy	ETL	51
William	ETL	48

Name	County	Page
LAY, Bery	BRK	269
Burrell	PUL	61A
Elijah	FTE	112
George	FTE	107
Hannah (Crossed Out)	WTY	118A
Hannah	WTY	113A
Jesse, Jr. (Crossed Out)	WTY	118A
Jesse	WTY	113A
Jessee	WTY	113A
John	JEF	65
John	SCT	118A
Nancy	UNN	149
Stephen	BRK	269
William	FTE	107
William	FTE	107
William (Crossed Out)	WTY	118A
William	WRN	47A
William	WTY	113A
LAYER, Conrad	TOD	129A
George	TOD	129A
James	WYN	80A
LAYMON, Jonithan	GSN	142A
Michael	GSN	142A
LAYNE, Daniel, Jr.	HRY	200
Johnson	GRD	107A
Joseph	HRY	200
Larkin	GRD	102A
Sally	GRD	113A
William	GRD	108A
LAYSON, Hannah	BBN	106
Isaac	BBN	136
John	BBN	118
John	BBN	132
John	BBN	132
LAYTON, ----h?	DVS	10A
--nin?	DVS	10A
Conrod	FTE	108
Danl.	BBN	110
David	SCT	111A
Jerry	GRD	122A
John	HAR	192
John	GRD	93A
Nicholas C.	OHO	10A
Robert	HAR	140
Spencer	BBN	140
Thomas	BNE	46
Thomas	HAR	194
William	GRT	146
William	GRD	110A
LAZARETH, Jessee	ADR	20
LE GRAND, Abner	FTE	58
LEA, Lewis	MAS	52
Mary	BTH	156
LEAC-?, Joseph	HAR	164
LEACH, Widow	LVG	16
Asel	HRT	162
Benjamin	NCH	106A
Charlott	BKN	13
Daniel	SHE	176
Elijah	ADR	62
Fanny	FTE	93
Hezekiah	BBN	118
James	JEF	36
James	CWL	39
James B.	HAR	214
Jer	ADR	32
John	HRT	163
John	BTH	178
Jos.	CWL	39
Joseph	OHO	8A
Leonard	OHO	7A
Mathew	ADR	3
Mathew	ADR	64

Name	County	Page
LEACH, Richard	HRD	10
Saml.	ADR	32
William	LVG	16
Wm.	OHO	5A
Wm.	OHO	5A
Wm.	OHO	7A
LEACHAM?, Wm.	BKN	13
LEACHMAN, -----?	DVS	9A
Anne	MER	101
Geo.	MAS	54
Leonard	GTN	130
LEAD?, Joseph	HAR	164
LEADENHAM, Peter	FLD	37
LEAF, John	BRK	269
LEAGUE, Richard	MER	101
LEAH, Ezekiel	BNE	24
Hiram	BNE	22
James	JEF	68
LEAK, Christopher	NSN	214
John	NSN	214
Rafl.	WAS	71A
Richard	WAS	56A
Walter	MAS	56
LEAMAN, --vid?	DVS	12A
Jacomiah	UNN	154
John	DVS	12A
Richd.	MAS	61
LEAN, Bradford	WYN	83A
LEANEY, Calbert	SPN	17A
William	SPN	17A
LEAPER, Andrew	HAR	134
LEAR, John	BBN	140
Thomas M.	BBN	102
William	SPN	25A
Wm.	BBN	116
LEAR?, David?	BBN	96
LEAREBAUGH?, Jacob	BBN	104
LEARS, Jesse	WTY	121A
Joseph	ALN	102
LEARY, Samuel	LVG	16
LEASTON, James	MAD	158
LEATHERMAN, David	SHE	115A
Michael, Jr.	JEF	37
Richard	JEF	49
LEATHERS, Benjamin	CBL	4A
Chs.	FKN	138
James	FKN	138
John	CBL	6A
Joshua	SCT	137A
Moses	JEF	57
Paul	HND	11A
Polly	JEF	65
William	NSN	210
LEATHERS?, James	WAS	49A
LEATON, Polly	JEF	53
William	SPN	7A
LEATON?, William	WRN	62A
LEAVEL, James	MAD	128
LEAVELL, Ben	TOD	130A
Edwd.	TOD	131A
Lewis	TOD	130A
LEAVEY, William	FTE	61
LEAWRIGHT, Wm.	BBN	130
LEAZER, Henry	HRD	22
LEBO, Daniel	WTY	124A
LECKEY, John	CLK	100
Nathan	CLK	84
LED-IDGE?, Joseph	HAR	204
LEDAN/ LEDAU?, John	NSN	183
LEDBETTER, Micajah?	CWL	32
LEDEBOTTOM?, John	CLK	84
Joseph	CLK	84
LEDFORD, Carter	JEF	51
Elias	HRL	112

LEDFORD, James BTH 182
John BTH 172
Joseph TRG 5
Solomon LVG 7
LEDGER, John BNE 22
LEE, (See See?) MTG
-----? DVS 8A
Abner HAR 188
Abraham LNC 29
Adam FLG 68A
Alexr. FLG 23A
Ambrose LNC 29
Anar.? MAS 65
Andrew HRL 112
Barton LWS 97A
Benjamin LWS 93A
Braley JEF 33
Buford BLT 196
Chs. PUL 39A
David CWL 55
Drewry PUL 57A
Edmund LGN 22
Edward PND 31A
Edward WYN 80A
Edwd. S. MAS 52
Elijah MAD 106
Ephraim LGN 31
Fanny BTL 325
Francis MAD 110
Frank LNC 29
George LGN 32
George BRK 269
George, Sr. LNC 27
Gersham GTN 125
Gersham, Sr. GTN 125
Greenbury PUL 53A
Grissum MAD 138
Henry BRN 18
Henry MAS 74
Henry, Sr. BLT 156
Henry WRN 40A
Henry WAS 76A
Isaac ALN 122
Jacob C. FLG 70A
James ALN 140
James KNX 300
Jane, Mrs. WYN 102A
Jas. JEF 23
Jesse NSN 214
John WDF 94
John CLD 152
John BLT 153
John BLT 156
John HRT 162
John HAR 194
John BTL 325
John, Jr. BLT 149
John FLG 76A
John WYN 81A
John A. WDF 112A
John B. PUL 56A
John H. WDF 112A
John N. FLG 79A
John R. FLG 70A
Jos. FLG 46A
Joseph BRN 18
Joseph BRN 19
Joseph MAD 180
Joshua JEF 41
Joshua GRN 78
Jubal SHE 174
Lewis MAD 108
Margaret BLT 196
Noah MAD 138
Permit, Junr. CLD 153
Permit, Senr. CLD 153
LEE, Peter MAS 79
Randolph FLG 73A
Richard LNC 29
Richard MNR 207
Richard WAS 53A
Richard R. FLD 47
Richd. H. LNC 7
Robert WRN 59A
Robt. SCT 131A
Robt. P. GRN 72
Rowland JEF 35
Saml. JEF 54
Saml. FLG 76A
Samuel NSN 194
Samuel MNR 209
Samuel NSN 214
Sarah OHO 7A
Seaton PUL 55A
Shadrach CLD 152
Stephen MAS 60
Stephen HRL 112
Stephen MNR 207
Susanah FLG 45A
Tarlton SHE 168
Thomas L. WDF 112A
Thos. JEF 35
Thos. R. FLG 77A
William LGN 31
William ETL 39
William BLT 158
William NSN 214
William LWS 92A
William G. BTH 186
Willis A. FKN 122
Willis D. FLG 73A
Wm. ADR 54
Wm. MAD 138
Wm. PUL 36A
Wm. C. GRN 61
Wm. C. FKN 100
Wm. F. LNC 7
Wm. P. JEF 25
Zachariah FKN 110
LEECH, Edward LNC 41
Enoch BLT 178
James HOP 252
Jerry SCT 118A
Matthew LNC 21
Reuben LNC 21
Will. B. SCT 129A
William BTH 180
LEECHMAN, James GRT 142
LEEFORD?, Wen/ Werr? BLT 174
LEEK, Anthony FLG 38A
Ignatius SCT 97A
James SCT 120A
LEEMEN, Josiah SHE 136A
LEEPER, ----? N. LVG 9
Amyteer BRN 19
Andrew FLG 33A
George LNC 11
James NCH 113A
Robert LVG 11
Robert BRN 19
Samuel HOP 254
William BRN 19
LEER, Jacob NCH 129A
LEESON?, Isaac WTY 118A
LEET, Joseph WRN 57A
LEEWRIGHT, John BLT 192
LEFA---?, George (Crossed Out) HAR 144
LEFAVORS, Samuel GTN 125
LEFEVERS, Andrew WYN 92A
Catherine, Mrs. WYN 92A
LEFEVERS, David WYN 92A
LEFLER, Christopher WAS 48A
LEFON, Nicholas WDF 107A
LEFORCE, George HAR 146
Jane CLK 79
Polly SCT 118A
Reyney CLK 78
Robert WTY 119A
Saml. SCT 118A
Saml. SCT 121A
William B. WDF 119A
LEFORGY, Ayers FLG 57A
Jessee FLG 61A
LEFTOR, Uriah MAS 73
LEFTREDGE, Sally BRK 269
LEFTRIGE, Wm. GNP 168A
LEFTWICK, Creed LGN 27
Robert LGN 23
LEG, Ambose SHE 134A
John LNC 9
LEGATE, John SHE 127A
LEGG, George SHE 137A
Isaac SHE 139A
Jonathan SHE 137A
M. JEF 24
LEGGEN?, William GTN 120
LEGGETT, Hannah MTG 277
LEGIN, Charles HRY 228
George HRY 230
John HRY 230
LEGIT, Sarah, Mrs. CLK 95
LEGRAND, Joel ALN 124
John HRD 42
Lucy WRN 58A
Wm. HRD 56
LEIGH, Samuel WAS 34A
Stephen WAS 76A
LEIPEN, Joel LGN 47
LEIPER/ LEIPES?, Robt. CWL 41
LEIPOR?, Saml. BKN 14
LEISLY?, James JES 72
LEISTER, Robert MNR 191
Sarah MNR 191
Thomas MNR 191
LEITCH, John W. LWS 89A
LEMAR?, Benj. BRK 269
LEMARR, Alexander LGN 28
LEMASTER, Abram SHE 170
Frances FLD 19
Richard HRY 202
Westly HRY 234
LEMASTERS, Abraham HRY 200
Eliazer FLD 36
Fielding HRY 222
John FLD 35
John FLD 36
Lewis FLD 22
Mikael FLG 47A
LEMASTERS?, Zachariah HRY 200
LEMAY, Lewis BRN 19
LEMMON, Elisha MNR 199
George HAR 198
John HAR 198
John SHE 127A
Reubin WYN 98A
Thomas C. LGN 39
William HAR 198
LEMMON?, Benjamin HAR 140
LEMMONS, David HAR 146
Elizabeth SHE 159
Philip WRN 41A
LEMMS, Elenor WAS 66A
James WAS 53A

Name	County	Page
LEMMS,		53A
John	WAS	55A
Mark	WAS	76A
Rodolph	WAS	56A
LEMON, James	FTE	56
Jno.	JEF	55
John, Sr.?	SCT	109A
John	SCT	122A
Joseph J.	FTE	56
Marth	SCT	118A
Robt.	SCT	103A
Will.	SCT	135A
LEMONS, Abraham	HRT	163
Abram	GRN	68
Jacob	BRN	18
Jacob	BRN	19
James	BNE	24
John	HRT	163
Rebecca B.	FTE	93
Rudian	BRN	18
LEMSON?, Willis	GRN	71
LEMSSCON?, Polly	WAS	55A
LENARD, Jas. T.	ADR	30
LENDRUM, Isham	MAD	120
LENDSEY, David	MAS	78
LENEER?, John C.	JES	92
LENER?, Soloman	JES	72
LENNIN, Chas. D.	BBN	144
LENNON, John	BBN	94
LENNUM, Charles	BTH	164
LENNUX?, Saml.	BBN	106
LENOIR, John	HRL	112
LENOX, Charles, Jr.	ETL	49
Charles, S?	ETL	41
George	ETL	41
LENREY?, Neville	HOP	252
LENT?, William	NSN	198
LENTHECUM, Thomas	BLT	158
LENTICUN?, Rice B.	LVG	10
LENTNY, Jacob	MAS	71
Jno.	MAS	71
Joab	MAS	71
LENTON, Moses	WAS	86A
Wm.	WAS	66A
LENTON?, William	WRN	62A
LEO, Samuel	GRN	60
Wesley	GRN	56
Wm., Sr.	GRN	64
LEONARD, David	MER	100
James W.	SHE	117A
Jno.	FKN	58
John	MER	100
Valentine	HAR	196
LEPOSS?, Will	MAS	59
LERSON?, William	GRD	116A
LESLEY, John	MER	101
Robert	FLD	34
LESLIE, David	NSN	192
John	NSN	192
Joseph	MTG	265
Solomon	NSN	192
Solomon	NSN	192
LESLY, Vachel	WYN	103A
LESSE, Michael	LNC	53
LESSENBERRY, Robt. P.	BRN	18
LESTER, Abner	FLD	26
James	GTN	128
Thos.	ADR	32
Wm.	ADR	32
LETCHER, A. R.	GRD	97A
Archibald	HRD	36
Ben	GRD	112A
R. P.	GRD	83A

Name	County	Page
LETCHER, Ste. G., Jr.	GRD	83A
Stephen G.	MER	117
Wm.	FKN	90
Wm. R.	MAD	180
LETCHWORTH, Joseph	WDF	121A
LETHERMAN, George	SHE	138A
Henry	SHE	138A
LETORA?, Lewis	MNR	205
LETT, Balam	OWN	99
Danil	OWN	101
James	CBL	6A
LETTERAL, James	GRD	107A
LETTON, Michael	NCH	124A
LETTY, (Free)	CLD	162
LEURANA, Jno.	MAS	66
LEURMON?, William	HAR	162
LEUVALL?, Notley	MAS	74
LEVAN?, Abraham	WRN	45A
John	WRN	45A
William	WRN	45A
LEVEE?, Benjamin	BTL	325
LEVEL, John	SHE	137A
LEVELEREN?, Samuel	JES	71
LEVERIDGE, John	MAD	134
John	GRD	120A
LEVI, John	BKN	20
Judas	MAS	77
Willis	BKN	20
LEVI?, Elias	MAS	59
Hugh	HAR	162
LEVIER, James	WTY	121A
LEVIL, Stephen	LNC	67
LEVILL, Benj.	GRD	105A
Ed	GRD	110A
John	GRD	120A
LEVIN, Charles	GRN	64
LEVINGSTON, Thos.	ADR	4
LEVIRNGER?, Peter	LVG	13
LEVISLOW, Thomas	MER	101
LEWALLEN, Clara	HRD	76
Jabes	OHO	3A
Stely	JES	76
LEWALLYN, Abednigo	HOP	252
LEWARANCE, See Lwrance	WAS	21A
LEWELLAN, Richd.	JEF	46
LEWELLEN, Charles	CSY	212
Jesse	WAS	26A
Saml.	JEF	27
LEWES, Henry	NSN	187
LEWES?, Saml.	GRD	99A
LEWIS, --ml.?	CWL	32
Aaron	CHN	39
Aaron	WRN	43A
Abijah	NSN	214
Abner	HRL	112
Abner	CLY	115
Abraham	BRN	18
Addison	GTN	130
Alexander	HAR	134
Alexander, Snr.	HAR	136
Ann	JES	89
Anne	MER	101
Aron	WDF	97
Asa K.	CLK	103
Augustine	OWN	102
Benjamin	FLD	27
Benjamin	GRN	79
Benjamin	CLD	159
Benjamin	SHE	161
Bracken	FLD	23
Buford	CWL	44
Charles	FLD	4
Charles	BRN	18
Charles	CLD	160

Name	County	Page
LEWIS, Chas.	SHE	141A
Christopher	ADR	32
Coleman	HRD	68
Covington	PUL	48A
Craddock	GTN	130
Daniel	JES	89
Daniel	MAD	114
Daniel	NSN	205
Daniel	HRY	253
David	CLY	114
David	CBL	2A
David	GNP	173A
David J.	BRK	269
Edmd. H.	JEF	20
Edward	WDF	99A
Elizabeth	FTE	107
Fanny	BTH	192
Fielding	SHE	159
Fielding,	WDF	96A
Francis	FLD	9
Fredderick	HRL	112
G.	JEF	24
Gabriel	LGN	27
George	PND	31A
Gideon	FLD	19
Hannah E.	BRK	267
Harry	FKN	158
Harry	FKN	160
Harry (A Free Negroe)	CLK	103
Hector P.	FTE	92
Henry	CWL	32
Henry	JEF	32
Henry	GTN	128
Henry	PUL	37A
Hiram	HAR	136
Hudson	BRN	18
Isaac	FKN	114
Isaac	SHE	152
Isaac	HRY	253
Isaac	WAS	47A
Isaac O.	WRN	43A
J. F. P.	LNC	31
Jacob	JEF	19
Jacob	SHE	151
James	JEF	39
James	CLY	114
James	CLY	127
James	SHE	159
James	NSN	187
James	WDF	96A
James	GSN	142A
James	GNP	176A
James A.	BTL	325
James G.	LGN	39
Jane	FKN	58
Jane	FTE	100
Jane	SPN	5A
Jaqulin A.	CSY	210
Jas., Sr.	CLY	127
Jas.	RCK	78A
Jasper	CLD	167
Jeremiah	GRN	80
Jeremiah	WYN	103A
Jesse	SHE	161
Jesse	NSN	196
Jno.	FKN	114
Jno.	HRY	268
Jno.	PUL	36A
Joab	SPN	3A
Job	PUL	49A
John	BKN	5
John	FLD	9
John	HND	13
John	CLK	93
John	WDF	97

LEWIS, John FTE 98
John HRL 112
John GTN 130
John CLY 131
John GTN 133
John CLD 154
John NSN 214
John SPN 4A
John SPN 23A
John Coons HRY 224
John W. MER 101
Jonas LVG 4
Jonathan HRD 68
Joseph BKN 6
Joseph BRN 19
Joseph CLY 127
Joseph SHE 174
Joseph NSN 177
Joseph WRN 42A
Joseph PUL 62A
Josiah CHN 29A
Leonard SPN 23A
Lewis PND 31A
Lilburn LVG 3
Marthy KNX 280
Mary MAS 58
Mat. PUL 36A
Messenger CLY 114
Mical WAS 80A
Moses FKN 92
Nancy HND 12
Nancy JES 83
Nat GRD 110A
Nat GRD 118A
Nathan CLY 131
Nathan MAD 132
Neriah SPN 21A
Patsey BBN 108
Peter FTE 61
Peter BBN 116
Peter B. FLG 49A
Reuben BBN 60
Richard GTN 130
Richard CLD 149
Richd. PUL 49A
Robert CHN 33
Robert FKN 140
Robert, Senr. CHN 36A
Robert T. LNC 9
Robert W. BRN 18
Robt. GNP 168A
Robt. G. FLG 50A
Robt. W. JEF 56
S--s? NSN 200
Salley SPN 19A
Sally BRN 18
Sally LGN 32
Samuel UNN 154
Samuel HAR 182
Samuel WDF 113A
Sarah SHE 151
Simeon BRN 19
Simeon B. HRT 162
Soloman SCT 112A
Stephen BKN 5
Stephen CLK 93
Stephen FKN 122
Thadius CLY 115
Thomas FLD 9
Thomas BRN 18
Thomas FLD 27
Thomas CLY 131
Thomas NSN 197
Thomas NSN 200
Thomas NSN 214
Thomas CBL 11A
LEWIS, Thos. BRK 269
Thos. HND 9A
Vincent NSN 205
Vincent SPN 6A
Warner W. LGN 27
William FLD 9
William BKN 13
William BRN 19
William FLD 19
William FLD 21
William JEF 38
William CLK 68
William JES 81
William JES 81
William JES 95
William CLY 130
William SHE 161
William CLD 166
William WRN 58A
Willis FTE 105
Wm. ADR 64
Wm. HRD 66
Wm. BRK 269
Wm. BRK 269
Wm. WAS 51A
Wm. GNP 175A
Wm. GNP 178A
Wm. GNP 179A
Yelberton? WDF 97
Zachariah FKN 102
LEWIS?, David RCK 78A
E. A. CHN 40A
Henry HRD 32
LEWMAN, Elijah FLG 48A
Leah? FLG 48A
LEWMAN?, John FLG 28A
Sally FLG 23A
LEXSON, William,
Jr. WTY 124A
LEXSON?, Isaac WTY 118A
LEYMOUR, Ebenezer GTN 124
LIBBEY, Silas CBL 20A
LIBLY?, Leonard HRY 230
LICHLITER, Jacob MER 101
LIDENER?, John FTE 93
LIDINER?, Martin CLK 99
LIDWELL, Elisha BBN 112
John BBN 120
Nathan MAS 61
LIGGETT, Robt. MAS 78
LIGGIN?, William GTN 120
LIGHT, Anthony FLG 25A
David MER 101
Samuel MER 101
Tom MER 114
LIGHTBURN, Tempy SCT 102A
LIGHTFOOD,
Goodrich PND 17A
LIGHTFOOT, Edward JEF 46
Henery ADR 32
Henry WRN 70A
Jno. MAS 64
John WRN 70A
John B. FLG 31A
Meredith ALN 106
Phillip BRK 227
Richd. PND 30A
Robt. FLG 31A
Ruben ADR 32
William ALN 98
William H. BTH 186
Wm. PND 18A
LIGHTNER, William FTE 92
LIGON, Judith HND 10
Leonard WDF 124A
LIKENS, James WRN 39A
LIKENS, William WRN 39A
LIKES, Jas. FLG 55A
Wm. FLG 52A
LILE, Daniel GRN 61
Jacob GRN 71
James GRN 54
John HND 9
John HND 12
Mary HND 9
Mrs. GRN 71
Peter GRN 66
Robert HND 12
William GRN 54
LILES, Saml. BBN 130
Vincent CLD 141
LILEY, Wilson JEF 58
LILLARD, Benjamin WDF 100
Christopher FKN 162
David BNE 24
Dilley MAD 108
Ephraim FKN 162
James, Esq. MER 101
Jno. FKN 138
John MER 101
Joseph MER 101
Thos. FKN 142
LILLETT?, Wm. BBN 106
LILLEY, Aaron CBL 17A
Gabriel HND 9
LILLY, David SHE 168
John SHE 171
John NSN 221
Kesiah HAR 158
Pleasant NCH 112A
Thomas GTN 134
Thomas NSN 221
William ETL 41
LILLY?, David CLK 77
LILY, Tho. ALN 114
LIMEBACK, Salley GTN 121
LIMELLE?, Wm. RCK 81A
Worley RCK 81A
LIMRICK, Tho. MAS 66
LIMSTALL?, Thos.
M. BBN 120
LINBOTTOM, Isaac HRY 192
LINBY?, (See
Linley) CLK 89
LINCH, Andrew PUL 60A
Cornelius BBN 114
Daniel BTH 194
Denis GSN 142A
Elija WAS 31A
Hugh WAS 78A
Meridith WAS 84A
LINCOLN, Abraham GSN 143A
George FTE 103
Mordica GSN 142A
Thos. FKN 102
LINDELL, Jacob J./
S.? NSN 212
LINDER, Abrm. HRD 18
Andrew HRD 58
Anne WTY 116A
Daniel, Junr. HRD 52
Danl., Sr. HRD 24
Izarel HRD 32
Jacob HRD 96
Nathaniel HRD 8
Saml. HRD 58
Thomas BRN 19
LINDEY, Jehu CHN 29
LINDLAY, John CHN 35A
LINDLEY, Daniel OHO 7A
David MAS 77
Jacob HOP 254

Name	County	Page
LINDLEY, Jonathan	HOP	254
Jos.	MAS	60
Thomas	CHN	36
LINDON, Mary	ETL	46
LINDSA, Thos.	MAD	152
LINDSAY, Andrew	MTG	297
Archibald	CHN	32
Jane	FKN	62
Jesse	GTN	127
Nathaniel	OWN	101
Richard C.	GTN	127
Thomas	BNE	24
William	GTN	127
Wm.	CHN	44A
LINDSEY, Alfred	TRG	7A
Allen	JES	82
Calip	GSN	143A
Carleton	TRG	8A
David?	DVS	17A
Geo.	BRK	271
George	CBL	7A
Hayten?	GSN	143A
Henry C.	SCT	105A
Jacob	BBN	74
James	FTE	107
James	HAR	152
James	TRG	4A
James	TRG	8A
James	CBL	22A
James	WRN	48A
John	TRG	7
John	HAR	134
John	CBL	2A
John	FLG	69A
John	SCT	120A
Joseph	WDF	94A
Joseph	SCT	99A
L.	TOD	132A
Landy	WDF	126A
Nancy	HAR	152
Nathaniel	WDF	95
Nimrod L.	BBN	74
Reuben	BBN	104
Richard	CBL	15A
Robert	JES	85
Robt.	SCT	120A
Sterling	TRG	8A
William	WDF	94
William	FTE	107
William	WRN	47A
LINDSY, John	GSN	142A
Olander	HRY	251
Thos.	HRY	267
LINEBAUGH, Daniel	LGN	23
Samuel W.	LGN	23
Thomas W.	LGN	23
LINEBURY, Frederick	LNC	27
LINESTALL?, Thos. M.	BBN	120
LINEY, John	JEF	48
LINGAMPTTER?, John	GTN	125
LINGENFELTER, David	CLK	89
Jacob	CLK	105
John	FTE	111
Valentine	CLK	105
LINGINFELTER, Daniel	WDF	96A
George	FTE	111
LINGUMFELTER, George	HAR	214
Jacob	HAR	212
LINGUMFETTER, John M.	HAR	190
LINGUNFETTER, Mich	HAR	190
LINK, Andrew	ADR	32
Catharine	FTE	94
Henery	ADR	30
Jacob	BBN	122
Joseph	BKN	15
Joseph	BRK	269
LINK?, Diason?	WAS	19A
LINKORN?, Ezakel	CSY	216
LINLEY, Hugh	CLK	89
Hugh	CLK	89
William	CLK	89
LINN, Adam	WDF	103
Alexr.	JEF	33
Ebenazer	MAS	74
Israel	BRN	19
James	HND	13
James	BRN	19
James	ADR	32
John	BRN	19
John	CLK	89
John, Sr.	HND	13
Jonathan	HND	13
Lewis	MAS	62
Patrick	BTH	198
Timothy	NCH	118A
Widw.	CWL	38
William	HND	13
William	BTH	200
LINN?, William M.	UNN	154
LINNEY, Henderson	MER	101
LINNIGER, William	SHE	171
LINNY, George	BTH	208
LINSEY, Abram	BTL	325
Amos	BTL	325
Marcas	WAS	43A
Walter	GRN	77
LINSLEY, Edward	ADR	3
LINTELL, George	DVS	18A
LINTHECUM, Thomas	BLT	176
LINTHECUMB, C.	MAS	64
J.	MAS	64
LINTHICUM, Priscilla	NSN	197
Thomas	NSN	179
LINTON, Benj.	BRK	267
Mary	BTH	202
William	HND	4A
LINUM/LINURN, Lee	BTH	192
LINUM/LINURN?, Andrew	BTH	184
Richard	BTH	182
LINUM, Francis	HAR	178
LINVILL, James	BTH	162
Josiah	BTH	162
Sarah	BTH	160
LINVILLE, Jas.	HRD	74
John	HRD	66
LINWELL?, Aron	BKN	8
John	BKN	4
Lewis	BKN	4
LINYFORD?, Rob.	HRY	188
LINZY, Anthoney	HRY	253
Eliz.	HRY	253
Jno.	HRY	240
Joshua	HRY	240
LION, Ephrim	BRK	269
Hinson	SHE	176
Paul	BRK	267
LIPSCOMB, Anderson	CBL	17A
George	CBL	12A
Joel	CBL	12A
John, Sr.	CBL	17A
John	CBL	16A
Marcus	CBL	16A
Nathan	MAD	158
Richard	CBL	12A
LIPSCOMB, William	CBL	16A
LIPSY, John	PUL	59A
LISBY, Henry	SHE	113A
LISENBY, Abraham	MNR	193
Williama M.	MNR	211
LISLE, James	CLK	90
John	CLK	77
Peter	CLK	96
Samuel	CLK	91
LIST, Geo.	HRY	257
Jac.	HRY	262
Jacob	HRY	251
LISTER, Elias	MER	100
Jane	BBN	88
LITCHER, Jos. & Co.	GRD	82A
LITCHFIELD, David	CWL	46
James	CWL	34
James	CWL	43
LITERAL, Benjamin	WRN	58A
Jeremiah	WRN	58A
John	FTE	81
Robert	WRN	58A
Thomas	WTY	121A
Wm.	GSN	142A
LITERELL, Joseph	JES	78
LITEY, James	GSN	142A
John	GSN	142A
LITHER, Ste.? G., Sr.	GRD	83A
LITLE, John	SHE	142A
Wm.	BKN	2
LITLEFORD?, John D.	FTE	63
LITSEY, Anthony	HRD	40
Mathew	HRD	54
LITSEY?, Randolph	WAS	45A
LITTEL, Thos. G.	MAD	180
LITTELL, Robbert	CBL	3A
William	GRT	146
Wm.	FKN	62
LITTEN, Ralph	BBN	144
LITTEN?, Burton	ADR	32
Daniel	UNN	154
LITTER?, John	JEF	35
LITTERAL, John	CLD	158
Roadham	WDF	97A
LITTESTON, R. C.	MAS	76
LITTESTON?, J. W.	MAS	76
LITTLE, Abram	FLG	26A
Edwd.	CLY	131
Elizabeth	MER	101
Francis	LVG	11
Henry	TOD	128
Henry	SHE	173
Isaac	FLD	40
James W.	FLD	40
John	JEF	33
John	GRD	94A
Nathl.	FLG	60A
Peter	FLD	11
Phillip	SCT	116A
Rob./ Pet.?	HRY	240
Robert	LNC	49
Robt.	LVG	3
Will.	SCT	133A
William	FLD	40
William	NSN	194
LITTLEJOHN, Charles	PUL	67A
Jno.	MAS	74
John	WRN	51A
Morris	SHE	135A
Voluntine	GNP	175A
LITTLEPAGE, Amy	HOP	254
Epps?	HOP	252

Name	County	Page
LITTLEPAGE, James	HOP	252
Nancy	MBG	139A
Richard	HOP	254
Samuel B.	OHO	6A
LITTLETON, John	FLG	52A
John	GNP	169A
Jos.	FLG	51A
LITTON, Burton	WTY	123A
Caleb	BBN	82
John	BBN	72
Solomon	WTY	119A
Thomas	LVG	16
Thomas	LVG	16
LITTRALL, John	FLD	35
LITTREL, John	GTN	127
Rodeham	GTN	117
LITTRELL, Joshua	CSY	226
Thos.	TOD	131
William	CSY	226
LITTRELL?, Richard	CSY	226
LIVELEY, Mark	HRT	162
Tucker	SHE	126A
LIVELY, Cannon	HRT	163
Gilliam	SHE	127A
Henry	GRN	74
John H.	GRN	74
Mark	GRN	69
Richd.	GRN	80
Shadrach	CBL	21A
LIVERS, Robert	NSN	184
Thos.	WAS	44A
LIVES, John	SHE	119A
LIVINGOOD, Peter	HAR	206
Philip	NCH	103A
LIVINGSTEN, David	BKN	15
LIVINGSTON, Barbary	HRT	163
James	JES	93
Jessee	JES	78
John	JES	87
Robert	WYN	95A
Stephen	FKN	76
William	CBL	2A
LIZENBY, William	WDF	99A
LIZER, Peter	HAR	176
LLOYD, James	NSN	221
Joseph	NSN	221
Nancy	BBN	132
Robert	MTG	231
William	MTG	267
LNASBURY?, Benjn.	BBN	128
LO--IL?, John	SCT	123A
LOAN, Jos. W.	BRK	227
LOAR?, David?	BBN	96
LOARDON?, Oliva	HRY	224
LOB, Reuben	HRT	162
LOBB?, Chapman	GRN	57
LOCEY, Solomon	CBL	15A
LOCH, James	GRD	122A
LOCHART, James	WYN	95A
Robert	WYN	93A
Thomas	WYN	93A
LOCHER, Allen	WYN	91A
LOCHLIN, John, Sen.	WYN	87A
LOCK, Jacob, Jr.	BRN	19
James	BKN	14
Nancy	SHE	176
Richard	BTH	170
Will	BBN	62
Wm.	HRT	163
LOCKARD, Andw.	PUL	36A
Thomas	CLY	114
LOCKE, David, Ser.	BRN	18
David,, Jr.	BRN	18
Jacob, Senr.	BRN	19
LOCKE, John D., Jr.	JEF	50
Peter	JEF	41
Richard	BRN	18
LOCKEBIE?, Geo.	JEF	20
LOCKER, Jessee	MAD	168
John	GRD	113A
LOCKER?, G. L.	CHN	46
LOCKERIDGE, Joseph	WRN	69A
LOCKERT, Silas	JES	78
LOCKET, Benjamin	CLK	92
Danl.	ADR	16
Francis	WDF	104A
William	WYN	89A
LOCKETT, Archibald	PUL	66A
James	MBG	141
Joseph	LNC	55
Josiah	PUL	64A
Milton W.	MBG	141
LOCKETTE, Francis	HND	11
LOCKHART, David	LNC	13
Isaac	TRG	11
James	CHN	32A
John	CHN	36
Jonas	LNC	35
LOCKHEART, David	DVS	16A
Elisha	FKN	138
Jesse	DVS	16A
LOCKLIN, Roger	MTG	287
LOCKMAN, John B.	MER	101
LOCKRIDGE, Andrew	HOP	252
James	MTG	241
James	NCH	118A
John	MTG	225
John	MTG	261
John, Sr.	NCH	114A
Jones	BTH	154
Robert	MTG	225
Robert	NCH	118A
William	BTH	172
William	NCH	112A
LOCKWOOD, Ben.	PND	22A
Isaac	PND	20A
Jacob	GNP	168A
John	FTE	64
Junoce?	BNE	22
Saml.	PND	30A
Syllomen	CHN	43
Wm.	PND	15A
LOCLART, Charles	HAR	134
James	HAR	135
LOCLE, John D.	JEF	50
LODGE, Henry	LGN	23
LODUSK, John	WAS	63A
LODUSKEY, Nancy	WAS	65A
LODUSKY?, Jacob	WAS	34A
LOE, Caleb	WRN	52A
David	WRN	58A
Edw.	WAS	84A
George	HAR	208
John	WAS	52A
William, Junr.	WRN	52A
William	WRN	52A
LOE?, William	GTN	131
LOFLAND, Smith	LGN	44
Wm.	CHN	45A
LOFTER?, Bar.	RCK	83A
LOFTIES, Wm.	FLG	40A
LOFTON, -----?	CWL	41
LOFTUN, John	TRG	14A
LOGAN, Alexander	SHE	159
Alexr.	SCT	112A
Allen	LNC	15
Archabald	JES	95
Benj.	SHE	133A
Blakely	KNX	302
LOGAN, Cyrus	LNC	13
David	BRN	18
David	FTE	73
David	GRD	99A
George	LNC	53
Hugh	JEF	38
Hugh	LNC	53
Hugh	PUL	53A
Hugh	GRD	93A
James	FLD	22
James	LNC	35
James	LNC	79
James	FTE	95
James	SHE	159
James	CLD	160
James	HOP	252
James	KNX	308
John	LNC	53
John	SHE	168
John	HRY	184
John	KNX	302
John	GRD	94A
John	SHE	143A
Jos.	MAS	65
Jos.	HRY	256
Joseph	BKN	26
Lewis	CSY	226
M. C.	LNC	13
Margaret	HAR	220
Martin	FTE	93
Mary	FTE	108
Michael	BBN	70
Robert L.	ALN	102
Saml.	MAD	178
Saml.	KNX	288
Samuel	SHE	159
Samuel	MTG	225
Samuel	SPN	8A
Samul?	FTE	75
Timothy	GRD	93A
Tobias	FLG	46A
Will., Jnr.	KNX	310
Will., Sr.	KNX	304
William	FTE	69
William	FTE	108
William	MTG	275
Willm.	LNC	69
Wm.	BKN	24
Wm.	JEF	44
Wm.	BBN	70
Wm., (Clerk)	BRN	18
Wm.	FLG	45A
Wm.	SHE	129A
LOGE, Susannah	BKN	10
LOGHLIN, John W.	HAR	178
LOGIN, Baty	WAS	39A
Mathew	WAS	39A
LOGINS, Joseph	FLD	8
LOGSTON, Edward	MAD	92
Edward	MAD	124
Hiram	HRT	162
James	MAD	94
James	HRT	163
James	HRT	163
James	WYN	93A
John	MAD	94
John C.	HRT	163
John K.	HRT	162
Joseph	MAD	106
Joseph	HRT	162
Joseph	HRT	163
Joshua	WYN	99A
Peter	HRD	22
Polley	HRT	163
Saml.	HRT	163
Susan	MAD	106

LOGSTON, Thomas HRT 162
Thomas S. HRT 163
Ussilla HRT 163
William HRT 162
William WYN 93A
Wm. HRT 163
LOGUE, James FTE 62
LOK, Abraham HRL 112
LOLLARD, Richard FTE 80
LOLLER, Henry CLD 160
James CLD 161
Reuben CLD 163
Robert NCH 111A
LOLLOW?, James SHE 170
LOMA--?, Thomas WRN 45A
LOMAX, Elijah WRN 60A
LONARGEN, Joseph JEF 24
LONCEFORD, Nelly LNC 55
Rodam LNC 67
William LNC 79
LONDON?, John NCH 114A
William NCH 125A
LONES, Henry ETL 40
LONES?, Thomas BBN 142
LONEY, Hugh FTE 68
Thomas FTE 68
LONG, Aaron SHE 175
Abner WRN 47A
Abner SHE 125A
Adam FTE 89
Alexr. SCT 105A
Alexr. SCT 107A
Anderson SHE 175
Anderson WRN 40A
Andrew HRD 50
Andrew GRN 64
Ann GSN 142A
Anthony FKN 136
Aquilla CHN 36
Avery NCH 117A
Benj. SCT 125A
Benjamin JEF 59
Benjamin FKN 114
Benjn. ALN 130
Betssey LNC 43
Briton ALN 142
Brumfield ALN 132
Burril ALN 142
Charles CHN 29
Daniel OHO 6A
David JEF 35
David MAD 110
Edmd. MAS 68
Edward MAD 108
Eliakim NCH 117A
Elijah MAD 108
Francis FTE 93
Gabriel GTN 119
Garret HRY 270
George HND 6
Hardin PUL 38A
Harvy H. SHE 175
Henry FTE 108
Henry BTH 206
Henry GNP 169A
Isaac FTE 105
James MAD 136
James SHE 167
James NSN 182
James WRN 48A
James C. WDF 96
Jane CHN 36
Jane JES 75
Jas. SCT 128A
Jeremiah SHE 160
Jesse MER 100
LONG, Joel MAD 168
Joel WYN 88A
John HND 5
John LGN 38
John CLK 66
John MAD 98
John, Jr. WDF 104A
John, Sr. WDF 104A
John CHN 36A
John WRN 42A
John PUL 55A
John PUL 59A
John WDF 116A
John SHE 126A
John D. MAD 168
John S. LGN 28
Jones MAD 168
Jos. TOD 128A
Joseph MTG 225
Laurence FKN 136
Martin GNP 169A
Melind? GNP 169A
Nathan SHE 127A
Nicholas FTE 74
Nicholas SCT 133A
Nimrod WDF 109A
Peter GSN 142A
Polly CLD 147
Reubin WDF 102A
Richard MAD 164
Richard P. FTE 76
Richd. FKN 114
Robert WDF 103
Robert MTG 229
Robert WRN 59A
Saml. HRY 253
Saml. PND 26A
Saml. NCH 111A
Samuel FTE 64
Samuel WYN 88A
Samuel C. MBG 140
Solomon CLD 149
Tho. HRY 190
Thomas CHN 28
Thomas HAR 216
Thomas NCH 117A
Thos. JEF 24
Thos. CWL 46
Thos. JEF 53
Thos. FKN 60
Thos. SHE 134A
Thos. P. FKN 98
Viney MAD 130
Widow BBN 94
William CHN 36
William FTE 79
William MER 100
William MER 101
William OWN 101
William FTE 105
William CLD 146
William SHE 167
William OHO 8A
William M. WDF 96
Willis HRY 264
Willis SHE 134A
Winney MAD 170
Wm. FKN 96
Wm. MAD 110
Wm. B. WDF 121A
LONG?, Wm. CHN 42
LONGDON, Beverly SCT 135A
Thos. SCT 139A
LONGE?, Anthony JEF 22
LONGENKENER?, A----? PND 25A
LONGLY, James PND 30A
LONGMOOR, Sarah BBN 80
LONGNECKER, David MTG 253
LONHART, Joseph FTE 111
LONRY?, Andrew BRN 18
LONTZ, Curtis LWS 94A
LOOFBOURROW, Thos. V. FKN 60
LOOMAN, Aaron LWS 91A
John LWS 93A
Rezin LWS 87A
Samuel LWS 87A
LOONAMAKER, G. H. JEF 42
LOONEY, Alfred SCT 17A
Peter LWS 94A
LOORD, Christian BBN 88
John BBN 90
LOPER, James GNP 175A
LOPP, Andrew JEF 32
LORANCE, Henry LGN 29
William OWN 105
LORD, James WAS 26A
John BKN 15
Wm. WAS 84A
LORING, Fredk. BBN 146
LORRAIN?, Wm. RCK 83A
LORRANCE?, Wm. RCK 83A
LORREL?, Garrot WAS 81A
LORTON, Jacob WYN 95A
John WRN 45A
Thomas WRN 45A
LOSS, John WRN 62A
LOSSON, Davd? GRD 98A
Willis SHE 134A
LOTH, William CLK 85
LOTSPRICK?, Benjamin FTE 59
LOTT, Aron DVS 18A
Mary SHE 131A
Susanna MBG 135
LOUDAN, Josh. HRY 240
LOUDEN, David FTE 89
LOUDENBACK, William SHE 157
LOUDER, Jefferson WYN 81A
Joshua BTH 200
Nancy GNP 172A
LOUDERBACK, Abraham WDF 110A
John GTN 122
LOUDON, James WRN 64A
Jno. HRY 258
Robt. HRY 254
Terressy HRY 268
LOUDON?, John NCH 114A
William NCH 125A
LOUGH, Daniel MNR 209
Jacob MNR 217
LOUGHLIN, Wm. GNP 173A
LOUGHSON, John GNP 173A
Thomas GNP 169A
LOUGHSON?, John GNP 170A
LOUIS, Isaiah MER 101
LOUNSDALE, Jas. MAS 64
LOURY, Jno. MAS 76
LOVE, -----? DVS 13A
--dw.? E. CWL 39
--rt--? CWL 40
Andrew LVG 7
Arthur LVG 7
Chas. PND 30A
David SHE 157
Edmund BRN 18
Elisabeth FKN 54
G. N. (Inn Keeper) CLY 126

Name	County	Page
LOVE, James	LVG	7
Jas.	CLY	111
Jno.	FKN	160
John	BNE	22
Joseph	SHE	156
Joseph	PUL	56A
Mark	BTH	172
Mathew	JEF	39
Phillip	FTE	94
Samuel	BNE	22
Samuel	HAR	206
Samuel	BTH	208
Thomas	CBL	11A
William	CLD	142
William	HAR	206
William	GSN	142A
Windell	BNE	46
LOVE?, Hugh	HAR	162
LOVEALL, Jonathan, Senr.	PUL	63A
Jonathan	PUL	59A
Jonathan	PUL	63A
Thomas	PUL	61A
Zachariah	PUL	40A
LOVEGROVE, George	HOP	254
LOVEJOY, William	CBL	3A
LOVEL, William	SPN	21A
LOVELACE, Colmore	HRD	66
George	LVG	16
Hazall?	HAR	176
Hillary (Crossed Out)	BLT	196
John	MBG	136
Leonard	BLT	176
William	MBG	136
Zododc?	NSN	214
LOVELACE?, Hillary	BLT	170
LOVELESS, -----?	DVS	7A
Andrew	BTL	325
Archibald	OHO	7A
Elias	BTL	327
George	WYN	99A
Isaac	BTL	327
James	BTL	325
James	CBL	17A
John, Jr.	CBL	17A
John, Sr.	CBL	17A
John	PUL	58A
Reason	SHE	136A
Samuel	CBL	17A
Sarah	WDF	123A
William	WYN	96A
LOVELL, Geo.	FLG	51A
James	BRN	18
Michael	MBG	141A
LOVELY, Jno.	MAS	77
Jno. V.	MAS	76
LOVEN, Isaac	RCK	84A
LOVET, Edom	WTY	116A
LOVIA?, ---ky?	CWL	36
LOVIACE?, Walter	LVG	16
LOVING, Daniel	CBL	5A
John	HOP	252
John	WRN	44A
Joseph	HOP	254
William	LGN	27
William	HOP	252
William	SPN	9A
LOVIT, James W.	ALN	112
LOVLIND?, George	LVG	16
LOVRIL?, John	SCT	123A
LOW, Anna	FTE	91
Elijah	MER	101
Isah	BTH	194
James	ALN	124
John	CLK	65
LOW, John	PND	22A
Nancy	PND	24A
Richard	NSN	214
Saml.	PND	22A
Saml.	PND	31A
Thomas	LNC	81
Thomas	CLD	141
William	LVG	6
William	BTH	194
LOW?, Lot	BTL	325
LOWARD?, Richd.	MAS	75
LOWDER, John	BBN	142
Nathan	WYN	97A
William	ETL	46
LOWDER?, Betsey	BBN	140
LOWDERBACK, Andrew	HAR	188
Jno.	FKN	78
LOWDON, John	GTN	126
LOWE, Isaac	NCH	115A
James R.	GTN	124
John	GRT	145
John	GNP	167A
John F.	SPN	24A
Moses	SHE	112A
Ralph	LGN	42
Stephen	FLD	30
Thomas	CSY	204
William	SPN	24A
LOWELL, Armstead	MNR	195
LOWEN, Benjamin	JES	79
Francis, Jnr.	JES	79
Francis, Snr.	JES	79
LOWER?, Andrew	CLY	112
LOWERY, Betsey	SCT	103A
G. L.	JES	84
Jeremiah	JEF	32
John	JES	94
John	FTE	112
John	SCT	99A
Matthew -.?	MAD	130
Nathan	MAD	158
Robert	JES	91
Thos.	BRK	269
Wilvell	JES	94
Wm.	MAD	106
Wm.	BRK	269
LOWHEAD?, Lewis	GTN	135
LOWMAN, John	FTE	69
LOWREY, Enoc	CLK	73
James	CLK	73
Jno.	FTE	61
John (In Town)	FTE	61
Lud?	CLK	73
Sam	TOD	129A
Wm. G.	FLG	40A
LOWRY, Allen	WRN	76A
Elender	MNR	209
Elijah	MAD	106
James	FTE	58
Jas.?	CWL	39
John	LGN	45
John	FTE	110
John	CLD	150
John	WRN	52A
John	GNP	171A
Nancy	CWL	55
Overton	MNR	209
Rachel	MTG	275
Stephen	WRN	53A
Thos.	LVG	3
William	HAR	144
William	WRN	64A
LOWRY?, -----	CWL	40
----. S.	CWL	40
Andrew	BRN	18
James	FTE	58
LOYAL, James	GRN	57
LOYD, Mrs.?	MAS	66
Dixson	MAS	68
Isaac	MAD	182
James	BRN	19
James	MAD	100
James	WYN	81A
Lemuel	FLG	55A
Nancy	BBN	118
Phitias	LVG	8
Rhodes	FKN	110
Saml.	MAD	100
Sarah	FLG	55A
Simeon	SCT	109A
Thompson C.	CLD	144
Thos.	SCT	101A
Will	MAS	72
William	FTE	100
Wm.?	MAS	66
LOYED, Hannah	GRD	119A
Mulky	GRD	98A
LOYED?, Moses	GRD	119A
LOZANCE?, Jacob	LGN	29
LUALLEN, John	OHO	5A
LUCAS, Abraham	HRD	36
Charles	WRN	46A
Cornelus	HRD	46
Cornelus	HRD	86
George	OWN	100
Henry	NSN	193
Igs.	WAS	62A
Ingram	LVG	7
Jas.	HRD	20
Jno.	NSN	193
John	CSY	204
John	OHO	8A
John	WRN	46A
John	WAS	55A
John W.	WRN	75A
Lindors	NSN	207
Manoah	SCT	106A
Reubin	CBL	11A
Richard	GRT	146
Robert W.	WRN	46A
Saml.	MAS	76
Samuel	LVG	16
Samuel	LVG	16
Sarah	FTE	94
Sarah	WRN	46A
Thos. C.	BBN	64
William	LNC	49
William	LWS	90A
Zackariah	CLK	103
LUCE, William	MBG	136
LUCE?, Benjamin	BTL	325
LUCES?, William	GRD	110A
LUCEY, Thos.	SCT	104A
LUCH, Burton	SCT	133A
Martial	SCT	102A
LUCK, Cagaby	SCT	103A
Henry	SCT	108A
Joseph	SCT	117A
LUCKER, Benjamin	UNN	150
LUCKET, Hezekiah	WAS	56A
Samuel	BRN	18
Wm.	BRN	19
LUCKETT, Benj.	FKN	82
C. P.	JEF	19
David L.	HRY	184
Ignatius	LGN	28
Jeremiah	FKN	82
Jerry	FKN	96
Saml.	FKN	90
Saml. N.	JEF	50
Thos.	FKN	88
William G.	SHE	176

LUCKETT, Wm. PND 17A
Wm. PND 23A
LUCKEY, John MAD 158
LUCKIE, Clohe. Collerd Free Woman BBN 70
Joseph BBN 64
Robt. BBN 64
LUCKY, Geo. MAS 79
Hugh F. HRY 178
James GSN 142A
Jane ADC 68
Samuel GSN 142A
LUCUS, Benedick BRK 267
Elijah BNE 22
Elijah SCT 122A
John SCT 121A
Richard CLY 126
Stephen SCT 127A
Wm. BKN 5
LUCUS?, Guy BRK 269
LUCUST, J. G.? SHE 136A
Wm. SHE 121A
LUDLOW, Nathaniel JEF 60
Wm. H. JEF 24
LUDOWECK?, Christopher NSN 211
LUDWICK, John MER 101
LUDY?, Philip ETL 53
LUFLOW, Jacob SHE 160
LUGAN?, James BBN 124
LUKE, John SCT 104A
John SCT 127A
LUKINS, Peter FLG 24A
LUMBARD, Jessee CBL 7A
LUMES, Ephraim GNP 167A
LUMMIS, Reubin CBL 18A
LUMPKIN, John FTE 107
Tho. M. ALN 92
LUMPSON, Solomon MAS 55
LUMPTON, John MAD 172
LUN?, John D. BLT 184
LUNA?, Robert FTE 106
LUNAR?, Samuel ALN 116
LUNCE, Ephraim CLY 130
Fany RCK 83A
LUNCEFORD, Peter SHE 125A
LUND, Isaac PUL 49A
LUND?, Robert FTE 106
LUNDRY, Joseph SCT 135A
Simon HRD 64
LUNELLE?, Wm. RCK 81A
Worley RCK 81A
LUNES?, Nancy OHO 10A
LUNG, Jacob MER 101
LUNSDILL?, W? TOD 128A
LUNSFORD, Moses FLD 3
William SHE 152
LUPER?, -----? N. LVG 9
LUPIN?, Barbary NSN 193
Lewis NSN 185
LUPKIN, Benjamin FTE 103
LUPORS?, Thos. BBN 102
LURE?, John D. BLT 184
LURTON?, Will SCT 136A
LURTY, Robert BKN 4
Wm. B. BKN 4
LUSBY, John H. FTE 86
LUSE?, John RCK 79A
LUSH, Wm. HRD 48
LUSH?, Wm HRD 76
Wm., Junr. HRD 76
LUSK, Hugh HRD 60
James JES 85
John HRD 58
John CLK 105
LUSK, Lirus/ Sirus? CLK 82
Saml. HRD 44
Samuel CLY 121
William, Sr? GRD 105A
William GRD 114A
LUSK?, Wm HRD 76
Wm., Junr. HRD 76
LUSS, Adam MAD 180
LUSTER, Augustus GTN 123
Barbara, Mrs. WYN 103A
James PUL 59A
Jesse MER 100
John GTN 123
John PUL 63A
John GNP 169A
Vincent, Jr. PUL 58A
Vincent, Senr. PUL 63A
William JEF 64
William PUL 58A
Zachariah PUL 58A
LUSTON?, Will. SCT 136A
LUSTRE?, -----? CWL 36
LUTCH?, John W. LWS 89A
LUTES, Benjamin NSN 201
Danl. HRY 182
Henry ETL 53
John ETL 53
William NSN 192
LUTHAND, Saml. MAS 54
LUTRALL, John UNN 148
LUTTERAL, Nancy ADR 32
LUTTERLL, George GTN 122
LUTTREL?, Rodham, Jr. GTN 133
LUX?, John D. BLT 184
LWELLING, John MER 101
LWRANCE, Sollomon WAS 21A
LYCAN, David FLD 9
Isaac FLD 10
Jeremiah FLD 10
John FLD 10
William FLD 10
William FLD 10
William FLD 10
LYDICK, Barbary FTE 77
Elizabeth BBN 110
Harry (Free Man) BBN 136
LYEN, William UNN 147
LYLE, David FTE 78
David SHE 158
Joel R. BBN 146
John FTE 79
John, Rev. BBN 146
Sarah SCT 138A
LYLE?, Joseph G. SCT 94A
LYLES, James UNN 149
LYLN, Lewis BBN 110
LYMAN, Abner HRD 84
David JEF 44
LYMES, Frances CSY 204
Zachariah CSY 208
LYMORE, Jonas MAS 63
LYN?, Jacob RCK 83A
LYNCH, B. J./ I.? SCT 139A
Charles SHE 163
George H. LGN 35
Henry MAD 166
James ETL 50
James H. WYN 87A
John HRY 226
John PUL 62A
Joseph NSN 196
Joshua JES 91
Lawrence KNX 282
Nancy WRN 71A
LYNCH, William SPN 23A
Wm. RCK 75A
LYNCHARD, Prudence OWN 102
LYNE, George HND 11
Leonard H. HND 11
Timothy LGN 37
LYNE?, Thomas WDF 97
LYNN, -----? DVS 9A
-----? DVS 9A
Adam TRG 7
Adam CBL 9A
Charles TRG 7
David SCT 115A
Frances CLD 161
Gasham MBG 137
Hannah FTE 84
Henry MBG 141A
James TRG 11
James HOP 252
Jas. SCT 115A
John LNC 23
John OWN 105
John ALN 122
Joseph JEF 31
Nancy TOD 127A
Pehhyt WRN 59A
Pitts HOP 252
Priscilla LNC 23
Robt. SCT 115A
Rubin TRG 7
Samuel CLD 155
William CSY 216
William, Junr. MBG 141A
William, Senr. MBG 137
William NCH 119A
LYNTHYCUM, Tho. LNC 27
LYON, -----? CWL 40
Chas MAS 67
Chittenden CWL 46
David BRN 19
E., Mrs.? MAS 67
Elijah LGN 37
Elijah SHE 114A
Elly RCK 80A
George BRN 19
Henry SHE 142A
Hezakiah GNP 175A
Hezekiah JEF 54
Humphrey HAR 210
James MAS 52
Jas HRD 38
Jas. CLY 111
John ADR 32
John LGN 37
John BBN 124
Joshua ALN 98
Lawson HAR 168
Lucy LGN 45
Mathew, Jr. CWL 46
Mildred SHE 142A
Milley FKN 108
Nathl. SCT 92A
Richd. BBN 144
Samuel SHE 142A
Thomas WRN 37A
Valentine SHE 133A
William FLD 19
William F. GTN 118
Wm.? E. MAS 67
Zac SHE 142A
LYONS, Abraham LGN 43
Elijah GTN 117
Ezekiel MER 101
George LNC 39
Hannah CBL 22A
James MER 101

LYONS, John BNE 22
John LGN 37
John LGN 44
John MER 101
John FLG 55A
John WAS 59A
Jonathan GTN 117
Joseph MER 101
Robert MER 101
Samuel MER 101
Stephen MER 101
Stephen MER 101
Thomas GRD 118A
Thos. WAS 59A
Thos. WAS 60A
Wm. HRD 50
LYONS?, John BBN 120
Zecheriah ALN 94
LYSLE, John E. CLK 79
LYSMAN?, John HOP 254
LYSTER, Cornelius MER 100
John MER 100
Peter MER 100
Stephen MER 100
LYTEN?, Caleb HOP 252
LYTER, John JEF 44
John, Jr. BBN 110
John, Senr. BBN 110
Jonas JEF 65
LYTER?, Henry BBN 110
Henry, Rev.? BBN 110
Jacob BBN 110
LYTLE, John GRD 86A
William FTE 106
LYTTE, Jacob JEF 33

M-----?, John GRN 62
M----, Robert BNE 26
M----?, -----? HRT 164
-----? HRT 164
M--CUM, Daniel ALN 116
M--F--D?, Richd. J.? HRT 164
M--RS, Micah WAS 46A
M--RY?, John GTN 132
M-IRE?, James CLK 86
MA----, John ADR 34
MA-Y?, Alex. FKN 104
Gustavus FKN 104
MABAN, James LGN 41
John LGN 46
MABEN, A. TOD 129
MABRY, John TRG 13
MAC CONN?, John MER 103
Moses MER 101
MAC COUN, John MER 103
Joseph MER 103
Samuel MER 104
MACATEE, Abednago BBN 72
MACATEE?, Elisha UNN 152
MACBRIDE?, David CSY 216
MACCOUN, James FTE 59
MACEY?, Chs. FKN 98
MACGOWAN, Julia FTE 67
Thomas FTE 59
MACHEN, Henry CWL 37
MACHER?, William FTE 105
MACHIN, E., Miss MAS 81
MACHLIN, Hugh FKN 86
MACK, Randolph MER 102
MACK?, Robert MTG 281
MACKALL, John J. LGN 41
MACKAY, Jas. MAS 61
MACKBEE, Isaac CLD 137
MACKEE, Jane MAD 134
MACKENLIRE, Elizab MER 101
MACKENTIRE, John BBN 80
MACKEY, David SHE 157
John LWS 93A
Will MAS 66
Wm. FKN 162
MACKINTERE, James CHN 39
MACKLIE?, Hendon BKN 16
MACKLIN, Jno. MAS 56
Wm. MAS 56
MACKLIN?, Hendon BKN 16
MACKY, Geo. M. BKN 24
James CLD 153
MACUM, Jas. BBN 84
MACURDY, Allen F. FKN 58
MACY, Alexander B. LGN 42
MADARES?, Charls ADR 36
MADCALF, Kimble MAD 136
Mary MAD 136
MADCAP, James WAS 57A
Norris CHN 35
MADDEN, Elizabth FLD 14
Jere. FLG 73A
John OWN 101
John FLG 73A
Jos. FLG 73A
Lina SCT 119A
Walter WAS 42A
MADDERA, Jno. LVG 3
MADDEX, Nathaniel FLD 22
MADDIN, Elisha BTL 327
Jane HRD 90
MADDISON, John MAD 150
Susanna WRN 46A
MADDON, Thomas BNE 26
MADDOX, -----? DVS 5A
Baylor BBN 118
Benett NCH 120A
Benjamin BBN 66
Bennet HRY 259
Charles CBL 17A
Dan SHE 165
David SHE 165
Elijah SHE 166
Ellis JEF 31
George FLD 8
Gordin JEF 64
Henley NCH 123A
Hezekiah CBL 17A
James OWN 103
Jno. HRY 259
John SHE 158
John, Junr. OHO 9A
John, Senr. OHO 9A
Luke PND 20A
Michael GTN 129
Nath. HRY 260
Posey SHE 117A
Robert SHE 165
Sherwood OWN 103
Sherwood GTN 119
Stephen H. SHE 154
Susana GTN 119
Thomas OWN 102
Thomas WDF 103A
William SHE 165
Wilson SHE 155
Wilson SHE 162
Wilson HRY 241
Wm. FKN 78
Wm. HRY 260
Wm. OHO 9A
MADDUX, Benj. FLG 30A
Geo. B. FLG 26A
John FLG 30A
Mathew FLG 32A
Walter FLG 61A
MADIRE, Nathan GNP 170A
MADISON, Bowland MER 102
Francis BRN 20
James, Jr. BTL 327
James, Sr. BTL 327
Leroy OHO 5A
Moriah JES 73
Robert HAR 162
MADOX, Catharine WAS 40A
MAFFEE, William NSN 212
MAFFET, William NSN 221
MAFFETT, John NSN 221
MAFFIT, Henry HAR 206
John HAR 208
Matthew HAR 208
MAFFITT, Thomas HAR 208
William HAR 208
MAGEE, Giorge? MAD 166
Henry MAD 108
Humphrey SHE 151
John MAD 106
Merriman FLD 40
Ralph MAD 104
Ralph MAD 110
MAGERS, Alexander SPN 7A
Elijah SPN 7A
John, Jr. WYN 94A
John WYN 94A
MAGGARD, John HRL 114
Samuel HRL 114
MAGGARDS, Peggy GNP 172A
MAGGART, Jacob BRN 19
MAGILL, Andrew UNN 152
James LNC 15
James LNC 19
Jno. FKN 128
John LNC 61
Margarett LNC 17
Mathew E. FKN 128
Saml. FKN 128
Saml. P. GRD 105A
Willm. LNC 53
Wm. LNC 19
MAGNOR, William LGN 25
MAGOFFIN, Beriah MER 114
Nathaniel MER 115
MAGOWAN, David FTE 70
James S. MTG 295
MAGOWEN, Abram FLG 42A
Susanah FLG 32A
MAGOWIN, William BTH 186
MAGREGG, Emeriah A. SHE 154
MAGREGOR, Ann FTE 68
MAGRUDER, Ezekiel NSN 192
John NSN 180
MAGUER?, John NCH 124A
MAGUIR?, William NCH 127A
MAGUIRE, Edward FTE 74
MAHAFFEY, Alexander FTE 63
MAHAN, Alexander MNR 191
Alexander WRN 40A
Geo. FLG 48A
Hesek. KNX 302
James LVG 8
James SHE 166
James KNX 278
James WAS 35A
James WTY 118A
John MER 102
John MER 102
John FLG 25A
John WTY 126A
Margarett HAR 164
Peter LVG 8

Name	County	Page
MAHAN, R. S.	HAR	166
Saml.	LVG	7
Saml.	FLG	48A
Thomas	WTY	123A
Will.	LVG	8
William	WDF	97
William	BLT	190
MAHANEY, John	FLG	54A
MAHANY, Clerimond	MNR	199
William	BTH	170
MAHERN?, Lucas	ALN	114
MAHEUR?, Alexander	GNP	168A
MAHEW?, Alexander	GNP	168A
MAHON, Alexander	FTE	110
William	LGN	31
MAHONE?, Dennis	BTL	327
MAHONEY, James H.	SCT	91A
Richd. B.	SCT	112A
MAHORNEY, Ben.	HRY	267
Dennis	HRY	253
Field.	HRY	255
Lloyd	HRY	253
Talifaro	SHE	166
Wilbern	BLT	194
MAHORNY, Ben.	HRY	262
MAHOW?, Dennis	BTL	327
MAHU, Murry	GNP	177A
MAHUE, Walter	WRN	42A
MAHUGH, Alexan.	ALN	104
Bryant	FLG	61A
Moses	ALN	104
Moses	ALN	114
MAHUGH?, Jas.	ALN	112
MAHURAN?, Elias	SHE	113A
MAHUREN, Othoniel?	SHE	116A
Samuel	SHE	114A
MAIDE, Meridith	LGN	45
MAIDEN, Isaac	RCK	80A
MAIL, Freak	NSN	182
MAINER, Christopher	FLD	33
Christopher	FLD	33
MAINER?, David	FLD	26
MAINES, George	BKN	15
Jacob	BKN	15
Levi	BKN	13
Peter	BKN	14
MAINGALT, Benjamin	JEF	31
MAINOR, James	FLD	33
James	FLD	34
Jesse	FLD	34
Lewis	FLD	34
Mark	FLD	34
Moses	FLD	34
William	FLD	34
MAINS, George, Sr.	BKN	6
Phillip	BKN	22
MAIRE/MAISE?, William	BTH	200
MAIZE, William	WTY	114A
MAJOR, Arthurs	BNE	50
Benj.	CHN	40
Dav.	HRY	241
Francis	FKN	122
Geo.	FKN	124
James	FKN	76
Jno.	CHN	39
Jno.	FKN	126
Jno., Jr.	FKN	126
Joseph	CHN	39
Lewis R.	FKN	80
Littleton	FKN	132
Thos.	FKN	76
Thos.	FKN	126
Weden	FKN	126
Wm. T.	CHN	39
MAJORS, Alexander	HOP	256
James	HND	6
James	HOP	254
Robert	WRN	52A
Saml.	HND	6
William	HOP	258
William	WRN	52A
MAKEMSON, Andrew	HAR	134
Jos.	HRD	40
Thomas	HAR	134
William	HAR	134
MAKERN?, Lucas	ALN	114
MAKEY, Alesander	LWS	96A
MAKIMSON, Andrew	HAR	140
MAKINZIE, Mark	KNX	292
MAKWELL, Jas.	FLG	42A
MALADA?, John	BNE	24
MALCOM, William	ALN	116
MALCOMB, Leven	WDF	114A
Robert	WDF	114A
MALDEN, Richard	LVG	16
MALES?, Enoch	HAR	144
MALIN, John	HOP	254
John	BRK	277
MALL-RY?, Geo.	SCT	117A
MALLAHAM?, James	WAS	18A
MALLARD, Elizabeth	CHN	34A
MALLEREY, Wm.	CHN	40A
MALLERY, Timothy	HAR	182
William	SPN	16A
MALLET, William	CLY	126
MALLETT, Thomas	FLD	13
Thomas	FLD	13
MALLIN, Isaac	HRY	240
J.	HRY	228
Job P.	BTL	327
Owen	HRY	240
Saml.	HRY	252
MALLONE, Wm.	MAD	94
MALLORY, Ambrose	FTE	93
D.	JEF	20
Elijah	MAD	134
James	MAD	150
Jno., Jr.	CHN	40A
Jno., Snr.	CHN	40A
John F.	BRN	19
Lucy	LNC	71
Mary	SCT	118A
Nancy	BBN	104
Roger	FTE	94
Roger	MAD	134
Samuel	FTE	94
Stephen	BBN	84
Thos.	CHN	40A
Thos.	CHN	40A
MALLOTT, Elias	JEF	37
MALLOY?, James	ALN	122
MALOAN, Andrew	MTG	257
MALON, J. T.	BNE	52
MALONE, Banister	ADR	3
Benjamin	MNR	211
C. Williamson	MNR	211
Saml. P.	BRN	20
William	HAR	188
William	MNR	191
Wm.	MAD	162
Wynn	BRN	20
MALONEY, Robert	BLT	168
MALONY, John	ETL	45
MALOT, Joseph	MAD	146
MALOTT, Hiram	JEF	40
MALOY, Marcus	CWL	44
MALRINE?, Edw.	BKN	24
MALTIS?, William	JES	77
MALTZ, Jacobson &?	JEF	27
MALVANIN, Sally	BRK	275
MAMAN?, Liddy?	MAD	150
MAN, Jesse	BTL	327
John	HND	10
Robert	HND	10
MAN?, John, Jr.	GRN	66
Joseph, Sr.	GRN	66
Mary	GRN	66
Moses	GRN	65
MANAFEE, James	LNC	71
Reuben	LNC	71
MANCEL?, Nancy	MTG	241
MANCY?, John	WRN	74A
MANDLY?, John H.	JES	69
MANECA, Amelia	NSN	198
MANEES, Jno.	LVG	4
MANEN?, Cornulus?	TRG	7A
MANER?, Jonathan	BTH	216
MANEY?, John	WRN	74A
MANGARD?, John	JEF	45
MANGRUM, Lewis	CBL	16A
MANI-?, Abraham	ALN	138
MANIARD, John	BRN	21
Richd.	HRY	270
MANIER, John	FLG	29A
John	FLG	45A
MANIFEE, Larkin	SCT	98A
Larkin	SCT	112A
MANING, Elisha	PND	31A
John	SCT	98A
MANION, Francis	MAD	152
MANION?, Jas.	TOD	133
MANKINS, Peter	FLD	23
Walter	FLD	23
MANKSFIELD, David	LGN	38
Elijah	LGN	38
Rebecca	LGN	37
MANLEY, Ephram	GSN	144A
Isaac	LWS	88A
Jonathan, Jr.	WRN	56A
Thomas	BRN	19
MANLEY?, Saml.	FLG	58A
MANLY, Ann	FTE	113
Cornelius	WRN	56A
James	BTH	166
MANLY?, Wm.	FLG	59A
MANN, Benjamin	CBL	14A
Chas. E.	TOD	126A
Eligah	CBL	14A
Elisha	CHN	31
Francis	HAR	202
George	CHN	31
Henry	BBN	118
Jackson	MER	102
Jacob	NCH	111A
Jesse	TOD	133
John	JEF	30
John	ETL	54
John	TOD	125
John	HAR	202
John	NCH	111A
Peter	BKN	18
Peter	NCH	111A
Phill	MAS	73
Richd.	PND	16A
Robert	CLD	155
Samuel	FLD	5
Thomas	MER	101
Thomas	SHE	152
Thomas	CBL	14A
William	FLD	5
William	CBL	14A
Wm.	BRN	20
MANN?, Ben	GRD	83A
MANNAN, Andrew	HRL	114
John	FLD	12
Samuel	HRL	114

MANNER?, Adam BBN 130
MANNIN?, Polly HRY 214
MANNING, Miss JEF 26
Henry BTH 174
John MAD 156
John BTH 196
Meredith BTH 174
Richard WDF 100A
William WDF 112A
William WTY 122A
MANNON, Ambrose MNR 199
Asa WRN 46A
Jas. MAS 54
Jno. MAS 54
Jno., Jr. MAS 54
Nancy WRN 60A
Stephen WRN 57A
MANOR, Jeremiah HAR 194
John MER 104
MANSEL, Ann SCT 94A
MANSEL?, Nancy MTG 241
MANSF----?, -----? HRT 164
MANSFIELD, G. W. ALN 132
J. TOD 125A
J. S. TOD 125A
James BRN 21
James CWL 37
Jesse BRN 21
John CBL 8A
John GRD 93A
R. TOD 125A
Saml. BBN 110
Samuel WAS 53A
Shelton GTN 120
Thos. BRN 19
Wm. BRN 21
Wm. MAD 118
MANSON, Amos? O. BKN 10
MANT?, Sandell LGN 44
MANUEL, Catharine FTE 96
William FTE 95
MAPLE, David LWS 96A
George LWS 96A
John LWS 96A
Sally JEF 33
MAPPIN, Carr BTH 208
Dabney BTH 216
John BTH 216
Margaret BTH 182
MARAMAN, Frances BLT 190
MARCH, Abraham VID 96
Absolam CLK 76
Jacob CLK 72
John CLK 72
Laurence JES 87
Rudolph MAD 112
William LGN 43
Wm. MAD 150
MARCH?, Wm. BKN 20
MARCHALL, James WAS 52A
MARCUM, James FLD 45
John GRN 66
John CLY 114
Thomas CLY 115
William FLD 42
MARCY?, Alex. FKN 104
Gustavus FKN 104
MARDIS, Elizabeth CBL 12A
James CBL 12A
Will. KNX 314
William CBL 12A
MARDIS?, Roby GRN 75
MAREK?, Wm. BKN 20
MARES, Saml. NCH 108A
MARGHAM?, Blanch LGN 36
MARGURSON, John OWN 105
MARION, William CBL 16A
MARION?, George CBL 16A
John CBL 16A
MARK, Elijah FLG 30A
John W. FLG 25A
Samuel HRL 114
Wm. BBN 128
Wm. FLG 25A
MARK?, Robert MTG 281
MARKAM, Archibald WYN 82A
Edmund WYN 82A
James WYN 102A
Thomas WYN 102A
MARKER, John BTL 327
Timothy JES 74
MARKER?, William FTE 105
MARKEY, Jonas BBN 110
MARKHAM, Allen UNN 152
John UNN 152
William BBN 108
MARKLAND, Alley BNE 26
Jessee BNE 26
Mathew CLK 69
Matthew ETL 39
MARKLAND?, Mathew BTH 180
MARKLEY, Jno. A. FKN 56
Thomas CLK 88
MARKS, ----h? DVS 14A
Benjamin HND 11A
George NSN 196
Hasteen? CLK 94
Isaah HND 12
Jessee HND 13
John, Jr. HND 13
John, Sr. HND 13
Rachel HND 12
Sarah NSN 196
Sarah DVS 14A
MARKSBERRY, John GRT 143
John SHE 161
Samuel GRT 143
Samuel GRT 145
Sophia, Miss GRT 143
Willis GRT 145
MARKSBURY, Isaac GRD 91A
Richd. GRD 114A
MARKSBURY?, William GRD 86A
MARKSPILE, William MER 103
MARKUM, Wm. ALN 112
MARKWELL, Elias BLT 188
Geo. JEF 45
Henry FLG 75A
Hurst FLG 54A
John BLT 186
Wm. JEF 45
Wm. FLG 58A
MARLER, Luke MNR 209
MARLOW, Dory WAS 43A
Edward OHO 6A
Geo. SCT 106A
John WYN 96A
Margaret OHO 10A
Mark CLD 153
Saml. SCT 102A
Will. W. SCT 108A
William CLD 155
Wm. B. OHO 5A
MARLOWE, B. BBN 138
MARMADUKE, Samson SHE 165
MARMON, John JES 97
MARMON?, Joseph WRN 44A
MARMOOD, George JES 89
MARONA, Henry MNR 209
MAROON?, Jacob HRD 88
MARPLES, Ben WAS 30A
John ADR 38
MARQUES, Wm. SHE 137A
MARR, James HAR 134
John BRN 20
Richd. GRN 70
MARR?, David WAS 84A
John, Jr. GRN 66
Joseph, Sr. GRN 66
Mary GRN 66
Moses GRN 65
MARRER?, Jonathan BTH 216
MARRICLE, Fredderic HRL 114
Fredderick HRL 114
James HRL 114
John HRL 114
MARRION?, Jas. TOD 133
MARRIOTT, Jas. HRD 46
Will SCT 97A
MARRS, A. T. MNR 215
Alexander SHE 164
David SHE 163
Henry M. MER 103
Hugh LGN 47
Hugh BTL 327
Hugh, Jr. BTL 327
John BTL 327
John SHE 133A
Mary LGN 47
Samuel MNR 217
William LGN 47
William, Jr. LGN 47
MARRT?, Sandell LGN 44
MARS, James JES 81
James JES 87
Jno., Sr. JEF 50
John, Jr. JEF 50
MARSDON, James BLT 158
John BLT 158
Jonathan BLT 158
Mary BLT 196
MARSELL, John ADR 62
MARSH, Achd. BKN 20
Beal BBN 112
Catherine FTE 70
Charles MER 102
David HAR 150
Henry MNR 209
James HAR 150
James HAR 218
Jno. HRY 241
Jonathan HAR 146
Joseph MNR 207
Margaret HAR 178
Mary CBL 3A
Mene JEF 23
Nathaniel CLK 76
Samuel MBG 136
Thomas CBL 15A
Thos. CWL 43
Thos. BBN 86
MARSHAK, Martin BKN 16
MARSHAL, Alexander BNE 24
Benjamin FTE 61
Christiana CHN 40A
Isral CHN 40A
James BNE 24
James HAR 140
James HAR 194
Jno. CHN 40A
John LVG 16
John BNE 26
John HAR 192
Joseph BNE 26
Lewis WDF 94A

MARSHAL, Lucy HND 11
Ralf HAR 194
Robert FTE 107
Timothy P. NSN 204
William BNE 24
William MER 102
William HAR 194
William HAR 198
Wm. HRY 241
Wm. CHN 40A
MARSHALL, A. K. MAS 58
Anarchy FTE 108
Benj. BKN 20
Benjamin MNR 197
Bennett HND 4A
Beverly GRN 64
Carter HRY 186
Dd. BBN 128
Eliza GRN 64
Elizabeth BBN 104
F., Mrs. MAS 81
Francis MTG 297
George CWL 40
George SHE 150
George BLT 186
George HAR 198
George WAS 19A
Henry MAS 77
Hugh NCH 103A
Humphrey FKN 66
James BNE 26
James JES 75
Jane/ Jam? GRD 105A
Jas. JEF 28
Jas. BRK 273
Jno. MAS 58
Jno. MAS 65
Jno. FKN 66
Jno., Jr. MAS 69
John FLD 5
John HRD 64
John MTG 253
John B. GRN 56
Joseph BBN 128
Joseph H. GRN 51
Josiah LGN 28
Josiah NSN 200
Lewis LGN 42
Margaret NSN 200
Mark HRD 30
Martin P. MAS 81
Mary Ann FTE 86
Maryann HRY 266
Mason LGN 30
Polly MNR 201
Polly? MAS 55
Reuben FLD 5
Reuben LNC 73
Robbert CBL 12A
Robt. HRD 74
Rubin CWL 44
Samuel BRN 19
Samuel LGN 30
Samuel GRN 51
Samuel GRN 61
Samuel HAR 194
Samuel MNR 195
Stephen SCT 93A
Steven PND 22A
Thomas OWN 104
Thomas MTG 231
Thomas LWS 96A
Thomas A. BBN 142
Thos. FKN 112
Thos. HRY 259
Timothy NSN 213
MARSHALL, Will MAS 59
William JES 87
William JES 88
William CLK 94
William OWN 102
William CBL 18A
William WRN 34A
Wm. JEF 19
Wm. FKN 64
Wm. MAS 76
Wm. BRK 275
MARSHEL, Samuel SHE 131A
MARSHELL, John HRL 114
MARSTELLER, John FLG 75A
MARSTON, James OWN 99
William OWN 104
MARTAIN, Dabney CSY 208
Moses CSY 208
Simeon CSY 206
William CSY 214
MARTEN, Saml. MAS 54
MARTHIS?, Conrad NSN 183
MARTIAL, George MAD 146
Henry MAD 156
MARTIN, Mrs. MAS 77
Mrs. MAS 78
--ncent? DVS 14A
-ewis? CWL 42
-i--s? BRK 277
Abner HOP 254
Abraham SHE 113A
Alex. CWL 34
Alexander HAR 134
Andrew MER 101
Ann TOD 130
Anna TRG 13A
Archibald WRN 67A
Asael FLG 52A
Azeriah ETL 42
Benj. SCT 122A
Benjamin JES 94
Benjamin MER 101
Benjamin WRN 30A
Benjamin WRN 58A
Benjamin WYN 96A
Benjamin SHE 124A
Blackstone CBL 13A
Charles BRN 21
Charles FTE 104
Charles SPN 23A
Daniel SHE 122A
Danl. BRK 277
David LVG 5
David FLD 43
David CLD 140
David GRD 102A
Edmund NCH 128A
Edward BRN 21
Edward HAR 208
Elexander SHE 128A
Elijah OWN 104
Elijah GTN 128
Elijah MTG 233
Elizabeth CHN 38
Elizabeth KNX 302
Elizabeth SHE 124A
Elizah BRK 273
Enoch SHE 170
Evi? LVG 12
Frederick HRD 48
French FLG 23A
Garld. BRN 20
Geo. FKN 88
George FLD 47
George CLK 72
George CLD 141
MARTIN, Gibson WRN 29A
Gideon WRN 29A
Hannah FKN 60
Harry MAS 72
Henery CBL 21A
Henry WDF 94A
Henry SHE 143A
Hezekiah BBN 126
Hosea FKN 130
Hudson CLK 77
Hudson MAD 162
Hudson WRN 61A
Hugh JEF 50
Hutson JES 87
Hutson MBG 142A
Isaac BRN 20
Isaac TOD 128
Isha FTE 107
Isham MNR 195
Jacob NCH 107A
James ADR 14
James LVG 16
James BRN 21
James BNE 26
James JEF 37
James FLD 43
James JES 83
James FKN 88
James JES 88
James GTN 135
James HAR 188
James MNR 211
James MTG 239
James HOP 254
James HOP 256
James OHO 5A
James SHE 112A
James SHE 120A
James A? JES 79
Jane CBL 14A
Jarvis WDF 94A
Jas. LVG 6
Jas. CHN 38
Jas. HRD 58
Jas. BRK 277
Jeremiah MAS 59
Jilson MTG 291
Jno. HAR 170
Jno. PUL 40A
Job WYN 83A
Joel FLD 43
John HND 13
John LNC 75
John CLK 102
John BBN 128
John GTN 133
John HAR 140
John HAR 194
John MNR 195
John HAR 196
John MNR 207
John BTL 327
John BTL 327
John BTL 327
John, Jr. CLK 77
John, Majr. CLK 102
John, Sr. WYN 94A
John (Tailor) CLK 92
John -.? GRN 60
John DVS 18A
John WRN 33A
John WAS 43A
John WAS 58A
John WRN 58A
John WRN 71A
John WYN 86A

MARTIN, John NCH 107A
John SHE 123A
John G. BBN 146
John G. FLG 27A
John L. FTE 74
John P. CLK 64
John S. SHE 124A
Johnson PUL 36A
Jonah HAR 198
Jonas LNC 55
Jonothan HRD 34
Jos. MAS 53
Jos. SHE 124A
Jos. M. SHE 139A
Joseph TRG 4
Joseph GRN 68
Joseph, Jnr. HAR 176
Joseph, Snr. HAR 176
Joseph CBL 13A
Joseph SCT 108A
Joshua HND 12
Josiah SHE 161
Larkin HRY 264
Lawr. WAS 58A
Leroy FTE 99
Levi PUL 40A
Lewis ADR 36
Lindsey CWL 55
Littleton BRK 277
Lydia FTE 98
Lyman GTN 119
Manoah SHE 170
Margaret FTE 99
Martin F. LVG 16
Martwell GRN 80
Mary CWL 44
Mary ALN 108
Mary ALN 114
Michael HOP 256
Moses CLY 121
Moses GTN 133
Moses MNR 211
Moses OHO 10A
Moses SHE 112A
Nathan TOD 129
Nathan WRN 58A
Nathaniel MNR 217
Nehemiah NCH 106A
Nelson JES 85
Nicholas LNC 5
Nicholas JEF 39
Obadiah LNC 5
Obadiah MER 101
Obadiah OHO 5A
Peter WAS 80A
Peter SHE 124A
Phebe WRN 39A
Philip LGN 34
Philip LGN 46
Philip HAR 156
Pleasant MER 101
Pleasant WRN 37A
Polly MTG 249
Prudence HOP 256
Reuben BRK 277
Robert HRD 16
Robert MAD 120
Robt. BKN 14
Robt. HRY 250
Russel B. FKN 126
Ruthy TOD 128
Sam FKN 124
Sam ALN 130
Saml. BRN 21
Saml. BRN 21
Saml. HRD 96
MARTIN, Samuel, Capt. WYN 90A
Samuel, Jr. WDF 102A
Samuel, Sr. WDF 102A
Samuel LWS 87A
Samuel D. CLK 106
Sarah HAR 156
Sarah WDF 110A
Sarah SHE 128A
Sary HRL 114
Saul CHN 41
Silvester WRN 29A
Simeon BKN 16
Smith TRG 10
Solomon MNR 211
Stephen BRK 275
Stephen HND 10A
Stephen WRN 32A
Susan GRD 112A
Thomas FTE 95
Thomas GTN 128
Thomas HAR 134
Thomas, Jnr. HAR 140
Thomas OHO 5A
Thomas DVS 17A
Thomas WRN 28A
Thomas WDF 93A
Thomas SHE 119A
Thos. HND 12
Thos. HRY 250
Thos. BRK 273
Thos. BRK 277
Thos. SHE 120A
Thos. SHE 123A
Tilman CWL 37
Valentine CLK 93
Welcome MNR 211
Wilford WAS 62A
Will. LVG 7
Will. LVG 9
William FLD 9
William ETL 43
William CLK 77
William GRN 79
William GRN 80
William MER 101
William MER 102
William GTN 133
William HAR 138
William CLD 143
William SHE 150
William UNN 151
William CLD 153
William BTH 174
William MNR 193
William NSN 195
William MNR 205
William, Jr. WDF 94A
William, Sr. NSN 195
William, Sr. WDF 94A
William CBL 5A
William SPN 5A
William CBL 6A
William DVS 18A
William WRN 30A
William FLG 46A
William MBG 139A
William MBG 142A
William C. WRN 67A
William C. WTY 119A
Winston WRN 65A
Wm. BRN 20
Wm. CHN 38
Wm. HRD 42
Wm. FKN 90
Wm. MAD 172
MARTIN, Wm. HRY 244
Wm. HRY 263
Wm. BRK 275
Wm. CHN 35A
Wm. TOD 126A
Wm. SHE 131A
Wm. GNP 169A
Wyatte DVS 17A
MARTIN?, Betsey FKN 92
Chas. MAS 55
Jno. FKN 86
Will. SCT 104A
MARTINE, Dav. HRY 258
MARTINI, Ernestus? HRY 267
MARTON, Ellen WDF 96
James BBN 136
Margret GRN 57
Samuel NSN 218
MARTON?, Sarah WDF 98
MARTS?, George HAR 152
MARTTIN, Luther JEF 33
MARVELL, Eli LVG 12
MARVEY, Jas. HRD 20
MARWOOD?, George JES 89
MARYMAN, Reuben SCT 135A
MARYWETHER, Garret CHN 40
MASAN, Isbell MAD 170
MASBY, Samuel MER 115
MASDEN, Elias MAS 62
MASDON?, Elijah MAS 69
MASEN?, Wilson ALN 98
MASENER?, Adam BBN 130
MASEY, James WAS 79A
John BRK 275
Wm. BRK 273
MASEY?, Robt. BRK 273
MASH, Claibourn CLD 148
Groomer MAD 164
Henry WYN 97A
John WYN 97A
Joseph H. MAD 152
Stephen WYN 100A
MASHAM, William TRG 6
MASINER?, Christopher JES 83
MASON, Abraham CSY 214
Benjamin S. NSN 205
Caswell CWL 39
Chas. (Free Man) BBN 76
David BTL 327
E. JEF 23
Edwine MAD 136
Elijah BRN 21
Elisha GRD 115A
Enoch BBN 62
George LGN 25
George FTE 62
George JES 90
Hugh LNC 25
J. T. LGN 25
J. T. BBN 96
J. T. GTN 134
J. T. GRT 147
J. T. BRK 309
J. T. OHO 12A
J. T. PUL 50A
Jacob HAR 132
James MTG 271
James KNX 286
James HND 4A
James CHN 44A
Joel WYN 104A
John BNE 24
John LGN 30
John HRD 48
John MAD 130

MASON, John UNN 147
John, Jr. MTG 255
John OHO 3A
John GRD 106A
Jos. BRK 273
Levi (Free Man) BBN 76
Levin JEF 41
M. FTE 103
Martain CSY 214
Mary NSN 177
Nathaniel BLT 192
Peter FTE 107
Peter BTH 206
Peter MTG 263
Rashel HAR 132
Rice C. BTL 327
Richard HOP 258
Richd. GRN 50
Robt., Jr. KNX 286
Robt., Sr. KNX 286
Sally BBN 136
Sam FTE 60
Sarah BBN 120
Sarey CSY 220
Thomas CSY 208
Thomas B. CSY 212
Will. KNX 286
William LNC 23
William BNE 24
William CLK 99
William CSY 210
William BTL 327
William WYN 104A
William D. WRN 62A
William W. NSN 204
Winney FTE 61
MASON?, John T. FTE 64
Sary FKN 162
Thompson LVG 16
Wade ALN 98
MASONER?, Christopher JES 83
MASSACH, Abraham CHN 39
MASSACK, Lydy MAD 120
MASSEE, Benjamin OWN 102
Edward BNE 28
John BNE 24
John ADR 36
Jonathan BBN 146
Thos. ADR 36
Thos., Jr. ADR 14
William OWN 100
William R. CLK 105
MASSEY, Eli PUL 46A
Elizabeth HAR 138
Henry JES 74
Israel MER 103
Jno. HAR 166
John CBL 2A
Jonathan ALN 118
Sary HRL 114
Silvestus MAD 92
Thomas GRD 122A
William HRL 114
MASSIE, David MTG 273
Henry JEF 47
Nancy FKN 138
Will. SCT 98A
William GRT 140
William SPN 5A
MASSLEY?, Duncan BKN 6
MASSON, Peter CBL 21A
MASSY, Abram PUL 46A
James MER 104
MASTEN?, Chas. MAS 55
MASTERS, Charles WRN 62A
MASTERS, Curtis MAD 168
John ADR 36
John MAD 96
Moses MAD 108
Richard WRN 61A
Thos. MAD 168
MASTERS?, John GRN 53
Joshuay WAS 74A
MASTERSON, Aaron MTG 225
Caleb BBN 92
Charles SHE 150
Charles NSN 218
Chas. MAS 68
James FTE 84
James GRT 140
Jas. HRD 16
John GRT 141
John, Jr. NSN 218
John, Sr. NSN 218
John O. NSN 218
Jonathan MTG 225
Joseph NSN 218
Lazarus LGN 29
Patrick ETL 53
Polly SCT 99A
Richd. MAS 54
Sarah GTN 123
Wesley GTN 123
William MER 102
William FTE 109
Zachariah NSN 218
MASTIN, Betsey FKN 92
Peter NCH 122A
MASTIN?, Jno. FKN 86
MASTON, Lew. HRY 261
MATAX, George MAD 102
MATCHEL?, John FLG 51A
MATCHLEY, Benjamin GTN 130
MATEER?, Robert MTG 285
MATENY?, John ADR 34
MATHENY, Abisha MER 101
Michael HRD 40
Micheal JES 96
Moses BBN 112
Robert CLD 153
MATHERLEY, Israel MER 101
MATHERLY, Alisha WAS 81A
Bazil HRY 190
Lemuel HRD 90
MATHERS, Gavin NCH 129A
James, Jr. NCH 123A
James NCH 127A
Richard HRD 50
Thomas NCH 127A
William, Jr. NCH 123A
William, Sr. NCH 123A
MATHERSON, Aaron FTE 77
MATHES, John ADR 36
Nugan? HAR 152
Richd. HAR 148
MATHESS, Martin UNN 147
MATHEWS, Absalom T. SHE 124A
Chitester BNE 26
Henry JEF 52
James BNE 24
Jesse TRG 8
John TRG 8
John CBL 23A
Jonas BNE 50
Levi BKN 23
Thomas TRG 8
Thomas CLK 105
William BTH 188
William N. WDF 102A
MATHIAS, James WTY 123A
MATHIAS, John ETL 39
Marquis BNE 26
MATHIS, Anthony WYN 98A
Conrad NSN 193
George NSN 193
Hopkins GSN 145A
Joel WAS 48A
John GRN 65
John SHE 150
Richd. GRN 65
Wm. GRN 71
MATHOLY, John ETL 41
MATHUS, Josiah TRG 8
MATHUS?, William TRG 7A
MATHWIN?, James CWL 35
MATIANGLY, Ignatius MAD 178
MATINA, Jona. HRY 218
MATINGLEY, Barnet GSN 145A
Bennit GSN 145A
MATKINS, James WRN 51A
MATLOCK, -zch.? CWL 42
Absalom WRN 65A
David CLD 164
Nathan LVG 16
Wm. J. MAS 79
MATOX, Daniel GNP 169A
MATSAN, Andrew, Sr. MTG 225
MATSON, Asa MAS 75
Elezebeth HAR 156
James BBN 122
Thomas BBN 108
MATT?, John CWL 37
MATTENGLY, Bazzle WAS 61A
Edwd. WAS 60A
MATTENGLY?, Mary WAS 42A
MATTEY?, John GRN 54
MATTHERLY, William PUL 64A
MATTHEWS, Amos V. GTN 125
David HOP 254
Edward MBG 143
Eggleston HND 11
Geo. FLG 34A
George BRN 33
George OHO 6A
James BRN 19
James HOP 256
James OHO 6A
Jas. FLG 32A
Jeremiah FKN 156
John BRN 21
John HOP 256
John CHN 29A
Joseph CLD 160
Oliver MNR 211
Peter M. HOP 256
Pleasant BRN 33
R. Lot CLD 160
Reuben FLD 33
Samuel FTE 90
Samuel MNR 211
Thomas FLD 33
Wm. BRK 229
Wm. FLG 45A
MATTHIAS, George HRD 18
MATTHIS, David NSN 193
Henry NSN 198
MATTING, Lenard WAS 62A
MATTINGLEY, And? MAS 63
Barton BRK 271
Barton WAS 43A
Ghals BRK 275
Jas. BRK 273
John BRK 277
Mary MBG 141

MATTINGLEY,
Richard BRK 277
Richd. MAS 63
Stephen HRD 88
Townley MAS 63
Zac BRK 273
MATTINGLY, Barnet WAS 85A
Bazzel WAS 62A
Benedict NSN 193
Benj. WAS 57A
Charles WAS 62A
Gabriel WAS 70A
George WAS 60A
Igs. WAS 62A
Jeremiah WAS 73A
John WAS 42A
John WAS 71A
Joshuay WAS 61A
Lenard WAS 62A
Lewis WAS 43A
Lewis? BRK 277
Luk WAS 42A
Luke WAS 56A
Luke WAS 62A
Margret WAS 56A
Philip NSN 189
Phill. WAS 35A
Richard NSN 210
Sarah HRD 88
Thos. WAS 44A
William WAS 87A
MATTIX, Thos. BRK 275
MATTOCK, William MER 103
MATTOCKS, Edmond HAR 198
Tobias HAR 198
MATTOX, -----? DVS 11A
----tine? DVS 11A
---uel? DVS 11A
Absolem KNX 282
Christopher ALN 114
David T. LVG 14
John G. SHE 126A
Nelson SHE 134A
Smalwood LNC 55
Tho. B. GRD 99A
Thomas LNC 49
MATTOY, James ALN 122
MAUGHAM?, Blanch LGN 36
MAULD--?, Mary? CHN 31
MAULDING, West. LGN 22
MAULEY?, Saml. FLG 58A
MAULY, Edward WRN 55A
Jonathan WRN 55A
MAULY?, Wm. FLG 59A
MAUPIN, Barrell/
Banell? FLG 59A
Daniel MAD 132
Daniel MAD 170
Gabriel MAD 160
Garland D. MAD 114
Gartin B. HOP 258
James MAD 128
Jessee FTE 83
Joel WRN 40A
R. A. JEF 20
Robert D. BRN 34
MAURICE, Dabnah LNC 67
John LNC 59
MAURY, Leonard H. BRN 20
MAUSKFIELD?, James WRN 51A
MAUX, John MER 104
MAUXLEY, Henry WRN 45A
MAUZEE, Henry LGN 31
James LGN 31
Lewis LGN 45
MAUZEY, Henry LGN 23
MAVITY?, John MTG 235
MAWMAN, John WRN 28A
MAXCEY, Edward BRN 19
MAXEY, Bennet FKN 100
Caleb CLD 148
Edward WRN 31A
Ephraim HRT 163
James WRN 75A
Joel LGN 47
Nathal. BRK 273
Sally GRN 73
Saml. GRD 93A
William WRN 33A
William C. WRN 33A
MAXEY?, Elizabeth HRT 164
MAXFIELD, Daniel CBL 6A
George CLK 81
Jas. PND 18A
Moses BNE 26
MAXI, Asa BTH 190
MAXLEY, Job MTG 281
MAXNER?, Adam BBN 130
MAXWELL, -----? CWL 41
---.? CWL 41
Alexander CLK 89
Archibald MTG 259
Bazzel WYN 98A
Hugh MTG 293
James LGN 33
James CWL 38
James WRN 42A
James GRD 93A
Jane WRN 47A
Jas. GSN 145A
John HRY 184
John CBL 18A
Joseph BTH 152
Joseph WAS 68A
Sally SCT 113A
Thomas LGN 33
William OHO 4A
William CBL 19A
MAXWILL, Thos. MAD 174
MAXY, Boaz LNC 33
Bradford MNR 215
William MNR 213
William, Jr. MNR 213
MAY, -----? DVS 13A
Abagail MER 103
Abraham LVG 5
Abraham LVG 9
Allen GTN 124
Andrew LNC 25
Andrew LWS 97A
Benj. LNC 25
Bennett GTN 118
Caleb FLD 1A
Calep SPN 23A
Coleman LGN 34
David R. ETL 40
Deborah MER 101
Gabriel GTN 124
George LVG 11
Henry MER 102
Henry NSN 222
Hester MAD 122
Humphrey MER 102
Humphrey NSN 221
Jacob LVG 10
Jacob, Jr. LNC 27
Jacob, Sr. LNC 25
James ETL 48
Jesse GTN 120
Jessey MAD 130
Jno. LVG 9
John FLD 29
MAY, John MER 101
John NSN 208
John DVS 17A
John DVS 18A
John SPN 23A
John LWS 97A
John C. WRN 34A
John C. WRN 61A
Joseph DVS 18A
Lemuel SPN 23A
Mary NSN 175
Nancy PUL 62A
Peter WYN 88A
Pleasant BRN 20
Richard HRD 36
Richard L. OHO 6A
Rolland LNC 31
Sally LGN 29
Sally CLY 128
Samuel FLD 29
Smith NSN 181
Stephen NSN 179
Stephen NSN 207
Thomas FLD 40
Will. LVG 9
William GTN 117
William HAR 160
William NSN 209
William, Jr. MER 101
William, Sr. MER 102
William DVS 17A
William DVS 18A
Wm. JEF 25
MAYALL, Daniel CBL 22A
Nancy CBL 22A
MAYBERRY, Braxton CLD 153
Maximillian CLD 153
William WRN 31A
MAYBOURNE, James LGN 38
MAYBRIER, Jacob HAR 196
MAYBURGH, John J. BKN 23
MAYBURY, John BTH 206
Joseph BTH 206
MAYERS, Adam FLG 37A
MAYES, Elijah GRN 61
John GRN 61
Richd. GRN 69
Saml. FLG 68A
Samuel FLD 28
MAYFEILF, Isaac CSY 222
MAYFIELD, Burdett GTN 129
Cates B. JEF 58
George HRT 164
Gideon MNR 217
Hannah GTN 129
Isaac BRN 20
James BRN 21
James JEF 44
James GRD 108A
John BRN 21
John, Jr. BRN 20
Joshua GTN 130
Levi JEF 54
Mc Cagy JEF 62
Patsey WTY 126A
Polly PUL 39A
Robert WTY 126A
Sud GRD 90A
Thomas BRN 33
Will GRD 88A
MAYHALL, Benjamin FKN 128
Jno. FKN 126
Timothy FKN 118
Wm. FKN 126
Wm. FKN 140
MAYHAN, James CSY 210

MAYHAN, James V. WAS 28A
MAYHUGH, Perry FLG 65A
MAYNARD, Henry CLD 150
Joel BLT 182
MAYNER, Hannah CLD 153
Stephen NCH 105
MAYNIARD, Wm. BRN 19
MAYNOR, Richard FTE 64
MAYO, Daniel CBL 3A
Hiram WRN 38A
Mial? FLD 17
Moses SPN 23A
William WDF 104A
Wilson FLD 29
MAYO?, William J./ I.? FLD 29
MAYORS, John FLG 58A
MAYS, Abraham CLY 120
Abraham WYN 103A
Daniel CHN 27A
David CLY 120
David WYN 101A
Drury HRL 114
George SPN 16A
Henry B. FLD 47
James FLD 11
James FLD 25
James GRN 67
John WRN 72A
John G. WAS 46A
Joseph WYN 83A
Joseph WYN 103A
Lewis HRY 202
Lindsay JES 87
Richard BRK 273
Robert LGN 33
Robert HOP 258
Robt. GRN 62
Sandy SPN 24A
Thomas HRL 114
William FLD 40
William JES 85
William CLY 120
William SPN 14A
Wilson MER 117
Wm. CHN 40A
MAZE, Solomon WTY 125A
MC FADAN, Elias B. WRN 71A
MC ----?, John RCK 78A
MC ----Y, John ALN 94
MC ---CON, John FTE 62
MC --ICKOR, Anna BTH 196
MC -ERAN?, John SHE 176
MC ACKRAN, James HRY 188
MC ADAMS, Armstrong BBN 144
Geo. CHN 43
MC ADAMS?, -----? WTY 111A
MC ADON?, Samuel MNR 215
MC AFEE, Ann BKN 22
Anne MER 103
Clarke, Esqr. MER 103
George LNC 77
James MER 103
John MER 103
John FTE 106
John GRD 122A
Robert MER 104
Robert FTE 106
Robert B., Col. MER 104
Samuel, Esq. MER 103
Wm. WAS 35A
MC AFFEE, Mary BRK 275
MC AHRON, William BLT 156
MC AIN, James BLT 170
MC ALANNY?, Samul ADR 36
MC ALEE?, Ebednigo FTE 111
MC ALEXANDER, David MAD 132
MC ALFRESH, Abner FLG 51A
MC ALISLER, John CHN 33
MC ALISTER, Angus LVG 11
Ben. CHN 39
Garland CHN 39
Hector LVG 8
James GNP 175A
John GNP 175A
Jos. PUL 49A
Jos. H. CHN 40
Pleasant LVG 8
Robt. PUL 43A
MC ALL, John CLY 117
MC ALLA, W. L./ S.?, Revd. BKN 24
MC ALLESTER, James LWS 89A
MC ALLISTER, Daniel SHE 154
Jas. SCT 136A
Nathaniel PUL 59A
MC AND?, Saml. CHN 29A
MC ANDRE, Bunyan FKN 80
MC ANDREW, Jno. HRY 258
Reuben HRY 249
MC ANE?, Joseph BKN 9
Saml. BKN 19
MC ANELLY, John MER 102
Mary MAS 68
Wm. NCH 105
MC ANNALLY, James CBL 6A
MC ANNELLY, Henry MAS 66
MC ANULTY, Jane NCH 113A
MC ARNE, Jno. LVG 4
MC ART, John BTH 214
MC ARTHUR, Peter CBL 3A
MC ARTY, Thos. BKN 5
MC ATEE, Benjn. MAS 63
Geo. SCT 97A
George NSN 179
Hezekiah TRG 13A
James WAS 70A
John TRG 13A
Richd. SCT 97A
Richd. SCT 97A
Walter NSN 179
MC ATEE?, Ebednigo FTE 111
MC AUD?, Saml. CHN 29A
MC AUDE, Jno. MAS 57
MC AUL, Benjn. J. HRT 163
MC AUTHER, John BLT 188
MC AVOY, & Dougan JEF 25
MC AWLEY, Chas. HRD 32
MC BANE, Elizabeth MAD 126
MC BARRE?, Thos. MAD 92
MC BATH, Wm. ADR 38
MC BEAN, Gillis BTH 204
William FTE 65
MC BEE, Philip GTN 122
William BTH 192
MC BRAYER, Alexander FKN 72
Andrew FKN 146
James FKN 162
James, Sr. FKN 148
Jane FKN 154
MC BRIDE, Ann WAS 45A
Chs. FKN 142
Daniel HND 4A
Elisabeth FKN 126
George LWS 87A
James MAD 124
Jno. FKN 142
MC BRIDE, Jos. TOD 126A
Saml. LVG 4
William WDF 120A
MC BROOM, ---es? DVS 13A
Joseph FLD 30
Robert MNR 213
Westly HRY 206
MC BROYER, Ichabod FLD 43
MC BURNEY, Thomas FTE 62
MC C----?, James CHN 30
MC C--LL?, Arthur? LVG 16
MC CABE, Fanny JES 76
Jas. SCT 118A
Jas. SCT 132A
John JEF 44
John JES 96
John CBL 3A
Josiah NCH 107A
Ruth FLG 69A
MC CAFFERY, Thos. BRK 275
MC CAFFRY, James CLD 147
MC CAIN, James CLK 96
James BTH 178
MC CALA, John SCT 133A
MC CALF, James KNX 314
MC CALISTER, Bartlett FKN 142
Joel FKN 142
MC CALL, Duncan CLK 74
James GNP 171A
John CLK 94
John BBN 126
John FLG 64A
Nancy, Mrs. CLK 94
Ross ETL 53
William FTE 82
Wm. MAS 76
MC CALLA, Andrew FTE 68
George PND 18A
James FTE 112
Jenney FTE 61
John M. FTE 70
Joseph HAR 190
Rachel FTE 60
Thomas HAR 192
MC CALLESTER, Daniel WAS 66A
MC CALLEY, John FTE 67
John WAS 58A
MC CALLIE, John FTE 111
MC CALLISTER, Danl. JEF 24
Dave. RCK 80A
John CBL 9A
MC CALLY, Wm. T. ADR 66
MC CALOP?, Catharine LGN 42
MC CALY, Mires? JES 89
MC CAMEL, Andrew SHE 154
George W. SHE 159
Saml. SHE 159
MC CAMISH, Adam BTH 162
MC CAMISH?, Isam BRK 277
MC CAMMAN, Classa MAD 152
MC CAMMEL, James SHE 171
John SHE 159
Saml. SHE 175
MC CAMMEN, John KNX 312
MC CAMMON, William MBG 135A
MC CAMON, James HRT 164
MC CAMPBELL, James JES 87
John SHE 125A
Wm. SHE 142A
MC CAMPBELL?, David JES 83
David MBG 140A

MC CAN, Joseph GTN 128
Martha PUL 65A
MC CANBREE, Arthur JEF 20
MC CAND?, Ann WAS 43A
S. L. WAS 17A
MC CANDLESS,
Alexr. HRD 86
James PND 24A
John HRD 66
Robert PND 17A
Wm. HRT 164
MC CANDLIS, Mary GRN 74
MC CANE, James HND 10A
Jno. HRY 267
MC CANE?, Isaac JES 92
MC CANEL?, S. L. WAS 17A
MC CANICK?,
(Blank) JEF 22
MC CANLASS, John LWS 98A
MC CANLESS, James
(Crossed Out) PND 25A
William HAR 176
MC CANLIS, Alexr. BRN 21
John BRN 21
MC CANN, Hezikiah BBN 104
James SHE 169
John BBN 144
John FLG 65A
Neal FTE 95
Patrick PND 22A
Patrick FLG 51A
Polly, Mrs. CLK 101
Robt. JEF 32
Thomas CSY 204
Thos. FLG 60A
William CSY 206
William LWS 99A
Wm. FLG 65A
MC CANNISH?, Isam BRK 277
MC CARDY, Alex. HRY 210
MC CAREY?, Charles UNN 154
MC CARGO, Radford CLK 84
MC CARMACK,
Stephen WRN 37A
MC CARROLL, James WDF 105
MC CART, Mrs.? JEF 22
Carthn.? FLG 77A
MC CARTA, Ezekia BTH 214
James ETL 37
MC CARTER, David HAR 178
Samuel HAR 178
MC CARTIE, William HAR 182
MC CARTNEY, James WRN 76A
Jas. CHN 44A
Thomas MBG 135A
MC CARTY, Aaron HRD 60
Adam PND 29A
Chany? MER 102
Charles BNE 26
Chas. CHN 42A
Cornelus HRD 60
Daniel MTG 255
Danl. MAS 56
David MAS 74
David FLG 38A
Dennis WDF 124A
Edward PND 15A
Edward CHN 42A
Eneas HRD 84
Ezekiel CLK 64
Felix FLG 39A
Henry BNE 26
Henry SHE 142A
James HRD 22
James BNE 26
James MTG 255
MC CARTY, Jno. ADR 34
John CWL 44
John B. FTE 63
Jos. JEF 52
Joseph CLK 64
Milburn WAS 29A
Nathl. MAS 56
Reubin PND 16A
Reubin PND 26A
Saml. PND 26A
Saml. SHE 136A
Thos. HRD 60
Thos. FLG 39A
Widow BBN 86
Widw.? CWL 42
William BNE 26
William CLK 66
William MER 101
William MER 102
MC CARULL, John CHN 27A
MC CARVER,
Archibald WYN 94A
Campbell FKN 102
MC CARY, Robt. WAS 48A
MC CARY?, Robt. ADR 34
MC CASLAND, J. P. JEF 20
Jas. JEF 32
MC CASLIN, ---ny? CWL 32
Andrew SHE 175
David SHE 169
Hugh CWL 33
James CWL 33
MC CASTUN, Robt. WAS 17A
MC CAUGHAN,
Alexander TRG 11A
James TRG 11A
John TRG 11A
MC CAULEY, Jas. SCT 101A
John LVG 17
Priscilla CLD 156
Thomas FLD 31
MC CAULL, John MER 103
William MER 104
MC CAULY, Robt. SCT 134A
MC CAWLEY, Benjn. OHO 6A
Jas. JEF 39
Joshua JEF 37
Joshua G. JEF 32
Sarah OHO 6A
Tabner? OHO 10A
Thos. JEF 37
MC CAWLY, James LVG 16
MC CAY, William BNE 28
MC CAY?, Alexander BNE 28
Willian BNE 50
MC CELVAIN,
William SPN 9A
MC CHENY?, James BTH 168
John BTH 166
MC CHESNEY, Samuel WRN 47A
MC CHESNY?, Walter CWL 39
MC CHISTEY, Peter ADR 38
MC CHORD, John FTE 102
MC CHRISTY, James ETL 52
MC CINDEY, William LGN 30
MC CINZY, Aquis WDF 95A
MC CLAIN, Betha HAR 154
Danl. PND 23A
Jacob HRY 198
James GTN 129
James LWS 93A
John BNE 24
John ADR 34
John CHN 30A
Johnathan HAR 154
Joseph HAR 154
MC CLAIN, Joseph CHN 35A
Mordecai WYN 82A
Neil CHN 30A
Samuel HAR 152
MC CLAIR?, Patk. JEF 25
MC CLALAND, Mary HRY 265
MC CLANACHAN,
Robt. BRN 20
MC CLANAHAM, Hugh BKN 13
MC CLANAHAM?, John BKN 2
MC CLANAHAN,
Andrew SPN 3A
James NCH 117A
Marshal WDF 102A
Thomas MER 102
Thomas BBN 142
Thomas SPN 9A
William NCH 129A
MC CLANCY, Mathew FLG 25A
MC CLANE,
Alexander NCH 120A
Arthur HAR 154
Charles WAS 52A
Charles NCH 120A
Danl. SCT 108A
Isaac WAS 57A
Jack HRY 244
Jas. HRY 243
Jno. HAR 162
John B. WAS 72A
Nancy HRY 267
Richard MAD 150
Wm.? HRY 243
MC CLANNAHAM, Wm. MAD 178
MC CLANNAHAN,
George HND 12
Tos., Jr. BBN 120
MC CLANNIHAN,
Elijah FTE 103
MC CLARILY, Saml. BRK 227
MC CLARN, William GTN 126
MC CLARY, John FLG 32A
Samuel NCH 108A
MC CLATCHEY, Saml. MAS 78
MC CLAY, Thomas BNE 24
MC CLEAN, James FTE 70
Wm. FKN 140
MC CLEASE, Danl. GNP 171A
MC CLEESE, John FLG 58A
Thos. FLG 58A
MC CLELAND, Susan BTH 180
MC CLELLAN, Joseph
G. WAS 77A
Rmon. BRN 21
MC CLELLAND,
Alexr. MTG 261
Benjn. SCT 108A
Dan SHE 133A
James BBN 110
James B. SHE 171
Joseph SHE 133A
Keziah HRY 188
Sarah HRY 202
Uriah BRN 20
Will. MAS 59
William JES 79
William FTE 100
William HRY 202
MC CLENAND, Thos. JEF 41
MC CLENDEN, John HOP 254
MC CLENDENEN, Jas, JEF 19
MC CLENDON, Briant HND 6A
John HND 6A
William WYN 88A
MC CLENEHAN,
Elijah PND 17A

MC CLEUR,
Nathaniel MER 102
William MER 102
MC CLEWER?, John FLG 59A
MC CLINN/MC CLUM?,
Moses ALN 142
MC CLINTIC, James BBN 108
MC CLINTICK,
Alexander OWN 105
Alexr. BBN 128
John FLD 9
Joseph BBN 134
Robert FLD 9
Samuel FLD 10
William FLD 8
MC CLINTOCK,
Daniel HAR 212
Hugh NCH 126A
Joseph NCH 126A
Thomas NCH 110A
William NCH 109A
William NCH 123A
MC CLISH, Absalom MER 103
MC CLLAND, Elisha BBN 92
James BBN 90
Robt. BBN 90
MC CLOLIE?,
Archab., Jr. BRK 277
MC CLONELL, Saml. BBN 130
MC CLORE, John BBN 86
Moses BNE 26
MC CLORE?, Ridley? BBN 96
MC CLOSKEY, Daniel BNE 24
Makael FLG 78A
MC CLOSKY, Michael BBN 126
MC CLOUD,
Archibald BBN 104
Gov. BBN 112
John BBN 104
John HRL 114
John, Jr. BBN 104
William BBN 104
MC CLOWER, Jas. FLG 24A
MC CLUER, John CHN 31
MC CLUNG, Charles WRN 41A
Eleanor PUL 41A
Tho. MAS 75
MC CLURE, -----? HND 13
Alexander CLK 72
Alexander GRT 140
Alexander UNN 154
Alexander OHO 5A
Alexander WDF 116A
Andrew MTG 233
Cathn. CWL 52
Daniel? KNX 314
David HND 12
David UNN 154
Henry FLG 78A
Holbert RCK 75A
Hugh CLD 143
James BBN 128
James FKN 130
James CLD 157
James HAR 164
James SHE 129A
Jane SCT 107A
John MTG 265
John CBL 2A
John WAS 66A
Margaret BBN 128
Nathaniel BNE 24
Nathaniel WDF 103
Robert LNC 71
Saml. CWL 52
Saml. JEF 53
MC CLURE, Samuel CLK 106
Sarah HAR 134
Will. SCT 107A
William FLD 21
William NSN 195
MC CLURE?, Nath. RCK 77A
Thos. MAD 140
MC CLURG, Jas.,
Jr. FLG 47A
Jas., Snr. FLG 47A
MC CLUSKY, John ADR 20
Mark CLD 159
MC COD?, John JEF 19
MC COGG, Saml. JEF 45
MC COGLIN, Thos. WAS 36A
MC COHORN?, Andrew MER 103
MC COLESTER, Tempy SPN 11A
MC COLGAN?, James CLD 141
MC COLGIN, John GRN 77
William GRN 77
MC COLISTER, James ALN 136
John ADR 64
MC COLLEM, William TRG 3
MC COLLESTER, Jno. ADR 34
MC COLLISTER,
Aeneas HND 7
Allen MER 103
Archibald HRY 182
Charles MER 103
David PUL 67A
James SHE 113A
John WRN 75A
MC COLLOM, Asa CBL 13A
Asa CBL 15A
Isaac WYN 94A
James, Jr.? WYN 102A
James, Sr. WYN 103A
James CBL 6A
James WYN 103A
John CBL 12A
Sarah CBL 13A
Thomas, Sr. WYN 94A
Thomas CBL 11A
Thomas WYN 103A
MC COLLOUGH,
Esther BTH 154
Jonathan BTH 212
Samuel CLK 76
MC COLLUM, Abraham TRG 7A
Daniel CLY 111
Robert TRG 3
Saml. CLY 111
Thomas BRN 19
Wm. BRN 20
MC COLLUM?, Danl.,
Jr. CLY 116
MC COLPIN, J. TOD 132
J. TOD 132A
Jos. TOD 133
MC COMAS,
Nathaniel LWS 94A
William MNR 211
MC COMB, John JEF 33
MC COMBS, Henry TRG 13
Hugh BRN 21
John BRN 20
MC COMMICK, Andrew CHN 43A
MC COMMON, John WRN 57A
William WRN 57A
MC CONAHAY, John NCH 124A
MC CONALD?, R. GRD 83A
MC CONATHEY, Jacob FTE 67
MC CONELL,
Archibald CLK 70
John D. CWL 39
John M. GNP 178A
MC CONN, Also See
Mc Coun MER 103
James CLK 103
MC CONNAUGHAY,
Jas. BBN 78
MC CONNAUGHHAHAY?,
David BBN 74
MC CONNEL, Adam JES 69
Andrew JES 96
Edwd. BBN 120
James MBG 136
James, Sr. WDF 103
James WDF 116A
John ETL 51
Jonathan CSY 206
Mathew JES 96
Robt. SCT 106A
William JES 95
MC CONNELL, Jesse BRN 19
John BBN 108
John BBN 114
John SHE 157
John MBG 141A
Joseph BBN 108
Joseph BBN 122
Robert JEF 43
Robert FTE 67
Saml. BBN 110
Sampson BBN 108
Samuel SPN 5A
Wm. BBN 122
MC CONNOL, Alexr. SCT 116A
MC COOL, Adam,
Junr. WRN 63A
Adam SPN 19A
Adam WRN 63A
Andrew HOP 256
Thomas WRN 63A
MC COOMGER?, Js. HRL 114
MC CORCLE, John GRN 62
Saml. GRN 62
MC CORD, David FLG 38A
James LVG 12
James LGN 42
James MAD 152
Jas. FLG 38A
John MAD 112
John, Snr. FLG 39A
John CHN 34A
John FLG 38A
John WAS 69A
Mickael FLG 38A
Robert MAD 114
Samuel CHN 34
Wm. CHN 34
Wm. MAD 152
Wm. FLG 37A
Wm. K. FLG 38A
MC CORKLE, John FLG 70A
Jos. FLG 26A
MC CORMAC, C. TOD 128
J. TOD 127A
Jane SHE 160
Joseph LNC 9
Joseph LNC 27
MC CORMACK, Danl. LNC 63
George HND 9A
George LWS 87A
James LWS 90A
James SHE 109A
Jas. J. LVG 5
John GTN 129
Joseph SHE 163
Joshua LNC 2
Robt. CBL 5A
Wm. LNC 9

MC CORMACK, Wm. LNC 63
MC CORMIC, John HOP 256
MC CORMICK, Abraham MER 103
Adam MTG 229
Eliza JEF 31
Francis OWN 103
George SHE 138A
Ignis. BRK 271
James LVG 12
James BBN 60
James NCH 111A
John MTG 233
John OHO 4A
John E. BKN 23
John S. CSY 210
Leannah LGN 27
Patk. JEF 20
Richard SHE 121A
Thos. LVG 16
Walter NCH 128A
Will. MTG 239
Wm. SHE 117A
MC CORY?, David HRY 204
MC COTRY, William UNN 152
MC COUBREE?, Arthur JEF 20
MC COULLOUGH, John BTH 212
MC COULLUM, Isaac TRG 4
MC COUN, Alexander FLD 35
Hannah LGN 32
James T. WDF 102A
Joseph MBG 140A
Nancy WYN 81A
Thomas LGN 30
Thomas LGN 43
MC COUN?, Samuel, Maj. MER 103
MC COVINGER?, Js. HRL 114
MC COWAN, Alexander NSN 175
Robt. JEF 36
MC COWN, Betsey, Mrs. WYN 94A
Catherine JEF 41
Isaac SPN 22A
Lawrence SPN 22A
MC COY / MC COW?, Tabner DVS 19A
MC COY, Alexr. GRD 114A
Andrew NCH 126A
Daniel FLD 31
Daniel, Jr. WDF 92
Daniel, Sr. WDF 92
Daniel DVS 18A
Daniel NCH 126A
Danl. BBN 138
Danl. GRD 105A
Edward C. BTL 327
Elenor HOP 254
George GNP 167A
Heny? NSN 184
Hugh GRD 96A
James MER 103
James GNP 173A
Jeremiah CLD 151
John BNE 24
John FLD 31
John WDF 102
John OWN 103
John SHE 160
John HRT 164
John HOP 254
John, Jr. MER 103
John, Sr. MER 103
John NCH 116A
MC COY, John NCH 124A
John GNP 167A
Joseph FTE 77
Joseph, Jr. MER 103
Kenneth GRD 105A
Margaret BBN 132
Mary FLG 77A
Mosey HRY 243
Neal FTE 112
Patsey MAD 142
Richard FLD 31
Robt. MAS 57
Ruben GNP 167A
Samuel FLD 39
Samuel DVS 18A
Thos. BRK 273
William FLD 31
Willis BTL 327
Wm. JEF 37
Wm. JEF 42
Zacheriah PND 16A
MC COY?, Alexander BNE 28
William BNE 28
William BNE 50
MC CRACKEN, ---n? DVS 13A
David BBN 72
John JEF 26
John FLD 32
Milley FKN 88
Osbern FKN 88
Ovid HRD 84
Seneca? FKN 82
Thomas FTE 64
William GTN 134
MC CRACKIN, James GTN 134
MC CRADY, George BKN 15
Jas. MAS 62
MC CRAKEN, Wm. HRY 258
MC CRAKIN, Cyrus WDF 122A
John FTE 106
MC CRARRY, John WYN 100A
MC CRARY, Rebecca MGB 137A
Robert HND 5
William GTN 126
MC CRARY?, Eli ADR 34
MC CRAY, Isaac MER 103
MC CREERY, ----t? DVS 14A
Charles OHO 3A
Elijah DVS 15A
James ETL 49
MC CROCKLIN, Jessee NSN 214
Wm. SHE 132A
MC CROHAN, Chas. P. WRN 74A
MC CRORY, James BBN 134
MC CROSKY, -----? CWL 40
David FTE 86
Jas. SCT 112A
John GNP 176A
Saml. SCT 115A
MC CROY?, John CWL 36
MC CRUCHEN, Chas. FLG 59A
MC CRUM, James ETL 39
Jas. JEF 34
MC CRURY, Robert ETL 49
William ETL 49
MC CUBBEN, James HRT 164
Zacheriah HRT 164
MC CUBBIN, John SPN 4A
MC CUCHINGS, Samuel SPN 14A
MC CUDDY, Isaac WDF 103
William WDF 103
MC CUE, James NSN 182
John NSN 175
MC CULLA, Jos. GRD 84A
MC CULLAM, James HRD 18
Sally HRD 72
Wm. HRD 40
MC CULLEY, Samuel HAR 138
MC CULLOCH, Alexander LGN 23
MC CULLOCK, John BNE 26
MC CULLOUGH, Alexr. FLG 66A
James MTG 263
Jas. FLG 61A
Jno. PUL 42A
John GRT 139
John SHE 148
Lawson FTE 67
Peter FLG 66A
Robt. PUL 42A
Simeon MTG 259
William MTG 241
Wm. PUL 42A
Wm. FLG 66A
MC CULLY, George CLD 150
MC CUMSLEY?, Wm. JEF 45
MC CUNE, Gavin NCH 127A
Jas. M. SCT 113A
John NCH 127A
Joseph JES 76
Margaret JES 80
Margarett JES 89
Miles MAD 92
Robert NCH 114A
Robert NCH 127A
Samuel NCH 109A
Wash G. ALN 140
MC CUNE?, Isaac JES 92
MC CURDY, Catherine JEF 66
Dolly TOD 129
James LGN 45
Thomas LGN 43
MC CURTY, Justin WAS 30A
MC CUTCHELL, Chs. JEF 30
MC CUTCHIN, Hugh LGN 37
John LGN 45
Marga. LNC 79
William LGN 45
MC CUTCHON, Thomas BBN 114
MC DADE, Edward JEF 37
John BBN 60
Josh. FKN 114
MC DANEL, Alexr. FLG 30A
Eanos BBN 118
Robt. BBN 116
Sally FLG 41A
Wm. WAS 57A
MC DANELL, Jane FLG 64A
Jas. FLG 54A
Mary FLG 54A
Thos. FLG 64A
Ze--? FLG 64A
MC DANIEL, (also see MCDANIEL)
-----? DVS 11A
-----? DVS 11A
-----? DVS 11A
-----? DVS 11A
----an? DVS 11A
----h?, Jr. DVS 11A
---.? CWL 53
Aaron GTN 126
Aaron MBG 139A
Alexander LVG 10
Alexander MTG 271
Alexander? DVS 13A
Ambrose D. LWS 90A
Andrew SHE 128A

MC DANIEL,
Archibald LWS 90A
Barney HRY 263
Boon FTE 99
Charles FTE 67
Colins GSN 144A
Daniel BTH 168
Daniel NSN 208
David GRN 66
Duncan LGN 29
Elizabeth CLK 101
Francis CLK 69
Geo. JEF 56
Geo. CLY 118
Geo., Sr. CLY 118
George CLK 83
George FTE 108
George GSN 144A
Henry GTN 126
Henry BTH 198
Hiram LVG 11
Isabella SHE 140A
J. TOD 128A
James BKN 9
James CLK 68
James CLK 101
James GTN 117
James GTN 126
James GSN 143A
Jas. HRD 50
Jas. JEF 62
Jesse SCT 109A
Joel JEF 62
John BKN 6
John BRN 19
John LGN 32
John ADR 36
John GRN 54
John HRD 80
John CLK 101
John GTN 123
John GTN 125
John BLT 168
John LWS 87A
John WYN 89A
John LWS 90A
John SHE 121A
Josephus BLT 190
Judson MTG 229
Judson MTG 273
Marcus SHE 131A
Margaret CBL 8A
Marshal SHE 136A
Mary BRN 19
Mary FTE 99
Mary CHN 43A
Matthew BRN 20
Miles BLT 152
Nely GRN 58
Peter BLT 168
Richd. NSN 222
Robt. BKN 9
Ruth FTE 99
Samuel CLK 101
Shadrack FLD 3
Shadrick CLY 124
Spencer, Jr. PUL 64A
Spencer, Senr? PUL 64A
Spencer PUL 64A
Stacy LVG 16
Thos. CLY 118
Wayne GTN 126
William CLK 85
William CLY 121
William BLT 168
William BLT 192

MC DANIEL, William BTH 200
William PUL 64A
William MBG 142A
Wm. ADR 3
Wm. ADR 34
John LWS 88A
MC DANIEL?,
Jeremiah CLY 116
MC DANIELD, Jane CSY 228
MC DANNOLD, Reuben MTG 245
MC DANNOLD?, John,
Jr. MTG 279
John, Sr. MTG 279
MC DAUELL?, (See
Mc Danell) FLG 64A
MC DAVID, James SHE 128A
MC DAVITT, Basil WDF 108A
MC DAWELL?, -----? CWL 40
MC DAY?, Hugh GRD 122A
MC DERMALL?, Jesse NSN 176
MC DERMENT, John GTN 117
MC DERMIT, Sarah,
Mrs. WYN 106A
MC DERMOT, Patrick HND 7A
MC DOLD, Alexander GTN 125
Andrew GTN 125
James GTN 126
Robert GTN 125
William GTN 125
MC DOLE, Catherine HAR 140
Josiah BBN 86
Peggy LGN 39
William LGN 39
MC DONAL,
Alexander WAS 41A
James WAS 42A
Joseph WAS 53A
Nancy GRD 114A
Thos. WAS 60A
Will, Sr.? GRD 94A
Will GRD 114A
William GRD 92A
MC DONALD, A. GRD 120A
Alex? BNE 26
Alexander HAR 200
Alexander, Jr. NCH 107A
Alexander NCH 107A
Angnes GRD 103A
Eli NCH 109A
Francis HAR 156
Francis HAR 200
Henry HAR 206
Hugh NCH 116A
James? CWL 36
John MER 101
John NCH 105
John WRN 37A
John NCH 119A
Jonathan HAR 202
Joseph HAR 200
Mordecai NCH 119A
Morgan TRG 8A
Peter NCH 115A
Polly NCH 105
R. GRD 83A
Rot.? GRD 92A
Samuel M. FTE 80
Thomas NCH 114A
William HAR 200
MC DONALL, Redmon NSN 210
MC DONELL?, John JES 95
MC DONNALD, Allen WRN 37A
Angus WRN 38A
Elizabeth WRN 47A
William WRN 39A
MC DONNALL, Daniel NSN 181

MC DONNALL, Joseph NSN 209
MC DONNEL, Nancy MAD 154
Rowland BBN 116
MC DONNOL, John SCT 126A
MC DONNOLD, Edwd. MAS 69
Wm. MAS 69
MC DONOLD,
Charrity HRT 164
Jno. FKN 86
Jno. FKN 98
John FKN 82
Osbern FKN 100
MC DONOUGH, Hugh OWN 105
Patrick JEF 31
Peter SCT 132A
Simon NSN 208
MC DOOGLE, Joseph CBL 4A
Tho. TOD 131
MC DOUGAL, Alexr. HRD 82
MC DOUGH, Widw. CWL 39
MC DOWAL, Alexr. NSN 221
MC DOWALL, Abraham NSN 210
Will HRY 218
MC DOWEL,
Alexander SHE 141A
Deborah FKN 54
Edwd. PUL 36A
Elizabeth BRK 275
Ephraim, Dr. MER 102
Ephraim, Dr. MER 116
John SHE 130A
Joseph, Maj. MER 102
Rachel SHE 130A
Thomas BKN 10
MC DOWELL, -----? CWL 40
Ann- BKN 4
Benj.? ADC 68
Danl. BBN 132
Dorcas SHE 154
George LVG 12
Horatio NCH 107A
J. TOD 131A
James FTE 101
James NCH 107A
Jas. PUL 36A
Jno. PUL 36A
John BKN 4
John FLD 20
John ADR 34
John HRD 68
John FTE 78
John HRD 90
John FTE 97
John BLT 156
John SPN 6A
John NCH 111A
John G. LWS 87A
John L. FTE 101
Joseph BKN 4
Margaret NCH 119A
Mathew ADR 34
Richard FTE 85
Saml. BBN 106
Saml. J./ I.? WRN 75A
Samuel JES 84
Samuel MTG 269
Samuel WRN 68A
Tho. MAS 53
Thomas CLK 77
William LGN 36
William FTE 85
William NCH7117
William WRN 68A
Wm. PUL 36A
Wm. GNP 168A
MC DUFFEE, Enoch HAR 192

Name	County	Page
MC DUFFEE,		
Fielding	HAR	190
Gabriel	HAR	194
Robert	HAR	192
Robert, Jnr.	HAR	192
MC DUNNERD?,		
Daniel	JES	71
MC ELDER, John	SCT	110A
MC ELROY, Abraham	CHN	38
Fasler?	ALN	108
Hugh	UNN	146
James	ALN	100
James A.	WAS	69A
James C.	WAS	28A
James P.	WAS	69A
John	WAS	53A
Samuel	WAS	17A
William	WAS	19A
William	WAS	19A
Wm.	WAS	70A
MC ELROY?, Abraham	WAS	35A
Alex	WAS	84A
James	WAS	33A
Samuel	WAS	33A
MC ELUR?, Thos.	MAD	140
MC ELVAIN, Thomas	MBG	135A
MC ELWAIN, John		
S.?	WRN	61A
William	CLK	85
MC ELYEA, Jas.	CWL	53
MC ELYEA?, John	LVG	16
MC ENALLY, Bassel?	WAS	24A
MC ENTIER?, Joseph	WAS	73A
MC ENTIRE, John	MER	101
MC ENTUR, Thos.	WAS	52A
MC EWEN, Archibald	MER	102
David	MER	103
James	mER	103
James	CLD	153
Thomas	CLD	153
MC FADDEN, Jas.?	CWL	35
Wade	WRN	29A
MC FADDIN, Isaac	TOD	133
J.	TOD	133
James	GRD	91A
Jesse	KNX	310
Jno.	JEF	59
John	WRN	40A
Wm.	GRD	104A
MC FALL, Danl.	ADR	34
David	HAR	220
Jno.	PUL	40A
John	BRK	277
MC FALL?, Jno.	ADR	34
MC FALRIDGE?, John	WDF	97
MC FARDLAND, Wm.	TOD	131A
MC FARLAN, Robert	TRG	14
Thomas	TRG	10
MC FARLAND,		
(Blank)	JEF	28
-----?	DVS	7A
-----?	DVS	7A
-----?	DVS	7A
-----?	DVS	7A
-----?	DVS	8A
---ky?	DVS	8A
A.	TOD	130A
Ben	ADR	36
Benja.	JEF	33
Benjn.	GRT	139
Duncan	KNX	308
George	KNX	308
James	HAR	198
John	ADR	34
John R.	NSN	175
Jonathan	ALN	124

Name	County	Page
MC FARLAND, Jos.	KNX	310
Joseph	JES	75
Marthy	CHN	44
Nathaniel	HAR	208
Patk.	JEF	25
Rachael	KNX	308
Robert	PUL	65A
Thomas	HAR	194
William	nAR	202
Wm.	TOD	130A
MC FARLEN, Peggy	BTH	170
MC FARLIN, Berry	GRD	97A
Charles	OWN	102
Elizabeth	OWN	105
Jerry	GRN	80
William	FTE	91
William	BTH	172
MC FARREN?,		
Catharine	MAS	57
MC FATRICK?,		
Ababgail	MER	104
Andrew	MER	104
MC FEARCON, John	WAS	42A
Wm.	WAS	42A
MC FEE, Michael	JEF	21
MC FEETERS?,		
Alexander	JES	88
MC FERRAN, John	BRN	21
Wm. R.	BRN	34
MC FERRIN, John	MTG	249
Jonathan	MTG	249
Patk.	SCT	133A
Thos.	JEF	50
MC FERSON, Stephen	BTH	190
MC FINCH?, George	CSY	206
MC FIRN, Robert	OHO	5A
MC FLOWERS, Thomas	LWS	89A
MC G---S?, W.	RCK	82A
MC GAFFICK, Wm.	FLG	47A
MC GAHAN?,		
Archibald	WYN	89A
MC GAHEN, William	WYN	89A
MC GALLIARD, Will.	MAS	79
MC GALLIARD?, Jno.	MAS	81
MC GANERY?,		
Michael	NSN	216
MC GANNEL, James,		
Sr.	WDF	103
MC GARY,		
Christenah	HOP	272
Daniel	ETL	44
Daniel	HOP	254
James	HOP	254
Jessee	HOP	254
Mary	HND	4A
MC GAUGHEY, Arthur	FKN	130
Arthur, Jr.	HRT	164
Arthur, Sr.	HRT	163
Daniel	SHE	140A
John	SHE	140A
John	SHE	143A
MC GAUGHLIN, Hugh	CLK	85
MC GEE, Abel	BRN	21
Asa	JEF	56
Benjamin	TRG	11
David	CLK	84
David	MER	104
David W.	CLK	84
James	SHE	117A
James	SHE	135A
Jas.	CHN	43
John	JES	75
John	MER	103
John	CHN	43A
John	WRN	68A

Name	County	Page
MC GEE, John B. F.	SHE	119A
John M.	CLK	84
Joseph	MER	103
Joseph L.	NSN	185
Molly	MER	104
Patrick	NSN	218
Robert	MER	103
Robinson	HAR	214
Sally	WRN	52A
Samuel	WDF	94
Seth	JES	75
Thomas	JES	83
Thomas	HAR	204
Thomas R.	HAR	214
Thos.	JEF	20
Thos.	CWL	53
Washington	HRY	214
William	MER	101
William	OWN	101
William	HAR	204
William L.	HRD	12
Wm.	CHN	43
MC GEEHE, Benjamin	MTG	225
William	BTH	184
William	BTH	184
MC GEEHEE, Chas.	MAS	56
Jesse	MAS	56
MC GEHEE, John	WYN	83A
MC GELL?, Thomas	NSN	196
MC GEORGE, James	HRL	114
Thomas	HRL	114
MC GHEE, L. A.	MAS	76
William	WTY	125A
MC GHEE?, Ben	CWL	53
MC GILL, Alexander	NCH	122A
Alexn.	BBN	104
David	NSN	205
David	BRK	271
James	FTE	68
James	NSN	176
John	FTE	110
Jos.	BRK	271
Richard	BRK	271
Robert	WDF	93A
Robt.	SCT	99A
Rosannah	OHO	9A
Thos.	BRK	271
MC GILL?, James	BKN	15
MC GILLIS?, John	RCK	84A
MC GINITS?, John	HRY	224
MC GINNES, Wm.	ADR	36
MC GINNES?, Jos.	ADR	32
MC GINNESS, Dory	MAS	70
Elijah	NCH	121A
James	NCH	121A
John	BBN	118
John	NCH	122A
Samuel	NCH	111A
Samuel	NCH	122A
Thomas	FTE	97
Thos.	MAS	60
MC GINNIS, David	BNE	24
Elizabeth	WRN	32A
Greenbury D.	MER	102
Jesse	MER	102
John	MER	102
John	MER	103
John L.	MER	102
Mary	MER	102
Nathaniel	TRG	11
Patsey	BNE	24
Samuel	BNE	24
Samuel	MER	102
Samuel	MER	102
Thomas	MER	102
Thomas	MER	102

MC GINNIS, Thomas MER 102
William MER 102
Wm. BRN 20
Wm. FKN 146
MC GLASSON, James CLD 147
James CBL 9A
John CBL 9A
Joseph CLD 146
Paschal MAS 70
Sophia CLD 146
William CLD 147
William CLD 149
William CBL 7A
Wm. BNE 26
MC GLATHLIN, John MAD 136
MC GLAUGAHLIN, Mrs.? MAS 68
Wm.? MAS 68
MC GLAUGHLIN, Patk. JEF 47
Thos. BBN 120
MC GLAUGHLIN?, D. MAS 73
MC GLAUHLIN, Ann MAS 65
MC GLOCKLIN, Charles WAS 56A
MC GLONE, Mary FTE 61
MC GLONE?, Owen GNP 174A
MC GLOUGHLIN, James BLT 184
MC GLOUHLAND?, Edward BTH 188
MC GOHAN, Danl. BKN 8
MC GOHORN, Mark MER 103
MC GOHORN?, William MER 103
MC GONEGAL, James SHE 143A
MC GOODWIN?, Daniel LGN 43
MC GOVERN, Edward HRD 34
MC GOWEN, Jno. MAS 72
Robert HRY 234
Samuel WRN 34A
MC GOWIN, Alexander WYN 92A
John WYN 93A
Patk. SCT 128A
Sally, Mrs. WYN 93A
Samuel WYN 101A
Solomon WYN 93A
MC GRATH, Laurence JES 96
Robert SHE 110A
MC GRAUT?, Jesse GNP 168A
MC GRAW, Cornithe? HAR 180
John HAR 186
John HND 9A
John WRN 43A
John L. WRN 74A
Josiah MAS 54
Maddie V.? JEF 20
William MER 102
MC GREAVY, Danl. JEF 22
MC GREEN, George BLT 188
MC GREENWOOD, Wm. BRK 275
MC GREGGER, Jas. FLG 51A
MC GREGGOR, William HOP 256
MC GREGOR, Thomas CBL 3A
MC GREUDER, Dorah BNE 24
Richd. BNE 24
Thos. BNE 24
MC GREW, Jno. CHN 46
John CWL 53
Jos. SHE 132A
Read? GSN 143A
Thomas CBL 19A
Thos. CWL 43
MC GRUDER, Acquilla JEF 52
Archibald BLT 194
Dennis HRY 261
Elias HRY 255
Enoch JEF 50
Felman JEF 27
Granderson JEF 32
Hezekiah MTG 226
Josiah SHE 150
Levi BLT 176
Nathaniel SHE 150
Robt. SCT 139A
Thomas SHE 150
Thos. HRY 257
MC GRUE/ MC GRICE?, Moses HRY 264
MC GUA?, John GRD 108A
Wm. GRD 108A
MC GUDDY?, John, Sr. WDF 96
MC GUE?, James BKN 15
MC GUERRY?, Eliz. GRD 111A
MC GUFFEE, James? CBL 22A
MC GUFFIN, Jarrel BRK 271
John FTE 80
MC GUIDER?, Thos. BRK 275
MC GUIER?, Jonathan GTN 127
MC GUIN, Zelic HRY 228
MC GUINESS, John BBN 70
Neill MAS 73
MC GUINNESS, Sarah MAS 66
MC GUIRE, Allen HRY 194
Alxr. ADR 36
Andrew G. CLD 137
Archibald ETL 53
Campbell BRN 20
Daniel BRN 21
David BRN 19
Esther FLD 33
George MTG 251
James FLD 9
James FKN 148
James, Jr. ETL 54
James, Sr. ETL 53
James FLD 1A
James GNP 170A
James GNP 172A
Jesse HRT 164
John HAR 188
John MTG 239
John GNP 174A
Jos. HRY 249
Luke HRY 249
Nathan SPN 21A
Owen SPN 21A
Samuel MTG 239
Solomon FLD 33
Squire BRN 21
William ETL 53
William SPN 8A
William SPN 13A
MC GUYRE, John WDF 99
MC HARGUE, Agnes KNX 308
John WTY 115A
Saml. KNX 306
Will. KNX 298
Will., Sr. KNX 308
MC HATTEN, Jas. SCT 102A
MC HATTON, Alexr. SCT 112A
Alexr. SCT 136A
David SCT 111A
Jas. JEF 49
John BNE 24
Mathew BNE 26
MC HATTON, Robt. SCT 127A
Saml. SCT 137A
Wm. BBN 136
MC HELVIN, Solomon BTH 196
MC HENDRY, James LGN 32
MC HENRY, Aron FLD 42
Barnabas WAS 76A
Isaac MAD 142
John WYN 88A
William WYN 88A
MC HENRY?, Wm. CWL 38
MC HERAN?, John SHE 176
MC HERINE?, Stephen GSN 144A
MC HINNEY, George CSY 218
MC HISNEY, David HRT 163
MC HITS?, John BTH 168
MC ILFRESH, Henry FLG 52A
MC ILHANEY, Felix HAR 176
MC ILROY, ----? CWL 41
Isaac? B. CWL 36
James LVG 14
John CWL 37
Thomas FTE 73
Wm.? CWL 41
MC ILROYE, John HND 6A
MC ILVAIN, Alexr. FLG 55A
Archibald FTE 83
David SHE 176
Hugh LWS 86A
James LNC 3
Sally WDF 93A
Samuel HAR 198
Wm. M. BBN 144
MC ILVOY, Daniel MER 116
MC ILWAIN, Alexander LGN 30
Frances LGN 42
Michael LGN 42
MC INNY, John GSN 144A
MC INTEER, Haman SHE 110A
William BRN 20
MC INTIRE, Alexander BTH 156
Alexr. MAS 71
Aron FLG 27A
Aron FLG 53A
Danl. FLG 55A
David BLT 190
E. BBN 128
Hue CLK 71
Isaac FLG 37A
Jacob BTH 160
Jas. FLG 45A
John FLG 44A
John FLG 44A
John NCH 128A
Jos. / Jas.? FLG 68A
Joseph L. MBG 135
Lucy NCH 116A
Mary HRD 70
Nicholas HRD 16
Polly FTE 75
Robert TRG 13A
Saml. LVG 5
Thos. FLG 28A
William GTN 132
Wm. FLG 72A
Wm. GSN 144A
MC INTIRE?, --nas? DVS 13A
MC INTOSH, Bazle WRN 30A
Frederick BTH 194
J. D. FTE 63
James CLY 127
John BNE 26
John ETL 41

Name	County	Page
MC INTOSH, John	SHE	176
Joshua	WRN	66A
Lloyd	LGN	44
Nimrod	CLY	127
Richd.	CLY	127
Saml.	CLY	127
Solomon	LGN	31
Thomas	BTH	194
Walter	LGN	37
William	CLY	131
William	BTH	194
William	BTH	216
MC INTURF, Emanuel	PUL	49A
MC INTUSH, John	LVG	16
MC INTUSH?, Charles	LVG	16
MC ISAAC, Isaac	FTE	110
James	FTE	104
John	NSN	175
MC IVAIN, Geo.	FLG	65A
MC JILTEN?, Thos.	CLY	111
MC JIMMERSON?, David	FLG	59A
MC JUNKINS, John	SPN	8A
MC KAIN?, Wm.	ADR	34
MC KAM?, Wm.	ADR	34
MC KANCE, Alexr.	HRD	18
John	HRD	68
MC KANE, John	LVG	16
MC KAUGHAN, George	PUL	53A
MC KAY, Enoch	NSN	212
George	WAS	78A
Jemima	WAS	26A
John	NSN	200
John	CBL	7A
Richard	NSN	211
Richard	NSN	212
Robbert	CBL	6A
Samuel	NSN	211
William	NSN	205
William	CBL	5A
MC KEE, Archibald	FTE	85
Archibald	MER	103
Darias	GRD	87A
David	JES	88
David	HAR	134
Elizabeth	MNR	209
G--an?, Jr.	FLG	66A
Guyan	FLG	62A
Henry	BBN	136
Henry	FKN	138
Hugh W.?	GRD	87A
James	FTE	83
James	GTN	121
James	SCT	123A
Jane	WDF	113A
Jno.	FKN	150
John	JES	94
John	BBN	130
John	MTG	271
John	FLG	58A
John	FLG	62A
John	SHE	115A
John	SCT	123A
John	TOD	131A
Joseph	CLK	97
Joshua	CLK	97
Mary	FTE	83
Polly	WTY	122A
Rebecka	HAR	134
Robt.	SCT	123A
Sam	GRD	111A
Saml.	HAR	134
Saml.	FKN	150
Samuel	MTG	285
Thos.	TOD	129

Name	County	Page
MC KEE, Will. H.	KNX	282
Wm.	FLG	62A
Wm.	TOD	131A
MC KEHAN, Benj.	KNX	288
MC KENDRICK, Polly	FKN	162
Wm.	FKN	150
MC KENLEY, Wm.	SHE	132A
MC KENLY, Wm.	SHE	122A
MC KENNEY, Jamey	MAD	94
John, Sr.	WDF	117A
John	CBL	2A
MC KENNON, Daniel	BNE	26
MC KENNY, Daniel	UNN	154
George W.	UNN	146
Hannah	UNN	149
William	UNN	148
MC KENRY, James	WYN	88A
MC KENSEY, Andrew	CHN	43A
MC KENZIE, Richard	GRT	141
MC KENZY, John	LWS	94A
Thomas	LWS	99A
MC KER?, Nancy	HRY	230
MC KERLY, Moses	GRD	98A
MC KERNAN, Joseph	UNN	150
MC KERNON?, Lawrence	UNN	150
MC KETTERICK, James	WAS	82A
John	WAS	82A
John	WAS	82A
Wm.	WAS	82A
MC KEVER, John	JEF	24
Kenith	CHN	44
MC KEY, Alexd.	KNX	288
Hannah	JEF	42
James	BBN	126
James	FKN	152
John	BBN	90
John	BBN	138
Polly	KNX	304
MC KIE, Bill (A Man Of Color)	WAS	35A
MC KIM, Abram	BNE	24
Joseph	BBN	90
MC KINDLEY, James	WYN	104A
Jno.	HAR	134
Sally, Mrs.	WYN	92A
MC KINEY, Raney	ADR	4
MC KINEY?, Edmund	CHN	33A
MC KINLEY, David	SHE	136A
James	SHE	118A
James	SHE	139A
Richard	SHE	120A
Wm.	SHE	122A
MC KINLY, Jonas	GRT	147
MC KINNEY, Archibald	GTN	126
Archibd.	LNC	19
C.	TOD	128
Chas.	CHN	30A
D.	TOD	128
Daniel F.	WYN	85A
David	FTE	74
Dennis	LNC	15
Francis	ETL	43
Francis	PND	29A
James	MBG	143A
Jas.	PUL	47A
John	LVG	7
John	GRN	61
John	GTN	130
John	BTL	327
John, Jr.	WDF	104A
John	CHN	30A
John W.	WAS	49A
Middleton	HND	12

Name	County	Page
MC KINNEY, Nelly	CLD	146
Rane	WYN	80A
Richard	ETL	51
Robert	CLK	84
Rody	WDF	119A
Susan	LNC	29
William	BTL	327
Williams	GRN	58
Wm.	PUL	39A
MC KINNEY?, (See MCKINNEY & Mc Hinney)		
James	WDF	104
MC KINNY, Charles	MER	103
Francis	BBN	92
Hardin	MER	103
Henry	HOP	256
Hugh	CLK	93
James	DVS	17A
Jas.	HRY	250
John	MER	101
Joseph	JES	69
Lewis	FLG	67A
Micajah	MER	103
Nancy	MER	104
Thos.	JEF	55
W.	ADR	20
Wiley	MAD	160
William	HOP	256
Wm.	HRY	263
MC KINNY?, John	FLG	61A
Thos.	FLG	77A
MC KINSEE, James, Junr.	CHN	30
James, Senr.	CHN	30
MC KINSEY, Aron	MAD	150
Asa	PUL	48A
Davd.	PUL	49A
David	SHE	127A
Isaac	FLD	9
James	WRN	76A
John	ETL	44
John P.	NSN	213
Joseph	BBN	104
Mordecia	BKN	4
Sarah	OHO	11A
Thomas	GTN	119
MC KINSEY?, John	FLG	61A
Thos.	FLG	67A
MC KINSTER, Ambrose	FLD	45
MC KINSY?, Edmund	CHN	33A
MC KINY, John	RCK	84A
MC KINZE?, John M.	GRD	111A
MC KINZEE, John	WRN	37A
Mordica	SCT	102A
MC KINZEY, Jno.	PUL	43A
MC KINZIE, Allex.?	LNC	21
MC KINZY, John	HRY	226
MC KIRBY, John	LGN	42
MC KIVER, Danl.	SHE	155
MC KNIGHT, Andrew	WDF	124A
James	WRN	76A
Jean	BRK	271
Virgil	WDF	105
MC KOY, John	WRN	58A
Robt.	MAS	68
MC KUMBER, Phebe	CBL	19A
MC KUREY?, Charles	BTH	204
MC L ENNEY?, John C. W.	BBN	104
MC LACY?, Franklin	GRD	111A
MC LAIN, Hanah	BTH	218
John	BTH	202
John	BTH	218
Patsy	BTH	190
Polly	BTH	218

MC LAIN, William BTH 200
William BTH 218
MC LAINE, Elijah FTE 93
Solomon BTH 202
MC LANAHAM, Jas. BKN 6
Wm. BKN 11
Wm. BKN 19
MC LANAHAN, Jas., Jr. BKN 20
Washington BKN 11
MC LANATHAN, William HOP 254
MC LAND?, Ann WAS 43A
MC LANE, Alexander SHE 121A
Andrew SHE 114A
David SHE 117A
Francis BKN 13
George HRT 163
George MTG 247
James BTH 216
James HND 7A
Jesse SHE 121A
John BKN 10
John MAD 138
John HRT 164
John SHE 113A
John SHE 122A
Marget GRD 118A
Sarah MAD 144
Thomas MTG 257
Thomas SHE 114A
Wm. SHE 113A
MC LANIHAN, James BTH 206
MC LANNY?, Hugh ADR 34
MC LARD, Daniel MNR 213
MC LARDY, Alexander LGN 42
MC LAREN, Michael MNR 211
MC LARNING, Hugh ADR 36
MC LARNY?, Hugh ADR 34
MC LARRY?, Hugh ADR 34
MC LARY?, Franklin GRD 111A
Robt. ADR 34
MC LAUGHLIN, B. MAS 65
Corn., Snr. LVG 9
Cornelius, Jr. LVG 9
Geo. BBN 110
George PND 18A
James MBG 143
Jas. LVG 2
Jas. H. CHN 45
Jno. JEF 53
John CWL 37
John MTG 247
John HOP 258
Susan PND 15A
Zominie SCT 120A
MC LEAN, Alney MBG 143
Daniel HOP 254
Elizabeth LGN 31
Ephraim MBG 143
George LGN 37
James TRG 5
John LGN 37
Lee LGN 37
Mary LGN 23
Michael UNN 153
Samuel MBG 141
Samuel NSN 177
Thomas TRG 6A
Thomas TRG 6A
William NSN 218
MC LEAR, Chas. JEF 22
MC LEAS?, Thomas GNP 174A
MC LEIN, John FTE 105
MC LELAND, Josiah MNR 195
MC LEMAR, Jno. JEF 59
MC LEMORE, Gillum RCK 77A
Tempe LGN 30
MC LENORE, Right RCK 83A
MC LERAY?, Eli ADR 34
MC LERVER, Thomas BTH 158
MC LERVER?, Mathew BTH 150
MC LIN, Henry GRD 107A
MC LINEY?, Mark? HRY 234
MC LINN?, William UNN 154
MC LINTICK, Eliza? LVG 16
MC LOCHLIN, William LVG 13
MC LONEY, D. SHE 109A
MC LONEY?, Danl. HAR 168
Jno. HAR 162
MC LOUGHLIN, Wm. GNP 165A
MC LOURY?, Jno. HAR 162
MC LUNE, Wm. BKN 10
MC LURE, Greenup SHE 160
Jean BTH 168
Jediah GSN 143A
John SHE 157
John GSN 143A
Robt. HRD 42
Samuel BTH 168
Widdow HRD 70
MC LUSKY, Alexr. LVG 12
David LVG 12
John LVG 12
Will. LVG 5
MC LWAYN, Andrew BTH 178
MC MACHEM?, James FTE 95
MC MACHERN?, James FTE 95
MC MACKIN, Jas. HRY 255
Nancy NSN 175
MC MAHAN, Abraham CLY 129
Alexander GRN 59
Andrew GRN 54
James HAR 180
James HND 9A
Jessey MAD 158
John CHN 30A
Moses ETL 43
Robert NCH 112A
Sarah JEF 43
MC MAHELL, John NCH 110A
Robert NCH 120A
Thomas NCH 117A
Wm. NCH 116A
MC MAHON, ---s.? CWL 42
John FTE 69
John HRD 84
MC MAINES, Robert WDF 123A
MC MAINS, Abraham OWN 101
Andrew OWN 101
James OWN 104
MC MAKIN, Charles NSN 205
Elisabeth BTL 327
John BTL 327
William NSN 200
MC MAN, Danl. SHE 154
MC MANAMA, James BNE 24
MC MANAMY, Samuel SHE 142A
MC MANIHAN?, Edward JEF 31
MC MANIS, Samuel GTN 126
Wayen GRD 97A
MC MANNES, Charles BLT 166
MC MANNIAN?, C. D. BKN 23
MC MANNING?, Mary NSN 178
MC MANNIS, Nancy SHE 126A
Wm. RCK 82A
MC MANNIS?, Mary NSN 178
MC MAUHAN?, Edward JEF 31
MC MEEKINS, Archi FTE 111
MC MEEKINS, Robert FTE 111
Samuel FTE 111
Samuel FTE 112
MC MELLEN, Alexander SHE 114A
MC MELON, John GNP 168A
MC MERRY, James ALN 132
MC MICHAEL, James FKN 144
Robert FKN 144
MC MICKEN, Robt. FTE 68
Will. LVG 5
MC MICKLE, Mrs. JEF 28
MC MILLAN, Andrew HRD 34
Francis HOP 256
James CLK 85
James MTG 235
John MTG 299
William CLK 82
MC MILLEN, Grace MNR 193
James MNR 211
James, Jr.? PND 28A
John BKN 26
John MNR 193
Joseph MAD 134
Joseph GTN 135
Joseph M. ADR 32
Susanah SCT 114A
MC MILLER, Wm. HRD 66
MC MILLIAN, John LGN 43
MC MILLIER?, Canada HAR 156
MC MILLIN, Andrew F. HAR 218
Elizabeth HAR 220
Ester HAR 144
James PND 28A
Mary HAR 158
Robt. SCT 136A
MC MILLON, George WRN 73A
MC MINIMY, Peggy WDF 105
MC MINN, John FTE 97
MC MINN?, Will A. LVG 16
MC MONIGALE, Aaron ETL 52
Barnett ETL 49
MC MORIS, David WAS 52A
MC MULLEN, --than? DVS 8A
Jane FTE 64
Jno. MAS 75
Neal BRK 277
William BTL 327
MC MULLENS, James GRT 139
MC MULLIN, Andrew HAR 142
Arch BRK 273
Duncan BLT 186
Geo. BKN 24
James SHE 155
John HND 10
John BRN 20
Samuel GRD 85A
Wm. JEF 31
Wm. GRD 115A
MC MULLINS, Arthur MAD 108
John LNC 41
Rice? LNC 21
Thomas LNC 31
MC MUNN, Alexr. SHE 167
MC MURDY, Francis, Capt. MER 103
MC MURRAY, John LVG 6
Michael LVG 6
Samuel WRN 28A
Simpson CLK 76
William WRN 57A
MC MURRY, Elizibeth WAS 27A
James WAS 27A

Name	County	Page
MC MURRY, John	LNC	9
John	CLK	76
John	WAS	28A
Tho.	LNC	9
Thomas	UNN	148
MC MURTER?, Robt.	BRK	277
MC MURTEY, Sarah	GRD	117A
MC MURTREY, James	MNR	211
Samuel	HAR	204
William	MER	101
MC MURTRY, Alexr.	GRD	120A
David	FTE	74
James	HAR	134
James	UNN	154
Joseph	HRD	82
Katharine	MER	114
Stephen	HRD	54
MC MURTRY?, Jemima	MER	103
William	MER	103
MC NAB, Andrew	BTH	188
James	BTH	180
John	BTH	160
MC NAB?, Abner	HAR	154
MC NABB, Alias	TRG	7
John W.	TRG	14
MC NAIR, Jane	FTE	100
MC NALLY, Wm.	MAD	96
MC NAMAR, Phillip	DVS	16A
MC NARY, Anna	MBG	139A
Jno.	MAS	70
John	MBG	133A
MC NATH?, Alexander	BKN	4
MC NAY, Saml.	PND	28A
MC NEAL, Archibald	FTE	88
Dorothy	CHN	36A
John	GTN	120
Joseph	MER	102
Prior	CHN	33
MC NEAL?, David	UNN	154
MC NEALL, Rebecca	BNE	26
MC NEAR, James	NCH	112A
MC NEELY, Esther	CLD	150
Samuel	HOP	256
Wm.	ADR	36
MC NEES?, Abraham	HAR	176
Alexander	HAR	176
MC NEILL, Danl.	HRD	66
James	KNX	280
John	KNX	314
Johnathan	KNX	280
MC NEILL?, D.	MAS	79
MC NELL, Wilson	FKN	56
MC NETT, George	BNE	26
MC NEW, -----?	DVS	9A
MC NIGHT, James	CHN	34
Jno.	MAS	72
MC NIT, Sarah	LWS	95A
MC NITE?, John	BTH	168
MC NITT, Robert	FTE	65
Wm.	MAS	72
MC NORTON?, William	CBL	15A
MC NUS?, (See Mc Nees?)	HAR	176
MC NUTT, Thomas	BLT	154
MC OLISTER, Jane	BTH	170
MC ORMIC, Blencha	BTH	172
MC PHAIL, Allen	TOD	129
Neal	SPN	15A
MC PHEETERS, Charles	FTE	97
MC PHERIN, James	LNC	55
MC PHERREN, James	OWN	106
John	OWN	106
MC PHERSON, Aaron	MNR	201
MC PHERSON, Alex.	BNE	24
Alexander	BNE	24
Evan	LGN	39
George	MNR	201
Jehu	MNR	197
Jesse	BTH	168
Jessee	MGB	137A
John	MBG	141A
Joshua	MNR	205
Mark	BNE	24
Mark	LNC	49
Merdock	LGN	28
Robt.	BNE	24
Sarah	MNR	201
Thos.	PND	31A
MC PHETERS, William	WRN	42A
MC PHIERSON, A.? G.	CHN	45A
MC PIKE, Edd.	HRY	255
Joseph	CBL	3A
MC QUA?, John	GRD	108A
Wm.	GRD	108A
MC QUAID, Henry	HOP	256
MC QUAIT, Thomas	FTE	69
MC QUARY, Wm.	GRD	104A
MC QUE, William	MER	103
William	FTE	104
MC QUEEN, -? L. A.	MAS	60
Dise	ETL	43
Joshua	MAD	152
William	ETL	46
MC QUEEN?, Edward	MAD	156
MC QUENN, John B.	MAD	116
MC QUERRY, Danl.	LNC	63
MC QUERRY?, Eliz.	GRD	111A
Jos.	GRD	102A
MC QUIDDY?, Benjamin	WDF	102A
James	WDF	96A
John, Jr.	WDF	96A
MC QUIDER?, Thos.	BRK	275
MC QUIE, Alexander	BRN	21
MC QUILLAN, Thomas	FTE	69
MC QUINCH?, Samuel	CSY	208
MC QUINN/ MC QUIM?, Carles	FLD	6
MC QUINN, Baxter	FLD	6
Jas.	JEF	59
MC QUINTON, Jane	TOD	129A
MC QUISTON, Jas.	TOD	130
MC QUN?, John	CLY	129
MC QUOIN, Lawrence	NCH	118A
MC QUOWN, William?	NSN	175
MC RACKEN, John	BKN	6
MC RACKIN?, Hugh	CWL	46
MC RADY, Alex	BKN	5
MC RAINY, Robert	MER	103
MC RAINY?, John	MER	104
MC RAIZON?, Lewis M.	GNP	166A
MC RAMY?, John	MER	104
MC RAY, Danl.	BBN	110
MC REA, Thos.	CWL	56
MC REYNOLDS, Archibald	LGN	32
Benjamin	LGN	32
Jane	LGN	32
Saml.	SHE	125A
MC ROBERTS, Andrew	LNC	65
Charles	LNC	53
David	HRD	50
George	LNC	53
Isaac	LNC	53
Jas.	FLG	58A
John	LNC	51
MC ROBERTS, John	FLG	58A
Margery	FLG	55A
Saml.	SCT	112A
Thomas	CLY	120
MC ROBY?, Jas.?	CWL	58
MC ROINALDS?, Edward	ALN	120
Jno.	ALN	140
John	ALN	116
John	ALN	118
Robt.	ALN	120
Roley	ALN	140
MC ROSKY?, Joseph	BLT	172
MC ROYNALDS?, James	ALN	120
MC ROYRY, Thomas	LVG	14
MC SHANE, Daniel	HAR	206
MC SHEELERS?, Adam	FTE	87
MC SORLEY, James	GNP	167A
MC SPADDIN, Jos.	KNX	286
MC SWANE, Thos. M., Jr.	MAD	132
Thos. M., Sr.	MAD	132
MC SWENEY, Geo.	JEF	19
MC THONY, Sim?	CWL	57
MC ULLY, Hugh	GSN	145A
MC UNE, Sophia	HAR	190
MC VAY, --gh?	CWL	41
Jas	HRD	78
John	TOD	130
Jordan?	CWL	35
Patrick	MAD	160
T. R.	TOD	132
MC VAY?, Hugh	GRD	122A
MC VEIGH, Danl.	KNX	292
MC VEY, John	BRK	275
John	NCH	122A
Martin	WRN	42A
Sarah	NCH	127A
MC VICKOR, Anna	BTH	196
MC WADE, James	SHE	127A
MC WAIN, John W.	FTE	61
MC WANE?, Saml.	ADR	34
MC WATERS, John	TRG	12A
Moses	TRG	12
William	TRG	6A
MC WATERS?, Hugh	CWL	57
MC WAUGH?, Samuel	NCH	116A
MC WERTHY, Elias	CWL	46
Elvin?	CWL	36
James	CWL	36
MC WHARTER, Robert	WRN	66A
MC WHIRTER, Elijah	CLY	125
Moses	LGN	30
Robt.	KNX	280
MC WHURTER, Abner	PUL	65A
MC WILLIAM, Rebekah	MAD	128
MC WILLIAMS, Alexander	MAD	128
David	MAD	150
David	SHE	163
James	MAD	124
James H.	MAD	166
Jas.	LVG	5
Jas.	HRD	62
John	HRD	46
John	CLK	80
John	MAD	124
John	MAD	166
John C.	MAD	122
Reacha / Beacha?	CHN	44A
Samuel	SHE	163
Wm.	HRY	261
MCDANIEL, Jane, Mrs.	CLK	101

Name	County	Page
MCGEE, John	JES	75
MCKINNEY, Gerrard	FTE	64
Jos.	PUL	42A
ME---?, Jacob	CHN	34
MEAD, Benj.	GRD	115A
Eli	FLD	32
Moses	FLD	28
Rhodes	FLD	32
Robert	FLD	32
Samuel	FLD	29
Samuel	FLD	29
William	FLD	42
MEAD?, Benjamin	GNP	177A
MEADE, David	JES	81
Richard B.	JES	81
Will	HRY	184
MEADERS, Allin	WYN	104A
Isaiah	WTY	123A
Thomas M.	WTY	124A
MEADLOCK?, Isham	CSY	218
MEADLY, Geo.	MAS	71
MEADOR, John	SHE	160
MEADORS, Edward	WTY	113A
MEADOWS, Andrew	WYN	83A
Archibald	HAR	188
Henry	WRN	54A
Jacob	WYN	91A
Jacob B.	ETL	52
James	WRN	54A
John	WRN	54A
Lacy	ALN	94
Thos.	BRK	273
William	ETL	52
Wm.	BRK	273
MEADOWS?, John	WTY	118A
MEADS, Saml.	MAS	55
MEAKER, David B.	FLG	43A
MEALERS?, Allen	ALN	114
MEALS, Widw.	CWL	35
MEALY, Igs.?	WAS	75A
Thos.	WAS	71A
MEANS, Benjamin	CLD	150
George	WAS	47A
George	LWS	92A
James	MNR	215
James	MTG	226
Jas.	JEF	62
John	MNR	191
John	MTG	265
John	LWS	95A
John	LWS	98A
Jos.	CHN	45
Robert	LWS	98A
Thomas	MNR	191
William	MTG	261
Wm., Jr.	CHN	42
Wm., Snr.	CHN	42
MEARIT, Isaac	CSY	210
MEARS, Andrew	LWS	86A
James	GRN	56
John	GRN	78
Moses	GRN	77
Thomas	GRN	77
MEASON, Benjamin	SHE	127A
MECHUM, Susannah	GSN	145A
MEDAUGH, James	GNP	170A
MEDCALF, Barnett	FTE	58
Benjn.	OHO	5A
Elisha	FTE	83
John	FTE	62
John	NSN	188
John K.	NSN	188
Thomas	FTE	62
MEDDORS, Reuben	WTY	114A
MEDDOWS, Saml.	WAS	49A
MEDLEY, Elizebeth	WAS	70A
MEDLEY, James	GTN	117
John L.	HRD	16
Philip	NSN	213
Reuben	NSN	200
Thos.	WAS	50A
MEDLIN, Sally	NCH	122A
MEDLOCK, James	SHE	135A
MEDLY, Elizebeth	WAS	44A
MEDORS, Thomas	WTY	121A
MEECHINS, John	FTE	86
MEED, Jesse	CLY	118
MEEDS, Solimon	GSN	144A
Wm.	GSN	145A
Wm.	GSN	146A
MEEK, Adam	SCT	134A
Baz., Sr.	HRY	270
Bazil, Jr.	HRY	253
James	GNP	175A
Jer.	HRY	253
Jesse	HRY	253
Jno.	HRY	253
Jonath.	HRY	253
Samuel	GTN	134
Samuel	PUL	64A
Thomas	WRN	56A
Will	SCT	119A
William	PUL	64A
MEEK?, (See Mick?)	GTN	124
James	WDF	103A
Jessee	GTN	134
MEEKES, John	CSY	226
MEEKS, Edward	CBL	9A
James	LVG	8
James	FLD	24
James	NCH	107A
John	NCH	107A
Pridy	HRT	164
Silvanus	MER	102
William	OHO	6A
William	NCH	107A
MEESE, (See Muse)	PUL	46A
Christopher	PUL	65A
George	PUL	60A
Joseph	PUL	62A
MEFFORD, C., Mrs.?	MAS	58
Elizabeth	BBN	120
Jacob	LGN	39
Jacob	FKN	94
John	LGN	39
Philip	FKN	94
MEFFORD?, Joseph	SCT	116A
MEGGINSON, John	SPN	7A
MEGINNIS, Elizabeth	BTH	150
Pyrhus	BTH	152
William	BTH	152
William	BTH	214
MEGLASSON?, Mathew	ADR	36
MEGOWAN, Charles	FTE	100
MEHOLM, Mn.? M.	MAD	140
MEHONEY, Daniel	ALN	124
MEIGG, Benjamin	NSN	204
John	NSN	204
MELDRUM, James	SHE	122A
Mw.	SHE	122A
MELEN, Isaac	OHO	9A
MELICAN, Patrick	FLG	55A
MELLENDER, Wm.	HRD	80
MELLON, Zachariah	BBN	116
MELLON?, Sam	ALN	128
MELNER, Luke	HAR	144
MELON, Job.	OHO	7A
MELONE, Drury	SHE	130A
James H.	SHE	142A
MELONEY, John	HND	6
MELSON, Elijah	WYN	101A
MELTON, Absalom	CLD	144
Charles	HRD	16
Early	WYN	83A
Elijah	NSN	206
Garland A.	HRT	163
James	HRT	164
Jesse	BRN	20
Jessee, Jr.	HND	10
Jessee, Sr.	HND	10
John	HND	11
John	WYN	85A
John	SHE	123A
Josiah	HND	11A
Mary	NSN	206
Michael	HRD	24
Moses	OHO	4A
Richard	NSN	206
Saml.	HND	11A
Terry	HRL	114
Thomas	LNC	39
Thos.	SHE	123A
MELTON?, Pleasant	CSY	220
MELVIN, Hugh	BBN	132
John	BKN	10
N.	JEF	26
MELVIN?, George C. S.	MER	103
MENAFEE, Joseph R.	SCT	96A
	TOD	130A
MENARY, Chas., Jr.	BBN	70
Chas., Senr.	BBN	70
MENDAY?, Mirntree?	ADR	34
MENEFIELD?, Samuel	NSN	212
MENIFEE, Ben. P.	CHN	42A
MENIX, Alexr.	MAS	73
Jas.	MAS	65
MENIX?, Charles	FLD	32
MENNAFEE, Gerrard	FTE	77
MENSER, Catharine	HOP	256
Daniel	HOP	256
John	HOP	256
Jonas	HOP	256
MENTELLE, Waldemar	FTE	112
MENTLO, James	BRN	20
MENZUS?, Wm. A.	BBN	102
MERANDA, R., Mrs.	BKN	26
S., Mrs.	BKN	26
Saml.	BKN	26
Thos.	BKN	26
MERCER, C.	JEF	23
Carver	JEF	46
David	MBG	142A
George	WAS	17A
Hosey	MAD	154
Howard	MNR	215
James	CWL	44
James	WYN	86A
James	SHE	135A
John, Jr.	CWL	42
John, Senr.	CWL	42
John	WYN	86A
Joseph	LVG	12
Martin	MBG	141A
Nicholas	WYN	86A
Nicholas M.	WYN	86A
Sarah	SHE	135A
MERCER?, Catherine	WAS	83A
MERCHANT, Milton	BNE	28
Thomas	FTE	108
Wm.	HRY	264
MEREDAITH, Obediah	FLG	40A
MEREDITH, Absm.	BBN	130
John	BBN	130
Joseph	WDF	113A
Rebecca	LWS	90A
Samuel	FTE	74

MEREDITH, Theodrick? ALN 122
Thos. BBN 130
Thos. FLG 40A
William MER 101
William WRN 44A
William L. WRN 43A
MEREDY?, James WYN 100A
MERES, Moses MNR 191
MERETTE?, Lewis BLT 176
MEREWETHER, Thos. WAS 36A
MEREWITHER, David JEF 31
Richd. SHE 167
Sarah JEF 31
Thos. H. JEF 65
William JEF 38
MERGERSON, Saml. WAS 31A
MERIDETH, John GSN 144A
MERIDITH, Allexandr. GSN 143A
Charles GSN 143A
Daniel PUL 53A
David LGN 31
David BNE 50
Edward B. WDF 104
Elish FTE 94
Elisha PUL 64A
Frederick GSN 144A
Jno. ALN 124
Joseph GSN 143A
Joseph GSN 145A
Thos. GSN 145A
William PUL 64A
MERINGO, Joseph HAR 138
MERIT, John KNX 296
MERITH, Francus JES 92
MERITT, John ALN 130
MERIWETHER, H. TOD 127
James SHE 162
MERIWITHER, James B. SHE 176
MERLIN, Daniel HRD 92
George HRD 20
John HRD 14
MERNON?, (See Marion?) CBL 16A
Elizabeth CBL 16A
MERREFIELD?, Samuel NSN 212
MERREL, Douglas SPN 5A
John M. BNE 26
Timothy SPN 22A
MERRELL, Andr. MAS 67
Benjamin FTE 89
Reuben MAS 61
Ruth FTE 109
MERRET, James BNE 24
Stephen BRN 21
MERRICK, Jno. MAS 64
MERRIL, David SCT 107A
MERRILL, Andrew ETL 49
Jno. CWL 55
Nicholas CLK 64
Peggy GRD 93A
William ETL 49
William FTE 109
MERRIMAN, Jesse CWL 55
MERRION?, (See Mernon?) CBL 16A
MERRIT, Richard WRN 65A
Richd. GRD 102B
Thomas WYN 101A
MERRITT, Archilaus JEF 41
Jane HRD 78
John GRD 110A
Peter GRD 103A
MERRIWEATHER, Valentine WRN 37A
MERRIWETHER, C. TOD 127
Wm. HRY 241
MERRY, Amelia BRK 227
Elizabeth CHN 38
James BRN 33
Jno. CHN 38
MERRYDITH, Salley HRT 164
Wm. HRT 164
MERRYFIELD, John TRG 11
John HRD 82
Thos. HRD 68
MERRYMAN, Allen RCK 75A
Amos SCT 118A
John NSN 182
Lyman SCT 118A
Reuben SCT 118A
MERSHAM?, Danl. FLG 66A
MERSHON, Andrew GRD 87A
Benj. FLG 61A
James GRD 102A
Job FTE 83
John GRD 102A
Rob. GRD 83A
William GRD 83A
MERSHON?, Cornelius CLK 105
Cornelius FLG 56A
Wm. BKN 23
MERTON, Alexander LGN 22
William I. LGN 23
MERVIN, Daniel HRD 46
Delancy NSN 194
Patk. HRD 14
MERVIRS?, Darias BLT 158
MESMORE?, George CHN 34
MESSACK, Saml. JEF 55
MESSEN / MESSER?, Rachiel FLG 65A
MESSEN?, Peter ADR 34
MESSER, Benj. KNX 294
John KNX 294
Sion KNX 294
Stephen KNX 294
Will. SCT 137A
MESSER?, Peter ADR 34
MESSICH?, Nathl. FLG 64A
MESSINNER?, Henry JEF 50
MESSON/ MESSORE?, Joseph GRN 65
MESSUCK, Saml. JEF 35
METCALF, ----am? DVS 13A
Allen DVS 17A
Ann JES 97
Charles NSN 180
Charles NSN 211
Charles SHE 130A
Enoch HOP 256
George, Jr. DVS 17A
George, Sr. DVS 17A
Ignatus NSN 198
Isaac HOP 256
James NSN 187
John HOP 254
John, Sen. WYN 89A
Jos. SHE 142A
Joseph NSN 222
Thomas FTE 78
Thomas HOP 256
William FTE 89
William, Jnr. HOP 258
William, Snr. HOP 258
William F. HOP 258
METCALFE, Alfred FLG 37A
Eli FLG 42A
METCALFE, James SHE 172
John SHE 172
Thomas NCH 107A
William SHE 173
METEER, Thomas BTH 162
METGAR, D. O. FTE 66
METTON, Francis WAS 30A
METTON?, Pleasant CSY 220
METTS, Cyrus BTH 166
John GRT 140
METTZ?, Moses NSN 221
MEWHORTER?, John CSY 206
MICALS, Silvia? WAS 59A
MICHAEL, John MBG 143
Robert HAR 150
MICHAELS, George HRD 80
Jacob WYN 81A
John WYN 82A
MICHAM, Harrison JES 95
MICHEL, Harry RCK 75A
James CWL 33
Maclin CWL 38
Thomas BBN 144
MICHELL, Ann BBN 138
Daniel WAS 47A
John BBN 134
John GRD 105A
John GRD 111A
Nelly GRD 115A
William TRG 3
William GRD 119A
Wm. M. MAS 52
MICHELL?, Robert B. WAS 46A
MICHIL, Obed OHO 3A
MICK, John FLG 79A
MICK?, James GTN 124
MIDDLETON, Adam SHE 170
Charles HRD 36
David SHE 168
Elijah HRD 50
Elizabeth SHE 169
H. GRD 106A
Hanson BRN 21
Henley HRD 64
Henry LNC 73
Horatio HRY 268
James FKN 140
James SHE 169
Jno. M. HRY 270
John BLT 196
John NSN 221
Joseph JEF 21
Micajah HRD 86
Robert WRN 37A
Thomas BLT 196
Thomas WRN 40A
Walter HRL 114
MIDDLETON?, Thomas BLT 166
MIDEGATE?, Jno. MAS 77
MIDGETT, Christ--? CWL 58
Micajah CWL 58
MIDLETON, Martin GRD 108A
Mathew GSN 144A
Robt. ADR 38
MIERICK?, George BKN 23
MIERS, Daniel BRN 19
Daniel (Barren Fork Of Beaver Creek) BRN 20
Henry BRN 19
Michael BRN 19
MIFFORD, Jacob CBL 23A
Saml. MAS 58
MIFFORD?, Joseph SCT 116A
MIFORD, Benjn. SCT 137A

MIKLEBOROUGH, James CLK 79
MILAM, Ambrose CLD 140
Benjamin LGN 31
George SHE 123A
Jno. FKN 120
Johnson WDF 105
MILBONNER?, Ewell WAS 87A
MILBURN, Andrew WYN 91A
David WAS 21A
Izzeral WAS 21A
John WAS 21A
Jonathon WAS 21A
Joseph MER 102
Nancy WAS 29A
William PUL 64A
Wm. JEF 52
Wm. WAS 31A
MILBY, John GRN 52
William R. CLK 77
MILDER, Thos. CLY 122
MILDRUM?, John H. GTN 125
MILEHAM, John GRT 140
MILEHAM?, Eben. PND 27A
MILES, Alexd. WAS 47A
Benjamin SHE 175
Benjamin SHE 131A
David FKN 102
Edward B. NSN 212
Edwd. WAS 64A
Gabriel HAR 166
Geo. MAS 81
George SHE 153
Henry NSN 179
Hillery ADR 14
Isaac WDF 124A
Jack GSN 143A
James SHE 174
James SHE 176
James BRK 275
James J./ I.? FKN 56
Jesse WAS 57A
Jno. HRY 259
Jno., Sr. HRY 269
John ADR 36
John GRN 60
John CLK 106
John SHE 161
John SHE 163
John NSN 179
John, Sr. SHE 172
John WAS 56A
Jonas SHE 140A
Mary HRL 114
Moses BLT 154
Nathan BLT 156
Nicholas NSN 182
Philip GSN 145A
Richard SHE 152
Ruben SHE 128A
Saml. JEF 41
Samuel SHE 151
Samuel SHE 174
Thomas NSN 217
Thomas PUL 56A
Wilford CSY 220
William FTE 102
William SHE 161
William CBL 19A
Wm. MAD 174
Wm. WAS 56A
MILES?, Adam HAR 168
J---? WAS 38A
MILHOLLAND, John CHN 32A
MILICAN, Frances MAD 102
MILIGEN, James GNP 175A
MILION, Elijah MAD 114
George MAD 102
Rodney MAD 150
MILLAN, Thomas MTG 231
MILLAR, Abraham LNC 59
Armstead LNC 11
Henry MNR 217
Jacob LNC 45
John LNC 65
Thomas MNR 197
William MNR 213
MILLAY, ---as? DVS 17A
MILLBANKS, John SCT 110A
MILLECAN, Lewis WRN 43A
MILLEN, George MAD 106
MILLEN?, Jas HRD 80
Jas. CHN 38
MILLER, -----? DVS 10A
Aaron FKN 108
Aaron CLD 156
Aaron MTG 293
Abm. BBN 124
Abraham CLK 74
Abraham HAR 202
Abraham, Jnr HAR 202
Abrm. HRD 78
Absalom BRN 21
Absolem MBG 142
Adam ADR 36
Adam LGN 38
Adam HRD 94
Adam HAR 182
Adam BTL 327
Adam WRN 37A
Adam GSN 143A
Adam GSN 145A
Alexander NSN 209
Alexander HOP 256
Alexander LWS 94A
Alexander LWS 99A
Alexnder BBN 126
Alexr. FLG 23A
Alexr. FLG 31A
Alxr. ADC 68
Aminedab? SHE 130A
Anderson JEF 23
Anderson GRN 64
Andrew BNE 24
Andrew HRD 26
Andrew HRD 48
Andrew WYN 83A
Anthony HND 4A
Anthony WRN 40A
Anthony C. FKN 72
Archibald BRN 20
Aron HAR 154
Barney, Sr. BRK 271
Benj. P.? GRN 52
Benjamin FLD 15
Benjamin FLD 28
Benjamin BLT 154
Benjamin WRN 40A
Beverly UNN 146
Buckner MER 102
Caleb MER 103
Christian NSN 217
Christopher TRG 6
Christopher HRD 70
Christopher GSN 144A
Conrod SHE 115A
Coonrod WYN 104A
Cornelius CBL 22A
Dabney SHE 134A
Daniel HRL 114
Daniel MAD 120
Danl. PUL 43A
MILLER, Danl. GRD 86A
David KNX 290
David OHO 3A
David SPN 7A
David WRN 40A
David WAS 60A
David GSN 144A
David GSN 144A
David C. HRY 206
Edward FLD 21
Edward HAR 170
Edward SHE 138A
Elijah SHE 155
Elizabeth CLD 140
Elizabeth MTG 293
Ephram HRY 188
Ezekiel SHE 123A
Federick MAD 180
Fleming SHE 123A
Francis JES 85
Frederic, Sr. WYN 99A
Frederick JEF 36
Frederick MBG 140
Frs. S. HRY 182
Geo. PUL 41A
George LGN 38
George GRN 56
George NSN 207
George SPN 8A
George WAS 48A
George WYN 99A
George F. MBG 138A
George P. SHE 176
George? GTN 126
Hannah CLD 156
Henry BRN 34
Henry BNE 46
Henry HRD 48
Henry JEF 58
Henry ALN 102
Henry GTN 128
Henry FKN 148
Henry NSN 197
Henry HOP 256
Henry BRK 271
Henry BRK 277
Henry BTL 327
Henry WRN 59A
Henry SHE 114A
Henry SCT 121A
Herald KNX 304
Hugh HAR 136
Isaac JEF 39
Isaac CHN 44
Isaac HAR 220
Isaac CHN 41A
Jacob LGN 36
Jacob JEF 58
Jacob CLK 74
Jacob ALN 100
Jacob BBN 140
Jacob HRT 164
Jacob BLT 168
Jacob HAR 168
Jacob NSN 192
Jacob, Jr. ETL 54
Jacob, Sr. ETL 45
Jacob WRN 38A
Jacob WDF 101A
Jacob GRD 102A
Jacob SCT 114A
Jacob SHE 114A
Jacob SCT 138A
Jacob GSN 143A
Jacob GSN 144A
Jacob GSN 144A

MILLER, Jacob GSN 145A
James ADR 3
James BRN 33
James JEF 39
James CLK 82
James BBN 126
James HAR 136
James HAR 154
James SHE 161
James HRT 164
James MTG 253
James MTG 289
James SPN 7A
James WRN 40A
James CHN 41A
James WRN 51A
James WYN 99A
James NCH 113A
James GSN 144A
James C. SPN 21A
Jane GRD 83A
Jas. HRD 26
Jas. HRD 50
Jas. HRD 80
Jas., Sen. ADR 34
Jas. B. SCT 93A
Jas. M. BBN 94
Jason BNE 28
Jessee MBG 135
Jessee WYN 99A
Jno. CWL 55
Jno. HAR 162
John ADR 3
John HND 10
John JEF 21
John JEF 24
John BRN 33
John ADR 34
John CWL 37
John JEF 40
John JEF 44
John ETL 45
John JEF 55
John GRN 57
John JEF 63
John JEF 65
John CLK 88
John BBN 92
John WDF 94
John BBN 120
John CLD 150
John MAD 154
John CLD 156
John SHE 163
John CLD 166
John HAR 170
John HAR 182
John NSN 192
John HAR 206
John BRK 273
John OHO 5A
John SPN 22A
John PND 29A
John WAS 48A
John FLG 49A
John FLG 62A
John WRN 64A
John FLG 65A
John RCK 81A
John SCT 99A
John NCH 114A
John SCT 121A
John GSN 144A
John GSN 145A
John GSN 145A
John GNP 176A
MILLER, John A. SCT 102A
John A. NCH 125A
John B. JES 82
John J./ I.? MAD 178
Jos. MAD 136
Jos. SHE 140A
Joseph FKN 80
Joseph CLK 82
Joseph BBN 126
Joseph SHE 167
Joseph HAR 192
Joseph NSN 214
Joseph, Jr. ADR 3
Joseph OHO 5A
Joseph GSN 144A
Joseph GSN 144A
Joseph GSN 146A
Joseph E. FKN 80
Joshua HRL 114
Katherine SHE 128A
Killy HAR 136
Leonard BRK 273
Levi JEF 33
Lewis MAD 118
Lewis NSN 180
Lewis CBL 21A
Lewis WAS 60A
M. W. JEF 24
Machael MAD 160
Margaret BNE 28
Martin MBG 140
Mary BTH 174
Mathew SPN 4A
Matthias CSY 224
Michael HRD 72
Michael CLK 96
Micheal JEF 36
Michel BRK 273
Michel, Jr. BRK 275
Morris ALN 108
Morris L. JEF 45
Nancy GRD 120A
Nat ADR 64
Nathan ADC 66
Nathaniel NSN 214
Nicholas HRD 14
Nicholas JES 76
Nicholas HAR 152
Nicholas SHE 153
Noah CLK 96
Oliver FLG 62A
Oliver FLG 65A
Olly GNP 174A
Peter JEF 41
Peter HRD 46
Peter MAS 78
Peter FKN 134
Peter BLT 168
Petor MAD 166
Philip FLD 21
Philip HRD 26
Philip HRD 36
Phillip GRN 52
Phillip MBG 138A
Polley SCT 112A
Polly CLY 131
Polly SCT 99A
Rachael WTY 126A
Reubin JEF 51
Rice HAR 154
Richard CLD 141
Richard MNR 191
Robert BRN 19
Robert FLD 21
Robert JEF 32
Robert MER 101
MILLER, Robert MER 103
Robert SHE 151
Robert MAD 156
Robert SHE 116A
Robt HRT 164
Robt. BBN 128
Robt. BBN 132
Robt. KNX 284
Robt. N. JEF 39
Ruben WAS 82A
Ruth OHO 10A
Saml. CHN 44
Saml. MAS 63
Saml. HRD 78
Saml. CLY 132
Saml. HAR 156
Saml. GSN 145A
Saml. Sn. GSN 145A
Samuel GRN 57
Samuel NSN 195
Samuel GSN 144A
Samuel A. CHN 27A
Stephen BBN 82
Stephen CLY 118
Stephen NCH 123A
Thomas ETL 48
Thomas HRD 68
Thomas HAR 154
Thomas HOP 258
Thomas GNP 171A
Thomas GNP 174A
Thomas D. FTE 99
Thompson SHE 137A
Thos. GRN 51
Thos. MAS 59
Thos. B. JEF 48
Thos. T. FLG 29A
Vincent HAR 148
Warrick JEF 38
Widw. CWL 38
William GRN 50
William GRN 62
William OWN 101
William CLK 102
William BBN 126
William CLY 132
William BTH 174
William HRY 206
William BRK 227
William HOP 272
William KNX 288
William, Col. MER 116
William GRD 101A
William NCH 114A
William K. DVS 16A
William P. TRG 8A
Windle JEF 36
Wm. ADR 56
Wm. HRD 64
Wm. BBN 126
Wm. FKN 148
Wm. MAD 148
Wm., Jr. BBN 126
Wm., Snr. FLG 29A
Wm. FLG 34A
Wm. FLG 62A
Wm. SHE 134A
Wm. GSN 144A
Wm. GNP 174A
Wm. GNP 176A
Wm. T. FLG 29A
Wm.? CWL 36
MILLER?, Alexander MAD 126
Jas. CHN 38
John Harris WDF 103
MILLES, Edward CSY 212

Name	County	Page
MILLES, John	CSY	222
Walter / Watter?	CSY	210
MILLES?, James	WRN	50A
MILLICAIN, Soloman	CSY	208
MILLICAN, Charles	SPN	7A
Hugh	LGN	36
James	SPN	7A
James	WRN	43A
Spencer	SPN	10A
William	LGN	30
MILLICUN, John	WRN	39A
MILLIGAN, James	MBG	135A
John	NSN	211
Joseph	NSN	211
William	FTE	92
William	MER	103
MILLIKIN, Archibald	NCH	106A
James	SHE	167
MILLIN, A.	TOD	128
Robin	TOD	133
Wm.	TOD	130
MILLION, Benson	MAD	90
Birrel	MAD	112
Elsey	MAD	100
Geo.	SCT	119A
John	MAD	102
Robert	MAD	100
Squire	MAD	90
William	JES	78
William	FTE	85
MILLION?, Hammon	HAR	152
MILLIOR?, Hammon	HAR	152
MILLIR, Delany	GRD	96B
Peter	CHN	38
William	BTL	327
MILLIS, William	OHO	5A
MILLIS?, Jas.	SCT	102A
MILLON, Isam	HAR	158
Travis	MAD	112
MILLR, George	ADR	36
MILLR?, John	ADR	34
MILLS, A., Mr.	JEF	28
Adam	TOD	129
Alexander	LNC	3
Ambros	TRG	4A
Andrew G.	BBN	82
Benjamin, Senr.	BBN	82
Caleb	WYN	86A
Charles	FKN	104
Charles	NSN	189
Chas	TOD	126
Edwd.	FLG	52A
Eli	NSN	206
Elisha	GTN	130
Elizabeth	JEF	34
Even	FLG	35A
Geo.	CHN	43A
Ignatious W.	TRG	5A
Jacob	ADR	38
James	ADR	34
James	NSN	185
James	NSN	197
James	KNX	294
James	OHO	8A
James	GNP	177A
Jesse	CLD	145
Jessee	GRN	54
Jno.	PUL	45A
John	ADR	38
John	JES	81
John	CLK	107
John	TRG	4A
John	SPN	16A
John	FLG	34A
John	WAS	40A
MILLS, John	WYN	79A
John	GSN	143A
John S.	HRD	14
Martin	FLG	53A
Moenan	CHN	33
Nathan	BBN	108
Robert	WYN	86A
Robert	GSN	146A
Sarah Ann	CLD	145
Thomas	FTE	68
Ulyses	WYN	86A
William	SPN	23A
William	WRN	50A
William	PUL	52A
Willis -?.	WAS	85A
Wm.	JEF	63
Wm.	PUL	36A
MILLS?, Harvy?	NCH	105
J----?	WAS	38A
John	ADR	34
Joseph L.	WAS	38A
MILLSPAUGH, Robert	LGN	47
MILLSPAW, Daniel	SPN	9A
MILLY, Nathan S.	LVG	16
MILNER, Jane/ Isac?	GSN	43A
John	LNC	11
MILONE, Isaac	WAS	23A
John	WAS	26A
Meshack	WAS	28A
Richd.	WAS	27A
Ruben	WAS	26A
MILROY?, James	BTH	164
MILSAPS, Thomas, Jr.	WYN	94A
Thomas, Sr.	WYN	94A
MILSTEAD, Jonatious	BNE	24
MILTON, Elenor	SHE	131A
Elijah	FTE	108
John	BNE	28
MILTON?, John S.	BLT	164
MILUM, John	BRK	271
MIMMS, Linah	CHN	42A
Robert	LGN	36
Shadr.	TOD	128A
MIMS?, James	WTY	122A
MINDAY, George	ADR	36
Mintree?	ADR	34
Samel?	ADR	36
MINDY, Christopher	ADR	36
MINER, Bartley	FLG	51A
John	SHE	124A
Nicholad	BRK	277
Thomas	SHE	159
MING?, Mary	JEF	20
MINGAS?, Wm.	BKN	13
MINGES, George	HRD	46
Philip	HRD	82
MINGIS?, Peter	BRK	275
MINGS, Joseph, Jr.?	WYN	96A
Joseph	WYN	81A
MINISH, Richard	GTN	129
MINKS, Nicholas	RCK	80A
MINNER, Richd.	LVG	9
MINNIX, Abner	GRD	86A
Jesse	GRD	96B
MINOR, Alvin	GTN	132
Anselm	MER	102
Daniel	FTE	74
Edmd.	SCT	101A
Elliott	BNE	26
Elzabeth	NSN	200
George	SCT	101A
Henry L.	NSN	212
MINOR, James	PUL	41A
Jeremiah	SCT	116A
John	MER	102
John	NSN	179
Josep	SCT	133A
Joseph	MAD	98
Joseph, Jr.	GTN	120
Joseph, Sr.	GTN	120
Larkin	GRN	53
Priscilla	MER	102
Sarah	MER	102
Spencer	NSN	212
Thomas	JES	91
Waller	PND	19A
William	CSY	218
MINOR?, Jacob	CSY	218
MINT--?, Hugh	FTE	89
MINTER, Edward	FKN	80
Elizabeth	SHE	125A
Gabriel	JES	89
Jacob	CBL	12A
John	SHE	129A
Joseph	JES	94
Thos.	JEF	66
Will	ADC	66
William	HAR	200
MINTON, -----?	DVS	8A
---as?	DVS	7A
Cader	WRN	36A
Gilferd	HND	9
Isaac	WYN	100A
Jackson	GRN	50
Peggy	MNR	207
Philip	PUL	67A
Willis	TRG	12
MINYARD, George	MAD	166
MINZES, Samuel	WDF	93A
MIRANDA, Saml.	BKN	24
MIRES, Benjamin	MER	102
George	CHN	33
George	FTE	79
Henry	CHN	30
Jacob	BNE	26
Jacob	JES	69
John	BTL	327
Jonathan	CLK	98
Peter	MER	102
MIRICK, Green	CHN	40
MIRITTE?, Lewis	BLT	176
MIRS, Jacob	JES	89
MIRTLE, Wm.	JEF	32
MISE, Benjamin	BRN	20
David	BRN	20
Isaac	BRN	20
Wm.	BRK	273
MISHLER, Catherine	MBG	139
MISICK, Jobe	SCT	96A
MISKELL, Thomas	GRN	72
MISNER, Jno.	FKN	156
Jno.	FKN	156
Joel	FKN	72
MISSACH, Isaac	CHN	39
MISSHSO, Charles L.	HND	6A
MISSICK, Gorge	SCT	96A
MISSNER, Christopher	FTE	66
MITCALF, Norris	RCK	81A
MITCHAM, Sarah	HND	6A
MITCHEAL, Margret	HRL	114
MITCHEALL, Benjamin	BNE	26
Jacob	BNE	26
Wahington	BNE	26
Wesley	BNE	26
MITCHEL, Agnes	SHE	109A

Name	County	Page
MITCHEL, Alexr.	GRD	101A
Anna	TRG	13
Asa	GTN	133
B.	CHN	30A
David	TRG	12A
David	WDF	122A
Dudley	GTN	128
Edward	HRY	220
Edward	CHN	30A
Edward	WDF	102A
Elijah	BRN	21
Elijah	TRG	12A
Frederick	WDF	124A
Garret	TRG	12A
Gurtavus?	WDF	102
Harris?	WDF	99A
Hiram	FTE	65
James	MAD	136
James	BTH	172
James	BTL	327
John	MAD	140
John	UNN	153
John	SHE	116A
John D.	WDF	122A
John P.	MAD	130
Joseph	GTN	132
Lucy	GTN	123
Marth	BTH	154
Michael	WDF	123A
Milly	WDF	102
Nathan	GTN	133
Pamelia	MER	102
Peyton	UNN	146
Phillip	FLG	27A
Polley	SHE	128A
Rebeckah	CSY	216
Robert	HAR	136
Robert	BTH	154
Robert	HAR	162
Robert	WDF	123A
S. P.	SHE	111A
Samuel	BTH	172
Sarah	GTN	128
Thomas	TRG	12A
Thomas	LWS	86A
Will.	KNX	304
William	BBN	60
William, Jnr.	HOP	254
William, Snr.	HOP	254
William	WDF	98A
William	WDF	123A
Willis, Jr.	ALN	132
Willis, Senr.	ALN	144
Willis, Senr.	ALN	145
Wm.	MAD	140
MITCHELL, -----?	TRG	7
Aaron	MAS	66
Adam	GRN	69
Agnus	LVG	12
Alex. J./ I.?	FKN	62
Alexander	ETL	51
Alexr.	MAS	69
Alexr.	FLG	63A
Andw.	HRY	265
Ann	BKN	4
Archibald	MTG	275
Arther	BTH	164
Asa F.	WRN	37A
Benjn.	ALN	118
Boswell	FTE	93
Braxton	MER	103
Charles	SHE	170
Clabourn	FTE	93
Daniel	LGN	35
Daniel	BBN	86
Daniel	SHE	150
MITCHELL, Dennis	JEF	32
Doctor	BBN	84
Dolly	MAS	61
Dora	BKN	4
Edward	FKN	108
Elijah	MNR	195
Elijah	NCH	109A
Elsey	ADR	34
Ezekiel	NCH	118A
Geo.	MAS	76
Geo.	BBN	134
Geo. K.	HRY	220
George	FTE	93
George	CBL	23A
Ignatious, Jun.	MAS	57
Isaac	LGN	44
Isaac	MER	103
Israel	MNR	207
J. Stewart	MNR	209
Jame	JES	83
James	LVG	3
James	LVG	13
James	LNC	57
James	GRN	66
James	..TG	225
James	MTG	269
James	WRN	31A
James	WRN	54A
James	NCH	109A
James	SCT	120A
James P.	MER	102
Jamima	WRN	54A
Jas., Sr.	MAS	72
Jas. G.	BBN	76
Jessee	JEF	30
Jno.	FKN	68
Jno.	MAS	76
Jno.	MAS	78
Jno.	FKN	110
John	LVG	12
John	GRN	53
John	BTH	148
John	SHE	148
John	CBL	22A
John	WRN	42A
John	WRN	54A
John D.	HRY	180
John P.	BBN	64
Joseph	BBN	112
Joseph	BBN	114
Margaret	TRG	6A
Martin	WRN	44A
Mary	MAS	73
Mary	NSN	221
Mary	WRN	54A
Mic?	HRY	234
Michael	LGN	29
Moses	WRN	51A
Polly	HRY	216
Rebecca	FKN	124
Rebecca	SHE	175
Rich?	ALN	132
Richard	LGN	29
Robert	SHE	150
Robert	BLT	164
Rosana	CBL	22A
Saml. H.	SHE	149
Samuel	BTH	210
Samuel	NSN	212
Sarah	BBN	64
Stanford	MAS	64
Stanley	LVG	16
Susanna	LGN	39
Tho. N.?	HRY	220
Thomas	GRN	54
Thomas	BLT	168
MITCHELL, Thos.	BBN	88
Will	MAS	55
Will	MAS	72
Will.	MAS	57
William	BLT	152
William	MTG	229
William	WRN	37A
William	WRN	51A
William	LWS	93A
William	NCH	112A
William I./ J?	SHE	172
Willis, Senr.	ALN	144
Wm.	GRN	69
Wm.	BBN	114
Wm.	FKN	122
Wm.	BBN	146
Wm.	FLG	63A
Wyatt	LGN	28
MITCHELLTEN/ MITCHELLTREE?, John	NCH	111A
MITCHERSSON?, ---d.	CWL	40
MITCHUM, Andrew	CHN	31A
Dudley	WDF	95A
Edmund	CHN	35
James	WDF	93A
John, Senr.	CHN	31A
John	WDF	95A
John G.	CHN	31A
Joseph	CHN	31
Willis	CHN	31
Wyott	CHN	31
MITCHUSSON, -----?	CWL	42
---.? E.	CWL	42
MITTEN, John	BRK	271
William	GRD	118A
MITTER?, George	FLD	26
MITTON, John	WDF	113A
Love	CSY	220
MITTS, Adam	HAR	140
Jacob	GRT	140
MIX, Enos	WDF	122A
MIZE, Dennis	ALN	108
Isaac	ETL	41
Jerh.	PUL	46A
Joshua	ETL	54
Moses	CHN	30
William	SPN	13A
MMORE, John	BBN	134
MO----?, Jno.	CHN	39
MO---LIN?, Right	LVG	16
MOAINI?, Jno.	CHN	39
MOBERLY, Benj.	MAD	114
Benjamin	MAD	132
Edward	MAD	156
Elias	MAD	136
Ephraim	MAD	126
John	MAD	108
John	MAD	120
John	MAD	126
John, Jr.	MAD	128
Richard	MAD	90
Saml.	MAD	168
Thomas J.	ETL	50
Wm.	MAD	94
MOBLEY, Ben	GRD	95A
Betssy	LNC	79
Clement, Senr.	WRN	29A
Clemment	WRN	29A
Ed	GRD	111A
Hezekeah	NSN	183
Isaiah	WRN	29A
Jno.	HRY	256
Joab	GRD	87A
John	ADR	50

Name	County	Page
MOBLEY, John	UNN	149
John	OHO	6A
Lewis	NSN	184
Nathan	SPN	6A
Nathan	TOD	126A
Rachael	TOD	127
Tho.	RCK	82A
MOCBEE?, Thomas	BTH	186
MOCK, Daniel	WAS	51A
Joseph	BNE	24
Margaret	BBN	142
Mary	BBN	142
Ruben	WAS	77A
Rudolph	BBN	140
MOCKBEE, Morene?	BKN	13
MOCKBIE, Henson?	BKN	20
MOCKBY, Mert.	MTG	255
MOCKIBY, Stephen	BTH	204
MOCKLE?, John M.	BKN	11
MOCQUEBY?, Nancy	ETL	54
MODOX, Notly	FTE	73
MODREL, Jno.	PUL	37A
MODRELL, Adam	PUL	56A
Robert, Junr.	PUL	56A
Robert, Senr.	PUL	56A
MODRIL, Andw.	PUL	37A
Robt.	PUL	45A
MOEBEE?, Thomas	BTH	186
MOFFETT, Bayles	FTE	99
Baylis	FTE	102
Benjamin	SHE	113A
Daniel	CBL	6A
Henry	WRN	30A
John	SHE	113A
Robert	WDF	114A
William	BTH	156
William	WRN	41A
MOFFIT, Bery	BRK	271
John	JES	80
MOFFITT, George	CHN	35A
James	BTH	156
MOFFORD?, Joseph	SCT	116A
MOFFUTT, James	WDF	93
MOHLY?, Wm.	BBN	110
MOIBEE, William	BLT	174
MOKLY?, Wm.	BBN	110
MOLAND, Ann	WAS	43A
MOLAND?, S. L.	WAS	17A
MOLEBIN?, John S.	BKN	6
MOLEN, Milou?	MAS	66
MOLER, Isaac	NCH	120A
Lewis	NCH	122A
MOLES, Joseph	NCH	122A
MOLES?, George	HRL	114
MOLETON?, Robt.	BKN	6
MOLIHON, Charles	GSN	145A
Wm.	GSN	143A
MOLIN, Aquila	PUL	37A
Jos.	PUL	47A
MONAN, Ambrose	MAD	152
Charles	MAD	128
MONARCH, Edward	WAS	61A
Elizebeth	WAS	57A
Francis	WAS	56A
James	WAS	40A
Joseph	WAS	61A
MONDAY, Ann	BRK	275
Geo.	BBN	134
Henry	GSN	145A
John	GSN	145A
Nath.	BRK	275
Samuel	GSN	143A
Thomas	WDF	102
Wm.	JEF	44
MONDAY?, George	LGN	40
Susannah	WDF	98A
MONEN, Rachael	LGN	34
MONEY, James	GRN	77
John	FLG	66A
MONEYMAKER, John	CHN	33A
MONIHON, William	OHO	6A
MONK, Daniel	HOP	256
MONKS, Richard	FTE	67
Richard	HAR	200
MONOHAN, Geo.	MAS	68
Will	MAS	68
MONROE, Alexr.	PND	20A
Benjamin	MNR	215
Danl.	LVG	6
David	BRN	21
George	PND	23A
Iredell	JEF	30
James	BRN	21
Jeremiah	PND	15A
John	BRN	134
John	CLD	142
John	BLT	168
John	MTG	265
John	WDF	108A
Johnson, Ser.?	BRN	21
Joshua	BNE	28
Liman	SCT	119A
Sanders	JEF	45
Thomas B.	BRN	133
William	BRN	19
Wm.	PND	16A
MONS?, Peter	BLT	180
MONSON, Thomas	NCH	128A
MONSON?, Samuel	NCH	112A
MONTAGUE, Cave	BNE	26
James M.	GTN	126
John	GTN	119
John	BRN	133
Peter	GTN	120
Seth	GTN	132
Thomas	FTE	101
William	BNE	26
William	GTN	119
MONTAGUE?, Johnath?	CWL	33
MONTFORT, Jno.	HRY	257
MONTG--RY?, Nat	ADR	34
MONTG--Y?, Frances	ADR	64
MONTGALL, Wm.	SHE	142A
MONTGOMERY, (See Montgomey & Mtgomry)		
----- J.	CWL	40
-----?	CWL	40
Adam	FKN	78
Ailsy	GRN	55
Alexander	SHE	111A
Allen	GRN	55
Allexandr.	GSN	143A
Anna	BLT	196
Austin	WAS	64A
Barton	WAS	74A
Bazzil	WAS	86A
Bend. E.	WAS	72A
Betsey, Mrs.	WYN	79A
Betsy	BRN	21
C. C.	LNC	7
Charity	MTG	243
David	FTE	64
Elisha	WAS	74A
Enos	GTN	120
Ezekiel	GRN	57
George	MTG	253
George	SHE	111A
George	SHE	111A
Hugh	GRN	64
Hugh	OWN	103
Hugh	SHE	110A
MONTGOMERY, James	LNC	13
James	MAD	138
James	MTG	231
James	MTG	291
James	WAS	47A
James	WAS	78A
Jas.	GRD	103A
Jery	WAS	73A
Jesse	MTG	285
Jno.	LNC	33
Jno.	RCK	77A
John	FLD	5
John	ADR	68
John	CLY	115
John	GTN	120
John	GTN	135
John	HOP	256
John, Jr.	SCT	99A
John	FLD	1A
John	OHO	6A
John	WAS	67A
John	WAS	73A
John	LWS	87A
John	SCT	139A
John A.	WAS	77A
Jos.	MAS	78
Joseph	MTG	253
Joseph	FLD	1A
Philip	MTG	226
Robert	GTN	132
Robert, Jr.	GTN	132
Robt.	ADR	34
Stephen	HRD	46
Stephen H.	SCT	97A
Tho.	LNC	11
Thomas	NSN	192
Thomas	NSN	209
Thomas	NSN	217
Thos.	WAS	74A
W.	ADR	34
Will.	LVG	4
Will.	SCT	139A
William	FLD	8
William	LGN	45
William	FTE	96
William	OWN	100
Wm.	LNC	7
Wm.	ADR	36
Wm.	HRD	60
Wm.	FKN	76
Wm.	SHE	111A
Wm. L.	LNC	7
MONTGOMEY, Thomas	GRN	77
William	BLT	160
MONTGOMEY?, Thomas	ADR	64
MONTGOMORY, Sarah	HRT	164
MONTGOMRY, James	HRY	230
John R.	BRK	275
MONTGOMY, Ezkial	ADR	36
John	ADR	36
John	ADR	36
Saml.	ADR	36
Thomas	ADR	68
MONTGONERY, Elenor	WAS	71A
MONTGONY, Ester	GRD	116A
MONTOOTH, William	GTN	117
MONDAY, Harrison	MER	103
Henry	MER	103
Stephen	MER	103
MONENTANGO?, Henry	LVG	16
MONTAGUE, James	MER	103
MONTGOMERY, Isaac	MER	102
James	MER	103
John	MER	103
Joseph	MER	103
Robert	MER	103

Name	County	Page
MONTGOMERY, William	MER	103
MOOD, John	JES	93
MOODY, Alexander	LGN	38
Blanks, Jr.	HRY	218
Blanks, Sr.	HRY	218
Burgess S.	UNN	146
Edmond	MNR	193
George	GRN	61
Henry	SHE	162
James	HRL	114
James	KNX	306
Jerry	CHN	40
John	GRN	54
John	CLD	141
John	HRY	190
John	SCT	114A
Joseph	MNR	193
Martin	ALN	110
Richard	HRY	218
Saml.	CHN	42
Saml. S.	MAD	132
Samuel	ALN	110
Stephen	MNR	193
Thomas	WAS	87A
Thos.	SCT	114A
Thos.	SCT	135A
Will	SCT	120A
William	MNR	193
Wm.	WAS	47A
MOOKS, Washington	BNE	28
MOON, Allen	WRN	56A
Elisha	WRN	56A
James	BBN	112
John	BBN	110
Joseph	GTN	132
Joseph, Senr.	WRN	56A
MOON?, Barton	BBN	134
Catharin	JEF	19
John	GTN	124
Juba	GTN	122
Robert	GTN	124
Shaderick K.	JES	92
MOONE, Daniel	HRY	182
MOONEY, Edward	HOP	256
James	SCT	105A
MOONNEY, Henry	HND	10
Susannah	HND	11A
MOOR, David	FKN	156
Elnathan	FKN	104
Garshorn	FKN	114
James	WDF	100A
Jno.	FKN	102
Jno.	FKN	110
John	GRN	54
John	GRN	62
Joseph	FKN	144
Joseph	BTH	160
Robt. A.	GRN	71
Samuel	BTH	162
Timothy M.	FKN	114
Timothy T.	FKN	110
Travis	GRN	69
MOORE, Mrs.	MAS	73
-----? M.	CWL	42
--dd.?	CWL	32
--fred?	CWL	32
Abner	BRN	19
Abram	SHE	160
Adn.?	TOD	131A
Alexander	BNE	26
Alexander	FTE	108
Alexander	NSN	181
Alexr.	HRD	68
Alexr.	FLG	47A
Alfred H.	HOP	256
MOORE, Andrew	FLD	43
Andrew	HAR	218
Andrew	WAS	35A
Andrew	WAS	39A
Anthony	CLK	91
Archer	HRT	164
Arn / Ann?	ADR	18
Aron	KNX	314
Asa	HRD	30
Austin	MER	101
Austin	HOP	256
Babel	MBG	141
Barton	BBN	118
Benj.	CHN	40
Benjamin	MAD	104
Benjamin, Junr.	LWS	90A
Benjamin, Senr.	LWS	90A
Bernard	ADR	34
Burtin? G.	CWL	34
Butler	FTE	112
Catharine	FTE	98
Charles K.	MAD	118
Charley	MTG	233
Charls	ADR	34
Charly	ALN	106
Chs.	RCK	78A
Chs.	RCK	81A
Corlems?	RCK	81A
Cristopher	FLD	21
Daniel	HRY	250
Danl.	JEF	48
David	JES	76
David	HRT	164
David	MAD	172
David	BTH	210
David	SPN	9A
David	TOD	131A
Deanna?	HRY	254
Elender	LNC	49
Elias	CLY	122
Elias	HND	7A
Elijah	MER	101
Elijah	HAR	214
Elijah	LWS	90A
Elisha	MTG	281
Elisha	LWS	87A
Elisha	WYN	89A
Elizabeth	JEF	38
Elizabeth	BBN	140
Elizabeth	HAR	196
Elizabeth	WRN	75A
Ephraigm	KNX	306
Evan	BLT	156
F. A.	JEF	21
Francis	LGN	28
Francis	LGN	46
Francis	FTE	93
Frederick	WAS	61A
Gabl.	CWL	55
Geo.	JEF	48
Geo. (R. M.)	BBN	116
Geo. E.	BBN	102
George	LNC	23
George	CBL	7A
George	WRN	31A
George	SHE	132A
George	SCT	138A
Green	LNC	23
Hanah	CHN	40A
Hannah	FTE	98
Harbin	BKN	28
Hector W.	JEF	32
Henby W. (At Farm)	LGN	28
Hendley W.	LGN	24
Henry	CHN	41
MOORE, Henry	HRY	194
Henry	PUL	55A
Hiram	JEF	31
Hiram W.	JEF	38
Hugh	BNE	24
Hugh, Junr.	WRN	67A
Hugh, Senr.	WRN	67A
Ire?	UNN	154
Isaac	BRN	20
Isaac	FLD	38
Isaac	KNX	290
Isham	HRT	164
Jacob	FLG	45A
James	LVG	13
James	FLD	20
James	BNE	28
James	CWL	34
James	JES	86
James	FTE	101
James	MAD	112
James	MAD	114
James	MAD	120
James	ALN	128
James	SHE	168
James	MNR	195
James	HAR	216
James	HOP	256
James	KNX	310
James, Jr.	BNE	28
James	SPN	24A
James	PND	25A
James	WRN	61A
James	SCT	100A
James	SHE	137A
James	GSN	145A
James F.	SHE	173
James H?	HAR	196
Jane	CHN	27A
Jarrot	ALN	98
Jas.	CHN	43
Jas.	JEF	53
Jas., Jr.	CLY	122
Jas., Sr.	CLY	122
Jas.	FLG	27A
Jere?	HRY	260
Jeremiah	LGN	37
Jeremiah	CWL	44
Jeremiah	MNR	197
Jesse	CWL	55
Jesse	MTG	293
Jesse	KNX	306
Jesse	KNX	312
Jno.	CHN	43
Jno.	HRY	263
Joab	CWL	34
Joel	JES	92
Joel	MNR	217
John	ADR	36
John	FLD	38
John	JES	78
John	FTE	85
John	MAD	90
John	FTE	101
John	MER	102
John	MER	103
John	CLY	122
John	BBN	126
John	MBG	140
John	BLT	164
John	HAR	198
John	BTH	200
John	CSY	212
John	HAR	220
John	MTG	263
John	MTG	281
John, As?	MNR	197

Name	County	Page
MOORE, John, Senr.	FTE	101
John	TRG	5A
John	FLG	41A
John	WAS	53A
John	WRN	55A
John	RCK	82A
John	SCT	100A
John	NCH	108A
John	NCH	121A
John	SCT	139A
John	GSN	145A
John A?.	JES	69
John G.	FTE	94
John G.	SHE	165
John L.	JEF	48
John L.	SPN	11A
John S.	WYN	106A
John W.	ETL	37
John W.	FTE	93
Johnathan	WYN	89A
Jonathan	BTH	212
Joseph	WRN	64A
Joseph	WAS	83A
Lambeth	MER	102
Lawson	MER	102
Ledie	FTE	62
Lemuel	WDF	120A
Leo/ Lev?	FLG	31A
Levi	BKN	22
Levi	MAD	138
Levi	MBG	141
Levi	KNX	306
Levi	WRN	49A
Lewis	ADR	36
Lewis	ETL	51
Lewis	BTH	148
Lewis	BLT	154
Little B.	MNR	211
Louis	MER	103
Mahlon	BRN	21
Maples	HRY	266
Margaret	FTE	94
Margaret	FTE	112
Margaret	SCT	120A
Martin	FTE	81
Mary	MAD	154
Mary	WRN	49A
Mary	LWS	89A
Mary	SHE	128A
Matthew	FTE	82
Matthew L.	SHE	109A
Maurice	MBG	142A
Michael	BTH	168
Mordicaih	CSY	204
Moses	FTE	101
Moses	HAR	206
Moses	KNX	312
Nancy	JES	78
Nathan	ADR	36
Nathan	WRN	50A
Nathaniel	FTE	100
Nathaniel	KNX	310
Nathaniel	SHE	109A
Nicholas	GNP	167A
Obadiah	SHE	158
Obadiah?	FLD	43
Patrick	MAD	114
Pheby, Jr.	MAD	154
Philiman	OHO	9A
Pleasant	FTE	92
Pleasant	PUL	61A
Reuben	FTE	73
Reubin	MAD	102
Reubin P.	FLG	46A
Richard	CLD	162
Richard	HRY	196

Name	County	Page
MOORE, Richd.	FLG	75A
Richd. K.	JEF	63
Robert	LGN	27
Robert	GRT	141
Robert	BTH	198
Robert	WRN	74A
Robt.	FLG	57A
Sam.	HRY	250
Saml.	CHN	43
Saml.	LNC	51
Saml.	LNC	57
Saml.	FLG	59A
Saml. T.	SCT	129A
Sampson	FLD	39
Samuel	BNE	26
Samuel	MER	103
Samuel	FTE	110
Samuel	CHN	34A
Samuel	LWS	96A
Samuel	WYN	103A
Samuel	NCH	118A
Sarah	TOD	129
Shadrack	CLD	142
Shadric	SHE	129A
Shadric	SHE	133A
Shattun	CWL	34
Simon	WRN	31A
Solomon	BTH	210
Solomon	SHE	130A
Stephen	MER	103
Syntha	MAD	154
T. P., Capt.	MER	115
Tavner	LWS	90A
Thomas	FLD	24
Thomas	BNE	26
Thomas	BNE	26
Thomas	LGN	32
Thomas	MER	102
Thomas	HRY	202
Thomas	BTH	216
Thomas	MTG	259
Thomas, Junr.	MER	103
Thomas, Senr.	MER	103
Thomas	CHN	27A
Thomas	WRN	47A
Thomas	NCH	121A
Thomas R.	CLK	102
Thos.	BKN	16
Thos.	JEF	35
Thos.	HRD	50
Thos.	HRY	262
Thos.	KNX	306
Verlinda	BBN	140
Warren	WRN	49A
William	LVG	13
William	FLD	45
William	FTE	93
William	WDF	101
William	MER	102
William	MER	102
William	CLY	122
William	BTH	180
William	BTH	208
William	MNR	211
William	CSY	220
William	HOP	256
William	HOP	258
William, Sr.	LVG	12
William	CBL	6A
William	HND	6A
William	WRN	55A
William	LWS	87A
William C.	BLT	156
William M.	MBG	135
Wm.	BKN	8
Wm.	CHN	31

Name	County	Page
MOORE, Wm.	CWL	34
Wm.	CWL	55
Wm.	GRN	71
Wm.	BBN	144
Wm.	HRY	262
Wm.	HRY	265
Wm., Sr.	HRY	254
Wm.	PND	25A
Wm.	PUL	45A
Wm.	RCK	81A
Yelly	FTE	99
Zeb	HRY	263
Zeb.	HRY	249
Zeba	FLG	44A
Zedekiah	NCH	107A
MOORE?, (See Moon?)	GTN	124
Barton	BBN	134
Elizabeth	MAD	172
Jno.	CHN	39
Juba	GTN	122
Shaderick K.	JES	92
MOOREHEAD, Armstead	MBG	138
Eli	BNE	46
John	ALN	126
MOORHEAD, John	CBL	11A
Mary	FLD	46
Samuel B.	FTE	67
MOORIFIELD, Alexr.	HRD	28
MOORMAN, Ab---	BRK	273
David	BRK	271
James	BRK	271
Jas. H. -.?	BRK	273
Jas. V.	BRK	273
Lewis	BRK	271
W., Jr.	BRK	271
Wm.	BRK	273
Wm.	BRK	275
Wm., Sr.	BRK	271
MOORNING, Edward	CBL	21A
MOOT, Calib	BTL	327
Randolph	WDF	105A
MOOTRY, Ann	CHN	32
Thophilus	CHN	32
MOPHET, Henry	MER	102
MOPING?, Cager	GRN	74
MOPPIN, Dabney	MAD	122
Daniel	GRN	73
Howard	CLY	124
Perry	CLY	125
Thos.	CLY	124
MORAN, And.	MAS	64
Anne	CLD	143
Barnet C.	MAD	174
Edwd.	MAS	62
Edwd. B.	BBN	106
Elijah	MAD	174
Gabriel	WYN	91A
John	ADR	60
John	MAD	174
Jonathan	MAS	54
Joseph	GRN	59
Joshua	MAD	174
Richd.	MAS	61
Will	MAS	68
William	BRN	20
Wm.	WAS	67A
MORDICA, Harry	FKN	54
MORE, ---er?	DVS	6A
Ephraim	CLD	139
James	MAD	116
James	MAD	172
James	BRK	277
James	BTL	327
Jeremiah	CLD	139

Name	County	Page
MORE, Jeremiah	GNP	174A
John	GNP	174A
Joseph	BTL	327
Peter	BRK	275
Pheby, Sr.	MAD	154
Samuel	BTL	327
Stephen	CLD	139
Thomas	BTL	327
MORE?/ MOSE?,		
James	HAR	154
William	HAR	154
MORE?, Jesse	HAR	148
Thomas	HAR	168
William	HAR	142
MOREDOCH, James	BRK	271
MOREHEAD, Amsted	ADR	16
Armd.	LGN	25
Armd.	LGN	25
Armistead	LGN	24
Aron	LNC	71
Charles	LGN	27
Danl.	LNC	71
Henry	WRN	44A
James	WRN	75A
James T.	WRN	74A
Joel	BBN	142
Joseph	SCT	100A
Mary	BRN	20
Presley	LGN	28
MOREHOUSE, James	LWS	86A
MORELAND,		
Alexander	DVS	19A
Enos	SHE	116A
Fielder	BBN	68
James	BBN	68
James	MTG	239
Jno. B.	HAR	136
John	SHE	171
Samuel	BTH	162
Thomas H.	ETL	44
William	MTG	267
Wm.	BBN	144
Wm.	SHE	117A
MORELEY?, Will B.	HRY	176
MORELY?, Ann	CHN	33
MOREMAN, Achills	HRD	32
Jesse	HRD	70
Jesse, Jr.	HRD	32
MOREN / MOREU?,		
John	FLG	68A
MORFORD, Danl.	BKN	10
James	BKN	20
MORFORD?, Danl.,		
Jr.	BKN	18
MORGAIN, John	CSY	208
William	CSY	208
MORGAN, -----?	DVS	5A
-----?	DVS	6A
-----?	DVS	6A
Abel	LGN	35
Abel	MTG	229
Allen	BNE	26
Ann	FKN	74
Anne	FLD	17
Armistead	LGN	35
Benoni	SPN	7A
Charles	BLT	176
Charles	SPN	23A
Charles	SCT	115A
Charles	MBG	139A
Chas.	SCT	100A
Daniel	FKN	140
Daniel, Jr.	WTY	117A
Daniel	WTY	117A
Danl.	TOD	128
Danl.	FLG	61A
MORGAN, David	BBN	86
Dennis	FTE	88
Elias H.	WRN	70A
Elijah	SHE	164
Elizabeth	CLK	79
Enoch	CBL	6A
Evan	MAS	56
Evan	FLG	65A
Geo.	FLG	70A
Henry	HRY	232
Hezekiah	NCH	107A
Isaiah	HAR	138
Jacob	UNN	154
James	LVG	8
James	FLD	40
James	CWL	55
James	BLT	196
James J.	FKN	140
Jared	FLD	25
Jas.	HRD	50
Jerdin	SPN	18A
Jeremiah	HAR	154
Jeremiah	SHE	164
Jno. D.	JEF	55
John	FTE	105
John	GTN	118
John	BTH	172
John	BTH	180
John	HRY	232
John	OHO	10A
John	CBL	11A
John	SPN	19A
John	FLG	65A
John	SCT	101A
John	MBG	139A
John	GNP	167A
Jonathan	CLD	146
Joseph	LGN	35
Joseph, Esq.	MER	114
Joshua C.	HRD	70
Lewis	PUL	62A
Luis?	OWN	103
Mary	FTE	70
Mary	MTG	241
Michael	LNC	41
Michael	NSN	180
Morgan	CLD	146
Moses	HND	4A
Nat	ADR	36
Nathaniel	FLD	9
Nicholas	FTE	102
Reese	NCH	122A
Reuben	MER	102
Reuben D. N.	BLT	174
Reuben Det?	BLT	174
Reubin	SPN	8A
Richd.	MAS	56
Robert	WRN	34A
Samuel	JES	73
Samuel	OWN	103
Samuel	SPN	12A
Sarah	NCH	113A
Tho.	MAS	56
Tho.	HRY	232
Tho., Jr.	HRY	232
Thomas	LGN	35
Thomas, Jr.	HRY	208
Thos.	BKN	8
Van	CLK	80
Wells	FLD	9
Will	MAS	59
Will	HRY	192
Will.	SCT	99A
William	LGN	38
William	CLK	79
William	CLD	149
MORGAN, William	SHE	165
William	BTH	184
William	NSN	205
William, Jr.	GTN	118
William, Sr.	GTN	118
William	WTY	115A
William	MBG	135A
Willis	MBG	143
Wm.	HRD	94
Zac	HRL	114
MORGEN, George	WAS	82A
MORGIN, James	JEF	41
John	WAS	49A
John	WAS	84A
Jubal	WAS	21A
Phill	WAS	76A
Sterling	WAS	84A
Wm.	WAS	21A
MORGISON, Elijah	ETL	52
MORGON, William	CLK	84
MORGUSON, Polly	CLK	65
MORIN, John	SCT	105A
MORINE?, Josiah	CHN	41A
MORIS, John	ALN	114
MORIS?, Abraham	ALN	138
MORISON, John	LNC	31
MORKLAND?, Mathew	BTH	180
MORN----, James	ALN	136
MORNBERRY, Daniel	BLT	154
MORNES?, John	CWL	32
MORNIN, Francis	JEF	35
MORNING, Charles	GRN	63
MORNING?, John	ADR	36
Rodger	GRN	70
MORRASS, Jessee	GRN	67
MORRILL, Michael	CBL	13A
Saml.	BKN	20
MORRIN?, Jas./Jos.	HRD	18
MORRIS, Abijah	WRN	65A
Abraham	CLY	125
Absolem	KNX	306
Arthur	HAR	150
B. Rubin	GSN	146A
Benj.	WAS	56A
Benjamin	FLD	20
Benjamin	FLD	41
Benjn.	OHO	5A
Bows	LVG	11
Charles	HRD	20
Christopher	MTG	293
Colmore	DVS	18A
Daniel	FLD	44
Daniel	BTH	204
Daniel	WRN	62A
Daniel	NCH	125A
David	MAS	67
David	ALN	118
David	WRN	62A
David	WYN	94A
Dickeson	BKN	10
Edin/ Edw.?	CHN	42A
Edmund	SPN	6A
Edmund W.	OHO	4A
Edward	CHN	45
Ezekiel	FLD	43
Geo.	FKN	142
George	ALN	106
George	CLY	115
George	MAD	158
George, Jr.	CLY	117
Gutherie	CLK	97
Henry	HRL	114
Henry	UNN	150
Holen	GSN	144A
J. S.	MAS	75
Jacob	TRG	4

MORRIS, Jacob BKN 5
Jacob MTG 237
Jacob MTG 261
Jacob SPN 6A
Jacob CHN 34A
James MAD 90
James CLY 125
James SHE 148
James MNR 201
James CSY 222
James PND 22A
James WDF 95A
Jas. MAS 63
Jesse LVG 4
Jesse WRN 58A
Jessee, Sr. GRN 73
Jessy FKN 54
Jno. MAS 75
Jno. FKN 106
John HND 5
John BRN 20
John FLD 44
John HRD 62
John GTN 121
John BRK 229
John KNX 296
John, Jr. BNE 26
John PND 16A
John WAS 60A
John H. GTN 131
John W. WDF 94
Jones BRK 271
Jones? BRK 277
Jos. BKN 16
Joseph BTH 210
Joshua NSN 193
Littleton HRL 114
Martha SCT 104A
Martin MNR 209
Mary FLD 41
Mary SHE 112A
Mertin BTL 327
Morris BBN 120
Morris NCH 129A
Moses CWL 55
Moses CBL 15A
Nathaniel JES 73
Nathl. G. MAS 52
Philip WRN 62A
Polley CSY 226
Polly ADR 38
Presley GRN 77
Richard BBN 120
Richard MNR 201
Richard SPN 17A
Richd. JEF 45
Robbert CBL 13A
Robert FTE 84
Robert CLY 116
Sally BTL 327
Saml. BRK 277
Saml. FLG 70A
Samuel ADR 34
Samuel LGN 42
Samuel CLK 72
Sarah KNX 284
Thales? ALN 114
Thomas SHE 110A
Thomas NCH 113A
Thos. MAD 162
Thos. L. BRN 20
W. V. MAS 64
Warren MAD 102
Weldon MAD 90
Widw. CWL 35
Will. SCT 100A
MORRIS, William BNE 26
William LGN 27
William WDF 96
William MER 103
William CLY 112
William SHE 170
William, Sr. CLY 113
Willoby HAR 148
Willson WRN 63A
Wm. JEF 56
Wm. BRK 273
Wm. G. BRK 277
Zackariah WRN 65A
MORRISON, Abner KNX 290
Archd. FLG 78A
Archibald WDF 113A
D? MAS 81
Daniel HAR 182
Daniel P? OHO 3A
David HAR 218
David FLG 78A
Ezra LNC 31
Fredrick FLG 53A
Gavin HAR 218
George JEF 27
Hamilton MER 102
Isaac HRD 8
Jacob BNE 46
James ADR 34
James FTE 55
James FTE 113
James UNN 148
James NSN 214
Jas. HRD 20
Jas. MAS 72
Jas. MAS 77
Jas. FLG 48A
Jesse HRD 8
Jno. O. BRN 21
Joel A. HRD 8
John HRD 8
John ADR 36
John BBN 118
John CBL 11A
John FLG 23A
John WAS 27A
John FLG 59A
John H. SCT 132A
Jos. FLG 26A
Jos. J. / I.? CHN 46
Joseph ADR 36
Major BBN 84
Martha FTE 98
Mary HRD 14
Robt. ADR 34
Robt. BTL 313
Robt. BTL 327
Robt. FLG 25A
Saml. CBL 2A
Steptoe BRN 21
Thomas HRD 34
Thos. JEF 34
Thos. SHE 141A
William WYN 103A
Wm. HRD 48
Wm. MAD 94
Wm. FLG 23A
MORRISS, David FTE 107
Jessee GRN 69
John GRN 79
John BBN 140
John, Senr. BNE 26
Luther GRN 73
Will. SCT 134A
MORRISSON, Hugh BBN 106
Thompson BBN 104
MORROW, Alexander BBN 144
Christopher CLK 81
Garnaway ADR 54
George LGN 29
James, Jr. LGN 33
James, Sr. LGN 33
Jas. FLG 64A
Jesse SPN 10A
John BKN 18
John BBN 60
John CLY 131
John TOD 132
John HAR 202
John WYN 79A
Mary WRN 35A
Mathew LGN 29
Mathew WYN 88A
Moses LGN 31
Richard WRN 29A
Riley BBN 60
Robert BTH 156
Saml. PUL 39A
Samuel WDF 95
Sarah BBN 60
Thomas LVG 16
Thomas LGN 31
Thomas CLK 79
Thomas CLK 100
Thomas HAR 200
Thomas C. CLK 68
Thos. FKN 106
William BLT 156
William HAR 202
Wm. BRN 21
Wm. CHN 35A
MORTENS?, John GRN 53
MORTER?, Jacob BRK 275
MORTIMORE, Fanios? FLG 28A
MORTIN, James WAS 38A
MORTON, Armstead MTG 283
Benjn. MAD 100
Charles S. FTE 73
David FTE 85
David DVS 19A
Geo. MAS 69
George SHE 117A
George W. FTE 79
Hezekiah MTG 285
Jacob ETL 40
James SHE 158
James MTG 283
James WRN 29A
James SHE 117A
Jeremiah WDF 105
Jno. MAS 78
John LGN 23
John CLK 78
John MAD 118
John SHE 117A
John GNP 170A
John H. FTE 62
Jonathan MAD 152
Joseph LGN 30
Joseph MER 102
Joseph FKN 142
Josiah GNP 172A
Murphy &? MAS 67
Nancy NSN 182
Nathl. LNC 17
Patrick UNN 153
Ricd. RCK 80A
Richard MAD 130
Richard OHO 3A
Samuel CLK 84
Tho. MAS 69
Thomas WDF 98

MORTON, Thomas HOP 258
William FTE 59
William WDF 105
William C. HOP 254
William J., Sr? LGN 47
William R. FTE 112
Willis MBG 139
Wm. ETL 40
MORTON?, (See Marton ?) WDF 98
James GNP 176A
Lutitia GNP 170A
MOSBEY, Daniel BNE 26
Robert BNE 26
MOSBY, Anne MER 102
Edward WDF 116A
James LGN 23
Joseph MER 103
Micajah MER 104
Nicholas WDF 115A
Robert MER 102
Robert, Jr. MER 102
Robert WDF 116A
Susanna WDF 116A
Thomas H. BRN 34
Will SCT 96A
William BRN 34
William MER 102
MOSBY?, Micajer ADR 34
Wm. ADR 36
MOSCUM?, Daniel ALN 116
MOSE?, See More? HAR
MOSEE, Peter FLG 63A
Thos. FLG 63A
MOSELBY, Susannah SCT 96A
MOSELEY, -----? DVS 7A
Daniel P. MTG 299
James LVG 13
James WDF 96A
John MTG 226
John H. CHN 36A
Rollen BTH 204
Thomas MTG 259
Thomas DVS 19A
William D. FTE 98
MOSELEY?, -----? DVS 7A
MOSELY, James CHN 33A
John O. O. CHN 29
Leonard SHE 166
Perrin? CLK 80
Sally KNX 288
Saml. CLY 115
MOSELY?, Ann CHN 33
MOSES, John WTY 118A
Joshua WTY 114A
MOSGRAVES, John MNR 211
MOSLEY, Blackman HND 10A
Hillery LGN 38
John FLD 3
John WRN 61A
Joseph SCT 96A
Robert LGN 38
Robert P. SHE 111A
Robt., Junr. OHO 3A
Robt., Senr. OHO 3A
MOSLEY?, William GTN 117
Wm. ADR 36
MOSLY, (See Musley) JES 92
John JES 92
Thomas JES 85
Thomas JES 90
MOSS, Alexander FKN 92
Benjm. T. GRN 65
Danl. FLG 75A
MOSS, David, Jr. GRN 53
Elizabeth WDF 117A
Francis FKN 98
Frederick BRN 20
Frederick, Jr. BRN 20
Fredrick GRN 61
Garret CWL 39
George SHE 137A
Israel FLG 37A
James CWL 39
James WDF 98
James WRN 38A
James SHE 139A
Jesse WDF 125A
John CWL 33
John GRN 64
John TOD 133
John HND 11A
John CHN 44A
John WDF 115A
Jonathan HND 6
Joshua HND 9A
Josiah BRN 34
Kendle FLG 24A
Mason? O. CWL 39
Meredeth LWS 89A
Moses FLG 68A
Nathaniel O. MTG 251
Patsey FKN 60
Ray JES 71
Right ADR 34
Robt. FKN 78
Stephen FLG 35A
Terry HND 8
Tho. TOD 124A
Thos. SCT 110A
Thos. S. T. GRN 51
Travis CWL 39
Will ADR 38
Will GRD 120A
William JES 86
William WDF 115A
Wm. CWL 38
Wm. CWL 39
Wm. FLG 35A
MOSSBERGER, Saml. HRD 42
MOSSING?, Cager GRN 74
MOSSIS, Martin MAD 142
MOTGOMEY, Alexander FLD 1A
MOTHERLES?, Danl. CHN 41A
MOTHERSHEAD, George SHE 117A
Jno. FKN 148
Minor BLT 178
Nathl. SCT 120A
MOTLEY, Edwin WRN 59A
Henry WRN 59A
John MTG 289
Joseph CWL 35
MOTLEY?, John GRN 54
MOTLY, Mathew WRN 59A
MOTON, Catharine WAS 70A
MOTON?, Lutitia GNP 170A
MOTT, Isaac HOP 254
James JES 91
Jno. MAS 73
John FLG 52A
Joseph JES 91
Randolph LVG 2
Steven MAS 73
Stokely MAD 98
Wm. MAD 144
MOTT?, John CWL 37
MOUHOLLAND?, Hugh WTY 123A
MOUNT, Elijah SHE 160
MOUNT, John SHE 160
John HRY 194
Thomas SHE 160
Thomas HRY 194
MOUNTAGUE, John SCT 118A
John SCT 127A
Thos. SCT 118A
MOUNTAIN, George SHE 124A
MOUNTJOY, Alvin PND 21A
Edmd. BBN 132
Edward FKN 146
Jared MTG 259
John PND 19A
Sarah BBN 130
Thos. MAS 59
William GRT 143
Wm. FKN 130
MOUNTS, John MTG 259
John, Sr. WYN 96A
William WYN 94A
MOUNTZ, John LNC 47
MOURINGO, James HAR 154
MOURNING, Joseph HAR 140
MOUSER, George HRT 163
MOUSER?, Frederick WAS 31A
MOUSON?, Samuel NCH 112A
MOW?, Jesse HAR 148
MOWREY, Adam HRY 208
MOXLEY, Agness FKN 82
Daniel SHE 120A
Elizabeth NSN 200
Joseph GTN 133
Penelope FTE 91
Spencer MTG 235
MOXLEY?, Will B. HRY 176
William GTN 117
MOYERS, Daniel WRN 31A
Jacob WRN 31A
Nicholas WDF 111A
Wm. FLG 31A
MOYORS?, Alexander BKN 4
MOZE, John MAD 136
MOZEE, Peter BBN 76
Wm. BBN 76
MTGOMRY, Alexander FLD 1A
MU-IN?, John TRG 5
MUCHON, Cornelus GRD 100A
MUCICK, Ephraim MAD 92
MUCKLEBERRY, David CBL 15A
MUD, Benjamin GSN 143A
Elizabeth GSN 145A
Francis SHE 123A
MUDD, Andrew WAS 40A
Andrew WAS 40A
Andrew WAS 70A
Daniel WAS 50A
Electious WAS 41A
Elias WAS 67A
Elizabeth NSN 195
Francis WAS 51A
Frank WAS 63A
Hezekiah WAS 50A
Richard UNN 147
Thomas NSN 187
Walter HRD 16
William UNN 149
Wm. WAS 40A
Zephaniah BRN 21
MUDY, Wm. JEF 49
MUER, Esely FTE 87
MUIR, George FTE 83
Jasper NSN 181
Jere. HRY 270
John FTE 84
Richard FTE 81
Robt. HRY 252

MUIR, William NSN 198
William, Sr. NSN 198
MUIRHEID, John MNR 201
MULBERRY, Jacob SCT 121A
Jas. SCT 117A
John SCT 121A
Will SCT 121A
MULBURY, John BTH 192
MULDROIS?, John WAS 87A
MULDROW, Andrew WDF 116A
George FTE 101
Wm. WAS 35A
MULDROW?, Andrew WAS 87A
MULER, Christian G. BTH 206
MULHALL, John SCT 116A
Thos. WAS 72A
MULHOLLAN, Jno. CHN 43
MULHOLN, Rebecca MTG 297
MULIGIN, Trisey WAS 80A
MULINS, Beverly GRD 95A
Samuel GRD 114A
MULKEY, John MNR 191
Jonathan MNR 193
Jonathan, Jr?. MNR 191
MULL, Anthony BBN 96
MULLEN, Asa HAR 186
James HAR 198
L. G. MAS 52
Thomas A. BTL 327
William HAR 198
MULLENS, Champ RCK 76A
David FLD 37
Gard? RCK 76A
Isaac CSY 218
John FLD 40
John WAS 23A
Morgan RCK 80A
Sherrard FLD 40
T-rry? RCK 80A
William FLD 37
MULLER, Jno. PUL 48A
MULLETT, Nathan FLD 22
MULLIGAN, Alexr. MAS 64
Benjn. MAS 66
William C. WRN 68A
MULLIKAN, Will HRY 180
MULLIKIN, Burton SHE 163
Jas. FLG 39A
John SHE 163
Judiah SHE 163
William SHE 155
William NCH 106A
Wm. FLG 39A
MULLIN, Fountain PND 18A
Fountain PND 27A
Gabl. PND 27A
John HAR 194
John HAR 206
Joshua HND 4A
Judas CHN 29A
Lindsey PND 27A
Michael HAR 192
Reubin PND 18A
Samuel HAR 192
Steven PND 17A
MULLIN?, Robert BKN 13
MULLINS, Booker FLD 37
Charles WYN 106A
Henry CLK 67
Isaac MER 102
Isham FLD 38
James FLD 40
James MER 102
John FLD 14
John FLD 37
MULLINS, John FLD 37
John FLD 40
Joseph BTH 216
Joshua FLD 14
Joshua FLD 37
Marshal FLD 38
Matthew MAD 158
Molly, Mrs. WYN 99A
Richard CBL 2A
Solomon FLD 37
Stephen MER 102
Thomas GRD 116A
Thos., Jr. WAS 24A
Thos., Sr. WAS 24A
William FLD 37
William FLD 38
William FLD 40
William CSY 218
William KNX 300
MULLUCE?, Ambrose ETL 45
MULNIX, Benjn. SCT 98A
MUNACH?, John NCH 125A
MUNCE, Jacob WAS 52A
MUNCEY, David CBL 13A
MUNCY, John CLY 116
Petery KNX 300
Sally KNX 304
MUNDAY, George BRN 20
James FTE 89
James MAD 114
Reubin MAD 100
Wm. ADR 36
MUNDER?, William LGN 43
MUNDY, Reubin FKN 136
MUNE?, John BTH 158
MUNFORD, Jeriah HRD 56
Richd. HRT 163
Thomas HRT 163
Wm. LNC 55
MUNN, William CBL 3A
MUNNETT, Isaac SHE 135A
MUNROE, Ann FTE 63
William nRY 204
MUNS?, Polly? BTH 168
MUNSEL, Allen SCT 121A
MUNSEY, James FLD 42
Samuel FLD 42
Samuel FLD 42
MUNSON, Allen SCT 100A
Eliasaph HAR 208
George HAR 194
Isaac HAR 196
Joel HAR 202
Samuel HAR 208
Will SCT 99A
MUNZINGO?, Benjamin BBN 118
MURAIN, William WDF 101
MURCER?, Davd. CWL 55
MURDOCK, Hants? FTE 110
Joseph H. BBN 138
Lewis TOD 128A
William FTE 87
Willis TOD 128A
MURE, James CLK 64
John CLK 64
Samuel BBN 108
MUREY?, Harry GRD 115A
MURFEY, Brice WAS 50A
James WAS 70A
Stephen ADR 34
Thed.? WAS 34A
William ALN 100
MURFREY, Charles TRG 3A
John ADR 38
Thos. ADR 38
MURFY, Mat WAS 50A
Peter ADR 32
MURGIS?, Peter BRK 275
MURL, Samuel LWS 89A
MURLEY, Daniel CLD 160
William MNR 213
MURPHEY, Ann JEF 21
Carles HOP 258
Charles MAD 168
Charles, Sr. NSN 205
Daniel BRK 271
David HND 9
Gabriel MNR 197
George W. NCH 116A
Henry MNR 197
Isaac CLK 99
Jeremiah FTE 58
Jeremiah OHO 9A
Jesse ETL 50
Jesse BRK 273
John FLD 11
John ETL 42
John CLY 113
John BLT 174
John, Jr. BRK 277
John FLG 50A
John NCH 113A
M. JEF 22
M. DVS 16A
Neale FLG 53A
Phillip NSN 206
Richard L. NSN 206
Robert NSN 182
Salley HOP 254
Stephen HOP 256
Thos. BBN 64
William FLD 11
William LGN 37
William LGN 39
William CLY 113
William NSN 211
William WRN 53A
MURPHREY, Felix/ Felise? CSY 222
Janney? CSY 222
Rennise / Rennix? CSY 222
MURPHY, Abram. H. JEF 33
Alexander CLD 148
Ben HRD 80
Clement CLD 140
Corneleus LNC 41
Eli PUL 57A
Francis CLD 143
Gabriel LNC 29
Gabriel NSN 221
Hays, Junr. CLD 150
Hays, Senr. CLD 167
Hezekiah NSN 181
Hosea WRN 52A
Isaac WRN 54A
James MER 103
James CLD 148
James CLD 162
James WTY 114A
Jas. CHN 39
Jas. HRY 270
Jenkins TOD 125
Jeremiah, Jr. FTE 57
Jessee MBG 138
Jno. MAS 56
John JEF 37
John LNC 41
John, Jr. JEF 39
John WRN 53A
John PUL 64A

Name	County	Page
MURPHY, John	GRD	110A
John	SHE	127A
Joshua	SCT	115A
Kendal	WAS	29A
Leander	SHE	127A
Miles	GTN	117
Nancy	FTE	84
Neal	CHN	39
Paul, Jr.	BRK	275
Rachel	WRN	53A
Robt.	PUL	44A
Spencer	BRK	277
T. B.	SHE	127A
Tho.	PUL	44A
Thomas	LNC	41
Thomas	LNC	65
Thomas	LWS	95A
Will	MAS	58
Will	MAS	80
William	JES	71
William	WYN	83A
Wm.	MAS	61
Wm.	TOD	132
Wm.	BRK	277
Wm., Jr.	MAS	61
Wm.	PUL	43A
Wm. T.	LNC	43
Zepeniah	CLY	118
MURR--?, Michael	MAS	71
MURRAH, Joseph	LGN	37
Joshua	LGN	43
William	LGN	40
MURRAY, -----?	CWL	41
Abraham	MER	102
Agness	LGN	35
Alexr.	BRN	20
Biarles	BRK	229
Charles	HRT	163
D. R.	BRK	227
Daniel	CLD	155
Eli	HRT	163
Fielden	JEF	50
Fountain	MER	102
Isaac	CBL	20A
James	FKN	82
Jas.	BKN	8
Jessee	JEF	60
Jno.	CWL	55
Jno.	FKN	90
John	OWN	100
John	BRK	273
John L.	JEF	21
Joseph	CLD	154
Robt.	BRK	227
William	TRG	3
William	CLD	155
MURREL, George	BRN	19
John	ADR	36
Samuel	BRN	21
Samuel	ADR	64
MURRELL, James	LNC	29
John	LNC	25
MURREY, Samuel	FLD	36
Thomas	FLD	36
MURRIL, Jessee	ADR	3
MURRILL, William	CHN	27A
MURROW, Chas.	MAS	59
Daniel	UNN	151
Hugh	LGN	43
Nicholas	MAS	59
Thos.	MAS	59
MURROW?, John	GRN	62
MURRY, ----?	GRN	75
Barnabas	PUL	65A
Darcus	NSN	211
Edward	LNC	33
MURRY, George	SCT	135A
James	HND	13
James	GRN	50
James	SHE	115A
Jerem.	CWL	55
Mathew	BTH	178
Nicholas	HND	10A
William	GRN	69
William	FTE	112
Wm.	GRN	52
MURTON, David	SPN	16A
MUSE, Christopher	PUL	65A
Geo., Jr.	FLG	47A
Geo., Snr.	FLG	49A
Jacob	PUL	46A
James	PUL	66A
Jas.	FLG	49A
John	PUL	54A
Richard	PUL	53A
Thomas	PUL	53A
MUSE?, Henry	PUL	46A
Jno.	PUL	46A
MUSECK, John	NCH	122A
MUSELY, Robert	JES	92
MUSEY?, Harry	GRD	115A
MUSGROVE, Anthony	SCT	97A
Cuthbert	WRN	41A
Gilbert	NCH	106A
Henry	BLT	176
Samuel	MBG	139A
MUSHGROVE, Obadiah	BTH	194
MUSHON?, Cornelius	FLG	56A
MUSIC, Sarah	BBN	108
MUSICK, Abraham	GSN	146A
Catherine, Mrs.	WYN	85A
David	WYN	85A
Thomas	NCH	122A
MUSICK?, John	GSN	146A
MUSSELMAN, Jacob	GRT	146
MUSSER, Jno.	PUL	48A
MUSSETT, James	BNE	26
MUSSIN, Adam	ADR	36
MUSSLET?, Christian	HAR	150
MUSSON, John	WAS	36A
MUSTER, John	SHE	119A
John	SHE	134A
MUSTINE, James W.	HRT	163
MUXLEY, George	FTE	96
MUZE, Elijah	BRK	271
MYARS, Christopher	BTH	216
Isaac	GRD	109A
Lewes	GRD	97A
Lucy	GRD	115A
MYATT?, Joanes	LVG	11
MYERS, Aaron	MTG	253
Abraham	NCH	118A
Andrew	GRT	142
Aron	LNC	67
Barbary	LNC	45
Barlard	JEF	36
Benjn.	OHO	11A
Betsey	MTG	243
Betssey	LNC	45
Catherine, Mrs.	GRT	146
Christian	NCH	115A
Daniel	CLD	144
Daniel	NCH	109A
David	LNC	45
David	LNC	55
David	NCH	118A
Frederick	ETL	49
Geo.	MAS	61
George	GRT	146
George	MTG	293
George	NCH	108A
MYERS, Henry	MAS	75
Henry	BTH	178
Henry	BTH	220
Henry, Jr.	MTG	241
Henry, Sr.	MTG	237
Henry	FLG	59A
Henry	LWS	94A
Henry	NCH	109A
Jacob	BBN	116
Jacob	GRT	139
Jacob	BTH	196
Jacob	LWS	98A
Jno.	MAS	61
John	BLT	170
John	BLT	188
John	MTG	243
John	MTG	249
John	FLG	46A
John	NCH	118A
Jonathan	MTG	261
Joseph	GRT	140
Joseph	BLT	194
Joseph	BTH	214
Joshua	LNC	65
Lewis	PND	18A
Lewis	NCH	108A
Lewis?	MTG	239
Margaret	NCH	118A
Michael	LWS	86A
Michal	OHO	11A
Pamelia	JEF	53
Peter	NCH	111A
Philip	LGN	46
Solomon	HAR	192
Solomon	MTG	253
Thomas	OHO	3A
William	GRT	140
William	CLD	156
William	WAS	18A
Wm.	PND	17A
Wm.	GSN	143A
MYERS?, Thomas	OHO	13A
MYERSBACK?, Sally	LGN	23
MYRES, ----y?	DVS	12A
Adam, Jr.	BTH	160
Adam, Sr.	BTH	160
Betsey	SCT	132A
David	GSN	143A
Jacob	MAD	142
Jacob	HRY	254
John	SCT	104A
Michael?	DVS	12A
Wm.	BRK	275
MYRES?, Thomas	MNR	191
MYRICK, Joseph	SCT	92A
Walter	HRD	68
N----?, -----?	HRT	164
-----?	HRT	164
N--?, Peter, Jnr	HAR	148
Peter, Snr	HAR	148
NA---?, Mary	FTE	105
NACCO, Francis	JEF	30
NAG, James	SHE	170
NAIL, James	LGN	31
John	LGN	31
John, Jr.	LGN	31
John	GNP	168A
NAILOR, Ben	ADR	32
John	JEF	60
Saml.	FLG	43A
NALE, Elizebeth	WAS	74A
Jonas	WAS	50A
NALE?, Lewis	SCT	127A
NALL, Charles L.	WDF	113A
Eleanor	WDF	114A

Name	County	Page
NALL, Elizabeth	HOP	258
Francis	WAS	74A
Gabriel	WDF	113A
James	WAS	74A
James T.	NSN	180
Jas.	HRD	60
John	HRD	10
John	NSN	196
Martin	FKN	86
Martin	WAS	20A
Rebeckah	CLD	145
Richard P.	OHO	13A
Wm.	WAS	74A
NALL?, Lewis	SCT	127A
Reuben	BTH	176
NALLEY, Henry	SHE	119A
NALLS, George	BTH	164
NALLY, Cloe	NSN	189
Dory	WAS	53A
Edward	LNC	53
Ralph	NSN	189
Theodore	NSN	222
NAME?, Peter	BRK	279
NAMEY?, Edmund	MBG	136
NAMKING?, Lewis	BKN	23
NANCE, Anne	MER	104
Buckner	CLD	141
Eaten	GRN	78
James	GRN	78
James	WRN	72A
Jenny	MER	104
Joel	SHE	168
John	CLD	141
Peter	SHE	162
Thomas	CLD	141
Thomas	SHE	171
Washington	GRN	78
Washington	GRN	80
NANCE?, Robt.	BRK	279
NANCY, John H.	ALN	98
NANEE?, Peter	BRK	279
NANNY, (Free)	CLD	162
Abel	CLD	139
Amos	CLD	139
John	MBG	136A
NANNY?, Abner	WRN	70A
Edmund	MBG	136
Hugh	WRN	70A
NANTZ, Fredrick	WAS	85A
Robert H.	WAS	77A
Tanner	WAS	75A
Thomas W.	LGN	24
Thomas W.	LGN	25
NAP, George	SHE	139A
John	SHE	136A
John	SHE	137A
Joshu	GNP	177A
Joshua	SHE	139A
Joshua	GNP	171A
Wm.	SHE	137A
NAPER, Raney	GRD	108A
NAPIER, Ben. W.	CSY	208
Edmund	HRL	116
James	HRL	116
John	WYN	84A
John F.	CSY	214
Joseph F.	CSY	212
Raney	CSY	206
Richard C.	CSY	214
Thomas	WTY	113A
William	CSY	210
NAPLE, Wm.	BBN	120
NAPP, Saml.	MAS	55
NAPPER, James	FTE	102
NARVIL?, Andrew	FLD	6
NASH, Abner	HOP	258
NASH, Amelia	JEF	52
Arthur B.	PUL	64A
Edwd.	FLG	27A
James	LWS	94A
Jeremiah	WDF	117A
John	LWS	90A
Joseph B.	WAS	30A
Marvel M.	LNC	43
Noble	SHE	160
Salley	SHE	143A
Sary	FKN	158
Tho.	WAS	30A
Will. M.	SCT	94A
William	WDF	95
William	WRN	73A
NATIAN, Christopher	GRT	147
NATION, Edward	FKN	118
George	SHE	115A
Hezakiah	FKN	118
Hezakieh	FKN	134
Isaac	BRN	22
Joseph	SHE	114A
Joseph	SHE	123A
William	SHE	115A
NATIS?, Mathew	BKN	2
NAUL?, Richard P.	OHO	3A
NAVE, Daniel	HRY	269
John	JES	76
Lenard	MAD	94
Peter	JES	76
Peter	JES	84
Saml.	HRD	34
NAY, Reubin	JEF	59
Saml.	JEF	57
Saml., Jr.	JEF	57
NAYLOR, E. B.	GRD	96A
Geo.	GRD	89A
Geo. T.	GRD	89A
James	ADR	38
James	GRN	50
James	PND	15A
John	GRD	89A
Jordan	FTE	81
Micajah	GRD	111A
Rezin	BRN	22
Samuel	FTE	76
NE-ERT?, John	WAS	56A
NEAFUS?, George	NSN	214
NEAGLE, James	WRN	52A
Loyd	WRN	55A
NEAL, Allen	WAS	43A
Barnet	SHE	154
Benjamin	BTL	327
Charles	FTE	106
Chas.	SCT	125A
Chas.	SCT	131A
Christo.	SCT	118A
Chs.	PUL	48A
Daniel	BBN	72
George	BTL	327
Jacob	BBN	70
James	BBN	60
James	BBN	92
James	FTE	104
James	BBN	112
James	SHE	155
James	SHE	170
James	MTG	277
Jessee	WYN	82A
John	BNE	28
John	FTE	73
John	GTN	122
John	BTH	174
John, Jr.	BNE	28
John, Senr.	BBN	126
NEAL, John	NCH	117A
John	SCT	125A
John W.	BBN	68
Joseph	BBN	92
Joseph	LWS	89A
Lewis	GTN	133
Mary, Mrs.	WYN	97A
Micajah	SHE	170
Nancy	LVG	9
Presly	FKN	82
Rebecca	BNE	28
Robert	BNE	28
Robert	MER	115
Robt.	FKN	88
Rodham	FTE	111
Rodham	SCT	128A
Sally	SCT	122A
Sampson	FTE	104
Tavner	BBN	82
Thomas	BNE	28
Thomas	GTN	133
Thomas	BTL	327
Thos.	BBN	92
William	BNE	28
William	FTE	104
William	GTN	122
William	SHE	176
William	NSN	221
William	BTL	327
William	BTL	327
Zach	RCK	78A
NEAL?, David M.?	UNN	154
NEALE, Adam	BNE	28
Joseph	FTE	76
Lewis	FTE	110
Richard D.	WRN	36A
Sarah	WRN	68A
Thomas	BNE	28
Thomas M.	WRN	74A
William P.	WRN	37A
NEALEY, James	SCT	98A
Nathl.	SCT	98A
NEALL, Charles	LGN	43
Elias	MAS	57
Tho.	MAS	57
NEALLE, Benjamin	LGN	35
Thomas	LGN	34
William	LGN	34
NEALY, ---es?	CWL	40
David	NSN	179
Wm. T.	GNP	165A
NEBORS, Jacob	CLD	162
John	CLD	162
NEDFUS?, Byer	NSN	184
NEEDHAM, Elias	HRD	84
Timothy	HRD	44
NEEDSPITH?, Davis	MNR	211
Gile	MNR	211
NEEL, (See Neet?)	ADR	38
(See Neet?)	JES	
Elijah	JES	82
Field.	HRY	262
Geo.	HRY	260
George	JES	80
George	JES	82
Lewis	HRY	264
Lewis	CBL	6A
Nancy	CLK	99
Sabree	LNC	7
Wm.	HRY	260
NEELE, Joseph	SHE	121A
Richard	SHE	120A
Samuel	SHE	121A
Wm.	SHE	137A
NEELE?, Moss?	ALN	92
NEELEY, Chas.	FLG	60A

NEELEY, David GTN 127
Jas. FLG 57A
John FLG 60A
Thomas LGN 33
NEELEY?, Thos. FLG 60A
NEELY, Abijah SPN 9A
C. H. LNC 69
Charles SPN 9A
Edward SPN 7A
Isaac PUL 35A
John ALN 114
NEET?, (See Neel)
George JES 79
Jacob ADR 38
Jacob JES 80
Jacob JES 83
John ADR 38
John JES 83
Reubin JES 74
Rheudolph ADR 38
NEEVE, Mildred HRY 258
Wm. HRY 252
NEEVE?, George WDF 125A
NEEVES, Danl. NCH 106A
Walter NCH 106A
NEFERS?, John HRD 50
NEFF, Francis MER 104
George HRD 46
Henry HRD 72
John MER 104
John HAR 210
Michael BBN 104
NEFFE, Jacob HND 12
NEFFS?, Samuel FLD 27
NEFUS?, John HRD 50
NEGLEY, Philip MER 104
NEGRO, Jack A. JEF 60
NEGROES, Rosses? JEF 22
NEICE, Austin CLY 120
NEIF, Joseph JEF 35
NEIGHBORS,
Elizabeth BLT 182
Thomas HRY 200
NEIGHBOURS,
Abraham GSN 146A
Nathan WRN 30A
NEIL, Andrew LVG 12
Andrew ETL 51
Corn. O. BKN 11
Daniel WTY 111A
Nancy LVG 12
NEILL, Solomon JEF 38
Thos. HRD 54
NEILL?, D. MAS 79
NELD, Rebecca MER 104
NELL, George ADR 38
John ADR 38
Philip ADR 38
NELLARSHALL?,
William GRN 53
NELLUMS, Thomas LGN 39
NELLY, Jos. M. MAS 76
NELSON, -----? DVS 13A
---liam? DVS 11A
Alexr. SCT 111A
Ambrose FTE 66
Benj. FKN 162
Betsy GRD 96B
Covington CBL 21A
Hayden CBL 9A
Imanuel FLD 22
James JEF 27
James LNC 69
James GRN 73
James FTE 81
James SHE 160
NELSON, James MTG 279
Jas. MAS 55
Jesse MNR 211
Joel MNR 217
John LGN 36
John FTE 66
John GRN 68
John GRN 73
John BBN 74
John BBN 78
John HRD 80
John FTE 97
John BBN 128
John BTH 202
John, Jr. MNR 197
John, Sr. MNR 211
John SCT 119A
Josep BTH 160
Joseph ADR 38
Juba HND 4
Matthew SHE 139A
Moses BBN 74
Moses BBN 78
Moses BTH 170
Moses NCH 120A
Rachel NCH 122A
Richard CBL 21A
Robinson HAR 154
Robt. SCT 103A
Samuel HRY 182
Samuel K. MER 104
Thomas BNE 28
Thomas FTE 66
Thomas CBL 19A
Thomas NCH 121A
Thos. BRK 279
Thos. TOD 127A
Wayd ADR 38
Widow BBN 60
Will SCT 119A
William MNR 193
William MTG 229
William CBL 9A
William WAS 23A
William WYN 91A
Wm. BKN 23
Wm. HRD 80
Wm. HRY 254
NEPPS?, Samuel FLD 27
NEREMON, David SPN 7A
NERMILLION, John BKN 19
NESBETT, Thomas NCH 123A
NESBIT, Hugh BTH 150
James HOP 258
Jeremiah HAR 204
Joseph BBN 126
Robt. BBN 130
Samuel HAR 216
Sarah BTH 170
William CLK 96
NESBITT, Sarah NCH 123A
William NCH 129A
NESEBUTT, John HAR 142
Robert HAR 132
Robert HAR 142
Saml. HAR 136
William HAR 136
NESS, Edward FLD 9
NETHATON?, Henry? HRY 226
NETHERLAND,
Benjamin JES 96
NETHERLY, Margaret CLD 154
Robert CLD 155
Samuel CLD 152
NETHERTON, Henry JEF 56
John JEF 54
NETHERTON, John,
Sr. JEF 64
NETTLE, Henry FTE 101
Thomas FTE 100
NEUSE, William MER 104
NEUSUM, William DVS 18A
NEW--?, ----y? CHN 31A
NEW, -----? DVS 13A
Anthony TOD 131A
George WDF 94A
Jacob GRT 146
Jacob PND 17A
James OHO 10A
Jethro GTN 120
John WRN 54A
Robert GTN 120
William GRT 142
Wm. B. TOD 131A
NEWAN, Catharine HOP 258
NEWBERRY, Levi BRN 22
NEWBOLD, Dd. BBN 138
George GRT 146
NEWBOLT, John WAS 33A
William BLT 176
NEWBY, Allen CWL 55
Allen MAD 106
Brian MAD 106
Edmond PUL 57A
Gamaliel PUL 65A
Henry SPN 8A
James WRN 36A
Jesse MAD 106
John LGN 33
John PUL 62A
Mathew SPN 10A
Zachus MAD 104
NEWCHURCH, Mary PUL 62A
NEWCOM, Joseph UNN 152
M. RCK 76A
NEWCOMB, Bennet HRD 20
Danl., Sr. FLG 70A
Danl. FLG 69A
Joseph LVG 7
Thos. FLG 62A
Wm. RCK 89
NEWCOME, Isaac GRN 53
James GRN 60
John B. GRN 60
NEWCUM, Mathew ADR 38
NEWEL, James HAR 152
Robert BRN 22
William BRN 22
William HAR 152
NEWELL/ NEVETT?,
James NSN 180
NEWELL, Hugh HAR 184
Hugh, Jnr. HAR 184
Jean MAS 69
John PUL 60A
John M.? PUL 58A
Landon? PUL 60A
Peter SPN 3A
Robert HAR 184
Robt. HRY 249
Samuel, Jr. PUL 63A
Samuel, Senr. PUL 55A
Stewart HRY 249
Wm. FLG 42A
NEWELL?, Joseph SHE 118A
NEWETT, Joseph SHE 118A
NEWGENT, Robt. BRK 279
Thomas GTN 126
Wm. BRK 279
NEWIL, John H. GTN 126
William GNP 169A
NEWIL?, John HRT 165

NEWILL, Jas. Jr. BRN 21
Jas./ Jos.? HRY 254
John BRN 22
John SHE 151
Joseph BRN 22
Thos. HRY 252
Wm BRN 22
NEWILLE, Oswell SHE 151
William SHE 161
NEWING, J./ I.? H. GRD 82A
NEWINS, George JES 82
John MER 104
NEWKIRK, Barnett ETL 40
Elias MTG 275
Elias CBL 20A
Henry PND 31A
Henry WYN 103A
Jacob JEF 52
Peter JEF 42
Tunis BLT 182
William BLT 162
Wm. JEF 33
NEWLAN, Hiram JEF 31
NEWLAND, Abraham MAD 148
Elizabeth BRN 22
Jno. A. BRN 22
John CLK 75
Wm. JEF 34
NEWLEN, Benoni S. SHE 128A
Margaret SHE 128A
Nancy SHE 128A
NEWLEN?, ---ah? HRT 164
NEWLIN, Abraham SHE 128A
Polley SHE 132A
NEWMAN, A./ N.? TOD 127A
Benjamin BRN 22
Christopher WDF 105
David JES 80
Edm. BRK 279
Elijah CLK 89
Ella JEF 43
George HRD 20
George KNX 292
George SHE 137A
Henry SHE 118A
Henry SHE 136A
Isaac MBG 133A
Jacob HND 13
Jacob NSN 192
Jacob PUL 63A
John FLD 33
John FLD 42
John CLK 89
John NSN 183
John BLT 188
John BTH 216
John SHE 136A
John F. MAD 146
Johnathan JES 80
Jonathan MNR 209
Joseph LVG 8
Joseph HOP 258
Martin CWL 44
Mary NSN 192
Obediah BRK 279
Simeon BNE 28
Susan HRD 80
Thomas MBG 141
Thomas BTL 327
Thos. BBN 70
Thos. BRK 279
Thos. FLG 66A
Thos. SHE 118A
William MTG 233
William CBL 8A
William CBL 21A
NEWMAN, William NCH 121A
William GNP 168A
Wilt BRK 279
NEWMANN, Joshua SCT 119A
NEWMANS?, John HOP 258
NEWMON?, David WRN 37A
NEWPORT, Joseph BNE 28
Pharroby WRN 45A
NEWSOM, Harrison FLD 37
NEWSUM, --nsey? CWL 36
NEWTEN, James FKN 96
NEWTHORN, Richd. GRN 63
NEWTON, -----? DVS 7A
---th? DVS 7A
Abraham HRD 92
Abraham MBG 137
Archebald NSN 188
Bennett SHE 143A
Charles GNP 169A
Cornelius NSN 188
Elias GRN 75
Elizabeth NSN 224
Emily FKN 152
Isaac WRN 74A
Isaac LWS 88A
Jacob BRK 279
James BLT 152
James OHO 5A
James WAS 44A
James GSN 146A
Jas., Jr. BRK 279
Jas., Sr. BRK 279
Jno. FKN 108
John HOP 258
John CBL 19A
John NCH 124A
John N. WAS 45A
Joseph FKN 96
Kenith A. MTG 235
Lewis GRN 74
Nace GRN 74
Peter BLT 168
Reubin HRD 22
Robert, Jr. HOP 258
Robert, Sr. HOP 258
Samuel SHE 167
Thomas ETL 53
Thos. BRK 279
William FLD 14
NEWTON?, -----? DVS 5A
NEWCOMB, Thomas LVG 11
William LVG 11
NEWTON, Benjamin MER 104
NEY?, Joseph HRY 226
NI-FONG?, Daniel? ALN 96
NIBBS, Jno. MAS 73
Mary MAS 73
NIBLACK, Hugh MBG 139A
NIBLAKE, John CLK 77
William CLK 62
NICE, Jessey MAD 174
NICHOL, James SPN 5A
Jas. CHN 41A
Wm. CHN 45A
NICHOLAS, Benj. JEF 20
Francis WYN 98A
Isaac MAD 130
James B HAR 210
John BRK 279
Jonathan SPN 11A
Joshua CLK 94
Mack P.? HRY 176
Shedreck BRK 279
Thomson WYN 99A
Thos. MAS 60
NICHOLASON, Tho. MAS 78
NICHOLASS, George, Sen. WYN 87A
NICHOLD, Robt. FLG 45A
NICHOLDS, Nancy JEF 59
Robt. SCT 125A
NICHOLDSON, Benj. HRY 255
Robt. BBN 136
Wm. FLG 41A
NICHOLL, (No Given Name) CHN 45A
NICHOLLES, Erasmus GTN 123
NICHOLLS, Abm. HRY 190
Hugh MBG 142
James MBG 135
Joseph BLT 154
Thomas GTN 123
Will HRY 190
NICHOLS, ----- CWL 35
---am? DVS 13A
-at.? CWL 35
Abner HAR 142
Abraham FTE 85
Andrew MER 104
Andrew SPN 22A
Benj. SHE 141A
Benjamin SHE 117A
Daniel PUL 67A
Edmund MER 104
Edward CLD 154
Frederic CLK 100
Frederick FTE 82
Garrett FTE 82
George CLK 81
Henry HRD 24
Henry NSN 198
Jacob UNN 148
Jacob MTG 239
James CLK 79
James SHE 153
James NSN 181
James GNP 177A
James H. MER 104
Jeremiah GRN 58
Jeremiah MER 104
Jerm. CWL 55
Jno. BRN 22
John BRN 22
John FTE 95
John MER 104
John SHE 162
John SHE 174
John TRG 3A
John GNP 167A
John F. FTE 95
Jonathan MER 116
Joshua MER 116
Matthew MER 104
Nathaniel MER 104
Nathl. CWL 35
Nathl.? CWL 32
Ned? HRT 165
Nicholas GNP 166A
Nimrod HAR 142
Noah HOP 258
Polly MER 104
Richard MER 104
Robert MER 104
Samuel WDF 118A
Simon GRT 140
Thomas WDF 103A
Thos. PUL 42A
William FTE 83
William SHE 153
William, Jr. MER 104
William, Sr. MER 104
Wm. BBN 138

Name	County	Page
NICHOLS, Wm.?	CWL	32
NICHOLS?, Margaret	MER	104
NICHOLSON, Alexander	SHE	115A
Bolin	PUL	68A
Jacob	WTY	111A
James S.	WDF	95A
John	WDF	100
John	GTN	127
Joseph	MTG	237
Marmaduke	UNN	149
Richd.	CLY	113
Robt.	JEF	25
Thomas	CLY	112
Wm.	HRD	82
Wm.	PND	17A
NICKASON, Mary	NCH	120A
NICKELS, Johnathan	WYN	94A
Simon	GRD	103A
NICKERSON, John	MAD	128
John	MAD	164
NICKLE, Andrew	FLD	11
Henry	FLD	11
Isaac	FLD	9
Jno.	FKN	78
John	FLD	8
John	FLD	11
John	FLD	11
Joseph	FLD	11
Robert	FLD	11
Robert	NCH	115A
Thomas	FLD	11
Thomas	WRN	68A
William	FLD	10
NICKOL, George	CHN	32A
James	CHN	32
Wm.	CHN	32A
NICKOLS, ---ddick?	CWL	32
NICLESON, James	GRD	93A
James	GRD	110A
John	GRD	109A
Wm.	GRD	92A
NICLY, Ann, Mrs.	CLK	101
NICOLAS, James	HAR	206
NICOLDS, John	ALN	122
Joseph	SCT	129A
Susanna	ALN	122
Tho.	ALN	122
NICOLL, Isaiah	MTG	247
NICOLS, James	BRN	22
NIELD, Charles	LNC	43
John	LNC	13
NIELLSON, -----?	DVS	13A
NIESS, Ann	FKN	56
NIFONG, Michael	MER	104
NIGHT, David	WTY	115A
Ephraim	CSY	228
George	WTY	119A
Jerem.	HRY	262
John, Jurn.	CHN	34
John, Senr.	CHN	34
John	HND	10A
Nelly	WTY	110A
Sarah	HND	9A
NIGHT?, Willis	HRY	252
NIGHTINGALE, Mathew	CSY	206
Matthew	OWN	103
NIGLEY, George	HND	9A
NILE, Darcus?	HAR	156
Thomas	HAR	146
NILES, Charles	HAR	190
NILEY?, Saml.	SCT	102A
NIMAN, Elias	HAR	190
NIMROD, (No Other Name Given)	BTH	194
NISBIT, John	BBN	118
Martha	BBN	130
NISBIT?, James?	LVG	16
NITE?, Ele	TRG	14A
NIVINS, Henry	MER	104
Susannah	MER	104
NIX, James	ALN	132
John	FLD	30
John	KNX	308
Will.	KNX	310
William	CHN	29
NIX?, James	WAS	21A
NO--SE?, Charles	NSN	175
NOAH, George	NCH	124A
Sally, Mrs.	CLK	99
NOAKS, George	LNC	73
John	LNC	47
Thomas	LNC	39
NOBLE, Adam J./I.?	GRD	85A
Curtis	CWL	55
Elijah	FTE	67
Elizabeth	BNE	28
Enoch	CLY	130
James	MER	115
Jas.	HRD	40
John	NCH	125A
Littlebury	BNE	28
Nathan	CLY	131
Peter	GTN	131
Peter	NSN	187
Robt.	BRK	279
Thos.	FKN	162
William	LGN	30
William	CLY	130
Winney, Miss	BBN	102
Wm.	FKN	132
Wm.	MAD	164
NOBLES, Jonathan	SPN	23A
NOE, Aquila	LGN	35
David	HRL	116
Elizabeth	HRL	116
Evi	HAR	210
George	NCH	120A
James	MER	104
James	BTH	158
John	HRL	116
John	HRL	116
John M.	SCT	107A
Landron?	CLK	69
Randolph	HRL	116
Samuel	GRT	146
Shaderick	HRL	116
Susan	FTE	81
NOEL, Alxr.	ADR	38
Armstrong	TRG	7
Barnard	MER	104
Benjamin	MER	104
Bernard	GTN	131
Dudley	MER	104
Edmd.	JEF	51
Edward?	TRG	6A
Garnett	BNE	28
Harris	MER	104
James	BNE	28
James	SHE	152
Joel	MER	104
John	BNE	28
John	GTN	131
John	SHE	153
Joseph	NSN	178
Loftus	FKN	58
Lonceford R.	LNC	79
Lucy	ALN	132
Moses	WAS	84A
Moses	GRD	85A
NOEL, Oliver	LNC	39
Philip	FKN	118
Silas M.	FKN	160
Smallwood	MER	115
Tabitha	LNC	37
Thos.	JEF	57
William	HOP	272
Wm.	WAS	54A
NOEL?, Samuel	MER	104
NOELL, Taylor	GRD	104A
NOFSINGER, John	MBG	139
John	MBG	138A
Samuel	MBG	136A
Susanna	MBG	133A
NOGGLE, John	SHE	138A
NOINS?, Mordica	WAS	17A
NOLAN, Elizabeth	MAD	120
Hannah	MAD	120
John	HRL	116
John	MAD	120
Smallwood V.	MAD	174
Wm., Jr.	MAD	120
Wm., Sr.	MAD	120
NOLAND, Ashford	ETL	43
Francis	ETL	42
Henry	ETL	43
James	ETL	42
James	HAR	168
Jesse	HRY	200
Jessee, Jr.	ETL	43
Jessee, Sr.	ETL	52
John	ETL	53
John	FTE	84
John	CLD	152
Joshua	ETL	43
Ledeton?	ETL	54
Nicholas	ETL	53
Pleasant	ETL	54
Rasha	ETL	43
Smalwod	ETL	52
Stephen	ETL	54
Thomas	ETL	53
Thos.	FKN	74
William	ETL	54
William P.	ETL	42
NOLBY?, Thomas	NSN	222
NOLEN, Eliza	JEF	22
Stephen	GNP	169A
NOLES?, Winney	GRD	121A
NOLIN, Isaac	FLD	31
Sinai	FLD	31
William	FLD	31
William	OWN	100
NOLING, James	PND	26A
NOLLEY, Daniel	GRN	50
John	GRN	69
Richd.	GRN	64
Wm.	WAS	51A
NOLLEY?, Thomas	NSN	222
NOOL?, Zephaniah	BBN	118
NOONON, James	JES	94
NOONON?, Patrick	JES	93
NOORE?, Elizabeth	MAD	172
NOOT?, Zephaniah	BBN	118
NOREL?, Landlon	MER	115
NORFLET, David	PUL	63A
James	WYN	79A
John	PUL	58A
NORIL, Nathan	KNX	312
NORINGTON?, Abra.	JEF	43
NORIS, Josiah	ALN	142
NORMAN, Abner	SHE	135A
Benjamin	BNE	28
Berryman	CLK	75
Caleb	BNE	28
Isaac	SHE	135A

NORMAN, Jesse B. SHE 174
Margarette LWS 91A
Ooliver FLG 27A
Reubin BTL 327
Thomas WYN 80A
William HRY 202
William MNR 211
NORRELD?, Ludamon? JES 97
NORRELI?, Ludamon? JES 97
NORRES?, Joseph NSN 199
William NSN 191
NORRINGTON, Jno. JEF 46
NORRIS, Barton MAS 66
Benjn. MAS 58
Claibourn CLD 148
David BTH 216
Enoch HRD 52
Gilbert BTH 206
Henry NSN 188
Henry WRN 41A
Hugh BRN 22
Jacob BTH 180
James BKN 28
James, Jr./ Sr.? MAS 68
James WRN 41A
Jas MAS 68
Jno. MAS 65
John BKN 15
John CLK 88
John CLD 141
John NSN 183
John NSN 188
John NSN 217
John BTH 220
John FLG 48A
Jos. MAS 53
Joseph BKN 20
Joseph BNE 28
Joseph BBN 86
Joseph S. SCT 137A
Joshua CLY 125
Leah LGN 33
Moses GSN 146A
Nancy MTG 285
Nath. BKN 26
Nathan CLD 165
Richard HRD 64
Samuel CLD 141
Samuel WRN 41A
Soloman WRN 41A
Thomas PND 17A
Thos. WAS 30A
Thos. R. JEF 34
Will MAS 53
Will MAS 69
William BRN 22
William CLK 89
William CLD 141
Wm. HRD 52
Zebulon CLD 141
NORRIS?, Igs. WAS 85A
Mordica WAS 17A
NORRISH, Robert MAD 180
NORTH, Abijah HAR 132
Abraham UNN 153
Abraham SPN 4A
Anthony GRN 56
John GTN 118
John ALN 126
John TOD 132A
William FTE 66
William L. BLT 160
NORTHAM, Eli SPN 6A
William SPN 6A
NORTHARTT, Benjamin CBL 5A
NORTHCRAFT, Arasmis WAS 37A
NORTHCUT, Arther WAS 30A
Benj. FLG 54A
Benjamin BBN 120
George BBN 126
Hannah, Mrs. WYN 103A
Hozea MTG 279
Jeramiah CBL 11A
Will BBN 62
William CBL 11A
NORTHCUTT, Archabald CSY 210
Geo. BBN 140
George CBL 10A
John HAR 148
Thomas CBL 11A
William CSY 224
Wm. BBN 102
NORTHCUTT?, Royal BLT 170
NORTHERN, Reuben BLT 184
Saml. PUL 48A
William LGN 47
NORTHINGTON, Jno. CHN 41
Samuel TRG 4A
NORTON, Alexander NSN 185
Asbury MER 104
Bradshaw MER 104
George FTE 59
George GRT 139
Henry GRT 143
J./ I.? P. FTE 69
James FKN 154
Jeremiah BRK 279
John FTE 59
John GRT 139
Joseph GTN 119
Nancy BBN 110
Sarah BBN 114
William LGN 23
William NSN 180
NORTON?, -----? HRT 164
James GNP 176A
NORVEL, Jarvis WDF 101A
NORVELL, Francis FKN 84
Thos. FKN 84
NORVILL, Lipscomb TRG 8
NORWEL?, M. J. FTE 55
NORWELL, Hugh BRN 22
NORWOOD, Charless WDF 104A
Frederick FTE 63
Jas. FLG 24A
NORWOOD?, Charles FTE 63
NOTHERN, Jonathan LGN 28
NOTHERN?, Jeremiah NSN 221
NOTHINGTON, Andrew CHN 43
Mikel CHN 45
NOTLEY?, Francis WAS 72A
NOTT, David MAS 69
Jos. MAS 71
NOURSE, Robert LGN 41
Wm. N. BRN 34
NOWEL, Ezekiel HAR 168
George HAR 168
James MER 117
John GTN 127
NOWERS, Alexr. MAS 70
Jas. MAS 71
NOWLEN, Nelson SHE 122A
NOWLES, Thos. HRY 265
NOWLS, S. HRY 261
NOWNING, William GTN 123
NOX, Elizabeth BTH 198
Will BBN 60
NOX?, George BTH 178
NOYES, Thompson HRD 74
NOYES, William T. FTE 56
NUBB?, Francis HAR 154
NUBERRY, Tho. MAS 69
NUBLE?, Francis HAR 154
NUCKELLS, Rodes (Crossed Out) WTY 117A
NUCKELS, Rhodes WTY 112A
NUCKOLDS, Lewis SCT 136A
NUCOLS, Andrew BRN 22
David BRN 22
Pouncy BRN 22
NUCOMB, John GRD 97A
NUDIGATE, Edwd. MAS 77
NULE, Wm. ALN 102
NULE?, Moss? ALN 92
NULIG?, Susanna MAD 110
NULT, John GRD 115A
NUMAN, John BTH 208
John FLG 51A
NUMON, Alexander BNE 28
NUN, Waters CLD 140
NUNAM, John SCT 120A
NUNLY, Jeremiah BTH 208
NUNN, Hugh HND 8
Ilais BBN 88
Ira LVG 8
James LGN 44
John MGB 137A
Saml. LVG 8
Wm. BRN 22
NUNN?, Thomas LGN 36
NUNNALLY, Will B. SCT 109A
NUNNELLY, Anderson PUL 56A
Bernard BRN 22
Josiah BRN 22
Robert BRN 22
Robt. SCT 109A
NUNNEMAKER, Barbara CBL 6A
NUNS, Mother Anns Congregation Of WAS 42A
NUNUM, Daniel OWN 104
NUR?, Peter, Jnr. HAR 148
Peter, Snr. HAR 148
NUTAFEE, George SHE 119A
NUTALL, Price HRY 270
NUTGRASS, Gray SHE 115A
William SHE 116A
NUTON?, Nancy GRD 120A
Walter WAS 83A
NUTT, James SHE 123A
NUTTER, David FTE 76
David SCT 101A
Hewitt SCT 113A
John SCT 122A
Thomas FTE 76
NUTTER?, George FLD 26
O BANNION?, James CLD 138
William CLD 140
O BANNON, Elias SHE 150
Isham SHE 158
James SHE 150
Mary FLG 30A
Permenas SHE 158
Presley N. LGN 23
William SHE 162
William WDF 94A
Wm. B. FLG 29A
O BANON, Danl. GRD 100A
O BRACKEN, John WAS 63A
O BRAKEN?, Edward WAS 22A
O BRIAN, Saml. JEF 27
O BRIANT, Thos. SHE 122A
O BRIEN, Wm. WAS 56A

O BRYON, Adam GNP 177A
O CALUM?, Thomas ETL 40
O CULUM?, Thomas ETL 40
O KELLY, Patk. JEF 25
O NEAL, (See Odyneal) SPN 23A
Danl. FLG 31A
Henry FLG 31A
John FLG 31A
John SHE 124A
Joseph JEF 41
Lewis BBN 74
Willis OHO 7A
O NEELE, Baley SHE 125A
Briant SHE 125A
O NEIL, Francis FTE 62
Timothy LVG 7
O NEILL, A. J. MAS 81
O ROBY?, Joseph WAS 63A
O SPRAKE?, Thomas FTE 113
O'BRIAN, Benedect NSN 191
Herrell FLD 22
John NSN 185
Joseph NSN 184
Lewis NSN 181
William NSN 201
O'BRIANT, Thomas TRG 11A
O'BRYAN, James BLT 194
O'CONNELL, Philip NSN 176
O'CONNER, Richard NSN 205
Thomas NSN 179
Thomas NSN 208
O'HARA, John CWL 43
O'HARRA, Kean FKN 122
O'HAVER?, David FTE 67
O'NEAL, Geo. BBN 128
John NSN 205
Lewis BBN 96
Thos. BBN 114
Widw. CWL 33
O'NEIL?, James BKN 18
O'VAN?, Clempston? FKN 112
Dennis FKN 112
Thos. FKN 112
Wm. FKN 112
O---IL?, James BKN 18
OAKASON, John FLG 59A
OAKELY, Christopher BTH 200
John P. BTH 200
OAKERSON, Isaiah BNE 28
John MTG 259
OAKES, Nancy HRL 116
OAKLEY, John FLD 12
John MTG 247
Plesant FLG 60A
Will. FLG 61A
OAKLY, Cesialo? BTH 204
Edmund BTH 190
OAKS, Samuel? WTY 126A
Thos. WAS 50A
OAKY?, John HRT 165
OATES, David MBG 142A
Jessee MBG 142A
Jos. TOD 128A
William MBG 142A
OATS, Bryan HOP 258
Jethro HOP 258
OATTS, Roger WYN 106A
OBANAN, Susan HAR 188
OBANION, George LNC 55
Jacob OWN 101
Susan OWN 101
OBANNION, Ben. LNC 5
OBANNON, Wm. HRY 269
OBBURN, Alesander LWS 96A
OBOUSOUR?, Luke GTN 123
OBRIAN, Daniel MER 116
Henry BRK 279
James FLD 23
Matthew MER 116
Thomas HOP 258
OBRIANT, Gustavos FKN 84
OBRIEN, Sary FKN 150
OBRYAN, Allin HOP 258
Redick HOP 258
Turner HOP 258
OBURNE, John JEF 22
ODAGHERTY?, Bernard NSN 224
ODAR, Thomas HAR 218
ODD, Zachariah NSN 213
ODEAN, John, Esq. WYN 96A
ODELL, Armstead MER 104
Jno. FKN 162
John MER 104
William MER 104
William MNR 211
ODEN, Hezekiah BBN 122
Leonard WRN 32A
Wm. FKN 64
ODER, James HAR 152
Joseph HAR 154
Joseph, Jnr. HAR 170
Joseph, Snr. HAR 152
Joseph GRD 92A
Martin HAR 154
Tho. C. GRD 92A
ODER?, Barnett HAR 138
Mariah MAD 176
William HAR 150
ODLE, Richd. WAS 51A
ODLE?, James BRK 281
ODUM, -----? DVS 4A
-----? DVS 7A
-----? DVS 8A
ODYNEAL?, James SPN 23A
OELLE?, James BRK 281
OESLER?, John JES 71
OFFICER, James SCT 107A
OFFICIAL, Elizphen BTH 166
Lemuel BTH 160
OFFOND, John M. JEF 30
OFFORD, John BBN 112
OFFORT, Samuel JES 88
Samuel JES 88
OFFOT, Andrew SHE 123A
Z. B. SHE 123A
OFFSETT, Zadock SCT 114A
OFFUT, Henry C. FTE 108
OFFUTT, Alexr. SCT 137A
Archid. SCT 123A
Barruch SCT 128A
Esley LGN 46
George H. WDF 112A
H. J. SCT 129A
Hugh SCT 129A
James LGN 46
Jas. D. SCT 136A
Otho SCT 106A
Sabrett? SCT 128A
Singleton SCT 139A
Thos. CHN 42
Thos. O. SCT 122A
Tilghman LGN 37
Warren WDF 112A
Will. T. SCT 123A
Zedekiah SCT 113A
OGBURN, Henry GTN 123
OGDEN, Aquilla CLK 69
Benj. BKN 16
Benj.? CWL 42
OGDEN, David CLD 140
Elizabeth CLD 139
Henry BKN 8
Jesse FLD 6
John W. NSN 223
Mary HAR 190
Robert G. WRN 76A
Stephen FLD 11
Zachariah GSN 146A
OGDLE, John JES 90
OGDON, George GTN 118
James LGN 27
Jas. ADR 38
John LGN 27
Masterson SHE 161
Otho LGN 27
Thomas LGN 27
William GTN 118
OGG, Wm. MAD 160
OGLE, Absolum SCT 137A
Alexander TRG 11
Jesse HAR 182
OGLEBY, Humphry F.?/ T.? MAS 62
OGLES, James FLD 23
OGLESBY, Ellis SHE 156
Jacob JEF 40
Jacob JEF 44
Jesse SHE 154
Jessy GRD 97A
John MAD 98
Joseph JEF 31
Macajah JEF 64
Nathan LVG 6
Richd. JEF 55
Samuel SHE 120A
Talton MAD 176
Washington SHE 156
William SHE 156
Wm. JEF 46
OGLESVY, Constant, Junr. CHN 30
Constant, Senr. CHN 30
Jacob CHN 30
Jane CHN 30
John CHN 30
Wm. CHN 30
OHUIR, Thomas GNP 169A
OISLER?, John JES 71
OLD, James CLK 68
John MAD 112
Wm. MAD 120
OLDAHAN, Jacob ADR 38
OLDER, John LNC 79
OLDES?, Reuben LNC 39
OLDFIELD, Jesse FLD 12
OLDHAM, Abner MAD 152
Absolem ETL 50
Caleb MAD 92
Charles BRN 23
Conaway JEF 40
Daniel GSN 146A
Dera ETL 41
Ezekiah MAD 130
Ezekiah MAD 154
George SCT 122A
George SHE 139A
Henry BLT 174
J./ I. HRY 234
James T. SHE 128A
James T. SHE 139A
Jesse SCT 121A
John ETL 43
John ETL 50
John MAD 166
John MNR 193

OLDHAM, John GSN 146A
John K. MAD 158
Moses MAD 106
Moses MAD 156
Nathaniel MAD 156
Newport MTG 293
Richard MAD 174
Richard MTG 289
Richard, Jr. ETL 49
Richard CBL 2A
Saml. JEF 46
Saml. MAD 152
Tapley BRN 23
Thomas CBL 13A
Tyree PND 20A
Will MAS 56
William MNR 193
William B. CLK 78
Wm. JEF 45
Wm. MAD 160
Wm. PND 18A
OLDHAM?, John HRT 165
Richard, Sr. ETL 40
OLDOM, George HOP 258
Hiram HOP 258
James HOP 258
OLDRIDGE, Joshua JES 71
OLDRIGE, John GNP 167A
OLDRUM, George BNE 28
OLDS, Jessee JEF 45
Moses HRY 254
William JES 96
OLFORD, Kildess CSY 218
OLHAM, Goodman RCK 89
OLIPHANT, Obadiah BRN 23
William BRN 23
OLIVE, Abel TRG 5A
Abel TRG 5A
Jubel? TRG 5A
OLIVER, Archibald NCH 117A
Benja. JEF 38
Carter JES 73
Charles CBL 13A
David LNC 33
David JEF 54
Eli TOD 131
Eli CBL 14A
Elijah FTE 69
Henry GNP 169A
Isaac, Jr. CLK 75
Isaac, Senr. CLK 75
James GTN 121
James HRY 186
Jno. FKN 96
Jno. FKN 96
John FTE 110
John HRY 182
John HAR 188
John, Jr. CLK 75
John, Senr. CLK 75
John SPN 15A
Joseph CBL 14A
Joshua CLY 126
Josiah BBN 78
Laven BBN 78
Laven, Senr. BBN 78
Lee CBL 14A
Leon. CWL 33
Levin CWL 33
Lewis CBL 11A
Martin CWL 55
Nancey FKN 108
Nathn. CWL 33
Nicholas BBN 106
Phillis FTE 103
Pleasant FKN 138
OLIVER, Presley FTE 110
Presly HRY 180
Presly HRY 182
Presly HRY 188
Richard CLK 73
Saml. BBN 130
Saml. CHN 30A
Shadk. CWL 32
Tho. ALN 122
Tho. ALN 128
Thomas OWN 105
Thomas LWS 99A
Thos. FKN 128
Walter CWL 33
William CLK 74
William HRY 188
Wilson WTY 116A
Wm. BBN 78
OLIVER?, William ALN 122
OLLER, ---d.? HRT 165
John GSN 146A
OLLIVER, Isaac CSY 212
John FLG 58A
Thos. FLG 57A
OLMSTEAD, Moses GTN 130
Moses GTN 130
OLNER, Nicholas L. HRY 176
OLSTOT?, Polley CSY 214
OLVERSON, Pleasant JES 90
OLVEY, Bazel GSN 146A
James GSN 146A
OMEDER?, Mathew RCK 75A
OMEHANY?, Wm. TOD 126
OMER, Danl. JEF 41
Danl. JEF 53
OMERLRANY?, Wm. TOD 126
OMSBY, George HND 11
ONAN, John SHE 120A
John SHE 123A
ONANN, Jas. HRY 265
ONANN?, P. HRY 261
ONEAL, Bennett BRN 23
Briant NSN 223
Charles NSN 211
Chas. BBN 88
Eleanor NSN 211
Henry MNR 201
James MNR 215
Jno. JEF 23
John ALN 118
John MAD 132
John NSN 211
Jonas WAS 21A
Joseph JEF 24
Stephen UNN 154
Thornton ALN 116
William BNE 28
ONSLOT, Nicholas GRD 102A
OOFFICE?, Harald SPN 10A
OOLEY?, David HRT 165
Peter HRT 165
OOR, John GRD 100A
OORR?, Daniel FTE 110
OOTEN?, Will KNX 284
OOTZ, Alsey SCT 119A
OPATRICK?, Martin (Free) LGN 31
ORAM, Saml. BRK 281
ORCHARD, Alexander MAD 128
James BTL 329
John MAD 152
John MAD 160
Thos. MAD 154
ORCHEN?, Wm. HRT 165
ORCHER, James HRT 165
ORCOTT, Joseph GTN 123
ORCUTT, James LWS 86A
ORD, John UNN 147
ORE, Robert LNC 33
OREAR, Benjamin CLK 70
Daniel MTG 237
E. C. FLG 79A
Jeremiah C. MTG 257
John MTG 261
John, Sr. MTG 225
Robert MTG 261
ORENDEN?, William MNR 215
ORFIELD, Jane GNP 171A
John GNP 171A
ORGAN, Archabald JES 81
Joel JES 77
Micajah JES 77
Thomas CBL 11A
ORICK, John FLG 61A
Wm. FLG 61A
ORLEN, Ann HOP 260
ORME, Jeremiah BLT 194
Morris BLT 194
Nathaniel BLT 194
Philip BLT 158
ORMES, Mathew BKN 4
Moses, Junr. LWS 99A
Moses LWS 99A
Nicholas LWS 99A
ORMSBERRY, Otis? CBL 3A
ORMSBY, Peter Burson? JEF 21
Robt. G. JEF 20
Stephen JEF 60
ORNDERFF, Esau? LGN 38
ORNDORFF, Christian LGN 45
Christopher LGN 38
ORR, A. D. MAS 64
Alex CWL 40
George CBL 16A
Hugh CWL 40
James GRN 68
James HAR 178
James PND 19A
Jessee? ADR 38
John UNN 151
John NCH 111A
Richard GTN 120
Robt. ADR 38
Samuel TRG 3
Samuel P. TRG 3
Thos. BKN 24
Will. SCT 136A
William LGN 24
William MER 104
William GTN 118
Wm. BRN 22
Wm. BKN 23
Wm. BBN 88
Wm. MAD 114
Wm. MAD 156
Wm.? CWL 40
ORREL?, James NSN 201
Margery NSN 201
ORRIL?, John WAS 50A
ORSBURN, Andrew HRL 116
Ephram? HRL 116
George HRL 116
James HRL 116
Margret HRL 116
Soloman HRL 116
ORTEN, Thomas HOP 260
ORTKIES, Henry LNC 55
Henry, Sr. LNC 55
John NSN 197
ORTON, Robert HOP 258

ORTON?, Will KNX 284
ORUM?, James ADR 38
ORUN?, Elly ADR 38
OSBERN, Elias JES 90
Nich. RCK 80A
OSBERRY, Wm. JEF 51
OSBORN, Benjamin MNR 195
Reuben WRN 60A
OSBORNE, Elijah CSY 226
Morgan HND 8
Randolph HND 10
Squire HND 13
Susanna P. HND 8
OSBURN, Benjn. SCT 137A
Bennet SCT 138A
Bennett SCT 99A
Danl. HRT 165
David, Jnr HAR 190
David, Snr HAR 190
Edward SHE 155
Fielding CBL 14A
George CLK 77
George SHE 168
Isaac NSN 182
Isham CWL 33
James ETL 39
James GNP 173A
Jane LWS 92A
Jesse FLD 19
John SCT 100A
John SCT 109A
Richard OWN 104
Sherrard FLD 37
Solomon FLD 40
Squire CLY 126
St. Clair CBL 12A
Susanah SCT 107A
Theodore NSN 184
Thomas BTH 192
Thomas? BLT 170
Thos. SCT 94A
Will SCT 99A
Will. SCT 123A
Will. SCT 134A
William CLK 62
Wm. JEF 30
Wm. GNP 173A
OSBURNE, Abner SHE 136A
Benjamin BLT 184
John BLT 184
OSCIER, James MTG 293
OSINTON, Samuel GNP 172A
OSLEY, Nathan LVG 11
OSNABACK, Jacob CWL 37
OSTEN, Saml. MAD 116
OTEY, James WRN 28A
OTIS, Johnathan BTH 186
OTRELL, Naoma FTE 76
OTSTOT?, Polley CSY 214
OTT, David PUL 65A
Nancy RCK 83A
Sarah RCK 84A
OTTRELL, William FTE 76
OTWELL, Francis SCT 96A
OUSELY, Ebsworth HRD 18
OUSLEY, Joel, M. D. CLD 167
OUSNER, F. TOD 126A
OUTAN, E. MAS 76
OUTHOUSE, Robert SHE 156
OUTLING?, Thomas TRG 8A
OUTON, Isaac MAS 78
Jacob MAS 77
OUTS, Abra. JEF 64
OUTTEN, Levi FTE 109
Thomas FTE 109
OVER, George BLT 196
OVERALL, Dorcus HRD 68
Mary HRD 42
Nancy BLT 194
Robert BLT 194
Whitledge BLT 194
OVERBAY, Henry NCH 106A
OVERBY, James ALN 138
OVERFIELD, John HND 11
OVERHOLTS, Mark MBG 139
OVERLEY, Peter NCH 115A
OVERLY, Jacob FLG 69A
Jessee FLG 66A
John FLG 66A
John FLG 74A
Wm. FLG 69A
OVERPECK, Jacob GTN 129
OVERSHINER, Gideon CHN 35
John CHN 36A
OVERSTAKE, Benjamin HAR 144
OVERSTREET, Benjamin MER 104
Charles JES 90
Charles WYN 99A
G. JEF 23
Gabriel JEF 57
George JES 90
Henry JES 90
Henry MER 104
J. H. JEF 19
James JES 71
James JES 86
James MER 104
James WYN 98A
John MER 104
John SHE 131A
Micheal JEF 59
Micheal, Jr. JEF 59
Moses MER 104
Robert JES 88
Saml. JEF 57
Thomas JES 74
Thomas JES 86
Thomas MER 104
Thomas MER 104
Thos. JEF 27
William JES 90
William WYN 98A
OVERTON, Bevily FKN 96
Ely OHO 6A
Ephraigm KNX 286
Francis E. FTE 95
George HRD 60
John HRD 60
John C. HRD 60
Lewis SHE 168
Milley GTN 129
Patsey ADR 38
R. B. SHE 111A
Reubin CBL 6A
Saml., Sr. NSN 224
Samuel NSN 179
Waller FTE 103
Will. G. SCT 131A
William OHO 6A
OVERTON?, Bartlet FTE 105
OVERTURS?, Conrod BKN 26
OWELL, Margarett LNC 61
OWEN, Barrel FKN 90
Daniel BRK 279
David LVG 2
David BRN 22
David GTN 125
Edmund MBG 140A
Edward JES 81
OWEN, Edward OHO 9A
Elisha RCK 77A
Elizabeth HRD 78
George PND 23A
Grant BRK 279
James BRN 22
James, Jr. BRN 22
Jeremiah MER 104
Jno. JEF 38
John JEF 31
John, Jr. BRN 22
John, Sr. BRN 22
Johnson BRN 22
Joseph UNN 153
Martha SHE 129A
Nancy FKN 106
Nelson HRY 208
Richard BRN 22
Robert SHE 127A
Robt. FKN 114
Robt. BRK 279
Shapley JEF 59
Thomas HRL 116
Thomas GTN 124
Thos., Jr. BRK 281
Thos., Sr. BRK 281
Timothy HRD 8
Will. LVG 10
William BRN 22
William FTE 108
William SHE 175
Wm. HRD 34
Wm. FKN 108
OWENN, James D. BKN 8
OWENS, Aaron LWS 91A
Alfred LWS 87A
Allen RCK 76A
Aquilla BLT 192
Asael FLG 31A
Banister MER 104
Barnett MAD 114
Benjamin BRN 22
Berton/ Buton? RCK 78A
Bethal MAS 60
Chas. SCT 114A
David RCK 78A
David RCK 84A
Easrum? SCT 111A
Edmund MBG 143A
Edward KNX 2/8
Edwd. CWL 55
Eli FLD 30
Elijah GRT 146
Even FTE 83
Felix BLT 178
Hanson MAS 69
Harroway SCT 100A
Henry HRY 256
Henson MAS 60
Isaac PND 23A
James CBL 10A
James WRN 68A
Jerry SCT 126A
Jno. MAS 60
Jno. HRY 243
Jno. HRY 247
Jno. 2nd CWL 57
Jno. PUL 45A
John ETL 50
John BLT 192
John HRY 212
John FLG 28A
John PUL 37A
John WRN 58A
John WRN 75A
John LWS 92A

OWENS, John SCT 100A
John SCT 121A
Johnathan RCK 79A
Jordin GRN 54
Joseph HRT 165
Joseph WYN 84A
Joshua MAS 80
Lawrance HRY 210
Levey SCT 136A
Ludwell MAS 53
Luther JEF 30
M. CHN 29A
M. RCK 76A
M. W. MAS 80
Martin PUL 59A
Mason HRY 267
Nathan MAS 54
Nathan GRN 77
Obadiah WRN 59A
Owen FLD 32
Owen SCT 100A
Owin WYN 104A
Peter HRT 165
Reubin HOP 260
Richard GRT 143
Robert CLD 147
Robt. SCT 139A
Saml. ADR 38
Saml. MAS 64
Saml. HRY 241
Saml. KNX 300
Samuel LGN 23
Samuel FLD 29
Sanford HRY 268
Thomas FLD 28
Thomas FLD 32
Thos. BKN 16
Thos. HRY 268
Thos. WAS 68A
Thos. SCT 111A
Unis? RCK 83A
Washi. KNX 300
Will MAS 54
Will. SCT 104A
William LGN 24
William FLD 28
William GRT 147
William HOP 258
William, Senr. PUL 56A
Wilsy? RCK 83A
Wm. CWL 38
Wm. CWL 55
Wm. ADC 68
Wm. FKN 80
Wm., Jr. CWL 55
Wm. PUL 37A
OWENS?, Charles R. HRT 165
John CSY 220
OWENSBY, Thos. ADR 38
OWIN, Fleming JES 69
OWING, John MTG 293
OWINGS, Armsted ETL 43
Edwd. C. BBN 96
Elihue BTH 208
George SPN 4A
Henry SPN 4A
Isaac JEF 44
John ETL 37
John CLK 65
John, Sr. CLK 87
John NCH 112A
Joshua FTE 89
Joshua BBN 144
Nancy MTG 293
Nathaniel NSN 213
Oratio CLK 74
OWINGS, Richard BTH 164
Robert BBN 122
Ruth BTH 208
Samuel NCH 109A
Thomas HAR 164
Thomas D. BTH 200
Thomas D. BTH 200
Thomas D. BTH 200
Thomas D. BTH 200
Thos. D. BTH 186
Thos. Deye? BTH 223
Zecheriah HAR 148
OWINS, Arthur WYN 98A
Barney MAD 162
Benjm. GRN 70
Enoch WYN 95A
John WYN 99A
Reubin, Esq. WYN 103A
Richard SPN 13A
Stephen WYN 95A
Wm. G. GRN 58
OWLEY, David GRN 71
Jeremiah GRN 65
Sarah GRN 65
Thomas GRN 70
William GRN 62
OWNBY?, Elizabeth SHE 153
OWNEY, Joseph GSN 146A
OWNLEY?, Elizabeth SHE 153
OWSLEY, Anthony LNC 77
Bryan Y. LNC 2
Catharine LNC 77
Daniel LNC 77
Henry LNC 51
John LNC 53
John CLK 90
Newdigate SHE 133A
Tho. RCK 75A
Thomas LNC 3
Thomas LNC 7
Thomas CLK 73
William LNC 71
William GRD 85A
OXENDINE, Stephen MBG 135A
OXFORD, Jacob CLY 128
OXIER, Barbary MTG 293
James GNP 167A
Simeon GNP 167A
OXLEY, Cleare FTE 111
Everd FTE 110
Joseph SCT 104A
Micajah FTE 110
Wm. FLG 67A
OYLER, Henry S.? WRN 60A
OYSTER, Sarah HRD 96
OZEE?, Peter GTN 132
P-----, Wm. ALN 110
P----, Joseph GTN 125
P--BRECK, Fitz ALN 144
P--KEN, Hanah FTE 58
P--THWAIT?, Joseph LVG 16
P-R--?, Frances BTH 198
P-R-IN?, Jessee ALN 140
PA--TON?, Ja--? ADR 42
PACA?, John LGN 24
PACE, Daniel TOD 129
Edward CLK 96
Edward WRN 49A
James, Capt. CLK 96
James, Senr. CLK 97
Jesse MAD 122
Joel TOD 129
Joel WDF 107A
John CLK 96
John CLY 126
PACE, John MAD 134
John CLD 142
John WDF 108A
Joseph BRN 23
Langston CLD 137
Langston TOD 132A
Matthew CLY 120
Murray CLK 76
Murry, Senr. CLK 96
Robert CLY 120
Spencer TOD 129A
Susanna WRN 49A
Thomas WDF 120A
Wm. J. BRN 23
PACE?, Polley HRL 118
PACK, Charles FLD 24
George FLD 22
George FLD 46
Richard NSN 178
Samuel FLD 24
PACK?, Jno. HAR 162
PACKSTON, James FKN 136
PACKWOOD, Richard FLD 21
PACO?, Polley HRL 118
PADEN, James TOD 130
John TOD 130
PADGET, Danl. NCH 116A
Edward MER 105
James MER 116
John BRN 24
Lewis LNC 41
Wm. BBN 126
PADGETT, James SHE 149
Robt. FLG 44A
PADGIT, Henry BBN 94
Saml. WAS 71A
PADOCK, Saml. WAS 80A
Wm. WAS 80A
PAGE, Anderson CLD 141
Anderson MNR 203
Axel?, WRN 31A
Daburg? MER 105
David FLD 6
Dillard LNC 27
Dorcas CLD 141
Edmond CBL 9A
George MAD 176
George W. BRN 24
Harriet MER 105
James ADR 40
James MER 105
James MNR 193
James GRD 120A
Jesse LGN 32
John B. MNR 193
Johnston LGN 28
Jos. JEF 62
Katharine MER 105
Leonard LGN 28
Linsey WRN 63A
Mary ADR 40
Pleasant LGN 44
Robt. ADR 40
Saml. ADR 40
Samuel LGN 33
Samuel LGN 38
Tandy C. MAD 174
Thomas FTE 75
Will. LVG 4
William LGN 30
William LGN 36
Wm. BRN 23
PAGET, John HRD 56
John JES 91
Kitty HRD 82
Laka? HRD 76

Name	County	Page
PAGET, Philis	JES	95
Thomas	JES	92
William	FTE	76
William	JES	91
Wm.	HRD	42
PAGETT, Jno.	MAS	56
PAICE, Richard	SPN	22A
PAIGE?, Martin	HRT	165
PAIN, Charles	NSN	188
Francis	NSN	187
Gayus	PND	16A
Ignatus	NSN	188
John	NSN	209
John	OHO	4A
Ruben	ADR	42
William	NSN	209
Wm.	ADR	42
PAIN?, John	ADR	40
PAINE, Baldwin	BKN	22
Henry	SHE	170
PAINE?, James J.	CLK	84
PAINTER, George	CBL	22A
John	GSN	148A
Joseph	GSN	147A
Sol.	HRY	251
PAINTEZ, William	BRK	285
PAIR?, John	ADR	40
PAISLEY, Robert	LGN	39
Samuel	LGN	46
PALAMER, James	GRD	110A
PALEAR, Peter	CLD	146
PALLERSON, Rich	ADR	40
PALLY?, John	ADR	42
Wm. M.	ADR	42
PALMER, Burton	GRD	102A
Charles	SCT	97A
Daniel	MTG	247
Ed	MAS	74
Geo.	BBN	140
Henry	MNR	215
Isaac	SCT	98A
Isaac	SCT	123A
James	GTN	135
James A.	JEF	31
James W.	FTE	57
John	CWL	36
John	BBN	116
John	BBN	124
John, Jr.	GRD	85A
John	FLG	74A
John	GRD	110A
John	GRD	116A
Joseph	CBL	17A
Levina	LNC	71
Lott B.	SCT	115A
Lydia	BTH	170
Nathl.	PND	29A
Reubin	JEF	34
Richd.	HRY	254
Robt.	BBN	60
Sylvanus	CWL	46
Tho. A.	MAS	74
Thomas	BBN	140
Thomas J./ I.?	CBL	2A
Thos.	JEF	21
William	WDF	123A
William	MBG	135A
Wm.	BKN	10
Wm.	BBN	116
Wm.	PND	25A
Wm. H.	FLG	26A
PALMER?, Elihu H.	TOD	132A
PALMITEER, William	FTE	69
PALMMER, John	FTE	75
PALMORE, Bowling	WRN	30A
John R.	MNR	197
PALMORE, Permenias	WRN	28A
Sampson	WRN	30A
William	WRN	29A
PALSGROVE, Henry	HRY	265
Jac.	HRY	265
PALSON, Andrew	ADR	42
Wm.	ADR	42
PANE?, Saml.	ADR	40
PANELL, Robt.	HRY	230
PANKEE, John	LNC	61
Mary	LNC	63
PANNEL, Benj.	TOD	132
Wm.	TOD	133
PANTER, David	LNC	13
George	LNC	67
Joshua	LNC	67
PANTHER, Nancy	WTY	112A
PANUER?, Mary	FKN	88
PAPLETT?, Thompson	FLD	7
PARATOR, Benjm.	MAD	110
PARCELS, Wm.	HRD	96
PARCH?, Henry	WTY	114A
PARE, Jeremiah	MNR	199
John	LNC	57
Marcus	MNR	209
William	MNR	209
PARENT, David	CWL	44
David	FKN	68
Jno.	FKN	124
Saml.	MAS	61
Thos.	FKN	120
PARIN?, James J.	CLK	84
PARIS, Geo.	SHE	161
James	CLK	98
John	BLT	184
Robert	SHE	152
PARISH, Abram	NSN	221
Apie / Opie?	BTH	178
Augustin	MER	105
Barkley	NCH	115A
Barnett	CLK	65
Benjamin	FTE	67
Carter	MER	106
David	NCH	124A
Edward	MAD	156
Elizabeth	MAD	110
Ezekiel	CLY	115
Fielding?	MAD	160
James	WDF	94
James	MAD	116
John	CLK	93
John	BBN	114
John	CLD	145
John L	HRD	16
Jolly S?	MER	115
Judea	MER	105
Lewis	GTN	117
Luvinah	MAD	146
Mary	HOP	260
Mary, Mrs.	CLK	94
Mathew	CHN	42A
Nathaniel	BBN	116
Nicholas	MER	106
Parks	BRN	23
Peyton	LGN	25
Richard	HRD	92
Robt.	MAS	56
Saml.	MAD	178
Thomas	NSN	221
Thomas	HOP	260
Thomas	CBL	22A
William	LGN	41
William, Sr.	ETL	54
William	NCH	115A
Wm. D.	ADR	20
Woodson	PND	19A
PARISH, Zachariah	BRN	23
PARK, Caty	ETL	49
Charles	ETL	44
Ebenezer	ETL	43
Eli	MAD	118
Hugh	TOD	131
James	BBN	120
Jas.	CHN	44A
Jessey	MAD	118
John	ETL	51
Levy	ETL	49
Saml.	MAS	54
Saml.	FLG	37A
Will	MAS	52
Wm. C.	FLG	78A
PARK?, Adam	HAR	168
Philip	HAR	162
PARKAM, Wm.	TOD	128A
PARKE, Hugh	TOD	132
James	TOD	131A
John	FTE	66
John	MTG	271
Joseph	MNR	201
PARKE?, Moses	MNR	205
PARKER, Abraham	BKN	15
Abram	BNE	46
Acquilla	BBN	92
Alexander	FTE	55
Alexander	LWS	90A
Alvin	SPN	24A
Archibald	FKN	138
Aron	BKN	9
Asher	LWS	88A
Baily	CHN	36
Barzella	UNN	146
Ben	HRD	24
Ben	HRY	186
Charles	GRD	87A
Charles	NCH	109A
Edward	BTH	200
Elias	BKN	19
Elisha	HOP	260
Eliza J.	FTE	60
Eliza R.	FTE	68
Elizabeth	CHN	36
Elizabeth	HRD	88
Gabriel	FTE	80
Garland	LWS	87A
George	BBN	84
Hannah	BNE	30
Harry	LWS	86A
Henry	BBN	92
Hutchens	SCT	110A
Jacob	FLG	76A
Jacob	SCT	110A
Jacob	SCT	126A
James	CLK	76
James	CBL	20A
James	CBL	20A
James	WYN	83A
James	WYN	99A
Jas.	CLY	112
Jas.	FLG	72A
Jessee	JEF	57
Jessee	CBL	23A
Jno.	MAS	59
Jno.	FKN	156
Joel	BTH	200
John	BRN	23
John	CHN	29
John	HRD	64
John	BBN	84
John	BBN	88
John	HRD	92
John	FTE	101
John	CLY	118

PARKER, John MAD 142
John CBL 20A
John WYN 81A
John SHE 129A
John T. LWS 86A
Jonathan WRN 28A
Jonathan H. LVG 7
Joseph OHO 3A
Lemuel BBN 84
Levi BBN 92
Levi MAD 144
Maria FKN 64
Martin FKN 156
Mary FTE 96
Mary WRN 31A
Mary E. WDF 100
Nat ALN 114
North FTE 79
Obadiah CHN 29
Peter BBN 72
Peter HOP 260
Pleasant CLY 124
Reeves WRN 47A
Richard HOP 260
Richard KNX 298
Richard CBL 20A
Richd. MAS 57
Richd. MAS 67
Rob. CWL 43
Robert NSN 204
Robt. GNP 169A
Rowld. LWS 86A
Sally CLK 73
Sam ALN 142
Saml. JEF 41
Saml. SCT 110A
Samuel HRD 90
Semual BBN 112
Soloman FLG 71A
Solomon SPN 21A
Stephen HOP 260
Stiles HRD 18
Susan FTE 107
Thomas BRN 24
Thomas HAR 198
Thomas LWS 97A
Thomas GRD 105A
Thos. BBN 116
Thos. SCT 110A
W--? LVG 16
Warren GRD 91A
Wiat MAD 116
Wiley HOP 260
Will BKN 5
Will MAS 64
William HND 9
William OHO 5A
William CBL 20A
William SPN 22A
William GRD 111A
William B. LWS 86A
Wilson H. FTE 80
Winn MAS 60
Winslow LWS 86A
Wm. JEF 46
Wm. FKN 74
Wm. BBN 92
Wm. S. JEF 60
PARKEY, Jno. PUL 35A
PARKINS, Ben CWL 55
Jesse WRN 55A
PARKS, Allen GRD 112A
Amos MAD 130
Andrew MBG 140
Asa ETL 45
Benjamin HAR 144
PARKS, Benjamin HAR 156
Catharine LNC 67
Catharine MAD 174
David LGN 40
David BLT 182
Ebenezer MAD 120
Eliza LNC 49
George BTH 178
James ETL 51
James HRD 74
James GTN 124
James NCH 121A
Jas. SCT 112A
Joab MAS 60
Joab MAS 60
John BTH 194
John DVS 19A
Moses MER 105
Moses WTY 111A
Peter JES 82
Peyton LNC 67
Reuben LNC 67
Reuben WTY 119A
Richard MAD 142
Robt. GNP 167A
Samuel BRN 23
Samuel BRK 283
Solomon OWN 103
Steven MAD 116
Thomas SHE 156
Uriah WTY 121A
William BRN 23
William ETL 50
William GRD 112A
PARKSTON, James FKN 154
PARMAN, Jiles, Jr. KNX 288
PARMENTER, Thophalus HOP 260
PARMER, Edward CHN 41A
James CLK 68
James HRT 165
Jas. BBN 82
Joseph CLK 102
Legrand HRT 165
Mary CHN 43
Rolley CLK 86
Rufus HRT 165
Thomas CLK 68
Wm. BBN 82
PARMERLY, Ephraim LVG 12
PARMLEY, Garner WYN 98A
John, Sr. WYN 96A
Robert WYN 98A
PARMLY, John, Jr. WYN 98A
PARNELL, Thos. BBN 126
PARR, David B. MER 116
Edmund BRK 283
Mary HRY 251
Noah FTE 107
Robert MER 105
Smith BRK 283
William BRK 283
Wm. SHE 111A
PARRAK, James UNN 154
PARRANT, Thos. BRK 281
Wm. BRK 281
PARRENT?, Stephen SHE 123A
PARRET, Richd. GRN 76
PARRETT, William GRN 77
PARRIS, E. CLY 119
Hyrem M. BTH 172
Jno. MAS 78
Moses CLY 119
R. H. ALN 132
Saml. WAS 32A
PARRISH, Benjamin SHE 126A
PARRISH, Daniel WRN 41A
John G. MAD 92
Jonathan FTE 81
Littleberry HRT 165
Thos. BBN 74
PARRIT, Jos./Jas.? RCK 78A
PARROT, Armstead KNX 280
John HAR 218
Tyra CHN 34A
PARROTT, George WAS 75A
John H. WAS 41A
Rhodam WAS 67A
William GTN 128
Wm. WAS 50A
PARRUM, Thos. MAD 158
PARSLEY, Eleanah BBN 70
Thos. BBN 70
Wm. BBN 70
PARSLEY?, Mary CLK 98
PARSON, George MAD 90
James MAD 128
John BRK 281
PARSON?, Joseph HRY 200
PARSONS, Benj. RCK 76A
Benjamin CBL 23A
Clem. WAS 39A
Clemont WAS 34A
Gabriel FLD 25
Harrison RCK 75A
Harrison RCK 75A
Hartwell CLD 145
Henry WAS 34A
Henry WAS 39A
Isaac BBN 78
Isaac BBN 112
Isaiah FLG 72A
James WAS 39A
John PND 20A
Joseph LNC 63
Samuel LGN 41
Samuel HRL 116
Simeon FLD 22
Tandy WAS 27A
Thomas GRN 56
PARSSONS, Thomas SPN 14A
PART-OVE?, William JES 78
PARTEN, William WTY 112A
PARTER, John P. WDF 124A
PARTIN, Benjamin PUL 59A
Benjn. CWL 35
PARTIN?, John HRY 220
PARTLOW, Henry GTN 121
John NSN 206
Saml. HRD 84
Samuel HRD 12
PARTON, Sandford CLK 80
Shelton WTY 115A
PARTON?, William CLK 105
PARVIN, Arthur BBN 108
Henry BBN 110
Thomas BBN 108
PASCHAL, Thos. PUL 36A
PASH?, John NSN 223
PASKILL, Jno. MAS 60
PASLEY, Jesse MNR 197
John MAD 152
Robert MER 106
PASLY, John BRK 285
PASMORE, Isaac WRN 51A
Joseph MTG 231
PASSLETT?, Thompson FLD 7
PASSMORE, Elias MER 115
George MER 115
PASTON?, William CLK 105

PATE, Allen BRK 281
Benet BRK 281
Edward BRK 281
Jane OHO 4A
Jeremiah HRD 60
Jeremiah BRK 285
John HND 6
John HOP 260
John C. BRK 285
Saml. BRK 281
Samuel OHO 6A
William BRK 281
PATEN, Jacob FTE 108
Volantine OHO 3A
PATERN, Mary GSN 148A
PATERSON, Isaac WAS 79A
John GSN 146A
Joseph GSN 147A
PATES, Reuben SCT 105A
PATETEN?, Benjamin CSY 204
Thomas CSY 204
PATHER, Ross MAS 58
PATON, John W. WAS 47A
PATRAN, Wm. GRN 71
PATRIC, Enoc CLK 75
Jane? CLK 86
PATRICK, Alexander WDF 112A
Alexr., Jr. CLY 131
Andrew SHE 154
Charles FTE 90
Elias FLD 7
Elizabeth NSN 211
Hugh FLD 5
James FLD 5
James CLY 119
James WRN 61A
Jeremiah CLY 119
Jeremiah BTH 170
John FLD 5
John MAD 112
John TRG 4A
John WRN 31A
Joseph WDF 95
Lydia NSN 177
Martin (Free) LGN 31
Mears TRG 4A
Robert FLD 5
Robert SHE 164
Robert NSN 209
Rubin ADR 40
Ruebeen FLD 7
Sally CLK 78
Samuel BTH 218
Sarah WRN 61A
Thomas NSN 209
Thomas FLD 1A
Wiley WRN 61A
William FLD 7
William FLD 11
PATRICK?, Benjamin BLT 164
PATTAN, B. W. CHN 46
PATTEN, Alexr. GRN 67
Charles CLK 77
Francis WDF 97
Joseph BBN 130
Joseph, Jr. BBN 130
Robert CHN 31
William HAR 154
William BTL 329
Wm. ALN 128
PATTERAGE, Matthew BRK 281
PATTERN, John GRN 63
PATTERSON, Abraham BKN 5
Alexander HRD 62
Alexander WRN 32A
Allen BLT 178
PATTERSON,
Anderson BKN 19
Andrew HRD 62
Archibald MAD 98
Armstead MER 105
Arthur SHE 168
Benjamin BBN 140
Benjamin BRK 283
Caty BLT 182
Charles GRN 59
Christopher BTH 208
Chs. SCT 117A
Edward BKN 5
Francis WRN 63A
Geo. BKN 20
George BKN 18
George BKN 19
George HRD 88
Henry JEF 34
Henry FKN 162
Isam BRK 281
Israell FLG 44A
J. SHE 124A
J./ I.? GRD 119A
James BKN 10
James BKN 20
James BKN 20
James FTE 78
James FTE 79
James BBN 110
James WRN 64A
James SCT 106A
James MGB 137A
James W. SHE 127A
Jas. CWL 55
Jas. SCT 99A
Jas. SCT 135A
Jesse LVG 4
Jessey MAD 130
John BKN 24
John CWL 39
John ADR 40
John ADR 42
John ADR 42
John JEF 45
John JES 74
John FTE 78
John FTE 99
John FTE 109
John HRT 165
John CSY 208
John BRK 281
John TRG 11A
John LWS 98A
John L. WDF 126A
John S. FTE 64
Jonathan H. CSY 208
Joseph ADR 40
Joseph FTE 99
Joseph FTE 109
Joseph HAR 156
Joseph CBL 8A
Joshua SCT 102A
Judea MER 105
Lewis HRT 165
Lewis C. GRN 59
Mathew SCT 137A
Nathanil BKN 23
Peter HAR 148
Polly MER 105
Rebecca BKN 15
Richard FTE 80
Robert LGN 32
Robt.? CWL 40
Saml. MAD 140
Samuel GRN 59
PATTERSON, Samuel FTE 79
Samuel FTE 96
Samuel FTE 99
Thomas BKN 19
Thomas CBL 21A
Thos. CWL 39
Thos. HRD 62
Thos. MAD 122
William MER 105
Will SCT 121A
Will. KNX 294
Will. SCT 99A
William FTE 75
William JES 75
William FTE 80
William MER 105
William MER 106
William SHE 159
William HAR 210
William TRG 14A
Wm. HRD 32
Wm. ADR 40
Wm. HRD 58
Wm. MAS 78
Wm. WAS 21A
Wm. SHE 12/A
PATTERSON?,
Francis NCH 108A
Rich ADR 40
PATTEY, Jno. FKN 124
PATTIE, Don. /
Dom.? CHN 46
John BKN 26
PATTON, Andw. FLG 76A
Benjamine SPN 23A
Charles CLK 73
Charles BBN 134
Christopher FLD 31
Chs. RCK 79A
D. S. CHN 46
David GTN 129
Felix GTN 131
Florence FLD 44
George CLK 73
Henry FLD 44
James LNC 27
James JES 74
James HAR 216
James GNP 170A
Jas. FLG 36A
Jno. ALN 126
Jno. D. CHN 45
John LGN 31
John FLD 44
John KNX 278
John FLG 36A
John GNP 170A
Mat.?, Sen. CHN 46
Mathew CHN 38
Nancy MTG 299
Polly WTY 122A
R. B. LNC 17
Robt. ALN 130
Samuel FLD 44
Samuel HAR 216
Samuel BRK 281
Thomas BRN 23
Thomas LGN 23
Thos. BRK 281
Thos. FLG 36A
Willm. LNC 31
Wm. CHN 46
Wm. BBN 134
Wm. BBN 146
Wm. FLG 36A
PATTON?, Joseph JES 88

Name	County	Page
PAUGH, Solomon	NCH	108A
PAUL, Danl.	MAS	59
Drusilla	NCH	124A
George S.	BRK	283
Hugh	WDF	101
Jacob	GSN	147A
James	HRD	58
James	WDF	101
James	CBL	22A
Jno.	MAS	70
Jno.	HAR	166
John	CLD	145
John	GSN	147A
Jos.	MAS	73
PAUL?, Saml.	ADR	40
PAULDING?, James	LVG	12
PAULEY, Frances F.	GTN	124
James	HRL	118
Jas.	HRD	68
Jeremiah	NCH	122A
John, Senr.	HRD	68
Stephen	HRD	68
Zachariah	NCH	113A
PAULEY?, John	NCH	115A
PAULK?, Jehu	MNR	207
PAULSEL, Henry	GRN	55
PAUN?, Shadrack	WRN	65A
PAV-Y?, Samuel	CBL	11A
PAVEY, John	GTN	122
PAVY, Daniel	HAR	146
Peter	HAR	138
PAW, Mical	WAS	46A
PAWLEY, John	HRD	58
Wm.	HRD	50
PAWLING, Henry	GRD	82A
Issachar	MER	105
John L.	GRD	103A
Will	GRD	83A
PAXTON, Daniel	NCH	129A
David C.	WDF	123A
Edward L.	SHE	112A
Elizabeth	LNC	81
Ester	FTE	74
Hugh	GRN	67
James	SHE	133A
Jas. A.	MAS	80
Joseph	LNC	13
Josep	BRN	0
Joseph	NCH	129A
Robert	NCH	116A
Thos.	FKN	154
Willm.	LNC	13
PAXTON?, Ja--?	ADR	42
PAYEN, Edmund	WRN	63A
William C.	WRN	62A
PAYNE, Adam	HRD	68
Alf	ALN	132
Ambrose	GRD	99A
Asa	SCT	107A
Bailey	SCT	104A
Bazzel	WAS	61A
Beckey	FTE	58
Bennit D.	JEF	48
Berry	FLG	41A
Chas. F.	TOD	124A
Daniel	MNR	195
Daniel	WAS	77A
Danl.	FLG	51A
Danl. Mc C.?	FTE	59
Dennis	TOD	132
Edmund	BRN	23
Edward	FTE	101
Edward	FTE	112
Elijah	HRD	42
Elijah	KNX	282
Elisha	KNX	282
PAYNE, Fanny M.	HRY	234
Fleming	JES	96
George	HAR	216
George	WAS	58A
Henry	FTE	107
Henry C.	FTE	100
Henry R.	NCH	120A
Hezekiah	MNR	207
Hugh	FTE	99
Hugh B.	BKN	23
Isaac	CHN	41
James	MTG	263
Jas	HRD	70
Jas., Jr.	HRD	32
Jas.	CHN	42A
Jefferson	FTE	96
Jilson	MTG	235
John	BKN	16
John	FTE	79
John	BBN	86
John	GTN	121
John	UNN	147
John	MNR	205
John	MTG	261
John	SCT	105A
John	GRD	109A
John	SHE	119A
John	SHE	122A
John C.? (Erased)	BRK	281
John G.	FLG	39A
John W.	WYN	83A
John W.	WYN	89A
Jonathan	LGN	23
Jonathan	SHE	142A
Joseph	UNN	147
Joseph	KNX	280
Joseph M.	HRY	220
Josiah	TOD	129
Jubal	BRK	285
Lewis	HRD	70
Lurall?	MAS	75
Mary B.	SHE	136A
Merideth	WAS	58A
Nathaniel	FTE	101
Pheleomon	WYN	89A
Phil. G.	HRY	241
Pleasant	MNR	209
Reuben	LNC	67
Richard	WAS	58A
Richard	GNP	170A
Richd.	WAS	61A
Robert	LGN	39
Robert	WAS	86A
Robert D.	LGN	40
Robt.	MAS	77
Rubin	FLG	30A
Sam.	HRY	250
Saml.	FKN	152
Samuel	SPN	20A
Samuel	SHE	122A
Thos.	HRD	60
Thos.	FKN	154
Thos.	TOD	124A
Verpyle	WDF	114A
Warford	FKN	132
Will	MAS	64
William	JES	95
William	MTG	233
William P.	WRN	73A
William R.	WRN	73A
Wm.	FKN	126
Wm.	TOD	127
Wm.	FKN	150
Wm.	CHN	44A
Wm.	SHE	132A
PAYNE, Zadock	FLG	54A
Zenas	HAR	220
PAYNE?, Tully? R.	WRN	74A
PAYNS, John C.	BBN	82
PAYNTZ, N., (& Co..)	MAS	77
Wm. M.	MAS	77
PAYTEN, Elisha	GSN	147A
James	GSN	147A
Watty?	GSN	147A
PAYTON, Benjamin	SHE	171
Charles	HRD	52
Danl.	MAS	59
Gabriel	HRD	20
George	WDF	97
Guffy?	MAD	128
Jardon	WDF	95A
Jno.	MAS	59
John	BKN	18
John	SHE	175
Jonathan	CWL	58
Lockhart	SHE	129A
Ransford	HRY	266
Thomas, Jr.	WDF	97
Thomas, Jr.	WDF	97
Thos.	MAS	59
PEACE, Joseph	KNX	298
Leroy	KNX	300
Simon	GRN	66
PEACH, Eliza	LNC	11
PEACHEY, Benj.	FLG	50A
Benj.	FLG	52A
PEACOCK, Edmd.	JEF	31
Jacob	BLT	156
Wm.	MAD	178
PEACOCK?, Horatio	HOP	260
PEAK, Asa	BNE	30
Daniel	FKN	76
Daniel	BLT	160
Edward	HRD	52
Elizabeth	BNE	30
Elizebeth	WAS	44A
Francis	NSN	191
Hezekiah	OHO	7A
Hezekiah	SCT	102A
Jesse	LNC	11
Jessee	GTN	135
Joel	SCT	128A
John	ADR	42
John	SHE	168
John	OHO	11A
John	SCT	115A
John	SHE	122A
Joseph	SCT	118A
Katharine	SHE	133A
Levy	LNC	13
Mathew	BNE	28
Patk.	HRD	36
Presley	BNE	28
Presley	SCT	126A
Spencer	LNC	63
Thomas	BNE	28
Will	SCT	113A
William	LNC	9
William	BNE	28
Willis	GTN	117
Wm.	HRD	24
PEAKE, John	LGN	47
John	HRY	204
William	HRY	204
PEAL, Hugh	FTE	95
Thomas	FTE	86
PEARCE, Adam	WAS	65A
Arthur	CLD	152
Benjamin	GNP	170A
Burmy?	GRD	116A

PEARCE, Edward SHE 149
  Francis CLD 146
  George SHE 149
  Isaac CLD 146
  Isaac WAS 65A
  Jacob WAS 51A
  James GRN 66
  James A. JEF 40
  Jeremiah PUL 54A
  Jesse PUL 54A
  John FLG 67A
  John WAS 81A
  Lazerth WAS 46A
  Rewben PUL 59A
  Thos. WAS 65A
  William PUL 53A
  Wm. FLG 57A
PEARCEFIELD, Wm. GNP 168A
PEARCH, Jessee FLG 56A
PEARCY, George SHE 172
  Hugh SHE 171
  John SHE 152
  William SHE 171
PEARL, Doran HRD 56
  Edward LNC 69
  Henry LNC 69
  John RCK 78A
  John C. GTN 129
  William LNC 79
  William CLY 124
PEARMAN, Cebert? HRD 58
  John HRD 82
  Randolph HRD 56
  Saml. HRD 44
  Saml. HRD 82
  Thos. HRD 26
  Thos. JEF 26
  Thos. HRD 82
  Wm. HRT 165
PEARPOINT, Charles HRD 24
  Evan SHE 172
  Jere HRD 14
PEARSE, George SPN 5A
PEARSON, ----- DVS 10A
  Allen FTE 106
  Benj. SHE 120A
  Coleman HRY 200
  Edmd. B. FTE 68
  Isaac JEF 42
  Isaac SHE 132A
  Joel CLD 141
  John ALN 108
  John SHE 152
  John SCT 130A
  Joseph ETL 48
  Meshech SHE 174
  Molly FTE 78
  Parker MAD 178
  Patric SHE 128A
  Susanna SHE 138A
  Thos. JEF 35
  Will. SCT 131A
  William CLD 146
  William SHE 162
  William NSN 217
  Wm. B. CHN 33
PEARSONS, Samuel CHN 29
PEART?, James LGN 40
PEARWALL, Clemont WAS 36A
PEAY, George SHE 149
  John JEF 42
  Nicholas SHE 177
PEBLES, John BTH 154
PEBWORTH, Henry MTG 235
  Robert MTG 233
PEBWORTH?, Robert JES 97
PECHEMPANG, Henry BRK 281
PECK, Benjamin MER 105
  Benjn. SCT 117A
  Christian JEF 63
  Danl., Jr. FLG 71A
  Jacob BRN 24
  Jas MAS 64
  Jas. MAS 60
  Jno. MAS 58
  John FTE 65
  Joseph FLD 21
  Saml. MAS 80
  Tho. MAS 67
  Thomas SCT 117A
  Thos. CWL 38
  Thos. SCT 137A
  Will MAS 80
  Zepheniah SCT 117A
PECK?, John SCT 97A
  Peter CBL 22A
PECKS, Danl. FLG 35A
PEDAM?, Graves? ALN 128
PEDCOCK, Horatio HOP 260
PEDEN, John TOD 125
PEDERO, Levy HRD 66
  Phillip HRD 86
PEDIGO, John MNR 197
  John, Jr. BRN 24
  John, Ser. BRN 23
  Joseph BRN 24
  Leah BRN 23
  Mary BRN 23
  Robert MNR 197
  William BRN 23
  Wm., (Jo's Son) BRN 24
PEDIN, James BRN 24
  John BRN 24
  Moses BRN 23
  Thompson BRN 24
  Zilpah BRN 24
PEEBLER, Michael SPN 5A
PEECE?, Wm. FLG 29A
PEED, Gabriel LWS 93A
  Jas MAS 63
  Richd. MAS 53
PEED?, Wm. FLG 29A
PEEK, Jno. HAR 142
  John HAR 164
PEEK?, Abigal HAR 144
  John SCT 97A
  Peter CBL 22A
PEEL, Stephen TRG 12
PEERCE?, Thomas BTH 168
PEEREY, John CSY 226
PEERS, V. MAS 76
PEERY, Elizabeth CLD 155
  James CLD 155
PEERY?, James NCH 129A
PEGG, David FTE 69
  Lewis FTE 69
PEGGS, Joseph HRY 202
PEIRCE, Caleb MAS 52
  James GRD 99A
  Mordicai NCH 122A
  Stephen MAS 68
PEIRCE?, Jacob NCH 122A
PEKENPAW, George HRD 40
PEKINES?, Peter? GRN 79
PELFREY, Alexander FLD 35
  Daniel FLD 35
  William FLD 19
  William FLD 36
PELHAM, Ca-.? MAS 58
PELL, Henry LGN 31
  Nancy LWS 99A
  Richard LWS 91A
PELLY, Benjamin CBL 6A
  James ADR 42
  Ransdale FTE 98
  Soloman FLG 54A
PELMANT?, Jacob WRN 75A
PEMBERTON, Bennet FKN 122
  George CWL 35
  George WYN 99A
  Harry FKN 118
  Jesse CWL 35
  Jesse B. CWL 38
  Jno. LNC 29
  John BRN 23
  John WDF 111A
  Lewis BRN 23
  Reuben, Sr. HRY 228
  Reubon HRY 178
  Richard WYN 98A
  Richd. FKN 146
  Stafford FKN 118
  Stephen FTE 98
  Tho. LNC 31
  Thomas HRY 224
  Thos. ADR 3
  Thos. E. WAS 84A
  William LNC 63
  William SHE 148
  William WTY 125A
  Wm. BRN 23
PEMPERTON, Hennary CSY 212
PEN?, -dw. CWL 32
  Benj. RCK 79A
  Elizabeth BBN 140
  John CWL 32
  R. G. RCK 83A
PENCE, Adam LGN 39
  Adam SHE 164
  Adam SCT 133A
  Catharine LNC 81
  Conrad SHE 154
  Geo. SCT 133A
  George SHE 164
  Jacob HRD 8
  Jacob HRD 92
  Jno. PUL 43A
  John HRD 92
  John SHE 164
  John SCT 101A
  Nancey SCT 94A
  Phillip JEF 66
  Samuel MTG 275
PENDELL?, Richard FTE 62
PENDER, Thomas, Senr. OHO 6A
  Thos. OHO 9A
PENDERGAST, Jno. G. FKN 154
PENDERGRAF / PENDERGRASS?, Edmund CSY 216
PENDERGRAF, Edward NCH 119A
  Thomas CSY 220
PENDERGRAFT, John JEF 41
PENDERGRASS, Abijah PUL 59A
PENDERGRASS?, Edward NCH 119A
PENDERGRAST, Elizabeth JEF 37
  Mary JEF 25
PENDLETON, Able, Jr. CLY 126
  Alexander ETL 40
  Benjamin BTL 329
  Curtis TOD 127
  Edmund CLK 100

PENDLETON, James JEF 41
  James CLY 121
  James T.? NSN 175
  Jno. TOD 127
  John ADR 40
  John ADR 42
  John CHN 45
  John LNC 81
  John CLD 149
  Peter LGN 32
  Rice BTH 220
  Thacker BTH 220
  Thos. FKN 122
  William CLY 128
  William (Crossed Out) WTY 117A
  William WTY 112A
PENDLEY, James GSN 147A
PENEBAKER, John JEF 34
PENECK, Edward WAS 28A
PENELL, E--d.? JEF 56
  Jno. JEF 56
  John JEF 56
  Wm. R. JEF 57
PENELTON, Able CLY 127
PENERLY, Astin BTL 329
  Joseph BTL 329
PENEYBAKER, Samuel MER 105
PENIBAKER, Wm. GSN 148A
PENICK, Agness LNC 67
  Edward WAS 28A
  Jeremiah WRN 29A
  Robert BRN 24
  Will MAS 53
  William BRN 23
  Wm. ADR 40
PENICK?, Jesse GRN 54
PENINGSTON, John JES 83
PENINGTON, Ephraim FKN 78
  Francis JES 69
  Jas. GRD 94A
  Samuel JES 69
PENISTON, John JES 81
  Robert JES 81
PENISTON?, Thomas JES 73
PENIX, John BTH 148
  John BRK 283
  Thomas BRK 285
PENLAND?, Jas. FLG 35A
  Wm. FLG 52A
PENMAN, Jean LNC 55
PENN, Abram CHN 35A
  Benj. FKN 112
  Chs. FKN 112
  David BBN 106
  Eli BBN 102
  Gabriel LNC 27
  Geo. BBN 102
  Geo. TOD 132
  Henry SCT 106A
  James R. GRN 60
  John BBN 106
  Jos. HRY 265
  Joseph BBN 106
  S., Jnr JEF 21
  Saml. BBN 106
  Saml. SCT 117A
  Shedrick, Sr. SCT 96A
  Thomas GRN 70
PENNABAKER, Frederic BLT 194
PENNEL, Barnass CSY 214
  Pearce CSY 218
PENNELL, John WAS 23A
  Pearce B. CSY 214
PENNER, Christophe WRN 40A
PENNER?, John WRN 39A
PENNEY, Abner WDF 108A
  Will. SCT 129A
PENNINGTON, -----? CWL 40
  -----? CWL 40
  -.? HRL 116
  Aaron HRL 116
  Anthony MNR 217
  Daniel MNR 217
  Francis P. CHN 31
  J. HRL 116
  Jas. HRL 116
  Jesse MNR 197
  John SPN 8A
  Micajah HRL 116
  Partrick CSY 214
  Polly FTE 77
  Royal ADR 32
  Simeon MNR 197
  Stewart MNR 197
  W. HRL 116
  Wells WTY 120A
  Wm. GRD 103A
PENNINTON?, Joshua MNR 211
  Joshua MTG 211
PENNY, Jno. FKN 140
  Jno., Sr. FKN 154
  John LGN 30
  William MER 105
PENNY?, Rebecka HAR 136
PENNYBAKER, Peter NSN 182
PENORINTON?, Joshua MNR 211
PENROD, Catherine MBG 137
  George MBG 137
  Jonathan BTL 329
  Solomon LGN 31
  Tobias BTL 329
PENSON, Sarah MER 105
PENTECOST, John GRN 52
PENTER?, Vincent GRD 119A
  Will GRD 110A
PENTICOST, Darby CWL 55
  Jno. CWL 55
PENTLAND?, John FLG 50A
PENTLETON, John ADR 40
PENYBAKER, Wiann GSN 148A
PEOBLES, John GNP 167A
PEOPLES, Abraham HRT 165
  Bird HRT 165
  Hance SCT 106A
  John GSN 148A
  Saml. BBN 94
  William CLK 84
PEPKIN?, Jessee HOP 260
PEPPER, Elijah WDF 109A
  Jesse MAS 52
  Saml. BKN 2
  Saml. MAS 62
  Thomas CHN 31
  Will MAS 69
  Will MAS 73
  Wm. BKN 10
  Wm. H. MAS 64
  Jos. S. FLG 37A
PEPPERS, Danl. HRT 165
  Joseph HRT 165
PEPPLES, Hiram LNC 47
PERAT, James BTH 190
  John BTH 190
PERCALL, Joseph UNN 148
PERCEFULL, Jas. HRD 96
  Saml. HRD 68
  Saml. GSN 147A
PERCIVAL, John S. BNE 46
  Samuel BNE 30
PERCIVAL, Timothy BNE 30
PERDUE, Francis MNR 199
  William WYN 97A
PERDY, Henry WAS 17A
  Stephen WAS 17A
PEREGRINE?, James MTG 243
PERFECT, John BBN 136
PERIGO?, Thomas BLT 180
PERINE, Danl. MAS 57
  Jas. MAS 71
PERKE-I-?, John CWL 35
PERKIN, Jno. HRY 247
  Jos. HRY 243
PERKING, Levi BKN 5
PERKINGS?, Elisabeth HAR 142
PERKINS, -----? CWL 41
  Abram GRN 61
  Abrm. CWL 41
  Anthony MAD 106
  Aquilla HAR 160
  Asa MAS 54
  Barnibas FKN 116
  Benjamin LGN 46
  Benjamin N./ H.? MER 117
  Charler BRN 23
  Charles N. CSY 210
  Christopher CSY 208
  Cit? GRD 87A
  David SHE 152
  David GRD 99A
  Edmond BTH 184
  Edmund GRD 121A
  Edward SHE 161
  Elijah OWN 99
  Elijah BTH 182
  Elisha LNC 19
  Elizabeth SHE 167
  George FLD 21
  Isaac BTH 162
  James OWN 99
  James FTE 100
  James GRD 99A
  James H. BKN 13
  Jeremiah OWN 102
  Jessee GRN 61
  Jno. HAR 150
  Jo. GRD 111A
  John BKN 18
  John GRN 79
  John H. SHE 152
  Joseph BBN 74
  Joseph CLD 145
  Joseph SHE 161
  Joshua LNC 21
  Lewis FLD 13
  Mary GRD 121A
  Moses CWL 37
  Moses SHE 168
  Moses? CWL 41
  Nicholas BKN 15
  Reuben LNC 21
  Reuben LNC 21
  Reuben FTE 76
  Richard FTE 104
  Richard HAR 150
  Richard CLD 159
  Riller HAR 146
  Simon ADR 42
  Stephen FLD 21
  Stephen CWL 39
  Stephen WRN 31A
  Thomas BTH 184
  Thomas GRD 99A
  William FTE 77
  William JES 97

Name	County	Page
PERKINS, William	HAR	142
William	WRN	30A
William	WYN	101A
Wm.	MAD	112
PERKINS?, Peter?	GRN	79
PERMAN, Frathias	KNX	302
Jiles, Sr.	KNX	302
PERNELL, Francis	FLG	77A
John	FLG	74A
PERR?, Benj.	RCK	79A
Queller	GRD	107A
PERREL, George	GSN	148A
Thos.	GSN	147A
PERRIGE?, William	BRK	283
PERRIN, Archibald	LNC	49
Chas.	GRD	103A
James	GRD	110A
Josephus	HAR	176
Lettis	GRD	96A
Robt.	GRD	116A
Ruth	HAR	176
PERRINE, Christopher	FLG	34A
PERRISTON?, Thomas	JES	73
PERROTHTON?, Robert Y.	CHN	38
PERRY, A.	WDF	107A
Abraham	SHE	111A
Anthony	SCT	103A
Arnold	FLD	25
Bartlet	SCT	115A
Bartlett	HRT	165
Ben., Sr.	HRY	249
Benjn.	SCT	106A
Benjn.	SCT	115A
Binj.	HRY	249
Charles W.	BKN	5
Chas.	SCT	103A
Daniel	FTE	76
Daniel	CBL	9A
Daniel	GNP	174A
Danl.	SCT	106A
David	HRT	166
David	CBL	2A
David	CHN	43A
Edwd.	SCT	103A
Elenor	FLG	47A
Elij.	HRY	249
Elija	BTH	162
Elizabeth	SHE	176
George	ADR	40
George	GTN	129
George	CBL	2A
Henry	GTN	119
Henry	SCT	123A
James	LGN	23
James	LGN	29
James	GTN	127
James	WAS	58A
James?	CWL	32
Jas.	SCT	103A
Jas.	SCT	123A
Jno. T.	HRY	256
John	FLD	8
John	LGN	24
John	JES	72
John	JES	95
John	CBL	19A
John	SHE	111A
Jos.	TOD	128
Jos.	HRY	249
Joseph	BBN	80
Joseph	CBL	13A
Joseph B.	SCT	137A
Larkin	SCT	115A
Lewis	WDF	93A
PERRY, Minor	GTN	117
Minor	GTN	120
Moses	SHE	111A
Nancy	CHN	45
Nathan	CHN	43A
Obediah	GRN	77
Peter	CHN	43A
Pierce	SCT	107A
Randolph	SHE	162
Richard	BRN	24
Robbert	CBL	9A
Robert	WDF	98A
Roderick	WDF	107A
S.	WDF	107A
Samuel	LGN	46
Samuel	CBL	2A
Simeon	GTN	127
Tandy	CWL	37
Tandy K.	HND	9
Thomas	FLD	9
Thomas	LGN	29
Thomas	GRN	76
Thos.	MAS	72
Wm.	HRT	166
Wm.	HRY	255
Wm.	SHE	111A
PERRY?, -----?	GRN	80
Rebecka	HAR	136
PERRYMAN, Alxr.	ADR	64
Peter	CLD	147
Wm., Jr.	ADR	62
Wm., Sen.	ADR	64
PERVIS, John	BTH	212
John	FLG	44A
Thomas	BTH	210
Wm.	FLG	44A
PETER, (Free)	CLD	162
John	WAS	20A
Richard	SPN	16A
William	SPN	16A
Wm.	WAS	82A
PETERS, Christian	MBG	138A
David	LWS	88A
Elizebeth	WDF	96
Isaac	LWS	89A
James	WDF	94A
Jessi	WAS	83A
John	WDF	95
Lewis	WDF	94A
Nancy	WDF	94A
Peter	UNN	148
Samuel	LGN	28
William	WDF	96
Wm.	TOD	132
PETERS?, James	HRY	220
Lucy W.	TOD	134
PETERSON, Garrot	WAS	76A
Peter	MER	105
W. F. & Co.?	JEF	27
Wm. F., & Co.?	JEF	20
PETERSON?, Henry	WAS	55A
PETICORD, Caleb	BBN	86
Nathaniel	CLK	81
PETIT, Benjamin	GNP	173A
Daniel	KNX	288
George?	CWL	44
James	CBL	22A
Samuel, Jr.?	GNP	173A
Samuel	GNP	173A
PETITT?, Thomas	WAS	18A
PETRE, Alexander	WRN	57A
Hazzle	TOD	131A
John	WRN	57A
PETTAGE?, Esrael	CSY	212
PETTAGREW, James	CSY	222
PETTE--T?, Vincent	ADR	40
PETTENT?, Vincent	ADR	40
PETTET, Simon	SHE	112A
Thomas	SHE	112A
PETTETT, Benjamin	FTE	67
Betsey	SCT	122A
Elizabeth	SCT	98A
Hanah	LNC	15
PETTEY, Jas.	SCT	97A
Jessee	CBL	12A
PETTICORD, -----?	DVS	4A
E.	MAS	64
Jno.	MAS	64
M., Mrs.?	MAS	65
Wm.? M.	MAS	65
PETTIFORD, Fanny	MAD	146
PETTIT, Amos	PND	18A
Francis	CLD	167
George	GTN	127
James	GTN	127
James	PND	23A
Rebecca	FTE	100
Wm.	JEF	65
PETTITT, Nathaniel	FTE	95
Obadiah	SCT	121A
Thomas	MTG	251
PETTUS?, Lucy W.	TOD	134
PETTY, Dice	CHN	32
Edmond	FLG	56A
Ezekiel	GTN	121
Francis	ETL	41
Garton	CLD	163
Geo. B.	TOD	125
Gorten	GSN	146A
Harbin	MER	105
Isaac	FLD	37
Isham	GSN	147A
Jno.	FKN	140
Joseph	WRN	44A
Larkin	HOP	260
Ralph	BRN	24
Rodham	FKN	140
Saml. B.	WAS	47A
Theophilus	BTL	329
Thomas	CLK	68
Thophhilus, Jr.	BTL	329
William	BTL	329
Wm.	FKN	78
Wm.	FKN	92
Zacariah	LNC	57
PEU, Queller	GRD	105A
PEU?, -dw.	CWL	32
Elizabeth	BBN	140
John	CWL	32
PEUGH, Mary	OHO	3A
PEULAND?, Jas.	FLG	35A
PEUS, Joel	BNE	30
PEVELER, Siby	BTH	214
PEVEON?, Harvey	WRN	65A
PEVEOU?, Harvey	WRN	65A
PEVLER, Christopher	MER	105
Daniel	BTH	214
David	MER	105
Joseph	MER	105
PEVYHOUSE, John	WYN	94A
Joseph	WYN	98A
PEW, Andrew	WYN	82A
George	FTE	109
Richard	SHE	115A
Thos.	JEF	62
PEYDON, Adam	CBL	8A
Lucinda	CBL	8A
PEYSON?, Craven	BLT	172
PEYTON, Abner D.	FKN	80
Augusta	CSY	216
Benj.	FKN	110

PEYTON, Benjamin MER 105
Bewford CSY 212
Charles BBN 122
Chs. FKN 112
Daniel FLD 9
Elizabeth BRN 23
Elizabeth CSY 214
Hennery CSY 214
James BBN 134
James NCH 107A
Jessey MAD 104
John BBN 126
Joseph BBN 60
Joseph WDF 117A
Letty FKN 112
Macajah JEF 42
Mary BLT 186
Randolph LNC 31
Robbert CBL 3A
Saml. NCH 118A
Samuel NCH 107A
Stephen NCH 117A
Stephen NCH 127A
Thomas NCH 120A
Val. BBN 120
Valentine LNC 31
Vinston CSY 216
William NCH 105
William NCH 107A
William NCH 108A
Wm. BBN 130
Yelberton, Jr. MAD 172
Yelberton, Sr. MAD 162
PEYTON?, Craven BLT 172
PFESTER, John MAD 180
PHAR, Samuel TRG 5
PHARIS, John BLT 162
Saml. JEF 37
PHELIX?, John OHO 10A
PHELP, Garret MAD 114
PHELPS, -eding? CWL 35
Ambrose PUL 63A
Anson GTN 130
Anthony HRD 64
Avington JEF 57
Betsey LGN 35
David LGN 34
Edwin BLT 162
Edwin T.? BLT 180
Freeman PUL 48A
Guy? BLT 154
Harris JEF 58
James MBG 139A
Jno. PUL 43A
John BTL 327
John WRN 38A
John H. CWL 44
Joseph MAD 94
Julian BTL 329
Larkin PUL 39A
Micajah LVG 3
Nicholas BTL 329
Obed. PUL 39A
Obediah PUL 48A
Philip MAD 104
Richard LGN 34
Robt. M. BBN 64
Samuel BTL 329
Sha? ADR 40
Smith JEF 57
Thos. MAD 150
Tibitha? MAD 174
William LGN 35
William MER 117
William BTL 329
William BTL 329
PHELPS, Wm.? W. CWL 36
Zachariah FLG 46A
PHERIGO, James MER 106
John MER 106
William MER 115
PHIGLEY, -----? DVS 6A
PHILBERT, Luke CLK 85
Wharton B. CLK 85
PHILES?, Uriah HAR 142
PHILIBER, Wm. GNP 177A
PHILIP, Nathan CLK 76
PHILIPS/ PHILEPS?, Anthony MAD 90
PHILIPS, Aaron MER 105
Andrew UNN 151
Ben GSN 148A
Benjamine SPN 4A
Brannock MTG 287
Charles BNE 30
Charles OHO 10A
Dabner FKN 136
Daniel FLD 20
David JES 71
Edward GSN 147A
Elizabeth JES 90
Ellen HAR 136
George MER 105
George MER 106
Hannah JES 74
Harrison LNC 37
Henry BLT 172
Jacob MER 105
Jacob FKN 144
James LNC 77
James MER 105
James MAD 112
James NSN 179
James MTG 289
James GSN 147A
Jno. LVG 7
Jno. FKN 128
Jno. FKN 144
Joel FKN 64
John BRN 23
John FLD 23
John CHN 36
John MER 105
John MTG 287
John C. HRD 64
Joseph JES 75
Leonard NCH 105
Leroy? LVG 6
Lewis PND 27A
Marice? WRN 57A
Mark LVG 7
Martha HAR 184
Michael LNC 75
Moses SPN 4A
Nicholas MER 105
Nimrod CLK 89
Peggy MTG 265
Philemon MTG 287
Philip MER 105
Robert LVG 12
Robert B. CHN 36
Robins HAR 148
Sally MER 106
Samuel MTG 245
Solomon OHO 10A
Tafley? FLD 29
Thomas CLK 76
Thomas MTG 235
Thos. ADR 40
Thos. MAD 162
Thos. HRY 253
Thos. GSN 146A
PHILIPS, Wade PUL 42A
Will MER 106
Will. LVG 3
William MTG 229
William MTG 255
Wm. J. FKN 54
Wm. S. MAD 90
Zachariah FLD 34
PHILLEY, Abiah CWL 55
Cyrus CWL 55
Miles CWL 55
PHILLIP, Ricd. JEF 47
PHILLIPS, Aaron CLY 116
Amos SCT 110A
Benj. WAS 45A
Benj. WAS 55A
Benjamin M. BBN 66
Charles CSY 218
Chiles FLG 75A
Cornelius WYN 80A
Danl. MAS 54
Danl. MAS 60
Danl. MAS 61
Davey WAS 37A
David H. WRN 34A
Edwd. MAS 61
Francis GRN 68
Gabrial MAS 61
Geo. MAS 62
George CLY 129
George MNR 211
George CSY 228
George WAS 17A
George CBL 21A
George WAS 51A
Harry B. LWS 99A
Hennery CSY 224
Isaac WAS 45A
Isaac GRD 104A
Jacob MBG 139
James WDF 100
James CSY 224
Jas. SCT 94A
Jesse WAS 69A
Jno. MAS 54
John HRD 90
John CLY 130
John CSY 228
John, Junr. CLD 161
John, Senr. CLD 152
John WAS 27A
John WAS 45A
John GRD 112A
John SHE 116A
Jos. MAS 58
Joseph M. FTE 67
Joshua JEF 65
Junkin JEF 38
Lott GRN 68
Matamus HRD 92
Moses MAS 60
Moses MAS 61
Phill. MAS 58
Richard WAS 77A
Sally GRN 64
Sam WAS 44A
Saml. HRD 36
Saml. JEF 60
Samuel GRN 59
Sarah GRN 67
Thomas CLY 129
Thos. JEF 38
Thos. WAS 45A
Thos. WAS 45A
Thos. TOD 127A
Thos. S. LVG 8

Name	County	Page
PHILLIPS, W. B.	MAS	76
William	GRN	68
William	GRN	74
William	CSY	206
William	WAS	17A
Wm.	JEF	68
Wm.	BBN	102
Wm.	BBN	138
Wm.	WAS	27A
Wm.	WAS	45A
Wm. T.	WAS	77A
PHILPOT, John	CLD	148
Mary An	GRN	72
Samuel	BRK	283
Thos.	CLY	116
William	GRN	71
William	GRN	72
Zachariah	CLD	160
Zachariah, Senr.	CLD	143
PHILPOTT, Jose	MNR	201
PHIMISTER, Chas.	HRY	252
PHINGO?, Katharine	MER	105
PHIPPEN, Wm.	PUL	38A
PHIPPS, Amos	TOD	134
John	LGN	25
Joshua	GRN	55
Joshua	WYN	80A
Rolly	JEF	41
PHIPS, Aaron	JEF	31
Jeremiah	JEF	31
Peter	WYN	95A
Thomas	OHO	8A
William	OHO	9A
PHIRTER, Conrod	MAS	78
PHITCHPATK., Hugh	SCT	108A
PHULKINSON, Philip	OHO	4A
PIATT, Jacob	BNE	30
Robert	BNE	28
PICHFORD?, Daniel	ALN	142
Wm.	ALN	142
PICK?, Abigal	HAR	144
PICKELHIMER, Isaac	RCK	75A
PICKELHIMORE, John	BTH	214
PICKENS, Cornelius	CLD	150
Joseph	CLD	150
Thomas	CLD	150
PICKERAL, Wm.	FLG	42A
PICKERALL, Abel	SHE	117A
PICKERELL, David	HRD	80
Henry	FLG	55A
John	BKN	6
Saml.	HRD	80
Wm.	HRD	80
PICKERET, John	GRN	77
PICKERING, Betsy	LVG	11
Rob	JEF	22
William	LVG	10
PICKERRIN, Wm.	WAS	59A
PICKET, Hetty	WAS	76A
John	BRN	24
William	BRN	24
PICKETT, Beall	CBL	5A
Cassiah	HAR	214
George	FTE	82
George	HAR	216
Jas.	JEF	25
Jas.	MAS	79
Jeremiah	FTE	82
Jno.	MAS	53
John	FTE	103
John	FTE	103
John	FTE	103
Phillip	CBL	5A
Rebeca	JEF	43
Thomas	CLK	103
William	FTE	83
PICKETT, William	CBL	5A
Willis M.	DVS	19A
Wm.	JEF	26
Wm.	MAS	66
PICKFORD?, (See Pichford?)	ALN	142
PICKINGS, Nancy	LVG	6
Will.	LVG	5
PICKIRING, Malicai	CWL	35
PICKLEHIMER, H.	GRD	96A
PICKLESIMER?, Abraham	FLD	22
PICKLIHIMER, Jacob	GRD	96A
PICKRALL?, Orange	MAS	61
PICKRELL, David	BKN	15
Richd.	MAS	52
PICREE, William	GRT	143
PIERC, Waller/ Walter?	SHE	130A
PIERCALL, John	CLK	67
PIERCE, Absalom	SHE	140A
Alijih?	WDF	108A
Ben	GSN	148A
Charles	BTH	170
Eligah	CBL	16A
Ephran	ADR	3
G.	HRY	241
G. Wm.	GSN	147A
James	ADR	62
James	SHE	141A
Jas.	HRY	241
Joel	ADR	42
John	BRN	24
John	JEF	51
John	HRT	165
John	BLT	188
John	BRK	283
John	TRG	11A
Joseph	FKN	90
Margaret	BLT	184
Robert	OWN	103
Sarah	WDF	121A
Wm.	ADR	42
Wm.	BBN	102
Wm.	GSN	148A
PIERCE?, Jessee	CLK	88
PIERCEALL, Samuel	CLK	90
PIERCEY, James	WYN	94A
Wiley	WYN	101A
William	WYN	94A
PIERCIN, Robbert	CBL	6A
PIERCY, Jacob	BBN	68
PIERSON, Benjn.	ADC	68
Charles	KNX	304
George	HAR	204
John	UNN	152
Moses	NSN	216
Nat	ADC	68
Shadrac	BBN	76
Shedrick	BBN	72
Wm.	ADR	42
PIG, Will	SCT	120A
PIGG, Anderson	CLK	73
James	FLD	23
John	SHE	134A
Lewis	CSY	204
Mourning	HAR	170
Paul	CLY	125
William	CLY	125
William	CSY	224
PIGGMON, Obadiah	FLD	45
PIGMAN, John	OHO	5A
PIKE, Henry	SHE	119A
Hibert	ETL	41
James M.	FTE	59
John	CSY	210
PIKE, John	WAS	45A
Robert	ETL	41
Samuel	MTG	291
Thos.	ADR	42
William	ETL	41
Wm.	ADR	40
PIKE?, Job H.	FTE	59
PILCHARD, Thomas	BKN	15
PILCHER, Benja.	JEF	50
Benjamin	FTE	103
Edward	FTE	68
Fielding	FTE	68
Frederick	FTE	109
James	FTE	100
Lewis	FTE	102
Nancy	FTE	103
Richd.	JEF	22
William	FTE	103
Zachaus	SHE	164
PILCHER?, Louis	FTE	79
PILCHERS, John	FTE	102
PILE, Benj.	WAS	76A
Francis	BRK	283
Henry	BRK	283
Jas.	CHN	46
Richard	WAS	76A
Saml.	WAS	80A
Thomas	BRK	283
Thos. C.	ADR	40
Wm.	WAS	80A
PILE?, John	ADR	40
Wm.	ADR	40
PILES, ----uel?	DVS	11A
Burdet	CLD	167
Con.?	HRY	252
Leonard	MAS	73
William	GTN	124
PILKENNTON, Larken	BLT	154
PILKINGTON, Samuel	FTE	69
PILL?, John	ADR	40
Thos. C.	ADR	40
Wm.	ADR	40
PILMAN, Sarah	WRN	38A
PINCEL?, Mary	NSN	198
PINCKLEY, Michael	BRN	23
PINDLE, Jacob	HRD	26
Thos. H.	FKN	82
PINER, John	JEF	56
Judith	JEF	56
Presley	BNE	30
Thomas	BNE	30
Wm.	JEF	56
PINES, Larkin	BNE	46
Permelia	SCT	111A
PING, Bowlin	PUL	37A
Elizabeth	PUL	49A
Jno., Jr.	PUL	44A
Robt.	PUL	39A
Walker	PUL	40A
Wm., Sr.	PUL	44A
Wm.	PUL	37A
PING?, Jno., Junr.	PUL	35A
PINGSTON, Barwell	JES	87
PINICH?, William	GRN	69
PINKARD, Betsey	FTE	90
Stanfield T.?	BKN	13
PINKERTON, David	KNX	298
PINKHAM, David	JEF	27
PINKLEY, John	MNR	209
PINKSTON, -----?	DVS	11A
----ing?	DVS	11A
---ack?	DVS	14A
---iel?	DVS	11A
---us?	DVS	14A
--chariah?	DVS	11A
--wis?	DVS	14A

Name	County	Page
PINKSTON, Bazle	MAD	90
Bazle	MAD	160
Elias	MAD	156
Isham	ETL	48
John	MAD	96
John	MAD	168
John	DVS	18A
Moses	WYN	79A
Noah	MAD	108
Obadiah	DVS	13A
Saml.	MAD	96
Wiat?	MAD	108
PINSON, Aaron	FLD	34
Aaron	ALN	124
Allen	FLD	34
Henry	FLD	34
Jared	FLD	34
John	FLD	34
Lott M.	ALN	124
Thomas	FLD	34
William	FLD	34
Zepheniah	ALN	124
PINSTON, Peter	SPN	12A
PINTER, James	GRD	122A
Jon	ADR	40
Thos., Jr.	ADR	40
Thos., Sen.	ADR	40
PINTER?, Will	GRD	110A
PINTHUS, Arthur	BNE	30
PINTS, John	BNE	30
Luke	BNE	30
PIPER, Asa	ALN	138
Benjamin	BRN	24
James	NCH	108A
John	BRN	24
John, Jr.	BRN	24
John	LWS	93A
Marshall	BRN	24
Nancy	BBN	96
Nathaniel	SPN	7A
Robert	BRN	24
Robert	NCH	109A
Saml.	NCH	123A
Thomas	LGN	37
William	BRN	24
William	MER	105
PIPES, John	MER	105
John	MTG	251
Nathaniel	MER	105
Pleasant	SPN	3A
PIPKIN?, Jessee	HOP	260
PIPPIN, Benja.	LVG	4
Benjamin	LGN	34
Joseple?	ALN	136
Will.	LVG	9
PIRSEFIELD, Henry	HRL	116
John	HRL	118
Joseph	HRL	116
Mount?	HRL	116
Peter	HRL	116
PITCHER, Alexander	CLK	64
Henrietta	ETL	54
Jonathan	WDF	101
Thomas	BNE	30
William	ETL	54
PITCHFORD, Daniel	ALN	142
Eli	ALN	142
PITCHFORD?, Auguston	ALN	106
PITCOCK, Stephen	MNR	191
PITENGER, Abraham	SHE	134A
Elizabeth	SHE	134A
PITLY, Wm.	HRY	241
PITMAN, Ambrose	WDF	98A
Geo.	PUL	37A
Hardy	MBG	142
PITMAN, James	MBG	142
James	WYN	96A
Jessee	ETL	54
Jno.	HRY	267
John	BTL	329
Joseph	NSN	206
Lot	KNX	280
Lydda	KNX	314
Michael	ETL	42
Mitchell	WRN	28A
Robert	BTH	218
Samuel	NSN	204
Thomas	MER	105
Thos.	PUL	38A
PITMON, Moses	PUL	38A
PITT, Archibald	NSN	179
Benjamin	MBG	138
David	TRG	5A
Joseph	MBG	138
Legrand	NCH	117A
William	TRG	5
PITTES, Jos.	GRD	97A
PITTIS, Jno.	CHN	38
PITTMAN, Asa	ADC	68
Holland	KNX	314
James	SHE	150
Lewis	KNX	314
Wmson.	ADC	68
PITTS, Isaac	LWS	94A
John	LGN	39
John	FLG	53A
Joseph	LWS	88A
Sally	FKN	124
Will	FLG	49A
William	LWS	99A
Wm.	FLG	59A
Younger	SCT	108A
PITZER, Fred.	CHN	32A
Wm.	CHN	31
PLAIN, David	MBG	139
John	MBG	136
PLAINS, George	FTE	110
PLAISTERS, Isaac	LGN	37
PLANK, Andrew, Sr.	FLG	74A
Andrew	FLG	70A
Andrew	FLG	74A
Micale	FLG	74A
Mikael	FLG	68A
PLASTERS, John	JEF	38
PLATT, Jno.	HAR	142
Samuel	WAS	18A
PLAYLE, Richard	HOP	260
Thomas	SHE	159
PLEAK, Fielding	MTG	239
George	MTG	239
Matthias	MTG	249
PLEAKSTALVER?, John	MTG	229
PLEASANT, Titus	MAD	176
PLEASANTS, Benjamin F.	MER	105
Edward	LNC	71
Wm. G.	ADR	42
PLEU?, Albert	WAS	48A
George	WAS	48A
PLOUGH, Daniel	FKN	142
James	WDF	120A
PLOWMAN, Thomas	ETL	43
PLUCK?, Mary	BKN	8
PLUCKET, Reubin	FTE	102
PLUGH, Elias	NCH	113A
PLUMB, John	FLG	68A
PLUMBLY, David	HAR	188
PLUMER, Abija	WAS	32A
Jno.	JEF	65
John	GNP	172A
PLUMER, Joseph	SPN	18A
Sarah	BTH	170
Will	SCT	120A
PLUMMER, Abram	FLG	31A
Benj.	FLG	28A
Benj.	FLG	51A
Benj.	FLG	52A
Caleb	OHO	11A
Geo.	FLG	52A
Isaiah	FLG	56A
Joseph	OHO	3A
Reason	FLG	50A
Reubin	FLG	49A
Saml.	FLG	49A
Saml.	FLG	53A
Samuel	ETL	54
Sarah	FLG	50A
Wm.	FLG	31A
PLUNKET, William	BNE	30
William, Jr.	BNE	30
PLUNKETT, Jesse	SHE	152
Nancy	HAR	146
PLYMPTON, Charles	FTE	60
PO-LE?, Jiehonias P.	TRG	13A
POAG, Allen	GNP	177A
George, Jr.	GNP	177A
George, Ser.	GNP	177A
James	GNP	177A
James A.	GNP	177A
John	GNP	166A
Mary	GNP	177A
Thomas	GNP	166A
Thomas	GNP	177A
William	FTE	103
POAGE, John	HAR	208
John M.	SHE	176
POAGUE, Joseph	MBG	135
Robert	CLD	152
POARLE, Townsen	BKN	11
POCK?, Adam	HAR	168
Jno.	HAR	162
Philip	HAR	162
POCTER, William	GTN	124
POE, Benjamin	MNR	199
Britten	MAS	66
Edmund	NCH	109A
Edmund	NCH	112A
Edward	FKN	94
Jno.	MAS	70
Jno.	FKN	86
John	JEF	24
Johnson	MNR	199
Patrick	MAS	66
Tho.	MAS	66
Thomas	TOD	134
Virgil	FKN	90
POE?, William	MNR	199
POFF/ POFT?, Wm.	FKN	104
POFF, George	HAR	216
POGUE, Edwin	MAS	74
Henry	FTE	102
Jno.	MAS	74
John	KNX	282
Joseph	SCT	136A
Robt.	MAS	74
Sally	FTE	97
Thomas	FTE	97
POHON, William	BLT	168
POINDEXTER, David	CLK	75
James	HAR	132
John	LGN	25
John	FTE	84
John	HOP	260
Pet.	HRY	259
William	FTE	61

Name	County	Page
POINTER, Cornelius	CLD	153
Edmund	BRN	24
James	BRN	23
James	HRT	166
Jane	HND	13
John	GRN	68
John	HRT	166
Joseph	GRN	68
Saml.	FLG	68A
William, Jr.	BRN	23
Wm.	BRN	23
Wm.	PUL	46A
POINTEXTER, Archa.	MNR	213
James	MNR	211
POINTS, Arthur	SCT	96A
Edward	GRT	141
John	CBL	18A
Joseph	FTE	73
Nathl.	GRT	142
William	GRT	141
POLAND, Jas.	HRD	40
POLER, Mary	WAS	68A
POLES?, Winney	GRD	121A
POLICK, Garvin	LNC	67
POLK, Daniel	SHE	133A
Peggy	SCT	96A
POLKE, Edmund	NSN	201
James	NSN	201
POLLACK, Presly	CHN	40
POLLAND, Jno.	MAS	60
John	MER	105
Robt	TOD	124A
POLLARD, Absalom	GRD	96A
Ama?	SHE	175
Benjamin R.	SHE	172
Benjn.	MAS	61
Braxton	PND	19A
Edmond	HAR	146
Elij.	HRY	255
Elijah	SHE	162
Elizabeth	FTE	60
Green	GRD	96A
Henry	SHE	151
Henry	SHE	175
James	WRN	52A
Jesse	WRN	52A
John	HAR	178
John	WAS	57A
John	GRD	82A
Pleasant	WRN	48A
Rachel	SHE	175
Roger B.	SHE	162
Saml.	MAS	61
Thomas	MBG	143
Thomas	HAR	178
William	JES	84
Wm. C.	FKN	154
POLLEN, Charlote	FTE	60
POLLETT, Betsy	FLG	27A
David	LWS	91A
Geo.	FLG	23A
James B	HND	4
Josiah	FLG	24A
Levan	FLG	24A
POLLEY, David	FLD	25
Edward	FLD	4
Henry	FLD	3
James	SHE	123A
John	SHE	122A
Joseph	JEF	36
Merret	SHE	123A
Peter	SHE	135A
Sanford	SHE	132A
POLLOCK, Elizabeth	FTE	105
Geo.	TOD	124A
Guy	HRY	192
POLLOCK, Hiram	HRY	192
James	NCH	112A
Jas.	MAS	54
Jno.	HAR	160
John	FTE	112
John	HRY	192
Jos.	MAS	54
William	FTE	109
Wm.	BKN	15
Zephaniah	BKN	19
POLLS, Thomas	CLK	64
POLLY, James D.	BNE	30
Jessee	BNE	30
John	BNE	30
John	BRK	283
John	WTY	120A
Joseph	BRK	283
Perter	BRK	283
Willis	BNE	30
POLLY?, David	LWS	92A
John	ADR	42
Wm. M.	ADR	42
POLSGROVE, Geo	FKN	112
POMPEY, (Free Man)	BBN	90
POMROY, Frank	JEF	66
Geo. A. K.	JEF	48
George	SHE	140A
Isaac	SHE	142A
Jas.	JEF	48
POMTENNY?, Nancy	LGN	31
POND, Caty	GRD	116A
Joseph R.	MAD	170
PONDER, Nathl.?	CWL	35
PONDEXTER, Peter	JES	81
Robt.	FKN	134
Thomas H.	JES	87
Wm.	FKN	92
PONELL?, Onor?	CBL	5A
Sarah	CBL	23A
POOL, Abraham	CLD	149
Bird P.	BRK	281
Buener? P.	BRK	281
David	NSN	180
David	NSN	221
Henry	CHN	34
Jno.	MAS	65
Jno.	MAS	67
John	BRN	23
John	CLK	90
John	NSN	185
John	WRN	59A
Mary	UNN	154
Mathias	BKN	26
Nathaniel	BBN	62
Philip	CLK	106
R., Mrs.?	MAS	67
Richard	HND	9A
Robert P.	BRK	281
Samuel	CBL	16A
Stephen P.	BRK	281
Thomas	LWS	94A
William	SPN	5A
William B.	UNN	149
Wm.? R.	MAS	67
POOLAM, Jno.	ALN	126
Wm.	ALN	130
POOLE, Anthony	FTE	94
Joseph R. G.	UNN	147
Seth P.	TRG	13A
POOLE?, Jiehonias P.	TRG	13A
POOLEY, Jno.	ALN	128
POOR, Andrew	GNP	175A
Ann	GRN	73
Arthur	GRN	64
David	CBL	5A
POOR, Drewry W.	LGN	29
Jesse	WDF	101A
John	FTE	86
Judith	LGN	33
Robert	LGN	33
Susannah	WDF	101A
William	LGN	29
William	CLK	74
POORE, James	LGN	47
Samuel	BTH	216
POPE, Alemander	GRD	104A
Alexr.	JEF	23
Benjamin	BLT	154
Elijah	ALN	140
Geo. F.	BLT	199
George F.	BLT	174
George H.	LNC	65
Henry	WAS	65A
Humphry	BTL	329
Jacob	HAR	194
Jacob	GNP	172A
James	ALN	104
Jane / Jam?	ALN	112
John	ADR	40
John	JEF	63
John	FTE	64
John	HAR	190
John	WAS	79A
Joseph O.	WAS	52A
Michael	GTN	130
Nathan	ALN	112
Peter	HAR	192
Polly	LNC	45
Reuben	SHE	165
Tho., Sr.	GRD	115A
Thomas	LNC	37
Thos.	KNX	288
William	GRD	87A
Wm., Jr.	JEF	45
Worden	JEF	27
POPEJOY, Edward	KNX	304
Tarents	KNX	304
Will.	KNX	304
POPERWELL?, -----?	ADR	42
Eliz.	ADR	42
POPES, Hackey	WDF	101A
POPHAM, James	HRD	40
James	FKN	88
John	HRD	40
Thos.	HRD	40
Thos., Jr.	HRD	40
POPHAM?, Humfrey	WAS	48A
Jacob	WAS	48A
Job	HRD	8
Wm.	WAS	48A
POPLATE?, Thomson	GNP	168A
POPNWELL?, -----?	ADR	42
Eliz.	ADR	42
POPTALE / POPTATE?, Thomson	GNP	168A
PORCH, Ezekiel A.	KNX	296
Frederick	LNC	25
William	WTY	127A
PORCH?, Henry	WTY	114A
PORE, William	GRD	105A
PORE?, Moses	BTH	210
William	BTH	210
PORR?, Daniel	FTE	110
PORTEE, Isaac	LGN	33
James	LGN	29
Wilson	LGN	29
PORTER, A. B.	BTH	186
Alfred	SHE	118A
Andrew	HAR	214
Andrew	CBL	8A

PORTER, Andrew PND 15A
Benjamin BTL 329
Benjamin, Sen. BTL 329
Catherine BBN 108
Charles LVG 5
Charles B. SHE 120A
Charles C. MAD 180
David ALN 134
David SHE 163
David SPN 20A
Denton S. ALN 124
Edward ALN 124
Edward GSN 147A
Edwin GRD 95A
Eli HRY 253
Elias GSN 147A
Elias GSN 148A
Elias GSN 148A
Elijah BTL 329
Ep. HRY 266
Ephraim BNE 46
Ephram WDF 97A
Francis, Jr. BTL 313
Francis, Jr. BTL 329
Francis, Sen. BTL 329
George BNE 30
Hannah FKN 54
Harrison LNC 67
Henry MAD 116
Henry MAD 136
Hugh BTH 186
Hugh BTL 329
Ira JEF 26
Isaac CSY 216
James BNE 30
James FLD 39
James JEF 52
James JES 73
James FKN 78
James BBN 144
James SHE 150
James SHE 154
James SHE 163
James NSN 205
Jas. FLG 64A
Jeremiah GTN 125
Jno. MAS 64
Jno. MAS 80
John LVG 11
John FLD 33
John BTL 327
John PND 20A
John WRN 36A
John WRN 36A
John GSN 147A
John R. MTG 251
Jos. FLG 67A
Joseph FLD 39
Joseph PUL 52A
Josiah BLT 182
Lewellen FTE 89
Llewellyn BBN 144
Mary MAD 96
Mary NSN 195
Mary TOD 131A
Nancy GSN 148A
Nathaniel P. GTN 125
Nicholas JEF 33
Norman FTE 59
Oliver BTL 329
Oliver C. BTL 329
Philip SHE 123A
Polley FLD 39
Polly KNX 312
Richard NSN 210
Robert PND 17A
PORTER, Roley S. FLG 57A
Ruth GNP 168A
Sam TOD 127A
Samuel LVG 11
Samuel FLD 39
Samuel SHE 167
Samuel CSY 216
Samuel WDF 97A
Samule, Jr. CSY 216
Sarah HAR 158
Seth LWS 92A
Silas LVG 10
Stanfield HAR 196
Thomas LVG 2
Thomas BNE 30
Thomas BTH 186
Thomas BTL 329
Thomas GNP 168A
Thomas D. MNR 193
Thos. PND 16A
Tomzen GSN 147A
Walter CBL 2A
Watson HAR 190
Westley GRT 146
Will MAS 59
Will. SCT 100A
William LVG 16
William BNE 30
William FLD 36
William SHE 150
William BTL 329
William, Jr. BTL 313
William, Sen. BTL 329
Wm. CHN 44
Wm. FKN 76
Wm. FKN 78
Wm. TOD 131A
Wm. GSN 147A
Wm. W. PND 15A
Zekiel LVG 11
PORTERFIELD, J. TOD 132
Jno. PUL 47A
PORTEUS, John BNE 50
PORTIN?, John HRY 220
PORTLOCK, John ADR 42
PORTUS, William SPN 18A
PORTWOOD, John MAD 114
Saml. MAD 160
Saml. MAD 160
Thos. MAD 166
POSEY, Feyatte HND 7A
Horatio BRK 283
Humphrey HOP 260
James FKN 148
John LGN 37
John HND 11A
Lain W. MBG 136A
Price MAD 176
Sarah GRD 94A
William CLK 107
POSSER, Wm. ADR 42
POSSERWELL?, -----? ADR 42
Eliz. ADR 42
POSTLETWAITE, Joseph FTE 67
POSTLEWAIT, Wm. JEF 35
Wm. JEF 65
POSTLEWAITE, John FTE 62
POSTON, Temple HRD 42
POSY, Harrison ADR 42
POTEET, Benj. RCK 77A
POTENGER, Isaac WAS 55A
POTES, William WDF 96A
POTLOCK, Guy SHE 156
POTSON?, John GRD 119A
POTT, Geo. JEF 34
POTTER, --mas? DVS 13A
Abraham FLD 37
Austin KNX 308
Benjamin FLD 37
Daniel BRN 23
Felix WRN 56A
Frederick WRN 67A
Gordon SHE 169
John WRN 67A
Lemuel LNC 13
Levi FLD 37
Moses JEF 62
Nat GRD 113A
Stanford WDF 102
Thomas BKN 9
Thomas LNC 13
Thomas LNC 53
Thomas WRN 56A
Thomas WRN 67A
Thos. KNX 298
William LNC 3
William WDF 102
William WRN 67A
POTTES, Lewis WRN 46A
POTTINGER, Samuel, Jr. NSN 191
Samuel, Sr. NSN 191
POTTORFF, Geo. JEF 63
Simeon JEF 66
POTTS, David MER 105
David WRN 63A
Geo. JEF 49
George NCH 120A
Henry NCH 109A
Jeremiah UNN 147
John JEF 63
John WRN 73A
John NCH 126A
Jonathan WRN 61A
Margaret SHE 153
Milky DVS 19A
Saml. RCK 76A
Samuel MER 117
Stephen RCK 75A
Thomas LWS 94A
William NCH 109A
William N. JES 84
POU?, Moses BTH 210
William BTH 210
POUGE?, James GRN 71
POULSON, Aaron CLD 159
Absalom BRN 24
Israel CLD 149
POULTER, Bluford MER 106
John, Jr. MER 106
John, Sr. MER 106
POULTON, Isaac ETL 41
William ETL 43
POUND, Thomas CWL 57
Vineyard ALN 110
POUNDS, ---w.? E. CWL 41
Hezekiah JEF 53
Jno. JEF 53
Jonathan JEF 53
Joseph JEF 43
POURTWOOD, Lewis HRT 166
Loid HRT 166
POWE, Jos. GRD 99A
William BTL 329
POWE?, William GRD 87A
POWEL, Abraham BNE 30
Achillis SCT 113A
Armbrose SCT 96A
Asah GRN 58
Colby SCT 96A

POWEL, Edmond MAD 126
Henery GSN 148A
Honour SCT 113A
Jeremiah MAD 92
John MER 106
John NSN 184
Layer MER 105
Lindsey CSY 212
Louis MER 105
Marsha SCT 103A
Martha LNC 65
Obadiah MAD 92
Reuben SCT 100A
Rutha SCT 97A
Salley SCT 116A
Stephen HRT 165
Susan SCT 111A
Thomas BRN 23
Thomas MER 105
William WDF 96
William, Jr. MER 105
Willis SCT 111A
Wm. MAD 152
POWELL, Allen FLD 38
Armbrose CLK 62
Benjamin GNP 176A
Benjn. ADR 64
Cader FLD 38
Charles WAS 71A
Charles NCH 115A
Chester B. FTE 74
Davd.? CBL 23A
David LVG 7
Elijah CLY 112
Elisha HND 10A
Geo., Sr. TOD 128
Geo. TOD 128A
Harrison HND 12
Henderson HND 10
Hold ADR 26
Isaac TOD 128
Isaac WYN 95A
Isaac NCH 116A
James HND 12
James ADR 40
James ETL 40
Jas. TOD 128
Jeeremiah NCH 120A
Jno. ADR 40
John ETL 44
John GRN 69
John SHE 150
John SHE 152
John NSN 177
John HAR 188
John FLG 65A
John NCH 120A
John B. ETL 37
John W. WRN 73A
Joseph GNP 177A
Lazarus HND 12
Levi TOD 128
Lunsford HND 10A
Mary ADR 40
Mary WRN 46A
Peter WAS 71A
Richd. GRD 96A
Rob. HRY 212
Robert NCH 120A
Robt. ADR 40
Stephen FLG 56A
Stephen GNP 176A
Stephen GNP 177A
Thomas ETL 40
Thomas LGN 43
Thomas TOD 130
POWELL, Thos., Sr. TOD 129A
Vincent GNP 177A
Will MAS 56
William LGN 43
William HRL 116
William SHE 156
Willoughby, Jr. HND 11A
Willoughby, Sr. HND 12
Wm. BBN 114
Zeuus NCH 120A
POWELL?, Ambrose TOD 134
Onor? CBL 5A
Sarah CBL 23A
POWER, Absalum BTH 160
Betsy BTH 188
Briant BTH 168
Ellenor BTH 168
George BTH 168
George A. WDF 104
Halloway FLD 12
James BTH 168
Jeremiah BTH 178
John FLG 24A
John F. BKN 22
Joseph OWN 99
Joseph FLG 30A
Joseph SCT 131A
Josha. FLG 29A
Lewis FLD 8
Patsey FTE 86
Polly BTH 168
Richd. FLG 26A
Robt. FLG 30A
Robt. SCT 110A
Thos. BKN 15
Walter? NSN 188
POWERS, Anderson FKN 116
Campbell PND 24A
Charles WDF 110A
Clement SHE 155
Edw. H. FLG 45A
Elias WAS 39A
Henry WAS 39A
Henry FLG 45A
Jacob FLG 45A
James HAR 176
James mTG 261
James PND 19A
James GNP 166A
Jeramiah CBL 21A
John BNE 30
John OHO 11A
John WAS 39A
John SHE 124A
Jos. MAS 60
Joseph BKN 20
Joseph SCT 100A
Lewis SHE 111A
Patrick WYN 101A
Polly SCT 113A
Richard GNP 177A
Thomas HAR 176
W. E. JEF 26
Wm. ALN 120
Wm. TOD 124A
POWERS?, William LVG 16
POWLESS, Daniel WRN 36A
POYNTER, Jesse MTG 241
William MTG 243
PRAGUE, Samuel FTE 60
PRAT, Stephen WYN 102A
PRATER, Benjamin BBN 72
Eleanor BBN 68
Elihu BTL 329
Jeremiah BBN 70
John LWS 87A
PRATER, Jonathan BBN 68
Joseph BBN 68
Walter, Jr. BBN 72
Walter, Senr. BBN 72
PRATER?, William WRN 65A
PRATHER, Barrack NCH 115A
Basil NCH 121A
Easter FLG 38A
Edward PUL 57A
Gideon PUL 60A
Jacob MTG 277
James MAD 116
James MTG 235
James HOP 260
Jere. FLG 39A
Jereh. FLG 38A
John BRK 283
John, Junr. PUL 56A
John, Senr. PUL 64A
Jonithan BTH 152
Rease BRK 283
Reason? WAS 58A
Stephen HOP 260
Tho. MAS 58
Thomas FTE 87
Thomas HOP 260
Thomas BRK 283
Thos. JEF 21
Walter FTE 87
William BRK 229
William BRK 283
William NCH 115A
PRATOR, Archibald FLD 14
Archibald FLD 1A
Elijah FLD 8
Henry, Capt. MER 105
John FLD 8
Mary Anne MER 114
Philip MAD 166
Thomas FLD 6
Thomas FLD 44
William FLD 6
William FLD 8
William FLD 44
PRATT, Fielding JES 80
James BNE 30
James FLD 31
James GTN 130
John SCT 130A
Lot.? GNP 178A
Richard BLT 188
Stephen WYN 96A
Susan SCT 130A
Thomas GRN 54
William BNE 28
Wm. CHN 33
PRATT?, John CHN 29
PRAUL, John WDF 113A
PRAWL, Benjamin MER 105
PREBLE, James PND 31A
PREEDON, Peter CSY 224
Peter, Jr. CSY 224
PRENTICE?, Charles SCT 101A
PRENTIS, Daniel WYN 85A
PRENTISS, Nathl. FTE 64
Thomas FTE 100
Thomas M. FTE 68
PREPORS?, Thos. BBN 102
PRESCOTT, James M. CWL 46
John TRG 12A
PRESLEY?, Edward MNR 191
PRESSER, Henry BNE 30
Henry, Jr. BNE 28
William BNE 30
PRESTEN, John GSN 147A
PRESTIN, Robert GSN 148A

PRESTON, Bernard C. MAS 59
Daniel CHN 28
Eliphas FLD 23
Enoch GRD 108A
Frances FTE 91
Frankey CBL 12A
Gideon V. HRD 62
Gillion JES 71
Isaac FLD 21
Isaac FLD 23
James M. BNE 46
Jane MBG 136A
Jeoffery FLD 23
Jesse CLD 143
Jno. PUL 43A
John CLK 106
John ALN 114
Lewis JES 71
Moses FLD 21
Moses FLD 21
Moses WYN 100A
Nathan FLD 23
Patrick MER 105
Sarah RCK 84A
Thos. FLG 40A
Toliver JES 71
Walter CLK 94
William JEF 36
William JES 71
William HAR 162
Winefred WRN 70A
Wm.(Crossed-out) JEF 52
PRETHEROE, Samuel SHE 174
PREVO, Clark WYN 94A
John WYN 94A
PREWET, Tunstal SHE 141A
PREWETT, Beverly SHE 118A
Bird JES 95
Brite JEF 44
Easan PUL 41A
Eli JEF 68
Elijah WTY 115A
Elisha SHE 120A
Jas. JEF 68
John WTY 116A
Jos. SHE 131A
Joseph WAS 65A
Joshua JES 95
Nathaniel SHE 150
Obediah JES 82
PREWETTE, Dokes HND 8
Robert HND 8
PREWIT, John L. HRD 10
William OWN 100
PREWITT, --riah? FLD 44
Abraham KNX 278
Adenson/ Aderson? CBL 12A
Alfred FLD 44
Anthony MER 105
Coleman HRY 190
David MER 105
Elisha HRY 178
Francis MER 105
Henry H. SCT 127A
Isham, Jr. MER 105
Isham, Sr. MER 105
Job LVG 11
Joel BBN 144
John CBL 6A
John WAS 31A
Jonathan CLY 112
Joseph MER 105
Joshua HRY 208
Martha FTE 88
PREWITT, Michl. HRY 190
Robert MER 105
Robert MER 117
Robert C. HRY 210
Saml. PUL 36A
Sarah MER 105
Thos. CWL 42
Walter JEF 33
William WTY 123A
William C. FTE 96
Willis FTE 87
PRIACE?, John GRN 80
PRIAR, Hisekiah GRN 65
Jessee GRN 62
John GRN 64
PRIBBLE, John BKN 11
Saml. BKN 10
Thos. BKN 11
Wm. BKN 11
PRICE, ---as? DVS 12A
A--alon ETL 43
Aaron PUL 46A
Andrew SCT 113A
Andrew F. FTE 90
Betsey HRD 86
Bird BNE 30
Bird? FTE 94
Caroline LGN 41
Catharine LGN 45
Charity BTH 214
Daniel BRN 24
Daniel wDF 105
Daniel WRN 34A
Daniel B. JES 96
David LGN 45
Delilah HOP 260
Eady WTY 112A
Edmun? GNP 167A
Edmund NSN 192
Elisha FLG 75A
Evan FTE 111
Francis H. BLT 174
Fred SHE 130A
Gideon ADR 40
Hannah FKN 58
Hansford PUL 36A
Ignatus NSN 178
Irvin UNN 151
Isaac BLT 158
Isaac RCK 76A
Isaac SCT 101A
Isaac SCT 114A
Isaac SCT 126A
James MTG 225
James HOP 260
James PUL 37A
James WRN 71A
James LWS 99A
Jas. PUL 46A
Jesse FLD 24
Jno., Jr. FKN 84
Jno., Sr. FKN 84
Joel M. LGN 40
John HRD 16
John JEF 34
John LGN 46
John GRN 61
John FTE 66
John GRN 76
John CLK 94
John HAR 182
John BTH 214
John HAR 220
John (Red Head) LGN 29
John GRD 90A
John WYN 92A
PRICE, John SCT 98A
John SCT 113A
John MBG 133A
John M. GTN 123
John R. FTE 95
Jordan GRD 102B
Joseph NSN 176
Joseph WDF 100A
Larian? FTE 89
Lewis SHE 130A
Major J. LGN 44
Martin HRD 78
Mary FKN 62
Mary JES 74
Moses M. ETL 37
Nancy LGN 46
Nancy CLK 77
Nathan PUL 49A
Natten? HRD 78
Patsy HRD 78
Peggy CLD 167
Peu? BNE 30
Philemon WDF 103A
Phillip B. SCT 91A
Pugh LGN 35
Reason NSN 184
Richard FTE 105
Richard HRL 116
Robert GRN 66
Robert WRN 71A
Robert R. GRN 58
Robt. BKN 22
Sally FTE 61
Saml. HRD 20
Saml. PUL 46A
Saml. SCT 115A
Sampson GNP 165A
Sarah GRN 76
Stephen CBL 11A
Thomas FLD 25
Thomas LNC 51
Thomas BTH 214
Thomas WRN 56A
Thos. HRD 80
Thos. FLG 41A
Thos. PUL 46A
Thos. SCT 113A
Thos. SCT 118A
Thos. SCT 139A
Will SCT 99A
Will. SCT 129A
William LGN 45
William GRN 52
William GTN 133
William SHE 175
William CSY 226
William GRD 85A
William B. FTE 108
William C. UNN 149
Williamson FTE 85
Wilson SHE 122A
Winfree MTG 277
Wm. FKN 104
Wm. FLG 24A
Wm. FLG 75A
Wm. H. ADR 40
Thos. PUL 38A
PRICE?, Isaiah SCT 139A
Joseph GTN 125
Thomas? HRT 165
Willis FTE 105
PRICHARD, Jean MAS 60
John GNP 172A
Joseph KNX 298
PRICHART, William FTE 92
PRICHETT, John FLD 13

PRICHETT, William HAR 190
PRICKETT, Taplett BTH 208
PRIDMORE, John FLD 15
PRIER, James SPN 10A
Lucy GRD 117A
PRIER?, Mary BBN 108
PRIEST, -----? H. DVS 14A
Daniel LWS 86A
Elias MTG 226
George MTG 263
George MTG 281
James HRY 230
Jonas MTG 233
Nathaniel BRN 23
Peter BRN 23
Peter JEF 34
Redham LGN 41
William P. MTG 269
PRIGMORE, Basel GRN 72
PRIM, Josha MAD 138
PRIMA?, Ann JEF 39
PRIN?, Mary BBN 108
PRINA, Ann JEF 38
PRINCE, Elisha LGN 33
Enock LVG 8
Francis CWL 46
Jno. CWL 58
Nathan WRN 51A
Widw. CWL 44
William FLD 37
PRINDLE, Harde HRT 165
PRINE, Daniel MNR 199
Rhodum MNR 209
PRINE?, Thos.? CWL 40
PRINGLE, James FKN 104
Jas. LVG 3
William GRN 79
William HRY 196
William HRY 208
William, Jr. HRY 208
PRINT, John RCK 80A
PRIOR, Jack HRY 202
John BBN 112
Richard CBL 19A
Sanuel CBL 21A
Simon GSN 146A
PRITCHARD, Christopher TRG 7
Curtis HRY 186
Danl. HRY 184
James BBN 118
John SCT 110A
Js. HRY 184
Lures? HRY 180
PRITCHART, Lewis CLK 95
PRITCHELL?, Jesse MTG 233
PRITCHET, Isaac, Sr. MER 105
Jacob MER 105
PRITCHETT, Abraham MER 105
Alfred BBN 102
Benjamin HOP 260
Charles MBG 140
Elizabeth HOP 260
Gabrial MAS 63
Hannah MTG 281
Isaac, Jr. MER 105
John HND 12
John MTG 263
Penelope MTG 263
Zachariah FLD 25
PRITCHETT?, Jesse MTG 233
PRIVIT, Nolan PUL 49A
PROBES, Allexander GSN 146A
PROCTER, Elizabeth JES 72
Ezekiel JES 74
PROCTER, Georoge RCK 75A
James B. MAD 160
John JES 74
John BTL 329
Richard SHE 113A
PROCTER?, Samuel FLD 5
PROCTOR, Abra. MAS 55
Ben LGN 42
Benjn. SCT 96A
Catlett SHE 164
Charles LGN 46
George LGN 46
George FTE 96
Greenvill SHE 165
Hezekiah LGN 46
Jacob LVG 7
James HRD 42
James RCK 75A
Jane MNR 209
John LGN 44
John GRD 99A
Joseph ETL 54
Muhlenburg SHE 164
Simon HRD 10
Thomas LGN 46
Thomas MNR 209
Thomas S. GRD 83A
Will MAS 53
Wm. FLG 58A
Wm. FLG 59A
Wm. SHE 115A
Wm. B. MAD 160
PROE, John LVG 11
PROFATER, Christian BBN 92
PROFFIT, Joseph FLD 13
Silvester FLD 13
PROFIT, Mary MAD 120
PROFITS?, John MNR 217
PROPHET, Jesse CHN 33A
PROSISE, Tho. RCK 81A
PROSISE?, John RCK 76A
PROTHOROE, Samuel SHE 160
PROTSMAN, Jacob NSN 176
PROUSE, Zilpha MBG 143A
PROVINCE, Hiram WYN 97A
Thomas WYN 100A
PROVINE, Andrew MAD 176
Andrew (Crossed Out) MAD 182
PROW, Philip TOD 134
PROWEL-?, James ADR 40
PROWETT?, Henry FLD 31
PRUATE, Sarah HRT 166
PRUDY, Saml. PND 29A
PRUET, Davd. RCK 84A
Davd. RCK 84A
Ephraim CLD 161
Henry MAD 138
Jno., Sr. RCK 84A
John MAD 142
John MAD 144
John CLD 159
Jonathan BRK 283
Joshua BRK 281
Joshua, Sr. BRK 283
Lemuel BRK 283
Solomon MAD 138
Solomon CLD 161
Solomon, Senr. CLD 161
PRUETT, Irvine PUL 41A
James NSN 206
James W. FKN 60
Joel FKN 130
Phil CWL 55
Richd. WAS 30A
PRUETT, Richd. PUL 41A
PRUIT, John CWL 43
PRUITT, Salley WAS 23A
PRUM?, George FTE 76
PRUND?, Stephen RCK 81A
PRUNTY, John SCT 109A
Thomas WRN 71A
PRUOST?, Ab ALN 102
David ALN 102
Wm. ALN 110
PRUOSTE?, Wm. ALN 136
PRUTER?, William WRN 65A
PRY, Jessee HND 5
John HND 9A
PRYER, Samuel CLD 152
PRYOR, Saml. CHN 42A
Thornton BBN 120
PUACE?, John GRN 80
PUCKET, John K. / H.? BTL 329
Peter MER 105
Polley HRT 166
Thomas HRT 166
PUCKETT, Elizabeth FLD 1A
James E. MNR 215
John LVG 14
John SHE 170
Samuel ETL 52
William LGN 25
William SHE 111A
PUDMAN?, Thos. HRD 92
PUGH, David BTH 202
George HAR 180
John CHN 32A
Samuel BTH 210
PULAM?, Graves? ALN 128
PULEN?, Ruben WAS 63A
PULIS, David WDF 125A
PULLAM, Absalom GRD 117A
Ben GRD 121A
Drury FKN 160
J./ I.? A. GRD 122A
James FKN 80
Jno. ALN 136
Jno. FKN 152
Joseph FTE 88
Nancy FKN 128
Polly GRD 122A
W. W. GRD 117A
William GRD 107A
Woodson GRD 106A
Zachariah FKN 76
PULLEN, Edwd. SCT 92A
Henry SCT 94A
John OWN 102
Joseph OWN 102
Nelson WDF 102A
Richard BRK 229
William WDF 99A
Youd? SCT 95A
PULLEY, Devige? MAD 158
Lewis MAD 156
PULLIAM, Ann HRT 166
Barnabas BRN 23
Charles HRT 165
George? W. GTN 125
Gideon HRT 165
Lucy HRT 166
William SHE 113A
PULLIN, Abraham BRK 285
Edwd. J./ I.? SCT 95A
Fountain SCT 95A
George BRK 285
Isaiah BRK 285
James BBN 120
Samuel BRN 23

PULLIN, Thomas BBN 102
PULLINGTON, Samuel BKN 19
PULLUM, Benjamin UNN 151
Diry MAD 102
James MAD 96
Lofly? MAD 144
Mary UNN 151
Mosley MAD 100
Robt. J./ I.? SCT 124A
Robt. J./ I.? SCT 127A
Thomas UNN 151
Thos. SCT 93A
William WDF 119A
PULLY, Edwd., (Free Man) BBN 82
PUMPHREY, Gabriel D. BRK 283
Jno. PUL 35A
PUMPHRY, Elijah PUL 44A
Jno. PUL 42A
Larkin PUL 42A
PUNCH, John CBL 6A
PUNPHY?, Huy? RCK 83A
Lewis/ Linus? RCK 82A
PUNTENNY?, Mitchell LGN 47
Nancy LGN 31
Peggy LGN 47
PURA?, Thomas BTH 168
PURCE?, Jessee CLK 88
PURCEL, Thomas BRK 281
Wesley HRD 96
PURCELL, John BLT 160
Rihard CHN 29A
Roddy HRD 14
PURCIFIELD, Saml. CLY 113
Thos. CLY 114
PURCY, Joseph NCH 116A
PURDAIN/ PURDAM?, Elijah CSY 218
Marke CSY 218
Thomas CSY 218
PURDAM?, William CSY 216
PURDHAM, Betsey FLG 76A
PURDY, Alexander BBN 132
Edmond HRD 26
Hugh LGN 45
Isaac BBN 130
Izabell BBN 130
John WAS 35A
John WAS 68A
Presley WAS 61A
Robt. BBN 130
Wm. WAS 39A
PUREE?, Frances BTH 198
PURGIS?, James CWL 46
PURKEPILE, Christian CBL 12A
PURKILL, Ben CWL 57
Jacob CWL 57
Jno. CWL 58
Wm. CWL 57
PURKINS, David PUL 65A
Jabez WTY 125A
Jesse WTY 123A
Michael MAD 110
Mitchel MAD 102
Plesant MAD 102
Richard MAD 102
Saml. MAD 110
Solomon WTY 120A
Stephen H. MAD 96
Timothy WTY 121A
PURNELL, William LWS 91A
Wm. FLG 61A
PURSELL, Benjamin ETL 43
PURSELL, John ETL 50
Richard ETL 43
Thomas ETL 48
William HAR 138
PURSLEY, Alexander SHE 139A
Elijah NCH 105
Jane NCH 125A
John CHN 45
Thomas NCH 125A
William BRN 24
PURTLE, David CWL 39
Henry WAS 63A
Henry WAS 80A
Peter CWL 38
Uriah GSN 146A
PURVIS, Calvin PUL 37A
James PUL 45A
PUSLEY, Daniel MAD 156
PUSLEY?, William GRN 63
PUTHUFF, Henry GNP 166A
PUTMAN, Danl. K. FLG 28A
Henry MAS 62
Henry, Jr. MAS 62
Hiram MNR 215
James BKN 18
John GNP 169A
Simeon MNR 191
PUTNAM, Joseph FTE 70
Reding BTL 327
Wm. BKN 18
PUTOFF, John FTE 80
PUTT, Rosannah GSN 147A
Samuel GSN 147A
PUTTY, George NSN 178
PUVELER?, David BTH 208
PYAT, Volentine BTH 178
PYBURN, Richd. HRD 34
PYE, Thomas CBL 3A
PYKE, Saml. BBN 144
PYLE, Nicholas CHN 31
Nicholas CHN 36A
Wm. CHN 35
PYNES, Wm. BBN 138
QU--BERRY?, John MAD 154
QUAINTANCE, Jas. FLG 28A
Wm. FLG 26A
QUALLS, Cynthia SHE 160
Roland ETL 49
QUARLES, Ambros FKN 98
Roger FTE 76
Tunstall PUL 52A
Wm. E. FKN 102
QUARLES?, James WDF 93A
QUART, David CHN 31
QUARTER, Madisons FKN 84
QUEEN, Charles LWS 87A
Elijah FLG 54A
John JEF 21
Timmothy HND 7
QUELT / QUETT?, James NCH 126A
QUERTERMONS, Elisha JEF 37
QUERTERMOS, James JEF 43
QUERY, Catherine JEF 63
Wm. JEF 34
QUESBERRY, Aaron JEF 54
QUESENBURY, William CLK 62
QUESSENBERRY, Page BRN 24
Zac. BRN 24
QUICK, Abraham BLT 164
Andrew HRD 58
Benjn. MAD 134
Dennis BLT 164
QUICK, Elleanor SHE 162
Ephraim BLT 182
Jacob CBL 10A
James ETL 43
Mary ETL 44
Thomas BLT 180
QUIGGINS, Henry WAS 56A
Joseph WAS 56A
QUIGLEY, Elizabeth MER 106
James MNR 205
Lewis HRD 96
QUILL?, John OWN 105
John OWN 105
QUILLAN, Teague FLD 29
QUILLEN, Jesse MNR 193
QUILLS, Hany/ Harry? FTE 60
QUILTNER?, Barnet WDF 104A
QUIMBY, Ephraim JES 86
George JES 86
QUIN, Charles HAR 144
Wm. HRD 64
QUIN?, William GRD 111A
QUINCY, Soloman HRD 66
QUINLIN, Phillip BKN 5
QUINLY, Greenberry MAD 152
John HRY 196
QUINN, Aaron MAS 77
Abner W. ETL 37
Abr. GRD 95A
Auther BLT 176
Benjn., Senr. SCT 132A
Benjn. SCT 131A
Edmund MER 106
Ennis GRD 85A
Feelan? NSN 175
Isah. JEF 56
Isham MNR 207
Jas. FLG 23A
Jas. FLG 25A
Jno. MAS 56
John MNR 207
John FLG 25A
John RCK 76A
Joshua MAD 100
William MER 106
Wm. JEF 42
QUINN?, Hiram MAD 142
QUINTON, James CWL 36
Jane CSY 226
Littleton NSN 177
William CSY 226
QUIRE, Wm. FKN 74
QUISENBERRY, Jas. GSN 147A
Nicholas WRN 42A
Roger CLK 81
QUISENBURY, James CLK 70
Joel CLK 70
Tandy CLK 93
QUISENDARY, Edward S.? CHN 44A
QUISHENBERY, James GRN 62
QUISHENBURY, James H. OWN 101
QUISHINBERRY, George GRN 75
QUISHINGBURY, Elizabeth WRN 44A
John WRN 44A
QUNESS?, Wm. BBN 126
R----, ----- HRT 166
R----?, -----? LVG 18
-----? LVG 18
R---?, Hiram? LVG 18
Jesse LVG 18

RABLER, Ann BKN 18
RABLER?, John BKN 18
RABOURN, Henry W. FLG 46A
Reece MTG 229
RABOURND, William M. MTG 229
RABOURNE, John BKN 11
John MTG 233
Ralph MTG 241
Sally MTG 255
Terry MTG 273
RABUM, Thomas FTE 77
RABURN, John SPN 11A
Joseph SPN 11A
RABURN?, James MAD 156
RACHEL, (Not Free) BRK 229
RACHFORD, Hugh CBL 18A
RACKET, William WRN 35A
RADCLIFF, Francis MAD 116
Jane SHE 161
John SHE 161
Josiah SHE 125A
Samuel SHE 124A
RADCLIFFE, Elisha GRT 140
RADDIX?, William NSN 222
RADER, Alexander HAR 204
Alexr. BBN 132
George MTG 231
Henry CLY 126
Jesse MTG 237
John MTG 247
Thomas MTG 247
RADFORD, Benj. CHN 40A
Carlton BRN 25
George SHE 159
Harriot LWS 88A
Henry SHE 175
James BRN 25
James CLD 163
James W. CLD 153
Jno. B. CHN 41
John SHE 161
John, Sr. SHE 162
John HND 7A
Nancy SHE 151
Otson SHE 143A
Silas BRN 24
Wm. CHN 41
Wm., Jr. CHN 41
RADIKIN, John MTG 237
RADLEY, Christopher HRD 66
Ichabud HRD 22
James BNE 34
RADLIFF, Charles BLT 180
RAEZOR?, Fredric SHE 122A
RAFERTY, Malcolm LVG 10
Robert LVG 10
RAFFARDY, Richard SPN 6A
RAFFE, John NCH 110A
RAFFERTY, James GRN 74
James MTG 269
James DVS 18A
John BNE 32
John GRN 55
Joseph MTG 277
RAFFITY, Samuel SPN 10A
Thomas, Jr. SPN 10A
Thomas SPN 10A
RAFFORTY, William BNE 30
RAFINESQUE, C. S. FTE 70
RAFTY, William SPN 13A
RAGAN, Abner MER 107
Daniel LGN 22
Edward LGN 22
Hiram BRK 289
RAGAN, Jacob MTG 253
Jesse WRN 75A
Milly MTG 251
Robert MER 107
RAGAN?, Robert MAD 92
RAGEN, Mary FTE 84
Owen KNX 298
Spencer FTE 84
RAGENSTINE, John H./ A.? LWS 99A
RAGER?, Elijah JEF 20
RAGFIELD, William CLD 158
RAGIN, Mary BTH 190
RAGLAN, Gideon, Junr. HRD 90
RAGLAND, Benj. ALN 102
Benjamin CLK 76
Benjamin (H. C.) CLK 89
Dudley CLK 67
Gideon HRD 88
James R. CLK 69
Joel HRT 166
John CLK 82
John ALN 98
Joseph ALN 98
Nathaniel JEF 39
Nathaniel CLK 80
Richard BRN 25
Tucker CLK 92
RAGLEN, James WAS 24A
John WRN 57A
Richard WRN 57A
RAGLIN, David MTG 231
James BTH 200
Robert W. WRN 31A
RAGNESS, Rome GTN 123
RAGOR, William F. LGN 44
RAGSDALE, Daniel HRY 210
Frederic SHE 153
Gabriel LNC 23
Geo. HRY 212
Godfrey SHE 129A
Henry LNC 51
Lewis LGN 28
Rich HRY 234
Robert NSN 212
Stephen LGN 34
William SHE 156
William HRY 192
William HRY 216
RAGSDELL, David WRN 56A
Drury BKN 14
Robert WRN 56A
William WRN 56A
RAIBORN, John MAD 160
RAIBOURN, Henry FLG 44A
RAILESBACK, Daniel FKN 148
RAILEY, Charles WDF 119A
Elizebeth WDF 95
George WDF 123A
Judith WDF 104
Peter J./ I.? WDF 104
Randolph, Jr. WDF 118A
Randolph WDF 118A
RAILS?, Joseph HRY 224
RAILSBACK, E. MAS 71
Edward CLK 83
RAIM?, Nathanl. B. BBN 116
RAIMER, Abraham GSN 148A
Michael GSN 149A
RAIMEY, Butler BBN 76
Chas. BBN 72
Jacob BBN 64
RAIN, J. B. BBN 112
RAINBOLT, John WYN 81A
RAINDON, Samuel CBL 22A
RAINDON?, Jacob CBL 22A
RAINE, Thomas BTH 176
William BTH 156
RAINE?, Nathanl. B. BBN 116
RAINES, Christopher BNE 50
RAINEY, Enoch HAR 154
James PUL 65A
Nancy MBG 138
William H. FTE 89
RAINEY?, William MTG 299
RAINS, Henry MAS 79
Henry HRL 118
James CHN 30A
Jesse HRY 212
Jno. MAS 79
John WTY 125A
Walker MTG 277
RAINWATERS, Abraham PUL 57A
William PUL 65A
RAINY, William JES 87
RAIRDON, Thos. FLG 79A
RAISNER?, Leonard CLY 132
RAISOR, Geo. FLG 44A
Henry FLG 44A
RAIZON?, Lewis M. M. GNP 166A
RAKER, Michael CLK 65
RAKER?, Abraham NCH 119A
RALEIGH, Thos. TRG 10
RALEY, Benj. WAS 32A
Henry WAS 29A
Jonathan OHO 7A
Lewis WAS 33A
Lidia WAS 29A
Thos. WAS 28A
RALEY?, Chas. JEF 27
RALLS, Hebron BTH 166
Nathaniel BTH 168
Robert LGN 34
William LGN 45
William MTG 251
RALPH, Benjamin MTG 277
John HRY 210
Wm. SHE 128A
RALSTON, -----? MAS 70
Andrew BRN 25
David BRN 25
David CHN 28A
Joseph BRN 24
M.' TOD 132
Matthew BRN 25
William MTG 283
Wm. CHN 44A
Wm. J./ I.? MAS 70
RALY, Cornelious WAS 34A
Cornelious WAS 35A
Henry WAS 36A
Peter WAS 34A
Sally WAS 34A
RAMADGE, Daniel BLT 190
RAMAGE, James LVG 6
Jno. LVG 2
Jos. LVG 6
Josiah LVG 3
RAMAGE?, -----? LVG 18
RAMAN, William BLT 178
RAMAY?, Butler NSN 200
RAMCEY?, Butler NSN 200
RAME, John LGN 47
William LGN 46
RAMEY, Archabalde BTH 200
Archd. FLG 45A

Name	County	Page
RAMEY, Daniel	FLD	22
Davis	MTG	235
Isaac	CLY	127
James	FLD	22
James	FLD	38
James	MTG	241
Jarvis	WDF	97A
John	FLD	19
John	FLD	36
John	CWL	37
John	MTG	249
John, Jr.	MTG	265
Moses	FLD	38
Westley	HRT	167
William	FLD	36
William	FLD	38
Wm. P.	FLG	64A
RAMEY?, William	MTG	299
RAMIER?, John	CLK	67
RAMLEY?, John	GSN	148A
RAMSAY, Alexander	CLK	71
Alexander, Jr.	CLK	72
James	CLK	67
John	CLK	92
William	CLK	68
William	CLK	83
RAMSDELL?, Charles M.	WRN	73A
RAMSEY, Abraham	JEF	34
Alexr.	FLG	60A
Alexr.	GRD	110A
Bartholomew	BRK	285
Charles	UNN	148
Daniel	FLD	25
Danl.	RCK	78A
David	FLG	58A
Enos	FKN	76
Francy	RCK	76A
George	HOP	262
Hannah	JEF	55
Hugh	CWL	56
James	HOP	262
James	BRK	287
John	HRT	167
John	CHN	32A
John	WYN	82A
John	GRD	103A
Larkin	GRD	102A
Martin	FLD	41
Mary	FLG	60A
Moses	JES	91
Obediah	PUL	60A
Richard	MAD	142
Richard	WYN	94A
Robert	HND	5
Robert	WDF	93
Samuel	LNC	3
Samuel	MNR	201
Samuel	SPN	8A
Seth	WDF	109A
Thomas	GRD	98A
Thomas	GRD	102A
Will.	LVG	4
Williams	WAS	30A
Wm.	BRK	287
RAMSEY?, Jordain?	CSY	216
RAMSY, Francy	RCK	75A
RAMY, E., Mrs.?	MAS	67
John, Jr.	CWL	37
John, Sr.	CWL	37
Wm.? E.	MAS	67
RAMY?, Lucy	ALN	118
RANBARGER, Daniel	BLT	178
Daniel	BLT	178
Henry	BLT	180
William	BLT	178
RANDAL, Henry	SHE	135A
RANDALL, Olive	SHE	109A
Thos.	FLG	54A
RANDALPH, Ignatius P.	SHE	135A
RANDALS, Wm.	RCK	84A
RANDEL, Brice C.	FTE	73
Robt.	JEF	25
Tho.	ALN	140
Wm.	ALN	140
RANDELL, James	WRN	73A
Michael	WRN	72A
RANDELL?, John?	CWL	41
RANDLE, Joseph	ALN	140
Paul	CBL	6A
RANDLES, James	BRN	25
RANDOL, Jno.	HAR	164
Nathaniel	BTH	194
Richard	BTH	194
RANDOL?, Joseph	BBN	96
RANDOLPH, Absalem	GRN	70
Clarkson E.	MER	107
David	TRG	12
Enoch	HND	8
Geo.	PUL	36A
James	BTH	156
James	PUL	38A
Jno.	PUL	39A
John	UNN	149
Malachi	MER	106
Moses	FTE	76
Nimrod	PUL	60A
Payton	PUL	38A
Reubin	BTH	156
William	TRG	12
William	UNN	147
RANDOLS, Winny	GRD	119A
RANDSELL, Wharten	WRN	29A
RANER, John	BTL	329
RANEY, Aaron	PUL	44A
Lucy	ALN	118
Robt.	SCT	106A
Wm.	PUL	48A
RANEY?, Wm.	PUL	37A
RANFROW, John	LVG	12
RANGON, Benj.	FKN	78
RANKIN, Adam	FTE	67
Adam	FTE	99
Arthur	LNC	81
Benjamine	SPN	17A
David P.	SCT	132A
Elias	CWL	41
H. W.	SCT	94A
Hiram	LWS	96A
James	HAR	202
Jane	HAR	196
John	HND	8
John	CLK	62
John	SHE	176
John	HAR	178
John	MNR	197
John	NCH	125A
Mary	WDF	93A
Moses	NCH	107A
Nancy	FTE	99
Robert	HAR	178
Robert	SPN	12A
Samuel	FTE	57
Samuel	HAR	210
Samuel	WDF	102A
Susannah	HND	11
Thomas	HAR	216
Thomas	WDF	111A
Thos.	SCT	102A
Widw.	CWL	39
William	SHE	176
RANKIN, William	HAR	218
RANKINS, B. H.	MAS	52
James	BBN	102
Jno.	MAS	79
Moses	MAS	60
Reuben	BBN	102
Thos.	SCT	98A
Winny	MAS	63
Wm.	MAS	61
Wm.	FLG	48A
RANNECK, Wm.	BBN	104
RANNELLS, D. V.	MAS	80
Wm.	BBN	132
RANNELS, Margaret	BBN	134
RANNOLDS, Elis	HRY	254
RANSDAL, Christopher	FKN	58
RANSDALE, Fox.?	HRY	261
Jno.	HRY	244
John	SCT	97A
Presley	FTE	92
Thos.	HRY	244
RANSDALL, James	FKN	78
Wharton	HRY	194
Wm.	TOD	128A
Zachariah	FKN	88
RANSDELL, Ann	FKN	84
Benj.	FKN	86
Elizabeth	MER	107
Fis--ing?	MER	107
John	FTE	80
Noel	FKN	84
Wha---?	MER	107
William	FTE	93
Zachariah	FKN	84
Zachariah	WDF	114A
RANSEY, James	WAS	30A
RANSOM, Benjamine	BRK	287
Ignatious	MAD	130
James	ALN	144
Richard	ALN	138
RANSON?, Richard	BNE	34
RANT?, Rhoadham	WDF	93
RANY, Theodocia	SCT	112A
Will	GRD	97A
Williamson	GRD	113A
RAPEL?, Thomas (Crossed Out)	WYN	90A
RAPER?, Thos.	SHE	132A
RAPHAEL, Betsey	LGN	23
Southy	LGN	43
RAPIER, James	WYN	106A
Jesse	WTY	119A
William	NSN	188
RARDIN, Jessee	PND	31A
John	PND	31A
RASCO, William	CHN	45
RASH, John	BBN	66
Perry	PUL	47A
Saml.	BBN	122
Stephen	HOP	260
William	CLK	80
William, Jr.	CLK	81
RASNER, John	MNR	191
RASOE?, Isabella	MER	116
RASOR, Andrew	CHN	44
George	SHE	140A
RASSEE, Elliott	BNE	32
RASSER?, Lewis	KNX	314
RASY?, Martin B.	MNR	215
RATCHFORD, Robt.	HRD	30
RATCHIN?, Jos.	PUL	37A
RATCLIFFE, John	CHN	30
RATCLIFT, Saml.	MAS	62
Wm.	MAS	62
RATENKIN, John	MAD	176

Name	County	Page
RATHBONE, Thos. W.	HRD	82
RATLEFF, Ruben	GRN	73
William	GRN	73
RATLIF, Jeremiah	FLD	34
RATLIFF, ---.?	CWL	43
--lman?	CWL	43
Alexander	WDF	115A
Caleb	BTH	158
Charles	HRY	212
Harper	CLY	122
Henry	FLD	35
James	FLD	28
John	FLD	28
Joseph	WDF	115A
Margaret	BRN	25
Martha	WDF	116A
Minis	OWN	100
Richard	FLD	28
Silas	FLD	28
Stephen	BRN	25
Stephen	FLD	28
William	FLD	25
William	FLD	28
RATLIFF?, Charles	HAR	144
Zepheniah	BTH	168
RATTEN, Tarlton	CWL	36
RAUSEY?, Jordain?	CSY	216
RAVENSCRAFT, Thomas	HAR	212
Thos., Jr.	HAR	212
William	HAR	212
RAVIL?, Nancy	ADC	68
RAWBARTES, John	CSY	224
RAWLEY, James	HND	11A
RAWLEY?, John	GSN	148A
Saml.	BKN	24
Saml.	BKN	24
RAWLINGS, Aron	BRK	287
Aron	FLG	64A
Benjamin H.	ETL	37
Francis	FTE	67
Johua.	FLG	34A
Levi	HRY	208
Lewis	BLT	170
Presly	FLG	58A
Thos.	FLG	30A
Thos.	FLG	55A
Wm.	FLG	58A
RAWLINGS?, Aaron, Jr.	BRK	287
RAWLSTON, Jno.	MAS	61
RAY, Alex	JEF	58
Andrew	WRN	47A
Aron	MAD	90
Barton	MTG	287
Baxter	ALN	108
Berdett C.	HND	9
Caleb	OHO	8A
Charles	CLK	90
Chs.	JEF	66
Danl.	GRD	89A
David	JEF	26
David	GRD	89A
Elias	WAS	57A
Elisha	WAS	58A
Eliza	LNC	71
Elizabeth	MER	114
Foster	LGN	44
Fountain	WRN	47A
Frances	WAS	62A
Garland	WRN	47A
George	WAS	32A
George	WAS	66A
Hezk.	WAS	61A
Hickinson	WRN	49A
Isaac	LNC	49
RAY, Isham	MER	107
J./ I.? S.	GRD	93A
James	BRN	25
James	HOP	262
James, Gen.	MER	107
James	WAS	48A
Jer M.	ALN	126
Jeremiah	GTN	125
Jesse	MER	107
Jessee	ETL	50
Jno.	JEF	66
Jno.	FKN	138
Jno., Jr.	JEF	66
Joel	CLD	139
John	GTN	134
John	UNN	154
John	MNR	201
John	MNR	213
John	MTG	241
John	HOP	260
John, Dr.	JEF	66
John	WAS	66A
John	GRD	93A
John C.	BTH	176
John S.	WAS	87A
Jos.	GRD	87A
Joseph	LNC	73
Joseph	WAS	87A
Joseph	GRD	103A
Jubal	MER	107
Lord	WAS	54A
Margaret, Mrs.	WYN	85A
Mary	ALN	134
Mary	WAS	58A
Matthew	SHE	140A
Michl.	GRD	102A
Moses	MER	107
Nathaniel	ALN	108
Nicolass	WAS	37A
Prudence	WAS	62A
Reson	WAS	58A
Richard	WRN	47A
Richard	WAS	58A
Richd.	WAS	58A
Robert, Esq.	WYN	87A
Robert	LWS	95A
Saml.	JEF	66
Saml.	WAS	39A
Samuel	GRD	88A
Stephen	WAS	47A
Susan	WAS	58A
Thomas	LGN	38
Thomas	LGN	44
Thomas	GTN	119
Thomas	HRT	166
Thomas	WRN	47A
Thomas L.	BRK	287
Tilman	MTG	289
William	MER	107
William	GTN	119
William	CLD	138
William	GRD	84A
Willim	HOP	262
Wm.	JEF	66
Wm.	ALN	102
Wm.	FKN	140
Wm.	WAS	58A
Wm.	WAS	58A
Zachr.	GRD	104A
RAYBERN, Mary	FKN	56
RAYBON?, Francis	ADR	42
RAYBOUN?, Green	TOD	131
RAYBURN, George	PUL	64A
John	PUL	59A
Robert	GTN	126
William	NCH	125A
RAYFIELD, Elizabeth	MBG	135
Isaac	CLD	149
RAYMOND, Barbary	BLT	190
Jacob	BLT	178
John	BLT	190
Saml.	JEF	19
William	HAR	192
RAYNES, Newman	WYN	102A
Stephen	WYN	97A
Uriah	WYN	97A
William	WYN	102A
RAYNOLDS, Charles	GRN	69
Henry, Sr.?	GRD	118A
Henry	GRD	84A
Moses	GRD	118A
William	GRN	67
RAYNOLS, David	GRD	109A
Heny, Jr.?	GRD	100A
RAYS, John	CBL	7A
RAZER, Elizabeth	OWN	105
Jacob, Jr.	OWN	101
Jacob, Sr.	OWN	105
William D.	OWN	105
RAZER?, Elijah	JEF	20
RAZIN?, Thomas	TRG	8A
RAZOR, Adam	SHE	140A
Anthony	HRD	10
Anthony, Senr.	HRD	84
George	OWN	101
Haman	SHE	140A
Jacob	HRD	34
Jno.	HRY	263
Paul	HRD	84
Paul	SHE	140A
Peter	HRD	32
Wm.	SHE	140A
RAZOR?, Fredric	SHE	122A
RE--ASS?, Austen	BBN	136
REACE, John	CLK	67
Nancy	MAD	106
READ/ REDD?, Philip	NSN	179
READ, Berry	GRN	57
Bery	GRN	63
Caleb	CHN	42
David, Sr.	NSN	222
George	UNN	153
James	BTL	329
James	OHO	7A
Jane	RCK	81A
Mary	JEF	32
Nathaniel	BTL	329
Robt.	BTL	329
Samuel	BTH	210
Samuel	BTL	329
Thomas	HAR	148
William	WDF	120A
READ?, Nathanl.	GRN	75
READE, Frances S.	LNC	2
Phillip	BKN	18
READER, John	GNP	177A
Lewis	SPN	21A
Samuel	PUL	62A
READER?, Amelia	BKN	5
READING----?, Joseph	SCT	111A
READING/ REDDING?, Nicholas G.	FKN	64
READING, Geo.	FKN	124
Jno.	FKN	124
John W.	SCT	131A
Joseph	FKN	124
Joseph	SCT	119A
Martha	TOD	128A
Saml.	FKN	124

Name	County	Page
READMAN, John	BBN	118
Wm. T.	BBN	118
READMO--?, Geo.	BBN	132
READY, Isham	JES	85
Isom	HRD	64
Sally	GRN	70
William	LNC	3
REAGIN, Samuel	FLD	8
REAM, Adam	NCH	111A
REAMS, John	CLY	125
Robt.	HRT	166
REAMY, Aaron	CWL	34
REANS?, Mills	CHN	40A
REARDDEN, Henry	BLT	168
REARDEN, Dennis	WDF	121A
REARDIN, Berry	WDF	104
REARDON, Hiram	SHE	174
REASONER, William	BLT	180
REASOR, Fredk.	SCT	121A
Will.	SCT	138A
REATHERFORD, James	LNC	29
Robt.	ADR	42
Thomas	GNP	170A
REAVES, James	GRN	75
Jo.	CWL	56
John	MAD	112
Joseph	SHE	174
Thomas	HRT	167
Wm.	ALN	118
REAVES?, Mills	CHN	40A
REBELIN, Martin	NCH	122A
REBO, Bartholomew	GRN	50
REBURN, William	UNN	148
RECER, Josiah	SHE	134A
Mikel	SHE	122A
RECER?, Daniel	SHE	140A
RECORDS, Josiah	PND	31A
Laban	PND	31A
Spencer	PND	31A
RECORDS?, Charles	CBL	13A
RECTOR, Jacob	LNC	73
Joel	CBL	9A
Nataniel	BLT	182
REDD, Dudley	CHN	30A
Elizebeth B.	WDF	103
Jno.	JEF	52
Lucy	TRG	11A
Samuel	FTE	67
William	TRG	11A
REDDECK, William	CBL	14A
REDDECK?, William	NSN	199
REDDICK, David	TOD	134
Whitmel	TRG	12
REDDIFORD, Wm.	ADR	44
REDDIN, Joseph	SHE	155
REDDING, Eli W.	GTN	117
George	HAR	136
James	BKN	20
John	BKN	8
Reuben	SHE	161
Samuel	FKN	122
Timothy	SHE	168
William	HAR	136
REDDINGHOUR, John	PND	25A
REDDISH, Ransom	FKN	120
Silas	FKN	128
REDIN, Nehemiah	WDF	122A
REDING, John H.	WDF	92
Shedrick	BKN	15
REDISH, John	SHE	116A
Nancy	GSN	149A
REDMAN, Abraham	MNR	195
Bennett	SHE	165
Charles K.	FTE	73
Elizebeth	WDF	97
George, Jr.	SHE	172
REDMAN, George, Sr.	SHE	172
George W.	CLK	81
Isaac	JEF	34
Isaac	MTG	297
John C.	FTE	78
Joseph	SHE	135A
Ledstone	SHE	155
Levy	FTE	75
Phebe	WDF	125A
Reuben	FTE	74
Robert	CLK	70
Robert	BLT	186
Samuel	LWS	88A
Thomas	GRN	69
Thomas	SHE	113A
Vincent	SHE	116A
Will	GRN	52
William	CLK	72
William T.	CLK	82
Willis	WDF	126A
Wm.	SHE	116A
REDMON, Charles	HAR	214
Charles	MBG	140A
Felix	MBG	140A
John	NSN	216
John, Sr.	NSN	213
John	GSN	148A
Richard	NSN	211
Thomas	HAR	214
Thos.	LVG	2
REDMOND, Aron	ADR	44
Betsey	ADR	44
George	HRD	18
James	ADR	44
Jas.	HRD	94
John	WAS	49A
Robt.	ADR	44
Solomon	LGN	41
Thomas	LGN	41
Thos.	ADR	42
REDPATH, Charles	BNE	32
REDWINE, Frederick	FTE	70
REECE, Elisha	LVG	7
George	HAR	204
Isaac	HAR	200
Jas., Jr.	FLG	26A
John	BRN	25
John	MAD	142
John	SHE	127A
Joseph B.	HOP	260
Thos. -.?	HRY	270
William	WYN	84A
REECE?, (See Reed?)	FLG	26A
REECER, Fredric	SHE	134A
REED, Widow	LVG	16
-----?	CWL	40
A. F.	TOD	131A
Abraham	JES	85
Alexander	SHE	133A
Alexr.	PUL	48A
Alexr.	GRD	97A
Alfred	BBN	102
Anderson	MAD	158
Andr.	MAS	69
Andrew	GRD	110A
Archibald	HRD	50
Benjamin	FTE	79
Benjamin T. / A.?	CSY	206
Boose?	CBL	15A
Caleb	SHE	131A
Caleb C.	SHE	134A
Caty	BBN	110
Charles	BNE	34
REED, Christo.	SCT	136A
Daniel	CBL	2A
David	MER	107
Elasha	MAD	180
Elijah	MER	107
Fredk.	BBN	132
Gabriel	HRY	202
Garland	MAD	150
Geo.	BBN	110
George	BNE	34
George	HRD	80
Grace	FTE	64
Hankerson	FKN	148
Hannan?	WRN	55A
Hennery	CSY	206
Henry	LVG	6
Hensley	HRD	74
Hensley, Senr.	HRD	74
Isaac	CWL	44
Jacob	HRD	10
Jacob	LNC	79
James	JEF	23
James	BNE	34
James	CLY	111
James	MAD	128
James	GRT	143
James	SPN	23A
James	PUL	38A
James	GRD	113A
Jas.	JEF	48
Jas., Jr.	JEF	48
Jas., Senr.	FLG	57A
Jas.	FLG	56A
Jno.	MAS	65
Jno.	MAS	69
Jno. W.	LNC	27
John	LNC	65
John	CLY	111
John	MER	116
John	BBN	126
John	MBG	139
John	HAR	146
John	MAD	162
John	BLT	166
John	MAD	172
John	SHE	172
John	BLT	174
John	HRY	200
John	WAS	27A
John	WAS	36A
John	RCK	81A
John	LWS	94A
John	SHE	134A
Jonath.	LNC	55
Jonathan	BBN	80
Jos. C.	FLG	41A
Joseph	BRN	25
Kaye &?	JEF	26
Lewis	HRD	34
Lewis	MAS	56
Margaret	TRG	4A
Mary	MER	106
Mathias	WTY	122A
Noah	TOD	130A
Philip	ADR	44
Richmond	BKN	8
Robert	BLT	178
Robt.	JEF	66
Robt.	HRD	78
Robt.	SCT	94A
Samuel	MBG	139
Samuel	wTY	111A
Stephen	CLY	111
Thomas	FTE	66
Thomas	SHE	134A
Thos.	JEF	20

Name	County	Page
REED, Thos.	MAD	126
Thos.	PUL	44A
Walter	HRT	167
Walter	BRK	287
Will	MAS	54
Will	MAS	69
Will.	LVG	5
Will. B.	LVG	5
William	MER	106
William	BTH	220
Wm.	JEF	48
Wm.	BBN	60
Wm.	HRD	80
Wm.	MAD	162
Zachariah	BNE	32
REED?, Archibald H.	BNE	50
Isaac	FTE	61
Jacob	FLG	27A
James	MAD	132
Jas., Jr.	FLG	26A
John	WDF	102
John	GTN	121
John	FLG	30A
Stephen	FLG	27A
William	WDF	105
REEDE, Christo.	SCT	97A
Saml.	SCT	98A
REEDE?, James	BKN	14
REEDER, Jehu	HND	10
Joel	SPN	20A
Wm.	CWL	55
REEDS, Gabriel	LNC	13
REEDS?, James	GTN	131
REEDY, Charles	TRG	11
Isaac	TRG	11
REEL, Jacob	JEF	47
REEL?, Jacob	JEF	48
REES, Ephraim	TRG	11
Stephen	MAS	73
REESE, Danl.	MAS	73
David	HAR	206
David	CBL	19A
George	SHE	148
Isaac	WRN	36A
Jacob	WRN	44A
John	JES	74
John	CBL	16A
Joseph	WRN	37A
Robert	WRN	44A
Thomas	CBL	19A
Thos.	JEF	25
Watson	CBL	19A
REESER, Ebenezer A. E.?	WRN	47A
REEVE?, Isaac	FTE	61
REEVES, Asa	FLG	40A
Austin	MAS	58
Bartley	MAS	57
Ben	MAS	65
Benj.	FLG	54A
Benjn.	MAS	57
Caleb	CBL	19A
Chs.	FKN	112
Elijah	FLG	43A
Geo.	FLG	40A
Geo.	FLG	53A
George	WRN	28A
Isaac	FLG	40A
Isam	JEF	42
Jas.	HRY	259
Jno.	MAS	54
John	CHN	29A
John	FLG	41A
Nathaniel	MBG	135
Noah	FLG	43A
REEVES, Peggy	FLG	43A
Smith	MAS	58
Spencer	FLG	54A
Stacey	CBL	15A
Stacy	MAS	68
Thos.	FLG	48A
REEVES?, Jeremiah	RCK	77A
Saml.	MAS	64
REFFITT, Christopher	MTG	291
Daniel	MTG	291
James	MTG	291
John	MTG	293
Joseph	MTG	295
Samuel	MTG	293
REFITT, John	MTG	255
REGAN, Jno.	MAS	61
Jno., Jr.	MAS	61
REGGS, John	WAS	43A
REGNEERSON, Anne	MER	107
Jacob	MER	107
REGNEERSON?, Isaac	MER	107
REICE, Isaac, Jun.	BKN	9
REICE?, Joseph	CLK	67
REID, Alexander	ETL	37
Alxr.	ADR	42
Archibald	MTG	255
David	CLK	80
George	CLK	92
George	WRN	36A
James	BRN	25
James	CLK	84
James	NCH	107A
John	CLD	164
John	WAS	45A
Joseph	MTG	285
Josiah	BTH	164
Mary	CHN	28
Peter	BTH	204
Polly	BTH	206
Richard	MTG	226
Robert	ETL	52
Robert	CLD	151
Sampson	MTG	289
Samuel	WRN	36A
Spencer	MTG	259
Stephen	ETL	42
Thomas	BTH	148
Thomas	MTG	233
William	FLD	35
William	MTG	273
William, Junr.	LWS	98A
William, Senr.	LWS	98A
William, Sr.	MTG	285
Winny F.	CHN	33A
Wm. P.	MTG	271
REID?, Joseph	CLK	67
Theoph.	ALN	134
REIDE, Isaac, Sr.	BKN	9
Mary	BTH	202
REIDE?, George	BKN	9
REIGHBOWEN?, Wm.	FLG	27A
REIGHNEY, Napper	GSN	148A
REILEY, John	CBL	12A
John	CBL	21A
John	CBL	22A
Smith	CBL	22A
Thomas	CBL	9A
Thomas	CBL	12A
William	CBL	22A
REILY, John	CLD	139
REINEY, James	CLK	99
REINEY?, Lewis	CLK	95
Thomas	CLK	95
REINHART, Jacob	JEF	20
REINS, Allen	MER	107
REINS, James	MER	106
William	MER	107
REISE?, George	BKN	9
REISER, Frederick	MNR	193
REITZEL, Peter	HAR	188
RELEY, Alexander	MER	107
REMCY?, See Remey?	GTN	123
REMEY, Henry	GTN	128
Jonathan	GTN	128
REMEY?, Isaac	GTN	122
John	GTN	123
Moses	GTN	123
REMLEY, Henry	BKN	26
REMY, John	CLD	157
RENALT, John	WAS	33A
RENCY?, James	WAS	56A
RENDER, Archibald	CBL	7A
George	OHO	8A
Joshua	OHO	4A
Robt., Senr.	OHO	4A
Thomas	OHO	7A
RENDER?, Robert	OHO	4A
RENECOR?, John	HAR	146
RENESOR?, Adam	HAR	146
RENEY, Wm.	WAS	67A
RENFRO, Isaac	BRN	25
Jas.	CHN	40A
Jesse	BRN	24
John	BRN	24
William	BRN	25
RENFROE, James	BTL	329
Jane	BRK	287
John	BTL	329
Moses	BTL	329
Moses	GRD	96A
Peter	BTL	329
William	GRD	123A
RENFROW, Joseph	MAD	110
Mark	TRG	8
Peter, Jr.	MAD	104
Peter, Sr.	MAD	104
Saml.	MAD	104
Tho.	GRD	112A
RENICK, George	CLK	100
RENICK?, Jesse	GRN	54
RENN, Wm.	MAD	154
RENNET?, Thomas	WYN	82A
RENNEX, Alexander	WDF	95A
Lydia	WDF	94A
RENNICK, James	BRN	26
James	LNC	29
John	BBN	104
William	WRN	59A
Wm	BRN	26
RENNO?, John	CLD	153
RENO, Alfred	CWL	43
Baylis	FLG	35A
Jessee	MBG	140A
John	MBG	135
Lewis	MBG	135
Lewis	HAR	144
RENSHAW, Andrew	WRN	54A
Nancy	SPN	12A
RENTFRO, Ab.	RCK	76A
John	RCK	77A
Mark	RCK	76A
Mark	RCK	76A
Mary	RCK	80A
RENTFROM, Isaac	RCK	77A
RENTFROW, Margar.	LNC	61
RENY?, Bazzil	WAS	36A
REOMAN?, Richard	SHE	120A
REPLY, William	MAD	116
REPPETOE, Peter	ADR	42
REPPETTOE, W.	ADR	54
RESCIN, Bannister	CBL	11A

Name	County	Page
RESPASS, Frances	BBN	138
RESPASS?, Thomas	BBN	138
REST?, Adam	CBL	17A
RESTINE, Lewis	HRD	84
RETHERFORD, Archabald	JES	83
George	GRD	98A
Joseph	WDF	111A
Will	GRD	98A
Wm.	BRK	287
Wm.	WAS	32A
Wm.	WAS	52A
RETTINGER, Abraham	JEF	50
REUBANS, James	BKN	8
REUBY, Henry	LNC	3
James	LNC	69
REUCH, Aaron	JEF	35
REVALL?, Thomas	CBL	23A
REVALLE?, Sarah	CBL	23A
REVEAL, Joseph	NCH	117A
Michael	NCH	111A
REVEILL(E), (See Revall?	CBL	23A
REVES, Wm.	MAD	134
Wm.	MAD	172
REVIELLE?, James	CBL	3A
REWBARTS, Samuel	CSY	208
REXROT, Adam	ADR	44
John	ADR	44
REYNALDS, William	WTY	127A
REYNARD, Benj.	PUL	39A
REYNEERSON, Abraham	MER	107
REYNNO, Charles C.	BBN	116
REYNOLDS, A.	TOD	134
Aaron	HOP	262
Abraham	HRT	167
Admiral	WRN	71A
Ann	HOP	262
Barny	JES	89
Bartemas	HRT	166
Caleb	LNC	39
Caleb	HRT	166
Charles	LVG	6
Charles	CLD	151
Charles	HRT	167
Chs.	JEF	51
David	HRT	167
Dolly	LNC	17
Dolly	NCH	121A
Edwd.	FLG	79A
Elisha	CWL	56
Ewd.	HRT	166
Foutain	LNC	73
Francis	FKN	58
Francis D.	MAD	144
George	LNC	19
Henery	ADR	3
Henry	BBN	80
Hugh	NSN	184
Isaac	BKN	15
Isaac	MAS	73
James	BKN	23
James	LNC	29
James	CHN	34
James	HRY	206
James	WRN	54A
Jesse	PUL	39A
Jesse	PUL	40A
Joel	CHN	40A
John	LVG	10
John	BKN	13
John	LNC	21
John	LNC	41
John	CWL	46
John	JEF	56
REYNOLDS, John	FTE	109
John	MAD	120
John	MTG	249
John	MTG	267
John G.	TRG	10
John H.	TRG	11
Joseph	LNC	3
Joseph	HOP	262
Joseph	MBG	141A
Levi	MAD	168
Little	HRD	78
Matthias	HRT	166
Michael	CHN	34
Nancy	CWL	56
Nathanile	HRT	167
Nathl.	BRN	25
Perry	LNC	21
Pleasant	CLY	111
Richard	SHE	113A
Richard	NCH	115A
Richard	MGB	137A
Samuel	WRN	55A
Tandy	LNC	79
Tho.	MAS	55
Thomas	JES	78
Thomas	JES	89
Thomas	HOP	262
Thomas	BRK	285
Thomas	WRN	55A
Thos.	HRD	90
Thos.	MAD	168
Thos.	PUL	36A
Thos.	SHE	143A
Tobias	CLY	111
William	CHN	34
William	HRD	90
William	MTG	263
Wm., (Near Ep. King's)	BRN	26
Wm.	HRT	167
Wm.	PUL	46A
Z.	BBN	118
REYNONDS, Michael	CLK	101
REZER?, Philip J./ I.?	NSN	187
REZIN?, Thomas	TRG	8A
RHEA, Charles	LGN	25
Chas.	LGN	24
Jno.	LVG	8
Joseph	LVG	8
Thomas	GRN	52
William	GRN	57
RHOADDS, Bradford	MBG	139
RHOADES, Henry	CWL	56
RHOADS, Beacham	GSN	149A
Benjamin	MBG	142A
Daniel	MBG	136A
David	MBG	140A
Henery	GSN	149A
Henry	MGB	137A
Jacob	MBG	136A
Jacob	MBG	136A
Jacob	GSN	148A
Jacob	GSN	149A
Jesse	GSN	148A
John	MBG	137
John	GSN	148A
Josiah	GSN	149A
Samuel	GSN	149A
William	MBG	138
RHODES, ----?	CWL	32
Charles	GRN	66
Elias	BRK	287
Ignatus	NSN	189
James	MNR	199
John	HRD	22
RHODES, John	MBG	136
Joseph	MAD	166
Saml.	FLG	72A
Saml. E.	FLG	72A
Silas	NCH	118A
Solomon	MBG	136A
Wiley	CWL	56
RHONEY, James	SHE	157
Joseph	SHE	156
Joseph, Sr.	SHE	156
RHORA?, Jacob	FTE	69
RHORER, Henry	JES	85
RI-LY, Philip	FTE	70
RIAN, Elizabeth	MER	106
Solomon	MER	107
RIATHEE?, Hansford	CSY	208
RIATTREE?, Hansford	CSY	208
RIBLAND, John	MTG	226
William	MTG	229
Wm., Jr.	MTG	251
RICE, Abraham	FTE	94
Allen	LVG	2
Ann	CHN	40
Archibald	GNP	176A
Aron	FLG	42A
Bavil	FKN	154
Ben.	GRD	121A
Benj. G.	LVG	2
Benjamin	FTE	93
Benjamin	CBL	9A
Benjm.	GRN	57
Caleb	FTE	95
Campbell	BTH	198
Charles	LNC	75
Charles	HRL	118
Charles	SHE	169
Charles	BTH	198
Claiborne	MBG	143
Coonrod	FLD	39
David	GRN	69
David	WDF	97
David	CLY	128
David	HRY	200
David	MTG	261
David, Sr.	MTG	241
David M.	CSY	222
Delilah	CBL	9A
Edmond	JEF	46
Edmund	UNN	154
Elias	HRD	68
Elijah	GNP	165A
Ezekiel	BNE	32
Ezekiel	MBG	133A
Ezekiel	GNP	176A
Francis	LGN	44
Fredk.	FLG	46A
Gabriel	MER	116
Gabriel	GRD	121A
George	MER	107
George	BRK	285
George	GNP	176A
Henry	BTH	178
Hiram	NCH	114A
Holeman	BTH	198
Holeman, Snr.	BTH	190
Hudson	BKN	6
Isaac I./ J.?	MAD	128
J. / I.? H.	CHN	46
Jacob	JES	83
Jacob	JES	91
Jacob	SHE	160
Jacob	GRD	106A
James	LVG	10
James	BKN	20
James	LGN	44

RICE, James MAD 148
James BTH 202
James MTG 241
James WYN 84A
James MBG 143A
Jas. H. LVG 3
Jasper JES 75
Jefferson JES 69
Jeremiah LGN 47
Jesse SHE 150
Jessee MBG 143
Jessee H. MBG 141
Joel BNE 32
John FLD 38
John CLK 78
John JES 82
John MER 107
John SHE 150
John HRY 198
John BTL 329
John, Jr. HRY 228
John FLG 45A
John SHE 113A
John V. BKN 13
Jonath. HRY 244
Jonathan LGN 29
Joseph JES 82
Joshua BNE 32
Levi HRD 92
Lucy MER 116
Martin FLD 35
Mary GRD 104A
Matthew LNC 75
Micheal, Jr. JES 82
Micheal, Sr. JES 82
Morris LGN 39
Nancy MER 107
Patrick H. LVG 3
Phillip R. BKN 20
Phinias G. MER 116
Polly BBN 124
Polly MTG 261
Randolph GRN 70
Richd. GRN 70
Rowlett SHE 170
Sally FLG 43A
Saml. BKN 6
Samuel FLD 35
Samuel JES 77
Samuel MBG 143
Samuel HRY 198
Samuel L. BRK 289
Sarah MAD 148
Shelton MTG 287
Simon PND 29A
Thomas BRK 289
Thomas WYN 83A
William LVG 2
William BNE 32
William LNC 63
William JES 79
William FTE 109
William MBG 141
William SHE 174
William HOP 262
William CBL 8A
William WYN 80A
William WDF 95A
William NCH 116A
William B. CSY 212
William G. BTH 212
Wm. HRY 254
Wm. FLG 45A
Wm. FLG 68A
Wm. F. HRY 256
Wm. M. HRY 244
RICE?, Abram GNP 176A
Eliza GRN 75
Joseph SCT 93A
Lucy CLK 66
RICER?, Daniel SHE 140A
Joseph SCT 93A
RICH---?, Joshua ALN 102
RICH, Allen CBL 7A
Israel BNE 34
John CBL 6A
Joseph CBL 5A
Obediah CWL 56
Sam. HRY 254
Samuel CBL 11A
Samuel CBL 14A
Stephen CBL 11A
Warren WRN 37A
William MNR 217
Wm. CWL 56
RICHARD, Aberella NSN 197
Joseph, Sr. LGN 33
Robert CLK 72
Susanna NSN 197
RICHARDS, (Also See Richds.)
-m.? JEF 28
Abram ALN 98
Annes PUL 42A
Benjamin ADR 44
Caleb CSY 212
Elziphen LWS 99A
Geo. BTH 166
Henry JEF 39
Isaah MAD 118
Jacob ADR 44
James FLG 24A
James JES 77
James BTH 166
James CBL 23A
Jane LWS 95A
John LWS 99A
John LNC 25
John JEF 31
John ALN 112
John BBN 146
John FLG 24A
John FLG 45A
John LWS 99A
Leonard CSY 222
Leonard, Jr. CSY 210
Leonard, Jun. CSY 222
Lewis UNN 154
Polly BTH 212
Richard CLK 79
Robert BTH 212
Saml. LNC 25
Thomas OHO 10A
Thomas GNP 174A
Tomsy? BTH 212
Wm. JEF 39
Wm. LNC 59
Wm. GNP 171A
RICHARDSON, Allen MNR 215
Amos ETL 47
Amos HRD 84
Augustus CBL 12A
Benjamin ETL 48
Benjamin CSY 218
Benjamin CBL 2A
Betsey BRN 25
Bradley CLK 62
Charles PUL 57A
Daniel ETL 48
Daniel CHN 34A
Danl., Sr. HRD 12
Danl. S. HRD 40
Davd. PUL 47A
RICHARDSON, David ETL 48
David JES 79
David MER 106
David BRK 285
David BRK 287
Elijah FTE 88
Elijah MER 106
Eliza. KNX 302
Elizabeth FKN 128
Fisher SHE 138A
Francis CHN 41
George BRN 25
George FTE 79
George CLD 157
Hugh CBL 20A
Ishum HRT 167
Izarel HRD 48
James HND 9
James BBN 112
James M. MTG 281
Jamima WRN 51A
Jeremiah FTE 95
Jesse HRL 118
Jesse PUL 55A
Jno. PUL 46A
Jno. C. FKN 72
Jno. D. FKN 152
John HRD 22
John LNC 47
John ETL 48
John FTE 102
John MER 106
John MER 107
John, Jr. ETL 37
John, Sr. ETL 51
John CBL 16A
John WRN 38A
John WTY 114A
John C. FTE 78
John C., Jr. FTE 62
Jonathan PUL 39A
Joseph NSN 221
Joseph, Jr.? WYN 89A
Joseph WRN 55A
Joseph WYN 89A
Joshua SHE 138A
Landie MER 106
Landy MTG 281
Lewis BTH 204
Lewis MTG 239
Marquis FTE 112
Martin DVS 16A
Mary GRN 74
Mary MAD 126
Mary CBL 12A
Mary--? CLK 102
Morgan CLD 161
Moses BBN 112
Nat. FKN 126
Paten CLK 77
Pearson PUL 68A
Philip HRD 80
Philip T. CLK 93
Rian ETL 50
Richard WRN 28A
Robert CHN 31
Robt. R. FLG 65A
Salley MAD 148
Samuel WYN 89A
Shadrack CLD 157
Stephen JEF 37
Tho. MAS 62
Thomas ETL 53
Thomas JES 90
Thomas JES 90
Thomas MBG 135A

Name	County	Page
RICHARDSON, Thos.	MAD	148
Thos. S.	JEF	36
Wesley	CLK	64
William	ETL	53
William	CLK	66
William	FTE	74
William	MER	106
William	HAR	148
William	MAD	180
Willis	CLK	78
Wm.	HRD	44
Wm.	JEF	46
Wm.	HRD	74
Wm.	MAD	116
Wm.	HRT	167
Wm.	CHN	31A
Wm.	PUL	46A
Wm.	SHE	114A
Wm.	GSN	148A
RICHARDSON?, William	FTE	63
RICHARES?, Thomas	GNP	166A
RICHART, William	NCH	115A
RICHASON, John	GRN	71
William	GRN	70
RICHDS., Eliphalet	JEF	28
RICHE, Archabald	HAR	154
Mary	JEF	20
RICHEE, Tabitha	HRT	167
RICHERDS, Wm.	FKN	156
RICHERDSON, Isaac	WAS	86A
RICHERSON, Ames	GNP	176A
RICHESON, Baylor	GRD	102A
Danl.	GRD	118A
Joseph	GRN	60
Mary	HAR	140
Ste.	GRD	83A
Wm., Sr.?	GRD	98A
RICHEY, Alex	ALN	132
Alexander	ALN	130
Andrew C.	ALN	130
D. W.	MAS	79
Esau	NCH	103A
George	ALN	134
Henry	NCH	111A
Isaac, Jr.	NCH	110A
Isaac	NCH	110A
James	PND	19A
Jno.	ALN	130
John	ALN	100
John	FLG	27A
John	NCH	103A
John	NCH	103A
Noah	NCH	103A
Samuel	ALN	128
Solomon	NCH	110A
Will	MAS	81
William	BRK	289
Wm.	MAS	68
Wm.	ALN	130
Zachariah	NCH	110A
RICHIE, Alexander	WRN	57A
Andrew	BTH	172
Duncan	BTH	150
James	BTH	162
Stephen	WRN	46A
RICHISON, Amos	GRD	107A
William	GRD	85A
RICHMOND, David	WTY	118A
Ezra	FKN	76
Hathaway	CBL	2A
Jesse	HRY	214
Js.	HRY	214
William	WTY	119A
RICHY, Adam	HAR	194
Clocket	CLY	131
RICHY, Gilbert	HAR	194
Isaac	CLY	111
Robert	BRN	24
Samuel	BRN	25
RICK, Jeremiah	MNR	211
Robert	MNR	193
RICKEL, C. H.	ADR	42
RICKETS, Alexander	BNE	34
Betsey	MAD	142
Edwd.	FLG	64A
Ezekiah	MAD	162
John, Jr.	FLG	60A
John, Snr.	FLG	60A
Reubin	CLK	91
Thomas	WRN	63A
William	BNE	34
Zedekiah	WRN	63A
RICKETS?, Robert	CLK	71
RICKETT, Rebec.	JEF	21
RICKETTS, Elizabeth	MNR	215
Gerard	SHE	158
Jno.	MAS	71
Jonathan	BLT	158
Letty	WAS	30A
Levy	HND	4
Rulof	MAS	71
Thomas	JES	80
Thomas	MTG	267
RICKEY, David	MAS	65
Elizabeth	GRT	141
RICKHERT, Isaac	MBG	138A
Jacob	MBG	138
John	MBG	138A
RICKMAN, Tho.	ALN	122
RICKS, John	NSN	209
Jonathan	TRG	5A
Richard	TRG	5A
Thomas	NSN	209
William	NSN	209
RICLLES, Will	SCT	116A
RICTER, Samuel	WYN	81A
RIDDELL, Archibald	BNE	32
Isaac	BNE	34
James	BNE	30
James	BNE	34
Lewis	BNE	48
Neal	BNE	32
Valentine	BNE	30
William	BNE	30
Wm.	BBN	124
RIDDLE, Ben H.	HRD	64
Benjamine	BRK	287
Ebenezor	PND	22A
George	SHE	154
George	PND	21A
James	CLD	150
James	CBL	11A
Jas.	RCK	76A
Jeremiah	UNN	147
John	PND	18A
John	SCT	105A
Joseph	CLD	158
Lewis	BTH	196
Robt.	PND	19A
Saml.	SCT	133A
Samuel	SPN	19A
Stephen	FLG	24A
William	GTN	125
William	SCT	104A
RIDDLE?, Thos.	FKN	116
RIDDON, John	BNE	32
RIDELL, Aquilla	ETL	48
Robert	ETL	50
RIDEN, William	MTG	245
William	MTG	257
RIDENS, James	WRN	54A
RIDEOUT, Elijah	HND	6
RIDER, (See Riden)	MTG	245
Ben	HRD	90
Daniel	FTE	68
John	HRD	24
Joseph	HRD	90
Nancy	FTE	81
RIDGE, Jno.	JEF	36
Robertson	PUL	56A
William	CSY	212
RIDGEL?, John	KNX	282
RIDGELL, Lewis	BLT	178
RIDGES, William	MTG	226
RIDGEWAY, Mathew	FLG	71A
Osburn	LNC	25
Paul	HRD	20
Saml.	LNC	29
Samuel	BLT	162
William	BLT	178
Zackariah	CLK	80
RIDGLEY, Frederick	FTE	63
RIDGWAY, John	OHO	4A
Ninian	CLK	85
Rezin	CLK	71
Richd.	SHE	159
Samuel	SHE	173
RIDLEY, Edward	HOP	262
Thomas	HOP	260
RIDWAY, Josa.	FLG	40A
RIECE?, Benjamin	FLD	10
RIED, David	WRN	36A
Walker	MAS	80
RIELY, Charles	BKN	6
Isaac	BKN	9
Sam	FTE	60
RIFE?, Abram	GNP	176A
RIFFE, Christopher	CSY	206
Jacob	CSY	212
John	CSY	204
John, Jr.	CSY	204
RIFFEE?, Christopher	ADR	44
RIGDON, Jas.	FLG	63A
Wm.	BRN	25
Wm.	FLG	63A
RIGES?, Hiram?	RCK	82A
RIGG, Charles	GNP	166A
David	MER	107
George	LGN	35
Jno.	FKN	128
Jno.	FKN	132
Jonathan	FTE	89
Joseph	GNP	177A
Peter	FKN	130
Richard	FKN	146
Samuel	GNP	177A
Stephen	GNP	177A
Thomas	GNP	177A
Zachariah	GNP	177A
RIGGE, Isaac?	WAS	69A
Jacob	WAS	49A
RIGGEN, Edward	JES	80
RIGGEN?, Jesse	NCH	122A
RIGGINS, David	ADR	44
RIGGS, ----h?	DVS	7A
----m?	DVS	7A
Charles	MNR	199
Clement	MAS	55
Erasmus	NCH	127A
Greenberry	MTG	245
Isaac, Jr.	CBL	15A
Isaac	CBL	7A
Israel	TOD	131
Jacob	CWL	56
James	MAS	61

Name	County	Page
RIGGS, James	MTG	253
James	CBL	6A
John, Junr.	LWS	94A
John	CBL	7A
John	RCK	75A
John	LWS	94A
Levi	PUL	59A
Nancy	NSN	210
Nathl.	MAS	69
Saml.	MAS	55
Saml.	FLG	47A
Saml.	RCK	82A
Samuel	MTG	283
Sheldon	LWS	90A
Silas	RCK	78A
Stephen	WAS	43A
Wm.	WAS	43A
RIGHT, Benjamin	BTH	194
Carter	HRT	166
Charles	ALN	96
Guy	CBL	3A
Henry	ALN	100
Isaac	ADR	44
James	CBL	13A
Jarott	ALN	98
Jno.	JEF	59
John	ALN	96
John	HRT	166
John	SHE	140A
Joseph	ALN	142
Levi	HRT	166
Philip	ALN	96
Reubin	JEF	51
Tabitha	HRT	166
Thos.	MAD	104
Thos. S.	MAD	100
Wm.	HRT	166
RIGHT?, John A.	MAD	158
Willis	HRY	252
RIGHTLEY, Isaac	ALN	110
Philip	ALN	110
RIGLEY?, John	CLK	67
RIGNEY, Harrison	CSY	214
Jessee	GRN	59
Stephen	WAS	22A
RIGSBEY, James	ALN	126
RIGSBY, John	ALN	124
William	GRD	98A
RIKER, Charles	MER	106
RILEY, Louis	MER	107
RILAND?, Joseph	ALN	132
RILES, Isham	ALN	122
RILEY, -----?	DVS	3A
Abram	ADR	44
Amas	DVS	16A
Ann	HRD	52
Benjamin	FTE	100
Christopher	FTE	98
Delpa?	WRN	34A
Edward	MER	107
Edwd.	FLG	52A
Francis	HRD	52
George	MER	107
Henry	BNE	32
Isaac M.	CHN	35
James	FTE	97
James	CLY	129
Jas.	SCT	115A
Jer.	HRY	264
Jerrard	HAR	200
Joel	WAS	83A
John	ETL	50
John	MER	107
John	CLY	129
John	SHE	168
John, Sr.	CLY	129
RILEY, John	PND	15A
John	WAS	83A
John	NCH	119A
John C.	WAS	78A
John M.	BRK	227
Martha	WAS	24A
Michael	HRD	52
Moses	WRN	33A
Nimian	FTE	100
Ninian	HAR	200
Patrick, Jr.	CLY	132
Patrick, Sr.	CLY	111
Saml.	NCH	119A
Samuel	WDF	101
Samuel	LWS	88A
Smith	WAS	82A
Thomas	MTG	275
William	ETL	54
William	CLY	129
William	PUL	52A
William	LWS	86A
Wm.	CWL	56
Wm.	MAD	152
Wm.	MAD	164
Wm.	SHE	130A
Zachariah	CLY	129
RILY, Nancy	BRK	289
RIMCY / RIMCY?, See Remey?	GTN	123
RIME?, Jacob	RCK	84A
RIMER?, Silles	RCK	84A
RIMMINGTON, James	HAR	220
RINEHART, Michl.	LNC	17
RINEHEART, Peggy	WAS	65A
RINELLI?, James	CBL	3A
RINEN?, (See Rivers?)	RCK	79A
RINER, Christopher	FTE	67
RINERS?, John	RCK	79A
RINEY, B. John	GSN	148A
Clemont	WAS	72A
Jonathan	WAS	49A
Robert	WAS	73A
RINEY?, Francis	WAS	80A
Richd.	WAS	87A
RING, Eliza	TOD	125
Mary	TOD	125
RINGO, Burtes	FLG	48A
Cornelias	HRY	190
Cornelius P.	MTG	225
Cornelus	HRD	46
Jno. R.	FLG	32A
John	MAD	112
John	SHE	135A
Joseph	MTG	259
Major	HRY	190
Major	MTG	259
Peter	MTG	225
Richard	BTH	154
Robert	MTG	225
Samuel	MTG	231
RININ?, (See Riners?)	RCK	79A
RINKER, Geo.	JEF	31
RINSEY?, Zachariah	NSN	218
RION, David	MER	107
RION?, Noah	ALN	108
RIPERCLAN?, Abraham	MER	106
Frederic	MER	106
RIPEY, Joshua	FLD	3
RIPPETTOE, Wm.	ADR	44
RIPPLE, Jacob	LGN	46
Michael, Jr.	MGB	137A
Michael, Ser.	MBG	133A
RIPPY, James	CLY	121
RISING, Joseph	CLK	65
RISINGER, Danl.	JEF	36
Elizabeth	JEF	40
Martin	JEF	49
Sally	JEF	53
RISK, Betsey	SCT	100A
James	SCT	99A
John	SCT	100A
Robt.	SCT	99A
RISLEY, Elihu	BLT	186
James	BLT	184
James, Jr.	BLT	186
RISLEY?, Samuel	BLT	172
RISNER, Michael	FLD	5
RISTER, John	GNP	170A
Nancy	GNP	170A
RISTINE?, John	GTN	128
Richard	GTN	127
RISTON, John	CHN	30
N. G.	CHN	30
RITCHARDS, Burton	BBN	82
RITCHEE, James	BBN	124
Jane	FTE	63
RITCHEY, James	CLD	137
John	CLD	137
John	SCT	100A
Samuel	CLD	137
Stephen	SCT	102A
RITCHIE, Abram	SHE	135A
David	SHE	109A
Isaac	SHE	120A
Isaac	SHE	135A
James	CLK	99
James	FTE	106
James	SHE	132A
John	SHE	132A
Jordin	WDF	105A
Jos.	SHE	135A
Joseph	SHE	132A
Robert	SHE	135A
Robt.	CWL	38
Samuel	CLK	70
Samuel	FTE	106
Thos.	SHE	120A
Wm.	SHE	119A
RITE, Francis	SCT	123A
James	FTE	81
Richard	FTE	101
RITE?, Samuel	FTE	107
RITER, Jno.	JEF	55
RITMAN, John	WYN	103A
RITTENHOUSE, Sarah	CBL	5A
RITTER, Charles	FTE	66
Coonrod	JES	90
David B.	BRN	24
George A.	FTE	93
Isaac	BRN	26
Joel	BRN	25
John	BRN	24
John	JES	86
Joseph	BRN	25
Micheal	JES	89
Preston	BRN	25
Richd.	MAS	72
Wilson	BRN	34
RITZGERALD, Philip	SHE	161
RIVERS, James	WAS	59A
Peggry	GRN	76
William	GRN	76
William	CLD	162
RIVERS?, Jacob	RCK	79A
RIYLEY?, John	CLK	67
RIZER, Jacob	NSN	175
Joshua	LGN	22
Mathew	WRN	75A
RO---?, Martin?	LVG	18

RO---T?, Mary FTE 55
ROACH, Amy MER 107
Baylor MAD 108
Bryan HOP 262
David J. MER 107
Gabl. TOD 127
H. Richard GSN 149A
Henery CBL 15A
Henry BTH 182
Isaac GRN 62
Isaac GRN 71
John JEF 34
John FTE 70
John JES 73
John MAD 136
John BTH 192
Littleberry MER 107
M. CWL 33
Stephen CWL 33
Thom CWL 56
Thom CWL 56
Thos. MAD 94
Thos. MAD 120
William MER 107
William MNR 199
Wm. CWL 43
ROADES, James NSN 217
ROADS, Andrew WTY 115A
Basel NSN 188
Benj. WAS 42A
Danl. HRT 166
Will. KNX 306
ROADS?, Robert WAS 38A
ROAN, Adam BTL 329
Elizabeth MER 115
George BTL 329
John BTL 329
ROARCK, John WAS 59A
ROARK, James CLY 122
John HRL 118
John HRL 118
John MBG 138A
Martin MBG 142
Patrick CWL 42
William MBG 142
ROBANS, Thomas BRK 285
ROBARD, William J./ I. BLT 174
ROBARDS, Archibald A. MER 107
George, Capt. MER 107
George S. BLT 174
Humphey BRK 285
Jesse MER 107
Joseph BRK 287
Robert MER 107
Squire BTH 164
Thomas JES 82
Thomas MER 107
Thomas BRK 287
William JES 81
ROBB, Frederick JES 69
Henry JEF 32
Henry JES 84
Hugh W. UNN 154
James JES 88
James JES 88
Jno. MAS 55
John JES 84
John LWS 95A
Joseph FTE 89
Joseph LWS 86A
Micheal JES 88
Robert, Senr. LWS 95A
Robert TRG 3A
Samuel FTE 70
ROBB, Will. H. LVG 7
William LWS 95A
ROBBETT, John WRN 51A
ROBBINS, Mrs. MAS 71
--? HRY 214
Abel HRY 222
Absolam HRY 226
Bartlett TRG 3A
Benjamine BRK 289
Charles HAR 216
George HRY 226
Jno. MAS 67
John HRY 230
Micajah HRY 226
Nancy SHE 167
Silas W. CLK 102
Will HRY 222
William HRY 214
ROBBISON, John BRK 285
ROBENITT, Joseph CLK 94
ROBERDS, Nancy BTH 160
Nicholas JES 78
William JES 85
ROBERS, Jonathan OHO 4A
ROBERSON, Andrew SHE 121A
Archer SHE 116A
Clarissa UNN 147
Daniel SPN 17A
David MBG 143
Elizabeth MER 106
Ezekiel FLD 32
George SHE 129A
Henry MER 107
Henry SHE 128A
Horatio SHE 137A
James ETL 39
James GRN 53
James GRN 69
Jessee ETL 49
John FLD 33
John SPN 5A
John SHE 109A
John SHE 126A
John D. MER 117
Maxamillion SHE 126A
Mills SHE 116A
Philip SHE 116A
Richard SHE 137A
Robert MBG 141A
Simeon JES 75
Solomon FLD 31
Thomas UNN 147
William ETL 45
Wm. SHE 135A
Zacheriah PND 25A
ROBERSON?, John LVG 18
ROBERTS, Aaron PUL 61A
Abner SCT 121A
Alex JEF 45
Alexander NCH 128A
Alfred LGN 44
Amos WYN 100A
Ardemas D. BRN 24
Azariah SCT 124A
Benj. PUL 40A
Benjamin LGN 45
Benjamin SHE 151
Benjamin HAR 170
Benjamin HRY 180
Benjamin, Jr. SHE 150
Benjamin DVS 15A
Benjn. SCT 104A
Billingsly BNE 34
Boanerges LGN 27
Charles LGN 34
Charles NSN 188
ROBERTS, Colburn GNP 173A
Cornelius FLD 40
Daniel BNE 34
Daniel MAD 100
Danl. G. HRT 166
David HOP 262
David PUL 65A
Deana NSN 194
Drury BRN 25
Edward MAD 100
Edward MAD 108
Edward FKN 114
Edward CSY 212
Edward MTG 251
Edward MTG 269
Edward MTG 275
Edwd. WAS 34A
Elijah BBN 116
Elijah BBN 120
Emanuel S. NSN 204
Evan FTE 92
Faris CLY 120
Feberick MAD 106
Frances LGN 34
Frances WAS 33A
Francis MTG 257
Frankey GNP 167A
George HND 6
George CLK 64
George CLK 74
George HRY 188
George WAS 77A
Gideon PUL 41A
Greenberry LGN 25
Hannah? BLT 190
Henley NCH 112A
Henry CWL 33
Henry FKN 116
Henry GTN 126
Henry DVS 16A
Henry WYN 95A
Henry R. HRY 256
Hugh HAR 160
Isaac BRN 25
Isaac FLD 42
Isaac GRN 78
Isabella NSN 192
J?. J?. SHE 133A
Jacob JEF 45
Jacob LNC 73
James FLD 4
James HND 6
James FLD 40
James MAD 96
James OWN 100
James TOD 125
James MAD 136
James, Jr. DVS 15A
James DVS 15A
James PUL 58A
James PUL 65A
James NCH 103A
James SHE 140A
Jane SHE 160
Jas. HRY 244
Jas. RCK 82A
Jas./ Jos.? HRY 250
Jas./ Jos? HRY 259
Jesse LVG 9
Jesse CLY 114
Jessee GRN 56
Jessee GRN 78
Jessey MAD 112
Jno. FKN 160
Jno. HRY 243
Jno. HRY 259

Name	County	Page
ROBERTS, Jno.	HRY	263
Joel	MAD	100
Joel	HAR	208
Joel	PUL	37A
John	FLD	15
John	LGN	23
John	CWL	43
John	BBN	74
John	MER	106
John	MAD	108
John	CLY	130
John	SHE	162
John	HAR	206
John	TRG	11A
John	PUL	55A
John?	DVS	19A
Jos.	HRY	259
Jos.	TOD	129A
Joseph	LGN	44
Joseph	CLY	112
Joseph	SHE	157
Joseph	CLD	161
Joseph	MTG	275
Joseph	BRK	285
Joshua	LGN	30
Laurence	MAD	108
Lewis	LGN	30
Lewis	LWS	89A
Mack	WRN	36A
Maning?	MAD	134
Margaret	MAD	108
Merry	DVS	16A
Moses	CLY	121
Naman	MAD	134
Nathan	MAD	96
Nathan	MAD	170
Peter	GTN	128
Philip	ETL	42
Philips	BNE	34
Redding	NCH	129A
Rich	RCK	79A
Saml.	FLG	26A
Samuel	GRN	53
Sarah	TOD	134
Shelton	MAD	170
Stephen	LVG	4
Swinkfield	CLY	120
Thomas	BRN	25
Thomas	FTE	101
Thomas	HAR	156
Thomas	HOP	262
Thomas	NCH	114A
Thos.	MAD	142
Thos.	HRY	254
Thos. C.	WAS	77A
Thos. H.	FKN	116
Thos. Q.	NSN	178
Wesley	BNE	48
Widw.	CWL	33
Will	SCT	122A
William	HND	5
William	BNE	34
William	FTE	65
William	CLD	143
William	SHE	151
William	SHE	159
William	CLD	162
William	NSN	188
William	MTG	229
William, Sr.	WYN	96A
William	DVS	15A
Willis	SHE	166
Willis	DVS	15A
Wm.	CWL	43
Wm.	MAD	102
Wm.	FKN	114
ROBERTS, Wm.	MAD	144
Wm.	HRY	251
Wm.	HRY	254
Wm.	HRY	260
Wm.	HRY	264
Wm.	WAS	31A
Wm.	RCK	78A
Wm. B./ R.?	HRY	256
Wm. S.	MAD	158
Zacheriah	OHO	8A
ROBERTS?, -----?	LVG	18
Henry?	WAS	38A
John	LVG	18
William	HAR	132
ROBERTSON, Abner	FKN	88
Agness	CHN	44
Alex.	CWL	34
Alexander	WRN	35A
Alxander	MAD	166
Andrew	SCT	121A
Benjamin	OWN	99
Benjamin	GTN	123
Benjamin	NSN	201
Bob/ Rob?	GRD	95A
Daniel	HRD	40
Daniel	CSY	218
Daniel	SPN	8A
David	MAD	166
David	SCT	96A
David	SCT	102A
Dick (A Free Negroe)	CLK	103
Dudley	WAS	77A
Duncan F.	LNC	81
Edward	PUL	66A
Elijah	SCT	114A
Elizabeth	SCT	100A
Fleming	WAS	87A
G. W.	GRD	83A
Galvin	MNR	191
Geo.	PUL	42A
George	HRD	38
George	HND	11A
George	WAS	22A
George	GRD	102A
Hanah	LNC	29
Henry	GRD	104A
Holcomb	PUL	66A
Hosey	LNC	53
J.	TOD	124A
James	BRN	24
James	JEF	42
James	LNC	53
James	MAD	118
James	MAD	138
James	SPN	21A
James	WYN	94A
Jas.	SCT	114A
Jas. F.	SCT	95A
Jeremiah	WRN	35A
John	BNE	34
John	LNC	67
John	CLK	81
John	MAD	96
John	BBN	116
John	MAD	132
John	BTH	172
John	NSN	183
John	HOP	260
John	HOP	260
John, Jr.	MNR	211
John, Sr.	MNR	195
John, Sr.	MNR	211
John	WRN	64A
John	SCT	125A
Johnan.	SCT	126A
ROBERTSON, Joseph	FKN	162
Joseph	HOP	260
Lawson	HOP	272
Leonard	HND	10
Leroy	ALN	110
Lewis	ADR	44
Littleberry	LGN	45
Louis	HOP	260
Luke	LNC	55
Martin	LGN	34
Mary	ADR	54
Mary	NSN	196
Mather	ADR	3
Nancy	WAS	27A
Neal C.	GTN	117
Owen	FKN	116
Randolph	WRN	69A
Richard	BTH	180
Richard P.	NSN	196
Robert	HOP	262
Roger	CLK	99
Sally	SPN	19A
Saml.	WAS	78A
Saml. B.	ADC	68
Samuel	MAD	170
Samuel	MNR	213
Samuel	WRN	63A
Samuel	NCH	115A
Sarah	MAD	174
Sarah	NSN	197
Sterling	WAS	17A
Steven	PUL	41A
Thomas	LNC	45
Thomas	CSY	228
Thomas	PUL	59A
Thos.	KNX	314
Toliver	SCT	116A
William	MER	107
Will? N.	NSN	224
William	LGN	46
William	CLK	69
William	CLK	74
William	GTN	121
William	NSN	180
William	MNR	201
William	MNR	217
William, Dr.	MER	115
Wm.	MAD	96
Wm.	FKN	128
Wm.	FKN	160
Wm.	HRT	166
Wm., Sr.	FKN	162
Wm.	WAS	49A
ROBERTSON?, Allan?	HRT	167
ROBESON, -----?	CWL	41
James	MER	107
Jane	MER	107
John	NCH	120A
Richard	WDF	120A
Robert	MER	107
Samuel	MER	107
Stephen	NCH	111A
ROBEY, Hezekiah	BBN	68
Owen	BBN	76
ROBINETT, Daniel	BBN	106
ROBINGSON, Laurance	HND	9A
ROBINS, Daniel	FLD	22
James	BTH	202
John	BBN	72
John	BTH	156
Richd.	GRN	62
Spencer	NCH	128A
ROBINSON, --.?	CWL	34
-awson	CWL	37
A.	CHN	31

ROBINSON, Absalom HAR 138
Allen FLG 76A
Andrew BBN 130
Arthur CLD 148
Bazel WRN 60A
Bazle WRN 69A
Ben HRD 38
Benjamin FTE 83
Benjamin FTE 93
Benjamin HAR 154
Benjamin HAR 204
Benjamin MTG 235
Braxton FTE 76
Charles LGN 37
Charles FTE 83
Chs. B. FKN 74
David H. LVG 6
Dudley FTE 93
Edwd. MAS 67
Erskin HRY 254
Francis HAR 148
Geo. LVG 2
Geo. MAS 60
Geo., Sr. LVG 8
George FTE 60
George MER 107
George CLD 149
George HAR 196
Griffin HAR 166
Harrison GRN 60
Henry FLG 51A
Israel MER 107
Jacob PND 17A
James CHN 31
James FTE 88
James FTE 93
James BBN 118
James BBN 130
James GRD 103A
James GRD 114A
James B. BKN 23
James M. LVG 6
James W. MER 115
Jesse, Mas. GRT 147
Jno. MAS 60
Jno. MAS 80
John FTE 93
John FTE 97
John FTE 99
John MER 106
John BBN 120
John HAR 142
John HAR 154
John SHE 159
John MTG 273
John SHE 119A
John M. MTG 259
John S. M. BBN 118
Joseph GRN 53
Joseph FTE 75
Joseph FTE 92
Joseph CBL 5A
Joseph WRN 71A
Landon BNE 32
Leonard SHE 159
Littleton HAR 142
M---? HAR 168
Michael HAR 134
Moses FTE 78
Nancy MER 107
Robert JEF 66
Robt. GRN 69
Robt. HRY 260
Saml. OHO 8A
Samuel FTE 107
Samuel E. MER 107
ROBINSON, Sarah HRY 267
Scarlet BBN 120
Simeon FLG 28A
Spencer FTE 78
Squire FTE 76
Squire C. SHE 160
Stephen LVG 5
Stephen BNE 32
Susanna FTE 90
Tho. MAS 68
Thomas GRN 65
Thomas MER 106
Thos. HRD 70
Uriah CLD 160
Walter LVG 5
Walthal CLD 147
Will. LVG 9
William FTE 64
William CLD 154
Wm. FLG 74A
Wm. FLG 77A
Zachh. FLG 76A
ROBISON, Andrew BRK 287
Asa CWL 55
Carter BRK 229
George CWL 38
George NCH 126A
James CWL 55
James CWL 56
James BRK 287
James, Sr. BRK 287
James (Sr.?) NCH 107A
James NCH 112A
Jane NCH 126A
John BLT 174
Jos. CWL 38
Joseph BRK 287
Kinsy CWL 38
Littlebery BRK 289
Mathew BRK 285
Nathaniel D. NCH 129A
Robt. GRD 104A
Samuel BRK 287
William BRK 285
William BRK 287
ROBNET, Moses BBN 60
ROBNITT?, John BBN 110
ROBY, Barton HRD 64
Catherine BLT 190
Jemima NSN 222
Laurence BLT 188
Owen JEF 36
Thos. FKN 92
Wm. H. OHO 7A
Josias NSN 222
Reason BLT 190
ROBY?, Francis? NSN 182
Isaac? NSN 182
Jas.? M.? CWL 58
Joseph O. WAS 63A
Rebecca OHO 6A
ROCHAL, Louis GTN 134
ROCHESTER, Nathl. CWL 44
ROCK, James OHO 7A
Sarah BRN 25
ROCKHOLD, Charles WTY 114A
ROCKMIRE?, Jacob NSN 175
ROCKWELL, Anny CLK 95
RODD, Jane NSN 199
RODDEN, Jas. MAS 61
RODES, Clifton BRN 25
Clifton MAD 174
James GRN 63
James UNN 153
James C. FTE 66
John BRN 25
RODES, John A. WAS 71A
Mary MAD 170
Will SCT 122A
RODESMITH, George ETL 49
RODGER, Thos. BBN 60
RODGERS, Ann BBN 84
Asa HRD 66
Chas. JEF 22
David TRG 5A
Elias HRD 14
Elias, Junr. HRD 90
George TRG 7A
George L. HRD 96
Jacob HRD 94
James BTH 170
John TRG 5
John HRD 22
John HRD 32
John CHN 44
John GRN 65
John GRN 67
Joseph BBN 60
Joseph BBN 84
Lewis HRD 36
Lydia SHE 113A
Martha BTH 188
Mathew HRD 38
Milly, (Free) BBN 80
Philip HRD 56
Robert TRG 14
Samuel BBN 64
Samuel BTH 182
Stephen LVG 5
Thomas H. FTE 66
Will BBN 76
RODMAN, Alexander CHN 39
John HRY 176
Mary JEF 59
Wm. JEF 59
RODMOND, Davey WAS 41A
RODUS, William MAD 116
ROE, Atha FLG 48A
Edward BTH 162
Edward BTH 198
Jacob MAS 61
James BTH 198
Jno. MAS 78
John WRN 45A
Nancy, Mrs. WYN 87A
Reuben ETL 40
Salley MAD 144
Thos. ADC 66
William WTY 111A
ROEBUCK, Geo. MAS 71
Tho. MAS 60
ROFER?, James FTE 83
ROGERS, ----d? DVS 6A
---m? DVS 8A
---ry? CWL 41
---se? DVS 12A
--s. CWL 32
Abigal MAS 67
Adam MAD 162
Andrew NSN 208
Andrew MTG 226
Andrew, Jr. NSN 208
Anne GTN 120
Atwell MTG 231
Barnet BNE 32
Bartlet CLY 115
Betsy KNX 308
Betsy KNX 316
Bird BRN 24
Burgess CLK 95
Daniel FKN 110
Daniel NSN 205

Name	County	Page
ROGERS, David	BRK	289
David	WDF	110A
Edmund	BRN	24
Eleanor	WDF	110A
Eli	FKN	110
Elias	SHE	161
Elijah	BNE	32
Elijah	FTE	93
Elizabeth	BBN	66
Elizabeth	BLT	180
Ezekiel	PUL	45A
Flemming P.	SHE	148
Geo.	MAS	63
George	BRN	34
George	ADR	42
George	FTE	96
George	CLY	115
George	HAR	134
George	SHE	160
George	WYN	80A
Green	NSN	180
Hannah	FLG	74A
Hanry W.	GTN	131
Henry	CLK	95
Henry	FTE	96
Hiram	MAD	120
Horace	MTG	269
Ivin	MER	106
Jack (Free Man)	BBN	62
James	BRN	26
James	ADR	38
James	FTE	80
James	BBN	114
James	HAR	138
James, Sr.	WTY	120A
James C.	OHO	3A
James M.	DVS	19A
Jeremiah	CLK	78
Jeremiah	FTE	90
Jno. S.	JEF	65
John	LNC	21
John	BRN	25
John	ADR	42
John	BBN	66
John	FTE	96
John	BBN	120
John	HAR	134
John	SHE	174
John	BTH	210
John	MTG	277
John	MTG	281
John, Sr.	LNC	21
John	OHO	3A
John	WRN	57A
John	SCT	118A
John	SCT	131A
John	GSN	149A
John C.	CLK	83
John W.	MTG	226
Jonathan	BRN	24
Joseph	BRN	25
Joseph	FTE	92
Joseph	FTE	96
Joseph	NSN	181
Joseph	SCT	129A
Lazarus	CHN	30
Lydia	HAR	138
Manson	LNC	21
Mathew	LGN	42
Mathew	MAS	79
Patrick	MTG	279
Patsey	MTG	279
Polley	GTN	118
Reubin	LGN	28
Robert	CHN	31A
Robt.	ADR	44
ROGERS, Rolland	LNC	21
Sam	TOD	127A
Samuel	HAR	138
Samuel	WTY	121A
Stephen	ADR	54
Stephen	WRN	35A
Tho.	MAS	72
Thomas	WRN	66A
Thos.	JEF	68
Wiley	TOD	132A
Will.	SCT	127A
William	FLD	14
William	BRN	24
William	BNE	32
William	ETL	52
William	CLY	131
William	BTH	176
William	OHO	8A
William	WTY	111A
William	WTY	127A
William	NCH	128A
Willis	NCH	105
Wm.	ADR	44
Wm.	WAS	83A
Wm.	TOD	132A
ROGERSON, James	SHE	131A
Wm.	SHE	119A
ROHEDES, John, Jr.	HRD	30
ROHRER, John	LGN	41
ROIALTY, Daniel	CLD	148
ROICE, Solimon	ADR	44
ROISTER, L.	TOD	133
ROITT?, Wm.	PND	25A
ROLAND, Archibald	CLD	143
Bedford	HOP	262
Gasper	SPN	4A
George	JES	94
George	CLD	140
George	CLD	143
Gilbert	CLD	140
Jesse	WRN	45A
Jesse P.	SPN	21A
Joseph	SPN	22A
Lewis	CWL	38
M.	MAS	77
Makajah B.	CHN	34A
Morgan	GRD	84A
Mortimer D.	BLT	194
Robert	SPN	21A
Unise	CLD	140
Widw. Ann	CWL	43
Wm.?	CWL	37
ROLANS, Moses	GRD	115A
ROLER, John	WAS	23A
Leonard	CWL	58
ROLEY, James	GNP	169A
ROLEY?, Barton	HRD	64
ROLF, Elizabeth	BLT	190
ROLIN, Richd.	CWL	36
ROLINS, Joshua	GNP	170A
ROLL?, Michael	HRD	56
ROLLE, Robert F.	FTE	78
ROLLENS, Alesander	WAS	32A
Anthony W.	MAD	180
ROLLIN?, John	LVG	18
ROLLING, Jacob	HAR	140
ROLLINGS, Nancy	PND	26A
Steph.	HRY	267
Stephen	BRK	285
ROLLINS, Benjamin	JES	93
Jesse	BBN	108
Jno.	CHN	39
John	BLT	152
John	SCT	110A
Joseph	TRG	11
Joseph	BNE	32
ROLLINS, Loyd	BBN	80
Sarah	JEF	66
Tho.	MAS	59
Thomas	FTE	110
Win.	SCT	106A
ROLLOW, Archibald	MAS	60
ROLLS, Nancy	FTE	58
Robert	FTE	108
ROLON?, Ben	GRD	83A
ROLSON, Mathew	WYN	87A
ROLSTON, John	BTH	182
Robt.	NCH	108A
Wm.	HRT	166
Wm. F.	HRT	167
ROLSTON?, John	HAR	160
ROLTON?, Polly	GRD	84A
ROLY?, Frances?	NSN	182
Isaac?	NSN	182
ROMAIN, Elizabeth	HRD	86
ROMAN, ----es?	DVS	12A
Isac	JES	81
Jacob	FTE	100
William	FTE	100
William	SHE	176
William	GRD	111A
ROMANS, Jacob	WRN	32A
James	WRN	32A
John	WRN	29A
Peter	WRN	32A
Philip, Senr.	WRN	32A
Philip	WRN	31A
ROMINE, Elias	LNC	2
James	SHE	111A
Samuel	SHE	112A
ROMINES?, Ludwell	FTE	107
ROMJUE?, John	HRY	178
ROMY?, G. D.	GRD	82A
RONEY, Patrick	WAS	36A
RONIMUS?, Joseph	JES	71
RONRY?, G. D.	GRD	82A
RONY?, Bazzil	WAS	36A
ROOF, Fnicholas	HRD	64
Martin	HRD	26
ROOK, Ebenezer	SHE	136A
Elizabeth	KNX	282
Joseph	LWS	92A
Severn	LWS	91A
ROOKS, Buckner	BRK	285
Thos.	WAS	30A
ROONEY, James	SHE	117A
Wm.	SHE	117A
ROOT, Charles C.	HAR	220
John	CLY	121
Samuel	HRD	12
ROOTS, Phillip	GRN	76
Willis	LVG	12
ROPER, Davd.	PUL	48A
David	LGN	35
David	CLD	160
David	SPN	16A
James	SPN	13A
John, Junr.	CLD	158
John, Senr.	CLD	158
Joseph	WDF	117A
William	HAR	218
Wm. P.	FLG	79A
ROPER?, James	FTE	83
Thos.	SHE	132A
ROPIER, Charles	NSN	184
ROPON?, Enoch	GRD	91A
RORHRER, David	JES	90
Henry	JES	93
Jacob	JES	90
Jacob, Jr.	JES	90
Peter	JES	93
Samuel	JES	93

RORITY, Timothy GRD 120A
ROSACRAUNCH, Benj. BRK 287
ROSE, Benj. WTY 127A
Benjamin MER 107
Benjamin MER 107
Charles MER 107
Charles GTN 133
David FLD 6
Debby HRL 118
Ezekiel MBG 133A
George FTE 102
Henery GSN 149A
James MAD 124
James HAR 150
James A. GTN 130
Jas. E. FLG 24A
Jesse HAR 200
John FLD 6
John KNX 298
John CBL 4A
John C. WRN 60A
Johnathan FLG 36A
Joshua FTE 106
Leroy FTE 101
Louis MER 107
Nathaniel ETL 42
Robert ETL 45
Robert MTG 253
Sarah MBG 133A
William GTN 130
William GTN 134
William GRD 106A
William GRD 108A
Willoughby WRN 69A
Wm. MAD 134
ROSE?, Allan JEF 66
Saml. MAD 132
ROSEBERRY, Charles SHE 169
Hugh BBN 78
Wm. BBN 80
ROSEBURY, Nancy BTH 174
ROSIER, John BBN 140
ROSS, Aaron MAS 78
Alexander BNE 34
Alexander CHN 43
Alexander FKN 56
Alexander MAD 144
Alexander HAR 194
Alexr. FLG 31A
Ambrose GRD 119A
Andrew GTN 133
Andw. CWL 56
Andw. FLG 40A
Angus WTY 114A
Benj. FLG 31A
Benjamin LGN 35
Benjamin BTH 172
Betsey LGN 38
Betsy BTH 196
Bowin CLY 118
Ca--? CWL 56
Caleb CWL 56
Catesby FLG 50A
Daniel BNE 32
Daniel JES 88
Daniel GTN 135
Daniel CSY 206
David FLD 19
David HAR 194
David, Jr. LGN 39
David, Sr. LGN 38
Edward JEF 34
Francis LGN 35
Frederick CBL 4A
Gabriel MAD 98
Garland LGN 38
ROSS, Geo. JEF 48
George BNE 32
George GRN 70
Green CWL 56
Hector BNE 32
Hetty RCK 81A
Jacob BTH 184
James HND 11
James BNE 34
James BNE 34
James HRD 74
James MAD 98
James FKN 108
James BBN 112
James A. BRK 287
Jas. HRD 74
Jas. TOD 132
Jas. FLG 27A
Jas. FLG 40A
Jessee BNE 34
Jessee BRK 289
Jno. CWL 56
Jno. MAS 59
John ADR 44
John JEF 48
John BBN 68
John MAD 144
John CSY 204
John MTG 263
John FLG 49A
John SHE 112A
John WTY 123A
John NCH 129A
Johnston FLG 35A
Joseph NSN 186
Joseph OHO 6A
Joseph FLG 34A
Joseph NCH 121A
Lawrence ETL 54
Lewis BNE 34
Lewis CHN 40A
Liddy MAD 98
Lydia HOP 262
M. J. LNC 69
Margaret HAR 202
Martin CWL 36
Martin CWL 46
Martin CLD 159
Matilda JEF 40
Moses JES 82
Nancy JEF 40
Nathl. HRY 212
Nely ADR 44
Nimrod FLG 48A
Phillip JEF 64
Reubin JEF 56
Richard GNP 171A
Robert BRK 289
Rubin FLG 42A
Sally BNE 34
Saml. SCT 125A
Saml. TOD 129A
Saml. W. MAD 138
Samuel BTH 174
Samuel WTY 120A
Simon HRD 42
Stephen LGN 34
Susanna JEF 40
Thomas BLT 180
Thomas OHO 6A
Thomas B HOP 262
Thos. JEF 45
Thos. MAS 58
Tilman NCH 106A
Vincent WDF 126A
William BNE 34
ROSS, William FTE 94
Wm. BBN 136
Wm. FLG 48A
ROSS?, Allan JEF 66
ROSSBERRY, Wm. JEF 66
ROSSEAN, Ezekial PUL 56A
ROSSEL, Charles FKN 96
Jno., Jr. FKN 152
Polly SCT 96A
ROSSEL?, Elijah SCT 96A
ROSSELL, Eli FTE 99
ROSSER, Richard GRD 114A
ROSSER?, James FTE 83
ROSSON, Benjamin FKN 114
Jesse BLT 180
Jno. FKN 114
Wm. FKN 108
ROSSON?, Enoch GRD 91A
ROSWELL, Wm. BBN 136
ROTCHESTER, John MER 117
Lititia MER 106
Robert MER 106
William H. MER 116
ROTERTSON, Jno. CHN 44
ROTHWELL, Kay JEF 25
ROTON?, Ben GRD 83A
ROTRAMMELL?, Henry LGN 45
John LGN 43
ROTRUCK, John MBG 143
ROTTON?, Polly GRD 84A
ROUCE, Daniel WYN 99A
ROUCH, Chs. FKN 112
ROUES?, John BNE 34
ROUINS?, Sophia BBN 108
ROUND-Y?, Jacob HRY 204
ROUND, Abraham CHN 40
ROUNDER, Joseph WAS 64A
ROUNDTREE, Dudley HRT 166
Turner HRT 167
ROUNTREE, Green F. WRN 51A
Henry BRN 25
James WRN 48A
John WRN 48A
Mary BRN 24
Richard BRN 34
Samuel BRN 34
ROUP?, Michael C. CLD 144
ROUS, James GNP 177A
Samuel GNP 166A
ROUSE, Aaron CBL 8A
Abraham BNE 32
Calvin LWS 90A
Elijah BNE 32
Elisha BNE 32
George BNE 32
Jacob BNE 34
Jeremiah BNE 34
Joel BNE 32
John BNE 32
John FTE 80
Joseph BNE 32
Joshua BNE 32
Julious BNE 32
Michael BNE 32
Michael BLT 190
Moses BNE 32
Moses BLT 162
Samuel BNE 32
Samuel BNE 32
Simeon BNE 34
Thomas BNE 30
William BNE 32
William SHE 143A
ROUSS?, Michael C. CLD 144
ROUSSEAU, John CLD 158
ROUT, George BTH 188

Name	Co.	Page
ROUT, John	GRD	86A
Wm.	FKN	160
ROUTIEN, Michel	GTN	123
ROUTON, Thomas	GRD	105A
ROUTSAW, Conrod	CSY	204
ROUTT, Daniel	CLK	73
Johan, Sr.	BKN	22
John	CHN	41A
John W.	BKN	22
Nimrod	BKN	20
Richard	CLK	73
William	CBL	3A
ROUTT?, George	BKN	16
ROVE-?, John	BNE	34
ROVE, Thos.	BKN	6
ROVE?, George	BKN	22
ROW, Anthony	ADR	44
Edmund	OHO	8A
Geo., Junr.	OHO	8A
George	OHO	8A
George	WYN	79A
Henry	BBN	132
Henry	MBG	133A
Jacob	BBN	142
James	SHE	127A
Jno.	PUL	49A
John	HRT	166
Nicholas	SHE	127A
Robert	OHO	9A
Thomas	OHO	8A
William	GRD	102B
ROWAN, John	NSN	223
Thomas	FLD	39
ROWDEN, Philip	LGN	37
ROWDON, Reuben	LGN	35
ROWE, James	FLD	25
James	FLD	26
James	HRY	220
James H.	MER	106
John	FLD	26
Solomon	FLD	26
Thomas	FLD	25
Thos.	LVG	4
Thos.	ADR	71
William	CLD	146
ROWIN, Andrew	BRK	229
Francis	BNE	32
ROWLAND, ----e?	DVS	12A
David	HRY	184
George	SHE	152
George	MAD	170
George, Jr.	HRY	184
George, Sr.	HRY	184
Henry	CWL	55
Henry	WDF	117A
Jacob	SPN	8A
James	LWS	96A
John	GRT	143
John	HRY	182
Rewben	CWL	55
Richard	WDF	119A
Sally	MER	106
Samuel	BLT	180
Thomas L.	CLK	85
ROWLET, Francis W.	UNN	149
Peter	HRT	166
Phillip	HRT	166
ROWLIN, Tho.	MAS	61
Wm.	SHE	127A
ROWLINGS, Aaron, Jr.	BRK	287
Robert	BRK	285
ROWLITT, William, Jr.	OWN	104
ROWS, James	HND	4
ROWTIN, Eliza	LNC	49
ROWTON, William	LNC	19
ROWZEE, Pheby	HRY	176
Saml.	HRY	176
ROWZY, Thomas	BRN	26
ROY, Asa	PUL	61A
Enos.	PUL	64A
John F.	FTE	75
Joseph	PUL	57A
Landy	KNX	304
Zachariah	PUL	57A
ROYAL, Isom	HRD	42
Jinnet	GSN	148A
ROYALTY, Charles	BRK	289
Samuel	BRK	289
Thomas	MER	106
ROYCE?, Thomas	BLT	166
ROYLE, Martha	FTE	108
Thomas	FTE	108
ROYSE, Henery	CBL	20A
ROYSTER, James	BNE	32
Mitchel	MAD	180
Wilkins	HND	10
ROYSTON, Will	GRD	104A
RUARK, Edward	GRN	55
John	GRN	71
Peter	PUL	39A
Timothy	PUL	38A
Zekiel	GRN	71
RUBEY, Jacob	WAS	82A
RUBISON, John	BLT	178
RUBLE, David	SHE	118A
George	ETL	50
Isaac	NSN	198
Jacob	SHE	118A
John P.	SHE	115A
Twinfield	GRD	118A
RUBY, Charles	WAS	51A
James	BRK	287
John	HAR	196
John	SHE	132A
John B.	HOP	262
Joseph	HAR	200
Mathew	HND	11A
William	BLT	192
Wm. H.	OHO	10A
RUCKBERRY, Jacob	JEF	58
Jacob, Jr.	JEF	58
RUCKER, --r-h.?	CWL	42
Ahmed	WDF	105A
Danl.	BBN	106
Elliott	SHE	126A
Elzephen	GNP	172A
Elzy	HRY	208
Ephraim	FKN	134
Isaac	JES	80
Isaac	WDF	114A
J-s.?	CWL	42
James, Jr.	CWL	40
James, Sr.	CWL	40
James	GNP	168A
James P.?	FTE	100
Jno.	FKN	160
John	SCT	104A
John S.	BNE	30
John?	CWL	40
Joshua	ADR	42
Lucy	SHE	168
Morning	FLG	54A
Paskal	BNE	32
Ruben	ADR	44
Saml.	GRN	68
William	WDF	96
Wisdom	MER	106
Wm. E.	BNE	32
RUCKERS, Abner	JES	95
Isaac	JES	95
RUCKLE, Henry	SCT	126A
RUCKMAN, Isaiah	BRN	25
RUD, George	HND	4
Samuel	WDF	92
William	WDF	93
RUD?, Archibald H.	BNE	50
John	GTN	121
RUDD, Christopher A.	WAS	78A
Jas.	JEF	25
John	WAS	76A
John H.	BKN	10
Joseph M.	BKN	5
Richard	NSN	178
Thos.	BKN	10
W., Mrs.	MAS	74
Wm.	WAS	63A
RUDDELL, George W.	HAR	186
Sarah	HAR	204
William	HAR	214
RUDDER, Charles	BTH	194
John	BTH	166
RUDDLE, Charles	GRT	139
Chas.	TOD	126A
Geo.	BBN	116
Mary	FLG	40A
Mary	FLG	56A
Steven	WDF	114A
Wm.	BKN	16
RUDE, Isaac A.	WRN	60A
Jas.	HRD	80
Wm.	HRD	80
RUDER, Joshua	ALN	108
Obediah	ALN	108
RUDER?, Rebicah	ALN	108
RUDULPH, T. H.	SCT	92A
RUDY, Danl.	JEF	46
Fred.	JEF	65
Geo.	JEF	35
Henry	JEF	46
Jacob	JEF	65
Jno.	MAS	78
RUE, Joel	FKN	134
Jonathan	MER	106
Joseph	MAD	168
RUELS?, Armstard	FKN	162
RUERD?, John	PND	31A
RUFF, Suky (Free)	CLD	162
RUFFIN, Jas.	CHN	42
RUFFNER, David	JES	79
Henry	HAR	158
Reuben	LNC	81
Samuel	JES	91
RUFLEY?, Catey	FLD	39
RUFS?, Aron	BTL	329
Daniel	BTL	329
RUGG, Luman	CBL	19A
RUGGELS, Enoch	LWS	91A
James	LWS	91A
John	LWS	91A
Jonathan	LWS	87A
Thomas	LWS	97A
RUGGER?, Richd.	CWL	38
RUGGLES, James	GNP	171A
Michael	GNP	171A
Nathaniel F.	HND	4
RUGLASS, William	MER	106
RUKE, Babel	LWS	90A
Jorden	LWS	91A
RULE, Andrew	FLD	36
Edward	PND	17A
Saml.	BBN	142
Saml.	NCH	128A
William	PND	17A
Wm. (Crossed Out)	PND	16A

RUMFORD, Betsy MAS 60
RUMINGER?, Christian LGN 28
RUMINGS?, Abram CLK 88
RUMMING, Abner FLG 25A
RUMMONS?, Aron FLG 48A
RUMSDELL?, Charles M. WRN 73A
RUMSEY, Charles FLD 24
Charles LWS 96A
Elijah FTE 101
James FTE 104
Thomas FTE 104
RUNNELS, William MER 107
RUNALDS, Pleasant ETL 54
Tobias ETL 43
RUNDEGGER, Sebastin FKN 60
RUNDLES, Thomas BTH 218
RUNELLS, Jessee CLK 88
RUNEY?, (See Reiney?) CLK 95
RUNION, Freeman CLD 141
Joseph GTN 119
RUNKLE, James MAD 130
RUNNA-, Larkin CSY 204
RUNNELLS, George CBL 3A
RUNNELS, Justice CBL 7A
RUNNER, John WRN 40A
RUNNINGS?, Abram CLK 88
RUNNION, Francis GTN 119
Henry FLD 39
Joseph FTE 77
Joseph FTE 109
RUNNOLDS, Jane BTL 329
Matthew PUL 54A
RUNNYAN, Spencer BNE 48
RUNYAN, Isaac MAD 94
John FLD 39
Peter G. BNE 32
RUNYON, A. R. MAS 64
Basefoot? BRN 25
Danl. MAS 52
David FLG 40A
Jas M. MAS 64
John FTE 77
Phineas BRN 25
RUPARD?, (See Russard) CLK 81
Erasmus CLK 76
Joseph CLK 76
William CLK 76
RUPE, Barnett LNC 47
RUPE?, Nicholas FKN 116
RUPEL?, Henry NSN 206
Henry NSN 212
Samuel NSN 206
RUPELL, Thos. WAS 54A
RUPERT, David CWL 34
M. Mace? FLG 36A
RUPLE?, Samuel CLK 83
RURKE, John CSY 214
RUSH, Abraham SHE 117A
Benjamin MNR 217
Coonrod JEF 43
Gabrial PND 17A
Geo. BBN 130
Grigsby LGN 29
Henry MER 106
Jacob SHE 121A
James MNR 217
James (Crossed Out) MNR 215
John HRD 10
John ALN 142
John, Jr. HRD 10
RUSH, Joshua MNR 217
Martha WAS 69A
Patrick FTE 92
Peter PND 18A
Robert JEF 37
Sanna SHE 121A
Simeon HRD 60
Thornton PND 15A
Thos. PND 22A
William MNR 217
Wm. PND 26A
RUSH?, Jeremiah CLD 161
John CLD 161
RUSHER, George BRK 289
Henry BRK 289
Heny, Jr. BRK 287
James BRK 289
William BRK 289
RUSK, Chs. PUL 38A
Eleanor NSN 175
James JES 83
John CBL 13A
John SCT 107A
Robt. SCT 107A
William CLK 69
RUSLE, Nancy BTH 172
RUSS?, Aron BTL 329
Daniel BTL 329
Nicholas BTL 329
RUSSAN, David LNC 13
RUSSARD?, Erasmus CLK 76
John CLK 81
Joseph CLK 76
William CLK 76
RUSSEAU, James WYN 89A
RUSSEL, Absalam CSY 228
Barny CLY 120
Birde CSY 224
David A. MER 117
Ephraim HND 13
Isaac MER 106
James BRN 25
Jane NSN 184
Jane NSN 199
Jarimiah CSY 216
John BRN 25
John BRN 25
Jordon MER 106
Joseph BBN 108
Joseph MNR 193
Louis MER 106
Phillip HND 4
Robert MER 117
Robert CSY 216
Robert CHN 31A
Robert SHE 121A
Seth TRG 7A
William GTN 119
Wm. WAS 62A
RUSSEL?, Henry NSN 206
Henry NSN 212
Samuel NSN 206
RUSSELL, Aaron MNR 207
Amasa FTE 75
Anderson MNR 207
Bazel WRN 29A
Benjamin BLT 186
Benjamin, Junr. WRN 38A
Benjamin, Senr. WRN 38A
Buckner MNR 201
Buckner, Sr. MNR 195
Const. JEF 48
Danl. JEF 43
David LGN 38
David N. LGN 23
Edmund LNC 27
RUSSELL, Edwd. TOD 132A
Elias WAS 60A
Franklin SHE 120A
Geo. MAS 54
George CWL 56
George MNR 201
George WRN 57A
George SHE 118A
Girvas? E. FKN 56
Haden SHE 120A
Hagman SHE 120A
Hezekiah JES 75
Hiram LGN 42
Isaah? GRN 72
James FKN 118
James HRY 234
James WAS 23A
James WRN 38A
James WAS 40A
James SHE 136A
James R. SPN 25A
James R. WRN 76A
Jno. CWL 56
John LNC 33
John TOD 134
John HAR 156
John HRY 234
John WYN 91A
John SHE 122A
John C. UNN 147
Joseph JEF 20
Joseph GRN 58
Judy LNC 11
Levi JEF 53
Mary O. FTE 70
Nancy WRN 38A
Nicholas BLT 186
Nicholas BLT 186
Rachel SHE 118A
Robert S./ L.? FTE 74
Samuel GRN 56
Samuel MBG 143
Sanders LNC 29
Seth ALN 100
Silias LNC 9
Tandy TOD 134
Thomas LGN 37
Thomas BLT 186
Thomas A. FTE 75
Thos. WAS 23A
William LNC 13
William FTE 75
Wm. WAS 40A
Wm. SHE 136A
Wm. B. JEF 60
Zachariah SHE 163
RUSSELL?, James LVG 18
RUSSLE, John KNX 278
Samuel WDF 92
RUSSLE?, Samuel CLK 83
RUSSUL, Elijah BRK 289
RUST, Abraham LGN 34
Ann LGN 34
David CBL 6A
Deborah HRD 54
George HRD 16
Isaac LGN 34
Isaac MBG 138
Jacob LGN 34
Jacob HRD 66
Jere HRD 18
John HRD 14
John LGN 34
John CBL 6A
John FLG 78A
Vincent WDF 98A

RUST, William CBL 7A
RUSTARD?, John JEF 21
RUT?, Adam CBL 17A
RUTH, David JEF 23
John WDF 111A
Saml. JEF 40
Tho. MAS 63
RUTHE, Tho. MAS 63
RUTHERFORD, Archd. LGN 32
Ben TOD 126A
Granvill BTH 186
Hugh WDF 99A
Isaac WDF 99A
Jacob WYN 85A
James FLD 42
James FTE 107
Jane LGN 31
Jessee FTE 97
Jessee FTE 107
John FLD 42
John GRN 70
John GTN 128
Joseph FTE 100
Polly BNE 30
Reyborn FLD 42
Shelon? JES 95
Stephen LGN 27
William LGN 32
RUTLAGE, Abraham HAR 146
RUTLEDGE, Fountain JES 77
Henry CLK 70
Henry CLD 158
Isaac HAR 196
Jacob CLK 69
Jessee? CBL 23A
John CLK 69
Joseph CLD 158
Rebecca SHE 142A
RUTLEGE, Joshua SHE 142A
RUTLIDGE, Robert HND 9
RUTON?, Nancy GRD 120A
RUTTER, Alexander HAR 210
Alexander, Jr. HAR 210
James LVG 6
John W HAR 210
Moses FKN 132
Richd. MAS 58
Tho. MAS 65
Wm. WAS 27A
RYAL, Rebeca RCK 81A
RYALS, Alexander BBN 118
RYAN, John BNE 32
Joseph HRD 52
Moses MAS 64
Robt. HRY 264
Wilson FKN 142
RYELY?, John JEF 36
RYLANDER, Mathew BKN 11
RYLE, Elijah BNE 32
James BNE 32
James BNE 32
John, Jr. BNE 32
John, Sr. BNE 32
Larkin BNE 32
William BNE 32
RYLEY, Erasmus HRY 264
RYMAN, John FTE 112
Rachel FTE 111
RYMARD?, Joseph JES 82
RYNEDISON?,
Christina NSN 213
RYNESON,
Christopher CSY 214
RYNESSON?, Garrard CSY 214
RYNNELS, William HAR 158
RYNNER, Wm. HRD 68
RYNOLDS, Henry PUL 35A
RYON, Betsey, Mrs. WYN 94A
Henry JEF 51
James WAS 19A
James CBL 22A
James WAS 85A
John CWL 42
John B. CLK 67
Joseph HRY 178
Leonard SPN 4A
Morris BRK 285
Philip CLK 70
Philip H. CLK 74
Richd. WAS 52A
Saml. WAS 33A
Thomas BRK 287
Thomas WYN 100A
William WYN 100A
Winney CLK 95
Wm. BBN 144

S----?, -----? LVG 18
-----? LVG 18
-----? LVG 18
Simon? LVG 18
S---S, Tho. ALN 126
S---S?, Tho. ALN 124
Tho. ALN 128
S---SER?, George HAR 142
S-ARNY?, Nancy NCH 103A
S-ON-E?, Robert GSN 149A
S-WRY?, George FTE 85
SA---E, John FTE 57
SABER, Samuel CLK 67
SACKETT, Charles JEF 51
SACRAY, James SHE 151
SACRE, Robt. FKN 92
SACRY, James W. GRN 54
SADD, Thomas GTN 134
SADDLER, Pleasant SHE 155
SADLER, A-? GRD 115A
Benjamin PUL 67A
Edmund GRD 118A
Edward NCH 111A
Edward GRD 115A
Francis PUL 67A
John MTG 271
Samuel PUL 58A
Thomas PUL 67A
William MTG 239
William GRD 95A
SAFFEL?, Joshua FKN 156
SAFFERN, Thos. FLG 61A
SAFFOON?, James FTE 97
SAFORN?, Richard JES 75
William JES 94
SAGACY, Daniel FTE 90
Jacob FTE 90
Jacob FTE 91
SAGE, Alex. WAS 21A
John JEF 58
SAGE?, Charles WTY 124A
Hennery CSY 210
SAGER, John BLT 178
SAGERS, Robert,
Junr. PUL 54A
SAGERSER,
Frederick JES 85
SAGESER?, Henry BBN 102
SAILER, Peter SHE 114A
SAILOR, John BTH 214
Manuel BTH 214
William BTH 214
SAIN, James FLD 30
James S. FLD 27
SAIN?, Samuel FLD 43
SAINTCLAR, Frances MAD 102
SAINTLAIR?, Henry JEF 43
SAKE?, Danl. HAR 152
SALE, Anthony JEF 57
Edmond JEF 44
James JES 79
James GTN 124
James H. GTN 131
Reuben HRY 226
Samuel MER 110
Will. JEF 24
SALEE, Asahil CHN 43A
SALENCRIS?,
William FLD 17
SALES, -es--? FTE 58
Leonard LGN 35
SALIER, Widw.? CWL 41
SALISBURY, John LWS 96A
SALLEE, Abraham BKN 28
Edward MTG 263
Henry? BKN 26
Jacob BKN 26
Jacob MTG 299
John MER 108
John, Junr. PUL 57A
John PUL 52A
Oliver MER 108
Rane Shat---? MER 108
William J./ I.? PUL 52A
SALLEY, Benjamin HAR 146
Nancy WAS 28A
Peter HAR 146
Phillip WAS 28A
Stephen MAD 96
Susan WAS 28A
SALLIE, Moses WYN 83A
SALLIERS, John SCT 110A
SALLING, Wm. HRT 167
SALLINGS,
Shederick GSN 151A
SALLY, Edward FTE 104
Isaac ADR 48
John GRN 65
Joseph, Capt. WYN 97A
Marymagdalane LNC 45
Oliver P. OHO 6A
William JES 82
SALLY?, William FTE 102
SALMERES?, Randal FLD 17
William FLD 17
SALMON, John MBG 143
SALMON?, Jacob BNE 36
John SHE 138A
SALMONS, James MER 108
John CLK 85
Nathan SPN 4A
Nathan SPN 22A
SALSBERRY, William FLD 43
SALSBURY, Thomas MBG 140
SALSER, John WRN 75A
SALTER?, Michael GRD 87A
SALTINGSTALL, G.
F. SCT 128A
SALTMARSH, Elijah JEF 31
SALTSMAN?, Grandy GRN 64
SALTSMON, George GSN 149A
Jacob GSN 151A
Moses GSN 151A
Peter GSN 151A
SALYARS, William FLD 5
SALYER, Benjamin HRL 118
Nelson HRL 118
SALYERS, Dunn LNC 41
Samuel MER 109
Zacariah LNC 41
SALYRS, James FTE 73

SAM--S?, Danl. BBN 130
SAMFIELD, Philena WAS 59A
SAMMONS, Joel SPN 20A
John BBN 132
Richard BLT 190
SAMMS, James CLD 162
SAMPELS, William WDF 123A
SAMPIER, Benjamin FTE 70
SAMPLE, John BRN 26
Mary SHE 112A
Polly NCH 114A
SAMPLES, Charles GRN 80
George GRN 64
James LVG 10
Matthew BRN 27
Saml. FKN 116
Saml. HRT 168
SAMPSON, Aquilla FLG 70A
Benj. FLG 77A
Cyrus FTE 74
David SCT 113A
Francis F. FLG 35A
Henry MNR 211
Isaac SHE 115A
Jacob FLG 56A
James BNE 36
Jessee FLG 77A
John BNE 34
John SHE 109A
Richard GTN 124
Richard MAD 180
Richard, Jr. GTN 124
Robert SHE 116A
Stephen CLD 167
Tinch T. FLG 56A
William GTN 124
William GRD 103A
Wm. SHE 109A
SAMPTON, James CLK 105
SAMS, James CLK 69
Jno. FKN 94
Joseph SCT 111A
SAMSON, Jacob LGN 29
Jno. HRY 247
SAMUEL, (Free) CLD 162
Andrew TRG 4A
Bill HRY 230
Catharine FKN 96
James MER 109
Jas. SCT 134A
Jn. HRY 241
Jno. MAS 69
John FTE 89
Larkin FKN 68
Martha SHE 129A
Minton HRY 226
Nicholas FKN 106
Reuben FKN 88
Reuben GRD 90A
Reubin TOD 133
Robt. FKN 96
Thomas MER 109
Thos. SCT 124A
Wm. FKN 78
Wm. SHE 129A
SAMUELL, Arm. C. HRY 218
Reub. HRY 218
Robert HRY 176
SAMUELS, James BLT 170
Josiah CHN 34A
Richard HAR 202
Robert BLT 160
Robert WRN 28A
William NSN 181
William HAR 202
SANASBURRY?, Wm. WAS 68A
SANCES, Isaac NSN 221
SANDEFER, Bennett HND 6
Bennitt, Snr HND 10A
Eliza GRN 75
John HND 9A
Richard HND 6
Samuel CSY 216
Tandy HND 6
SANDER, Nathaniel, Jr. GTN 130
SANDER?, Mich. RCK 78A
SANDERFER, James MER 108
James MER 108
John MER 108
Joseph MER 108
Louis MER 108
Polley CSY 222
Robert MER 108
Robert MER 109
Samuel GRN 76
SANDERFORD, Edward MER 108
SANDERS, Ab. RCK 80A
Abraham BRK 295
Agnes BTH 174
Alexander FTE 60
Christian BLT 166
Daniel J. / I.? BRK 289
David LGN 35
Edward LGN 28
Elijah GRN 74
Esther TRG 13
Ewd. HRT 167
George ADR 48
George BLT 174
George LWS 93A
George W. GTN 132
Henery GSN 150A
Henry GRN 76
Henry FTE 87
Henry BTH 182
Hezakiah BKN 5
Isaac BRN 28
Isaac MER 108
Isaac BRK 295
Isaac D. BNE 34
J. D. TOD 132A
Jacob FLD 17
Jacob BRK 295
James ADR 48
James FTE 103
James GTN 117
James BLT 164
James BTH 176
James, Sr. NCH 113A
James OHO 6A
James WAS 59A
James NCH 109A
Joel WDF 93A
John ADR 16
John FLD 17
John LGN 24
John BRN 26
John LGN 33
John ADR 48
John OWN 104
John CLY 117
John GTN 132
John HRT 168
John MAD 176
John, Sen. WYN 84A
John WAS 49A
Jonathon WAS 60A
Joseph BLT 162
Joseph HRT 168
Josua GSN 150A
Julius FTE 88
SANDERS, Lewis TOD 131
M. TOD 132A
Moses KNX 296
Nancy GTN 122
Nathaniel, Sr. GTN 130
Nathaniel P. BLT 176
Nelson A. BRN 27
Patsy MER 108
Peter OWN 100
Polly MER 109
Presley MER 108
R. M. TOD 127A
Rachel MAD 140
Raymond JEF 30
Ress? MAD 110
Richd. SCT 135A
Sally FTE 105
Saml. HRT 168
Samuel CLY 111
Samuel GTN 133
Stith BRK 291
Susan WAS 21A
Thomas FLD 17
Thomas LGN 40
Thomas OWN 99
Thomas GTN 133
Thomas BLT 180
Thomas, Jr. BLT 180
Thomas GNP 170A
Thos. MAD 98
Thos. HRY 259
Walker SCT 129A
Wiley MAD 98
Will HRY 222
William GTN 122
William GRT 139
William BLT 182
Wm. BRN 26
Wm. HRT 168
Wm. HRY 259
Wm. (Near Alexander Davidson's) BRN 27
Wm. GNP 169A
SANDERS?, James MAD 136
Joel FTE 102
SANDERSON, John JEF 27
Mary NCH 126A
William FTE 75
SANDFORD, Alfred CBL 5A
Chas. HRY 270
Hamlet MAS 63
Lawrence BNE 36
Margaret CBL 3A
Thomas CBL 6A
Willoughby BBN 60
SANDIDGE, Wm. B. MAS 52
SANDIFER, William GRN 75
SANDLIN, Lewis CLY 112
SANDORS?, James MAD 136
SANDRIDGE, John LNC 61
Larkin LNC 61
SANDRIGE, Pleasant GRN 65
SANDS, Benjamin N. HAR 216
William L. LGN 24
SANDS?, James GSN 149A
SANDUSKEY, Andrew BBN 88
Ephraigm JES 75
Jacob, Jr. JES 75
SANDUSKY, Abraham BBN 88
Anthony CLD 146
Emanuel WYN 90A
Isaac BBN 86
Jacob BBN 88
Jacob, Sr. JES 75
Mary BBN 88

SANDUSKY, Widow BBN 94
SANDY, (No Other Name) FTE 58
SANFORD, Dan HRY 247
Henry B. MTG 283
James WDF 124A
John MER 110
Joseph BTL 331
Laurance HRY 247
Letty CHN 29A
Stewart FKN 112
William SHE 158
Young S. FTE 85
SANGATE?, Dixon GRT 145
SANGSTER, John TOD 130
SANHAM, Pleasant CSY 206
SANNER, Isaac HND 13
Thos. HND 10A
SANSBURY, Benjn. BBN 128
SANTEE, Joseph SCT 114A
SANTER?, Benjamin HAR 150
SANTERN?, Jacob HAR 152
Larkin HAR 152
SAP, (See Sass) WAS 68A
Amanuel GSN 149A
James BBN 132
Nathan BBN 132
Noah BBN 132
Levi BBN 132
SAP?, James WAS 67A
SAPINGTON, John CHN 45
Richard CLK 72
Silvester CLK 69
SAPINTON, James MAD 156
SAPLER, John GTN 124
SAPP, Danl. FLG 67A
Jacob FLG 67A
John CBL 22A
SAPPIINGTON, Sylvester FTE 85
SAPPINGTON, John MTG 231
SARBIT?, David FLG 53A
SARCY, Allen MAD 146
Barlet? MAD 156
Jeremah MAD 172
Jessey MAD 152
Joseph MAD 118
Polley MAD 154
Richard MAD 154
Richard MAD 156
SARGEANT, Robert WDF 108A
SARGENS?, Wm. BKN 18
SARGENT, Aaron PUL 64A
John GNP 165A
William MER 114
SARJANT, Abreham HRL 118
SARK, John ALN 126
SARLES, Elijah GTN 125
SARTER, Dianna MER 109
SARTIN, Elijah GRD 82A
Joel BRN 28
John GRD 109A
SARTON, Claburn GNP 170A
James GNP 171A
SARVER, John ALN 114
SARVIS, William SHE 159
SASS, (See Sap) WAS 68A
Dory WAS 32A
James WAS 32A
Nathan WAS 32A
SASSEEN, -ewis? CWL 42
SATERDAY, Jacob WAS 48A
SATERFIELD, --nes? CWL 44
Clement HAR 208
Isaac ALN 122
SATERFIELD?, Henry ALN 122
SATERWRIGHT?, Jno. HRY 249
SATTER?, Michael GRD 87A
SATTERFIELD, Archibald WRN 61A
Eli WRN 71A
Ephraim WRN 71A
John WRN 59A
Moses WRN 60A
SATTERWHITE, James GRN 68
Martha FTE 65
SATTLE, Henry BRK 295
SATTS?, John BKN 14
SATURFIELD, Jesse MNR 209
SATURWHITE, Jno. FKN 132
Philip FKN 126
Walker FKN 74
SAUMERS?, John RCK 79A
SAUNDERS, Abm.? CWL 41
Ackley FLG 55A
Aron FLG 67A
Benjamin MTG 281
Cyrus FLG 67A
Elizabeth FLG 56A
Gunnel FLG 67A
Gunnell, Sr. FLG 67A
Henry FKN 134
Hugh FKN 102
James CWL 31
James FKN 126
John CHN 43A
John WRN 52A
John PUL 66A
John FLG 67A
John SHE 142A
Joshua CBL 15A
Lewis FKN 84
Moses FLG 67A
Oliver FLG 68A
Reuben SHE 111A
Robt. CWL 37
Robt. CHN 43A
Silvanus FLG 67A
Simon CWL 31
Stephen CWL 31
Thos. FLG 67A
William SHE 110A
Wm. FLG 67A
Zephorah HRD 56
SAUNDERSON, Robt. FLG 58A
SAUNNERES?, Thos. GNP 168A
SAUTHER, John BNE 36
Joshua BNE 36
SAVAGE, Chas. JEF 22
Edward GNP 176A
Hamilton MNR 211
Jane HND 11A
Jas. MAS 64
John WYN 102A
John GNP 176A
John P. LWS 86A
Littlebury WRN 45A
Marmaduge CHN 34
Martin CHN 34
Martin MNR 211
Pat D. WAS 37A
Pleasant M. LWS 88A
Richard, Senr. CHN 34A
Richard, Junr. CHN 34A
William CLD 142
Wm. BRN 26
SAVAREE?, Amos HRD 24
SAVETEER?, William NCH 122A
SAVICY?, James GTN 135
SAVIER, Isaac MER 108
William MER 108
SAVILLS, Thomas TRG 12A
SAVILLS?, Absalom TRG 12
Cornelius TRG 12
Daniel TRG 12
SAVIRN?, John BTH 218
SAWARD, Elisha MAS 65
SAWYER, Benjamin LGN 42
Charles CLD 146
Chas., Senr. HRD 58
Cyrus LGN 33
David LGN 41
Jno. HRD 58
John GSN 151A
William LGN 43
SAWYERS, Ab. RCK 76A
Elizabeth SHE 150
Elizabeth SHE 157
James LGN 32
Richard MBG 142
Robert, Senr. PUL 65A
SAXTON, Beverly CWL 57
Daniel LWS 98A
SAYE?, Alexander HRY 224
Alexandra CSY 212
SAYERS, Henery CBL 10A
Samuel CBL 10A
Stephen PUL 68A
William CBL 10A
SAYESER?, Henry BBN 102
SAYLOR, John HRL 120
Joseph HRL 120
Martin HRL 120
Solomon HRL 120
SAYRE, David A. FTE 62
Joseph FTE 64
SAYRES, James H. BNE 36
SAYWELL, Ellener HAR 136
SCAGGS, Aarcha ADR 48
Aron GSN 151A
Charles ADR 48
Henery GSN 151A
Henery GSN 151A
James GSN 150A
James GSN 151A
Jeremiah GSN 151A
Jno. CWL 56
Joseph WRN 66A
Martin GSN 150A
Richard GSN 151A
Wm. GSN 150A
Wm. GSN 150A
SCALLEN, James CWL 39
SCAMAHORN, Jacob JEF 63
SCANDRETT, William GTN 124
SCANER?, John WDF 94
SCANLAND, Robert GTN 133
William GTN 123
SCANTAND, Jane GTN 127
SCANTLAND, James WDF 119A
SCANTLIN, James FTE 111
James WAS 67A
John WAS 52A
John WAS 67A
SCANTLING, Ben HRD 58
Edmund FKN 160
William WDF 101A
SCANTTINGS?, Elizabth CLK 88
SCARBROUGH, Caty? RCK 81A
John TOD 127
SCARCE, David WDF 98
Henrietta WDF 98
James SHE 170
Laban WDF 98
Nathan SHE 169
Robert WDF 98
Robert WDF 98A

SCARCE, William WDF 95
SCARSE, Henry SHE 169
SCAYDEN, John HND 7
SCEARCY, Alexandeer ETL 50
SCECRETS, Wm.? FLG 66A
SCHA-SFIELD?, Jas. TOD 125
SCHAFFER, John HRD 84
SCHAMIHORN, Nathl. HRD 30
SCHANNEL, Jeremiah H. MER 109
SCHENE, Micajah LNC 57
SCHILER, John GRD 108A
SCHOLL, John CLK 75
SCHOOLAR, Benj. BBN 102
Joseph H. GRN 50
SCHOOLCRAFT, John HOP 262
SCHOOLER, (Blank) JEF 22
Benj. GRD 85A
Charles HAR 140
John MAD 98
Lewis CLK 94
Richard HAR 184
Robert CLK 68
Whorton FTE 96
William CLK 82
William HAR 140
Younger CLK 94
SCHOOLEY, James FTE 69
SCHOOLFIELD, John BKN 23
SCHOOLING, Joseph BLT 152
Joseph WAS 81A
Robert WAS 84A
SCHOTT, George CBL 10A
James CBL 7A
John CBL 11A
Solomon CBL 19A
William CBL 10A
SCHOUSH, Jacob MTG 287
SCHROYER, Jacob SCT 121A
SCHRYOCK, Mathias FTE 70
SCHULER, Malinda GRD 116A
SCHULL, Jessee CLK 81
Joseph CLK 76
Peter CLK 70
Septimus CLK 76
William CLK 76
SCHURING, John JEF 23
SCHUYLER, Jno. FKN 60
Wm. HRT 167
SCHWARTZWELDER, Peter NCH 129A
SCHWING, Saml. JEF 25
SCIDMORE, Henry GNP 165A
SCIFERS, Matthias NSN 222
SCIFERS?, Jacob NSN 222
SCISCOE, William WYN 86A
SCISSON, Abner JEF 31
Lawson BKN 23
SCOBEE, Daniel CLK 97
Dolly, Mrs. CLK 96
John CLK 96
Robert CLK 67
Stephen, Jr. CLK 96
SCOEFIELD, Martha SCT 96A
SCOFIELD, Jesse BTL 331
Saml. KNX 282
SCOGGINS, Nancy TOD 127
SCOLES, John CBL 12A
SCOMP?, Henry MER 108
John MER 108
SCONCE, John CLD 160
SCONCE?, Robert GSN 149A
SCONCES, John BBN 88
SCONSE, Elizabeth BBN 94
James BBN 94
SCOOLING, James WAS 81A
John WAS 81A
SCOOT, Elleaner CSY 222
SCOOTT, Robert MNR 207
SCOT, Samuel BTL 331
SCOTT, Widow LVG 18
-----? DVS 8A
--bbard? P. CWL 32
Aaron T. GTN 123
Abram HND 4
Absalom CLD 151
Alexr. FLG 58A
Amey FTE 61
Amos SCT 123A
Anderson HRD 48
Andrew FTE 91
Andrew SHE 122A
Arthur FTE 91
Arthur SHE 113A
Asa HRY 243
Benj. WAS 34A
Benj. WAS 53A
Benjamin MBG 138A
Catharine FKN 54
Catharine HOP 262
Christian BNE 34
Clement CLD 163
Colegate MBG 138A
Cosby HRD 26
Cyrus MER 108
Daniel ADR 44
Daniel UNN 153
Danl. MAS 76
Danl. FLG 75A
David LGN 23
David CWL 34
David CWL 40
David LGN 43
Earley SCT 134A
Edward FTE 59
Edward BTH 218
Elias BTH 152
Elija WAS 59A
Elijah ADR 48
Elisha HRY 180
Eliz. HRY 243
Elmore CBL 6A
Evan MAD 92
Ezekiel F. SCT 120A
Frances BBN 102
Francis BRN 27
Geo. HRY 180
George BBN 88
George MAD 136
Hanna SHE 169
Harding GRN 78
Harding GRN 80
Henry SHE 149
Henry HOP 262
Hugh ADR 46
Jacob CLD 161
Jacob LWS 89A
James FLD 7
James CWL 34
James HRD 42
James GRN 56
James MAS 68
James CLK 99
James MAD 130
James SHE 159
James NSN 195
James BTH 218
James MTG 283
James, Sr. MAD 136
James, Sr.? GRD 107A
James WAS 53A
SCOTT, James WAS 59A
James WYN 92A
James GRD 101A
James GRD 101A
James D. BBN 108
Jane MAD 136
Jas. MAS 72
Jas. HRY 243
Jas. RCK 78A
Jeduthen WYN 81A
Jeremiah CLD 163
Jno. C. MAS 77
Jno. G. MAS 61
Jo. GRD 120A
Joel SCT 93A
John JEF 21
John HRD 30
John JEF 39
John ADR 46
John GRN 52
John ADR 54
John CWL 56
John FTE 57
John GRN 57
John JES 74
John LNC 81
John FTE 91
John FTE 91
John WDF 97
John GTN 132
John BTH 150
John CLD 161
John HRY 182
John HAR 184
John BTH 194
John BTH 196
John BTH 206
John, Sen. WYN 84A
John -? JES 85
John PND 19A
John WAS 23A
John FLG 26A
John WRN 39A
John NCH 113A
John SHE 124A
John SHE 143A
John W. TOD 127A
Jonathan NCH 125A
Jos. CHN 41
Jos. FLG 70A
Joseph HRD 34
Joseph MAD 138
Joseph SHE 164
Joseph FKN 54
Joseph GRD 120A
Joseph? RCK 77A
Josiah NCH 128A
Kemp MNR 213
Levi HRY 243
Levi, Sr. HRY 184
Levi L. HRY 176
Lynard? WYN 84A
Marget GRD 113A
Marshall HRD 48
Marshall HRD 80
Martha JES 91
Martin ADR 3
Mary CLK 99
Mathew T. FTE 89
Matthew MAD 136
Matthew HAR 208
Matthew MTG 271
Moses BNE 36
Moses ADR 54
Moses SPN 15A
Moses SHE 116A

SCOTT, Moses SHE 122A
Nancy BBN 108
Nancy CLD 149
Nancy HAR 178
Nathan WRN 52A
Nathan WYN 91A
Nathan MBG 138A
Nathaneel CLD 161
Nathl. GRD 101A
Nathl. NCH 114A
Nelly WDF 105A
Nicholas BRK 295
Nimrod CLD 163
Oliver CWL 34
Pleasant BLT 166
Polly BNE 34
Reuben MNR 213
Richard CHN 29A
Richard WAS 59A
Robert CLK 98
Robert GTN 126
Robert HAR 180
Robert WAS 59A
Robert SHE 109A
Robt. CHN 41
Robt. BBN 114
Robt. FLG 75A
Robt. C. BBN 102
Rody? TRG 5
Rubin ADR 44
Salley MAD 136
Sally GRN 66
Sally CLD 158
Saml. MAS 56
Saml. HRY 198
Saml., Jr. MAS 56
Samuel TRG 5
Samuel BRN 28
Samuel CLD 149
Samuel HOP 262
Samuel BRK 295
Samuel WRN 55A
Samuel WYN 91A
Shadrack CLD 161
Susannah WDF 93
Thomas FLD 7
Thomas TRG 8
Thomas LNC 63
Thomas JES 74
Thomas LNC 81
Thomas FTE 91
Thomas FTE 91
Thomas HAR 134
Thomas MBG 138
Thomas CLD 149
Thomas NSN 206
Thomas HAR 208
Thomas MNR 215
Thomas GRD 90A
Thomas NCH 108A
Thomas SHE 113A
Thomas GNP 171A
Thomas B. JES 89
Thos. CHN 41
Will BBN 62
Will MAS 81
Will HRY 180
Will. MAS 58
William TRG 5
William FLD 34
William JES 74
William FTE 91
William FTE 93
William CLD 142
William HAR 142
William SHE 148
SCOTT, William CLD 160
William HAR 184
William MNR 195
William NSN 195
William MNR 207
William MTG 255
William, Jr. JES 74
William, Sr. WYN 97A
William WRN 51A
William WYN 79A
William NCH 108A
William GRD 112A
William SHE 113A
Wm. CHN 41
Wm. CHN 43
Wm. HRD 62
Wm. BBN 106
Wm. BBN 106
Wm., Jnr. SHE 141A
Wm. PND 29A
Wm. CHN 40A
Wm. B. TOD 126A
Wm. D. SHE 114A
Wm. Mercht. BBN 144
SCRANTON, David GNP 176A
SCREECHFIELD, Mary BBN 84
SCRIBNER, Abner HRD 84
SCRIDDER, Lemuel JEF 21
SCRIMINGER, John BRN 27
SCRINSHER, John, Esqr. OWN 104
SCRITCHFIELD, Isaac LNC 59
Nathl. LNC 59
SCRIVNER, James ETL 37
John MAD 118
Joseph ETL 50
SCRIVNER?, Thomas BRN 26
SCROGGAN, Joseph GTN 132
SCROGGEN, John BBN 136
Robert WDF 102A
SCROGGIN, -----?
P. HAR 166
Harriss WDF 93
John BBN 116
Thomas C. WDF 110A
SCROGGINS, Geo. BBN 138
Mary FTE 97
Robt. BBN 138
Samuel FTE 109
SCROGGS, Ebenezer FLG 48A
SCROGHAHAN, J. SHE 124A
SCROGHAM, Daniel FTE 104
Joseph FTE 81
William FTE 104
SCROGHAN, George SHE 124A
Wm. SHE 124A
SCROGIN, Billey? GTN 119
SCRUGGS, Henry C. KNX 288
James KNX 288
Jas. SCT 92A
John KNX 278
Thos. SCT 125A
Thos. B. SCT 125A
Will. SCT 136A
Wm. WAS 25A
SCRUGS, John GTN 120
Will GRD 115A
SCRUGSS, Micajaah MTG 235
SCUDDER, Charles WRN 75A
Chas MAS 66
SCUMMETT?, Jacob NCH 110A
SCURLOCK, George LNC 31
SCURRY, John MAD 90
SCYKES, George HRD 80
SCYPHERS, Jacob HRD 38
SCYPHERS, Jas. HRD 68
Matthias HRD 68
SEA, Garrett FLD 41
SEABOLT?, Geo. JEF 49
SEAMONS, Samuel CSY 224
SEARCEY, Lemuel MTG 285
SEARCY, Benj. FKN 156
Edmund FKN 156
Edmund HRY 176
Henry FKN 156
Howel MAD 100
John GTN 120
John WDF 121A
Richard MAD 114
Saml. MAD 154
Taylor GTN 120
SEARCY?, Elijah WDF 108A
Leonard WDF 109A
SEAREY, Richard WDF 121A
SEARGEANT, Sarah WRN 48A
SEARLES, James FTE 69
James CBL 22A
SEARS, Abram TOD 129
Abram TOD 133
Asa GNP 173A
Christian JEF 54
David LGN 36
David SPN 25A
Jacob SPN 3A
John LGN 36
John CLK 65
John KNX 288
John WRN 60A
Philip WRN 71A
Samuel SPN 24A
William LGN 36
William CLK 75
William WTY 124A
SEARS?, Henry ALN 130
Tho. ALN 128
SEATMAN, (No Given Name) JEF 51
SEATON, Geo. JEF 49
George BRK 293
Jas. K. JEF 49
Sarah JEF 63
Thomas PUL 65A
Wm. BRK 293
SEATS, John NSN 221
John, Jr./ Sr.? NSN 221
SEAWRIGHT, Andrew BBN 132
SEAY, Jacob WAS 66A
Saml. SHE 136A
SEAY?, Saml. WAS 64A
SEBASTIAN, Chals. BRK 229
Elijah SCT 109A
John JEF 26
John SCT 109A
Lewis SCT 134A
Saml. SHE 135A
Will SCT 106A
Will SCT 109A
Wm. SHE 130A
SEBASTIN, Ben GSN 151A
John CLY 121
Miles MAD 94
Wm. GSN 151A
SEBERT, John WAS 52A
SEBILL, Jno. FKN 122
SEBLES?, Will ADR 48
SEBORN, Cornelius SHE 155
SEBOURN, Harry P. SHE 165
Phebe SHE 165
SEBREE, Reuben BNE 36
Richard, Jr. OWN 102
Richd. SCT 130A

SEBREE, Thos. SCT 130A
Uriel BNE 36
William SCT 92A
SEBREE?, Laban OWN 104
SEBUE?, Martin I./ J.? FKN 92
SEBURN, Jacob CLY 131
SECIL, Samuel WYN 99A
SECRAY, John FTE 103
SECREST, William NCH 129A
SECRETS, William JES 69
SECRICH, Charles GRT 139
SECRIST?, Jacob FTE 97
SECRRITS?, Jos. FLG 55A
SEE, Austin MER 110
Federick SPN 16A
George BBN 70
George MTG 255
Jas. BBN 70
Joseph MTG 261
Leonard MER 110
Widow BBN 70
SEE?, Andrew MTG 267
Conrad MTG 261
John MTG 261
SEEATON, Kener. JEF 49
SEEING?, Stephen CHN 30
SEELY, Seth W HRD 12
SEERS?, John NCH 121A
Tho. ALN 124
Thos. ALN 126
SEGNIOURS, Daniel CBL 16A
SEGRAVES, Joseph HRL 118
Mary ALN 120
Rebecah ALN 120
SEGRO, Abijah HOP 264
SEIGNIOUR, John CBL 12A
SEIGNIOURS, Bryant CBL 12A
Phillip CBL 12A
SEIGNROUS?, Phillip CBL 12A
SEINER?, David P. GNP 165A
SEISTER, David LVG 6
SELBY, Barkley NCH 114A
Green? ADR 46
Hasty NCH 110A
Henry NCH 128A
Isaac NCH 128A
James BKN 24
John BBN 90
John HAR 192
Joseph HRL 118
Joshua HAR 192
Major NCH 110A
Major NCH 128A
Richard WAS 74A
William NCH 111A
SELCER, Hardin BRN 27
SELCH, Nicholas MER 108
Peter MER 109
Samuel MER 109
SELDEN, Olive, Mrs. BBN 128
SELF, Chamook? FTE 105
Danl. ADR 32
Joel CLD 156
John CLD 160
John HRT 168
Lawson SHE 174
Presley FTE 105
Presley MTG 239
Robert CLD 160
Salley HRT 168
William FTE 97
SELF?, Isaac WDF 97A
SELLARS, Joseph WDF 99A
SELLARS, Leonard BKN 28
Thomas W. WDF 101A
SELLARS?, W--? LVG 18
SELLERS, Elisabeth HAR 160
Elizab. RCK 81A
Isham HND 11A
James GRD 102B
John BKN 6
John HAR 168
John, Jun. BKN 9
John WYN 95A
Lewis KNX 314
Mary HAR 146
Orman HND 11
Phillip BKN 13
Rebecca UNN 146
Thomas BNE 34
SELLHEART, John BLT 172
SELLORS, Michael BKN 5
SELLORS?, Geo. BKN 9
SELLY, Wm. S. BBN 126
SELREE?, Martin I./ J.? FKN 92
SELVY, Lewis FLG 68A
Nicholas CLD 144
SEMOORE, Clabourn MER 108
SEMPLE, John W. CLD 152
SENNETT, John OHO 5A
SENOR, Henry JEF 49
Wm. JEF 66
SENT?, John GRD 92A
SENTER, J. H. LNC 17
SENTON?, Margret GRN 70
SEPPLES, Alexr. SCT 116A
SERATT, Hiliary CWL 56
SERET?, John BKN 10
SERGEANT, Dabney DVS 16A
John CBL 16A
SERGEANTS, Rodee PND 27A
SERVANT, William MER 108
SERVIN, Malaci GNP 177A
SERVING?, Caleb CBL 16A
SESSENY, Robert CHN 30A
Stephen CHN 30A
SESSION, Vincent JEF 43
SESSIONS, Solomon BTL 331
SESSON, John JEF 40
SESSON?, Phillip JEF 36
SETON, James BRK 291
SETT, John BTH 212
SETTLE, Bennet FKN 78
Charles BRN 26
Franklin BRN 26
Jno. FKN 100
Jno. M. FKN 134
John BRN 27
Martin SCT 96A
Simon BRN 26
Thornton BRN 28
Willis BRN 28
SETTLES, Abram GRN 70
Benj. ADR 46
Benjm. GRN 66
SETTLES?, James NSN 187
Joel NSN 187
Susanna NSN 187
SEURLOCK?, Thomas WDF 100
SEUT?, John GRD 92A
SEVEER, Enoch HND 7A
SEVEIR, Hannah CLD 164
John CLD 164
SEVER, John MBG 142
Michael MGB 137A
SEVERIDGE, Joseph MAD 138
SEVERIDGE?, John MAD 134
SEVERS, Henry FLG 52A
SEVINDLERS, Clayton MER 109
SEWALL, James MTG 283
SEWARD, Austin MAD 182
John S. HRD 72
Thos. MAD 130
Wm. HRD 42
SEWARDS, Daniel, Jr. GRT 144
Daniel, Sen. GRT 143
SEWEL, Abraham PUL 35A
Dawson, Jr.? PUL 35A
Isaac PUL 39A
SEWELL, Jas. CLY 122
Joseph FLD 8
Joseph CLK 83
Samuel CLK 76
SEWELL?, Mary JEF 22
SEXSON, Free WTY 111A
Jacob WTY 110A
James WTY 111A
Lemuel WTY 111A
William, Jr. WTY 125A
SEXTON, Benjamin, Jr. BTH 206
Benjamin, Sr. BTH 206
Jeremiah BTH 206
John FLD 40
John BTH 206
Lewis CWL 38
William BTH 208
SEXTON?, Margret GRN 70
SEYBOLD, Jasper FLG 29A
John FLG 24A
SEYER?, Phillip JEF 36
SH---?, Henry HRL 118
SH--?, John SHE 126A
SHA--?, Isaac LVG 18
SHACCLEFORD, Henry HRL 118
SHACKELET, Blanest? HRD 30
SHACKELETT, Jesse HRD 70
John HRD 70
SHACKELFORD, B. CHN 29A
Jeremiah SHE 164
John SHE 164
Richard CSY 228
Sterling SHE 163
Wm. S. FLG 36A
SHACKELITT, Ben HRD 14
SHACKELSWORTH, Allen WAS 34A
SHACKLEFORD, Abner T. CLK 73
B. C. LNC 19
Beverley WDF 126A
Edmd. LNC 7
Edmund LNC 31
Francis MAD 178
Geo. MAS 57
Henry MER 109
James CLK 102
James CSY 208
James GRD 98A
Jas MAS 57
John HRD 36
John, Sr. HRD 8
Marquis LNC 81
Ned GRD 97A
Robinson WRN 50A
Saml. LNC 25
Tarlton WRN 51A
Thos. HRD 30
W. B. MAS 78
William WRN 51A
William W. NSN 183

SHACKLEFORD, Wm. LNC 65
Zachariah MER 109
SHACKLETT, Wm. SHE 123A
SHAD?, John SCT 135A
SHADBUNE?, William NSN 176
SHADBURN, Jane JEF 37
Richard JEF 40
SHADBURNE, Thomas NSN 175
SHADD, David HAR 140
James HAR 136
Samuel HAR 140
Samuel HAR 140
Thos. HAR 138
SHADDIC, Thomas BLT 158
SHADOIN?, Wm. PUL 37A
SHADOWINS, John SPN 13A
SHADRIC, John SHE 124A
SHADWICK, Jno. HRY 265
SHADWICK?, Ben. HRY 261
Jas./ Jos.? HRY 261
Thos. NSN 199
SHAFFAT?, Littleton CSY 226
SHAFFORD?, John BBN 142
SHAHAN, John CWL 38
SHAIFF, Anthony BBN 126
SHAIN, Able BLT 196
David BLT 164
James GSN 150A
John GSN 150A
John B. BLT 162
Thomas LWS 88A
William BLT 194
William LWS 89A
SHAKE, Adam JEF 64
Jacob JEF 56
John JEF 45
Wm. JEF 56
SHAKELFORD, Hiram SHE 168
SHAKELIFF?, Thomas NSN 196
SHAKER?, Family (With Sam White) LGN 29
SHAKESPEAR, Edward MER 109
SHAKLEFORD, Jas./ Jos.? HRY 250
John MAD 118
SHAMWELL, Zakereah UNN 153
SHANAR?, Peter BBN 134
SHANE, Thomas GNP 171A
SHANE?, David GNP 172A
SHANK, Adam MBG 139
Jacob GTN 133
Thomas GTN 133
SHANK?, Thomas LVG 18
SHANKLEN, Sarah BLT 180
SHANKLIN, Alexander LGN 31
Andrew BTH 158
Benjamin NCH 119A
Edwd. TOD 132
F. TOD 129A
Gordan FLG 28A
James JES 76
Jas. MAS 74
John BLT 162
John WRN 49A
John FLG 66A
John NCH 119A
Josiah MAS 80
Lydia LGN 31
Madgaline JES 81
R. TOD 132
Richard BLT 160
Sally NCH 119A
Samuel CSY 214
SHANKLIN, Thomas LGN 42
Thomas JES 84
Wm. JEF 37
SHANKLING, Andrew LNC 33
SHANKS, Archild. LNC 3
Charles WAS 73A
David LNC 73
David BBN 88
Edward M. BBN 90
Elizabeth BLT 194
Henry WRN 75A
John BBN 72
John MAD 152
John BRK 291
Robert SHE 149
Samuel SHE 149
Sarah LNC 69
Thomas SHE 149
Thomas NSN 188
William SHE 149
SHANNAN, Thomas CSY 220
SHANNON, Absolem LNC 59
Alexander SHE 158
Alexr. SCT 107A
Andrew A. SHE 176
Ann LNC 33
Ann SHE 172
Arthur FTE 79
George FTE 64
Hugh SHE 174
Jacob FTE 77
James FLD 21
James FKN 62
James WRN 61A
James SHE 129A
Jane GNP 165A
John FTE 77
John, Jr. NCH 105
John, Sr. NCH 105
John WYN 88A
John SCT 98A
John SHE 109A
John NCH 120A
Jos. HRY 251
Jos. HRY 260
Joseph LGN 47
Joseph WDF 112A
Nathl. SCT 134A
Robt. HRY 260
Robt. SCT 98A
Saml. JEF 63
Saml. FKN 130
Saml. FKN 130
Saml. B. SHE 129A
Samuel ADR 46
Samuel NCH 126A
Samuel SHE 129A
Sidney BBN 86
Thomas SHE 168
Thomas R. WRN 35A
Will. SCT 131A
William HAR 158
Wm. MAD 126
Wm. HRY 255
Wm. SHE 129A
SHAPPELL, Ballard? BLT 170
SHAREWOOD, Nancy SHE 130A
Robert JES 75
SHARKLEFORD, Green WDF 100
SHARL?, John A. BRK 291
SHARLEY, George MAD 156
SHARMAN, Thomas GRN 68
SHARNEY, Henry SPN 9A
SHARP, Aaron ETL 39
Abraham MER 110
Abraham FKN 148
SHARP, Abraham WRN 28A
Absalom CHN 27A
Anderson FTE 82
Benjamin FTE 97
Benjamin SHE 172
Ebenr. BBN 146
Edward WYN 96A
Elias FTE 83
Elizabeth BBN 68
Elizabeth BTH 150
Ensteen HRT 167
George FTE 81
George HAR 212
Henry LNC 51
Horatio NSN 177
Isaac HRY 263
Isaac KNX 290
Isaac NCH 113A
Isham ADR 46
James MBG 135
Jno. HRY 250
John ADR 44
John GRN 68
John FTE 97
John HAR 212
John BTL 331
John, Sr. WTY 122A
John SPN 3A
John SCT 139A
John F. WTY 124A
John H. BNE 36
John T. NCH 111A
Leander J./ I.? WRN 74A
Linchfield FTE 88
Linsfield SCT 139A
M., Dr. CHN 27A
Moses ETL 50
Noah FKN 148
Richard FTE 66
Richard BTH 150
Richard SHE 156
Richard NCH 121A
Soloman P. WRN 74A
Solomon MER 110
Stephen FTE 81
Stephen JES 89
Stephen BBN 138
Stephen BTH 150
Thomas WTY 115A
Vincent BBN 68
Widow BBN 68
William LVG 18
William JES 75
William FTE 81
William, Esq. MER 110
William WDF 97A
Wm W. HRY 244
Wm. T. SHE 139A
SHARPE, Adam SHE 126A
Benjamin CSY 208
Caty PND 30A
Deborah SHE 137A
John SHE 126A
John SHE 138A
Thomas BKN 26
William CSY 220
William SHE 120A
SHARR?, Lewis NCH 110A
SHARRER, Henry BTL 331
SHARRER?, Jacob BTL 331
SHARRON, Hugh SCT 100A
Jas. SCT 100A
SHARRY, William WRN 69A
SHASTEEN, William LNC 9
SHATTEEN, Jessee WYN 83A
SHAVER, Andrew JEF 33

SHAVER, Benjamin HRD 12
Frederick PND 24A
George BNE 34
George HAR 152
Jacob JEF 39
Jno. HAR 138
John BNE 34
Peter MBG 138A
Wm. HRD 70
SHAVERS, David FLG 43A
SHAW, --ner? CWL 40
Aaron GTN 122
Aaron PND 31A
Arch. CHN 45A
Benjamin SHE 132A
David LVG 11
Elizabeth MER 108
Hiram FTE 69
Jacob DVS 16A
James GTN 130
James CBL 22A
James CHN 35A
John JEF 48
John FTE 100
John FTE 105
John BBN 118
John BBN 130
John GTN 130
John SHE 152
John TRG 8A
John P. SHE 114A
John W. MER 116
Joseph BKN 26
Joseph SHE 110A
Leonard TRG 6
Margaret NCH 127A
Mich. HRY 257
Polly CHN 42
Rebecca JEF 51
Robbert CBL 21A
Robt. LVG 9
Samuel BBN 128
The? WAS 23A
Thomas BNE 36
Thomas BBN 116
Thos. ADR 46
Thos. (Crossed Out) SCT 101A
Thos. SCT 94A
William CHN 35A
Wm. HRD 60
Wm. BBN 116
Wm. HRY 260
Wm., Snr. GSN 151A
Wm. GSN 149A
SHAW?, Hesekiah ALN 100
Jacob CSY 206
Lewis NCH 110A
SHAWHAN, Danl. PND 21A
SHAWHORN, Josep HAR 156
SHAWLER, Mary BLT 196
SHAWLER?, Anthony BLT 158
SHAWLEY, John NSN 186
SHAWN, Peter, Senr. OHO 10A
SHAWN?, Jerrimiah N. CHN 42
SHAY?, Widow? LVG 18
SHE-WATERS?, Danl. BBN 134
SHEALDS, Dur? WAS 52A
SHEALES?, Tho. ALN 100
SHEALS, Elijah ALN 96
SHEANON?, Charles CSY 218
SHEAPARD, Jos. MAS 55
SHEARER/SHEAVER, Andrew ADR 48
SHEARER, Daniel WYN 82A
Jacob WYN 82A
Martha MAD 154
Thos. MAD 134
Wm. MAD 174
SHEARLY, Tolifer BKN 28
William MER 108
SHEARMAN, Shadrack BBN 140
SHEARR?, Margaret MAD 112
SHEARS?, Ephraim ALN 116
SHEARWOOD, Charles CBL 3A
Thomas CSY 222
SHECKELS, Levi FLG 53A
SHECKLES, John HRD 76
Sarah HRD 76
Thomas HRD 24
SHEDEL, John J. FTE 69
SHEELEY?, Herman / Harrison? FTE 64
SHEELS?, B. Thos. GSN 150A
SHEELY, Horace FTE 93
John FTE 73
SHEELY?, David JES 95
SHEEN, John CSY 226
SHEENE?, David GNP 172A
SHEERWOOD, John FLG 40A
SHEETON?, (See Shelton) GTN
SHEETS, (See Shuts) FKN 104
Andrew BNE 36
Henry BRK 291
Henry H. OWN 104
Wm. HRY 260
SHEETS?, (See Shuts) FKN 84
Abraham CBL 9A
Frederick GTN 126
J. J. (I. I.?) CHN 46
SHEFFER?, Mary HND 11
SHEFFIELD, George ETL 49
SHEHAN, John WAS 18A
Mary NSN 193
SHEHON?, John BBN 142
SHEILDS, James BTH 196
Saml. CWL 56
William LWS 93A
Wm. BBN 116
SHELBERN?, John NSN 221
SHELBOURN, Jno. PUL 37A
SHELBURNE, Benjamin SHE 138A
Dioniscus SHE 119A
Jane SHE 115A
Robinson SHE 119A
Spencer SHE 132A
SHELBY, Aron UNN 148
Edward MAD 180
Evan LNC 59
Isaac, Jr. LNC 59
Isaac, Sr. LNC 59
James FTE 79
Sarah LVG 12
Smith LVG 18
Soloman HRD 10
Thomas LVG 13
Thomas H. FTE 84
Thos. LVG 5
SHELEY, John, Junr. SCT 108A
John SCT 108A
Singleton SCT 108A
SHELHOUSE, ----s? CWL 32
SHELL, Henry HAR 190
SHELLERS, John SCT 92A
William SCT 91A
SHELLIDAY, Caleb SHE 162
SHELLIE, John SHE 130A
SHELLY, Daniel CLD 161
David CLD 161
George CLD 165
John CLD 161
Mary BBN 80
Nathan WTY 110A
Peter, Junr. CLD 161
Peter, Senr. CLD 161
SHELMAN, Adam BRK 293
Lewis BRK 295
Martin BRK 293
SHELO-?, William JES 81
SHELTON/ SHETTON?, John JES 81
SHELTON, Abednigo BTL 331
Abraham HND 11
Abraham BTL 331
Asher TOD 129
Buckner TRG 3A
Daniel GTN 118
David OWN 99
David BTL 331
Elijah HND 13
Ezekiel WYN 102A
G--ne? W. GTN 127
George HND 11
George BTL 331
George, Jr. WDF 100A
George, Sr. WDF 100A
Hall LGN 45
Hannah HND 11
Henry HRD 22
Hugh GTN 118
Jacob GTN 129
Je---? CWL 56
Jeremiah BTL 331
Jno. MAS 60
John HRD 56
John GTN 128
John MGB 137A
Josiah CHN 36
Liberty CSY 226
Mackey BRN 26
Medley, Jr. GTN 129
Medley, Sr. GTN 129
Medley WDF 115A
Micajah SPN 17A
Nancy FTE 90
Reddick MBG 141
Robert TRG 5
Robert WYN 104A
Robert WDF 116A
Robt. HRY 250
Rutherford GTN 118
Samuel MER 108
Stephen JES 83
Tho. MAS 72
Tho. MAS 77
Thomas FTE 98
Thomas HRY 202
Thomas, Jr. BTH 190
Thomas, Snr. BTH 190
Thomas WDF 100A
Thos. FKN 84
Thos. MAD 144
William CHN 36
William BLT 170
William WDF 97A
Wyatt TOD 130A
SHELTON?, Cuthbert MBG 137
Thos. MAD 144
SHELY, Benjamin FKN 76
SHEMWELL, Jas. TOD 130A
Sam TOD 130A

Name	County	Page
SHENELL, Wm.	GRN	52
SHEPARD, A. F.	SCT	92A
B. John	GSN	150A
Ezekiel	SCT	131A
Jno.	MAS	55
John	LWS	91A
John	SCT	107A
Joseph	GSN	150A
Saml.	SCT	139A
Soloman	LWS	91A
Wm.	GSN	150A
SHEPHARD, Geo.	MAS	65
SHEPHERD, Andrew	ADR	46
Ann	FLG	65A
Atkinson	HRD	20
Christo.	HRY	206
David	SHE	167
Elizh.	FLG	27A
Enoch	CBL	17A
George P.	CHN	28A
Hiram	BRK	291
Isaac, Jr.	WYN	83A
Isaac, Senr.	WYN	80A
James	CLK	73
James	BLT	194
John	BNE	50
John	HRL	118
John	SHE	168
John	SHE	117A
John	WDF	124A
John	TOD	129A
Jonathan	HRD	64
Joseph	NCH	121A
Lewis	ADR	50
Pleasant	SHE	167
Rachael	BLT	156
Samuel	BLT	158
Silas	WYN	79A
Stephen	ADR	46
Thos.	BBN	128
William	SHE	158
William	HRY	206
Wm.	CHN	43
Wm.	ADR	52
Wm.	HRD	58
Wm.	HRY	258
SHEPHERDSON, Elijah	CWL	44
SHEPHRD, William	ETL	47
SHEPPARD, Henry	WAS	72A
SHEPPERD, Dickey	FTE	106
Geo.	CHN	42
SHERER, Jacob	BBN	144
SHERIDAN, John	CHN	33
William	HRY	212
SHERILL, Jacob	CHN	41
SHERILL?, Frederick	JES	74
SHERKLIFF?, Thomas	NSN	196
SHERLEY, John	FLG	46A
Samuel	HOP	266
Wm.	JEF	54
SHERMAN, Chs.	JEF	48
Edward	CHN	39
SHEROD, Thomas	TOD	130
SHEROLD?, Asom	WAS	63A
SHERRARD, Polly	HRD	54
SHERRELL, John, Sr.	GRN	50
SHERRELT?, Ambros	GRN	57
SHERRIL, Isaac	WYN	81A
John	WYN	103A
Thomas	WYN	101A
SHERRILL, Johnathan	WYN	82A
SHERROD, James	LGN	27
SHERROD, Robert	LGN	27
SHERRON, Isaac	GRD	106A
SHERROW, Jacob	JEF	24
SHERWOOD, Daniel	JES	89
SHERY, John	ALN	104
SHETFORD?, Wm.	CWL	33
SHEVELL?, Frederick	JES	74
George	JES	89
SHEVELY, Jacob	GRN	71
Michel	GRN	71
SHEVIL?, John	FTE	69
SHEWMAKER, Cornelious	WAS	84A
Elisabeth	BTH	188
Evan?	WAS	82A
John	WAS	82A
Sam	WAS	84A
Wm.	WAS	47A
Wm.	WAS	83A
SHEWSBERRY, Drury	HRD	64
SHIALES?, Tho.	ALN	96
SHICKLE?, Rebecca	MTG	277
SHICKLES, Loid / Lord?	NCH	129A
SHIE?, John	SHE	126A
SHIELD, David	ADR	48
SHIELDS, Archibald	HAR	166
James	JES	91
James	MER	109
Jno	FKN.	132
Jonathan	MAS	65
Joseph	CWL	56
Mary	MER	109
Patrick	FTE	68
Patrick	FTE	106
Thomas	MTG	231
William	MER	109
Wm.	CWL	56
Wm.	BBN	146
SHIFLET, Harden	WRN	61A
Haston	MAD	126
Joshua	MAD	126
Thos.	MAD	126
SHIGH, Leiper	CLD	156
Margaret	CLD	157
SHIKLE, Peter	BRN	26
SHILBINS, John	JEF	45
SHILLINGER?, Gabl.	HRY	188
SHILTON, James	BTL	331
SHIMP?, John	CWL	38
SHINDLEBOWER, Henry	HAR	204
SHINGLEBOWER, Ann	FTE	74
SHINGLER, George	SHE	117A
George	SHE	134A
SHINGLETON, Jonathan	SCT	108A
Strother	SCT	138A
Thos.	SCT	108A
SHINKEN, John	FTE	79
SHINN, B--.?	BNE	52
SHINN?, Betsey	BBN	106
SHIP, Ambros	GRN	75
Anderson D.	SCT	93A
Edmund	MER	116
Elijah	CLK	74
Fielding	CLK	73
James	CLK	64
John	GRN	76
John	PND	21A
Labin	CHN	40A
Richd.	GRN	67
Thomas	GRN	76
William	GRN	76
SHIPHERD, David	FLD	5
SHIPHERD, Jacob	FLD	5
SHIPLEY, Benjamin .	WYN	86A
Elias	MAS	62
James	FTE	87
James?	ALN	136
Nat	ALN	136
Noah	MAS	57
Reason?	MAS	57
Reuben	MNR	215
Richard	FTE	87
Richard	FTE	104
Robt.	ALN	136
Robt.	ALN	138
Samuel	MNR	191
Thomas	LNC	51
SHIPMAN, David	BRN	28
David	SHE	125A
Isaiah	SHE	148
John	SHE	169
William	SHE	172
SHIPP, Colby	OWN	99
Dudley	FTE	96
Ewell	JEF	22
Richard D.	WDF	113A
Thos.	JEF	22
SHIPPARD?, David	MAD	126
SHIPTON, John	MAD	94
SHIRE, John	TRG	5A
SHIRIDEN, Eugine?	JEF	30
SHIRKLIFF, John	NSN	181
SHIRLEY, Benjamin	WRN	53A
Caleb	BRN	26
Danl.	HRT	168
Easther	SCT	103A
Edmund	OWN	105
Ezekiel	SCT	131A
Isaac	WAS	48A
John	BRN	27
John	BBN	132
John	OHO	10A
John	GRD	91A
John W.	ADR	3`
Joshua	BLT	166
Paul	BRN	34
Polley	ADR	18
Polly	BRN	27
Richard	BRN	27
Richd. W.	BRN	28
Robert	BLT	176
Thomas, Jr.	BRN	28
Thomas, Ser.	BRN	26
Thomas	WRN	69A
Thomas W.	BRN	28
William	HAR	180
Wm. A.	BRN	34
SHIRLEY?, William	HAR	192
SHIRLY, Armstead	MAS	81
George	ADR	48
SHIRRELL, James H.	GRN	53
SHIRTS, John	HAR	200
SHITE, Leonard	NSN	194
Pierce	HRD	78
SHIVE, George	CLD	143
SHIVELEY, Phillip	JEF	38
SHIVELY, Christian	JEF	38
Cutprint	JEF	42
Henry	JEF	38
Henry	SHE	131A
Jacob	MTG	243
John	GRN	75
John	GRT	147
William	JEF	38
SHIVERY, George	FTE	100
SHOALFIELD, Isaac R./ B.?	BKN	8
SHOARES, Peter	TOD	129

Name	County	Page
SHOASS?, William	WYN	82A
SHOAT?, Gabriel	WYN	82A
SHOATE, Augustin	BTH	208
SHOBE, Jacob	WRN	53A
Martin	WRN	53A
SHOCK, John	FTE	77
SHOCKENSY, John	HRY	190
Richard W.	HRY	190
SHOCKEY, Jacob	FLG	77A
Jas.	FLG	70A
John	FLD	28
John	FLG	70A
John	FLG	77A
SHOCKLEY, David	BRN	27
James	LNC	11
Jas.	FLG	73A
Kendall	MTG	245
Lemuel	BRN	27
Purnell	FLG	63A
Saml.	FLG	63A
Thos.	FKN	62
Willis	MNR	209
Wm., Jr.	FLG	73A
Wm., Sr.	FLG	73A
Wm.	WAS	22A
SHOCKTON, James	WDF	101A
SHOEMAK, Roderick	NSN	213
SHOEMAKE, Fielding	MER	108
Jas.	BBN	102
John	PUL	57A
Joshua	MER	108
SHOEMAKER, -----?	DVS	7A
Henry	SHE	130A
Jereh.	CWL	56
Jessee	GRN	62
John	LVG	18
John	GRN	77
John	SHE	118A
William	WYN	94A
Wm.	CWL	56
SHOEMATE, Baler	HRL	118
John	HAR	152
Laky	PND	30A
Stephen	HAR	146
SHOFNER, Charles	GRN	67
David	GRN	78
Henry	GRN	79
Robert	GRN	77
SHOLDERS, Cader	WRN	34A
SHONS?, Jno.	FKN	160
SHOOFSTALL, Florance	MAS	76
SHOOTS, Federick	MAD	180
James	FTE	87
John	FTE	85
William	FTE	82
SHOPTAN?, Erasmus	BLT	168
SHOPTAW, John	BRK	295
Thomas	BRK	295
SHOPTOOLL, Jacob	MAS	53
SHORE, Susanna	FTE	110
SHORES, Frederic	CLD	137
Wilson	BRN	26
SHORT, -unnel?	SCT	118A
Aaron	FLD	20
Adam	FLD	40
Aner?	WAS	84A
Aron	LNC	43
Benjamin	FLD	37
Calap	WAS	59A
Charles	FLD	37
Charles W.	CHN	28
Coleman	NCH	127A
David	MBG	138A
Elias	SPN	13A
Elizabeth	GRN	59
SHORT, Fleming	BRN	26
George	MER	109
George	MBG	139
Henson	WAS	83A
Horatio	GRN	53
Jacob	HAR	150
Jacob	MBG	138A
James	GRN	60
James	GRN	73
James	MER	109
James C.	LNC	2
John	BBN	122
John	GTN	127
John	WDF	119A
Joseph	GRN	76
Landman	MNR	209
Leroy	MER	109
Moses	HRT	168
Obediah	SCT	118A
Peyton	FKN	82
Saml.	HRT	168
Samuel	PUL	55A
Samuel	MBG	138A
Scion	MNR	209
Will	BBN	64
William	FLD	37
William	MER	110
William	HRL	118
Wm.	GRN	73
Wm.	WAS	53A
Zack	GRD	113A
SHORT?, John A.	BRK	291
Joshua	GRN	73
Wm.	CWL	56
SHORTER?, Jane	FTE	60
SHORTRIDGE, Andw.	PUL	39A
Charles	MTG	279
Eli	MTG	225
Samuel	MTG	279
Will.	SCT	129A
William	MTG	281
SHORTRIGE, Geo.	HRY	270
George	GNP	167A
SHORTWELL, Lewis	CBL	6A
SHOTE, Peter	JEF	49
SHOTTON?, Christopher	WDF	95A
SHOTWELL, Daniel	KNX	308
Jabaz	MAS	74
Jno.	MAS	64
Jno.	MAS	66
Nathan	MAS	57
Will	MAS	74
SHOULDERS, Allin	TRG	6A
Joshua	TRG	6A
SHOULER?, Jane	FTE	60
SHOULS, Christian	GNP	171A
SHOULTH, Jacob	SPN	17A
Joseph	SPN	18A
SHOULTS, Henry	SPN	21A
SHOUSE, Daniel	SHE	140A
SHOUSH, Henry	MTG	241
SHOUTTES, Jacob	CSY	224
SHOWARD, Levin	FTE	74
SHOWER, Henry	WDF	98
Samuel	WDF	93A
William	WDF	98
SHOWER?, Jane	FTE	60
SHOWLEY, Lewis	NSN	205
SHOWN, Edward	DVS	18A
SHOWN?, Peter, Junr.	OHO	6A
SHOWRD?, -----?	DVS	11A
SHRADAR, Conrod	BBN	102
Tobias	BBN	106
SHRADER, George	OHO	4A
SHRADER, John	WRN	37A
Mary	WRN	37A
Mrs.	BBN	146
Philip	BBN	120
SHREACH?, Sam.?	CHN	46
SHREADER, Adain	JEF	50
Jacob	JEF	56
Jacob, Jr.	JEF	60
John	JEF	56
John, Jr.	JEF	64
Wm.	JEF	68
SHREAVE, Abner	GRN	75
Israel	BNE	36
SHREVE, Henry M.	JEF	31
Leven L.	FTE	56
SHREWSBERRY, Abel	WYN	79A
Benjamine	BRK	289
Nathaniel	WYN	80A
SHREWSBURY, John	BRK	291
Nathan	BRK	291
Rule	BRK	293
SHRIEVE, Thomas T. / F?	JES	96
William	JES	74
William	GRN	75
SHRITE, John	CLK	81
SHRIVE, Josh	TOD	128
SHROADER, Frederick	WRN	43A
Nicholas	WRN	43A
William	WRN	43A
SHROCK, John	FTE	60
SHRODES, Elisabeth	BTL	331
SHROPSHIRE, Abner	BBN	136
B. N.	BBN	136
Edward	CLK	101
George	CLK	67
James	FLD	9
James	HAR	136
John	CLK	101
John	BBN	118
Joseph	BBN	118
Mary	CLK	101
Waller?	HAR	168
William	HAR	168
SHROUT?, Saml.	FLG	45A
SHROYER, John	SCT	92A
SHRYACH, William	BTH	208
SHRYER, Jno.	CHN	42
SHRYHOCK, Adam	WDF	99
William	WDF	105
SHRYOCK, John	BNE	36
John	FTE	90
John F.	FTE	90
SHUBART, Nicholas	BTH	216
SHUBERT, Lewis	MTG	253
SHUCK, Andw.	HRY	257
Barbary	WAS	35A
Corneluis	SHE	172
Cumel./ Cunnel.?	HRY	260
Jno.	HRY	257
John	SHE	158
Matt.	HRY	265
Michael	BLT	160
Wm.	HRY	257
SHUCK?, George	CSY	214
John	CSY	214
John	WAS	36A
SHUEH?, George	CSY	214
John	CSY	214
SHUFF, Isaac	SCT	113A
Jacob	SCT	126A
SHUFFET, Jacob	BRN	26
SHUFFETT, Michael	HAR	168
SHUFFIT, Jacob	BTH	160
SHUGERS, Eli	CLD	165

SHULDTS, Charles OHO 7A
Matthias OHO 4A
SHULER?, Christian WYN 82A
SHULEY?, David HAR 194
William HAR 192
SHULL, Jonathan MGB 137A
Peter MBG 138
SHULS?, B. Thos. GSN 150A
SHULT, A. ALN 112
SHULTS, Jacob ADR 50
John ADR 46
John BTH 190
SHULTZ, Abraham NCH 121A
Christian MAS 76
Henry MTG 225
Mark MTG 253
Mark NCH 121A
Peter NCH 121A
SHUMAKER, Will LVG 18
SHUMATE, Bailey NCH 126A
Danl. GRD 105A
Jesse BBN 76
Michel GRD 110A
Peyton NCH 129A
SHURLEY, Uriah MBG 142A
SHURN?, Henry HRL 118
John OWN 99
SHURRY, William GRD 108A
SHUTES?, J. J. (I. I.?) CHN 46
SHUTS, Ben FKN 84
David BTH 168
Henry FKN 84
Martin FKN 104
SHUTS?, Abraham CBL 9A
Frederick GTN 126
SHUTT, Abraham MBG 138
Henry MBG 142
Jacob, Junr. MBG 138
Jacob, Senr. MBG 138
SHWADER, Christopher GSN 151A
SHWIN, Wiley FTE 82
SHY, Jesse MER 108
William MER 109
SHYE, Jacob BBN 136
James BBN 140
SHYE?, Simeon BBN 116
SIBERT, Danl. CLY 126
SIBERT?, Peter WAS 85A
SIBLEY, Isaac UNN 148
Lemuel G. WRN 43A
SICELY, (No Other Name) FTE 60
SICINY?, Stephen CHN 30
SICK, Martin WRN 35A
SIDDENS, James BRN 26
Joseph BRN 26
SIDDLE, Joshua LGN 39
SIDDONS, Wm. BRN 26
SIDEBOTTOM, Peter PUL 45A
Ray OWN 107
SIDEBOTTOM?, John CLK 84
Joseph CLK 84
SIDENER, Conrod FTE 94
George P. FTE 94
Henry FTE 94
Jacob FTE 94
Jacob MTG 241
John MTG 239
SIDENER?, John FTE 93
SIDINER?, Martin CLK 99
SIDLE, Christian HAR 210
SIDNER, Martin BBN 110
SIDNER?, Robert HAR 160
William HAR 160
SIDWELL, Jno. MAS 68
John CLD 152
Joseph CLD 154
Nathen MAS 68
William CLD 154
William CLD 154
SIDWELL?, Hugh BBN 120
SIGLER, George HOP 264
Jacob HOP 264
SIGLER?, Isaac ALN 100
SIGNER, John HAR 176
SILBER?, Aron UNN 148
SILCOCK, John GRN 55
SILCOX, John BTH 218
SILENER?, Edmd. HRY 250
SILES, Jane WRN 31A
SILKMAN, Henry NSN 201
SILKWOOD, Mary HOP 266
Matilda HOP 266
Thomas HOP 266
SILL, Asemith SHE 170
Beeda JEF 46
James SHE 170
Register SHE 175
William CBL 23A
SILLS, Abraham SHE 136A
John CBL 4A
SILVER, Thos. HND 4
SILVER?, Aron UNN 148
SILVERS, Charles CLD 149
Jane WDF 100A
Jno. MAS 60
Wm. PUL 45A
SILVERTOOTH, George MER 108
SILVESTER, Jeremiah W. ETL 39
SILVEY, George GRD 105A
SILVY, Edward MBG 135
James LWS 93A
Robert LWS 91A
SILWELL, Will MAS 67
SIMES, Benjamin MNR 193
John MNR 193
SIMMERMAN, Airhart CLD 142
Peter CLD 166
SIMMONS, ----?, Jr. HRD 26
Abraham OHO 4A
Adam HAR 144
Benj. W. WAS 75A
Benja. JEF 38
Benjamin LGN 32
Betsey HRD 70
Ceaphus OHO 5A
Daniel CBL 8A
David WRN 41A
Eli ETL 42
Elisha BLT 192
Eliza FTE 61
George WRN 48A
Greenberry LGN 47
Griffin BLT 180
Isham MNR 197
James TRG 11
James BLT 192
James MNR 197
Jas. HRD 70
Jno. MAS 73
John LGN 33
John CSY 226
Jonathan BLT 154
Jonothan, Senre. HRD 70
Joseph BLT 154
Ledwick? BLT 156
Levi BLT 166
SIMMONS, Manson BBN 116
Mary HOP 264
Nancy MNR 199
Peter HAR 144
Richard HRD 62
Richard P. BLT 174
Robert BLT 192
Robt. HRD 70
Roland WRN 48A
Rutha ADR 48
Saml. HRY 196
Samuel BLT 154
Samuel BLT 190
Thomas BLT 178
Thomas W. BLT 182
Tyler HRD 70
William HND 4
William BLT 154
William BLT 168
William MNR 195
William WRN 41A
Wm. TOD 125A
Wm. C. OHO 10A
SIMMS, Ambrose BBN 90
Ann HOP 266
Armstead MER 108
Augustine MNR 213
Benjamin CLK 83
Caleb MER 108
Charles NSN 179
Francis BLT 196
Francis WAS 41A
Garland MER 108
Garland CHN 36A
George CLD 140
James BBN 62
James L. WAS 78A
Jas. FLG 40A
John BBN 128
John MNR 213
John CHN 29A
John FLG 41A
Parrish MNR 211
Rachel, Mrs. WYN 102A
Richard CHN 36A
Saml. WAS 69A
Sterling HOP 266
William, Sr. MNR 213
SIMON, John M. SCT 93A
SIMONS, Burnett FLG 45A
George LGN 36
Isaiah ALN 142
Jacob TOD 134
John MAD 158
Jonathan MAD 158
Mary LGN 36
Peter TOD 134
Sam ALN 142
Zach TOD 134
SIMPKINS, George FLD 9
Wm. SHE 133A
SIMPSON, Aaron BBN 124
Abbengton WYN 101A
Abraham FTE 82
Abram GTN 132
Agnes SHE 133A
Anderson GRT 144
Andrew MTG 273
Azel WRN 43A
Bend. WAS 57A
Benjamin CBL 8A
Bernard ADR 48
Catharine FTE 110
Christopher WYN 89A
Daniel HAR 178
David LGN 38

SIMPSON, David SHE 133A
Delpha BNE 36
Edmond GRT 146
Edwin SHE 124A
Elijah GRD 84A
Erasmus SHE 164
Fanney CBL 11A
Francis CLK 81
George WRN 44A
George GRD 88A
George SHE 139A
George A. HAR 162
George H. HRT 167
Greenbury GTN 126
Heaton BNE 36
Henry BRN 28
Hugh WRN 34A
Ignatious CBL 14A
J. P. BTH 186
James ADR 48
James JES 83
James CLK 85
James GTN 117
James GTN 126
James HAR 150
James WAS 47A
James PUL 58A
Jane, Mrs. CLK 65
Jas. TOD 127A
Jesse GRD 116A
Jno. HAR 156
John LGN 32
John LNC 77
John GTN 122
John MAD 180
John HND 8A
John CHN 34A
John PUL 63A
John GRD 101A
John M. LGN 43
Johnson FTE 74
Jonathan NSN 175
Joseph CWL 35
Joseph ADR 48
Joshua WRN 41A
Langhorn ETL 42
Levi BBN 64
Lewis GRT 145
Lewis M. GRT 146
Martha WAS 21A
Mary BRN 27
Mary WAS 28A
Nathaniel FTE 66
Oliver JEF 26
Peter JES 72
Polly MER 109
Polly, Mrs. CLK 106
Reubin, Jr. WYN 102A
Reubin, Sr. WYN 101A
Reubin WYN 89A
Richard MAD 134
Richard WAS 72A
Richard B. MAD 126
Robert JES 84
Robert MER 110
Robet SPN 14A
Robt. ADR 50
Rodham CHN 28A
Samuel HRL 118
Samuel GRT 146
Samuel WYN 82A
Sarah LGN 34
Sarah ADR 50
Shelby SHE 155
Solomon SHE 157
Thomas GTN 133
SIMPSON, Thomas GRT 140
Thomas WYN 85A
Thos. CWL 39
Walter GTN 126
Walter NSN 224
William LVG 12
William GTN 122
William BBN 138
William TRG 5A
William WRN 42A
William WRN 42A
Willian I.? LWS 86A
Wilson CBL 8A
Wm. MAD 128
Wm. TOD 129
Wm. MAD 156
Wm. CHN 33A
SIMRALL, James SHE 169
Jos. SHE 142A
Mary SHE 176
SIMS, Allen MAD 108
Aloysus GSN 150A
Anderson WRN 47A
Anthony GSN 150A
Eli BRN 26
Elijah MAD 120
Ignatius R. MAD 162
John HRT 168
Nathaniel MAD 92
Randolph MAD 106
Richard FKN 146
Thos. FKN 84
William HAR 136
William GRD 110A
Wm. MAD 106
SIMSON, James GSN 150A
SINART?, Saml. NCH 117A
SINATT, Joseph P. WAS 18A
SINCLAIR, Amos SCT 110A
Armstead FKN 92
Benjn. SCT 110A
Elias SCT 103A
Jas. SCT 96A
Jas. SCT 135A
John SCT 110A
Morehead SCT 103A
Nancy SCT 101A
Robt. SCT 103A
Sally SCT 103A
SINCLEAR?, Robt. ALN 96
SINDER, John BNE 36
SINETHER, William BNE 34
SINGELTON, Allen GRD 111A
SINGER, Danl. HRY 232
George GTN 130
George HRY 232
John GTN 130
Joseph FTE 107
William GTN 130
Wm. JEF 45
SINGLETON, Abe GRD 111A
Allen HRD 62
Ben HRD 34
Christ LNC 21
Daniel JES 73
Frederick R. LWS 86A
Hannah LWS 90A
James W. LWS 90A
Jeremiah JES 73
John LNC 19
John MER 110
Joshua LWS 91A
Juhonius? WDF 96A
Lewis JES 69
Mary LNC 21
Mason JES 73
SINGLETON, Merrit RCK 76A
Moses JES 75
Nancy LNC 21
Phillip CLY 131
Richard LNC 21
Richard ETL 46
Richd. CLY 129
Robert WYN 83A
Robert H. LNC 21
Sarah LNC 41
Stanley BRK 229
Tho. LNC 41
V. TOD 125A
William LNC 79
William GRD 122A
Wm. HRD 44
Wm. MAD 144
SINKHORN?, William CSY 216
SINKHOUR?, Rachel CSY 216
SINKLEAR, George BBN 66
SINKLEN/SINKLER?, Alxr. ADR 44
SINKLER, George BRK 291
Isaac BRK 291
Joseph BRK 289
Waman BRK 291
William BRK 291
Wm. D. BRK 291
SINKORN?, Ezakel CSY 216
SINLEY?, Emily KNX 306
SINNET, Richard MER 108
SINNET?, John FLG 57A
SINNONIS?, Jno. FKN 114
SINTH?, Diason? WAS 19A
SINWELL?, John BKN 4
Lewis BKN 4
SIPEO, Duvall GSN 151A
SIPES, Henry BRK 293
Henry BRK 293
William BRK 291
SIPLEE, Asahel GTN 123
SIPOLE, Jesse WAS 86A
Jesse WAS 86A
Robert WAS 86A
SIPPLE, John GRT 142
SIRLS, Joseph GSN 150A
SISE?, William CBL 23A
SISELL, James GRD 120A
Richard GRD 121A
SISEMONT?, George ADR 50
SISK, Absolem HOP 262
Andrew, Jr. HOP 262
Andrew, Sr. HOP 262
Asa HOP 264
Barnaba HOP 262
Ebenezer HOP 264
Hezekiah HOP 264
Lourana HOP 262
Meredith HOP 264
Pendleton HOP 264
Plunght WDF 109A
Robert HOP 264
Thomas HOP 262
Timothy, Jr. HOP 264
Timothy, Sr. HOP 264
Willis HOP 264
SITERS?, Henry CLK 94
SITES, David HND 11A
Jacob HND 11A
John BBN 112
SITTER?, Daniel UNN 154
SIVIMAN?, John BTL 331
SIVLY, Jos. CHN 45
SIX, David BTH 176
John BTH 172
Mary BTH 172

SIZEMORE, Burgess TRG 14
Edwd. CLY 124
George CLY 113
Henry CLY 119
James CLY 120
John CLY 113
William CLY 113
SK----N?, Clayton? GTN 133
SKAGGS, Abraham WRN 69A
Charles BRN 27
Daniel WRN 65A
Elizabeth HRT 168
Fredk. CWL 56
Henry BRN 27
James HRT 167
James WRN 65A
John FLD 19
John BRN 26
Lewis FLD 20
Matthew HRT 167
Nancy HRT 167
Peter FLD 19
Richard BRN 27
Richd. HRT 168
Sarah HRT 167
Solomon FLD 19
Solomon FLD 20
Wm. BRN 27
SKAGGS?, -----? FLD 42
SKEAREMEKORN, Joseph WAS 52A
SKEEGS, Jas. HRD 88
Jeremiah HRD 88
Wm. HRD 88
SKEEN, Henry WTY 124A
James WTY 124A
SKEGGS, Elizabeth GRN 73
Margret GRN 79
Moses GRN 59
Richd. GRN 79
William GRN 65
William, Jr. GRN 59
SKELTON, Jeremiah LVG 14
Powell SHE 165
SKETERS, David BNE 36
James BNE 36
Josiah FTE 97
SKETOE, John MBG 136
Polly MBG 136
William MBG 136
William MBG 141
SKEYS, Ann HRD 92
James HRD 92
SKIDMERE, Samuel GNP 169A
SKIDMORE, James FLD 17
James LNC 17
James LNC 19
Jas./ Jos.? HRY 258
Jno. HRY 258
John FLD 45
Joseph LNC 17
Joseph GNP 169A
Mary HRY 258
Sarah LNC 19
SKIELDS?, Francis NSN 221
SKILES, Christian GTN 120
Henry WRN 68A
SKILLEN, Wm. WRN 76A
SKILLMAN, Christopher BBN 64
Isaac BBN 62
John BBN 64
Thomas T. FTE 63
SKILMAN, John BRK 295
Joseph SCT 124A
Richard BRK 291
SKIMBERLIN?, John WAS 35A
SKINER, Daniel TRG 5
Samuel TRG 5
SKINER?, Amy TRG 5
SKINMEN?, Benjamin ETL 42
SKINNER, Allen TRG 5
Benjamin HOP 264
Brice WAS 31A
Clark ETL 50
Coatland ETL 44
Cornelius CLK 93
Cornelius BLT 160
Elijah BLT 156
Ferris FLG 69A
Frederick UNN 151
H. CWL 34
Isaac BLT 166
Isaac W. SCT 121A
James ETL 48
James BBN 124
James UNN 151
Jesse UNN 151
John ETL 42
John MAD 146
John HOP 264
Richard NSN 185
Richard? BLT 154
Richd. WAS 30A
Richd. FLG 61A
Samuel UNN 147
Will SCT 119A
William ETL 48
William UNN 152
SKINNER?, Benjamin ETL 42
SKIPPER, Richard MNR 215
SKIRVIN, Absalom GRT 146
Joel GRT 147
John GRT 147
SKIRVIN?, George HAR 142
SKIRVIS, John, Jr. GRT 147
SKIVIN?, George HAR 142
SKOGGINS, Jonas R. TOD 126
R. TOD 126
SLACK, Elijah GNP 165A
John HRD 84
John WAS 53A
John W. LGN 23
Joseph BLT 156
Randolph HRD 30
Reubin HRD 74
Richd. HRD 14
Wm. HRD 20
Wm. G. WAS 47A
SLADE, Samuel SCT 97A
William HAR 186
SLAGEL, John WYN 94A
Peter WYN 94A
SLAGNER/SLAYNER, Jeremiah BTL 331
SLAPP?, Will GRD 111A
SLATEN?, Ben HRY 216
Rane/ Bane? CLD 158
SLATER, Josep CLD 0
Mary BNE 34
SLATON, Tho. ALN 120
SLATON?, (See Staton?)
Arthur ALN 120
George HRY 216
John ALN 122
Joseph HRY 192
Moses ALN 120
Thomas R. GRN 65
SLATTEN?, James ADR 46
SLATTER, Teri? ADR 44
SLATTIONS?, Aaron TRG 12
SLAUGHTER, Arthur LGN 47
Augustin MER 109
Bartholomew NCH 123A
Ed'd. HRY 263
Edgcomb FKN 158
Elias HRY 228
F. G. NSN 178
Frances R. JEF 45
Francis WDF 119A
Frank FKN 138
G., Col. FKN 66
Gabriel, Col. MER 109
James LGN 43
James NSN 191
James, Jr. NSN 175
James P. NSN 186
Jesse MER 110
Jno. H. RCK 81A
Jno. W. JEF 43
John H. MER 109
Lewis FKN 138
Matthew CSY 210
Philip C. LGN 25
Philip C. NSN 180
Robert MER 109
Robert CHN 27A
Robert F. WRN 76A
Robt. C. HRD 14
Sarah MER 108
Sarah MER 110
Thomas P. LGN 23
Thos. K. BRN 26
William B. MER 110
SLAUHTER, Charles GTN 117
SLAVEN, John GRD 97A
Will GRD 97A
SLAVENS, Isaiah MTG 271
John BTH 186
Reuben MTG 269
SLAVEY, Richard WYN 100A
SLAYDEN, Arthur HOP 262
Daniel HND 9A
Edmond HOP 266
Elizabeth BRN 28
James HOP 264
John FTE 110
John HOP 262
SLAYTON, Arthur FTE 112
Joseph WAS 33A
Washborn HRY 268
SLAYTON?, Wm. BKN 10
SLEDD, Sarah NCH 125A
SLEDGE, Miles C. ALN 100
William WRN 64A
SLEED, Charles JEF 37
SLEET?, Desilly GRD 87A
SLEMMONS, Washington BRN 26
SLEMONS, E. S. HRT 167
SLEWDER, Randolph LNC 27
SLICKEN?, John FTE 60
SLIGAR, David SCT 109A
SLIGER, David BLT 182
Lucas BLT 192
SLINKER, Fredrick GRN 57
Henry GRN 57
Henry GRN 67
John BRN 27
Joseph GRN 57
Lewis BRN 27
William BRN 27
SLINKER?, John GRN 61
SLIPP, Geo BBN.104
John BBN 104
SLITT?, James NCH 116A
SLOAN, Briant NSN 214

SLOAN, David PUL 63A
James HOP 264
James, Sen. WYN 85A
John SHE 168
Joseph HOP 262
Reubin WYN 93A
Thompson PUL 62A
William PUL 67A
William WYN 96A
SLOHATT?, George ALN 110
SLONE, George FLD 25
Hiram FLD 43
Isham FLD 43
Shadrach FLD 44
Shadrack FLD 26
Temperance SHE 124A
Thomas HRL 118
Wm. PUL 47A
SLOOP, James NCH 118A
Margaret NCH 103A
SLOSS, Alexander SPN 13A
Joseph SPN 14A
Thomas SPN 13A
SLOUGHTER, Saml. GNP 166A
SLOVER?, Mingo FTE 60
SLOWN, Benj. PUL 40A
SLUDER, David CSY 204
SLUSHER, Jacob FLD 32
SLUT?, Desilly GRD 87A
SLUTER, Henry FTE 59
SLY, Ben HRD 26
Ben HRD 40
Ebenezer HRD 40
SLYSHER, Phillip HRL 118
SMACK, Godliff LNC 45
James MER 109
SMALL, Catharine WRN 32A
Danl. MAS 69
David MAS 70
George BTH 150
George GRD 106A
Henry BLT 154
Ignatius JEF 49
Jas. MAS 74
Jno. CHN 39
John LGN 30
John BBN 134
John MBG 137
John BTH 174
Richd. JEF 48
SMALLEGE?, Josiah CHN 42A
SMALLEY, Abner CLD 154
Abner CLD 155
Andrew CLD 154
Jacob BBN 66
James BBN 66
John MTG 277
Joshua BBN 66
SMALLWOOD, Been / Ben? BTH 168
Cloe JEF 63
Elinor HRD 74
Heze HRD 20
Hezeciah, Sr. HRD 42
James MTG 247
John FTE 87
John SHE 118A
Saml. HRD 68
Saml., Jr. HRD 24
William BTH 168
Wm. SHE 134A
SMALLY, Andrew BKN 14
SMALWOOD, Randolph ETL 52
SMAR, Robt. SCT 110A
SMARR, Saml. MAS 54
SMART, David MTG 226

SMART, Elisha MTG 233
Glover MTG 233
Henry P. MER 109
Humphrey NCH 108A
James CWL 39
James FKN 126
James P. FKN 120
John MTG 263
John NCH 118A
Steven CWL 56
Thos. FKN 118
William MTG 237
SMART?, Saml. NCH 117A
SMARTE, Edmund BTH 198
SMATHERS, Andrew BTH 198
Joseph BTH 158
SMEDLEY, Aron, Jr. NCH 129A
Aron, Sr. NCH 129A
Christean HND 4
Christopher FTE 109
John FTE 109
John MER 115
Samuel FTE 74
Samuel FTE 110
SMEDLY, Daniel BBN 144
SMELCER, Isaiah HRT 168
Jacob HRT 168
SMELGER?, John BBN 114
SMELLERY, Nathanl. BBN 130
SMELLING?, Lowery BBN 134
SMELLY, Samuel NSN 175
SMELSER, Jacob BBN 130
SMELUR?, Paulur? CWL 56
SMELZER, Adam BBN 134
John BBN 118
SMICK, Godheart MER 108
SMILEY, Alex. CWL 33
Daniel CLD 137
Henry NSN 207
James NSN 178
James SHE 115A
Robert NCH 112A
SMILEY?, Lyn- NSN 221
SMISER?, Jacob JEF 47
Jacob, Jnr. JEF 47
SMITH, ----- CWL 34
-----? DVS 10A
----.? CWL 42
---. S. CWL 35
---.? CWL 37
---ac? CWL 32
Aaron CWL 43
Aaron FTE 95
Aaron MBG 136A
Abben G. MAD 178
Abe GRD 117A
Abigail SHE 126A
Abner CWL 31
Abraham BKN 11
Abraham JEF 44
Abraham BBN 64
Abraham JEF 64
Abraham BTH 176
Abraham SHE 143A
Abraham L. CSY 216
Abram WTY 127A
Absolem LNC 73
Absolem GNP 167A
Adam JEF 33
Adam HOP 264
Adam GSN 151A
Alexander BBN 130
Alexander CLD 144
Alexander Nai? LGN 22
Allen ADR 64
Allen WDF 102

SMITH, Ambrose LGN 38
Amos NSN 193
Andrew TRG 5
Andrew ADR 48
Andrew WYN 99A
Ann WAS 35A
Ann WAS 83A
Anthony MER 114
Any BNE 36
Aquilla LWS 91A
Archer GTN 119
Archibald CBL 19A
Arthur M. HOP 264
Asa SCT 91A
Augustin HOP 264
Augustus GTN 131
Austin GRD 95A
B. D. TOD 127
Barnet WDF 101
Bart. WAS 75A
Bartho. WAS 73A
Basel NSN 189
Ben. CWL 34
Benj. SHE 143A
Benja. JEF 64
Benjamin BRN 26
Benjamin FTE 89
Benjamin FKN 116
Benjamin CLY 128
Benjamin CLD 160
Benjamin MAD 176
Benjamin NSN 209
Benjamin CBL 22A
Benjamin PND 28A
Benjamin WYN 88A
Bennet MAD 92
Berry PUL 47A
Berry? HRT 168
Berryman SCT 120A
Bird FTE 56
Bradford D. SCT 126A
Britton SPN 10A
Catherine JEF 51
Charles JEF 45
Charles ADR 48
Charles CLY 117
Charles HAR 138
Charles MAD 158
Charles GNP 177A
Charles A. HAR 212
Chas, Jr. CHN 43A
Chas. TOD 125
Chas. D. SCT 101A
Christian? WYN 102A
Clemen FTE 73
Cyrus MER 109
Daniel HND 13
Daniel BRN 34
Daniel WRN 44A
Danl. JEF 26
Danl. JEF 55
Danl. BBN 128
Danl. HRT 168
Danl. PUL 36A
Dav., Jr. HRY 257
David BKN 5
David BRN 26
David HRD 42
David GRN 54
David JES 69
David FTE 77
David MAS 78
David TOD 125
David HRY 210
David HRY 257
David CBL 22A

SMITH, David WRN 40A
David WRN 66A
David GSN 150A
David T. LGN 29
Davis L.? WRN 48A
Drewry KNX 298
Drury BRN 27
Drury? CWL 32
Ebeneezar, Jr. CBL 15A
Ebeneezar, Sr. CBL 15A
Edmd. GRD 105A
Edmund GRD 117A
Edward MER 108
Edward UNN 147
Edward SHE 175
Edward BRK 295
Edward WRN 30A
Edwd. B. WAS 73A
Eleanor MER 109
Eleazer LVG 13
Elhanan W. HOP 264
Elias LNC 49
Elias HRL 118
Elias SHE 169
Elias HOP 266
Elias G. MBG 140
Elias P. BBN 112
Elias W. WAS 60A
Elijah FLD 35
Elijah FTE 104
Elijah HAR 134
Elijah MTG 241
Elijah RCK 80A
Elisha LVG 3
Elisha RCK 89
Eliza TOD 127
Elizabeth LGN 24
Elizabeth ALN 106
Elkanah MTG 231
Enoc CLK 71
Enoch BBN 108
Enoch, Jr. MTG 269
Enoch, Sr. MTG 271
Enoch M. FTE 64
Ephraim BRK 293
Ephram GRD 96A
Eunice BLT 166
Ezekiel BRN 28
Fanney ALN 124
Fortune WTY 122A
Frances NSN 179
Francis HRY 222
Francis PND 26A
Frederic CLD 160
Frederick BRN 26
G. W. JEF 20
Gabriel FKN 78
Gabriel GSN 151A
Garland LNC 79
Garland HOP 266
Geo. JEF 66
Geo. FKN 78
Geo. BBN 118
Geo. PUL 42A
George BKN 15
George ADR 46
George GRN 74
George JES 90
George WDF 100
George CLY 130
George CLD 147
George SHE 149
George SHE 169
George KNX 298
George CBL 18A
George WDF 101A
SMITH, George SHE 117A
George SHE 125A
George SHE 126A
Gilbert MAS 65
Godfrey GNP 170A
Godfrey? WRN 44A
Green H. LWS 89A
Greenberry FTE 84
H. MAS 76
Hanah LNC 31
Hannah CBL 3A
Hannah SPN 11A
Hardin FLD 6
Hardy TRG 12A
Henery ADR 44
Henery ADR 64
Henery CBL 18A
Henry LGN 39
Henry MAS 52
Henry CLK 101
Henry MER 109
Henry HRL 118
Henry SHE 172
Henry BTH 180
Henry MTG 297
Henry, Sr. MTG 259
Henry FLG 68A
Henry FLG 76A
Henry WYN 100A
Henry GRD 104A
Henry WDF 114A
Henry G. BNE 50
Hester MAS 66
Hezekiah NCH 107A
Hiram PUL 55A
Hiram WYN 98A
Howel ALN 106
Hubbard B. GRT 139
Hugh BRN 26
Hugh, Jr. MER 110
Hugh, Sr. MER 109
Isaac BKN 9
Isaac BRN 27
Isaac ETL 40
Isaac JEF 44
Isaac JEF 59
Isaac BBN 76
Isaac HRD 84
Isaac ALN 120
Isaac CSY 216
Isaac BRK 295
Isaac CBL 5A
Isaac WRN 36A
Isaac LWS 97A
Isaac SCT 121A
Isaiah GTN 123
Isom? CLY 117
Israel CBL 22A
J. M. LNC 57
J. W. N. TOD 125
J./ I.? R. GRD 87A
Jabel CLY 113
Jacob BRN 26
Jacob JEF 33
Jacob BBN 62
Jacob BBN 76
Jacob CLK 97
Jacob, (Spring Lick) BRN 27
Jacob GTN 121
Jacob BBN 142
Jacob HRY 176
Jacob BTL 331
Jacob WRN 43A
Jacob WRN 43A
Jacob WDF 105A
SMITH, Jacob SCT 108A
Jacob GNP 170A
James LNC 23
James CWL 31
James FLD 31
James LGN 31
James JEF 37
James LGN 38
James ETL 46
James ADR 48
James CWL 56
James JEF 61
James GRN 63
James FKN 90
James FTE 91
James JES 91
James BBN 106
James MER 108
James GTN 123
James HAR 136
James CLD 147
James MAD 150
James CLD 160
James MAD 170
James HAR 202
James NSN 214
James NSN 216
James HAR 218
James MTG 225
James HOP 264
James KNX 306
James, Sr. LGN 33
James (Benjamin's Son) BRN 27
James PND 17A
James PND 28A
James PND 29A
James GRD 102A
James WDF 105A
James NCH 107A
James NCH 126A
James MBG 135A
James C. GRT 139
James D. BRN 28
James D. WDF 104
James H. MER 110
James T. MER 110
James T. KNX 290
James W. MER 109
James W. MAD 112
Jane MER 109
Jane BBN 136
Jane SCT 112A
Jared, Sr. OWN 102
Jarrel G. LWS 86A
Jas HRD 20
Jas MAS 63
Jas. HRD 24
Jas. HRD 80
Jas. HAR 136
Jas., Junr. HRD 62
Jas. FLG 32A
Jas. FLG 57A
Jas. GRD 95A
Jas. SCT 131A
Jas./ Jos.? HRY 265
Jasper FTE 112
Jeremiah FLD 34
Jeremiah CLY 128
Jeremiah KNX 310
Jesse LGN 30
Jesse FTE 74
Jesse CLD 138
Jesse CLD 148
Jesse, Capt. MER 108

Name	County	Page
SMITH, Jesse (F)	WRN	62A
Jesse	GRD	102B
Jesse	WRN	34A
Jesse F.	UNN	146
Jesse W.	UNN	152
Jessee	MAD	142
Jessee	CBL	14A
Jno.	MAS	55
Jno.	MAS	65
Jno.	MAS	67
Jno.	FKN	78
Jno.	HAR	138
Jno.	NSN	177
Jno.	PUL	35A
Jno. P.	ADR	48
Jno. W.	JEF	56
Joab	ALN	92
Joel	GTN	133
Joel, Esq.	CWL	43
Joel	WDF	110A
John	BKN	10
John	HRD	24
John	JEF	25
John	BRN	26
John	JEF	30
John	LGN	31
John	FLD	32
John	JEF	33
John	JEF	45
John	ADR	46
John	ADR	48
John	ADR	48
John	GRN	52
John	HRD	56
John	GRN	59
John	GRN	60
John	JEF	60
John	CLK	64
John	CLK	67
John	CLK	67
John	FTE	68
John	GRN	68
John	BBN	72
John	HRD	72
John	GRN	74
John	BBN	76
John	JES	80
John	JES	82
John	JES	88
John	JES	91
John	ALN	92
John	JES	92
John	MER	108
John	MER	109
John	CLY	112
John	CLY	112
John	CLY	117
John	CLY	129
John	MAD	130
John	MAD	138
John	CLD	141
John	BBN	144
John	HAR	146
John	MAD	148
John	BLT	154
John	CLD	158
John	HAR	158
John	SHE	158
John	CLD	159
John	HRT	167
John	BLT	176
John	NSN	181
John	BTH	194
John	HAR	194
John	HAR	202
John	HRY	208
SMITH, John	HAR	210
John	CSY	212
John	MTG	253
John	HOP	264
John	MTG	269
John, Capt.	MER	109
John, Jr.	OWN	100
John, Jun.	MGB	137A
John, Rev.	MTG	263
John, Senr.	MBG	142A
John, Sr.	OWN	100
John (Hugh's Son)	BRN	27
John (M)	GRN	72
John (Crossed Out)	HRD	72
John (Near Ro. Stockton's)	BRN	26
John	GRD	102B
John	OHO	4A
John	CBL	10A
John	SPN	15A
John	SPN	19A
John	PND	21A
John	FLG	32A
John	WAS	43A
John	WRN	43A
John	WRN	53A
John	FLG	74A
John	SCT	93A
John	LWS	97A
John	WYN	100A
John	WYN	102A
John	WYN	102A
John	SCT	105A
John	NCH	114A
John	SCT	115A
John	SCT	118A
John	WDF	119A
John	WDF	119A
John	TOD	125A
John	MBG	139A
John	GSN	151A
John	GNP	178A
John	GNP	179A
John B.	MBG	140
John B.	SPN	20A
John B.	FLG	71A
John C.	OWN	100
John C.	BLT	178
John C.	WRN	53A
John D.	KNX	282
John G.	ADC	68
John G.	MAD	116
John G.	OHO	5A
John H.	WDF	116A
John J./ I.?	WRN	43A
John J./ I.?	WAS	73A
John M.	CLK	65
John M.	WDF	95
John O.	SHE	151
John R.	GRN	52
John S.	MAD	180
Johnson	GTN	131
Johnson	HND	11A
Jonathan	LGN	33
Jonathan	LGN	34
Jonathan	ETL	46
Jonathan	CLD	153
Jonthan	HRL	118
Jos./ Jas.?	HRY	243
Joseph	HRD	8
Joseph	LGN	33
Joseph	LGN	42
Joseph	GRN	60
Joseph	MER	108
SMITH, Joseph	CLD	147
Joseph	HAR	164
Joseph	CSY	204
Joseph	HRY	230
Joseph	MTG	241
Joseph	MTG	291
Joseph	BTL	331
Joseph	OHO	3A
Joseph	WAS	57A
Joseph	WRN	68A
Joseph	LWS	97A
Joseph	WDF	97A
Joseph	WTY	124A
Joseph	GSN	150A
Joseph S.	WRN	76A
Josiah	CLD	141
Josiah C.	BRN	28
Jurdan	GSN	150A
Landford A.	JES	95
Lane	MTG	241
Larkin	PND	21A
Larkin B.	WAS	79A
Leberty	GRD	102B
Lemuel	HRD	60
Letitia	FTE	103
Lewis	MAD	96
Lewis	FKN	98
Lewis	SCT	103A
Lewis H.	FTE	62
Lydia	HAR	162
Ma---y	ADR	64
Margaret	MAS	74
Margarett	BTH	164
Mariah	MTG	255
Martain	CSY	214
Martin	FLD	11
Martin	ETL	40
Martin	ADR	48
Martin	HAR	210
Martin	SCT	130A
Martin	GNP	169A
Mary	BRN	27
Mary	JEF	27
Mary	JEF	43
Mary	BBN	130
Mary	MAD	172
Mary	NSN	176
Mary	WAS	69A
Mathew	CLD	140
Matthew	FTE	79
Matthew	WAS	73A
Mich.	HRY	270
Michael	BTH	194
Michael	HAR	212
Michael	CBL	22A
Milly	CLD	140
Mitchell	NCH	111A
Morgan	SHE	134A
Moses	ADR	54
Moses	CLD	143
Moses	SPN	10A
Moses	CBL	16A
Moses	SCT	115A
Moses R. D.	FLD	46
Moses Seabolt	JEF	23
Nancy	BBN	72
Nancy	HRT	168
Nancy	HRY	230
Nancy	SPN	10A
Nancy	WAS	39A
Nancy	PUL	62A
Nancy	GRD	105A
Nathan	BNE	36
Nathan	BBN	136
Nathan	HND	7A
Nathan	NCH	127A

SMITH, Nathaniel CLD 150
Nathaniel WTY 123A
Nathl. LNC 79
Ned FKN 90
Nehemiah PND 29A
Nelson SCT 111A
Nich. HRY 269
Nicholas BBN 140
Nicholas SHE 170
Nicolass WAS 41A
Noah ADR 48
Noah HRD 82
Noah SCT 103A
Obadiah HND 4
Obadiah HND 11
Obedience FKN 80
Owin CHN 45
Oziel GRT 146
Patterson CLK 76
Paul HAR 206
Payten WRN 55A
Payton SHE 122A
Peggy BTH 216
Peter MAS 69
Peter JES 84
Peter BBN 120
Peter BLT 182
Peter MTG 241
Peter, Sr. BLT 162
Peter WRN 41A
Peter WRN 43A
Philip LGN 42
Philip NCH 113A
Philip J. JES 74
Phillip JEF 66
Phillip MBG 137
Phillip CLD 144
Phillip SCT 108A
Polley FTE 89
Polley CBL 22A
Polly LGN 31
Polly, Mrs. WYN 100A
Polly GNP 172A
Presley C. WAS 18A
Quillin RCK 82A
R. &? C. JEF 21
Rachael GNP 169A
Randle, Jr. GNP 174A
Randle GNP 174A
Rawley OWN 102
Rebecah LNC 31
Reuben FLD 4
Reuben BNE 36
Reuben MAS 55
Reuben SCT 128A
Reuben SHE 139A
Reuben B. SHE 129A
Reubin HRD 62
Rice FTE 75
Richard MER 109
Richard BBN 118
Richard CLY 121
Richard B. GRT 150
Richard L. CSY 224
Richd. MAS 52
Richd. WAS 40A
Robert HND 9
Robert LNC 31
Robert CLY 126
Robert CLD 138
Robert CLD 151
Robert NSN 192
Robert HAR 194
Robert HRY 196
Robert B. GRT 143
Robert T. MTG 297
SMITH, Robt. FKN 80
Robt. HRY 252
Robt. HRY 265
Robt. HRY 266
Robt. GNP 166A
Rodes SCT 130A
Rosannah JEF 61
Rutha OWN 105
S. B. SHE 129A
Sally BRN 26
Sally LNC 57
Sally GRN 68
Saml. JEF 30
Saml. CWL 56
Saml. MAS 67
Saml. MAS 69
Saml. MAS 70
Saml. WAS 43A
Saml. WAS 70A
Saml. GRD 88A
Saml. SHE 130A
Saml.? CWL 37
Samuel LGN 44
Samuel GRN 61
Samuel GRN 61
Samuel HRD 78
Samuel FTE 89
Samuel FTE 108
Samuel CLD 155
Samuel CLD 158
Samuel BLT 174
Samuel SHE 175
Samuel SHE 175
Samuel MNR 193
Samuel BLT 194
Samuel DVS 19A
Sarah HND 9
Sarah ALN 120
Sarah MBG 138
Sarah HAR 196
Scarlett LNC 75
Silvy GRN 74
Simeon JES 88
Soloman WRN 37A
Solomon MNR 209
Solomon? CWL 32
Spencer? CWL 34
Spephen, Sr. SHE 158
Steph. HRY 256
Stephen, Jr. SHE 159
Sum? ALN 128
Susanna WDF 107A
Susanna MBG 143A
Terner WAS 84A
Tho. HRY 176
Tho. HRY 222
Thomas LGN 29
Thomas BNE 36
Thomas GRN 56
Thomas FTE 57
Thomas GRN 63
Thomas GRN 74
Thomas FTE 76
Thomas JES 92
Thomas CLK 93
Thomas CLD 137
Thomas CLD 142
Thomas CLD 142
Thomas HAR 206
Thomas HAR 218
Thomas BRK 293
Thomas, Sr. CLY 129
Thomas (Fallen Timber) BRN 27
Thomas (Near Spring Lick) BRN 27
SMITH, Thomas OHO 3A
Thomas OHO 4A
Thomas CBL 15A
Thomas PND 23A
Thomas PND 28A
Thomas WRN 53A
Thomas PUL 55A
Thomas WYN 100A
Thomas NCH 126A
Thomas GNP 174A
Thomas P. BBN 142
Thos. CHN 43
Thos. MAS 62
Thos. HRD 68
Thos. FKN 86
Thos. CLY 128
Thos. MAD 170
Thos. HRY 250
Thos. HRY 266
Thos. PND 17A
Thos. FLG 32A
Thos. GSN 151A
Valentine CWL 35
Vardiman ALN 114
Vilet MER 109
Washington HRD 32
Washington ALN 128
Washington WRN 58A
Weather BBN 124
Weedon LNC 37
Will HRY 176
Will T. SCT 92A
Will. KNX 308
Will. SCT 97A
Will. SCT 108A
Will. SCT 126A
William HND 4
William HND 12
William FLD 14
William FLD 26
William BRN 28
William LGN 31
William LGN 34
William LNC 37
William LGN 46
William CLK 62
William GRN 74
William GRN 78
William FTE 79
William FTE 89
William FTE 90
William FTE 112
William CLY 119
William CLY 125
William CLY 131
William CLD 138
William CLD 150
William CLD 152
William CLD 158
William SHE 176
William BLT 186
William HAR 192
William HAR 194
William MTG 225
William MTG 243
William, Esq. RCK 74
William, Jr. CLY 128
William, Sr. WTY 113A
William PND 20A
William SPN 21A
William WRN 29A
William WRN 34A
William WRN 34A
William WRN 40A
William WRN 53A
William PUL 59A

SMITH, William PUL 66A
William PUL 67A
William WYN 88A
William WYN 100A
William WDF 102A
William NCH 106A
William WDF 107A
William NCH 109A
William GRD 121A
William WTY 127A
William MGB 137A
William B. WRN 52A
William C. GRN 60
William L. MBG 143A
William M. FLD 46
William W. MBG 136A
Willington? CWL 32
Willis R. CLK 102
Wm. HRD 32
Wm. LNC 37
Wm. CWL 38
Wm. ADR 48
Wm. JEF 49
Wm. ADR 50
Wm. ADR 50
Wm. JEF 52
Wm. JEF 54
Wm. LNC 69
Wm. RCK 89
Wm. ALN 110
Wm. BBN 114
Wm. TOD 134
Wm. FKN 146
Wm. BRK 293
Wm. PND 19A
Wm. PND 22A
Wm. PUL 47A
Wm. FLG 50A
Wm. RCK 75A
Wm. WAS 82A
Wm. SHE 138A
Wm. SHE 141A
Wm. SHE 143A
Wm. GNP 170A
Wm. GNP 174A
Wm. B. MAS 62
Wm. H. FLG 66A
Wm. J. BRK 291
Woodson HND 9
Zachariah MER 109
Zadock BBN 112
SMITH?, Diason? WAS 19A
Elijah RCK 76A
SMITHA, Fielding SHE 154
SMITHE, William CBL 3A
SMITHER, James OWN 104
Leonard OWN 104
Noel OWN 105
Richard WDF 101A
Robert OWN 104
Samuel WDF 114A
Thomas SHE 119A
William OWN 104
William WDF 95A
William WDF 116A
SMITHERS, James DVS 16A
John A. SCT 91A
Polly DVS 16A
Thos. PUL 49A
Thos. T. ADC 66
SMITHEY, John WDF 112A
Robert MER 110
Thomas MER 110
SMITHMERMAN?, W. B. MAS 81
SMITHON, John M. BBN 138
SMITHY, Reubin JEF 62
William WDF 100
SMITSON?, Henry BKN 4
SMOCK, Abraham MER 108
Catherine BLT 186
Henry JEF 45
Henry MER 108
Henry MER 109
Isaac MER 110
Jacob MER 109
Jacob SHE 154
James BLT 186
John MER 109
John SHE 154
John SHE 164
John WAS 55A
John B. MER 108
Mathew SHE 158
Peter WAS 75A
Simon SHE 158
Wm. WAS 55A
SMOOT, Alexr. JEF 32
Alexr., Jnr. JEF 32
Barton FLG 52A
Clabourn FLG 64A
Coleman BTH 196
Geo. FLG 52A
Saml. MAS 70
Stephen FLG 57A
William R. OWN 105
SMOTE, John HRT 167
SMOTHERS, Hugh FLD 7
John FLD 7
SMOTHSON, Tho. LNC 55
SMUTHERS, Daniel WAS 32A
James WAS 30A
SMYES?, Zachariah CSY 208
SMYSER, Henry SHE 156
Michael SHE 156
SMYTHE, John CBL 9A
Samuel CBL 9A
William CBL 15A
SNADERS, J. H., Dr. BBN 128
SNAP, Daniel NCH 110A
George, Jr. NCH 111A
George NCH 110A
Matthew MAD 106
Saml. NCH 110A
SNAP?, -----? NCH 126A
SNAPE, James GTN 120
SNAPP, Laurence GRN 54
Lewis BLT 172
SNAWSNELL, Wm. JEF 41
SNEAD, Elijah CWL 58
Wm. WAS 27A
SNEAN?, Hamon NSN 207
SNEDAGAR, Mary FLG 60A
SNEDIGER, James GNP 174A
SNEED, Aechilles FKN 62
Alexr. GRD 87A
Billy BRN 26
Charles PUL 63A
Charles? WTY 127A
Harrison LNC 7
James JEF 39
John HRD 64
John PUL 56A
John GRD 108A
Landon FKN 116
Mary SPN 15A
Polley GTN 120
Susannah MER 109
Wm. FKN 154
SNELING, Alexander WDF 92
Jesse WDF 92
SNELING, John WDF 92
SNELL, Betsey SCT 101A
Calvine BRK 295
Cumberland SCT 136A
James PND 15A
Jesse OWN 100
John OWN 103
John SCT 129A
Joseph HAR 212
Loudon SCT 136A
Mary HAR 156
Robert M. GRT 142
Robt. FKN 108
Will SCT 109A
Willis SCT 135A
Wm. JEF 57
SNELLAN, Enoch HRD 54
SNELLEN, Benjn. SCT 105A
SNELLIN?, William BTH 158
SNELLING, -----? CWL 36
---nt? CWL 36
Alexander BRK 295
Benjamin BTH 160
Benjamin, Snr. BTH 162
John BRK 295
SNELLINGBARGER, John BLT 162
SNELSON, Bartlett OWN 103
John T. OWN 103
SNIDER, Abram FLG 32A
Adam SHE 113A
Adam SHE 114A
Backslet BRK 291
Christopher SHE 114A
Frederic WTY 119A
Gabriel SHE 113A
Geo. BBN 144
George SHE 142A
Henry JEF 61
Henry TOD 127A
Jacob NSN 207
James LWS 89A
Jeremiah UNN 147
John JEF 64
John, Jr. BRK 295
John, Sr. BRK 295
John DVS 19A
John WAS 48A
John WDF 107A
John SHE 113A
John GSN 149A
Jonas SHE 138A
Joseph JEF 42
Joseph MER 109
Michael BNE 36
Mildred JEF 64
Peter FLD 44
Peter ALN 104
Peter CLK 106
Phillip DVS 19A
William ALN 102
SNIDER?, Hamon NSN 207
SNIFFER, David KNX 288
SNITH, Nehemiah PND 29A
SNIVEL, Samuel SPN 9A
SNODDEN, Geo. TOD 125A
SNODDY, Daniel BRN 27
Saml. MAD 126
Sophia BRN 26
SNODEN, Charles ETL 42
David ETL 45
David, Sr. ETL 42
James ETL 53
Wm. WAS 31A
Wm. TOD 131A
SNODGRASS, Benjamin HAR 192

SNODGRASS, David HAR 192
  David BTL 331
  Isaac RCK 83A
  James BRN 27
  Jas. PUL 47A
  Jno. HAR 144
  John JES 75
  John HAR 192
  John CBL 5A
  Joseph BBN 68
  Robert HAR 132
  Robert HAR 144
  Robert HAR 192
  Samuel BBN 130
  Thomas HAR 142
  William HAR 144
  William HAR 182
SNODLY?, Jacob RCK 79A
SNODY, Furgus BBN 76
  John BBN 76
SNOOK, Martin SHE 174
SNORGRASS?, Robert CSY 222
SNOW, Aquilla LVG 7
  Frostin LNC 25
  Isaac PND 31A
  Jean LNC 7
  Jonathan CBL 13A
  Martin LNC 33
  Nichodemus WRN 64A
  Robert BNE 34
  Samuel WYN 104A
  Susanna MNR 209
  William CLD 155
  Wm. PND 30A
SNOWDE-?, Thomas BLT 168
SNOWDEN, Francis JEF 50
  John JEF 39
SNOWDEN?, Joseph BLT 152
SNULGER?, John BBN 114
SOAPER, Chas. BBN 72
  James MER 108
  William HND 4
SOCK?, Peter HRY 240
SODUSKY?, Jacob WAS 34A
SOESBY, Thomas BTH 176
  Thomas, Jr. BTH 176
SOFIELD, Israel CBL 14A
SOLKENS?, Clem? HRL 118
SOLKIM?, Clem? HRL 118
SOLLOW?, James SHE 170
SOLMON?, Jacob BNE 36
  John SHE 138A
SOLOMAN, El. FTE 60
SOLOMON, Aaron MBG 143A
  Abraham KNX 302
  Elijah LGN 44
  Josiah UNN 146
  Will. KNX 302
  William SPN 3A
SOLOMON?, Lewis MBG 142
SOLSBURY, Allen GRD 91A
  Nat GRD 92A
SOMERSALL, John MTG 299
SOMES?, William LVG 18
SONE, Wm. GSN 149A
SOOK?, Peter HRY 240
SOOL?, Thomas BRK 291
SOOT?, Thomas BRK 291
SOPER, Benjamin JES 80
  Chas. GRD 99A
  James JES 80
SOPRICE?, Christ ALN 124
SORREL?, Richard NSN 189
SORRELL, Elisha BTH 178
  Elisha BTH 210
  Joseph BTH 210
SORRELS, David BTL 331
  James BTH 204
  John BTL 331
  Joseph BTH 204
  Thomas WRN 51A
  William WRN 33A
SORTER, Jacob, Jr. MER 110
  Jacob, Sr. MER 109
  Lambert MER 109
SORTER?, John MER 108
SOTHARD, Isaac GRD 118A
SOTT, Wm. BBN 144
SOUDER, Peter RCK 75A
SOUDER?, D. RCK 77A
  Mich. RCK 78A
SOUDERS, Henry BTL 331
SOURLEY?, Geo. D. FLG 69A
SOUSLEY, Jacob FLG 72A
  Phillip FLG 72A
SOUSLEY?, George BLT 182
  Jacob BLT 182
SOUTH, Benjamin MAD 146
  Elizabeth FTE 88
  Reamon FLG 65A
  Sam, Gen. FKN 64
  Thos. BBN 80
  Weldon BBN 80
  Wm. HRD 58
  Wm. MAD 146
  Wm., Senr. HRD 58
SOUTHARD, James PND 19A
  John PND 30A
  Micah MTG 253
SOUTHARD?, Lewis GTN 135
SOUTHER, Abraham BNE 36
  Henry JEF 60
  Jacob JEF 56
  Jacob CBL 11A
  Joseph BRN 34
SOUTHERLAND,
  -----? CWL 36
  Daniel LGN 47
  Daniel KNX 308
  George KNX 296
  Jalan FKN 142
  Jas. SCT 128A
  Jno. FKN 142
  John LGN 31
  Jos., Jr. RCK 80A
  Joseph RCK 80A
  Levi RCK 79A
  Philip KNX 300
  William LGN 31
  William WYN 79A
SOUTHERLANE,
  Jessee BKN 23
SOUTHERLIN, Hosea MER 110
  Mordeca HND 12
  Samuel CSY 216
SOUTHERLIN?,
  William CSY 216
SOUTHERLING, James MER 108
SOUTHERN, Stephen MER 109
  William MER 109
SOUTHGATE, Richd. CBL 2A
SOUTHLAND?, John?,
  Sr. PND 23A
SOUTHWOOD, John WYN 81A
SOUTHWORTH, Robert OWN 101
  William OWN 102
SOWARD?, Elisha MAS 69
SOWARDS, Leticia FLD 28
SOWDER, John GSN 149A
SP---?, John SCT 134A
SP---S?, Henry HRY 184
SPAIN, Hiram GRN 77
SPAIN, James GRN 77
  James MNR 211
  James D. GRN 56
  John D. GRN 55
  Peter D. GRN 58
  Soloman GRN 79
  William GRN 77
SPAINHOWARD, John CSY 228
  John CSY 228
  Thomas CSY 228
SPAINHOWARD?,
  Warrin CSY 224
SPAINHOWDS?,
  Hennery CSY 224
SPALDING, Aaron CBL 20A
  Aron WAS 36A
  Bend. WAS 36A
  Bend.? WAS 37A
  Charles WRN 43A
  D. MAS 76
  Igs.? WAS 74A
  James WAS 37A
  Joseph WAS 55A
  Lewis WAS 36A
  Nancy WAS 74A
  Peter NSN 185
  Richd. WAS 36A
  Thos. WAS 39A
  William UNN 146
  Wilson FKN 134
  Wm. HRY 261
SPALDING?, James NSN 211
SPAN, Thos. LVG 4
SPANARY?, Joseph NSN 177
SPANES?, Walter HRY 218
SPANGLER, Daniel BNE 50
  Federick BNE 50
  John GTN 119
SPANN, Sol. GRD 93A
  Tho. ALN 94
SPARKES, Daniel SHE 136A
  James MAD 120
  Richard SHE 136A
  Wm. FLG 72A
SPARKMAN, Henry LVG 18
  Wm. CWL 38
SPARKS, Absalom HRL 120
  Anderson LNC 61
  Anthony OWN 104
  Benjamin BLT 178
  Caleb NCH 121A
  Catharine NCH 121A
  Catharine NCH 125A
  Caty ETL 51
  Davd. PUL 41A
  Elenor FTE 67
  Eli TRG 4
  Elihu ADR 44
  Ephram JEF 48
  Ezra JEF 43
  George ETL 51
  George MER 108
  George NCH 117A
  Hampton JEF 53
  Henry, Sr. OWN 104
  Humphrey OWN 104
  Isaac ETL 45
  Isaac GNP 173A
  James BNE 34
  James CBL 8A
  Jas. SCT 133A
  John ADR 48
  John GNP 173A
  Jos. HRY 251
  Joseph LWS 94A
  Madison OWN 104

Name	County	Page
SPARKS, Martin	OWN	104
Robt.	HRY	261
Ruth	ETL	51
Samuel K.	BLT	186
Thomas	BNE	36
Thomas	CHN	34A
Thos.	HND	6
Thos.	HRD	26
Valentine	SHE	131A
William	FTE	85
William	HAR	144
William, Jr.	ETL	51
William, Sr.	ETL	51
Wm.	ADR	48
Wm.	JEF	48
Wm.	BBN	142
Wm.	HRY	251
SPARKY, Walter?	JEF	43
SPARROW, Dennis	MER	108
Elias	LGN	27
Henry	MER	108
James	MER	108
Peter	CSY	218
SPARTS, Catherine	BBN	140
SPASHMAN, William R.	TRG	7A
SPATES, Robert	FTE	95
Saml.	BBN	118
SPATES?, Thomas	BBN	134
SPAULDEN, Francis	FLD	21
John	FLD	24
SPAULDIN, George	MER	109
SPAULDING, James	WDF	99A
Jonathan	WDF	100A
Kirtlett	SHE	151
Polly	HRD	62
Robison	WDF	99A
Watker	WDF	101A
William	WDF	100A
SPAULDING?, James	LVG	12
Stephen	WAS	54A
SPAW?, Jacob	CSY	206
SPEACE, Frederick	BKN	11
George	BKN	11
SPEAGH, Philip	BNE	34
SPEAGLE, John	HAR	196
Martin	HAR	194
Samuel	HAR	196
Samuel, Jnr.	HAR	192
SPEAK, John	ADR	48
Jos.	MAD	114
SPEAK?, Bazzel	WAS	28A
SPEAKE?, Joseph	FTE	89
SPEAKMAN, Fanny	MNR	197
William	MNR	197
SPEAKS, Hezekiah	BBN	142
James	NSN	222
John	JEF	25
John	NSN	187
Thomas	NSN	222
SPEAR, Abm.	BBN	134
John	GRN	56
John D.	GRN	63
Saml.	GRN	65
Solloman	GRN	54
Thomas	GRN	71
SPEARMAN, John	CLD	163
Susanna	CLD	163
SPEARS, Abigal	LNC	33
Abraham	CLD	159
Andrew	SHE	156
Benjamin	CLD	159
David	LNC	33
David	WAS	77A
Dorman	MNR	211
Geo.	JEF	42
SPEARS, George	GRN	54
Isaac	CLD	159
Jacob	GRN	55
Jacob	BBN	142
Jacob	HRY	218
James	GRN	55
James	MER	108
Jno.	JEF	55
John	GRN	54
John	FTE	102
Joseph	CLD	159
Levi	MNR	211
Mary	HAR	158
Noah	HAR	136
Robert	FKN	136
Solomon	BBN	132
Will	HRY	180
William	CLD	159
William	PUL	55A
Wm.	ALN	116
SPEARS?, Ephraim	ALN	116
SPECK, Danl.	BBN	134
SPECK?, Jacob	CLD	153
SPEED, Henry	MER	109
John	JEF	40
John	MER	108
John, Jnr.	JEF	32
Lewis	JEF	32
Mathew, Jr.	CSY	216
Mathias	CSY	216
Robert	HND	4
Thos.	NSN	198
SPEEK?, Jacob	CLD	153
SPEER, John	CLD	158
SPEERS, Robert	FLD	33
Thomas	FLD	33
SPEICE?, Frederick	BKN	20
SPELIC?, Joseph	GSN	151A
SPELING, William	GRN	71
SPELL, Lucy	LVG	4
SPELMAN, Mary	GTN	126
Robert	GRN	53
SPELMON, Benj.	GRN	50
SPELU?, Joseph	GSN	151A
SPENCE, Henry	FKN	64
James	SHE	153
John	LVG	18
John	OHO	8A
Joseph	LWS	97A
William	GRN	55
William	BTH	210
SPENCE?, John	SCT	134A
SPENCER, -----?	DVS	4A
Abraham	MAD	150
Absolem	ALN	102
Amasa	PUL	67A
Andrew	SCT	133A
Barksdale	LGN	40
Benj.	FLG	75A
Bernard	GRT	142
Chas.	FLG	41A
David	JES	78
Edward	BNE	36
Edward	GRT	142
Eli	BNE	36
Elijah	CLY	119
Flor.	RCK	82A
Francis	BNE	36
Francis	OWN	105
Henry	FLG	42A
Isaac	MAS	59
Isaac	FLG	40A
James	PUL	59A
James?	BLT	192
Jas.	FLG	42A
Jno.	ALN	130
SPENCER, John	LVG	17
John	ADR	46
John	BBN	78
John	BTH	164
John	BTH	204
John	WYN	93A
John	SHE	122A
Joseph	BNE	36
Joseph	HRD	64
Joseph	MAD	114
Joseph	GRT	141
Margaret	SHE	122A
Moses	JES	72
Richard	HND	10
Sally	OWN	103
Samuel	BRN	26
Samuel	GTN	126
Samuel	PUL	59A
Sharp	HRD	48
Tho.	RCK	81A
Thomas	CLD	158
Thomas	NSN	221
Will	SCT	121A
Willa	BLT	192
William	CLK	94
William	BLT	192
Wm.	ADR	50
Wm.	ALN	110
Wm.	SHE	126A
SPENCER?, Thomas	FLD	46
SPENSER, John	BRK	293
SPENSOR, Saml.	GSN	150A
Samuel	BRK	291
SPERLING, George	GRN	63
William	GRN	69
SPERRY, Samuel	GNP	166A
SPHAR, Daniel	CLK	85
James	CLK	71
SPHARE, Henry	NCH	117A
SPHARE?, Jacob	NCH	106A
SPICER, ---ser?	BBN	94
Cain	OWN	100
John	CLY	113
John	SCT	124A
Wm.	BBN	94
SPICKARD, John	BBN	104
SPICKLEMIRE, Abraham	WYN	93A
SPIDEL, Jacob	HND	4
John	HND	4
SPIER, Elizabeth	OWN	99
SPIERS, John	LNC	33
John	LNC	43
Joshua	OWN	104
William	LNC	43
SPIKEMAN, William	CLY	122
SPILLARD, Andw.	CWL	46
SPILLER, Carven	MTG	249
Philip	MTG	249
SPILLMAN, James	ALN	134
James	ALN	134
Jno.	ALN	134
Mary	ALN	134
Robt.	ALN	136
SPILMAN, Benja.	LVG	3
Benjamin	CBL	19A
Charity	MAD	140
Charles	HRY	198
Charles	GRD	108A
Chas., Jr.?	GRD	107A
Frances	CBL	18A
George	HRY	178
Henery	CBL	18A
Jacob	HRY	178
James	CLK	106
James	GTN	128

Name	County	Page
SPILMAN, Sarah	CBL	20A
Tho.	GRD	108A
Thomas	GTN	126
Thomas	CBL	18A
Zachariah	GTN	126
SPINCER, John	FLG	70A
SPINGATE, John	MER	110
SPINKS, Francis	WAS	75A
Ignatius	HRD	14
Ralph	WAS	74A
Thomas	WRN	39A
SPINNET, David	MER	110
John	MER	110
SPINX?, John	CWL	38
SPIRES, Catharine	FTE	102
Greenberry	FTE	97
Jeremiah	FTE	102
Noah	FTE	81
Samuel	FTE	81
Susannah	JES	83
SPIRGIN, David	BBN	84
Sarah	BBN	84
SPITLER, Adam	HRD	84
SPIVY, Zadoc	CLY	117
SPLASTER, William, Sr.	SHE	175
SPOICE?, Christian	BKN	2
SPONHIMER, Adam	LNC	51
SPONHIMORE, Jacob	LNC	67
SPOON, Barbary	SCT	113A
Coonrod	SCT	111A
George	CLD	140
Jacob	SCT	111A
John	SCT	111A
SPOONER, Thos.	MAS	59
SPOONHIMER, Elender	LNC	47
SPOTSWOOD, Alxr. W.	BBN	108
SPOTTESWOOD, Alexr. E.	BRN	27
SPOTTLE?, Danl.	BKN	11
SPOWL, Maryann	HRY	252
SPRADLIN, James	FLD	35
John	FLD	35
Joseph	FLD	35
Micajah	FLD	43
Robert	FLD	35
SPRADLING, James	WRN	52A
James	WYN	96A
Jessee	WYN	96A
Polly	FKN	102
SPRAGAINS, James	CSY	214
SPRAGINS?, Isaac	JEF	66
SPRAGUE, Jesse	UNN	153
John	UNN	148
Jonathan	UNN	153
SPRAIG, Danl.	HRD	40
SPRAKE, Thomas O.	FTE	113
SPRAKE?, Joseph	FTE	89
SPRATT, Andrew	MTG	226
James	MNR	215
John	GRD	100A
Robert	MTG	297
Thomas	GRD	113A
William	LNC	2
William	MTG	235
SPRAWL, Letitia	FTE	111
SPRAY, ----1?	DVS	8A
SPRDLIN, Benjamin	FLD	36
SPREAKE, John O.	FTE	67
SPRIG, Daniel	BRK	293
SPRIGGS, Able D.	FKN	58
John	HRD	28
Robert	FLD	34
Thos.	HRD	46
SPRIGGS?, Levin	HRD	10
SPRINER, Ezekiel	MNR	211
SPRINGATE, William	MER	110
SPRINGER, Abner	JES	88
David	MER	116
Edwd.	SCT	105A
Ezekiel	TRG	3
Ezekiel	MNR	217
Francis	FTE	106
Gabl.	SCT	105A
George	JES	81
Jacob	JES	79
John	JES	79
John	MNR	215
John	WAS	30A
Jonathan	MNR	193
Richard	BNE	36
Will.	SCT	105A
SPRINGLE, Elizabeth	FTE	64
SPRINKLE, Jacob	HND	4
Michael	HRD	10
SPROUCE, Geo.	TOD	127A
SPROUL, Jane	CLD	153
Joseph	CLD	152
William	WYN	100A
SPROUSE, James	GTN	127
SPROUT, William	LGN	40
William	LGN	47
SPROUT?, John	LGN	39
SPROWL, Alexr.	GRN	80
Joseph	LNC	47
Oliver	MAD	136
SPROWLS, John	WAS	26A
SPROWT, John	GRN	63
SPRY, -----?	DVS	9A
SPUNIER?, Jas.	HRD	30
SPURER, Will M.	JEF	22
SPURGEN, David	BBN	112
Jeremiah	LWS	89A
Samuel	LWS	88A
SPURGEON, Amos	LWS	94A
James	HRY	208
John	LWS	97A
Moses	LWS	97A
William	HRY	208
SPURGIN, Asaac	CBL	19A
Eli	ADR	48
Samuel	MTG	297
SPURLING, Hanson	CLK	92
SPURLOCK, Daniel	BRN	28
David	FLD	17
Frances	FLD	47
Hiram	FLD	17
Jesse	CLY	132
John	HRL	118
Matthew	FLD	31
Will	HRL	118
SPURR, Daniel	FTE	105
James	FTE	84
William	FTE	81
SPURRIER, Hosy	GSN	151A
Jarret	MAS	65
Jas.	MAS	61
Wm.	GSN	150A
SPURRIER?, Jas.	HRD	30
SPURRIOR, Geo.	MAS	62
SPUTSMAN, Jacob	MER	109
SQUIRES, Caleb	OWN	105
George	ADR	44
John	BRK	293
Levi	ADR	48
Margaret	NCH	124A
Thomas	BRK	291
Thos.	ADR	3
Uriah	ADR	50
SQUIRS, John	ETL	46
John	ADR	48
SQURIS?, Urriah	ADR	46
SRO-E?, Adam	MAS	68
SROUT?, Abrm.	BBN	68
Isaac	BTH	166
Rebecca	BTH	210
ST---?, John	LVG	18
ST. AUBAINE?, George	LVG	10
ST. CLAIR, Jehu	MTG	277
Waugh	BBN	140
ST. JOHN, Saml	CLY	113
STA--EUM?, George	LWS	98A
STACEY, Simon	FLD	13
STACK, Jacob	MAS	52
Randolph, Senr.	HRD	54
Richard	HRD	54
STACKS, Amos	WDF	120A
STACY, Benj.	CLY	125
George	CLY	121
Jessey	WYN	91A
John	GRN	78
Peter	PUL	53A
Simon	PUL	53A
William	FLD	13
William	WYN	90A
STADE, William	MNR	193
STADER, Adam	HRD	46
Jacob	HRD	46
John, Sr.	HRD	36
Peter	HRD	46
Wm.	HRD	24
STADLER, Jacob	BBN	90
John	BBN	66
STADLEY, Wm.	BBN	72
STAFFORD, James	FLD	36
James	JES	80
James	JES	80
James	CLD	149
Jas.	SCT	123A
John	FLD	24
John	LNC	55
Martin	GTN	117
Stuard?	CWL	44
Thos.	JEF	43
William	GTN	126
William	HAR	136
STAGG, Daniel	MER	108
James, Jr.	MER	110
James, Sr.	MER	109
Wm.	BKN	16
STAGGS, Jas.	FLG	50A
Joseph	LWS	99A
STAGNER/STAYNER, Jeremiah	BTL	331
STAGNER, Andrew	WRN	30A
Barney	MAD	136
George	SPN	18A
Jessey	MAD	94
John	MAD	94
John	MAD	174
John	SPN	21A
John	WRN	33A
Thos.	MAD	162
STAHL, David	WRN	61A
Magdalin	WRN	62A
STALCUP, Isaac	CLD	138
Martha	FLG	40A
Moses	CLD	140
STALEY, Adam	CBL	22A
Christian	LWS	90A
Jacob	LWS	90A
Samuel	LWS	90A
STALKER, Wm.	MAD	106
STALKUP, Elias	LWS	88A

STALKUP, John LWS 88A
Matthias LWS 88A
Rebecca LWS 99A
STALLARD, David NSN 221
James NSN 217
James NSN 221
Walter NSN 221
STALLING, --orer?/ ----oses? CWL 32
STALLINGS, Hez. WAS 67A
Walter N. WAS 67A
Will W. WAS 67A
Wm. WAS 68A
STALLIONS, Elisha LVG 3
Henry BLT 162
John BLT 164
Samuel BLT 164
Samuel BLT 168
Simon LVG 3
Thomas BLT 180
STALLSWORTH, Jesse BRN 28
STALON?, John WAS 25A
STALVER?, John Pleak? MTG 229
STAM--?, Charles ALN 94
Mildred ALN 94
STAMBACK, Robt. TOD 124A
STAMBAUGH, John FLD 44
Philip, Jr. FLD 43
Philip, Sr. FLD 43
STAMBURY, Saml. KNX 310
Sol. KNX 310
STAMES?, Conrad PUL 43A
STAMFIELD, Thos. WAS 59A
STAMPER, Jacob OWN 103
James CLY 122
James, Sr. CLY 121
Jesse OWN 103
Joel CLY 118
John BTH 182
Jonathan FLD 12
Jonathan OWN 103
Joshua CLK 99
Richd. CLY 120
Sarah WDF 118A
William CLY 122
STAMPS/STAMPR?, Charles ALN 94
Mildred ALN 94
STAMPS, Larah? ALN 112
Wm. BBN 142
STAMS?, John RCK 82A
STAN?, Jacob MER 109
STANARD, Henry SPN 9A
STANART, Daniel SPN 5A
STANDARD, ----s.? CWL 43
Bazil CWL 37
Jas. CWL 33
Wm. CWL 56
STANDEFORD, David SHE 142A
John SHE 176
STANDELIFT?, Joseph BTH 212
STANDERFORD, Geo. FLG 38A
Mary BBN 144
STANDFORD, Lucus SPN 4A
Lyman HRD 20
STANDIFORD, David SHE 163
Elisha JEF 38
Ephram HRD 90
Francis SHE 165
Izarel HRD 90
James JEF 37
James JEF 42
James SHE 163
James NCH 118A
STANDIFORD, John W. HRD 22
William JEF 37
STANDLEY, James LVG 14
STANFIELD, John WTY 110A
Sampson WTY 114A
Shered (Crossed Out) WTY 118A
Shered WTY 113A
STANFORD, James WDF 119A
STANHOPE, Robert FTE 83
STANIBAUGH, Jacob TRG 14
STANLEY, Andrew WTY 126A
Eligah CBL 16A
James HOP 264
John SHE 168
John MBG 142A
Julius LGN 30
Moses BBN 70
Moses HOP 266
Sarah CBL 19A
Spencer HOP 264
William FLD 40
William HOP 262
Wm. HRY 263
STANLEY?, Sally LGN 34
STANLY, Anderson WRN 34A
Elijah TRG 6A
Nathan MAD 170
Solomon SPN 14A
STANNFER?, Gabriel FKN 106
STANSBERRY, Benjamin BLT 188
Nathan WYN 95A
STANSBERY, Benjamin BLT 170
STANSBURRY, Nancy BTH 210
STANSILL, Nicolass WAS 77A
STANTON, Andrew JES 73
Jeremiah GNP 171A
Thomas CSY 206
Thomas PUL 61A
William CSY 206
William GRD 99A
STANUP, William FTE 109
STANZ?, Hooper BLT 172
STAP, John HND 7A
STAPLENS, William JES 75
STAPLES, Joshua JES 72
Saml. SHE 128A
STAPLETON, David JES 72
Edward CLY 113
Joseph WYN 96A
Joshua FLD 36
Thomas CLY 113
STAPP, Akillis SCT 138A
Elijah ADR 46
Elijah SCT 92A
Jno. FKN 64
John MAD 170
Joseph ADR 48
Wm. ADR 48
STAPP?, Will GRD 111A
STAR?, Jacob MER 109
STARES, Mary SHE 123A
STARK, Abner HRY 188
Daniel ALN 128
Danile BLT 158
James ALN 126
Jerrimiah ALN 126
Jessee ALN 126
John BBN 114
John NCH 113A
Joseph BBN 64
Phillip HRY 192
Raleigh ALN 126
STARK, Sarah BBN 64
Tho. ALN 126
Thomas NCH 113A
Thos. BBN 64
STARK?, Caleb HRY 210
Reuben HRY 210
STARKE, Aaron SHE 134A
Elijah SHE 134A
Haden SHE 132A
James MER 114
James SHE 130A
Jas. HRD 66
Nancy MER 115
Reuben TOD 129A
STARKEY, Jessee CBL 5A
Josua CBL 5A
STARKS, Berry SPN 8A
George LGN 35
Jesse TOD 129
John FTE 85
John CHN 28A
Wm. MAD 160
STARKY, Nathan FLG 32A
Stacy FLG 32A
Wm. B. FLG 31A
STARKY?, Rachall BBN 110
STARLING, George GRN 63
STARN, Frederic MER 110
STARNES, Thomas CSY 212
STARNES?, Conrad PUL 43A
STARNS, Isaack MAD 146
STARR, Abraham CLK 100
Adam CLK 100
Jacob BBN 62
John CLD 154
START, Joseph CLD 145
STATEN, Elizabeth ADR 60
Hanner WAS 69A
James BTH 208
John BTL 329
Obed. WAS 69A
Solomon BTH 210
Thomas BTH 210
STATEN?, Rane/ Bane? CLD 158
STATIN, Benjamin BTH 210
STATIONS, Reuben HOP 264
STATON, John ADR 50
John BTL 331
Peter WAS 34A
Reuben ADR 50
William GRN 64
Wm. ADR 50
STATON?, George GRN 70
John WAS 25A
Joseph HRY 192
Thomas R. GRN 65
Thomas R. GRN 70
STATTIONS, Aaron TRG 12
STAYLOR, James SHE 167
STAYTON, Chas. CWL 56
John CWL 56
William SHE 167
Wm. CWL 56
Wm. HRY 247
Wm. WAS 17A
STAYTON?, (See Slayton) HRY 268
STEADAM, Mary MAS 77
STEADWIN?, Silis ALN 122
STEAL, Volentine WAS 83A
Wm. G. WAS 78A
STEAN, Nathan HOP 266
STEAN?, William H. WRN 74A
STEAPLES, Sarah H. BRK 293
STEARMAN, ----as? DVS 14A

STEARNS, Alex MAS 81
STEARS, John NCH 117A
Mathew BNE 36
William HAR 132
William HAR 140
STEARS?, William BNE 34
STEDMAN, Ebenezer SCT 95A
STEEDMAN?, Thomas FTE 69
STEEL, Andrew GSN 151A
Basel NSN 208
Basil NSN 204
Bruce FTE 100
Cahterine BBN 124
Campbell JES 91
Elizabeth BNE 36
Elzabeth NSN 208
Henry WDF 95
Jacob BTH 186
Jacob WYN 98A
James CWL 33
James FLD 43
James BLT 188
James BRK 291
John ADR 50
John FTE 105
John MER 108
Joseph BBN 118
Joseph HND 8A
Katharine MER 109
Lucretia LNC 13
Rachel MAD 102
Reuben MER 108
Robt. ADR 46
Robt. PND 30A
Samuel BRN 27
Samuel FTE 108
Samuel WTY 125A
Samuel D. MER 117
Stephen P. HRD 60
Susan CHN 27A
Thomas BTH 154
Thomas NSN 221
Will ADR 46
William FLD 31
William GRN 75
William WTY 126A
Wm. BBN 128
STEEL?, David WDF 101
Robert FKN 102
Wm. FKN 110
STEELE, Adam SHE 143A
Andrew JEF 50
Andrew GRN 54
Archibald CHN 41A
Henry MTG 255
Isaac LGN 36
Jesse MTG 231
John LVG 14
John SHE 159
John BTH 198
John, Capt. WDF 114A
John PND 30A
John FLG 70A
John SHE 137A
Nicholas FLG 44A
Ranken SHE 114A
Richd. JEF 21
Saml. JEF 65
Saml. BBN 86
Saml. SHE 137A
Samuel SHE 118A
Soloman FLG 70A
Solomon BTH 198
Susanah FLG 44A
Thomas JES 94
Thomas WDF 114A
STEELE, Will. SCT 117A
William, Col. WDF 119A
Wm. CHN 32
Wm. SHE 118A
STEELE?, Andrew JES 95
STEELY, Isaiah HRL 118
Josiah HRL 118
STEEN, Joseph MNR 215
STEEN?, William GRD 106A
STEEPLES, Benjamin NCH 122A
STEERMAN, Foxall LGN 30
STEERMAN?, Valentine NCH 126A
STEERS, Holiday MTG 279
Hugh BNE 34
John BNE 34
STEERS?, Tho. MAS 55
STEGER, Wm. CHN 43A
STEGERS, John, Jr. GTN 131
Samuel GTN 120
Thomas GTN 132
STEGERS?, John GTN 131
STEIN, Betsy GRD 118A
STEIN?, Charles GTN 117
STEINBRIDGE, William MBG 133A
STELY, John PUL 54A
STEMMONS?, Jacob LGN 34
STENERS?, Edward GTN 119
STENNET?, Absalom GRD 106A
Daniel GRN 62
STENNETT, William GRD 89A
STENNETT?, Robt. GRD 106A
STENNITT, Charles WAS 20A
STEP, James HRL 120
Margaret BTL 331
STEPENS, John BNE 36
STEPH, Barnett FLD 6
STEPHEN, J. L. BBN 128
John FTE 68
Samuel BBN 130
STEPHENS, Abdengo JES 73
Alphred WRN 64A
Asae JES 84
Benj. S?. SHE 133A
Benja. LVG 4
Benjamin BNE 34
Benjamin OWN 104
Benjamin CBL 8A
Benjn. BBN 138
Charles MAD 178
David CLY 114
David H. HOP 264
Ely JES 83
Gabriel BBN 130
George CBL 8A
George W.? WRN 36A
Gilbert FLD 19
Harvey? WRN 28A
Henerietter FTE 61
Henry BNE 36
Henry OHO 8A
Henson JEF 33
Isaac WRN 28A
Isaac WYN 85A
Jacob BNE 50
Jacob MAD 142
Jacob BTH 206
James CWL 35
James MAD 116
James, Jr. HRY 224
James, Sr. HRY 224
James CBL 18A
James WRN 64A
James WYN 83A
Jesse CWL 31
STEPHENS, Jno. FKN 76
Jno. S. JEF 30
John BNE 34
John JES 81
John CLY 113
John BTH 206
John, Junr. OHO 11A
John TRG 5A
John OHO 11A
John CBL 13A
John CBL 22A
John E. MNR 193
Jos. FLG 61A
Joseph BBN 146
Joseph CBL 14A
Joseph H. WRN 32A
Leoniard? CBL 8A
Lewis F. FKN 62
Martin CBL 13A
Mathias BTH 218
Mathl. HRY 224
Obediah ADR 46
Price SCT 96A
Richard ETL 41
Richard JES 91
Richard BRK 295
Richard OHO 3A
Richard WRN 73A
Robert CSY 204
Robert BRK 293
Sampson MAD 100
Samuel BNE 36
Samuel GRT 147
Samuel BTL 331
Stephenan PUL 65A
Thomas OHO 7A
Thomas CBL 13A
Thomas CBL 18A
Thomas WRN 28A
Uriah HAR 218
W. D. BBN 60
William JES 73
William FTE 101
William HAR 176
William BTH 184
William BTH 218
William CBL 8A
William HND 9A
William CBL 14A
William PUL 55A
Wm. CWL 35
Wm. ADR 46
Wm. OHO 11A
STEPHENS?, Edward CBL 10A
STEPHENSON, Aaron CBL 17A
Ann BNE 50
Betsey CBL 10A
Dudley CBL 17A
Edward LWS 94A
Elizabeth NCH 113A
George NCH 122A
Hugh LGN 41
J. TOD 130
J., Jr. TOD 129A
Jacob CHN 43
James, Sr. JEF 37
James SPN 13A
James SPN 13A
James CBL 17A
James CBL 23A
James LWS 94A
John BNE 36
John MAD 150
John, Esq. WYN 83A
John SPN 13A
John WRN 32A

STEPHENSON, John LWS 94A
John NCH 113A
Joseph NCH 115A
Joseph H. MAD 98
Lindsay FKN 78
Moses CHN 43A
Nathan H. MAD 124
Nathen MAS 67
Rebeckah NCH 113A
Reuben CBL 17A
Richard GNP 173A
Robert LGN 46
Robert NCH 114A
Robert NCH 125A
Samuel CLK 68
Samuel HOP 264
Thomas NCH 129A
Will, Sr. / Jr.? HRY 222
William HOP 266
William CBL 11A
William NCH 113A
William NCH 113A
Zedock BNE 34
STEPHINS, Martin BBN 134
STEPNEY, (Free) CLD 162
STEPP, Frederic CLK 100
George CLK 68
Michael CLK 100
Rewbin? MAD 104
STERETT, John BRK 289
John BRK 310
STERGES, Jonathan LNC 51
STERGIN, John BRK 293
STERGIS, Mary SHE 161
STERLING, Edmund FKN 58
Henry SHE 115A
Jno. MAS 72
John GTN 133
Wm. FKN 66
STERMON, Andrew SPN 10A
STERNE, Susanah PND 26A
STERNS, Jesse TRG 7
Mary TRG 3A
Sydney BNE 36
William TRG 3A
STERRET, Joseph BTL 331
Thomas WRN 40A
STERRETT, James WRN 75A
STERRITT, Betsey SCT 101A
Betsey SCT 123A
Jas. SCT 123A
STETH?, Richard BRK 291
STEUMAN, Joshua LGN 35
STEVEN/STEVERS, Wm. L. ADR 50
STEVEN/STEVERS?, Dudley ADR 50
John ADR 50
Welcome ADR 50
Wm., Sen. ADR 50
Wm. B. ADR 50
STEVENS, ----.? CWL 40
----h? CWL 42
Abram SHE 148
Caty MNR 205
Edmond FKN 136
Edward WDF 120A
Elisha PUL 35A
J./ I.? L. GRD 96B
James FKN 106
James MTG 243
Jas. HRD 52
Jas. SCT 114A
John CLK 84
John MTG 243
John, Jr. MNR 201
STEVENS, John MNR 201
John GRD 96B
John PND 21A
John D. CWL 32
Johnethn.? CWL 42
Joseph HRD 12
Joseph CLK 101
Joseph MNR 199
Joseph DVS 15A
Joshua MNR 205
Joshua PUL 41A
Meriman WDF 111A
Moses CWL 56
Moses PUL 41A
Robert HRD 62
Sally LNC 41
Saml. MAS 67
Saml. MAS 70
Susanna MNR 199
Syntha ADR 50
Tho. ALN 130
Tho. PUL 50A
Tho. P. GRD 96A
Thomas FTE 76
Thos. HRD 24
Vincent HRD 54
Will GRD 96B
William MNR 217
William MTG 249
Wm. JEF 41
STEVENSON, -----?, Jr. CWL 40
--ry? CWL 40
Alexander WDF 93A
Alexr. CWL 40
Allen WAS 72A
Benjamin, Jr. WDF 94
Benjamin, Sr. WDF 96
Charles CLK 81
David WDF 104A
Geo. GRD 83A
Henry SCT 107A
Hugh CWL 39
Isaac CLK 82
James JEF 41
James CLK 84
James OWN 103
James, Jr. WDF 94
James, Sr. WDF 94
James H. LNC 17
James M. CLK 72
Jas., Sr. SCT 107A
Jas. CHN 43A
Jas. SCT 136A
Jas. H. LVG 5
Jobe SCT 91A
John CLK 82
John WDF 94
John UNN 154
John LWS 89A
John A. HRD 72
Jonathan OWN 102
Jos. MAS 57
Jos. MAS 60
Mary WDF 122A
Mathew CWL 46
Reuben (Crossed Out) SCT 95A
Reuben SCT 92A
Robert WDF 102A
Samuel WDF 93A
Susannah WDF 94A
Tho. MAS 67
Thomas HRD 12
Thomas LNC 71
Thomas FTE 73
STEVENSON, Thomas WDF 104
Will SCT 104A
William CLK 72
William CLK 72
William, Jr. WDF 93A
William WDF 94A
Williamson CLK 72
Wm. CWL 39
Wm.? CWL 39
STEVER, George CLY 115
Rossel P. CLY 113
STEVERSON, John MER 109
STEVINS, Thomas PND 25A
STEVINS?, Lewis PND 25A
STEWARD, Abram GRN 64
Andrew SHE 126A
Charles OHO 7A
Chas. SHE 124A
Daniel CBL 23A
George MER 108
Jacob OHO 7A
James FLD 30
James SHE 119A
James SHE 134A
John MER 108
Joseph SPN 18A
Nancy JEF 51
Peter MAD 94
Richard OHO 11A
Thomas FLD 33
Thomas FLD 37
Thomas SHE 128A
William OHO 3A
William WRN 74A
STEWART, Abel NCH 111A
Alan HRY 252
Alex JEF 55
Alexander BRN 27
Alexander FTE 93
Alexander OHO 5A
Alexandra CSY 216
Alexr. KNX 284
Ans.? BBN 138
Asa HRY 255
Bob/ Rob? GRD 100A
Caldwell PUL 52A
Charles BRN 27
Charles JEF 40
Charles KNX 296
Charles SCT 99A
Charles GNP 166A
Charles GNP 166A
Charles GNP 172A
Charles E. MNR 207
Chas. HRY 252
Chas. SCT 125A
Daniel GRT 142
Danl. K. HRD 12
David JEF 23
David ALN 142
David MTG 245
David PUL 65A
Debora SCT 125A
Elisha BBN 116
Elizabeth HAR 202
Ezekiel MTG 285
Frederick LGN 43
George MTG 265
Gravinis? CHN 44A
Hiram KNX 280
Hugh BNE 36
Hugh JEF 39
Hugh BLT 184
Hugh TOD 127A
Isaac JEF 22
Isaac KNX 284

Name	County	Page
STEWART, James	JEF	38
James	JEF	40
James	CWL	56
James	CLK	65
James	FTE	67
James	CLK	83
James	MAD	114
James	BBN	122
James	GRT	145
James	CSY	212
James	MTG	243
James	KNX	294
James	PUL	37A
James	SCT	99A
James	GNP	165A
Jas.	FLG	65A
Jas.	FLG	78A
Jas.	TOD	127A
Jas./ Jos.?	HRY	252
Jno.	HRY	250
Jno., Sr.	HRY	252
Joel	HRY	253
John	LVG	13
John	HRL	120
John	GRT	141
John	ALN	142
John	NSN	201
John	HAR	210
John	MTG	226
John	MTG	241
John	KNX	280
John	FLG	65A
John	SCT	118A
John	GNP	177A
John G.	CLK	79
John H.	FTE	94
Jos.	GRD	115A
Joseph	HAR	202
Joseph	KNX	280
Joshua	JEF	35
Levan	MAS	77
M.	JEF	21
Mathew	JEF	39
Mathew	GNP	166A
Merchant	JEF	34
Milly	GRD	95A
Milton	LVG	7
Mitchel	GNP	165A
Polly	MTG	263
Quinton	CHN	35
Rachel	PUL	54A
Ralph	GNP	165A
Reuben	MAD	116
Robert	FTE	81
Robert	NSN	182
Roboert	HAR	210
Robt.	JEF	48
Robt.	FLG	57A
Roy	CLK	80
Roy	GRD	95A
Solomon	MAS	74
Stephen	CHN	30
Stephen	ETL	54
Stephen	MTG	287
Stephen	WRN	32A
Thomas	BLT	188
Thomas	BTH	216
Thomas	BTL	331
Thomas	NCH	109A
Thos.	JEF	24
Thos., Sr.	JEF	28
Washington	LVG	8
Will.	LVG	5
Will.	LVG	9
William	LGN	23
William	FTE	74
STEWART, William	CLK	87
William	FTE	93
William	MER	116
William	HAR	178
William	HAR	200
William	MNR	209
William	HAR	220
Willis	JEF	23
Wm.	CHN	35
Wm.	MAS	64
Wm.	FKN	72
Wm.	HRD	82
Wm.	BBN	118
Wm.	BBN	122
Wm. K.	TOD	124A
STEWART?, Moses	BNE	38
Willoby	NCH	105
STEWELL, Ely	JEF	25
STEWERT, Thos.	PND	23A
STHRESHLEY, Thomas	FTE	89
STICE, David	WRN	48A
Philip	WRN	48A
STICKELL, Jacob	LWS	88A
STICKEN?, John	FTE	60
STICKLES, Isaac	BLT	196
STID, Jacob	BRK	293
James	BRK	293
STIDGER, Martha	NSN	175
STIFF, James	BRK	293
Thomas	ADR	54
Wm.	BRK	293
STIFFE, John	BRK	295
STIFFEY, Herman	SCT	95A
STIFLER, Adam	SCT	120A
STIGALL, Thomas	PUL	54A
STIGER, Henry	BBN	136
STIGHTS?, Asel	CWL	58
Jonas	CWL	58
STILES, Ann	FKN	60
Charles	NSN	218
David, Jr.	NSN	213
John	HRD	40
Lewis	NSN	213
Polly	MER	108
Richard	HND	4
Richard	NCH	113A
Saml.	BKN	22
Wm.	PND	20A
STILES?, Abram?	CHN	27A
Aron	BKN	4
David	NSN	186
Wm.	BKN	8
STILFIELD?, John	FTE	65
STILL, Claborn	WRN	36A
Jessee	MAD	144
John	LGN	38
John	MAD	170
William	WRN	36A
STILL?, Hugh	NCH	126A
James	NCH	116A
STILLE, Samuel	BBN	66
STILLMAN, Jonathan	JEF	35
STILLS, Ruth	LGN	27
STILLS?, B. B.	MAS	76
STILLWELL, Isaac	HRD	78
Jeremiah	SHE	164
Jno.	HRY	243
John	SHE	164
John	GNP	174A
Joseph, Jr.	CBL	15A
Joseph, Sr.	CBL	15A
Obadiah	GNP	174A
STILWELL, Absolem	ADR	46
Daniel	SHE	134A
Elijah	ADR	46
John	SHE	137A
STILWELL, John	SHE	139A
Jos.	SHE	135A
Thos.	SHE	136A
STILWELL?, Mary	HAR	194
STIMMONS, Stephen	MER	108
STIMMONS?, Martin A.	NSN	224
STINC?, Jacob	LNC	35
STINE, Jacob	LNC	67
STINE?, Jacob	LNC	35
STINGER, Jacob	FKN	68
STINKER?, John	GRN	61
STINNETT, Ruben	GRD	114A
Shadrack	MTG	251
STINNITT, James	GRN	63
STINSON, Andrew	LVG	5
Andrew	LVG	8
Auther	LWS	98A
Benoni	WYN	86A
Edward	MAD	140
George	WYN	97A
Jas.	PUL	38A
Jessee	MAD	140
Jos.	MAS	70
Joseph	MNR	199
Lewis	WYN	86A
Lovell	MNR	199
Martin	WYN	86A
William	WYN	85A
Wm.	GSN	149A
STINSONS, Jos.	MAS	61
STINSTON?, James	MAD	140
STINTSON, Richd.	JEF	46
STIPE, Frederick	JES	87
Henry	JES	87
John	JES	88
STIPHENS, Daniel	OHO	11A
STITES?, Abram?	CHN	27A
Aron	BKN	4
STITH, Benjamin	HRD	20
John	HRD	10
John	FTE	95
Jos.	HRD	42
Joseph	MTG	261
Richard	HRD	42
Richd., Jr.	HRD	44
Thomas	GNP	168A
Thos. H.	HRD	70
Wm.	HRD	42
Wm. B.	HRD	10
STITT, Creed	WRN	30A
STITT?, Hugh	NCH	126A
James	NCH	116A
STIVARD?, Samuel/ Lemuel?	GRN	79
STIVERS, Daniel	MAD	90
Edward	ETL	51
Edward	FTE	85
James	FTE	103
John	FTE	83
John	MAD	162
Reubin	FTE	104
Richard	MAD	92
Robert	FTE	104
William	ETL	51
STIVERS?, William	GTN	119
STO, Joel	WTY	116A
STOAKLY, Jacob	ETL	44
STOBALE, Tho.	ALN	122
STOBALL, George	ALN	124
John	MBG	141A
Nancy	ALN	128
Wm.	ALN	126
STOBUCK, Adam	HOP	264
John	HOP	264
Rebecca	FLD	45

STOCKARD?, James LVG 18
STOCKDALE, Jas., Jr. FLG 37A
Jas. FLG 37A
Milton FLG 42A
Simeon FLG 56A
Wm. FLG 37A
STOCKDELL, William FTE 75
STOCKDON, Nathaniel SPN 13A
STOCKER, E. JEF 24
STOCKHAM, John LWS 89A
John LWS 89A
STOCKMAN, John H. JEF 45
STOCKTON, D. K. FLG 79A
Edward MTG 295
Geo. FLG 78A
J./ I.? D. FLG 79A
James, Jr. WDF 100A
Jesse CLD 147
Josa. FLG 78A
L. D. FLG 70A
Lemuel CLD 145
Michael CLD 146
Newberry BRN 28
Peggy CLD 147
Polly CLD 145
Reuben B. WRN 73A
Robert BRN 28
Robert MTG 297
Susanna BRN 28
Thomas CLD 147
Thomas, Ser. BRN 28
Wm. W. GRN 58
STOCKTON?, John HRY 220
STOCKWELL, Jas. FLG 55A
John BNE 36
Joseph BNE 36
Mary H. FLG 79A
Michael BBN 66
Saml. FLG 78A
Sarah HRD 94
STODART, Ben GSN 151A
STODE?, John FLG 77A
STODGEL, Thomas SHE 114A
STODGHILL, Jacob FKN 94
Mary HOP 266
Reuben FKN 94
Saml. FKN 100
STOE, Abram WTY 110A
STOGDON, James WYN 101A
Mesheck WYN 81A
Peter H. WYN 103A
William WYN 82A
STOGSDIL, Shadh. PUL 46A
STOGSDILL, Danl. PUL 48A
Edward PUL 64A
Tho. PUL 50A
Wm. PUL 46A
STOKELY, Isaac MTG 253
STOKER, Edward BBN 88
Edward, Jr. BBN 88
Jas. H. BBN 90
Joseph BBN 88
Sally MTG 275
STOKES, Absalom CWL 56
Benjamin HOP 264
Benjamin NCH 124A
Berryman MTG 231
David TOD 127
James BRK 291
James TOD 126A
Joel HRT 168
Larkin TOD 126
Mary, Mrs. CLK 96
Matthew TOD 127
STOKES, Robert MTG 245
Stephen LGN 32
Thomas HOP 266
Thomas NCH 123A
STOLE?, John WYN 90A
STOLT?, George SHE 109A
STOM?, Henry MBG 140
STON?, Moses ADR 46
Spencer ADR 46
STONAFFER?, John CBL 6A
STONCIFFER/ STONDIFFER?, John CBL 6A
STONE, --ih-.? CWL 43
Aaron GSN 149A
Andrew SCT 99A
Archibald FLD 25
Asa SCT 131A
Baley WAS 61A
Barton W. SCT 106A
Benjamin BRK 293
Benjamin WRN 76A
Caleb LNC 75
Caleb MAD 94
Caleb, Jr. CWL 39
Caleb. CWL 34
Catharine WDF 125A
Charles BTH 178
Coleman SHE 159
Cuthbert FLD 43
Daniel WRN 43A
Davis NSN 200
Dudley MAD 146
Edward BBN 94
Eli H. NSN 180
Elias LNC 39
Elijah BBN 112
Elisha GTN 119
Elizabeth ALN 98
Elizabeth MER 109
Elizabeth WDF 126A
Enoch FLD 43
Enoch MER 109
Ezekiel FLD 35
Francis ETL 40
Gabriel JEF 56
George FTE 105
George LWS 95A
George WDF 125A
Henry WDF 125A
Hosy? GSN 149A
Jacob FTE 102
James FLD 25
James MER 109
James MAD 166
James SHE 166
James WYN 79A
James SHE 118A
James H. SHE 162
James M. BBN 114
Jane FTE 105
Jas. MAS 72
Jereby GSN 149A
Jesse BBN 74
John HRD 12
John FLD 34
John LNC 37
John CWL 38
John ADR 46
John BBN 60
John FTE 102
John BBN 134
John UNN 154
John HRT 168
John NSN 200
John WRN 34A
STONE, John SCT 135A
John SCT 136A
Joshua NCH 109A
Josiah JEF 42
Josiah UNN 149
Kinsey BBN 60
Levey? HND 13
Levi CWL 56
Lewis CLD 163
Manoah ADR 46
Mary BBN 132
Mary BLT 188
Micajah FTE 108
Milley HRD 94
Moses GSN 149A
Peter LVG 7
Reubin WYN 100A
Robert BTH 176
Saml. MAD 178
Saml. HRY 206
Samuel WRN 40A
Silas BNE 34
Smith GRD 116A
Solomon FLD 43
Spencer LNC 75
Stephen ADR 54
Stephen GRD 90A
Susanna NSN 199
Thomas GTN 119
Thomas BBN 134
Thomas NSN 185
Thomas, Senr. CLK 73
Volentine BTH 178
Wilderoy BRN 27
Will ADR 46
Will. SHE 124A
William CLK 73
William FTE 89
William FTE 106
William SHE 162
William WRN 54A
Wm. CWL 43
Wm. ADR 50
Wm. MAD 162
Wm. SHE 119A
Wm. H. BRN 27
STONE?, Ja--? ADR 54
Spencer ADR 54
STONER, Jerge W. MAD 164
William BLT 196
STONESTREET, Butler JEF 61
Henry JEF 61
James CLK 94
STONG, John SCT 94A
STONSIFER, Abraham BNE 34
STONSTREET, Benjamin JES 94
STONUM, Fortunatus TRG 8
STOOPS, James NCH 119A
John NCH 119A
Moses NCH 118A
Philip NCH 119A
William NCH 119A
William NCH 119A
STOPER, Henry MER 109
STOPHER, Peter MER 109
STORDENT, Stephen FTE 64
STORM, Jacob WDF 104
STORMAN, S. TOD 129A
STORMES, Coonrod GRD 97A
Peter GSN 149A
STORMS, Nathan GRD 91A
STORTS, James SHE 159
STORY, Elijah FLG 60A
Henry FKN 148

STORY, Isaac CLD 154
Jas., Snr. FLG 60A
Jas. FLG 60A
Jno. FKN 72
John CWL 38
John CWL 56
John FTE 74
John MTG 251
John GNP 168A
Jos. FLG 60A
Lewis FLG 64A
Phoebe HAR 218
S., Dr. BBN 128
Smith WDF 125A
Thomas CBL 7A
Thos. FLG 60A
Will SCT 92A
Will. FLG 61A
STOTSTON, Benj. MAD 100
STOTT, George SHE 109A
Jno. MAS 55
Thos. HND 7
Thos. FKN 146
STOTT?, Lewis L. FKN 158
STOTTS, Andrew ADR 50
James ADR 48
John FLD 39
John ADR 46
John PUL 63A
Johnson ADR 44
Thos. ADR 46
Will ADR 48
STOUT, Aaron SHE 128A
Amos WDF 103A
Anthony FTE 77
Aron SHE 135A
Benjamin FTE 65
Benjamin SHE 128A
David HRD 60
David FTE 65
David FTE 98
Elijah FTE 98
Elijah SHE 128A
Enoch SHE 137A
Ira BNE 36
James LNC 57
James SHE 117A
James SHE 138A
Jams? SHE 134A
John FTE 77
John SHE 128A
Jonathan MAD 178
Jonathan SHE 134A
Jos. SHE 130A
Joseph SHE 131A
Judith FTE 109
Peter SHE 134A
Phillemon SCT 133A
Platt MAS 77
Rachel MAS 67
Reuben SHE 134A
Saml. MAS 67
Sampson SHE 110A
William NCH 122A
Wm. FLG 37A
Wm. SHE 132A
Zebulan MAS 62
STOVALL, Eliza GRN 54
George J. LGN 35
Wm. BRN 28
STOVEALL, Hezekiah HRD 62
Ralph HRD 48
Wm. HRD 44
STOVER?, Mingo FTE 60
STOVERS, Mathias MAD 122
STOWERS, Jeremiah GTN 127
STOWERS, John BRK 295
Patrick SHE 156
Richard HAR 204
Samuel BRK 295
William SHE 154
Wm. PND 19A
STRA-S?, Joseph CLK 74
STRABOE, Fre?. MAS 71
STRADE, Patsey MNR 193
STRADER, Francis HRD 48
Jess HRD 28
Joseph GRN 58
Nancy SPN 24A
STRAHAN, David FLG 60A
Jas. FLG 59A
STRAHEN, John BTH 194
STRAHERN?, David ALN 114
STRAIGHT, David ALN 134
Wm. ALN 124
STRAMBLER, Daniel WRN 73A
STRANGE, A. A. ADR 46
Ann MTG 285
Bird HRT 168
Caty HRD 76
Ignatius HRD 76
Jas. HRD 76
Jeremiah WDF 97A
John MTG 285
John WRN 50A
John SHE 119A
Parrum BRN 26
Perry MTG 229
Washington GRD 103A
STRANY/ STRANG?, James BLT 164
STRANY, Mary SCT 117A
STRATFORD, Gowins FKN 60
STRATTEN, David WAS 29A
James JEF 46
Seregah HRD 68
STRATTON, Aaron LWS 87A
Absalom WRN 70A
Benjamin LGN 44
Edithe LGN 44
Hannah FLD 33
Harry FLD 27
Henry SPN 11A
James FLD 27
Jos. SHE 128A
Richard FLD 27
Salley FLD 27
Seth SHE 130A
Tandy? FLD 27
Wm. SHE 112A
Wm. SHE 131A
STRAUBE, Geo. BKN 10
Jacob BKN 19
STRAUGHAN, Benjamin ETL 37
Jacob MAD 152
STRAUGHN, Joseph MAD 158
STRAWMET?, John? CWL 41
STRAWN, James SHE 116A
John SHE 109A
Larkin SCT 108A
STRAWS, Elisa FKN 64
Gooly FKN 64
STRAYDER, Henry GRN 58
John GRN 58
John GRN 69
Lewis GRN 69
Richd. GRN 67
STREET, Anthony SHE 114A
Antony WAS 84A
David SHE 111A
George TRG 11A
STREET, James M. BBN 124
Jno. TOD 133
John S. OWN 101
Joseph, Sr. SHE 112A
Joseph SHE 119A
Mary LNC 45
Nathiel LNC 45
Rachel SHE 111A
William MER 108
STREETER, Jonathan CBL 20A
STREIGOR, John CBL 8A
STRESHLY, Robt. B. HND 11
STRETFORD?, Wm. CWL 33
STRIBLIN, Saml. SCT 107A
STRIBLING, Benjamin LGN 47
Thomas LGN 43
STRICKLER, John BNE 50
John SCT 128A
STRICKLIN, Saml. ADR 4
STRIGLER, Jacob HRD 96
STRING, Jeremiah BBN 90
STRINGER, Davd. PUL 38A
Edmond BLT 184
Edward MNR 205
Isaac MBG 136
James MTG 263
Jesse PUL 64A
Joel MTG 255
John GRN 56
John BLT 184
Leonard TRG 5
Polly, Mrs. WYN 102A
Richard BLT 188
Tennessee PUL 52A
Thomas BLT 184
Thos. WAS 66A
William MTG 255
William PUL 62A
William H. WTY 119A
Wm. ADR 44
STRINGFELLER, John W. FTE 64
William GTN 124
STRINGFELLOW, Geo. FKN 102
Henry FKN 102
STRINGFIELD, James BRN 28
STRIPLIN, Nancy CLK 103
STRODE, Amos WRN 41A
Jahue WRN 48A
James WRN 47A
Jereh. FLG 41A
John CLK 69
Saml. MAS 53
Saml. MAS 54
Saml. MAS 56
Saml. MAS 58
Susanna MNR 207
Tho. MAS 68
William, Sr. MNR 207
STROGHN, John CBL 16A
STRONG, Amos C. MBG 138A
Chas. P. SHE 139A
Edward CLY 119
Elizabeth CLD 161
John CLY 122
John SCT 106A
Moses CLY 132
Samuel MNR 197
Synthia MAD 146
William CLY 125
STRONGER, Lary MBG 136
STROTHER, Daniel JEF 60
Eleanor BBN 118
George GTN 129
James BBN 142

STROTHER, John D. NSN 217
Robt. GNP 167A
Samuel BRN 26
STROUD, Ansel PUL 61A
Eli LGN 27
Isaac CHN 31
Isaac CHN 31A
Joel LGN 40
John MBG 135
Lot MBG 135
Mark FLD 41
Thomas P. BTL 331
Wm. CHN 31
STROW, John TOD 132A
STROWBRIGE, Job, Sr. HRT 167
STRUNK, Peggy WTY 120A
STRUNK?, Daniel WTY 114A
STRUTTON, John MER 110
STRUTTON?, William GTN 128
STUARD, Daniel CLY 128
John CLY 114
Mary HOP 266
William CLY 117
STUARD?, Thos. E. MAD 178
STUARR?, Margaret MAD 112
STUART, Alex BBN 66
Alexander WRN 42A
Barnett MBG 139
Charles TRG 12A
Charles WRN 42A
Chas. CHN 42
Chs. RCK 75A
Daniel MBG 139
David MAD 118
Elijah GTN 131
Elisha GTN 131
Ezekiel MAD 120
James GTN 131
James WRN 32A
James MBG 139A
John BBN 66
John BBN 78
John WRN 49A
Joseph BBN 84
Joshua MBG 139
Peter GTN 131
Richard GTN 131
Robert WRN 58A
Robt., Jr. PUL 48A
Robt. PUL 48A
Saml. MAD 118
Sarah WRN 45A
Simpson RCK 75A
William WRN 39A
William D. GTN 130
STUART?, William NCH 108A
STUBBINS, John SHE 155
Saml. HRY 241
STUBBLEFIELD, Alexr. MAS 68
B. TOD 130A
Beverly P. LWS 93A
Cath. CHN 28A
Thomas LGN 32
William CLK 106
STUBBS, Thomas GRN 56
William FTE 73
STUBELFIELD, Robt. ALN 96
STUCK, Peter MER 108
STUCKER, John WDF 122A
STUCKY, Emanuel JEF 36
Geo. JEF 36
Martin JEF 36
William BTH 210
STUDMAN?, Thomas FTE 69
STUFFLEBEEN, Andrew ETL 52
James ETL 53
Jno. FKN 68
John ETL 52
Michael ETL 54
William ETL 54
STUFFY, Joseph BRN 27
STUL?, Robert FKN 102
Wm. FKN 110
STULL, Jesse NCH 114A
John HOP 264
STULL?, Andrew JES 95
STULTS, Richard ADR 46
Wm. ADR 46
STULTS?, Georg ADR 54
STULTZ, John HRY 212
STULY?, John WRN 60A
STUMP, Christopher GNP 171A
David MBG 141A
Federick BNE 36
George CBL 9A
George WAS 45A
George GNP 166A
Jacob HAR 178
Leonard HAR 134
STUN?, William GRD 106A
STURGEION, Robert JEF 61
STURGEON, Esquire HRT 168
James HRT 168
James HRT 168
Jeremiah BRN 27
Jeremiah GRT 144
John JEF 62
John HRT 168
Saml. HRY 266
Simpson SHE 148
Thos. JEF 62
Thos., Snr. JEF 61
STURGUS, Robert A. MAD 164
STURMAN?, Valentine NCH 126A
William MER 117
STUTE / STULE?, Joseph GTN 121
STUTIVILL, Charles GSN 150A
STUTTS?, Georg ADR 54
STWEART?, John HRT 167
Polley HRT 168
Richd. E. HRT 168
SUARDENER?, Edmund PND 27A
SUBLET, Charles J. BTL 313
Charles J./ I.? WRN 30A
Charles T.? BTL 331
James MAD 114
John HND 4
Samuel WRN 28A
SUBLETT, Abraham LNC 69
Abram GRN 72
Allen LNC 5
Benjamin B. WRN 32A
James HRY 226
Joseph GRN 69
Lewis, Jur. WDF 116A
Lewis WDF 117A
Littleberry WDF 118A
Samuel GRN 61
Samuel D. WRN 33A
Wm. GRD 91A
SUDDARTH, Benjamin MER 109
SUDDETH, Francis NCH 121A
George WDF 121A
Henry LGN 42
Henry WDF 124A
Thornton WDF 124A
SUDDITH, Baylor LNC 63
SUDDITH, George L. LNC 65
John LNC 33
Robert LNC 65
William M. BTH 186
Willm. LNC 7
SUDDUTH, Ann, Mrs. CLK 97
Hen. HRY 258
James CLK 85
Jas. HRY 253
John CLK 97
William CLK 103
SUET, Elijah BRK 293
SUFFIETT?, John JES 86
SUFFORRANS, Jno. CHN 45A
SUFFRUTT?, John JES 86
SUGAN?, James BBN 124
SUGART, John MAD 136
SUGG, Allin J. HND 11A
Calvin HND 11
Joel BTL 313
Joel BTL 331
Patience HND 11
Simon HND 11
William UNN 148
Wyly HND 11
SUGG?, Rachael BBN 146
SUGGETT, Edgcomb P. SCT 92A
Jas. SCT 104A
John, Junr. SCT 127A
John, Senr. SCT 131A
Thos. SCT 104A
Will. SCT 129A
SUING?, Stephen CHN 30
SUISEBAUGH?, Adam WRN 72A
SUITER, Jno. FKN 90
John SHE 158
Tabitha BBN 82
SULAVIN, Jos. FLG 37A
SULEVAN, Rachel HRT 168
SULIVAN, James WDF 94
Spencer LNC 55
Stephen CWL 39
SULLARDS, Samuel FLD 45
SULLARDS?, John FLD 27
SULLAVEN, Richard WAS 86A
SULLAVIN, Daniel GRN 59
John GRN 59
Samuel GRN 61
William GRN 74
SULLENGER, Jno. HRY 258
John MAD 180
Robt. HRY 258
Robt., Jr. HRY 258
SULLER?, William HRD 8
SULLIAN, Uriah MBG 135
SULLINGER, James HRY 206
Thos. GSN 150A
SULLINS, Peter, Jun. WYN 86A
Peter, Sen. WYN 86A
SULLIVAN, Abel MBG 135
Burges HRY 250
D. TOD 134
Daniel NSN 221
David FLD 15
David FTE 91
Dennis HRY 228
Eleanor WTY 124A
Gabl. MAS 57
Henry HRD 94
James FTE 103
James WTY 119A
Jas. SCT 91A
John W. WTY 119A
Jos. HRY 208

SULLIVAN, Lewis WDF 96
Lewis MBG 135
Nathan MER 108
Peter FLD 15
Price HRD 92
Randolp MAS 57
Robert MAD 158
Rodney MAS 57
Saml. MAD 180
Will MAS 57
William BNE 36
William FTE 94
Wilson FLD 46
SULLIVANT, Charles UNN 152
SULUR?, William HRD 8
SUMALT, (See Sumwalt) HAR 164
SUMALT?, Philip HAR 144
SUMERS, Joseph NCH 124A
Saml. MAS 72
Soloman CHN 40
SUMET?, John FLG 57A
SUMIT, John JES 89
SUMLOLT, (See Sumwalt) HAR 164
SUMMER?, Isacc TRG 6
SUMMERHILL, Jas. JEF 55
SUMMERS, Abraham WYN 80A
Adam WDF 92
Ann MAS 59
Archibald MTG 269
Benj. FLG 34A
Benjamin BNE 36
Benjamin BLT 164
Cald. FTE 88
Caleb FTE 88
Caleb MTG 289
Carter FLG 34A
Charles BTH 178
Charles MBG 140A
Cornelius MTG 287
David MBG 142A
Elijah MAS 68
Elijah SHE 120A
Elijah M. SHE 120A
Francis BRK 295
George S. SHE 119A
Henry CHN 39
Hiram WYN 83A
Isaac HAR 214
Jacob WYN 81A
Jessee FLG 35A
Jno. MAS 53
Jno. MAS 54
Jno. CWL 58
John HRD 40
John GRN 57
John MAD 156
John MNR 201
John MTG 285
John WAS 19A
John FLG 34A
John WYN 82A
John SHE 120A
John C. GRN 51
Levy GRN 62
Lewis FLG 35A
Mikael FLG 34A
Nancy MNR 201
Richard WYN 83A
Robert BNE 36
Saml. MAS 63
Samuel WYN 84A
Sanford MTG 229
Thomas BNE 36
Thomas BLT 196
SUMMERS, Thomas H. NSN 197
Thos. CHN 40
Thos. FLG 36A
Thos. L. BKN 6
Waitman WYN 90A
William CLK 93
William NSN 196
William, Capt. WYN 84A
William, Sen. WYN 84A
Wm. BKN 6
Wm. FLG 34A
SUMMERS?, Samuel NSN 196
William, Sr. NSN 196
SUMMERVILL, John, Jr. FLG 73A
John FLG 73A
Jos. FLG 73A
SUMMINS?, Will. KNX 308
SUMMITT?, George NCH 122A
James NCH 110A
SUMMNER, Nehennah? WTY 121A
SUMNER, George WTY 122A
James WTY 122A
Jessee MBG 137
John FLD 3
John MBG 136A
Lieurena KNX 280
Saml. KNX 282
Thomas MBG 136A
SUMNER?, Isacc TRG 6
Samuel FLD 25
SUMPKINS, William DVS 15A
SUMPTER, Fielding WYN 91A
James WYN 96A
John WYN 84A
Samuel WRN 40A
William WRN 40A
SUMRALL, J. K. MAS 77
SUMRALLA, Jno. MAS 77
SUMWALT?, Christian HAR 164
Jno. HAR 164
SUN?, -----? CWL 40
SUNNS?, John BRN 28
SUNRALT?, Philip HAR 144
SUNS?, Eli BRN 26
SURBER, Adain PUL 38A
Adam, Jr. PUL 38A
Adam, Sr. PUL 49A
Isaac PUL 40A
Jos. PUL 39A
SURBO, Jacob LNC 73
SUREFIELD?, Jno. FKN 124
SURLEN, Jacob PUL 66A
SURLOTT, George LNC 3
SURLS, Luther LWS 90A
SURLS?, Samuel CLK 97
SURMMETT?, Jacob NCH 110A
SURRINEY?, David BTH 198
SURVEAR?, James CSY 222
SURVY, Christopher LNC 75
SUTER, Andrew OWN 103
George BRN 28
George FTE 70
John BRN 28
Rebeckah OWN 103
Thomas WDF 112A
William WDF 92
William M. OWN 103
SUTER?, John WRN 44A
SUTFIELD, Richard M. MER 115
SUTFIN, Gilbert SCT 100A
Gilbert SCT 109A
John SCT 137A
Low SCT 113A
SUTHERD, Benjn. OHO 9A
SUTHERLAND, Enus MER 109
Frederic CLK 98
George BRN 28
James ADR 62
Jo. GRD 96B
John CSY 212
Lee CBL 19A
Owen CSY 210
Thomas BRN 27
Thomas CLK 75
Travis HRY 256
Walter E. CLK 75
Will ADR 50
William NSN 181
Wm. BRN 27
Wm. MAS 76
SUTHERLEN, Howard SHE 116A
SUTLIFF, John FKN 80
John HAR 202
SUTPHON?, John BKN 23
SUTSTON, Salley SCT 134A
SUTT, Christopher SHE 114A
SUTTERFIELD, Edward MER 109
James GTN 129
SUTTERS, Uriah NCH 117A
SUTTLES, Henry BBN 106
Lewis ADR 46
Uriah JEF 59
SUTTLY, Abraham JEF 32
SUTTON, -----? HND 13
A. GRD 88A
Amos FLG 50A
Ann GRD 114A
Ben GRD 87A
Benjamin CLK 66
Benjamin HAR 164
Benjamin CBL 19A
David FTE 55
David FTE 78
David, Capt. MER 115
David GRD 82A
Edmond WAS 43A
Elij. HRY 255
Elijah SCT 121A
Fielding OHO 8A
Geo. FLG 57A
Isaac MER 110
Jame? JES 94
James LNC 39
James OHO 5A
James SCT 98A
James GRD 105A
John JEF 19
John LGN 27
John BRN 28
John, Sr. SCT 122A
John GRD 101A
John GNP 171A
Johna. FLG 76A
Jonas LNC 39
Joseph BRN 28
Joseph SCT 122A
Leroy JES 91
Leroy WDF 101A
Moses HND 13
Moses CBL 15A
Oliver FTE 92
Philip C. GNP 165A
Richd. FLG 50A
Richd. F. WAS 59A
Robt. SCT 107A
Roland GRD 88A
Rowland BBN 140
Samuel MTG 249

Name	County	Page
SUTTON, Samuel	CBL	19A
Samuel	WTY	125A
Tho.	ALN	92
Thomas	ALN	145
Toliver	BBN	138
Will	GRD	114A
William	JES	75
William	HAR	158
William	WYN	87A
William	GRD	104A
William J./ Jno.?	GRD	101A
Wisdom	MER	109
Wm.	FKN	136
Wm.	BBN	140
Wm.	SHE	123A
SUTTON?, Oliver	FTE	87
SUTZER, Elizabeth	HRD	72
John	HRD	72
SUWALT?, Jno.	HAR	164
SWAGER, Joseph	JEF	22
SWAGGARD, John	GTN	119
SWAIN, Cornelius	CLD	156
Henry	BTL	331
Jas.	MAS	54
Nathan	FLG	39A
Wm.	FLG	39A
SWALES, Will.	LVG	3
SWAN, Edward	NSN	194
Geo.	MAS	63
George	LVG	18
Jacob	FKN	96
James	SPN	8A
John (Cold.)	BLT	176
Philip	CHN	28A
Phillip	JEF	63
Richd.	SCT	127A
Robert	CLD	159
Samuel	SPN	4A
Thomas	HRD	50
Will.	LVG	9
SWANEY, Edward	BTH	158
Miles	BTH	150
SWANGO, Abraham	FLD	6
Abram	GTN	133
James	GTN	135
Levi	GTN	135
Samuel	FLD	6
William	GTN	133
SWANK, David	HRD	74
Jacob	HRD	66
SWANN, David C.	HRD	84
Wm	HRD	84
SWANSEY, Jno.	LVG	5
SWANSON, Levi	FLD	41
SWART?, George	NCH	106A
SWARTS, Henry	LWS	94A
SWARTZ, John	BBN	84
SWATSWELFER?, Saml.	BBN	144
SWEARENGEN, Hezekiah	NCH	127A
Josiah	NCH	127A
SWEARENGIN, Abraham	LWS	96A
Bartlett	LWS	97A
Charles	LWS	96A
John, Junr.	LWS	97A
John	LWS	96A
Marmaduke	LWS	87A
SWEARINGEN, Andrew	MTG	241
Daniel	LWS	88A
Elemelake	BLT	180
Elemelake	BLT	192
Jesse	BLT	184
Rachael	BLT	184
SWEARINGIN, Saml.	JEF	40
Van	SHE	169
SWEASEY?, William	NSN	210
SWEAT, Izarel	HRD	40
SWEATMAN, Neni?	FLD	20
William	CBL	12A
SWEENEY, Eliza	LNC	63
James	HAR	204
Jesse	LNC	39
Wm.	PUL	43A
SWEENY, Danl.	PUL	44A
James	ADR	46
Steven	PUL	40A
Thos.	PUL	44A
SWEET, Catherine, Mrs.	WYN	98A
Jas.	FLG	33A
John	WYN	98A
Margaret	GNP	170A
Nathl.	FLG	33A
Thos.	FLG	66A
Wm.	FLG	33A
SWEETEN, Absolum	CLY	128
SWEETLAND, Jas.	JEF	20
SWEETS, Michael	NSN	177
Peter	NSN	176
Thomas	NSN	177
SWEIGART, Samuel	FTE	63
SWEM, Jacob	HAR	200
SWENEY, Moses	WRN	64A
Saml.	BRN	28
Thomas	NCH	127A
SWERENGIN, Jos.	SHE	136A
SWERINGEN, Abijah	JEF	49
SWESEY?, Joseph	WAS	49A
SWETESER, Samuel	BNE	36
SWETMAN, William	BTH	162
SWETNAM, Geo.	SCT	134A
SWEZEY?, Joseph	WAS	49A
SWIFT, Elijah N.	SCT	91A
Henry	BBN	90
Jno.	CWL	56
John	JEF	51
John	CLD	144
Thomas	SHE	165
William	WTY	119A
SWIGATE, Edward	ADR	50
SWIGGATE?, James	CSY	214
SWIGLEY, Joseph	GRN	57
SWILOVEN?, John	ALN	112
SWIM?, Michael	GNP	171A
SWIMAN?, John	FLG	47A
Margret	FLG	47A
Trumbo	FLG	53A
Vincent	FLG	48A
SWIMEN?, Jane	FLG	71A
SWIMM, Anthony	FLG	29A
Nathl.	FLG	29A
SWIMM?, Jane	FLG	71A
John	FLG	47A
Margret	FLG	47A
Trumbo	FLG	53A
Vincent	FLG	48A
SWINDLE, John	BNE	34
SWINDLER, Jessee	JEF	39
Jonathan	SHE	149
SWINE, Valintine	JEF	52
SWINE?, Michael	GNP	171A
SWINEY, Daniel	WAS	84A
Joseph	WAS	51A
Moses	WAS	52A
SWINEY?, Wm.	WAS	45A
SWINFORD, Hezekiah	HAR	176
James	HAR	176
Jno.	HAR	138
Jno.	HAR	138
SWINFORD, Joshua	HAR	138
Thankful	HAR	176
SWING, Mary	CBL	13A
SWINGLE, George	LWS	87A
John	ETL	51
John, Sr.	ETL	39
SWINK, George	BRK	293
Leonard	PUL	36A
SWINNEY, Bartlett	SHE	153
Charles	CSY	208
Elizabeth	SHE	153
Henry	SHE	153
Job	CSY	210
Joel	CSY	222
John	ETL	39
John	SHE	153
Josiah	CSY	212
Josias M.	WRN	63A
Lewis	SHE	153
Robert	SHE	153
Sheppard	CSY	224
SWINNY, Austin	SHE	153
Edward	WRN	28A
James	WRN	68A
Jennet	BTH	168
John	SHE	153
John A.	ALN	106
SWINSEN?, John	FLG	47A
SWISHER, Voluntine	FKN	96
SWITSER, Danl.	HAR	146
SWITZER, Abraham	BTH	160
SWOAPS, George	WDF	110A
SWOPE, Archibald	CLD	152
David	LNC	67
George	CLD	146
George	SHE	135A
Jacob	LNC	5
John	GRD	117A
Jos.	SHE	135A
Joseph	ETL	39
Martin	LNC	47
Michael	SHE	135A
Saml.	GRD	98A
SWOPES, Susan R.	MAD	104
SWORD, John	FLD	28
SWORE?, Hay	RCK	83A
SYCK, Jacob	FLD	28
SYKES, George, Jr.	HRD	26
SYLER, Adam	WTY	112A
Jacob	WTY	112A
John	MBG	135
John	WTY	112A
William	WTY	127A
SYLVIA, (Free)	CLD	162
SYMES, John	CSY	204
SYMMS, John	MTG	245
Josiah	MTG	279
SYMPSON, William	GRN	73
SYMS, Garland	OWN	101
Jno. P.	HRY	269
John	CBL	3A
SYRA, Martha	BRN	28
SYRUS, Joel	FKN	130
SYX, Abraham	OHO	5A
David	OHO	8A
Jno.	OHO	6A
Jno.	OHO	8A
T BALL?, John	HRL	120
T------?, Zach	WAS	70A
T-----?, John	UNN	150
T---T?, Jesse	HRY	265
TABB, Bailey S.	HRD	92
Edmond C.	HRD	92
Edward	LVG	14
Edws.	MAS	58

Name	County	Page
TABB, John E.	HRD	8
Richd.	MAS	53
Robt.	HRD	90
Robt. H.	HRD	90
TABER, Amasa	BRK	297
Henry?	ALN	120
Isaac	ALN	110
TABERT, Pardon	OHO	5A
TABOR, David	JES	84
TABOTT?, Thomas	GNP	165A
TABOU-?, Jacob	ALN	124
TACKET, Balis	BTH	168
TACKETT, Archibald	MTG	235
Frances	FLD	37
James	WTY	110A
Lewis	FLD	35
Thomas	FLD	19
Thomas	HRL	120
William	FLD	37
TACKETT?, George	FLD	40
TACKSON, Amy	SPN	20A
TADE, James	MNR	195
John	MNR	211
TADLOCK, Carter	MER	110
Edward	HRD	86
John	TRG	12
John	HOP	266
Sevier	TRG	10
TAFT?, Benjamin	CBL	18A
TAGART, Margaret	SHE	128A
TAGNE?, George	HRY	196
George	HRY	196
John	HRY	196
Joseph	HRY	196
Robert	HRY	198
TAGUE?, (See Tagne?)	HRY	
TAILOR, Ellis	TRG	5
John	BRK	297
Simon	BBN	78
William	BTH	170
TAIPLEY, Wm.	HRD	10
TAIT?, Elizabeth	BBN	106
Saml.	MAS	60
TAITE?, Charles	CSY	210
TALBORTS?, John	CLK	95
TALBOT, Aquilla	BBN	122
Cyrus	NSN	196
Danl.	BBN	126
Elizabeth	NSN	195
Elizabeth, Sr.	NSN	195
Enoch	UNN	153
George	MER	114
Henley	NSN	195
J. M.	JEF	21
John	BBN	138
John B.	SCT	114A
Paul	MTG	251
Richard	OWN	103
Thomas	OWN	102
William	SHE	141A
TALBOTT, Abm. R.	BBN	106
Benjamin	HND	10
Benjamin	SHE	172
Benjamin	HAR	212
Charles	BBN	126
Daniel	NSN	195
Danl.	BBN	128
David	SHE	157
Demoval	BBN	124
Edmund	HND	9
Edward	SHE	172
Edward	SHE	175
Edward, Sr.	SHE	172
Edwd.	JEF	50
Geo.	BBN	126
TALBOTT, Geo.	BBN	128
George	JES	73
Henry	BBN	116
Hugh	BBN	126
James	FTE	75
James	SHE	158
James	DVS	19A
James S./ L.?	GTN	132
Jane	CLD	144
John	JEF	44
John	JEF	57
John	SHE	172
John	CBL	9A
Margaret	HAR	214
Mason	BBN	122
Nathaniel	SHE	163
Nicholas	BBN	104
Othniel	SHE	157
Peter	PND	18A
Preston	JES	83
R.	CHN	27A
Rachael	BBN	110
Reason	BBN	128
Samuel	BBN	124
Tabitha	BBN	122
Theodore F.	FTE	62
Thomas	WRN	44A
William	BBN	126
William	CLD	144
Wm.	CHN	27A
TALFARO, William	CSY	204
TALIAFERRO, Hay	CLK	92
John W.	UNN	149
William	CLK	92
TALIFERRO, Anne	CBL	23A
Francis	JEF	65
John	CBL	3A
TALKINGTON, John	LGN	27
Jos.	TOD	126
TALKINTON, S.	TOD	127A
TALL, Samuel	FTE	102
TALLEY, Charles	MAD	154
Sarah	CLD	150
TALLIFERRO, Robt., Dr.	BBN	146
TALLY, Clabron	BTH	156
David	CHN	45A
James	CWL	37
John	FTE	102
Martin	TOD	132A
Overton	HAR	184
TALLY?, William	FTE	102
TALMON, James	OHO	11A
William	OHO	11A
TAMER?, Lucias	HRY	220
TAMERLIN, Lewis	TOD	130
TAMPLER?, Dixson	CWL	38
TAMPSON, William	SHE	163
TANAHILL, Andrew	CHN	43A
TANCIL, Francis	SCT	120A
TANDY, Achillas	FTE	96
Gabriel	BNE	48
Gabriel, Maj.	MER	114
Jackson	TOD	132
John	GTN	122
Mary	GTN	127
Miles	CHN	45
Moses	HRY	206
Ralph	CHN	44A
Roger	CWL	37
Roger	GTN	128
Sary	FKN	58
William	GTN	127
Wm.	CHN	45
TANGATE?, Dixon	GRT	145
TANGET, Ephraim	GRT	143
TANKERSLY, Edward	BRK	299
TANKESLY, Charles	BRK	297
TANNEHILL, Niman	LGN	44
TANNEHILL?, John	LGN	30
TANNER, -----?, Jr.	DVS	6A
-----?, Sr.	DVS	6A
-----?	DVS	6A
Aaron	BNE	38
Archilaus	CLK	72
David	CLK	77
Ephraim	BNE	38
Federick	BNE	38
Frederick	BRN	29
Frederick	OHO	10A
George	JES	72
Jacob	BNE	38
James	MBG	142
John	FTE	99
M.	RCK	78A
Moses	BNE	38
Nancy	BNE	38
Richd. M.	BBN	80
Saml.	HRY	232
Samuel	MBG	139
Simeon	BNE	38
Thomas	OHO	10A
Thomas	MBG	139A
William	LVG	18
William	LNC	41
William	FTE	102
TANNER?, Branch	CLK	81
Creed H.	HRY	232
Edward	ALN	100
Mathew	HRY	232
TAP?, Wm.	JEF	56
TAPP, Burkett	BRN	29
Elizabeth	MTG	239
Ellias	MAS	78
John	MTG	281
Lewis	JES	80
Lucinda	MTG	239
Major	MTG	231
Nelson	FTE	74
TAPSCOTT, ----iam?	DVS	11A
TARANCE, James	HOP	266
TARANTS, Rubin	GRD	113A
TARASCON, John A.	JEF	30
TARBIT?, David	FLG	53A
TARBURTON?, Henry?	LVG	18
TARETON, Jeremiah	JEF	30
TARLTON, Alfred	SCT	105A
Caleb	MAS	55
Calip?	SCT	135A
George	SCT	97A
Hatton	BNE	38
Jas.	SCT	137A
Jeremiah	SCT	105A
Jerry	SCT	129A
Leo	SCT	91A
Ralph	SCT	128A
TARR, Charles	SHE	165
Charles	NCH	123A
George	JEF	63
Jno.	MAS	60
Lydia	BBN	108
William	SHE	165
TARRANCE, Ann	SPN	13A
John	FLG	39A
TARRANT, Terey?	CWL	57
TARRENCE, Mino-?	WRN	67A
TARROWMAN, Mary	MAS	59
TARROWMAN?, Tho.	MAS	57
TART, John	BNE	48
TARTER, Christley, Jr.	PUL	57A

Name	County	Page
TARTER, Christly	PUL	54A
Jacob	PUL	54A
Jesse	PUL	57A
John, Senr.	PUL	66A
John	PUL	58A
Peter, Senr.	PUL	66A
TARVIN, Joseph	CBL	22A
Thomas	CBL	21A
TARVIN?, Geo.	FLG	71A
Richard	CBL	14A
TATE, Benjamin	SHE	157
Elsey	GRD	118A
Hugh	HND	8A
Isaac	GRN	69
James	BRK	297
James	WAS	81A
Jesse M.	HRD	46
John	GRN	68
Robt.	PUL	41A
Saml.	PUL	41A
Samuel	BRK	297
Waddy	CLK	93
William	LNC	27
William	CLK	93
William	GTN	120
William	HAR	192
William	BRK	297
William	PUL	67A
TATE?, Richard	JEF	37
TATMAN, John	MTG	271
John	FLG	26A
Jos.	FLG	33A
Louder	FLG	63A
Nancy	FLG	33A
Stephen	FLG	34A
Vincent	FLG	57A
TATSPAW, George	BNE	50
TATUM, Alfred	LGN	46
John	GRD	113A
N. S.	GRD	84A
Saml.	GRD	93A
Thomas	LGN	29
William	LGN	30
TAUL, Jonathan	MTG	233
Levi	MTG	283
Micha	CLK	106
TAUL?, Benjamin	CLK	82
TAUSEY?, Moses	BNE	38
Thomas	BNE	38
Zerah	BNE	38
TAWLER, Henry	WDF	94
TAYLER, Colby H., Col.	CLK	96
Hubbard, Jr.	CLK	102
James	FLD	42
Joseph	BTL	331
Peter	BTL	331
TAYLON?, Thomas	BTL	331
TAYLOR, -----?	DVS	3A
-----?	DVS	6A
-----?	DVS	6A
-----?	DVS	9A
----d?	DVS	16A
-manuel?	DVS	7A
Adam	PND	31A
Allen	WRN	38A
Anderson	WDF	113A
Andrew	HRT	169
Andw.	CWL	57
Ann	ADR	52
Anthony	MAD	124
Argle	WDF	96A
Armstead	NSN	185
Aron	DVS	18A
Ayers	FLG	66A
Ben	HRY	192
TAYLOR, Benj.	JEF	20
Benj.	FKN	82
Benj.	WAS	75A
Benj.	WAS	75A
Benjamin	MAD	106
Benjamine	SPN	16A
Bertholamew	BKN	26
Betsey	SCT	110A
Beverly	SHE	156
Britan?	WTY	114A
Brooken	FKN	126
Caleb	LWS	93A
Carter	BNE	38
Chapman	LGN	32
Chapman	WDF	118A
Charles	BTH	172
Charles P.	BRN	34
Chas.	FLG	35A
Christiana	HAR	196
Clifton	MAD	102
Comodore	JEF	57
Cranson	SHE	150
Curnelious?	HRL	120
Daniel	LGN	46
Daniel	SPN	3A
Dav.	HRY	250
David	HRL	120
David	MAD	162
Edmond	BRK	297
Edmund	LGN	31
Edmund	FKN	120
Edmund H.	JEF	65
Edward	BNE	38
Edwd.	HRY	234
Elizabeth	FTE	61
Elizabeth	MER	111
Elizebeth	WDF	105A
Fanny	SCT	104A
Fanny	SCT	113A
Fauchee T.	LNC	59
Francis	JEF	44
Francis	MAS	63
Francis	MER	110
Francis	MTG	237
Geo.	BKN	24
Geo., (Free Man)	BBN	128
Geo., Jr.	CLK	66
Geo.	FLG	35A
Geo.	FLG	55A
George	LGN	31
George	JES	72
George	HAR	132
George	HAR	188
George	PND	31A
George	NCH	125A
George G.	CLK	93
Gibson B.	UNN	147
Gile	MER	115
Giles	LVG	10
Gorge, Jr.	ADR	52
Gorge, Sen.	ADR	52
Grooms	MAD	168
Hancock	JEF	39
Hannah	FTE	78
Hannah	FTE	88
Harrison	OHO	3A
Harrison	OHO	8A
Henry	JES	83
Henry	FLG	25A
Henry	WAS	40A
Henry	WAS	84A
Henry	SHE	140A
Hillory	HAR	180
Hubbard, Senr.	CLK	102
Humphrey E.	OWN	100
Isaac	CLD	166
TAYLOR, Isaac	HRT	169
Isaac	WTY	125A
J. W.?	SHE	143A
Jack	GSN	152A
Jacob	HRD	46
Jacob	MAS	52
Jacob	BRK	299
James	LNC	27
James	JEF	44
James	BBN	80
James	MAD	98
James	MER	111
James	FKN	118
James	MAD	124
James	MAD	148
James	HAR	208
James	BRK	297
James	BRK	297
James	CBL	2A
James	OHO	3A
James	WRN	32A
James	WRN	63A
James	GRD	83A
James	GRD	107A
James	SHE	140A
James L.	UNN	150
James W., Atty.	CLD	166
Jams?	SHE	135A
Jarvis C.	BNE	38
Jas.	ADR	52
Jash.?	CHN	43
Jefferson	WRN	73A
Jery	WAS	84A
Jesse	MTG	233
Jessee	CLK	105
Jessee	WYN	79A
Jno.	CWL	57
Jno.	FKN	82
Jno.	FKN	108
Jno.	HRY	256
John	BRN	29
John	LNC	51
John	JEF	52
John	HRD	70
John	FTE	78
John	FTE	87
John	WDF	98
John	MER	111
John	SHE	156
John	BTH	158
John	HRT	169
John	BLT	188
John	HAR	190
John, Jnr.	HAR	188
John, Jr.	NCH	128A
John, Sr.	MAD	96
John	OHO	3A
John	OHO	4A
John	CBL	14A
John	WAS	33A
John	WAS	55A
John	FLG	61A
John	RCK	78A
John	WAS	81A
John	RCK	83A
John	WAS	84A
John	NCH	110A
John	SCT	112A
John	NCH	125A
John	SHE	132A
John	TOD	132A
John	SHE	133A
John G.	JEF	46
John M.	FTE	96
John P.	SHE	155
John Y.	GRN	78

Name	County	Page
TAYLOR, John?	PND	31A
Jonathan	HND	5
Jonathan	CLK	103
Jonh.	GRD	95A
Joseph	FKN	56
Joseph	BBN	90
Joseph	WDF	100
Joseph	MAD	104
Joseph	GTN	120
Joseph	GTN	130
Joseph	OHO	5A
Joseph	LWS	98A
Joseph	WTY	113A
Joseph P.	MAD	104
Josephus	FTE	67
Joshua	LVG	11
Joshua	LGN	32
Joshua	WRN	50A
Kenly	WAS	24A
Larking	ETL	41
Leonard	FTE	70
Leonard	CSY	208
Leroy	GRD	107A
Levi T.	WYN	94A
Luke	MNR	211
Malcolm	LVG	8
Margarett	OWN	99
Mary	BTH	196
Mary	OHO	7A
Matthew	BBN	90
Michael	LVG	18
Milley	FTE	58
Moses	WRN	32A
Nancy	MAD	170
Nancy	FLG	30A
Nat.	HRD	78
Nathan	BBN	130
Nathan	GRD	82A
Nineon	HRT	168
Norman	GRD	97A
Petor W.	MAD	180
Philip	FKN	62
Philip W.	SHE	131A
Phillis	NSN	216
Prysilla	HRT	169
R., Col.	FKN	64
Rebecka	BBN	102
Reding	BTL	331
Reubin	JEF	65
Reubin	FTE	96
Richard	JEF	46
Richard	MTG	273
Richard	OHO	4A
Richard	OHO	7A
Richard	WDF	107A
Richardson	LGN	25
Richd.	FKN	122
Richd. A.	GRN	50
Robbert	CBL	14A
Robert	FTE	100
Robert	LWS	97A
Robert	WDF	112A
Robt.	JEF	63
Robt., Jr.	PND	23A
Robt.	PND	16A
Robt.	PND	19A
Robt. Jr.	MAS	80
Robt. L.	FKN	64
Sally	GRN	65
Saml.	ADR	52
Saml.	MAS	52
Samuel	BNE	38
Samuel	MER	111
Samuel	HAR	204
Samuel	LWS	90A
Samuel M.	CLK	102

Name	County	Page
TAYLOR, Sarah	FTE	75
Sarah	MTG	273
Sarah	CBL	14A
Sarah	WRN	38A
Season	BKN	18
Seaton	LNC	51
Silvester	WRN	60A
Simeon	HRT	169
Simon	MBG	140
Solomon	BKN	20
Starky	MER	111
Stephen	BKN	20
Stephen	RCK	84A
Tapley	HAR	184
Tarpley	FLG	41A
Tatton?	MAD	110
Teakle	FKN	148
Thomas	LGN	31
Thomas	BNE	38
Thomas	LGN	43
Thomas	CLK	92
Thomas	MER	117
Thomas	HRL	120
Thomas	SHE	155
Thomas, Senr.	OHO	12A
Thomas	OHO	3A
Thomas	OHO	7A
Thomas	OHO	9A
Thomas	LWS	98A
Thomas W.	WRN	66A
Thompson	JEF	62
Thompson	NSN	186
Thos.	MAD	106
Thos.	WAS	21A
Thos.	GSN	152A
Uriah	ADR	52
Uriah	MER	111
Vincent	CLD	162
Warren	BRK	297
Washington	WRN	73A
William	BNE	38
William	FTE	84
William	HRL	120
William	HAR	134
William	CLD	151
William	SHE	154
William	HRY	182
William	MNR	213
William	CSY	218
William	CSY	220
William	MTG	247
William	OHO	7A
William	WAS	19A
William	WRN	32A
William	WRN	35A
William	WDF	115A
William H.	MER	111
William M.	MER	111
Wittes?	WAS	84A
Wm.	JEF	19
Wm.	JEF	39
Wm.	JEF	55
Wm.	JEF	65
Wm.	BBN	82
Wm.	MAD	102
Wm., Snr	JEF	28
Wm.	FLG	25A
Wm.	PUL	42A
Wm.	FLG	74A
Wm.	WAS	82A
Wm.	RCK	84A
Wm.	SHE	109A
Wm.	SHE	121A
Wm.	GSN	152A
Wm. F.	MAD	90
Zachariah	WDF	103A

Name	County	Page
TAYLOR, Zachriah	JEF	46
Zack	ADR	52
TAYLOR?, -----?	DVS	6A
Judah	JES	78
TAYTON/ TAYTOR?, John	JES	94
TAYTON?, Judah	JES	78
TAYTOR, Dudley	GRD	88A
TEAG, Joshua	WTY	112A
William	WTY	112A
TEAGUE, Abel	LVG	6
Edward	HOP	266
Van S.	HOP	266
William	HOP	266
Wm.	CHN	29
TEAL, Henry	BTH	208
TEALMAN?, Thos.	BKN	20
TEAR?, Samuel	UNN	153
TEASLEY, Jonathan	LNC	65
TEAT, Jacob	ALN	118
TEATER, Robt.	HRY	242
TEATHAM, Isaac	CSY	224
TEATUM, Seath?	CSY	226
TEBBS, Danl.	MAS	61
TEBBS?, Jesse	WRN	63A
TEBLES, Jos.	MAS	71
TEDELL?, Jno.	CWL	57
TEE?, John, Jr.	BKN	18
John, Sr.	BKN	18
TEEFORD?, Wen/ Werr?	BLT	174
TEELE, Isaac	JEF	43
TEER?, Wm.?	CWL	36
TEETER, Jonath.	HRY	269
Polly	HRY	269
Samuel	FTE	110
TEGAR, Adam	LWS	92A
John	LWS	92A
TEGARD, John	GRD	111A
TEGARDEN, Jeremiah	BKN	24
Susan	FTE	112
Wm.	CHN	45
TEISON?, Jacob	CWL	33
TELFORD, Jams?	ADR	52
TELL, Simon	MAS	60
Solomon	MAS	74
TELLEY, Laz.	SHE	138A
Moses	GTN	132
TEMPE, Catharine, Mrs.	GRT	145
TEMPLE, Benjain	LGN	45
Burrel?	ALN	142
Jessee	BKN	22
Jessee	CBL	2A
Margaret	LGN	41
Robert	LNC	35
Robert W.	LGN	43
William	BLT	190
Wyatt	LGN	25
TEMPLEMAN, Henry	FTE	102
Lewis	BTH	194
Matthew D.	FKN	154
Roy	GSN	152A
TEMPLETON, George	WYN	88A
James	CLY	120
John	MER	110
TENIL, Edward	NSN	222
TENISON, Shadrach	SHE	151
TENNANT, Richd.	MAS	56
TENNELL, Josepeh	MAD	102
TENNEY, John	NCH	110A
TENNIC?, John	UNN	150
TENNINGS, Stephen	OHO	9A
TENNIS, John	CBL	5A
Robt.	MAS	70
Saml.	MAS	70

TENNON?, Abner LGN 237
Kerry LGN 238
TENTON, Richd. FLG 35A
TERAULT?, John BLT 196
TEREL?, Michael NSN 180
TEREY, Joseph CLK 86
TERHOON, Isaac SHE 154
TERHUNE, Albert FLG 72A
Barnett MAS 68
David FLG 64A
Drul.? FLG 37A
Garrett FLG 60A
Garrot, Jr. MER 111
Garrot, Sr. MER 110
Garrote MER 111
Isaac MER 110
Isaac FLG 64A
Jable? FLG 65A
Jacob FLG 77A
John MER 111
Luke MAS 68
Saml. FLG 66A
Stephen MER 110
William MER 110
TERIL, (See Terril/ Tevel) MAD 158
TERMON?, Abner LGN 41
Kerry LGN 40
TERPIN, Jeremiah BBN 88
Nathan HRT 169
TERREL?, Archabald WDF 102A
TERRELL, John WAS 55A
M. C. SHE 137A
Oliver GRD 93A
Robert WAS 39A
Thomas LNC 37
Timothy BTH 206
Zachariah SHE 113A
TERRELL?, Jas. RCK 84A
TERRIL, (See Tevil/ Teril) MAD 158
David JES 71
Harry GRD 118A
Jos. GRD 118A
Presley WDF 93A
Wm. MAD 158
TERRILL, Abner CBL 19A
Harry GRD 86A
John BBN 94
John GRD 104A
John J. BBN 128
Lynch HRY 188
Robt. GRD 107A
Solomon KNX 302
Will KNX 302
TERRY, Aaron HRD 30
Champion LVG 3
Elijah GSN 152A
George HOP 266
Isaac FLD 20
Jasper HRD 26
Jno. LVG 6
Joseph LGN 23
Joseph JEF 39
Josiah GSN 152A
Josiah GSN 152A
Leonard FLD 44
Micajah LGN 32
Mildrid TOD 125
Miles FLD 19
Nathaniel TOD 125
Nathl. BRN 29
Reuben NCH 128A
Robert HND 5A
Stephen LNC 15
Stephen TOD 125
TERRY, Stephen TOD 132A
Thomas BRN 28
Thomas HRT 168
Thos. LVG 9
Thos. BBN 60
Thos., Sr. LVG 3
W. T. CHN 46
William FLD 29
Wm. M. TOD 131A
TERRY?, Robert HND 10A
TETER, Nancy GRD 84A
Paris GRD 88A
Paris GRD 118A
TEUME, George MER 110
John, Sr. MER 110
John I./ J.? MER 111
Kimple MER 110
William MER 110
William W. MER 110
TEURTOY?, Michael HAR 216
TEVEL, (See Teril/ Terril) MAD 158
TEVIS, Josiah MAS 60
Samuel SHE 176
TEVIS?, Robert SHE 158
THACKER, Abner BRN 29
Absalom FLD 25
Allen BRN 29
Holt TRG 11A
Joel FKN 138
Lewis FKN 138
Nathl. BRN 29
Tilman SHE 127A
Wm. PUL 45A
THACKER?, Edward ALN 100
THACKSTON, Tho. ALN 112
THAD?, John SCT 135A
THAKER?, Family (With Sam White) LGN 29
THARP, -----? DVS 6A
Alexander MAD 126
And. MAS 71
Geo. HRY 243
Green B. HRT 169
Jamess WAS 51A
Jane HRT 169
Jane SCT 109A
Jeremiah MAD 92
Jesse HAR 168
John SHE 174
John WAS 23A
Peggy MAD 126
Perry WAS 24A
Robt. SCT 109A
Ruth HRT 169
Salley SCT 109A
Samuel BNE 38
Will. SCT 109A
Wilson MER 111
Wm. WAS 23A
Zachariah MAD 150
THATCHER, Daniel BBN 108
John BBN 108
John P. SHE 114A
Jos. BKN 8
Joseph SHE 118A
Wm. BBN 102
Zedic D. SHE 118A
THAY---?, Thos. CWL 46
THEABALD, Clement GRT 139
Griffin P. GRT 139
James GRT 139
Moses GRT 139
THECKER?, Ellen CLD 144
THEOBALD, G. Phil. GRT 149
THEOBALD, William HAR 218
THEOBALDS, Saml. SCT 93A
Thos. SCT 93A
Will. SCT 137A
THERMAN?, William GRN 63
THERMON, Elisha LVG 9
THERSTON?, Joseph BLT 152
THETFORD, Elizabbeth TRG 14A
Gabriel TRG 14A
Simon TRG 13
THICKSTON, Jacob MER 110
THILMAN?, James MNR 197
THINTON, John JEF 33
Lewis JEF 33
THIOBALDS, F. JEF 22
THOMAS--?, Andrew FLG 66A
THOMAS, (See Thos.) MAD ~~112~~
----- Senr. CLD 160
-eridith? CWL 36
Abner S. GNP 173A
Abraham ETL 54
Amos HRY 251
Andrew FTE 60
Ann FKN 54
B-yn? NSN 204
B. P. MAS 54
Bartholomew NSN 218
Basle CBL 17A
Benedict SCT 93A
Benj. WAS 22A
Benjamin CBL 18A
Cealy LNC 75
Chalphan GTN 128
Charles CLD 159
Chas. MAS 67
Clarissa BNE 38
Cullan TRG 6
Daniel BBN 88
Daniel WRN 42A
Daniel LWS 99A
David MAS 71
David BBN 72
David FTE 73
David FTE 79
David BTH 176
Ed. HRY 241
Edmund G. MER 111
Edward HOP 266
Edward NCH 111A
Eleaser NSN 186
Eli BBN 122
Elias PUL 65A
Elijah FLG 47A
Elisha WYN 89A
Elizabeth MER 111
Elizabeth BBN 122
Enoch MER 111
Enoch CBL 12A
Ervin PUL 64A
Ethelrod? TRG 4A
Ezekiel TRG 6A
Fielder MAD 118
Fran. HRY 265
Franklin MAS 57
Geo. JEF 55
George BBN 108
George WAS 67A
George LWS 86A
Hambleton WAS 36A
Hardin HRD 70
Hardin CSY 224
Harrison CSY 224
Henry BKN 26
Henry MAS 57
Henry WAS 74A

THOMAS, Henry WRN 76A
Henry H. MAD 158
Isaac JEF 53
Isaac HRD 60
Isaac MAS 71
Isaac MBG 142
Isaac NSN 186
Isaac GSN 152A
Israel LWS 86A
Ivan WYN 90A
J. CLY 111
Jack GSN 152A
Jacob MAS 77
James TRG 6
James JEF 53
James FTE 102
James CLK 105
James HRL 120
James HAR 136
James GRT 141
James WRN 52A
James WRN 67A
James GSN 152A
James O. W. BNE 38
Jas. HRD 68
Jas. FLG 27A
Jas. FLG 45A
Jas. FLG 46A
Jas. FLG 49A
Jeremiah WRN 45A
Jesse FTE 73
Jesse WRN 45A
Jno. MAS 59
Jno. W. NSN 191
Joel MAD 172
Joel BTH 176
John HRD 24
John BKN 26
John ADR 52
John LNC 61
John ALN 104
John OWN 105
John MER 110
John BBN 122
John CLD 160
John BTH 192
John BTH 216
John CSY 224
John SPN 12A
John SPN 16A
John WRN 45A
John WYN 88A
John LWS 92A
John NCH 111A
John SHE 129A
John SHE 139A
John GNP 177A
John D. CLK 105
John H. MAD 92
John J. BKN 11
Jordan FKN 112
Jos. HRD 30
Jos. HRD 34
Joseph BBN 124
Joseph HAR 152
Joseph HRY 190
Joseph PUL 57A
Joseph GSN 152A
Josiah GNP 177A
Lewis WAS 43A
Lica? OHO 3A
Lucy LNC 81
Luke TRG 12A
Marcus MTG 295
Margaret MAS 59
Margarette MTG 241
THOMAS, Mark NSN 204
Martain CSY 224
Mary MAD 172
Mary FLG 35A
Mathew MAD 122
Matthew HOP 266
Meredith LVG 7
Michael BKN 24
Middleton NSN 204
Moses HRD 18
N. JEF 21
Nancy LNC 75
Nancy NSN 189
Nathan WRN 36A
Nathaniel OHO 9A
Nichademus GSN 152A
Norborne K. JEF 58
Organ BRN 29
Oswell SHE 166
Owen FLD 3
Pendleton HRD 14
Pendleton MER 111
Philip BNE 38
Plummer LWS 88A
Presley MAD 112
Presley N. BRN 29
Presly GRT 141
Priscilla GTN 127
R. N. MAS 52
Redmon G. NSN 204
Richard TRG 3
Richard LGN 29
Richard WDF 102
Richard NSN 222
Richd. JEF 57
Richd. BBN 66
Robert ADR 54
Robert CLD 159
Robert HRY 184
Robert MTG 231
Robert WTY 114A
Robt. HRD 60
Ron HRY 218
Rosil NCH 123A
Rowland LWS 88A
Ruben ADR 64
Rubin GRD 83A
Saml. BKN 24
Saml. HRD 34
Saml. BBN 124
Samuel BLT 190
Samuel WRN 58A
Sarah LGN 27
Soloman LWS 86A
Spencer FKN 112
Talbert MNR 217
Thirten? BKN 18
Thomas BBN 138
Thomas GRT 140
Thomas BRK 297
Thomas CBL 18A
Thomas P. BKN 19
Thompson FKN 132
Thos. HRD 28
Topley? WDF 98
Walter ALN 134
Walter W. NSN 180
William BKN 26
William CLK 76
William OWN 105
William HAR 142
William HAR 164
William BTH 192
William CSY 224
William CBL 17A
William PUL 68A
THOMAS, William WYN 91A
Wm. BKN 8
Wm. BBN 104
Wm. BBN 122
Wm. CHN 40A
Wm. WAS 41A
Wm. WAS 87A
Z. MAS 65
Zachariah WRN 59A
Zadock TRG 12
THOMAS?, Francis W.? BLT 156
John ADR 54
THOMASAN, Salley SCT 131A
THOMASON, Abner MTG 239
Jas. SCT 105A
John SCT 106A
Joseph SCT 127A
Landy NCH 109A
Saml.? SCT 126A
Will SCT 106A
THOMASSON, John H. BBN 90
John J./ I.? BLT 174
Samuel OWN 99
William HOP 266
THOME, Arthur BKN 23
THOMIS, Charles ADR 52
THOMISON, Alice CBL 19A
James CBL 17A
Poyn. HRY 218
THOMMASSON, David H. HOP 266
Samuel D. HOP 266
THOMPKINS, Gabriel WDF 122A
THOMPSON, -----? DVS 7A
----h? DVS 14A
---im? DVS 14A
Abra. MAS 68
Adam TRG 13A
Alexander SHE 164
Alexander PUL 63A
Alexd. CWL 57
Allen SPN 19A
Ambrous WAS 20A
Anderson WDF 108A
Andr. MAS 68
Andrew FLD 45
Andrew MER 111
Andrew UNN 151
Annis WAS 83A
Anthony LWS 89A
Anthony WDF 107A
Archibald MER 111
Austin WAS 53A
Balam? ALN 104
Barnett WAS 40A
Batton NSN 187
Ben HRY 194
Ben. CHN 29
Betsy BTH 210
Bowen LVG 13
Bowen MTG 237
Carter BTL 331
Charles NSN 181
Charles NSN 218
Charles CHN 36A
Charles WAS 63A
Chs. R. FKN 80
Colbert JEF 62
D. MAS 52
Daniel WAS 77A
Daniel NCH 110A
Daved, Sr. GRD 115A
Daved GRD 115A
David BRN 29
David CLK 83

THOMPSON, David WDF 124A
Davis GRD 108A
Drury GRN 79
Ebenezer BKN 18
Ebenezer PUL 52A
Edward BNE 38
Edward BNE 38
Edward WRN 48A
Elijah BKN 4
Elizabeth FTE 69
Elizabeth WRN 63A
Elizh. HRY 216
Evan SHE 170
Frank LNC 79
Gabrial WAS 53A
Gabrial WAS 74A
George FLD 45
George MTG 259
George, Col. MER 111
George WAS 43A
George WRN 66A
George B. BKN 4
George B. MER 115
George W., Capt. MER 111
Gid. TOD 129A
Greenberry SPN 19A
Henry BBN 144
Henry NCH 126A
Horatio BRN 29
Horatio MTG 263
Hugh BRK 297
Hugh D. MTG 295
Isaac BRK 297
James BKN 5
James TRG 10
James BKN 24
James CHN 31
James BNE 50
James JEF 52
James CLK 83
James MER 110
James MER 111
James FKN 134
James HRY 194
James HRY 220
James BRK 297
James BRK 297
James DVS 14A
James PUL 63A
James WRN 65A
James WAS 73A
James GRD 86A
James H. NCH 114A
James M. CHN 34
Jas. CWL 57
Jas., Jr. HRD 18
Jas., Sr. HRD 46
Jas. TOD 124A
Jeremiah WRN 65A
Jno. MAS 59
Jno. MAS 60
Jno. FKN 142
John HND 8
John HRD 14
John BKN 15
John LVG 18
John BRN 29
John CHN 33
John JEF 33
John JEF 37
John JEF 46
John JEF 47
John JEF 63
John MER 111
John BBN 138
John MAD 160

THOMPSON, John BLT 164
John SHE 170
John, Col. MER 111
John, Ser. BRN 28
John OHO 9A
John CBL 13A
John WRN 29A
John CHN 34A
John PUL 35A
John LWS 88A
John SCT 92A
John LWS 98A
John WDF 117A
John NCH 125A
John B. MER 115
John B. GTN 132
John C. BTL 331
John P. BKN 5
John R. CHN 33A
John S. SHE 133A
Jonas LGN 31
Jos. MAS 53
Jos. FLG 37A
Jos. PUL 39A
Josep BTH 206
Joseph JES 89
Joseph MER 110
Joseph NSN 187
Joseph BTH 200
Joseph MTG 237
Joseph MTG 255
Lawrence MAD 152
Lawson CHN 36
Lefford MAS 78
Lloyd MTG 245
M. TOD 126A
Mathew BKN 14
Mathew CLK 83
Matthew LWS 88A
Matthew LWS 89A
Mike GRN 78
Moses FLG 52A
Nancy LNC 3
Nancy HRT 168
Nancy TRG 13A
Nancy WRN 65A
Nathan GRN 63
Nathaniel WDF 108A
Nelson A. LNC 31
Peggy BLT 190
Phillip DVS 19A
Polly MTG 263
Rader MER 111
Ralf MAS 79
Ratliff GRN 79
Reeves UNN 150
Reuben MAS 70
Rhuhama HRY 218
Richard FLD 45
Richard CLK 105
Richard MER 111
Richard BTH 178
Richard NSN 178
Richard SPN 21A
Richard SPN 24A
Richd. WAS 60A
Ro----? MNR 193
Robert L. HRT 171
Robt. BTL 331
S. TOD 133
Saml. LVG 4
Saml. MAS 65
Samuel CHN 34
Samuel LGN 41
Samuel FLD 45
Samuel HRY 190

THOMPSON, Samuel HAR 204
Samuel HRY 218
Samuel CBL 19A
Sarah BLT 190
Sarah WAS 44A
Sarah NCH 117A
Sarah SHE 141A
Stephen WAS 50A
Susan NCH 120A
Susanna FLD 31
T. V., Jr.? TOD 125
Thomas NSN 185
Thomas NSN 189
Thomas NSN 196
Thomas BTL 331
Thomas LWS 98A
Thomas W. NSN 183
Thos. PUL 43A
Thos. A. BBN 128
Thos. G. WAS 54A
Valentine NSN 216
Waddy BRN 29
Wall JEF 23
Will NSN 178
Will. LVG 3
Will. MTG 299
William CHN 29
William GTN 123
William GTN 134
William SHE 164
William NSN 183
William HRY 190
William BTH 198
William HAR 200
William CSY 206
William MTG 255
William, Jr. CBL 21A
William, Sr. NSN 217
William HND 5A
William CBL 21A
William WRN 68A
William LWS 88A
William SHE 123A
Wm C. CHN 27A
Wm. BKN 13
Wm. GRN 70
Wm. HRT 169
Wm. CHN 32A
Wm. SHE 143A
Wm. G. GRD 99A
Wm. L.? JEF 21
Wm. W. BRN 29
THOMPSON?, -----? HND 13
THOMS.?, Wakefield GRN 72
THOMSON, Asa FTE 96
Chas. SCT 132A
Clifton FTE 96
David SCT 126A
Dickerson WYN 93A
Edmond FLG 45A
Eliza SCT 97A
Franky SCT 113A
Fulton FTE 106
Gilbert SCT 106A
James ALN 134
James HAR 142
James NCH 108A
James GNP 167A
Jarvis SCT 135A
John HAR 136
John SCT 128A
John SHE 130A
John GNP 171A
Laurance FLG 58A
Leonard WYN 92A
Martin PND 25A

Name	County	Page
THOMSON, Peter	SCT	105A
Richard	MBG	142A
Robt.	SCT	110A
Rodes	SCT	130A
Salley	SCT	117A
Saml.	NCH	120A
Saml.	SCT	136A
Thomas	HAR	154
Thomas	MBG	135A
Thomas	GNP	168A
Walter	GNP	173A
Will. H.	SCT	125A
William	FTE	98
William	NCH	114A
William	MBG	141A
William Z.	FTE	77
THORMAN, John	LWS	91A
Samuel	LWS	91A
THORN, Anthony	JEF	49
Hanabal	FTE	58
Henry	JEF	40
Henry	JEF	42
Jas.	SCT	103A
John	SHE	165
M., Mrs.	MAS	72
Michael	HRY	240
Saml.	LNC	55
Saml.	HRY	244
Thos.	HRY	263
Thos.	SCT	128A
THORN?, Wakefield, Sr.?	GRN	72
THORNBERRY, Ben	HRD	44
John	BLT	176
Samuel	BLT	176
Seth B.	BLT	180
William	LGN	28
William	UNN	154
William	BLT	196
THORNBURG, Isaac	MTG	291
THORNBURRY, Elijah	SCT	136A
THORNHILL, Reuben	GRT	144
THORNLEY?, Enoch	HAR	150
THORNSBERRY, James	JEF	46
Winnefrey	HND	10A
THORNSBURY, Jno.	MAS	72
Z.	MAS	72
THORNTON, Aaron	WRN	41A
Ann	BBN	124
Anthony	CLD	167
Anthony	HAR	212
Benjamin	BBN	70
Charles	LNC	17
Charles	GRN	68
Charles	CBL	5A
Chs.	JEF	57
F.	JEF	57
George	LNC	31
George	JES	71
James	PND	22A
James	WRN	41A
James	WDF	114A
Jeremiah	MER	111
Jno.	HRY	270
John	JES	86
Jos.	MAS	63
Jos.	MAS	72
Kissey?	GRN	57
Lewis	BBN	138
Mark	CWL	43
Nathl.	SCT	111A
Sarah	PND	27A
Thos.	BBN	70
Thos.	WAS	27A
Toliver	OWN	99
William	BBN	126
THORNTON, Wm.	JEF	44
Wm.	MAD	164
Wm., Sen.	MAS	63
THORNTON?, Elizebeth	WAS	68A
Samuel	ALN	130
THORP, Alexr.	MAS	64
Benjamin	JEF	60
George	HRD	62
John	OHO	3A
THORTON, John	FTE	86
THOS., Athlamus	MAD	114
James	MAD	112
THRAILKILL, Daniel	MER	111
George	MER	111
William	MER	110
THRALEKILL, Dan.	HRY	261
Danl.	BKN	18
THRALKILL, Thos.	HRY	269
THRASHER, Eli	BRK	297
John	BRK	297
John	CBL	16A
Joseph	PND	27A
Josiah	PND	27A
Rosanna	CBL	18A
Stephen	PND	27A
THRAULS?, Isaac	NSN	188
Joseph	NSN	214
THREET?, Isham	CWL	57
THREFT, Charles	CHN	42
Chas.	CHN	41
THREILKILL, Daniel	UNN	148
Tho.	ALN	128
THRELDKILL, Ann	FLG	35A
John	FLG	35A
Wm.	FLG	35A
THRELKELD, Aron	LVG	9
Elijah	OWN	101
Gabriel	LVG	3
John	SHE	172
Thomas	SHE	169
William	SHE	169
THRELKILL, Geo.	SCT	118A
Peter	BRN	29
Thomas	HAR	158
Will.	SCT	139A
THRESHER, William	CLD	151
THRIFT, Charles	CHN	35A
Saml. M.	CHN	35A
Tobitha	FTE	86
THROCKMORTON, Jas. E.	LVG	2
John	NCH	126A
Thomas, Jr.	NCH	105
Thomas, Sr.	NCH	105
THROGMORTON, Aris?	BBN	144
Feby	FKN	56
Wm.	GNP	173A
THRONHILL, John	GRT	142
THRUSTON, Bartlett	LNC	15
Benjamin	BRN	29
Fitzhughs J?.	JEF	20
THUILT?, Jno.	HRY	268
THUMAN?, William	GRN	63
THURBY, James	MNR	197
Robert	MNR	197
THURMAN, Andrew	CLD	165
Andrew	SHE	173
Anny	ALN	116
Baze	NSN	218
Charles	CLD	142
Charles	CLD	164
Edmund	SHE	131A
Fountain	WDF	92
Henderson	MAD	132
James	MER	110
THURMAN, John	GRN	52
John	MER	110
John	MAD	122
John	CLD	164
Joshua	GRD	87A
Littleberry	CLD	150
Nathan	CLD	150
Richard	MAD	122
William	CLD	165
William C.	CLD	166
Wm.	ALN	116
THURMON, Benj.	PUL	47A
Bennett	LNC	35
John C.	LNC	3
THURMOND, Charles	LNC	81
Henry	LNC	81
Martha	LNC	35
Philip	LNC	35
Phill	WAS	28A
Thos.	WAS	51A
Wm.	WAS	36A
Wm.	WAS	51A
THURSTON, (No Given Name)	JEF	23
Ezekiel	SHE	169
Leonard	SHE	125A
Robt.	HRY	263
William	WRN	36A
Wm. P.	BBN	120
TIBBATTS, Thomas	FTE	58
TIBBITTS, George	CBL	19A
John	CBL	20A
TIBBS, ----m?	DVS	9A
Ben	JEF	22
Danl.	MAS	69
George	GRN	62
James	MAS	53
James	WRN	67A
John	GRN	62
Wm. T.	FLG	32A
TIBBS?, Jesse	WRN	63A
TIBBY, Saml.	FLG	68A
TICEAN, Maclin	SCT	98A
TICHENER, James	NSN	207
Peter	NSN	211
TICHENOR, Daniel	NSN	211
Daniel	OHO	7A
Jared	OHO	8A
Jonas	OHO	7A
Joseph	NSN	213
Thomas	NSN	211
William	NSN	211
TICHENORE, Timothy	OHO	9A
TICHNOR, Silas	NSN	211
TIDNOE, Elizabeth	WTY	116A
Nancy	WTY	116A
TIDWELL?, Hugh	BBN	120
TIERNAGE, James	WRN	36A
TIFFEE, Chas.	SCT	101A
TIFFEY, Catlet	SCT	116A
TIFFINE, Robert	BRK	297
TIGG, Benj.	SHE	121A
TIGLER, William	LGN	25
TIGNER, Benjamin	DVS	17A
TILFORD, Alexr.	SCT	128A
Andrew	OHO	11A
Andrew	GSN	152A
James	MER	111
Jeremiah	OHO	3A
John	BRN	29
John	FTE	55
Robert	FTE	55
TILL, John	JEF	31
Wm.	JEF	22
TILLER, (Free)	CLD	162
James	WRN	34A

TILLER, James WDF 117A
Jno. FKN 106
John HRY 210
TILLERY, William WDF 99
William, Jr. WDF 116A
TILLET, John MAD 92
TILLETT, John BBN 108
TILLETT?, Wm. BBN 106
TILLEY, Aaron SHE 112A
John ALN 94
Laz. SHE 113A
Wm. SHE 126A
TILLMAN, G. CHN 28A
TILLOTSON, William WTY 127A
TILLY, Benjamin JES 78
TILMAN, Geo. TOD 132
TILMAN?, D. TOD 127
TILMON, J. B. ADR 52
TILTON, Peter FTE 70
TIMBELECK?, John WAS 61A
TIMBERLAKE, George W. HAR 218
Henry BBN 148
Heny/ Herry? BBN 144
Joseph CLD 157
Oba S. GNP 178A
Oba S. GNP 179A
Phillip CLD 157
Phillip CBL 11A
Thornton CBL 15A
TIMBERLICK, John MAD 92
William MER 111
TIMBERLOCK, Joseph GRN 76
TIMBLE?, Robert MTG 229
TIMENS, Abner HOP 268
Betsy HOP 268
Elijah HOP 266
Fielding HOP 268
George HOP 268
John HOP 266
Stephen HOP 268
Toliver HOP 268
TIMMONS, Nimrod MER 111
Wm. OHO 9A
TIMMS, William, Jr. MNR 213
TIMONS, Wm. CHN 38
TIMPY, Jacob FTE 106
TINALL?, John BNE 38
TINCHEN/TINCHER?, John ETL 53
TINCHER, (See Fincher?) CLY 116
Robert MAD 120
Samuel MAD 120
William BTH 210
TINDAL, Jas. CHN 42A
Samuel MER 111
TINDALL, Moses CWL 39
TINDELL, Polly HRD 14
TINDER, Elijah SHE 151
James OWN 99
James WDF 124A
Jas. SCT 125A
William S. WRN 74A
TINDLE, John BRK 297
Susannah BRK 299
TINERAL?, Robert CLK 95
TINGLE, Edd. HRY 250
Jas. HRY 258
Jeptha SCT 105A
Jessee FTE 104
Jno. HRY 258
Kindal HRY 258
Lit. HRY 255
Littleton HRY 252
TINKER, Ralph HRD 30
TINLEY, Samuel MTG 237
Wm. SHE 112A
TINLEY?, Emily KNX 306
TINNEY, Charles GRD 91A
TINSLEY, Caleb FKN 134
Coleby BRN 29
David ADR 52
Elijah ALN 136
Enoch FLG 49A
Henry FKN 134
James LNC 35
James, Jr. LNC 35
James MBG 135A
Jane BRN 29
Jas. FLG 54A
John TRG 5
John BRN 29
John LNC 43
John FTE 75
John SHE 150
Joseph GNP 174A
Mary SHE 110A
Polly CLK 78
R. TOD 131
Sam. SHE 116A
Samuel SHE 110A
Samuel MBG 135A
Steph. F. LNC 35
Thomas MTG 267
Thos. KNX 286
William BRN 29
William HRL 120
Wm. TOD 131
Wm. SHE 110A
TINSLY, Charles NSN 187
TINSTALL, Bell &? JEF 22
TIPES, Jacob SCT 110A
TIPPET, Alice CBL 12A
Jas. BBN 72
John HAR 184
TIPPETT, John CBL 9A
TIPPITT, Jo. GRD 96B
TIPTON, Alexis MTG 259
Daniel MAD 134
Daniel MAD 138
Elizabeth MAD 174
Esram? MTG 295
John MTG 265
Mitchell MTG 229
Reuben S. ETL 43
Samuel ETL 49
William LVG 18
William ETL 41
William MTG 231
TIRPIN, Nathan JES 78
TISDALE, Henry MAS 52
John LNC 51
Sarah HAR 132
William LNC 51
Willm., Sen. LNC 51
TISDELL, Jno. CWL 58
Sussanna MAD 130
Wilson MER 110
TISSON?, Gowen? CWL 35
TISTER, Daniel O. WRN 73A
TITCHENOR, Jacob SHE 134A
James SHE 134A
Lewis SHE 134A
TITCHINER, John MER 110
TITES, Wm. MAD 94
TITSWORTH, John LVG 13
TITSWORTH?, William LVG 18
TITTERINGTON, Adam CLD 150
TITTERTON, Richard MGB 137A
TITTERTON, Thomas MGB 137A
TITTLE, Henery CBL 19A
TITUS, Ebinezar MAD 92
George GTN 119
Harris NCH 107A
John GTN 119
TIVIS, Jeremiah MAD 148
Jessee MAD 180
Nancy MAD 136
Robert MAD 130
Thomas S. BNE 38
Thos. MAD 90
TIVIS?, Robt. BKN 8
TOADVINE?, Purnal HAR 184
TOALY, George ADR 54
TOBBLE?, Geo. MAS 77
TOBIN, George CLD 166
Joseph H.,, M.d. CLD 143
Robert CLD 142
TOD, William FTE 66
TODD, Abraham WDF 107A
Anderson PUL 40A
Andrew SHE 153
Andrew GRD 93A
Ann MAD 170
Benjamin LGN 42
Benjamin BBN 112
Benjamin MAD 160
Benjamin WRN 59A
Benjamin L. HOP 266
Chs. FKN 70
Daniel MAD 118
Elizabeth PUL 68A
Geo. FKN 68
Henry MAD 166
Isaac MAD 126
Jeremiah MAD 128
Jesse BBN 120
Jessey MAD 124
Jno. JEF 50
Jno. FKN 68
John FTE 103
John BBN 108
John MAD 124
John MTG 225
John, Jr. FLG 64A
John WRN 45A
John FLG 63A
Johnston SHE 119A
Jonathan HOP 266
Joseph MAD 156
Joseph CBL 2A
Joshua HOP 266
Levi L. MTG 299
Levin BBN 138
Mary BBN 146
Mary SHE 126A
Peter MAD 124
Peter MAD 128
Polly CLY 111
Robert SHE 176
Robert WRN 72A
Robert S. FTE 58
Robt. JEF 41
Robt. ADR 52
Samuel GTN 121
Samuel GTN 132
Samuel CBL 21A
Samuel SHE 121A
Thomas HOP 266
Thos. FKN 56
Thos. MAD 126
Thos. FLG 64A
William FTE 112
William PUL 61A
Wm. HRD 42

Name	County	Page
TODD, Wm.	MAD	148
Wm.	MAD	166
TODD?, Richd.	SCT	125A
Sally	FTE	99
TODHUNTER, Jacob	JES	83
John	JES	73
TOIRENCE, Elbert	HRD	50
TOLAND, Morgan	CLK	92
TOLBERT, Benjamin	BTL	331
James	LVG	18
Joshua	BTL	331
Thos.	JEF	66
TOLBOT, Gasway	SCT	117A
TOLER, Christopher	GNP	166A
Robt.	GNP	167A
William P.	JES	89
TOLES, Henry	BBN	64
TOLIFER, James	BNE	38
TOLIN, Alexander	MTG	283
Elias	FLD	15
Elias	MTG	271
Porterfield	MTG	283
TOLIVER, Edmond	MAS	81
Joel	FLD	12
TOLL, Will. G.	MAS	78
TOLLE, Jeremiah	LWS	93A
John	LWS	92A
Joseph	LWS	93A
Matthias	LWS	92A
Stephen	LWS	93A
Susanna	LWS	92A
TOLLEY, Isaac D.	FLD	6
James	FLD	6
Jane	MER	110
Nelson	MER	111
Sally	MER	110
William, Jr.	MER	110
William, Sr.	MER	110
TOLLS, Stephen	MAS	62
TOLLS?, Reuben	MAS	61
TOLLY, Jno.	LVG	10
Samuel	FLD	6
William	FLD	6
TOLOMON, Lewis	MBG	142
TOLOVER, Francis	GRN	61
TOLSON, Thomas	FLD	3
TOLSTON?, Thos.	MAD	104
Wm.	MAD	100
TOMASON, Robt.	SCT	125A
Stephen	SCT	123A
TOMBERLIN, Lewis	LGN	27
TOMBLIN, Ambrose	MAD	130
George	MAD	92
Jas.	SCT	132A
Jeremiah	MAD	92
Joel	MAD	150
Will.	SCT	132A
TOMBS, Agnes	SHE	111A
Ambrose	LNC	17
Gabriel	JEF	65
John	SHE	111A
Sally	PUL	67A
TOMES, Jesse	LNC	7
TOMES?, William	HRY	214
TOMKINS, Robt.	HRD	50
William	CLD	152
TOMLIN, Christian	PND	28A
TOMLINSON, Ambrose	FTE	80
Elizabeth	FTE	80
Hamilton	JES	81
James	MNR	211
James	HAR	220
Jas.	CWL	57
John	BNE	38
John A., Dr.	MER	115
William	BNE	38

Name	County	Page
TOMLINSON, Wm.	BKN	23
TOMPKINS, Archibald	BTH	204
Christopher	BRN	29
Edward	LNC	67
Elias	MER	111
G--yn? R.	FTE	77
Grisham	CLY	122
Jame	CBL	8A
James	HOP	268
John	JES	84
John	BRK	297
Nathan	HAR	216
Robt.	JEF	47
William	HOP	268
TOMPSON, Harrey/ Haney?	CLK	95
Hiram	PUL	40A
James	WAS	47A
John	CLK	70
Jos.	RCK	77A
Joseph	CLK	71
Mary	GSN	152A
Mr.	RCK	76A
Nancy	MAD	144
Squire	RCK	79A
William	BNE	38
Wm.	RCK	79A
TOMS, Anderson	GSN	152A
TOMSON, John	GTN	127
TONCRA?, Ezra	LWS	93A
TONCRAY, Daniel	NSN	207
Elizabeth	SHE	122A
TONEY, Jesse, Jr.	BRN	29
Joab	BRN	34
Tarlton W.	BTH	198
TONEY?, John	HAR	216
TONG, Joseph F.	NSN	196
TONGET?, Ephraim	GRT	143
TOOD, David	FKN	130
Joseph	ADR	54
TOOD?, Richd.	SCT	125A
Sarah	GRN	76
TOOL, Daniel	SHE	177
Dennis	NSN	195
John	MAD	122
William	BTL	331
Wm.	MAD	94
TOOLEY, Arthur	MNR	191
James	MGB	137A
John	MBG	137
Patsy	MGB	137A
William	MNR	191
TOOLEY?, James	GRD	102A
TOOLY, Polley	MAD	124
TOOLY?, John	DVS	15A
TOOMY, Jno.	HRY	262
Mathew	SCT	135A
TOON, Stanishlaus	WAS	18A
TOON?, Benjamin	GTN	117
John	GTN	117
Josiah	GTN	117
TOOPMERE?, John	BRK	297
TOOTON, Jo.	GRD	118A
TOPASS, James	SCT	104A
John	SCT	111A
TOPING, Saml. W.	SHE	143A
TORBET, Samuel	WDF	93A
TORBIT, James	WDF	95A
Robert	WDF	99A
TORIAN?, Jacob	TRG	4A
TORRENS, James	BTL	331
TORROWMAN?, Tho.	MAS	57
TORYAN, Peter	CHN	41A
TOSH, John	MNR	191
TOSON?, George	SCT	91A

Name	County	Page
TOTH?, William	FTE	56
TOTLY?, William	WRN	57A
TOTSTON, James	MAD	150
TOUBT, Basil	FLG	62A
Benj.	FLG	62A
Wm.	FLG	62A
TOUSEY?, Moses	BNE	38
Thomas	BNE	38
Zerah	BNE	38
TOUSLY, John	JEF	45
TOUSO, C.	JEF	26
TOUT, Abram	FLG	29A
TOUYAN?, Geo.	CHN	42A
TOWER, Matthew	HRD	38
TOWL?, Jonathan	BBN	136
TOWLER, Elisha	BRN	29
Luke	NCH	112A
William	BRN	28
TOWLES, George	GRN	72
Joseph	GRN	70
Larking S.	HND	5A
Raughley T.	WDF	100A
Thos.	HND	11A
TOWNES, Henry	HND	11A
TOWNLEY, Jno.	FKN	76
TOWNLY, Mann	CHN	38
TOWNS, Baxter D.	HOP	272
TOWNSAND, John, Jr.	ADR	52
John, Sen.	ADR	52
Wm.	ADR	52
TOWNSEN, ----?	MAD	166
Edwin	MER	111
Thos.	MAD	160
TOWNSEND, Elizabeth	WRN	47A
George	LGN	38
George	GSN	152A
James	ETL	40
James	UNN	146
John	OHO	3A
Joseph M.	NCH	116A
Joshua	NCH	128A
Light	LGN	44
Light, Jr.	LGN	38
Mary	LGN	45
Peter	NCH	116A
Thomas	LGN	38
William	NCH	116A
William	NCH	128A
Wm.	SHE	140A
TOWNSIN, Peter	WAS	80A
TOWNSON, Henry	SHE	153
TOWSON, Mary	FKN	160
TOY, Joseph	BTL	331
TR---, Thos.	ADR	52
TR---L?, John	GTN	126
TRABU-?, Robt.	ADR	52
TRABU?, Danl.	ADR	52
TRABUE, George W.	BRN	34
Haskins	LGN	32
Jane	WDF	119A
Robert	ADR	71
Stephen	LGN	32
TRACE?, Henry	LVG	18
TRACENRIDER, Coonrod	JEF	36
Samuel	JEF	36
TRACEY, Jeremiah	FKN	118
Jno.	FKN	108
TRACY, Asa	CLK	66
Charles	CLK	66
Elsey	GRD	117A
Erasmus	BRN	29
Geo.	GRD	121A
Hetty?	GRD	121A

Name	County	Page
TRACY, Isaac	BRN	29
Isaac	ALN	140
Isaac	LWS	90A
James	ALN	140
James	HRY	208
Jessee	LWS	98A
John	HRY	206
Jonathan	LWS	87A
Sebert	GRD	109A
Soloman	LWS	90A
Solomon	MAD	164
William	HRY	200
Wm.	GRD	121A
TRAGG?, William, Senr.	CLD	150
TRAHOON?, Steph.	HRY	257
TRAIL, Elizabeth	ALN	96
Solomon	SPN	4A
TRAIL?, John	CBL	10A
TRAILER, George	CLD	147
James	SHE	127A
John	CWL	33
Nancy	FLG	44A
Wm.	CWL	33
TRAILOR, Cary	FLG	52A
Lawson	FLG	73A
TRAINER, Elizebeth	WDF	103A
TRAINNER, James	SPN	20A
John	SPN	21A
TRAINUM, John	LNC	19
TRAMELL?, David	LVG	18
TRAMSIL?, William	WDF	99
TRANER?, James	CBL	3A
TRANNELL, John	BLT	166
TRANSEL, John	ALN	120
Sampson	ALN	118
TRAPNET?, Philip	MER	111
TRAVELSBUCK, Wm.	ALN	102
TRAVELSTREET?, Frederick	ALN	104
Jno.	ALN	106
TRAVERS, Charles	ALN	92
Henry	ALN	94
James	ALN	92
John	ALN	92
Tho.	ALN	92
TRAVIS, --hn?	DVS	9A
Barba	SPN	8A
James	LVG	18
James	SHE	161
James, Jr.	LVG	13
John	LVG	13
John	SHE	158
Jos.	SHE	124A
Martha	LVG	13
Phebe	LGN	46
Sinclair	MER	114
William	LVG	7
TRAVY, Christian	CBL	7A
TRAWDRIDGE?, Silas	BNE	38
TRAYLOR, Agnes	BTH	196
Cary	BTH	180
Joel	BTH	212
John	BTH	204
John	BTH	212
Nicholas	BTH	198
Rubin	BTH	212
TREACLE, Mrs.	MAS	80
TREADWAY, John	MTG	289
John, Sr.	MTG	271
Moses	MTG	291
William	CLK	86
William	CLK	88
TREANOR, Abraham	HRD	86
Wm.	HRD	48
TREBLE, Andrew	MAD	174
TREBLE, Harris Jeremiah	BRN	29
Peter	MAD	174
Silas	MAD	160
TREFSNER?, Jacob	GRD	111A
TRELL?, John	NCH	123A
TREMBLE, Alexr.	FLG	48A
TREMSHOW?, Adam	BBN	104
Geo.	BBN	104
TRENT, Alexander	BRN	29
Alexander	HRT	169
Benjamin	HRD	10
Henry	BRN	29
James	WAS	49A
John	HRD	54
John	LWS	94A
John H.	BRK	297
Lyda	FLD	39
Nancy	BRN	29
Nicholas	BRK	297
Robert	WYN	82A
Williamson	GRN	53
TRENTS?, Joshua? -.?	GRN	51
TREPNER?, Jacob	GRD	111A
TRESSNER?, Jacob	GRD	111A
TREWITT, Andrew	SHE	157
TRIBBLE, -----?	DVS	3A
Andrew	SHE	164
Orson	CLK	76
Samuel	CLK	80
William	GRN	62
TRIBBY, Benj.	FLG	56A
Jacob	FLG	47A
Jason	FLG	71A
John	FLG	78A
Jos.	FLG	74A
Wm.	FLG	56A
TRIBEN/ TRIBEW?, Robert	BBN	136
S. H.	BBN	136
TRIBUE?, Ephraiam	JES	95
TRICE, Dabnah	HOP	266
Patsy	MNR	213
William	MNR	213
TRICKLE, Thos.	FLG	28A
TRIGG, Alanson	BRN	28
Allen	BBN	126
Danl.	JEF	50
Mary	JEF	50
Simeon	HOP	266
Stephen	ETL	47
Thomas	NCH	111A
Wm.	JEF	50
Wm., Jr.	JEF	44
TRIGSBY?, Susanah	FLG	48A
TRIM, Chas.	CWL	43
TRIMBLE, David	MTG	253
David	MTG	257
Elizabeth	BBN	128
Forgis	BBN	66
Hugh	MTG	263
Isaac	MTG	243
James	HAR	136
James	HAR	216
James	MTG	295
James	WYN	89A
Jno.	HAR	136
John	LGN	36
John	JES	87
John	FTE	106
John	MTG	255
John	FLG	53A
Mark	FLD	11
Robert	BBN	108
Robt.	GRT	150
TRIMBLE, Thomas	BBN	104
Thos.	FLG	51A
William	FLD	11
William	LGN	47
William	CLK	100
William, Senr.	PUL	66A
William	PUL	54A
Wm.	FLG	69A
Wm. C.	FLG	69A
TRIMBLE?, Robert	MTG	229
TRIPLET, Cajah	ADR	62
Frederick	HRD	56
Hedgeman	MAS	57
Jas.	BBN	72
Joel	ADR	52
John	ADR	62
Lewis	ADR	52
Nimrod	ADR	62
Sennet	SCT	125A
Thos.	ADR	52
Thos.	BBN	122
Wm.	ADR	62
TRIPLETT, Chs.	FKN	80
George	BLT	188
Hedgerman	FKN	84
Hedgman	FKN	98
Jas.	FLG	56A
Jno.	MAS	60
John	WDF	113A
Laurance	FLG	51A
Phillip	DVS	19A
Robert	DVS	19A
Thomas	BTH	182
Thomas	MTG	299
TRIPPELETT, Lewis	HRD	70
TRIPTER, Wm.	ADR	52
TRISTER, Abraham	JES	90
Jacob	JES	90
TRISTER?, Abraham	JES	85
TRITE?, Eli	TRG	14A
TROBER, Henry	LGN	39
Henry, Junr.	LGN	39
Michael	LGN	39
William	LGN	40
William, Junr.	LGN	39
TROBRIDGE, Jonathan	CLK	70
TROMPT, Frederick	LGN	44
TROOP, Geo. L.	SCT	91A
TROOP?, John	CWL	46
TROSEWELL, Peter	WYN	94A
TROSPER, Elijah	KNX	282
James	KNX	302
John	KNX	302
Nichol.	KNX	280
Robert	KNX	278
TROTT, Saml.	SCT	139A
TROTTER, Charles	HRT	169
David	WDF	93A
Eliza	FTE	63
George, Senr.	FTE	55
James	FTE	101
Jas.	SCT	117A
Joseph	BBN	82
Nancy	BBN	82
Polly	CLD	153
Robert M.	SHE	138A
Samuel	FTE	55
Widow	BBN	82
Wm.	FKN	100
Wm.	HRT	169
TROTTER?, Joseph	BKN	19
TROTWELL, Agness	BBN	94
TROUP, Jacob	GRD	96B
TROUT, Daniel	GTN	130
Daniel, Senr.	GTN	127

TROUT, Jeremiah GTN 129
John FLD 29
Wendle FKN 94
TROUTMAN, Abraham BLT 164
Isaac BRK 299
Jacob FTE 90
Jacob BLT 156
John HOP 268
Leonard NSN 180
Leonard P. NSN 217
Peter BBN 110
Philip B. BLT 156
TROWBRIDGE, Ebenezer LNC 21
Isaac LNC 15
TROWDRIDGE?, Silas BNE 38
TROWEN / TROWER?
Henry MER 111
Samuel MER 111
Solomon, Jr. MER 111
Solomon, Sr. MER 111
TROWER?, (See Trowen) MER 111
TROXEL, Frederick OHO 5A
Frederick GSN 152A
Henery GSN 152A
John OHO 5A
TROXEL?, John GTN 126
TROXWELL, Daniel WYN 101A
Jane, Mrs. WYN 98A
TROY, Michael SCT 106A
TRUAX, Edward NSN 222
TRUAX?, Edward NSN 185
TRUE, Benjn. MAS 57
Henry MAS 54
James JES 73
James FTE 94
James FTE 94
Jas. MAS 53
John FTE 94
John SCT 94A
John SCT 123A
John F. FTE 69
Robbert CBL 17A
Robert JES 92
Robert JES 92
Robert FTE 110
Robert G. OWN 102
Simeon SCT 131A
Thomas FTE 102
William E. FTE 94
TRUEMAN, Henry HRD 60
TRUESDALE, Jessee LWS 95A
William GTN 121
TRUET?, Jese HRY 265
Thomas NCH 126A
TRUETT, Jos. MAS 54
Tapman SCT 118A
Will MAS 60
TRUGSDALE?, Mary CBL 8A
TRUITT, John B. LGN 41
Mary FLG 24A
Sax. FLG 24A
TRULOVE, Timothy GRD 96B
Will A. GRD 96B
TRUMAN, Aron LVG 13
Bemona JEF 57
Jesse SHE 168
John SHE 171
Walter NSN 183
Walter, Jr. NSN 213
William SHE 161
TRUMBO, Andrew BTH 194
Andrew, Snr. BTH 194
Jacob BTH 196
TRUMBO, John BTH 196
TRUMP, Roda HRT 169
TRUNNELS?, Daniel BBN 130
Hester BBN 144
TRUNYON?, Evan? MAS 65
TRUSSELL, John LWS 92A
TRUSTY, William FLD 22
Wm. GNP 169A
TRUYSDALE, Solomon CBL 22A
TRYN?, Elijah RCK 82A
TRYSDALE, John CBL 22A
TUBBS, Cyrus GTN 122
TUBS, Jessey MAD 132
TUCKER, Alexander HRY 228
Allen CHN 38
Amy HAR 134
Archibald CLK 65
Arin CHN 40A
Asa CLK 65
Benjamin NSN 222
Boothe HRY 228
Charles CBL 19A
Chas. CHN 31A
Clarke HRD 18
Dabney ADR 54
Dandridge ADR 54
Daniel UNN 148
Edward BKN 4
Edward SHE 141A
Eli BKN 4
Elias BBN 140
Elitia HRY 269
Ezekiel HND 6A
George CWL 57
George HRY 228
Henry UNN 154
Hiram SCT 111A
Isaac LNC 59
Jacob HRD 84
Jacob, Junr. HRD 84
James CLK 65
James UNN 148
James BLT 194
James H. WAS 29A
James L. WAS 26A
Jas. HRY 256
Jno. MAS 71
Jno. B. HAR 156
John BKN 10
John BBN 140
John NSN 200
John NSN 204
John BRK 297
John CHN 31A
John SCT 110A
Joseph BBN 120
Josh TOD 128
Joshua SHE 119A
Kelsy CLK 82
Larinion? LVG 18
M. TOD 132A
Martha ADR 54
Mary HRY 206
Mary CHN 31A
Mathew GRN 77
Meshack NSN 204
Moses WRN 49A
Nathan CLK 72
Nathan, Senr. HRD 72
Paskel GRN 53
Philip LNC 47
Rebecca WRN 50A
Robert FTE 106
Robert CSY 208
Saly LNC 35
Saml.? CHN 30
TUCKER, Samuel HAR 156
Samuel NCH 115A
Thomas BKN 4
Thornton MAS 72
Thos. WAS 86A
Thos. SHE 134A
Truman NSN 198
William FTE 61
William BBN 140
William HAR 212
William BRK 299
William CBL 15A
Wm. ADR 54
Zacariah LNC 35
Zackariah CBL 20A
TUDER, Daniel MAD 98
Daniel MAD 98
Henry BRN 29
John BRN 29
John, Jr. MAD 98
John, Sr. MAD 98
Nancy BRN 29
Saml. MAD 98
Saml. MAD 116
Thos. MAD 148
Valentine MAD 94
TUDER?, John E. LVG 10
TUDOR, John FTE 80
Slathel? FTE 73
Thomas FTE 65
TUEL, Joseph WAS 77A
Redrick NSN 217
Roderick NSN 211
TUEL?, Michael NSN 180
TUGGLE, Benj. KNX 300
Charles CLK 75
Ebenezer FLG 51A
Griffin WDF 95
Henry WYN 80A
Jas., Sr. KNX 288
Margaret PUL 42A
Thos. KNX 296
William CLK 69
William PUL 55A
TUGMAN, Edwd. CLY 111
TULEY?, John BLT 170
TULFER?, Hannah CLD 146
TULL, Andrew GRT 141
Handy WDF 122A
Handy NCH 127A
James JEF 34
Jessee NCH 128A
John NCH 123A
Levi BKN 9
Samuel FTE 105
Samuel GRT 141
Samuel CBL 18A
TULLEY, Saml. SCT 133A
TULLUST?, Jane CBL 11A
TULLY, John LWS 87A
Leonard FLG 34A
William WRN 46A
William LWS 87A
TULTON?, James GNP 165A
TULY, Elizabeth JEF 55
TUMBLESTON, Sarah SCT 95A
TUMEY?, Samuel SHE 173
TUMLINSON, John ETL 39
TUMMELSON, John PUL 52A
Nathaniel PUL 68A
TUMY?, John MNR 215
TUNE?, Henry OWN 105
TUNGATE, Akillas WAS 27A
John GRD 98A
Peter GRD 109A
TUNLY, John JES 76

TUNNEL, John WDF 125A
TUNNELL, Daniel NSN 206
  John MNR 207
  Nicholas MNR 217
  Stephen MNR 215
TUNSTAL, Joseph T. BRN 29
  Leonard H. BRN 28
TUNSTALL, John O.? LVG 18
  John P. JEF 25
  Milicent FKN 68
  Richard MAD 162
  William I./ J.? SHE 176
TUNSTATO?, H. R. JEF 25
TUNSTEL?, Richard, Sr. MAD 134
TUPENAIR?, Wm. ADR 52
TUPENAN?, Wm. ADR 52
TUPMAN, Thomas CBL 19A
TURBAVILLE, James HOP 266
TUREMAN, Thomas WDF 109A
  Wm. MAS 76
TURK, Robt. HRY 270
  Thos. ADR 52
TURLEY, Aaron ALN 128
  Charles MTG 297
  Charles B. NCH 121A
  David MTG 261
  John CLD 159
  John MTG 251
  Sampson HRD 56
  Samson CHN 45A
  Samuel MTG 263
  William MTG 229
  William HOP 268
TURMAN, James HOP 266
TURMAN?, James CHN 29
  John FLD 47
TURNACE, Thos. SHE 142A
TURNBO, John HRD 90
TURNBULL, James FTE 95
  Sarah, Mrs. CLK 103
TURNER, Adin BRN 29
  Alfred HND 12
  Ann LNC 9
  Ann FLG 28A
  Arthur HRY 260
  Asa HND 9
  Barrey MAD 112
  Bartholomew G. WTY 112A
  Beevins? CBL 4A
  Berry HRL 120
  Caleb LNC 67
  Catharine WDF 95A
  Charles MER 111
  Chas. CWL 57
  Dabney BRN 29
  Daniel MER 111
  David BNE 38
  David CLY 112
  Edward BKN 14
  Edward FTE 101
  Edward MAD 116
  Edward CLY 121
  Elias HND 9
  Ezekial HAR 198
  George MTG 295
  George WYN 87A
  George E. FTE 83
  George P. CLD 141
  Hannah HRY 198
  Isaac GRT 139
  Jabe- ADR 52
  James BKN 9
  James TRG 14
  James FLD 30
  James LGN 35

TURNER, James ADR 52
  James GRN 59
  James MAD 90
  James CLY 127
  James CLD 140
  James CLD 147
  James, Jr.? WYN 90A
  James WYN 90A
  James GRD 115A
  James GRD 120A
  James GSN 152A
  Jas. CLY 120
  Jas. CHN 41A
  Jeremiah CLD 141
  Jesse, Sr. CLY 120
  Joel FLG 28A
  John BNE 38
  John CLY 120
  John HRL 120
  John, Sr.? PND 26A
  John SPN 15A
  John PND 18A
  John PND 31A
  John WRN 62A
  John WYN 89A
  John WYN 91A
  John WDF 98A
  John WDF 101A
  John WYN 102A
  John A. BTH 186
  Joseph HRL 120
  Joseph MAD 178
  Joshua HRY 252
  Josiah WAS 70A
  Larken CLD 140
  Levi LGN 24
  Levi LGN 45
  Levi WRN 76A
  Lewis FLG 28A
  Lewis E. FTE 107
  Lynch MAD 162
  Martin MAD 150
  Mary LNC 37
  Mathew JES 87
  Mathew BRK 297
  Meshack NSN 199
  Nathan WTY 125A
  Nelson FTE 94
  Philip MAD 116
  Polley MAD 98
  Polly LGN 35
  Polly MAD 154
  Reuben CLD 146
  Reubin CBL 10A
  Reubin PND 15A
  Rich ADR 52
  Richd. BBN 144
  Robert LGN 28
  Robert BBN 124
  Robert BBN 130
  Robert BTH 182
  Robert NCH 127A
  Robt. JEF 42
  Robt. CHN 44
  Robt. BBN 88
  Roger CLY 120
  Roger, Jr. CLY 121
  Rubin GSN 152A
  Sally HRD 58
  Sally WDF 94A
  Sam. HRY 268
  Samuel CLK 99
  Samuel GTN 124
  Sarah SHE 138A
  Smith ADR 52
  Squire MAD 180

TURNER, Starling MER 110
  Suddith D. FLD 31
  Thom CWL 57
  Thomas CLY 120
  Thos. MAD 112
  Thos. MAD 150
  Thos. MAD 164
  Thos., Sr. CLY 120
  Thos. PND 29A
  Thos. SCT 130A
  Tillden L. GRN 54
  William HND 12
  William LGN 40
  William GRN 54
  William GRN 62
  William CLY 120
  William HRL 120
  William BLT 162
  William WYN 88A
  William WDF 95A
  William GRD 97A
  William C. WRN 74A
  Willis LGN 35
  Willis CWL 57
  Wm. BKN 20
  Wm. ADR 52
  Wm. BBN 88
  Wm., Sr. GRD 102A
  Wm. SHE 138A
  Wm. GNP 165A
TURNER?, Edd. HRY 244
  Fountain MAD 90
  Jno. HAR 170
  Joseph ADR 52
  Thos. ADR 52
TURNEY, Daniel BBN 126
  Daniel WRN 75A
  David SCT 94A
  John HAR 214
  Peter BBN 90
TURNEY?, Samuel SHE 173
TURNHAM, David SHE 133A
  George SHE 131A
  Joel JES 82
  John SHE 137A
TURPEN, Philip GSN 152A
TURPIN, Aaron, Jr. WYN 88A
  Aaron, Sr. WYN 88A
  Abraham MTG 275
  Ann GRD 90A
  Danl. GRD 114A
  Hez.? GRD 114A
  Hugh GRD 102A
  Isaac MTG 279
  James GRD 104A
  John MAD 158
  Magdalin PUL 41A
  Martin, Jr. WYN 89A
  Martin, Sen. WYN 84A
  Martin PUL 66A
  Moses GRD 110A
  Polly PUL 64A
  Saml. PUL 36A
  Solomon MAD 154
  Solomon, Jr. WYN 84A
  Solomon, Jun. WYN 87A
  Solomon PUL 36A
  Thomas HND 5
  Thomas GRD 101A
  Thos. ADR 52
  William, Jr. HND 6A
  William, Snr. HND 5
  William GRD 102A
  Wm. MAD 104
  Woodson GRD 122A
TURRANCE, Terry WRN 37A

TURREL, George BNE 38
James BNE 38
John BNE 38
Robert BNE 38
TURTLE?, John KNX 298
TURVEY, William HAR 190
TUSSEY, Jonathan BRN 28
TUSTON?, Betsey, Mrs. WYN 104A
TUTCHER?, Wm. FKN 108
TUTT, Burket G. WDF 110A
George H. WDF 110A
Hansford WDF 110A
James WDF 110A
Mary WDF 113A
TUTTLE, Benj. CLY 131
Peter CLY 119
Peter NCH 115A
Thos. CLY 128
Thos. SHE 143A
William CLK 64
TUTWILER, John MAD 166
Jonathan MAD 166
TUYMAN, Leo HRD 96
TWAILS, Polly FTE 99
TWAIT?, Saml. MAS 75
TWAITS, Elizabeth FTE 73
TWAT?, Saml. (Crossed Out) MAS 62
TWATES, Mace WDF 95
TWEEDY, David HAR 210
TWIDDLE, Silas GRD 108A
TWIDWELL?, Wm. ADR 52
TWIDY, James ADR 54
TWIFORD, William, Sr. WYN 90A
TWIG, Daniel WTY 111A
TWINER, Thos. JEF 57
TWYMAN, Abraham BRN 28
Charles M. BRN 29
Jas. SCT 132A
John BRN 28
Mildred BRN 29
Reubin WDF 125A
William BRN 29
TWYMAN?, Buford WDF 120A
TYDINGS, Edward BNE 38
TYE, Elizabeth KNX 298
George WTY 127A
Henry WTY 125A
Joshua WTY 125A
TYGART, Isabella WRN 32A
James WRN 32A
Jane WRN 32A
TYGER, Samuel WRN 66A
TYLER, Abel SHE 173
Absalom JEF 49
Allen JEF 49
Benjamin FTE 108
Charles OWN 105
Charles MBG 140
Chas. HRY 265
David E. BLT 186
E. JEF 25
Edward JEF 49
George FTE 110
James BTL 313
James BTL 331
James W. JEF 41
Jno. JEF 52
Joseph GTN 133
Levi JEF 24
Magdalin BTL 331
Moses, Jnr. JEF 63
Moses, Sr. JEF 49
Soloman WRN 29A
TYLER, Stephen MER 111
William CHN 38
William FTE 108
William SHE 173
Wm. JEF 49
TYLEY, James ETL 39
TYLOR, Benjamin SHE 138A
Rebert? SHE 124A
TYMAN, Elijah HRD 22
TYRE, Betsey MAD 120
Daniel FLD 3
John HRY 198
TYREE, Andrew GRD 94A
Isham HAR 202
John GRT 145
TYREE?, Thos. HRD 22
TYRRELL, William MNR 209
TYSON, Edward JES 73
Ezekiel MBG 139A
U---DERWOOD?, Easter FTE 61
UBANK, John MNR 207
Jonathan ALN 108
UDEN?, James BKN 10
UIM?, Michael ALN 104
ULARD, Samul/ James? WAS 19A
ULETT, Wm. FLG 54A
ULETT?, John FLG 58A
ULIN, Benjamin GNP 170A
ULRICK, Saml. NCH 106A
ULRY, Peter BTH 180
UMBLE, Uriah BBN 118
UMPHLET, Levi PUL 37A
UMPHLETE, James KNX 282
UMPHREY, Owing BTH 182
Wm. BKN 22
UMPHRIES, James ADR 54
UMPHRIS, William HND 12
UNDERHILL, John BNE 40
Thomas BNE 40
William BNE 40
UNDERWOOD, Ambrose? HRY 178
Austin GRD 109A
Bennet BBN 138
Caleb GRN 77
Chester GRN 77
Francis HAR 168
Garret GRD 109A
Gideon FKN 82
Hiram GRN 77
Hisekiah GRN 77
Jacob SHE 169
James GRN 77
James BTH 166
Jehue BTH 166
John SHE 152
John MAD 168
John CHN 36A
Joseph SHE 170
Joseph R. BRN 34
Js. HRY 202
Lewis MAD 168
Mathew OHO 9A
Nathan JEF 51
Nathanl SHE 152
Peter GRN 77
Reubin BTH 160
Saml. CHN 36
William GRN 77
William, Sr. GRN 77
UNGLES, John BKN 4
UNSELD, John NSN 198
Margaret NSN 175
UNSELL, Abraham MBG 135A
Ann MBG 137
Federick MBG 135A
Henry MBG 140
Henry MBG 140A
UPCHURCH, Geo. WYN 100A
John ALN 100
Shadrick WYN 100A
UPDIKE, Major FTE 109
UPP, Jacob HND 7A
UPPHRES, Patrick H. MAD 148
UPTHEGROVE, Joseph LNC 17
UPTIGROW?, Elijah ALN 116
UPTON, Benjamin WYN 88A
Daniel HRD 92
Daniel, Senr. HRD 92
Edward HRD 92
Elijah WRN 38A
Jesse DVS 19A
URSREY, Larkin SPN 4A
URTON, Henry GRD 109A
Peter GRD 89A
URVIN, Ananias GRD 101A
David GRD 106A
URY, Sally CLK 73
US--ER?, Luke FTE 57
USHER, ---as? DVS 12A
David CHN 42
Jno. FKN 148
USSARY?, Thomas CSY 216
USTLER?, Luke FTE 57
UTELL?, John FLG 58A
UTERBACK, John NCH 121A
UTEY, William JES 73
UTINGEN?, William JES 84
UTINGER, Jacob FTE 102
Joshua JES 88
UTLEY, David FTE 87
Jacob CWL 57
Jacob MBG 142
John FTE 81
John FTE 81
Merrill CWL 57
UTLY, John R. JES 89
Josiah MER 111
William MER 111
UTT, John Frederick FTE 65
UTTER, John B. HRT 169
UTTERBACH, Lewis WDF 118A
UTTERBACK, Adam BNE 40
Ben GSN 152A
Benj. FKN 118
Benjamin WDF 117A
Benjamin NCH 121A
Chs. FKN 156
Covington NCH 121A
Elij. HRY 257
Elijah WDF 98A
Elijah GSN 152A
Hankerson BNE 40
Harman NCH 121A
Harmon BTH 164
Henry WDF 116A
Jno. FKN 158
Joel CHN 40
Martin GSN 152A
Nimrod FKN 158
Peyton BTH 164
Reuben BBN 72
Thompson GRD 122A
Wm. FKN 156
UTZ, Aaron BNE 40
Elizabeth BNE 40
Ephraim BNE 40

UTZ, Fielding BNE 40
Jonas BNE 40
Jonathon BNE 40
UZZEL, Bennet B. HOP 268
UZZELL, Elisha MBG 140A
Thomas MBG 142A

V--DIN?, James ALN 122
VAIL, John P. BBN 112
VALANCE, Saml. GNP 170A
VALANDINGHAM,
James FTE 89
Richard CLK 102
VALENTINE, A. CHN 45A
Abram? CHN 28
Henry MAS 59
Jesse KNX 282
Lucy NSN 195
Thos. FLG 64A
VALLANDEGHAM,
Lewis SCT 135A
VALLANDIGHAM, Asa SCT 91A
Thos. D. SCT 126A
VALLANDINGHAM,
George B. OWN 101
James OWN 106
Richard OWN 105
Robert OWN 101
S.? TOD 128
W. TOD 128
VALLENCE, William LVG 18
VAN BUSKIRK, C. JEF 21
VAN DOZIER, John LGN 35
VAN PELT?, Samuel FTE 67
VAN WINKLE, Saml. JEF 21
William JEF 30
VANADER?, Martin HND 8A
VANARSDAL,
Cornelius SHE 140A
VANASDALE,
Cornelius MER 112
VANASDALL, Abraham MER 112
Alexander MER 112
Cornelimus B. MER 112
Cornelius A. B. MER 111
Cornelius C. MER 112
Cornelius O. MER 112
Elizabeth MER 112
Isaac MER 112
Isaac MER 112
Isaac MER 112
Isaac B. MER 112
Peter MER 112
Simon MER 112
Simon J./ I.? MER 111
VANAT?, Henry WDF 120A
VANATTAN,
Ferdinand FLG 42A
VANBIBBER, Jacob GNP 176A
James GNP 167A
John GNP 176A
Peter GNP 176A
VANCAMP, Jno. MAS 63
Levi MAS 64
Levi MAS 69
VANCE, Benjamin WRN 75A
Catharine FTE 92
David ADR 54
David MAS 76
David FTE 106
Ely UNN 154
Henry H. WRN 60A
Isaac BNE 48
Jacob GRD 108A
James JEF 34
James FTE 79
VANCE, James FTE 100
James TOD 130
Jane FTE 107
John CLK 82
John TOD 126A
Joseph SCT 122A
Louis FTE 73
Martha MNR 205
Patrick FTE 79
Richd. GRN 61
Richd. GRN 63
Robert FTE 79
Robt. W. JEF 50
Saml. JEF 23
Saml. JEF 52
Samuel CLD 152
Samuel PUL 38A
Solomon WDF 124A
Thomas LNC 7
Thomas BNE 40
Tobias HRY 212
Will. SCT 100A
William SHE 151
VANCE?, Benjamin WDF 103
Joseph GTN 124
VANCENEN?, Barnard BBN 130
VANCLEAVE, Aaron SHE 155
Aaron SHE 157
Benjamin SHE 155
Benjamin SHE 165
David SHE 169
Jesse SHE 155
Joel MBG 136
John SHE 165
Joseph SHE 155
Ralph SHE 157
Saml. SHE 155
Saml. SHE 162
Siras SHE 155
Thomas SHE 157
VANCLEVE, John B. WAS 43A
Rachel WAS 44A
VANDAGRIFT,
Christ. HRY 244
Elij. HRY 249
VANDAVERD, Ashbury CSY 206
Burrey CSY 226
Charles CSY 206
Charles, Sr. CSY 206
George CSY 226
John L. CSY 226
William CSY 228
VANDDER, Martin HND 9
Martin JEF 9
VANDEAVERMAN,
Jacob NSN 207
VANDEGRAFF, Abram SCT 108A
VANDEGRAFT, David NSN 196
VANDEREN, Jesse M. HAR 218
Joseph HAR 218
Stephen HAR 210
VANDEREN?, James HAR 196
Jodfrey HAR 204
VANDERIPE,
Cornelius MER 111
Katharine MER 112
VANDERPOOL, J. M. RCK 76A
VANDERSON,
Abraham, Sr. CBL 7A
Abraham CBL 6A
Abraham CBL 7A
Isaac CBL 7A
Robbert CBL 6A
VANDERSON?, Isaac CBL 4A
VANDERVAN?, Wright PND 18A
VANDERVEER, Garrot MER 112
VANDERVEER, Henry MER 111
Henry MER 112
Isaac MER 111
Peter MER 111
Peter, Jr. MER 112
Sarah MER 112
VANDEVENTER, James SHE 115A
John SHE 114A
Josiah SHE 115A
VANDEVIER, John HAR 134
VANDEVOIR, Jno. CWL 57
VANDIGRAFT, Samuel HRD 58
VANDIGSAFT?,
Samuel HRD 56
VANDIKE, Domonic MAS 62
Elijah SHE 110A
Garrot MER 112
Mary WAS 24A
Peter SHE 131A
Richard SHE 131A
VANDIVER, James MNR 205
John SHE 173
Nancy MBG 138A
VANDLENDINGHAM,
John BTH 196
VANDUSON?, Isaac CBL 4A
VANERGLER, Waller JEF 26
VANFLEET, Henry MER 112
William MER 112
VANH--ER?, Jacob WYN 83A
VANHICE/VANHICE?,
Jas./ Jos.? HRY 267
VANHOOK, Abner HAR 202
Archilaus HAR 170
Benj. PUL 39A
Lawrence PUL 57A
Martin HAR 188
Mary HAR 184
Samuel PUL 57A
Sarah HAR 194
VANHOOKE, John LGN 39
VANHOOSE, James FLD 23
John FLD 24
John FLD 35
Levi FLD 21
VANHORN, Jessee CBL 4A
Keziah GTN 124
VANHOSER, Sampson WYN 86A
VANIER, Jno. FKN 54
VANKIKE, John CSY 224
VANKIRK, ----d? DVS 12A
Matthias MTG 275
Thos. KNX 286
VANLANDIGHAM,
George FTE 88
Nelly FTE 86
VANLANDINGHAM,
Elizabeth BBN 118
Geo. MBG 136A
George WDF 102A
Jas. BBN 136
Jas. BTH 184
Joshua BTH 196
Polly BTH 196
Susan FLG 64A
Thomas HAR 150
Wm. FLG 60A
VANMATRE, Abisha HRD 48
Abraham HRD 84
Abraham GSN 153A
Isaac HRD 8
Jacob HRD 10
Jacob HRD 48
Jacob HRD 72
John HRD 8
John HRD 84

VANMATRE, John GSN 153A
Jonathan HRD 36
Joseph HRD 84
Washington HRD 8
VANMETER, Eliza SHE 133A
Isaac CLK 87
Jacob WRN 74A
Nathan HRT 169
VANNESE, Charles MER 112
VANNEST, Peter MER 112
VANNISE, Abraham MER 117
Isaac MER 112
Mary MER 112
Peter MER 112
VANNORMAN, Benjamin GTN 129
VANNOY, Brazalla A. MER 112
Joel KNX 300
Mason MER 117
Peter KNX 304
Saml. KNX 296
Will. KNX 296
VANNUYS, Henry SHE 158
John SHE 155
Tunis SHE 173
VANOLE?, Margaret BLT 196
VANOVER, Cornelimus MNR 193
Henry ALN 140
Henry WAS 82A
Wm. WAS 82A
VANPELT, John GTN 119
Joseph GTN 120
Samuel GTN 129
William FTE 109
VANSHIKE?, Rubin FLG 56A
VANSKIKE, Robt. MAS 73
VANSKIKE?, Rubin FLG 56A
VANSKOCKE, Josiah NCH 116A
VANSKORKE?, Josiah NCH 120A
VANT, Fielding ALN 126
VANTREESE, Fredk. FLG 41A
Jacob GSN 153A
VANTREESE?, Keziah FLG 34A
VANVACTOR?, Ben HRD 56
VANWINKLE, Abraham WYN 83A
Benjamin MAD 132
David GTN 125
Isaac WYN 98A
James MAD 134
Joel WYN 97A
Joel WYN 99A
John WYN 98A
Micajah WYN 84A
VANWY?, John GNP 175A
VANZANT, Isaiah SCT 93A
John SCT 105A
VAR--, John ALN 112
VARBLE, George HRY 226
George HRY 226
Henry, Sr. HRY 228
Jacob FTE 97
Phillip FTE 97
VARBLE?, Daniel HRY 194
VARDAMAN, Morgan LNC 65
VARNER, Adam HAR 178
Andrew FKN 116
Conrad HAR 178
Henry CLD 155
Jamaes HND 10A
John FTE 94
John HAR 208
John, Jnr. HAR 182
VARNEY, Alexander FLD 39
VARNON, John BBN 128
VARNUM, John MER 116
VARROW, Benjamin BBN 128
VARVIL?, Daniel FLD 11
VARVILL, Philip MTG 287
VASTINE, Abraham PND 19A
VAUGAN, Widw. CWL 46
VAUGHAN, ---.? CWL 32
A. JEF 26
Ayres FLD 33
Ayres? FLD 27
Benjamin MNR 207
Chesley GRN 59
Chesley GRN 78
Daniel LVG 4
Edmund HND 10
Elisabeth FKN 74
Gabrial FLD 27
James FTE 112
James CHN 35A
James NCH 115A
John GRN 67
Obediah MNR 209
Patrick FLD 30
Phillip GRN 69
Phillip W. GRN 67
Rhody CHN 28A
Ruben GRN 55
Sally FTE 64
Saml. HRY 188
Samuel MNR 211
Thomas GRN 60
Thomas CLD 143
Thomas CHN 35A
Thos. GRN 67
Walker FKN 132
William CLD 158
William MNR 207
VAUGHEN, John WAS 66A
VAUGHN, Abram BNE 38
Allen CHN 45
Allen MER 114
Cathrn. FLG 79A
Clabern WAS 46A
Cornelius FTE 112
Danl. T. PND 29A
Edmd. FKN 74
Elenezar FTE 98
Eli CLK 79
Elijah CLK 73
Elisha LNC 71
Enn--- ADR 54
George MER 111
Griffith CBL 3A
Henry SHE 130A
James LNC 71
James FTE 80
James HOP 268
Jesse SCT 119A
Joel BLT 156
John WDF 100A
Jos. SHE 131A
M. FTE 98
Nancy LNC 21
Nancy SHE 112A
Newman LNC 77
Ruben WAS 25A
Saml. ADR 54
Saml. WAS 25A
Saml. WAS 25A
Thomas LNC 71
Thomas UNN 151
Thos. MAD 150
W., Revd. BKN 23
William SHE 177
William WYN 100A
Wm. FKN 74
VAUGHT, Christopher PUL 62A
Harrison LNC 69
Henry, Sr.? PUL 48A
Henry, Sr? PUL 45A
Henry PUL 40A
Henry PUL 48A
Jacob PUL 48A
Jacob PUL 60A
John PUL 60A
Wm. PUL 45A
VAUGHTON, Jessee JES 74
VAUGN, John UNN 152
William UNN 152
VAUTERS, Winny GRD 102A
VAUTTER, E. TOD 131A
VAWN, James ALN 108
VAWN?, David ALN 96
VAWTER, Flimg? BNE 48
Richard FTE 68
William BNE 38
VAWTERS, Jessee JES 82
VEACH, Alex. JEF 35
Asia C. JES 91
Elijah CWL 57
Jeremiah JES 91
Nathan CWL 57
Nathaniel WDF 97A
Otia? WDF 101
Sarah WDF 97A
VEAL, (See Neal) FTE 104
John WRN 48A
Thomas GTN 121
VEAMOUNT, Lewis BBN 128
VEANY, Joseph (Free Black Man) BBN 140
VEARS, Will M. GRD 112A
VEATCH, James HAR 134
Jeremiah HAR 214
Jno. HAR 162
Samuel HAR 206
Thomas HAR 206
VEDER, Anthony SHE 144A
VEECH, Benjamin SHE 131A
Elliott SHE 128A
Gorge SHE 131A
Jesse SHE 117A
John SHE 128A
VEEK, James SHE 130A
VEEL, James FTE 85
William FTE 82
VEERS?, John LGN 34
VEINOU?, Richard WRN 42A
VEITCH, Thomas LWS 89A
VELINT?, Francis GRD 98A
VELLARS, Matthew BLT 156
VENABLE, Abraham FTE 101
Darkey MAD 104
Hampdon S. MAD 180
James ALN 92
James FTE 98
James ALN 145
James SHE 175
Jno. ALN 134
Joseph ALN 94
Joseph SHE 162
Joseph SHE 168
Phillip HRY 222
VENATTIN, Cherie FLG 43A
Danl. FLG 43A
VENORSDALL, Luke SHE 176
VENOSDALE?, Isaac? NCH 121A
VENRY, Henry BNE 40
VENT, Joshuay WAS 50A
VENTERS, Jesse FLD 41

VENTERS, John FLD 41
VENZANT, Wm. FLG 52A
VERBRICK, Barna MER 112
  William MER 112
VERBRIGHT, John WRN 75A
VERCH, Ishmael WRN 34A
VERDEN, James WRN 59A
  Ma--ex? FTE 65
  William MNR 215
VERDIN, Hugh BTH 170
VERMILLIAN, Josiah MER 111
  Nichademus MER 111
VERMILLION, Burch MER 112
  Henderson MER 112
  Robert CLD 159
VERNON, Anthony HRD 50
  William S. JEF 34
VERNOY, Francis FLG 38A
VERT, Jacob MTG 259
  Jacob BRK 299
  Jno. FKN 58
  William MTG 225
VERTREES, Thos. HRD 90
VERTREESE, Charles HRD 20
  Isaac HRD 94
  Jacob HRD 32
  Jacob HRD 50
  John HRD 24
  Jos. HRD 42
  Wm. HRD 22
VESSAR, Peter ETL 42
VESSELLS, Charles WAS 55A
VESSELS, James WAS 58A
  Wm. WAS 58A
VEST, Caleb HRY 186
  Chistley WDF 100A
  Edward GRD 119A
  George BNE 38
  George BNE 38
  George HRY 202
  Henry WAS 63A
  James CSY 228
  John BNE 38
  John GRN 65
  . Littlebury WAS 25A
  Phillip GRN 65
  Ruben WAS 63A
  Squire BNE 38
  Thomas BNE 38
VESTILL, David MTG 226
  William MTG 226
VETTELOW?, Daniel NSN 195
  Samuel NSN 195
  Stephen NSN 186
VETTINAGE,
    Christor. FTE 66
VIBBERT?, James CLD 163
VICARUS, Riley HND 10A
VICE, Aaron BTH 188
  Aquilla ETL 53
  Aquilla CLY 129
  Edmund BTH 150
  Edmund BTH 176
  Eligah CBL 13A
  Enoch BTH 176
  Esom BTH 176
  George CBL 14A
  John BTH 188
  John BTH 202
  John CBL 14A
  Luvenee? BTH 184
  Moses BTH 188
  Mourning BTH 176
  Robert BTH 172
  Robert, Jr. BTH 176
  Uriah CBL 14A
VICE, William BTH 188
  William, Jr. BTH 150
  William, Jr. BTH 188
VICERY, William OHO 7A
VICK, Arthur LVG 8
  Rhoda MBG 133A
  Stephen MBG 143
VICKERS, Adam WYN 83A
  Alvis HOP 268
  Charles HOP 268
  Jacob MBG 138A
  James CBL 11A
  John BNE 38
  John HOP 268
  John MBG 138A
  Jos. MAS 77
  Nancy CBL 6A
  Ralph, Junr. MBG 138A
  Ralph, Senr. MBG 138A
  William BNE 38
VICTOR, James NCH 123A
  John BTH 194
  John NCH 128A
  Littleton BBN 128
  Samuel V. LWS 87A
  William NCH 128A
VICUS?, Samuel WRN 55A
VIERS, Elisha HRD 34
  John HRD 22
  Nathan HRD 62
VIGIS?, Zach ADR 54
VIGLE, Mathias JEF 46
VIGRIS, Charles T. WDF 111A
VIGUE?, Dorsey NSN 198
VIGUS?, Jabez FTE 58
VILES?, Thomas OHO 10A
VILESET?, Luces? GRD 105A
VILEY, Willa SCT 134A
VILEY?, Saml. SCT 102A
VINCEN, &? Hollis JEF 47
  David MAD 98
VINCENT, Alf CHN 30A
  Allen CLD 157
  Andrew LNC 43
  Asa CLD 155
  Azariah HOP 268
  Barten GSN 153A
  Charles MBG 142A
  Chas. FLG 29A
  David ? ADR 54
  Edwin CLD 157
  Ezekiel TRG 7
  Gillis BKN 24
  Hessa FLG 30A
  James WDF 102
  John MBG 142
  Joseph SHE 153
  Nancy UNN 150
  Thomas LWS 93A
  Thomas MBG 139A
  Zack GRD 113A
VINCINER?, John HRY 232
VINEYARD, Jno. HAR 168
  William LGN 41
  William HAR 162
VINSEN, Darkey MAD 168
VINSON, Eli GTN 129
  Peggy MER 111
VINYARD,
    Allexander LNC 43
  Martha LNC 45
VINZANT, Aven FLG 66A
  Elisha FLG 57A
  Garrett BRN 29
  Jacob BRN 29
VIOLET, Edmd. JEF 51
VIOLET, Jno. HRY 240
VIOLETT, Henson WDF 101
  John T. GTN 134
  Thomas WDF 102
VIRGIN, John GNP 175A
  Reason HAR 202
  Rezin GNP 175A
  Thomas GNP 172A
VISAGE, Thos. LVG 9
VISE, David CLY 121
VISEN, Theophelus MAD 168
VITTELOW, Samuel NSN 185
VITTILAW, Danl. HRD 16
VITTILAW?, Thos. HRD 28
VITTILOE, Daniel DVS 18A
VITTILOW, William NSN 194
VITTILOW?, Stephen NSN 186
VIVEON, Flavel CLK 83
VIVION, Thomas CLK 85
VOATAW, Margt. KNX 306
VOGAN, Saml. FLG 71A
VOGLE, John JEF 31
VOIRES, John LWS 87A
  Robert LWS 88A
VOIRES?, James HRY 176
VONOR?, Salley/
    Lalley? CSY 220
VOORHIES, Abraham MER 111
  Elijah MER 112
  Isaac MER 112
  Jacob MER 112
  James MER 112
  John MER 112
  Koart? MER 112
  Luke MER 112
  Peter G. FKN 106
VORIS, Albert SHE 158
  Corneluis SHE 173
  James HND 5A
VORISE, P. H. HRY 243
VORISE?, Francis HRY 252
  Jno. HRY 257
VOSS, Thos. CHN 44A
VOUGHT, Elizabeth MBG 136A
  Gilbert MBG 140
  John MBG 136A
  Simeon MBG 136A
VOULS, Thos. WAS 60A
VOUTREES?, Samuel WRN 69A
VOUTZ?, Mary NSN 191
VOWLS, Henry WAS 61A
  Thomas NSN 195
W-----, Abra. H. JEF 54
W-----?, James PUL 57A
W----, ----- CWL 31
  ----- BNE 52
W----?, Carter T.? CHN 28
  Elizabeth JES 73
  John LVG 18
W----T?, John LVG 18
W---, James FTE 63
W--HOMAS?, Francis BLT 156
W--LIN?, Elizabeth BKN 15
WA--LD, Elisha FTE 56
WADDLE, Asa BBN 68
  David HRT 170
  Eve FLG 72A
  Henry PUL 45A
  Henry PUL 60A
  Jane MAS 63
  Jas MAS 66
  Jas. FLG 72A
  Jno. MAS 63
  Jno. PUL 46A
  John BLT 168

WADDLE, John NCH 109A
John S. BTL 333
Joseph NCH 124A
Kisiah HRT 170
Robt. BBN 130
Will MAS 66
Wm. PUL 37A
Wm. PUL 46A
WADDY?, Samuel SHE 117A
WADE, Balenger CLD 140
Balenger OHO 3A
Bartlett MNR 199
Betsy LNC 35
Daniel LVG 18
David FKN 62
David CLK 83
David R. MTG 249
Dawson MTG 235
Elisha WYN 103A
Hampton TRG 6A
James CLD 139
James BTH 178
James MTG 245
Jeremiah JEF 21
Jeremiah LNC 61
Jeremiah GTN 133
John CLK 97
John ALN 128
John WAS 59A
John WRN 70A
John WAS 79A
John WYN 103A
John GNP 176A
Joseph WYN 90A
Joshua NSN 218
Obadiah BRN 30
Pearce CLD 137
Pierce BRN 31
Richard CLD 139
Royal, Sr. SHE 174
Thomas CLK 97
Thomas SHE 174
Tignal ALN 130
William JES 86
William NSN 213
William MTG 281
William, Col. MER 113
William WRN 65A
Willm. LNC 17
WADE?, Richard, Sr. WYN 104A
WADER, Banister CWL 57
WADES?, Richard, Sr. WYN 103A
Richard, Sr. WYN 104A
WADKIN, Saml. BBN 76
WADKINS, Abrose ALN 106
Anstet? BRK 301
Benjamin FLD 13
Ezekiel LNC 7
James MAD 162
James GSN 154A
Mary HRT 170
Rachel GSN 155A
Thomas FLD 44
Thomas CLD 162
Wm. BBN 76
WADLE?, Charles ALN 104
WADLEY, Rob. CWL 31
Wm. HRD 22
WADLINGTON, -----? CWL 42
--e-cus? CWL 38
Ferdinand TRG 11
James CWL 40
Thomas TRG 11
Thos. CWL 32
WADLINGTON, Warner W. CWL 44
Wm. CWL 44
WADSWORTH, Adney? MAS 76
WAFERS, Francis CWL 33
WAGENOR, George GSN 154A
WAGERS, Moses FLD 7
WAGES, Francis ETL 50
WAGGENER, Alxr. ADR 3
Bargess ADR 60
Catharine ADR 58
Ed ADC 66
H., Jr. ADR 60
H. G., Sen. ADR 60
John ADR 58
W. W. ADR 60
WAGGENER?, Andrew ADR 56
WAGGERMON, John JES 93
WAGGLE, Adam ALN 114
George ALN 116
WAGGLIN?, Andrew ADR 56
WAGGONER, Christian HAR 194
Daniel BRK 303
David MBG 141
Dennis BRK 301
Edmond ALN 118
Ephraim ALN 118
George ALN 94
George MBG 142
Henry BRN 32
James JEF 38
John HRD 8
John MBG 141
John CLD 147
John HAR 194
John HOP 268
John BRK 303
John C. GTN 135
Michael LGN 36
Nancy ALN 118
Peter ALN 118
Thos. CHN 43A
WAGLE, Isaac MAD 156
John MAD 150
WAGNON, John P. MNR 205
WAGO, Abraham OWN 105
WAGONER, Andrew UNN 146
Danl. JEF 27
Nancy UNN 154
Thos. SCT 127A
WAHOOP, William MER 113
WAID, Brent LGN 28
Catharine HOP 270
David NSN 207
Joseph ADR 58
Richd. LGN 28
Stephen GRN 57
William NSN 204
Zachariah HOP 270
WAIDE, David JEF 43
Josiah LGN 44
WAIGHT, Joseph SPN 15A
WAILS, -ev.? CWL 39
WAIN, John WAS 42A
WAINE, John C. WAS 41A
John W. BBN 128
WAIR, Dudly GRD 93A
Henry GRD 103A
WAIT, William PUL 52A
WAITS, David FKN 112
John HAR 206
William HAR 206
William CBL 22A
WAKE, Alexander JES 96
WAKEFIELD, Daniel NSN 207
WAKEFIELD, Elizabeth NSN 206
John NSN 206
Ruth NSN 199
William NSN 199
WAKELIN, Jno. OHO 7A
John OHO 9A
Mary OHO 9A
Wm. OHO 7A
WAKER, Joseph HAR 162
WALBERT, David ADR 60
WALBERT?, Charity ADR 54
WALCH?, -----? ALN 92
WALCUT?, John BTH 150
WALDAN, Jno? JEF 60
WALDEN, Austin MAD 92
Benjamin WTY 111A
Jno. MAS 62
John GRD 123A
Joseph WDF 121A
Mary PUL 66A
Nathan HND 9A
Richard MNR 203
Richard HND 5A
Thomas HAR 146
William HND 11
William BRN 32
William FTE 63
WALDIN, James MAD 160
WALDING, Wm. FKN 68
WALDREN, Richd. HRY 228
WALDREN?, John HRY 196
WALDROP, David MNR 191
Wiet HRT 170
WALDROPE, Jas. TOD 134
Reace HRT 170
Sion HRT 170
WALDRUP, William WYN 100A
WALEN, James MER 114
WALER, John? HND 10A
WALES, Adam KNX 288
Benjamin BBN 118
George BRK 303
Martin BRK 301
Widow BBN 92
WALIS?, John LVG 18
William LVG 18
WALKER, -enelder? (Crossed Out) WTY 117A
Alexander FTE 79
Alexander MER 113
Alexander HAR 216
Alxr. ADR 56
Alxr., Sen. ADR 58
Alxr. S. ADR 58
Andrew FTE 63
Anselm JEF 25
Aurelius FLG 51A
Benjamin WDF 98A
Bennet NSN 185
Betsey, Mrs. WYN 101A
Betsey, Mrs. WYN 104A
Charles NSN 185
Christ. KNX 294
Clarissa MER 113
Coleman MER 113
Cyrus ADC 68
Daniel HRD 10
Daniel NSN 201
Daniel MTG 237
Daniel, Jr. HRD 10
Davey WAS 20A
David ADR 58
David ALN 132
David J./ T.? JES 81
Edward CLD 157

WALKER, Edward WDF 98A
Edward WDF 102A
Elijah CHN 29A
Elijah GRD 90A
Elisha CWL 37
Elizth. GRD 97A
Francis FTE 68
Francis E. HND 10A
George CWL 34
George FTE 88
George W. WAS 78A
Gideon BLT 186
Gideon WYN 85A
Gillum WYN 95A
Harrison MER 116
Henry FTE 86
Henry WDF 96
Henry GTN 128
Henry NSN 187
Henry BRK 299
Henry FLG 23A
Hugh ADR 58
Ignatus NSN 187
Isaac HRY 186
Isaac W. MAD 100
Isbell HND 6
Jacob FTE 81
Jacob HRY 184
James HND 6
James LVG 8
James TRG 8
James BNE 42
James ADR 56
James ADR 56
James ADR 58
James JES 72
James JES 89
James CLK 95
James HRY 210
James CSY 226
James MTG 283
James, Jun. WYN 85A
James, Sr. WYN 85A
James B. MAD 178
James E. BTH 158
James V.? LGN 28
Jas. MAS 65
Jas., Jr. FLG 23A
Jas., Sr. FLG 23A
Jeremiah WYN 95A
Jesse WTY 113A
Jno. FKN 158
Jno. RCK 82A
John TRG 8
John BKN 22
John JEF 48
John ETL 54
John ADR 58
John JES 77
John HRD 80
John WDF 98
John CLY 112
John MER 117
John FLD 11
John MBG 141
John HOP 270
John KNX 284
John CBL 20A
John FLG 23A
John PND 24A
John WAS 35A
John WDF 122A
John SHE 132A
John C. JES 97
Jona. HRY 214
Jones MBG 142
WALKER, Jos. CHN 40A
Jos. SHE 136A
Joseph ADR 3
Joseph ADR 58
Joseph FTE 63
Joseph BTH 158
Joseph NSN 182
Joseph, Sen. ADR 58
Joshua CLK 76
Kemp GRD 92A
Lewis HRD 38
Lewis HRD 80
Lucy MAD 170
Mariun? ADR 58
Martha WAS 41A
Mary MAD 132
Mary WAS 38A
Mary WRN 46A
Mary FLG 57A
Mathew JES 69
Mathew FTE 89
Morgan ETL 37
Moses LVG 11
Moses JES 94
Musin/ Mersin? GRD 94A
Nancy ALN 144
Nancy MAD 172
Nathaniel GTN 117
Phebe ALN 140
Philip MER 113
Phill WAS 22A
Polly LNC 15
Rachael GNP 168A
Rachel, Mrs. WYN 95A
Randall FKN 160
Randol JES 73
Rebeckah MAD 110
Reneldec? WTY 112A
Richard HRD 10
Richard HRD 72
Richard WDF 99
Richard CBL 17A
Richard SPN 17A
Richard L. OHO 3A
Roachee ETL 49
Robert BNE 42
Robert FLD 47
Robert MER 113
Robert MTG 271
Robert WRN 46A
Robt., Jr. FLG 23A
Robt. FLG 23A
Robt. FLG 33A
Robt. FLG 51A
Rosannah WDF 99
Sally BRK 303
Sally GRD 97A
Saml. MAS 74
Saml. MAS 75
Saml. HRY 194
Saml. SCT 113A
Saml. GNP 169A
Samuel TRG 7A
Samuel W. WTY 116A
Sanders BRN 30
Shedrick WRN 35A
Stanley B. HRD 24
Susanah SCT 94A
Tho. RCK 80A
Tho. GRD 118A
Thomas WAS 19A
Thos. MAD 118
Ths. JEF 47
Travis WDF 115A
Washington FTE 88
West WYN 95A
WALKER, Widw. CWL 37
William BRN 30
William BNE 42
William LGN 46
William JES 79
William WDF 100
William MAD 116
William GTN 117
William GTN 121
William BTH 208
William HAR 216
William HAR 220
William, Jun. LWS 91A
William, Senr. LWS 91A
William SPN 16A
William SPN 17A
William WYN 79A
William LWS 88A
William? HND 10A
Willis WRN 42A
Winston BBN 138
Wm. HRD 10
Wm. ADR 56
Wm. FKN 102
Wm. ALN 112
Wm. MAD 144
Wm. FLG 33A
Wm. FLG 48A
Wm. GSN 154A
Zep. HRY 180
WALKINS, Hutson WAS 27A
Joseph HAR 142
WALKINS?, Wm. BRK 305
WALKUP, James MER 113
Jon ADR 58
Joseph ADR 58
Mathew ADR 58
Saml. MAD 138
Saml., Jr. MAD 138
WALL, -----? DVS 8A
---ter? DVS 10A
Benjamin HND 10A
Caleb OHO 6A
Frances CSY 204
Gabriel CSY 204
Garrett SCT 129A
Isaac CSY 204
Jacob CSY 204
Lydia MAS 70
Polly LGN 39
Ransom WRN 52A
Ransom WRN 68A
Reuben BTH 184
Saml. JEF 61
Saml. SCT 130A
Stephen SCT 108A
William K. HAR 218
Wm. SHE 133A
WALL?, Reuben BTH 176
WALLACE, A. H. LVG 6
Abra. H. JEF 54
Andrew LNC 11
Andrew BBN 84
Andrew JES 96
Andrew BBN 114
Andrew MAD 162
Arthur OHO 11A
Benj. FLG 42A
Benjamin TRG 4
Benjamin UNN 152
Charles OHO 3A
Colson O. MBG 135
Geo. HRY 250
Graham PND 16A
H. LVG 6
Henry WDF 103

WALLACE, Hurbert TRG 3
Jame MAD 124
James TRG 3
James LNC 11
James HAR 132
James MAD 138
James UNN 151
Jas. HRY 250
John CHN 34
John JES 79
John FTE 86
John GTN 132
John MAD 144
John HRY 194
John OHO 11A
John PND 19A
John WRN 41A
John SCT 105A
John NCH 106A
John GNP 165A
Joseph LNC 11
Joseph JES 89
Joseph BBN 126
Joseph OHO 11A
Joseph WDF 103A
Joshua HRY 250
Margaret BBN 144
Martha B. LGN 25
Nancey FKN 60
Patrick BNE 42
Robert, Jr. JEF 41
Robert WRN 53A
Robert B. OHO 10A
Robt. JEF 23
Robt. HRY 250
Saml. MAD 174
Samuel ETL 43
Samuel M. WDF 98A
Sarah NCH 106A
Simon LGN 32
Stephen BBN 110
Thomas LVG 18
Thomas FTE 66
Thomas JES 75
Thos. LVG 6
Thos. FLG 78A
William TRG 3
William WDF 103
William WRN 53A
Wm. JEF 34
Wm. -. FKN 72
WALLEDGE, Peter GRD 86A
WALLER, Allen SCT 106A
Aron UNN 147
Benjamin GTN 129
Dempsey UNN 148
Edmd. BBN 140
Edmond JES 95
Frances BRN 30
George SHE 133A
Jacob FLD 45
James W. GTN 125
Jesse FLD 33
John FTE 88
John UNN 154
John SCT 126A
Nathan FLD 29
Richard SHE 143A
Stephen SHE 138A
Thomas UNN 147
Thomas V. WDF 110A
Thos. JEF 53
Valentine NCH 120A
William GTN 125
Wm. S. FKN 152
WALLER?, John PND 16A
WALLERS, Mary, Mrs. CLK 92
WALLES, Jacob WAS 51A
Josiah GRD 93A
Richd. MAS 56
WALLICE, Jane, Mrs. WYN 82A
John WYN 95A
WALLING, Jas. LVG 6
WALLINGEFORD, Benjn. MAS 62
WALLINGFORD, Jas. FLG 24A
Joel FTE 62
Jos. MAS 69
N? MAS 69
Richd. FLG 25A
WALLINGTON, John FLG 24A
WALLIS, Allen GRD 100A
Andrew MNR 209
Edward LWS 89A
James FTE 74
John MER 113
Robert FTE 74
Thomas GRN 68
Thomas FTE 74
Thomas GRD 84A
William GRN 57
William FTE 75
William GRD 85A
WALLIS?, John GRN 62
John PND 16A
WALLS, Benjamin BNE 40
David BNE 40
Edward FKN 158
James BBN 122
John MTG 251
John WRN 56A
Joseph FLG 31A
Joshua BRK 299
Leven D. BRK 303
Margaret WRN 71A
Moses H. JES 84
Nathan BNE 40
Samuel BRK 299
Susan BNE 40
Wm. HRD 38
WALLS?, Jobe BRK 301
WALMSLEY, Uriah MTG 267
WALSH, B. JEF 22
David UNN 152
James MTG 253
Robert JEF 43
Thomas MTG 293
WALSTON, Charles LWS 96A
John MBG 139A
Joseph WAS 33A
Obd. WAS 33A
Widw.? CWL 42
Wm. WAS 33A
WALTER, Benjamin MER 113
Jacob JEF 51
Katharine MER 113
William FLD 20
WALTER?, Jacob JEF 27
Levi BKN 22
WALTERS, (See Watters?) JES
(See Watters?) PND 28A
Abraham CHN 41
Absolem GNP 179A
Andrew HRD 20
Barnabas BRN 32
Champness? JES 78
Conrod HRD 64
Conrod, Senr. HRD 82
Coonrod BRN 32
WALTERS, David JES 78
Elizabeth JES 95
George CLY 117
Isaac SHE 142A
Jacob BRN 32
Jacob JES 77
Jacob GTN 133
James BNE 42
James JES 77
Jas. CLY 112
Jedeia? HRD 88
Jno. JEF 54
John BRN 30
John BNE 42
John HRD 50
John JES 77
John JES 77
John JES 77
John JES 78
John MER 113
John WYN 94A
John SHE 125A
Luke JES 77
Michael CHN 44A
Perry LGN 33
Robert CLY 116
Sally BRN 31
Samuel JES 78
Thomas JES 94
Thos. PUL 38A
William JES 77
William CLY 131
Wm. HRD 86
WALTERS?, Asolem GNP 178A
Elisabeth FLD 3
Isaac FLG 63A
Robert KNX 296
Thomas JES 85
William JES 86
William KNX 298
WALTHAL, Richard CLD 142
WALTHALL, Thos. S. CHN 43A
WALTON, Barr, & MAS 81
Claibourn BRN 32
Edward ETL 42
Elijah HND 5
Francis SPN 19A
Isaac BTH 210
James CBL 19A
Jno. MAS 68
Joel MAD 134
Joel MAD 138
John GTN 133
John HAR 210
Josiah C. BKN 14
Margret FLG 55A
Sally FLG 55A
Sanion? MAS 67
Simon BKN 15
Will MAS 67
William HND 11A
William CBL 19A
Wm. FLG 52A
WALTRESS?, Luke BRK 303
Michael BRK 303
WALTRIP, -----? DVS 8A
WALTZ, Frederick FTE 111
Jacobson &? JEF 27
WAMACH, Wm. ADR 62
WAMACK, Abner BTL 333
James BTL 333
Jesse BTL 333
Lewis BTL 333
WAMAK, David UNN 148
WAMMACK, John SHE 135A
Mossanello SHE 135A

WAMOCK, Isaac CHN 41A
WAMOK, Jacob CLD 162
WAMUCK, Thos. HRD 54
WAN, William S. WYN 101A
WAN?, Alexander WYN 81A
William WYN 83A
WANCH?, James BTL 313
WAND, James LGN 23
James BTL 333
Pegy? BTL 333
Thomas WRN 28A
Thomas WRN 30A
WANER?, David MER 112
WANNMER?, James ADR 60
WANSEAT?, Felix NSN 188
WANT?, William NCH 128A
WANTLAND, Thomas WRN 66A
WANTON, Richmond NSN 176
WARD, Abm. BBN 146
Andrew HAR 206
Andrew NCH 106A
Archibald GTN 122
B. TOD 129
Benjamin HAR 144
Benjn. SCT 101A
Beverley BNE 40
Blanford SHE 177
Brent LGN 44
Chas. MAS 69
Conrod LGN 27
Cyrus MTG 249
David L. JEF 40
Demsey CWL 57
Dillenham MTG 249
Elisha WAS 86A
Evan SCT 107A
Ezl. GRD 96B
Flan MBG 137
Fredrick HND 10
Geo. CHN 42
Geo. W. BBN 146
George CWL 57
George MER 112
George S. WDF 97
Green WAS 60A
Hugh BTH 206
Jacob SCT 130A
James FLD 24
James FLD 41
James JEF 44
James CWL 57
James BBN 90
James HAR 204
James, Jr. GNP 178A
James WYN 86A
James Ser. GNP 172A
Jas. MAS 63
Jesse HRY 206
Jilson ETL 53
Jno. JEF 51
Jno. FKN 56
Jno. HAR 144
John HRD 20
John HRD 26
John CLK 106
John MER 113
John MTG 245
John GRD 84A
John SCT 101A
John R. NCH 129A
Jonathan SPN 3A
Joseph GTN 122
Joseph HAR 160
Joseph MTG 249
Joseph LWS 97A
Joseph R. GNP 178A

WARD, Joshua SPN 9A
Lawrence ETL 51
Mary MAS 66
Melzar? MTG 283
Mitchel SCT 136A
Molly KNX 290
Nathan BBN 90
Nathon WAS 49A
Racael ALN 108
Richd. BBN 86
Richd. BBN 90
Richd. BBN 134
Robt. J./ I.? SCT 130A
Salley SCT 100A
Sandy WAS 49A
Sarah JEF 41
Shadrack FLD 24
Soloman HRD 46
Solomon FLD 24
Susanna MBG 133A
Thomas ADR 58
Thomas GTN 132
Thomson GNP 165A
Will SCT 102A
Will. SCT 99A
Will. SCT 129A
Will. SCT 130A
William FLD 20
William FLD 24
William ETL 39
William GRN 78
William GRN 79
William CLY 118
William GRD 84A
William GRD 102A
Wm. TOD 129
Wm. GNP 172A
WARDE, Benjn. OHO 6A
Edmund OHO 10A
John OHO 3A
Joseah OHO 3A
WARDEMAN, Thomas WDF 117A
WARDEN, Benjn. OHO 8A
Joseph OHO 8A
Peter FLD 35
Richd. MAS 77
Robert NSN 175
Walter MAS 63
WARDER, John BRN 30
Joseph, Jr. BRN 32
Joseph, Ser. BRN 32
William BTH 204
WARDIN, Elisha ALN 124
WARDLIN, Andrew WRN 46A
WARDLOW, James FTE 94
John FTE 94
Joseph NCH 112A
WARDON, Byram LGN 47
Philip LGN 33
WARE, Andrew -? SHE 131A
Annice PUL 68A
Caleb CLK 90
Charles SHE 112A
Charles WDF 124A
Iverson SHE 125A
James SHE 138A
Jno. HRY 264
John FTE 90
John SHE 113A
John SHE 133A
Jos. CHN 46
Lewis SHE 129A
Nicholas SHE 133A
Presley CLK 91
Rice PUL 68A
Robert CLK 86

WARE, Thompson BBN 136
Thos. BKN 5
Wm. SHE 138A
WARE?, Abram SCT 106A
Wm. FKN 76
WARFIELD, Benjamin HAR 206
Caleb HRT 170
Jarret HRY 266
Jno. MAS 75
N., Dr. BBN 144
Reason KNX 278
Ruth HAR 220
Shadrach HAR 214
Vachel FKN 110
Walter FTE 57
WARFORD, -arret? CWL 39
Abraham ETL 42
Ben. PND 29A
David WDF 97
Garret? CWL 39
James LVG 10
John WAS 48A
Joseph SHE 126A
Pery? WAS 48A
Simeon ETL 50
WARIL?, William NCH 128A
WARMAN, Joseph LNC 17
WARMOUTH, Thaddues MAD 176
WARNEN, Jacob GRD 85A
WARNER, Dennis MTG 265
Elijah FTE 63
George BTH 196
Henson SHE 177
Jack, (Free Man) BBN 78
Jacob BTH 190
Jane MTG 263
John ETL 53
John JES 81
Martin MAS 57
Moses (Crossed Out) WTY 117A
Moses WTY 113A
Nathl. S. GNP 167A
Peter CWL 39
Richard OHO 10A
William ETL 53
William FTE 104
William BTH 190
WARNICK, James OWN 99
Saml. MAS 57
WARNIER, Jacob CSY 216
WARNUCK, Jesse GSN 155A
WARREN, Avery GRN 77
Benj. LNC 73
Charles BBN 106
Charles BRK 303
Chs. PUL 47A
Davd. PUL 38A
David BRN 32
Drury GRD 88A
Drury SHE 137A
Edwd. SCT 111A
Fedrick GRN 70
Hedgewood CHN 28A
Isaac WDF 122A
James LNC 61
James LNC 65
James NSN 201
James WAS 75A
James R. LNC 3
John LNC 57
John CLK 67
John LNC 73
John MAD 144
John BTH 212
John PUL 38A

WARREN, John WAS 74A
John GRD 109A
John WDF 123A
John B. BTH 206
Jos. GRD 119A
Joshua WDF 123A
Nathaniel WYN 82A
Peter PUL 38A
Reuben FLD 32
Reubin WYN 82A
Robert BTH 206
Saml. LNC 59
Thomas LNC 39
Thomas CLK 98
Thos. FKN 90
Thos. MAD 94
Will SCT 92A
William CHN 28A
William GRD 84A
William E. MER 117
Willm. LNC 61
Wm. LNC 59
Wm. W. BRN 34
WARREN?, Mathias BKN 5
WARRENER, Carter CLD 143
Iverson? CLD 160
Robert CHN 32
Wm. GRN 53
WARRENTON, Thomas CBL 16A
WARRICK, Severn JEF 38
WARRIN, Hiram PUL 38A
Thos. B. CHN 43A
WARRINE?, Jacob CSY 216
WARRINER, Jacob CSY 224
WARRING, Bazil, Ser. GNP 174A
Bazil GNP 178A
Clemant GNP 173A
Francis GNP 166A
James H., Jr.? GNP 173A
James H. GNP 174A
Jno. JEF 42
Thos. T. G. GNP 178A
WARRINGTON, Wm. MAS 76
WARRMER?, James ADR 60
WARSON, Robert SHE 153
WARSON?, Mary FTE 106
WARTH, Abraham HAR 156
WARTHAM, Charles GSN 153A
Jas. GSN 153A
Samuel GSN 153A
WARTON, John BNE 42
WARWICK, Wilson CBL 13A
WASBURN, Isaac PND 31A
WASBURNE, Elias BKN 4
WASH---?, Tho., Exors. Of LGN 31
WASH, Benj. FKN 162
George CHN 32A
Jas. SCT 134A
John LGN 31
John CLD 137
Lucious FKN 98
Thomas CLD 143
WASHAM, Cannon WYN 84A
Charles WYN 79A
Lucy HOP 270
WASHBOURN, Benjn. SHE 162
Nancy FLG 69A
WASHBURN, Delany JEF 46
Gabl. CWL 58
Isaac SPN 12A
Jas. B. JEF 65
John HAR 178
Saml. F. JEF 35
WASHBURNE, Jer. SHE 129A
WASHER, George NSN 211
Heny NSN 211
Jacob NSN 211
WASHINGTON, Fairfax LGN 40
Francis LGN 39
Henry JEF 44
John LGN 25
John JES 81
John WAS 73A
Robt. W. BRK 227
Whiting LGN 25
Whiting LGN 36
WASKOM, Pearson SHE 148
William SHE 148
WASSON, Alexander SHE 149
Andrew ETL 42
Andrew CBL 6A
Chas. BBN 80
Jas. BBN 82
John BBN 66
John SHE 149
Joseph HAR 166
Robert SHE 149
Saml. BBN 106
Saml. R. BBN 82
William SHE 149
WAT, Joseph GSN 155A
WATERFIELD, Jesse TRG 14
Macajah JEF 31
WATERMAN, Jonathan CLK 98
WATERS, Aaron SHE 176
Beverly CLD 141
Caswell BTL 333
Daniel GTN 132
Dory D. WAS 74A
Edson MER 114
Elijah WYN 96A
Henry ETL 40
Henry ETL 43
Hezekiah B. BLT 160
James GRN 76
Joe WDF 93
John BNE 40
John HRT 169
John HRY 182
John CSY 210
John, Sr. ETL 41
John WYN 85A
John F. ETL 49
Joseph CSY 208
Joseph E. CLD 141
Josephus BNE 40
Julia FTE 65
Levy ETL 42
Major JEF 34
Mason MAS 72
Mathew SPN 3A
Mathews WRN 38A
Nathan LNC 35
Patssey LNC 63
Phebe B. WAS 43A
Philmamon WAS 17A
R. L. MAS 54
Richard WDF 97A
Richard D. SHE 173
Saml. LNC 17
Sampson MAD 106
Seeley? ETL 40
Soloman WDF 97A
Solomon FTE 63
Will MAS 54
William CLK 71
William CLK 99
William BLT 154
William SPN 4A
WATERS, Wm. HRT 170
WATERS?, Hugh M.? CWL 57
Silas BBN 94
WATHALL, Francis M? JEF 39
WATHAN, Feben? HRD 76
Gabriel HRD 96
Thos. HRD 96
Thos. B. HRD 76
WATHAR?, Thomas NSN 217
WATHE-?, Benedict NSN 210
WATHEN, Benj. WAS 37A
Edward WAS 76A
Nicolass WAS 64A
Thomas UNN 154
WATHEN?, Nicolass WAS 75A
Sarah WAS 56A
Thomas NSN 217
WATHER, Henry H. WAS 28A
WATHERSPOON, Jas. ALN 102
WATHUR, Henry NSN 184
Wilford NSN 179
WATKINS, Andrew HRY 216
Benjamin WDF 117A
Chapman KNX 310
Edmund MBG 143
Elijah HRT 170
Ephraim LGN 32
Francis WDF 105
George GRN 60
Henry LGN 32
Henry JES 73
Henry WDF 99
Isaac MAS 72
Isaac SHE 176
Isaac HRY 218
Isham L. LGN 23
James HRT 170
Jno. HRY 190
Joel LGN 30
Joel A. WTY 123A
John LGN 37
John BBN 102
John HRT 170
John HAR 184
John LWS 91A
John W. CWL 44
Joseph GRN 59
Joseph WRN 53A
Joseph LWS 97A
Lewis MBG 139
Luke, Jr. KNX 310
Luke, Sr. KNX 310
Margret FTE 63
Miles WAS 29A
Overlow? MER 112
Peter MBG 135
Pleasant MAD 172
Rachl. HRY 218
Sally FLG 39A
Saml. HRD 32
Saml. CWL 34
Saml. HRT 170
Samuel WDF 98
Samuel WRN 58A
Stephen MBG 142A
Thomas SHE 120A
Tureene? DVS 19A
William LGN 37
William LWS 97A
Wm. FKN 86
Wm. WAS 25A
WATKINS?, Horace D.g. HND 10A
Joseph HAR 142
Wm. BRK 305

WATON, Nathan N. WRN 50A
WATS, Edward FKN 134
  Fielding CLK 96
  Francis BBN 110
WATSON, ---nas? DVS 9A
  Abner FKN 118
  Alkeno? MAS 73
  Amos LVG 6
  Anna FLD 11
  Asa MAS 75
  Authur FLG 28A
  Bartholomew SHE 160
  Bassett HRY 180
  Ben GRD 117A
  Ben. MAS 68
  Ben. MAS 70
  Benjamin GSN 154A
  Cain MAS 56
  Cloe HAR 220
  Daniel NSN 211
  Daniel NSN 214
  Davey WAS 26A
  David MAD 132
  David MAD 166
  Eliazer FLG 50A
  Elizabeth CSY 206
  Evan WRN 62A
  Flavill LGN 44
  Frances LGN 42
  Hezekiah FLG 46A
  Hugh LVG 18
  Isac ALN 138
  Israel LVG 10
  Jacob FLG 63A
  James FLD 5
  James FKN 62
  James BBN 138
  James BLT 160
  James HAR 190
  James NSN 197
  Jas. RCK 78A
  Jeptha FLG 49A
  Jesse WRN 62A
  Jessee ADR 56
  Jno. FKN 158
  Joab MTG 275
  Joab WRN 48A
  Joel ADR 60
  Joel RCK 82A
  John HRD 42
  John ADR 60
  John MAD 102
  John GTN 120
  John SPN 14A
  John FLG 38A
  John W. PND 25A
  Johnson ADR 58
  Jos. MAS 70
  Jos. FLG 49A
  Joseph MAD 118
  Joseph MAD 126
  Joseph PND 17A
  Joshua CLD 158
  Mary CWL 39
  Mary FTE 97
  Milley LGN 43
  Nancy JEF 44
  Nathan FKN 146
  Nathaniel SPN 18A
  Parson CLY 120
  Patk. SCT 117A
  Patrick JES 96
  Patrick HAR 190
  Paul MAD 126
  Phebe MNR 197
  Polly, Mrs. WYN 104A
WATSON, Polly RCK 83A
  Robin CHN 43
  Saml JEF 35
  Saml. CWL 57
  Saml., Jr. JEF 52
  Saml. FLG 49A
  Saml. B. CHN 43
  Saml.? CWL 39
  She--? LVG 10
  Stanton RCK 82A
  Susan JEF 39
  Thos. MAD 140
  Thos. FLG 49A
  William BKN 4
  William LGN 44
  William FTE 111
  William HAR 168
  William NSN 205
  William, Sr. LGN 39
  William SPN 13A
  Wm. MAD 102
  Wm. PUL 47A
  Wm. GNP 169A
  Zepheniah MAS 70
WATSON?, Robert S. FTE 75
WATT, Charles, Jr. CBL 15A
  Charles, Sr. CBL 15A
  Gabriel WRN 41A
  James CLK 107
  John WRN 41A
WATTER?, Jacob JEF 27
WATTERMAN, George HRD 12
WATTERS, (See
    Walters) JES 77
  Jackson WRN 33A
  Pleasant JES 77
  Richard JES 93
  Stephen JES 89
WATTERS?, (See
    Walters?) KNX
  (See Walters) CHN 44A
  (See Walters?) FLG
  Asolem GNP 178A
  John PND 28A
  Thomas JES 85
  William JES 86
WATTS, Abraham MTG 291
  Alson TRG 13
  Barnett FTE 106
  Benjamin BRK 301
  Bledsoe WDF 121A
  Charles SPN 15A
  David FTE 82
  Deborah MAS 78
  Drury ALN 102
  Ezekel ALN 110
  Francis BBN 92
  Francis BRK 301
  George FLD 14
  George FTE 76
  George CLK 77
  George MAD 116
  Henry FTE 68
  Holland KNX 290
  Jacob SHE 111A
  James GRN 56
  Jer. SHE 109A
  Jno. FKN 136
  Jno. HRY 241
  John CLK 74
  John CLK 77
  John CLK 96
  John FTE 106
  John B. HRD 60
  Julian CLK 66
  Peter, Capt. MER 113
WATTS, Philip SHE 171
  Philip SHE 142A
  Richard WAS 75A
  Samuel JES 89
  Samuel WRN 41A
  Thomas SHE 165
  Thomas HOP 268
  Thurman SHE 109A
  William TRG 10
  William MER 112
  Wm. MAD 170
  Wm. WAS 76A
  Wm. C. CHN 27A
WATTS?, Agnes? BBN 96
  Jobe BRK 301
WATTSON,
    Greenberry HND 12
  John HND 11A
  Mary BBN 86
  Polley HND 12
  Tarlton HND 9
  Thos. HND 6A
WATZON, John JEF 35
WAUGH, George GNP 166A
  Jacob FLG 32A
  John FLG 49A
WAUGH?, Samuel M.? NCH 116A
WAVER?, David MER 112
WAW?, Eliza MAS 73
  Henson MAS 76
  Jno. MAS 73
WAX, Henry GRN 52
WAY, Charles M. WAS 78A
  Mary JEF 33
  Mary BBN 138
  Saml. SCT 109A
WAYLAND, John HRY 182
  Joseph CBL 6A
  Joshua GTN 128
  Joshua SHE 150
  Willis GTN 128
WAYMAN, Aaron CBL 5A
  Harman CBL 12A
  John WAS 25A
  Moses CBL 4A
  Simeon CBL 12A
  Solomon CBL 11A
  Wm. BNE 42
WAYNE, Benjamin MTG 281
  Francis BRK 303
  Isaac DVS 15A
WEADMAN, Wm. GSN 155A
WEAGLE, Jacob MTG 237
  John MTG 237
  Thomas MTG 293
WEAKLEY, George HRD 52
  John HRD 44
  Stephen SHE 175
WEAKLY, Abraham NSN 188
  Jeremiah SCT 115A
  Thomas SHE 169
WEAKS, Lewes OHO 3A
WEARD?, James BBN 92
WEARE?, James BBN 92
WEARNING, John U. WRN 73A
WEARY, George HAR 220
WEATHERBY, D. JEF 23
  D. JEF 23
  Jno. FKN 80
WEATHERED, William FTE 84
WEATHERFORD, Abel SHE 177
  Archibald LNC 51
  Burrel CSY 214
  David LNC 51
  George CSY 214
  Hardin M. SHE 177

WEATHERFORD, Joel CSY 214
John WAS 26A
WEATHERHEAD, Thos. MAD 156
WEATHERHOLT, Jacob BRK 301
WEATHERINGTON, Benjn. ADR 60
Joseph ADR 60
Mark BKN 19
Mathew ADR 58
Richard ADR 58
Wm. BKN 18
Wm. ADR 58
WEATHERLY?, Wm. WAS 44A
WEATHERS, Benjamin HAR 168
Charles HRT 170
H. B. CHN 46
James FTE 91
James WAS 86A
John JEF 33
John JES 93
John SCT 121A
Nicolass WAS 49A
Thomas HAR 212
W. A. SCT 127A
WEATHERSPOON, Isaac HOP 268
James HOP 268
Major ALN 110
Wiley ALN 110
WEATHINGTON, John BKN 10
WEATHURS, William M. SHE 165
WEATKONSPONS?, Hardy ALN 122
WEATT, John JES 76
WEAVER, Abram BTH 176
Ambrose WYN 86A
David KNX 312
David SHE 136A
Eli FLG 51A
Elijah PUL 54A
Geo. BBN 116
Hesek. KNX 312
Jacob SHE 157
James SHE 171
James WYN 86A
Jas. MAS 73
Jeremiah NSN 186
John ALN 122
John SHE 172
John FLG 33A
John CHN 34A
Moore SHE 152
Peter KNX 310
Peter FLG 47A
Phillip FLG 33A
Saml. KNX 310
Simeon PUL 53A
Simon FLG 60A
Susanna SHE 133A
Thomas LWS 96A
Valentine CHN 33
William SHE 172
Wm. BKN 9
WEB, John HRT 170
M. James GSN 154A
Martin HRT 170
Richard GTN 126
Susanna MAD 154
Wm. MAD 146
WEBB, Aaron WDF 111A
Alexr. PND 27A
Amasa GRN 57
Augustine BLT 164
Augustine SHE 141A
Benjamin FLD 4
WEBB, Benjamin LGN 47
Charles NCH 103A
Edmond BRK 301
Elijah BBN 112
Elizabeth WRN 67A
Ezekiel NSN 192
George CLK 106
Hallifax MAD 140
Henry CLK 70
Isaac FTE 92
Jacob ADR 58
James HRL 120
James HRY 184
Jane SHE 150
Jas. JEF 54
Jeremiah WRN 33A
John FTE 106
John SHE 150
John MAD 172
John NSN 181
John HRY 184
John MNR 205
John BRK 301
John OHO 3A
John PND 27A
John V. SCT 133A
Jonathan SHE 141A
Jos. SHE 141A
Joseph CLK 70
Joseph WRN 63A
Lewis BNE 40
Lewis MER 113
Martin WRN 48A
Mary FTE 91
Merry WRN 48A
Moses HAR 134
Nancy WRN 50A
Nehemiah NSN 223
Plesent GNP 165A
Polly CLY 121
Richard BRN 30
Robert WRN 48A
Robt. BBN 92
Robt. HRY 255
Samuel CLK 70
Samuel PND 27A
Samuel SHE 115A
Theophilus BRN 31
Thos. MAD 160
Walter HRY 240
William FLD 33
William CLK 80
William WRN 52A
Willis LGN 40
Wm. FKN 102
Zachariah FKN 102
WEBBER, A., Dr. CHN 27A
Archabald JES 84
Chalc. W. BRK 229
George Adam FTE 73
Henry JES 80
John JES 74
Philip SHE 171
Polly GTN 121
William SHE 171
WEBER, Jones ETL 40
Orson ETL 40
WEBSTER, Achillas FTE 98
Agness FTE 99
Allen JEF 31
Archd. GRN 58
Beverly FTE 98
Bright B. FTE 97
Cornelius BNE 42
Daniel BNE 42
Daniel GRT 140
WEBSTER, Dudley GRT 140
Dudley MAD 178
Elijah CSY 218
George GTN 124
Haniah? HND 5A
Hannah JES 91
Henry FKN 86
Henry FLG 62A
Isaac NCH 127A
Jacob FTE 84
James BNE 42
James FTE 98
James GTN 125
John FTE 99
John FTE 99
John GTN 124
Larcan? FTE 99
Leroy FTE 90
Margett GTN 131
Martin FTE 90
Mary JES 72
Nelson FTE 63
Thomas FTE 84
Thomas FTE 98
Thos. BKN 24
Tillman FTE 98
William FTE 99
William CSY 214
William CSY 218
WEDDING, George OHO 11A
Henry NSN 191
Thos. C. WAS 69A
WEDDLE, Daniel PUL 64A
James MER 113
John MER 113
John PUL 57A
WEDEMAN, Christopher GSN 154A
John GSN 153A
WEDINGTON, Henry FLD 28
WEEKLEY, Enoch SCT 134A
WEEKS, -----? R. CWL 41
Elijah BLT 188
James BLT 188
Payton BTH 170
Tempy TRG 12A
Wm. L. SHE 136A
WEEVER, John ADC 70
WEIGART, David FTE 68
Jacob FTE 57
Philip A. FTE 67
WEILY, Able MAS 56
WEIR, Aaron FTE 97
Alexander, Jr. CBL 9A
Alexander, Sr. CBL 10A
Daniel CBL 20A
Israel CBL 20A
James MBG 143
James CBL 8A
Robbert CBL 20A
Saml. HRT 169
Samuel MBG 136A
WEIR?, Benjamin GNP 177A
WEIRE?, Abram SCT 106A
WEIRICK?, Nicholas BKN 24
WEISGER, Daniel, Jr. FKN 104
WEISIGER, Daniel, Sr. FKN 104
Joseph, Dr. MER 117
WELBORN, Joshua MNR 205
Peggy MNR 205
William MNR 205
WELCH, -----? ALN 92
Elizabeth FTE 96
Ephraim CLD 159

Name	County	Page
WELCH, George	BBN	66
George	BTH	208
George P.	JES	96
Harry	NSN	191
James	LNC	51
James	CLK	73
James	FTE	96
James	CLD	156
James	MNR	201
James H.	SHE	142A
Jas.	TOD	134
John	JES	77
John	LNC	77
John	FTE	96
John	MNR	195
John	WAS	31A
Joseph	WAS	30A
Joseph	WAS	50A
Nathaniel	JES	77
Noble	FLG	77A
Ozias	MBG	136
Richard	CLD	156
Richard	MNR	197
Sherod	GTN	127
Solomon	CLD	156
Thomas	MBG	139
Thomas	BTH	174
Thomas	NSN	183
William	LNC	53
William	BLT	152
William	BLT	166
Wm.	HRY	264
Wm.	SHE	141A
WELCHER, Charles	LNC	77
WELCHER?, John	CSY	212
WELDIN, James	BKN	24
WELDON, Abraham	CLK	83
Andrew	BKN	23
Andrew	GRD	94A
Isaac	BNE	40
Jeseph	HND	8A
John	GNP	175A
Nancy	HND	8A
Rachael	BKN	23
Thos.	HND	8A
William	BNE	40
WELINGTON, Joel	MAD	180
WELKER, John	BTH	204
WELL, Benj.	WAS	64A
Henry	MAD	120
John, Sr.	MNR	205
WELLDON, John	LNC	41
WELLER, Christian	LGN	22
Coonrod	GSN	155A
Daniel	NSN	182
David	NSN	175
Frederick	LGN	22
George	BRK	303
Henry	NSN	175
Heny	NSN	184
John	HND	7A
Jonathan	NSN	193
Joseph	NSN	201
Margaret	NSN	186
Philip	NSN	182
Philip	NSN	194
Samuel	NSN	195
William	BRK	303
William	HND	7A
WELLER?, Sampson	HRL	120
Thomas	BLT	160
WELLES?, John	LVG	18
Thomas	BLT	160
WELLETT, Thomas	NSN	189
William	NSN	189
WELLING, Joseph	WAS	55A
WELLING, Thomas	BRK	303
WELLINGTON, Thos.	HRD	62
WELLMAN, Bennett	FLD	46
Cornelius	FTE	67
Lewis	FLD	45
Michl.	PND	30A
WELLMEN, Michale	FLD	46
WELLMON, Elisha	FLD	46
James	FLD	46
Jeremiah	FLD	46
Joseph	FLD	46
William	FLD	45
WELLS, (See Wills?)		
Abner	BRN	30
Absalom	BTH	218
Ambrose	OWN	102
Ann	BTH	204
Bazel	PND	17A
Ben.	PND	18A
Benja.	JEF	35
Benja.	JEF	62
Benjamin	BTH	190
Betsy	BTH	214
Catherine	JEF	55
Catherine	JEF	62
David	MAD	104
David	MTG	271
Edmond	FLD	11
Edmond	HAR	132
Edmond	PND	24A
Elijah	LNC	23
Francis	BKN	23
Francis/Frances?	MBG	143A
Geo.	JEF	51
Geo. P.	JEF	62
George	NSN	218
Haden	HRY	266
Hasten	MTG	251
Henry	LGN	39
Henry	MAD	116
Herbett	HAR	138
Isaac	FTE	103
Isaac	MTG	245
Jacob	MER	112
Jacob	BLT	180
James	BBN	64
James	BRK	301
James	BRK	303
James H.	MTG	251
Jane	BRN	31
Jesse	BRN	30
Joel	CLD	154
John	FLD	7
John	ETL	42
John	HRT	169
John	SHE	169
John	NSN	204
John	MTG	285
John, Senr.	CLK	71
John	WTY	115A
John	MBG	143A
John H.	JEF	35
Johnston	MBG	143A
Joseph	FKN	120
Joseph	BTH	210
Joseph	WRN	56A
Lewis	HRT	170
Littleberry	HRY	212
Micajah	MBG	140A
Nathan	NCH	106A
Newman	SHE	132A
Peter	CLK	88
Peter	MTG	287
Phillip	HRT	170
Richard	CBL	8A
WELLS, Robt.	BKN	22
Ruth	NCH	106A
Saml.	MAS	74
Saml.	PND	29A
Samuel	JES	92
Samuel	SHE	165
Solomon	CLD	158
Solomon	CLD	160
Thomas	CLK	73
Thomas	BLT	160
Thomas	HRT	170
Thos.	PND	21A
Thos.	WAS	86A
Will	HRY	222
Will.	KNX	300
William	FLD	7
William	CLK	83
William	CLK	98
William	HRT	170
William	HOP	270
William	WRN	57A
Wm.	MAD	92
Wm.	MAD	110
Wm.	FLG	77A
Wm.	WAS	83A
Wm.	SHE	132A
Wyatt	MBG	143A
Zackeriah	KNX	300
WELLS?, James Q.?	NCH	115A
Jesse	NSN	192
Thomas	NSN	192
Thos.	MAS	68
William	NSN	192
Willis	LGN	27
WELMAN, Andrew	JEF	59
Jeremiah	JEF	59
Thos.	JEF	59
WELSH, Elenor	JEF	33
Elenor	JEF	37
James	UNN	152
Jas.	JEF	19
John	HRD	82
John D.	JEF	60
Michael	BBN	128
Robt.	JEF	20
William	JEF	41
WELSON?, Thos.	BRK	303
WELTHAL, Archibald	CLD	162
WELTON?, Michael	CLK	68
WELTY, Abraham	SPN	20A
Peter	SPN	21A
WENETTA, Saml. A.?	SHE	124A
WERD/WERE?, James	ADR	56
WERNALL?, Thomas	CLK	99
WERT, George	SHE	116A
Thos.	SCT	132A
WERT?, Jas.	SCT	126A
Jas.	SCT	134A
WERTHINGTON, Thos. F.	WAS	42A
WERTMAN?, Benjamin	CBL	9A
WESIGAR, Sally	LWS	96A
WESINGTON?, Thompson	BBN	104
WESLEY, Thomas	CSY	208
WEST, Abner	HOP	268
Adam	NCH	108A
Alexander, Maj.	WYN	87A
Alexander	WYN	89A
Alexr.	GRD	98A
Allen R.	WYN	106A
Amos	NCH	127A
Amos S.	SPN	9A
Ann	LGN	47
Benony	GRD	89A
Bransford	MAD	170

WEST, Carey NCH 110A
Catherine BLT 194
Charles BKN 22
Charles CHN 31
Charles JES 76
Claborun CHN 43A
Edward FTE 66
Edward GTN 119
Elijah NCH 123A
Elizabeth FLG 77A
Elizabth BBN 106
Ephraim CWL 34
Fieling SPN 9A
George CBL 21A
Henry MAS 60
Henry BTL 331
Isaac WYN 87A
Isaac NCH 119A
Isaiah BKN 19
James MAD 144
James HRT 170
James SPN 7A
James LWS 93A
James H. JEF 39
Jane NCH 112A
Jas. MAS 73
Jeptha CHN 31A
Jesse MAS 61
Jesse MAS 73
Jesse CHN 31A
Jo. GRD 112A
John LGN 47
John FTE 79
John NCH 105
John MAD 126
John HRT 170
John CHN 31A
John LWS 92A
John SCT 124A
Jon MAS 69
Jonathan MAD 162
Josep BRN 0
Joseph, Sen. WYN 85A
Joseph GNP 177A
Joshua FKN 96
Joshua PUL 54A
Josiah MAS 70
Leonard SPN 9A
Lisander GRD 113A
Luke MAD 162
Lynn SCT 92A
Marun D. GTN 119
Mathew SPN 7A
Nancy LGN 35
Nath. GNP 177A
Nicholas ETL 39
P. GRD 112A
Payton GRD 95A
Philip NCH 119A
Philop CHN 31A
Polley MAD 112
Rebecca CLY 128
Reubin BTL 331
Rezein? OWN 99
Richard ETL 51
Richard JES 76
Richard CHN 31A
Richd. BKN 8
Robert D. CLK 101
Rodger P. LGN 33
Roland HAR 184
Saml. SCT 107A
Samuel ETL 49
Semian MAS 74
Solomon, Sen. WYN 87A
Sophy GRD 102A
WEST, Susan FKN 96
Temple CHN 33
Thomas CHN 30
Thomas NCH 105
Thomas BBN 126
Thomas HRT 170
Thos. CHN 42
Thos. MAS 65
Thos. PND 31A
Ven. S. OWN 100
Walker GRD 84A
William LNC 19
William ETL 50
William FTE 55
William CLY 128
William SHE 175
William SPN 10A
William WYN 89A
Wm. FKN 94
Wm. FKN 100
Wm. FKN 108
Wm. MAD 172
Wm. GNP 177A
Zury? PUL 41A
WEST?, Jas. SCT 126A
Jas. SCT 134A
Peter BLT 162
WESTBROOK, Demcy MBG 139
Elijah WRN 29A
WESTBROOKS, Thomas CLK 89
WESTCOAT,
Elizabeth NSN 193
WESTE, John BTH 148
John BTH 212
WESTER, Benjamin LGN 41
Elizabeth TRG 5A
John LGN 43
WESTER?, Jacob,
Jr. FLG 29A
WESTERFIELD,
Cornelious OHO 5A
Isaac MER 113
James MER 113
James, Esq. MER 113
Widw. CWL 35
WESTFALL,
Cornelieus GSN 154A
Danl. HRD 38
Hezekiah BLT 190
John BLT 162
Vincent HRD 38
WESTHERFORD, Jonas NCH 120A
WESTLEY, John PUL 67A
Rovbert PUL 60A
WESTON, Elisabeth
& Daughter FKN 60
WESTOVER, Samuel BRK 301
WET-ELL?, Jesse OWN 99
WET-ILL?, Jesse OWN 99
WETHERFORD,
Jackson MER 114
Patsey SHE 125A
WETHERS, John G. SHE 143A
WETHERSPOON,
George LVG 14
WETHINGTON,
James?, Jr. LVG 18
WEVER, William ALN 122
WEYMAN, William CLK 94
WEYMOUTH, Jno. SHE 133A
WHALEN,
Bartholomew NSN 208
Bartholomew NSN 210
Henry HAR 180
John NSN 210
John WAS 20A
WHALEN, John WRN 40A
John W. NSN 180
Mary HAR 180
Patrick NSN 209
Patrick WRN 40A
Westley WRN 40A
WHALEY, Ann GRD 104A
Benjm. BBN 128
Edward BBN 60
Elijah HAR 210
Ellender CBL 13A
James FTE 84
James FTE 85
James BTH 176
John NCH 105
John GTN 134
John CBL 13A
Johnson BTH 178
Leland BBN 116
Vincent BTH 180
William BTH 176
WHALIN, Valentine BTL 333
WHALING, Wm. CHN 33
WHALY, John BBN 128
Nicholas ADR 60
WHARIN?, Abraham CBL 3A
WHARTON, John TRG 10
WHAYLIN, James WAS 20A
WHEALEY?, Benjamin FTE 58
WHEALY, Thos. MAS 59
WHEAT, Bazle ADR 56
Eli MER 114
Handon? WDF 108A
Hezekiah BBN 120
John ADR 56
John GRN 70
Joseph ADR 56
Joseph MER 114
Levi ADR 56
Oathy ADC 68
Perry CLK 101
Will BBN 108
Zacheriah BBN 106
WHEATLEY, Bend. WAS 70A
Bernard NSN 218
Daniel FTE 90
Edwd. WAS 73A
Francis WAS 73A
James BRK 301
John HAR 134
John WAS 72A
John WAS 75A
Joseph GTN 120
Thomas NCH 106A
William LGN 32
WHEATLY, Francis CHN 45A
Francis WAS 54A
James WAS 69A
Jno. MAS 74
John GSN 153A
Josep NSN 0
Leonard BRK 301
Thomas BRK 301
WHEELER, Aarch,
Jr. ADR 56
Allen GRD 84A
Allen GRD 106A
Basle CBL 5A
Benj. ADR 56
Benj. MAD 168
Benjamin NSN 189
Bond BRN 32
Charles WYN 87A
Clement W. GTN 135
David BRN 31
Drummond PND 21A

WHEELER, Etheldred PUL 62A
Frances BRN 30
George FTE 106
George F. GRT 145
Henry LVG 13
Hezekiah PND 24A
Ignatius PND 24A
Ignatus JEF 43
Itius? LVG 4
James LVG 9
James FLD 20
James FLD 20
Jno. LVG 7
Joel BRN 32
John JEF 22
John BRN 30
John JEF 44
John ADR 58
John MAD 92
John UNN 149
John HRY 208
John NSN 208
John CHN 33A
John FLG 70A
John WRN 70A
John GRD 100A
John B. BLT 180
John N.? PND 30A
Joseph BTH 210
Joseph NCH 106A
Joshua BRN 32
Laurance MAS 56
Leonard BRK 301
Nancy BRK 303
Nathan WRN 70A
Robert BLT 184
Saml. ADR 56
Samuel MTG 273
Sarah KNX 298
Sibern GSN 155A
Solomon LVG 14
Stephen FLD 20
Tedick BKN 15
Thomas HAR 184
Warren FTE 112
William FLD 19
William LGN 40
William WRN 55A
William GRD 84A
William NCH 119A
Wm. ADR 56
Wm. L. BBN 134
Zachariah BRN 31
Zediach ADR 3
WHEELER?, Arch, Sen. ADR 60
WHEELOR, Stephen FLD 23
WHEET, Saml. MAS 62
WHELAN, Grace WAS 74A
Lititia MER 116
WHELDON, Cornelius PUL 39A
WHELER, Garlant GSN 154A
Polly GNP 169A
WHELLEAYS?, -----? BLT 166
WHELLER, John PND 26A
WHERITT, Henry JES 96
WHERITT?, Samuel JES 73
WHERLY, Frail BRK 299
WHERRITT, Margarett JES 95
WHERRY, Susan CBL 2A
WHETER, William BRK 299
WHETING, Ann WDF 120A
WHETSEL, Christopher HOP 270
WHETSTONE, Peter HRD 66

WHIGHT, Jno. MAS 64
Wm. LNC 29
WHILETMOST?, James CLK 99
WHILLINGTON, William WRN 63A
WHILLOCK?, John WRN 33A
WHINGER?, George JES 88
WHIP, Adam UNN 146
WHIPPLE, Arty M. JEF 41
WHIPS, Denton JEF 58
Jno. MAS 54
Jno., Sr? MAS 54
John JEF 40
Will MAS 69
WHIRLEY, William BNE 42
WHISNER?, Jacob BTH 176
WHISTLER, Mary NCH 119A
WHISTON, James HAR 214
WHITAKER, David BTL 333
Elijah GTN 132
George W. LGN 23
Henry LGN 30
Henry BTL 333
Isaac CLY 122
James S. SHE 176
Jno. PUL 50A
John GTN 126
John CLD 153
John HAR 190
John W HAR 198
Joseph BKN 23
Joshua WYN 91A
Josiah HAR 198
Mark BTL 333
Peter HAR 190
Price FLD 44
Squire OHO 10A
Thomas BTL 333
Thomas MBG 143A
Thos. MGB 137A
Washington NSN 196
William M. LGN 28
William W. LGN 25
WHITE---TON?, James WAS 66A
WHITE, ----.? CWL 41
Aaron GTN 131
Able GNP 173A
Abner FKN 88
Abraham BLT 168
Alex. BKN 8
Alexr. CLY 129
Ambros FKN 104
Ameh? FTE 100
Andrew ADR 60
Andrew GRN 66
Andrew HAR 188
Andrew MNR 193
Ann FKN 106
Ann HRL 122
Aquilla MTG 291
Archabald MNR 193
Archd. FLG 33A
Arnel MAD 122
Auctin BTH 208
Austin FTE 92
Awuilla ETL 54
Balen? NSN 224
Barret CLD 163
Bartholomew SPN 19A
Benjamin SHE 177
Benjm. SPN 25A
Benson HRD 52
Britain BLT 182
Brockman FTE 109
C. W. CLY 130

WHITE, Carr FLG 36A
Carter SPN 5A
Charles FLD 39
Charles MTG 249
Conyers CBL 18A
Daniel GRN 68
Daniel FTE 79
Daniel MNR 209
Daniel HRY 254
Daniel, Jr. GRN 51
Danl. JEF 39
Danl. B. SCT 129A
Dav. HRY 241
Davd. PUL 35A
David MAD 122
David ALN 138
David SHE 177
David GNP 168A
David P.? WRN 64A
Delia LGN 37
Demcy WTY 110A
Dempsy CWL 34
Duret MAD 142
Easter ETL 52
Ebenezer NCH 103A
Edmund BRN 32
Edward ETL 47
Edwd. SCT 132A
Elizabeth BRN 31
Felix HRD 60
Fendel WAS 67A
Francis CLK 75
Galion MAD 128
Geo. MAS 68
George HRD 38
George GRN 65
George HAR 142
George SHE 151
George CSY 218
George GSN 153A
Gilbert PUL 43A
Harrison WTY 127A
Henderson LGN 46
Hendrick WTY 127A
Henrey ADR 3
Henry JEF 40
Henry CLK 75
Henry MAD 112
Henry MTG 241
Henry OHO 10A
Henry DVS 15A
Hezekiah MER 113
Hugh CLY 126
Iliff, Ser. FLG 34A
Iliff FLG 25A
Isaac BLT 152
Izaac CSY 226
Jac. HRY 254
Jacob HOP 270
Jacob, Jr. CBL 18A
Jacob, Jr. CBL 20A
Jacob CBL 20A
Jacob GNP 167A
Jacob S. MAD 180
James ETL 37
James BNE 42
James GRN 54
James MAD 118
James MAD 128
James MAD 160
James SHE 163
James SHE 165
James SHE 166
James CSY 226
James MTG 293
James, Col. WYN 88A

WHITE, James, Jr. GRN 69
James, Sr. GRN 69
James CBL 16A
James G. CLD 145
James J./ I.? FKN 102
James P.? MAD 176
Jas.? HRY 267
Jemima MNR 217
Jeremiah FTE 91
Jessee MAS 55
Jessee ADR 56
Joel BNE 40
Joel PUL 44A
John LGN 44
John LGN 46
John GRN 53
John GRN 67
John JES 83
John JES 91
John MAD 96
John OWN 101
John FTE 103
John MAD 112
John GTN 126
John GRT 146
John HRY 214
John HAR 216
John HRY 226
John MTG 229
John MTG 243
John HOP 268
John, Jr. WTY 126A
John, Sen. ADR 58
John, Sr. WTY 120A
John CBL 16A
John PND 22A
John FLG 26A
John FLG 37A
John FLG 46A
John WRN 53A
John GRD 99A
John NCH 106A
John GSN 153A
John GNP 173A
John A. WRN 64A
John B. NSN 214
John B. CHN 29A
John C. ADR 58
John D. WDF 99A
John H. WRN 38A
Jonathan WAS 64A
Joseph BRN 32
Joseph FTE 61
Joseph GRN 69
Joseph GTN 122
Joseph MNR 207
Joseph HOP 268
Joseph, Sr. GRN 69
Joseph CBL 5A
Joseph B. WDF 126A
Joshua WRN 62A
Labourn GSN 154A
Lambert PUL 37A
Larking HND 8
Lewis BTL 333
Luther CBL 22A
Margaret BNE 40
Margaret JEF 61
Margaret BBN 126
Mary JEF 44
Mary TOD 127A
Michael MAS 61
Michael SCT 92A
Minon JEF 35
Nancy GNP 168A
Nathl. FLG 46A

WHITE, Nelson FLG 34A
Nicholas BTH 152
Nicholas WYN 80A
Obadiah BRN 30
Peter SHE 134A
Philip FKN 154
Polly BBN 110
Polly SHE 163
Presley FKN 142
Reason FLG 34A
Reason B. GRD 122A
Richard BNE 42
Richard WTY 120A
Richard S. WAS 71A
Robert GTN 132
Robert SHE 165
Robert HRY 198
Robt. CWL 37
Robt. BNE 40
Saley JEF 32
Salley MAD 170
Saml. GRN 68
Saml. MAD 156
Samuel GRN 60
Samuel (Incl Shaker? Family) LGN 29
Samuel LWS 94A
Samuel W. SHE 164
Seth GNP 173A
Simeon BRN 32
Smith HAR 160
Stephen NCH 103A
Stewart HRY 198
Susan ADR 60
Thomas SHE 170
Thomas BTH 186
Thomas MNR 205
Thomas, Sen. ADR 56
Thomas OHO 10A
Thomas WDF 121A
Thos. JEF 21
Thos. CWL 38
Thos. HRY 259
Thos., Jr. ADR 3
Thos., Sen. ADR 3
Timothy NSN 186
Truman JEF 53
Warren SHE 168
Westly PUL 46A
Whitfield FKN 142
William ETL 52
William JES 73
William JES 77
William FTE 84
William GTN 131
William BTH 154
William SHE 163
William MNR 207
William BTH 214
William WRN 38A
William WDF 110A
William GRD 122A
William P. GRN 60
Willis MTG 293
Wm. JEF 55
Wm. PUL 48A
Wm. WAS 73A
Wm. GNP 168A
Wm. D. JEF 35
Wm. G. JEF 44
Wm? JEF 30
Zachariah FKN 120
Zephh. FLG 23A
WHITE?, Peter ALN 112
Wm. GRN 51
[also see Whitt/White?]

WHITECOTTON, Isaac PUL 41A
WHITECRAFT, John BTH 170
John, Jr. BTH 170
WHITEHEAD, Armstead HAR 214
John FTE 107
John GTN 128
John HAR 186
John NSN 191
Joseph WAS 42A
Joseph WAS 70A
Polley GTN 128
Richard GTN 132
William HRL 122
Wm. HRD 76
Wm. J. HRD 76
WHITEHOME?, Cornelious WAS 22A
WHITEHORN, Wm. GSN 153A
WHITEHOUSE, Benjamin MER 113
Charles MBG 133A
James MER 113
Joel GSN 155A
John MER 113
Sally MER 113
Thomas MER 113
WHITEING?, Lewis BRK 301
WHITEKER, B. K?. SHE 129A
Chas. SHE 134A
Elijah SHE 129A
Elijah SHE 132A
Isaac BRK 299
John SHE 127A
John SHE 129A
John SHE 133A
John SHE 133A
Livi? SHE 129A
Martha SHE 129A
Seth SHE 129A
Susanna SHE 129A
WHITELEDGE, Thos. HND 9
WHITELEY, William WTY 120A
WHITELY, Alexander FLD 10
Andrew HRY 222
John GSN 153A
Joshua HRY 190
Thomas PUL 65A
WHITEMAN, Chardlon/ Chardlow? FLG 54A
John SHE 156
WHITENECK, Abraham, Jr. MER 112
Abraham, Sr. MER 112
Henry MER 112
John MER 112
WHITENHALL, John OHO 6A
WHITERS?, Jeremiah GSN 154A
WHITESCARVER, Cornelius LGN 30
Robert LGN 42
WHITESEY, C. JEF 28
WHITESIDES, ----- CLD 158
Elizabeth, Mrs. WYN 85A
Elizabeth WRN 33A
Ephriam CLK 81
Isaac SHE 130A
James HRY 224
James H. LNC 25
John CLK 82
John HOP 268
Joseph CLK 69
Joseph HRY 224
Martin HRY 224
Samuel HOP 268

WHITESIDES, Samuel WRN 33A
William WYN 89A
WHITEWORTH, Abram BRK 301
WHITFIELD, Bryant HOP 268
WHITFILL, Joseph GSN 153A
WHITFORD, John B. GTN 133
WHITHER?, Elisha WRN 59A
WHITICAR, Nimrod HRY 200
WHITICK, George LGN 36
Jacob LGN 38
John LGN 39
Samuel LGN 46
WHITIKER, Isaac BRK 303
Jas. MAS 66
Jessee BRK 303
Thomas BNE 40
William BNE 40
WHITING, Jerremia? ALN 136
Richard CHN 46
William FTE 92
WHITLAGE?, Juriah BLT 180
WHITLEDGE?, John BLT 180
WHITLEY, Daniel HAR 190
Nimrod WRN 54A
Robert WRN 59A
Rubin GRN 66
William LNC 73
Wm. FLG 48A
WHITLOCK, Charls ADR 56
Jno. R. CHN 41
John WRN 70A
Robert SPN 17A
Thomas CLD 157
Thos. GRN 66
William BNE 42
Wm. ADR 60
WHITLOCK?, John WRN 33A
WHITLOW, Britton MAD 98
Greenville CLD 138
Jessee ALN 130
John MAD 98
John MER 112
Pleasant BRN 30
Solomon CLD 138
WHITMAN, Christopher HRT 170
Henry HRY 192
Isaac BRK 303
Richd. HRT 169
Thomas HRT 170
William HRY 182
Wm. HRT 169
WHITMER, Jacob MBG 141
John MBG 139
John MBG 139
Vallentine MBG 140
WHITMIRE, John JES 80
WHITMORE, Chas. SHE 129A
WHITNEY, ---cy? CWL 40
Ann ALN 136
Elijah TRG 6A
Hiram TRG 3
Jno. ALN 136
John SCT 92A
Laomi BRN 30
Mary FTE 64
Robert BLT 176
Tho. ALN 136
WHITROATH, William MNR 213
WHITSELL, James MTG 239
Ralph MTG 245
Rebecca MTG 289
WHITSERE?, Abram JEF 49
WHITSILL, Isaac, (Free) LGN 22
William LGN 33
WHITSON, James MNR 217
John MNR 217
Jonathan MNR 193
Nathan JEF 64
Reuben MNR 215
William HAR 138
WHITSON?, Thomas RCK 80A
WHITT/ WHITE?, Richard FLD 25
WHITT, Bauman FLD 44
WHITTAKER, Mark PUL 57A
WHITTEAYR?, O------? BLT 166
WHITTEKER, Francis FLD 5
Joseph HRL 120
WHITTEMORE, John KNX 294
Mathew KNX 310
WHITTEN, James GSN 155A
Jeremiah GSN 154A
Jeremiah GSN 155A
John GSN 155A
Noel WAS 83A
Samuel WYN 83A
Thos. GSN 153A
Wm. CWL 46
WHITTEN?, Charity WRN 59A
Elisha WRN 59A
WHITTIER?, Charity WRN 59A
Elisha WRN 59A
WHITTIMORE, William G. TRG 12A
WHITTINGHAM, C. JEF 22
WHITTINGTON, Isaac WDF 104
John WRN 66A
Joshua MAS 78
Littleton, Jr. WDF 123A
Littleton WDF 123A
William WDF 124A
WHITTINTON, Charles BTH 186
WHITTLE, John CSY 210
Robert WYN 91A
WHITTON, George BTH 152
Robert JES 84
WHITWORTH, Willis CLD 140
WHOBERRY, Jacob MER 113
Michael MER 113
WHORTON, Eli NCH 126A
George JES 92
John GRD 122A
Joseph NCH 128A
Reubin JES 96
WHURRL?, Thos. JEF 59
WIAT, Sally MAD 140
Thomas TOD 127
WIATT, John NSN 200
Jourden ETL 43
Mark ETL 42
Wm. G. TOD 132
WIATT?, James ETL 44
WICKER, Elizabeth TRG 13A
WICKERSHAM, Daniel MER 112
Elizabeth MER 112
Jacob MER 112
William CBL 16A
WICKHAM, Peter NSN 193
WICKINGHAM, Benjamin WDF 99
WICKLIFFE, Charles FTE 55
Charles A. NSN 176
Martin H. NSN 176
Moses MBG 141A
Nathaniel NSN 176
Robert FTE 62
Robert MBG 138
Sarah MBG 140
WICKOFF, John MER 113
Nicholas MER 113
WICKS, Wm. CHN 32A
WICKWARE, Samuel WRN 29A
WICKWIRE, Alphius LGN 33
Elisha LGN 33
Susanna LGN 42
WICLEY?, Elijah BKN 22
WICLIFFE, Catharine MBG 139
WICLY / WIELY?, Eli BKN 6
WICOFF, James PND 19A
John CBL 14A
WIDENER, George GTN 119
WIELEY?, Elijah BKN 22
WIELY, Elisha BKN 14
WIER, Hazle FLG 35A
Henry FTE 60
James FTE 64
James, Jr. FTE 60
John MER 113
John, Jr. FLG 78A
John, Snr. FLG 23A
Turner UNN 151
William R. HOP 268
WIETT, Dickerson BNE 40
WIGAL, John? JEF 56
WIGGANS, Enoch M. HAR 204
WIGGART?, Johanna FTE 66
WIGGENTON, James BLT 172
William BLT 174
WIGGINGTON, John CHN 34A
WIGGINS, Absolum SCT 131A
Alexander LGN 38
Frederick LGN 40
George HND 8A
Jas. MAS 55
John SCT 99A
John NCH 107A
Simon BNE 42
Thomas MBG 138
William NCH 107A
WIGGINTON, Elijah NSN 214
Jacob WYN 95A
John W. B. WRN 76A
Rogers BNE 42
Seth BLT 186
Wm. G. BLT 199
WIGGLESWORTH, James HAR 132
John HAR 132
John BTH 178
Tomkins HAR 132
William CLK 77
WIGGS, Hiram HRY 194
Richard WDF 95
Wheeler HRY 180
WIGHAM, John MER 113
John MER 113
Joseph MER 113
WIGHT, Elizabeth NSN 193
Geo. FKN 152
George BNE 42
James FKN 62
James GNP 165A
Jane FLG 29A
Thomas T. NSN 193
Thos. N. WAS 37A
WIGINGTON, Henry BBN 108
Presley HND 10
Roger GTN 126
William BBN 108
WIGINS, Jonas MBG 138A
WIL--?, Alexander MAD 168
WILBANKS, Reubin WRN 69A

WILBERTON, Tho. MAD 122
WILBORN, James MBG 133A
WILBOURN, Edward CLD 163
Samuel CLD 159
Tabitha BRN 30
William CLD 163
WILBURN, Jane MAS 73
John GRD 119A
William GRD 119A
WILCLUS, Elijah WRN 55A
WILCOX, ---.? CWL 42
George BRN 30
Isaac SHE 163
Isaac NSN 207
James BRN 31
Jane FKN 120
John LNC 35
Joseph SHE 109A
Sarah SHE 166
William BTH 198
WILCOXEN, Alfred ETL 45
Daniel CLK 89
Elijah ETL 45
George CLK 75
Isaac CLK 86
Izreal CLK 86
Jessee CLK 91
John CLK 86
Samuel, Sr. ETL 45
Squire ETL 53
WILCOXON, Daniel WDF 117A
Josiah NCH 127A
Lewis BLT 192
Lewis PND 31A
Thomas H. BLT 162
WILDER, Burrel ALN 96
Janey CSY 206
Jas. HRD 48
Joseph CLY 120
Nancy HRL 122
Sampson WTY 121A
WILDER?, Sampson HRL 120
WILDINEL?, Edmund FKN 106
WILDS, Felix CLY 115
Henry CLY 115
John CLY 128
John PUL 60A
Joseph PUL 60A
WILER, Jacob JES 84
Pheby JES 73
WILES, Ben GRD 121A
Jno. MAS 68
John GRD 121A
WILEY, -----?, Snr. DVS 3A
Ann C. GRD 119A
Ben. HRY 259
Benjamin WRN 33A
Benjn. MAD 136
David BRN 31
David CHN 31
Elizabeth GSN 154A
Harry SCT 116A
Henry SHE 112A
Hezekiah FLD 24
Hugh NCH 114A
Jacob MBG 139
James LWS 88A
James GSN 154A
Jas. H. SCT 124A
Jean FLD 24
John LVG 10
John CWL 46
John LNC 65
John SHE 170
John MTG 263
WILEY, John, Sr. LVG 10
John SHE 112A
Joseph SCT 125A
Margaret LVG 10
Mary HRD 62
Mary HRY 249
Mathew JES 88
Matthew BRN 31
Nathl. SCT 116A
Patrick HOP 270
Robert NCH 114A
Stephen MBG 138A
Thomas SHE 112A
Washn. LNC 5
William, Jr. MTG 265
William, Sr. MTG 265
Willsam HRY 214
WILEY?, (See Wiles) GRD 121A
Alexander MAD 168
WILGUS, Asa LGN 40
John LGN 46
John, Senr. LGN 40
WILGUS?, William FTE 80
WILHAM, Thomas MER 114
WILHAM?, Cornelius MER 112
William MER 112
WILHELMS, Alexr. BRN 31
George BRN 31
John BRN 31
WILHITE, Elias WYN 87A
George WYN 85A
Joel WYN 85A
Jos. HRY 264
Micheal WDF 94A
Nicholas MER 113
Ob. HRY 264
William WYN 87A
WILHOIT, Caleb BNE 42
Joel LNC 77
Lewis LNC 55
William BNE 42
WILHOITE, Aaron JEF 68
Allen JEF 50
Ben. JEF 46
Danl. JEF 63
Elijah JEF 64
Elliott JEF 64
Evan JEF 56
Jeremiah JEF 54
Jessee JEF 56
Jos. JEF 51
Julious JEF 60
Larkin JEF 56
Lewis JEF 56
Noah JEF 68
Simeon JEF 58
Thos. JEF 59
Umphrey JEF 59
Wm. JEF 44
Zachr. JEF 50
WILKENS, Jonas MBG 139A
Michael, Senr. MBG 139A
William Jun. MBG 133A
WILKENSON, Batley BRN 31
James CSY 210
John CSY 208
Richd. BRN 31
Tarlton CSY 212
William BRN 31
Wm., Senr. BRN 31
WILKERS?, Jennings HAR 158
WILKERSHAM, James HAR 142
WILKERSON, Abram MTG 299
Brice ETL 47
Drury ADR 56
WILKERSON, Elitha MTG 287
Henry MTG 251
James SPN 14A
Job BTL 333
John MTG 279
John BRK 299
Joseph CLK 67
Joseph BRK 299
Joseph WAS 78A
Joseph WAS 82A
Meredith HRY 232
Miray SPN 14A
Newton ADR 58
Ross ETL 53
Thomas MBG 142
William CLK 83
William MBG 142
Wm. MTG 279
Wyatt WRN 29A
WILKES, Izarel HRD 62
WILKINGHAM?, Benjamin WDF 99
WILKINS, Alexander HND 9
Benj. CHN 40
Charles FTE 62
Hugh TOD 128A
James MBG 139
Jas., Jr. TOD 127A
Jas., Sr. TOD 127A
Jesse SPN 10A
John MBG 139
Michael MBG 140
Nancy MBG 139
Peregrine HRD 80
Robt. LVG 18
Saml. LVG 18
Solomon GTN 123
Thomas TOD 132A
Thos. HRD 80
William MBG 142A
WILKINSON, Benja. JEF 55
Job WRN 39A
John D. MAD 146
Lydia LNC 49
Robt. HRT 169
Robt., Sr. HRT 170
Snelling JES 83
Spotswood TRG 10
Will. LNC 51
Will. KNX 308
William WRN 34A
WILKISON, Presley CLK 93
WILKNSON, George NSN 208
George NSN 208
WILKS, Coleman JEF 48
Jesse CWL 43
Jesse? CWL 32
Mifls? BNE 40
Saml. JEF 53
Wm. JEF 48
WILKY, Mary JEF 26
Rebecca BRN 30
WILL.?, Woods SCT 121A
WILL, Robert WAS 51A
WILLARD, John MER 113
Phillip JEF 42
Reuben LGN 23
WILLBARGER, John BBN 64
WILLBORN, Robert MBG 141A
WILLBOROUGH, Jas. HRD 90
WILLBURN, Isaac MAS 55
WILLCOCKS, Ezra HRD 88
Plesant CHN 41
Zera HRD 72
WILLCOM, Hardin CLY 119
WILLCOX, Benjm. GRN 52

WILLCOX, Ephraim GRN 57
Jacob GRN 57
William GRN 68
WILLCOXON, William GRN 57
William FTE 98
Wm. GRN 58
WILLEFORD, Jas. CLY 116
John HRL 120
WILLES, Matthew G. MBG 133A
WILLESS, James CSY 214
Robert CSY 220
WILLET, Richard BRK 301
WILLETH/ WILLETT?,
Edmd. BBN 128
WILLETT, Chas. MAS 60
Geo. FLG 25A
Griffin NSN 218
Jas. MAS 67
Jas. MAS 70
Jas. FLG 24A
John SHE 168
Jonathan BBN 134
Richd. MAS 70
Samuel UNN 153
Samuel NSN 218
WILLHIGHT, J. TOD 127A
WILLHITE, Abraham WDF 115A
Ann WDF 115A
Jesse WDF 125A
Larkin WDF 126A
WILLHOIT, John OWN 99
Lewis OWN 100
Tobias OWN 99
WILLIAM, Croswhite HAR 138
Eliott LVG 18
Isaiah BKN 20
Knight GTN 117
Wharton WDF 93A
Woods HAR 160
WILLIAM?,
Cornelius MER 112
William MER 112
WILLIAMS, -----? DVS 9A
----.? CWL 43
----? FLG 66A
----y? DVS 11A
Aaron ADR 60
Abra. JEF 64
Abra. MAS 68
Abraham MAD 142
Abraham NCH 106A
Absalom FKN 132
Alexander FLD 24
Alexander OWN 104
Alexr. HRD 24
Alfred HND 11A
Amos MTG 243
Amos BRK 301
Amos WRN 55A
Andrew FKN 86
Andrew GRD 106A
Anley? CBL 8A
Anson CWL 57
Arthur CWL 57
Arthur TRG 5A
Asa BBN 140
Austin CWL 57
Basil FLG 37A
Baylis PUL 49A
Bazil HND 5A
Ben JEF 44
Ben FTE 58
Benjamim TRG 14A
Benjamin BRN 30
Benjamin JES 74
Benjamin NCH 124A
WILLIAMS, Benjn. BBN 94
Benn. JEF 47
Bennet NSN 184
Bennet PUL 38A
Bennett GRT 143
Beverly MER 112
Brittain CLY 128
Burwell HND 5
Burwell HOP 270
C., Mrs.? MAS 58
C. J. JEF 23
Caleb FTE 57
Caleb CLD 164
Catron TRG 3A
Charles HRD 32
Charles JES 74
Charles JES 92
Charles OWN 104
Charles HAR 164
Charles NSN 186
Chas. P. SCT 133A
Cloe GRD 103A
Coleman FLD 4
Daley SHE 111A
Daniel HRD 56
Daniel JEF 60
Daniel GRN 72
Daniel MAD 94
Daniel MBG 137
Daniel J./ I.? WDF 96A
David FLD 19
David LNC 25
David LGN 42
David CLK 75
David FKN 154
David BRK 303
David, Capt. MER 113
Dudly CHN 40A
Edward NSN 199
Edward, Senr. OHO 7A
Edward OHO 7A
Edward K. SPN 17A
Edward P. SHE 113A
Edwd. WAS 48A
Eli MTG 265
Eli FLG 37A
Eliabeth FLG 52A
Eligah CBL 8A
Elijah ALN 118
Elijah OHO 4A
Elijah PND 17A
Elijah GRD 90A
Elijah LWS 92A
Elisabeth HAR 140
Eliza CBL 10A
Elizh. FLG 76A
Ellison CBL 7A
Ephraim CLD 138
Evan JEF 38
Evan NSN 186
Ezra MER 117
Frederic PUL 56A
Gabriel WDF 110A
Garrard FLG 35A
Garret CLD 143
Geo. BBN 140
Geo. J./ I.? FKN 124
George BRN 30
George LNC 37
George CWL 43
George ALN 114
George, Jr. CLK 78
George CBL 9A
George WAS 48A
George WRN 55A
Hardy CLY 127
WILLIAMS, Henry HRD 36
Henry CWL 57
Henry MAS 59
Henry ALN 130
Henry GTN 131
Henry HOP 270
Henson FTE 106
Hiram KNX 300
Howard MAD 178
Hubbard BBN 128
Hugh R. BRK 303
Irwin HRD 60
Isaac FLD 8
Isaac FLD 9
Isaac LNC 21
Isaac OHO 8A
Isaac WDF 103A
Jacob JEF 44
Jacob GRT 146
Jacob CHN 32A
Jacob GSN 154A
James LGN 30
James CHN 31
James JES 74
James FTE 78
James BBN 94
James CLY 129
James MAD 138
James GRT 145
James CLD 152
James BTH 164
James BTH 194
James KNX 312
James, Jr. LGN 30
James (Near Jas. Jolliff's) BRN 30
James SPN 7A
James SPN 17A
James PND 20A
James GNP 171A
James R. JEF 38
James W. HOP 270
James W., Junr. HRD 54
Jane WDF 98
Jane SCT 112A
Janeage BRK 303
Jas. HRD 30
Jas. FLG 59A
Jas. FLG 69A
Jas. FLG 71A
Jas. GSN 153A
Jerry JEF 46
Jesse LGN 41
Jesse HRY 182
Jesse GRD 90A
Jno. CWL 57
Jno. MAS 59
Jno. HRY 240
Joel MER 113
Joel P., Capt. MER 115
John TRG 3
John FLD 10
John HND 11
John LGN 29
John LGN 30
John BRN 32
John FLD 33
John HRD 36
John CWL 40
John CWL 44
John HRD 54
John ADR 62
John CLK 64
John FTE 64
John FTE 73
John LNC 77

WILLIAMS, John OWN 104
John MER 112
John MAD 130
John CLD 144
John BTH 152
John CLD 152
John BLT 170
John SHE 171
John BTH 188
John HRY 196
John HAR 210
John HAR 210
John MNR 213
John HAR 216
John HRY 222
John MTG 231
John HOP 270
John MTG 299
John, Esq. WYN 101A
John, Jr. WDF 95A
John, Ser. BRN 30
John, Sr. WDF 95A
John & Co. GRD 82A
John CLY 124
John FLD 1A
John OHO 4A
John CBL 8A
John SPN 10A
John CBL 15A
John SPN 17A
John SPN 22A
John PUL 60A
John FLG 62A
John NCH 109A
John WDF 110A
John NCH 125A
John SHE 128A
John GSN 153A
John F. SCT 135A
John G. HAR 178
John T. MNR 205
Johnothan GRN 73
Jonas BRN 30
Jonathon WAS 64A
Jos. MAS 60
Jos. CHN 44A
Joseph BRN 30
Joseph CLK 93
Joseph MAD 152
Joseph SHE 155
Joseph CSY 208
Joseph BTH 216
Joseph BTH 218
Joseph WAS 81A
Joshua FLD 9
Josiah MAS 53
Josiah GRN 79
Josiah GTN 128
Josiah UNN 148
Keeling WYN 100A
L. BBN 126
L. Wm. GSN 153A
Langston ALN 100
Lawrance, Snr. FLG 37A
Lawrance FLG 41A
Lemuel CLD 137
Levi FKN 86
Levi MAD 162
Lewis JES 74
Lewis JES 92
Lewis CLY 127
Lewis PND 29A
Lewis GNP 176A
Luther MAS 53
Margret FTE 69
Martha JEF 39
WILLIAMS, Martin ALN 110
Martin MER 112
Mary LNC 19
Mary GTN 130
Mary SPN 19A
Mary FLG 55A
Masey GRD 106A
Mason FLD 1A
Mathew JEF 44
Matthew BRN 32
Matthias GTN 129
Merriet SCT 134A
Meshack MER 113
Michael JEF 21
Milly SHE 163
Milton WDF 98A
Mordica FLG 70A
Mordica GNP 167A
Morgan CSY 212
Morris HAR 208
Moses JEF 33
Moses MTG 261
Nancy LVG 18
Nancy HRD 62
Nancy MAD 180
Nancy MTG 273
Nancy PUL 66A
Nancy SHE 126A
Nathan MAD 118
Nathan NCH 106A
Nathaniel LGN 38
Nathaniel GTN 129
Noris BRK 303
Otha? BRK 299
Owen PND 16A
Peter SPN 5A
Philip FLD 19
Philip HRD 62
Philip OHO 7A
Phillip BTH 212
Pleasant CLD 161
Polly BBN 140
Polly UNN 151
Pope PND 20A
Presley CBL 8A
R., Genl. BBN 112
Raleigh MTG 269
Ralph PUL 69
Ralph ALN 92
Ralph PUL 52A
Reece? FKN 148
Ri-? BTL 333
Richard BRN 30
Richard FLD 36
Richard FTE 83
Richard OWN 104
Richard CLD 158
Richard CHN 33A
Richard PUL 56A
Richard SHE 138A
Richard G. MAD 178
Richd. FTE 67
Robert HND 5
Robert LGN 29
Robert LGN 30
Robert MBG 143
Robert MTG 263
Robt. CWL 57
Robt. SCT 114A
Sally FKN 118
Samil ALN 118
Saml. LNC 31
Saml. JEF 55
Saml. MAD 128
Saml. MAD 130
Saml. SHE 155
WILLIAMS, Saml., Sr. HND 13
Saml., Sr. HRY 196
Saml. WAS 54A
Saml. GRD 91A
Saml. SCT 114A
Saml. GSN 153A
Sampson GTN 127
Samuel FTE 87
Samuel BBN 116
Samuel CLD 139
Samuel HAR 140
Samuel CSY 208
Samuel HOP 270
Samuel, Jr. HND 13
Samuel LWS 92A
Samuel NCH 128A
Samuel L. MTG 261
Sanford BBN 136
Sary FKN 92
Seth CLD 139
Shadrick MAD 148
Simon BBN 74
Smith PUL 55A
Solomon CWL 58
Solomon ALN 94
Ste. GRD 103A
Stephen ETL 40
Stephen UNN 151
Stephen OHO 4A
Susan SHE 155
Tabitha CLD 138
Thadeus MTG 269
Tho. MAS 76
Tho. PUL 43A
Tho. PUL 47A
Thomas HRD 8
Thomas FLD 22
Thomas BRN 30
Thomas CWL 57
Thomas HRD 74
Thomas CLD 139
Thomas MNR 195
Thomas CSY 208
Thomas HOP 268
Thomas HOP 268
Thomas PND 16A
Thomas PUL 52A
Thomson SCT 114A
Thornton FLD 9
Thos. HRD 24
Thos. CWL 57
Thos. HRD 64
Thos. HRD 66
Thos. MAS 80
Thos. WAS 23A
Thos. WAS 40A
Thos. FLG 70A
Toy CLD 144
Walter HRD 38
Warren PUL 42A
Warren PUL 49A
Washington JEF 56
Wesley SCT 114A
Westly BBN 146
Will HRY 184
Will B. MAS 70
Will. SCT 135A
William HND 10
William BRN 31
William FLD 34
William LGN 37
William LGN 40
William CLK 65
William CLY 119
William GTN 127

WILLIAMS, William MBG 137
William MTG 285
William BRK 301
William BTL 333
William HND 11A
William WRN 60A
William WDF 124A
William H. LGN 35
William J./ I.? SPN 20A
William J./ I.? NCH 116A
Williamson FTE 110
Winifred WDF 98A
Winny BRN 30
Wm. HRD 16
Wm. CHN 29
Wm. JEF 60
Wm. MAD 114
Wm. ALN 118
Wm. MAD 140
Wm. MAD 174
Wm. FLG 38A
Wm. FLG 70A
Wm.? C. MAS 58
Zachh. FLG 29A
Zealy/ Bealy? BLT 160
Zedekiah MTG 253
Zephaniah GRN 51
WILLIAMSON, ----.? CWL 42
Abram SCT 122A
Albert FLG 65A
Alden FLD 41
Alexander HRD 16
Alexander FTE 84
Benjamin FLD 39
Charrity SHE 133A
Christopher LGN 45
Christopher LGN 47
David BTH 208
David SCT 137A
Deborah BNE 40
Elisabeth FLD 41
Fedrick GRN 57
Garrett FTE 78
Haman FLD 34
Hannah LVG 8
Henry LGN 30
Henry CWL 57
Henry R. SPN 23A
Hiram FLD 41
Hugh LGN 28
Isaac FTE 78
Jacob LGN 47
Jacob MAS 66
James LVG 8
James LGN 31
James HRT 170
James SPN 18A
Jno. LNC 57
Jno. SCT 138A
John LGN 28
John FLD 34
John FLD 39
John JEF 60
John GRN 62
John FLG 74A
John SCT 129A
John P. NSN 194
Joshua LGN 31
Joshua LGN 41
Leonard SHE 121A
M. BRK 303
Parkey MAD 158
Patrick GRD 97A
Rany GRD 94A
Samuel GNP 165A
Sarah JEF 27

WILLIAMSON,
Stephen TRG 14
Thomson SCT 99A
Thos. CHN 34
Thos. M. GRN 51
Tucker SPN 3A
Wm. BNE 40
Wm. FLG 62A
WILLIAN, William,
M. D. CLD 159
WILLIFORD, Britain BNE 42
WILLIFORD?, Jorden MAD 146
Nathan MAD 146
WILLINGHAM,
Deloney HND 9A
Elijah HND 8A
Isaac HND 8A
Jarrald HND 8
Jarrald, Jr. HND 8A
John HND 8
Susannah HND 8
Wm. HND 8
WILLINGS, Henry PUL 63A
WILLIS, Abner WDF 96A
Alxr. ADR 58
Amos HOP 270
Anthony ADR 56
Benjamin G. BNE 42
Britain MBG 143
Burrel CLD 159
David OHO 8A
David LWS 94A
David GNP 172A
Drury JES 69
Drury MAD 104
Edward MER 112
Eleanor GRD 96A
Frances ADR 58
George BRN 31
George B BRN 31
Henry MAD 108
Henry MER 117
Henry PUL 61A
Jacob MBG 141A
James CLK 85
James MAD 92
Jerediah BRK 303
John JEF 21
John LGN 27
John BNE 42
John CLD 159
John SHE 126A
John L. WYN 82A
Joseph BRN 31
Joseph, Capt. MER 113
Joseph GNP 171A
Lemuel SHE 124A
Lewis BNE 42
Lewis PUL 68A
Lewis GSN 153A
Major OHO 4A
Mary MER 113
Mc Kinsy MAD 158
Merry GRN 67
Owen GSN 153A
Pearson SHE 124A
Peggy ADR 58
Peter JEF 37
Price C. SHE 110A
Richard JES 69
Robert BNE 40
Sally MAD 108
Samuel CBL 2A
Sterling LGN 27
Thomas MAD 96
Thomas MBG 141A

WILLIS, White BNE 40
William BNE 42
William ADR 56
William ADR 58
William JES 69
William JES 72
William NSN 211
William SPN 16A
Wm. HRY 253
Wm. T. GRN 72
Wright W. HOP 268
Zadick BRK 299
WILLIS?, Elizabeth JES 73
WILLISON, James CBL 19A
Sarah CBL 19A
WILLISS, William CSY 220
WILLIT, Martin F. PND 15A
WILLITT, Jas. MAS 71
Wm. SHE 143A
WILLKERSON, David MBG 143
WILLLIAMS, Saml. HRY 196
WILLMORE, Jacob JES 76
James JES 96
John JES 90
WILLOBY, Ann MTG 267
Benjamin MTG 293
Elijah MTG 267
Enoch MTG 267
James MTG 267
Nehemiah WRN 59A
William MTG 267
WILLOBY?, Stewart NCH 105
WILLOCK, David GRN 68
Robt. GRN 76
WILLOUBY, Andrew ALN 102
WILLOUGHBY,
Alexander JES 77
Wm. LNC 33
WILLOWBY, Benjamin GTN 123
Samuel ALN 100
WILLS, Agnus FLG 64A
Andrew FLG 64A
Benjn. BBN 144
Charles F. SHE 126A
Durrit SCT 121A
Frederick ETL 52
Geo. FLG 46A
Henry H. MAD 136
James FLD 6
James MTG 247
Jas. FLG 60A
Jas. FLG 60A
Jno. ALN 132
John GRN 60
John JES 69
John JES 78
John CLD 139
John MTG 295
John FLG 64A
John NCH 118A
John SCT 119A
John SCT 122A
John SCT 128A
Nathan BLT 180
Rich. HRY 234
Robert JES 80
Robert NCH 118A
Saml. FLG 64A
Samuel GSN 153A
Thomas CLD 139
Thomas MTG 281
Thomas MTG 295
Thornton CLK 68
Thos. FLG 65A
Washington CLK 72
William MTG 287

WILLS, William MTG 295
Wm. GRN 53
WILLS?, (See Wells?)
David NCH 114A
Henry LVG 18
James Q.? NCH 115A
Thos. MAS 68
William LVG 18
William LVG 18
WILLSON, Abner ADR 60
Abraham LNC 27
Alexander BBN 84
Alexr. FLG 61A
Allexdr. LNC 17
Bird JES 91
Daniel BLT 164
Danl. FLG 66A
David JES 83
Elizabeth BBN 76
George LVG 18
Gorge GRN 60
Gustavos FLG 70A
Hammelton BBN 76
Henry BBN 72
Hugh GRN 54
Hugh FLG 44A
Isaac LVG 18
Isaac GRN 53
Isaac MBG 137
Isaac FLG 28A
James LVG 9
James ADR 60
James BLT 180
Jas. HRD 96
Jas. FLG 53A
Jeremiah BBN 68
Jesse BLT 160
Jno. E. LVG 9
John ADR 56
John JES 84
John, Sr. HRT 169
John FLG 25A
John WRN 46A
John C. BBN 72
John F. BBN 76
John H. BLT 164
Johnson GRN 79
Jonathan WRN 39A
Jonothan HRD 68
Josiah HOP 268
Levi FLG 70A
Lewis BBN 72
M. CHN 27A
Margot GTN 125
Matthew LNC 37
Matthew BLT 174
Moses ADR 56
Moses ADR 60
Moses ADR 60
Moses JES 91
Moses FTE 92
Nat ADR 60
Nathan JES 95
Richd. BBN 72
Robert FTE 75
Robt. LVG 9
Robt. A. FLG 62A
Saml. FLG 25A
Saml. FLG 47A
Saml. FLG 56A
Samuel JES 84
Samuel BLT 184
Samuel WRN 29A
Spencer LNC 33
Thomas ADR 60
WILLSON, Thomas LNC 65
Thomas JES 95
Thomas BLT 178
Thomas WRN 40A
Thomas WRN 57A
Thomas Q. BLT 174
Thos. BBN 68
Thos. FLG 25A
Thos. T. HRD 38
Will BBN 72
William GRN 56
William JES 94
William HRT 169
William HOP 268
William WRN 38A
William WRN 67A
Wm. FLG 66A
WILLYARD, Henry HRD 42
WILMOT, James WAS 79A
Robt. FKN 68
Robt. H. SCT 93A
Wm. FKN 60
WILMOTH, Cressett BLT 192
WILMOTT, Charles BBN 110
John BBN 130
Robt. BBN 110
WILMOUTH, George NSN 194
WILMUT, Erasmus GRD 83A
Saml. GRD 82A
WILSON, -----? LVG 12
---ick? HND 10A
---uel? LGN 28
Aaron HND 5A
Abner FTE 92
Abner BTH 148
Absolom WDF 97A
Absolum GSN 154A
Alex. CWL 38
Alexander TRG 3
Alexander FTE 73
Alexander MER 112
Alexander FKN 120
Alexander GNP 175A
Ambrose UNN 150
Amos FKN 120
Andrew FLD 6
Andrew FLD 11
Andrew CSY 206
Ann JEF 21
Ann BNE 52
Antony WAS 50A
Aquilla CBL 8A
Asa MNR 193
Barclay &? JEF 21
Benami LWS 94A
Benj. JEF 24
Benjamin TRG 6
Benjamin WDF 103
Benjamin CLD 157
Benjamin NCH 117A
Benjamin NCH 127A
Betsey LGN 30
Betsy MER 114
Bird PUL 60A
Brackston G. FTE 69
Caroline MAS 78
Catharine NCH 121A
Charles OHO 6A
Charles WTY 110A
Charles NCH 123A
Christopher GSN 154A
Christy HRT 170
Cumberland? LGN 22
D. W. SHE 143A
Daniel JEF 22
Daniel HOP 270
WILSON, Danl. JEF 33
David CLK 74
David FTE 74
David FTE 92
David MER 113
David GTN 124
David GRT 144
David HAR 144
David MTG 275
David KNX 288
David, Snr. HAR 144
David CBL 20A
David NCH 121A
David WTY 123A
Deborah MTG 277
E. M. CHN 46
Ebenezer ETL 49
Edward HRD 10
Edward CLK 100
Edward SHE 113A
Edwd. MAS 56
Edwd. BBN 110
Eli B. ETL 43
Elijah UNN 146
Elijah NSN 200
Eliza. SHE 149
Elizabeth BRN 31
Ellis OWN 104
Ely SHE 149
Ezra BTH 148
Feelan? NSN 175
Francis MER 113
Garret HAR 206
Garrod CLK 94
Geo. JEF 30
Geo. MAS 59
George BRN 30
George HRD 46
George ALN 100
George CSY 218
George GRD 102B
George LWS 94A
George GSN 154A
George B. BTL 331
Gholson WYN 92A
H. William BRN 31
Hanner WAS 66A
Harris FLD 44
Henry BBN 144
Henry NSN 200
Henry MTG 275
Hosea BRN 31
Hugh MTG 261
Hugh WAS 58A
Humphrey B. WAS 18A
Isaac LGN 40
Isaac ETL 54
Isaac JEF 55
Isaac FKN 84
Isaac NSN 205
Isaac CBL 2A
Isaac SCT 111A
Isaiath? MAS 77
Jacob BRN 30
Jacob CLK 72
Jacob BBN 140
Jacob, Junr. BRN 31
Jacob CBL 8A
James TRG 6
James HRD 10
James LGN 36
James LGN 44
James LGN 45
James FTE 73
James FTE 92
James OWN 101

WILSON, James CLK 103
James FKN 104
James WDF 104
James MER 113
James GTN 117
James GTN 133
James GRT 141
James GRT 144
James HRT 170
James SHE 177
James HAR 188
James NSN 205
James HAR 208
James MNR 213
James MTG 241
James, Jnr. HAR 182
James, Jr. BKN 5
James, Jr. HOP 270
James, Sr. BKN 6
James, Sr. HOP 270
James HND 5A
James PND 15A
James PUL 55A
James WAS 84A
James WYN 87A
James WTY 119A
James GSN 154A
James D. BBN 138
James K. MTG 226
James? MNR 213
Jane FTE 97
Jane CLK 100
Jane HRT 170
Jane MTG 293
Jas. JEF 19
Jas. MAS 58
Jas. JEF 59
Jas. HRD 94
Jas. RCK 82A
Jas. RCK 83A
Jeremiah LVG 11
Jeremiah WDF 99
Jeremiah HRT 170
Jeremiah NCH 122A
Jesse FTE 74
Jesse NCH 125A
Jesse GSN 154A
Jessee WYN 79A
Jno. LVG 7
Jno. MAS 55
Jno. MAS 56
Jno. MAS 79
Jno. FKN 150
Jno. A. MAS 57
Joel TRG 11
Joel TRG 13
John TRG 6
John HND 11
John LGN 23
John JEF 24
John BRN 31
John ETL 44
John CWL 46
John FTE 73
John FTE 89
John FTE 99
John FTE 112
John MER 112
John CLY 114
John MER 117
John GTN 121
John HRL 122
John MBG 140
John GRT 141
John GRT 142
John GRT 144
WILSON, John UNN 147
John UNN 152
John BTH 158
John BTH 158
John BTH 164
John MNR 191
John MNR 199
John NSN 206
John NSN 207
John MTG 226
John MTG 233
John MTG 255
John HOP 270
John KNX 288
John KNX 290
John KNX 298
John BTL 313
John BTL 333
John, Sr. CBL 12A
John (J.) MTG 271
John (Near Poplar Log Meeting House) BRN 30
John (Virginia) BRN 30
John CBL 21A
John PUL 58A
John RCK 77A
John WDF 100A
John NCH 115A
John NCH 119A
John SCT 127A
John GSN 154A
John GNP 175A
John G. UNN 154
John H. WAS 18A
John S. LGN 32
John S. BTH 198
John? BNE 42
John? BNE 44
Jonas PUL 68A
Jonathan CLY 115
Jonathan, Junr. LWS 91A
Jonathan, Senr. LWS 90A
Joseph BNE 40
Joseph MER 113
Joseph ALN 116
Joseph BTH 148
Joseph NSN 183
Joseph NSN 196
Joseph MTG 241
Joseph, Sn. GSN 154A
Joseph SCT 108A
Joseph GSN 154A
Joseph GSN 154A
Joseph G. NSN 201
Joseph N. MTG 239
Joseph T. ALN 116
Joshua BRN 32
Joshua WDF 101
Joshua RCK 75A
Joshua RCK 83A
Josiah MER 112
Jubal BRN 31
Judith, Mrs. GRT 140
Laurence WDF 100A
Lewis FKN 128
Margaret HAR 208
Martin BNE 42
Mary LVG 10
Mary GNP 175A
Mason FTE 87
Mathew HRD 46
Matthew TOD 129
Matthew HAR 210
Matthew MTG 239
Matthew SHE 131A
WILSON, Michael KNX 288
Moses BNE 42
Moses MTG 277
Moses WYN 93A
Nancy MTG 241
Nancy GRD 112A
Nancy GRD 114A
Nathaniel BTH 154
Nathaniel SHE 133A
Perry FTE 73
Peter KNX 288
Phillip CLY 115
Phillip, Sr. CLY 114
Pleasant CLY 113
Presley MTG 231
Rachael CHN 31
Ralph GRT 144
Reid FTE 80
Rice WYN 93A
Richard LGN 30
Richard BRN 31
Richard HRL 120
Richard MTG 239
Richd. SCT 127A
Robert ETL 46
Robert FTE 67
Robert FTE 74
Robert GRT 142
Robert NSN 180
Robert HAR 184
Robert HAR 208
Robert, Jr. JEF 58
Robt. BKN 5
Robt. JEF 33
Robt. JEF 46
Robt. MAS 58
Robt. MAS 63
Robt. MAS 64
Robt. MAS 81
Sam. HRY 261
Saml. LVG 7
Saml. PND 15A
Sampson ETL 43
Samuel LGN 34
Samuel LGN 39
Samuel LGN 46
Samuel MER 113
Samuel GRT 147
Samuel BTH 176
Samuel MNR 213
Samuel MTG 245
Samuel MTG 277
Samuel SPN 15A
Samuel LWS 94A
Samuel WDF 100A
Samuel GSN 153A
Seybert BRN 31
Simmeon HRL 120
Singleton SHE 126A
Solomon WTY 119A
Spires? MTG 235
Stephen NCH 103A
Susanna WDF 115A
Tabitha HND 5A
Teler? NSN 177
Thomas LGN 31
Thomas LGN 32
Thomas MER 113
Thomas MER 114
Thomas GRT 144
Thomas HOP 268
Thomas BRK 299
Thomas BTL 333
Thomas, Clo-? B. WDF 100A
Thomas CBL 8A
Thomas OHO 8A

WILSON, Thomas CBL 10A
Thomas CBL 13A
Thomas WYN 93A
Thomas LWS 94A
Thomas WDF 115A
Thomas GSN 153A
Thomas GNP 177A
Thornton UNN 147
Thornton J. BBN 138
Thos. MAS 58
Thos. GRT 145
Thos. WAS 64A
Thos. P. SHE 143A
Turner NSN 177
Uriah MTG 275
Uriah NCH 125A
Vance MER 114
Wedeman? GSN 154A
Wesley/ Wyley? CBL 5A
Widw. CWL 37
Wiley TRG 13A
Will MAS 63
Will MAS 63
Will S. BKN 15
Will. D. SCT 113A
William LGN 34
William CLK 87
William FTE 92
William CLK 100
William WDF 100
William OWN 102
William MER 113
William GTN 133
William HAR 144
William HAR 180
William HRY 180
William MNR 191
William NSN 212
William MTG 233
William CBL 5A
William OHO 5A
William CBL 23A
William GRD 82A
William LWS 87A
William WDF 100A
William C. MNR 213
William G. LWS 94A
William H. LGN 22
William H. ETL 49
Willis WDF 103
Wm. CHN 31
Wm. MAD 90
Wm., Senr. BRN 31
Wm. PUL 41A
Wm. GSN 154A
Wm. E. WAS 37A
Wm. E. SHE 125A
Wm.? BNE 42
Wm.? BNE 44
WILSON?, Widow LVG 18
Thos. CWL 44
Thos? BRK 303
William LVG 18
WILT, James HRT 170
WILTBERGER, Joseph W. HRT 169
WILTSHIRE, Reuben BRN 30
Thomas WYN 80A
WILY, John HRY 200
WILY?, Cyrus HRY 249
David NCH 114A
WIM--?, Thomas C. CHN 34A
WIMBERLEY, John TRG 12
WIMBERLY, James TRG 14A
WIMBLEDOFF, Danl. LVG 13
WIMBLEY, Noah ALN 96
WIMER, Martin FTE 100
WIMMS, Saml. TOD 128A
WIMP, Danl. HRD 70
Ephraim HRD 70
John HRD 70
WIMP?, John HRD 32
WIMPERLY, Thos. FLG 44A
WIMPEY, Obediah LGN 41
WIMSEAT?, John NSN 189
WIN, Harmon WYN 97A
Josiah WYN 97A
Thomas GRN 78
WIN?, Benjamin GNP 167A
WINANS, James PND 19A
WINBURN, John V. MAD 146
Saml. MAD 114
WINCFORD, Nowel WRN 56A
WINCLECLACK?, John MTG 265
WINCLER, David ETL 44
Henry ETL 51
Henry, Jr. ETL 42
Lewis ETL 48
William ETL 47
WIND---?, Elizabeth ALN 96
WINDER, John TOD 134
John, Jr./ Sr.? TOD 133
Seth CBL 16A
WINDERS, George LVG 12
Jas. HRD 82
WINDLE, Sarah HND 13
WINDSER, Newman HND 10
WINDSOR, James FTE 107
Thomas LGN 44
WINEBRINER, Geo. FKN 62
WINEGAR, Saml. HRD 70
WINEHERTER?, Rebecca JEF 46
WINELAND, Federick BNE 40
WINER, John SCT 136A
WINES, James BRN 31
Mary SHE 175
WINET, Sarah MAD 136
WINFREE, Fanny CLD 159
Nancy WRN 55A
William CLD 160
WINFREY, Charles HND 8A
Hennery CSY 224
James ALN 108
John ADR 56
Nicholas CSY 224
Philip ADR 60
Thomas ADR 58
Wm. ADR 56
WINFRY, Archabald ADR 60
WING, Charles F. MBG 143
John MBG 143
WINGATE, Cyrus OWN 106
Elias MER 113
Henry FKN 68
Isaac FKN 84
John MER 113
John C. SHE 164
Joseph FTE 64
Joseph OHO 5A
Joseph PND 21A
N. S. HRY 251
Smith GTN 120
William BNE 40
WINGET, Reuben TRG 5A
WINGFIELD, Jacob WRN 54A
John WRN 42A
WINGYARD, George CBL 20A
WINIFRED, Ennis GTN 128
WININGS, Jacob GRT 146
WINISEAT?, Felix NSN 188
WINISEAT?, John NSN 189
WINKFIELD, Henry HRY 264
Jas./ Jos.? HRY 259
WINKLER, -----? DVS 10A
---n? DVS 10A
Adam DVS 17A
WINKLES/ WINKLER?, David FLD 10
Mary FLD 1A
WINLOCK, Fielding SHE 176
George GRN 55
Joseph BRN 34
Joseph SHE 110A
Wm. C. SHE 142A
WINN, Adam FTE 85
Braxton B. BRN 34
Daniel MAD 156
Daniel HAR 176
Dudley CHN 30A
George FTE 86
James MAD 180
Jessee FTE 90
John CWL 32
John CBL 11A
Mary FTE 85
Minor CLK 70
Minor MER 114
Minor HAR 186
Nathaniel FTE 83
Nathaniel FTE 85
Philip B. CLK 94
Sally, Mrs. CLK 102
Saml. MAS 62
Stephen J. CLK 82
Susan FTE 86
Thomas BRN 31
Thomas GTN 135
Thomas WDF 120A
Thos. MAS 60
Widw. CWL 43
William FTE 83
Willis FTE 81
WINSCOT, Adam SPN 21A
Richart SPN 19A
WINSCOTT, Caty OWN 105
John OWN 103
John C. OWN 99
Rebecca GTN 126
Richard OWN 105
Solomon OWN 99
William OWN 101
WINSEAT, John NSN 179
WINSETT, Joseph WAS 17A
WINSLOW, Henry GTN 123
Stephen J.? FTE 56
Thomas BKN 14
William GTN 124
WINSON, Will MAS 63
WINSTEAD, ----n? H. DVS 10A
Burkard D. HOP 270
Cowtance HRT 169
Maley HOP 268
WINSTON, Bickerton GRN 53
John BNE 40
John CBL 12A
John T. GRN 68
Joseph CBL 14A
Nicholas J. GRN 61
WINTER, David FKN 64
Elisha J. FTE 55
WINTERS, Frederick MNR 193
George SCT 108A
Gorge SCT 96A
Henry CLD 138
Jacob SCT 122A

WINTERS, James NSN 184
  Jno. MAS 68
  John BNE 40
  John BNE 42
WINTERSMITH, Horatio G. HRD 96
WINTRS?, John BNE 40
  Wm. BNE 40
WINTWORTH, Levi SHE 174
WIRE?, Benjamin GNP 177A
WIREMAN/ WISEMAN?, Abraham FLD 33
WIREMAN, (See Wiseman) FLD 44
WIRGHT, Mary HRY 188
  Wm. HRD 16
WIRK, John FTE 57
WIRS, Elender ETL 52
WIRT, John SHE 177
WISAR, K. JEF 42
WISDOM, Francis CLD 143
  James ADR 58
  John, Junr. CLD 140
  John, Senr. CLD 140
  Thomas ADR 60
  Thomas CLD 140
  Wm. ADR 60
WISE, Abram GTN 127
  Adam HRD 94
  Calep BLT 160
  Daniel GTN 129
  Daniel SHE 122A
  David GTN 129
  Elijah GRN 74
  Elizabeth GTN 129
  Ellener BTH 210
  George SHE 166
  George SHE 122A
  Henry JEF 45
  Henry GTN 132
  Jas. SCT 135A
  John LNC 43
  John GRN 74
  John JES 81
  John GTN 127
  John MTG 233
  Peter JEF 48
  Richard BLT 182
  Samuel JES 79
  Thos. H. HRD 68
  Tobias OHO 8A
  William BLT 174
WISE?, Peter BLT 162
WISEHART, Conrod BRK 229
  Henry NSN 196
  Jacob NSN 193
  John NSN 193
  Wm. HRD 60
WISEHEART, John JEF 62
WISEMAN, Abner ETL 51
  Benjamine SPN 23A
  Jacob FLD 44
  Jacob HAR 212
  James CWL 31
  John NSN 194
  Martin ALN 104
  Rachel NSN 194
  Thomas NSN 194
  William FTE 66
  William CLD 144
WISEMAN?, John FLD 31
WISER, David CSY 214
WISER?, Danul CSY 214
WISHARD, Abram FLG 72A
  Elizh. FLG 71A
  James MBG 141A
WISHARD, John FLG 71A
  Samuel NCH 107A
  Wm. FLG 72A
WISHON, Adam CLD 155
WISINGTON?, Peter BBN 104
WITBY?, Tarlton OHO 6A
WITCHER, Josiah WRN 54A
WITCHER?, John CSY 212
WITCKER?, John CSY 212
WITE?, Eli TRG 14A
WITESLER, Nelson BNE 40
WITHAM, James CLD 153
  Joseph CLD 153
  Peter CLD 153
WITHEROE, John WAS 32A
  Stephen WAS 36A
WITHEROL, Joseph WAS 60A
WITHEROW, William FTE 69
WITHERS, Allen SCT 126A
  Bejah GRD 115A
  Benjamin BLT 196
  Charles WDF 109A
  Fountain SCT 102A
  Gideon HRD 20
  Hiram HRD 82
  Hugh GRT 142
  James LNC 37
  James NSN 198
  John LNC 55
  John LNC 65
  John HRD 84
  John GRD 120A
  John? CWL 36
  Joseph LNC 53
  Lewis HRD 60
  Mathew K. HRD 22
  Mathew K. FTE 94
  Silas HRD 84
  Sophy BLT 192
  Thomas NSN 176
  Thomas WDF 123A
  William BLT 164
  William NSN 198
  Wm., Junr. HRD 60
  Wm., Senr. HRD 74
WITHERS?, Jennings HAR 158
WITHERSPOON, John FTE 73
WITHINGTON, James, Sr. LVG 18
WITHINGTON?, William LVG 18
WITHROW, Isaac WRN 49A
  Jas. CWL 57
  Priscilla MNR 211
WITSON, Sanford MTG 235
WITT, Abner ETL 49
  Aris KNX 288
  Charles ETL 47
  Charles GRN 68
  Christopher R. LGN 25
  Elisha, Sr. ETL 41
  Jno. FKN 150
  John LGN 27
  John WAS 49A
  Mills LGN 25
  Nancy ETL 43
  Robert LGN 40
  William LGN 40
  William, Jr. ETL 50
  Wm. FKN 152
WITTEN/ WITTON?, Thomas FLD 27
WITTENBY?, Solomon ALN 120
WITTER, Samuel GSN 154A
WITTIT, John WAS 50A
WITTMAN?, Rich ALN 134
WITTS, Elezebeth HAR 148
WITTUN/ WITTUR?, Peter JES 94
WITTY, Carran / Carvan? CHN 40
  Ezekiel BRN 31
WIZE, Jno. MAS 63
  Solomon MAS 63
WOHNER, George LNC 37
  Peter LNC 37
WOKMAN, Jacob BBN 66
WOLBANKS, Berrimon SPN 19A
WOLDRIDGE, Jos. TOD 126A
  S. TOD 126A
  Seth TOD 126A
WOLDROPE, Younger HRT 170
WOLF, --ilding? CWL 36
  Caleb BRN 31
  Geo. TOD 127A
  Jacob FTE 105
  Jno. HAR 154
  Lewis? HAR 146
  Peter HRD 50
  Robert CSY 204
WOLFE, Henry MTG 279
  Jesse LGN 27
  Michael LGN 43
WOLPH?, Philip ALN 118
WOLPLE?, Philip ALN 118
WOLSEY, George PUL 61A
WOMACK, Jesse MER 113
  John FTE 64
WOMATH, Tho. GRD 92A
WOMOCK, Charles GNP 175A
  Tignal GNP 175A
WOMOCK?, Robt. FLG 78A
WOMOTH, Gethin? GRD 93A
  Thadias GRD 91A
WONER, Jacob GRD 107A
WONER?, David MER 112
WOOD--?, Bealle HRY 210
WOOD, A., Mrs. MAS 74
  Abner MER 114
  Abner GTN 119
  Abraham HRD 38
  Abraham SPN 19A
  Amos WDF 108A
  Andr. MAS 75
  B. J.? CHN 45A
  Basil LGN 29
  Benj. SHE 136A
  Benjamin BNE 42
  Benjamin CBL 3A
  Benjamin WDF 95A
  Benjm. MAS 54
  Bennett SPN 10A
  Brewer LGN 44
  Charles LWS 98A
  Chilton PUL 36A
  Daniel LWS 92A
  David MAS 61
  David MAS 79
  David MER 113
  David SHE 122A
  Edmund, Jun. CSY 222
  Edmund, Jur. CSY 210
  Edward WDF 93
  Edwd. FLG 37A
  Edwd. SCT 110A
  Eli MAS 64
  Elias SHE 141A
  Eliot MAD 170
  Fielding BBN 82
  Fielding SCT 130A
  Francis MAD 146
  Geo. MAS 80

Name	County	Page
WOOD, George	FTE	69
George, Jr.	OWN	103
George, Sr.	OWN	99
George	WRN	66A
George	NCH	124A
Gideon	OWN	102
Gideon P.	SHE	155
Harris	JEF	58
Harry	MAS	65
Henry	BLT	196
Henry?	RCK	82A
Howard?	MAD	170
Isaac	GTN	119
Isaac	SCT	107A
Jacob	OHO	11A
James	BKN	22
James	BRN	32
James	CWL	37
James	CLK	73
James	FTE	89
James	FTE	109
James	MAD	110
James	MER	113
James	ALN	130
James	GTN	133
James	CLD	149
James	SHE	172
James (Near Jas. Level's)	BRN	30
Jarimiah	CSY	222
Jesse	MER	113
Jesse	MNR	195
Jessee	HRT	170
Jno.	JEF	56
Jno.	FKN	62
Jno.	MAS	77
Jno.	CHN	42A
John	JEF	38
John	BNE	42
John	LNC	51
John	GRN	67
John	CLK	100
John	MAD	110
John	CLY	112
John	MER	113
John	GTN	133
John	CLD	144
John	NSN	183
John	NSN	197
John	NSN	199
John	KNX	314
John, Jr.	JEF	59
John	NCH	106A
John	NCH	124A
John	SHE	141A
Jonathan	NSN	182
Jonathan	NSN	198
Joseph	NCH	115A
Lewis	WRN	34A
Lydia	MAS	62
Malcom	BBN	82
Martin	BKN	20
Mary	BBN	138
Mary	MTG	251
Miller	WRN	34A
Moses	MAS	60
N. B.	SHE	132A
Nancy	MAD	98
Nimrod	NCH	117A
Noah	MAS	64
Otha	WRN	51A
Peter	BRN	30
Peter	JEF	35
Pleasant	BRN	30
Richard	SHE	172
Robert	MBG	133A
WOOD, Robt.	FLG	47A
Rodham	SCT	131A
Ruben	HRL	122
Saml.	BKN	8
Saml.	CWL	57
Saml.	MAS	65
Saml.	CLY	112
Saml.	MAD	148
Simion	HRY	249
Spencer	CWL	32
Stephen	FTE	102
Stephen	FTE	102
Tandy	LGN	44
Tho.	MAS	61
Thomas	MER	113
Thomas	CLD	148
Thomas	MNR	209
Thomas	OHO	3A
Thomas	CBL	12A
Thomas	WRN	68A
Thos.	CWL	39
Thos.	BBN	82
Thos.	PUL	41A
Timothy	JEF	52
Wiley	MAD	160
Will.	SCT	130A
William	BRN	31
William	CLK	81
William	CLK	95
William	NCH	105
William	GTN	119
William	GTN	126
William	GTN	127
William	GTN	134
William	CLD	148
William	MNR	209
William, Esq.	MER	113
William	SPN	22A
William	SPN	25A
Wm.	JEF	55
Wm.	FKN	56
Wm. I./ J.?	HRT	170
Zachariah	MAD	170
WOODALL, James	PUL	37A
John	LNC	73
John	MAD	148
Peggy	LNC	77
William	LNC	77
WOODARD, Abram	GRN	57
Edward	SPN	8A
George	GRN	50
James	CWL	57
James	JES	85
James	UNN	150
James	PND	28A
Joel	GRN	61
Julis	GRN	53
Richd.	GRN	59
Saml.	MAD	112
Stephen	CHN	39
William	LNC	65
WOODB--N, James	CHN	30
WOODCOCK, Stephen	PUL	59A
WOODDY, Thos.	MAD	138
WOODEN, John	HRY	194
Robert	JEF	68
Robt., Jr.	JEF	60
Thomas	GTN	117
WOODFILL, Joseph	GTN	120
WOODFORD, John, Col.	CLK	103
Thomas	BBN	96
Thomas	CLK	103
Thos.	BBN	74
WOODGATE, Jonathan	FTE	78
WOODLAND, Heth	ETL	52
WOODLEY, Samuel	WTY	126A
WOODMANSEE, Sarah	HAR	220
WOODMORE, William	WYN	86A
WOODPUOF?, Banjamin	MAD	166
WOODRAM, John	LNC	61
Obadiah	ADR	58
Stephen	ADR	58
WOODRIDGE, Jno. W.	FKN	56
WOODRING, Ben	HRD	44
John	HRD	86
Peter	LGN	31
WOODROW, Alexr.	JEF	42
Plesan	JES	93
Wade N.	KNX	290
WOODRUFF, Aaron	CWL	57
Aaron	FTE	58
David	ETL	37
David	HOP	268
Fielding	LGN	45
James	LNC	27
James	WYN	97A
John	HOP	270
Jos.	GRD	82A
Joseph	HOP	270
Mary	MAD	152
Samuel	HOP	270
WOODS, -----?	DVS	13A
Aaron	JES	87
Abijah	JES	74
Abraham	CSY	210
Adam	MAD	170
Adam, Jr.	MAD	164
Anderson	BRK	301
Andrew	CBL	14A
Archabald	JES	91
Archibald	MER	114
Archibald	MAD	166
Archibald	BTL	333
Archibald	WYN	83A
Avery	MBG	136
Caldwell	LNC	47
Carter T.	LVG	12
Catharine	FTE	109
Clement	CHN	36
David	LVG	2
Ebial?	PUL	52A
Edmund, Snr.	CSY	222
Elias	PUL	60A
Eliza C.	BLT	172
Ezekiel	CHN	35A
Frank	GRD	89A
Hannah	HAR	204
Harvey	MER	115
Hawkins	HRD	26
Henry	FTE	73
Isaac	MBG	137
Isaac	CBL	16A
James	MER	114
James	MBG	136
James	HAR	144
James	BRK	303
James	GRD	119A
James G.?	GRD	112A
James M.	WAS	78A
Jane	CBL	9A
Jas.	FLG	71A
Jas.	TOD	130A
Jno.	CWL	57
Jno.	PUL	47A
Joel	FKN	156
John	HND	8
John	LGN	37
John	MER	113
John	MBG	136
John	BBN	142

Name	County	Page
WOODS, John	MBG	143
John	MAD	162
John	SPN	17A
John	GRD	114A
Jonathan	SHE	157
Joseph	MER	114
Joseph	MBG	136
Joseph	CBL	12A
Mary	MER	114
Mical	SPN	4A
Nancy	FLD	20
Nancy	HRY	247
Polly	BRK	299
Richard	JES	74
Rob.?	CWL	41
Robert	WAS	64A
Samuel	CHN	36
Samuel	MER	113
Samuel	SPN	8A
Searight	SCT	126A
Susanna	MBG	137
Thomas	LGN	38
Thomas	JES	95
Thomas	FTE	97
Thomas	WYN	97A
Thomas	MBG	136A
Urban	GRD	109A
Will	GRD	91A
Will	SCT	129A
Will.	LVG	8
William	CHN	36
William	LNC	79
William	HAR	158
William	WDF	107A
WOODS?, Will.	SCT	121A
WOODSIDE, -----?	LVG	9
Mary	JEF	53
Mary	SHE	151
William	OWN	100
WOODSIDES, -----?	LVG	9
-----?	LVG	9
Robt.	LVG	9
WOODSMALL, George	SHE	131A
Jno.	JEF	45
WOODSON, David	SPN	22A
Elizabeth	CHN	40
Henry	CLY	129
Henry	KNX	296
James	SHE	173
Jno.	FKN	86
John	BRN	31
John S.	WDF	119A
Joseph A.	BRN	34
Richd.	CHN	41
Robt. S.	HRT	169
Samuel	BRN	31
Samuel	HOP	268
Samuel H.	JES	75
Shadrack	WRN	47A
Talton	MAD	152
Thomas	HRT	170
Thomas, Sr.	HOP	268
Tucker M.	JES	69
William	PUL	53A
WOODWARD, Asual?	MAS	54
Bend.	WAS	68A
Chesly	JES	85
Edward	ALN	94
Elizabeth	MTG	285
Elizh.	OHO	10A
Enos	BKN	6
George	WDF	97
George	CLK	105
H.	TOD	131
Henry	MTG	281
Joel	BKN	6
WOODWARD, John	SHE	156
John	MTG	229
John	SHE	126A
Joseph	MTG	283
Joseph	WAS	67A
Joseph C.	CLK	102
Richard	NSN	188
Robert	JES	85
Samuel	MTG	283
Silas	BKN	22
Thomas	OHO	10A
William	HND	11A
Willis	HND	11A
WOODWORTH, Gerrard	PND	15A
WOODY, Thomas	WYN	80A
Washington	PND	29A
WOODYARD, Jesse	LVG	8
Jesse	GRT	145
John	LNC	5
Lewis	PND	18A
Nancy	HAR	220
Strother	GRT	145
William	GRT	145
WOOFRUFFE, Nodar?	FKN	104
WOOLAMS?, Wm.	FLG	37A
WOOLBANKS, Merrium	TRG	11
WOOLCOT, Shelton	SHE	139A
WOOLDERIDGE, Wm.	GSN	154A
WOOLDRIDGE, Alxr.	ADR	56
Chesley	WDF	118A
Daniel	HRD	54
Daniel	CLD	142
Edward	TRG	8
Edward	HOP	270
Fleming	BBN	86
Isiah	HRY	190
James	ADR	60
Jessee	ADR	62
John	ADR	60
John	SHE	160
Phillip?	GTN	133
Powitan	CHN	43A
William	WDF	121A
Wm.	HRD	54
WOOLDRIGE, Peggy	GRN	70
Richd.	GRN	55
Thos.	HRY	254
WOOLEN, Leonard	HAR	208
WOOLERY, Ann	ETL	39
Francis	MAD	148
Joseph	HAR	178
Michael	HAR	212
WOOLETT, John	JEF	41
WOOLEY, Henry	GRD	92A
John	GRD	99A
Will	GRD	105A
WOOLEY?, Baret?	ALN	138
Isac?	ALN	138
WOOLF, Andrew	CBL	9A
Conrod	SCT	128A
David	SCT	122A
Geo.	SCT	128A
Henry	PND	17A
Jesse	SCT	109A
Jesse	SCT	122A
Margaret	SCT	109A
WOOLFOK, Thos.	MAS	80
WOOLFOLK, Austin	OWN	105
Edmund	JEF	50
Elijah	SCT	128A
George	SHE	168
John	FTE	75
John	OWN	101
Jos., Junr.	HRD	84
Joseph	SHE	148
Joseph	WDF	96A
WOOLFOLK, Lewis	SCT	109A
Ricd.	JEF	57
Robert	JEF	50
Samel	WDF	96
W. S.	SCT	139A
Wm.	JEF	57
WOOLFORD, Mr.	JEF	28
John	ADR	56
P.	JEF	23
WOOLFORK, Ellitt/ Ellin?	HRY	224
Fleming	HRD	84
James B.	HRD	14
Jos. F.	HRD	70
Sowell	FTE	104
Thomas	FTE	110
Will	HRY	226
WOOLLEN, John	OWN	102
Thos.	SCT	129A
WOOLLERY, Peter	MTG	243
WOOLLEY, John	FTE	111
WOOLLOMS?, Charles	CBL	17A
WOOLLUM, Jacob	HRL	122
James	HRL	122
Zachariah	OWN	102
WOOLLY, Esther	HRY	192
Richard	NSN	182
Thomas	NSN	182
WOOLMAN, Hernan	BNE	42
WOOLS, Catharine	MTG	251
Daniel	MTG	235
WOOLSEY, Eldridge	WRN	48A
George	OHO	10A
Joseph	JES	81
Richard	PUL	63A
William	WRN	50A
Zephaniah	CLD	144
WOOLSY, Isaac	MAD	118
Nathaniel	PUL	67A
Richard	JES	77
WOOLSY?, Baret?	ALN	138
Isac?	ALN	138
WOOLWINE, George G.	MAD	170
WOOLY, Will	HRY	180
WOOMBLE, Jorkin-?	FKN	128
WOONER, Henry	GRD	106A
John	GRD	106A
WOORLEY?, Francis	HRD	8
WOOSLEY, Joshua	HRT	170
WOOSLEY?, Thomas	TRG	13
WOOSLY, Thos.	GSN	155A
WOOTEN, Charles	GNP	166A
Joseph	BRN	30
WOOTON, George	FLD	21
John	NSN	222
Levi	FLD	40
Silas P.	FLD	24
WORD, Ezebella	FLG	43A
George	MAD	166
John	KNX	284
WORDALL, Benjamin	MTG	241
WORDDEN?, Bealle	HRY	210
WORDEN, Sarah	RCK	82A
WORICK, John	FLG	41A
WORK, Anne	WRN	30A
WORKMAN, Andrew	BTH	166
Bam.	BBN	112
Benjn.	ADR	56
George	BTH	162
John	ADR	56
John	NCH	121A
Joseph	SHE	149
Michael	CHN	33
Peter	BBN	120
Richard	GRT	143

WORKMAN, Saml. GRN 66
Samuel SHE 160
Samuel NCH 122A
Stephen CLK 97
Wm. ADC 68
WORKS, Andrew OWN 102
James CBL 8A
Jinney OWN 102
Joseph OWN 102
Thomas OWN 105
WORL?, Amos GRD 99A
WORLAND, Barnaby SCT 133A
Charles WAS 77A
Charles B. WAS 45A
Henry WAS 54A
Thomas FTE 79
WORLDLEY, John CSY 206
WORLEY, Alexander PUL 62A
Calob HAR 140
Danl. MAS 73
Danl. PUL 45A
David MER 113
George MER 113
Joshua FTE 108
Voluntine PUL 58A
Wiley WTY 121A
William WRN 39A
WORLEY?, Mary FTE 106
WORLIS, Sarah HAR 180
WORMAN, Tho. MAS 81
WORMLEY, Comfort MTG 243
John MTG 243
WORNALL?, Thomas CLK 99
WORNEL, Wm. GSN 155A
WORNER, George WAS 81A
WORNOCK, James GNP 178A
Johnson GNP 166A
Wm. GNP 170A
WORNOCK?, Robt. FLG 78A
WORRELL, (No Given Name Listed) BNE 40
WORREN, Tho. RCK 82A
Tho. RCK 82A
WORRILL, William CBL 5A
WORRMER?, James ADR 60
Joseph ADR 58
WORSLEY, William W. FTE 59
WORSTERS?, Hugh BKN 11
WORTH, John (Crossed Out) ADR 56
WORTHAM, Charles NSN 181
WORTHEN, Enoch HAR 220
WORTHERINGTON, T. T. MAS 68
Wm. MAS 52
WORTHINGTON, Andrew MBG 138A
Chares DVS 16A
Edward MER 113
Edward DVS 16A
Jacob FLG 56A
James T. MER 113
Nicholas DVS 15A
Thomas MBG 136
William MBG 136
William MBG 138A
WORTMAN, Abraham CBL 6A
Richard CBL 10A
WORTMAN?, Benjamin CBL 9A
WRAE, Thomas BRK 303
WRAGG, Samuel FTE 75
WRAGLIN, Pettis WRN 46A
WRATHWELL, Thomas BTH 218
WRAY, Amos MBG 138
Daniel MNR 195
WREN, Isaac BRN 31
James MAD 156
James MAD 166
James, Jr. MTG 225
James, Sr. MTG 295
James WRN 63A
Jno. JEF 66
John MTG 231
Sanford MTG 225
Wm. BBN 110
WRENCH, Michael NSN 185
WRENFRO, James KNX 284
WRENN, John FTE 84
WRIGGLESWORTH, Johna FTE 55
WRIGHT, -----? DVS 3A
---am? DVS 9A
Abner CLD 151
Alexander FKN 142
Allen HRT 170
Andrew BBN 144
Ann JEF 22
Asa CLK 92
Auauillar? CSY 206
B. C. LNC 15
Beldsoe FTE 111
Ben HRD 18
Benjamin NSN 183
Charles BNE 42
Charles CLK 99
Charles M. LGN 35
Christo. HRY 218
David HND 13
Easter HND 13
Edmond HOP 270
Edward OWN 100
Edward CLD 150
Edward NCH 124A
Elijah BBN 108
Elijah BLT 188
Ellis LNC 15
Esau CLD 150
Felix WAS 66A
Flemstedd BBN 68
Geo., Sr. HRY 200
George MER 114
George HRY 206
George HOP 268
George WRN 54A
Giddeon MAD 116
Harbert SPN 20A
Henry WDF 93
Hillary CLK 106
Isaac LNC 9
J. E. LNC 15
Jacob BRN 30
Jacob WRN 54A
James LNC 29
James BBN 104
James BBN 114
James FKN 142
James CBL 12A
James WAS 36A
James WDF 114A
James M. NSN 176
Jas. MAS 55
Jefferson HAR 220
Jesse HRY 198
Jessee WYN 85A
Jno. MAS 74
Jno. HRY 184
Joel CSY 206
John HND 13
John LNC 29
John OWN 102
John BBN 108
WRIGHT, John BBN 110
John MER 113
John GTN 120
John MBG 138
John HRY 218
John KNX 294
John, Junr. CLD 145
John, Senr. CLD 145
John CBL 21A
John WAS 27A
John WAS 29A
John CHN 30A
John CHN 32A
John WRN 45A
John WYN 85A
John SHE 117A
John MGB 137A
John SHE 141A
John W. HRY 208
John W. WRN 61A
Johnson SPN 6A
Jonathan HRD 92
Jonathan HOP 270
Jonathan, Junr. HRD 92
Jos. LVG 2
Joseph BBN 146
Joseph CLD 151
Joseph NSN 224
Joseph CBL 21A
Josiah GRN 57
Josiah MAS 72
Josiah WRN 29A
Laban HRD 74
Larkin LGN 27
Lewis CLD 144
Lewis CLD 144
Lewis PND 26A
Lewis WRN 52A
Lilbourne? LGN 22
Lindsey GTN 128
Mary MAS 63
Mary WAS 21A
Mary FLG 43A
Mary WAS 68A
Matthew PND 20A
Maurice LNC 17
Meridith JES 95
Morgan WAS 63A
Moses HRD 26
Moses, Capt. WYN 85A
Nelson HRY 200
Noah G. FLG 42A
Oliver MBG 136
Peggy JEF 61
Pettis R. GTN 119
Phillip CLD 145
Reuben FKN 92
Reubin NSN 177
Richard NSN 180
Richard NSN 210
Richard SHE 121A
Richd. GRN 62
Robert MER 114
Robert R. WRN 43A
Robt. BBN 92
Robt. WAS 25A
Sampson GRN 75
Samuel LVG 10
Samuel BBN 108
Samuel WRN 70A
Sarah BBN 110
Stephen MBG 141A
Tho. MAS 63
Thomas BRN 31
Thomas GRN 71
Thomas GRN 73

WRIGHT, Thomas GRN 78
Thomas CLK 99
Thomas MER 112
Thomas GTN 128
Thomas NSN 211
Thomas SHE 120A
Thos. WAS 68A
Thralkill CLK 90
Timothy CBL 20A
Vinson HRT 169
Walter MER 113
Widow BBN 94
William LGN 25
William OWN 100
William CLD 145
William, Jr. CLK 90
William, Senr. CLK 90
William HND 7A
William SPN 19A
William WRN 54A
William MBG 140A
William P.? LGN 22
Willis HRY 186
Wingfield FKN 134
Wm. BBN 114
Wm. WAS 24A
Wm. WAS 66A
Wm. WAS 71A
Wm. SHE 141A
Wm. M. MAS 52
Zephaniah SHE 152
WRIGHT?, Wm. MAD 134
WRIGLEY, John CLK 81
WRITE, Isum CHN 39
James SCT 97A
James SCT 120A
Jas. SCT 124A
John SCT 119A
John R. SCT 99A
Jonathan SCT 107A
Will SCT 107A
Wm. BRK 303
WRY?, Sally CLK 73
WUMS?, Mrs. JEF 28
WUNSEAT?, Felix NSN 188
John NSN 189
WURICH, Henry MAS 79
WURTS, Danl. JEF 24
WYAN, Jacob LNC 3
WYANT, Isaac GTN 119
Jacob GTN 119
WYAT, John BRN 30
Joseph BRN 31
WYATT, Amanuel? BBN 124
Charles HOP 270
Congue MNR 213
Frank MTG 243
George HOP 270
Gilbert CWL 57
Isum HOP 270
James KNX 294
John HRY 198
John KNX 294
John TOD 131A
Jonathan LVG 13
Jos. FLG 25A
Micajah FLG 26A
Norman GRD 87A
Richard BBN 124
Sally HOP 270
Saml. HRY 198
Saml. KNX 286
Thos. KNX 296
Turner BBN 124
Vincent KNX 286
Walter FTE 73
WYATT, William MTG 243
Woolford FLG 66A
Zadoc CWL 36
WYATT?, Joanes LVG 11
WYATTE, John HAR 216
WYBRANT, Hugh TRG 5A
WYCOFF, Ephraim NCH 121A
John BBN 114
Nicholas MTG 269
Urcella BBN 114
William CLK 66
WYETT, John WAS 64A
WYLEE, John GRD 95A
Sally GRD 119A
WYLEE?, Joshua GRD 91A
WYLER?, Joshua GRD 91A
WYMAN, ----? HRY 212
Aeles? HRL 120
Geo. JEF 57
John MTG 225
WYMER, John, Sr. MTG 241
WYMORE, Frederick OWN 103
George OWN 103
James OWN 101
John OWN 101
Samuel OWN 103
WYNE, Ben? ADC 68
WYOTT, William WRN 63A
YA-ON?, Matthew WAS 87A
YAGAR, Jacob HRY 247
Jessee JEF 56
YAGER, Absalom NSN 185
Annanias WAS 85A
Cornelious WAS 85A
Eligah CBL 9A
Elisha SHE 163
James MAD 146
James HAR 160
John CBL 8A
Jonas CBL 8A
Joseph CLY 118
Joshua MER 114
Saml. MAD 146
Stephen WAS 47A
Urijah PUL 53A
YAGER?, Ephraim GTN 128
YAJOR, Joel CBL 8A
YAJOR?, Simion CBL 8A
YAKER?, Harry GRD 96B
YAKEY, Fred. GRD 109A
YALCER?, Harry GRD 96B
YANCEY, David BRN 32
George SCT 105A
Joel BRN 32
Leyton MAD 104
Robert WDF 107A
Will SCT 105A
YANCY, G. L. TOD 133
Jaconias? LGN 28
Jane PUL 43A
John TOD 133
Philip GTN 119
Richard GTN 119
Robert MAD 104
Thomas GTN 118
YANDELL, Saml. CWL 57
YANDERS, Christey? PUL 37A
YANDLE, Henry WYN 99A
YANKEE, Jacob MER 114
YANTES, Jesse GRD 82A
YANTIS, Aaron SHE 131A
Amos MER 114
Enoch LNC 2
John GRD 85A
YAPP, Thomas LWS 98A
YARBOROUGH, Wm. BRN 32
YARBROUGH, Sally TOD 131
Thomas BTH 166
Wm. P. HRY 255
YARNALD, David HAR 132
Isaac HAR 136
YARNALD?, Saml. HAR 132
YARNELL, Isaac FTE 106
YATER/ YATES?,
Abram GRD 117A
Henry GRD 94A
YATES, Adial CBL 13A
Alesey NCH 111A
Alpheus BRN 32
Andrew FLG 67A
Charles MER 114
Elijah MAD 122
Frank ADR 62
George BRN 32
Henry GTN 133
Isaac BLT 178
Jacob GRD 105A
James BLT 186
James G.? ADR 62
Jno. PUL 39A
Joel MER 114
John ADR 62
John ADR 62
John MAD 90
John HRT 170
John HOP 270
John WYN 82A
John WYN 101A
John SCT 106A
John GSN 155A
Jos. FLG 73A
Mary WAS 71A
Michael FTE 95
Michael BBN 140
Polly WAS 71A
Robert WAS 71A
Sally MER 114
Saml. FKN 134
Samuel BRN 32
Stephen LVG 10
Thos. MAS 70
William MER 114
William CLD 150
William NSN 197
William, Sr. WYN 101A
William WRN 44A
Wm. MAD 150
YATES?, William JES 97
Wm.? WAS 38A
YAWEALL?, Thomas BNE 42
YAZLE, Jacob FLG 48A
John FLG 53A
Saml. FLG 53A
YEACON?, Thos. WAS 42A
YEAGER, Daniel LNC 77
Frederick LNC 75
Joseph LNC 45
Lewis HRY 222
Nicholas LNC 75
YEAGLES, Nicholass WDF 117A
YEAHER, Josiah H. HRD 14
YEAKER, Henery ADR 62
YEARGIN, Mark M. HND 13
YEARLY, John GSN 155A
Samuel GSN 155A
YEARNEST?,
Catherine HRL 122
YEAST, Jacob, Jr. MER 114
Jacob, Sr. MER 114
Leonard MER 114
YEATES, Benjamin SHE 150

Name	County	Page
YEATES, Enoch	MTG	271
George	MTG	225
Joel	CWL	57
Joshua	MTG	283
Joshua, Sr.?	MTG	271
William	MTG	283
YEATMAN?, Jno.	FKN	106
YEISER, Engleheart	FTE	69
George	ADR	62
Philip	MER	117
YEISER?, Frederic	MER	116
YELTON/ YELTOW?, Jesse	BBN	134
YERGAIN, John	SHE	141A
YESTERDAY, Louis	FKN	76
YEWELL, Humprey	WAS	26A
Leroy	WAS	28A
Wm.	WAS	27A
YEWMAN, Stokes	BTH	182
YINGLING, Joseph	BBN	78
YOCUM, Frank	MTG	293
George	MTG	237
George	MTG	253
Jacob	MTG	233
John	MTG	239
John	MTG	283
John	MTG	293
John, Jr.	MTG	293
Jonathan	MTG	255
Matthias	BLT	162
William	MTG	255
YOKE?, Elias	HAR	150
YONTS, Phillip	MBG	135A
Rudolph	MBG	135A
William	MBG	135A
YONTSEY?, (See Youtsey?)	CBL	
YORICK, Allen	HRD	88
Elizabeth	HRD	88
Lewis	HRD	88
YORK, Bartlett	MER	114
Benj.	BKN	8
Charles	BKN	4
Elijah	MAS	57
Ezekial	BTH	152
Jere	HRD	74
Jeremiah	CLY	128
Jesse	MAS	57
Jessee	BKN	11
John	FTE	109
Jos.	MAS	57
Joshua	MAS	57
Mary	BBN	68
Newman	FTE	107
YORK?, Armsted	BRN	32
YORKHAM, John	BTH	216
YOST, George	JES	76
YOTER?, Jacob	SHE	130A
YOUCUM, Anbros	GSN	155A
YOUKUM, Henry	LNC	23
Henry, Sr.	LNC	23
Liberty	LNC	23
YOUNG, -----?	DVS	9A
--s.?	CWL	34
Abijah	SHE	124A
Absolum	FLD	14
Adam	WAS	46A
Adam	WAS	80A
Alesander	LWS	96A
Alexander	FLD	29
Ambrose	FTE	88
Andrew	MTG	225
Aquilla	MTG	251
Archabald	JES	96
Aris	SHE	148
Aron H.	FLG	28A
YOUNG, Barney	GRD	83A
Benj.	FLG	32A
Benjamin S.	MBG	140A
Betsey	FTE	58
Betsey, Mrs.	WYN	99A
Brice	BKN	15
Catesby	SHE	148
Catesby, Jnr.	SHE	148
Charles	CSY	210
Charles	WYN	82A
Charles W.	FLD	33
Daniel	BTH	178
David, Jr.	WYN	91A
David, Sen.	WYN	82A
David	WDF	93A
Edward	BRN	32
Edwin	BTH	156
Elinor	FKN	134
Eliza	LNC	65
Elizabeth	HRD	92
Ephraim	MTG	257
Even	WAS	37A
Ezekiel	TRG	4
Fanny	JES	83
Ferdinand	TRG	11A
Frances	FTE	60
Fred.	JEF	54
George	ADR	62
George	GRN	63
George	MGB	137A
George H.	WRN	75A
Godfrey	PUL	60A
H.	JEF	28
Hannah	JES	92
Harvy	CHN	44A
Henry	CWL	34
Henry	HRY	200
Hiram	BBN	132
Hugh?	CWL	40
Ja-.	BKN	8
Jacob	SHE	149
Jacob	NSN	194
Jacob	BRK	305
Jacob	WAS	46A
Jacob	NCH	111A
James	FLD	29
James	BRN	32
James	CHN	33
James	CWL	34
James	CLK	68
James	CLK	81
James	JES	88
James	CLD	153
James	SHE	157
James	HAR	158
James	BTH	160
James	HAR	206
James, Jr.	MTG	251
James, Junr.	CLD	144
James, Senr.	CLD	144
James, Sr.	MTG	225
James	WRN	38A
James	WRN	38A
James C.	WRN	36A
James L.	HRY	178
James M.	LVG	3
James R.	FTE	101
Jane	LGN	38
Jane	WRN	39A
Jas.	MAS	56
Jas.	HRD	84
Jas.	FLG	32A
Jno.	LVG	8
Joel	WDF	97
John	TRG	3
John	TRG	4
YOUNG, John	BKN	19
John	BRN	32
John	LGN	32
John	FLD	33
John	CWL	34
John	CWL	34
John	LNC	57
John	ADR	62
John	BBN	76
John	CLK	80
John	JES	88
John	FTE	109
John	CLY	119
John	UNN	153
John	CLD	161
John	HRY	186
John, Sr.	CLY	124
John	TRG	11A
John	SPN	15A
John	WRN	39A
John	WAS	46A
John	PUL	60A
John	WYN	90A
John	SCT	99A
John	WYN	100A
John	WDF	104A
John	WTY	119A
John	SHE	129A
John	SHE	139A
John	GNP	175A
John D.	FTE	100
John L.	SHE	149
John W.	UNN	152
Johnson	ALN	130
Jonathan	CLD	144
Jonathan	CLD	155
Jos.	HRY	257
Joseph F.	CLK	68
Joshua	SHE	141A
Lathum	MER	114
Leonard	FTE	93
Leonard L.	BRN	32
Leven	FTE	60
Lewis	JES	73
Lucy	FTE	58
Lucy	FTE	97
Margaret	FTE	89
Martha	WDF	125A
Martin	JES	87
Martin	BRK	305
Mary	SPN	19A
Mary	SPN	20A
Mary	WRN	66A
Mathew	WRN	38A
Merit	CHN	42A
Minor	JES	95
Nathan	BBN	82
Nimrod	MER	114
Original	CLK	85
Original	BTH	212
Peter	UNN	152
Peter	NSN	213
Philip V.	BRN	32
Pleasant	CLY	124
Rachel	HRD	66
Ralph	WRN	38A
Randolph G.	SPN	19A
Reubin	JES	73
Richard	JES	74
Richard	JES	79
Richd.	HRY	259
Robbert	CBL	21A
Robert	LVG	11
Robert	FLD	20
Robert	GRN	73
Robert	FKN	136

YOUNG, Robert CLD 144
Robert L. GTN 122
Robt. BBN 70
Robt. HRY 268
Robt. PUL 41A
Ruth MNR 193
Sam. HRY 267
Saml. BKN 9
Saml. HRD 34
Samuel FLD 14
Samuel JES 83
Samuel MTG 229
Samuel WYN 82A
Samuel WYN 99A
Samul ADR 62
Sary FKN 134
Senate, Jr. BTH 178
Senate, Snr. BTH 166
Seonard FTE 90
Silas WYN 99A
Solomon PUL 60A
Stephen LVG 9
Stephen FTE 66
Tavender B. BTH 160
Thomas TRG 4
Thomas TRG 4
Thomas BBN 106
Thomas HRL 122
Thomas CLD 143
Thomas BTH 160
Thomas MTG 251
Thomas HOP 270
Thomas CBL 21A
Thomas WRN 28A
Vachal MAD 170
W. T. MAS 58
Walter JEF 41
Walter GRN 64
Washington WYN 99A
Will SCT 113A
Will. SCT 100A
William TRG 4
William BKN 26
William BRN 32
William FLD 36
William LGN 38
William CLK 69
William JES 87
William CLD 139
William BTH 162
William NSN 181
William MTG 235
William, Jr. TRG 11A
William OHO 7A
William TRG 11A
William MBG 135A
William MBG 135A
William D. WDF 118A
William? DVS 12A
Willis BBN 144
Wm. BKN 19
Wm. ADR 62
Wm. FKN 134
Wm., Junr. HRD 58
Wm., Senr. HRD 58
Wm. SHE 142A
Wm. GSN 155A
Wm. F. WAS 20A
Wm. L. HRD 64
YOUNG?, James BKN 16
YOUNGER, Danl. HRY 228
Henry BLT 158
Isaac BLT 160
John SHE 129A
Joshua NCH 125A
Kenard BLT 174
YOUNGER, Nimrod CLY 118
Peter HAR 154
Samuel LGN 41
William A. LGN 40
Willis HOP 270
YOUNGLOVE, Saml. CHN 28A
YOUNGMAN, Isaiah BKN 18
Jesse MAS 58
John CBL 19A
Susan CBL 19A
YOUNGS, Nathan CHN 28A
YOUNGS?, Caleb CHN 45
YOUNT, Jonathan SHE 172
Joseph SHE 171
YOUNTS, William FLD 15
YOURS, Charles GRN 63
YOUSE, Michael G. MER 116
YOUST, Nicholas MTG 257
YOUTSEY?, George CBL 16A
Jacob CBL 12A
John, Jr. CBL 16A
John, Sr. CBL 16A
YOWEALL?, Thomas BNE 42
YOWELL, James WAS 25A
James SHE 140A
John WAS 25A
Moses WAS 24A
YOWL, Cornelius GTN 123
YUNT, Geo. FKN 116
Geo., Jr. FKN 116
Jno. FKN 110
William GTN 134
Wm. FKN 110
ZACHARY, Jno. PUL 37A
Thomas BNE 42
Willis PUL 37A
ZACKARY, Benjamin PUL 68A
ZARING, Benja. JEF 64
Jacob JEF 64
John JEF 64
ZECKLIDGE, Wm. JEF 39
ZEIGLER, Amos CWL 33
David? CWL 32
George HAR 182
Jacob CWL 33
Nancy CWL 32
Wm. CWL 31
ZELL, Harrison E. LVG 11
Henry BNE 42
Mason E. LVG 11
ZIKE, Jacob JES 86
John JES 89
ZIKE?, David JES 85
ZILER?, Jacob NCH 117A
ZILHART, Geo. JEF 36
Phillip JEF 39
Phillip JEF 40
ZILN?, Jacob NCH 117A
ZIMMERMAN, Augustus JES 72
Chris. BNE 42
David JEF 42
David JEF 45
Federick BNE 42
Fredk. SCT 91A
John HND 11
John LNC 55
ZIMMERMAN?, Wm. FKN 162
ZIMMERMON, John SHE 124A
ZINK, Andrew FTE 56
ZINN, John GRT 145
Joseph GRT 147
ZOOK, Jacob FKN 122
Polly FKN 122
ZORIS?, Philip GNP 170A
ZORNES?, Wm. FLG 76A
ZORUS, Andrew, Ser. GNP 174A
Andrew GNP 174A
John GNP 173A
Martin GNP 174A
Martin GNP 174A
Thomas GNP 174A